THEOLOGICAL DICTIONARY
OF THE
OLD TESTAMENT

THEOLOGICAL DICTIONARY

OF THE

OLD TESTAMENT

EDITED BY

G. JOHANNES BOTTERWECK,

HELMER RINGGREN,

AND

HEINZ-JOSEF FABRY

Translated by

DAVID E. GREEN

Volume XI

עזז ־ פָּנִים

ʿzz — pānîm

WILLIAM B. EERDMANS PUBLISHING COMPANY
GRAND RAPIDS, MICHIGAN / CAMBRIDGE, U.K.

THEOLOGICAL DICTIONARY OF THE OLD TESTAMENT
Volume XI
Translated from
THEOLOGISCHES WÖRTERBUCH ZUM ALTEN TESTAMENT
Band VI, Lieferungen 1-6
Published 1987-1988 by
Verlag W. Kohlhammer GmbH, Stuttgart, Germany

Wm. B. Eerdmans Publishing Co.
255 Jefferson Ave. S.E., Grand Rapids, Michigan 49503 /
P.O. Box 163, Cambridge CB3 9PU U.K.

Printed in the United States of America

08 07 06 05 04 03 02 01   7 6 5 4 3 2 1

Library of Congress Cataloging-in-Publication Data

Botterweck, G. Johannes
Theological dictionary of the Old Testament
Translation of Theologisches Wörterbuch zum Alten Testament.
Translated by David E. Green and Douglas W. Stott
Includes rev. ed. of v. 1-2.
Includes bibliographical references.
1. Bible. O.T. — Dictionaries — Hebrew. 2. Hebrew language — Dictionaries — English.
I. Ringgren, Helmer, 1917 — joint author. II. Fabry, Heinz-Josef, — joint author.
III. Title.
ISBN 0-8028-2338-6 (set)

Volume XI ISBN 0-8028-2335-1

www.eerdmans.com

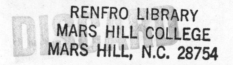

CONTENTS

		Page
Contributors		v
Abbreviations		xi
Transliteration		xxiv
עזז	*ʿzz;* עֱזוּז *ʿezûz;* עִזּוּז *ʿizzûz;* עַז *ʿaz;* עוֹז/עֹז *ʿôz/ʿōz;* מָעוֹז *māʿôz* **strength** (Wagner)	1
עָזַר	*ʿāzar;* עֹזֵר *ʿōzēr;* עֵזֶר *ʿēzer;* עֶזְרָה *ʿezrâ;* עֲזָרָה *ʿazārâ;* עַזִּיר *ʿaz(z)îr;* עָזַר II *ʿāzar* II **help; leader** (Lipiński; Fabry)	12
עָטַר	*ʿāṭar;* עֲטָרָה *ʿaṭārâ* **crown, wreath** (D. Kellermann)	18
עַיִן	*ʿayin* **eye** (Stendebach)	28
עַיִן	*ʿayin;* מַעְיָן *maʿyān* **spring** (Schreiner)	44
עִיר	*ʿîr* **city** (E. Otto)	51
עָכַר	*ʿākar;* עֵמֶק עָכוֹר *ʿēmeq ʿākôr* **restrain, hinder** (Mosis)	67
עֹל	*ʿōl* **yoke** (Schmoldt)	72
עָלָה	*ʿālâ;* מַעַל *maʿal;* מֹעַל *mōʿal;* מַעֲלֶה *maʿaleh;* מַעֲלָה *maʿalâ;* תְּעָלָה *teʿālâ;* עֱלִי *ʿelî;* עִלִּי *ʿillî;* עֲלִיָּה *ʿalîyâ* **go up, raise up** (Fuhs)	76
עוֹלָה/עֹלָה	*ʿōlâ/ʿôlâ* **burnt offering, sacrifice** (D. Kellermann)	96
עָלֶה	*ʿāleh* **leaves, foliage** (Beyse)	113
עָלַז	*ʿālaz;* *עַלִּיז *ʿallîz;* *עָלֵז *ʿālēz;* עָלַץ *ʿālaṣ;* עֲלִיצוּת *ʿalîṣûṯ;* עָלַס *ʿālas* **express joy** (Vanoni)	115
עֶלְיוֹן	*ʿelyôn* **Most High** (Zobel)	121
עלל	*ʿll;* עֹלֵלָה *ʿolēlâ;* עֲלִילָה *ʿalîlâ;* עֲלִילִיָּה *ʿalîlîyâ;* מַעֲלָל *maʿalāl;* תַּעֲלוּל *taʿalûl* **deal with** (Roth; Fabry)	139
עָלַם	*ʿālam;* תַּעֲלֻמָה *taʿalumâ* **(be) hidden** (Locher)	147
עַלְמָה	*ʿalmâ;* עֶלֶם *ʿelem* **young woman** (Dohmen; Ringgren)	154

עַם — *ʿam* **people** (Lipiński; Von Soden) 163

עָמַד — *ʿāmaḏ;* עֹמֶד *ʿōmeḏ;* עֶמְדָּה *ʿemdâ;* מַעֲמָד *maʿ^{a}māḏ;* מָעֳמָד *moʿ^{o}māḏ* **approach, stand** (Ringgren) 178

עַמּוּד — *ʿammûḏ* **pillar** (Freedman — Willoughby; Fabry) 187

עָמִית — *ʿāmîṯ* **kin** (Zobel) 192

עָמָל — *ʿāmāl;* עָמַל *ʿāmal;* עָמֵל *ʿāmēl* **affliction** (Otzen) 196

עֵמֶק — *ʿēmeq;* עָמַק *ʿāmaq;* עֹמֶק *ʿōmeq;* עָמֹק/עָמֵק *ʿāmēq/ʿāmōq;* מַעֲמַקִּים *maʿ^{a}maqqîm* **valley** (Beyse) 202

עֵנָב — *ʿēnāḇ;* אֶשְׁכּוֹל *ʾeškôl;* צִמּוּקִים *ṣimmûqîm* **grape** (Angerstorfer) 209

עָנַג — *ʿānag;* עֹנֶג *ʿōneg;* עָנֹג *ʿānōg;* תַּעֲנוּג *taʿ^{a}nûg* **be, make soft, delicate; pleasure** (Kronholm) 212

עָנָה — *ʿānâ* I; מַעֲנֶה *maʿ^{a}neh;* עִנְיָן *ʿinyān;* עֹנָה *ʿōnâ* **answer** (Stendebach) 215

עָנָה — II *ʿānâ;* עֲנָוָה *ʿ^{a}nāwâ;* עֱנוּת *ʿ^{e}nûṯ;* עֹנָה *ʿōnâ;* תַּעֲנִית *taʿ^{a}nîṯ;* עָנִי *ʿānî;* עָנָו *ʿānāw* **debase; misery; poor** (Gerstenberger) 230

עָנָן — *ʿānān* **cloud** (Freedman — Willoughby; Fabry) 253

עָפָר — *ʿāpār;* עפר *ʿpr;* אֵפֶר *ʾēper* **dust** (Wächter) 257

עֵץ — *ʿēṣ* **tree** (K. Nielsen; Ringgren; Fabry) 265

עָצַב — *ʿāṣaḇ;* עֶצֶב; *ʿeṣeḇ;* עֹצֶב *ʿōṣeḇ;* עָצֵב *ʿāṣēḇ;* עִצָּבוֹן *ʿiṣṣāḇôn;* עַצֶּבֶת *ʿaṣṣeḇeṯ;* מַעֲצֵבָה *maʿ^{a}ṣēḇâ* **mental suffering** (C. Meyers) 278

עָצָב* — *ʿāṣāḇ* **idol** (Graupner) 281

עָצֵל — *ʿāṣēl* **lazy, laziness** (Reiterer) 284

עָצַם — *ʿāṣam;* עָצוּם *ʿāṣûm;* עֹצֶם *ʿōṣem;* עָצְמָה *ʿoṣmâ;* תַּעֲצֻמוֹת *taʿ^{a}ṣumôṯ* **(be) numerous, mighty** (Lohfink) 289

עֶצֶם — *ʿeṣem;* עֹצֶם *ʿōṣem* **bone** (Beyse) 304

עָצַר — *ʿāṣar;* עֶצֶר *ʿeṣer;* עֹצֶר *ʿōṣer;* עֲצֶרֶת *ʿ^{a}ṣereṯ;* עֲצָרָה *ʿ^{a}ṣārâ;* מַעְצוֹר *maʿṣôr;* מַעְצָר *maʿṣār* **hold back** (Wright — Milgrom) 310

עקב — *ʿqb;* עָקֵב *ʿāqēḇ;* עֵקֶב *ʿēqeḇ;* עָקֹב *ʿāqōḇ* **heel** (Zobel) 315

עָקַר — *ʿāqar;* עָקָר *ʿāqār;* עֵקֶר *ʿēqer;* עִקָּר *ʿiqqār* **uproot** (Fabry) 320

עקשׁ ʿqš; עִקֵּשׁ ʿiqqēš; עִקְּשׁוּת ʿiqqᵉšûṯ; מַעֲקַשִּׁים maʿᵃqaššîm **twist, pervert** (Warmuth) · 323

עָרַב I ʿāraḇ I; עֲרֻבָּה ʿᵃrubbâ; עֵרָבוֹן ʿērāḇôn; עָרֵב ʿārēḇ; תַּעֲרוּבָה taʿᵃrûḇâ **stand surety** (Lipiński) · 326

ערב II/III ʿrb II/III; עֶרֶב I ʿereḇ I; עֶרֶב II ʿereḇ II; עָרֹב ʿārōḇ; עָרֵב ʿārēḇ **mix; be sweet** (Fabry — Lamberty-Zielinski) · · · · · · · · · · · 331

עֶרֶב ʿereḇ; עָרַב ʿāraḇ; מַעֲרָב maʿᵃrāḇ **evening** (Niehr) · · · · · · · · · · · · 335

עֹרֵב ʿōrēḇ **raven** (Angerstorfer) · 341

עָרָה ʿārâ; מוֹרָה môrâ; מַעַר maʿar; עֶרְוָה ʿerwâ; עֶרְיָה ʿeryâ **(be) naked, empty** (Niehr) · 343

עָרוֹם ʿārôm; עֵירוֹם ʿêrôm **nakedness** (Niehr) · · · · · · · · · · · · · · · · · 349

עָרַךְ ʿāraḵ; עֵרֶךְ ʿēreḵ; מַעֲרָכָה/מַעֲרֶכֶת maʿᵃrāḵâ/maʿᵃreḵeṯ **lay out, arrange** (Firmage — Milgrom) · 355

עָרַל ʿāral; עָרֵל ʿārēl; עָרְלָה ʿorlâ **foreskin, circumcise** (Mayer) · · · · · · · 359

עָרַם ʿāram; עָרוּם ʿārûm; עָרְמָה ʿārmâ **crafty** (Niehr) · · · · · · · · · · · · · 361

עֹרֶף ʿōrep; עָרַף ʿārap **(turn, break the) neck** (Zipor) · · · · · · · · · · · · 366

עֲרָפֶל ᵃʿrāpel **thick clouds, darkness** (Mulder) · · · · · · · · · · · · · · · · 371

עָרַץ ʿāraṣ; עָרִיץ ʿārîṣ; מַעֲרָצָה maʿᵃrāṣâ; עָרוּץ ʿārûṣ **terrify; terror** (Kedar-Kopfstein) · 376

עֶרֶשׂ ʿereś; מִטָּה miṭṭâ; יָצוּעַ yāṣûaʿ **bed** (Angerstorfer) · · · · · · · · · · · 379

עֵשֶׂב ʿēśeḇ **grass** (Maiberger) · 383

עָשָׂה ʿāśâ; מַעֲשֶׂה maʿᵃśeh **make; do; act** (Ringgren) · · · · · · · · · · · · · 387

עֶשֶׂר ʿeśer; עשׂר ʿśr; מַעֲשֵׂר maʿᵃśēr **ten** (North) · · · · · · · · · · · · · · · 404

עָשָׁן ʿāšān **smoke** (North) · 409

עָשַׁק ʿāšaq; עֹשֶׁק ʿōšeq; עֵשֶׁק ʿēšeq; עָשְׁקָה ʿošqâ; עָשֹׁק ʿāšōq; עֲשׁוּקִים ʿᵃšûqîm; מַעֲשַׁקּוֹת maʿᵃšaqqôṯ **oppress** (Gerstenberger) · · · · · · · · · 412

עָשַׁר ʿāšar; עָשִׁיר ʿāšîr; עֹשֶׁר ʿōšer **(be) rich; wealth** (Sæbø) · · · · · · · · 417

עשתרת ʿštrt (ʿaštōreṯ); *עַשְׁתֶּרֶת *ʿaštereṯ; עַשְׁתָּרֹת ʿaštārōṯ; עַשְׁתְּרָתִי ʿaštᵉrāṯî **Astarte** (H.-P. Müller) · 423

עֵת	*ʿēṯ;* עַתָּה *ʿattâ* **time** (Kronholm)	434
עַתּוּד	*ʿattûḏ* **goat** (Maiberger)	452
עתק	*ʿtq;* עָתִיק *ʿāṯîq;* עַתִּיק *ʿattîq;* עָתֵק *ʿāṯēq;* עָתָק *ʿāṯāq* **move forward** (Schmoldt)	456
עָתַר	*ʿāṯar;* עָתָר *ʿāṯār* **entreat** (Gerstenberger)	458
פֵּאָה	*pēʾâ* **side, edge, boundary** (Angerstorfer)	461
פאר	*pʾr;* תִּפְאֶרֶת *tip̄ʾereṯ;* פְּאֵר *p^eʾēr* **glory** (Hausmann)	464
פִּגּוּל	*piggûl* **filth, dung** (D. Kellermann)	468
פָּגַע	*pāgaʿ;* פֶּגַע *pegaʿ;* מִפְגָּע *mipgāʿ* **strike, hit** (Maiberger)	470
פָּגַר	*pāgar;* פֶּגֶר *peger* **corpse** (Maiberger)	477
פָּדָה	*pāḏâ;* פְּדוּת *p^eḏûṯ;* פִּדְיוֹן *piḏyôn* **redeem** (Cazelles)	483
פֶּה	*peh* **mouth** (García-López)	490
פוח	*pwḥ* **blow** (Reiterer)	504
פוּץ	*pûṣ;* תְּפוּצָה *t^epûṣâ;* נָפַץ *nāp̄aṣ;* פזר *pzr* **overflow; scatter** (Ringgren)	509
פַּח	*paḥ* **trap, snare** (D. Kellermann)	513
פָּחַד	*pāḥaḏ;* פַּחַד *paḥaḏ* I and II **tremble; (feel) dread** (H.-P. Müller)	517
פַּחַת	*paḥaṯ* **pit** (Mulder)	526
פָּטַר	*pāṭar;* פָּטִיר *pāṭîr;* פֶּטֶר *peṭer;* פִּטְרָה *piṭrâ* **release** (Niehr)	529
פלא	*plʾ;* פֶּלֶא *peleʾ* **(be) marvelous** (Conrad)	533
פָּלַג	*pālag;* פֶּלֶג *peleg;* פְּלַגָּה *p^elaggâ;* פְּלֻגָּה *p^eluggâ;* מִפְלַגָּה *miplaggâ* **wadi, watercourse** (Schunck)	546
פִּלֶגֶשׁ	*pileḡeš* **concubine** (Engelken)	549
פָּלַט	*pālaṭ;* מָלַט *mālaṭ;* פָּלִיט *pālîṭ;* פָּלֵ(י)ט *pālêṭ;* פְּלֵ(י)טָה *p^elêṭâ;* מִפְלָט *miplāṭ* **escape; deliver** (Hasel)	551
פלל	*pll;* תְּפִלָּה *t^epillâ;* פְּלִילִים *p^elîlîm;* פְּלִילָה *p^elîlâ;* פְּלִילִי *p^elîlî;* פְּלִילִיָּה *p^elîlîyâ* **pray; prayer** (Gerstenberger; Fabry)	567
פָּנָה	*pānâ* **turn** (Schreiner)	578
פִּנָּה	*pinnâ* **corner** (Oeming)	586
פָּנִים	*pānîm* **face** (Simian-Yofre)	589

ABBREVIATIONS

AAAS	*Annales archéologiques Arabes Syriennes,* Damascus
AANLR	*Atti dell'Academia Nazionale dei Lincei, Rendiconti,* Rome
AASOR	*Annual of the American Schools of Oriental Research,* New Haven, Ann Arbor, Philadelphia
ÄAT	Ägypten und Altes Testament. Studien zur Geschichte, Kultur und Religion Ägyptens und des ATs, Wiesbaden
AB	*The Anchor Bible,* ed. W. F. Albright and D. N. Freedman, Garden City, N.Y.
ABL	R. F. Harper, *Assyrian and Babylonian Letters,* 14 vols. (Chicago, 1892-1914)
ABLAK	M. Noth, *Aufsätze und biblischen Landes- und Altertumskunde,* 2 vols. (Neukirchen, 1971)
ABR	*Australian Biblical Review,* Melbourne
abs.	absolute
acc.	accusative
AcOr	*Acta orientalia,* Copenhagen, Leiden
act.	active
AcThD	*Acta theologica danica,* Århus, Copenhagen
adj.	adjective
ADPV	*Abhandlungen des Deutschen Palästinavereins,* Wiesbaden
adv.	adverb, adverbial
AfO	*Archiv für Orientforschung,* Graz
AHAW	*Abhandlungen der Heidelberger Akademie der Wissenschaften*
AHDO	*Archive de l'histoire du droit oriental,* Wetteren (Belgium)
AHw	W. von Soden, *Akkadisches Handwörterbuch,* 3 vols. (Wiesbaden, 1965-81)
AION	*Annali dell'Istituto Universitario Orientali di Napoli*
AJBA	*Australian Journal of Biblical Archaeology,* Sydney
AJBI	*Annual of the Japanese Biblical Institute,* Tokyo
AJSL	*The American Journal of Semitic Languages and Literatures,* Chicago
Akk.	Akkadian
ALGHJ	*Arbeiten zur Literatur und Geschichte des hellenistischen Judentums,* Leiden
ALUOS	*Annals of Leeds University Oriental Society*
Amhar.	Amharic
Amor.	Amorite
AN	J. J. Stamm, *Akkadische Namengebung* (1939)
AnAcScFen	*Annales Academiae Scientarum Fennicae,* Helsinki
AnBibl	*Analecta biblica,* Rome
AncIsr	R. de Vaux, *Ancient Israel: Its Life and Institutions* (Eng. trans., New York, 1961, repr. 1965)
ANEP	*The Ancient Near East in Pictures,* ed. J. B. Pritchard (Princeton, ^{2}1955, ^{3}1969)
ANET	*Ancient Near Eastern Texts Relating to the OT,* ed. J. B. Pritchard (Princeton, ^{2}1955, ^{3}1969)
ANH	G. Dalman, *Aramäisch-Neuhebräisches Handwörterbuch* (Göttingen, ^{3}1938)
AnOr	*Analecta orientalia,* Rome
AnSt	*Anatolian Studies,* Leiden

ANVAO	*Avhandlinger utgitt av det Norske Videnskaps-Akademi i Oslo*
AO	*Tablets in the Collection of the Musée de Louvre,* Paris
AOAT	*Alter Orient und AT,* Kevelaer, Neukirchen-Vluyn
AOB	*Altorientalische Bilder zum AT,* ed. H. Gressmann (Berlin, ²1927)
AO Beihefte	*Beiheft zum Alte Orient,* Leipzig
AOS	*American Oriental Series,* New Haven
AOT	*Altorientalische Texte zum AT,* ed. H. Gressmann (Berlin, ²1926, repr. 1953)
AP	A. E. Cowley, *Aramaic Papyri of the Fifth Century B.C.* (1923, repr. Osnabruck, 1976)
APN	K. Tallqvist, *Assyrian Personal Names. ASSF* 43/1 (1914, repr. 1966)
APNM	H. B. Huffmon, *Amorite Personal Names in the Mari Texts* (Baltimore, 1965)
APOT	R. H. Charles, ed., *Apocrypha and Pseudepigrapha of the Old Testament,* 2 vols. (Oxford, 1913)
Arab.	Arabic
ARAB	D. D. Luckenbill, *Ancient Records of Assyria and Babylonia,* 2 vols. (Chicago, 1926-27)
Aram.	Aramaic
ARM	*Archives royales de Mari. Textes cunéiformes,* Paris
ARW	*Archiv für Religionswissenschaft,* Freiburg, Leipzig, Berlin
AS	*Assyriological Studies,* Chicago
ASAW	*Abhandlungen der Sächsischen Gesellschaft der Wissenschaften,* Leipzig
ASSF	*Acta Societatis Scientiarum Fennicae,* Helsinki
Assyr.	Assyrian
ASTI	*Annual of the Swedish Theological Institute in Jerusalem,* Leiden
AT	Altes Testament, Ancien Testament, etc.
ATA	*Alttestamentliche Abhandlungen,* Münster
ATANT	*Abhandlungen zur Theologie des Alten und Neuen Testaments,* Zurich
ATD	*Das AT Deutsch,* ed. V. Herntrich and A. Weiser, Göttingen
ATDA	J. Hoftijzer and G. van der Kooij, *Aramaic Texts from Deir ʿAlla* (Leiden, 1976)
ATR	*Anglican Theological Review,* Evanston
ATS	*Arbeiten zu Text und Sprache im AT,* St. Ottilien, Munich
AuS	G. Dalman, *Arbeit und Sitte in Palästina,* 7 vols. (1928-42, repr. Hildesheim, 1964)
AUSS	*Andrews University Seminary Studies,* Berrien Springs
AzT	*Arbeiten zur Theologie,* Stuttgart
BA	*The Biblical Archaeologist,* New Haven, Ann Arbor, Philadelphia, Atlanta
Bab.	Babylonian, Babylonian Talmud
BAfO	*Beiheft zur AfO*
BAR	*Biblical Archaeology Review,* Washington
BASOR	*Bulletin of the American Schools of Oriental Research,* New Haven, Ann Arbor, Philadelphia, Baltimore
BASORSup	*BASOR Supplemental Studies*
BAT	*Die Botschaft des AT,* Stuttgart
BBB	*Bonner biblische Beiträge*
BBET	*Beiträge zur biblischen Exegese und Theologie,* Frankfurt, Las Vegas
BCPE	*Bulletin du Centre Protestant d'Études,* Geneva
BDB	F. Brown, S. R. Driver, and C. A. Briggs, *A Hebrew and English Lexicon of the OT* (Oxford, 1907; Peabody, Mass., ²1979)
BDBAT	*Beiheft zur Dielheimer Blätter zum AT*
Beeston	A. F. L. Beeston et al., *Sabaic Dictionary* (Louvain-la-Neuve, 1982)
Benz	F. L. Benz, *Personal Names in the Phoenician and Punic Inscriptions. StPohl* 8 (1972)

BeO	*Bibbia e oriente,* Milan
BethM	*Beth Miqra,* Jerusalem
BETL	*Bibliotheca ephemeridum theologicarum Lovaniensium,* Paris, Gembloux
Beyer	K. Beyer, *Die aramäischen Texte vom Toten Meer* (Göttingen, 1984)
BFCT	*Beiträge zur Förderung christliches Theologie,* Gütersloh
BHHW	*Biblisch-historisches Handwörterbuch,* ed. L. Rost and B. Reicke, 4 vols. (Göttingen, 1962-66; index and maps, 1979)
BHK	*Biblia hebraica,* ed. R. Kittel (Stuttgart, [3]1929)
BHS	*Biblia hebraica stuttgartensia,* ed. K. Elliger and W. Rudolph (Stuttgart, 1966-77)
BHT	*Beiträge zur historischen Theologie,* Tübingen
BibB	*Biblische Beiträge,* Fribourg
Bibl	*Biblica,* Rome
bibliog.	bibliography
Biella	J. Biella, *Dictionary of Old South Arabic, Sabaean Dialect. HSS* 25 (1982)
BietOr	*Biblica et orientalia,* Rome
BiKi	*Bibel und Kirche,* Stuttgart
BiLe	*Bibel und Leben,* Düsseldorf
BiOr	*Bibliotheca orientalis,* Leiden
BJRL	*Bulletin of the John Rylands Library,* Manchester
BK	*Biblischer Kommentar AT,* ed. M. Noth and H. W. Wolff, Neukirchen-Vluyn
BJS	*Brown Judaic Studies,* Missoula, Mont.; Chico, Calif.; Atlanta
BL	*Bibel-Lexikon,* ed. H. Haag (Einsiedeln, 1951, [2]1968)
BLe	H. Bauer and P. Leander, *Historische Grammatik der hebräischen Sprache des ATs* (1918-22, repr. Hildesheim, 1991)
BMAP	E. G. Kraeling, *The Brooklyn Museum Aramaic Papyri* (New Haven, 1953)
BN	*Biblische Notizen,* Bamberg
BOT	*De Boeken van het OT,* Roermond en Maaseik
BRL	K. Galling, *Biblisches Reallexikon. HAT* (1937, [2]1977)
BS	*Bibliotheca sacra,* Dallas
BSt	*Biblische Studien,* Neukirchen-Vluyn
BT	*The Bible Translator,* London
BTB	*Biblical Theology Bulletin,* Rome
BVC	*Bible et vie chrétienne,* Paris
BWA(N)T	*Beiträge zur Wissenschaft vom Alten (und Neuen) Testament,* Leipzig, Stuttgart
BWL	W. G. Lambert, *Babylonian Wisdom Literature* (Oxford, 1960)
BZ	*Biblische Zeitschrift,* Paderborn
BZAW	*Beihefte zur ZAW,* Berlin
BZRGG	*Beihefte zur Zeitschrift für Religions- und Geistesgeschichte,* Cologne et al.
ca.	about
CAD	*The Assyrian Dictionary of the Oriental Institute of the University of Chicago* (1956–)
CahRB	*Cahiers de la RB,* Paris
Can.	Canaanite
CAT	*Commentaire de l'AT,* Neuchâtel
CB	*Coniectanea biblica, OT Series,* Lund
CBC	*Cambridge Bible Commentary on the New English Bible,* Cambridge
CBQ	*Catholic Biblical Quarterly,* Washington
CBQMS	*Catholic Biblical Quarterly Monograph Series*
CD A, B	Damascus document, manuscript A, B
cf.	compare, see
ch(s).	chapter(s)

CH	Code of Hammurabi
ChW	J. Levy, *Chaldäisches Wörterbuch über die Targumim und einen grossen Theil des rabbinischen Schriftthums,* 2 vols. (Leipzig, 1867-68, repr. 1959)
CIH	*Corpus inscriptionum himyariticarum* (= *CIS,* IV)
CIS	*Corpus inscriptionum semiticarum* (Paris, 1881–)
cj.	conjecture
CML	G. R. Driver, *Canaanite Myths and Legends* (Edinburgh, 1956; ^{2}1977, ed. J. C. L. Gibson)
col.	column
comm(s).	commentary(ies)
Conc	*Concilium*
const.	construct
ContiRossini	K. Conti Rossini, *Chrestomathia arabica meridionalis ephigraphica* (Rome, 1931)
CRAIBL	*Comptes rendus des séances de l'Academie des Inscriptions et Belles Lettres,* Paris
CSD	R. Payne Smith, *A Compendious Syriac Dictionary* (Oxford, 1903, repr. 1976)
CSEL	*Corpus scriptorum ecclesiasticorum latinorum* (Vienna, 1866–)
CT	*Cuneiform Texts from Babylonian Tablets in the British Museum,* London
CTA	A. Herdner, *Corpus des tablettes en cunéiformes alphabétiques découvertes à Ras Shamra-Ugarit,* 2 vols. (Paris, 1963)
D	D (doubling) stem
DBS	*Dictionnaire de la Bible, Supplement,* ed. L. Pirot et al. (Paris, 1926–)
dir.	direct
diss.	dissertation
DJD	*Discoveries in the Judaean Desert* (Oxford, 1955–)
DN	deity name
DNSI	J. Hoftijzer and K. Jongeling, *Dictionary of North-West Semitic Inscriptions,* 2 vols. (Leiden, 1995)
Dtn	Deuteronomic source
Dtr	Deuteronomistic source
DtrH	Deuteronomistic historian
DtrN	nomistic Deuteronomistic source
DtrP	prophetic Deuteronomistic redactor
DTT	*Dansk teologisk Tidsskrift,* Copenhagen
E	Elohistic source
EA	Tell el-Amarna tablets
EAEHL	*Encyclopedia of Archaeological Excavations in the Holy Land,* ed. M. Avi-Yonah and E. Stern, 4 vols. (Englewood Cliffs, N.J., 1975-78)
Eb.	Eblaite
ed.	edition, editor
EdF	*Erträge der Forschung,* Darmstadt
EDNT	*Exegetical Dictionary of the NT,* ed. H. Balz and G. Schneider, 3 vols. (Eng. trans., Grand Rapids, 1990-93)
Egyp.	Egyptian
EH	*Europäische Hochschulschriften,* Frankfurt, Bern
EHAT	*Exegetisches Handbuch zum AT,* Münster
EMiqr	*Enṣiqlōpedyā miqrāʾit (Encyclopedia Biblica)* (Jerusalem, 1950–)
emph.	emphatic(us)
EncBib	*Encyclopaedia Biblica,* ed. T. K. Cheyne, 4 vols. (London, 1900-1903, repr. 1958)

EncJud	*Encyclopaedia judaica,* 16 vols. (Jerusalem, New York, 1971-72)
EnEl	Enuma Elish
Eng.	English
ERE	*Encyclopedia of Religion and Ethics,* ed. J. Hastings, 13 vols. (New York, 1913-27)
Erg.	Ergänzungsheft, Ergänzungsreihe
ErIsr	*Eretz-Israel,* Jerusalem
esp.	especially
EstBíb	*Estudios bíblicos,* Madrid
Eth.	Ethiopic
ETL	*Ephemerides theologicae lovanienses,* Louvain
ETR	*Études théologiques et religieuses,* Montpellier
ETS	*Erfurter theologische Studien,* Leipzig
EÜ	Einheitsübersetzung der Heilige Schrift (Stuttgart, 1974-80)
EvT	*Evangelische Theologie,* Munich
ExpT	*Expository Times,* Edinburgh
fem.	feminine
fig(s).	figure(s)
FolOr	*Folio Orientalia,* Krakow
fr(s).	fragment(s)
FRLANT	*Forschungen zur Religion und Literatur des Alten und Neuen Testaments,* Göttingen
FS	Festschrift
FThS	*Frankfurter theologische Studien,* Frankfurt am Main
FuF	*Forschungen und Fortschritte,* Berlin
FzB	*Forschung zur Bibel,* Würzburg
G	G (*Grund,* basic) stem
GaG	W. von Soden, *Grundriss der akkadischen Grammatik. AnOr* 33 (1952, ²1969 [with Erg., *AnOr* 47])
gen.	genitive
Ger.	German
GesB	W. Gesenius and F. Buhl, *Hebräisches und aramäisches Handwörterbuch über das AT* (Berlin, ¹⁷1921, ¹⁸1987–)
GesTh	W. Gesenius, *Thesaurus philologicus criticus linguae hebraecae et chaldaeae Veteris Testamenti,* 3 vols. (Leipzig, 1829-58)
Gilg.	Gilgamesh epic
Gk.	Greek
GK	W. Gesenius and E. Kautsch, *Hebräische Grammatik* (Halle, ²⁸1909) (= Kautsch and A. E. Cowley, *Gesenius' Hebrew Grammar* [Oxford, ²1910])
GLECS	*Comptes rendus du Groupe Linguistique d'Études Chamito-Sémitiques,* Paris
GSAT	*Gesammelte Studien zum AT,* Munich
GTTOT	J. J. Simons, *The Geographical and Topographical Texts of the OT. SFS* 2 (1959)
H	Holiness Code
Habil.	Habilitationschrift
HAL	L. Koehler, W. Baumgartner et al., *The Hebrew and Aramaic Lexicon of the OT,* 5 vols. plus Sup (Eng. trans., Leiden, 1967-96)
HAT	*Handbuch zum AT,* ser. 1, ed. O. Eissfeldt, Tübingen
HDR	*Harvard Dissertations in Religion,* Cambridge
Heb.	Hebrew
Herm	*Hermeneia,* Philadelphia, Minneapolis
Hitt.	Hittite

HKAT — *Handkommentar zum AT,* ed. W. Nowack, Göttingen
HO — *Handbuch der Orientalistik,* Leiden
HP — E. Jenni, *Das hebräische Piʿel* (Zurich, 1968)
HSAT — *Die Heilige Schrift des ATs,* ed. E. Kautsch and A. Bertholet, 4 vols. (Tübingen, ^{4}1922-23)
HSM — *Harvard Semitic Monographs,* Cambridge, Mass.
HSS — *Harvard Semitic Series/Studies,* Cambridge, Missoula, Chico, Atlanta
HTR — *Harvard Theological Review,* Cambridge, Mass.
HTS — *Harvard Theological Studies,* Cambridge, Mass.
HUCA — *Hebrew Union College Annual,* Cincinnati
Hurr. — Hurrian
IB — *The Interpreter's Bible,* ed. G. A. Buttrick, 12 vols. (Nashville, 1952-57)
ICC — *The International Critical Commentary,* Edinburgh
IDB — *The Interpreter's Dictionary of the Bible,* ed. G. A. Buttrick, 4 vols. (Nashville, 1962); *Sup,* ed. K. Crim (Nashville, 1976)
IEJ — *Israel Exploration Journal,* Jerusalem
ILC — J. Pedersen, *Israel: Its Life and Culture,* 4 vols. in 2 (Eng. trans., Oxford, 1926-40, ^{5}1963)
ILR — *Israel Law Review,* Jerusalem
impf. — imperfect
impv. — imperative
inf. — infinitive
in loc. — on this passage
Int — *Interpretation,* Richmond
Intro(s). — Introduction(s) (to the)
IPN — M. Noth, *Die israelitischen Personennamen im Rahmen der gemeinsemitischen Namengebung. BWANT* 46[III/10] (1928, repr. 1980)
J — Yahwist source (J^1, earliest Yahwist source)
JA — *Journal asiatique,* Paris
JAC — *Jahrbuch für Antike und Christentum,* Münster
JANES — *Journal of the Ancient Near Eastern Society of Columbia University,* New York
JAOS — *Journal of the American Oriental Society,* Baltimore, Boston, New Haven
JARCE — *Journal of the American Research Center in Egypt,* Boston
Jastrow — M. Jastrow, *A Dictionary of the Targumim, the Talmud Babli and Yerushalmi, and the Midrashic Literature* (1903; repr. 2 vols. in 1, Brooklyn, 1975)
JBL — *Journal of Biblical Literature,* Philadelphia, Missoula, Chico, Atlanta
JBR — *Journal of Bible and Religion,* Boston
JCS — *Journal of Cuneiform Studies,* New Haven, Cambridge, Mass., Philadelphia, Baltimore
JE — Yahwist-Elohist source
Jer. — Jerusalem (Palestinian) Talmud
JESHO — *Journal of Economic and Social History of the Orient,* London
JJS — *Journal of Jewish Studies,* London
JM — P. Joüon and T. Muraoka, *A Grammar of Biblical Hebrew. Subsidia biblica* 14/I-II (Eng. trans. 1991)
JNES — *Journal of Near Eastern Studies,* Chicago
JNSL — *Journal of Northwest Semitic Languages,* Stellenbosch
JPOS — *Journal of the Palestine Oriental Society,* Jerusalem
JQR — *Jewish Quarterly Review,* Philadelphia
JRH — *Journal of Religious History,* Sydney
JSHRZ — *Jüdische Schriften aus hellenistisch-römischer Zeit,* Gütersloh
JSJ — *Journal for the Study of Judaism in the Persian, Hellenistic and Roman Period,* Leiden

JSOT	*Journal for the Study of the OT,* Sheffield
JSOTSup	*Journal for the Study of the OT Supplement,* Sheffield
JSS	*Journal of Semitic Studies,* Manchester
JTS	*Journal of Theological Studies,* Oxford
Jud	*Judaica,* Zurich
K	*Ketib*
KAI	H. Donner and W. Röllig, *Kanaanäische und aramäische Inschriften,* 3 vols. (Wiesbaden, ^{2}1966-69, ^{3}1971-76)
KAR	*Keilschrifttexte aus Assur religiösen Inhalts,* Leipzig
KAT	*Kommentar zum AT,* ed. E. Sellin and J. Herrmann, Leipzig, Gütersloh
KBL	L. Koehler and W. Baumgartner, *Lexicon in Veteris Testamenti Libros* (Leiden, ^{1}1953, ^{2}1958, ^{3}1967–96)
KBo	*Keilschrifttexte aus Boghazköy. WVDOG* (1916–)
KD	C. F. Keil and F. Delitzsch, *Comm. on the OT,* 10 vols. (Eng. trans., repr. Grand Rapids, 1954)
KEHAT	*Kurzgefasstes exegetisches Handbuch zum AT,* ed. O. F. Fridelin (Leipzig, 1812-96)
KHC	*Kurzer Hand-Commentar zum AT,* ed. K. Marti (Freiburg, Leipzig, Tübingen)
KlS	*Kleine Schriften* (A. Alt [Munich, 1953-59, ^{3}1964]; O. Eissfeldt [Tübingen, 1962-79]; K. Elliger [*ThB* 32 (1966)]; E. Meyer [Halle, 1910-24])
KTU	*Die keilalphabetischen Texte aus Ugarit,* I, ed. M. Dietrich, O. Loretz, and J. Sanmartín. *AOAT* 24 (1976)
KuD	*Kerygma und Dogma,* Göttingen
Kuhn	K. G. Kuhn, *Konkordanz zu den Qumrantexten* (Göttingen, 1960); Nachträge, *RevQ* 4 (1963-64) 163-234
l(l).	line(s)
Lane	E. W. Lane, *An Arabic-English Lexicon,* 8 vols. (London, 1863-93, repr. 1968)
Lat.	Latin
LCL	*Loeb Classical Library,* Cambridge, Mass., and London
LD	*Lectio divina,* Paris
Leslau, *Contributions*	W. Leslau, *Ethiopic and South Arabic Contributions to the Hebrew Lexicon* (Los Angeles, 1958)
Leš	*Lešonénu,* Jerusalem
LexÄg	W. Helck and E. Otto, eds., *Lexikon der Ägyptologie* (Wiesbaden, 1975–)
LexHebAram	F. Zorrell, *Lexicon hebraicum et aramaicum Veteris Testamenti* (Rome, 1958, repr. 1968)
LexLingAeth	A. Dillmann, *Lexicon linguae aethiopicae* (Leipzig, 1865)
LexLingAram	E. Vogt, *Lexicon linguae aramaicae Veteris Testamenti documentis antiquis illustratum* (Rome, 1971)
LexSyr	C. Brockelmann, *Lexicon syriacum* (Halle, 1928, ^{2}1968)
LidzEph	M. Lidzbarski, *Ephemeris für semitische Epigraphik* (Giessen, 1900-1915)
Lisowsky	G. Lisowsky, *Konkordanz zum hebräischen AT* (Stuttgart, 1958, ^{2}1966)
lit.	literally
LOT	Z. Ben Ḥayyim, *The Literary and Oral Tradition of Hebrew and Aramaic amongst the Samaritans* (Jerusalem, 1957)
LQ	*Lutheran Quarterly,* Gettysburg, Pa.
LSJ	H. G. Liddell, R. Scott, and H. S. Jones, *A Greek-English Lexicon* (Oxford, ^{9}1940)
LThK	*Lexikon für Theologie und Kirche,* ed. M. Buchberger, 10 vols. (Freiburg, 1930-38); ed. J. Höfer and K. Rahner, 10 vols. and 3 sups. (^{2}1957-68, ^{3}1966-68)
LUÅ	*Lunds Universitets Årsskrift*

LXX	Septuagint (LXX^{A}, Codex Alexandrinus; LXX^{B}, Codex Vaticanus; LXX^{Or}, Origen; LXX^{R}, Lucianic recension; LXX$^{S[1,2]}$, Codex Sinaiticus, correctors 1, 2, etc.)
M	Masada (manuscript)
MAD	*Materials for the Assyrian Dictionary,* Chicago
Mand.	Mandaic
Mandelkern	S. Mandelkern, *Veteris Testamenti Concordantiae* (Tel Aviv, 1971)
MAOG	*Mitteilungen der Altorientalistischen Gesellschaft,* Leipzig
masc.	masculine
MdD	E. S. Drower and R. Macuch, *Mandaic Dictionary* (Oxford, 1963)
MEE	*Materiali epigrafici di Ebla,* Naples
Meyer	R. Meyer, *Hebräische Grammatik,* 4 vols. (Berlin, ^{3}1966-72)
MGWJ	*Monatsschrift für Geschichte und Wissenschaft des Judentums,* Breslau
Midr.	Midrash
MIO	*Mitteilungen des Instituts für Orientforschung,* Berlin
Mish.	Mishnah
Moab.	Moabite
MRS	*Mission de Ras Shamra,* Paris
ms(s).	manuscript(s)
MSL	*Materialen zum sumerischen Lexikon,* Rome
MT	Masoretic Text
MTS	*Münchener theologische Studien,* Munich
Mur	Wadi Murabbaʿat text(s)
Mus	*Muséon,* Louvain
MUSJ	*Mélanges de l'Université St.-Joseph,* Beirut
MüSt	*Münsterschwarzacher Studien*
n(n).	note(s)
Nab.	Nabatean
NBSS	T. Nöldeke, *Neue Beiträge zur semitischen Sprachwissenschaft* (Strassburg, 1910)
NCBC	*New Century Bible Commentary,* Grand Rapids and London
NEAJT	*Northeast Asia Journal of Theology,* Tokyo
NEB	*Die Neue Echter-Bibel,* Würzburg
NedTT	*Nederlands theologisch Tijdschrift,* Wageningen
NERT	*Near Eastern Religious Texts Relating to the OT,* ed. W. Beyerlin. *OTL* (Eng. trans. 1978)
NESE	R. Degen, W. W. Müller, and W. Röllig, *Neue Ephemeris für Semitische Epigraphik,* 1972-78
NGWG	*Nachrichten von der Gesellschaft der Wissenschaften zu Göttingen*
NICOT	*The New International Commentary on the OT,* Grand Rapids
NJB	New Jerusalem Bible (Garden City, N.Y., 1985)
no(s).	number(s)
NovTSup	*Novum Testamentum, Supplements,* Leiden
NRSV	New Revised Standard Version (New York, 1989)
N.S.	new series
NSS	J. Barth, *Die Nominalbildung in den semitischen Sprachen* (^{2}1894, repr. Hildesheim, 1967)
NT	New Testament, Neues Testament, etc.
NTS	*New Testament Studies,* Cambridge
NTT	*Norsk teologisk Tidsskrift,* Oslo
obj.	object
OBO	*Orbis biblicus et orientalis,* Fribourg, Göttingen
OBT	*Overtures to Biblical Theology,* Philadelphia, Minneapolis

obv.	obverse of a papyrus or tablet
OIP	*Oriental Institute Publications,* Chicago
OL	Old Latin (OL^S, Fragmenta Sangallensia Prophetarum)
OLP	*Orientalia lovaniensia periodica,* Louvain
OLZ	*Orientalistische Literaturzeitung,* Leipzig, Berlin
Or	*Orientalia,* Rome
OrAnt	*Oriens antiquus,* Rome
OSA	Old South Arabic
OT	Old Testament, Oude Testament, etc.
OTA	*Old Testament Abstracts,* Washington, D.C.
OTL	*The Old Testament Library,* Philadelphia, Louisville
OTS	*Oudtestamentische Studiën,* Leiden
OTWSA	*Ou testamentiese werkgemeenskap in Suid-Afrika,* Pretoria
p(p).	page(s)
P	Priestly source (P^G, Priestly *Grundschrift* ["basic material"]; P^S, secondary Priestly source)
PAAJR	*Proceedings of the American Academy for Jewish Research,* New York
Palmyr.	Palmyrene
Pap.	Papyrus
par.	parallel/and parallel passages
pass.	passive
PEQ	*Palestine Exploration Quarterly,* London
perf.	perfect
Pes.	Pesiqta
Phil.-hist. Kl.	Philosophische-historische Klasse
Phoen.	Phoenician
pl(s).	plate(s)
pl.	plural
PLO	*Porta linguarum orientalium,* Wiesbaden
PN	Personal name
PNPI	J. K. Stark, *Personal Names in Palmyrene Inscriptions* (Oxford, 1971)
PNU	F. Grondähl, *Die Personennamen der Texte aus Ugarit. StPohl* 1 (1967)
POS	*Pretoria Oriental Series,* Leiden
POT	*De Prediking van het OT,* Nijkerk
prep.	preposition
PRU	*Le Palais royal d'Ugarit,* ed. C. F.-A. Schaeffer and J. Nougayrol. *MRS*
ptcp.	participle
Pun.	Punic
PW	A. Pauly and G. Wissowa, *Real-Encyclopädie der classischen Altertumswissenschaft,* 6 vols. (Stuttgart, 1839-52); Sup, 11 vols. (1903-56); ser. 2, 10 vols. (1914-48)
Pyr.	K. Sethe, *Die altägyptischen Pyramidentexte,* 4 vols. (Leipzig, 1908-22)
Q	Qumran scroll (preceded by arabic numeral designating cave)
Q	*Qere*
Qat.	Qatabanian
QD	*Quaestiones disputatae,* Florence
QuadSem	*Quaderni di Semitistica,* Florence
r.	reverse (side of a tablet, coin, etc.)
R	Redactor (R^D, Deuteronomistic; R^P, Priestly; R^J, Yahwist)
R.	Rabbi
RA	*Revue d'assyriologie et d'archéologie orientale,* Paris
RAC	*Reallexikon für Antike und Christentum,* ed. T. Klauser (Stuttgart, 1950–)
RAI	*Rencontre Assyriologique Internationale,* Paris

RAO	*Recuil d'archéologie orientale,* Paris
RÄR	H. Bonnet, *Reallexikon der ägyptischen Religionsgeschichte* (Berlin, 1952, [2]1971)
RB	*Revue biblique,* Paris
REJ	*Revue des études juives,* Paris
repr.	reprint, reprinted
RES	*Répertoire d'épigraphie sémitique* (Paris, 1900–) (with number of text)
rev.	revised, revision
RevBibl	*Revista bíblica,* Buenos Aires
RevQ	*Revue de Qumrân,* Paris
RGG	*Die Religion in Geschichte und Gegenwart* (Tübingen, [2]1927-31, ed. H. Gunkel and L. Zscharnack, 5 vols.; [3]1957-65, ed. K. Galling, 6 vols.)
RHPR	*Revue d'histoire et de philosophie religieuses,* Strasbourg, Paris
RHR	*Revue de l'histoire des religions,* Paris
RIDA	*Revue internationale des droits d'antiquité,* Brussels
RivB	*Rivista biblica,* Rome
RLA	*Reallexikon der Assyriologie,* ed. E. Ebeling and B. Meissner (Berlin, 1932–)
RM	*Die Religion der Menschheit,* Stuttgart
RS	Ras Shamra text
RSF	*Rivista di studi Fenici,* Rome
RSO	*Rivista degli studi orientali,* Rome
RSP	*Ras Shamra Parallels: The Texts from Ugarit and the Hebrew Bible,* ed. L. R. Fisher et al., I, *AnOr* 49 (1972); II, *AnOr* 50 (1975); III, *AnOr* 51 (1981)
RSPT	*Revue des sciences philosophiques et théologiques,* Paris
RSR	*Recherches de science religieuse,* Paris
RSV	Revised Standard Version (New York, 1946, 1952)
rto.	recto, on the obverse of a papyrus or tablet
RTP	*Revue de théologie et de philosophie,* Lausanne
RVV	*Religionsgeschichtliche Versuche und Vorarbeiten,* Giessen
Ryckmans	G. Ryckmans, *Les noms propres sud-sémitiques,* 3 vols. (Leiden, 1934-35)
Sab.	Sabaic
Saf.	Safaitic
SAHG	A. Falkenstein and W. von Soden, *Sumerische und akkadische Hymnen und Gebeten* (Zurich, 1953)
Sam.	Samaritan
SANT	*Studien zum Alten und Neuen Testament,* Munich
SAOC	*Studies in Ancient Oriental Civilization,* Chicago
SAW	*Sitzungsberichte der Österreichischen Akademie der Wissenschaften in Wien,* Vienna
SB	*Sources bibliques,* Paris
SBAW	*Sitzungsberichte der Bayerischen Akademie der Wissenschaften in München*
SBB	*Stuttgarter biblische Beiträge*
SBFLA	*Studii biblici franciscani liber annus,* Jerusalem
SBL	Society of Biblical Literature
SBLDS	*SBL Dissertation Series,* Missoula, Chico, Atlanta
SBLMS	*SBL Monograph Series,* Missoula, Chico, Atlanta
SBLSBS	*SBL Sources for Biblical Study,* Chico, Atlanta
SBLSCS	*SBL Septuagint and Cognate Studies,* Missoula, Chico, Atlanta
SBLSP	*SBL Seminar Papers,* Missoula, Chico, Atlanta
SBS	*Stuttgarter Bibel-Studien*
SBT	*Studies in Biblical Theology,* London, Naperville
ScrHier	*Scripta hierosolymitana,* Jerusalem

SEÅ	*Svensk exegetisk Årsbok,* Lund
Sem.	Semitic
Sem	*Semitica,* Paris
ser.	series
Seux	J. M. Seux, *Epithètes royales akkadiens et sumériennes* (Paris, 1967)
SFS	*Studia Francisci Scholten memoriae dicata,* Leiden
sg.	singular
SHANE	*Studies in the History of the Ancient Near East,* Leiden
ShM	*Shnaton le-miqra ule-ḥeker ha-mizraḥ ha-kadum (Shnationian Annual for Biblical and Ancient Near Eastern Studies),* Jerusalem
SJLA	*Studies in Judaism in Late Antiquity,* Leiden
SNVAO	*Skrifter utgitt av det Norske Videnskaps-Akademi i Oslo*
SPIB	*Scripta Pontificii Instituti Biblici,* Rome
SR	*Studies in Religion/Sciences religieuses,* Toronto
SS	*Studi semitici,* Rome
SSAW	*Sitzungsberichte der Sächsischen Akademie der Wissenschaften zu Leipzig,* Phil.-hist. Kl.
SSN	*Studia semitica neerlandica,* Assen
SSS	*Semitic Studies Series,* Leiden
ST	*Studia theologica,* Lund, Århus
St.-B.	H. L. Strack and P. Billerbeck, *Kommentar zum NT aus Talmud und Midrasch,* 6 vols. (Munich, 1922-61)
StBoT	*Studien zu den Boğazköy-Texten,* Wiesbaden
STDJ	*Studies on the Texts of the Desert of Judah,* Leiden, Grand Rapids
StOr	*Studia orientalia,* Helsinki
StPohl	*Studia Pohl,* Rome
StudGen	*Studium Generale,* Berlin
subj.	subject
subst.	substantive
suf.	suffix
Sum.	Sumerian
SUNT	*Studien zur Umwelt des NTs,* Göttingen
Sup	Supplement(s) (to)
s.v.	*sub voce (vocibus),* under the word(s)
SVT	*Supplements to VT,* Leiden
SWBA	*Social World of Biblical Antiquity,* Sheffield
SWJT	*Southwestern Journal of Theology,* Seminary Hill, Texas
Synt	C. Brockelmann, *Hebräische Syntax* (Neukirchen-Vluyn, 1956)
Syr.	Syriac
Syr	*Syria. Revue d'art oriental et d'archéologie,* Paris
Targ.	Targum; Targ.^{J}, Targ. Jonathan from Codex Reuchlinianus
TAVO-B	*Tübinger Atlas des Vorderen Orients, Beihefte,* Wiesbaden
TBT	*The Bible Today*
TCL	*Textes cunéiformes du Musée du Louvre,* 31 vols. (Paris, 1910-67)
TDNT	*Theological Dictionary of the NT,* ed. G. Kittel and G. Friedrich, 9 vols. plus index vol. (Eng. trans., Grand Rapids, 1964-76)
TDOT	*Theological Dictionary of the OT,* ed. G. J. Botterweck, H. Ringgren, and H.-J. Fabry (Eng. trans., Grand Rapids, 1974–)
ThArb	*Theologische Arbeiten,* Berlin
ThB	*Theologische Bücherei,* Munich
ThS	*Theologische Studien,* Zurich
ThV	*Theologische Versuche,* Berlin
Tigr.	Tigriña

TLOT	*Theological Lexicon of the OT,* ed. E. Jenni and C. Westermann, 3 vols. (Eng. trans., Peabody, Mass., 1997)
TLZ	*Theologische Literaturzeitung,* Leipzig, Berlin
TM	Tell Mardikh-Ebla tablets
TOB	Traduction oecoumenique de la Bible
Tos.	Tosephta
TOTC	*Tyndale Old Testament Commentaries,* London, Downers Grove
TP	*Theologie und Philosophie,* Freiburg im Breisgau
TQ	*Theologische Quartalschrift,* Tübingen, Stuttgart
trans.	translation, translated by
TRE	*Theologische Realenzyklopädie,* ed. G. Krause, G. Müller, and H. R. Balz, 22 vols. (Berlin, 1977-92)
TRu	*Theologische Rundschau,* Tübingen
TS	*Theological Studies,* Woodstock, Md.
TSK	*Theologische Studien und Kritiken,* Hamburg, Gotha, Leipzig
TSSI	J. C. L. Gibson, *Textbook of Syrian Semitic Inscriptions,* 3 vols. (Oxford, 1975-82)
TTS	*Trierer theologische Studien*
TTZ	*Trierer theologische Zeitschrift*
TU	*Texte und Untersuchungen der altchristlichen Literatur,* Leipzig, Berlin
TUAT	*Texte aus der Umwelt des ATs,* Gütersloh
TWNT	*Theologisches Wörterbuch zum NT,* ed. G. Kittel and G. Friedrich, 10 vols. plus index (Stuttgart, 1933-79)
TynB	*Tyndale Bulletin,* London
TZ	*Theologische Zeitschrift,* Basel
UF	*Ugarit-Forschungen,* Neukirchen-Vluyn
Ugar.	Ugaritic
Univ.	University
Urk.	*Urkunden des ägyptischen Altertums,* ed. G. Steindorff (Leipzig, Berlin, 1903–)
UT	C. H. Gordon, *Ugaritic Textbook. AnOr* 38 (1965, ^{2}1967)
UUÅ	*Uppsala universitets årsskrift*
v(v).	verse(s)
VAB	*Vorderasiatische Bibliothek,* 7 vols. (Leipzig, 1907-16)
VD	*Verbum domini,* Rome
VG	C. Brockelmann, *Grundriss der vergleichenden Grammatik der semitischen Sprachen,* 2 vols. (1908-13, repr. Hildesheim, 1961)
vo.	verso, on the reverse of a papyrus or tablet
VT	*Vetus Testamentum,* Leiden
Vulg.	Vulgate
Wagner	M. Wagner, *Die lexikalischen und grammatikalischen Aramaismen im alttestamentlichen Hebräisch. BZAW* 96 (1966)
WbÄS	A. Erman and H. Grapow, *Wörterbuch der ägyptischen Sprache,* 6 vols. (Leipzig, 1926-31, repr. 1963)
WbMyth	*Wörterbuch der Mythologie,* ed. H. W. Haussig (Stuttgart, 1965–)
WbTigr	E. Littmann and M. Höfner, *Wörterbuch der Tigre Sprache* (Wiesbaden, 1962)
Wehr	H. Wehr, *A Dictionary of Modern Written Arabic,* ed. J. M. Cowan (Ithaca, 1961, ^{3}1971, ^{4}1979)
Whitaker	R. E. Whitaker, *A Concordance of the Ugaritic Language* (Cambridge, Mass., 1972)
WMANT	*Wissenschaftliche Monographien zum Alten und Neuen Testament,* Neukirchen-Vluyn

WO	*Die Welt des Orients,* Göttingen
WTM	J. Levy, *Wörterbuch über die Talmudim und Midraschim,* 4 vols. (Leipzig, ^{2}1924, repr. 1963)
WuD	*Wort und Dienst,* Bielefeld
WUS	J. Aistleitner, *Wörterbuch der ugaritischen Sprache. BSAW,* Phil.-hist. Kl. 106/3 (1963, ^{4}1974)
WZ Greifswald	*Wissenschaftliche Zeitschrift,* Greifswald
WZ Halle	*Wissenschaftliche Zeitschrift der Martin-Luther-Universität Halle-Wittenberg,* Halle
WZKMBeih.	*Beihefte zur Wiener Zeitschrift für die Kunde des Morgenlandes,* Vienna
ZA	*Zeitschrift für Assyriologie,* Leipzig, Berlin
ZÄS	*Zeitschrift für ägyptische Sprache und Altertumskunde,* Leipzig, Berlin
ZAW	*Zeitschrift für die alttestamentliche Wissenschaft,* Giessen, Berlin
ZBK	*Zürcher Bibelkommentare,* Zurich, Stuttgart
ZDMG	*Zeitschrift der Deutschen Morgenländischen Gesellschaft,* Leipzig, Wiesbaden
ZDPV	*Zeitschrift des Deutschen Palästina-Vereins,* Leipzig, Stuttgart, Wiesbaden
ZEE	*Zeitschrift für evangelische Ethik,* Gütersloh
ZNW	*Zeitschrift für die neutestamentliche Wissenschaft,* Giessen, Berlin
ZTK	*Zeitschrift für Theologie und Kirche,* Tübingen
→	cross-reference within this Dictionary
<	derived from
>	whence derived, to
*	theoretical form

TRANSLITERATION

VOWELS

◌ַ	a
◌ֲ	^{a}
◌ָ	ā
◌ָה	â
◌ָיו	āyw
◌ַי	ay
◌ָי	āy
◌ֶ	e
◌ֱ	^{e}
◌ֶי	ey
◌ֵ	ē
◌ֵי	ê
◌ְ	^{e}
◌ִ	i
◌ִי	î
◌ִיּ	îy
◌ָ	o
◌ֳ	^{o}
◌ֹ	ō
וֹ	ô
◌ֻ	u, ū
וּ	û

CONSONANTS

א	ʼ
בּ	b
ב	ḇ
גּ	g
ג	ḡ
דּ	d
ד	ḏ
ה, הּ	h
ו	w
ז	z
ח	ḥ
ט	ṭ
י	y
כּ, ךּ	k
כ, ך	ḵ
ל	l
מ, ם	m
נ, ן	n
ס	s
ע	ʻ
פּ	p
פ, ף	p̄
צ, ץ	ṣ
ק	q
ר	r
שׂ	ś
שׁ	š
תּ	t
ת	ṯ

עזז ʿzz; עֱזוּז ʿ*ezûz;* עִזּוּז *ʿizzûz;* עַז *ʿaz;* עוֹז/עֹז *ʿôz/ʿōz;* מָעוֹז *māʿôz*

I. 1. Etymology, Occurrences, and Meaning; 2. LXX. II. Verb. III. Nouns: 1. *ʿezûz, ʿizzûz;* 2. *ʿaz;* 3. *ʿōz;* 4. *māʿôz.* IV. Dead Sea Scrolls.

I. 1. *Etymology, Occurrences, and Meaning.* The root *ʿzz* is common Semitic. Ugaritic uses it as a verb, noun, and adjective in the sense of "be strong," "strengthen," "strong," "strength," etc.[1] Akk. *ezēzu/ezzu* means "be angry," "be powerful," "be(come) enraged."[2] OSA *ʿzz* means "fortify, strengthen," and *ʿzt* means "strength."[3] The meaning of Old Aram. *ʿzz/ʿzyz* corresponds to Ugaritic usage.[4] The root occurs also in Jewish Aramaic, Mandaic, and Ethiopic. The Qumran Scrolls use both verbal and substantival forms of *ʿzz.* The meaning is essentially constant: "be/become/make strong, powerful," "strength, power." There are 11 occurrences of the verb in the OT, all in the qal or hiphil. Intensive stems are found in other Semitic languages. In Hebrew a number of nouns derive from *ʿzz: ʿezûz,* "strength, power" (3 times); *ʿizzûz,* "powerful" (twice); *ʿaz,* "strength," "strong" (22 times); and *ʿōz,* "strength, power, might" (94 times), which can sometimes take on the meaning "(strong) defense," "(great) security," "refuge," "protection." The derivation from *ʿwz* of forms having this meaning has been suggested frequently but is difficult to prove etymologically.[5] The same is true of *māʿôz* (36 times), which means "refuge, fortress," but also "strength" (Ps. 27:1).[6] Several proper names appear in extrabiblical texts;[7] in the OT we find: *ʿuzzāʾ, ʿuzzâ, ʿāzāz, ʿazazyāhû, ʿuzzî, ʿuzzîyāʾ, ʿuzzîyāh(û), ʿazîʾēl, ʿuzzîʾēl, ʿazîzāʾ, ʿazzān,* and *maʿazyâ.*[8] We also find *yʿz,* a by-form of *ʿzz,* in the niphal ptcp. *nôʿāz* (Isa. 33:19).

ʿzz. Y. Avishur, "Biblical Words and Phrases in the Light of Their Akkadian Parallels," *ShM* 2 (1977) 11-19; W. Beyerlin, *Die Rettung der Bedrängten in den Feindpsalmen der Einzelnen auf institutionelle Zusammenhänge untersucht.* FRLANT 99 (1970); M. Dahood, "The Composite Divine Names in Ps. 89,16-17 and 140,9," *Bibl* 61 (1980) 277-78; D. Eichhorn, *Gott als Fels, Burg und Zuflucht. EH* XXIII/4 (1972); E. Gerstenberger, "עוּז *ʿûz* to seek refuge," *TLOT* II, 846-48; W. Grundmann, "δύναμις," *TDNT,* II, 284-317; idem, "ἰσχύω," *TDNT,* III, 397-402; V. Hamp, "Ps 8,2b.3," *BZ* 16 (1972) 115-20; P. Hugger, *Jahwe, meine Zuflucht. MüSt* 13 (1971); S. E. Loewenstamm, "'The Lord Is My Strength and My Glory,'" *VT* 19 (1969) 464-70; A. Malamat, "Josiah's Bid for Armageddon," *JANES* 5 (1973) 267-78; W. Michaelis, "κράτος," *TDNT,* III, 905-15; Y. Muffs, "Two Comparative Lexical Studies," *JANES* 5 (1973) 287-98, esp. 295-98; C. Toll, "Ausdrücke für 'Kraft' im AT mit besonderer Rücksicht auf die Wurzel BRK," *ZAW* 94 (1982) 111-23; A. S. van der Woude, "עזז *ʿzz* to be strong," *TLOT,* II, 868-72.

1. *ʿz, WUS,* no. 2021; *UT,* no. 1835.
2. *AHw,* I, 269-70.
3. Biella, 360.
4. *KAI* 26 has 6 occurrences; cf. *DNSI,* II, 835.
5. So van der Woude, 869. Cf. *HAL,* II, 806; Gerstenberger.
6. Cf. *DNSI,* II, 835. *HAL* (II, 610) is uncertain, citing Arab. *māʿāḏ,* "place of refuge," and proposing the cj. **māʿôzen* in Isa. 23:11; but cf. 1QIs[a].
7. *KAI; AP,* 297b; *BMAP,* 306b.
8. See *IPN.*

2. *LXX.* For ʿzz and its various derivatives, the LXX uses forms from the lexical field of *dýnamis, ischýs,* and *krátos;* for the semantic domain of "refuge," it uses *boēthós* or *hyperaspistḗs.*

II. Verb. Only in late texts do we find verbal forms of ʿzz with the meaning "be strong" (qal, 9 times) or "strengthen" (hiphil, twice). In the Dtr framework surrounding the stories of the book of Judges, the ascendancy of one personal entity over another is a commonplace: "Israel" is subjected to the tyranny of a foreign king, or the deliverer raised up by Yahweh triumphs over the tyrant. Twice this situation is represented by the expression "the hand of one was stronger than [NRSV 'prevailed over'] the hand of the other." First it is Othniel whose hand prevails over Cushan-rishathaim (Jgs. 3:10, *wattāʿōz yāḏô ʿal*), then it is the Midianites who prevail over Israel (6:2).

In other contexts (without *yāḏ*), too, people can grow strong. They may rebel against Yahweh by oppressing the poor and needy. The author of a postexilic lament fragment in Ps. 9/10 prays: *qûmâ yhwh ʾal- yāʿōz ʾ^{e}nôš,* "Rise up, Yahweh! Do not let mortals prevail" (9:20[Eng. v. 19]). Although it is difficult to assign Ps. 52 to a genre, it is clear that the beleaguered psalmist is speaking of his oppressor, after God has given him refuge and affirmation in the temple. From this position, the psalmist can even mock the conduct of the evil rich man, who did not take *māʿôz* in God but trusted in abundant riches (his influence) and became mighty (*yāʿōz,* v. 9[7]) in his wickedness. V. 7(5) voices the assurance that God's destruction will strike down the villain.

The lengthy Ps. 68 comprises both hymnic elements and petitions. The latter include a prayer that God will intervene forcefully on behalf of the faithful: "Your God has displayed might for you; show your strength, O God, as you have done for us before" (v. 29[28]; the first stich is often read "Summon your might, O God," with the versions; but the text makes sense without emendation).

These texts touch on Yahweh's power to guide history; Ps. 89:14(13) (in the context of vv. 10ff.[9ff.]) extols Yahweh's creative power, documented in victory over the forces of chaos (*tāʿōz yāḏ^{e}ḵā,* par. to "mighty arm" and "high right hand"). Personified Wisdom, present at God's individual acts of creation, witnessed the establishment of the fountains of the deep (Prov. 8:28, *baʿ^{a}zôz ʿînôṯ t^{e}hôm;* we would expect a hiphil or piel, par. with ʾmṣ piel).[9]

Other passages in wisdom literature use ʿzz in secular contexts. Eccl. 7:19 declares that wisdom gives strength to the wise *(haḥoḵmâ tāʿōz leḥāḵām),* indeed even greater strength than that of ten potentates *(šallîṭ)* in a city. The seductive woman against whom Proverbs warns is able to give her face a strong, firm, "provocative"[10] expression (Prov. 7:13, *hēʿēzâ pāneyhā*). That this text describes disapproved conduct is shown by the similar maxim in 21:29, which contrasts the *ʾîš rāšāʿ* to the *yāšār:* the former puts on a "strong" face *(hēʿēz . . . b^{e}pānāyw),* expressing the willpower to carry out wickedness. "Make one's face strong" has also been translated "make bold" or "inso-

9. Cf. K. Aartun, *WO* 4 (1968) 297: "when the fountains of the deep flowed" (Ugar. *ǵdd*).
10. O. Plöger, *Sprüche Salomos. BK* XVII (1984), 74.

lent." This meaning would be appropriate for the hapax legomenon *ʿam nôʿāz* (from *yʿz*, a by-form of *ʿzz;* see above), "an insolent people," in Isa. 33:19, in the context of a secondary oracle of salvation: on the day of salvation Israel will no longer have to look on the arrogant, impudent occupation forces.

Finally, Dnl. 11:12 uses *ʿzz* to describe the weakness of Ptolemy IV against Antiochus III: he will win victories but will not prevail *(lōʾ yāʿôz).*

Thus *ʿzz* is used in both theological and secular contexts. Theological contexts speak of Yahweh's *ʿzz* in history and the natural realm; secular contexts exhibit a tendency to associate strength and power more with violence and oppression than with safety and security.

III. Nouns.

1. *ʿᵉzûz, ʿizzûz.* The nouns *ʿᵉzûz* (3 times) and *ʿizzûz* (twice) predicate strength and power to the God of Israel; they can be exercised for the benefit of God's people, but nevertheless clearly reveal the ambivalence of the root, since they can also wreak havoc. The entrance liturgy of Ps. 24 includes the question: Who is *meleḵ hakkāḇôḏ?* The answer is: *yhwh ʿizzûz wᵉgibbôr,* further qualified by *gibbôr milḥāmâ.* This text uses *ʿizzûz* for Yahweh's victorious military power. In Deutero-Isaiah's message of salvation, the same victorious power of Yahweh finds vivid expression in the description of how, at the beginning of Israel's history, the hosts of Egypt are destined for destruction: Yahweh is absolutely and fundamentally superior to chariot and horse, army and warrior (Isa. 43:17, *ḥayil wᵉʿizzûz*). Isa. 42:18-25 speaks of the outpouring of the heat of Yahweh's anger on his people, manifested in the "violence of war" (*ʿᵉzûz milḥāmâ,* v. 25). The "historical" Ps. 78 uses *ʿᵉzûzô* to extol Yahweh's great and mighty deeds in history (v. 4; par. to *niplᵉʾôṯāyw*). Finally, we find the same statement in a hymn (Ps. 145:6) that juxtaposes "the might of your awesome deeds" *(ʿᵉzûz nôrᵉʾōṯeyḵā)* and "your great deeds" *(gᵉḏûllōṯeyḵā,* with *K),* which are to be proclaimed and declared *(ʾmr* and *spr).*

2. *ʿaz.* We find *ʿaz* used as both noun and adjective; the predicative use of the adjective exhibits prominent verbal government. The context is almost always secular. The earliest occurrence appears to be Gen. 49:7, in the so-called Blessing of Jacob, where the curse on Simeon and Levi is ascribed to their fierce anger and cruel wrath *(ʾārûr ʾappām kî ʿāz,* par. *qšh).* This harsh hostility in personal relationships is expressed sometimes with *ʿaz pānîm:* in Dt. 28:50, in response to the disobedience of the people, Yahweh unleashes a "grim-faced" foreign nation; in Dnl. 8:23 Antiochus IV Epiphanes is called *meleḵ ʿaz-pānîm.* Even without *pānîm, ʿaz* can mean "powerful" in a menacing sense: in Nu. 13:28 (J), e.g., the spies extol the land they have been exploring, but caution that the people living there are "strong" and their cities well fortified *(bᵉṣūrôṯ).* The territory of the Ammonites, who refuse to grant Israel passage and whose king is put to the sword in retaliation, is described nevertheless as strong and secure in the sense of being fortified (Nu. 21:24 [E]; many modern exegetes prefer the LXX reading: *yaʿzēr* as the name of a border point). Isaiah's oracle against Egypt declares that it will be delivered into the hand of harsh masters and a *meleḵ ʿaz* (Isa. 19:4).

Ps. 18:2-31(1-30) glorifies Yahweh (among other reasons) for delivering the psalmist from a strong enemy (v. 18[17] = 2 S. 22:18). At the eschaton, a thanksgiving hymn within the Apocalypse of Isaiah foresees that a strong people *('am-'āz)* will glorify Yahweh, and ruthless nations *(gôyîm 'ārîṣîm)* will fear Yahweh (Isa. 25:3). Even this passage preserves the notion that strength is menacing, although it must submit to one who is stronger still. For example, the persecuted psalmist complains that *'azzîm* are stirring up strife against him (Ps. 59:4[3], par. "enemies," "workers of evil," and "the bloodthirsty") and calls on Yahweh for help and deliverance. In an oracle of judgment in Trito-Isaiah that recalls preexilic prophecy, Isa. 56:11 castigates the mighty (here the leaders of the nation) as greedy dogs that never have enough (*'azzê-nepeš,* lit. "strong of life" or "strong of hunger").[11] In Ezekiel the arrogance of the strong comes under Yahweh's judgment (7:24, *gᵉ'ôn 'azzîm;* cf. Am. 5:9, where Yahweh "makes destruction flash out against the strong ['*az*]" [NRSV]).

In very different portions of the OT, the exodus tradition uses *'az* as an adjective to describe the violence of the natural elements. In Ex. 14:21 (J), for example, Yahweh drives the sea back by a strong east wind *(bᵉrûaḥ qāḏîm 'azzâ).* In Isa. 43:16 Yahweh is introduced as having total sovereignty over the natural elements: he makes a way in the sea and a path in the mighty waters *(bᵉmayim 'azzîm).* The postexilic historical summary in Neh. 9 speaks of the destruction of the Egyptians who pursued the Israelites escaping from Egypt: Yahweh threw them into the mighty waters like a stone (v. 11).

Finally, *'az* finds employment in wisdom aphorisms. Samson's riddle and its solution (Jgs. 14:14 and 18) are well known. In v. 14 *'az* is used as a personal noun: "the strong one"; in v. 18 it is used as a comparative adjective. The only text where *'az* appears as a feminine plural (used as an abstract noun) is Prov. 18:23 (possibly dating from the mid-monarchy), which contrasts the rich and the poor. The rich answer the entreaties of the poor with harshness *('azzôṯ);* in other words, they spurn them. The same collection contains another bicolon (21:14) that states that a bribe in secret averts violent anger *(ḥēmâ 'azzâ).* A numerical proverb (30:25) points to the ants, "a people without strength *('am lō'-'āz),*" who nevertheless understand the need to provide their food (for the winter) during the summer. Despite their weakness and humble station, they are endowed with wisdom (30:24). According to Cant. 8:6, love is as "strong as death," a statement set in parallel with "passion *(qin'â)* fierce as *šᵉ'ôl.*"

3. *'ōz.* a. *Psalms.* Of the 94 occurrences of *'ōz,* 44 are in the Psalms. The range of meanings is wide: "strength," "power," "might," but also "refuge." The noun appears occasionally in parallel with *mā'ôz* (Ps. 28:8). It can be used both literally and figuratively.

Creation hymns and texts that allude to the theology of creation extol Yahweh's creative power: it can bring to pass works of power and might and lend strength to both the people and the individual believer, making them strong. Somewhat obscure is the

11. → IX, 506.

"founding" (*ysd* piel) of *ʿōz* from the mouths of babes and infants (8:3[2]), an *ʿōz* that prevails against enemies like a bulwark.[12] The praise that resounds in the sanctuary takes place at the point of contact between heaven and earth, so that we hear the summons *hallᵉlûhû birqîaʿ ʿuzzô,* "praise him in the firmament of his power" or "praise him in his mighty firmament" (150:1). With his might *(bᵉʿozzᵉḵā)* he divided the sea in the act of creation (74:13); with his mighty arm *(bizrôaʿ ʿuzzᵉḵā)* he scattered the forces of chaos (89:11[10]). His commanding voice is "a mighty voice" (*qôl ʿōz,* 68:34[33]; cf. Ps. 29). Power over nature and power over history are based on power in the skies, inaccessible to mortals (68:35[34], par. *gaʾᵃwāṯô,* "his majesty"). This universal power he gives *(nāṯan)* to his people (68:36[35], *ʿōz* par. *taʿᵃṣumôṯ,* as in 29:11). All creatures in heaven and earth are called on to acknowledge (by worshiping) this mighty God: *hāḇû lᵉyhwh kāḇôḏ wāʿōz,* "ascribe to Yahweh glory and strength" (29:1; cf. 96:7; 1 Ch. 16:28; Ps. 68:35[34], *tᵉnû ʿōz lēʾlōhîm*). This figure of speech probably does not refer to a cultic investiture of Yahweh but to confession and affirmation of the power and glory Yahweh inherently possesses. This affirmation (learned or heard, 62:12a [11a]) is common knowledge: *ʿōz* belongs to Yahweh (v. 12b[11b]). Nevertheless, a hymn to Yahweh as king can say that Yahweh has robed himself *(lāḇēš)* in majesty and girded himself (*ʾzr* hithpael) with *ʿōz* (93:1). The worshiper pouring out a lament in the sanctuary can look on God there and behold (physically) God's power and glory (63:3[2], *lirʾôṯ ʿuzzᵉḵā ûḵᵉḇôḏeḵā;* cf. 96:6, *ʿōz wᵉṯipʾereṯ bᵉmiqdāšô;* also 1 Ch. 16:27), so that it is reasonable to think of a visual representation. But the possibility of individual ceremonial acts cannot alter the fact that no one can give or bring Yahweh anything that he does not already have.

In laments the motif of trust leads to affirmation of Yahweh's greatness and power, on which one can rely; the poet also prays for a demonstration of God's power to save. In 62:8(7) the meaning of *ʿōz* modulates to the equivalent of Eng. "refuge," since the beset psalmist finds in Yahweh *ṣûr-ʿuzzî,* the "rock of my might" (or "my mighty rock"). In parallel are words like "salvation," "honor," and "refuge" (vv. 3,12[2,11]). The psalmist miraculously experiences Yahweh as a "strong refuge"; in this experience he himself is a kind of portent to many (71:7, *kᵉmôpēṯ hāyîṯî lᵉrabbîm wᵉʾattâ maḥᵃsî-ʿōz*). Another psalmist confesses: "You are my refuge *(maḥseh),* a strong tower *(migdal-ʿōz)* against the enemy" (61:4[3]). The persecuted supplicant sees in Yahweh a strong deliverer (140:8[7], *ʿōz yᵉšûʿāṯî*). Finally, the psalmist can pray for Yahweh to give his strength *(tᵉnāh-ʿuzzᵉḵā)* to his servant (86:16).

Yahweh can be addressed directly as "my strength" (59:10,18[9,17]; in v. 10[9] *ʿuzzô* should be emended to *ʿuzzî* with LXX, Targ., and Heb. mss., as well as the analogy of v. 18[17]; in both verses the parallel is *miśgāḇ*). At the same time, in the oath section of the lament *ʿuzzᵉḵā* can be objectified as the subject of praise (59:17[16], with *mānôs* and *miśgāḇ* in parallel). The speaker of a lament remembers the great and wonderful acts of Yahweh in nature and history (77:12[11]), acts that imbue the worshiper

12. H.-J. Kraus, *Psalms 1–59* (Eng. trans. 1988), 181-82; cf. Hamp; for another interpretation → VI, 108.

with confidence and trust. The psalmist also knows that Yahweh has made known (*yd'* hiphil) his *'ōz* among the peoples (v. 15[14]).

Lament and petition (and the supposed priestly oracle of salvation) are followed by praise and thanksgiving, in which God's saving power is proclaimed (e.g., 28:7-8[6-7]). In Ps. 30:8(7) the text should probably be emended to *lᵉharᵉrê 'ōz* (with Targ.) and the verb read as *he'ᵉmadṯānî:* "By your favor, O Yahweh, you have established me on a strong mountain [or: 'firm ground']." Here *'ōz* describes the nature of the firm foundation on which Yahweh has set the psalmist, whose life was threatened. The use of *'ōz* in 138:3 is not without its problems. Aquila (see also Jerome) has probably preserved the correct interpretation: *tarḥîḇēnî,* "you give me great space, in my soul [or: 'life'] there is strength."

As we would expect, hymns also extol the strength and power of God. Because of Yahweh's great power *(bᵉrōḇ 'uzzᵉḵā),* even Yahweh's enemies must ultimately do him homage (66:3; *kḥš* must be translated in this sense).[13] Yahweh is also praised for summoning his strength for his people (68:29[28]). This text is not easy to translate. The MT means: "Your God has summoned might for you [taking the suf. of *'uzzeḵā* as an objective gen.], the strength of God, which you have done [or: 'used'] for us." The phrase *'uzzâ 'ᵉlōhîm* should be emended to *'ōz hā'ᵉlōhîm;* the versions suggest reading *ṣawwēh* instead of *ṣiwwâ* and *'ᵉlōheyḵā* without a suffix ("Summon, O God, your might"); but *'uzzâ* can also be interpreted as an imperative: "Prove yourself mighty, O God, as you have done for us before."

The introduction to a hymn may contain predications that belong by nature in the body: "Let us sing aloud to God our strength" (81:2[1]). A different nuance appears in 89:18(17), which proclaims Yahweh as *tip'ereṯ 'uzzāmô,* "the glory of their strength" (the suf. refers to the people). Finally, 118:14 uses "strength" in parallel with "song" and identifies both entities with Yahweh (*'ozzî wᵉzimrāṯî yâ;* so also Ex. 15:2; Isa. 12:2).[14]

The royal psalms assume that Yahweh is strong; the king rejoices in that strength (21:2[1]) and the worshipers pray Yahweh to rise up in his strength and power to intervene against the enemy (21:14[13]). As part of the enthronement ceremonial, the scepter (*maṭṭēh-'uzzᵉḵā,* "scepter of your might" = "your mighty scepter") is conveyed to the king (110:2).

In the historical summaries, besides the general view that Yahweh shapes and governs history, we find certain events singled out as being inaugurated by Yahweh, e.g., the miraculous feeding during the wandering in the desert. For this purpose the (creative) power of Yahweh *(bᵉ'uzzô)* was invoked, bringing out the south wind (78:26), which together with the east wind drove flocks of birds toward the Israelites (v. 27). Ps. 78:61 says that Yahweh abandoned his sacred ark, identified as *'uzzô* and *tip'artô,* to captivity and into the hand of the foe (cf. 1 S. 4). This comports well with the descrip-

---

13. F. Crüsemann, *Studien zur Formgeschichte von Hymnus und Danklied in Isräel. WMANT* 32 (1969), 175 n. 5.

14. P. C. Craigie, *VT* 22 (1972) 145-46, citing Ugar. *'z* and *ḏmr* (see J. C. de Moor, *UF* 1 [1969] 179), translates "refuge and shelter."

tion of the ark as *ʾaʾrôn ʿuzzᵉkā* ("ark of your might" = "your mighty ark") in Ps. 132, which appears to speak of a procession with the ark (v. 8; cf. v. 7; 2 Ch. 6:41). In another historical summary the recapitulation of history is understood as "seeking Yahweh and his strength" (Ps. 105:4 = 1 Ch. 16:11).

In the Zion hymns the use of *ʿōz* does not vary from what we have observed already. Yahweh, who dwells on Zion, is celebrated and affirmed by the worshiping community as a refuge, strength, and help (46:2[1]); every pilgrim is happy whose strength is in Yahweh (84:6[5]).

It is not just God's help, mercy, and goodness that can be associated with *ʿōz;* the power of God's anger is also a reality in the OT, and Ps. 90:11 warns against underestimating it: "Who considers the power of your anger? Your wrath is great." It is therefore good to know that the strength of King Yahweh loves justice (99:4).

b. *Wisdom Literature.* In wisdom literature the secular usage of *ʿōz* predominates. For example, the description of Leviathan says that strength spends the night in its neck (Job 41:14[22]), and Job ironically characterizes Bildad's "wise counsel" as assistance by an arm without strength (26:2, *zᵉrôaʿ lōʾ-ʿōz*). The capable wife is not only diligent but physically strong and powerful (Prov. 31:17, *ḥāgᵉrâ bᵉʿôz moṯneyhā*, "she girds her hips with strength"; "strength and dignity [*ʿōz-wᵉhāḏār*] are her clothing," v. 25). Prov. 10:15 expresses the conviction that the wealth of the rich is (like) their fortress (*qiryaṯ ʿuzzô;* cf. also 18:11). A brother offended is more obdurate (and less approachable) than a fortified city (18:19). Prov. 21:22 appears to explain the superiority of wisdom to outward strength: "One wise person goes up against a city of warriors (*gibbôrîm*) and brings down the *ʿōz* in which they trust." Prov. 24:5 moves in the same direction: "A wise person is strength, and one with knowledge strengthens [increases] strength." The point of this saying is probably that the one who is wise is truly the one who is strong. By contrast, Eccl. 8:1 appears to view *ʿōz* in a negative light: "Wisdom makes one's face shine (*tāʾîr*), while *ʿōz* distorts one's face"; here *ʿōz* means "hardness," and no emendation is needed.

As an example of the theological use of *ʿōz* in wisdom literature, a typical wisdom commonplace may be cited: "In the fear of Yahweh there is strong confidence" (Prov. 14:26, *miḇṭaḥ-ʿōz*). We also find an element of the traditional *šēm* theology: "The name of Yahweh is a strong tower" (18:10, *migdal-ʿōz*). God's total power and freedom prevail over all human concepts of justice (Job 12:16, *ʿimmô ʿōz wᵉṯûšîyâ*, "with him are strength and success"). Finally, one of the discourses of Elihu speaks of the creative power of God, which controls the snow and the rain (Job 37:6; the text contains a dittography, and should be emended either to *wᵉlaggešem ûmāṭār,* in which case *ʿuzzô* should be read as the impv. *ʿōzzû*, "increase," or to *wᵉgešem māṭār ʿuzzô*, "and the shower of rain is his might").

c. *General Usage Elsewhere.* One of the earliest texts illustrating the general usage of *ʿōz* in the OT is Gen. 49:3, in the Blessing of Jacob, where Reuben as the firstborn is addressed as "my might" *(kōḥî)*, "the firstfruits of my vigor" *(rēʾšîṯ ʾônî)*, and "excelling in power" *(yeṯer ʿāz* [a by-form of *ʿōz*]). Also early is the Song of Deborah (Jgs. 5:2-31); vv. 19-21 describe the battle at Taanach, in which Yahweh intervened with the natural resources at his disposal. This may have occasioned the interpolated 1st-person summons in v. 21 to come forward with might, i.e., to participate in the promising battle (*tiḏrᵉḵî napšî ʿōz,* "May my soul come forward with might"; or, if we take *nep̱eš* in the sense of "neck," "You shall tread on the neck of the strong";[15] in either case *ʿōz* is connected with the military prowess of the combatants). Human ability and activity are reflected in David's dancing with all his might before Yahweh when the ark was brought to Jerusalem (2 S. 6:14, *bᵉḵol-ʿōz;* 1 Ch. 13:8 describes the scene differently: David and all Israel dance before God with all their might).

Material objects and localities may also be described as possessing *ʿōz,* e.g., a city (Isa. 26:1, *ʿîr ʿōz-lānû,* "We have a strong city" [with reference to Jerusalem]), a scepter (Jer. 48:17, *maṭṭēh-ʿōz,* expressing the strength of the Moabite domain, which is about to be shattered), or an inaccessible fortified height (Jer. 51:53, *mᵉrôm ʿuzzâ*) like that of Babylon, which will nevertheless be taken at Yahweh's judgment. Outward strength thus also symbolizes hubris. Ezekiel compares the royal house of Judah to a vine, whose sturdy stems could have been used for rulers' scepters but are now destroyed (Ezk. 19:11,12,14, *maṭṭēh-ʿōz*). When Tyre is destroyed, even the strong pillars *(maṣṣᵉḇôṯ ʿuzzēḵ)* will fall to the ground (26:11). Scholars dispute whether the *kᵉlê-ʿōz lᵉyhwh* with which the priests and Levites praised Yahweh during Hezekiah's Passover celebration were mighty (loud) musical instruments (2 Ch. 30:21).

That *ʿōz* can also refer abstractly to the power and might of a political entity is shown by Amos's prophecy of doom against Samaria (3:11): this power will be demolished.

Several texts use *gāʾôn* and *ʿōz* together in the sense of "insufferable pride or arrogance," which Yahweh will bring low (Lev. 26:19; Ezk. 24:21; 30:6,18; 33:28). Ezk. 24:21 speaks of the Jerusalem sanctuary as "your mighty pride" *(gᵉʾôn-ʿuzzᵉḵem).* This pride always involves elements of rebellion and sin against Yahweh, so that *ʿōz* moves imperceptibly from its secular to its theological usage.

d. *Theological Usage Elsewhere.* It appears that only in late texts did *ʿōz* acquire clearer theological overtones, again primarily in poetic passages (i.e., in formulaic expressions). In the Song of the Sea (Ex. 15:1-18) Yahweh is praised for the strength with which he guided his people to his holy abode (v. 13b). Hannah's hymn of praise (1 S. 2:1-10) expresses assurance that Yahweh will give strength to his king and exalt the horn of his anointed (v. 10). A similar notion appears in Mic. 5:3(4): the future ruler and savior will stand and feed his flock in the strength of Yahweh his God (the translation of *ʿōz* as "majesty" is not justified).

In Isa. 51:9 the prophet calls on the "arm of Yahweh" (a synecdoche in which the arm is already strong in principle; cf. Yahweh's oath by his mighty arm in 62:8) to awake and put on strength (*liḇšî-ʿōz;* cf. Ps. 35:23; 44:24[23]). If the text is correct in Isa. 52:1, which addresses the same summons to Zion, the reference can only be to the strength and power vouchsafed and guaranteed by Yahweh (the "beautiful garments" in v. 1b have led some exegetes to emend *ʿuzzēḵ* to *ʿeḏyēḵ,* "your jewelry"). A judgment oracle seeks to make clear that Yahweh alone is God and that every knee shall bow to

---

15. R. G. Boling, *Judges. AB* 6A (1975), 113.

him and every tongue affirm (45:23): "Only in Yahweh are acts of righteousness and strength" (*ṣᵉḏāqôṯ wāʿōz,* v. 24). The affirmation of the individual is the same, e.g., 49:5 (the servant of Yahweh declares, "and my God is my strength") or Jer. 16:19: "Yahweh is my strength and my stronghold, my refuge in the day of trouble" *(ʿōz* with *māʿōz* and *mānôs).*[16] Yahweh's power exhibited in his glorious theophany is extolled in Hab. 3. The list includes glory *(hôḏ)* and praise *(tᵉhillâ),* brightness, rays of light *(qeren),* and power (v. 4, *šām ḥeḇyôn ʿuzzōh,* "there is the cloak of his power"; there is no good reason for the general interpretation of this clause as a gloss: the phenomena accompanying the theophany are not themselves the power of Yahweh; cf. 1 K. 19:11-12).

But God's power also has destructive potential. In Ezr. 8:22, for example, a maxim states that "the hand of God is gracious to all who seek him, but his power and his wrath are against *(ʿuzzô wᵉʾappô ʿal)* all who forsake him" (the two nouns may be interpreted as a hendiadys for "his powerful wrath" or "his wrathful power").

4. *māʿôz.* The noun *māʿôz* involves the semantic elements of protection and refuge but also of security and strength, which may be imagined quite concretely in the form of an inaccessible stronghold or citadel on a rock. This meaning, in the first instance concrete and secular, can be abstracted and transferred to theological situations, which identify Yahweh with a *māʿôz* as a refuge for the persecuted, oppressed, and assailed.

Used in the general sense, *māʿôz* appears as a stronghold in the story of Gideon's call (Jgs. 6:26). Isa. 17:9, too, makes reference to "fortified cities" *(ʿārê māʿuzzôṯ),* which will be deserted and destroyed; Isa. 23:4 (actually an oracle against Tyre [cf. v. 5], but *māʿôz hayyām* must refer to Sidon) calls Sidon a "fortress by the sea," which will meet disaster. Behind this disaster stands Yahweh, who will destroy all the fortresses of Phoenicia (v. 11; reading *māʿuzzeyhā* with 1QIs[a]). Ezekiel's oracle against Egypt predicts that Yahweh's wrath will strike the Egyptian city of *sîn,* called *māʿôz miṣrāyim,* "the stronghold of Egypt" (30:15). In Nah. 3:11 the *māʿôz* ("[place of] refuge") Nineveh seeks (in vain) from the advancing enemy may be meant abstractly, but v. 12 probably refers to strongholds *(kol-miḇṣārayiḵ)* that will fall like ripe fruit into the mouth of the "devouring enemy." This uniformly concrete and secular meaning of *māʿôz* is maintained throughout the OT, in early and late traditions. Isa. 23:14 (cf. v. 1) calls Sidon a fortified and secure harbor *(māʿuzzᵉḵen),* over whose destruction the ships of Tarshish will wail (i.e., lament). Ezk. 24:25 shows that Jerusalem too was thought of as a *māʿôz: māʿuzzām* parallels such valued feelings as the joy of their glory and the delight of their eyes; cf. v. 21, which describes the temple as *gᵉʾôn ʿuzzᵉḵām,* "proud treasure."[17] The phrase *māʿôz rōʾšî* may be translated as "head protection" or "(military) helmet" (Ps. 60:9[7] = 108:9: "Ephraim is my helmet" [spoken by Yahweh]).

In addition to this concrete meaning, the OT contains a wide range of texts that use

---

16. W. Thiel, *Die deuteronomistische Redaktion von Jeremia 1–25. WMANT* 41 (1973), 195ff.

17. W. Zimmerli, *Ezekiel 1. Herm* (Eng. trans. 1979), 503.

māʿôz in a figurative and theological sense. In most cases it is Yahweh who is the refuge, haven, or sanctuary for those who flee to him. Isaiah castigates his people because they take refuge with Pharaoh instead of listening to Yahweh (Isa. 30:2, *lāʿôz bᵉmāʿôz parʿōh,* par. *laḥăsôṯ*). The Jerusalemites' forgetfulness of God (17:10a) serves as the justification for the oracle of disaster that follows (vv. 10b-11): "For you have forgotten the God of your salvation, and have not remembered the *ṣûr māʿuzzēḵ*."

Affirmation of Yahweh as *māʿôz* appears in Psalms of various genres. In all cases strong defense, protection, and refuge are the defining semantic elements. An individual hymn of confidence describes Yahweh as *māʿôz-ḥayyay* ("refuge of my life," possibly an objective gen.: "for my life"); therefore anxiety and fear are immaterial (27:1). The parallel characterizes Yahweh as light and salvation. The same affirmation in an individual hymn of thanksgiving (Ps. 28) speaks of Yahweh as strength for "his people" (v. 8, *yhwh ʿōz-lāmô;* reading *lᵉʿammô* with LXX, Syr., and several Heb. mss.), while for his *māšîaḥ* he is *māʿôz yᵉšûʿôṯ* (the one who provides refuge in acts of salvation). The same psalm calls Yahweh *ʿuzzî ûmāginnî,* "my strength and my shield" (v. 7). A lament prays urgently that Yahweh will be the petitioner's "rock of refuge" *(ṣûr-māʿôz,* 31:3[2]; the parallel stich has *bêṯ mᵉṣûḏôṯ*). The afflicted psalmist, praying for deliverance from the snare, is convinced that Yahweh is his refuge (v. 5, *kî-ʾattāh māʿûzzî;* cf. 43:2: "the God in whom I take refuge").

Didactic poetry influenced by wisdom shares this conviction. In the time of trouble, Yahweh is the salvation *(tᵉšûʿâ)* and refuge *(māʿûzzām)* of the righteous *(ṣaddîqîm)* (37:39). The maxims of Ps. 52 similarly reveal the influence of wisdom. V. 9(7) looks with disfavor on one who would not find *māʿôz* in God but trusts instead in abundant riches and proves strong in destruction *(yāʿōz bᵉhawwāṯô).*

The affirmation that God is a "strong refuge" *(māʿûzzî ḥāyil)* appears in hymnic texts, e.g., 2 S. 22:33 (Ps. 18:33[32] reads *hammᵉʾazzᵉrēnî ḥāyil,* "who has girded me with strength"; but in the context of v. 32 the MT of v. 33a makes good sense). Isa. 25:1-5 praises God as a shelter and refuge (twice in v. 4, par. *maḥseh*) to the poor and needy *(dal, ʾeḇyôn).* The force of 27:5 is somewhat obscure. Apart from the question of how v. 5 relates to vv. 2-4, this verse with the words *yaḥᵃzēq bᵉmāʿûzzî* appears to allude to the notion of asylum in the temple: someone whose life is threatened can flee to the temple and grasp the horns of the altar (1 K. 1:50). Affirmation, proclamation, and eschatological expectation of Yahweh's power to protect are heard, e.g., in Jer. 16:19: *yhwh ʿuzzî ûmāʿuzzî ûmᵉnûsî bᵉyôm ṣārâ;* Joel 4:16(3:16): *wᵉyhwh maḥᵃseh lᵉʿammô ûmāʿôz liḇnê yiśrāʾēl;* and Nah. 1:7: *ṭôḇ yhwh lᵉmāʿôz bᵉyôm ṣārâ.*

From the concrete meaning "stronghold" through the personification of refuge and strength in Yahweh, the usage of *māʿôz* finally reaches the level of abstraction, as in the great sermon of Ezra (Neh. 8:10), which calls joy in Yahweh strength *(kî ḥeḏwaṯ yhwh hîʾ māʿuzzᵉḵem),* or in Prov. 10:29, where for the blameless (reading *lattam*) the "way of Yahweh" is a defense, refuge, and stronghold (contra most comms., which translate the text as "a refuge for one who walks blamelessly," or the like). The "way of Yahweh" may be the code of conduct observed by the devout or the way shown by Yahweh (ordained destiny).

Dnl. 11 contains seven occurrences of *māʿôz.* In vv. 7, 10, and 19, the word denotes the fortress in the literal sense, while in v. 31 it refers to the Jerusalem sanctuary *(miqdāš),* thought of as a fortress. Who the "god of the fortresses" *('ᵉlōah mā'uzzîm)* in v. 38 might be is unclear. V. 39 returns to the notion of fortified sites *(mibṣᵉrê mā'uzzîm)* or garrisons. Only in v. 1 do we appear to have figurative usage; the text of the MT, however, is out of order.[18] The reference is probably to Michael, who stands beside God as "support and protection" in the battle with the angelic princes.

IV. Dead Sea Scrolls. In the Dead Sea Scrolls most of the occurrences of derivatives of *'zz* are in the Thanksgiving Scroll. Only a handful are verb forms: *lᵉhā'îz bᵉkôaḥ* (1QH 7:17,19), "to strengthen with power" (formally, derivation from *'wz* is also possible); *yā'ōz libbām* (CD 20:33), "let their heart be strong," referring to the hearts of the men belonging to the community, who hearken to the instruction of the Teacher of Righteousness. Most instances are nouns *('ōz* or *mā'ôz),* in either secular or theological contexts: *rûḥôṯ 'ōz,* "mighty winds" (1QH 1:10, creation theology); God as a "strong wall" (3:37; cf. 6:26-27); a "strong wall" (among other things) constituting a prison for the devout (5:37), but "strong bars" for protection against enemies (6:28); God's "strength" as a support for the faithful (7:6; cf. 18:13); "a strong tower and a high wall" symbolizing the secure believer (7:8; cf. 1QSb 5:23); the "rock of my strength" is with God (9:28); the works done by God's "strong right hand" are praised (17:18; cf. 18:7). At Qumran *mā'ôz* appears to have a wider range of usage than in the OT: a rootstock retains its "vigor" even in the heat (1QH 8:24); the lamenting believer finds no "refuge" (8:27); "strength" has departed from the body of the lamenter (8:32); declining "strength of the loins" symbolizing weakness (8:33); rejection of possessions as a place of "refuge" (10:23); and finally *mā'ôz* as a "place of refuge on high" (10:32).

The Manual of Discipline speaks of "strong justice" (*mišpaṭ 'ōz,* 1QS 10:25). The way of the steps of the devout leads over a "mighty rock," identified with God's truth (11:4).

The War Scroll extols God's great "strength" (1QM 11:5; 14:11,16; l. 16 prays that God will rise up in "might"; cf. Ps. 21:14[13]; Isa. 51:9).

The Rule of the Blessings also speaks of the "power of God's mouth" *('ōz pîḵā),* with which God establishes his dominion among the nations (1QSb 5:24). A noteworthy usage occurs in 4Q175 (4QTest) 26, which calls the fortification of Jerusalem the "bulwark of wickedness" *('ōz reša').* There are still other occurrences of forms of *'zz,* e.g., in 1Q27 4:1; 1Q35 1:1; 4Q403 (4QshirShabb[d]) 1:25; 4Q494 (4QM[a]) 13; and 1QH 2:2 (without context). It can be seen that, although there is increasing blending among the individual terms, their meanings do not essentially go beyond OT usage.

Wagner

18. See *BHS* and the comms.

עָזַר *ʿāzar;* עֹזֵר *ʿōzēr;* עֵזֶר *ʿēzer;* עֶזְרָה *ʿezrâ;* עֲזָרָה *ʿᵃzārâ;* עזיר *ʿaz(z)îr;* עָזַר II *ʿāzar* II

I. 1. The Roots *ʿzr* I and II; 2. Occurrences. II. *ʿzr* I: 1. Verb; 2. Nouns; 3. Names. III. *ʿzr* II: 1. Verb; 2. Nouns. IV. Dead Sea Scrolls.

I. 1. *The Roots* ʿzr *I and II.* Heb. *ʿzr* reflects two distinct Semitic roots, *ʿḏr* > *ʿzr* I and *ǵzr* > *ʿzr* II. Originally, they had only the radical *r* in common; in the course of phonetic development, however, they coalesced after the 2nd millennium B.C.E. and finally became homophones and homographs.

The verbal root *ʿḏr* > *ʿzr* I is attested in the Amorite onomasticon, in Ugaritic, Hebrew, Aramaic, and Phoenician, in North Arabian anthroponymy, and in Arabic, South Arabian, and Ethiopic. It normally means "help." In South Arabian, however, it occurs also in the idiomatic syntagm *ʿḏr bʿm/bʿly* PN (*ʿḏr* "against" someone) *b-* ("for" a misdeed), which in fact means "requite someone for something," e.g., *lʿḏrn bʿmhmw bhwt ḏrn,* "to pay them back for this war."[1] In Sabaic, however, the reflexive Št stem of the causative means "ask forgiveness,"[2] from the etymological meaning "cause oneself to be helped." This meaning corresponds exactly to that of stem X of Arab. *ʿḏr (istaʿḏara).* In Classical Arabic the meaning of stem I (*ʿaḏara)* is "forgive," ultimately a semantic derivative of "help." The root *ʿḏr* is not attested in Akkadian, which instead uses derivatives of *rêṣu,* "help."

The root *ǵzr* is intransitive. The stative means "be abundant"; the active means "come together (in a group), form a mass, assemble." This root is attested in Hebrew (*ʿzr* II) and Arabic *(ǵazura);* the noun *ǵzr* occurs in Amorite, Ugaritic, and Minaean.

2. *Occurrences.* In the MT the verb *ʿāzar* occurs 56 times in the qal (with an additional 19 occurrences of the ptcp. *ʿōzēr*), 4 times in the niphal, and once in the hiphil. The subst. *ʿēzer* occurs 21 times and *ʿezrâ* 26 times (3 times with the directional enclitic *-â*).

ʿāzar. B. Q. Baisas, "Ugaritic *ʿḏr* and Hebrew *ʿzr* I," *UF* 5 (1973) 41-52; U. Bergmann, "עזר *ʿzr* to help," *TLOT,* II, 872-74; G. Brin, "The Roots *ʿzr* — *ʿzz* in the Bible," *Leš* 24 (1959/60) 8-14; M. Dietrich and O. Loretz, "*ḫāšeruḫuli* — 'junger Dienstmann, Bursche,'" *WO* 3 (1964-66) 189-91; M. Heltzer, "*ḪZR* in den Verwaltungstexten aus Ugarit," *UF* 12 (1980) 410-12; E. Lipiński, *Le poème royal du Psaume LXXXIX 1-5, 20-38. CahRB* 6 (1967), esp. 35-42; P. D. Miller, "Ugaritic *ǴZR* and Hebrew *ʿZR* II," *UF* 2 (1970) 159-75; A. F. Rainey, *"Ilānu rēṣūtni lillikū!" Orient and Occident. FS C. H. Gordon. AOAT* 22 (1973), 139-42; V. Sasson, "Ugaritic *ṯʿ* and *ǵzr* and Hebrew *šôwaʿ* and *ʿōzēr,*" *UF* 14 (1982) 201-8.

1. *CIS,* IV 308, 22.
2. *CIS,* IV 568, 4.

II. *ʿzr I.*

1. *Verb.* The verb *ʿzr* I, "help," conveys the notion of protection, as the noun *ʿᵃzārâ* ("enclosure") shows. God is frequently the subject, and a phrase denoting the believer or the people of God the direct object. For example, the Blessing of Jacob says of Joseph: "The God of your father will help you, and El Shaddai will bless you" (Gen. 49:25). When Samuel sets up the Ebenezer stone, he says: "Thus far Yahweh has helped us" (1 S. 7:12). As here, in 2 Chronicles the reference is often to help in battle: Asa cries to God as the only one who can help, praying "Help us" (14:10); Jehoshaphat cries out to God, and God helps him (18:31); God helps Uzziah against the enemy (26:7); Hezekiah says: "Yahweh our God is with us, to help us and to fight our battles" (32:8). An interesting text is 25:8: "God has power to help or to overthrow *(hikšîl).*" Authors of laments pray to Yahweh for help: "Help us, O God of our salvation *(yēšaʿ)* . . . deliver *(hiṣṣîl)* us, and forgive us our sins" (Ps. 79:9); "Help me, save *(hôšîaʿ)* me" (109:26); "I am persecuted, help me" (119:86). Or the text says that Yahweh helps the righteous and rescues (*plṭ* piel) them (37:40 [also with *hôšîaʿ*]), that he will help the holy city when morning dawns (46:6[Eng. v. 5]), or that he helped the psalmist, who was being pushed hard to the point of falling (118:13). In the salvation oracle of Deutero-Isaiah, we find such statements as: "Do not fear, for I am with you . . . I will strengthen (*ʾmṣ* piel) you, I will help you, I will uphold *(tāmak)* you with my right hand" (Isa. 41:10; cf. vv. 13,14).

Other subjects include the gods, who are called on ironically for help (Dt. 32:38); the gods of Aram, who helped their worshipers and to whom Ahaz wishes to turn (2 Ch. 28:23); the hand of God (Ps. 119:173); the ordinances *(mišpāṭîm)* of God (Ps. 119:175); and the angel Michael, who comes to help Daniel (Dnl. 10:13). In the secular domain, the subject may be a warlord or warrior (1 K. 20:16; Josh. 1:14; 10:4,6,33; Ezr. 8:22; 1 Ch. 12:18,20,23[17,19,22]) or even Egypt, whose help, however, is useless (Isa. 30:7; cf. 31:3: both the helper [*ʿōzēr*] and the one helped [*ʿāzûr*] will fall [*kāšal, nāpal*]). Outside military contexts, the verb can denote moral or social support (Isa. 41:6, the makers of idols "help" each other; Ezr. 10:15), or assistance in performing a task (2 Ch. 32:3).

We also find the construction *ʿāzar lᵉ*, which likewise means "help, come to the aid of": Job 26:2 (Job says ironically to Bildad, "How you have assisted the weak!"); cf. also 2 S. 8:5 (par. 1 Ch. 18:5: in battle); 2 S. 21:17 (Abishai comes to David's aid and kills the Philistine); Isa. 50:7,9 (God helps the servant of Yahweh); Zec. 1:15 (the pagan nations helped Yahweh in his anger against Israel); 1 Ch. 22:17 (David orders the leaders of Israel to help Solomon); 2 Ch. 19:2 ("Should you help the wicked?" par. "love those who hate Yahweh"); 26:13 (helping the king against the enemy); 28:16 (Ahaz asks Assyria for help). The syntagm *ʿāzar lᵉ* can be compared to the use of *hôšîaʿ lᵉ* (e.g., Ezk. 34:22; Ps. 86:16; 116:6). Since several of the texts in question are relatively late, the use of *lᵉ* before the direct object may reflect Aramaic influence. If the verb *ʿāzar* is followed by a circumstantial expression introduced by *min* (e.g., Ezr. 8:22), it effectively means "save." This meaning is confirmed by Gk. *sǭzō* in Ps. 119:173; Ezr. 8:22; 2 Ch. 14:10(11); 18:31; 32:8. The usual translation is *boēthéō,* "help."

Only in 2 Ch. 14:10(11) is *ʿzr* constructed with *bên . . . l*ᵉ*;* this usage is explained by instances in Mishnaic Hebrew and especially in Sir. 42:5. Examination of the parallels shows that *ʿāzar bên raḇ l*ᵉ*ʾên kōaḥ* means "help the rich or the poor," i.e., help whomever one wishes.

The only occurrence of the hiphil is the participle in 2 Ch. 28:23 (see above; possibly to be read as a qal). The meaning of the niphal is passive in Ps. 28:7 ("I was helped") and Dnl. 11:34 (the wise among the people receive a little help) but reflexive in 2 Ch. 26:15: "for he [Uzziah] did wonders to help himself, until he became strong."

In 1 Ch. 5:20 Driver interprets *ʿzr* as *ʿzr* II; probably, however, the form should be interpreted as the niphal or qal of *ʿzr* I.[3] Ullendorff cites the Ethiopic version of Jgs. 15:9, where Heb. *wayyinnāṭ*ᵉ*šû* is translated by the reflexive form of *ʿzr.*[4] Although Dillmann here translates with *"impetum facere,"*[5] which might suggest *ʿzr* II, the context, which has to do with vengeance, suggests comparison with South Arabian *ʿḏr,* "requite." In 1 Ch. 5:20 the reflexive reading *wayyēʿāz*ᵉ*rû ʿ*ᵃ*lêhem,* "they helped each other against them," is possible; this was the interpretation of the Masoretes. But the South Semitic evidence suggests the reading *wayyaʿz*ᵉ*rû ʿ*ᵃ*lêhem,* "and they took vengeance on them." The style of 1 Ch. 5:20 is so reminiscent of certain South Semitic inscriptions that it would not be surprising if an Arabic text served as the Chronicler's model.

2. *Nouns.* The noun *ʿzr* is sometimes vocalized as *ʿēzer,* sometimes as *ʿōzēr;* it is therefore not always possible to decide whether we are dealing with the noun "help" or the ptcp. "helping, helpful." The textual tradition does not clarify the problem; cf. Ps. 124:8 (MT *ʿēzer,* 11QPsᵃ *ʿôzēr*); Isa. 44:2 (MT *yaʿz*ᵉ*reḵā,* 1QIsᵃ *ʿôzēr*). It therefore appears proper to disregard the Masoretic vocalization and compare the substantival usage of *ʿzr* with that of *ʿezrâ* and its archaic or archaizing form *ʿezrāṯ,* likewise meaning "help, support," where such confusion is impossible. The nouns *ʿēzer* and *ʿezrâ/ʿezrāṯ* are equivalents, as the synonymous phrases *ʿēzer miṣṣār* (Dt. 33:7) and *ʿezrāṯ miṣṣār* (Ps. 60:13[11]; 108:13[12]) show.

It is necessary, however, to distinguish *ʿezrâ,* "help, support" (Lam. 4:17), from the noun *ʿ*ᵃ*zārâ,* "enclosure, court," which appears in Isa. 31:2; Job 31:21 (despite the Masoretic vocalization *ʿazrāṯî*); 2 Ch. 4:9 (twice); 6:13; Sir. 50:11. The latter word is also used for the "ledge" of the altar (Ezk. 43:14,17,20; 45:19; see IV below).

The syntagm *b*ᵉ + *ʿezrâ* occurs in Nah. 3:9; Ps. 35:2; with *ʿēzer* in Ex. 18:4; Dt. 33:26; Hos. 13:9; Ps. 146:5; and with *ʿōzēr* in Ps. 118:7 (reading *b*ᵉ*ʿezrî*). It is always God from whom help is expected, except in Hos. 13:9, which says that there will be no one to help when Yahweh destroys Israel, and Nah. 3:9, where the Libyans served as "helpers" of Thebes in Egypt.

The syntagm *l*ᵉ + *ʿezrâ* occurs 11 times, frequently with reference to help in battle. The inhabitants of Meroz are to be cursed because they did not "come to the help of Yahweh"

---

3. G. R. Driver, *CML,* 142 n. 17.
4. E. Ullendorff, *JSS* 7 (1962) 347; → נטשׁ *nāṭaš.*
5. *LexLingAeth,* 1003.

(Jgs. 5:23); the inhabitants of the coastal cities have looked to Egypt and Cush for help, and deliverance *(hinnāṣēl)* from Assyria (Isa. 20:6; cf. also 31:1); Pharaoh's army set out unsuccessfully to help Israel (Jer. 37:7); Ahaz gives the king of Assyria all his treasures, but it does not help him (2 Ch. 28:21). According to Isa. 10:3, the unjust judges will find no help when the enemy comes. The Psalms repeatedly call on God to "make haste to help" *(ḥûšâ leʿezrâ); ʿezrâ* always has a pronominal suffix. In parallel, twice we find "do not be far" (22:20[19]; 71:12[11]) and twice *hiṣṣîl,* "deliver" (40:14[13]; 70:2[1]); once God is addressed as "my salvation" (Ps. 38:23[22], *tešûʿāṯî*).

In Isa. 30:5 we find *leʿēzer* and in 1 Ch. 12:19(18) *leʿōzēr.* In the latter verse, however, the vocalization should be *leʿezreḵā;* in the last line of the tricolon, similarly, *ʿezreḵā,* "your help," should be read. The MT reads: "Peace *(šālôm)* to you / and peace to your helpers! / For your God helps you *(ʿazāreḵā).*" In Isa. 30:5 we could read *laʿzōr* instead of *leʿēzer* so as to have two infinitives; 1QIs^a, however, reads: "not as a help *(leʿezrâ),* and you will not profit *(tôʿîl)* from it." This variant shows that *ʿzr/ʿzrh* is a substantive; since the LXX omits *lōʾ lehôʿîl, hôʿîl/tôʿîl* may be considered a gloss.

A third syntagm *hāyâ* + *ʿzr/ʿzrh* + suffix or *lî* ("to me") or *miṣṣar* ("from the enemy") occurs with *ʿezrâ* in Ps. 27:9 (par. "God of my salvation [*yēšaʿ*]") and 63:8(7) (par. "shadow of your wings"), with *ʿēzer* in Dt. 33:7 (against the enemy), and with *ʿōzēr* in Ps. 10:14 (God is the helper of the orphan) and 30:11(10) ("Hear . . . be a helper to me"). In these texts God is the help expected. This syntagm may be placed alongside nominal clauses in which God is the subject and *ʿzr/ʿzrh* the predicate: with *ʿezrâ* in Ps. 40:18(17) ("my help and my deliverer [*mepallēṭ*]") and 46:2(1) (par. "refuge"), with *ʿezrāṯâ* in Ps. 94:17 ("If Yahweh had not been my help"), with *ʿēzer* in Ps. 33:20 (help and shield); 70:6(5) (help and deliverer); 115:9-11 (help and shield), and with *ʿōzēr* in 54:6(4) (par. "upholder [*sāmaḵ*] of my life [*nepeš*]").

The syntagm *ʾên ʿōzēr,* "there is no helper," describes a desperate situation. When Israel had no helper, God sent Jeroboam (2 K. 14:26). When God had no helper in his wrath, his own arm helped *(hôšîaʿ)* him, and his wrath sustained *(sāmaḵ)* him (Isa. 63:5). The speaker of a lament says that trouble is near and there is no one to help (Ps. 22:12[11]). The wretched, whom God bowed down with hard labor, fell down with no one to help (Ps. 107:12). Devastated Jerusalem has no one to help (Lam. 1:7). The king delivers those who have no helper (Ps. 72:12). The king of the North has no one to help him and comes to his end (Dnl. 11:45). Similar is *lōʾ-ʿōzēr* in Job 29:12 (Job delivered the orphan who had no helper) and 30:13, where the text may be corrupt (possibly reading *ʿōṣēr:* no one restrains the enemy [NRSV]). Job 6:13 is clearly corrupt and probably must be read *hēʾ mēʾayin ʿezrāṯî ʾāḇî,* "Behold, from where will I obtain my help?" (cf. Ps. 121:1).[6]

The participle means "auxiliary troops" or "adjutants" bound to the person of a warlord. This applies to the "helpers of Rahab" in Job 9:13, who correspond to the "gods, helpers" of Kingu;[7] it applies also to the "auxiliaries" of King Zedekiah in Ezk. 12:14

---

6. Against this emendation see G. Fohrer, *Das Buch Hiob. KAT* XVI (1963), 161.
7. EnEl IV, 69.

(reading *ʿōzᵉrāyw*). In Ps. 89:20(19) (reading the ptcp. *ʿōzēr*), *ʿzr* I is used with *gibbôr* (cf. Ezk. 32:21; 1 Ch. 12:1 [possibly *ʿzr* II]; see III.1 below}. Jer. 47:4 may also refer to "auxiliary troops." Ezk. 30:8 prophesies that the "helpers" of Egypt *(ʿōzᵉreyhā)* will be broken. In Isa. 31:3 the participle is involved in a play on words between *ʿōzēr* and *ʿāzûr* (see II.1).

In poetry the noun *ʿēzer* may modify *māgēn,* "shield" (Dt. 33:29) or parallel it (Ps. 33:20; 115:9-11); both terms stand metaphorically for God. Here the meaning of *ʿēzer* is closer to "protection." By contrast, in Ps. 20:3(2); 121:1-2; 124:8, *ʿēzer* means the "help" expected from God. In Gen. 2:18,20, *ʿēzer,* "help," concretely denotes the woman, who is meant to be a help to the man. This specialized meaning of *ʿēzer* recalls Sab. *(d̲-)ʿd̲r,* which refers to female relatives.[8] In Dnl. 11:34 *ʿēzer* is the internal object of *ʿāzar* niphal: "bring help."

3. *Names.* The verb *ʿzr* I is very common in the Semitic onomasticon. It is used to form theophorous names that give thanks for a happy event, perhaps the birth of a child or the happy outcome of a difficult delivery. The root appears frequently in Amorite personal names expressing trust in a deity: *yaʿd̲ar-ʾil, yaʿd̲ir-ʾil,* or *yaʿd̲ur-ʾil,* "God has helped"; *yaʿd̲ur haddu,* "Haddu has helped"; etc.[9] We also find the act. ptcp. *ʿād̲iru: ʾilī-ʿād̲irī,* "My God is my helper" or "My God, my helper!"[10] Also frequent is *ʿad̲ru,* "help": *ʿad̲rī-haddu, ʿad̲rī-ʾaḫī, ʾabi-ʿad̲rī,* etc. Some of these names appear later at Ugarit.[11]

The great majority of Phoenician and Punic names with the element *ʿzr* are composed of the noun *ʿazr* followed by a theophorous element (e.g., *ʿzrbʿl, ʿzrmlqrt*) or a divine name followed by a perfect (e.g., *ʾšmnʿzr, mlqrtʿzr*).[12] Used by itself, *ʿzr* is either a pet name or a thanksgiving name: *ʿa(z)zūr,* "helpful."[13]

In Aramaic the noun *ʿid̲r/ʿēd̲r,* "help," appears particularly as a predicate in theophorous names, e.g., *hadad-ʿid̲ri, ʿattar-ʿid̲rī, ʿidr-ʾilī* (cf. *ʿad̲rî-ʾēl* in 1 S. 18:19; 2 S. 21:8).[14]

A theophorous name with the verbal predicate *ʿād̲ar* is found also in Nabatean *(qwsʿdr),* as the Greek transcription *Kosadaros* shows.[15]

The verb *ʿāzar* appears also in the Ammonite PN *ʾlʿzr.*[16] Finally, the element *ʿd̲r* is very frequent in North Arabian names.[17]

The Hebrew proper names using *ʿzr* I fit quite naturally into this broader context and

---

8. Beeston, 13.

9. I. J. Gelb, *Computer-Aided Analysis of Amorite. AS* 21 (1980), 256, 259f.

10. *AN,* 215. Cf. also *šamaš-ḫāzir* (*APN,* 193).

11. *PNU,* 107.

12. Benz, 375-76.

13. Cf. *a-zu-ri* (*APN,* 49a).

14. *APN,* 265b.

15. *LidzEph,* II, 339-40; *CIS,* II, 923.

16. K. P. Jackson, *The Ammonite Language of the Iron Age. HSM* 27 (1983), 95.

17. G. L. Harding, *An Index and Concordance of Pre-Islamic Arabian Names and Inscriptions* (1971), 412, 617, 675.

reflect the same tendency as in Aramaic (*ʾelîʿezer, yᵉhô-ʿezer, ʿᵃzar-yâ,* etc.). Outside the Bible, Hebrew names with *ʿzr* appear in cuneiform Neo-Assyrian and Neo-Babylonian texts, in the Aramaic papyri, and in the legends of Palestinian seals. According to 1QM 4:13, the name *ʿzrʾl,* "help of God," was borne by one of the standards of the victorious sons of light.

III. *ʿzr II.*

1. *Verb.* The verb *ʿzr* II probably appears only in 1 K. 1:7; 1 Ch. 12:22(21); and 2 Ch. 20:23. The contexts and comparison with Arab. *ġazura,* "be abundant," suggest some such meaning as "come together (in a group), form a mass, assemble." The syntagm *ʿāzar ʾaḥᵃrê X,* "join someone, support someone" (1 K. 1:7), appears nowhere else.[18] Another hapax legomenon occurs in 1 Ch. 12:22: *ʿāzar ʿim,* which might be translated "join forces with." In 2 Ch. 20:23 we find *ʿāzᵉrû ʾîš bᵉrēʿēhû lᵉmašḥîṯ,* "they joined together, the ones against the others, to (their own) destruction."

2. *Nouns.* The noun *ġzr* appears frequently in the mythological and epic texts of Ugarit as a "Homeric" epithet for gods and heroes. On the basis of Arab. *ġazīr,* "abundant," scholars agree that *ġzr* should be translated "hero" or "leader." Indeed, the contextual meaning of *ġzr* suggests comparison with words like *ʾabbîr,* "strong"; *ʾaddîr,* "mighty"; *kabbîr,* "great"; and *šallîṭ,* "ruler." This comparison would argue for a form *ġazzīru,* with the Hebrew equivalent *ʿazzîr.* Identification of *ġzr* with *ẖzr* is inappropriate, since the latter is connected with Arab. *ẖazara,* "look on with suspicion," and means rather "superintendent."[19] The Hurrian name *ẖa-še-ru-ẖu-li* should also not be associated with *ʿāḏiru* or *ġazzīru.*[20] It is based on *ẖašširum,* "container," and denotes a maker of vessels.[21]

The noun *ġzr* > *ʿzr* (pronounced *ʿāzîr* or *ʿazzîr*) is attested in 2 S. 18:3 and Ps. 89:20(19). This interpretation would also yield a clearer sense than MT *ʿōzēr* in Ezk. 32:21 and 1 Ch. 12:1, possibly also in Jer. 47:4 and Ezk. 30:8. In 2 S. 18:3 we have the only text with the plene reading *ʿzyr,* preserved by *K:* "It is better that you serve as our leader from the city" (NRSV "send us help"). If Ps. 89:20(19) was written originally as a purely consonantal text, it could be read as *št ʿzr ʿl gbr* (cf. 4QPs 89), "I have set *(šattî)* a leader *(ʿazzîr)* at the head of *(ʿal)* the army *(gᵉḇūrâ)*" (cf. Gen. 41:33; Isa. 3:25), or "I have set *(šattî)* a leader *(ʿazzîr)* against a warrior *(gibbōr),*" probably a reference to Goliath. The expression *ʿzry hammilḥāmâ,* "leaders in battle(?)," in 1 Ch. 12:1 may be compared to *gibbôr(ê) milḥāmâ* (Ps. 24:8; 2 Ch. 13:3) and *ʿᵉzûz milḥāmâ* (Isa. 42:25; cf. Ps. 24:8). In Ezk. 32:21 the *ʿzryw* correspond to the *(ʾēlê) gibbôrîm* and are therefore also "leaders." This meaning would also be appropriate in Ezk. 30:8 and Jer. 47:4, but the context is too vague to be certain.

Lipiński

---

18. *HAL,* II, 811, assigns it to *ʿzr* I.
19. Cf. Heltzer.
20. Alalakh 269, 22; contra Dietrich and Loretz.
21. Tell al-Rimah, no. 126, 21.

IV. Dead Sea Scrolls. To date the root *ʿzr* I appears some 30 times in the Dead Sea Scrolls: 10 times as a verb, 11 times as the noun *ʿēzer,* and 9 times as the noun *ʿezrâ* (the last only in 1QM and 11QT). The distribution carries little significance; the concentration in the *milḥāmâ* literature is not surprising.

Syntactic usage is approximately the same as in the OT. As the distribution would suggest, the texts speak most often of God's helping his community. He supports his holy ones (1QM 1:16) and makes use of his angels for help (1QS 3:24; 1QM 13:10,14; 17:6; 4Q177 [4QCatena[a]] frs. 12-13 1:7; cf. 9). Belial likewise helps the sons of darkness (1QM 16:11; cf. 1:2), but this help does not endure (1QM 1:6; 1QpHab 5:11). The Essene community at Qumran celebrates the help of their God (1QM 13:13) and the help of God's deliverance (4QM[a] [4Q491] fr. 11 2:14; 4QM[e] [4Q495] 2:2); it sees this help realized in the continued existence of the community and understands the community as the agent of God's help (1QM 12:7; 13:8). The degree to which this divine help is understood militarily is illustrated by the mention of a battle standard named *ʿēzer ʾēl,* "help of God" (1QM 4:13; see above). The devout worshiper probably has concrete assistance in mind when he says that he has been "helped" (= delivered) by God from the hand of the one stronger than he (1QH 2:35; cf. 5:6; 7:23). Finally, the "marriage ritual" 4Q502 records the benediction *bārûḵ ʾēl yiśrāʾēl ʾašer ʿāzar* [. . .], "blessed by the God of Israel, who helps [. . .]" (24:2).[22]

The noun *ʿazārâ* appears in 11QT only in the construct phrase *ʿazraṯ mizbēaḥ,* which denotes the narrow "altar ledge" to be sprinkled with sacrificial blood in the course of the various sacrificial rites (16:03,17; 23:13,14; 37:4). It is unclear whether this explicit construct phrase represents a semantic shift from the use of *ʿazārâ* alone in Ezk. 43:14,17,20.

Fabry

---

22. J. M. Baumgarten, *JJS* 34 (1983) 125-35.

עָטַר *ʿāṭar;* עֲטָרָה *ʿaṭārâ*

I. 1. Etymology; 2. Occurrences; 3. Meaning; 4. LXX; 5. Dead Sea Scrolls. II. Lexical Field: 1. *nēzer;* 2. *zēr;* 3. *ṭûrîm;* 4. *liwyâ;* 5. *lᵉwāyôṯ;* 6. *ṣᵉpîrâ;* 7. *keṯer.* III. Ancient Near East: 1. Egypt; 2. Mesopotamia; 3. Greece and Rome. IV. OT: 1. Royal Crown; 2. Material; 3. Crown of the High Priest; 4. Marriage Crown; 5. Names; 6. Metaphorical Usage.

ʿāṭar. J. Abeler, *Kronen, Herrschaftszeichen der Welt* ([5]1980); K. Baus, *Der Kranz in Antike und Christentum. Theophaneia* 2 (1940); M. Blech, *Studien zum Kranz bei den Griechen. RVV*

I. 1. *Etymology.* The root *'ṭr* is not widespread in Semitic. Apart from Hebrew, a verb *'ṭr* and a noun *'ṭrt* are found only in Phoenician and Punic. The so-called wreath inscription from Piraeus states that the Sidonian colony decided to donate a golden wreath *(l'ṭr . . . 'ṭrt ḥrṣ)* to *šm'b'l bn mgn* for his services during the building of the temple, to inscribe this decision on a stele, and to set this stele up in the vestibule of the temple.[1] This decision reflects a custom borrowed from the Greeks. Similarly a Latin-Punic bilingual on the funerary stele of a Numidian says that the departed was "possessor of a wreath" *(dl 'ṭrt)* and "possessor of a name of heroism" *(dl šm t'ṣmt).*[2] A Neo-Punic inscription from Maktar uses *'ṭrt* in a different sense; the phrase *'ṭrt 'drt'* probably refers to the magnificent facade of the temple.[3] Line 6 of an inscription from Carthage was thought to read *wt'rt w['ṭrt]t,* but the actual reading is *wt'rt k[t]tb.*[4] The end of the line, however, clearly reads *br'š 'ṭr,* which Ferron translates "au sommet du fronton."[5] As in *KAI* 145, then, we are dealing with an architectural feature.

Citing Guillaume, *HAL* refers to Arab. *'ṭr,* but this is based on a typographical error.[6] Guillaume compares the Arabic root *'ṭr,* "bend, twist," to Heb. *'ṭr.*[7] The Arabic verb might correspond to the Hebrew semantically, but not phonetically.

The connection to Akk. *eṭru,* "headband," goes back to Bezold;[8] the translation is probably based on association with Heb. *'ᵃṭārâ* More recent lexicons enter it under *idru* B (or *itru, iṭru*), "strap or band," or *id/tru,* III, "band."[9] It is not possible to establish its precise meaning from an occurrence in a list of gifts given to Amenophis IV.[10] It is not impossible that an Akkadian word *iṭru* or *eṭru* is related to Heb. *'ᵃṭārâ,* but the evidence

---

38 (1982); R. M. Boehmer, "Hörnerkrone," *RLA,* IV, 431-34; H. Bonnet, "Kronen, Krönung," *RÄR,* 394-400; A. Brekelmans, *Martyrerkranz. Analecta Gregoriana* 150 (1965); R. Delbrueck, "Der spätantike Kaiserornat," *Die Antike* 8 (1932) 1-21; L. Deubner, "Die Bedeutung des Kranzes im klassischen Altertum," *ARW* 30 (1933) 70-104; O. Fiebiger, "Corona. 1)," *PW,* IV, 1636-44; R. Ganszyniec, "Kranz," *PW,* XI, 1588-1607; W. Grundmann, "στέφανος, στεφανόω," *TDNT,* VII, 615-36; H.-D. Kahl, "Weihekrone und Herrscherkrone" (Habil., Giessen, 1964); J. Köchling, *De coronarum apud antiquos vi et usu. RVV* 14/2 (1914; vol. 1 = diss., Münster, 1913); L. Löw, "Kranz und Krone," *Gesammelte Schriften,* III (1893, ²1979), 407-37; C. Meister, "Kranz Krone," *BHHW,* II, 999-1000; C. Strauss, "Kronen," *LexÄg,* III, 811-16; *Quinti Septimi Florentis Tertulliani Opera ex recensione Aemilii Kroymann. CSEL* 70 (1942), 153-88 (De corona); E. Unger, "Diadem und Krone," *RLA,* II, 201-11; H. Waetzoldt and R. M. Boehmer, "Kopfbedeckung," *RLA,* VI, 197-210.

1. *KAI* 60, quotation l. 3.
2. *KAI* 165.6.
3. *KAI* 145.3; see J. G. Février, *Sem* 6 (1956) 17-18.
4. *RES* 13 = *CIS* 6000 (bis).
5. J. Ferron, *Studi Magrebini,* 1 (1966), 67-80 and pl. 1.
6. *HAL,* II, 815.
7. A. Guillaume, *Abr-Nahrain* 3 (1961/62) 6.
8. C. Bezold, *Babylonisch-assyrisches Glossar* (1926), 26, with a question mark. Still cited by *KBL*², 698.
9. See, respectively, *CAD,* VII, 10b; *AHw,* I, 364b.
10. EA 14, III, 16.

is not clear enough for it to serve as an etymology of the Hebrew root *ʿṭr.*[11] The word *eṭēru(m),* "take away, rescue,"[12] cited by *GesB* and *BDB,* can hardly have anything to do with Heb. *ʿṭr.*

In Jewish Aramaic the primary meaning is "surround," in Middle Hebrew, "wreathe."

2. *Occurrences.* The verb *ʿāṭar* occurs just twice in the qal, with the meaning "surround": 1 S. 23:26 reports that Saul and his followers set out to entrap David by encirclement; Ps. 5:13(Eng. v. 12) says that Yahweh's favor surrounds the righteous like a longshield. There are four occurrences of the piel, which means "'make crowned' . . . as a permanent condition."[13] Since the "performance of the action itself" is attested in the qal with the meaning "surround," neither the piel nor the hiphil should be considered a denominative verb.[14]

The piel appears in Cant. 3:11: the bridegroom is crowned by his mother with a wreath or crown. It also appears three times in the Psalms. Ps. 8:6(5) speaks of the individual whom Yahweh crowns "with grace and mercy" (*ḥeseḏ wᵉraḥᵃmîm;* cf. the very similar expression in 11QPsᵃ 19:8). Ps. 65:12(11) declares that Yahweh has crowned the year with his goodness; the fertility of the land is ascribed to Yahweh's intervention, here a "circuit," "a progress through the land by God in person";[15] v. 12b(11b) says, "Your wagon tracks overflow with riches." Ps. 103:4 says that God crowns the soul of the psalmist with steadfast love and mercy.

The hiphil is a hapax legomenon. The MT of Isa. 23:8 contains the fem. ptcp. *hammaʿᵃṭîrâ,* describing Tyre. The same passage in 1QIsᵃ reads *hmʿṭrh,* probably a piel or pual participle. The Syr. and Vulg. provide passive readings: "crowned." The interpretation of the passage is disputed. Since Duhm, exegetes have tended to replace Tyre with Sidon, the "bestower of crowns," the founder of numerous monarchic city-states in such areas as Cyprus.[16] In short, Isa. 23:8 predicts that the Phoenician city will be disgraced even though she wears a crown or even though she bestowed crowns and wreaths, installing client rulers in many of her colonies.[17]

The noun *ʿᵃṭārâ* occurs 23 times in the OT; with the exception of 2 S. 12:30 par. 1 Ch. 20:2 it appears only in poetic texts: 5 times in Proverbs, 4 times in Isaiah, 3 times in Ezekiel, twice each in Zechariah and Job, and once each (besides 2 Samuel and 1 Chronicles) in Jeremiah, Psalms, Song of Songs, Esther, and Lamentations. Finally, it occurs in the Hebrew text of Sirach: 45:12a (ms. B); 50:12c (ms. A); 6:31b (ms. A = 2Q18). The verb occurs in 45:25-26 (ms. B) and 6:31b (ms. A = 2Q18). The absolute

---

11. Personal communication from R. Borger.
12. *AHw,* I, 264; *CAD,* 4, 401-4.
13. *HP,* 205.
14. Cf. *BDB,* 742-43; cf. *HAL,* II, 815.
15. H. Schmidt, *Die Psalmen. HAT* I/15 (1934), in loc.
16. See also O. Kaiser, *Isaiah 13–39. OTL* (Eng. trans. 1974), 160, 162, 166.
17. W. Rudolph, "Jesaja 23,1-14," *FS F. Baumgärtel. EF* A/10 (1959), 166-74, esp. 172; similarly H. Wildberger, *Isaiah 13–27* (Eng. trans. 1997), 428-29.

form *'ᵃṭārâ* appears only twice (Ezk. 21:31[26]; Cant. 3:11); the construct form is *'ᵃṭereṯ*. This form used absolutely should probably replace the plural form *'ᵃṭārôṯ* in the three texts where it occurs (Zec. 6:11,14; Job 31:36); it is also conceivable that *-ôṯ* should be interpreted as an archaic or archaizing singular ending.[18] It is possible, however, that the form should be treated as a plural of magnitude (see IV.3 below).

3. *Meaning.* The word *'ᵃṭārâ* covers a fairly broad range of meanings. The basic sense of the root is "surround, encircle"; from it develops the meaning "wreath" of flowers, leaves, or twigs, in other words, a botanical crown. This meaning then gives rise to the general meaning "crown," a metallic wreath. As parallelisms show, *'ᵃṭārâ* can refer to a wide variety of head coverings or ornaments, e.g., *ṣᵉp̱îrâ* (Isa. 28:5), *ṣānîp* (Isa. 62:3), *miṣnepeṯ* (Ezk. 21:31[26]), *liwyâ* (Prov. 4:9, etc.). Presumably the diadem *(nēzer),* which is part of the royal insignia, can also be called *'ᵃṭārâ.* In other words, *'ᵃṭārâ* can denote not just the royal crown of gold but also the cloth cap decorated with precious stones, the diadem, or the head covering recalling the Assyrian tiara, decorated with ornate bands.[19]

4. *LXX.* The LXX regularly uses *stéphanos* to translate *'ᵃṭārâ;* its semantic range is astonishingly similar to that of the Hebrew word: *stéphanos* can refer to an encirclement, a city wall, a wreath, or a crown (of twigs or flowers as well as metal). There are 50 occurrences of *stéphanos* in the LXX,[20] 23 of which translate *'ᵃṭārâ;* in addition, there are 9 occurrences in Sirach, 7 in 1 Maccabees, 1 in 2 Maccabees, 2 in Judith, and 1 in Baruch 6 (= Letter of Jeremiah). Once (Isa. 22:21) *stéphanos* represents *'aḇnēṭ,* twice (Lam. 2:15; Ezk. 28:12) *kālîl,* and twice (Prov. 1:9; 4:9) *liwyâ.* It has no Hebrew equivalent in Isa. 22:18 (but cf. 22:21) and Ps. 65:12(11), where the noun *stéphanos* represents the verb *'iṭṭartā.* In four passages (Ps. 5:13[12]; 8:6[5]; 103:4; Cant. 3:11) the verb *stephanóō* translates *'āṭar;* it appears also in Jdt. 15:13; 3 Mc. 3:28; and 4 Mc. 17:15.

5. *Dead Sea Scrolls.* The root *'ṭr* does not play an important role in the Dead Sea Scrolls. In 1QSb 4:3 the priest is promised that "eternal blessings" will be the crown of his head; 11QPsᵃ 19:7-8, adapting Ps. 103:4, says of Yahweh: *m'ṭr ḥsydyw ḥsd wrḥmym,* "who crowns his faithful with steadfast love and mercy." The Temple Scroll uses *'ṭrh* twice (17:1 [restored]; 40:11) for an architectural feature.

II. Lexical Field. The terms "wreath," "crown," and "diadem" translate several Hebrew words, the specific meanings of which need to be distinguished.

1. *nēzer.* The noun → נזר *nēzer* refers to the royal diadem. When the text refers to the royal headdress, *'ᵃṭārâ* can subsume *nēzer.*

---

18. E. Lipiński, *VT* 20 (1970) 34-35.
19. Cf. Barrois, *Manuel d'archéologie biblique,* II (1953), 55-56.
20. Grundmann (624 n. 57) counts only 49.

2. *zēr.* The golden wreath *(zēr)* around the ark of the covenant is to be thought of as an ornate golden molding (Ex. 25:11; 37:2); it is also mentioned in connection with the table (25:24-25; 37:11-12) and above all the incense altar (30:3-4; 37:26-27).

3. *ṭûrîm.* According to *GesB,* the *ṭûrîm* (1 K. 7:18, etc.) are "decorations joined together to form a wreath." The description of the metalwork for the temple is not detailed enough, however, to permit definite conclusions in the case of each individual word. Noth proposes for *ṭûr* the meaning "plate, panel," "from which the meanings 'course' and then 'row' could have developed."[21]

4. *liwyâ.* The noun *liwyâ,* "garland" (Prov. 1:9; 4:9; 14:24 cj.; and possibly 1 K. 7:29), derives from a verb *lāwâ* III, "twist, turn," attested in Hebrew only in its nominal derivative.[22] Prov. 1:9 says the instructions of parents are "a fair garland" *(liwyaṯ ḥēn)* on the head of their son and a "necklace" *(ʿᵃnāqîm)* around his neck. According to 4:9, wisdom will place on the head of one who hearkens to her "a fair garland" *(liwyaṯ-ḥēn)* and thus bestow "a beautiful crown" *(ʿᵃṭereṯ tipʾereṯ).* In 14:24, too, *liwyaṯ* must be read in parallel with *ʿᵃṭereṯ,* so that the proverb reads: "The crown of the wise is their wisdom, but folly is the garland of fools."

5. *lᵉwāyôṯ.* In the description of how to make the ten stands for the ten basins in the temple, the MT uses the form *lōyôṯ* (1 K. 7:29,30,36). This form would derive from a sg. *lōyâ,* otherwise unattested. In all likelihood, however, the form should be *lᵉwāyôṯ,* so that here we would have the pl. of *liwyâ* (see II.4 above). The text clearly refers to some kind of "wreaths" (cf. NRSV) firmly attached to the stands.[23] To date, the phrases *mēʿēḇer ʾîš lōyôṯ* in v. 30 and *kᵉmaʿar-ʾîš wᵉlōyôṯ* in v. 36 defy interpretation.

6. *ṣᵉpîrâ.* On the evidence of Isa. 28:5, where *ṣᵉpîraṯ tipʾārâ* ("a garland of glory") parallels *ʿᵃṭereṯ ṣᵉḇî* ("a diadem of beauty"), *ṣᵉpîrâ* means "garland, wreath, crown." The occurrence of this word in Ezk. 7:7,10, however, remains unexplained.[24]

7. *keṯer.* Heb. *keṯer* occurs only three times in the OT: Est. 1:11; 2:17; 6:8. Each time it is qualified by *malḵûṯ.* In the first two texts, *keṯer* denotes the headdress of a queen (Vashti in 1:11, Esther at her enthronement in 2:17); in 6:8 it refers quite remarkably to the adornment of a horse's head. The noun derives from a verb *ktr* II (piel), "surround" (cf. *ʿāṭar*). The LXX translates with *diádēma* (cf. Vulg. *diadema*), identifying *keṯer* with the diadem denoted elsewhere in the OT by *nēzer.* In the book of Esther *keṯer* refers to the tall, rigid tiara that adorned the head of the Persian king (Gk. *kídaris = tiára orthḗ*), the "crown" worn only by the great king, singling him out from all others. Since it can be shown that the consorts of Hellenistic kings wore

21. M. Noth, *Könige. BK* IX/1 (1968), 150-51.
22. → VII, 475.
23. See also Noth, *BK* IX/1, 144.
24. See W, Zimmerli, *Ezekiel 1. Herm* (Eng. trans. 1979), 195; J. Reider, *VT* 4 (1954) 278.

the diadem,[25] the interpretation of the LXX and Vulg. is correct; the author of the Hebrew text clearly used *keṯer* in a broader sense. Crowning with the diadem appears not to symbolize installation as coregent but recognition as lawful consort.

According to the MT of 6:8, Haman proposes that the king adorn the one he wishes to honor with royal robes that the king has worn and with a horse "that the king has ridden, with a royal diadem [or: 'royal tiara,' *keṯer malḵûṯ*] on its head." Since it is impossible to picture a horse wearing either the tiara of the great king or the diadem of the queen,[26] we should accept the suggestion of Gerleman and translate: "and a horse like that on which the king rode when the royal diadem was placed on his head."

There is one occurrence of a denominative verb (hiphil) derived from *keṯer* in Prov. 14:18, with the meaning "crown oneself": "The simple are adorned[27] with folly, but the clever crown themselves *(yaḵtirû)* with knowledge."

III. Ancient Near East.

1. *Egypt.* The outstanding adornment of Egyptian deities was their headdress, the attribute by which they are most easily recognized. A crown was not just decorative, being above all a symbol expressing the nature of the god: gods of the heavens and of light wore crowns adorned with the sun disk, gods whose realm is the air wore feathered crowns, gods whose animals were horned had a pair of horns symbolizing their strength. Like all symbols, crowns were also vehicles of power, in which the attributes and forces they represented were effectively present. The crowns of the king and queen mediated and guaranteed the divine power they claimed; therefore the royal crowns enjoyed their own cult. The earliest crowns were those of the two lands. The white crown was a tall headdress terminating in a knob; its wearer represented the territory of Upper Egypt. The red crown was a cap, the back of which rose steeply, with an upwardly coiled "wire" in front. It symbolized the territory of Lower Egypt. The two crowns, representing the principle of dualism, were first associated with the ruler of both lands on the Narmer palette. In the late period we find flamboyant composite crowns. Since the New Kingdom, the cult of the dead allotted the departed a wreath, usually of olive leaves, as a sign of vindication in the final judgment. This "wreath of vindication"[28] was worn like a crown by the departed. Christianity later borrowed it as the "crown of life."

2. *Mesopotamia.* The usual Akkadian word for "crown, tiara" is *agû(m),* a mark of sovereignty denoting both the tiara of the gods and the headdress of the king.[29] The form was not critical; what mattered was that the *agû* expressed the power and function of its wearer. The term therefore served to denote any headdress of a deity or of the

---

25. G. Gerleman, *Esther. BK* XXI (1973), 64.

26. Ibid., 116-17; for a different view see H. Bardtke, *Das Buch Esther. KAT* XVII/4-5 (1963), 348.

27. G. R. Driver, *Bibl* 32 (1951) 181.

28. D. Jankuhn, *LexÄg,* III, 764.

AHw, I, 16-17; *CAD,* I/1, 153-57.

king, be it a band, a circlet, or a cap. In every era, of course, there were prescribed forms for the tiaras of individual deities and for the "crown" of the king. A crown, cap, or helmet with the horns of a bull, however, always symbolized divinity. As a rule, such a headdress was worn only by a god, but in a few cases also by the divinized king. Interpretation confronts the difficulty that pictorial representations show changes in fashion that cannot be integrated with the texts because much of the terminology remained the same, although the words probably referred to different forms of headdress in different eras and regions. For example, the word *kubšu,* denoting a soldier's cap, can refer both to the king's crown and (with horns) to the tiara of a god.[30] A total of 115 distinct forms of headdress have been found in pictorial representations.[31]

3. *Greece and Rome.* In the Greco-Roman world, wreaths found their place primarily in the cult. They adorned priests, altars, those who offered sacrifice, sacrificial animals, and seers. The symbolism indicated that the person or object so adorned was separated from the profane world. From this cultic usage derived the use of wreaths at banquets and athletic competitions, in triumphal processions, and in the cult of the dead. Wreaths were symbols of divine favor and protection. The close connection between cultic and political life led to holders of public office wearing wreaths as a sign of their dignity. Over time, these wreaths developed into a variety of crowns. To wear the victor's crown in an athletic contest was considered the highest form of earthly happiness. The wreath also found employment in the private sphere, adorning singers, for example. Wreaths were used to express joy and honor. Wreaths of precious metal served as votive offerings and tokens of honor. Aristophanes makes fun of the multiplication of wreaths in his *Equites (Knights):* when a sausage dealer informs the council that anchovies are the cheapest they have been since the outbreak of war, he is awarded a wreath as a bearer of good news. Weddings were also occasions for coronation, and the guests at banquets and symposia were crowned with wreaths. Finally, wreaths were used in the funerary cult and to honor the dead. The use of wreaths in the Roman cult for the most part probably echoed Greek usage. The diadem, which signified sovereignty and encircled the tiara worn by the Achaemenids, formed part of the Hellenistic royal ornaments since the time of Alexander the Great. Beginning with Ptolemy IV, the diadem was represented on coins as a rayed wreath. At Rome the diadem — a hated symbol of despotism — did not come into use until the late period.

When we move from the Greco-Roman world and the Hellenistic Near East to the OT world, we are struck by the little use made of crowns, wreaths, and coronation. Only in the later strata of the OT do the terms come to be used more often, primarily figuratively. The reserve of the OT shows that Israel rejected the cultic and magical use of the wreath (a botanical crown), from which developed the crown proper, a metal wreath, customary among its neighbors.

---

30. *AHw,* I, 497-98.
31. R. M. Boehmer, *RLA,* VI, 204, 206, 209.

IV. OT.

1. *Royal Crown.* It is striking that the crown of Saul, the first king of Israel, is mentioned for the first time in the story of his tragic death. The Amalekite who brought David the news of Saul's death concludes his account: "Then I took the crown *(hannēzer)* that was on his head and the armlet that was on his arm, and I have brought them here to my lord" (2 S. 1:10). It is nowhere stated that David wore the crown or diadem of Saul. We do read in 2 S. 12:30 that, after defeating the Ammonites, David took "the crown of their king *('ᵃṭereṯ malkām)* from his head . . . and it was placed on David's head." A particular problem is presented by the statement that its weight was a talent of gold (some 80 lbs.) — possibly a measure of its value, unless attendants held it over the king's head. A further complication is the parallel in 1 Ch. 20:2, where the Vulg. and possibly the LXX read *milkōm,* a reference to the imperial deity of the Ammonites.[32]

Nothing is said of a coronation of Solomon or his successors. Not until Joash are we told once more of a coronation: the high priest Jehoiada sets the diadem (once again *nēzer*) on his head (2 K. 11:12 par. 2 Ch. 23:11).[33] In the case of the kings of the northern kingdom, we can only theorize that they wore a crown or diadem, perhaps following the example of their neighbors, the kings of Phoenicia, and of the Aramaic rulers. The so-called Black Obelisk of Shalmaneser III represents Jehu as wearing a pointed cap, possibly decorated with precious stones. The "proud garland [or: 'crown']" of Isa. 28:1,3 may be seen as a reference to the royal house, which failed to distance itself from the doings of the upper class of Samaria. The threat addressed to the king and the "lady" (*gᵉḇîrâ,* i.e., the king's mother) indicates that each wore a magnificent crown (*'ᵃṭereṯ tip'ereṯ,* Jer. 13:18; cf. similarly Ezk. 21:31[26]).

Herod the Great was buried with a diadem on which was set a golden crown.[34] We read in 1 Mc. 11:13 that Ptolemy VI Philometor wore two crowns: the crown of Egypt and the crown of Asia.

2. *Material.* Even in the ancient world, crowns were generally made of gold (see *'ṭrt ḥrṣ* in the Phoenician wreath inscription),[35] as we can see from 2 S. 12:30 par. 1 Ch. 20:2 *(kikkar-zāhāḇ)* and Est. 8:15 (the crown of Mordecai, *'ᵃṭereṯ zāhāḇ gᵉḏôlâ*). Ps. 21:4(3) and Sir. 45:12 also speak of an *'ᵃṭereṯ paz,* a crown of fine gold (if *paz* actually means "fine gold"). In Sir. 45:12 the crown *('ṭrt)* is one of the ornaments of the high priest, but we can conclude from Ps. 21:4(3) that the royal crown of Israel was a golden diadem (elsewhere usually called *nēzer*), which, as Ezk. 21:31 teaches, was probably studded with precious stones (cf. 2 S. 12:30) and was worn over the turban *(miṣnepeṯ).* As elsewhere in the ancient Near East, the king received the crown from the hand of the deity (cf. Ps. 21:4[3]). The royal power and dignity symbolized by the king's crown

32. See W. Röllig, *WbMyth,* I, 299.

33. For a discussion of the coronation ritual, see → נזר *nāzar,* II.3; → עוד *'wd,* IV.1.b; → עמוד *'ammûḏ.*

34. Josephus *Ant.* 17.8.3 §197.

35. *KAI* 60.3.

were bestowed by God. The crown was presumably worn on state occasions and perhaps also when the king engaged in battle (cf. 2 S. 1:10, *nēzer*).

There is plentiful evidence that Israel's neighbors believed that the king was ultimately crowned by the deity. This idea is attested also in Ps. 21:4(3): it is Yahweh who bestows blessings and success on the king and sets the crown on his head.

3. *Crown of the High Priest.* Only gradually did the royal ideology of the high priest develop and find acceptance. This development is graphically illustrated in Zec. 6:9-14: Zechariah is commanded to collect silver and gold brought back by the returning exiles and to make *ʿaṭārôṯ* to set on the head of the high priest Joshua son of Jehozadak. V. 14 says that the crown(s) are to remain as a memorial in the temple of Yahweh. The pl. *ʿaṭārôṯ* has caused problems since time immemorial; for example, the Targ. interprets it as a plural of magnitude ("a large crown"). Others have suggested that the form refers to a composite artifact: a multiple crown like the papal tiara or crown described in Rev. 19:12.[36] Rudolph is probably correct, however, in assuming that we are dealing here with an archaic singular ending *-ôṯ* < *-āṯ* and that obviously only one crown is meant. Since it is unreasonable to assume that Joshua wore the crown at all times, v. 14 also creates no problems. When the crown was not being used on an official state occasion, it was deposited in the temple, where it both recalled the founders and evoked constant recollection of Yahweh's steadfast love and mercy. Since the crown was a symbol of royal dignity, while the high priest originally wore a turban (*miṣnepeṯ,* Ex. 28:4, etc.), many exegetes substitute Zerubbabel for Joshua in v. 11. Rudolph is right not to follow this lead: Zec. 6:9-14 for the first time legitimizes Joshua as a royal high priest and descendant of David. Sir. 45:12, too, is probably dominated by the notion of the royal high priest. This ideal became a reality under the Hasmoneans. Each of the eight heads of this house, from Jonathan to Antigonus, was both high priest and the secular leader of the Jewish people.

4. *Marriage Crown.* Since the bridal couple is celebrated as king and queen, the wreath or crown plays an important role in the marriage ceremony (as in the Greco-Roman world).[37] To the accompaniment of music (1 Mc. 3:39), the bridegroom, crowned by his mother (Cant. 3:11), approached the bride. The allegory in Ezk. 16 shows that the bride was also adorned with a beautiful crown (*ʿaṭereṯ tip'ereṯ,* Ezk. 16:12), in this case by her father; bridal wreaths might be made of myrtle, roses, or gold.[38] A lover would also present a beautiful crown to a prostitute (Ezk. 23:42). According to 3 Mc. 4:8, during a persecution in Alexandria young Jewish couples had ropes wrapped around their necks instead of wreaths on their heads. During Vespasian's war, an edict prohibited the crowning of the groom; during the war of Quietus (governor of Judea in 117 C.E.), the crowning of the bride was prohibited.[39]

---

36. E.g., L. G. Rignell, *Die Nachtgesichte des Sacharja* (1950), in loc.
37. See, e.g., Euripides *Iphigenia in Aulis* 905-6.
38. St.-B., I, 508-9.
39. Mish. *Soṭa* 9.14.

5. *Names.* In one text (1 Ch. 2:26) *ʿᵃṭārâ* is the name of a woman, the second wife of Jerahmeel. This name reflects "joy over a daughter who adds to the number of children."[40]

Several toponyms are based on the pl. of *ʿᵃṭārâ;* they are understood either in the sense of "enclosure" or "cattle pen,"[41] or as a plural of differentiation: stones forming a kind of crown around a ring of hills.[42] (1) The *ʿaṭrôṯ bêṯ yôʾāḇ* in Judah of 1 Ch. 2:54 has not been identified. (2) The *ʿaṭrôṯ šôpān* in Gad mentioned in Nu. 32:35 has likewise not been identified, if it is not to be equated with Khirbet ʿAṭṭārūs/z (see below). (3) The *ʿᵃṭārôṯ* in the southern region of Ephraim (Josh. 16:2) is probably the same as *ʿaṭrôṯ ʾaddār* on the border with Benjamin (16:5; 18:13); it may be identical with Khirbet ʿAṭṭāra at the southern foot of Tell en-Naṣbeh. (4) The *ʿᵃṭārôṯ* on the northern or eastern border of Ephraimite settlement (Josh. 16:7) may possibly be identified with Tell Sheikh ej-Jiab in the Jordan Valley northwest of Phasaelis. (5) The most famous site is the *ʿᵃṭārôṯ* east of the Jordan (Nu. 32:3,34), which appears also in the inscription of King Mesha of Moab *(ʿṭrt);*[43] despite the final consonant, which mocks the principles of phonetic equivalence, it is probably to be identified with Khirbet ʿAṭṭārūs/z, some 6 mi. northwest of Dibon. (6) The Targ. to Jgs. 4:5 mentions an *ʿṭrwt* between Ramah and Bethel. (7) Eusebius was familiar with two sites named Ataroth near Jerusalem; the names suggest identification with Khirbet ʿAṭṭāra at the foot to Tell en-Naṣbeh and Khirbet ʿAṭṭara (= Khirbet el-Kharāba).[44] (8) The modern village of el-ʿAṭṭāra north of Jīfna may represent an ancient Ataroth by chance unrecorded in the OT.

6. *Metaphorical Usage.* Wisdom literature frequently uses the image of a wreath or crown. A good wife is her husband's wreath (Prov. 12:4). Grandchildren are "the wreath of the aged," and the glory of children is their fathers (17:6). The gray hair of the aged is "a glorious crown" (*ʿᵃṭereṯ tip̱ʾereṯ,* 16:31), and "rich experience is the crown [or: 'ornament'][45] of the aged" (Sir. 25:6). A father's instruction and a mother's teaching are "a fair wreath" *(liwyaṯ ḥēn)* on their son's head (Prov. 1:9). Above all, however, wisdom herself is the power that brings honor. "She will place on your head a fair wreath *(liwyaṯ ḥēn);* she will bestow on you a beautiful crown *(ʿᵃṭereṯ tip̱ʾereṯ)*" (4:9; cf. also 14:24). Thus the fear of God can be understood as a crown of wisdom (Sir. 1:18; LXX *stéphanos sophías* almost surely represents *ʿᵃṭereṯ ḥoḵmâ,* not *nēzer*).[46] Wisdom can be worn like a glorious robe and put on like a splendid crown (Gk. *stéphanon agalliámatos,* Sir. 6:31).

---

40. J. J. Stamm, *Hebräische Wortforschung. FS W. Baumgartner. SVT* 16 (1967), 327-28. Cf. the allegorical interpretation in Jer. *Sanh.* 2.20b.

41. See, respectively, K. Elliger, *BHHW,* I, 144; *HAL,* II, 815.

42. E. König, *Hebräisches und aramäisches Wörterbuch zum AT* (1936), s.v.

43. *KAI* 181.11.

44. *Onomasticon* 26.15-16.

45. G. Sauer, "Jesus Sirach," *Historische und legendarische Erzählungen. JSHRZ* III/5 (1981), 567.

46. Ibid., 508 n. 18a.

On the other hand, loss of a wreath represents loss of human glory and honor; it means suffering and abject misery. Job (19:9) says of himself: "He has stripped my glory from me, and taken the crown from my head." Jeremiah utters the same threat against the king and the king's mother (Jer. 13:18), referring to their imminent deportation: "Take a lowly seat, for your beautiful crown has come down from your head." In Lam. 5:16 the Israelites themselves declare, "The wreath has fallen from our head."

Finally, crowns and wreaths represent sharing in the coming kingdom of glory. When Isa. 62:3 says, "You shall be a wreath of glory *(ʿᵃṭereṯ tipʾereṯ)* in the hand of Yahweh and a royal diadem [reading *ûṣᵉnîp mᵉlûḵâ*] in the hand of your God," the reference is to Jerusalem of the eschaton; but Wis. 5:15-16 extends this vision to all the elect: "The righteous shall live forever, and their reward is with the Lord; the Most High takes care of them. Therefore they will receive from the hand of the Lord a glorious kingdom and a beautiful diadem *(tó diádēma toú kállous)*."

D. Kellermann

עַיִן *ʿayin*

I. The Word. II. Ancient Near East: 1. Egypt; 2. Mesopotamia; 3. Ugarit. III. OT: 1. Sensory Organ; 2. Locus of Personality; 3. Idioms; 4. Metaphors; 5. God's Eye. IV. Deuterocanonical Texts. V. Dead Sea Scrolls.

I. The Word. The word *ʿayin* occurs 866 times in the Hebrew OT with the meaning "eye," 23 times with the metaphorical meaning "spring." It occurs 5 times in the Aramaic portions of the OT.

ʿayin. M. Dahood, "Zacharia 9,1, *ʿÊN ʾĀDĀM,*" *CBQ* 25 (1963) 123-24; E. Dhorme, *L'emploi métaphorique des noms de parties du corps en hébreu et en akkadien* (1923, ²1963), 75-80; E. Ebeling, "Auge," *RLA,* I, 313; idem, "Blick, böser," *RLA,* II, 55; C. Edlund, "Auge," *BHHW,* I, 153; H. Goeke, "Das Menschenbild der individuellen Klagelieder" (diss., Bonn, 1971), esp. 214ff.; W. Helck, "'Augen des Königs,'" *LexÄg,* I, 560; E. Jenni and D. Vetter, "עַיִן *ʿayin* eye," *TLOT,* II, 874-80; A. R. Johnson, *The Vitality of the Individual in the Thought of Ancient Israel* (²1964); O. Keel, *Deine Blicke sind wie Tauben. SBS* 114/115 (1984); idem, *Jahwe-Visionen und Siegelkunst. SBS* 84/85 (1977); H.-J. Kraus, "Hören und Sehen in der althebräischen Tradition," in *Biblisch-theologische Aufsätze* (1972), 84-101; M. Lurker, *Wörterbuch biblischer Bilder und Symbole* (²1978); L. Malten, *Die Sprache des menschlichen Antlitzes in der Antike. FuF* 27 (1953); W. Michaelis, "ὀφθαλμός," *TDNT,* V, 375-78; P. H. Middendorf, "Gott sieht" (diss., Freiburg, Breslau, 1935); F. Nötscher, *"Das Angesicht Gottes schauen" nach biblischer und babylonischer Auffassung* (1924, ²1969); A. L. Oppenheim, "'The Eyes of the Lord,'" *JAOS* 88 (1968) 173-80; E. Otto, "Auge," *LexÄg,* I, 559-60; S. C. Reif, "A Root to Look Up? A Study of the Hebrew *nśʾ ʿyn,*" *Congress Volume, Salamanca 1983. SVT* 36 (1985), 230-44; A. E. Rüthy, "'Sieben Augen auf einem Stein,' Sach. 3,9," *TZ* 13 (1957) 523-29; F. J. Stendebach, "Theologische Anthropologie des Jahwisten" (diss., Bonn, 1970); H. W. Wolff, *Anthropology of the OT* (Eng. trans. 1974).

The word is probably a primary noun, found in all the Semitic languages: Ugar. *'n;*[1] Akk. *īnu/ēnu;*[2] the Canaanite glosses in the Amarna texts have the suffixed form *ḫinaia;*[3] Phoen. *'n;* Aramaic dialects *'yn* (Jewish Aram. *'ênā'* or *'aynā';* Syr. *'aynā*);[4] Arab. *'ayn;* OSA *'yn;*[5] Eth. *'ayn.* An Egyp. *'yn* is attested only in written characters; the normal word for "eye" is *ỉr.t.*[6]

Apart from the primary noun, the qal participle of a denominative verb *'yn* occurs once in the OT (1 S. 18:9 *Q*), with the meaning "look upon with suspicion." Denominative verbs are found also in Ugaritic,[7] Jewish Aramaic, and Middle Hebrew. A poel participle has been conjectured in 1 S. 2:29,32.[8]

Finally, several personal names derive from *'ayin,* including *'elyô'ênay,* "my eyes are with [or: 'toward'] Yahweh," which imitates an Akkadian pattern.[9]

In the LXX the Greek equivalent *ophthalmós* occurs almost 700 times; it is used almost exclusively to translate *'ayin.*[10] The lexical field includes → חזה *ḥāzâ* and → ראה *rā'â.*

II. Ancient Near East.

1. *Egypt.* In Egypt the eye plays an important role as the organ by which light and the physical world are perceived; it is also expressive of personal power. The significance of the eye as a human organ is illustrated by the use of the phrase "every eye" to mean "everyone." A major metaphorical use of "eye" is in the epithet "eyes of the king of Upper Egypt," used (together with "ears of the king of Lower Egypt") as an honorific title of high officials, especially in the Eighteenth Dynasty. Egypt is called "eye of Re" and "healing eye" *(wḏ3.t).* An "evil eye" is in part an apotropaic force, in part a harbinger of affliction.

In mythological thought the sun and moon were the eyes of Horus, god of the heavens. Later we read also of the "eyes of Re"; the sun god is said to illuminate the land with his two eyes.[11] Usually, however, the sun is the "eye of Re" and the moon the "eye of Horus." Horus loses his eye in his battle with Seth; Thoth brings it back and heals it (a mythological representation of the phases of the moon). Therefore the healed eye or *udjat* eye *(wḏ3.t)* is a symbol of life and strength, often used as an amulet with apotropaic powers. Drawn on a coffin, a pair of eyes serves in part to avert the forces of evil, in part to let the dead person look out from the tomb.[12] The solar eye can be sent

---

1. *WUS,* no. 2055; *UT,* no. 1846.
2. *AHw,* I, 383; *CAD,* VII, 153-58.
3. *BLe,* §2m.
4. *DNSI,* II, 839.
5. Biella, 363.
6. See, respectively, *WbÄS,* I, 189, 106-7.
7. *WUS,* no. 2055a; *UT,* no. 1846.
8. H. J. Stoebe, *Das erste Buch Samuelis. KAT* VIII/1 (1973), 116-17.
9. *IPN,* 163, 216.
10. Michaelis, 376.
11. H. Ringgren, *Liber amicorum. FS C. J. Bleeker* (1969), 141.
12. *RÄR,* 854-56.

forth by the sun god for various purposes. More often, however, texts speak of the angry solar eye, separated from the deity, which must be appeased and brought back. Under these circumstances, it is often identified with a divinized wild lioness.[13]

The identification of the divine with light is paralleled by the receptivity to light of the human eye. The relationship between divinity and humanity is that of sight. Blindness is separation from God. Just as the divine eyes are undamaged, so the eyes of human beings are to be whole.[14]

2. *Mespotamia.* In Mesopotamia *īnu namirtu* means both "bright eye" and "happy face." A sharp eye was considered a sign of a sharp mind. The eye expresses both approval and displeasure. Someone who has won favor is described as *ša īn* PN *maru,* "pleasing to the eye of PN." Goodwill and the like are indicated by the expression *niš īnē,* "raising of the eyes." The moon is referred to metaphorically as the eye of heaven and earth. Reproductions of eyes were presented as votive offerings and used as amulets.[15] Also metaphorical is the expression *^{aban}īnu (= ^{ná}IGI),* "eye-stone," referring to a jewel set in a piece of jewelry (cf. Ezk. 1:4,7,16,22).[16] There was a widespread belief in the effect of the evil eye, based on the notion that the eye can function as an independent force. For protection against the evil eye, we find amulets such as miniature hands with outstretched fingers made of imitation lapis lazuli.

3. *Ugarit.* A small tablet in Akkadian with an incantation against eye diseases has been found at Ugarit.[17] The similarity of the poetic language of Ugarit to that of the OT is illustrated, e.g., by the comparison of an eye to a pool. Both also speak of the "spring of the eye." In each case there is probably a play on the double meaning of *'n,* "eye" and "spring."[18] The combination of *yn* and *'n,* literally "wine of brightness," refers to sparkling wine.[19] We find *'n* and *riš* in parallelism.[20] The combination of *'p'p,* "pupil" (not "eyelash"[?]), and *'n* is found only in Ugaritic and Hebrew.[21]

III. OT.

1. *Sensory Organ.* In the first instance, "eye" denotes the physical organ that enables people to see. Relatively few texts, however, limit the meaning of the eye to this function, and most of these speak of a defect: a blemish in the eye (Lev. 21:20), failure (*kilyôn,* Dt. 28:65) or dimming (*khh,* Zec. 11:17; Gen. 27:1; Dt. 34:7) of the eyes; weak (*rkk,* Gen. 29:17) or "heavy" eyes (*kbd,* Gen. 48:10); eyes that have grown weak *(khh)*

13. *RÄR,* 733-35.
14. E. Otto, *Gott und Mensch. AHAW* 1964:1, 47ff., 101-5.
15. Ebeling, *RLA,* I, 313.
16. Boson, *RLA,* II, 270.
17. W. von Soden, *UF* 1 (1969) 191.
18. M. Dahood, *RSP,* I, 149-50, no. 123, citing Cant. 7:5(Eng. v. 4).
19. Ibid., 209, no. 247, citing Prov. 23:31.
20. Ibid., 299, no. 435, citing Jer. 8:23.
21. Ibid., 301, no. 440, citing Jer. 9:17(18); Ps. 11:4; 132:4; Prov. 4:25; 6:4; 30:13; Job 41:10(18).

or fixed (*qûm,* 1 S. 3:2 *Q;* 4:15; cf. 1 K. 14:4); weary eyes (*dll,* Isa. 38:14); eyes that rot (*mqq* niphal, Zec. 14:12), are darkened (*ḥšk,* Ps. 69:24[23]), fail (*klh,* Job 11:20; cf. 17:5), or are wasted (*klh* piel, Lev. 26:16; cf. 1 S. 2:33); redness of eyes (*ḥaḵlilûṯ,* Prov. 23:29); cf. also Prov. 15:30.

Ex. 21:16 requires an Israelite who knocks out *(nkh + šḥt)* the eye of a male or female slave to release that slave. In Jgs. 16:21 the Philistines gouge out (*nqr* piel; cf. 1 S. 11:2) Samson's eyes. In 2 K. 25:7 Nebuchadnezzar has Zedekiah's eyes put out (*'wr* piel; cf. Jer. 39:7; 52:11). In the context of a threat oracle, Ezk. 6:9 speaks of crushing *(šbr;* cf. *BHS)* the eyes that turned after idols. We note in such texts that both honor and disgrace find expression in the body, so that disgrace may be effected by destruction of the latter, e.g., by putting out the eyes[22] — an illustration of how fluid the boundary is between the eye as a physical entity and its personal connotations. The same principle applies to positive statements: the eyes of the blind see (Isa. 29:18) or are opened (35:5; cf. 42:7).

The eye appears in the talion formula in Ex. 21:24; Lev. 24:20 *('ayin taḥaṯ 'ayin);* Dt. 19:21 *('ayin bᵉ'ayin);* cf. Jgs. 16:28.[23]

The eye as the organ of vision is also meant in the idiom that speaks of vanishing from someone's eyes (Jgs. 6:21; cf. Nu. 11:6). An eye that sees can also testify on someone's behalf (Job 29:15; the verbal action of the sensory organ is noteworthy; cf. also Prov. 25:7b,8).

Another group of texts sees in the eyes the part of the body in which sleep has its home. Sleep flees from *(ndd min)* the eyes (Gen. 31:40); David allows his eyes no sleep (Ps. 132:4; cf. Prov. 6:4; Eccl. 8:16); someone who has been sleeping opens his eyes (Job 27:19). In Ps. 77:5(4) the psalmist laments, "You have taken hold of my eyelids," probably meaning that God refuses to let the author sleep. In these texts, too, the personal connotation is unmistakable. Also in this context belongs the idiom "lays one's hand on someone's eyes" (Gen. 46:4) — a description of the final service done for someone who is dying.

Jer. 8:23(9:1) calls the eye a fountain of tears *(mᵉqôr dim'â);* cf. Jer. 9:17(18); 13:17; 14:17; Ps. 116:8; 119:136; Jer. 31:16; Lam. 1:16; 3:48-49; 3:51 (see *BHS*); 2:11; cf. Job 16:20.

Just as the shutting of eyes is associated with death, so the opening of eyes is associated with awakening to new life (2 K. 4:35, preceded in v. 34 by the magical act in which Elisha lays his eyes upon the eyes of the dead child). The element of life is also present when the tribal oracle says that Judah's eyes are dark *(ḥaḵlîlî)* with wine (Gen. 49:12), or when Jonathan's eyes are described as brightening at the taste of honey (1 S. 14:27[*Q*],29; cf. Ezr. 9:8). Excessive vitality, noted with disapprobation, is indicated by the statement that someone's eyes swell out with fatness (*yāṣā' mēḥēleḇ,* Ps. 73:7).

David is described as having beautiful eyes (1 S. 16:12). Such beauty can be empha-

---

22. *ILC,* I-II, 241.
23. A. Alt, *KlS,* I, 341-44; K. Elliger, *Leviticus. HAT* I/4 (1966), 335.

sized by makeup (2 K. 9:30; Jer. 4:30; Ezk. 23:40). Conversely, a bandage over the eyes can serve as a disguise (1 K. 20:38,41).

In Ex. 13:9,16; Dt. 6:8; 11:18, the phrase "between the eyes" is a periphrastic reference to the forehead. All these texts appear in the context of Dtn or Dtr paraenesis, which calls observance of the Feast of Unleavened Bread a "reminder" (Ex. 13:9) and the sacrifice of the firstborn or the words of the *tôrâ* an "emblem" (→ טוטפות *ṭôṭāpôṯ*, Ex. 13:16; Dt. 6:8; 11:18) on the forehead.

The same expression appears in Dt. 14:1, where the Israelites are forbidden to make a bald spot "between the eyes" when in mourning, and in Dnl. 8:5,21, which describe a male goat with a horn "between its eyes."

In polemic against idols, we find the statement that idols cannot see even though they have eyes (Ps. 115:5; 135:16).

The eyes of animals are mentioned in Gen. 30:41; Job 28:7; 39:29; 40:24; 41:10(18); Prov. 1:17; Jer. 14:6; cf. Dnl. 8:5,21.

Finally, we find the fundamental statement that Yahweh made the eye (Prov. 20:12; Ps. 94:9). These words "withdraw hearing and sight from the sphere of absolute human sovereignty" and emphasize human responsibility for the gifts of creation[24] — another instance of the personal significance of what in essence is just a bodily organ.

2. *Locus of Personality.* In most texts the eye is the locus of personal perception and knowledge. In the eye the human "soul" is revealed.[25] Gen. 3:5 and 7 clearly illustrate this personal admixture. The snake declares that the eyes of the man and the woman will be opened as the result of their eating of the tree in middle of the garden, so that they will be like God (v. 5); v. 7 confirms that their eyes are indeed opened — but with the consequence that they both recognize that they are naked.[26] In 21:19 God opens Hagar's eyes so that she sees the well (cf. Nu. 22:31). In 2 K. 6 Elisha prays that Yahweh will open the eyes of his servant (v. 17) and of the Arameans (v. 20); both prayers are answered. In Ps. 119:18 the psalmist asks Yahweh to open his eyes that he may behold the wondrous things in Yahweh's law. Yahweh's "enlightening" (*'wr* hiphil) the eyes implies renewal or preservation of life (Ps. 13:4[3]; 19:9[8];[27] cf. Prov. 29:13; 15:30).

Prov. 20:13 takes us into the sphere of practical everyday wisdom: "Open your eyes, and you will have plenty of bread." Perception thus presupposes an inward disposition not necessarily available at will but frequently experienced as a gift. It is rooted in encounter with objects, with human beings, and with God.[28]

On the other hand, the eyes of the people are shut as the effective result of Isaiah's message — a collective blindness that nullifies the disposition to perceive (Isa. 6:10; cf. 32:3; 44:18). In these passages the eye is associated with the heart. The eye is ac-

24. Kraus, 87.
25. Stendebach, 263.
26. Cf. Stendebach, 130-34.
27. Kraus, *Psalms 1–59* (Eng. trans. 1988), 274.
28. Stendebach, 263-64.

cordingly a concentrated expression of the personality, of people's disposition toward God, human beings, and the world about them.[29] In a similar vein, 43:8 speaks of the people as being blind, though they have eyes, and 29:10 says that Yahweh has closed the eyes of the prophets.

The personal nature of perception is likewise evident in Ezk. 40:4 and 44:5: "See *(rā'â)* with your eyes"; cf. Gen. 45:12; Dt. 3:21; 4:3,9; 7:19; 10:21; 11:7; 21:7; 29:2-3(3-4); Josh. 24:7; 1 S. 24:11(10); 2 S. 24:3; 1 K. 1:48; 10:7; 2 K. 7:2,19; 22:20; Isa. 6:5; 30:20; 33:17,20; 64:3; Jer. 20:4; 42:2; Mal. 1:5; Ps. 35:21; 91:8; Job 7:7,8a; 10:18; 13:1; 19:27; 20:9; 28:10; 42:5; Eccl. 11:9; 2 Ch. 9:6; 29:8; 34:28. In all these passages, *'ayin* is associated with a verb of seeing or perceiving; the concentration of this usage in Deuteronomy and Dtr texts is striking (in 2 S. 16:12 read *bᵉ'onyî;* see *BHS*).

An aspect of direct personal encounter and perception is expressed by the idiom "eye in eye" (*'ayin bᵉ'ayin,* Nu. 14:14; Isa. 52:8), in the sense of a real, personal revelation of God (cf. Jer. 32:4; 34:3).[30]

In this context, too, belong the words Moses addressed to Hobab, who was familiar with the country the Israelites were about to enter: "You will serve as a pair of eyes *(lᵉ'ênayim)* for us" (Nu. 10:31; cf. Job 29:15).

Isa. 11:3 also presupposes that the eye is the agent of perception. The future king will not judge by what his eyes see *(lᵉmar'ēh 'ênāyw),* which the context describes as an unrighteous (because superficial) judgment. In 1 S. 16:7, contrariwise, the eye is the object of perception: human beings look on the eyes, the outward appearance, while Yahweh looks on the heart.[31] The expressions *bᵉ'ênê* in Lev. 13:5 and *mar'ēh 'ênê* in 13:12 refer to examination of lepers by a priest.

The language of prayer in the Psalms likewise treats the eye as the agent of perception. The psalmist sees Yahweh's steadfast love before his eyes (26:3) — possibly a reference to a manifestation of Yahweh's love occurring in the course of worship;[32] the wicked have no fear of God before their eyes (36:2[1]); the sinner's guilt is set before his eyes (50:21). The speaker of 101:7 declares that no liar shall continue before his eyes; his eye seeks out instead the faithful in the land (v. 6).

Job curses the night on which he was conceived because it did not hide trouble from his eyes (Job 3:10). According to 28:20-21, wisdom is hidden from the eyes of all the living.

In Prov. 4:21 the wise teacher cautions the listener not to let his words escape from his eyes. Prov. 20:8 describes a king as "winnowing" (*zārâ* piel) all evil with his eyes, separating the evil from the good as grain is winnowed during threshing. Eccl. 5:10b(11b) states that the eyes of the rich must look on as their wealth is consumed. Eccl. 2:14 observes that the wise have eyes in their head, whereas fools walk in darkness.

The eyes also serve as the agents of aesthetic appreciation (Gen. 3:6; 1 K. 20:6;

---

29. Edlund, 153.
30. Nötscher, 55.
31. Stoebe, *KAT* VIII/1, 301, conjecturing a secondary correction in v. 12.
32. Kraus, *Psalms 1–59,* 327.

Lam. 2:4). Ezekiel's wife is described as attractive, the "delight of his eyes" (Ezk. 24:16; cf. vv. 21,25). Eccl. 11:7 observes that it is pleasant for the eyes to see the sun.

Thus the eye can also be the agent of affect and emotion, longing and desire (Prov. 27:20;[33] cf. Eccl. 1:8; 2:10; 4:8). Rachel says to her father: "Do not let [anger] flare up in the eyes of my lord" (Gen. 31:35; cf. 45:5). In Ezk. 23:16 (Oholibah's lusting after the Babylonians), the eyes are the instigators of sexual desire (cf. Isa. 3:16). Ezk. 20:7-8 speaks of idols as abominations *(šiqqûṣ)* on which the eyes feast (cf. 20:24). Conversely, Job says (31:1) that he has made a covenant with his eyes not to look on a virgin; in v. 7 he says that his heart has not followed his eyes (cf. Nu. 15:39). In the Song of Songs, on the other hand, the man sings the praises of his beloved for making his heart beat (*lbb* piel) with a glance of her eyes (4:9). And the woman says that in the eyes of her lover she has become as one who finds *šālôm* (8:10).

A broad spectrum of inward states can find expression in the eyes, for the "soul" reveals itself in the face and its expression. If the "soul" is vigorous and healthy, the eyes are bright. The psalmist who is weak and has lost his vigor laments that the light of his eyes has departed from him (Ps. 38:11[10]).[34] Thus the eye can be the locus of respect or disrespect. Job 15:12 speaks of eyes that "flash" (*rzm;* some mss. have *rmz;* LXX reads *y^{e}rumûn;* cf. *BHS*), i.e., roll in anger.[35] According to Est. 1:17, the conduct of Queen Vashti will make all the husbands of the realm contemptible (*bzh* hiphil) in the eyes of their wives (cf. 3:6; Neh. 6:16). The expression "honor in the eyes of" *(kabbēḏ b^e)* appears in 1 Ch. 19:3.

Isa. 2:11 speaks of "eyes of pride" (cf. 5:15; 10:12; Ps. 18:28[27]; 101:5; Prov. 6:17; 21:4; 30:13; 2 S. 22:28 [cf. *BHS*]; 2 K. 19:22 = Isa. 37:23; also Ps. 131:1). In Job 22:29 "downcast" *(šaḥ)* eyes are a sign of humility.

Prov. 21:10 observes that people find no mercy in the eyes of the wicked (cf. Ps. 10:8; 15:4; 54:9[7]; 92:12[11]). Prov. 22:9 speaks of a good eye, 23:6 of a malicious eye (cf. 28:22; Dt. 15:9; 28:54,56).

The expression "Do not let your eye be saddened (→ חוס *ḥûs),*" i.e., "show no pity," has a marked affective accent (Gen. 45:20; cf. Ps. 88:10; Job 31:16). It occurs in Dt. 7:16 in the context of the destruction of the peoples and in 13:9(8); 19:13,21; 25:12 in the context of legal proceedings (cf. also Isa. 13:18; Ezk. 9:5; 16:5). Eyes "waste away" *('šš)* with grief (Ps. 6:8[7]; 31:10;[36] cf. Lam. 5:17, *ḥšk*).

Dt. 28:32 threatens the disobedient Israelites that their eyes will grow weak *(klh)* with straining in vain to see their deported sons and daughters (cf. Ps. 69:4[3]; 119:82,123; Lam. 4:17).

To direct one's eyes toward someone (*'ênayim 'al,* 1 K. 1:20; 2 Ch. 20:12) or to look upon someone (Isa. 17:7) signifies concentration of attention on the part of the subject in hope and expectation (also Ezk. 18:6,12,15; 23:27; 33:25; Ps. 121:1; 123:1; Dnl. 4:31[34] [Aram. *nṭl*]; cf. also Ps. 25:15; 119:148; 123:2; 141:8; 145:15). Wandering

33. O. Plöger, *Sprüche Salomos. BK* XVII (1984), 326.
34. *ILC,* I-II, 174-75.
35. G. Fohrer, *Das Buch Hiob. KAT* XVI (1963), 270.
36. L. Delekat (*VT* 14 [1964] 52-55) proposes the meaning "swell up."

eyes, on the contrary, betray a lack of attention (Prov. 17:24).[37] Therefore the eye (lit. "the daughter of the eye," the pupil; see below) should not rest (Lam. 2:18). Negatively, Jer. 22:17 says that Jehoiakim's eyes are set solely on his own dishonest gain. A voluntative accent is present when the psalmist vows never to set anything that is base before his eyes (*šîṯ lᵉneged*, Ps. 101:3). Mic. 4:11 says that the eyes of the enemy look on (*ḥāzâ bᵉ*) Zion with satisfaction, gloating over her destruction (cf. Mic. 7:10).[38]

Job says that his eye pours out tears to God (Job 16:20), spends the nights in bitterness (17:2), and grows dim (*khh*) from grief (17:7).

In Prov. 4:25 the sage counsels: "Let your eyes look directly forward," for "eyes that are easily diverted lose sight of the word of truth."[39] Prov. 4:21 advises the disciple not to let the words of the teacher escape from sight. The eyes should instead delight in the ways of the teacher (23:26). The eyes of a fool roam to the ends of the earth (17:24), "because a fool has no goal."[40] Therefore we find the prayer that Yahweh will turn aside the eyes of the devout psalmist from looking at vanities (Ps. 119:37).

An extremely personal and deliberate mode of seeing is denoted by the expression "raise (*nāśā'*) one's eyes" (e.g., Gen. 13:10; Dt. 4:19; Josh. 5:13; Isa. 40:26; 49:18; 51:6; 60:4; Jer. 3:2; Ezk. 8:5; Zec. 2:1,5[1:18; 2:1]; Ps. 121:1; Job 2:12; Dnl. 8:3; 10:5; 1 Ch. 21:16). This idiom usually denotes an introductory action followed by *rā'â*, frequently followed in turn by *wᵉhinnēh*, "and behold." But it can also express desire, longing, dependence, etc.[41] Kraus speaks of a "heightened mode of seeing," in which the perception of outward form is permeated with its initial interpretive experiences. The word *hinnēh* is meant to alert the reader truly to perceive a situation or a person.[42]

The expression takes on a special accent in Gen. 13:14, where Yahweh commands Abraham: "Raise your eyes now, and look." These words may reflect the ancient legal practice of taking effectual ownership of land by a visual survey (cf. Dt. 3:27; 34:4).[43] More specifically, ownership of land was transferred by its owner's taking the new owner to an elevated site to show the extent of the property.[44]

In Nu. 24:2 the raising of Balaam's eyes means that he conveys a blessing.[45] In Gen. 39:7 the expression has an erotic connotation (cf. Isa. 3:16).[46] In Gen. 44:21, similarly, the expression *śîm 'ênayim* conveys a sense of personal favor (cf. Jer. 39:12; 40:4).

---

37. Johnson, 47.

38. On the text see I. Willi-Plein, *Vorformen der Schriftexegeses innerhalb des ATs. BZAW* 123 (1971), 87.

39. O. Plöger, *BK* XVII, 49-50.

40. Ibid., 206.

41. Jenni and Vetter, 876-77.

42. Kraus, 85.

43. D. Daube, *Studies in Biblical Law* (1947, ²1969), 34-35.

44. D. Daube, "Rechtsgedanken in der Erzählungen das Pentateuchs," *Von Ugarit nach Qumran. FS. O. Eissfeldt. BZAW* 77 (²1961), 32-41, esp. 35; idem, *Journal of Roman Studies* 47 (1957) 39-52, esp. 39-40.

45. Stendebach, 66, 266.

46. Wildberger, *Isaiah 1–12* (Eng. trans. 1991), 149.

Conversely, in Cant. 6:5 the young man says to his bride: "Turn your eyes away from me, for they overwhelm (*rhb* hiphil) me."

Deliberate refusal to take notice of something is expressed by the words "close (*'lm* hiphil) the eyes to" (Lev. 20:4; 1 S. 12:3; Isa. 33:15 [*'ṣm*]; Ezk. 22:26; Prov. 28:27; cf. Lev. 4:13; Nu. 5:13 [niphal]; 15:24 [simply *mē'ênayim*]). A bribe is called a "covering" (*kᵉsûṯ*) of the eyes (Gen. 20:16).[47] To motivate a prohibition against accepting bribes, Dt. 16:19 cites a maxim that clearly belongs to the wisdom tradition: "A bribe blinds the eyes of the wise."[48]

Intention is conveyed by the idiom "set one's eyes to . . ." (*šîṯ lᵉ*, Ps. 17:11).

Scorn and derision are expressed by narrowing *(qrṣ)* the eyes (Ps. 35:19; Prov. 6:13; 10:10), secret planning by closing them (*'ṣh,* 16:30).[49]

Prov. 30:17 says: "The eye that mocks *(l'g lᵉ)* a father and scorns *(bûz lᵉ)* the aging *(ziqnaṯ)* of a mother will be pecked out by the ravens of the valley and eaten by the vultures."

Prov. 23:5a cautions against striving after wealth: "When your eyes light upon it, it is gone." This involves a play on words with v. 25b, which says that wealth flies like an eagle toward heaven.[50]

Eccl. 6:9 teaches: "Better is the sight of the eyes than the wandering of the gullet *(hᵃloḵ-nāpeš),*" i.e., "Better to have something in view than hungry jaws." Does this convey the traditional wisdom that a bird in the hand is worth two in the bush? Or better alive than dead (cf. 6:7)? Or having to look on the good fortune of others is still better than being dead (cf. 5:10[11])?[51]

Prov. 15:30 reflects psychosomatic relationships: "The light of the eyes rejoices the heart."

Visionary sight is the subject of Nu. 24:3-4. Balaam is called a man with an opened *(šᵉṯum)* eye and uncovered *(gᵉlûy)* eyes;[52] cf. vv. 15-16. In Job 4:16 Eliphaz says that in a vision a form stood before his eyes.

Johnson is therefore correct in saying that the eye is associated with a wide range of "psychical" activities, so that at times the use of *'ayin* is almost synonymous with *nepeš* and *pānîm* (cf. Job 24:15).[53]

3. *Idioms.* Some very common idioms also have a personal aspect. For example, approval or liking is expressed by the words "good in the eyes of" *(ṭôḇ* or *yṭb bᵉ);* examples include Gen. 16:6; Dt. 1:23; Josh. 22:30,33; Jer. 26:14; 40:4; Zec. 11:12; Est. 1:21; 2:4,9; 3:11; 8:5,8; 1 Ch. 21:23.

---

47. → VII, 263-64.
48. G. von Rad, *Deuteronomy. OTL* (Eng. trans. 1966), 115.
49. But see *BHS;* Plöger, *BK* XVII, 188, 196.
50. Cf. Amenemope, chap. 7 (col. 10, 4-5; *AOT*², 40; *ANET,* 422).
51. Lohfink, *Kohelet. NEB* (1980), 48.
52. On *šᵉṯum* see Noth, *Numbers. OTL* (Eng. trans. 1968), 190; Stendebach, 265 n. 194; → סתם *stm.*
53. Pp. 47-48.

The expression "right in the eyes of" *(yāšār bᵉ)* occurs in Dt. 12:8; Josh. 9:25 *(ṭôḇ + yšr);* Jgs. 14:3,7; 17:6; 21:25; 1 S. 18:20,26; 2 S. 17:4; 19:7(6); 1 K. 9:12; Jer. 18:4; 26:14; 40:4,5; Prov. 12:15; 21:2; 1 Ch. 13:4; 2 Ch. 30:4.

Disapproval or dislike is expressed by "bad/evil in the eyes of" *(r'' or ra' bᵉ):* Gen. 21:11-12; 28:8; 48:17; Ex. 21:8; Nu. 11:10; Josh. 24:15; 1 S. 8:6; 18:8; 29:7; 2 S. 11:25; Jer. 40:4.[54]

The presence of someone as an eyewitness is expressed by "before the eyes of" *(lᵉ'ênê),* e.g., Gen. 23:11,18; Lev. 20:17; 25:53; 26:45; Nu. 19:5; 20:8,12,27; Dt. 1:30; 4:6,34; 6:22; 25:9; 28:31; 1 S. 12:16; Isa. 13:16; 52:10; Jer. 16:9; 19:10; Ezk. 4:12, etc.; Hos. 2:12(10); Joel 1:16 *(negeḏ);* Zeph. 3:20; Ps. 79:10; 98:2; Job 21:8; Ezr. 3:12 *(bᵉ);* Neh. 8:5; 1 Ch. 28:8; 29:10,25; 2 Ch. 32:23. The frequent use of the expression in Ezekiel is noteworthy.

Another common expression is "find *(māṣā')*/give *(nāṯan)* favor *(ḥēn)*[55] in the eyes of": Gen. 30:27; 32:6(5); 33:8,10,15; 34:11; 39:4,21; 47:25,29; 50:4; Ex. 3:21; 11:3; 12:36; Nu. 32:5; Dt. 24:1; 1 S. 1,18; 16:22; 20:3,29; 25:8; 27:5; 2 S. 14:22; 16:4; 1 K. 11:19; Prov. 3:4 *(ḥēn wᵉśēḵel-ṭôḇ);* Ruth 2:2,10,13; Est. 2:15 *(nś');* 5:2 *(nś');* 5:8; 7:3.[56] This usage probably originates in the realm of aesthetic perception; the eye thus shifts from being the locus of aesthetic judgment to being the locus of moral judgment.[57] This holds true for both judgment of others and judgment of oneself. In this context belong the many warnings of wisdom literature against being wise in one's own eyes, i.e., considering oneself wise (Prov. 3:7; 26:5,12,16; 28:11; 30:12; cf. also 12:15; 16:2; 21:2; Job 32:1; Isa. 5:21).

Other examples: "be slight *(qll)* in the eyes of" (Gen. 16:4 [cf. v. 5]; Dt. 25:3 [*qlh* niphal]; 1 S. 18:23 [*qll* niphal]; cf. also 2 S. 6:22 [*šāp̱al*]); "be hard *(qāšâ)*" (Dt. 15:18); "act like one who jests (*ṣḥq* piel)" (Gen. 19:14); "make their reputation stink (*b'š* hiphil)," i.e., "bring into disrepute" (Ex. 5:21);[58] "appear like one who mocks (*t''* piel)" (Gen. 27:12); "be great *(gāḏôl)* in the eyes of" (Ex. 11:3; cf. Josh. 3:7; 4:14); "be like grasshoppers" (Nu. 13:33; cf. 1 S. 15:17); "disguise one's mind = dissemble (*šnh* piel)" (1 S. 21:14[13]); "have a precious *(yāqār)* life" (1 S. 26:21; cf. v. 24 [*gdl*]; 2 K. 1:13-14; Ps. 72:14); "be like a bearer of good news *(mᵉḇaśśēr)*" (2 S. 4:10); "wish to honor someone" (2 S. 10:3); "be difficult (*pl'* niphal) to do" (2 S. 13:2); "be worthless *(šāw')*" (Ezk. 21:28[23]);[59] "be a burden *('āmāl)*" (Ps. 73:16); "be unclean *(ṭmh)*"[60] (Job 18:3); "become thorns" (Nu. 33:55; cf. Josh. 23:13).

In Jer. 7:11 the inhabitants of Jerusalem are asked accusingly, "Has this house . . . become a den of robbers in your eyes?" (cf. Hag. 2:3). Zec. 8:6 asks rhetorically whether something that seems too wonderful in the eyes of the inhabitants of Jerusalem

---

54. Cf. III.5 below with reference to God.
55. → חנן *ḥnn.*
56. See III.5 below with reference to God.
57. Stendebach, 74, 265; Johnson, 47-48.
58. See *HAL,* I, 107.
59. See W. Zimmerli, *Ezekiel 1. Herm* (Eng. trans. 1979), 438.
60. A by-form of *ṭm';* or cj. *ṭmm* niphal, "be blocked, be silent": Fohrer, *KAT* XVI, 297.

must also seem too wonderful (*pl'* niphal) in the eyes of Yahweh (cf. Ps. 118:2). Prov. 17:8 calls a bribe a "magic stone" (*'eḇen ḥēn)* in the eyes of the giver: it is like a magic charm that guarantees success.

In the light of this evidence, it seems odd that Wolff discusses the eye only cursorily in his *Anthropology of the OT.* It is impossible to support his statement that the priority of the ear and speech for truly human understanding is clear.[61] The eye and the ear stand rather in a relationship of equivalence. Kraus describes the situation more accurately: "No organ of the human body reflects the totality of life more impressively than does the eye. . . . All the motions and emotions of the inner life are manifested in the eye."[62]

4. *Metaphors.* The eye appears also in metaphorical contexts. In 2 S. 12:11, e.g., we find the "eyes of the sun" used in the sense of "broad daylight."

The eye of a metallic substance *(ḥšml)* is its luster (Ezk. 1:4,7,27; 8:2; Dnl. 10:6; etc.). Nu. 11:7 says that the "eye" of the manna was like the "eye" of gum resin — i.e., its appearance was similar. According to Jenni and Vetter,[63] these examples belong under the general category of "the visible."

Ezk. 1:18 speaks of "eyes" on the rims of the wheels. Zimmerli sees in them decorative wheel ornaments, which, however, are to be understood in a deeper sense as symbolizing Yahweh's all-seeing presence.[64] Ezk. 10:12 adds that the bodies of the cherubim, including their hands and wings, were covered with eyes. Zimmerli views this description as a secondary elaboration of the text; here too, he maintains, only the rims of the wheels were involved.[65] Keel thinks these "eyes" were reinforcements (made of nails?), which were (once again?) common on Mesopotamian chariots since the time of Ashurbanipal. He also cites Egyptian Bes figurines, which in the period of the New Kingdom were occasionally covered with copper nails, but in the late period were sewn with "eyes." The Ezekiel passage also refers to eyes in the literal sense. They are the counterpart to the faces of the four living creatures; like these, they establish omnipresence. In 10:12 we already find the "wheels" thought of as independent angelic beings; such figures play a role in prerabbinic and rabbinic literature.[66]

Prov. 7:2 compares the teachings of the instructor to the pupil (*'îšôn)* of the eye — "vulnerable but precious."[67] Prov. 10:26 says that the lazy are like smoke to the eyes of their employers — useless and annoying.[68]

In the light of Ps. 17:8, where *baṯ* is probably a gloss on *'îšôn,* the phrase *baṯ-'ênēḵ*

---

61. P. 118.
62. P. 84.
63. P. 878.
64. Zimmerli, *Ezekiel 1,* 129. See *BRL*², 252; *ANEP,* no. 11; *AOB*², 567; cf. Zec. 4:2,10b.
65. *Ezekiel 1,* 227.
66. Keel, *Jahwe-Visionen,* 268-69.
67. Plöger, *BK* XVII, 76.
68. Ibid., 129.

in Lam. 2:18 should be in interpreted as meaning "eyeball." The attempt by Robertson to read it as a poetic image for "tears" on the basis of Arab. *bint al-ʿain* is wide of the mark.[69]

Zec. 3:9 speaks of a "single stone" with seven eyes that Yahweh has set before Joshua. Galling thinks this refers to a precious stone of a sort familiar from seals. The "eyes" are an engraved wreath of seven small circles — ע *(ʿayin)* being a circle in Old Hebrew script. The reference is to the single precious stone in the frontlet *(ṣîṣ)* of the high priest (Ex. 28:36ff.).[70] Rüthy suggests that the text of Zec. 3:9 (like that of 5:6) is corrupt and should be read *ʿwnym.*[71]

The MT of Zec. 9:1 reads: "For to Yahweh belongs [or: 'Toward Yahweh is directed'] the eye of man." While Elliger follows the MT, Rudolph proposes reading *'ᵃrām* instead of *'āḏām,* interpreting the "eye of Aram" as a laudatory reference to Damascus.[72] This interpretation is certainly preferable to translating *ʿayin* as "substance" or "spring" in the sense of "offspring," or interpreting *lᵉ* as emphatic and translating "truly Yahweh is the eye."[73] Dahood interprets *ʿên 'āḏām* as "surface of the earth," citing Prov. 30:14b; Gen. 16:12; Job 36:28; Jer. 32:20; Zec. 13:5.[74] In this case *ʿên 'āḏām* would be equivalent to *ʿên hā'āreṣ* in Ex. 10:5,15; Nu. 22:5,11.

In Cant. 1:15; 4:1; 5:12, the eyes of the bride and bridegroom are likened to doves. Keel finds here a stereotyped metaphor or simile and proposes translating *ʿênayim* as "glances," arguing that the Hebrews did not think of the eye as a form but in terms of actions like glowing and sparkling (cf. Prov. 23:31; Ezk. 1:7; Dnl. 10:6). The point is the dynamic quality of the eyes (cf. Isa. 3:16). The *tertium comparationis* of the metaphor is the dove's mobility and function as a messenger (cf. Ps. 55:7[6]; Gen. 8:8-12; Ps. 56:1; 68:12ff.[11ff.]).[75] As messenger of the goddess of love, the dove conveys love and tenderness. The metaphor should be translated: "Your glances are messengers of love."[76]

Cant. 7:5(4) compares the eyes to pools: they are "dark and deep as two pools." Dnl. 10:6 says that the eyes of the angel were like flaming torches, a variation on the theophany imagery of Ezk. 1:26-27.[77]

In Nu. 16:14 Dathan and Abiram ask whether Moses wants to put out (*nqr* piel) the

---

69. E. Robertson, *JTS* 38 (1937) 59. Cf. W. Rudolph, *Das Buch Ruth-Das Hohe Lied-Die Klagelieder. KAT* XVII/3 (1962), 220.

70. K. Galling, *Verbannung und Heimkehr. FS W. Rudolph* (1961), 93-94.

71. P. 527.

72. K. Elliger, *Das Buch der zwölf kleinen Propheten II. ATD* 25 (⁷1975), 144-45; cf. idem, *ZAW* 62 (1949/50) 63ff.; Rudolph, *Haggai-Sacharja 1–8-Sacharja 9–14-Maleachi. KAT* XIII/4 (1976), 168.

73. See, respectively, E. Lipiński, *VT* 20 (1970) 47; G. Gaide, *Jérusalem, voici ton roi. LD* 49 (1968), 59-60; P. J. van Zijl, *JNSL* 1 (1971) 59ff.

74. M. Dahood, *CBQ* 25 (1963) 123-24. Cf. *LidzEph,* I, 42.

75. For a different interpretation see H.-P. Müller, *Vergleich und Metapher im Hohenlied. OBO* 56 (1984), 13.

76. Keel, *Deine Blick,* 53-62.

77. Plöger, *Das Buch Daniel. KAT* XVIII (1965), 148.

eyes of the men, i.e., blind them "with the unfulfilled promise of bringing Israel into a pleasant and fertile land."[78]

In 2 S. 20:6 David orders Abishai to pursue Sheba, lest the latter reach the fortified cities and thus "tear out *(nṣl* hiphil) our eyes." Hertzberg suggests the translation "snatches away our eyes."[79] In either case, the image is of something irreplaceable.

Dnl. 7:8 describes a small horn growing up among the ten horns of the fourth beast: there were eyes like human eyes in it (cf. v. 20). The interpretation of the vision in vv. 23-27 makes no mention of these eyes, which recall the eyes of Ezk. 1:18.[80] In Ezekiel they signify the all-seeing omnipresence of Yahweh; here they probably allude to the arrogant insolence of the satanic power.

5. *God's Eye.* When anthropomorphic language speaks of God's eye, the emphasis is on the eye's function as the locus of personal attitudes and actions. For instance, numerous texts speak of finding favor *(māṣā' ḥēn)* in the eyes of Yahweh: Gen. 6:8; 18:3; 19:19; Ex. 33:12,13,16,17; Nu. 11:11,15; Jgs. 6:17; 2 S. 15:25 (see III.3 above).

Other texts speak of someone or something as being wicked or evil *(ra', r'')* in the eyes of Yahweh, i.e., displeasing Yahweh: Gen. 38:7,10; Nu. 22:34; Dt. 4:25; 17:2; Jgs. 2:11; 3:7,12; Isa. 59:15; 65:12; 66:4; Jer. 7:30; Ps. 51:6(4); Prov. 24:18; 1 Ch. 2:3; 21:7; 2 Ch. 21:6.[81] There is a notable concentration of this usage in Deuteronomy, the Dtr corpus, and Chronicles.

Ex. 15:26 calls on Israel to do what is right *(yāšār)* in Yahweh's eyes; cf. also such passages as Nu. 23:27; Dt. 6:18; 12:25,28; Jer. 27:5; 34:15; 2 Ch. 14:1(2) *(ṭôḇ + yšr).* As in the case of *ra',* this usage is concentrated in Dtn (Dtr) texts and the associated material in Chronicles, especially in the stereotyped verdicts concerning kings.

The expression "good *(ṭôḇ, yṭb)* in the eyes of Yahweh" appears in Lev. 10:19; Nu. 24:1; Dt. 6:18; 12:28; Jgs. 10:15; 1 S. 3:18; 2 S. 10:12; 15:26; 1 K. 3:10; 2 K. 20:3 = Isa. 38:3; Mal. 2:17; 1 Ch. 19:13; 2 Ch. 14:1(2).

Saul's life is precious in the eyes of David; so too is David's in the eyes of Yahweh: 1 S. 26:24; cf. Isa. 43:4; 49:5; Ps. 116:15; Job 11:4; 15:15; 25:5). Conversely, something can also be small (i.e., insignificant) in the eyes of Yahweh (2 S. 7:19 = 1 Ch. 17:17; cf. 2 K. 3:18).

In 2 S. 22:25 = Ps. 18:25(24), the worshiper declares that Yahweh has recompensed him according to his cleanness in *(l^eneḡeḏ)* Yahweh's eyes. In his prayer at the dedication of the temple, Solomon prays that Yahweh's eyes may be open toward this house — an expression of Yahweh's gracious care and solicitude (1 K. 8:29 = 2 Ch. 6:20; cf. Dt. 11:12; 1 K. 8:52; 9:3; 2 K. 19:16 = Isa. 37:17; Zec. 9:8;[82] 12:4; Dnl. 9:18; Ps. 33:18; 34:16[15]; Job 24:23;[83] 2 Ch. 6:40; 7:15,16; Neh. 1:6). Yahweh's beneficent

---

78. Noth, *Numbers,* 125.
79. *I and II Samuel. OTL* (Eng. trans. 1964), 369.
80. Plöger, *KAT* XVIII, 116.
81. See III.3 above with reference to humans.
82. But cf. *BHS;* Rudolph (*KAT* XIII/4, 169) retains the MT, contra Elliger, *ATD* 25[7], 145.
83. See Fohrer, *KAT* XVI, 370.

presence is expressed superlatively in Ps. 139:16, where the psalmist declares that Yahweh's eyes saw him even when he was an embryo *(gōlem)*. The same love and favor are described in 2 Ch. 16:9: Yahweh's eyes range (*šûṭ* piel) throughout the whole earth to help his faithful ones (cf. Ezr. 5:5 [Aramaic]). God promises the psalmist that he will make his eye watch over him (*'āleykā 'ênî,* Ps. 32:8). Elihu instructs Job that God does not withdraw *(gāra')* his eyes from the righteous (Job 36:7). Jer. 24:6 says that Yahweh will set his eyes on *(śîm 'al)* the exiles for good.

The idiom has negative force in Am. 9:4, an oracle describing the wrathful gaze of God. Here the preposition is *'al* instead of the more common *b^e;* beneficence is usually expressed by the prep. *'el* (e.g., Ps. 34:16-17[15-16]).[84] Yahweh can hide compassion from his eyes (Hos. 13:14) or hide (*'lm* hiphil) his eyes (Isa. 1:15). In Ezekiel we read with surprising frequency that Yahweh's eye will not pity, will not spare (*ḥûs,* 5:11; 7:4,9; 8:18; 9:10; cf. 20:17). Job indicts his God: "Your eyes are against me, and I shall be gone" (Job 7:8). Here God's enmity toward Job is concentrated in God's eye (cf. 16:9). In 10:4 Job asks whether God has "eyes of flesh," the eyes of a mortal, because God persecutes him so; cf. also Jon. 2:5(4); Ps. 31:23(22).

The notion of Yahweh as an eyewitness to human actions appears in Isa. 1:16 (cf. Isa. 65:16; Jer. 16:17).

In Jer. 5:3 the prophet asks Yahweh rhetorically, "Do your eyes not look for truth?" The question reflects Yahweh's personal interest in the conduct of Israel.

Yahweh's omnipresence and omnipotent judgment find expression: "Though they hide from my eyes[85] at the bottom of the sea, there I will command the sea-serpent, and it shall bite them" (Am. 9:3; cf. Jer. 16:17; 32:19; Am. 9:8; Ps. 66:7; Job 34:21; Prov. 15:3).

Hab. 1:13 says that Yahweh's eyes are too pure to behold evil. Zec. 8:6 emphasizes that in Yahweh's eyes nothing is too wonderful (*pl'* niphal), i.e., nothing is impossible.

The connotation of judgment is present in Ps. 5:6(5), which says that the boastful will not stand before Yahweh's eyes. Human ways are under the eyes of Yahweh; he sees them clearly (Prov. 5:21; cf. also Ps. 11:4; Job 14:3).

An element of appraisal can be heard in Ps. 90:4, where the psalmist avows that a thousand years in Yahweh's eyes are like yesterday when it passes (or, with LXX and Syr., "is past"; see *BHS*).

Prov. 22:12 says: "The eyes of Yahweh keep watch over knowledge." This means that Yahweh's eyes not only see but penetrate to the heart of all that takes place.

Isa. 3:8 says that the inhabitants of Jerusalem and Judah defy the eyes of Yahweh's glory. The text is problematic. One solution is to delete *'ny* (see *BHS*). Wildberger suggests emending *'ny* to *p^enê* or reading it as a corruption of original *'im.*[86]

The eye of God appears also in metaphorical contexts. For example, Dt. 32:10 says that Yahweh guards Israel as the pupil *('îšôn)* of his eye (similarly Zec. 2:12[8]; Ps. 17:8).

---

84. Nötscher, 128-29.
85. Scholars consider *minneged 'ênay* to be secondary; see *BHS*.
86. *Isaiah 1–12,* 125.

In Zec. 4:10b a mythological allusion lies behind the interpretation of the seven lamps of the lampstand (4:2) as the eyes of Yahweh ranging (*šûṭ* piel) through the whole earth. Behind this language lies the Mesopotamian notion of the seven planets, which the Sumerians considered "transmitters of orders" of the most high god, representing the universal sovereignty of this god in its totality.[87] According to Keel, the "seven eyes," like the four faces in Ezekiel, signify not simply omniscience but effectual omnipresence.[88] In the ancient Near East, identification of the eye with a lamp is not a kind of allegory; it expresses a profound inward kinship between the two entities, for *'ayin* means both "eye" and "brightness." "Bright" eyes characterize the living (Prov. 29:13; Ps. 13:4[3]; 1 S. 14:29). Keel notes also the eye of Horus, depicted with a lamp in many illustrations of the Nineteenth and Twentieth Dynasties. Thus the great lampstand with its seven times seven lamps proclaims the inexhaustible vitality of Yahweh, whose effectual omnipresence the pusillanimous community will experience shortly. Seybold sees in the light symbolism of Zec. 4:10b "the presence of God as lord over all the earth."[89] Behind the "eyes" of Yahweh stands the secret service of the Persian state (cf. also 2 Ch. 16:9).[90]

IV. Deuterocanonical Texts. Deuterocanonical texts paint the same picture. The eye *(ophthalmós)* as a physical organ appears in Tob. 2:10 (LXX^{BA}; LXX^{S} differs); 3:17 (S); 5:10 (S); 6:9 (BA; S differs); 7:6; 11:7,8,11,12 (BA; S differs); 11:16 (S); 14:2 (S). Sir. 17:6 emphasizes that God made human eyes; 22:19 cites a proverb: "One who pricks the eye brings tears." Sir. 43:4 (H) observes that the burning sun inflames the eyes.

Here too, however, the personal element predominates. In Tob. 3:12 (BA; S differs), Sarah declares that she has raised her eyes to God — an expression of hope and trust. Tob. 3:17 (S) reports the healing of Tobit, "so that he might see God's light with his eyes" — here the eye is an agent of perception and knowledge (cf. Tob. 5:21 [S]; Jdt. 7:27; Add. Est. 4:17i[LXX = 13:18 NRSV]; Wis. 3:2; Sir. 16:5 [H]; 17:13; 30:20 [H]; 38:28; 51:27 [H]; 2 Mc. 8:17).

The notion of presence as an eyewitness is expressed by the phrase "before the eyes" (*apénanti tṓn ophthalmṓn,* Sir. 27:23; cf. 1 Mc. 2:23).

In Tob. 4:7,16 (BA), the eye reflects the inner disposition (cf. Sir. 14:8). Sir. 23:24 speaks of haughty eyes (cf. also 26:9, with erotic connotations); 26:11 cautions against an impudent eye; 35:10 (= 32:10 LXX) is an exhortation to worship the Lord with a good and upright eye.

The eye appears in a metaphorical context in Tob. 10:5 (BAS), where Anna calls her son Tobias the light of her eyes (cf. Tob. 11:13 [S]; Bar. 3:14). Sir. 20:14 says that a fool has many eyes, not just one — probably an image of instability and greed.

---

87. F. Horst, *Die zwölf kleinen Propheten. HAT* I/14³, 231.
88. *Jahwe-Visionen,* 316-17.
89. K. Seybold, *Bilder zum Tempelbau. SBS* 70 (1974), 34.
90. Ibid., 83, citing A. L. Oppenheim, "The Eye of the Lord," *JAOS* 88 (1968) (= *FS E. A. Speiser*) 175.

As in Hebrew, we also find formulaic expressions with personal connotations: "good in the eyes" (Jdt. 3:4 [cf. 12:14]; Wis. 9:9; 1 Mc. 1:12); "find favor in the eyes" (Sir. 45:1); "raise the eyes" (1 Mc. 4:12; 5:30; 9:39).

An erotic element is present when Judith is described as making herself beautiful "to entice the eyes of all the men" (Jdt. 10:4;[91] cf. 16:9). Therefore Sir. 9:8 admonishes: "Turn away your eyes from a shapely woman."

The eye as agent of aesthetic perception appears in Sir. 40:22 (H, supplemented by LXX): "Grace and beauty delight the eye, but the flowers of the field more than both" (cf. also 43:8 [H]; 45:12 [H, with LXX]).

Sir. 4:1 admonishes not to keep needy eyes waiting. Bar. 2:18 speaks of failing eyes. According to Sir. 4:5, one should not avert one's eye from the needy (cf. 27:1).

The connotation of valuative judgment is present when Sir. 8:16 (LXX + H) says that blood counts as nothing in the eyes of the quick-tempered. In the eye reside guile and deception (12:16), greed (14:9), and grudging charity (14:10). Sir. 17:8 is difficult to interpret: "He has set his eye on their hearts."[92]

Sir. 18:18 observes that the gift of a grudging giver makes the eyes dim. Sir. 20:29 states that favors and gifts blind the eyes of the wise (cf. Dt. 16:19). It is God, however, who gives light to the eyes (Sir. 34:20 [= 31:29 LXX]; cf. Bar. 1:2).

Sir. 23:19 says that a fornicator's fear is confined to the human eyes of those who can catch him, rather than the eyes of the Lord.

Sir. 27:22 cautions against people who wink. Sir. 31:13 (H; = 34:13 LXX, differently) warns: "Remember that an evil eye is evil; God hates the evil of an eye; God has created nothing more evil."

Some texts also speak of God's eyes. For example, Sir. 10:20 says that those who fear God are honored in God's eyes; 11:12 states that the eyes of the Lord look kindly on the poor (cf. 15:19).

Israel's ways are not hid from God's eyes (Sir. 17:15; cf. 39:19 [H]). According to 17:19, God's eyes are ever on the Israelites. God's eyes are ten thousand times brighter than the sun (23:19). The eyes of the Lord are on those who love him (34:19).

V. Dead Sea Scrolls. In the Dead Sea Scrolls, too, the personal meaning of the eye predominates. The physical organ is mentioned in the context of a simile in 4QpIsa^{d} 1:1, which speaks of eye makeup (cf. also 11QT 48:8 and the talion formula in 61:12). The eye is associated with the erotic and sexual realm in 1QpHab 5:7; 1QS 1:6; CD 2:16. Blind eyes in the metaphorical sense are mentioned in 1QS 4:11; cf. 1QS 5:5. Formulaic expressions with personal reference also appear, e.g., *l'yny* in the sense of being present as an eyewitness (1QS 5:8; 1QH 14:16; 15:20; 18:7; CD 9:18; 11QT 63:6; cf. 1QS 10:11; 1QM 11:15; 17:2; 1QH 11:1,19; 1QSa 2:7; 4QpHos^{b} 2:13). The phrase "right *(yšr)* in the eyes of" appears in CD 3:6; 8:7; 19:20. In 1QS 11:3,6, the eye

91. On the text see Zenger, "Das Buch Judith," *Historische und legendarische Erzählungen. JSHRZ* I/6 (1981), 496.

92. Sauer, "Jesus Sirach," *JSHRZ* I/6, 547.

is the agent of perception and knowledge. In 1QH 5:34 the worshiper's eyes have become dull with sadness (cf. 1QH 7:2; 9:5). The eye is compared to a moth in a furnace in 1QH 9:5. In 1QH 18:19 we learn that the worshiper relies on God's opening his eyes (cf. CD 2:14). In 1QH 2:31 the worshiper avows that God's eyes have been over him to protect him. The "good/evil in the eyes of God" is found in 1QH 14:18; 16:18; 17:24; 11QT 55:16.

Stendebach

עַיִן *'ayin;* מַעְיָן *ma'yān*

I. Occurrences, Etymology; II. Significance; III. Geography; IV. Creation and Sacred History; V. Figurative Usage; VI. Dead Sea Scrolls.

I. Occurrences, Etymology. The noun *'ayin* denotes a spring 19 or 23 times in the OT, depending on whether it is interpreted as a toponym or as a reference to a spring in Jgs. 7:1; 1 S. 29:1; 1 K. 1:9; Neh. 2:13.[1] The noun *ma'yān,* with preformative *m-,* occurs 23 times in the OT; strictly speaking, it means "spring site," but it is usually used simply in the sense of "spring." This usage takes a word that refers primarily to an organ of the human body and applies it to a geographical phenomenon; there are other examples. The etymology is discussed in the preceding article. This transference is found in all Semitic dialects, including Akkadian and Ugaritic; it appears also in other languages.[2]

When a spring is called *'ayin,* "eye" (the OT also uses → מקור *māqôr*), it is reasonable to assume that springs are thought of as "eyes on the face of the earth" or as the eyes of a monster dwelling in the depths, in the waters under the earth.[3] There is, however, no evidence of such a conception in the OT. The rare phrase "eye of the (whole)

'ayin. G. Bienaimé, *Moïse et le don de l'eau dans la tradition juive ancienne: Targum et Midrash. AnBibl* 98 (1984); T. Canaan, "Haunted Springs and Water Demons in Palestine," *JPOS* 1 (1920) 153-70; A. Causse, "Le jardin d'Élohim et la source de vie," *RHR* 81 (1920) 289-315; J. A. Emerton, "'Spring and Torrent' in Psalm lxxiv 15," *Volume du Congrès, Genève 1965. SVT* 15 (1966), 122-33; P. van Imschoot, "L'ésprit de Yahvé, source de vie dans l'AT," *RB* 44 (1935) 481-501; T. J. Jones, *Quelle, Brunnen und Cisternen im AT* (1928); O. Keel, M. Küchler, and C. Uehlinger, *Orte und Landschaften der Bibel,* I (1984); A. Legendre, "Fontaine," *DB,* II (1899), 2302-6; S. Lehming, "Massa und Meriba," *ZAW* 73 (1961) 71-77; J. Obermann, "Wind, Water, and Light in an Archaic Inscription from Shechem," *JBL* 57 (1938) 239-53; P. Reymond, *L'eau, sa vie et sa signification dans l'AT. SVT* 6 (1958); A. Schwarzenbach, *Die geographische Terminologie im Hebräischen des ATs* (1954); W. R. Smith, *Religion of the Semites* (repr. [2]1956), 165-84; E. Zolli, "*'Eyn 'ādām* (Zach. IX 1)," *VT* 5 (1955) 90-92.

1. For the former see Mandelkern; for the latter, Jenni, *TLOT,* II, 874-75; *HAL,* II, 817.
2. See *AHw,* I, 383; *WUS,* no. 2056; Schwarzenbach, 55.
3. For the former see Schwarzenbach, 55; for the latter, Jones, 2.

earth" (*'ên hā'āreṣ,* Ex. 10:5; Nu. 22:5,11) refers to the surface of the earth or land. The *'înôṯ tᵉhôm* ("springs of the deep") are mentioned only in Prov. 8:28 (cf. Dt. 8:7, *'ᵃyānōṯ ûṯᵉhōmōṯ*) in the context of creation; the expression does not reflect a mythological background, but simply represents an attempt to portray the heights and depths of the whole world. The deluge narrative, where the mythological coloring is generally quite clear, speaks of the *ma'yᵉnōṯ tᵉhôm* in Gen. 7:11; 8:2; this phrase can refer only to the springs of the primal deep, not to the eyes of a chaos monster. The use of *'ayin* in conjunction with "water" refers to the bright play of light on a spring, as in the expressions *'ên hammayim* ("bright water," Gen. 16:7; 24:13,43) and *'ênôṯ mayim* (Nu. 33:9); again, there are no mythological overtones. Especially in bright sunlight, a spring bubbling out of the earth gleams like an eye. The LXX frequently uses *gḗ* to translate *'ayin,* "spring," and *ma'yān* even in toponyms and in the disputed text Dt. 33:28.

II. Significance. In the Near East, especially at the edge of the desert, water is precious. Springs are generally rare; with their fresh, bubbling, and hence "living" water,[4] they are preferred to cisterns and are very important for the water supply. Even in the Nile Valley, where the river provides the needed water, the single major fresh-water spring not far from Heliopolis was highly esteemed since time immemorial. Its importance was less economic than mythological and theological: "The Egyptians considered the water of this spring to be the milk of the heavenly ocean in which the sun god was wont to bathe his countenance."[5]

With no major river to provide water for irrigation, Palestine was dependent on rainfall; here the economic significance of springs was primary and had theological implications. Especially in time of war, the availability of springs was important: a besieged city had to have access to a spring with its reliable flow of water (as illustrated by the water supply systems of Jerusalem, Hazor, and Megiddo); an army invading a foreign territory had to find springs. It was not without good reason that religious ceremonies were performed at springs during the military campaigns of Mesopotamian rulers.[6] For the same reason, it was important to block the flow of springs outside a city in the face of an approaching enemy (2 Ch. 32:3-4). When an enemy was to be annihilated totally, all the springs were stopped up (2 K. 3:19), removing or sharply restricting one of the necessities of life.

During periods of drought, when even the cisterns were exhausted, springs and the brooks they fed constituted the last hope for saving humans and animals from dying of thirst (1 K. 18:5). The enormous importance of springs is also illustrated by the precept of Lev. 11:35-36: "Everything on which a carcass [of an unclean animal] falls is unclean. . . . But a spring or a cistern holding water shall still be clean." This stipulation probably reflects the notion that the cleansing element itself cannot be rendered unclean; fundamentally, however, it embodies the necessity of preserving the vital water supply.

---

4. → IV, 333.
5. A. Wiedemann, *Das alte Ägypten* (1920), 16.
6. B. Meissner, *Babylonien und Assyrien,* 2 vols. (1920-25), II, 87.

Of course there were not enough natural springs flowing from a hillside or rising from a valley floor to provide sufficient water for human beings and their flocks and herds. People had to search out underground watercourses by digging wells. When water rose in a well, when the "brightness" of the water was seen, the well could also be called an *ʿayin,* "spring." In either case, the groundwater of the subterranean ocean issued forth. The same narrative can therefore use *ʿayin* and → באר *beʾēr* interchangeably (Gen. 24 uses *ʿayin* 7 times, *beʾēr* twice; Gen. 16 uses each twice). It is also possible that natural springs were enclosed to collect and protect their water; then they could be considered wells. The Spring Gate of Neh. 2:14 and 32:15 was possibly a structure protecting the spring that supplied Jerusalem with water.

III. Geography. Springs were very special places in the regions occupied by nomads as well as in Palestine, where they were not plentiful. In the steppe, people collected around them with their animals, families, and whole clans; the inhabitants of a town collected around a nearby spring. Of course, the spring was the primary given; it came first. The settlement was secondary; it came later. Springs had been given names since time immemorial; the name was then transferred to the adjacent settlement. Seventeen such names are listed in *HAL;*[7] it is unclear in many cases whether the name belongs solely to the spring or to the adjacent settlement as well. To the extent that the names can be interpreted, they provide information about notions associated with the springs. Some evoke their economic necessity: *ʿên gannîm,* "spring of gardens" (Josh. 15:34, in the lowland; 19:21 and 21:29, in Issachar); *ʿên rōgēl,* "spring of the fuller" (Josh. 15:7; 18:16; etc.); *ʿên rimmôn,* "spring of the pomegranate tree" (Neh. 11:29; cf. Josh. 19:7); *ʿên tappûaḥ,* possibly "spring of the apple tree" (Josh. 17:7); probably also *ʿên-dōʾr,* "spring of the settlement" or "spring of the former generation" (Ps. 83:11[Eng. v. 10]; 1 S. 28:7, *ʿên dôr*). Some springs are associated with fauna: *ʿên geḏî,* "spring of the kid" (Josh. 15:62, etc.), as well as *ʿên haqqôrēʾ,* "spring of the partridge" (Jgs. 15:19), if this interpretation is correct. The Spring of the Kid might be so named because its water "leaps" like a kid. More likely, however, this name derives from a widespread ancient popular belief, still current among Palestinian Arabs,[8] that "murmuring" springs, which change their appearance by daylight and dark, are inhabited by spirits, usually beneficent; people perhaps imagined that a demon in the form of a goat dwelt in this spring. The name "Dragon's Spring" *(ʿên hattannîn)* in Neh. 2:13 may reflect the same belief, especially since the "Serpent Stone" was located there (1 K. 1:9).[9] The name *ʿên šemeš,* "spring of the sun" (Josh. 15:7; 18:17), may fall into the same category. It is possible, too, that *ʿên haqqôrêʾ* means "spring of the one who calls"; unlike the situation in Jgs. 15:19, it is unclear who this was — perhaps a demon?

The Hagar narrative (Gen. 16) still alludes clearly to a numen residing at a spring.

---

7. *HAL,* II, 819-20.
8. See Canaan.
9. See *HAL,* II, 820.

Fleeing from Sarai, Hagar comes upon a spring in the desert (v. 7); there she finds the "angel of Yahweh" *(mal'ak yhwh),* who speaks to her and gives her a promise of offspring. "So she named the name of Yahweh, who had spoken to her: 'You are *'ēl rō'î'*. . . . Therefore the well was called *b^e'ēr laḥay rō'î*" (vv. 13-14). In the light of the phrase *'ēl rō'î,* this difficult name is often interpreted as meaning "well of the living one who looks upon me." In any case, at or near this spring people worshiped a deity whose original name is obscure; this etiological narrative, using the *mal'ak yhwh* and perhaps the *'ēl rō'î* as a preliminary stage, identifies the deity with Israel's God Yahweh.

Jgs. 15:18-19 also contains an etiological narrative, intended to explain the name of the spring flowing from the cave at Lehi, which is not named for the legendary jawbone of a donkey with which Samson killed a thousand Philistines (vv. 15ff.). Indeed, v. 17 does interpret the toponym etiologically with reference to this jawbone. The preceding story of Samson's victory over the Philistines provided an opportunity to associate the "caller" (see above) in the name of the spring with the exhausted Samson. In contrast to Gen. 16, the original presence of a numen has been totally erased. The OT preserves only traces of the belief — not unknown in Israel — of divine beings dwelling in and around springs. In the OT, springs are not sacred sites in this sense.

While people could move or desert their settlements, springs were fixed points on the map, beyond human influence. They could be used to find one's bearings with assurance or define boundaries meant to endure into the distant future. This is probably why place-names containing *'ên* appear frequently in the allocation of the tribal territories (Josh. 15–19) on the basis of concrete observations, claims, and theoretical calculations. Yahweh assigns the territories by lot. He also uses springs as important reference points.

IV. Creation and Sacred History. Among the marvelous works of the creator God, springs are singled out occasionally on account of their importance for all things living. For example, Ps. 104:10ff. speaks of springs that gush forth in the valley and give drink to the wild animals. They appear in the first place in the description of the water supply established by the creator. Prov. 8:24-30 speaks of depths and springs, mountains and hills, earth and fields, the heavens, clouds and springs emerging from the primal sea, the sea and the foundations of the earth. The observer's gaze moves from the depths to the heights and back to the depths. When God created the primal sea, he caused it to serve his purposes, making it the source of springs and streams (Ps. 74:13ff.). And when water gushes forth from the rock at Yahweh's command, it is a demonstration of his creative power (114:8), which his people experience in the desert. It is springs and rain that render the land fertile; they are a sign and a gift of divine blessing (84:7[6]), prayed for by pilgrims going up to Jerusalem through a dry valley (v. 8[7]). Yahweh can also use his creative power to punish sinful humanity: this power opens and shuts the springs of the primal sea (Gen. 7:11; 8:2), so that the waters of the deluge inundate the earth and extinguish all life on it. In order that the new exodus through the desert may succeed, Yahweh gives his promise to the people in exile: "I will open rivers on the bare heights, and springs in the midst of the valleys" (Isa. 41:18).

This prophetic oracle is not the first occasion on which springs play a role in the history of Yahweh's people. Here the prophet of the exile alludes to the narratives concerning Israel's wanderings in the wilderness after the exodus from Egypt. But already in the patriarchal period, sites associated with springs are important. "In the wilderness by a spring on the way to Shur," Hagar receives from the "angel of Yahweh" the promise crucial for Ishmael and his descendants (Gen. 16:7). Springs are sites of deliverance. At the spring outside the city of Nahor (Gen. 24), Abraham's servant learns and experiences that Yahweh has granted his mission success (v. 56); here he meets Rebekah and is able to bring the future matriarch back to his master Isaac. After the exodus, the people who have escaped from Egypt under Moses' leadership arrive at Elim on their journey to Sinai; there are twelve springs there, reason enough to encamp (Ex. 15:27).

Even more important for Israel's wilderness period, however, is the region of Kadesh and its springs. The people went there directly (according to Jgs. 11:16) and stayed there a long time (Dt. 1:46). There were located the "spring of judgment" (*'ên mišpāṭ,* Gen. 14:7) and the waters of Meribah (Nu. 27:14), where disputes were settled by judicial judgment. This spring was certainly already sacred and the site of a tribunal before the Israelites. Nomadic tribes probably met here and shared their traditions. The so-called Moses band may well have received its roots of law and order here (Ex. 18). This group probably established contact here with related tribal groups already living in Palestine (see the narrative of the spies in Nu. 13–14) and laid the groundwork for the occupation of Canaan (Dt. 9:23). In Josh. 14:6-7 Caleb appeals to a divine oracle received through Moses in Kadesh in which he and his descendants are promised possession of the land (Nu. 14:24). Kadesh, its location fixed by its springs, is an important site. It plays an important role in defining the southern boundary of the land bestowed by Yahweh (Nu. 34:4) during the conquest under Joshua (Josh. 10:41). Even in Ezekiel's scheme for the allocation of the land (Ezk. 47:19; 48:28), the southern boundary runs "from Tamar as far as the waters of Meribath-kadesh."

But for Israel the significance of this spring region, the "waters of Meribah," was not exclusively positive. An invasion of the promised land attempted against the will of Yahweh proved a disaster (Nu. 14:40-45; Dt. 1:41-46). This interpretation of the failed undertaking linked the theme of rebellion and murmuring with Kadesh. In an etiological narrative associated with Kadesh that seeks to explain the name of the spring (Nu. 20:2-13; cf. Ex. 17:1-7), the word *m^e^rîḇâ,* "contention," was associated with the rebellion of the whole people together with Moses and Aaron against Yahweh: "These are the waters of Meribah, where the people of Israel quarreled with Yahweh, and by which he showed his holiness" (v. 13). Ps. 81:8(7) says that God tested Israel at the waters of Meribah — unless the text should be emended to read *tiḇḥānēnî,* "you [Israel] tested me," to agree with the content of the tradition elsewhere (cf. also Ps. 106:32). Because of its great importance, it was natural for Kadesh to be included in the list of Israel's encampments in the wilderness (Nu. 33:36-37).

Dt. 8:7ff. vividly describes the goal of Israel's pilgrimage: "a good land, a land with flowing streams, with springs and underground waters welling up in valleys and hills." The springs are among the primary blessings of the promised land. But they also play a role in the subsequent history of Israel. The toponym *ʿên dôr* merely denotes the place where Saul met the medium (1 S. 28:7). But in the story of the Davidic succession, critical events take place at springs in the vicinity of Jerusalem: Adonijah celebrates beside En-rogel (1 K. 1:9), and at David's behest Solomon is anointed king at Gihon (vv. 38-39). Without trying to define the role Gihon played subsequently in the royal ritual (see the discussion of Ps. 110:7), we may safely assume that both springs were sacred at the time of David. Located outside Jerusalem, Gihon provided an accessible source of water; later a conduit was built to bring its water into the city. In Isa. 8:6 it represents Yahweh's dependable care for his people: he will save Jerusalem even if this spring ceases to flow (cf. 2 Ch. 32:3-4,11; → גִּיחוֹן *gîḥôn*). This notion then occasions the eschatological prophecy of the miraculous spring issuing from the temple (Joel 4:18[3:18]), yielding fertility and blessing.

The prophecy in Joel is related to the vision of the temple spring in Ezk. 47; this text does not use the word *ʿayin,* but speaks of water flowing from below the threshold of the temple and swelling to become a mighty river, bringing fertility and vitality to the region. This theme is developed further in Zec. 14:8: when the land is restored at the eschaton, living water will flow from Jerusalem, half to the western sea and half to the eastern sea.

V. Figurative Usage. The OT milieu associates springs with fertility and life, a nexus of ideas reflected in similes and figurative language. A tree beside flowing water must be particularly luxuriant (Ps. 1:3). Gen. 49:22 likens the tribe of Joseph to a fruit tree by a spring. This same image probably lies behind the oracle of judgment against Ephraim in Hos. 13:15: although Ephraim prospers and flourishes, Yahweh will send a violent east wind that will cause its wells to dry up and its springs to be parched. The Lord will take away the resources by which the people live. This figurative language recalls places like En-gedi, where vegetation flourishes in the midst of a desert (cf. Cant. 1:14; Sir. 24:14).

Human beings, the source of life for others in the literal and figurative sense, can also be compared to springs. A wife and mother is the wellspring of the family. In the language of love, she is called "a garden spring, a well of living water, and flowing streams from Lebanon" (Cant. 4:15). The bride is accordingly "a garden locked, a spring sealed" (4:12). A woman is a fountain of life and of all kinds of benefits for her husband (cf. Prov. 31:10-31), a notion that can be expressed in the image of a spring. This is probably the idea behind the obscure question of 5:16: "Should your springs flow in the street, your streams in the open places?" This is quite possibly a warning to a man not to squander his resources on a "strange woman" *(ʾiššâ zārâ),*[10] leaving himself without offspring, or wasting on her the resources he lives on. In context, however, the "springs" belonging to the man are clearly an image of his wife. A spring can also symbolize the vital social role played by the righteous (25:26). If they give way, they are like a polluted spring, worthless. Finally, when Zion is spoken of as a mother (Ps. 87:5-6), the metaphor of a spring is ready to hand. Possibly, however, v. 7 ("All my

---

10. → IV, 56.

springs are in you") reflects instead the notion of Ps. 46:5(4), the streams of blessing issuing from Zion, the "springs of salvation" (Isa. 12:3) set there by God, the divine source of all prosperity.

Another difficult text, Dt. 33:28 ("So Israel settled in safety, the spring of Jacob alone"), may also be an example of figurative language, if *ʿên* is not emended to *ʿān,* "dwelt."[11] God's blessings bring fertility in the promised land. Zec. 9:1 ("For to Yahweh belong *ʿên ʾāḏām* and all the tribes of Israel") is another much-debated text, translated variously and often emended; its interpretation probably has to do with *ʿayin* meaning "eye" rather than "spring."[12]

VI. Dead Sea Scrolls. The noun *ʿayin* with the meaning "spring" does not occur in the Dead Sea Scrolls. There are 11 occurrences of *mʿyn,* 6 in parallel with *mqwr,* which appears more often. Two texts are so fragmentary that they convey little: "wellspring of life" (1Q35 2:1); "wellspring of knowledge" (1Q36 12:2).[13] God is often referred to metaphorically as a spring, as is God's antagonist, the "angel of darkness" (1QS 3:21): "With the wellspring *(mʿyn)* of light is the source of truth, but from the fount *(mqwr)* of darkness comes the source of evil" (lQS 3:19), the fundamental statement of the advice to the teacher on distinguishing spirits and giving instruction. The prayer in 1QS 10:12 addresses God: "Founder of my well-being, fount *(mqwr)* of knowledge and wellspring *(mʿyn)* of holiness, height of majesty and all-powerful one of eternal glory." The suppliant expresses the dependence of his well-being on God, from whom come revelation and the ethical qualities that bring and are the condition of salvation. In 1QS 11:7 we should probably read *mʿwn,* "place" (of glory), although the preceding line reads "fount *(mqwr)* of righteousness." The latter is apparently the knowledge bestowed by God. In 1QH 1:5 God is apparently referred to as "wellspring of stre[ngth]"; no more of the damaged text can be reconstructed. In 5:26 the speaker — probably the Teacher of Righteousness — says that God has hidden the wellspring of understanding and the counsel of truth from his enemies on account of their wickedness: God refuses to bestow understanding on these enemies and bars them from the "community of the new covenant." In 6:17-18 we read of the fire of judgment that issues from God, destroying the men of wickedness and all sinners: God is the source of light and the eternal fount *(mqwr)* of the fire that devours the wicked. In 8:6 the speaker gives thanks to God for calling him into the community, which he uses the image of a plantation to describe. Its members draw from the "mysterious fount," the revelation of God, which flows within the community. In an allusion to paradise, 8:12 speaks of the "fount of life" that provides holy water — undoubtedly divine revelation. In 12:13 the speaker thanks God for opening to him the fount of his strength (cf. 1:5). In all these passages, God is the wellspring from which knowledge, power, and life issue for the teacher and his community.

Schreiner

---

11. *HAL,* II, 818, citing an otherwise unattested *ʿwn* III.

12. W. Rudolph, *Haggai-Sacharja 1–8-Sacharja 9–14-Maleachi. KAT* XIII/4 (1976): the eye of Aram; NRSV: the capital of Aram.

13. J. T. Milik, *DJD,* I, 137, 139.

עיף *ʿyp* → יעף *yʿp*

עִיר *ʿîr*

I. Ancient Near East: 1. Mesopotamia; 2. Egypt; 3. West Semitic Region. II. Etymology and Meaning. III. History: 1. Bronze Age; 2. Premonarchic Period; 3. Monarchic Period; 4. Persian Period; 5. Hellenistic Period. IV. OT Tradition: 1. Early Narratives; 2. Learned Reflection; 3. Prophetic Criticism; 4. Zion; 5. Apocalypse of Isaiah; 6. Wisdom. V. Qumran. VI. LXX.

ʿîr. R. M. Adams, *The Heartland of Cities* (1981); G. W. Ahlström, *Royal Administration and National Religion in Ancient Palestine. SHANE* 1 (1982); idem, "Where Did the Israelites Live?" *JNES* 41 (1982) 133-38; A. Alt, "Festungen und Levitenorte im Lande Juda," *KlS,* II (1953), 306-15; idem, "Jerusalems Aufstieg," *KlS,* III (1959), 243-57; idem, "Der Stadtstaat Samaria," *KlS,* III (1959), 258-302; N.-E. Andreasen, "Town and Country in the OT," *Encounter* 42 (1981) 259-75; M. Atzler, "Erwägungen zur Stadt im Alten Reich" (diss., Leipzig, 1968); A. N. Barghouti, "Urbanization of Palestine and Jordan in Hellenistic and Roman Times," in A. Hadidi, ed., *Studies in the History and Archaeology of Jordan,* 1 (1982), 209-29; J. Barr, "*Migraš* in the OT," *JSS* 29 (1984) 15-31; D. C. Benjamin, "Deuteronomy and City Life" (diss., Claremont, 1981); A. Ben-Tor, "Tell Quiri," *BA* 42 (1979) 105-13; M. Bietak, "Stadt(anlage)," *LexÄg,* V (1985), 1233-50; idem, "Das Stadtproblem im Alten Ägypten," *150 Jahre DAI 1829-1979* (1981), 68-78; idem, "Urban Archaeology and the Town Problem in Ancient Egypt," in K. R. Weeks, ed., *Egyptology and the Social Sciences* (1979), 97-144; F. Braemer, *L'architecture domestique du Levant à l'Age du Fer. Ed. Recherche sur les civilisations* 8 (1982); B. Brentjes, "Zum Verhältnis von Dorf und Stadt in Altvorderasien," *WZ Halle* 17 (1968) 9-42; G. Buccellati, *Cities and Nations of Ancient Syria. SS* 26 (1967); W. Caspari, "Tochter-Ortschaften im AT," *ZAW* 39 (1921) 174-80; A. D. Crown, "Some Factors Relating to Settlement and Urbanization in Ancient Canaan in the Second and First Millennia B.C.," *Abr-Nahrain* 11 (1971) 22-41; W. G. Dever, "Monumental Architecture in Ancient Israel in the Period of the United Monarchy," in T. Ishida, ed., *Studies in the Period of David and Solomon* (1982), 269-306; H. J. Dreyer, "The Roots *qr, ʿr, ġr* and *ṣ/ṭr* = 'Stone, Wall, City,' etc.," *FS A. van Selms. POS* 9 (1971), 17-25; M. M. Eisman, "A Tale of Three Cities," *BA* 41 (1978) 47-60; B. Z. Eshel, "The Semantics of the Word *ʿîr* in the Language of the Bible," *BethM* 18 (1972/73) 327-41, 423-24; D. G. Evans, "'Gates' and 'Streets,'" *JRH* 2 (1962) 1-12; R. Feuillet, "Les villes de Juda au temps d'Ozias," *VT* 11 (1961) 270-91; L. R. Fisher, "The Temple Quarter," *JSS* 8 (1963) 34-41; A. Fitzgerald, "*btwlt* and *bt* as Titles for Capital Cities," *CBQ* 37 (1975) 167-83; R. G. Fox, *Urban Anthropology* (1977); F. S. Frick, *The City in Ancient Israel. SBLDS* 36 (1977); V. Fritz, "The 'List of Rehoboam's Fortresses' in 2 Chr. 11:5-12," *ErIsr* 15 (1983) 46-53; C. H. J. de Geus, "Agrarian Communities in Biblical Times," *Les communautés rurales, II, Antiquité. Receuils de la Société Jean Bodin pour l'histoire comparative des institutions* 41 (1983), 207-37; idem, *De israëlitische Stad. Palaestina Antiqua* 3 (1984); R. Gonen, "Urban Canaan in the Late Bronze Period," *BASOR* 253 (1984) 61-73; J. M. Halligan, "A Critique of the City in the Yahwist Corpus" (diss., Notre Dame, 1975); W. W. Hallo, "Antediluvian Cities," *JCS* 23 (1970/71) 57-67; M. Hammond, ed., *The City in the Ancient World* (1972); R. Hanhart, "Die jahwefeindliche Stadt," *Beiträge zur alttestamentliche Theologie. FS W. Zimmerli* (1977), 152-63; B. Hartmann, "Mögen die Götter dich behüten und

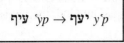

I. Ancient Near East.

1. *Mesopotamia.* Sum. *uru* (sometimes *unug*) and Akk. *ālu(m)* refer to a settlement in contrast to the unsettled steppe (Sum. *edin,* Akk. *ṣēru[m]*). The terms apply to both the open village with (if one includes *uru.še*) its surrounding fields and the fortified city or town, in contrast to the unfortified settlement (Sum. *maš-gan,* Akk.

---

unversehrt bewahren," *Hebräische Wortforschung. FS W. Baumgartner. SVT* 16 (1967), 102-5; M. Hengel, *Judaism and Hellenism* (Eng. trans. 1974); Z. Herzog, "Enclosed Settlements in the Negeb and the Wilderness of Beer-Sheba," *BASOR* 250 (1983) 41-49; idem, "Israelite City Planning, Seen in the Light of the Beer-Sheba and Arad Excavations," *Expedition* 20 (1978) 38-43; idem, *Das Stadttor in Israel und in den Nachbarländern* (1986); D. C. Hopkins, *The Highlands of Canaan. SWBA* 3 (1985); I. W. J. Hopkins, "The City Region in Roman Palestine," *PEQ* 112 (1980) 19-32; idem, *The Urban Geography of Roman Palestine* (1965); A. R. Hulst, "עִיר *ʿîr* City," *TLOT,* II, 880-83; A. J. Jawad, *The Advent of the Era of Townships in Northern Mesopotamia* (1965); W. Johnstone, "OT Technical Expressions in Property Holding," *Ugaritica* 6 (1969) 309-17, esp. 315-17; A. H. M. Jones, *The Cities of the Eastern Roman Provinces* (1971); B. J. Kemp, "The Early Development of Towns in Egypt," *Antiquity* 51 (1977) 185-200; idem, "Temple and Town in Ancient Egypt," in P. Ucko et al., eds., *Man, Settlement and Urbanism* (1972), 657-80; A. Kempinski, *The Rise of an Urban Culture. Studies of the Israel Ethnographic Society* 4 (1978); idem, *Syrien und Palästina (Kanaan) in der letzten Phase der Mittelbronze II B-Zeit (1650-1570 v. Chr.). ÄAT* 4 (1983); K. M. Kenyon, *Digging Up Jerusalem* (1974); idem, *Royal Cities of the OT* (1971); F. Kolb, *Die Stadt im Altertum* (1984); C. H. Kraeling and R. M. Adams, eds., *City Invincible* (1960); P. Lampl, *Cities and Planning in the Ancient Near East* (1968); N. P. Lemche, *Early Israel. SVT* 37 (1986); W. J. van Liere, "Capitals and Citadels of Bronze-Iron Age Syria in Their Relationship to Land and Water," *Annales archéologiques de Syrie. Revue d'archéologie et d'histoire* 13 (1963), 107-22; S. F. Loewenstein, "The Urban Experiment in the OT" (diss., Syracuse, 1971); R. A. F. Mackenzie, "The City and Israelite Religion," *CBQ* 25 (1963) 60-70; A. Mazar, "Three Israelite Sites in the Hills of Judah and Ephraim," *BA* 45 (1982) 167-78; B. Mazar, *Cities and Districts of Israel* (1976) (Heb.); T. L. McClellan, "Town Planning at Tell en-Naṣbeh," *ZDPV* 100 (1984) 53-69; L. M. Muntingh, " 'The City Which Has Foundations'," *FS A. van Selms. POS* 9 (1971), 108-20; N. Na'aman, "Hezekiah's Fortified Cities and the *LMLK* Stamp," *BASOR* 261 (1986) 5-21; E. Neufeld, "The Emergence of a Royal-Urban Society in Ancient Israel," *HUCA* 31 (1960) 31-53; E. W. Nicholson, "Blood Spattered Altars?" *VT* 27 (1977) 113-17; M. Noth, "Jerusalem and the Israelite Tradition," *Laws in the Pentateuch and Other Studies* (Eng. trans. 1966), 132-44; D. Oates, "The Development of Assyrian Towns and Cities," in P. Ucko et al., eds., *Man, Settlement and Urbanism* (1972), 799-804; P. J. Olivier, "In Search of a Capital for the Northern Kingdom," *JNSL* 11 (1983) 117-32; A. L. Oppenheim, "Land of Many Cities," in I. M. Lapidus, ed., *Middle Eastern Cities* (1969), 3-18; E. Otto, "Gibt es Zusammenhänge zwischen Bevölkerungswachstum, Staatsbildung und Kulturentwicklung im eisenzeitlichen Israel" in O. Kraus, ed., *Regulation, Manipulation und Explosion der Bevölkerungsdichte. Veröffentlichung der Joachim Jungius Gesellschaft der Wissenschaften Hamburg* 55 (1986), 73-87; idem, *Jerusalem* (1980); P. Parr, "Settlement Patterns and Urban Planning in the Ancient Levant," in P. Ucko et al., *Man, Settlement and Urbanism* (1972), 805-10; A. Parrot, *Samaria, the Capital of the Kingdom of Israel* (1958); D. N. Pienaar, "The Role of Fortified Cities in the Northern Kingdom during the Reign of the Omride Dynasty," *JNSL* 9 (1981) 151-57; A. de Pury, *La ville dans le ProcheOrient Ancient. Actes du Colloques de Cartigny 1979. Cahiers du Centre d'Étude du Proche-Orient Ancien, Université de Genève* (1983), 219-29; H. Reviv, "Early Elements and Late Terminology in the Descriptions of Non-Israelite Cities in the Bible," *IEJ* 27 (1977) 189-96; idem, "Jabesh-Gilead in I Samuel 11:1-4," *The Jerusalem Cathedra* 1 (1981) 4-8; idem, "On Urban Representative Institutions and Self-Government in

maškānu[m]). The further differentiation of the semantic field of *ālu(m)* as a fortified center *(ālānišu dannūti)*[1] surrounded by satellite towns *(ālāni seḫrūti ša limētišunu),*[2] royal residence *(ālu šá šarri),*[3] regional administrative center,[4] garrison city *(āl maṣṣarti),*[5] and fortress reflects the functional variety of the Mesopotamian city. Its social complexity is reflected in the *ālu(m)* terminology of urban districts (*ālu eššu,* "new city"; *āl ilāni,* "city of the gods") and quarters assigned to various professions, social classes, and ethnic groups, as well as of the subject of city-related administrative functions (*mala dīn ālim,* "according to the decision of the city").[6]

In contrast to the OT, cuneiform literature from the 3rd millennium until well into the 1st holds cities in high esteem, which can reach the point of deification (e.g., in the Sumerian hymns extolling Kish, Babylon, and Nippur and the Akkadian hymns to Babylon, Arba'il, and Ashur); few negative voices are heard.[7]

Syria-Palestine in the Second Half of the Second Millennium B.C.," *JESHO* 12 (1969) 283-97; L. Rost, "Die Stadt im AT," *ZDPV* 97 (1981) 129-38; O. Rössler, "Ghain im Ugaritischen," *ZA* 54 (1961) 158-72; C. Schäfer-Lichtenberger, *Stadt und Eidgenossenschaft im AT. BZAW* 156 (1983); K. L. Schmidt, *Die Polis in Kirche und Welt* (1939); Y. Shiloh, "Elements in the Development of Town Planning in the Israelite City," *IEJ* 28 (1978) 36-51; idem, *Excavations at the City of David I, 1978-1982. Qedem* 19 (1984); idem, "The Four-Room House, Its Situation and Function in the Israelite City," *IEJ* 20 (1970) 180-90; idem, "The Population of Iron Age Palestine in the Light of a Sample Analysis of Urban Plans, Areas, and Population Density," *BASOR* 239 (1980) 25-35; G. Sjoberg, *The Preindustrial City: Past and Present* (1960); W. von Soden, "Tempelstadt und Metropolis im Alten Orient," in H. Stoob, ed., *Die Stadt* (1979), 37-82; L. E. Stager, "The Archaeology of the Family in Ancient Israel," *BASOR* 260 (1985) 1-35; J. J. Stamm, "Ein ugaritisch-hebräisches Verbum und seine Ableitungen," *TZ* 35 (1979) 5-9; E. Stern, *Material Culture of the Land of the Bible in the Persian Period 538-332 B.C.* (1982); H. Strathmann, "πόλις," *TDNT,* VI, 516-35; H. Tadmor, "Some Aspects of the History of Samaria during the Biblical Period," *Jerusalem Cathedra* 3 (1983) 1-11; idem, "Temple Cities and Royal Cities in Babylonia and Assyria," in *City and Community, Proceedings of the 12th Conference of the Israel Historical Society* (1968), 179-205; V. Tcherikover, *Hellenistic Civilization and the Jews* (Eng. trans. 1959); idem, "Die hellenistischen Stadtgründungen von Alexander dem Grossen bis auf die Römerzeit," *Philologus* Sup 19 (1927), 1-216; W. Thiel, *Die soziale Entwicklung Israels in vorstaatlicher Zeit* (²1985); J. A. Thompson, "The Israelite Village," *Buried History* 19 (1983) 51-58; idem, "The 'Town' in OT Times," *Buried History* 19 (1983) 35-42; T. C. Vriezen, *Jahwe en zijn stad* (1962); G. Wallis, "Jerusalem und Samaria als Königsstädte," *VT* 26 (1976) 480-96; idem, "Die Stadt in den Überlieferungen der Genesis," *ZAW* 78 (1966) 133-47; M. Weber, *Ancient Judaism* (Eng. trans. 1952); idem, *Economy and Society,* 2 vols. (Eng. trans. 1978), II, 1212-1372; H. Weippert, "Stadtanlage," *BRL*², 313-17; J. V. Kinnier Wilson, "Hebrew and Akkadian Philological Notes," *JSS* 7 (1962) 173-83, esp. 181ff.; E. Wirth, "Die orientalische Stadt," *Saeculum* 26 (1975) 45-94; G. E. Wright, *Shechem* (1965); Y. Yadin, *Hazor. Schweich Lectures,* 1970 (1972).

1. *OIP* 2, 164, I, 36.
2. *OIP* 2, 164, I, 37-38.
3. *ABL* 895:4.
4. *CAD,* I/1, 382.
5. EA 76:36.
6. *TCL* 4, 79:24.
7. Erra Epic, I, 46-60; Hallo, 57.

2. *Egypt.* Egyp. *nîw.t (nww)* means "city,"[8] in contrast to *wḥy.t,* "village, family-based community." These meanings of *wḥy.t* preserve an echo of the predynastic structure of society; the growth of cities during the Old Kingdom is associated with the monarchy. City planning in the initial stages of urban development is reflected in the ideogram *nwt,* "settlement," which shows a circular settlement like that found at el-Kab,[9] with main streets in the form of a cross. The ideogram *ḥwt* represents royal urban foundations rectangular in shape (e.g., at Abydos) beginning in the Old Kingdom; this form remained influential well into the New Kingdom in rectangular temple and fortress cities.

3. *West Semitic Region.* The meaning "city" for Ugar. *ʿr,* pl. *ʿrm,* is established by its use in parallel with *pdr* I.[10] Derivation from a verb *ʿyr* or *ǵyr* cannot be established, since the existence of a verb *ǵyr* alongside *nǵr* is not certain.[11] In Phoenician the expression *ʿr shrw* appears in the inscription of Eshmunaton.[12] The aspect of fortification becomes primary in the meaning of OSA *ʿr,* "citadel."[13]

II. Etymology and Meaning. Heb. *ʿîr* occurs 1,092 times in the OT;[14] outside the Bible, it occurs as *hʿyrh,* "to the city [Jerusalem]," in the fourth Lachish ostracon.[15] Its feminine gender is explained by the function of the city as mother and nurturer of her inhabitants (2 S. 20:19).[16] The pl. *ʿārîm* derives from the lexeme *ʿar* > Aroer (Nu. 21:15; Dt. 2:9; 4:48; Josh. 12:2), which still occurs in proper names.[17] The plural ending *-îm* can express the collective identity of a city and its satellites.[18] It is likely that the noun *ʿîr* is associated with a verb **ʿr,* "protect" (Dt. 32:11; Job 8:6).[19] That the aspect of protection is central to the semantic field of *ʿîr* is shown by the terms used antithetically. Lev. 25:19 and 31 contrast *ʿîr* as a settlement fortified by a wall with → **חצר** *ḥāṣēr,* "village." In 1 S. 6:18 the fortified city *(ʿîr mibṣār)* is distinct from the open rural settlement *(kōper happᵉrāzî).* In Nu. 13:19 the statement of the spies' mission uses *ʿîr* as an inclusive term covering both *maḥᵃneh* and *mibṣār;* the clear semantic connotation of *ʿîr* prefigures the report of the spies (v. 28) that they found fortified cities: forti-

---

8. R. Faulkner, *Concise Dictionary of Middle Egyptian* (1962), 125.
9. Bietak, *LexÄg,* V, 1234-35.
10. For the singular see *KTU* 1.4, VII, 9. For the plural see 1.4, VII, 7; 1.14, III, 6; IV, 49; 1.16, V, 47. For parallels with *pdr* I, see 1.4, VII, 8, 10; 1.14, III, 7; IV, 50; see *UT,* nos. 1847, 2019.
11. Contra Hartmann, 102ff. See M. Dahood, *RSP,* I, 307-8; A. F. Rainey, *UF* 3 (1971) 157.
12. *CIS,* I, 113.
13. Biella, 385.
14. *TLOT,* II, 880-81.
15. *KAI* 194.7.
16. D. Michel, *Hebräische Syntax,* I (1977), 76; for a different explanation (*ʿîr wᵉʾēm* = city and clan), see A. Malamat, *UF* 11 (1979) 535-36.
17. *GK,* §96.
18. Michel, *Syntax,* I, 40; criticized by Conti, *AION* 41 (1981) 152-53.
19. Stamm, 5ff.

fication is semantically proper to *'îr,* distinguishing it from an unfortified settlement. The settlements to which *'îr* refers range in size from small refuges to fortified cities (2 K. 17:9; cf. also Dt. 3:5,19).

III. History.

1. *Bronze Age.* The political structure of Bronze Age Palestine was defined by the concurrent existence of numerous city-states controlling small areas of only a few square miles;[20] the organization of territorial states such as Shechem in the Late Bronze Age remained episodic. The cities were concentrated in the fertile plains along the coast, the plain of Jezreel, and the Shephelah. The intensity of urban settlement varied: there were high points in the Early Bronze (EB II-III) and Middle Bronze (MB IIB) periods and a marked drop-off in the Late Bronze period, accompanied in the 14th through 12th centuries B.C.E. by a breakdown of long-distance commerce, the violent destruction of many urban settlements, and the reduction of most Canaanite settlements to villages.[21] These events also put an end to the dimorphic structure reflected in the patriarchal narratives of Proto-Israelite pastoral clans and Canaanite city-states, thus laying the foundation for the establishment of Israel as a tribal society of shepherds who gradually shifted to subsistence agriculture, a way of life independent of the culture of the Canaanite city-states.[22]

The OT preserves hardly any traditions embodying historically reliable memories of the political structures and forms of sovereignty typical of the pre-Israelite cities. Among the many OT references to pre-Israelite kings and royal cities, only Jgs. 5:19 can be considered an immediately reliable tradition concerning the pre-Israelite period.

In Jgs. 4:4-22*, the representation of Hazor as a royal city is traditio-historically secondary, accomplished by the introduction of Jabin in vv. 2 and 17. Josh. 11:1-9 is dependent on Jgs. 4:2,17; Josh. 10*. The motifs of Jericho (Josh. 2:2; 8:2), Ai (Josh. 8:2,14,29), and Heshbon (Nu. 21:25-26) as pre-Israelite royal cities, as well as the story of Makkedah (Khirbet el-Qom),[23] which originally involved only anonymous Amorite kings, are not historical, since these sites were not settled in the Late Bronze Age. Dtr theology paints the cities of the indigenous population as *'ārîm gᵉḏōlôṯ ûḇᵉṣûrōṯ baššāmayim* (Dt. 1:28; 9:1) with walls, gates, and bars (3:5) in order to represent the occupation of the land as God's gracious gift. Along the same lines, Josh. 10:1-5,23b,29-39 uses a city list from the time of Solomon to summarize the occupation as a string of victories over city kings (cf. Dt. 7:24).[24] This line of interpretation is continued in Neh. 9:24 and Gen. 14.

The OT does not preserve any recollection of a democratic form of government in

20. Buccellati, 25ff.

21. For EB II-III see M. Broshi and R. Gophna, *BASOR* 253 (1984) 41ff. For MB IIA see Broshi and Gophna, *BASOR* 261 (1986) 72ff. For Late Bronze see Gonen, 61ff.

22. E. Otto, *BN* 23 (1984) 68ff. For the patriarchal narratives see M. B. Rowton, *JNES* 35 (1976) 13-20.

23. D. A. Dorsey, *Tel Aviv Journal* 7 (1980) 185-93.

24. V. Fritz, *ZDPV* 85 (1969) 136-61.

the pre-Israelite cities.[25] The motif of the *yōšeḇê giḇʿôn* negotiating with Joshua (Josh. 9:3-4) presupposes the prohibition against making a *berîṯ* (Ex. 34:12, *pen-tiḵrōṯ berîṯ leyôšēḇ hāʾāreṣ;* etc.). The point of 1 S. 5:9-10 is to recount the effect of the ark on the entire population of Beth-shemesh and their reaction.

Non-Israelite in origin, however, is the motif of oligarchic hegemony exercised by the *baʿalê (migdal) šeḵem* (Jgs. 9:6ff.,46-47), associated with Manasseh, during the Early Iron Age.[26]

The scarcity of historical data on the political structure of pre-Israelite cities does not support the theory that Israel's origins are to be sought in the social conflicts of urban civilization during the Late Bronze Age in Palestine.

2. *Premonarchic Period.* Preexilic strata of the OT interpret premonarchic Israel after the model of the later period as a structure of fortified cities (1 S. 9). There is no archaeological evidence of Early Iron Age fortifications at Shiloh or Hebron, which 1 S. 4:13,18; 2 S. 3:27 describe as fortified cities with gates.[27] Jgs. 19 pictures Gibeah as a city with an open square (Jgs. 19:15,17) and probably a gate (v. 16), quite unlike the modest village of the Early Iron Age.[28] The same applies to the description of the village of Early Iron Age Jericho as a "city of palms" (Jgs. 1:16; 3:13). Exilic and postexilic strata of the OT reinforce the retrojection of urban features into the early history of Israel (Nu. 32:16-17,34-36; Dt. 3:19; Jgs. 11:26; 18:28b; 21:23b; 1 S. 8:22; 18:6; etc.), especially in the description of early Israel by means of city lists (Josh. 13:17-20,25,27; 15:21-62; 19:35-38; etc.) from the period of the monarchy.

Against the background of the numerous unfortified cities of the Late Bronze Age,[29] the characterization of premonarchic settlements as *ʿārîm* is based on the astonishing use of free-standing walls to reinforce early Israelite cities,[30] the circular arrangement of houses in Beer-sheba and other settlements in the Negeb,[31] as well as Ai and Megiddo,[32] and refuge towers like the one at Penuel (Jgs. 8:17) and Janoah.[33] There were also unfortified settlements like Tell Masos and Khirbet Raddana.[34]

The first stages of Israel's urbanization were also marked by the emergence of extensive town sites from the villages typical of the Early Iron Age, with areas of as little as half an acre to over two acres. The average population density was 40 to 50 persons

---

25. Contra Schäfer-Lichtenberger, 209ff.
26. H. Reviv, *IEJ* 16 (1966) 252-57.
27. For Shiloh see I. Finkelstein et al., *Qadmoniot* 17 (1984) 15-25; for Hebron, *BRL*², 145.
28. Cf. Rost, 131-32; P. W. Lapp, *BA* 28 (1965) 2-10.
29. Gonen, 69-70.
30. Beth-zur: R. W. Funk, *The 1957 Excavation at Beth-zur. AASOR* 38 (1968), 6-7; Giloh: A. Mazar, *IEJ* 31 (1981) 1ff.; Mizpah: McClellan, 54; Bethel: J. L. Kelso, *The Excavation of Bethel. AASOR* 39 (1968), 16-17.
31. Herzog, "Enclosed Settlements," 41ff.; cf. also Braemer, 28ff.
32. Shiloh, "Elements," 36ff.
33. E. Otto, *ZDPV* 94 (1978) 108-18.
34. On the former see Z. Herzog, *Beer-Sheba,* II (1984), 80-81; on the latter, J. A. Callaway and R. E. Cooley, *BASOR* 201 (1971) 1-19.

per dunam (= 1,000 sq. m., about ¼ acre):[35] Beer-sheba (stratum VII), with an area of 4 dunams, had 160-200 inhabitants; Giloh, with 6 dunams, had 240-300; Ai, with a bit more than 10 dunams, had 400-500; Khirbet Radana, with under 5 dunams, had fewer than 250; ʿIzbet Sarta, with under 2 dunams, had fewer than 100. Large towns like Tell Mosas (stratum II) housed 1,400 to 1,800 inhabitants on 35 dunams, Tell en-Nasbeh (stratum I) 800 to 1,000 on 20, Khirbet el-Kheibar (coordinates: 1954. 1764) 1,400 to 1,750 on 35, and Megiddo (stratum VB) 1,600-2,000 on 40.[36]

Political leadership of the settlements was in the hands of the assembly of the *ʾanšê hāʿîr* (Jgs. 19:22, etc.) and the *ziqnê hāʿîr* (1 S. 16:4), whose respective jurisdictions can no longer be determined; this structure is identical to that of family organization of the clan. A settlement and the *mišpāḥâ* living there can be considered as a unit (cf. Jgs. 6:24; 8:32, *ʿoprâ* [*ʿopraṯ*] *ʾᵃḇî hāʿezrî*).[37] (Fictive) genealogies made it possible to incorporate non-Israelite localities such as Shechem and Tirzah into the Israelite tribal system (Nu. 26:28-34; 27:1-11; 36:10-12; Josh. 17:1-6; 1 Ch. 7:14-19; for toponyms represented as descendants of an ancestor, see 1 Ch. 7:8; 8:36; as ancestors of clan eponyms, see 1 Ch. 8:37). Hostility within Israel between city and countryside is alien to the early period of Israel's history. Only in 1 S. 11:1-4, in the special circumstances of Transjordan, do we find initial attempts of settlements to achieve independence.[38] Relationships between Israelite tribes and Canaanite city-states ran the gamut from Asher's vassalage to Acco through the formal treaty of Benjamin with the Gibeonite tetrapolis to military conflict (Jgs. 5); they cannot be reduced uniformly to hostility between city and countryside, but involved a wide range of sociohistorical and religious factors.

3. *Monarchic Period.* With the formation of the Davidic state, the network that bound settlements together in a structure of genealogically defined communities retreated in favor of a hierarchical alignment, both territorial and political, of administrative districts (1 K. 4:7-19) with a capital city.[39] In the Davidic period, these districts still were based on the tribal boundaries (2 S. 15:2); in the period of Solomon, however, they incorporated both Israelite and Canaanite territories[40] and became disengaged from the genealogical integration of premonarchic society. Now a new form of integration was needed; it was found in the hierarchy of governmental administration, based on power. The new administrative structure was reflected in a hierarchy of cities and rural settlements, from which the social tensions in Israelite society could cause conflict between city and countryside to arise.[41] Subordinate to the royal capital were the provincial capitals, in which the governors of the provinces resided. For the third,

---

35. Shiloh, "Population."
36. Otto, "Gibt es Zusammenhänge," 81ff.
37. On the ending *â/aṯ* see A. F. Rainey, *BASOR* 231 (1978) 4.
38. See Reviv, "Jabesh-Gilead."
39. H. W. Rösel, *ZDPV* 100 (1984) 84-90.
40. G. E. Wright, *ErIsr* 8 (1967) 58*-68*.
41. See IV.1 and 3 below.

sixth, and seventh provinces, Arubboth, Ramoth-gilead, and Mahanaim are named (1 K. 4:10,13-14); Megiddo was probably the center of the fifth province and Hazor of the eighth province, Naphtali. Subordinate to the provincial capitals were the provincial towns (1 K. 4:13). The city lists in Josh. 15–19 are administrative documents drawn up to aid in the assessment of taxes[42] and the organization of the militia (Am. 5:3); they reflect the urban structure of Judah during the monarchy.[43] The towns functioned as centers for the surrounding villages (*ḥᵃṣērîm,* Josh. 15:32,36,41; etc.). It is impossible to reconstruct a more precise differentiation in the administrative hierarchy involving the towns and villages.

During the exilic period, the motif of daughter cities *(bᵉnôṯeyhā),* which has its traditio-historical roots in the hierarchy of non-Israelite settlements (1 S. 6:18; 27:5-6), was extended literarily to cities outside Israel (Nu. 21:25,32; 32:42; Josh. 17:11; Jgs. 1:27; 11:26; Jer. 49:2; Ezk. 26:6); in the late postexilic period, under the influence of the Persian administrative structure, it became the organizing principle of Judahite settlements (Josh. 15:28; 1 Ch. 7:28; 8:12; Neh. 11:25; etc.).

The royal cities were the focus of the settlement hierarchies: Jerusalem in the south and, after the division of the kingdom, Shechem, Penuel, Tirzah, and Samaria in the north. Increasingly Jerusalem became quite simply *the* city (*hā'îr,* 2 S. 15:25; 1 K. 8:44,48; Neh. 2:3; 11:9; Isa. 36:15; 37:33,35; Ezk. 7:23; 9:4,9; Zeph. 3:1).[44]

The theory that Jerusalem was the personal property of the Davidides on the basis of a *ius expugnationis,* extending the Canaanite concept of the city-state,[45] finds no support in the use of the expression *'îr dāwîḏ* with reference to Jerusalem. In 2 S. 5:7,9, this phrase is applied to part of the city, identical with the acropolis,[46] the *mᵉṣuḏaṯ ṣîyôn* (see also 1 K. 8:1; 9:24); it does not refer to the city itself (2 S. 6:10,12,16; Isa. 22:9-10). In 1 K. 20:30 and 2 K. 10:25, too, *'îr* refers to the citadel of a city; it is not restricted to the temple precincts.[47] Even less likely is the theory that Samaria constituted a city-state.[48] The administration of the capital cities Jerusalem (2 K. 23:8) and Samaria (2 K. 10:5), including police powers (1 K. 22:26), was in the hands of a *śar ('al)-hā'îr,* who, as a late preexilic seal confirms, was one of the royal officials.[49]

The original function of the city was to serve as a protected settlement for families engaged in agriculture. Now, going beyond the immediate protection of its inhabitants, the city took on certain military functions of the state. As early as the time of David, Dan and Beer-sheba were probably fortified border outposts.[50] Solomon secured important travel

---

42. O. Bächli, *ZDPV* 89 (1973) 1-14.
43. P. Welten, *Die Königsstempel. ADPV* (1969), 93-102.
44. See also *KAI* 194.7.
45. Alt, "Jerusalems Aufstieg," 254; Buccellati, 31ff.
46. On the excavations see Shiloh, *City of David,* 15ff.
47. Contra Fisher.
48. Alt, "Samaria"; see more recently S. Timm, *Die Dynastie Omri. FRLANT* 124 (1982), 142ff.
49. See Avigad, *IEJ* 26 (1976) 178-82; U. Rüterswörden, *Die Beamten der israelitischen Königszeit. BWANT* 117 (1985), 38ff.
50. Y. Aharoni, *IEJ* 24 (1974) 13-16.

and trade routes by means of fortified cities in densely settled areas and by chains of strongholds elsewhere (1 K. 9:15,17-19). Fortification of Hazor, Megiddo, and Gezer with casemate walls and six-chambered gates[51] secured the major travel artery between Egypt and Syria; fortification of Beth-horon secured the link between the coast and the mountains of central Palestine; and a chain of strongholds secured the road from Judah to Eilat.[52] Many other cities were fortified to serve as garrison cities (*'ārê hāreḵeḇ, 'ārê happārāšîm,* 1 K. 9:19; 10:26) and to strengthen the security of the region.[53]

After the division of the kingdom, the security of the heartland of Judah was increased against attack from the south (2 Ch. 11:5b,6-10aβ) by a ring of fortified cities (*'ārîm lᵉmāṣôr),* while Asa secured the north of Judah by building Geba and Mizpah (1 K. 15:22).[54] This system of fortifications was reinforced by an additional ring of strongholds around Jerusalem.[55]

For the northern kingdom, the scanty literary references to fortifications (1 K. 12:25; 15:17; 16:24,34; 22:39) are compensated for by a wealth of archaeological evidence from urban centers along major travel routes, such as Dan, Hazor, Kinneret, Megiddo, Tirzah, Shechem, and Samaria, as well as from towns far from these routes, such as Khirbet el-Marjameh.[56]

In the hierarchical political and social structure of Israel, the cities became intermediaries of governmental administration, as is attested archaeologically by the Iron Age palaces of Lachish, Megiddo, and Hazor, and the storehouses *(miskᵉnôṯ)* of Arad, Beer-sheba, Lachish, Beth-shemesh, Shechem, Megiddo, and Hazor.[57] The *'ārê hammiskᵉnôṯ* (1 K. 9:19) served to collect taxes and provide supplies for the garrisons.[58]

The urbanization of Israel, which began in the 10th century, radiated from the capital city; the result was the centralized direction of city planning, based on a layout that developed from the round village of the Early Iron Age: a circular city wall and main street, with houses arranged radially, together with a public square associated with the gate area.[59] This plan was utilized at Tell Beit Mirsim, Beth-shemesh, Tell en-Nasbeh, Megiddo, and probably at Jokneam.[60]

---

51. Dever, 269ff.

52. Z. Herzog, *Beer-Sheba II* (1984), 83.

53. On the fortifications see N. L. Lapp, *BASOR* 223 (1976) 25-42. For an archaeological discussion see de Geus, *Stad,* 76-81.

54. On the former see Y. Yadin, *BASOR* 239 (1980) 19-23: Rehoboam; Na'aman, 5ff.: Hezekiah; Fritz, 46ff.: Josiah; see also D. Ussishkin, *Tel Aviv Journal* 10 (1983) 171-72. On the latter see S. Timm, *ZDPV* 96 (1980) 22-23.

55. A. Mazar, *ErIsr* 15 (1981) 229-49.

56. See also *KAI* 181.10-11, 18-19. On travel routes see Pienaar, 151ff. On Kinneret see V. Fritz, *IEJ* 33 (1983) 257-59. See also Mazar, "Three Israelite Sites," 171ff.

57. On the palaces see V. Fritz, *ZDPV* 99 (1983) 22ff.; on the storehouses, Z. Herzog, "The Storehouses," in Y. Aharoni, ed., *Beer-Sheba I* (1973), 23-30.

58. J. Naveh in Y. Aharoni, ed., *Arad Inscriptions* (1981), 142-48.

59. On urbanization see B. S. J. Isserlin, *VT* 34 (1984) 169-78. On city planning see Herzog, "City Planning," 38-43. On the radial arrangement of houses see Shiloh, "Town Planning"; McClellan. On the square and gate area see Herzog, *Stadttor,* 160ff.

60. A. Ben-Tor et al., *IEJ* 33 (1983) 30ff.

The urbanization of Israel was reflected linguistically in the increased use of the expressions *yṣʾ mikkol-ʿārê yiśrāʾēl* (1 S. 18:6) and *šûḇ/hlk ʾîš leʿîrô* (1 S. 8:22; Ezr. 2:1; Neh. 7:6; cf. 1 K. 22:36). It also exerted increasing influence on the social structure of Israel. In the rural villages most of the population were engaged in agriculture, making their living, as the many silos and presses for wine and oil show, by working the land belonging to the settlement (*śeḏēh hāʿîr,* Josh. 21:12; *migrešê heāʿrîm,* Nu. 35:5).[61] In the capital cities, however, distinct quarters housed different classes of craftspeople (Jer. 37:21; Neh. 3:32) and merchants (1 K. 20:34).[62] Among the provincial cities, the textile industry was concentrated in Lachish and Tell Beit Mirsim, the wine industry in Gibeon, and metallurgy in Tell Deir ʿAllā.[63] The process of urbanization and division of labor was accompanied by a social differentiation into poor and wealthy strata (2 S. 12:1-4),[64] which led to slum areas such as those found at Tirzah, Shechem, and Jerusalem,[65] as well as a general impoverishment of the country villages during the period from the 8th through the 6th century.[66]

Another consequence of urbanization was an increasing shift of Israelite legal and judicial institutions to the cities. In Dt. 13:13-19; 19:1-13; 20:10-20; 21:1-9, urban legal traditions have entered the stream of Israelite legal history.[67] These traditions, unknown to the Covenant Code, underscore the growing importance of cities as the sites where legal cases were decided,[68] especially after the legal reform of Jehoshaphat (2 Ch. 19:5-11). In Dt. 12–26 *ʿîr* and → שׁער *šaʿar* can be used interchangeably (cf. 13:13ff. [Eng. 13:12ff.]; 17:2ff.).[69] Dt. 19:2a,3b,4bα,5b illustrate how before Dtn the asylum function shifted from the local sanctuary (Ex. 21:13-14) to three special cities.

4. *Persian Period.* The lists preserved in Ezr. 2:21-35; Neh. 3:2-22; 7:25-38; 11:25-35 provide information concerning the settlement pattern in the province of Yehud during the Persian period. The territory described in these lists, the extent of which is confirmed by finds of coins and official seals, was limited to the region bounded by Mizpah to the north, Beth-zur to the south, Jericho and En-gedi to the east, and Azekah and Gezer to the south. The province was divided into at least five districts, whose centers were Beth-zur, Beth-haccherem, Keilah, Jerusalem, and Mizpah (Neh. 3:1-22). Gezer and Jericho were probably the centers of two additional districts.[70] Neh. 11:25-35 reveals an administrative hierarchy of district capital, its subordinate towns, and their "daughter" villages. This hierarchy was focused on Jerusalem, whose signifi-

---

61. See Feuillet, 275ff.; on *migraš* see Barr.
62. I. Mendelsohn, *BASOR* 80 (1940) 17-21.
63. See Frick, 127ff. On Tell Beit Mirsim cf. D. Eitam, *Tel Aviv Journal* 6 (1979) 150ff.
64. D. Michel, *TRE,* IV, 72ff.
65. See, respectively, R. de Vaux, *AncIsr,* I, 72-73; Wright, 154-55; Shiloh, *City of David,* 28-29.
66. C. H. J. de Geus, *ZDPV* 98 (1982) 54ff.
67. Benjamin, 177-348.
68. Z. Herzog, *Stadttor,* 163-64.
69. C. M. Carmichael, *The Laws of Deuteronomy* (1974), 261-62.
70. Stern, 245ff.

cance was increased by Nehemiah's program of fortification and enforced repopulation (Neh. 2–7; 11).[71]

For the province of Samaria (Neh. 2:10,19; 4:1[7]), the evidence is scantier. The only cities for which there is literary evidence are Samaria and Shechem.[72] These towns of central Palestine appear quite modest when compared to the great coastal cities of Acco, Dor, Jabneh, Ashdod, and Ashkelon, under the sovereignty of Tyre and Sidon.[73] Herodotus describes Gaza as holding its own in the company of Sardis.[74] At Shikmonah and Tell Abu Hawam we find the beginnings of orthogonal city planning.[75] The foci of the Persian military infrastructure, which was aimed at Egypt, were fortresses and supply depots along the coast road (Shikmonah, Tell Qasile, Ashdod, Tell Jemmeh, Tell el-Farʿa [south]) and in the Negeb (Tell Seraʿ, Beer-Sheba, Arad, Khirbet Ritma, Kadesh-barnea, Tell el-Kheleifeh).

5. *Hellenistic Period.* The classic Greek polis was a single entity constituting both city and state.[76] Externally, it was characterized by political and economic autonomy, including the right to strike coinage; internally, it was characterized by self-governance of the *dḗmos* in *ekklēsía* and *boulḗ* and by legal and cultic independence. The polis survived transformed in the Hellenistic Near East, becoming integrated into the concept of a territorial state ruled by a monarch. Alongside the administrative units of Coele-Syria, representing ethnic groups like the Judeans and the Idumeans, intensively hellenized areas were home to such semi-autonomous cities with a polis form of government. In line with the classical notion of the polis, Hellenistic political theory could treat these cities as "allies" of the king. Despite their organization as poleis after the classical model, however, their administration and economy were controlled by officials of the king.[77] In actual practice, loss of political freedom changed the nature of the Hellenistic polis markedly from that of the Greek polis. Theoretically, however, the polis was still the highest constitutional concept, distinguishing such a settlement from others that did not enjoy this right (villages, colonies).

The Phoenician and Palestinian coast, already urban in the Persian period, became a center of Hellenistic poleis. Acco-Ptolemais was probably the capital of the Ptolemaic province "Syria and Phoenicia." Other regions with cities established as Hellenistic poleis or hellenized by renaming and the introduction of a polis constitution included northern Transjordan and the land around Lakes Gennesaret and Semechonitis, forming a wall against the Arabs.[78] These foci of Ptolemaic urban hellenization (including

---

71. Otto, *Jerusalem,* 100ff.
72. Josephus *Ant.* 11.8.6 §§340-45. For Samaria see Tadmor, "Samaria," 8ff.; for Shechem, N. L. Lapp, *BASOR* 257 (1985) 19-43.
73. See Pseudo-Scylax; K. Galling, *ZDPV* 61 (1938) 83ff.
74. *Hist.* 3.5.
75. Stern, 230.
76. Kolb, 58ff.
77. Hengel, 23.
78. Tcherikover, *Hellenistic Civilization,* 90ff.

Ptolemais, Scythopolis, Philadelphia, Rabbat-Moab, Gerasa, Gadara, Hippos, Abila, and Philoteria) supported a policy of controlling the Mediterranean ports and the trade routes between the ports, the Persian Gulf, and the Arabian Peninsula.[79] By contrast, Seleucid hellenization (represented by such cities as Antioch, Laodicea, Apamea, Beroea, Dura Europus, and Damascus) was guided by the desire to establish a homogeneous culture.[80] These disparate goals resulted in substantial differences between Ptolemaic and Seleucid city planning.[81] Ptolemaic planning concentrated on the acropolis or citadel; residential areas were structured only superficially by main streets, with secondary streets branching off from them. Seleucid planning was more concerned with the total form of the city, using a hippodromic street plan that included an agora and adorning the residential quarters with public buildings.

No new Hellenistic cities were founded in Judea; the influence of urban Hellenism was also slight in Samaria and Idumea, despite the Macedonian colony in Samaria[82] and the small rural cities Marissa and Adoraim. Southern Palestine was defended militarily against the desert by a chain of fortresses from the Dead Sea (including En-gedi) through Arad to Beth-zur. Jerusalem played a special role as the Ptolemaic temple city Hierosolyma and the heart of the temple state Judah. Attempts to hellenize Jerusalem as a polis during the Seleucid period, however, remained unsuccessful.[83] The slight influence of the Hellenistic polis idea in Judea as well as in the Ptolemaic heartland of Egypt is reflected also in the depoliticized and therefore de-hellenized use of the term *pólis* in the LXX (see VI below).

IV. OT Tradition.

1. *Early Narratives.* Patriarchal narratives preserving memories of the dimorphic way of life of the proto-Israelite pastoral families reflect a critical attitude on the part of shepherds toward urban population centers, with which they necessarily came into contact. Gen. 26:1-11 pictures the city as a center of political power that seeks to subject the shepherds to its will; the shepherds in turn experience the city as a source of legal insecurity and conflicts (cf. also Gen. 34).[84] Gen. 19 and Jgs. 19 present the city as an inhospitable place of moral corruption; it is a source of the disintegration of the rural ethics of family solidarity. These two narratives enshrine the criticism of the city by the countryside.[85]

2. *Learned Reflection.* Gen. 4:1,(2),17-18 is a fragmentary history of civilization originating in learned Judahite circles. Exhibiting a positive estimate of cities, it links agriculture with urban civilization in a pattern of cultural progress that sees cities

---

79. M. Rostovtzeff, *Caravan Cities* (1932).
80. M. Hadas, *Hellenistic Culture* (1959), 24ff.
81. Barghouti, 209-29.
82. Tcherikover, "Stadtgründungen," 73-74.
83. Tcherikover, *Hellenistic Civilization,* 117ff.
84. E. Otto, *Jakob in Sichem. BWANT* 110 (1979), 169-81.
85. De Pury, 219-29.

emerging from agricultural civilization. In Gen. 10:8-12, a traditio-historically related reflection on the history of civilization, the origin of kingdoms and empires is traced back to the urban center of Babylon; the founder of the city is identified as a despot. Philo of Byblos has a similar account.[86]

The story of the Tower of Babel in Gen. 11:2-5,6aαγb,8 puts a negative face on the connection between imperial and urban ideology. The claim of an urban metropolis of a Mesopotamian empire to be the center of humanity, it suggests, does not unite humanity but divides it. This Israelite narrative probably criticizes the interdependence of political power and urban culture in Israel.

The theology of the Tetrateuch, reflecting the views of rural Judah, borrowed these positive and negative traditions to illustrate the ambivalence of urban culture as an element of human civilization. Once the protective security of paradise was lost (Gen. 2:4b–3:24), creative labor became a necessity to secure the necessities of life; humankind, having fallen from the security of Yahweh's protection into a yearning for autonomy, turns on its head every vital cultural achievement, abusing urban civilization (4:17) as a triumphal attempt to take heaven by storm (11:1-9). Gen. 12:1-3 offers the alternative: not through the grandiose organization of a metropolis but through the blessing of Abraham, in which all the families of the earth share through Israel and toward which neutrality is impossible, is the unity of humanity realized.

In Dt. 6:10-13 (see also 19:1),[87] the Dtn tradition presents a positive assessment of the urban structure of Israel as a cultural element borrowed from the indigenous population, but warns against the danger of self-assurance, trusting in the security of the fortified cities, which is an affront to Yahweh. Incorporation of 6:10-13 into the Dtr context ratifies this perspective as applying also to the new Israel of the postexilic period. Under prophetic influence, this warning was expanded to include danger of idolatry, promoted by the city (6:14-19; cf. also 13:13-19; see IV.3 below).

The Chronicler's History records a positive assessment of cities and the urban organization of the land, not only in the detailed description of Nehemiah's efforts to fortify Jerusalem but also in the favorable verdict on preexilic kings conveyed by statements concerning city building.[88]

3. *Prophetic Criticism.* The prophetic movement in the northern kingdom does not criticize cities per se, leveling social criticism only at epiphenomena of urban culture. Prophecy in the southern kingdom, however, incorporates the criticism of cities associated with rural Judah that is reflected in the Tetrateuch. This criticism is directed specifically against Jerusalem: the city is built on bloodguilt and iniquity (*dāmîm* and *ʿawlâ,* Mic. 3:10; Hab. 2:12; cf. Ezk. 22:2). It is a place of oppression

---

86. Eusebius *Praep. evang.* 1.10.9,12-13,35.

87. Benjamin, 136ff.

88. P. Welten, *Geschichte und Geschichtsdarstellung in dem Chronikbüchern. WMANT* 42 (1973), 9-52.

(*ʿōšeq,* Jer. 6:6; *yônâ,* Zeph. 3:1) and perversity (*muṭṭeh,* Ezk. 9:9), of tumultuous pleasure and inappropriate carousing (Isa. 22:2; cf. Jer. 7:34). This criticism reflects the social differentiation that accompanies urbanization and interferes with the administration of justice (Mic. 3:9-11; 6:9-16). The theological critique preserved in the Judahite interpretation of the Hoseanic tradition (Hos. 8:14b) sees the city as an expression of aspirations for security that flout the creative power of Yahweh. Mic. 1:13 views the city as the fountainhead of *ḥaṭṭāʾṯ* and *pešaʿ,* breaking Israel's bond with Yahweh. In the Jeremianic tradition (Jer. 2:28) and the Dtr tradition dependent on Jeremiah (Jer. 7:17-18; 11:12; 2 K. 23:5; etc.), which borrows Hoseanic motifs while giving them a Judahite interpretation, the city is a hotbed of idolatry. As a consequence, its destruction is predicted (Mic. 1:8-16; 3:12; Jer. 2:15; 5:17; etc.); its walls cannot protect it (Dt. 28:52). In the perspective of Isaianic theology (Isa. 32:19), destruction of the mighty city that arrogantly turns its back on God can be an element of the salvation to come. For Jeremiah, the protective function of the city is turned on its head (Jer. 8:14): the only survivors will be those who voluntarily leave the city and surrender to the enemy (21:9; 38:2).

4. *Zion.* Prophetic criticism has its theological antipode in the theology of Zion and the Jerusalem cult. With the help of mythological motifs, Jerusalem is pictured as the city of God (*ʿîr ʾelōhîm*[*-hênû*], Ps. 46:5[4]; 48:2[1]), the place of God's presence (Ps. 46; 48; 76) chosen by Yahweh (132:13), where the forces of chaos are shattered and from which peace goes forth throughout the world (46:10-11[9-10]). In the view of this theology, the fortifications of Jerusalem are themselves an empirical expression of God's presence and of the power and security of the city they provide. By the same token, other fortified cities besides Jerusalem can also be cities of God (*ʿārê ʾelōhîm,* 2 S. 10:12) protected by Yahweh (Ps. 127:1).

In the exilic period, the motif of Jerusalem's election was combined with that of cultic centralization (1 K. 8:16ff.; etc.) in a Dtr reform program for the postexilic period. The Deutero-Isaianic tradition transferred the cultic conception of the sacredness of the sanctuary to the city of Jerusalem as *ʿîr haqqōḏeš* (Isa. 48:2; 52:1). In the postexilic period, this motif became widely influential (Neh. 11:18; Dnl. 9:24; 1 Mc. 2:7; 2 Mc. 1:12; 3:1; 9:14; etc.). As the city chosen once more by Yahweh, Jerusalem will overflow with the prosperity that promotes life (Zec. 1:17). Yahweh will dwell in the midst of her as *ʿîr-hāʾemeṯ* (Zec. 8:3).

5. *Apocalypse of Isaiah.* Prophetic and cultic interpretations come together in the Apocalypse of Isaiah (Isa. 24–27). Despite substantial differences among scholars in the identification and dating of its literary strata,[89] there is general consensus that Isa. 24–27 reflects a lengthy process of continual reinterpretation.

Isa. 24:7-12(13); 25:1-5; 26:1-6 constitutes a self-contained unit interpreting the traditions recorded in 24:1-6,14-20,23; 25:6-7,8*,9-10a; 26:7-21. Isa. 24:7-12(13)

89. See H. Wildberger, *Isaiah 13–27* (Eng. trans. 1997), 447ff.

elaborates the prophecy of doom in 24:1-6 in terms of the destruction of urban life; the prophetic hymn of thanksgiving in 25:1-5 associates the revelation of Yahweh as king in Jerusalem with the destruction of a metropolis; and the antithesis between Jerusalem and the metropolis destroyed by Yahweh informs the hymn in 26:1-6, which builds on 25:9-10a, especially the motif of the mountain of God.

This interpretive stratum associates the doom and deliverance of the age to come with the respective fates of a metropolis that represents paradigmatically the world falling prey to destruction and Jerusalem, which represents the coming age of salvation. The metropolis will be destroyed by Yahweh despite its military might as *qiryâ b^eṣûrâ* (25:2) and *qiryâ niśgāḇâ* (26:5). It will become a desolation (*ʿîr šammâ,* 24:12) and a heap of stones (*gal,* 25:2). Riotous hedonism, music, and wine stand for the way of life of this city (Isa. 24:8-11). The towering city stands for the attitude of its inhabitants: they are insolent *(zēḏîm)* and violent *(ʿārîṣîm).* With their ruthless blasts, they represent the chaos that overwhelms the poor and needy (25:4-5).

This interpretive stratum does not criticize cities in general: in contrast to the false triumphalism of the metropolis, it presents a different reality in the image of the new Jerusalem. It too will be a strong city (*ʿîr ʿaz,* 26:1). But it will be Yahweh who sets up its walls and bulwarks. Its inhabitants are a *gôy ṣaddîq* (26:2). Instead of the raging of the violent and arrogant, there will be steadfast trust in Yahweh. Instead of humiliation and destruction, Yahweh will establish peace for the inhabitants of the new Jerusalem (26:3). The destitute will triumph over the arrogant. In the contrasting descriptions of the doomed metropolis and the new Jerusalem, the universalistic mythological tradition is fleshed out with concrete details drawn from urban life. The contrast between the conduct of the violent and arrogant and that of those who trust steadfastly in Yahweh represents the contrast between the age of disaster and the age of deliverance. To interpret the motifs associated with the godless city as reflecting concrete historical events is to ignore the intent of this stratum.

The concrete historical dimension appears only in the subsequent redactions that introduce the themes of Moab (25:10b-12) and hope for reunification (27:6-11). The urban symbolism was already so central to the material that these later redactions could not help associating their additions with the somewhat inappropriate motif of the destroyed city (25:12; 27:10-11).

6. *Wisdom.* Wisdom tradition uses the city as a symbol of the attitude that relies on power and strength rather than wise conduct. Trust in the strength represented empirically by a fortified city is inferior to a life guided by wisdom, the source of true strength (Prov. 21:22). Self-control and self-mastery are superior to the brute force demonstrated by conquest of a city (16:32). In contrast to the cultic theology associated with Jerusalem, wisdom does not see a city's strength as an expression of Yahweh's mighty presence. Neither does it follow prophetic criticism in attacking triumphalistic self-assurance apart from and therefore hostile to Yahweh. For wisdom, the fortified city represents an unauthentic externality in contrast to the inward heart, the authentic site of the distinction between strength and weakness.

V. Qumran. The word *ʿîr* appears some 90 times in the Dead Sea Scrolls; the majority of occurrences (55) are in the *pesharim,* the Damascus Document, and the Temple Scroll.[90]

In 1QpHab prophetic criticism of cities is applied to the writer's present situation. Social criticism takes a back seat to religio-political controversy. The motif of the bloody and iniquitous city (Hab. 2:12) is interpreted as referring to the prophet of lies, who leads many astray in order to build a *ʿyr šww* (1QpHab 10:10), which 1QpHab 12:7, combining Hab. 2:17 with 2:12, sees as a reference to Jerusalem. The act of bloody violence against the city is interpreted as the desecration of the temple by the wicked priest, the violence against the countryside as his dispossession of the poor in the cities of Judah. Similarly, 4QpNah 2:2 interprets the motif of the *ʿyr dmm* (Nah. 3:1) as a reference to the *ʿyr ʾprym* in the hands of those who "seek after smooth things." In interpreting Hab. 2:12,17, the criticism of 1QpHab 12:6b-10 evinces a conception of graduated holiness inherent in the temple, the temple city, and the outlying cities of Judah. This conception of varying degrees of holiness inherent in different regions of the holy land with its houses and cities — a three-day journey, an inner zone with a radius of some 4 mi., each centered on the temple city as the sacred focal point of the land, the temple mount, and finally the temple itself with its own gradations — becomes explicit in the Damascus Document and especially the Temple Scroll. Jerusalem as temple city is called *ʿyry* (11QT 47:15,18; 52:19), *hʿyr* (46:13,17), *ʿyr hmqdš* (CD 12:1,2; 11QT 45:11-12,16-17), *ʿyr hqdš* (CD 20:22), *ʿyr mqdšy* (11QT 47:9,13), *hʿyr ʾšr ʾny šwkn btwkh* (45:13-14), *hʿyr ʾšr ʾqdyš lškyn šmy wmqd(šy btwkh)* (47:3-4), *hʿyr ʾšr ʾnwky mškn ʾt šmy wmqdšy btwkh* (47:10-11), and *ʿyry ʾšr ʾnwky mqdš lśwm šmy btwkh* (52:19-20).[91]

The notion of holiness finds concrete expression in the application of the pentateuchal regulations governing the purity of the camp (cf. Nu. 5:2-3) to Jerusalem and the cities of Israel (CD 12:1-2,19,22-23; 11QT 47:2-7), a development that can appeal to Isa. 52:1 (cf. Rev. 21:27). The temple city demands a celibate life (CD 12:1-2; 11QT 45:11-12; 51:5-10). Women, lepers, and the physically handicapped are excluded from the city (45:12-18). Defilement through excrement is prevented by a *mqwm yd* 3,000 yards northwest of the city (46:13-16). Josephus's information about the Essene Gate and Bethso in his description of the "first wall" may indicate that this is not simply a literary fiction but may reflect Essene practice in Jerusalem.[92] Meat from animals slaughtered under secular auspices must remain outside the city (47:7-18). The cities throughout the countryside, too, are governed by holiness regulations, less stringent than those governing the temple city (CD 12:19; 11QT 47:3). In particular, these regulations forbid burial within a city and require special cemeteries for every four cities (48:12-14).

---

90. Yadin, *Temple Scroll,* 3 vols. in 4 (1983), II, 453.
91. Ibid., I, 280.
92. *BJ* 5.4.2 §145; see Otto, *Jerusalem,* 124-25; see also B. Pixner, "An Essene Quarter on Mount Zion?" *Studia Hierosolymitana* 1 (1976) 245-85.

VI. LXX. The LXX uses *pólis* to translate *ʿîr.*[93] In the LXX *pólis* occurs approximately 1,600 times, including some that render *qiryâ, šaʿar* (Dt. 14:21), *māqôm* (Dt. 21:19), *bîrâ* (Est. 1:2,5; etc.), or *ʾarmôn* (Isa. 34:13). The passages where *ʿîr* is translated by *kṓmē* (Josh. 10:39; 1 Ch. 27:25; 2 Ch. 14:13[14]; Isa. 42:11) are probably meant to clarify the postexilic hierarchy of settlements. Texts that could not be interpreted on the basis of the postexilic urban geography were liable to misinterpretation: in Josh. 10:2, e.g., *ʿārê hammamlāḵâ* is translated *mētrópoleōs.* The translation of *ʿîr dāwîḏ* as *hē ákra Dauid* reflects the architectural history of Jerusalem in the Hellenistic period.[94]

The theoretical political implications of the term *pólis* are not reflected in the LXX. The words *politeúesthai, politeía,* and *políteuma* appear only in those parts of the LXX without a Hebrew prototype.[95]

The depoliticizing of the term *pólis* in the LXX[96] can hardly be an expression of deliberate rejection of Hellenism; it is more likely due to the modest influence of the polis notion not only in Judea but also in Egypt, the Ptolemaic heartland.[97]

E. Otto

93. Strathmann, 522.
94. Otto, *Jerusalem,* 115ff.
95. For a discussion of the texts see Schmidt, 96-97.
96. Strathmann, 523.
97. Tcherikover, *Hellenistic Civilization,* 25.

עָכַר *ʿāḵar;* עֵמֶק עָכוֹר *ʿēmeq ʿāḵôr*

I. General: 1. Statistics; 2. Cognate Languages and Ancient Versions; 3. Basic Meaning. II. Biblical Usage: 1. Verb; 2. Valley of Achor.

I. General.

1. *Statistics.* The root *ʿkr* appears in the OT both as a verb and as an element of a toponym and of personal names. There are no other nominal derivatives. The verb occurs 14 times (not counting Job 6:4 cj., where the emendation of *yaʿarḵûnî* to *yaʿaḵrûnî* is unnecessary;[1] and Jgs. 11:35 cj., where the emendation of *krʿ* hiphil to *ʿkr* hiphil is

ʿāḵar. H.-D. Neef, "Die Ebene Achor — das 'Tor der Hoffnung,'" *ZDPV* 100 (1984) 91-107; J. J. Stamm, "Das hebräische Verbum *ʿākar,*" *Or* 47 (1978) 339-50.

1. *HAL,* II, 824.

also unnecessary, the more so since *'kr* hiphil is otherwise unattested). In Sir. 37:12 *'kr* is uncertain;[2] in 7:10 *'kr* hithpael should probably be emended to *'br* hithpael.[3] The form *ybkr* should probably be read in Lachish ostracon 2:5.[4]

Of the 14 occurrences of the verb in the MT, 12 are in the qal, 2 in the niphal. The other stems, in particular the piel (see I.3 below), are not found. It is noteworthy that of the 12 occurrences of the qal, 6 are participles (see I.3 below).

There are 5 occurrences of the toponym *'ēmeq 'āḵôr,* "Valley of Achor"; the same name occurs twice in the Copper Scroll from Qumran (3Q15 1:1; 4:6).[5] There are 5 occurrences of the PN *'oḵrān* (all in the phrase "Pagiel son of Okran"; the association of this name with *'kr* is uncertain);[6] there is a single occurrence of the PN *'āḵār* (1 Ch. 2:7, a secondary wordplay associating the name *'āḵān* with the verb *'kr;* cf. *Ácharos* in Josephus;[7] also *Achar* in LXX^{B} consistently and in LXX^{A} Josh. 7:24 for Heb. *'āḵān*).

The OT occurrences of the verb, the toponym, and the personal names are generally assigned to the same root. Nonetheless, since the connection of the name *'oḵrān* with the verb *'kr* is uncertain and the assimilation of the name *'āḵān* to the root *'kr* is secondary and artificial, the personal names can have no bearing on the meaning of OT *'kr.*

2. *Cognate Languages and Ancient Versions.* Middle Hebrew and Jewish Aramaic use the root *'kr* with the basic meaning "make (a liquid) turbid." In some passages (e.g., Gen. 34:30), early Jewish exegesis uses this metaphor to interpret OT *'kr.*[8] The root has the same meaning in Mandaic, Samaritan, and Christian Aramaic.[9] In a similar vein, the Vulg. generally uses *(con-, per-) turbare* to translate *'kr.* For the Valley of Achor, Jerome cites a traditional interpretation *tumultus atque turbarum,* "tumult and throng."[10] In seven passages the Syr. uses *d^{e}laḥ,* "disturb, make (water) turbid," to translate OT *'kr,*[11] but it retains the Hebrew consonants, probably with the meaning of Syr. *'kr* (see below), in 1 Ch. 2:7 or interprets the word as meaning "destroy, damage" (*'bd,* Prov. 11:17; 15:6,27; *hrr* aphel, Gen. 34:30). In Jgs. 11:35 LXX^{A} translates *'kr* with *tarássō* (as do Aquila, Symmachus, and Theodotion in 1 S. 14:29). Elsewhere it displays a striking lack of consistency in its treatment of Heb. *'kr.*[12] The Targ. (Pentateuch and Prophets) does not translate but uses Heb. *'kr* as a loanword.

In Syriac, *'kr* means "hold back, hinder."[13] It is related to Mand. *akr* I, "detain, re-

---

2. D. Barthélemy and O. Rickenbacher, *Konkordanz zum hebräischen Sirach* (1973), 298.
3. I. Levi, *The Hebrew Text of the Book of Ecclesiasticus. SSS* 3 (1904), in loc.
4. *KAI* 192.5; Stamm, 342; *DNSI,* II, 842.
5. See also Eusebius *Onomasticon* 84.18-21; F. Wutz, *Onomastica Sacra. TU* 41, 2 vols. (1914-15), s.v. Achor and Ἄχωρ.
6. M. Noth, *IPN,* 253.
7. *Ant.* 5.1.10, 14 §§33, 44.
8. Levy, *WTM,* III, 647-48; Jastrow, 1079.
9. See *MdD,* 18: *akr* II; *HAL,* II, 824.
10. *Epistula 108 ad Eustochium,* 13 (*CSEL* 55 [1912], 306-51).
11. Brockelmann, *LexSyr*^{2}, 155.
12. Stamm, 344.
13. Brockelmann, *LexSyr*^{2}, 523.

tain, hold back, restrain, obstruct."[14] OSA *'kr,* "contradict, raise objections, act in a hostile manner," "contest (a claim), refuse (a request)," clearly belongs here as well.[15] The only occurrence of Pun. *'kr* means "destroy."[16] Finally, Mandaic and Old South Arabic have a root *'kr* with the respective meanings "plow, dig, cultivate," and "become pregnant, be fertile."[17] The root *'kr* is not found in Ugaritic or Akkadian.

The various meanings of *'kr* can hardly be related to each other, and so we must distinguish three homonymous roots: *'kr* I, "push back"; *'kr* II, "make turbid"; and *'kr* III, "be fertile."

3. *Basic Meaning.* Because in Josh. 6–7 and 1 Ch. 2:7 *'kr* appears in conjunction with → חרם *ḥrm,* "ban, devote, devoted thing," some have proposed for *'kr* the basic meaning "declare taboo, make unavailable to others."[18] But neither the meanings of *'kr* in cognate languages nor the ancient versions support this interpretation. Furthermore, if this resultative sense were actually present, we would expect that *'kr* would occur also or even primarily in the piel.[19] The significantly frequent use of the qal participle, in at least one instance (1 K. 18:17)[20] almost as a fixed "title" or technical term, also speaks against this understanding. Above all, in several OT passages this translation would make no sense.[21]

Most scholars assume an exclusively metaphorical use of *'kr* II, "stir up, make turbid" (see I.2 above), translating the qal of OT *'kr* as "confuse, trouble, disturb" and the niphal as "be confused, be disturbed."[22] The OT, however, displays no trace of the supposed basic literal meaning "make turbid."[23] In addition, the more general meaning "injure, trouble," required by the various contexts, is hard to derive from the supposed basic literal meaning; at the very least, an additional specialized meaning must be assumed for Ps. 39:3(Eng. v. 2).[24]

All the OT occurrences of the verb *'kr* are easy to interpret, however, if OT *'kr* derives from *'kr* I (see I.2 above), with the concrete literal basic meaning "hold together, restrain, push back (with effort, with violence, or with hostile intent)," extended to the more general meaning "hinder, beset, treat with hostility, injure."

For the toponym *'ēmeq 'āḵôr,* it is reasonable to postulate an original association with *'kr* III, "be fertile" (see I.2 above).

---

14. *MdD,* 17-18; associated by *HAL,* II, 824, with Arab. *'aqara.*
15. For the former definition see Biella, 363-64; for the latter, Beeston, 14-15.
16. *DNSI,* II, 842.
17. See, respectively, *MdD,* 18: *akr* III; Beeston, 14-15.
18. E.g., *KBL*[2], 703, following F. Schwally, *Semitische Kriegsaltertümer,* I (1901), 41ff.
19. *HP,* 123ff.
20. T. Dozeman, "The 'Troubler' of Israel: *'kr* in I Kings 18,17-18," *Studia Biblica et Theologica* 9 (1979) 81-93.
21. Stamm.
22. Cf. *HAL,* II, 824; cf. *GesB,* 585; *LexHebAram,* 595; König, *Hebräisches und aramäisches Wörterbuch zum AT,* 327; Stamm.
23. As Stamm also observes.
24. Stamm, 349-50.

II. Biblical Usage.

1. *Verb.* In Ps. 39:3(2) almost all modern translations and commentators treat the words *ûḵᵉʾēḇî neʿkār* as standing in adversative contrast ("but," "nevertheless"; cf., however, LXX *kaí,* Vulg. *et*) to v. 3aβ(2aβ), which it follows syndetically, linking it in (synonymous) parallelism (contrary to the MT pointing) with the following asyndetic clause in v. 4aα(3aα), and translate accordingly.[25] But the noun clause in v. 3b(2b) is a circumstantial clause concluding the two preceding verbal clauses in v. 3aαβ(2aαβ);[26] it must describe a state occasioned by refusal to give voice to inward distress. Ps. 39:3b(2b) should be translated: "while my distress remained suppressed" (niphal ptcp. of *ʿkr*). The same participle in Prov. 15:6b should be interpreted similarly: "but the income of the wicked is kept down" — in other words, in contrast to the righteous described in v. 6a, the wicked receive no return.

Derivation of OT *ʿkr* from *ʿkr* I also accounts for the six occurrences of the finite verb in the qal. By making their father odious (*bʾš* hiphil) to the inhabitants of the land, Simeon and Levi "frustrated" him, i.e., they made it impossible for him to lead a successful life among the Canaanites (Gen. 34:30). Saul's unfortunate order "frustrated" the land, preventing success in battle (1 S. 14:29). By transgressing the ban, Achan made the Israelite camp itself an object for destruction and thereby "frustrated" it, preventing it from achieving its goal of capturing Ai (Josh. 6:18). Because Achan "frustrated" the Israelites under Joshua's leadership, "obstructing" their success, Yahweh "obstructs" him: he is stoned by the people (7:25). Elijah rejects Ahab's rebuke: it is not the prophet who has "frustrated" Israel to its detriment, but the king and his father's house (1 K. 18:18).

For the qal participle, too, the basic privative meaning of *ʿkr* I is clear: "hinder, obstruct (with hostile intent), trouble." In all six occurrences it is construed as a noun rather than a verb (*nomen regens* in a construct phrase). It is a kind of appellative or epithet characterizing the subject in question primarily as the possessor of an attribute rather than as the performer of a particular action (cf. the ptcps. *ʾōyēḇ, gōʾēl, ʾōhēḇ,* and *mašḥîṯ*). In 1 Ch. 2:7 the event recounted in Josh. 6–7* has become the distinguishing feature of its central figure: Achan now bears the nickname and title "the troubler of Israel" (*ʿôḵēr yiśrāʾēl* [determined!]). Ahab does not accuse Elijah of having troubled Israel through a specific list of actions but of being himself "the troubler of Israel" (*ʿōḵēr yiśrāʾēl* [determined], 1 K. 18:17). Jephthah's daughter, too, became one of his "troublers" and enemies (*wᵉʾatt hāyîṯ bᵉʿōḵᵉrāy* [determined], Jgs. 11:35). In Proverbs the determined qal participle occurs twice in parallel with other nominalized participles. Here too, however, it probably functions as a kind of technical term or title characterizing the personal nature of the subject rather than the name of that subject's actions. One who is cruel is "his own enemy" (*ʿōḵēr šᵉʾērô,* 11:17). One who takes a bribe is "the enemy of his own household" (*ʿōḵēr bêṯô,* 15:27). And one who is "the enemy of his own household" (*ʿôḵēr bêṯô*) will inherit wind (11:29).

---

25. See also *BHK* and *BHS*.

26. *GK,* §§156, 141e, 142d; D. Michel, *Tempora und Satzstellung in den Psalmen* (1960), 75, 185.

2. *Valley of Achor.* In a secondary literary development, the story of Achan in Josh. 6–7* has been linked to the narrative of the capture of Ai in Josh. 7–8.* The figure of Achan was originally not associated traditio-historically with the Valley of Achor; the evidence includes the two different names *'kn* and *'kr.*[27] The Achan material was reshaped secondarily to provide an etiology for the name of the valley, with the verb *'kr* I serving as the link (Josh. 6:18; 7:24-26; see II.1 above). This clearly secondary association of the toponym with the verb *'kr* I does not prevent deriving it from *'kr* III, "be fruitful." The use of the name in Isa. 65:10 and Hos. 2:17(15) supports this etymology. This would argue in favor of identifying the Valley of Achor with Wadi en-Nuwe'ime rather than Buqei'a.[28]

In Isa. 65:10 "Valley of Achor" appears in parallel with "Sharon"; like the latter (33:9; 35:2; cf. Cant. 2:1; 1 Ch. 27:29), it denotes a fruitful, almost paradisal region. Sharon to the west and the Valley of Achor to the east comprehend the whole land, so that the two names together signalize the fertility of the whole land (cf. Isa. 65:9: "inheritor of my mountains"). The allocation of herds (of cattle) to the Valley of Achor and flocks (of sheep and goats) to Sharon is not intended to denigrate Sharon,[29] but has a stylistic explanation: the merism "flocks and herds" is divided between the two fertile valleys that mark the eastern and western borders of the land. In the admittedly late text 65:9-10, there is no hint of the troubling of Israel that links the story of Achan in Josh. 6–7* with the Valley of Achor. Josh. 15:7 likewise mentions the Valley of Achor in a neutral sense with no negative overtones as a location on the northern border of Judah. It also appears neutrally in the Copper Scroll from Qumran (3Q15 1:1; 4:6).

In Hos. 2:17(15), in the context of a new entrance into the promised land from the wilderness, Yahweh promises to espouse Israel once more and to restore her vineyards to her; in parallel, he will make the Valley of Achor a door of hope *(peṯaḥ tiqwâ).* Modern commentators find in the name "Valley of Achor" an allusion to the Achan story.[30] But there is nothing in Hos. 2:16-17(14-15) to support this interpretation; indeed, such a connotation would appear to be out of the question, since it contradicts the message of the text. In parallel with the gift of the vineyards and mentioned immediately after them, the Valley of Achor must be understood as the first portion and quintessence of the fertile land that opens in this valley.[31] In the context of the new entrance into the promised land, the Valley of Achor symbolizes not Achan's troubling of Israel but the gift of the fertile land.[32] It is reasonable to suppose that the "Valley of Achor" played this entirely positive role, recalling the first exodus, in the occupation traditions of the northern tribes, centered on Jericho and Gilgal, and that Hosea, preaching in the northern kingdom, is alluding to this tradition of Achor and the entrance into the promised land.

Mosis

---

27. M. Noth, *Josua. HAT* I/7 (^{3}1971), 43ff.; Neef, 92-93.

28. For the former see F. M. Abel, *Géographie de la Palestine,* I (^{2}1933), 406; H. W. Wolff, *ZDPV* 70 (1954) 76-81; Neef, passim. For the latter, Noth, *HAT* I/7^{3}, in loc., etc.

29. Neef, 103.

30. See also Neef, 97-101.

31. As noted also by Neef, 100.

32. F. I. Andersen and D. N. Freedman, *Hosea. AB* 24 (1980), 275.

עֹל *ʿōl*

I. Etymology. II. Ancient Near East. III. OT: 1. General; 2. Draft Animals; 3. Forced Labor; 4. Foreign Domination; 5. Positive Symbolism. IV. LXX.

I. Etymology. While *KBL*[2] still derived the word *ʿōl* from *ʿll* II, "put in," *HAL* treats it as a primary noun, attested in Ugaritic and Canaanite *(ḫul[l]u),* as well as Imperial Aramaic, Jewish Aramaic, Palmyrene, and Nabatean (cf. Arab. *ǵullu,* "neck ring of prisoners").[1] The Akkadian word for yoke is *nīru* (cf. Syr. *nîrā*) or (in literary contexts) *abšānu.*

II. Ancient Near East. Texts from Mesopotamia and Amarna-age Palestine use the yoke as a metaphor of political and religious subordination and subjection. The king lays the yoke of his overlordship on those he has subjugated;[2] as obedient subjects, they bear the yoke of their overlord.[3] To rebel against an overlord is therefore to "break the yoke."[4] Sometimes "bearing the yoke" is equated explicitly with forced labor, but it can also be — from the perspective of the overlord — a metaphor for stable government.[5] Since the kings of Mesopotamia considered their actions to be commanded by the gods, the deity was thought of as the agent who imposed the yoke on conquered peoples; to rebel was to shake off the yoke of the deity.[6] The king can also describe himself as bearing the yoke of the deity.[7] One Babylonian myth recounts that Marduk created humans to "bear the yoke," to serve Marduk instead of other gods.[8] This religio-political metaphor is not found in Egypt, perhaps because, in the Egyptian view, the stability of the world depended not on the obedience of the people to the king and the obedience of the king to the gods, but on the presence of the king, who was also god.[9]

III. OT.

1. *General.* The word *ʿōl* occurs 40 times in the OT (including 15 times in 1 K. 12 par. 2 Ch. 10, and 7 times in Jer. 17–28), always in contexts dealing with some other

ʿōl. C. L. Tyer, "The Yoke in Ancient Near Eastern, Hebrew, and NT Materials" (diss., Vanderbilt, 1963).

1. See *KTU* 4.749; EA I, 257:15; 296:38; *DNSI,* II, 842.
2. *ANET,* 297.
3. *ANET,* 314; EA 257:15; 296:38.
4. *ARAB,* II, 27, 218.
5. For the former see *ANET,* 287, 316; for the latter, 286.
6. For the former see *ANET,* 297, 383; for the latter, 291, 292.
7. *ANET,* 307.
8. *ANET,* 99; Tyer, 27.
9. Tyer, 35-36.

topic; *ʿōl* is never the subject of a narrative. Therefore the OT provides no information about what an ancient yoke looked like, although it can hardly have differed greatly from the yoke of today. This consists of a beam joining two animals (the OT mentions only cattle; see III.2 below) to pull a plow or cart; on both sides of the neck of each animal there are pegs to which cords *(môsērôṯ)* are attached; these are tied together under the necks of the animals.[10]

2. *Draft Animals.* In three texts (always in a negated clause), *ʿōl* refers to an agricultural instrument. "Water for purification" is to be prepared from the ashes of a red heifer *(pārâ)* without defect, "on which no yoke has been laid *(ʿlh)*" (Nu. 19:2). For purification in case of murder at the hands of a person unknown, a young heifer *(ʿeglaṯ bāqār)* "that has not pulled *(mšk)* in the yoke" is to be killed over flowing water (Dt. 21:3). The Philistines want to be rid of the ark and are advised to prepare a new cart and two milch cows *(pārôṯ)* "on which a yoke has never been placed *(ʿlh)*" (1 S. 6:7). Use of the cows as draft animals would render them profane.

The simile in Hos. 11:4 also refers to a yoke on an animal's neck: "I was to them like those [= like one of those] who ease the yoke on their jaws." The proposed emendation of *ʿōl* to *ʿûl* ("and I was like one who lifts an infant to his cheeks") is not persuasive.[11] And it is probably unnecessary to introduce a yoke in 10:11: "and Ephraim was like a trained heifer *(ʿeglâ)* that loved to thresh; and I passed over *(ʿāḇar + ʿal)* her fair neck; I wanted to harness Ephraim." Objections to the proposed emendation "and I placed (*ʿbr* hiphil) a yoke on her fair neck" include the need to assign a specialized meaning to the verb *ʿāḇar.*[12]

3. *Forced Labor.* The word *ʿōl* is central to the account of Rehoboam's negotiations with the representatives of Israel (1 K. 12 par. 2 Ch. 10), in which the lexeme → כבד *kbd* in particular describes the "heaviness" of the yoke. The representatives of Israel say: "Your father made our yoke hard (*qšh* hiphil); now therefore lighten *(qll* hiphil + *min)* the hard *(qāšâ* service of your father and his heavy *(kāḇēḏ)* yoke that he placed *(nāṯan)* on us, and we will serve you" (1 K. 12:4 = 2 Ch. 10:4). Rehoboam turns to the "young men who had grown up with him," citing in abbreviated form the words of Israel's representatives: "Lighten the yoke that your father put on us" (1 K. 12:9b = 2 Ch. 10:9bβ). Rehoboam moderates the words of Israel's representatives by omitting the first clause and the "hard service" and not describing the yoke as "heavy." The young men cite the same words, again somewhat altered: "Your father made our yoke heavy (*kbd* hiphil), but you must lighten it for us" (1 K. 12:10aβ = 2 Ch. 10:10aβ). That the young men cite these words in fuller form than they were recounted by Rehoboam is probably due to the "anecdotal nature" of the account.[13] They advise Rehoboam to answer: "Now, whereas my father laid on *(ʿms + ʿal)* you a heavy *(kāḇēḏ)* yoke, I will add

---

10. On the whole subject see Dalman, *AuS,* II, 93-105; *BRL,* 428; *BRL*², 253, 255.
11. Cf. *BHS.*
12. Cf. *BHS;* → עבר *ʿāḇar* III.2.d.(4).
13. M. Noth, *Könige. BK* IX/1 (1968), 270.

to *(ysp* hiphil + *ʿal)* your yoke" (1 K. 12:11a = 2 Ch. 10:11a). Rehoboam follows their advice: "My father made your yoke heavy, but I will add to your yoke" (1 K. 12:14aβ; somewhat different in 2 Ch. 10:14, where *ʿōl* appears only in the first clause).

The same usage appears in Neh. 5:15 if we accept the proposed emendation of *hiḵbîḏû ʿal* to *hiḵbîḏû ʿōl ʿal* ("the former governors . . . laid a heavy yoke on the people").[14]

4. *Foreign Domination.* In Jer. 27–28 a yoke plays a role in a prophetic symbolic action. The yoke itself is referred to by the word *môṭâ/mōṭôṯ* (27:2; 28:10,12,13[twice]), while *ʿōl* is used figuratively for the "yoke of the king of Babylon" (27:8,11,12; 28:2,4,11,14). The two chapters did not originally form a unit: ch. 27 is a 1st-person account, while ch. 28 is in the 3rd person. Jeremiah is commanded by Yahweh to make straps and yokes *(mōṭôṯ)* (v. 2a), put them on his neck (v. 2b), and send them to five neighboring kings (v. 3). There is an accompanying message to the kings: a threat against the nations that will not put *(nāṯan)* their neck under the yoke of the king of Babylon (v. 8) and a promise for those that will bring (*bô'* hiphil) their neck under the yoke of the king of Babylon (v. 11). The oddity that Jeremiah puts the yokes on his own neck and (then?) sends them is usually resolved by eliminating the suffix in v. 3a,[15] making the text read: "And send (word) to the king of. . . ." In this reading, however, the message is remarkably abstract: the kings in question are to accept the call to bear their yokes while the yokes themselves are in Jerusalem. It makes more sense to keep the MT in v. 3a (so that Jeremiah sends several yokes) and treat v. 2b as a secondary addition to establish a link with ch. 28 (see below). In 27:12 the prophet surprisingly changes the addressee of the message (perhaps vv. 12-22 are secondary)[16] and says to Zedekiah: "Put your neck under the yoke of the king of Babylon."

Ch. 28 describes the conflict between Jeremiah and Hananiah, who frames his prophecy of deliverance with the words: "Thus says Yahweh Sabaoth . . . I have broken the yoke of the king of Babylon . . . for I will break the yoke of the king of Babylon" (vv. 2,4b). The change from the afformative conjugation *(šāḇartî)* to the preformative *('ešbōr)* reflects the genre of the prophecy: the prophecy of deliverance here follows the model of prophecies of doom.[17] Then Hananiah takes the yoke (*môṭâ;* not previously mentioned in ch. 28) from Jeremiah's neck, breaks it, and says in the name of Yahweh: "This is how I will break the yoke of King Nebuchadnezzar of Babylon from the neck of all the nations within two years" (v. 11a). Jeremiah responds: "You have broken wooden yokes *(mōṭôṯ)* only to forge iron yokes *(mōṭôṯ)* in place of them. . . . For thus says Yahweh, I have put an iron yoke *(ʿōl)* on the neck of all these nations" (vv. 13aβ-14aα). The meaning of v. 13 can only be guessed at: "by his action Hananiah has invoked an even greater, unshatterable yoke, perhaps from Jahweh himself."[18]

---

14. See *BHS; HAL,* II, 456.
15. E.g., W. Rudolph, *Jeremia. HAT* I/12 (^{3}1968), 176.
16. W. Thiel, *Die deuteronomistische Redaktion von Jeremia 26–45. WMANT* 52 (1981), 8.
17. K. Koch, *Growth of the Biblical Tradition* (Eng. trans. ^{2}1988), 207.
18. Ibid., 206.

Also striking is the change from *môṭâ,*[19] the yoke borne by Jeremiah (vv. 10,12), to *mōṭôṯ* (v. 13, as in 27:2). In 27:2 the reference is probably to several yokes (see above), and in 28:13 we may have a "general plural."[20] Wanke proposes a different analysis: "When the narrative speaks of making a yoke, it uses the plural '(yoke) bars'; the singular 'yoke' denotes the finished yoke resting on the neck of Jeremiah."[21] Comparison with other texts using *môṭâ/mōṭôṯ* — always in a figurative sense — does not help. The plural appears also in the phrase *mōṭôṯ 'ōl* and in Ezk. 30:18 (where the correct reading is probably *maṭṭôṯ,* "staffs");[22] in 1 Ch. 15:15 *mōṭôṯ* means the "poles" used to carry the ark. The sg. *môṭâ,* "yoke," appears in Isa. 58:6(twice),9, and Nah. 1:13, where the odd suffixed form *mōṭēhû* may suggest the reading *maṭṭēhû.*[23]

The phrase *mōṭôṯ 'ōl* occurs twice. The first concludes Lev. 26:4-13, a promise of blessing if Israel keeps the laws: "I am Yahweh your God who brought you out of the land of Egypt. . . . I have broken the *mōṭôṯ* of your yoke" (v. 13). Lev. 26:4-13 served as the model for Ezk. 34:25-30,[24] a description of the age of salvation in which the recollection of Yahweh's act of deliverance (Lev. 26:13) was reshaped into a promise of deliverance to come and was made the focus of the passage: "And they shall know that I am Yahweh, when I break the *mōṭôṯ* of their yoke" (Ezk. 34:27b).

In contrast to general OT usage, which treats *môṭâ/mōṭôṯ* as a parallel term synonymous with *'ōl* (see above), these passages appear to use *mōṭôṯ* for the wooden bars from which the yoke was constructed.[25]

Contrary to the traditional interpretation, Isa. 9:3(4) *('eṯ-'ōl subbᵒlô . . . haḥittōṯā)* should probably be understood as referring not to the future but to the past ("for the yoke of their burden . . . you have broken"), to the departure of the Assyrians from the northern region west of the Jordan in the last third of the 7th century.[26] In Isa. 10:27a ("his burden will be removed from your shoulder, and his yoke will be destroyed from your neck") and — similarly — 14:25b we find two late actualizations of 9:3(4).[27] Jer. 30:8 ("I will break the yoke from off his [MT 'your'] neck, and I will burst his bonds") probably belongs to the same category.[28] According to Gen. 27:40, Esau (Edom) will throw off the overlordship of Jacob (Israel): "You shall break his yoke from your neck." Once (Dt. 28:48) Yahweh threatens to put an "iron yoke" (foreign overlordship) on the neck of Israel if the people are disobedient. The statement of Isa. 47:6 is unique: the prophet charges "virgin daughter Babylon" with cruel treatment of the elderly: "You

19. → VIII, 153.
20. Rudolph, *HAT* I/12, 180.
21. G. Wanke, *Untersuchungen zur sogenannten Baruchschrift. BZAW* 122 (1971), 24.
22. See *BHS;* see further below.
23. W. Rudolph, *Micha-Nahum-Habakuk-Zephanja. KAT* XIII/3 (1975), 159.
24. F. L. Hossfeld, *Untersuchungen zu Komposition und Theologie des Ezechielbuches. FzB* 20 (²1983), 273-76.
25. R. Hentschke, *BHHW,* II, 869.
26. H. Barth, *Die Jesaja-Worte in Josiazeit. WMANT* 48 (1977), 148, 173-74.
27. H. Wildberger, *Isaiah 1–12* (Eng. trans. 1991), 441; *Isaiah 13–27* (Eng. trans. 1997), 79-80.
28. Rudolph, *HAT* I/12, 191.

made your yoke exceedingly heavy on *(kbd ʿal)* the aged." The text of Isa. 10:27b ("a yoke before fat") is corrupt; so possibly is the text of Lam. 1:14 ("the yoke of my sins").

5. *Positive Symbolism.* It is rare for a yoke to convey a positive sense. In Jer. 2:20 it symbolizes Yahweh's tutelage ("long ago you broke your yoke and burst your bonds"); the wording of 5:5 is similar. It can also represent ennobling hardship: "It is good for one to bear *(nāśāʾ)* the yoke in youth" (Lam. 3:27).

IV. LXX. The LXX has no problems with *ʿōl,* which it translates 27 times with *zygós/zygón,* and 10 times with *kloiós.*

Schmoldt

עָלָה *ʿālâ;* מַעַל *maʿal;* מֹעַל *mōʿal;* מַעֲלֶה *maʿaleh;* מַעֲלָה *maʿalâ;* תְּעָלָה *teʿālâ;* י . עֶל *ʿelî;* עִלִּי *ʿillî;* עֲלִיָּה *ʿalîyâ*

→ עֹלָה *ʿōlâ,* → עָלֶה *ʿāleh,* → עֶלְיוֹן *ʿelyôn*

I. Etymology. II. Ancient Near East: 1. Egyptian; 2. Canaanite; 3. Ugaritic; 4. Akkadian. III. OT: 1. Occurrences; 2. Synonyms and Antonyms; 3. Verb; 4. Nouns. IV. 1. Dead Sea Scrolls; 2. LXX.

ʿālâ. F. Asensio, "Observaciones sobre el 'holocausto' y el sacrificio 'pacifico' en el culto de Israel," *Studia Missionalia* 23 (1974) 191-211; W. B. Barrick, "The Meaning and Usage of RKB in Biblical Hebrew," *JBL* 101 (1982) 481-503; J. B. Bauer, "Der 'Fuchs' Neh 3,35 ein Belagerungsturm," *BZ* 19 (1975) 97-98; L. Boisvert, "Le passage de la mer des Roseaux et la foi d'Israël," *Science et Esprit* 27 (1975) 147-59; G. Brin, "The Formulae 'From . . . and Onward/Upward' (והלאה/ומעלה . . . מ)," *JBL* 99 (1980) 161-71; H. A. Brongers, "Das Zeitwort *ʿālā* und seine Derivate," *Travels in the World of the OT. FS M. A. Beek* (1974), 30-40; M. Dahood, "The Divine Name ʿElî in the Psalms," *TS* 14 (1953) 452-57; S. Daniel, *Recherches sur le vocabulaire du culte dans la 'Septante,' Études et Commentaires* 61 (1966); M. Delcor, "*ʿālâh* (Gen 31, 10) sensu sexuali, sicut etiam *slq* aram.," *QuadSem* 5 (1974) 106-7; G. R. Driver, "Hebrew *ʿal,* ('High One') as a Divine Title," *ExpT* 50 (1938/39) 92-93; J. H. Eaton, "Some Misunderstood Hebrew Words for God's Self-Revelation," *BT* 25 (1974) 331-38; I. Ephʿal, "The Assyrian Ramp at Lachish," *Zion* 49 (1984) 333-47; H. J. Fabry, "'Ihr alle seid Söhne des Allerhöchsten' (Ps 82,6)," *BiLe* 15 (1974) 135-47; J. A. Fitzmyer, "The Aramaic Inscriptions of Sefire I and II," *JAOS* 81 (1961) 178-221; idem, *The Aramaic Inscriptions of Sefîre. BietOr* 19 (1967); W. Gross, "Die Herausführungsformel," *ZAW* 86 (1974) 425-53; J. D. Heck, "The Missing Sanctuary of Deut 33:12," *JBL* 103 (1984) 523-29; J. Hoftijzer, "Der sogenannte Feueropfer," *Hebräische Wortforschung. FS W. Baumgartner. SVT* 16 (1967), 114-34; W. H. Irwin, "The Punctuation of Isaiah 24:14-16a and 25:4c-5," *CBQ* 46 (1984) 215-22; N. M. Loss, "La terminologia e il tema del peccato in Lev 4–5," *Salesianum* 30 (1968) 437-61; S. M. Paul, "Two Cognate Semitic Terms

I. Etymology. The root *ʿlh* is found in all Semitic languages: Akk. *elû(m);*[1] Ugar. *ʿly;*[2] Can. *ʿly;*[3] Arab. *ʿlw/ʿly;*[4] OSA *ʿly,* "be high, prominent"[5] (in PNs: *d̲mrʿly, smhʿly,* and *ʿlym* or *ʿlyn*[6]); Eth. *laʿala,* "be high, superior";[7] cf. Egyp. *ʿ(r)/ʿry.*[8] The root is usually assumed to have three radicals: **ʿly.* There are morphological and historical reasons, however, for considering a two-radical primary noun *ʿl* with the meaning "that which is above, height." The verb *ʿlh* would then be a *tertiae infirmae* denominative with a basic meaning indicating movement upward: "go up." The noun forms are secondary derivatives of the verbal stem.

II. Ancient Near East.
1. *Egyptian.* Egyp. *iʿ(r)* (*ʿry* after the Middle Kingdom), "go up," is found as early as the Pyramid Texts: go up to a place, go up to something, or go up to someone (a person of high rank).[9] Causatively, it means "bring someone or something up."[10] Both forms of the verb can also express the goal, with the meaning "arrive."[11] We also find the figurative meaning "approach (a person)."[12]

2. *Canaanite.* In extrabiblical Hebrew, the hiphil appears in a Lachish ostracon: "Shemayahu took him and brought him up to the city."[13] In Phoenician inscriptions the nominal prep. *ʿl/ʿlt* is common. The verb *ʿly* is relatively rare; it appears as a military term in the Ahiram inscription: "If a king from among the kings or a governor from

---

for Mating and Copulation," *VT* 32 (1982) 492-94; J. Reider, "Etymological Studies in Biblical Hebrew," *VT* 2 (1952) 113-30; idem, "Substantival *ʿal* in Biblical Hebrew," *JQR* 30 (1939/40) 263-70; B. Renaud, "Osée ii 2: *ʿlh mn hʾrṣ:* essai d'interprétation," *VT* 33 (1983) 495-500; R. Rendtorff, *Studien zur Geschichte des Opfers im Alten Israel. WMANT* 24 (1967); L. Rost, "Erwägungen zum israelitischen Brandopfer," *Von Ugarit nach Qumran. FS O. Eissfeldt. BZAW* 77 (1958), 177-83; L. Ruppert, "Erhöhungsvorstellungen im AT," *BZ* 22 (1978) 199-220; K. Rupprecht, "עלה מן הארץ (Ex 1, 10; Hos 2, 2) 'sich des Landes bemächtigen'?" *ZAW* 82 (1970) 442-47; J. F. A. Sawyer, "Hebrew Words for the Resurrection of the Dead," *VT* 23 (1973) 218-34; S. Shibayana, "Notes on ירד and עלה," *JBR* 34 (1966) 358-62; G. Wehmeier, "עלה *ʿlh* to go up," *TLOT,* II, 883-96; J. Wijngaards, "הוציא and העלה, a Twofold Approach to the Exodus," *VT* 15 (1965) 91-102.

1. *AHw,* I, 205-10; *CAD,* IV, 110-35.
2. *WUS,* no. 2030; *UT,* no. 1855.
3. *DNSI,* II, 853.
4. Wehr, 658.
5. Biella, 365.
6. On the first see Jamme, no. 552, 4; on the second, no. 555, 1, 4; on the last, no. 689, 4; 745, 2; 575, 2.
7. Dillmann, *LexLingAeth,* 54ff.
8. *WbÄS,* I, 41.
9. For the first see *Pyr.* 369; cf. *Amduat* I, 28; with *r: Theban Tomb,* no. 66; *Edfu,* I, 315. For the second, *Pyr.* 452. For the third, *Pyr.* 1455, 1773; cf. the formulaic usage in *Urk.,* I, 121, etc.
10. For the former see *Edfu,* I, 513, 579; for the latter, *Dend Mar,* III, 54; IV, 27a.
11. *Pyr.* 452.
12. Book of the Dead, 189; *Theban Tomb,* no. 36; cf. *Edfu,* I, 315.
13. *KAI* 194.7.

among the governors or the commander of a camp goes up against Byblos and exposes this sarcophagus, may the staff of his power be stripped of its leaves."[14] The causative stem is used as a sacrificial term: "Everyone who offered a burnt offering or a *minḥâ* in the sanctuary";[15] this text also uses the noun *ʿlt,* "burnt offering." The only other nominal form attested is *mʿl,* "upper portion," with the prep. *l* or *l-m.*[16] A unique usage appears in a formula for testamentary adoption: "who has taken his place *(ʿlt)* as a son."[17]

In Aramaic inscriptions *slq* generally replaces *ʿly.*[18] The occurrence of the latter in the Sefire inscriptions is interpreted by Degen as a form of *ʿll,* "enter."[19] We do find *ʿly* used as a military term: "[and the king] who goes up and captures LBKH or H[. . .]" (text damaged). Besides the prep. *ʿl,* we find the noun form *ʿly(t)* with the meaning "upper portion": "[with the kings] of Upper Aram and Lower Aram";[20] "On the day when he doe[s] so, may the gods overthrow [th]at ma[n] and his house and all that is in [it], and may its lower part become its upper part."[21] In both cases, the antonym is *tḥt.*

3. *Ugaritic.* Ugar. *ʿly* appears frequently in connection with the offering of sacrifices and the ascent of the gods to Zaphon, the mountain of the gods. In everyday usage *ʿly* means "climb (into bed), go to bed."[22] At the behest of El, KRT mounts the platform of the tower to offer sacrifice.[23] With a silver bowl full of wine and a golden bowl of honey he mounts the platform of the tower to offer sacrifice to his father El.[24] The ascent of the gods to the mountain of the gods is recounted frequently: ʿAnat "goes up to Mount Mslmt, to Mount Tliyt, and she goes up weeping to Arr, to Arr and to Zaphon";[25] "And Baal ascends to the heights of Zaphon."[26] "Baal ascends (to the mountain)" should be interpreted in the same way.[27] ʿAṯtar ascends to the peak of Zaphon in an unsuccessful attempt to sit on the throne of Baal.[28] The causative *šʿly* can denote the offering of a sacrifice; it occurs also in the expression "offer a *pgr* sacrifice."[29] ʿAnat bears *(šʿly)* the body of Baal to the crest of Zaphon.[30] The phrase *ʿly nʿm* appears as an epithet for Baal.[31]

---

14. *KAI* 1.2.
15. *KAI* 159.8 (Punic).
16. *KAI* 14.12; 145.14.
17. *KAI* 124.3.
18. *KAI* 222A.5.27, C.4; 224.14-16; cf. *HAL,* II, 828.
19. *KAI* 222B.35; R. Degen, *Altaramäische Grammatik* (1969), 73 n. 67.
20. *KAI* 222A.6.
21. *KAI* 222C.24.
22. *KTU* 1.17, I, 38; probably also I, 4, 14.
23. *KTU* 1.14, II, 20; cf. II, 21 (probably dittography).
24. *KTU* 1.14, IV, 2.
25. *KTU* 1.10, III, 28-30.
26. *KTU* 1.4, IV, 19.
27. *KTU* 1.10, III, 11.
28. *KTU* 1.6, I, 57.
29. For the former see *KTU* 1.19, IV, 23, 30. For the latter, 6.13-14; M. Dijkstra and J. C. de Moor, *UF* 7 (1975) 175.
30. *KTU* 1.6, I, 15.
31. *KTU* 1.16, III, 6-9; see Dahood and III.4.c below.

4. *Akkadian.* Akk. *elû(m)* is the closest equivalent to Heb. *ʿlh* in its range of meanings, its wealth of nominal derivatives, and its widespread use. One nominal form, *elû* I, means "high" in both the literal and figurative senses. Examples of literal usage include: "who conquers the high mountains"; "strong cedars grown in the high mountains"; "their high citadels, as solidly founded as mountains"; "I love your tall stature"; in oil augury and similar contexts, e.g., "if the central part of the oil is high [= stands out] and does not level out with the surface of the water."[32] Figuratively, *elû* may mean "exalted": "the singer sings 'Exalted Ea'"; cf. such Old Babylonian PNs as *A-li-a-at-KA-Sin,* "Exalted is the Word of Sin," and *E-li-e-re-sa,* "Exalted is her [= the goddess's] desire."[33] It may also mean "proud": "the gods vouchsafed me to walk with my head high, full of joy and happiness."[34]

A second nominal form, *elû* II, means "upper," often with an antonym in the immediate context: "have I not sealed with my seal the lower house and the upper house?"[35] Examples of topographical usage are: "I climbed the upper mountains and crossed the lower mountains"; "on the upper gate of X"; "the upper river (district) and the lower river (district)."[36] Sometimes *elû* serves as a geographical name: "the decision concerning the expedition against the upper country is being made"; "I ruled over the cities of the Upper Sea [= the Mediterranean or Lake Urmia]."[37]

The verb *elû* covers such a wide range of meanings that we must content ourselves here with a few comments of particular importance for Heb. *ʿlh.*[38] The primary use of *elû* is to denote movement to a higher place: "he went up [from Ur] to Babylon and spent the night there."[39] Many texts speak of going up to court or to the king or palace: "come up to me, you and the elders of the land you rule, for a conference"; "as many as ten times we went up to the prince."[40] People speak also of going up to a temple: "I went up to Emašmaš to offer sacrifice."[41] We often find *elû* used as a military term: "I will lead the troops and go up against X"; "PN went up and conquered both cities."[42] Many texts speak of ascending into the heavens: "whether we ascend into the heavens or descend into the underworld"; "let us ascend into the heavens like smoke"; "we cannot ascend to you, nor can you descend to us"; cf. "Ishtar descended into the under-

---

32. See, respectively, *VAB,* 4, 234, i, 10; *VAB,* 4, 138, ix, 4; *TCL,* 3, 260; *VAB,* 4, 140, ix, 53; *CT,* 5, 5, 39.

33. See, respectively, H. Zimmern, *Beiträge zur Kenntnis der babylonischen Religion. Assyriologische Bibliothek* 12 (1901), no. 60, 15; *CAD,* IV, 111; *CT,* 6, 48b, 22.

34. L. W. King, *Letters and Inscriptions of Hammurabi,* 3 vols. (1898-1900), I, 98:96.

35. *Babylonian Inscriptions in the Collection of J. B. Nies* (1944), VI, 20:7.

36. For the first see *CT,* 13, 42, 15. For the second, *ARM,* 2, 87, 7; cf. *TCL,* 12, 13, 203, 2. For the third, A. G. Lie, *Inscriptions of Sargon II* (1929), 98.

37. For the former see *ARM,* 1, 53, r. 6; for the latter, *CAD,* IV, 113.

38. For a full treatment see *AHw,* I, 206-10; *CAD,* IV, 114-35.

39. *KAR,* 43, 26.

40. *TCL,* 17, 76, 23.

41. For the former see *TCL,* 19, 75, 7; for the latter, *CAD,* IV, 117.

42. For the former see *ARM,* 1, 53, 5; for the latter, EA 81:46; cf. 114:18.

world and never rose again."[43] By contrast, Dumuzi ascends from the underworld.[44] Note the proverbial statement: "When they are happy, they [human beings] speak of ascending to the heavens; when they are sad, they speak of descending to the underworld."[45]

III. OT.

1. *Occurrences.* a. *Verb.* The verb *ʿālâ* occurs 890 times in the OT.[46] There are 612 occurrences of the qal: Genesis, 44; Exodus, 36; Leviticus, 4; Numbers, 23; Deuteronomy, 24; Joshua, 48; Judges, 57; 1 Samuel, 48; 2 Samuel, 22; 1 Kings, 38; 2 Kings, 52 (including 2 K. 16:12); Isaiah, 34; Jeremiah, 41 (including Jer. 46:8); Ezekiel, 18; Hosea, 6; Joel, 7; Amos, 5; Obadiah, 1; Jonah, 3; Micah, 2; Nahum, 1; Habakkuk, 1; Zechariah, 6; Psalms, 12; Job, 6; Proverbs, 6; Ecclesiastes, 2; Ruth, 1; Song of Songs, 5; Lamentations, 1; Daniel, 3; Ezra, 8; Nehemiah, 10; 1 Chronicles, 11; 2 Chronicles, 25. The niphal occurs 18 times: Exodus, 3; Numbers, 7; 2 Samuel, 1; Jeremiah, 2; Ezekiel, 2; Psalms, 2; Ezra, 1. The hiphil occurs 255 times: Genesis, 7; Exodus, 23; Leviticus, 10; Numbers, 12; Deuteronomy, 8; Joshua, 7; Judges, 14; 1 Samuel, 22 (including 1 S. 28:11a); 2 Samuel, 13 (including 2 S. 15:24); 1 Kings, 15 (including 1 K. 8:4b; 10:5); 2 Kings, 7; Isaiah, 6 (including Isa. 40:31); Jeremiah, 20 (including Jer. 52:9); Ezekiel, 19 (including Ezk. 19:3); Hosea, 1; Amos, 6; Jonah, 1; Micah, 1; Nahum, 1; Habakkuk, 1; Psalms, 9 (including Ps. 51:21[Eng. v. 19]); Job, 2; Proverbs, 1; Lamentations, 1; Ezra, 5; Nehemiah, 3; 1 Chronicles, 13; 2 Chronicles, 27 (including 2 Ch. 5:5a). The hophal occurs 3 times: Jgs. 6:28; Neh. 2:8 (text uncertain; see *BHS*); 2 Ch. 20:34. The hithpael occurs twice: Jer. 51:3 (text uncertain); Ps. 37:35 (with *BHS* reading *wmtʿlh* instead of *wmtʿrh*).

The verb is found in every book of the OT except Zephaniah and Malachi. Usage is concentrated in the Dtr History (377 occurrences) and the Tetrateuch (169 occurrences). The Chronicler's History lags well behind with 104 occurrences. The verb occurs with surprising frequency in Judges (72), 1 Samuel (70), and Jeremiah (64); several of the occurrences in Jeremiah can be ascribed to the Dtr redaction of the book.

b. *Nouns.* Of the nominal forms derived from *ʿlh,* the first is the basic word *ʿal,* "height": 1 S. 2:10; 2 S. 23:1; Isa. 59:18;[47] 63:7; Ezk. 19:11; Hos. 7:16; 11:7;[48] *mēʿāl* in Gen. 27:39; 49:25; Ps. 50:4 is probably not a miswriting of *mimmaʿal.*[49] Other derived nouns are: → *ʿāleh* (18 times); → *ʿōlâ* (287 times); *mōʿal* (Neh. 8:6); *maʿaleh* (19 times: Nu. 34:4; 4 in Joshua; 2 in Judges; 1 S. 9:11; 2 S. 15:30; 2 K. 9:27; Isa. 15:5; Jer.

---

43. See, respectively, EA 246:15; *KBo,* 1, 3, r. 2; EA 264:15: Nergal and Ereshkigal; *CT,* 15, 46, r. 5.

44. *CT,* 15, 47, r. 56-57; cf. "whether you are spirit that has ascended from the underworld," *CT,* 16, 10, iv, 42-43.

45. Ludlul, II, 46.

46. *HAL,* II, 828-30; Wehmeier, 884-85: 888 times.

47. Klostermann; cf. H. Gunkel, *Schöpfung und Chaos* (1895), 108: "amount."

48. But cf. Wolff, *Hosea. Herm* (Eng. trans. 1974), 108, 192-93.

49. As suggested by König, *Hebräisches und aramäisches Wörterbuch zum AT* ([7]1936); against König, see *GesB,* 585; cf. *HAL,* II, 824.

48:5 [*Q*]; Ezk. 40:31,34,37 [all *Q*]; Neh. 9:4; 12:37; 2 in 2 Chronicles); *maʿᵃlâ* (47 times: Ex. 20:26; 2 in 1 Kings; 8 in 2 Kings; 5 in Isaiah; 9 in Ezekiel [including 40:6,31,34,37 *Q*]; Am. 9:6 *Q;* 15 in Psalms [pl. in superscriptions]; Ezr. 7:9; 2 in Nehemiah; 1 Ch. 17:17; 2 in 2 Chronicles); *teʿālâ* (Jer. 30:13; 46:11); *ʿelî* (Prov. 27:22); *ʿillî* (Josh. 15:19; Jgs. 1:15); *ʿᵃlîyâ* (20 times: 4 in Judges; 2 S. 19:1; 2 in 1 Kings; 4 in 2 Kings; Jer. 22:13,14; Ps. 104:3,13; 2 in Nehemiah; 1 Ch. 28:11; 2 in 2 Chronicles); → עֶלְיוֹן *ʿelyôn* (53 times); *ʿalwâ/ʿalyâ* (Gen. 36:40; 1 Ch. 1:51); *ʿalwān/ʿalyān* (Gen. 36:23); *ʿēlî* (1 S. 1:3–4:16; 14:3; 1 K. 2:27; cf. 1 Ch. 24:3); *ʾelʿālēʾ* (Nu. 32:3,37; Isa. 15:4; Jer. 48:34).

2. *Synonyms and Antonyms.* Because the verb is widely used in many different ways, we find a wealth of synonyms in the immediate and extended context.

Movement in general: → עבר *ʿābar* (Mic. 2:12-13); → בוא *bôʾ* (Gen. 45:25; Ex. 7:28; Dt. 1:24); → הלך *hālak* (Ex. 33:1; Jgs. 11:16; 2 S. 17:21; Isa. 2:3; 8:7; Mic. 4:2); → יצא *yāṣāʾ* (1 K. 10:29); → קום *qûm* (Gen. 35:1,3; Dt. 17:18; Josh. 8:1,3); → רום *rûm* (1 S. 2:1,7); → פנה *pānâ* (Dt. 1:24; 3:1); → נגשׁ *nāgaš* (Josh. 8:11).

Military contexts: *lāḥam* niphal (Dt. 1:41-42; Josh. 10:36; 19:47; Jgs. 1:3; 1 K. 12:24; 20:1; 2 K. 12:18[17]; 2 Ch. 11:4; → מלחמה *milḥāmâ*); → צור *ṣûr* (1 K. 20:1; 2 K. 6:24; 16:5; 17:5; 18:9; Isa. 21:2); *tāpaś* (2 K. 16:9; 18:13; Isa. 36:1); *nkh* hiphil (Josh. 7:3; Jgs. 8:11); *bāqaʿ* (Isa. 7:6); *ḥānâ* (1 S. 11:1); → חרב *ḥārab* (Jer. 50:21); → חרם *ḥāram* I hiphil (Jer. 50:21); → ירשׁ *yāraš* (Dt. 9:23); *šādad* (Jer. 49:28); → שׂרף *śārap* (Jgs. 15:6).

Sacrifice: → זבח *zabaḥ* (Ex. 24:5; Dt. 27:6-7; Josh. 8:31; 1 S. 6:15; 10:8); *qṭr* (Jer. 33:18; 48:35; 2 Ch. 29:7); *ngš* hiphil (Ex. 32:6); *ʿāśâ šelāmîm* (1 K. 3:15); *ʿāśâ zebaḥ* (Jer. 33:18).

The verb → ירד *yārad* functions as a direct antonym, as is clear from texts that use both verbs in parallel to express movement in opposite directions (Gen. 24:16; 28:12; Ex. 19:24; Nu. 20:27-28; Dt. 28:43; Jgs. 14:1-2,19; 16:31; 2 K. 1:4,6,16; Jer. 48:18; Ps. 104:8; 107:26; Job 7:9; Prov. 30:4; Eccl. 3:21; 2 Ch. 18:2).

3. *Verb.* Drawing on the basic meaning of its nominal root *ʿl,* "height," *ʿālâ* denotes movement toward an elevated goal. From its use in highly differentiated contextual settings, the verb can represent a wealth of semantic aspects.

a. *Physical Movement.* In everyday usage the basic meaning of *ʿālāh* qal is "move to a higher location from a lower."[50] Abraham goes up from Egypt into the Negeb (Gen. 13:1). Joseph's brothers go up from Egypt into the land of Canaan (Gen. 45:25). The Israelites' journey from Rameses to Succoth (Ex. 12:37) is interpreted in v. 38 as "going up." The route from Egypt to Canaan or to an intermediate station was clearly considered an "ascent" (Ex. 13:18; Nu. 20:19; 32:11; Jgs. 11:13,16; 19:30; 1 S. 15:2,6; 1 K. 9:16; Isa. 11:16; Hos. 2:17). By the same token, the journey from the desert into Canaan was described as an ascent (Ex. 33:1; Nu. 13:17,21,30; Dt. 1:21,26,41; by con-

---

50. *GesB,* 589, following Graf.

trast, Job 6:18 speaks of caravans that "go up into the waste" [*tōhû*], because, like the sea viewed from the harbor, the desert waste appears to be higher). It is therefore necessary to consider in each case whether and to what extent there is a reference or an allusion to one of the exodus formulas. Such an allusion is clearly likely when the return of the exiles is described as "going up" or "coming up" (Ezr. 2:1,59; 7:6,7,28; 8:1; Neh. 7:5,6,61; 12:1; cf. d below). In any event, this usage became such a standard feature of the language that topographic references can be omitted entirely (Gen. 44:17,24,33-34; 45:9; 50:5-7,14). In the immediate context, travel in the opposite direction, from Canaan to Egypt, can be expressed by *yrd* (44:23,26; 45:9). The hypothesis of a specialized meaning for *ʿālâ,* "go north," after the analogy of Akk. *elû,* is therefore unnecessary.[51]

Whenever the terrain permitted, cities were situated on elevations; therefore *ʿālâ* frequently refers to going up to or entering a city. Judah goes up to Timnah to shear his sheep (Gen. 38:12,13); Saul and his servant go up to the town (1 S. 9:11,19). After Solomon is anointed king at Gihon, he and his retinue go back up to the city (1 K. 1:35,40,45).

In geographical lists *ʿālâ* serves to describe a boundary following rising terrain (Josh. 15:6,8; 18:12; 19:11,12)[52] or the terrain itself (11:17; 12:7; 15:3,6-8; 16:1).

In specialized contexts *ʿālâ* can express a wealth of nuances, but they all can be understood as involving upward movement.[53] For example, according to Gen. 49:4, Reuben's sin consists in having gone up onto his father's bed; in a dream Pharaoh sees seven ears of grain growing up on one stalk (41:5,22); in his dream Jacob sees angels ascending and descending *(yrd!)* on a heavenly ladder (28:12); the dawn rises (19:15; cf. 32:25,27: Jacob wrestles until the dawn rises); a cloud rises from the sea (1 K. 18:44; cf. Jer. 10:13; 51:16; Ps. 135:7); a snare springs up from the ground (Am. 3:5); a razor passes over the head (Jgs. 13:5; 16:17; 1 S. 1:11); the lot comes forth (from the vessel) and falls on someone (Lev. 16:9; Josh. 18:11; 19:10); a wound heals (Jer. 8:22); flesh covers bones (Ezk. 37:6,8); goats cover the sheep (Gen. 31:10,12);[54] locusts cover the land (Ex. 10:12,14); frogs come up (qal) out of the Nile, frogs that Aaron, at Yahweh's command, causes to come up (hiphil) and cover the land (Ex. 8:1-3[5-8]); Yahweh will inflict (hiphil) on Israel all sorts of maladies and afflictions if Israel does not observe his instructions (Dt. 28:61), The element of bringing or carrying up is also central to the other texts that use the hiphil of *ʿālâ:* the bones of Joseph (Gen. 50:25; cf. Ex. 13:19; Josh. 24:32) and Saul (2 S. 21:13) are carried up; so too are vessels (Ezr. 1:11; cf. Jer. 27:22), wood (2 Ch. 2:15), chariots (2 Ch. 1:17), tithes (Neh. 10:39), and tribute (2 K. 17:4). The tabernacle is provided with a lampstand on which seven lamps are set up (Ex. 25:37); the Israelites are to prepare pure oil so that a lamp may be set up

---

51. So W. Leslau, *ZAW* 74 (1962) 322-23: Shibayana; contra G. R. Driver, *ZAW* 69 (1957) 74-77.

52. Bächli, *ZDPV* 89 (1973) 6-7.

53. Wehmeier, 888.

54. Cf. Paul.

to burn regularly (Ex. 27:20; cf. 30:8). Finally, the hiphil of *ʿālâ* can refer to animals' chewing the cud (Lev. 11:3-6,26; Dt. 14:6-7).

The words of admiration spoken by the lover in Cant. 7:7-10(6-9) use *ʿālâ* metaphorically: the intimacy of the lovers is compared to the climbing of a palm (v. 9[8]). The prophetic oracle of judgment in Jer. 4:5-31 likens the foe from the north advancing against Israel to storm clouds rising (v. 13) and a lion that goes up from its thicket (v. 7). A contrasting image compares Yahweh to a lion coming up from the thickets of the Jordan to put the enemy to flight, bringing deliverance to Israel (50:44). This image has been incorporated secondarily into the oracle against Edom: the disaster about to befall Edom will mount up and swoop down like an eagle (49:22).

b. *Figurative Usage.* The verb *ʿālâ* is often used figuratively. One "goes up" to a person of high rank. Contrary to general usage (one usually "goes down" to Egypt), Joseph "goes up" to Pharaoh in Egypt (Gen. 46:31). The same notion lies behind Hos. 8:9, which states the reason for Israel's affliction: "They have gone up to Assyria." The sons of Eliab refuse to go up to Moses (Nu. 16:12,14). The word is also used in forensic contexts: the Israelites go up to Deborah for judgment (Jgs. 4:5); people go up to the judgment of the elders in the gate to obtain a judicial decision (Dt. 17:8; 25:7; Ruth 4:1).

Gen. 49:9 compares Judah to a young lion going up from the prey — in other words, Judah will be great and powerful. According to Dt. 28:43, aliens will ascend above Israel while Israel sinks *(yrd)* lower and lower. The panegyric that concludes the book of Proverbs extols the capable wife as surpassing all (*ʿālâ ʿal,* Prov. 31:29). Contrariwise, the image of rising balances signifies worthlessness (Ps. 62:10[9]).

Figurative usage can also describe anger (2 S. 11:20; 2 Ch. 36:16; Ps. 78:21,31; Prov. 15:1 [hiphil]) or cries of distress (Ex. 2:23; 1 S. 5:12; Jer. 14:2) as rising, and picture human wickedness as coming up before Yahweh (Jon. 1:2; cf. Ps. 74:23).

c. *Idioms and Technical Terminology.* Among idioms and technical terminology using *ʿālâ* (apart from formulas associated with the exodus; see d below), we may note the following:

ʿālâ ʿal-rûaḥ or *ʿal-lēḇ*. The use of *ʿālâ* with *rûaḥ* occurs 5 times (with minor variations) in Ezekiel, 4 times with reference to Israel. The hidden thoughts and secrets of the heart rise up and are revealed. According to 11:5; 14:3,7, Israel has its inmost heart set on apostasy from Yahweh; its mind is set on the *gillûlîm.* It is not clear whether 20:32, a late text, refers to willful idolatry[55] or to an awareness brought about by God's judgment that Israel faces an empty future without Yahweh and must therefore turn to alien cults like the other nations. Postexilic prophets of salvation adopt the expression, replacing *rûaḥ* with *lēḇ,* probably taking Jer. 31:33 as their cue. According to Isa. 65:17, the coming of salvation will mean that the afflictions of the past will not be remembered (→ זכר *zāḵar);* they will no longer arise in the heart. With fourfold repetition, Jer. 3:16 says that the "ark of the covenant of Yahweh," the embodiment of the law (Ex. 25:16; cf. Dt. 10:1-5; 1 K. 8:9), will not come to mind, will not be remem-

55. Van den Born, in loc.

bered *(zkr),* will not be missed, will not be made again. It is superfluous, because in the age of salvation the law of Yahweh will be written on people's hearts (Jer. 31:33).

The expression *ʿālâ ʿal-śᵉpaṯ lāšôn,* found only in Ezk. 36:3, means "become an object of gossip."

As Ludlul II, 46 shows, *ʿālâ haššāmayim(â),* "mount up to heaven," is a proverbial expression (see I.4 above). In Ps. 107:26 it is purely metaphorical. In Isa. 14:13,14; Jer. 51:53, it expresses human hubris; in Am. 9:2 it describes the futility of any attempt on the part of the wicked to escape Yahweh's clutches (cf. Ps. 139:8 with *slq*). Finally, Dt. 30:12 states that it is totally unnecessary to do any such thing in order to receive Yahweh's commandment.

In 1 K. 10:29 *ʿālâ* is used as a technical commercial term: a product "comes to" (i.e., costs) a certain amount.

In 1 K. 5:27; 9:15; 9:21 = 2 Ch. 8:8, the hiphil is used for the conscription of forced labor.

In its frequent use as a military term *ʿālâ* means "attack" (qal) or "bring against" (hiphil).[56] In Josh. 7:2 Joshua sends spies up to Ai before attacking and capturing the city (8:1,3,10 [Dtr],11). The same Dtr hand as in 8:10 probably framed the account of the successful attack on Jericho by the "people" (6:5,20), as well as the summary in Jgs. 1:1-4. In Jgs. 6:3 the Midianites and Amalekites attack Israel; in 15:10 the Philistines do the same. In 1 K. 14:25 = 2 Ch. 12:9, Shishak attacks and takes Jerusalem; in 1 K. 15:17 = 2 Ch. 16:1, King Baasha of Israel attacks Judah; etc.

In these and similar texts, *ʿālâ* is constructed with *ʿal* (Jgs. 18:9; 1 K. 20:22; 2 K. 12:18[17]; 17:3; 18:13 = Isa. 36:1; 2 K. 18:25 = Isa. 36:10; 2 K. 23:29; Jer. 50:3,21; Ezk. 38:11,16; Joel 1:6; Nah. 2:2; 1 Ch. 14:10), *ʾel* (Nu. 13:31; Josh. 15:15; Jgs. 1:1; 12:3; 20:23,30; 1 S. 7:7; 2 S. 5:19; 2 K. 16:9; Jer. 35:11; 49:28,31), or *bᵉ* (Isa. 7:6). A variety of phrases express the same meaning: *ʿālâ lᵉhillāḥem,* "go up to fight" (2 K. 3:21; 2 Ch. 35:20); *ʿālâ lammilḥāmâ* (1 K. 20:26; 2 K. 16:5; Isa. 7:1) or *bammilḥāmâ* (1 S. 29:9), "go up to battle"; *ʿālâ bammaḥᵃneh* (1 S. 14:21). Analogously, the hiphil of *ʿālâ* means "bring against" (Jer. 50:9; Ezk. 16:40; 23:46; 26:3; 2 Ch. 36:17). In the immediate and extended context we naturally find many examples of military terminology (see III.2 below). Termination of battle or retreat is expressed by *ʿālâ mēʿal* (1 K. 15:19 = 2 Ch. 16:3; 2 K. 12:19[18]; Jer. 21:2; 34:21; cf. 1 S. 14:46; 2 S. 23:9). In Ex. 1:10 and Hos. 2:2(1:11), *ʿālâ min-hāʾāreṣ* may mean "take possession of the land" or "withdraw from the land."[57]

Prophetic oracles of judgment interpret the enemies attacking Israel as the declared and inexorable judgment of Yahweh. In the symbolic description of the judgment on the harlot Jerusalem in Ezk. 16, Yahweh summons all her lovers to desecrate the faithless city (v. 37) and gather (*ʿālâ* hiphil) an assembly against her to condemn and punish her (cf. the secondary inclusion of the same image in 23:46). In Jer. 5:7-11, an oracle of

---

56. R. Bach, *Die Aufforderungen zur Flucht und zum Kampf im alttestamentliche Prophetenspruch. WMANT* 9 (1962), 63.

57. For the former translation see Wolff, *Hosea. Herm* (Eng. trans. 1974), 24, 28; Wehmeier, 887; for the latter, Rupprecht; *HAL,* II, 829.

Yahweh, v. 10 (a late interpolation) compares Jerusalem to a vineyard attacked and laid waste by the enemy. Joel 1:5-14 summons the people to a communal lament in response to a plague of locusts; v. 6 compares the locusts to a powerful enemy nation invading the land of Yahweh.

Basing their message on the earlier oracles against the nations, exilic and postexilic prophecies of salvation transform the function of the enemy motif. The preexilic (!) oracle against Nineveh in Nah. 2:2-14(1-13)[58] may have served as the stimulus: an unnamed enemy (Yahweh?) comes up against *(ʿālâ ʿal-pᵉnê)* the city (v. 2) and destroys it utterly. According to Jer. 48:12, Yahweh himself will dispatch (*šlḥ* piel) the destroyer of Moab to go up against the land and its towns (v. 15).[59] Against Babylon Yahweh leads (*ʿālâ* hiphil) "a company of great nations," which will attack and conquer it (Jer. 50:9); cf. Ezk. 26:3, where Yahweh hurls "many nations" against Tyre. Yahweh turns the advance of Israel's enemies around, making them attack themselves, so that they will be destroyed and Israel will be delivered. The secondary prophecy of the gathering and deliverance of Jacob in Mic. 2:12-13 speaks of a champion who will go up *(ʿālâ)* before the remnant of Israel and eliminate every obstacle that stands in the way of entry into Jerusalem.[60] V. 13b names Yahweh himself as this champion, going at the head of his people.

d. *Theological Usage.* Of theological significance are the phrases and formulas using the qal or hiphil of *ʿālâ* in recalling the exodus from Egypt, in the cultic contexts of pilgrimage and sacrifice, and in conjunction with the notion of exaltation or rapture and ascension.

(1) *Exodus.* The OT speaks with astonishing frequency of the exodus from Egypt, using a wide variety of idioms and formulas, directly or by allusion. For the event of the exodus itself, the OT uses two verbs: → **יצא** *yāṣāʾ* (76 times) and *ʿālâ* (42 times). According to Noth, we are dealing here with a primary credal statement, fixed at an early date; it referred originally to the miracle at the Sea of Reeds and became the nucleus around which all the rest of the pentateuchal narrative crystallized. He considers the alternation between *yāṣāʾ* and *ʿālâ* to be quite random.[61] Humbert sees in *yāṣāʾ* an expression of a juridical and political element emphasizing deliverance from captivity and thus the sociological aspect of the exodus, while *ʿālâ* conveys the geographical and military aspect.[62] Wijngaards restricts the formulas using the hiphil of *yāṣāʾ* to the message of deliverance from slavery. By contrast, the formula with the hiphil of *ʿālâ* is cultic in nature; it often refers to the occupation of Canaan, and was associated with the sanctuaries of the northern kingdom. For Lubsczyk, *yāṣāʾ* and *ʿālâ* mark priestly and prophetic exodus traditions, each with its own theological significance.[63] According to Richter, the *yāṣāʾ* and *ʿālâ* formulas are of equal antiquity and developed in the north-

58. Deissler, *Zwölf Propheten. NEB* (1984), II, 203ff.
59. On the text see *BHS.*
60. T. Lescow, *ZAW* 84 (1972) 46-85.
61. Noth, *History of Pentateuchal Traditions* (Eng. trans. 1972), 46-51.
62. P. Humbert, *TZ* 18 (1962) 357-61.
63. H. Lubsczyk, *Der Auszug Israels aus Ägypten. ETS* 11 (1963).

ern kingdom.[64] The *ʿālâ* formula was associated with the tabernacle, while no concrete *Sitz im Leben* can be identified for *yāṣāʾ*. Zenger theorizes that the *yāṣāʾ* formula had its *Sitz im Leben* in the conception of Yahweh as king.[65] The *ʿālâ* formula is earlier, referring primarily to the event of the exodus; Jeroboam used it as a presentation formula. The contradictory conclusions of current scholarship make it advisable to examine separately the theological function and *Sitz im Leben* of the *ʿālâ* formulas and their contexts.

(a) The hiphil of *ʿālâ* in the relative clause: "Here is your God, O Israel, who brought you up out of the land of Egypt" (1 K. 12:28); "these are your gods, O Israel, who brought you up out of the land of Egypt" (Ex. 32:4,8); "this is your God, who brought you up out of Egypt" (Neh. 9:18). Neh. 9:18 proves to be secondary; it is dependent on Ex. 32 in its singular construction of God and in the omission of "land." In 1 K. 12 we have a pre-Dtr account antedating 722; it originated in Jerusalem. Ex. 32 is probably dependent on this account.[66] The general agreement in the wording of the formulas supports the possibility that they reflect an ancient cultic formula from Bethel, adopted by Jeroboam as a presentation formula. In other preexilic texts using the hiphil of *ʿālâ* in a relative clause, Moses is always the subject (Ex. 32:1,7,23; 33:1). This formula was borrowed by the Dtr corpus and reshaped in narrative form (1 S. 12:6; 2 K. 17:36; Jer. 16:14; Am. 3:1[?]).

(b) The hiphil participle of *ʿālâ:* "I am Yahweh your God, the one bringing you up out of the land of Egypt" (Ps. 81:11[10]). This is unquestionably a preexilic text enshrining a liturgical formula; it echoes the beginning of the Decalogue and appears in the context of prohibition of other gods. A cultic *Sitz im Leben* is also likely for the pre-P conclusion of the law in Lev. 11:45: "I am Yahweh, the one bringing you up out of the land of Egypt." Both formulas have God speaking in the 1st person; both appear in legal contexts.

In Josh. 24:17 and Jer. 2:6 the situation is different. The former is probably pre-Dtr; it reads: "Yahweh our God, he is the one bringing us up from the land of Egypt"; cf. Jer. 2:6: "Where is Yahweh, the one bringing us up from the land of Egypt?" This passage comes from the first scroll. Josh. 24:17 may well be based on a credal formula, the precise wording of which can no longer be determined. By contrast, Jer. 2:6 could reflect a liturgical formula. The same may also be true of Dt. 20:1: "Yahweh your God, the one bringing you up from the land of Egypt, is with you." Boecker sees here support for his theory that the formula is closely associated with the Yahweh war.[67] Dt. 20:1 is probably, however, not an element of the ancient war code but a paraenetic bracketing introduced by Dtr redaction (cf. 2 K. 17:7). This also argues against the theory of Richter that the redaction of the Dtn laws took place in the northern kingdom.[68]

---

64. W. Richter, "Beobachtungen zur theologischen Systembildung in der alttestamentlichen Literatur," *Wahrheit und Verkundigung. FS M. Schmaus,* 2 vols. (1967), I, 175-212.

65. E. Zenger, *ZDMG* Sup 1 (1969), 334-42.

66. Gross, 433; C. Dohmen, *Der Bilderverbot. BBB* 62 (1985), 102ff.

67. H. J. Boecker, *Die Beurteilung der Anfänge des Königtums in den deuteronomistischen Abschnitten des 1. Saumuelbuches. WMANT* 31 (1969), 42.

68. Richter, *FS Schmaus,* 184.

(c) Infinitive *baʿ^{a}lô̱t* + "from Egypt": this and the following formulas are formulaic indications of time. "Israel, on coming from Egypt, took away my land," says the king of the Ammonites to the messengers of Jephthah. The reply of the messengers uses the same formula (v. 16). It appears again in a similar context in 1 S. 15:2, in words spoken by Yahweh: "I will punish the Amalekites for what they did to Israel, by opposing them on their coming out of Egypt." In the same context Saul advises the Kenites to withdraw, "for you showed kindness to all the people of Israel on their coming out of Egypt" (v. 6). The texts using this formula are early (preexilic) and exhibit no trace of Dtr language. The context indicates that they refer to the situation of the wilderness; the use of *ʿālâ* emphasizes the element of journeying.

(d) The phrase *yôm ʿ^{a}lô̱t* (inf.) + suffix indicating the human subject: "There she [Israel] shall go as in the days of her youth, as on the day of her coming out of Egypt" (Hos. 2:17[15]). The same formula appears in Isa. 11:16: "So there shall be a highway for the remnant of the people left by the Assyrians, as there was for Israel on the day of its coming from the land of Egypt." While Hos. 2:17(15) is preexilic and non-Dtn, Isa. 11:16 is probably from the hand of a late redactor. The formula does not refer to the exodus and wilderness experience in general, but accentuates clearly the event of the flight from Egypt.

(e) The phrase *(l^{e})mîyôm* + *ʿ^{a}lô̱t/haʿ^{a}lô̱t* + *ʿaḏ hayyôm hazzeh:* in Jgs. 19:30 the Levite whose concubine was killed by the Benjaminites commands his emissaries to ask the tribes of Israel: "Has such a thing ever happened from the day of the Israelites' coming up from the land of Egypt until this day?" In Yahweh's words to Nathan forbidding David's building of the temple, 2 S. 7:6 says: "I have not lived in a house since the day of my bringing up the people of Israel to this day" (cf. the variant in 1 Ch. 17:5). Both passages are early and pre-Dtn. The context of Jgs. 19:30 probably points to the tradition of the wars of Yahweh, associated with the northern kingdom,[69] while 2 S. 7:6 is clearly associated with the southern kingdom and Jerusalem. The other occurrences of this formula are Dtr (Dtr) or are dependent on this material (cf. 1 S. 8:8; Jer. 11:7). Of the two early texts, 2 S. 7:6 probably represents the source of Dtr usage.

All the temporal formulas and formulaic idioms are secondary relative to the 1st-person liturgical formulas with God as subject of *ʿālâ* hiphil. They show that already in the preexilic period and before Deuteronomy a wide variety of formulaic expressions could be used to refer to the exodus. Their *Sitz im Leben* cannot be determined; their actual setting is literary. Although it is possible to discern certain semantic distinctions and to identify usages that are characteristic of P or Dtr material, it is hardly possible to decide whether and why a particular formula was used in every instance. They all can be used to refer to the exodus.

We can determine a *Sitz im Leben* for two other formulas, to the extent that they may be considered independent and not reformulations or variants of the formula *ʿālâ* hiphil with divine subject. In 1 S. 10:18 we read: "Thus says Yahweh, the God of Israel: I brought up Israel out of Egypt." In v. 19 Samuel shifts without transition to direct dis-

---

69. Ibid.

course and speaks of the "sons of Israel"; it is therefore reasonable to conclude that v. 18 is quoting a formula (cf. also Jgs. 6:8). In both cases we are dealing with an independent adaptation of a formula deriving from prophetic discourse.[70] This pre-Dtn formula also gave rise to the exodus formula in question. The late texts Am. 9:7 (cf. 2:10); 3:1 (all Dtr); and Mic. 6:4 (postexilic)[71] confirm this conclusion, each in its own way. The *Sitz im Leben* of this formula is the prophetic *rîḇ* or lawsuit.

The postexilic redactor of the book of Jeremiah sees the return of the exiles as a parallel to the exodus from Egypt. He finds the new demonstration of Yahweh's power so extraordinary that it causes the foundational event of the exodus to be forgotten: "It shall no longer be said: 'As Yahweh lives, who brought Israel up out of the land of Egypt,' but: 'As Yahweh lives, who brought Israel up out of the land of the north and out of all the lands where he had driven them'" (Jer. 16:14-15; cf. 23:7-8). The postexilic community was clearly familiar with the credal affirmation of the exodus in this form, so that they could use the contrasting motif to awaken new hope. Since it is unlikely that the formula came into being in this period, it appears to reflect an earlier formula, which may possibly recur in Jgs. 6:13: "Did not Yahweh bring us up from Egypt?" If so, we may in fact be dealing with an ancient credal formula.[72]

In the narrative sections of the Pentateuch, the hiphil of *ʿālâ* is used extensively to develop the theme of the exodus, albeit without any apparent fixed association with any of the exodus formulas. It is hard to decide whether individual texts represent allusions or free formulations. In alluding to the exodus formulas, J uses the hiphil of *ʿālâ* but varies the formulation freely (Ex. 3:8,17 [divine subj.]; 33:1; Nu. 16:13 [human subj.]; and, if the pre-Dtn portions of Ex. 32 can be assigned to J, 32:1,23 [human subj.]). To the extent that independent E texts can be identified at all, E does not use any of the formulas but does allude to them (Gen. 46:4; 50:24 [divine subj.]; Ex. 17:3; Nu. 21:5 [human subj.]).

The *ʿālâ* hiphil formulas have been associated with the northern kingdom and its sanctuaries.[73] This theory is connected with the assumption that the formulas using *ʿālâ* were repressed because they conveyed overtones of cultic politics and went out of use entirely after the exile; the *yāṣāʾ* formulas prevailed because they had no such overtones.[74] We may note, however, that in the exilic and postexilic period — apart from the Dtr History, which stands in the Dtn (Dtr) linguistic tradition and uses *ʿālâ* only when incorporating traditions of the northern kingdom — the use of *ʿālâ* is not infrequent: Lev. 11:45; Jer. 16:14; 23:7 (postexilic); Jer. 11:7 (Dtr); Mic. 6:4; Isa. 11:16; Nu. 14:13; 32:11; also the secondary Amos texts 2:10; 3:1. Furthermore, both *yāṣāʾ* and *ʿālâ* are used side by side in Jer. 31:32 (cf. 2:6), by the Dtr Jeremiah text 11:4 (cf. 11:7), as well as by the author of the Dtr History (1 S. 12:6; cf. 12:8). At

70. W. Richter, *Die Bearbeitungen des "Retterbuches" in der deuteronomischen Epoche. BBB* 21 (1964), 105-9.

71. T. Lescow, *ZAW* 84 (1972) 187.

72. Wijngaards, 99-100.

73. Wehmeier, 894-95, following Wijngaards, 100.

74. See also Richter, *Bearbeitungen,* 108.

most, we may conclude that in this later period the distinction between *yāṣāʾ* and *ʿālâ* had faded.

(2) *Pilgrimage.* Many texts use *ʿālâ* to describe the encounter with God, who dwells in heaven, in terms of going up to the sanctuary or the mountain of God, so that in these contexts the verb becomes a technical term for "go on pilgrimage." The complex traditional web of the Sinai pericope often speaks very concretely of Moses as going up or receiving the command to go up the mountain to God (Ex. 19:3) or to Yahweh (24:12,15,18; 32:30; cf. Dt. 10:1); other texts speak of Moses and Aaron (Ex. 19:24) or Moses, Aaron, Nadab, and Abihu, together with seventy of the elders of Israel, although Moses alone is allowed to approach God (24:1,9). According to 24:13, Moses goes up the mountain of God, while in 34:2 he is commanded to go up the mountain and present himself before Yahweh on its top (cf. 34:4, where he carries out the command). By contrast, the people are forbidden to go up Mt. Sinai (19:23). In Nu. 20:27 (P), Moses goes up Mt. Hor with the son of Aaron, who is wearing the vestments of his father as a sign of succession; according to a later P text (33:38), Aaron himself goes up Mt. Hor to die.

The premonarchic and early dynastic period knew a series of local sanctuaries, the goal of regular pilgrimages by individual families or clans. They are usually provided with secondary familial etymologies. For example, Jacob goes on pilgrimages from Shechem to Bethel to set up an altar and a pillar there (Gen. 35:1-9,14-15 [E]). In its present context, this account presents itself as the fulfillment of the vow made in 28:20ff.; in fact, however, we are dealing with a narrative doublet based on 28:10-22 (JE) and repeating the etymology of 28:18-19. According to 12:8 (J), Abraham had already built an altar there. Later the Israelites go up to Bethel to inquire of God (Jgs. 20:18) and to offer sacrifice (20:26ff.; cf. 21:2). On his way to Gilgal, Saul meets men who are "going up to God at Bethel" (1 S. 10:3). Year by year, Elkanah would go up with his family to Shiloh to pray before Yahweh and to offer sacrifice (1 S. 1:3,7,21,22; 2:19). Isaac goes up to Beer-sheba, where Yahweh appears to him (Gen. 26:23-25 [JE or Dtr]). According to Jgs. 21:5,8, the Israelites go up "to Yahweh at Mizpah." Elijah goes up to the top of Carmel to pray to Yahweh (1 K. 18:42).

With the building of the Jerusalem temple, the significance of the local sanctuaries decreased, a development encouraged by the monarchy on religio-political grounds to establish Jerusalem as the central metropolis of the state and the temple as the national sanctuary. To this end, David had a solemn procession transfer the ark, which had been brought up (*ʿālâ* hiphil) from Beth-shemesh to the house of Abinadab (1 S. 6:21; 7:1), to the city of David (2 S. 6:2,12,15), whence Solomon finally had it brought into the temple. According to the pre-Dtr narrative underlying 1 K. 8:1-11*,[75] this was done in a great procession. Ps. 47:6(5) may reflect a liturgical representation of such an ark procession.

According to Ps. 122:4, it is obvious that the tribes should make a pilgrimage up to Jerusalem to praise Yahweh, for "so it was decreed for Israel." Depending on the date

75. Hentschel, *1 Könige, 2 Könige. NEB* (1984), 55.

of this psalm, the poet is referring either to the pre-Dtn "pilgrimage stratum" (Ex. 34:22,23,24b,26a),[76] which requires Israel to go up three times each year to appear before Yahweh (34:24b), or to the Dtn summary of the obligatory annual festivals (Dt. 16:16-17).[77] The acceptance of the Jerusalem pilgrimage is illustrated negatively by 1 K. 12:27-28, where Jeroboam seeks to prohibit the northern tribes from going on this pilgrimage, saying: "You have gone up to Jerusalem long enough!" By contrast, Hos. 4:15 (borrowing from Am. 5:5) warns Israel sternly against entering (→ בוא *bô'*) into Gilgal and going up to Beth-aven (= Bethel; cf. already Am. 5:5).

In the exilic period, a prophetic oracle (Jer. 31:6) promises the exiles renewed cultic communion with the temple of Zion: as pilgrims they will go up to Zion, to Yahweh their God. In a postexilic Zion hymn of unknown authorship (Isa. 2:2-4 = Mic. 4:1-3), which has affinities with Isa. 56:3-7; 66:18-23; Zec. 8:20-23, the horizon expands. Not just the Israelites scattered among the nations but all the nation themselves will arise and make pilgrimage to Zion, to encounter Yahweh in his sanctuary and to receive instruction from him (cf. Zec. 14:16-19).

(3) *Sacrifice.* The hiphil of *'ālâ* is used 77 times for the offering of sacrifice, 61 times in conjunction with → עלה *'ōlâ.* There is no consensus as to whether the hiphil is meant to express the placing of the sacrifice upon the altar or its rising in smoke. The former interpretation is supported by several passages that use the qal of *'ālâ* with sacrificial victims to mean "ascend the altar." According to 1 K. 18:29, the prophets of Baal prophesy until the grain offering "goes up" (is offered). Isa. 60:7 says that sheep and rams "will go up to acceptance on my altar." In Lev. 2:12 and Ps. 51:21(19), it is also possible to read the hiphil. Less conclusive are the passages that describe the king or a priest as going up to the altar to offer sacrifice (1 K. 12:32-33; 2 K. 23:9; Isa. 57:7). The latter interpretation is supported by the association with *'ōlâ* and the fact that a sacrifice to the deity was not considered consummated until it had been burned.

Of course the hiphil of *'ālâ* can be used for other types of sacrifice as well, "esp. various types mentioned in sequence whose purposes are not clearly distinguished"[78] (Ex. 30:9; 40:29; Lev. 14:20; Josh. 22:23; Jgs. 20:26; 21:4; 2 S. 6:17; 24:25 = 1 Ch. 21:26; 1 K. 9:25; 1 Ch. 16:2; 2 Ch. 35:14; Jer. 14:12; Am. 5:22). It is impossible to sustain Wehmeier's hypothesis that in various passages that do not include more specific language the hiphil of *'ālâ* has the general meaning "to sacrifice," since the immediate contexts of all the passages he cites (except 2 S. 15:24) speak explicitly of burnt offerings.[79]

It is noteworthy, nevertheless, that the P texts differ significantly from the earlier tradition in their use of sacrificial terminology. In the earlier texts, the hiphil of *'ālâ* clearly predominates; with few exceptions (Ex. 30:9; 40:29; Lev. 14:20; 17:8), P avoids this expression. The Chronicler turns out to be surprisingly independent of the P terminology; here once again the hiphil of *'ālâ* predominates, not only where earlier

---

76. J. Halbe, *Das Privilegrecht Jahwes. FRLANT* 114 (1975), 206-9, 316-17.
77. Braulik, *Deuteronomium 1–16,17. NEB* (1986), 120.
78. Wehmeier, 889.
79. Ibid.

sources are incorporated but also in passages composed by the Chronicler without a model in the sources (1 Ch. 16:40; 23:31; 29:21; 2 Ch. 23:18; 29:7,27; Ezr. 3:2-3,6).

(4) *Exaltation, Ascension.* The hiphil of *'ālâ* is used in texts that speak of the exaltation or ascension of human beings. Since the two notions have different religio-historical origins, I shall discuss them separately.

The hymnic predications of Yahweh in the Song of Hannah (1 S. 2:1-10) speak of God's exaltation of human beings: "Yahweh kills and brings to life; he brings down to Sheol and raises up. Yahweh makes poor and makes rich; he brings low and also exalts (→ רום *rûm* polel). He raises up (→ קום *qûm* hiphil) the poor from the dust; he lifts up (*rûm* hiphil) the needy from the ash heap" (vv. 6-8).[80] This very general theologoumenon of exaltation appears in a hymn of thanksgiving, i.e., not (yet) in a statement about human beings but in the context of praise of Yahweh. Vv. 7-8 describe the group exalted by Yahweh as comprising the poor (→ דל *dal*) and needy (→ אביון *'eḇyôn*). Here exaltation means the social rehabilitation of the weak and oppressed. The statement of v. 6 is more general, praising Yahweh as lord over life and death. The exaltation he performs is understood as deliverance from death or the fear of death occasioned by serious illness or affliction caused by enemies. As a rule, deliverance from enemies is expressed by the hiphil of *rûm* (e.g., Ps. 3:4[3]; 92:11[10]), whereas statements using the hiphil of *'ālâ* suggest deliverance from the danger of death caused by serious illness. In Ps. 30:4(3) the psalmist gives thanks: "Yahweh, you have brought up my soul from Sheol," in parallel with "You have healed me" (v. 3[2]). Ps. 71:20 describes deliverance from the assaults of enemies and from deadly disease as being brought up "from the depths of the earth." Other texts use different terminology, such as *rûm* polel (Ps. 9:14[13]), *qûm* hiphil (41:11[10]; cf. 40:3[2]), or *śgb* piel (Ps. 69:30[29]). Deliverance from deadly disease is probably also behind Ps. 40:3(2): "He drew me up from the desolate pit, out of the miry bog," although the psalm does not mention disease explicitly until vv. 13-18(12-17). These verses, however, probably represent an independent lament (cf. Ps. 70). In Jon. 2:3-10(2-9), a secondary psalm of thanksgiving, the speaker depicts his deadly peril: he is sinking in deep waters and descending into the earth (vv. 6-7a[5-6a]). In contrast, he describes Yahweh's saving intervention: "You brought up my life from the Pit" (v. 7b[6b]). Deliverance from deadly disease is depicted in mythological images, all of which describe the realm of death. The psalmist identifies the most profound reason for his suffering as God's having deserted him, so that he is cut off from all possibility of life. Only the direct intervention of God can end his affliction. The image of descending into Sheol that describes the psalmist's illness is transformed into its opposite: God intervenes to deliver the psalmist, bringing him up, exalting him.[81]

In the strict sense, the rapture or ascension of a human being is mentioned only in connection with the death of Elijah (2 K. 2:1, *'ālâ* hiphil; 2:11, *'ālâ* qal); cf. the use of

---

80. See T. J. Lewis, *JBL* 104 (1985) 105-8.

81. C. Barth, *Die Errettung vom Tode in den individuellen Klage- und Dankliedern des AT* (1947), 53ff.

→ לקח *lāqaḥ* in 2:3,5 and the rapture of Enoch in Gen. 5:1-4.[82] According to 2 K. 2:11, Elijah ascends (*ʿālâ* qal) into heaven in a whirlwind. The whirlwind and the "chariots and horses of fire" in the same verse are traditional elements associated with theophanies (Ps. 68:18[17]; 77:17ff.[16ff.]; Hab. 3:8; Zec. 6:1-8; Isa. 66:15). In the midst of a theophanic event, Elijah enters the sphere of God. The agent of the event is Yahweh, as the redactional introduction 2 K. 2:1a makes clear. The notion that human beings who enjoy special friendship with the gods ascend into heaven was widespread in the ancient world. Here its formulaic and mythological language elaborates the simple fact that Elijah died. The extraordinary personality of the prophet accounts for this euphemism. His exceptional status is documented even in his death. While other mortals must go down into Sheol, he may rise up into heaven.

Most religions look on heaven as the dwelling place of the gods. Israel, too, from the earliest times viewed heaven as the dwelling place of Yahweh (e.g., Dt. 4:39; 10:14; 26:15; 1 K. 8:23; Ps. 2:4).[83] Thence Yahweh descends to make himself and his instruction known to human beings, and thither he returns. So many texts speak of Yahweh's descending that in such contexts → ירד *yārad* without further qualification becomes virtually a technical term for "come down from heaven"; texts that speak of his ascending into heaven, however, are rare (cf. esp. J).[84]

Twice (Gen. 17:22; 35:13) P mentions briefly the ascent of Elohim to his heavenly dwelling place. Gen. 17:1-22 is a narrative totally characterized by the language and theology of P; it is constructed in imitation of the earlier patriarchal traditions and is presented as an alternative to them. This narrative culminates in the establishment of a *bᵉrîṯ ʿôlām.* The introduction (v. 1a) speaks of God's coming to Abraham, using the niphal of → ראה *rāʾâ,* commonly used to denote a prophetic revelation. The narrative concludes with the words "And Elohim went up from *(ʿālâ* qal + *mēʿal)* Abraham" (v. 22). The text does not identify the location of this ascent, nor does it mention the destination *(haššāmayim),* as usage elsewhere would lead one to expect. Gen. 35:13 is equally vague: "Then God went up from him at the place where he had spoken with him." Once again, the text uses the niphal of *rāʾâ* for the coming of God. "P clearly expresses his religious aversion to entangling the supernatural God in the things of the world."[85] For P all the emphasis is on the content of Elohim's revelation; the accidental trappings of the revelatory process are not significant.

An ascent of Yahweh is spoken of in Ps. 47:6(5) and 68:19(18). Ps. 47 is a hymn celebrating the kingship of Yahweh.[86] Its similarity to 1 K. 8:1-9 in language and substance leads Kraus to claim with assurance that *ʿālâ* describes the ascent of the ark to Zion.[87] "Shouting" and the "sound of trumpets," however, are associated with the proclamation and enthronement of an earthly king (2 S. 15:10; 1 K. 1:34,39; 2 K. 9:13;

---

82. See A. Schmitt, *Entruckung, Aufnahme, Himmelfahrt. FzB* 10 (^{2}1976).
83. M. Metzger, *UF* 2 (1970) 139-58.
84. E. Zenger, in E. Haag, ed., *Gott, der Einzige. QD* 104 (1985), 49.
85. H. Gunkel, *Genesis* (Eng. trans. 1997), lxxxii.
86. H. J. Kraus, *Psalms 1–59* (Eng. trans. 1988), 465ff.
87. Ibid., 468.

etc.). According to ancient tradition, Yahweh's throne is both on Zion and in heaven (Ps. 11:4; 103:19). His ascent establishes his hegemony as lord over all the world, as is clear from the epithets *meleḵ* and *'elyôn* (47:3,8-9). The correspondence between *'elyôn* and *'ālâ* suggests strongly that this passage refers to Yahweh's ascent to his heavenly dwelling place, where he reigns as king (Isa. 14:14), exalted (*'ālâ* niphal) above all gods (Ps. 97:9).[88]

Ps. 68:19(18) speaks of Yahweh's ascending the heights *(mārôm).* The reference is probably to neither Zion nor Sinai: the mention of the "captives" and "gifts" that accompany Yahweh's ascent suggest instead his ascent into heaven.[89] In the background stands the ancient Canaanite notion of the ascent of the gods to Zaphon, echoes of which appear in vv. 16-18(15-17). Concretely, the words "you ascended the heights" (v. 19[18]) refer to Yahweh's ascent to the mountain of God described in vv. 16-17(15-16), which is identical with his heavenly dwelling place.

However one interprets the details, these texts express Israel's conviction of Yahweh's universal sovereignty. He is exalted (*'ālâ* niphal) both "over all the earth" (Ps. 47:3[2]), i.e., over all the rulers of the earth, and over all gods (97:9).

4. *Nouns.* a. *ma'ălâ.* The basic meaning of *ma'ălâ* derives from that of the verb: "journey up." In Ezr. 7:9 it refers to the return of the exiles. In the technical sense it means "that on which one climbs," "step": the stairs leading to the city of David (Neh. 3:15; 12:37); the steps of a throne (1 K. 10:19-20; 2 Ch. 9:18-19), a gate (Ezk. 40:6,22,26,31,37), a vestibule (Ezk. 40:49), or an altar (Ex. 20:26; Ezk. 43:17); and finally the divisions of a sundial (2 K. 20:9-11; Isa. 38:8).

The meaning of the phrase *šîr hamma'ălôṯ* in the superscriptions of Ps. 120–134 (*lamma'ălôṯ* in Ps. 121) is disputed. Some have interpreted it as referring to the rhetorical figure of anadiplosis, the repetition of the final word of a verse or strophe at the beginning of the following verse or strophe. Others, citing Ezr. 7:9, think these psalms were sung by the exiles on their return journey. Still others, noting Mishnah *Middot* 2.5, think they were sung by the Levites on the fifteen steps of the Nicanor Gate. An interpretation of these psalms as pilgrimage or processional hymns, which stays close to the meaning of the verb, is probably preferable. This group of psalms constitutes a small collection of songs sung during the pilgrimage to Jerusalem and/or its final act, the procession to the sanctuary.

b. *ma'ăleh.* The noun *ma'ăleh* denotes the place where one goes up, the "way up": in general (Ezk. 40:31,34,37; Neh. 12:37), the path leading up to a city (1 S. 9:11), the Mount of Olives (2 S. 15:30), or the tombs of David's descendants (2 Ch. 32:33). In conjunction with toponyms, it means "ascent" or "pass": *m. 'ăḏummîm* (Josh. 15:7; 18:17), possibly present-day Kal'at ed-Dam in the desert between Jerusalem and Jericho; *m. 'aqrabbîm,* the so-called Ascent of Scorpions (Nu. 34:4; Josh. 15:3; Jgs. 1:36);

---

88. As noted already by R. Kittel, *Die Psalmen. KAT* XIII (^{4}1922), 175; E. J. Kissane, *The Book of Psalms,* I (1953), 206.

89. Contra E. Podechard, *RB* 54 (1947) 509 (Zion); and M. Dahood, *Psalms II: 51–100. AB* 17 (1968), 143 (Sinai).

m. bêṯ-ḥôrōn (Josh. 10:10); *m. heḥāres* (Jgs. 8:13); *m. hallûḥîṯ* (Isa. 15:5; Jer. 48:5). Most of these ascents and passes can no longer be identified with certainty.

In Neh. 9:4 *maʿaleh* appears to function as a technical term denoting a dais, podium, or platform for the Levites.

c. *Personal Names.* The priest at Shiloh is named *ʿēlî* (1 S. 1:3-4,18; 14:3; 1 K. 2:27). The etymology and interpretation of this name are disputed. Old South Arabic personal names containing the element *ʿly* may suggest that *ʿēlî* is a hypocoristicon (see I above). The PN *yhwʿly* appears in the Samaria ostraca,[90] so that it is possible that the name of the priest derives from this form. There is a possibility that Ugar. *ʿly* should be interpreted as a divine name synonymous with *ʿlyn.*[91]

The form *ʿalwān* (Gen. 36:23) or *ʿalyān* (1 Ch. 1:40) is the name of a clan attached genealogically to the Horites, the original inhabitants of the mountainous region of Seir.[92] The name *ʿalwâ* (Gen. 36:40) or *ʿalyâ* (1 Ch. 1:51) denotes an Edomite clan or its chief. Since the Edomites overran the territory of the Horites and assimilated the indigenous population, it is not impossible that these names refer to one and the same clan.

d. *Other Nouns.* Other nominal formations include: *maʿal,* "above," used frequently in combination with *min* or *he locale* as an adverbial modifier;[93] *mōʿal,* "lifting up (of hands)," is found only in Neh. 8:6; *ʿāleh,* "that which sprouts, foliage," is discussed at → עלה *ʿāleh;* in Prov. 27:22 *ʿelî* probably means "pestle" (cf. Akk. *elit urṣî*); *ʿillî* (cf. Akk. *elû*) means "upper": Caleb gives his daughter the upper and lower springs as a farewell gift (Josh. 15:19 = Jgs. 1:15); *ʿalîyâ* is an upper chamber or loft (Jgs. 3:20,23,25; 1 K. 17:19,23; 2 K. 1:2; 23:12; Jer. 22:13-14), metaphorically a "chamber above the waters," the chambers of the heavens (Ps. 104:3,13); finally, *teʿālâ* refers to what covers over a wound, abstractly "healing" — impossible for Israel in Jer. 30:12-15 (v. 13) and for Egypt in Jer. 46:2-12 (v. 11).

IV. 1. *Dead Sea Scrolls.* The Dead Sea Scrolls use the qal and hiphil of *ʿālâ* as well as its nominal derivatives much like the OT. We find everyday usage, for example, in the law of the sabbath: "A living person who falls into a water-hole or into a [. . .] place no one shall lift out" (CD 11:16-17). Military usage appears in 1QM 1:3: the sons of light go up to battle against the Kittim (cf. CD 3:7, "Go up and take possession [of the land]"). It can also be used for retreat from battle (1QM 14:2). CD 4:18 may also reflect this usage: Israel is trapped in the three nets of Belial (fornication, wealth, pollution of the sanctuary); whoever escapes (*ʿlh* qal) from one is caught by the other.

Figurative and theological usage is commoner. Abraham is esteemed (*ʿālâ + ʾōhēḇ*) as a friend (of God), i.e., God regards him highly (CD 3:2). Whoever enters (→ עבר *ʿāḇar*) the covenant is upgraded (*ʿālâ* hiphil) in the hierarchy of the commu-

90. W. F. Albright, *CBQ* 7 (1945) 31.
91. *KTU* 1.16, III, 6-9. On the discussion see Dahood; → עליון *ʿelyôn.*
92. Scharbert, *Genesis 12–50. NEB* (1986), 235.
93. The formula "from . . . and upward," is discussed by Brin.

nity after an annual testing of his insight and the perfection of his path (1QS 5:24). The men of sin, i.e., those who have not entered into the covenant, by their conduct have "aroused" (*ʿālâ* qal) God's wrath, bringing judgment (1QS 5:12). God will "lead" (hiphil) the wicked priest to judgment (1QpHab 10:4) but will "raise" (hiphil) the merciful poor from the mire (1QH 5:22). Whether the latter statement refers to deliverance from oppression or suggests already a kind of resurrection remains an open question. A hope for resurrection is probably behind 1QH 3:20: "You have saved (→ פדה *pāḏâ)* my life from the pit, from Sheol you have lifted me up (*ʿlh* hiphil) to an everlasting height."[94] Sacrificial terminology appears in the general prohibition against placing anything on the altar on the sabbath (CD 11:17). The meaning of CD 5:5 is not entirely clear: David's deeds "were lifted up, except for Uriah's blood, and God allowed *(ʿzb)* them to him." This probably means that David's deeds were esteemed, were considered just.

The Temple Scroll presents a different picture. Here nouns predominate, mostly technical architectural terms. 11QT 6:6; 31:6,7 speak of a loft *(ʿalîyâ)* reached by a staircase (*maʿalâ,* 7:6; cf. 32:11), a flight of stairs around the structure (*msbyb ʿwlh mʿlwt,* 30:10), or a circular or spiral staircase (*ʿwlym msbwt,* 42:8). A stairwell is to be installed to the side of the walls in the porch, in which one may spiral upward (hiphil ptcp.) to the second and third porches and to the roof (42:7-9). The elders, the chiefs, and the princes are to go up and take their places there during the "offering" (hiphil inf.) of the sacrifices (42:15-16).

Sacrificial terminology appears in a few other passages. According to 26:5, the high priest is to slaughter the he-goat chosen by lot *(ʿlh hgwrl)* and lift (*ʿlh* hiphil) its blood in a golden bowl (cf. 23:11; 33:14). The offering of sacrifice is also mentioned in 18:9 and possibly 32:6 (the text is damaged). The meaning of *tʿlh* in 32:12 is unclear. After the analogy of 1 K. 18:32, the text may refer to a kind of trench around the altar. In 11QT 61:14 we find the exodus formula with the hiphil participle. In contrast to the parallel in Dt. 20:1, the divine subject that introduces the formula is absent here *(ʾnky yhwh ʾlhyk).* In its place we find the assurance of support *(ʾnky ʿmk),* which concludes the sentence in Dt. 20:1. A unique intensive form appears in the expression *ʿlwt dbrym,* "attribute culpability to someone" (11QT 65:7,12).

2. LXX. The LXX usually uses *anabaínein* to translate *ʿlh;* the semantic spectrum of the Greek word is similarly broad, so that only in the case of a few technical terms did the translators need to have recourse to other expressions.

Fuhs

---

94. See H. Lichtenberger, *Studien zum Menschenbild in Texten der Qumrangemeinde. SUNT* 15 (1980), 219-27.

עֹלָה/עוֹלָה *ʿōlâ/ʿôlâ*

I. 1. Etymology; 2. Occurrences. II. OT: 1. P; 2. Outside P; 3. Prophetic Polemic against the Cult; 4. Ezekiel; 5. Psalms; 6. Chronicler's History; 7. The King's *ʿōlâ;* 8. Human Sacrifice; 9. Altar of Burnt Offering; 10. Problematic Texts; 11. Apocrypha; 12. Origin and Meaning. III. 1. Elephantine; 2. LXX; 3. Dead Sea Scrolls.

I. 1. *Etymology.* The theory that *ʿōlâ* is connected with the Arabic root *ġalā (ġly),* "bubble up, boil, seethe," goes back to Hommel, who refers to "bubbling fleshpots" and the meaning of the participle, "fatty meat."[1] But König already stressed that this Arabic root cannot cast any light on the etymology of *ʿōlâ,* because — in contrast to the *zeḇaḥ* (cf. 1 S. 2:13-14) — kettles and pots play no role in the burnt offering.[2] According to the rules of Hebrew grammar, the form *ʿōlâ* can be analyzed as a qal fem. sg. ptcp. of *ʿālâ,* "rise up," with the meaning "that which rises up." Köhler attempted to treat *ʿōlâ* as an abbreviation of *hamminḥâ hāʿōlâ,* "the rising offering," citing Lat. *aqua tincta* (ink) as a parallel, although he was unable to cite any OT analog to such an ab-

---

ʿōlâ. A. van den Branden, "Lévitique 1–7 et le tarif de Marseille, CIS I 165," *RSO* 40 (1965) 107-30; R. Dussaud, *Les origines cananéenes du sacrifice israélite* (1921, [2]1941); H. Gese, "Ezechiel 20, 25f. und die Erstgeburtsopfer," *Beiträge zur alttestamentlichen Theologie. FS W. Zimmerli* (1977), 140-51; idem, "The Atonement," *Essays on Biblical Theology* (Eng. trans. 1981), 93-116; G. B. Gray, *Sacrifice in the OT* (1925; repr. 1971); H. Haag, "Das Opfer im AT," in F. J. Zinniker, ed., *Bibel und Liturgie. BibB* 1 (1961), 17-27; B. Janowski, "Erwägungen zur Vorgeschichte des israelitischen *šᵉlamîm*-Opfers," *UF* 12 (1980) 231-59; idem, *Sühne also Heilsgeschehen. WMANT* 55 (1982); O. Kaiser, "Den Erstgeborenen deiner Söhne sollst du mir geben," *Denkender Glaube. FS C. H. Ratschow* (1976), 24-28 = his *Von der Grundbedeutung des ATs* (1984), 142-66; B. A. Levine, *In the Presence of the Lord. SJLA* 5 (1974), esp. 22-23; L. Moraldi, "Terminologia cultuale israelitica," *RSO* 32 (1957) = *FS G. Furlani,* 321-37, esp. 326-27; W. O. E. Oesterley, *Sacrifices in Ancient Israel* (1937); A. F. Rainey, "The Order of Sacrifices in OT Ritual Texts," *Bibl* 51 (1970) 485-98; R. Rendtorff, *Studien zur Geschichte des Opfers im Alten Israel. WMANT* 24 (1967); H. Ringgren, *Sacrifice in the Bible. World Christian Books* 42 (1962); L. Rost, "Erwägungen zum israelitischen Brandopfer," *Von Ugarit nach Qumran. FS O. Eissfeldt. BZAW* 77 (1958), 177-83 = *Das kleine Credo und andere Studien zum AT* (1965), 112-19; idem, "Fragen um Bileam," *FS W. Zimmerli* (1977), 377-87; idem, "Opfer I. Im AT," *BHHW,* II, 1345-50; idem, "Ein Psalmenproblem," *TLZ* 93 (1968) 241-46; idem, *Studien zum Opfer im Alten Israel. BWANT* 113 (1981); idem, "Zu den Festopfervorschriften von Numeri 28 und 29," *TLZ* 83 (1958) 329-34; H. H. Rowley, "The Meaning of Sacrifice in the OT," *BJRL* 33 (1950/51) 74-110 = *From Moses to Qumran* (1963), 67-107; N. H. Snaith, "Sacrifices in the OT," *VT* 7 (1957) 308-17; W. B. Stevenson, "Hebrew ʿOlah and Zebach Sacrifices," *FS A. Bertholet* (1950), 488-97; R. de Vaux, *AncIsr,* II, 415ff.; idem, *Studies in OT Sacrifice* (1964), 27-51; R. K. Yerkes, *Sacrifice in Greek and Roman Religions and Early Judaism* (1952).

1. F. Hommel, *Die altisraelitische Überlieferung in inschriftlicher Beleuchtung* (1897), 279. A similar approach is taken by J. Barth, *Wurzeluntersuchungen zum hebräischen und aramäischen Lexicon* (1897), 297; and F. Zorell, *LexHebAram,* 601a.

2. E. König, *Hebräisch und Semitisch* (1901), 92.

breviation.[3] How the "rising" is to be understood is also unclear. One might think of the sacrifice rising in smoke and fire, or its rising aroma, or the sacrificial animal mounting the altar, or the ascent of a worshiper to an elevated site such as a high place (→ במה *bāmâ),* a tower, a wall, or the roof of the temple, to offer sacrifice there.[4]

An Ugaritic text describes KRT as climbing a tower and the shoulder of a wall to offer sacrifice; Dussaud connects this scene with 2 K. 3:27, which says that King Mesha of Moab offered his firstborn son "as a burnt offering on the wall."[5] Dussaud therefore theorizes that the *ʿōlâ* was a "tower sacrifice."[6] That Ugar. *šʿly,* like the hiphil of Heb. *ʿālâ,* can mean "sacrifice" might suggest linguistic and pragmatic affinities.[7] In the early days of Ugaritology, scholars already suggested that the Ugaritic sacrificial term *šrp* corresponds to Heb. *ʿōlâ.*[8] Since the meaning of the root makes it certain that Ugar. *šrp* means "burnt offering," the parallel to Heb. *ʿōlâ* cannot be rejected out of hand, even though the Ugaritic texts say next to nothing about the ritual of a *šrp* offering.[9]

Some have interpreted the consonant sequence *mʾhbʿlt* in the Proto-Sinaitic inscriptions as a PN, "Beloved of Baalat";[10] Albright, however, analyzed it as *mʾ hb ʿlt* and translated: "Swear to bring a sacrifice."[11] Whether *ʿlt* in these texts has some connection with Heb. *ʿōlâ,* as Albright would have it, must remain uncertain,[12] for the call to offer sacrifice is exceptional in a pilgrimage inscription.

In Imperial Aramaic the burnt offering (Heb. *ʿōlâ*) of the Jews at Elephantine is written as *ʿlwh* rather than the expected *ʿwlh;* the emphatic form is *ʿlwtʾ.* Ungnad suggests the simple possibility of metathesis.[13] The word *ʿlwh* does not occur elsewhere in Aramaic, with the exception of the pl. *ʿ^alāwān* in Ezr. 6:9. In Syriac, however, we find *ʿ^elāṯāʾ,* pl. *ʿ^elāwāṯā,*[14] with the meaning "burnt offering," as the equivalent of Heb. *ʿōlâ.* More often, however, it means "altar" (cf. 1 Mc. 2:25, where it stands for Gk. *bōmós*). The Jewish Aramaic word is *ʿ^alāṯāʾ;* its only meaning is "burnt offering." In Palmyrene

---

3. L. Köhler, "Hebräische Vokabeln I," *ZAW* 54 (1936) 287-93, esp. 292; idem, *OT Theology* (Eng. trans. 1957), 184.

4. D. Conrad, "Studien zum Altargesetz, Ex 20:24-26" (diss., Marburg, 1968), 114ff. (Excursus: The Cult on the Temple Roof).

5. *KTU* 1.14, IV, 2ff.; R. Dussaud, *CRAIBL* (1941), 534.

6. *Syr* 23 (1942/43) 39-41; not C. Schaeffer, as stated by B. A. Levine in his introduction to G. B. Gray, *Sacrifice,* xliii. See also H. L. Ginsberg, *Legend of King Keret. BASORSup* 2-3 (1946), 37.

7. *KTU* 1.19, IV, 23, 30; 6.14; also 1 K. 12:32-33.

8. Janowski, "Erwägungen," 232.

9. *KTU* 1.39, 4; 1.46, 7; 1.109, 10 (all in conjunction with *šlmm;* 1.65, 16: *b šrp il.* See M. Dietrich and O. Loretz, *UF* 13 (1981) 87. For a different view see J. F. Healey, *UF* 15 (1983) 48.

10. G. R. Driver, *Semitic Writing* (1948; ³1976), 97.

11. W. F. Albright, *The Proto-Sinaitic Inscriptions and Their Decipherment. HTS* 22 (1966), 17, 19-20, 42. See also idem, *BASOR* 110 (1948) 6-22, esp. 16-17 with n. 52, suggesting the reading *ʿālîtu* or *ʿôlîtu.*

12. H. P. Rüger, *BRL²*, 292a.

13. A. Ungnad, *Aramäische Papyri aus Elephantine* (1911), 4.

14. *LexSyr,* 526b/527a.

the only meaning of *ʿlt* is "altar."[15] This may be because the altar itself was a consecrated offering.[16] Since one inscription from Palmyra that uses the word was written by Nabateans, we may conclude that Nabateans also used the word *ʿlt* in the sense of "altar," if they did not simply conform to local usage when they were in Palmyra.[17]

In terms of meaning, the Hebrew word → כליל *kālîl,* "whole offering," could be taken as synonymous with *ʿōlâ.* Many scholars think that *kālîl* was the earlier term for a whole burnt offering and was later replaced by the term *ʿōlâ.*[18] The few texts where *kālîl* appears as a sacrificial term (Lev. 6:15-16[Eng. vv. 22-23]; Dt. 13:17[16]; 33:10; 1 S. 7:9; Ps. 51:21[19]) and the fact that in 1 S. 7:9 *ʿōlâ* and *kālîl* stand side by side without connection and are linked in Ps. 51:21(19) with *waw (explicativum?)* suggest instead that *kālîl* is a secondary attempt to hebraize the "foreign" term *ʿōlâ* (cf. also Dt. 33:10); the attempt did not succeed because the term *ʿōlâ* was already established in the ritual and in popular speech. There is also a Phoenician-Punic word *kll* that appears frequently in sacrificial tariffs in parallel with *šlmm;* its relationship to Heb. *kālîl* is problematic.[19]

One passage in the Elephantine papyri uses *mqlw,* an Akkadian loanword (*maqlû,* "incineration, roasting furnace"), for *ʿōlâ.*[20] There is a Lihyanite word *ḥmm,* which Caskel vocalizes as **ḥummat,* pl. *ḥumam,* and translates as "burnt offering";[21] whether it represents a mode of sacrifice comparable to the *ʿōlâ* must remain an open question.

The single Neo-Punic occurrence of *ʿlt* for burnt offering is not as unambiguous as scholars suggest.[22] It appears in a votive inscription from Altiburus, to whose seven easily legible lines two lines have been added in a different script that is hard to decipher. If the reading in *KAI* is correct, these two lines have no connection with the preceding text; they say that someone offered a burnt offering or a grain offering in the sanctuary to fulfill a vow. This text would be relevant only to the survival of *ʿōlâ* in a later period.

In summary, I must say that the precise meaning and etymology of the word *ʿōlâ* are obscure. On cogent grounds Rost points out that the term *ʿōlâ* is neither Greek nor Semitic in origin.[23] The burnt offering probably grew out of a ritual practiced by a population stratum living south of the Taurus, later displaced by Greeks and Semites; the Israelites then borrowed the *ʿōlâ* from the Canaanites.

---

15. *DNSI,* II, 851.

16. J. Teixidor, *The Pantheon of Palmyra* (1979), 66; he writes *ʿallatha.*

17. G. A. Cooke (*Text-Book of North-Semitic Inscriptions* [1903], no. 140A/B; B 2.10) speaks of several altars.

18. See R. Rendtorff, *Leviticus. BK* III/1-3 (1985-92), 27; A. Kapelrud, *TDOT,* VII, 184.

19. Rendtorff, *BK* III, 27; A. Kapelrud, → VII, 183-84; Janowski, "Erwägungen," 254-55; O. Kaiser, *TUAT* I/3, 264.

20. *AP* 33:19. See *AHw,* II, 607b; cf. S. A. Kaufman, *The Akkadian Influences on Aramaic. AS* 19 (1974), 70.

21. See *JS,* 77; W. Caskel, *Lihyan und Lihyanisch. Arbeitsgemeinschaft für Forschung des Landes Nordrhein-Westfalen, Geisteswissenschaften* 4 (1954), 92, 117, 134.

22. M. Lidzbarski, *Handbuch der nordsemitischen Epigraphik* (1898), I, 341; *DNSI,* II, 851; *KAI* 159.

23. Rost, "Erwägungen," 180-81 (116).

2. *Occurrences.* The *ʿōlâ* is the form of sacrifice most frequently mentioned in the OT. Even-Shoshan counts 286 occurrences, others 287.[24] The occurrences are distributed as follows: Genesis 7, Exodus 17, Leviticus 62, Numbers 56, Deuteronomy 6; thus 148 occurrences, more than half of the total, appear in the Pentateuch, 126 of them in P. Occurrences elsewhere: Joshua 6, Judges, 6, 1 Samuel 10, 2 Samuel 5, 1 Kings 8, 2 Kings 9, 1 Chronicles 14, 2 Chronicles 30, Ezra 8, Nehemiah 1, Job 2, Psalms 7, Isaiah 5, Jeremiah 7, Ezekiel 19, and Hosea, Amos, and Micah 1 each. The word does not appear in most of the Minor Prophets (Joel, Obadiah, Jonah, Nahum, Habakkuk, Zephaniah, Haggai, Zechariah, Malachi), in the Megillot, in Proverbs, or in Daniel. In the Hebrew text of Sirach, *ʿlh* appears only once, in 45:16b of ms. B. In the Aramaic sections of the OT, only the pl. *ʿᵃlāwān* occurs (Ezr. 6:9). The plene form appears only 48 times. The altar of burnt offering *(mizbaḥ hāʿōlâ)* is mentioned 19 times (Ex. 30:28; 31:9; 35:16; 38:1; 40:6,10,29; Lev. 4:7,10,18,25[twice],30,34; 1 Ch. 6:34; 16:40; 21:26,29; 2 Ch. 29:18). The regular daily burnt offering *(ʿōlaṯ hattāmîḏ)* appears 20 times (4 times as *ʿōlaṯ tāmîḏ*).

II. OT.

1. *P.* The distinctive characteristic of the *ʿōlâ* is that the entire animal is consumed by fire; nothing is left for either the person offering the sacrifice or the priest.

a. *The Ritual.* The customary performance of an *ʿōlâ* at the time when P was composed can be described on the basis of Lev. 1. First, the layperson offering the sacrifice brings *(hiqrîḇ)* the animal to be sacrificed. It is noteworthy that in Lev. 1:2 (twice) and 3a the verb *hiqrîḇ* describes what the layperson does, whereas other P texts often use this verb for what the priests do in the sacrificial act. As the next act, the sacrificer places his hand on the head of the victim (1:4). This *sᵉmîḵâ* is mentioned whenever an animal is to be sacrificed. Its meaning is disputed (→ סמך *sāmaḵ*). Gese is probably correct in citing the notion of "identification" by way of explanation.[25] The purpose is not "exclusive substitution," in which the victim is slain as the bearer of sin that has been transferred to it. Instead, "in the cultic atonement the sacrifice of the victim's life is a substitute that includes the one bringing the sacrifice."[26] Since none of the early texts mentions a *sᵉmîḵâ* in connection with an *ʿōlâ,* this act was probably not an original element of the *ʿōlâ* ritual.[27] The third action is the slaying of the sacrificial animal (1:5a,11a), which is slaughtered "before Yahweh" by the sacrificer himself. Several texts mention "the spot where the *ʿōlâ* is slaughtered" (4:24,29,33; 6:18[25]; 7:2; cf. 14:13). It is to be noted that in the ritual of Lev. 1 it is the sacrificer who slaughters the victim, whereas in Ex. 29:16 and Lev. 8:19 Moses, functioning as a priest, takes over the slaughtering; in Lev. 9:12 Aaron slaughters and sacrifices the *ʿōlâ* for himself. In Lev. 14:19 the priest is probably the subject of *šāḥaṭ* (cf. LXX, which adds *ho hiereús*).

---

24. Cf. A. Even-Shoshan, *A New Concordance of the Bible* (Eng. trans. 1985); *TLOT,* II, 885; *HAL,* II, 830.

25. H. Gese, "Atonement"; similarly Janowski, *Sühne,* 219-20.

26. Gese, "Atonement," 106.

27. Rendtorff, 97; more guardedly in *BK* III, 47-48.

Ezk. 44:11 says that the Levites are to slaughter the *ʿōlâ* for the people. The Chronicler's description in 2 Ch. 29:20ff. is not entirely clear. V. 22a does not say explicitly who slaughters the *ʿōlâ*. If the Chronicler had been thinking of the Levites (on the basis of Ezk. 44:11), we would expect that he would not have missed this chance to assign them new functions and rights. It is therefore more likely that the slaughtering was done by the laypeople offering the sacrifice, as in Lev. 1:5,11.

The rituals dependent on Lev. 1 regularly mention the sprinkling (→ זרק *zāraq)* of the blood of the *ʿōlâ* (Ex. 29:16; Lev. 8:19; 9:12). Rendtorff is probably correct in supposing that this sprinkling was not an original element of the *ʿōlâ* ritual; its real purpose was ritually to withhold the blood from human use, a process of particular importance in the case of the *zeḇaḥ* and *šᵉlāmîm,* in which portions of the sacrificial animal were eaten (cf. also Dt. 12:6,23; 15:23, which permit the secular slaughtering of animals so long as the blood is poured on the ground).[28] Whereas the priest clearly sprinkles the blood on the walls around the altar, using a bowl (*mizrāq;* cf. Zec. 9:15), the sacrificer has to remove the skin of the animal himself (but cf. 2 Ch. 29:34); Lev. 7:8 assigns this skin to the priest as a perquisite. The sacrificial tariffs from Carthage make varying provisions on this point. In one text the skin of the victim belongs to the sacrificer; in another the skin is allotted to the priest.[29] For Carthage, therefore, we must envision a variety of regulations applying to different temples or different periods. For Israel, too, we can therefore envision a development of sacrificial practice, with differing regulations and with changes in the individual rituals as time passed. The next act consists in the division of the animal into its natural parts (*nittaḥ,* "carve, cut up," 1:6b).[30] Then the priests are to arrange the sacrificial portions — including the head, which was cut off, and the fat[31] — on the wood piled up on the blazing altar. The sacrificer meanwhile has been engaged in washing the entrails and legs (1:9a), so that nothing unclean will be placed on the altar. Finally, the priest lays these parts, too, on the fire, thus (as v. 9b emphasizes explicitly) making the whole *ʿōlâ* go up in smoke *(hiqṭîr),* an offering of an appeasing odor to Yahweh.

b. *Birds.* The ritual of the bird *ʿōlâ* (Lev. 1:14-17), a later addition, occupies a special place, for 1:2b speaks only of cattle, sheep, and goats. The ritual itself is different: there is no *sᵉmîḵâ* and no separate act of killing; everything is done at the altar, and therefore everything is done by the priest. Lev. 1:15-17 describes the offering: the priest wrings off the bird's head and burns it, drains the blood against the side of the altar, removes the crop with its contents[32] and discards it near the altar, tears the bird open by its wings without severing them, and finally burns the bird on the altar. From 5:7 and 12:8 we learn that a bird *ʿōlâ* represents a concession in case poverty prevents

---

28. *Studien,* 99ff.; *BK* III, 54.

29. For the former see *KAI* 69.4, 6, 8, 10; for the latter, 74.2, 3, 4, 5.

30. Cf. Mish. *Tamid* 4.2.

31. Following Elliger's translation *(Schmer)* of *peḏer,* found only in Lev. 1:8,12; 8:20; *HAL,* III, 914: "suet."

32. H. P. Rüger, "'Dann entfeint er seinen Kropf samt desssen Federn,'" *Wort und Geschichte. FS K. Elliger. AOAT* 18 (1973), 163-72.

the sacrificer from sacrificing a larger animal; a bird *'ōlâ* is thus always a private offering. Lev. 1:14 specifies a turtledove or pigeon. The sacrifice of Noah (Gen. 8:20 [J]) is described expressly as an *'ōlâ* of "every clean bird." Other P texts speak of a bird *'ōlâ* as a purification offering in the context of certain rituals: Lev. 12:8 (a woman who has given birth, if she cannot afford a sheep); 14:22,30-31 (someone cleansed of leprosy, again in case of penury); 15:14-15 (a man made unclean by a discharge of semen); 15:29-30 (a woman made unclean by a discharge of blood); Nu. 6:10-11 (a nazirite made unclean by the sudden death of someone nearby). "Initially a substitute for a more expensive offering (cf. 5:7; 12:8; 14:21-22), during the course of the postexilic period the offering of a pigeon changed from an exception conceded the poor, reflecting the transition from a rural to an urban civilization with its negative consequences, to the rule itself."[33]

c. *Animals Sacrificed.* Rendtorff lists the animals sacrificed.[34] His analysis reveals a pattern in P. Lev. 1 distinguishes two basic groups of domestic animals: herds (cattle) and flocks. The latter are subdivided into sheep and goats. In the calendar of sacrifices in Nu. 28–29, however, the basic animal sacrificed in an *'ōlâ* is a lamb. In the regular morning and evening *'ōlâ,* two lambs a year old are offered (Nu. 28:3ff.; cf. Ex. 29:38); the same is true for the sabbath *'ōlâ.* The combination of bullocks *(pārîm bᵉnê-bāqār),* rams, and lambs (in numbers depending on the occasion) is characteristic of P. It appears, e.g., in the list of the offerings of the twelve tribal chiefs at the dedication of the altar (Nu. 7). Nu. 15, however, which regulates supplementary sacrifices, lists the three groups of animals in a different sequence: lamb, ram, bull (vv. 5ff.). The same animals appear in the new moon offering of the *nāśî'* in Ezk. 46:6: one bull, six lambs, and a ram. But we can also observe a more precise distinction among the sacrificial animals. A lamb is often mentioned in the context of an *'ōlâ* offered by an individual (Lev. 12:6; 14:10; Nu. 6:14), a ram appears in the *'ōlâ* of the priests (Ex. 29:15ff. = Lev. 8:18ff.; 9:2; 16:3), and a bull is offered in an *'ōlâ* for the whole community (Nu. 15:24).

There are exceptions to this pattern: in Lev. 9:3 an *'ēgel* and a *keḇeś* are offered in an *'ōlâ* of the Israelites, in Lev. 16:5 a ram is offered for the whole community, and in Nu. 8:8 a bull is offered as an *'ōlâ* for the Levites. There are also exceptions in Ezk. 40ff.: in 46:4 six lambs and a ram are required for the sabbath offering of the *nāśî';* in 43:23 and 45:23 there is an *'ōlâ* of bulls and rams.

The earlier texts agree with P in always specifying domestic animals, with the possible exception of the comprehensive language in Gen. 8:20. Many texts give the impression that an *'ōlâ* could involve whatever animals were available, such as suckling calves (*pārôṯ 'ālôṯ:* 1 S. 6:10,14), oxen (2 S. 24:22), or sheep, goats, and oxen (Ex. 20:24). Bullocks *(par)* are mentioned with some frequency (Jgs. 6:26; 1 S. 6:14 [fem.]; 1 K. 18:30ff.; Ps. 50:9 [cf. Gen. 22:13]). We also find rams (*'ayil,* Isa. 1:11), bullocks and rams together (*par* and *'ayil,* Nu. 23:1-2,14,29-30; Job 42:8), calves (*'ēgel,* Mic. 6:6), sheep (*śeh,* Gen. 22:7-8; Isa. 43:23), suckling lambs (*ṭᵉlēh ḥālāḇ,* 1 S. 7:9), and

33. K. Elliger, *Leviticus. HAT* I/4 (1966), 37; cf. Mk. 11:15-16 and Mish. *Qinnim.*
34. *Studien,* 115-18.

kids (*gᵉḏî 'izzîm,* Jgs. 13:15). Ps. 66:15 lists fatlings *(mēḥîm),* rams *('êlîm),* bulls *(bāqār),* and goats *('attûḏîm).* "It would appear impossible to draw any conclusions from these disparate texts concerning the animals customarily offered or even stipulated for an *'ōlâ,*" although it may be that "there were specific regulations stipulating the animals to be offered in the regular sacrifices at the individual sanctuaries."[35]

d. *Daily 'ōlāh.* According to the regulations of P (Nu. 28:3-8; Ex. 29:38-42; cf. also Lev. 6:2), two male lambs a year old are to be sacrificed every day as a regular burnt offering; Nu. 28:3 requires them to be without blemish. One is sacrificed in the morning, the other at twilight. Nu. 28:6 calls this regular offering *'ōlaṯ tāmîḏ.* The passages that follow dealing with the festival sacrifices (Nu. 28:10,15,24,31; 29:6,11,16,19,22,25, 28,31,34,38) emphasize that they are additional to the *'ōlaṯ hattāmîḏ.* The only exception is the formulation in Nu. 28:23, which states that the sacrifice on the first day of the Feast of Unleavened Bread is additional to the morning *'ōlâ ('ōlaṯ habbōqer);* this morning *'ōlâ* is qualified by the addition *'ᵃšer lᵉ'ōlaṯ hattāmîḏ.* We may therefore conclude that *'ōlaṯ habbōqer* is the earlier expression.

In 1 K. 18:29,36, the hour of an offering is referred to twice: "the time of the offering of the grain offering *(→ minḥâ)*"; v. 29 adds "as midday passed." The use of → מנחה *minḥâ* to designate the evening sacrifice — as is still the practice today in the afternoon prayer of the synagogue, which takes place at the ninth hour (3 p.m.)[36] — reveals a practice earlier than that documented by P: the evening sacrifice was not a lamb but a bloodless offering. This earlier practice appears also in the liturgical measures of King Ahaz (2 K. 16:10-28): in addition to all the other sacrifices, the king commands the priest Uriah to offer on the new altar the "morning burnt offering" *('ōlaṯ habbōqer)* and the "evening grain offering" *(minḥaṯ hā'ereḇ).*

In Ezekiel, too, in an appendix to the regulations governing the sacrifices offered by the *nāśî'* (46:13-15), we find instructions for the daily sacrifices. Here a single yearling lamb without blemish is to be offered as an *'ōlâ* "morning by morning." Only in the postexilic period is there evidence for the daily morning and evening sacrifices required by P (1 Ch. 16:40; 2 Ch. 13:11; esp. Ezr. 3:3). That in a period of economic distress the offerings given to God were not reduced from what they had been but were rather increased, as Ezr. 3:3 attests, illustrates the devotion of the returning exiles. This devotion left its mark on the sacrificial cult. The "evening *minḥâ*" nevertheless continued to be used to designate the time of day: Ezra speaks his penitential prayer at the time of the evening *minḥâ* (9:5), and the angel Gabriel appears to Daniel at this hour (Dnl. 9:21); cf. also Jdt. 9:1. This usage shows that the old terminology was preserved even when the bloody evening sacrifice had long since been introduced.

e. *Special Occasions.* In addition to the daily *'ōlâ,* the regulations governing festival sacrifice in Nu. 28–29 stipulate that the *'ōlâ* is the fundamental festival sacrifice for sabbath and new moon as well as for all the following festivals.[37] The *'ōlâ* appears to

35. Ibid., 117.
36. Mish. *Pesaḥim* 5.1; cf. Acts 3:1; 10:3,30.
37. Rendtorff, *Studien,* 77.

be a secondary interpolation in the purity laws of Lev. 11–15. Nu. 15:22-26 shows that in case of an unwitting transgression the whole community must sacrifice a bullock as an *'ōlâ.*[38] It is reasonable to suppose "that originally Nu. 15:22-26 spoke of the *'ōlâ* in the context of a public confession of sin, perhaps in the setting of a communal lament."[39] Such a rite may also be suggested by Jgs. 20:26; 21:2-4; 1 S. 7:6,9-10; Jer. 14:12. In the story of the judgment between Yahweh and Baal on Mt. Carmel (1 K. 18:30ff.), the *'ōlâ* appears as a sacrifice to Yahweh pure and simple.

2. *Outside P.* Josh. 22:10ff. reveals that there was "a separate Gileadite cult of Yahweh at Gilgal, specifically at the Gileadite altar of Gilgal," where sacrifice was offered with *'ōlôṯ, zᵉḇāḥîm,* and *šᵉlāmîm.*[40] The Israelite majority to the west considered this cult apostasy from the cult of Israel. Finally, in a "reinterpretation of the traditio-historically late form of Josh. 22:10ff.," it was construed as being no longer practiced, serving as nothing more than a sign and witness to the fact that the Gileadites adhered to Yahwism.[41]

In a perceptive analysis of the sacrifices offered by Gideon (Jgs. 6) and Manoah (Jgs. 13), Rost has succeeded in demonstrating that here what was originally an offering of food for the deity has been turned into an *'ōlâ.*[42] These two narratives show that introduction of the burnt offering in the time of the judges was a decisive step in the history of Israel's religion. It is significant that both texts speak of a rock as the locus of the sacrifice and that no priest is needed. "Neither Gideon nor Manoah was the ancestral founder of a priesthood; they were and continued to be laypersons."[43] The transformation of Gideon's and Manoah's offering of food into an *'ōlâ* may be viewed as an etiology of this sacrifice. At the same time, the two texts reveal that it was only after the Israelites had settled in Canaan that they came to know the *'ōlâ* as a form of sacrifice and adopted this Canaanite practice.

Several OT passages mention an *'ōlâ* offered not to Yahweh but to Baal. Already Gideon's action in Jgs. 6:25ff. reveals clearly that Gideon's father Joash was the custodian of a Baal sanctuary, where sacrifice was probably offered in the form of an *'ōlâ.* Naaman, too, offered burnt offerings and sacrifices to other gods (2 K. 5:17). In the scene on Carmel in 1 K. 18, the burnt offering of the prophets of Baal and that of Elijah are prepared in the same way. The meaning of the story requires this to have been the regular form of a sacrifice to Baal. The episode of the temple of Baal in 2 K. 10:18-27 also presupposes that Jehu follows the Canaanite ritual, including sacrifices and burnt offerings (*zᵉḇāḥîm wᵉ'ōlôṯ,* v. 24; cf. also Jer. 19:5; 2 K. 3:27).

---

38. D. Kellermann, "Bemerkungen zum Sündopfergesetz in Num 15,22ff.," *FS Elliger,* 107-13.

39. Rendtorff, 83.

40. H. Gese, "Jakob und Mose," *Tradition and Re-Interpretation in Jewish and Early Christian Literature. FS J. C. H. Lebram* (1986), 38-47, quotation: 45.

41. For a different interpretation see J. S. Kloppenborg, *Bibl* 62 (1981) 347-71.

42. *Studien,* 17ff.

43. Ibid., 27.

3. *Prophetic Polemic against the Cult.* Apart from Ezk. 40ff., when the prophetic books mention the *'ōlâ,* usually in conjunction with other forms of sacrifice, the message is polemical in nature. It is probably safe to say that, despite all the bitter polemic, the prophets never in principle rejected the cult itself and its sacrifices; they condemned either perversions of conduct or a mistaken interpretation ("the more the better") with its resulting false sense of security. It is noteworthy that such texts always mention the *'ōlâ;* as the most important form of sacrifice, it appears either alone (Mic. 6:6; Jer. 19:5; Isa. 40:16, which says that all the animals of Lebanon would not be enough for an *'ōlâ* of Yahweh) or in conjunction with other forms (Isa. 1:11; Hos. 6:6; Jer. 6:20; 7:21-22; 17:26; Isa. 43:23).

In Am. 5:22 Wolff deletes v. 22aα as a gloss, interpreting *minḥâ* not as "grain offering" but as an inclusive term for "offering."[44] Rudolph is probably correct, however, in assuming that something has been lost from the text, so that here too in Amos's polemic the *'ōlâ* appears first as the most important form of sacrifice.[45]

4. *Ezekiel.* In Ezekiel's blueprint for a restored Israel (Ezk. 40–48),[46] a secondary section mentions a vestibule in which the burnt offering is washed *(dwḥ)* and tables on which the animals are slaughtered (40:38,39,42). At the consecration of the altar (43:18-27), the sin offering is followed by the offering of a bull without blemish and a ram without blemish as an *'ōlâ* (vv. 23-24); here the sin offering already comes first. According to 44:11, the Levites are to take over the function of slaughtering the burnt offerings for the people as part of their ministry. But this expansion of the Levites' functions clearly remained theoretical. The ancient practice of having the sacrificer slaughter the sacrificial animal (1 S. 14:32-35) could not be supplanted. Lev. 1:5a, too, has the sacrificer slaughter the victim.[47] The section Ezk. 45:10-17 deals with accurate weights and measures and amounts to be offered. In contrast to 44:30a and Nu. 18, the rule for the *t^erûmâ* of grain, oil, and flocks (sheep and goats) is not based on a tithe; in the case of flocks, e.g., one animal is to be offered from a flock of two hundred. It is unusual that the *minḥâ* precedes the *'ōlâ* in vv. 15,17. The major festivals and the offerings of the *nāśî'* are treated in 45:18-25. In addition to the other offerings, every day during the seven days of Passover and the Feast of Unleavened Bread the *nāśî'* is required to offer a burnt offering of seven bulls and seven rams. Here too the sin offering comes first, followed by the *'ōlâ,* the *minḥâ,* and the offering of oil. The same sequence appears in the observance of the autumn festival (45:25). The personal sacrifices offered by the *nāśî'* are the subject of 46:1-12. According to v. 2, his sabbath offering is to be an *'ōlâ* and a *š^elāmîm* offering. The *š^elāmîm* offering is not mentioned in the detailed explication in vv. 4-5; instead, the *minḥâ* appears in conjunction with the *'ōlâ.* The same is true in the description of the new moon offering in vv. 6-7. Both *'ōlâ* and *š^elāmîm* are mentioned in the so-called east gate tradition.

44. H. W. Wolff, *Joel and Amos. Herm* (Eng. trans. 1977), 259 note c.
45. W. Rudolph, *Joel-Amos-Obadja-Jona. KAT* XIII/2 (1971), 206.
46. Analyzed by Gese, *Der Verfassungsentwurt des Ezechiel. BHT* 25 (1957).
47. For the later period see Josephus *Ant.* 3.9.1 §§224-27; Mish. *Zebaḥim* 3.1.

5. *Psalms.* Only five psalms mention the *ʿōlâ,* two twice: 20:4(3); 40:7(6); 50:8; 51:18,21(16,19); 66:13,15. In 51:21(19) *ʿōlâ* and *kālîl* appear together, in that order; both constitute an explanatory gloss, not an organic part of vv. 20-21(18-19), themselves a secondary appendix to the psalm. Ps. 66:15 speaks of *ʿōlôṯ mēḥîm,* burnt offerings of fatlings; in 20:4(3) the psalmist prays that Yahweh will declare his burnt offering fat *(diššēn)* — emphasizing that in this case Malachi's reproof (1:7-8) concerning the offering of inferior animals does not apply.[48] While Ps. 20:4(3) prays for gracious acceptance of grain offerings and burnt offerings (probably offered by the king), 40:7(6) and 51:18(16) polemicize in the manner of the prophets against a misconstrued sacrificial cult. Ps. 50:8 also belongs here: Yahweh, lord of the universe, does not need to be "nourished." The rarity of *ʿōlâ* in the Psalms shows clearly that "not only are the Psalms meant for laypeople, they are also an expression of lay spirituality."[49]

6. *Chronicler's History.* The Chronicler's History often expands or modifies material from earlier sources dealing with sacrifice, and also supplies additional information about sacrifice. The *ʿōlâ* is the sacrifice mentioned most often. In 1 Ch. 16:1-2, e.g., the account of the *ʿōlôṯ* and *šᵉlāmîm* offered when the ark was brought to Jerusalem is incorporated from 2 S. 6:17-18. Echoing 2 S. 24:22-25, 1 Ch. 21:23-26 speaks of the sacrifices offered by David at the threshing floor of Araunah. It is noteworthy that v. 23 adds "wheat for a *minḥâ,*" thus assimilating the tradition of P, which regularly associates the *minḥâ* with the *ʿōlâ.* Solomon's cultic observance in 2 Ch. 8:12-13 expands substantially on 1 K. 9:25 (see II.7 below). Independently of any earlier source, 1 Ch. 16:39-40 records that David appointed Zadok and his kindred — i.e., the rightful priests of the later temple — to offer the daily morning and evening sacrifices (again reflecting Nu. 28:3ff. and Ex. 29:38ff.). The function of the Levites in the regular *ʿōlâ* is stressed in 1 Ch. 23:31, and 2 Ch. 13:10-11 emphasizes that it is the duty of priests and Levites to offer the *ʿōlâ* every morning and evening. According to 2 Ch. 23:18, Jehoiada restored to the priests their ancient function in offering the *ʿōlâ.* The description of Hezekiah's cultic reforms mentions the *ḥaṭṭāʾṯ,* but the primary emphasis is on the *ʿōlâ* (2 Ch. 29:21-24,27-29,31-35; in v. 21 *lᵉʿōlâ* should be added, as v. 24 shows; see *BHS*). Ezr. 3:2-3 reports that the priests began their sacrificial ministry once more after the altar of burnt offering was rebuilt in Jerusalem. Besides freewill offerings, the text speaks only of *ʿōlôṯ.* In 2 Ch. 2:3(4) (expanding on 1 K. 5:19), we read that the planned temple will serve primarily for the offering of *ʿōlôṯ.* In 2 Ch. 24:14 we are told that during the lifetime of the priest Jehoiada the *ʿōlâ* was offered regularly; in 2 Ch. 29:7 Hezekiah reproaches the ancestors for failing to offer incense and burnt offerings in the temple. These texts show that for the author(s) the *ʿōlâ* was the all-important sacrifice; its offering could represent the whole sacrificial cult. The Chronicler's History clearly displays a great interest in the *ʿōlâ.*

The use of the word *ʿōlâ* in 2 Ch. 35:12,14,16 is hard to explain. The text recounts

---

48. Rost, "Psalmenproblem," 245.
49. Ibid., 246.

Josiah's Passover observance. V. 11 mentions the slaughtering of the Passover animals; *hā'ōlâ* in v. 12 cannot refer to living animals intended for a burnt offering, distinct from the Passover animals. Furthermore, nowhere else in the OT are burnt offerings mentioned in connection with Passover. Rudolph is therefore probably correct in viewing this as a unique usage: *hā'ōlâ* denotes "the portions to be burnt, i.e., as v. 14 notes correctly, the fat parts of the Passover animals."[50]

7. *The King's 'ōlâ.* According to 1 K. 9:25, Solomon offered up *'ōlôṯ* and *šᵉlāmîm* three times a year. The number three clearly refers to the three annual festivals (cf. Ex. 23:14-17): the Feast of Unleavened Bread (Passover), the Feast of Weeks, and the Feast of Booths. Now they are celebrated in the Jerusalem temple as well. These offerings are probably not the general festival sacrifices but special additional sacrifices offered by the king.

According to 1 K. 10:5, the queen of Sheba marveled at the burnt offerings Solomon offered in the temple. The parallel text 2 Ch. 9:4 says that the queen was left breathless when she saw the various manifestations of Solomon's magnificence, including (strangely) "his upper chamber" *('ᵃlîyāṯô)* to which he went up in the house of Yahweh. This may recall 2 Ch. 3:9, which speaks of upper chambers of the temple overlaid with gold. The LXX, Syr., and Vulg. harmonize the text with 1 K. 10:5, seeing here too a reference to Solomon's burnt offerings that evoke the queen's wonderment. It was probably, however, neither burnt offerings nor an upper chamber that impressed the queen, but rather the king's procession from the palace to the temple. The noun should be pointed as *'ᵃlôṯô* (qal inf. with suf.), or else the MT pointing is to be explained after the analogy of Modern Heb. *'ᵃlîyâ,* "ascent." It is reasonably certain that both 1 K. 10:5 and 2 Ch. 9:4 speak of Solomon's procession, not his burnt offerings or upper chamber.

That the king offered sacrifice can also be inferred from 2 K. 16:15: the burnt offering of the king (*'ōlaṯ hammeleḵ;* only here in the OT) is to be offered on the altar that Ahaz ordered built after the model of the altar at Damascus. An offering of the king is mentioned also in 2 S. 6 and 1 K. 8 (v. 5 and vv. 62-64, a secondary addition). David offers sacrifices in 2 S. 24:25. A survival of the tradition of royal sacrifice can be seen in the regulations governing the offerings of the *nāśî'* in Ezk. 45-46. The Chronicler, too, frequently emphasizes the king's responsibility for sacrifices. 2 Ch. 8:12ff. elaborates considerably on 1 K. 9:25. The latter passage mentions only the three great annual festivals, while the former, following P (Nu. 28–29), includes the sabbath and new moon offerings. Surprisingly, only *'ōlôṯ* are mentioned (2 Ch. 8:12). Rudolph maintains that the daily offerings are not mentioned, but this is not true: the expression *ûḇiḏḇar yôm bᵉyôm* in v. 13 should be translated "according to the precepts governing each day," as noted by Rendtorff.[51] One may also cite 2 Ch. 29:20ff. and 31:3, which stress that Hezekiah — clearly as a new Solomon — contributed to the regular burnt offerings from his own wealth. In all these passages it is difficult to say whether the

---

50. *Chonikbüchern. HAT* I/21 (1955), 327.
51. Rudolph, *HAT,* I/21, 221; Rendtorff, *Studien,* 80.

king was exercising the religious privileges of the head of a family, inherited from the distant past, or was claiming his rights on the basis of a Near Eastern ideology of royal priesthood.

8. *Human Sacrifice.* Students of comparative religion have a theory that the sacrificial animal is a substitute for a human being, concluding that humans were originally sacrificed.[52] One cannot deny that some OT texts speak of human sacrifice as an *'ōlâ* (Jgs. 11:30-40, Jephthah's daughter; Jer. 7:31, children of both sexes sacrificed to Yahweh at Topheth in the valley of Hinnom). Jer. 7:31 does not use the word *'ōlâ,* but *liśrōp̄ bā'ēš* suggests a burnt offering; the connection is strengthened by the fact that *šrp* is the Ugaritic equivalent of *'ōlâ.* Jer. 19:5 speaks of children sacrificed as *'ōlôṯ* to Baal (cf. Ps. 106:38). The sacrifice of the Moabite king's only son as a burnt offering (2 K. 3:27) must be considered exceptional, an act of desperation. Gese has shown that it is out of the question that the idea behind the commandment to redeem every firstborn male could ever have led to a general practice of sacrificing firstborn children in Israel. The sacrifice of firstborn animals, however, could take the form of an *'ōlâ:* "the firstborn, whose return is required by God, could in fact be considered the primary element of the *'ōlâ* sacrifice."[53] The story of Abraham's sacrifice, in which Isaac, intended as an *'ōlâ,* is replaced by a ram, could be an etiological narrative explaining and justifying the substitution of an animal for a human sacrifice. "The author of Gen. 22 was never in doubt that God could require it of a human being; but he was convinced that God does not demand it as a human act."[54]

9. *Altar of Burnt Offering.* A special characteristic of the *'ōlâ* is its close association with "altar." Narrative texts frequently describe the building of an altar and the offering of an *'ōlâ* (Gen. 8:20; Nu. 23:1-2,14,29-30; Jgs. 6:26; 2 S. 24:25; cf. also Gen. 22:9). Legal texts likewise often mention *'ōlâ* and altar together (Ex. 20:24; Dt. 27:5-7; Josh. 8:30-31; also Dt. 12:27a). The combination is not unknown to P. According to Ex. 29:38ff., the essential purpose of the altar appears to be the offering of the *'ōlâ* (cf. Ex. 28:43; Lev. 6:5). The point is even clearer in Ezk. 43:18ff. It is therefore not surprising that the phrase *mizbaḥ hā'ōlâ* should occur 19 times. Remarkably, the account of Solomon's building of the temple does not go into detail concerning the altar of burnt offering, nor do postexilic texts. Neither is it possible to reconstruct the altar built by Ahaz (2 K. 16:10ff.). Attempts to draw conclusions concerning the altar of the Solomonic temple or that of the postexilic period from the description of the altar in Ezk. 43:13-27 are hardly justifiable.[55]

The description of the altar of burnt offering in Ex. 27:1-8 and 38:1-7 shows that it was made of acacia wood. The boards were covered with bronze (*mizbaḥ hannᵉḥōšeṯ,* 38:30;

---

52. Kaiser; Gese, "Ezechiel 20,25f."

53. Gese, "Ezechiel 20,25f.," 148.

54. Kaiser, 48 (= 166).

55. T. A. Busink, *Der Tempel von Jerusalem,* II (1980), 730-36; W. Zimmerli, *Ezekiel 2. Herm* (Eng. trans. 1983), 423-28.

39:39); the mention of a bronze grating *(miḵbar hannᵉḥōšeṯ)* might suggest a large gridiron or grill on which the offering was burned (cf. 1 K. 8:64; 2 K. 16:15, which also mention a movable bronze altar that could be put in a new location [2 K. 16:14]). Perhaps the description of this altar in 1 K. 6–7 was suppressed on the grounds that it was alien to the law and customs of Israel (cf. Ex. 20:24ff.), although such an altar was a standard feature of the Syro-Phoenician cult, as two Phoenician-Punic inscriptions show.[56] The Chronicler supplied the omission, ascribing to Solomon the building of a bronze altar (2 Ch. 4:1). When Ahaz had Uriah build an altar of burnt offering in Jerusalem analogous to the one in Damascus, the old bronze altar was moved to the north side of this new altar (2 K. 16:14). Whether there had been an earlier altar of burnt offering made of stones or earth within the temple precincts of Jerusalem we do not know.

10. *Problematic Texts.* The form *ʿōlâ,* the qal fem. act. ptcp. of *ʿālâ,* "go up," is identical to the noun *ʿōlâ;* it occurs 16 times in the OT (Jgs. 20:31; 21:19; 1 K. 18:44; Eccl. 3:21; Cant. 3:6 = 8:5; Ezk. 20:32; Dnl. 8:3; 1 Ch. 26:16 [see below]). The pl. *ʿōlōṯ* occurs only in Gen. 41:2,3,5,18,19,22,27.

The pointing of certain other forms would allow derivation from *ʿōlâ* if the context did not rule it out. In Isa. 61:8 *ʿôlâ* should be vocalized as *ʿawlâ* (cf. 59:3), with the translation "I hate wicked robbery." This interpretation is supported by the ancient versions with the exception of the Vulg.; following Bab. *Sukka* 30a and Rashi, where MT *ʿôlâ* is defended, Jerome translates: *ripam in holocausto.* In Job 5:16 *ʿawlāṯâ,* "wickedness," has been monophthongized to *ʿôlāṯâ.* In Ps. 92:16(15), similarly, the *Ketib (ʿlth)* is explained by the *Qere (ʿawlāṯâ).* In Ps. 58:3(2) and 64:7(6), *ʿôlōṯ* is the pl. of *ʿawlâ* and therefore has nothing to do with burnt offerings.

In Ezk. 40:26 the *Qere* is *ûmaʿᵃlôṯ šiḇʿâ ʿōlôṯāyw;* the *Ketib ʿlwtw* is unusual, as is the feminine form of the numeral. The form *ʿlwtw* can be interpreted as either an infinitive or a participle *(Q).*[57] But most likely we are dealing with a simple scribal error: *h* has been written for *m,* and the correct reading should be *šbʿ mʿlwtyw.* Like the east gate in 40:22, the south gate is reached by "seven steps."[58]

Only Lisowsky includes the form *ʿōlâ* in 1 Ch. 26:16 under "burnt offering." It is conceivable that there was a special road along which sacrificial animals were brought to the temple. The usual translation "on the ascending road" is preferable, however, since no other text mentions a "burnt offering road."

For a discussion of 2 Ch. 9:4, see II.7 above.

11. *Apocrypha.* The books of the Apocrypha rarely mention burnt offerings (Gk. *holokaútōma* or *holokaútōsis*). According to Bar. 1:10, the exiles send money to buy burnt offerings, sin offerings, incense, and grain offerings. This obviously reflects a desire to participate at least indirectly in the cult and share in its blessings. Jdt. 16:18 says

---

56. *KAI* 10.4; 66.1; → VIII, 219.

57. P. Wernberg-Møller, *ZAW* 71 (1959) 57.

58. Zimmerli, *Ezekiel 2,* 340.

that after their victory the people offered burnt offerings in Jerusalem, although Judith herself finds fear of the Lord more important than any offering or the fat of any whole burnt offering (v. 16). We may note also Wis. 3:6 (the righteous are accepted like a burnt offering) and Sir. 45:16 (Aaron was chosen to offer the daily sacrifice).

Some references to burnt offerings appear in Maccabees. In 1 Mc. 1:45 Antiochus IV Epiphanes forbids burnt offerings, sacrifices, and drink offerings in the temple, thus profaning all festivals. In 4:44ff. we read how Judas Maccabeus and his brothers tore down the profaned altar of burnt offering and stored the stones on the temple hill "until a prophet should come to tell what to do with them." Then they build a new altar like the former one out of unhewn stones (v. 47; cf. Ex. 20:25). The dedication of the altar lasted eight days and was celebrated joyfully with burnt offerings. In 2 Mc. 2:9 the situation is raised to the level of the miraculous. After the victories in Galilee and Gilead, too, the people offered burnt offerings in thanksgiving that no one had fallen in battle (1 Mc. 5:54). According to 2 Mc. 4:41, the ashes of the burnt offerings were used (together with blocks of wood and stones) as a weapon against the forces of Lysimachus who were despoiling the temple.

12. *Origin and Meaning.* "It is out of the question — and, we may add, in spite of the reference to Jethro the priest [Ex. 18:12] — that the Israelites became acquainted with the burnt offering in the wilderness period."[59] To all appearances, the Israelites borrowed the burnt offering from the Canaanites. This is suggested not only by the story of Gideon's sacrifice (Jgs. 6)[60] but also by 1 K. 18, which describes the prophets of Baal and Elijah as preparing the burnt offering in the same manner. The slaughter of the priests of Baal by Jehu (2 K. 10:18-27) also presupposes that Jehu was following the Canaanite ritual when he offered sacrifices and burnt offerings (v. 24). As the term *'ōlâ* shows, the Canaanites probably borrowed this type of sacrifice from a population group south of the Taurus; for the word appears to go back to a people antedating both Greeks and Semites.[61] The *'ōlâ,* a sacrifice in which the offering is totally consumed by fire, might have originated in a culture that cremated the dead. In Greece the evidence indicates that a sacrifice like the *'ōlâ* was offered only to chthonic deities; it could therefore have originated as a vicarious sacrifice on behalf of someone near death, whose deliverance the offering of an *'ōlâ* was hoped to effect. But when the Canaanites and subsequently the Israelites adopted this type of sacrifice, its original meaning had been long forgotten.[62] Ugarit probably mediated the borrowing.

The image of the *'ōlâ* remains remarkably constant throughout all stages of the OT tradition. In all periods it is a sacrifice burned in its entirety on the altar; this burning was the essential element of the ritual.[63] It is difficult to define precisely the meaning

---

59. Rost, *Studien,* 66.
60. Ibid., 17ff.
61. See I.1 above, and L. Rost's discussions: "Erwägungen," 116 = 180-81; *BHHW,* 1345-46; "Fragen," 378ff.; also Janowski, "Erwägungen," 250-51.
62. Rost, *BHHW,* 1350.
63. Rendtorff, *Studien,* 235.

and significance of sacrifice, especially the *ʿōlâ,* in the OT: although the OT contains detailed instructions for offering the various sacrifices, there are no explicit explanations of how they were understood. Furthermore, the prayers, hymns, and recitations (cf. 2 Ch. 29:25ff., where v. 27 says: "When the burnt offering began, the song in honor of Yahweh began also") associated with the sacrifices are no longer preserved in their original context.

The OT preserves remnants of the notion of nourishing the deity by offerings of food (and drink). For example, Ezk. 44:7 puts the term *laḥmî,* "my food," into Yahweh's mouth to describe the offerings in the temple. The word is used in the same sense in Nu. 28:2, at the beginning of the sacrificial calendar.[64] The sacrifices offered by Gideon and Manoah in Jgs. 6 and 13 also show that there was nothing strange about the notion of offering food to the deity.[65] Only Hos. 13:8, however, speaks anthropomorphically of Yahweh's eating. Other gods devour sacrifices (Dt. 32:38; cf. vv. 27-28 of the debunking Letter of Jeremiah), but Ps. 50:12-13 rejects the notion of appeasing Yahweh's hunger (cf. also Isa. 40:16).

When a sacrifice is consumed by burning, it is "transfer[red] by fire into the sphere of *pneuma,* which was conceived as immaterial";[66] the notion of feeding is excluded (cf. Jgs. 13:16). Since everything we possess comes from God, it is only meet and right to "render tribute to God, as a subject pays tribute to his king, or a tenant to his landowner."[67] In a certain sense, every sacrifice has the nature of a gift or offering. Lev. 1:2 refers to the *ʿōlâ* as *qorbān lᵉyhwh,* showing clearly that the sacrifice was considered an offering to Yahweh.

It is noteworthy "that in P not only do the sin offerings bring atonement but all sacrifices do. The whole sacrificial system serves to atone and finds its meaning in the atoning function of sacrifice itself."[68] The offering of the *ʿōlâ* makes atonement for Israel, its representatives, the individual, and the sanctuary.[69] That the *ʿōlâ* in particular serves the purpose of atonement is shown by the translation of Lev. 6:2(9) in Targ.ᴶ: the burnt offering is intended to atone for a sinful nature. As the Targ. says, an *ʿōlâ* can atone not just for trespasses, not just for wicked plans never carried out (cf. Job 1:5, which says that after every feast Job offered burnt offerings according the number of his children, thinking "It may be that my children have sinned and cursed God in their hearts"), but for the very disposition that fails to satisfy the demands of Yahweh.

III. 1. *Elephantine.* As is well known, the Jewish military colony of Elephantine (probably established in the 6th century B.C.E.) built a temple for Yahweh. Probably in 410 B.C.E., at the urging of the Egyptian priests of the god Khnum, the Egyptians succeeded in destroying the temple of YHW. The Jews thereupon turned to their homeland

64. W. Herrmann, *ZAW* 72 (1960) 205-16, esp. 213; → VII, 521-29.
65. Rost, *Studien,* 17ff.
66. Gese, "Atonement," 101.
67. De Vaux, *AncIsr,* II, 451.
68. Gese, "Atonement," 103.
69. Janowski, *Sühne,* 190ff.

and asked for help. In the first letter detailing their grievances,[70] ll. 13-14 report that the Egyptian priests refuse to allow the Jews to offer grain offerings, incense, and burnt offerings (*mnḥh wlbwnh w'lwh* [in part reconstructed]). A later letter,[71] addressed to Bagohi, the governor of Judah, requests his intervention on behalf of the Jews of Elephantine; l. 19 of this letter states that a first letter (possibly *AP* 27) has gone unanswered and that the community has observed the rites of mourning and has ceased to offer "grain offerings and incense offerings and burnt offerings" in that temple. If the governor should grant permission to have the temple rebuilt, then the community would offer grain offerings and incense offerings and burnt offerings on the altar of the god YHW in the name of the governor as before (l. 25). To bring more pressure to bear, the letter advances the argument that with such permission the governor would gain merit, "more than one who offers him [YHW] burnt offerings and sacrifices worth thousands of talents" (l. 28). The brief reply contains permission to rebuild the temple "and to offer grain offerings and incense offerings upon that altar, as was previously the custom."[72] Yet another letter says (obviously with sagacious insight) that after restoration of the temple "[only] incense offerings and grain offerings . . . but not sheep, cattle, and goats as burnt offerings *(mqlw)* may be offered."[73]

In summary, we can say that the Jews of Elephantine offered burnt offerings *('lwh, mqlw)* to Yahweh, consisting of sheep, cattle, and goats (if that is the correct translation of *qn twr 'nz*).[74] The sequence *mnḥh–lbwnh–'lwh*[75] may indicate that the *'ōlâ* was no longer considered the most important form of sacrifice. Above all, the restriction of the offerings to *minḥāh* and incense after the rebuilding of the temple illustrates respect for the Egyptians and the cult of their god Khnum.[76] At the same time, from the perspective of Jerusalem it was a good opportunity to restrict the sacrificial cult of Elephantine: if bloody sacrifice could no longer be offered, no one could speak of competition with the universal sacrificial cult of the Jerusalem sanctuary.

2. *LXX.* The LXX translators faced a problem in finding an equivalent for *'ōlâ,* because in Greek sacrificial practice the burning of an entire animal was an annihilating sacrifice reserved for chthonic deities in the cult of the dead. The translators therefore could not make use of an existing Greek word.[77] The closest equivalent to Heb. *'ōlâ* as a sacrifice in which the entire animal is consumed would be *enagismós* or *enágisma,* "offering to the dead."[78] An etymological solution would have to have taken as its starting point the verb *'ālâ* (qal, hiphil/hophal), often rendered in the LXX by forms of the

70. *AP* 27.
71. *AP* 30, duplicate *AP* 31.
72. *AP* 32.
73. *AP* 33. On *mqlw* see I.1 above.
74. *AP* 33:10.
75. *AP* 30:2.
76. *AP* 33:9.
77. Yerkes, 201.
78. J. Casabona, *Recherches sur le vocabulaire des sacrifices en grec des origines à la fin de l'époque classique* (1967), 206.

verb *anaphérein.* In fact, the noun *anaphorá* is used (albeit only once) to translate *ʿōlâ* or *kālîl* in Ps. 51:21(19).[79] The usual LXX translations of *ʿōlâ, holokárpōma,* "that which is offered," *holokaútōsis,* "total burning," or (more rarely) *holokárpōsis,* "total offering," or *holokaútōma,* "that which is burned totally," are neologisms that successfully convey the meaning of *ʿōlâ;* the homophonic beginning of all four makes this approach especially convincing.

Most of the biblical books use *holokárpōma* and *holokaútōsis* promiscuously, without any apparent distinction; in some texts, however, the LXX goes its own way. In Ex. 10:25 and Josh. 23:23, the order of sacrifices is changed without apparent reason. Daniel has shown, however, that there is a meaningful explanation for the different translations of *ʿōlâ* in the Balaam story — *thysía* in Nu. 23:3 (twice, once in an LXX addition to MT) and 23:15, but *holokautōmata* in 23:6 and *holokaútōsis* in 23:17.[80] When Balaam is speaking with Balak, the king of Moab, the translators place in his mouth a common word for "offering"; outside direct discourse, they use the normal translations *holokaútōma* and *holokaútōsis.* In the book of Job the word *ʿōlâ* occurs only twice: once at the beginning (1:5) and once at the end (42:8). When the LXX translates *ʿōlâ* with *thysía* in 1:5, this might indicate that the reader is being offered a familiar word; it might also reflect the fact that Job and his friends are not Israelites and do not live in the Israelite heartland.[81]

Jerome, borrowing from the LXX, uses *holocaustum,* an apt neologism.

3. *Dead Sea Scrolls.* The word *ʿōlâ* appears 4 times in the Dead Sea Scrolls (1QS 9:4; 1QM 2:5; CD 11:18,19); there are also 2 occurrences in 1QapGen (21:2,20) and 58 in the Temple Scroll (including Yadin's reconstructions). In 1QS 9:4 righteousness and upright conduct are contrasted with the flesh of burnt offerings and the fat of sacrifices. This passage does not, however, suggest a fundamental hostility to sacrifice, but rather the substitution of life in the Qumran community for sacrifice.[82] The eschatological ordinances in 1QM 2:5 call on the whole community to assemble for burnt offering and sacrifice, that atonement may be made for the community, thus underlining that the Qumran community was not hostile in principle to the cult. On the basis of Lev. 23:38, CD 11:18 stipulates that on the sabbath no sacrifice may be offered on the altar other than the sabbath burnt offering; 11:19 adds that no one who is unclean may bring burnt offerings, grain offerings, incense, or wood to the altar. Here, as in the LXX and Vulg. translations of Lev. 23:38, *mlbd* appears to be understood as being exclusive, so that even festival sacrifices may not be offered when they fall on the sabbath. The two precepts appear to presuppose that the members of the community were still participating in the Jerusalem cult, at least to the extent of

---

79. For an explanation of this translation, see S. Daniel, *Recherches sur le vocabulaire du culte dans la Septante. Études et commentaires* 61 (1966), 249, 269-70.

80. Ibid., 245-46.

81. Ibid., 248.

82. J. Maier, *Die Texte vom Toten Meer,* 2 vols. (1960), II, 32; G. Klinzing, *Die Umdeutung des Kultus in der Qumrangemeinde und im NT. SUNT* 7 (1971), 40-41.

sending tribute to the temple.[83] These ordinances may date from a period when there was as yet no hostility toward the Jerusalem temple.

Upon the rebuilt altar at Bethel, according to 1QapGen 21:2, Abraham offered "burnt offerings and a *minḥâ* for El Elyon" (cf. Gen. 13:3-4). According to 1QapGen 21:20, he also built an altar at Mamre and offered "a burnt offering and a *minḥâ* for El Elyon" (cf. Gen. 13:18). The pl. *ʿlwʾn* in 1QapGen 21:2 is probably to be vocalized as *ʿalāwāʾn* (cf. Ezr. 6:9); the sg. *ʿlʾ* in 1QapGen 21:20 is attested only here in this form. It is striking that, in contrast to the Genesis account, at both Bethel and Mamre Abraham offers an *ʿōlâ* or *ʿōlôṯ* along with its accompanying *minḥâ*. This shows that the sacrificial regulations laid down by P were known and observed.

Like the OT, the Temple Scroll speaks of two altars of burnt offering: on the one hand a bronze altar (3:14ff.; cf. Ex. 27:4ff.; 38:1ff.), on the other the great altar of burnt offering (11QT 12:8ff.). It is not clear how the author of the Temple Scroll conceived the relationship between the two altars. He was probably guided by an attempt to harmonize the different descriptions in the OT. It is a special concern of the Temple Scroll to give the sin offering priority over the burnt offering. I have already noted the trend in the OT for the sin offering to supplant the burnt offering; in the Temple Scroll this trend becomes the rule. According to Mishnah *Zebaḥim* 10.2, e.g., only the blood of the sin offerings must be sprinkled on the altar before the burnt offering.[84]

The content and significance of the sabbath burnt offering liturgy at Qumran in 4QShirShabb are discussed elsewhere.[85]

D. Kellermann

---

83. See Josephus *Ant.* 18.1.5 §19.

84. J. Maier, *The Temple Scroll. JSOTSup* 34 (Eng. trans. 1985), 77.

85. J. Strugnell, "The Angelic Liturgy at Qumrân," *Congress Volume, Oxford 1959. SVT* 7 (1960), 318-45; C. Newsom, *Song of the Sabbath Sacrifice. HSS* 27 (1985).

עָלֶה *ʿāleh*

I. Occurrences. II. OT Usage: 1. Literal Usage; 2. Figurative Usage. III. Dead Sea Scrolls and LXX.

I. Occurrences. The noun *ʿāleh,* "leaves, foliage," occurs 13 times in the OT, once in Sirach, and 3 times in the Dead Sea Scrolls. It has not been found in other West Se-

---

ʿāleh. M. Zohary, *Plants of the Bible* (Eng. trans. 1982).

mitic languages. The Akkadian noun *elû,* "shoot," derives from the verb *elû,* "go up."[1] This meaning confirms the derivation of the Hebrew noun *ʿāleh* from the verb → **עלה** *ʿālâ.*[2]

II. OT Usage.

1. *Literal Sense.* The singular of the noun *ʿāleh* is used collectively. In one-third of its occurrences, it is used literally to denote the leaves of certain kinds of trees. In the garden of Eden, e.g., Adam and Eve made loincloths out of fig leaves to cover their nakedness (Gen. 3:7). Westermann believes that this is a statement "of great significance in the history of civilization."[3] By contrast, the mythological interpretation of the fig tree as the tree of death is probably off track.[4] The discussion of the fig leaf in Dillmann's commentary on Genesis is still enlightening.[5]

The dove sent forth from the ark by Noah returns with a fresh olive leaf, showing that vegetation has begun to grow on the earth once more (Gen. 8:11). The image of a dove with an olive branch as a symbol of peace derives from this story.[6] Nehemiah commands the citizens of Jerusalem: "Go out to the hills and bring leaves from the olive tree and branches of pine[7] and leaves of myrtle and palm and oak[8] to make booths, as it is written" (Neh. 8:15). In Ezekiel's vision evergreen fruit trees grow on the banks of the miraculous river that issues from the Jerusalem temple; their leaves have healing power (Ezk. 47:12).

Driven, withered leaves *(ʿāleh niddāp)* play a baneful role in Lev. 26:36, the curse that concludes the Holiness Code (Lev. 17–26); the passage might be understood as a counterpart to the blessing in 26:6b: "The survivors of the catastrophe, living in a foreign land, are still in terror, so that even rustling leaves can plunge them into panic."[9]

The examples of *ʿāleh* in the Talmud and Midrash cited by Levy lead us for the most part to the botanical realm.[10] One text describes the growth of plants, which put forth 6 leaves after 60 days and 60 leaves after another 6 days; another speaks of the healing power of certain leaves placed upon the eyes.[11] Levy cites only one instance of figurative usage: "'If there were no leaves, the grapes would not survive'; in other words, without the support of ordinary people, there can be no scholars."[12]

---

1. *AHw,* I, 206b; attested only in a list of synonyms.
2. Barth, *NSS,* §9c; *GesB,* 591; *GesTh,* II, 1024: "folium, a crescendo dictum"; G. Wehmeier, *TLOT,* II, 884.
3. C. Westermann, *Genesis 1–11* (Eng. trans. 1984), 251-52.
4. See B. Pipal, *Křestanská Revue* 29 (1962) 38-39.
5. A. Dillmann, *Genesis,* 2 vols. (Eng. trans. 1897), in loc.
6. See also H. Gunkel, *Genesis* (Eng. trans. 1997), in loc.
7. Zohary, 114.
8. E. Bertheau, *Die Bücher Esra, Nechemia und Ester. KEHAT* XVII (1862), 215-16.
9. K. Elliger, *Leviticus. HAT* I/4 (1966), 377.
10. *WTM,* III, 650.
11. Jer. *Shebiit* 5.35d; *Shabbat* 109a.
12. Bab. *Ḥullin* 92a.

2. *Figurative Usage.* The metaphorical usage of *ʿāleh* in the prophetic and wisdom traditions of the OT is theologically eloquent; it continued to exert its influence well after the OT period (see III below). In conjunction with → נבל *nāḇēl,* withered leaves serve as an image for the people who are in distress on account of God's judgment (Isa. 1:30; 64:5).[13] In contrast, the negated *lō'-yibbôl* in Ps. 1:3 (Jer. 17:8, *ʿāleh raʿᵃnān*) uses the image of a tree whose leaves never wither to describe those who enjoy Yahweh's blessing (cf. Prov. 11:28, "The righteous will flourish like green leaves"). In Job 13:25 the image of windblown leaves (used literally in Lev. 26:36) serves to symbolize a person whose life has been destroyed by disaster (par. *qaš yāḇēš*). In Sir. 6:2-3 dried and withered leaves do not symbolize downfall: instead, they are devoured by passion (represented as an animal), and as a result the tree withers.

Like Isaiah's Song of the Vineyard (Isa. 5:1-7), Jer. 8:13 compares the disobedient people of God to a vine or fig tree with withered leaves, bearing no fruit. The prophecy of universal judgment in Isa. 34:4 uses an image not found elsewhere in the OT: the dissolution of the starry sky is likened to the rolling up of a scroll and the withering of leaves on the vine and figs on the tree.[14]

III. Dead Sea Scrolls and LXX. Figurative use of *ʿāleh* is found also in the Hymn Scroll from Qumran. In 1QH 10:25 we read: "But you have made me a verdant tree beside the streams, with luxuriant foliage and many branches"; the image recalls Ps. 1:3 and Jer. 17:8. In 1QH 8:8,26, the community is represented as a shoot on whose green leaves (*nēṣer ʿāleh*)[15] all the animals feed; the leaves wither, however, when the Teacher of Righteousness withdraws his hand, causing the life-giving spring to dry up.

The usual translation of the LXX is *phýllon.*

Beyse

---

13. → IX, 154.
14. For a discussion of the context see H. Wildberger, *Jesaja 28–39. BK* X/3 (1982), 1341-42.
15. → IX, 550-51.

עָלַז *ʿālaz;* *עַלִּיז *ʿallîz;* *עָלֵז *ʿālēz;* עָלַץ *ʿālaṣ;* עֲלִיצוּת *ʿᵃlîṣûṯ;* עָלַס *ʿālas*

I. 1. Forms; 2. Versions; 3. Textual Problems; 4. Etymology; 5. *ʿālas.* II. 1. Syntax; 2. Lexical Fields; 3. Meaning.

ʿālaz. G. Bertram, "'Hochmut' und verwandte Begriffe im griechischen und hebräischen AT," *WO* 3 (1964/66) 32-43; J. Bright, "Jeremiah's Complaints: Liturgy, or Expressions of Personal Distress?" *Proclamation and Presence. FS G. H. Davies* (1970), 189-214; G. Brunet, *Essai sur l'Isaïe de l'histoire* (1975); J. A. Emerton, "Notes on Some Passages in the Book of Proverbs,"

I. 1. *Forms.* The roots *ʿlz* and *ʿlṣ* are usually treated as synonymous variants; in the OT they appear only in poetic contexts. The qal of *ʿlz* occurs 16 times, the verbal adj. *ʿālēz* once, and the adj. *ʿallîz* 7 times; the qal of *ʿlṣ* occurs 8 times, and the subst. *ʿalîṣûṯ* once. The adj. *ʿallîṣ* has been conjectured in Ps. 37:35 on the basis of the LXX (not convincingly; cf. the LXX rendering of *ārîṣ* in Isa. 13:11). The hiphil of *ʿlṣ* appears in Sir. 40:20.

2. *Versions.* The ancient versions vary widely in their renderings of *ʿlz/ʿlṣ* and their derivatives. One striking feature is the proportion of translations that convey the meaning "be strong."[1] The divergent translations have led scholars to various hypotheses, in the realm of both textual criticism (different original texts, conjectural emendations; see I.3 below) and lexicography (homonyms; see I.4 below). The translations used by the LXX include *agalliáomai* (6 times), *(kata)kaucháomai* (4 times), *chaírō, hýbris/hybrízō,* and *phaúlisma/phaulístria* (twice each).

3. *Textual Problems.* Scholars have proposed textual emendation for some occurrences of *ʿlz/ʿlṣ: ʿlz* in Jer. 11:15;[2] 51:39;[3] Ps. 60:8(Eng. v. 6) par. 108:8(7);[4] *ʿālēz* in Isa. 5:14;[5] *ʿlṣ* in Prov. 28:12.[6] Except for Jer. 51:39, where the pual of *ʿlp* should be read with most versions (König suggests that the MT is an instance of metonymy),[7] the case for these emendations is not persuasive. For 1 S. 2:1, it has been suggested that the LXX represents a different Hebrew text.[8] De Boer, however, considers the translation of the versions an "accurate interpretation."[9]

4. *Etymology.* For some occurrences of *ʿlz/ʿlṣ,* scholars have proposed meanings reflecting different etymologies. Rabin connects *ʿlz* with Arab. *ġalīẓ,* "thick," and postulates the meaning "be proud" for the majority of its occurrences.[10] Emerton associates

---

JTS 20 (1969) 202-20; A. Guillaume, "Hebrew and Arabic Lexicography, A Comparative Study, I," *Abr-Nahrain* 1 (1959/60) 3-35; C. Hardmeier, *Texttheorie und biblische Exegese. BEvT* 79 (1978); G. Mansfeld, "Der Ruf zur Freude im AT" (diss., Heidelberg, 1965); A. R. Millard, "עלז 'to exult,'" *JTS* 26 (1975) 87-89; C. Rabin, "Etymological Miscellanea," *ScrHier* 8 (1961) 384-400; E. Ruprecht, "שׂמח *śmḥ* to rejoice," *TLOT,* III, 1272-77; G. Vanoni, "Das Problem der Homonymie beim althebräischen *ʿLZ/ʿLṢ,*" *BN* 33 (1986) 29-33.

1. Vanoni, 30-31.
2. *BHS;* W. Rudolph, *Jeremia. HAT* I/12 (^{3}1968), 78; G. Wilhelmi, *VT* 25 (1975) 121.
3. *BHS.*
4. C. R. North, *VT* 17 (1967) 242-43; *BHS.*
5. J. A. Emerton, *VT* 17 (1967) 135-42, esp. 137ff.
6. *BHS;* cf. Emerton, "Notes," 216.
7. *Hebräisches und aramäisches Wörterbuch zum AT* (1936), 330.
8. For example, H. P. Smith (*Samuel. ICC* [1899], 15) suggests *ʾmṣ;* H. J. Stoebe (*Das erste Buch Samuelis. KAT* VIII/1 [1973], 101) suggests *ʿṣm.*
9. P. A. H. de Boer, *Beiträge zur alttestamentlichen Theologie. FS W. Zimmerli* (1977), 54. See the discussion of the problem in I.4 below.
10. Pp. 396-97.

ʿlṣ with Arab. *ǵaluẓa,* "be strong."[11] For *ʿālēz,* Driver proposes a relationship with Arab. *ʿaliza;* Zorell connects *ʿᵃlîṣûṯ* with Arab. *ǵalīẓ,* "ferocity"; other etymologies suggest such meanings as "throat" or "shelter."[12] But the theory of homonyms does not explain either the evidence of the ancient versions (see I.2 above) or the alternation of *ʿlz* and *ʿlṣ* (cf. Ps. 68:4,5[3,4]; 96:12 [*ʿlz*] par. 1 Ch. 16:32 [*ʿlṣ*]; also unproven are the proposals of G. Siegfried and B. Stade [*ʿlṣ* is a "late by-form" of *ʿlz*] and *BLe* [different regional dialects]).[13] The same applies to proposals that are not based on homonyms but assign pejorative meanings to the variant *ʿlz* (*ʿālēz* = "pride," *ʿallîz* = "haughty").[14] Comparison with other Semitic languages suggests a different solution.

The root *ʿlz/ʿlṣ* expressing exultation appears in other Semitic languages besides Hebrew: Ugar. *ʿlṣ,* "rejoice" (context unclear); OSA *mʿlṣ,* "joy"; Akk. *elēṣu,* "swell; rejoice, exult."[15] Uncertain are the Amorite name *alazum* and Pun. *ʿlṣ.*[16] The only suggestion of an etymon behind the meaning "rejoice" is in the Akkadian meaning "swell." In this connection, however, we must note that other Hebrew (and non-Hebrew) words denoting expressions of joy involve verbs that function primarily to express a condition or movement.[17]

This evidence suggests the following conclusion: Heb. *ʿlz/ʿlṣ* has an invariant semantic core: "express joy." More specific features ("self-confidently," etc.) and valuative connotations do not depend on the choice of sibilant *(z/ṣ)* or the form *(qaṭṭîl)* but only on the specific context. The ancient versions do not reflect etymological familiarity with Hebrew or Arabic but simply a general familiarity with the terminology of rejoicing in the languages of the translators.[18]

5. *ʿālas.* Many lexicons associate *ʿls* with *ʿlz/ʿlṣ.* But *ʿls* does not appear in the word clusters typical of *ʿlz/ʿlṣ* (see II.2 below). Among the ancient versions, only the Targ. on Job 20:18 supports identification of the two roots. The root *ʿls* is associated with (1) Arab. *ʿalasa* (Job 20:18, qal; Prov. 7:18, hithpael) or (2) Arab. *ʿaliza* (Job 39:13, niphal) and means "share pleasure" (1) or "move wildly" (2).

---

11. "Notes," 216-20.

12. See G. R. Driver, *Von Ugarit nach Qumran. FS O. Eissfeldt. BZAW* 77 (1958), 42-43; see I.5 below; Zorell, *LexHebAram,* 602; see also W. Rudolph, *Micha-Nahum-Habakuk-Zephanja. KAT* XIII/3 (1975), 238.

13. Siegfried and Stade, *Hebräisches Wörterbuch zum AT* (1893), 521; *BLe,* §2v.

14. Brunet, 291-92; but see Bertram, 37. Cf. H. G. Reventlow's discussion of Jer. 15:17, *Liturgie und prophetisches Ich bei Jeremia* (1963), 22-23; convincingly disproved by Bright, 200-203.

15. On Middle Heb. *ʿallîz, ʿᵃlîzâ, ʿālaṣ,* and *ʿᵃlîṣâ,* see Dalman, *ANH,* 314-15. For Ugaritic see *UT,* no. 1860. For OSA see Conti-Rossini, 207; but cf. Biella, 369: "battle." For Akkadian see *AHw,* I, 200; *CAD,* IV, 88.

16. J.-R. Küpper, *Les nomades en Mésopotamie au temps des rois de Mari* (1957), 94; *DNSI,* II, 863 ("rejoice" or par. Heb. *ʿlṣ;* cf. Emerton, "Notes," 218-19.

17. Vanoni, 31-32.

18. Similarly Bertram, 37 (LXX); and Millard, 88-89 (with bibliog. on the problem of homonymy).

II. 1. *Syntax.* For the most part *ʿlz/ʿlṣ* denotes imperfective situations (imperfective form, generally modal). The perfective occurs once (1 S. 2:1), the consecutive imperfective twice (Jer. 15:17; Ps. 28:7), the infinitive construct twice (Isa. 23:12; Prov. 28:12), and the imperative twice (Zeph. 3:14; Ps. 68:5[4]). The subject is usually animate; inanimate subjects refer to the "heart" or "kidneys" of the speaker (1 S. 2:1; Ps. 28:7; Prov. 23:16) or imply animate inhabitants (Ps. 96:12 par. 1 Ch. 16:32; Prov. 11:10). In the case of the nominal forms, the subject is also animate. Other syntagms are rare: a prepositional object denotes the object of rejoicing (always Yahweh) or (with *l*ᵉ) malicious pleasure: 5 times with *b*ᵉ (1 S. 2:1; Hab. 3:18; Ps. 5:12[11]; 9:3[2]; 149:5),[19] once with *l*ᵉ (Ps. 25:2), 4 times with *(mil)lipnê* (Ps. 68:4,5[3,4]; 96:12 par. 1 Ch. 16:32 [from the parallelism]); a free syntagm expresses intensity (Zeph. 3:14); an infinitive group with *b*ᵉ expresses the cause of rejoicing (Ps. 9:4[3]; Prov. 11:10; 23:16). The cause can also be expressed in an independent clause (Zeph. 3:15; Ps. 28:7; 68:6[5]; 96:13 par. 1 Ch. 16:33; negatively, 2 S. 1:19). In Ps. 60:8(6) par. 108:8(7), *ʿlz* may be functionalized.[20] In adjectival constructions the object of joy is expressed by the associated *nomen rectum* (Isa. 13:3, *gaʾ*ᵃ*wāṯî* [Yahweh's majesty]; Zeph. 3:11, *gaʾ*ᵃ*wāṯēḵ* [Jerusalem's majesty]) or possibly by a prepositional object (Isa. 5:14, *bâ* [or an expression of place?]).[21]

2. *Lexical Fields.* Several roots appear in parallel with *ʿlz/ʿlṣ: gyl* (Hab. 3:18), *zmr* (Ps. 9:3[2]; 68:5[4]), *rnn* (5:12[11]; 96:12 par. 1 Ch. 16:33; Ps. 49:5; Prov. 11:10), *rʿm* (Ps. 96:11 par. 1 Ch. 16:32), *śwś* (Ps. 68:4[3]), *śmḥ* (2 S. 1:20; Jer. 50:11; Zeph. 3:14; Ps. 5:12[11]; 9:3[2]; 68:4[3]; Prov. 23:15). In the extended context we find (a) expressions indicating joy: *gyl* (Ps. 96:11 par. 1 Ch. 16:31; Ps. 149:2), *ydh* hiphil (28:7, with change of tense), *zmr* (149:3), *ṣhl* (Jer. 50:11), *rwʿ* hiphil (Jer. 50:15; Zeph. 3:14; Ps. 60:10[8] par. 108:10[9]), *rnn* (Zeph. 3:14), *śwś* (Jer. 15:16; with *ʿallîz* in Isa. 24:8; 32:13), *śḥq* (Jer. 15:17), *śmḥ* (1 S. 2:1; Jer. 15:16; Ps. 96:11 par. 1 Ch. 16:31; Ps. 149:2; with *ʿallîz* in Isa. 24:7), *šyr* (Ps. 68:5[4]); (b) expressions indicating sadness: *ʾbl* (Isa. 24:7, with *ʿallîz*), *bkh* (2 S. 1:24; with *ʿallîz* in Isa. 22:4), *yll* (Isa. 23:14; with *ʿallîz* in 23:6), *spd* (32:12, with *ʿallîz*); (c) expressions related to dancing: *kinnôr* + *tōp̄* (Ps. 149:3; with *ʿālēz* in Isa 5:12; with *ʿallîz* in Isa. 24:8), *māḥôl* (Ps. 149:3). In the context of the adj. *ʿālēz/ʿallîz* we finds words in the semantic field of "self-confidence": *bṭḥ* (Isa. 32:11; Zeph. 2:15), *gʾh* (Isa. [13:3]; 23:9; Zeph. 2:10; 3:11), *hmh* (Isa. 5:14; 22:2; 32:14), *šʾh* (5:14; 22:2; 24:8). Other lexical fields are discussed below.

3. *Meaning.* a. *Secular Contexts.* When the context of *ʿlz/ʿlṣ* does not have negative implications, we may assume that the connotations are positive. This is demonstrated especially by passages that express the value of joy by mentioning the absence or ces-

19. König, *Historisch-kritisches Lehrgebäude des hebräische Sprach,* II/2: *Syntax,* §212d: *kāḇôḏ* refers to Yahweh; cf. M. Dahood, *Psalms III: 101–150. AB* 17A (1970), 356-57, 430.

20. See W. Richter, *ATS* 23 (1985) 77; cf. Dahood, *Psalms II: 51–100. AB* 17 (1968), 75: "Exultant, I will make."

21. See the discussion by Emerton, *VT* 17 (1967) 137.

sation of *ʿlz/ʿlṣ*. Jeremiah does not sit in the company of merrymakers but sits alone (Jer. 15:17). Prophetic oracles of destruction and exhortations to lament underline "the happy and peaceful life of the present in contrast to the coming devastation of battle"[22] (Isa. 22:2; 23:7,12; 24:8; 32:13; Zeph. 2:15; cf. Jer. 49:25; Lam. 2:15 [with *māśôś*]). In Isa. 5:14, in the context of a prophetic threat, *ʿālēz* has more negative overtones, although some of the associated motifs resemble Isa. 32:11-14 and Zeph. 2:14-15 ("trust," "pasture").[23] The threat in Jer. 11:15 is positive, envisioning future joy. Sir. 40:20 speaks of wine and friendship as sources of joy. Rejoicing on the part of the women *(bānôṯ)* at home when a victory is announced is mentioned in 2 S. 1:20 (negated) and Jer. 50:11 (ironic); Mansfeld believes that these texts reflect a "jubilation" genre: pl. impv. "rejoice" + vocative "*baṯ* + city name" + *kî* clause.[24]

In Proverbs *ʿlz/ʿlṣ* is categorized positively by adjectives and abstract nouns (11:10, *ṣaddîq, ṭûḇ;* 23:16, *mêšārîm;* 28:12, *ṣaddîq*). A disapproved subject (*rāšāʿ,* Ps. 94:3; Hab. 3:14 [cf. v. 13]; *ʾōyēḇ,* Ps. 25:2) lends other occurrences of *ʿlz/ʿlṣ* negative overtones. Such usage signals the transition to theological contexts; in these cases Yahweh is expected to intervene. This holds true also in Zeph. 3:11, where Yahweh predicts the removal (*swr* hiphil) of those who exult in their own greatness (*gaʾ*^{a}*wāh* par. *goḇhāh;* cf. the antithesis in v. 12: the humble and lowly seek refuge in Yahweh's name; similarly the *bṭḥ* of the psalmist in Ps. 25:2).

b. *Theological Contexts.* Unlike the proud in Zeph. 3:11, Yahweh's warriors in Isa. 13:3 are viewed positively, since they exult in Yahweh's greatness; the formal resemblance may indicate that this text is borrowed from Zephaniah.[25] The other texts cited here (primarily in the context of prayers) associate *ʿlz/ʿlṣ* with Yahweh's deliverance or judgment, usually depicted in very general terms with many abstract nouns. Ps. 5 contrasts the wicked (vv. 5-7,10-11[4-6,9-10]) with the righteous (vv. 8-9,13[7-8,12]); secure against enemies (v. 9[8]), the righteous can rejoice in Yahweh's protection (v. 12[11], *b*^{e} + Yahweh; the realm of Yahweh's presence or a shorthand way of saying "rejoice in Yahweh's act of deliverance").[26] The "wicked" (and "enemies") appear in other prayers in which the worshiper rejoices in Yahweh and Yahweh's salvation: 1 S. 2:1 ("my mouth opens wide against [NRSV 'derides'] my enemies" par. *śmḥ* + *y*^{e}*šûʿâ;* cf. v. 9); Hab. 3:18 (par. *gyl* + *yēšaʿ;* cf. v. 13); Ps. 9:3(2) (v. 4[3], "for my enemies turned back"; cf. v. 6[5]); 28:7 ("Yahweh is my strength and my shield . . . so I am helped [*ʿzr*]"; cf. v. 3); 68:4-5(3-4) (cf. vv. 2-3[1-2]). At the same time, 1 S. 2:10; Ps. 9:5,9(4,8); 68:6(5) also speak of God as "judge." The contexts of Hab. 3:18 and Ps.

22. Bertram, 37. See Hardmeier, 215, 351, 361-62, 369.

23. H. Wildberger, *Isaiah 1–12* (Eng. trans. 1991), 204.

24. P. 25; cf. 11-47.

25. Rudolph, *KAT* XIII/3, 297; on Yahweh's warriors see H. Wildberger, *Isaiah 13–27* (1997), 18ff.

26. For the former see H.-J. Kraus, *Psalms 1–59* (Eng. trans. 1988), 157; for the latter, Ruprecht, 1275-76. The institutional background of Ps. 5 is discussed by W. Beyerlin, *Die Rettung der Bedrängten in den Feindpsalmen der Einzelnen auf institutionelle Zusammenhänge untersucht. FRLANT* 99 (1970), 90-95.

68:4(3) include theophanies. Willis finds in 1 S. 2, Hab. 3, and Ps. 68 an ancient genre, the "song of victory."[27] With other texts to be discussed below, Ps. 68 speaks of God as king (v. 25[24]; cf. also Ps. 5:3[2]).[28] The "shout of joy" in Zeph. 3:14 has "daughter Zion" rejoicing over the retreat of the enemy and the entrance of King Yahweh (v. 15).[29] Ps. 96:12 par. 1 Ch. 15:32 summons the entire natural realm to welcome with joy the king of the universe (v. 10 [according to Mansfeld a late interpolation]).[30] In Ps. 96:13 *špṭ* means "rule."[31] Ps. 149:5 has the faithful rejoice in the *kāḇôḏ* of Yahweh their king (v. 2), who brings salvation (*yᵉšûʿâ,* v. 4) to the humble.

Mansfeld views the contexts of Ps. 68:4-5(3-4); 96:12 par. 1 Ch. 15:32; Ps. 149:5 as late imitations of a genre "song of welcome" associated with the report of victory; its form is imperative ("sing") + *kî* clause + jussive ("rejoice").[32] Like the imitation of the "jubilation" genre in Zeph. 3:14-15 (see II.3.a above), they are postexilic attempts to keep alive the imminent eschatological hopes of Deutero-Isaiah; cf. the "jubilations" in Isa. 44:23; 45:8; 48:20; 49:13; 52:9; 54:1 and "song of welcome" in 42:10-11 (all without *ʿlz/ʿlṣ*). Crüsemann sees a different genre in the texts assigned by Mansfeld to the "jubilation" genre: "assurance of well-being in the context of the sexual fertility cult."[33] Mansfeld's theory is the more likely.[34]

c. *Theological Usage.* Only in the salvation oracle Ps. 60:8(6) par. 108:8(7) is God the subject of *ʿlz,* again in the context of victory: the mighty God (v. 9, *māʿôz;* cf. *ʿzz* in 28:7-8, *ḥyl* in 1 S. 2:4; Hab. 3:19) celebrates his victorious triumph (cf. the framing of the oracle with *ʿlz* and *rwʿ* hithpael [v. 10(8)]) and divides the spoil.[35]

Vanoni

---

27. J. T. Willis, *CBQ* 35 (1973) 139-54.

28. → VIII, 365ff.

29. Mansfeld, 83-86. The concentration of terms expressing joy is discussed by Ihromi, *VT* 33 (1983) 106-10.

30. Mansfeld, 128ff.

31. W. H. Schmidt, *Königtum Gottes in Ugarit und Israel. BZAW* 80 (²1966), 38-39.

32. Pp. 102ff., 125-44.

33. W. Crüsemann, *Studien zur Formgeschichte von Hymnus und Danklied in Israel. WMANT* 32 (1969), 65.

34. Cf. Ruprecht, 1276-77.

35. A possible Canaanite background is proposed by Dahood, *AB* 17A, 94.

עֶלְיוֹן *ʿelyôn*

I. 1. Etymology and Meaning; 2. Occurrences; 3. LXX. II. OT: 1. Usage; 2. Connotations; 3. Origin; 4. *ʿāl?* III. Extrabiblical Texts: 1. Ugarit; 2. Sefire; 3. Philo of Byblos; 4. Summary. IV. Jerusalem: 1. Gen. 14; 2. Cult. V. Late Usage: 1. Daniel; 2. Dead Sea Scrolls; 3. Apocrypha and Pseudepigrapha.

ʿelyôn. W. W. Graf Baudissin, *Kyrios als Gottesname im Judentum und seine Stelle in der Religionsgeschichte,* III (1929); G. Bertram, "Theologische Aussagen im griechischen AT: Gottesnamen," *ZNW* 69 (1978) 239-46; idem, "ὕψιστος," *TDNT,* VIII, 614-20; P. A. H. de Boer, "Numbers VI 27," *VT* 32 (1982) 3-13; A. van den Branden, "Il Dio Eljôn," *BeO* 16 (1974) 65-85; G. Cooke, "The Sons of (the) God(s)," *ZAW* 76 (1964) 22-47; F. M. Cross, "Yahweh and the God of the Patriarchs," *HTR* 55 (1962) 225-59; M. Dahood, "The Divine Name *ʿēlî* in the Psalms," *TS* 14 (1953) 452-57; R. Dussaud, *Les découvertes de Ras Shamra (Ugarit) et l'AT* ([2]1941); O. Eissfeldt, "Baʿalšamēm und Jahwe," *ZAW* 57 (1939) 1-31 = *KlS,* II, 171-98; idem, "Jahwes Verhältnis zu ʿEljon und Schaddaj nach Psalm 91," *WO* 2 (1957) 343-48 = *KlS,* III, 441-47; idem, "Der kanaanäische El als Geber der den israelitischen Erzvätern geltenden Nachkommenschaft und Landbesitzverheissungen," *WZ Halle,* Gesellschafts- und Sprachwissenschaftliche 17 (1968) 45-53 = *KlS,* V, 50-62; idem, *Das Lied Moses Deuteronomium 32, 1-43 und das Lehrgedicht Asaphs Psalm 78 samt einer Analyse derer Umgebung des Mose-Liedes. Berichte über die Verhandlungen der Sächsischen Akademie der Wissenschaften zu Leipzig,* Phil.-hist. Kl. 104/5 (1958); idem, "Psalm 46," *KlS,* IV, 8-11; idem, "Eine Qumran-Textform des 91. Psalms," *Bibel et Qumran. FS H. Bardtke* (1968), 82-85 = *KlS,* V, 45-49; idem, "Silo und Jerusalem," *Volume du Congrès, Strasbourg 1956. SVT* 4 (1957), 138-47 = *KlS,* III, 417-25; H.-J. Fabry, "'Ihr alle seid Söhne des Allerhöchsten' (Ps 82,6)," *BiLe* 15 (1974) 135-47; H. Gese et al., *Die Religionen Altsyriens, Altarabiens und der Mandaer. RM* 10/2 (1970), 1-232; N. C. Habel, "'Yahweh, Maker of Heaven and Earth': A Study in Tradition Criticism," *JBL* 91 (1972) 321-37; T. Hanlon, "The Most High God of Genesis 14,18-20," *Scripture* 11 (1959) 110-18; R. Hillmann, "Wasser und Berg" (diss., Halle, 1965); P. Hugger, *Jahwe meine Zuflucht. MüSt* 13 (1971), esp. 164-67; E. O. James, *The Worship of the Sky-God. Jordan Lectures in Comparative Religion* 6 (1963); H.-J. Kraus, "Excursus 1. The Cultic Traditions of Jerusalem," *Psalms 1–59* (Eng. trans. 1988), 81-89; R. Lack, "Les origines de ʿElyôn, le Très-Haut, dans la tradition cultuelle d'Israël," *CBQ* 24 (1962) 44-64; G. Levi della Vida, "El ʿElyôn in Genesis 14,18-20," *JBL* 63 (1944) 1-9; Comte du Mesnil du Buisson, "Origine et évolution du panthéon de Tyr," *RHR* 164 (1963) 133-63; P. D. Miller Jr., "El, the Creator of Earth," *BASOR* 239 (1980) 43-46; M. J. Mulder, *Kanaäitische Goden in het OT. Exegetica* IV/4-5 (1965); H. S. Nyberg, "Studien zum Religionskampf im AT," *ARW* 35 (1938) 329-87; R. A. Oden, "Baʿal Šamēm and ʾĒl," *CBQ* 39 (1977) 457-73; U. Oldenburg, "Above the Stars of El," *ZAW* 82 (1970) 187-208; idem, *The Conflict between El and Baʿal in Canaanite Religion* (1969); M. H. Pope, *El in the Ugaritic Texts. SVT* 2 (1955); R. Rendtorff, "The Background of the Title ʾEl ʿEljon in Gen. XIV," *Fourth World Congress of Jewish Studies* I (1967), 167-70; idem, "El, Baʿal und Jahwe," *ZAW* 78 (1966) 277-92 = *ThB* 57 (1975) 172-87; H. Ringgren, *Religions of the Ancient Near East* (Eng. trans. 1973), esp. 127-44; D. Sanders, "The Names of God, Part 1: The OT," *Eternity* 34 (1983) 26-27; W. Schatz, *Genesis 14. EH* XXIII/2 (1972); H. Schmid, "Jahwe und die Kulttraditionen von Jerusalem," *ZAW* 67 (1955) 168-97; W. H. Schmidt, *Königtum Gottes in Ugarit und Israel. BZAW* 80 ([2]1966); idem, *Faith of the OT* (Eng. trans. 1983); E. C. Smith, "Hebrew Names of God," *Bulletin of the New York Public Library* 54 (1950) 555-60; F. Stolz, *Strukturen und Figuren im Kult von Jerusalem. BZAW* 118 (1970); B. Uffenheimer, "El Elyon, Creator of Heaven and Earth,"

I. 1. *Etymology and Meaning.* The adj. *'elyôn* is a denominative form derived from *'āl,* "height," by the afformative *-ôn.*[1] It has superlative force: "the most high."[2] The interpretation of this form as a reference to "god on high, that is, the god of the heavens,"[3] is probably too narrow. Since the divine epithet *'ly,* "the exalted one," is attested in Ugaritic, Gese thinks it possible "that Elyon derived from such an epithet," but he adds, "Of course, this is uncertain."[4]

2. *Occurrences.* The word *'elyôn* occurs 53 times in the OT: 22 times in secular usage to distinguish something above from something below (in 1 K. 9:8 = 2 Ch. 7:21, read *'iyîm* with *BHS*), 31 times as a divine epithet, "(God) Most High." Three conjectural emendations may increase the latter number. (1) In the tribal saying concerning Benjamin (Dt. 33:12), since Houbigant *'elyôn* has been substituted for *'ālāyw*[5] and connected with the following stich: "*'elyôn* surrounds him all day long." (2) In Ps. 106:7, too, emendation of *'al-yām* to *'elyôn* makes sense: "They rebelled against *'elyôn* at the Sea of Reeds."[6] (3) Finally, in 1 S. 2:10, in the song of Hannah, it is possible that *'ālāyw (K)* should be emended to *'elyôn:*[7] "*'elyôn* thunders in heaven." Stoebe, however, points out that *'ālāyw* more likely goes back to an ancient divine epithet *'āl,* "high, exalted," a theory also suggested (albeit less persuasively) in the case of Dt. 33:12 and Ps. 106:7.[8]

In the *'āl* of the last words of David (2 S. 23:1) we are also dealing with a divine appellative, whether we retain the MT *huqam 'āl,* "oracle of the man appointed by the Most High," or emend the text to *hēqîm 'āl,* "whom the Most High exalted."[9] In Hos. 7:16 and 11:7, too, it is reasonable to read, respectively, "they return to the Most High" and "to the Most High they call."[10] The proposals (still supported by Nyberg and Dahood) to interpret Isa. 59:18; 63:7; Ps. 7:9,11(Eng. 8,10); 57:3(2); 141(3) are unconvincing or problematic (see the comms.). Ceresko has proposed recovering the divine

---

ShM 2 (1977) 20-26; R. de Vaux, *Early History of Israel* (Eng. trans. 1978); idem, *AncIsr,* II; G. Wanke, *Die Zionstheologie der Korachiten in ihrem traditionsgeschichtlichen Zusammenhang. BZAW* 97 (1966), esp. 46-54; G. Wehmeier, "עלה *'lh* to go up," *TLOT,* II, 883-96; H.-J. Zobel, "Der kanaanäische Hintergrund der Vorstellung vom lebendigen Gott," *WZ Greifswald* 24/1975 (1977) 187-94.

1. *BLe,* §61pθ; see also Stolz, 134.
2. *GK,* §133g n. 3.
3. Stolz, 135.
4. P. 117.
5. Zobel, *Stammesspruch und Geschichte. BZAW* 95 (1965) 35 n. 37.
6. Cf. Ps. 78:17 and Kraus, *Psalms 60–150* (Eng. trans. 1989), 315.
7. Schmid, 183.
8. Stoebe, *Das erste Buch Samuelis. KAT* VIII/1 (1973), 102, as first proposed by Nyberg, 368-69 (see already his *Studien zum Hoseabuche. UUÅ* 1935:6, 58-60), and G. R. Driver, *ExpT* 50 (1938/39) 92.
9. Cf. *HAL,* II, 825.
10. J. Jeremias, *Der Prophet Hosea. ATD* 24/1 (1983), 91 n. 17, 144; for a different interpretation see H. W. Wolff, *Hosea. Herm* (Eng. trans. 1974), 108, 192; and W. Rudolph, *Hosea. KAT* XIII/1 (1966), 152, 212.

name Eli ("the Most High") in Job 29:4 and 31:35.[11] This *ʿāl* is explained as a hypocoristic form of *ʿelyôn,* an abbreviated form of Baʿal, or even an independent divine epithet.[12]

In addition to these texts, Aram. *ʿillāy,* "Most High," occurs as a divine appellative 10 times in Daniel; the pl. form *ʿelyônîn,* "Most High," occurs 4 times in Dnl. 7.

The word also appears frequently in the Apocrypha and Pseudepigrapha. There are 10 occurrences in 1QapGen and 6 additional occurrences elsewhere in the Dead Sea Scrolls.

The divine epithet *ʿlyn* occurs also in the Aramaic Sefire inscriptions (8th century B.C.E.), in the expression *ʾl tʿly,* "El Most High"; in Old South Arabic documents from the 2nd century B.C.E.; and in the phrase *Elioúm kaloúmenos Hýpsistos* in Philo of Byblos.[13]

We also find *ʿly* used as a divine epithet for Baʿal in Ugaritic; in one text the phrases *mṭr bʿl,* "the rain of Baʿal," and *mṭr ʿly,* "the rain of the Exalted One," appear twice side by side.[14] Another text G. R. Driver reconstructs as *ytnm qrt lʿly*[*nym*], "let glory be given to the exalted ones," but this remains questionable.[15] Finally, *ʿl* appears as an element of West Semitic personal names.[16]

3. LXX. The LXX invariably translates *ʿelyôn* as *(ho) hýpsistos,* confirming the generally accepted meaning "Most High."

II. OT.

1. *Usage.* The many questions and problems associated with the origin and interpretation of the divine epithet *ʿelyôn* make it methodologically advisable to begin with what is certain, the usage of *ʿelyôn* in the OT. It is of no small importance to note at the outset that in the Hebrew text of the OT our word appears only in poetry: 21 times in Psalms, twice in Lamentations, and once each in Num. 24, Dt. 32, 2 S. 22, and Isa. 14. The 4 occurrences in Gen. 14 do not alter the situation: this text, comprising blessing and praise, should be considered a stereotyped form. The conjectural emendations conform to these observations. This can only mean that there is a special affinity between the term *ʿelyôn* and poetry, an affinity that can be described with regard to both form and content.

Construct phrases speak of the "right hand" (*yᵉmîn,* Ps. 77:11[10]), the "shelter" (*sēṯer,* 91:1), the "steadfast love" (*ḥeseḏ,* 21:8[7]) of *ʿelyôn;* of the "face" and "mouth"

---

11. *Job 29–31 in the Light of Northwest Semitic. BietOr* 36 (1980), 12, 182; cf. the review of Zobel, *OLZ* 81 (1986) 168.

12. For the first see Stolz, 156 n. 33; cf. Wehmeier, 893. For the last see Jeremias, *ATD* 24/1, 91 n. 17.

13. See, respectively, *KAI* 222A.11; Oldenburg, *ZAW* 82 (1970) 189-200; Eusebius *Praep. ev.* 1.10.14.

14. *KTU* 1.16, III, 5-8. See *WUS,* no. 2030.

15. *KTU* 1.23, 3. Driver (*CML,* 120-21) is cited by Stolz, 135.

16. On the occurrences and their interpretation, see *PNU,* 42, 44; *APNM,* 194; Stolz, 135.

(pᵉnê, pî) of the Most High; of his "counsel" (*ʿᵃṣaṯ,* 107:11), as well as the "holiest of the dwelling places" (46:5[4]) and the "sons" (82:6) of *ʿelyôn.* For the most part these expressions are familiar from similar formulas associated with Yahweh: the "right hand of Yahweh" (Hab. 2:16; Ps. 118:15-16; cf. Ex. 15:6; Dt. 33:2; etc.), the "steadfast love of Yahweh/God" (Ps. 33:5; 52:3,10[1,8]; 103:17; etc.), the "counsel of Yahweh" (Isa. 19:17; Ps. 33:11; Prov. 19:21; cf. Isa. 46:10; etc.), "his shelter" (Ps. 18:12[11]) or the "shelter of [his] wings" (Ps. 61:5[4]), the "mouth of Yahweh" (Lev. 24:12; Nu. 9:23; Dt. 1:26,43; etc.), and the extremely common "face of Yahweh." Naturally it is also possible to speak of the "dwelling place" (Nu. 16:9; 31:30; Josh. 22:19; etc.) or even the "dwelling places" (Ps. 84:2[1]) of Yahweh, but not of any "sons of Yahweh." The similarity of usage points to the extensive congruence of Yahweh and *ʿelyôn,* but there is a certain difference between the two that cannot be blurred.

This phenomenon can be observed also in the structure of poetic parallelism: on the one hand, Yahweh and *ʿelyôn* occupy equivalent places in synonymous stichs; on the other, *ʾēl* also appears in parallel with *ʿelyôn,* taking the place of Yahweh. Examples of the former are Ps. 18:14(13) = 2 S. 22:14 ("Yahweh thunders in the heavens" par. "*ʿelyôn* utters his voice"), Ps. 21:8(7) ("the king trusts in Yahweh" par. "through the steadfast love of *ʿelyôn* he shall not be moved"), and Ps. 50:14 ("offer to Yahweh [MT *ʾᵉlōhîm*] thanksgiving" par. "pay your vows to *ʿelyôn*"). In Ps. 47:3(2) we even find the expression *yhwh ʿelyôn* (par. "a great king"), which expresses the complete identity of Yahweh and *ʿelyôn.*[17]

It is not always clear in these passages whether *ʿelyôn* is to be taken as a personal name or as an appellative ("the Most High"). In the following instances, *ʿelyôn* is clearly an appellative, being used in apposition with Yahweh: "They sinned against him, rebelling against the Most High" (Ps. 78:17); "They tested the Most High God" (v. 56), or better, "Yahweh the Most High";[18] "I will sing praise to the name of Yahweh, the Most High" (7:18[17]), or "I will sing praise to your name, O Most High" (9:3[2]); "It is good to give thanks to Yahweh, to sing praises to your name, O Most High" (92:2[1]); "Yahweh alone is the Most High over all the earth" (83:19[18]; cf. 97:9); "I cry to God [or better: Yahweh] Most High, El, who fulfills his purpose for me" (57:3). In these texts *ʿelyôn* appears in second place after "Yahweh."

We find *ʾēl* and *ʿelyôn* used in parallel in Ps. 73:11 ("How can El know? Is there knowledge in *ʿelyôn?*") and 107:11, where the expressions "commandments of El" and "counsel of *ʿelyôn*" appear in parallel. Here too belongs the introduction to the third oracle of Balaam (Nu. 24:16), which says that the seer hears the words of El and knows the knowledge of *ʿelyôn.* In this instance, too, we note that *ʾēl* appears first, followed by *ʿelyôn.* Their position suggests that El and Yahweh are identical. The oracle goes on to say that the seer sees the vision of Shaddai, falling down with eyes uncovered (Nu. 24:16; cf. also v. 4). There is no convincing way to distinguish three different entities

17. Cooke, 32.

18. According to many scholars "Elohim" has replaced an original "Yahweh" throughout the so-called Elohistic Psalter (Ps. 42–83). Hence in both Ps. 78 here and Ps. 57 below the preferable reading is "Yahweh."

ʾēl, ʿelyôn, and *šadday,* since we have already noted the poetic analogy and functional association linking *ʾēl* and *ʿelyôn.* It would appear more reasonable to define the relationship of the three names by saying that the first term, *ʾēl,* is elucidated by the following terms, *ʿelyôn* and *šadday.* It follows that the full forms of the two divine names were *ʾēl ʿelyôn* and *ʾēl šadday.*[19] Ps. 91:1 makes this same assumption if "shelter of *ʿelyôn*" and "shadow of *šadday*" are instances of synonymous parallelism. To interpret this as meaning that *ʿelyôn* and *šadday* are identical makes sense only if this identity is to be found in El.[20]

This survey leads to my first conclusion: in comparison to the parallelism of El and *ʿelyôn,* the parallelism of Yahweh and *ʿelyôn* represents a later stage, where the word *ʿelyôn* has become an appositional appellative. All the OT evidence suggests that the full divine name was originally *ʾēl ʿelyôn,*[21] and that this name enshrines a concept of God antedating Yahwism. This full form of the divine name *ʾēl ʿelyôn* is attested in Gen. 14:18-20 and Ps. 78:35; in Ps. 78 it appears in parallel with *ʾelōhîm* (or, better, *yhwh*), a usage that corresponds precisely to Gen. 14:22, where a redactor has clearly identified Yahweh with the *ʾēl ʿelyôn* of vv. 18-20, having Abraham swear, "I raise my hand to Yahweh *ʾēl ʿelyôn.*" The theory that *ʾēl ʿelyôn* was originally a god distinct from Yahweh is confirmed by Dt. 32:8-9 and Isa. 14:14 as well as by Gen. 14. Gen. 14 speaks of the god of Jerusalem before it was an Israelite city (cf. Ps. 87:5); Isa. 14 appears to reflect an ancient Canaanite myth of a revolt against this god and the dethroning of *ʾēl ʿelyôn;*[22] the Song of Moses (Dt. 32:8-9) appears still to be aware that Yahweh had formerly been subordinate to *ʾēl ʿelyôn.*

These observations based on form can be confirmed and supplemented by an examination of content. When we survey the genres of the passages containing *ʿelyôn* texts, the most frequent is the hymn of praise, represented by Ps. 46:5(4); 47:3(2); 87:5; 92:2(1); 97:9; because Gen. 14:20 is also poetic praise of God, it may be included in this category. Next most frequent is the lament, represented by Ps. 7:18(17); 57:3(2); 77:11(10); 83:19, as well as Lam. 3:35,38; perhaps the prophetic dirge Isa. 14:14 may also be included here. There follow wisdom poems (Ps. 73:11; 78:17,35,56; 91:1,9; and the Song of Moses [Dt. 32:8]), thanksgivings (Ps. 9:3[2]; 50:14; 107:11), royal hymns (18:14[13] = 2 S. 22:14; Ps. 21:8[7]), and judgment discourse (Ps. 82:6).

Even though our word is not associated preferentially with a psalm genre, it does appear primarily in cultic poetry.[23] This setting points to the special affinity of *ʾēl ʿelyôn* with the cult and thus with the temple, specifically the Jerusalem temple. If we note further that 10 of the 21 occurrences of our word in the Psalms are in eight psalms

---

19. Stolz, 158ff.

20. Eissfeldt, *KlS,* V, 46.

21. Schmidt, *Königtum,* 31 n. 7, 58ff.; idem, *Faith of the OT,* 138-39; Eissfeldt, *KlS,* III, 389 n. 1; de Vaux, *AncIsr,* II, 310; Wanke, 50; Stolz, 161. For a different interpretation see Dussaud, 112-13; idem, *Syr* 27 (1950) 332-33; idem, *Syr* 35 (1958) 408-9; Levi della Vida; Pope, 52-53.

22. Oldenburg, *ZAW* 82 (1970) 187-88; Preuss, → III, 253-54; see also Wildberger, *Isaiah 13–27* (1997), 67-68.

23. Wanke, 46.

of the Korahites,[24] this conclusion is confirmed. Wanke points out rightly that these Korahite psalms are associated with postexilic groups of temple singers.[25] It follows that the term *ʿelyôn* is among the traditions handed down for ages within the cult. This is suggested also by the observation above that the word *ʿelyôn* became associated ever more intimately with Yahweh, until it finally appeared as an attribute of or in apposition with Yahweh.[26] At the same time, we must remember that the postexilic and late postexilic period had a predilection for archaizing linguistic forms and that poetic texts in particular had a tendency to incorporate and preserve non-Israelite material.[27]

2. *Connotations.* If we inquire into the meanings associated with *ʿelyôn* in the OT, we find in first place the notion of the "highest god" inherent in the word itself. This notion can still be interpreted in a fully polytheistic sense as "the god [or El] of the gods" (Ps. 50:1; Josh. 22:22), which in fact means nothing other than "the lord over the gods." This meaning simultaneously implies the notion of dominion over the universe. The one who is "exalted far above all gods" is also "most high over all the earth" (Ps. 97:9; the latter expression appears also in 83:19), because he is sovereign over the national gods of the various lands and peoples (cf. Dt. 32:8-9). In Ps. 97 these words appear in the context of a hymn celebrating Yahweh's kingship; 47:3(2) states the logical connection between the universal dominion of the highest god and the royal title: "Yahweh *ʿelyôn* is awesome, a great king over all the earth." But if Yahweh holds dominion over the whole earth, he is also the guarantor of its order.[28] This is expressed by Ps. 82: because all the nations belong to God, he can rise up to judge the earth (v. 8). But this means that he is also judge of the gods, who sides with the poor and those who suffer (vv. 1ff.; cf. Lam. 3:35). If *ʿelyôn* is the correct reading in 1 S. 2:10, then this text also describes Yahweh as judge over the whole earth in the context of his rank as the highest god.

This cosmic setting of the *ʿelyôn* passages easily accommodates the texts that associate the highest god with the heavens, picturing him dwelling there or (better) reigning there as king. That *ʿelyôn* acts in the heavens and makes his voice resound there is presupposed by Ps. 18:14(13) (= 2 S. 22:14) and 1 S. 2:10 (as well as Ps. 57:3-4[2-3]). When Isa. 14:13-14 puts into the heart of the king of Babylon the desire to "ascend to heaven," "above the stars of El," "to sit on the mount of assembly on the heights of Zaphon," "to ascend to the tops of the clouds" and make himself "like the Most High," here too the heights of heaven are conceived of as the habitation of *ʿelyôn.* This conception does not contradict the assertion that the city of God is the holiest habitation of the Most High (Ps. 46:4[4]),[29] because the temple of the city of God is, as it were, the earthly counterpart of God's heavenly habitation. This notion also finds expression in

24. Ibid.
25. Ibid., 53.
26. Ibid., 53-54.
27. Wehmeier, 893.
28. Ottosson, → I, 394.
29. See Eissfeldt, *KlS,* IV, 8-11; Schmid, 182-83.

the statement that "*ʿelyôn* himself established (*kûn* polel) it" (Ps. 87:5). The root → כון *kûn* belongs to the terminology of creation; Ps. 87 therefore suggests that the city of God owes its existence to a creative act of *ʿelyôn.* This links us with Gen. 14:19, which describes *ʾēl ʿelyôn* as "creator of heaven and earth." Ps. 50 also illustrates the connection between *ʿelyôn* and the Creator; as H.-J. Kraus noted correctly, vv. 9-13 justify the command in v. 14: because all the wild animals are God's, the devout are to offer a sacrifice of thanksgiving to God and pay their vows to the Most High.[30] Finally, one might also argue that 95:3-5 uses creation language to expand on the title "great king" given the Most High in 47:3(2).

That it is fitting to give thanks and praise to such a God, the Most High sovereign over other gods, the God of the universe, the Creator (Ps. 7:18[17]; 9:3[2]; 92:2[1]; cf. also 50:14; 106:7 cj.; 107:11), is as obvious as the hope or expectation that he will help, protect, and shelter, as Ps. 91:1,9 assert when they speak of living "in the shelter of *ʿelyôn*" or in his "refuge"; these words probably do not refer to asylum in the temple[31] but to the security the psalmist finds in the Most High God. But the psalmist can also lament that "the right hand of *ʿelyôn*" has changed (Ps. 77:11[10]) because he has not helped, even though it is Yahweh *ʿelyôn* who champions the psalmist (57:3[2]) and whose steadfast love keeps the king secure (21:8[7]).

These statements are the utterances of individuals, although they do have an element of universality that opens the possibility of generalization. Two or three texts differ formally, associating *ʿelyôn* with a plural or collective entity. In Ps. 78 it is the Israelites, who remembered that "God was their rock and *ʾēl ʿelyôn* their redeemer" (v. 35) but nevertheless rebelled against *ʿelyôn* in the desert (v. 17) and rebelliously "tested God *ʿelyôn* and did not observe his decrees" (v. 56). In Ps. 106:7 it is "our fathers," who rebelled against *ʿelyôn* at the Sea of Reeds. The conjectural text of Dt. 33:12 in the Blessing of Moses says that the tribe of Benjamin rests in safety because *ʿelyôn* surrounds him all day long and he (Benjamin) rests between his shoulders.[32]

3. *Origin.* Beyond doubt all these *ʿelyôn* texts refer to Yahweh. For Israel, Yahweh is the Most High God. This includes the passages that speaks of the "counsel" (Ps. 107:11) and the "knowledge" (Nu. 24:16; Ps. 73:11) of *ʿelyôn.* It is not impossible, however, that some of the statements were associated originally with *ʾēl ʿelyôn* and were transferred to Yahweh when the deities coalesced. For the statement that *ʾēl ʿelyôn* was an independent deity is just as true as Eissfeldt's observation that *ʿelyôn* must be counted among the gods "of high moral rank."[33]

Convincing as the case for the coalescence of Yahweh with *ʾēl ʿelyôn* is, it remains striking that — except for the two passages that speak of Israel's rebellion against *ʿelyôn* at the Sea of Reeds (Ps. 106:7) and in the desert (78:17) — there are no references in the *ʿelyôn* material to the great historical traditions of Israel. Even in the later

---

30. *Psalms 1–59* (Eng. trans. 1988), 493-94.
31. As argued by Delekat, *Asylie und Schutzorakel am Zionheiligtum* (1967), 235ff.
32. → VII, 390-91; see J. D. Heck, *JBL* 103 (1984) 523-29.
33. *KlS,* II, 146.

period, this defining core of Israel's theology remained somewhat alien to the "Most High." This observation, too, supports an early development of belief in *ʾēl ʿelyôn* independent of Israel's notion of Yahweh. This stage is still reflected in Dt. 32:8-9 and Ps. 82:1-8.[34]

Both passages assume that from the outset *ʿelyôn* and Yahweh were two distinct deities, with Yahweh subordinate to the Most High God and a member of the latter's pantheon. In the Song of Moses *ʿelyôn* functions as the supreme god by assigning the nations to the individual national gods constituting his pantheon, the "sons of El" or "sons of God." As a result of this process, Israel became Yahweh's possession (vv. 8-9).[35] Not only is Yahweh distinct from *ʾēl ʿelyôn* in being subordinate; he also differs in that *ʿelyôn,* in contrast to the national gods (including Yahweh), is supranational.[36] That this text reflects so early a stage in the history of Israel's religion is also apparent in its language; departing from the general OT notion that Yahweh was the active party in the election of Israel (as in v. 10), and interrupting the flow of the narrative in v. 8, which describes the apportioning of the nations by *ʿelyôn,* v. 9 uses a cautious, neutral-passive construction: "Then Israel became Yahweh's portion."[37]

To some extent Ps. 82 confirms and expands on this picture. V. 1 speaks of a "council of El," in which Kraus sees the Canaanite divine pantheon, Eissfeldt (more accurately) "the council of the gods presided over by El";[38] again, *ʾēl ʿelyôn* ranks as monarch. Yahweh appears before this council; he is possibly a member of it. In any case he accuses the other gods, the "sons of *ʿelyôn*" (v. 6),[39] of injustice, resulting in the "total breakdown of order,"[40] and condemns them to die like mortals (v. 7). Thus he leaves no doubt that he alone is indeed the Most High God (some suggest that Ps. 82 is based on a Canaanite myth), just as the Song of Moses concludes with a rapturous hymn to Yahweh's unique status, which incorporates the sovereign power of *ʿelyôn:* "Praise, O heavens, Yahweh; worship him, all you gods" (Dt. 32:43).[41]

Both texts clearly assume that Yahweh and *ʿelyôn* are not identical; equally clearly, in both hymns Yahweh triumphs in the end over *ʿelyôn* and replaces him. We may therefore agree with Eissfeldt that these texts reflect a transitional period in which,

---

34. Ibid.

35. Following Eissfeldt, *Lied,* 9 nn. 2 and 3; also Wanke, 49; Haag, → II, 158-59; others read the passage differently: W. F. Albright, *VT* 9 (1959) 343-44; R. Meyer, "Die Bedeutung von Dt 32,8s,43 (4Q) für die Auslegung des Mosesliedes," *Verbannung und Heimkehr. FS W. Rudolph* (1961), 197-209; G. von Rad, *Deuteronomy. OTL* (Eng. trans. 1966), 196-97; M. Tsevat, *HUCA* 40/41 (1969/70) 123-37.

36. Stolz, 169.

37. Eissfeldt, *KlS,* III, 390.

38. Kraus, *Psalms 60–150,* 155-56 (cf. Cooke, 30); Eissfeldt, *KlS,* III, 390. Cf. Schmidt, *Königtum,* 41: "El's council of state."

39. So, correctly, Cooke, 30ff.; Schmidt, *Königtum,* 41; Gese, 117; Haag, → II, 158.

40. Eissfeldt, *KlS,* III, 390.

41. On Ps. 82 see Cooke, 34; Schmidt, *Königtum,* 42. On the text of Dt. 32:43 see Eissfeldt, *Lied,* 13, 14 n. 1.

"true to the cosmic mythological tradition," *'ēl 'elyôn* is still considered the highest God, while Yahweh "is the sole controlling power, soon to take El's place in the theoretical worldview of Israelite religion as well."[42]

Finally, Isa. 14:12-15 may be cited in support of distinguishing *'ēl 'elyôn* from Yahweh,[43] because this poem is likely based on a Canaanite myth recounting the rebellion of the deities Shahar and Shalim, manifestations of the Day Star Ashtar, against *'ēl 'elyôn* in an unsuccessful attempt to dethrone him.

Eissfeldt describes Ps. 91 as a "psalm of conversion," bearing witness to how a former devout worshiper of Elyon-Shaddai has turned to Yahweh and is assured by a priest of Yahweh that he stands in Yahweh's sure protection.[44] If this theory is correct,[45] then this text, too, may be taken as evidence that *'ēl 'elyôn* was originally an independent deity.

To sum up, we can say that the OT still shows knowledge of a Canaanite god named *'ēl 'elyôn;* on the basis of our discussion, we may assume that this deity represents a hypostatic embodiment of an attribute or, as Gese says, of "a particular aspect of El."[46] In this respect the name *'ēl 'elyôn* can be placed alongside other divine names in Genesis such as *'ēl 'ôlām, 'ēl shadday,* or *'ēl rō'î,* because they too are hypostases of El embodying specific qualities of the deity.

4. *'āl?* I shall briefly examine the substance of those passages that with some likelihood deal with the god *'āl.* The "last words" of David begin with a line resembling in some respects the introduction of the earlier Yahwistic Balaam oracles (Nu. 24:3-4,15-16): "Oracle of David, son of Jesse, oracle of the man appointed by *'āl*" (2 S. 23:1).[47] The appearance of El in v. 5 suggests that the god *'āl* is a hypostasis of El. Further, the mention of the "Spirit of Yahweh" in v. 2 indicates that this deity must be identical with Yahweh. The text also states that it was this deity who made David king, establishing the Davidic dynasty by making an "everlasting covenant" (v. 5). All this could well fit with what we have established about *'elyôn* and with the specific statement of Ps. 21:8(7).

This analysis, however, appears to be at odds with two Hosea texts (7:16; 11:7). However one interprets the word *'āl/'al,* it refers clearly to the god Baal, against whom Hosea is campaigning. The northern Israelites thus gave the title "Exalted One," "Most High," to this storm god, who governed the fertility of the fields and stock, on account of his enormous influence on human life. Hosea alludes to this title when he sees Israel's "devotion to the powerless god Baal (the 'Exalted One' who cannot 'raise' anyone)"[48] as apostasy and stigmatizes Baal as *lō' 'āl,* "Not Exalted," i.e., impotent. Thus

42. *KlS,* III, 390.
43. Wanke, 48-49; Oldenburg, *ZAW* 82 (1970) 187-88; Preuss, → III, 253-54.
44. *KlS,* II, 145-46; III, 441-47; *The OT: An Intro.* (Eng. trans. 1965), 126.
45. Contra Kraus, *Psalms 60–150,* 222, who calls the psalm an affirmation of trust.
46. P. 117.
47. Textual problems have been discussed above.
48. Jeremias, *ATD* 24/1, 144.

Ringgren is probably correct in his conjecture that we are dealing here with an epithet of Baal.[49]

III. Extrabiblical Texts.

1. *Ugarit.* If we follow up the hints in the OT concerning an independent deity *'ēl 'elyôn* and look for evidence of this deity outside the OT, Ugaritic literature stands in first place on account of its enormous value as source material for the early history of Canaanite religion. We must make clear, however, that the word *'lyn* is not attested in Ugaritic, although the word *'ly,* "the Exalted One, the Most High," does occur as an epithet of Baal. We must therefore differentiate between the texts referring to El and those referring to Baal.

First as regards El: his paramount role within the pantheon and the titles accorded him correspond in large measure to what we have seen to be the substance of the OT *'ēl 'elyôn* texts. Although the actual words are not used, at Ugarit El is the "highest god." The epithets of El — "friendly El, the kindly" *(lṭpn il dpid),* "bull El" *(ṯr il),* "lord" *(rpi),* "King El" *(il mlk),* "king of eternity" *(mlk 'lm),* "mighty and majestic" *(gṯr wyqr),* "creator of creation" *(bny bnwt),* "father of humankind" *('b 'dm),* "Judge El" *(il dn)* — demonstrate first the high rank of this god as lord of the pantheon, king of the gods and consequently of the world, and chief of the "assembly of the gods" *(pḫr ilm, pḫr bn ilm),* who are called "sons of El" *(bn il).* Second, his power is expressed by the epithet "bull," by being called "holy" and "possessor of eternal life," and by the title "judge," i.e., "supreme judge." Third, he is worshiped as a god who maintains justice and shows concern for those who have suffered wrong,[50] who is both kindly and wise, and whose word is auspicious for life. Fourth, although no cosmogony is recounted, El is clearly the creator god: he is given that title and is considered a living god.[51] He dwells "at the wellspring of rivers, the mouth of the deeps" *(mbk nhrm qrb 'pq thmtm),* or on the "mountain" *(ḫršn),* probably the cosmic mountain that is the navel of the earth. He is called "father of humankind"; he promises the desperate Keret the birth of seven sons and heals him of a deadly disease. El is the heavenly god who creates and sustains life.[52]

Baal is quite a different figure. His epithets are "most powerful" *('liyn),* "prince, lord of the earth" *(zbl b'l 'rṣ),* "lord of Mt. Zaphon" *(b'l ṣpn),* "rider of the clouds" *(rkb 'rpt),* "son of Dagon [the grain god]" *(bn dgn),* "lord of the springs of the fields" *(b'l 'nt mḥrṯt),* "the holy one," "the exalted one" *('ly),* whose rain *(mṭr)* brings delight to earth and field.[53] In addition, there are Ugaritic personal names with a Baal element,[54] narratives concerning Baal, and likenesses of him. All this material can be classified into three groups. First there is evidence of Baal's power and honor; next to El, he is the

49. Pp. 132-33.
50. *KTU* 1.17, V, 8; 1.16, VI.
51. Zobel.
52. Schmid, 178, 180; Schmidt, *Königtum,* 31 n. 7, 58ff.; Gese, 97-100.
53. *KTU* 1.16, III, 5-9.
54. See esp. *PNU,* 44.

most powerful god, to whom the earth is allotted as his specific realm. He did not create the earth, but he rules over it. Second, he dwells on Mt. Zaphon, the highest mountain in the vicinity of Ugarit, and is its lord. He lives there in his kingdom above the clouds. Third, Baal is a rain and storm god and hence the god of fertility. With regard to these functions, Mt. Zaphon "with its peak often shrouded by clouds is the proper dwelling place for a storm god."[55] This association is also illustrated by the picture of Baal riding on the clouds, ax or club in his right hand and lightning lance in his left, a storm god who feeds the springs of the fields and guarantees the fertility of the soil. When he dies, he takes his clouds, his winds, his team, and his showers with him to his grave.[56] As a result, finally, "bread *(lḥm)* vanishes from the jars" of the people, "wine *(yn)* departs from their wineskins and oil *(šmn)*."[57] Bread, wine, and oil are the specific gifts bestowed by Baal. All three classes of predicate are summarized by the epithet "the exalted one," accorded Baal as the giver of rain, the storm and fertility god of Ugarit.

2. *Sefire.* A particular problem is posed by the word *'lyn* in the treaty between Barga'ya, king of KTK, and Mati''el, king of Arpad (the Sefire stele).[58] The context is a list of the gods that have witnessed the making of the treaty and are therefore guarantors of the agreement. This list concludes with ll. 10-13: "[. . . in the presence of Hadad of A]leppo, in the presence of Sibitti, in the presence of 'El and 'Elyan, in the presence of Hea[ven and Earth, in the presence of (the) A]byss and (the) Springs, and in the presence of Day and Night — all the god[s of KTK and the gods of Ar]pad (are) witnesses."[59] It is clear that starting in l. 11 *wqdm* ("and in the presence of") introduces pairs of words: 'El and 'Elyan, Heaven and Earth, Abyss and Springs, Day and Night. Gese interprets this sequence by understanding Heaven and Earth as representing cosmic space, the Abyss and the Springs as representing the element of water, and Day and Night as representing the totality of time.[60] He accordingly explains the pair 'El and 'Elyan at the head of this list as "the gods that sustain the cosmos as a whole." But the point at issue is whether l. 11 refers to a pair of gods or to a single god,[61] i.e., whether 'El and 'Elyan are taken as two distinct deities, whether the words may be translated as "El who is 'Elyon,"[62] or whether we have here a double divine name, El 'Elyan, similar to other double Ugaritic divine appellatives such as *qd w'mrr* or *kṯr wḫss*.[63] One thing is certain: because l. 10 mentions Hadad, 'Elyan must refer to El

55. Eissfeldt, *Kanaanäisch-ugaritische Religion,* 80.
56. *KTU* 1.5, V, 5ff.
57. *KTU* 1.16, III, 12ff.
58. *KAI* 222A.11.
59. Translation of J. A. Fitzmyer, *The Aramaic Inscriptions of Sefîre. BietOr* 19 (1967), 13.
60. P. 116.
61. See Eissfeldt, *KlS,* II, 172 n. 4; Ringgren, 130; Schmidt, *Königtum,* 58ff.; idem, *Faith of the OT,* 139.
62. De Vaux, *AncIsr,* II, 310.
63. Fitzmyer, *Sefîre,* 37; *KAI,* II, 246.

rather than Baal. If so, it is more logical to interpret El and ʿElyan as the single deity El, one of whose essential features is being the highest god.[64]

3. *Philo of Byblos.* Finally, we must discuss a passage in Philo of Byblos that may contain the divine name *ʿelyôn,* as well as possible historical reminiscences from the time of Sanchuniathon.[65] The story runs as follows: A certain Elioun, called Hypsistos, and a woman named Berouth came into being and settled in the vicinity of Byblos. To them were born Epigeios Autochthon, later called Ouranos, and his sister Ge. Hypsistos, however, perished in an encounter with wild beasts and was deified. Then Ouranos took over the dominion of his father and with his sister Ge begot four sons, the first being Elos, also called Kronos.[66]

Most interpreters begin with the assumption that Elioun represents an original Phoen. *ʿelyôn* because of its translation into Greek as *hýpsistos,* "most high." Then the "generation of heaven and earth" means that this *ʿelyôn* would be understood as a creator god.[67] And because the genealogy of the gods lists Elos (= Kronos) as the grandson of Elioun, El and *ʿelyôn* must be considered two totally different deities.[68] Even if this argument is correct, the question remains whether the text reflects the situation in the time of Sanchuniathon (2nd millennium B.C.E.) or in the time of Philo of Byblos. Depending on the answer, other interpretations are possible. *ʾēl ʿelyôn* may originally have been a single entity, dividing into two deities with the passage of time in a manner comparable to the later hypostatization of Bethel and Olam.[69] Conversely, the single entity might be the result of an historical process.[70]

Furthermore, the account of Philo of Byblos is so confused that it is hardly possible to base reliable conclusions on it. First, the genealogy of the gods Elium, Uranos, and Elos is at best unusual and "itself needs elucidation" before it can be used to support further conclusions.[71] Eissfeldt is also correct in pointing out that the killing of Elium by wild beasts recalls the Adonis myth, while in the Ugaritic texts Baal appears as an Adonis figure; he goes on to suggest that Philo confused Baal's second name, Aliyan, with *ʿelyôn,* "most high."[72] It is also possible that the Ugaritic Baal epithet *ʿly,* "the exalted one," lies behind Philo's Elium.

4. *Summary.* Extrabiblical sources contribute little to our understanding of *ʿelyôn* or *ʾēl ʿelyôn.* The Ugaritic material bears witness to the high status of El, but explicitly calls Baal "the exalted one," ranking him at least very close to El in importance. That

64. Stolz, 133-37.
65. Excerpted in Eusebius *Praep. ev.* 1.10.14.
66. Ibid., 1.10.15-16.
67. See, e.g., de Vaux, *AncIsr,* II, 310; Schmid, 179.
68. Schmidt, *Königtum,* 58-60; idem, *Faith of the OT,* 139; Ringgren, 130.
69. Gese, 113, 203.
70. Schmidt, *Faith of the OT,* 139; also Dussaud, 182-83; idem, *Syr* 35 (1958) 408-9; Comte du Mesnil du Buisson; de Vaux, *History,* 275.
71. Eissfeldt, *KlS,* III, 389 n. 1.
72. *KlS,* II, 231-32. See also Bertram, *TDNT,* 616 n. 13; Stolz, 136-37; Gese, 116.

some Canaanite/Aramaic texts even rank Baalshamem or Hadad before El is due to special local or regional circumstances and does not conflict with the Ugaritic evidence.[73]

The Sefire inscription, too, shows that the term *ʿelyôn* is assigned to El. Both texts also agree in associating El with creation. At Ugarit El is the creator of the gods and humankind, in fact of all creatures; at Sefire *ʾēl ʿelyôn* is the one "who sustains the whole universe."[74] Furthermore, in a number of West Semitic inscriptions from Karatepe, Hatra, Leptis Magna, Palmyra, and Jerusalem, El is called *qn ʾrṣ,* "creator of the earth"; at Boghazköy we find the name ʾIlkuniršа.[75] But it would be wrong to conclude from this evidence that in the Canaanite sphere El was originally the creator of the earth and Baal the exalted *(ʿelyôn)* creator of the heavens,[76] because the god Baal — clearly distinguished from El — as Baalshamem is "lord of the heavens," not their creator; as *bʿl ʾrṣ,* "lord of the earth," he is not its creator; "as a vegetation god, he is the sustainer of creation."[77] The information provided by the extrabiblical evidence makes it more likely that already in the 2nd millennium B.C.E. *ʿelyôn* should be considered a particular aspect of El, the creator of heaven and earth, the gods, humankind, and possibly also the animal world.[78]

IV. Jerusalem. On the basis of this discussion, we can now address the special theme of *ʾēl ʿelyôn* of Jerusalem.

1. *Gen. 14.* The most important text is Gen. 14:18-20. In these three verses we have a self-contained theme, originally independent, which has been linked secondarily with Abraham.[79] A sequence of cultic events repeatable at any time (meal, blessing, praise, tithe) becomes a unique historical event in the life of Abraham, and an encounter with manifestations of a settled local cult has been introduced into his nomadic life. V. 22 is also part of the complex: it links the scene with the context, placing *ʾēl ʿelyôn* in apposition with Yahweh and thus identifying the two deities.

Gen. 14 is the only OT text where the full name *ʾēl ʿelyôn* appears, referring to a pre-Israelite deity who is clearly not Yahwistic. The question whether *ʿelyôn* stands in apposition to El or El ("god") is placed first as an appellative[80] can be answered in favor of the former, because here we are dealing with a pre-Israelite deity named "El, the most high." This also answers the next question: the two terms refer to one and the same deity.[81]

---

73. Cf. R. Rendtorff, *ZAW* 78 (1966) 282-83; Schmidt, *Königtum,* 61.
74. Gese, 116.
75. For a detailed discussion see R. Rendtorff, *ZAW* 78 (1966) 284-86; Stolz, 130-33; most recently Miller.
76. Rendtorff, *ZAW* 78 (1966) 285ff.
77. Schmidt, *Königtum,* 61-62.
78. Gese, 117; Stolz, 137.
79. Westermann, *Genesis 12–36* (Eng. trans. 1985), 203-4.
80. Eissfeldt, *KlS,* III, 389 n. 1.
81. Ibid.; see also de Vaux, *AncIsr,* II, 310; idem, *History,* 275.

A hymnic predication entitles this god "creator of heaven and earth" *(qōnēh šāmayim wāʾāreṣ)*. Only here does the OT use the root *qnh* as a technical term for creation (but cf. Prov. 8:22); outside the OT it occurs with some frequency.[82] This supports the authenticity of our text and is further evidence supporting its non-Israelite origin. As to the phrase "heaven and earth," our text gives no reason to suspect that it represents a conjunction of two originally independent elements.[83] Westermann is correct in calling this predication "a fixed cultic formula."[84] In fact, we are dealing here with a fragment of Canaanite religiosity.[85]

Other details of the text support this impression. It speaks of a king who is also a priest of *ʾēl ʿelyôn*. This dual role points to the institution of sacral kingship, which presupposes the existence of a sanctuary. The text mentions the giving of a tithe, a practice also attested for the sanctuary at Bethel.[86] The stranger is given bread and wine, natural gifts that symbolize the fertility of the land; eating and drinking establish a convivium (cf. Josh. 9:3-15; also Ex. 24:11).[87] Finally, Abraham is blessed in the name of the deity. This blessing differs from that in Gen. 12:1-3, however, for it is not a promise of blessing. It also differs from the other patriarchal blessings in Genesis, for it does not promise land or descendants.[88] The blessing does not have any historical reference point; it is totally unhistorical. In this lack of historical references, Gen. 14 resembles the other *ʾēl ʿelyôn* texts of the OT, which likewise make no reference to the great saving acts of God in history. Furthermore, this scene is associated with a particular place. The Salem of v. 18, which appears in parallel with Zion in Ps. 76:3(2), probably refers to Jerusalem. But in Gen. 14 this is not an Israelite site. Abraham passes it by, like the Levite later in Jgs. 19:1ff.

It is therefore highly likely that Gen. 14:18ff. testifies to the existence of a cult of *ʾēl ʿelyôn* in Jerusalem around the mid-2nd millennium B.C.E.[89] The association of this scene with Abraham serves the etiological purpose of tracing back to Abraham the special cult of Yahweh observed in Jerusalem since the time of David and thus legitimizing it.

Besides *ʾēl ʿelyôn*, scholars have found evidence for the deities Ṣadeq and Shalim associated with Jerusalem. Their mutual relationship and the possibility that they belonged to a triad constitute an obscure problem.[90] The triad of El, *ʿelyôn*, and Kunirsha postulated by Gese is unlikely.[91]

---

82. *HAL*, III, 1111-12.
83. Contra Levi della Vida; Pope, 52-53; for other approaches see Stolz, 149f.
84. *Genesis 12–36*, 205.
85. Cf. Ringgren, 130; contra Rendtorff, *ZAW* 78 (1966) 290-91.
86. Eissfeldt, *KlS*, IV, 166.
87. → VII, 524. See Å. V. Ström, "Kreis und Linie," *Hermeneutik eschatologischer biblischer Texte* (1983), 103-22.
88. Eissfeldt, *KlS*, V, 53-54.
89. Eissfeldt, *KlS*, IV, 165; see also Van den Branden.
90. Schmid, 176-77; Schmidt, *Faith of the OT*, 209-10.
91. Pp. 113ff.

2. *Cult.* Since, as we have seen, the *ʾēl ʿelyôn* passages are primarily in cultic texts, while Gen. 14:18 associates this deity with pre-Israelite Jerusalem, it is highly probable that the *ʿelyôn* texts as a whole are associated with the Jerusalem sanctuary of this deity, "the holiest of his habitations" (Ps. 46:5[4]). This gives us the right to treat them as a single unit.

Jerusalem did not become an Israelite city until its capture by David. Several scholars have suggested that this event marks the beginning of the process that integrated the *ʾēl ʿelyôn* texts into Yahwism.[92] But this theory overlooks the statement of the Benjamin saying in Dt. 33:12 that the tribe rests in safety through the protection of *ʿelyôn*. It is out of the question that *ʿelyôn* here should mean Yahweh;[93] it is also certain that the saying dates from the premonarchic period. It therefore bears witness that this process of integration was already underway in the period of the judges. Beyond doubt, the capture of Jerusalem strongly reinforced the process: Yahweh was the god of the victors and thus became the new god of the vanquished. If the transfer of the ark to Jerusalem was David's work, then its entrance into the city was a visible sign that from then on Yahweh Sabaoth, the god of the ark, would be the overlord of this city and of its god *ʾēl ʿelyôn*.

This process of integration was, however, probably not so quick and straightforward as it might appear. If Eissfeldt is correct in interpreting Ps. 91 as a conversion psalm,[94] then at least there was an occasional sense that Yahwism was irreconcilable with or distinct from the worship of *ʿelyôn*. Even David appears to have been forced to make serious concessions to the religious traditions of Jerusalem. If Zadok was the priest of *ʾēl ʿelyôn*, then David's giving him dominating precedence over Abiathar (2 S. 8:17) was a mark of respect for the ancestral rights of the Jerusalem priesthood and consequently also a sign of a certain reverence toward its god *ʾēl ʿelyôn*.[95] Nyberg points out that, unlike the sons born to David in Hebron, who bore names with the theophorous element Yahweh rather than El, none of the twelve or eleven sons born in Jerusalem was given a Yahweh name, whereas several received El names.[96] This early stage of integration is probably reflected also in the texts that acknowledge the preeminence of *ʾēl ʿelyôn* and integrate Yahweh into his pantheon, making Yahweh, as it were, "a hypostasis of Elyon."[97] Last but not least, this interpretation casts new light on the statement in 2 S. 23:1 that *ʿelyôn* (= *ʿāl*) was David's kingmaker.

In this process Yahweh ultimately gained the upper hand, regardless of whether the critical impulses came from the specifically North Israelite tradition of the ark[98] or from elsewhere. With this integration, conceptions of God of Canaanite-Jerusalemite

---

92. Esp. Schmid, 197; Cooke, 33; also Lack.
93. Zobel, *Klio* 46 (1965) 83-92.
94. *KlS,* III, 441-47, 498.
95. Eissfeldt, *KlS,* III, 421, 423; see also de Vaux, *AncIsr,* II, 310-11.
96. Pp. 373-74. See also Wanke, 52.
97. Eissfeldt, *KlS,* III, 447.
98. Ibid., 421.

provenance came to be incorporated into the conception of Yahweh. Outward signs of this process include the titles accorded Yahweh, such as king, creator of heaven and earth, gracious and merciful, and defender of widows and orphans.

These features can be traced easily to the *'ēl 'elyôn* theology of Jerusalem, because elsewhere, too, they were associated with El (cf. Ugarit). But several expressions raise particular questions because they are associated traditionally with the Canaanite conception of Baal or at least closely resemble this conception, whereas the poetry of the OT links them with the Jerusalemite *'elyôn*.

It has been pointed out repeatedly that Ps. 47:3,7,9(2,6,8) and 97:1,9 are evidence for an enthronement festival of Yahweh-*'elyôn*.[99] If this festival derives from the Canaanite cultic tradition of Jerusalem and was associated originally with *'ēl 'elyôn,* it cannot reflect a tradition specific to El, because there was no enthronement festival of El, whereas there probably was an enthronement festival of Baal.

Isa. 14:13 identifies Zion with Mt. Zaphon and says that *'elyôn* has raised his throne "high above the stars of El," is enthroned on the "mount of the assembly of the god" *(har-mô'ēḏ)* and "on the heights of Zaphon" *(bᵉyarkᵉṯê ṣāp̄ôn)*. Just as the assembly and Mt. Zaphon are associated with Baal, so are the "tops of the clouds" mentioned in v. 14 — Baal is the rider of the clouds. According to 2 S. 22:10-11 = Ps. 18:10-11(9-10), however, it is once more "the Most High" who "bowed the heavens and came down, who rode on a cherub and flew" (cf. Dt. 33:26; Isa. 19:1, where Yahweh rides on the clouds), and was seen on the wings of the wind. Ps. 48:3(2), too, calls Zion a "holy mountain" and "the joy of all the earth"; again in apposition to "Mt. Zion" we find "the farthest reaches of Zaphon [NRSV 'north']."

The situation is equally clear in the case of texts that describe the power of *'elyôn* as a storm god. In 1 S. 2:10 the language is still somewhat restrained: the Most High thunders in heaven.[100] In 2 S. 22:13ff. = Ps. 18:13ff.(12ff.), however, the theme is handled at length:

> Out of the brightness before him there broke through his clouds hailstones
> and coals of fire.
> Then Yahweh thundered "from" the heavens, and *'elyôn* uttered his voice.
> He sent out his arrows and scattered them, he flashed forth lightnings
> and routed them.
> Then the channels of the sea were seen, and the foundations of the world
> were laid bare.

Dark clouds, thunder and lightning, wind and hail — these are Baal's weapons in his battle with Yamm, the sea.[101]

That this psalm really reflects the Yahweh-*'elyôn* theology of Jerusalem is shown by

---

99. Schmid, 185-86, 190; Schmidt, *Königtum,* 31 n. 7.

100. See Ringgren, 133.

101. On the theme of the battle with chaos, see esp. V. Maag, *Gesammelte Studien* (1980), 203-20.

v. 7(6), where the temple of Yahweh is called *hêkāl,* a word that (except for Shiloh) is used only for the temple in Jerusalem. Similar descriptions of *'elyôn* appear in Ps. 77:17-20(16-19); 97:1-5. To survey the total extent to which descriptions of natural phenomena have been incorporated into the Psalter, we would have to include such texts as 65:10-14(9-13), one of the most beautiful passages of nature poetry in the OT.[102] If we recall that the elements of bread and wine Melchizedek brought out to Abraham appear also in the Ugaritic texts, in the same sequence,[103] and that at Ugarit (as in Hosea) bread, wine, and oil were considered exemplary offerings to Baal, then the conclusion is inescapable: the remarkable mixture of El and Baal language in these poems can hardly be the work of Israel;[104] it was present in the material Israel drew upon. But this means that a combination of El and Baal conceptions was already present in the *'ēl 'elyôn* theology of Jerusalem[105] and was borrowed by Israel. Nor is it without interest, finally, that Philo of Byblos's Zeus, equated with Beelsamen, is called *mégistos* and *hýpsistos.*[106]

Here we can see once more an important theological difference between Israel and Judah. The northern kingdom explicitly, vigorously, consistently, and fundamentally rejected Baal, the Most High; easily, effortlessly, and almost as a matter of course ideas associated with Baal infiltrated the Yahwism of Judah by way of *'ēl 'elyôn.* Because of the distinct El and Baal traditions, handed down separately, the alternative was clear and unambiguous in Israel: Yahweh or Baal. This choice could not be so formulated in Judah and Jerusalem, because there the traditions had already coalesced and Yahweh was associated with the "syncretistic *'ēl 'elyôn.*" Last but by no means least, this analysis helps explain why we can speak of a remarkable acceptance of Canaanite elements in Judah,[107] why polemic against Baal appears only in texts of the northern kingdom, and why we can speak of an independent Baal cult in Judah only after its promotion by Athaliah (2 K. 11:18; 21:1ff.; 23:4ff.).[108]

V. Late Usage. That language referring to Israel's "most high God" was rooted originally in the Jerusalem cult is the necessary factor for its being handed down and actively used over the centuries, thanks to the high status of Jerusalem. This also explains the continued use of our term in the late OT period and beyond.

1. *Daniel.* The book of Daniel uses *'illāy* 4 times as an adjective in the phrase "the Most High God" and 6 times as an appellative, "the Most High"; this usage is quite analogous to that of *'elyôn* in the OT. The difference consists in that our word now ap-

102. See also C. Gottfriedsen, *Die Fruchtbarkeit von Israels Land* (1985).
103. For example, *KTU* 1.6, VI, 42*-44*; 1.4, IV, 35-37; 1.23, 6.71.
104. As claimed by Schmidt, *Königtum,* 55-58, citing Ps. 29.
105. Schmid, 187-90; Stolz, 154, 165; but also J. A. Emerton, *JTS* 9 (1958) 225-42.
106. Eusebius *Praep. ev.* 1.10.7. See Eissfeldt, *KlS,* II, 175; Bertram, *TDNT,* VIII, 614-16.
107. H.-J. Zobel, *Stammesspruch und Geschichte. BZAW* 95 (1965), 74, 127; idem, → V, 497-98.
108. Mulder, → II, 195-96; cf. also Stolz, 154 n. 23.

pears exclusively in narrative texts and, within Daniel, only in the Aramaic portions. Dnl. 3:26,32(4:2) place it in the mouth of Nebuchadnezzar; he addresses the three young men as "servants of the Most High God" and speaks of the wonders "that the Most High God has worked" for him. This usage makes two points: the God of the Jews is the only god there is, and a Gentile confesses this God and acknowledges that the monotheistic claim of the Jews is justified. In Nebuchadnezzar's dream (4:14[17]), it is acknowledged that "the Most High is sovereign over the kingdom of mortals." Daniel's interpretation is called "a decree of the Most High" (4:21[24]); v. 22(25) repeats the assertion of v. 14(17). In v. 29(32) it is repeated again by a voice from heaven; at the conclusion the king blesses the Most High (v. 31[34]). The reference to God as the Most High supports the idea of God's uniqueness and incomparable sway over all humankind, an idea that even the Gentile king must acknowledge. This all returns in historical dress in 5:18,21: Daniel points out to Belshazzar that the Most High God gave his father Nebuchadnezzar the kingship and brought him to acknowledge that the Most High God has sovereignty over the kingdom of mortals.

"Most High" appears once again in 7:25 as an appellation for God. This chapter also says that power will be given forever to "the holy ones of the Most High" (*qaddîšê 'elyônîn,* vv. 18,22,25,27). This phrase probably means "the faithful Jews."[109]

2. *Dead Sea Scrolls.* This brings us immediately to the Dead Sea Scrolls, because the phrase "the holy ones of the Most High" occurs also in CD 20:8, probably referring to the members of the community, who are to curse the evildoer. The other occurrences are also typical of OT usage. Twice we find the full expression *'ēl 'elyôn* (1QH 4:31; 6:33); twice *'elyôn* parallels El (1QS 10:12; 11:15). "Knowledge of the Most High" is mentioned in 1QS 4:22; in 1QH 4:31 *'elyôn* is associated with righteousness, in 1QS 11:15 with majesty, and in 1QS 10:12 with a series of expressions that culminate in "highness of majesty" and "omnipotence for eternal glory." Finally, in 1QapGen 2:4 and 20:7, we find simply *'ly,* "the Most High"; elsewhere the same text uses *'ēl 'elyôn* (20:12,16; 21:2,20; 22:15,16,21). An oath is sworn by the Most High (2:4) or God Most High (21:21); he is praised as "lord of all the worlds" (20:12) and hearer of prayers (20:16), and to him sacrifices are offered (21:2,20). The text of Gen. 14:18ff. is echoed in 22:15ff. Taken as a whole, the Dead Sea Scrolls show that the title *'ēl 'elyôn* continued in use as an archaic appellation for God, possibly even gaining increasing favor because it gave expression to God's uniqueness.

3. *Apocrypha and Pseudepigrapha.* When we come to the Apocrypha and Pseudepigrapha, it is correct to say that the divine appellative *'ēl 'elyôn* is used "frequently."[110] Most of the occurrences are in Sirach. Baudissin counts 44 passages and concludes that "the notion of Yahweh's greatness is expressed with a vigor that could

---

109. Porteous, *Daniel. OTL* (1965), 115-16; cf. M. Noth, "The Holy Ones of the Most High," *Laws in the Pentateuch and Other Studies* (Eng. trans. 1966), 215-28.

110. St.-B., II (^{2}1956), 100.

hardly be surpassed."[111] Bertram agrees, noting that "after *kýrios,* then, *hýpsistos* is the most common divine name in Sir[ach]."[112]

Altogether we may say that in the Apocrypha and Pseudepigrapha the name of the Most High serves as a summary of the Jewish idea of God and can therefore legitimately substitute for the name Yahweh. This holds true especially in the Hellenistic material, where "Most High" becomes "the usual term for the God of the Jews."[113] This name is associated not only with the hopes and longings of the devout, but also with the apologetic and propagandistic goals of the Jews.

Zobel

---

111. P. 223.
112. *TDNT,* VIII, 618.
113. Wehmeier, 895, citing A. B. Cook.

עלל *ʿll;* עֹלֵלָה *ʿōlēlâ;* עֲלִילָה *ʿalîlâ;* עֲלִילִיָּה *ʿalîlîyâ;* מַעֲלָל *maʿalāl;* תַּעֲלוּל *taʿalûl*

I. Introduction: 1. Occurrences; 2. Organization. II. "Treat." III. "Gleanings": 1. Social Legislation; 2. Metaphorical Usage. IV. "Abuse." V. Other Nouns: 1. *ʿalîlâ;* 2. *ʿalîlîyâ;* 3. *maʿalāl;* 4. *taʿalûl.* VI. 1. LXX; 2. Dead Sea Scrolls.

I. Introduction.

1. *Occurrences.* The lexicons do not agree as to the number of roots represented by *ʿll: GesB* cites three, *HAL* two. This article deals only with the occurrences that assign to *ʿll* I, i.e., the verbal forms (20 times) together with the substs. *ʿōlēlâ* ("gleanings," 6 times), *ʿalîlâ* ("deed," 24 times), *ʿalîlîyâ* ("deed," once), *maʿalāl* ("deed," 41 times), and *taʿalûl* ("treatment," twice), for a total of 94 occurrences. According to *GesB,* the root is found in Arabic and Syriac; *HAL* adds Middle Hebrew. The doubling of the second radical indicates a transitive word or a word denoting an activity.[1] The general meaning "do, act" can be abstracted for the root, but as a rule the OT uses the root → עשׂה *ʿāśâ* and its derivatives for this concept. In summary one can say that the words derived from *ʿll* occur rarely in the OT; they are found generally in elevated language or in association with specialized contexts.

2. *Organization.* Of the 11 occurrences of the poel, 5 are used with the general meaning "treat"; I discuss these first, together with the poal and hithpoel, each of which occurs once. The other 6 occurrences belong to the technical terminology of vi-

---

1. *GK,* §67a.

ticulture and correspond to the subst. *ʿōlēlâ* (6 times), with which I discuss them below. Next I discuss the 7 hithpael forms, which are used in a special sense. I treat the remaining 4 substantives last.

II. "Treat." The occurrences of the poel in the sense of "treat, deal with" (Job 16:15; Lam. 1:22 [twice]; 2:20; 3:51), the poal (Lam. 1:12), and the hithpoel (Ps. 141:4) appear in poetic texts and belong to the domain of elevated language. Thus Job can say: "I have sewed sackcloth upon my skin and laid *(ʿll)* my strength [lit. 'horn'] in the dust." As is typical of such language, the verbal forms often appear with a word deriving from the same root *(figura etymologica),* so that reduplication emphasizes the word in its context (Lam. 1:22; 2:20; Ps. 141:1).

III. "Gleanings." The 2 occurrences of *ʿōlēlôṯ,* "gleanings," in the Pentateuch use the word in its literal sense to denote an aspect of viticulture; the other 10 (2 in Judges, 8 in the Prophets), use the same term figuratively.[2]

1. *Social Legislation.* Both the Holiness Code (Lev. 17–26) and the summary of the whole law by Moses before his death (Dt. 1–30) include an ordinance forbidding all Israelite landowners from gathering the gleanings of their vineyards (Lev. 19:10; Dt. 24:21); they must refrain from seeking out and collecting the grapes that during the harvest were overlooked or fell to the ground or were rejected because they were unripe or too small. Dalman suggests the translation "immature grapes," but also notes that it is difficult to determine the precise meaning of the expression.[3] In both passages the ordinance appears in the context of similar ordinances (e.g., governing reaping); they are all based on the stipulation that the food left behind is meant for "the poor and the alien" (Lev. 19) or "the alien, the orphan, and the widow" (Dt. 24). Lev. 19 concludes this group of ordinances with the self-presentation formula "I am Yahweh," while Dt. 24 promises Yahweh's blessing if the Israelites obey the commandments and also reminds them of their life as slaves in Egypt. Obeying the gleanings ordinance is thus not simply an aspect of charity toward the poor in Israel, but also and above all a profession of faith in Yahweh (Dt. 26:12-19; Lev. 19:33-34,37).

2. *Metaphorical Usage.* The ten texts that use the term figuratively (including all the texts using the noun) implicitly compare the people to a vineyard (cf. Isa. 5:1-7). The usage in the individual texts shows how the notion takes concrete shape in each. Jgs. 20:45 recounts how, after a victory over Benjamin, Israel pursued the fugitives and "gleaned" — i.e., slew — an additional 5,000 Benjaminites. Jgs. 8:2 tells how Gideon appeased the Ephraimites, who felt they had been ignored, with a rhetorical question: "Is not the gleaning of the grapes of Ephraim better than the vintage of Abiezer?" — in

2. See Kapelrud, *BHHW,* II, 1274.
3. *AuS,* I/2, 585.

other words, even after the victory of the Abiezerites, the tribe of Ephraim is considered superior.

The book of Isaiah uses the word figuratively in three contexts: 3:12; 17:6; 24:13. In 3:1-15 the root *ʿll* occurs 4 times (vv. 4,8,10,12), giving the passage a kind of tonal unity.[4] The poel participle describes the leaders of the people as forcing everything they can from them, like gleaners in a vineyard. Isa. 17:6 uses the image of gleaning to describe the humiliation of Jacob on the day of Damascus's fall, and continues the figure with the beating of "two or three olives from the top of the tree, four or five from the branches." Finally, Isa. 24:13 uses the image to describe the handful of people in the diaspora who, like the gleanings from a vineyard, still worship Yahweh.

The book of Jeremiah, too, uses the verb and noun metaphorically, once referring to Jerusalem (6:9) and once to Edom (49:9 [= Ob. 5]). The first passage (Jer. 5:20–6:30) is a meditation on "the foe from the north." The enemy is told to "glean thoroughly" (inf. abs. + finite verb) the remnant of Israel like a vine — i.e., destroy it totally. In similar fashion, 49:14-16 and 6:9-10 (cf. Ob. 1-6) speak of Edom, saying that the grape gatherers will be so thorough in initial harvest that there will be nothing left to glean. Edom will be destroyed at a single stroke.

Finally, in Mic. 6:9–7:20, 7:1 describes the prophet as despairing because the faithful and upright have vanished from the land. He compares himself to someone who has already both gathered and gleaned and therefore can find nothing more to eat.

IV. "Abuse." The 7 occurrences of the hithpael, with the meaning "abuse," are always followed by the prep. *bᵉ*, introducing the object of the action. They are widely dispersed: 2 are in the Pentateuch (Ex. 10:2; Nu. 22:29) and 3 in the Deuteronomistic History (Jgs. 19:25; 1 S. 6:6; 31:4 [= 1 Ch. 10:4]); the other is in Jer. 38:19. In two instances the grammatical subject is Yahweh, in three (four) a group of specific individuals, and in one Balaam's ass. The objects abused are also diverse: twice it is the Egyptians who are oppressing the Israelites, and four (five) times it is an individual: Balaam, the concubine of a Levite, Saul (twice), and Zedekiah. The narrative context shows in each case how the verb is to be understood. In Ex. 10:2 and 1 S. 6:6, the plagues with which Yahweh has inflicted the Egyptians are the substance of his sovereign action. According to 1 S. 31:4 = 1 Ch. 10:4, it is the feared mistreatment of Saul's corpse by the "uncircumcised" (i.e., the Philistines). In each case the reflexive meaning of the form is clear.[5] A translation that does justice to all the occurrences would therefore be: "abuse/mistreat someone."

V. Other Nouns.

1. *ʿᵃlîlâ.* The noun *ʿᵃlîlâ,* "deed," occurs 24 times. The feminine ending denotes impersonal objects or abstractions;[6] the word can refer to both a concrete "deed" or ab-

---

4. See also V.4 below.
5. *GK,* §54a.
6. *GK,* §83a-b.

stract "conduct." Its connotations are therefore more active than those of *ma'alālîm,* which it occasionally parallels (Ps. 77:13[Eng. v. 12]). It is like *ma'alāl* in that it (usually) occurs in the plural and refers quite generally to the deeds of God or human beings. In a prophetic book, the one term is used almost to the exclusion of the other.

a. Of the 16 occurrences with the meaning "human deeds," half are in the book of Ezekiel. The others are widely scattered. Two occurrences are in a formula of Dtn legislation; I discuss them (3) after the discussion of the related occurrences in Ezekiel and Zephaniah (1) and the other occurrences (2).

(1) Ezekiel has a predilection for *'alîlôṯ* similar to that of Jeremiah for *ma'alālîm.* Both words appear in theologically significant contexts. The five Ezekiel texts in which we find the eight occurrences are extended meditations on the fate of Jerusalem, Judah, and Israel: 14:22,23 (12-23); 30:43,44 (1-44); 21:29(24) (1-37[20:45–21:32]); 24:14 (1-14); 36:17,19 (16-38). In all these texts the word denotes the disobedient deeds of the people or a portion of them. This is clear, for example, in the extended composition 36:16-38. A retrospective introduction compares Israel's "ways and deeds" of cultic impurity to a woman in her menstrual period and blames them on the "heart of stone" within the house of Israel (vv. 17,26). The promised "new heart" and "new spirit" will enable the people to live obediently, so that they need no longer do the faithless deeds of the past. Here the message of the book closely resembles Jeremiah's message of circumcision of the heart.[7] The two occurrences in Zephaniah clearly evince this tension between yesterday and tomorrow: one day God's intervention will make the disobedient deeds of Jerusalem a thing of the past (3:7), so that the city will no longer be put to shame on their account (3:11).

(2) The Song of Hannah (1 S. 2:1b-10) praises Yahweh as a God of knowledge, "so great that [human] deeds do not [even] have to be weighed [by him to determine their motives]" *(K),* or "because by him deeds are weighed" *(Q)* (v. 3). This text uses the word in its simple, descriptive sense. Ps. 14:1 begins by citing the denial of God by those who stand outside the community of Yahweh, noting in summary that such fools are corrupt and abominable in their deeds (cf. 53:2[1]). Here and in 141:4 these people are identified with "those who work iniquity," i.e., those who have turned their backs on the veneration of Yahweh demanded by "law and prophets." The occurrence in 99:8 comes at the end of a hymn to Yahweh as king. God has answered their prayers but has also "avenged" their "deeds." This refers either to the wrongdoings of Israel (e.g., Nu. 13:1–14:45), or, less likely, to the wrongdoings of Israel's enemies (e.g., Ex. 7:9–15:21).

(3) The Dtn ordinance in Dt. 22:14,17 deals with a man's charges that his wife was not a virgin at the consummation of the marriage. Both verses use the phrase *weśām lâ 'alîlōṯ deḇārîm* to express the accusation. Since this formula occurs only here and is not used in similar situations (cf., e.g., Dt. 13:13-19[12-18]), we may assume that it is an expression used only in this (sexual) context; it may be translated "cause to be talked about."

---

7. See V.3 below on *ma'alālîm.*

b. The seven (eight) occurrences that refer to deeds of God appear in hymnic texts. Isa. 12:1-6 summons Jerusalem to give thanks to the God of Israel, to call on his name, and to make known his deeds among the nations (v. 4). This text clearly refers to the miraculous deliverance of the city, described in the book of Isaiah, from threatened subjugation by the Arameans, Ephraimites, and Assyrians in 701 during the Syro-Ephraimite War (7:1-9; 36:1-37,38). By contrast, Ps. 9:12(11) speaks summarily of Yahweh's "deeds," revealed in all his "wonders" (*niplāʾôṯ,* v. 2[1]), including his gift of the law (v. 5[4]). Ps. 66:5, in the Elohistic Psalter, identifies God's deeds with Israel's crossing of the Sea of Reeds and the Jordan (cf. Ex. 14:21-23; Josh. 3:14-17). In Ps. 77 and 78 *ʿalîlôṯ* (77:13[12]; 78:11) parallels *maʿalālîm* (77:12[11]; 78:7), from the same root, recalling God's "mighty deeds." It is noteworthy that the two passages are in a sense contradictory: in 77:13(12) (cf. v. 12[11]), the psalmist, sympathetic to Jacob and Joseph, "remembers" the mighty deeds of Yahweh, whereas the author of the other psalm says that the Ephraimites "forgot" the deeds of Elohim (78:9-11). These passages reflect the tension, attested elsewhere in the biblical tradition, between north and south, Joseph and Judah. Ps. 103:8 emphasizes that "Yahweh is merciful and gracious, slow to anger and abounding in steadfast love." Here this weighty formula (cf. Ex. 34:6; Joel 2:13; Jon. 4:2; Neh. 9:17) characterizes how God works in his deeds (Ps. 103:7). Finally, Ps. 105 shows how this word (v. 1) can refer to the totality of God's individually described "mighty acts" (vv. 6-44).

2. *ʿalîlîyâ.* The word *ʿalîlîyâ* appears in the OT only in the story of Jeremiah's purchase of a field. It is an abstract noun[8] used to described Yahweh as "great in counsel and mighty in deed," rewarding all according to their ways and "doings" (*maʿalālîm,* Jer. 32:19). The juxtaposition of two nouns derived from the same root emphasizes both the contrast and the relationship between the divine and human spheres and is a mark of liturgical style.[9]

3. *maʿalāl.* The noun *maʿalāl,* formed with a preformative,[10] occurs 41 times, always in the plural. Its most frequent synonym by far in the OT, *maʿaśeh,*[11] occurs some 230 times, but only once in parallel with *maʿalāl* (Ps. 106:39). By contrast, the nouns *pōʿal* (38 times) and *peʿullâ* (14 times),[12] similarly infrequent, appear twice in poetic parallelism with *maʿalāl* (Ps. 28:4; Prov. 20:11). The word *dereḵ,* "way," both singular and plural, appears 17 times in juxtaposition with *maʿalāl,* thus suggesting that the latter is an inclusive term. This interpretation is confirmed by other parallelisms: "foreskin of the heart" (Jer. 4:4), "(cultic) abominations" (Jer. 44:22), and "wickedness [i.e., apostasy]" (Hos. 7:2; 9:15). We also find such summary construct phrases as "the wicked-

8. Rudolph, *Jeremia. HAT* I/12 (^{3}1968), 210.

9. P. Volz, *Der Prophet Jeremia. KAT* X (^{2}1928), in loc.; cf. the quotation of the phrase "great in counsel and mighty in deed" in 1QH 16:8.

10. *GK,* §85e-g.

11. → עשׂה *ʿāśâ.*

12. → פעל *pāʿal.*

ness [apostasy that is a result] of your deeds" (11 times) and "the result [lit. 'fruit'] of his/their deeds" (4 times). In short, whether the word refers to human deeds or to the deeds of God (Ps. 77:12[11]; 78:7), it usually plays a summarizing role; see esp. the description of Nabal: "he was surly [lit. 'hard'] and ruthless [lit. 'evil'] in his deeds" (1 S. 25:3). In v. 25, playing on his name, Abigail calls his conduct *n^e^ḇālâ,* i.e., antisocial behavior.[13] In almost all cases, the grammatical or logical subject of the word is human; only Mic. 2:7; Ps. 77:12(11); 78:7 speak of God's or Yahweh's deeds.

a. The occurrences referring to human deeds are concentrated in the Prophets (31 of 38): there are three occurrences in the Psalms (28:4; 106:29,39), and one each in Deuteronomy (28:20), Judges (2:19), 1 Samuel (25:3), Proverbs (20:11), and Nehemiah (9:35). The distribution indicates a specific prophetic use. Thus in the epilogue to the prophetic canon one finds in the book of Zechariah, including its beginning, a look back to the message of the "former prophets" in this way: "Return from your evil ways and from your evil deeds" (1:4; cf. the repetition in v. 6). Among the 31 occurrences in the prophetic literature, 17 are in Jeremiah, 5 in Hosea, 3 each in Isaiah and Micah, 2 in Zechariah, and one in Ezekiel. The frequency of the noun in Jeremiah and Hosea and its rarity elsewhere suggest beginning our discussion with those two prophetic books.

(1) In Jeremiah three repeated syntactic combinations exemplify the summary character of the word: "the apostasy [lit. 'wickedness'] of your/their deeds" (7 times), "the result [lit. 'fruit'] of his/your deeds" (3 times), and the use of the word as the direct object of the transitive verb *yṭb* hiphil, "make good, amend," in the sense of "let your/their deeds be guided by Yahweh's instruction through the law and prophets" (26:3,13). Furthermore, the texts use the word either in summary evaluation of past deeds (e.g., 4:4; 25:5) or argumentatively in discussing actions that should be guided by a different standard (e.g., 7:5; 35:15). The addressees are generally the "men of Judah and inhabitants of Jerusalem" (4:4; 18:11) or those among them who appear in the temple (7:3; 26:3), or the people of Judah who have fled to Egypt despite Jeremiah's words (44:22). But the people of Israel as a whole can also be identified as the doer (32:19), or at least some of them: the royal house of Judah (21:12,14; 23:2), the disobedient prophets (23:22), or the "men of Anathoth" (11:18-23).

Synonymous words and phrases cast light on the conceptual usage of the word. The phrase "evil way(s)," corresponding to the equally broad expression "evil, wickedness" (11:18; cf. v. 17), in the sense of a behavioral norm governing all of life appears eleven times; Jeremiah uses this general expression concretely in various ways to mean "apostasy from Yahweh." Here is the list of four required or prohibited acts laid down in 7:5-6: act justly with one another; do not oppress aliens, orphans, and widows; do not shed innocent blood; and renounce other gods. These requirements may be compared with the summary demand to "act justly" (Dt. 16:18-20; 16:21-25:19), the commandment not to deprive of justice those without full rights (24:17-18), the requirement of two witnesses (19:15; cf. 17:2-7), and the condemnation of worship of other deities (8:19-

13. Roth, *VT* 10 (1960) 394-409.

20). Actions that are condemned can thus be described generally as "(religious) abominations" or "following other gods" (Jer. 25:5-6; 44:22).

Acts of apostasy include failure to obey God's instruction (26:3-4) and the baseless and therefore deceptive promise of peace and prosperity (23:22). Sometimes the actions of the royal house or the guild of prophets are condemned (23:2,23). At the same time others are attacked who trust in mortals rather than in Yahweh, for only the God of Israel "gives to all according to their ways, according to the fruit of their doings" (17:10; cf. Prov. 20:11). Finally, the doings of the inhabitants of Judah and Jerusalem, the fruit of disobedience, are compared to "sowing among thorns" and "uncircumcised hearts," in contrast to "breaking up fallow ground" (Jer. 4:4; cf. v. 3).

Several texts are theologically significant. It is clear, for example, that the actions of the people of Judah, Jerusalem, and Israel are judged by the criterion of the law and the message of the prophets, up to and including Jeremiah; every action that does not meet this criterion represents apostasy from Yahweh. Jeremiah's recourse to the distant past, comparing the fate awaiting Jerusalem to that of Shiloh, the ruins of a sanctuary dating from the end of the period of the judges (7:1–8:3; 26:1-24; cf. 1 S. 1:1–4:22), lends his words an unexpected topicality. Only Yahweh's special revelation makes clear to the prophet the true — i.e., faithless — nature of his opponents' attacks (Jer. 11:18-23). It is this profound sense of God's active involvement that grounds the prophet's call to his people to circumcise their hearts (2:1–4:4). These and parallel texts (9:24-25; Dt. 10:16; 30:6) offer a new possibility: the doing of the law now and in the future through a spiritualization given by God and freely accepted, overcoming the faithless disobedience of Israel's past "doings."

(2) The five occurrences in Hosea illustrate the word's importance for the prophet. Like Jeremiah, Hosea uses the phrase "the faithlessness [lit. 'wickedness'] of their deeds" (9:15) and employs the word in parallel with "ways" and "apostasy" (twice each). The doers of these deeds are the people of Ephraim or Israel; one text singles out the priests (4:9), and there is one allusion to the patriarch Jacob, whose deeds prefigure, as it were, those of his descendants (12:3[2]). Unique to Hosea is language that gives the deeds a life of their own: "they surround him" and "do not permit him to return to Yahweh" (7:2; 5:4).

(3) For the most part, the remaining occurrences use the word like Jeremiah and Hosea to refer to the faithless deeds of Israel, usually in the past. Zec. 1:1-6 is striking: in summary terms it describes Israel's disobedience ("ways," "deeds," v. 4), the dark folly that stands in such sharp contrast to the obedience of those who let their eyes and ears be opened by Yahweh (Dt. 29:1-20; Jer. 4:1-4). The exhortation to "remove the evil of your doings" appears not only in the prologue to the book of Isaiah (1:16) but also in the prophet's castigation of the leaders of Judah and Jerusalem, who are perverting justice (3:1-15; here the word is used both negatively [v. 8] and positively [v. 10]). Within a meditation on the restoration of Israel (Ezk. 36:16-38), v. 31 describes the people as looking back with loathing on their "deeds." Mic. 3:4 and 7:13 condemn the actions of the heads of Jacob/Israel in the past as well as those of the inhabitants of the land (but not the city of Jerusalem) in the present. A similarly broad perspective is reflected in Dt. 28:20; Jgs. 2:19; Ps. 106:29,39; Neh. 9:35.

In the text of Deuteronomy, failure to observe the law is censured as the root of "faithless deeds"; the other four passages show how this faithless disobedience was already manifested in the time of judges and even before, during Israel's wandering in the wilderness and finally also after it settled in Canaan. The word is used in an even more general sense in stating the fundamental principle that "faithless deeds" are done by those who do not know Yahweh's deeds and therefore engage in futile, idolatrous actions (Ps. 28:4; cf. v. 3). Finally, the maxim in Prov. 20:11 says that the actions even of young children show whether the principles of their "doing" are pure and right.

b. In Ps. 77:12(11); 78:7, *maʿalāl* refers to God's acts as demonstrations of his favor toward Israel (cf. the discussion above of *ʿalîlôṯ,* used in parallel in both texts). Mic. 1:2–2:13 in a sense extends the theme of Ps. 77 and 78 by pronouncing judgment on Judah as well. The word appears in a quotation from the prophet's opponents: "Is Yahweh's patience exhausted? Are these his doings?" (Mic. 2:7). The reference is to the destruction of Samaria, Jerusalem, and other cities described by the prophet. The double question underlines the clash of views: Micah's enemies see Yahweh as the unconditional guarantor of the peace and security of his people (cf. similar prophetic subversions of popular expectations of deliverance in Jer. 21:1-21; Am. 5:18-21).

4. *taʿalûl.* The noun *taʿalûl* occurs only in Isaiah (twice) and only as a plural. Its form suggests an abstract meaning,[14] something like "principles manifested in certain acts." Both occurrences appear in summarizing texts (3:4; 66:4); structurally, they bracket the book. In the first text the word parallels "boys," in the sense of "people unqualified to rule"; it refers to times when exile of the leadership leaves only simple, ignorant people to inhabit the land, so that violence prevails over justice (cf. 2 K. 25:4-12,18-26). In Isa. 66:4, by contrast, the word describes idolatrous acts that render those who do them deaf to Yahweh's call.

Roth

VI. 1. *LXX.* The LXX uses a great variety of words to translate *ʿll* I: besides *empaízein* (6 times for the hithpael), *kalamásthai* (4 times for the poel), *epiphyllízein* (3 [4] times), and *epanatrygán* (twice), several translations are used only once. The same variety appears in the translations of the nouns: *epiphyllís* is used 3 times for *ʿōlēlôṯ; epitḗdeuma* translates *ʿalîlâ* 10 times, while *hamartía, anomía, asébeia,* and other words are used once; *ʿalîlîyâ* is represented neutrally by *érgon; maʿalāl* is translated by *epitḗdeuma* 28 times, by *érgon* 4 times, and by *diaboúlion* 3 times, as well as by other words.[15]

2. *Dead Sea Scrolls.* In the Dead Sea Scrolls the word appears only in the noun forms *ʿōlēlôṯ,* which occurs 7 times, and *ʿalîlîyâ,* found only in 1QH 16:8: "Blessed are

14. *GK,* §85r.
15. See also Bertram, *TDNT,* V, 631.

you, Lord, great in counsel *(ʿēṣâ),* rich in *ʿalîlîyâ,* whose work *(maʿaśeh)* is all." The deeds of the wicked (*ʿalîlôṯ ʿawlâ,* 1QS 4:17; *ʿalîlôṯ rišʿâ,* 1QS 4:21; cf. 1QH 14:9; 15:24) are punished by God (CD 5:16) and cleansed by God's holy spirit. If God were to consider only these deeds, there would be no deliverance. But God looks with favor on the *ʿalîlôṯ* of the righteous.

Fabry

עָלַם *ʿālam;* תַּעֲלֻמָה *taʿalumâ*

I. General: 1. Occurrences; 2. Etymology. II. Usage and Meaning: 1. Semantic Field; 2. Cognitive Aspect; 3. Niphal; 4. Hiphil; 5. Hithpael. III. Theological Usage: 1. Hiddenness of God; 2. Refusal to Help. IV. LXX.

I. General.

1. *Occurrences.* The Hebrew verb *ʿālam* (= *ʿlm* I and II),[1] "be hidden," appears 28 times in the protocanonical OT; there are 5 additional occurrences in Sirach and 6 in the Dead Sea Scrolls. It appears only once in the qal (pass. ptcp.: "our secret," i.e., "our secret sins" [Ps. 90:8]). There are 16 occurrences of the niphal (11 in the protocanonical OT, 1 in Sirach, 4 in the Dead Sea Scrolls), 12 of the hiphil (10 in the protocanonical OT [including Isa. 57:11 (see II.4 below) and counting Lev. 20:4 as 1 occurrence], 2 in Sirach), and 10 of the hithpael (protocanonical OT 6, Sirach 2, Dead Sea Scrolls 2). Ignoring the Dead Sea Scrolls, we find 13 occurrences in the historical books, 5 in the Prophets, 5 in Psalms and Lamentations, and 10 in wisdom literature (including Sirach). Poetic texts account for 19 occurrences, prose texts for 14 (including 9 in legal contexts [Deuteronomy, H, P^S]). Most of the occurrences are probably postexilic; it is likely that Isa. 1:15; 1 S. 12:3 (if pre-Dtr); and Nah. 3:11 are preexilic. The forms in Dt. 28:61 and Jgs. 16:3,[2] as well as Isa. 63:11, derive from → עלה *ʿālâ.* Sir. 46:19 *(wenaʿal[ay]im)* is from → נעל *naʿal.*

ʿālam. S. E. Balentine, *The Hidden God* (1983), 1-21 (ch. 1), a revision of his "Description of the Semantic Field of Hebrew Words for 'Hide,'" *VT* 30 (1980) 137-53; S. Ben-Reuven, "עלם ועלמה במקרא," *BethM* 28 (1982/83) 320-21 (cf. *OTA* 7 [1984], no. 419); G. Gerleman, "Die sperrende Grenze," *ZAW* 91 (1979) 338-49; G. del Olmo Lete, "Nota sobre Prov. 30,19 *(wederek geber beʿalmâ),*" *Bibl* 67 (1986) 68-74; L. Perlitt, "Die Verborgenheit Gottes," *Probleme biblischer Theologie. FS G. von Rad* (1971), 367-82; H. Schult, "Vergleichende Studien zur alttestamentlichen Namenkunde" (diss., Bonn, 1967), 107; J. A. Thompson, "The Root *ʿ-L-M* in Semitic Languages and Some Proposed New Translations in Ugaritic and Hebrew," *Tribute to A. Vööbus* (1977), 159-66; G. Wehmeier, "סתר *str* hi. to hide," *TLOT,* II, 813-19.

1. *HAL,* II, 834-35.
2. Listed by Lisowsky, 1072, under *ʿlm* I.

The noun *taʿalumâ,* "secret,"[3] appears 3 times in the OT (sg. in Job 28:11; pl. in Ps. 44:22[Eng. v. 21]; Job 11:6); it is not found in Sirach or the Dead Sea Scrolls. There are no grounds for the conjectural form *taʿalumōṯēnû* in Ps. 64:7(6).

Other conjectural nominal forms should also be rejected: **naʿalām,* "bribe" (1 S. 12:3 par. Sir. 46:19 [see II.4 below]; for MT *naʿalāyim* in Am. 2:6; 8:6);[4] **ʿēlem,* "understanding" (Eccl. 3:11, MT *ʿôlām*);[5] **ʿelem,* "wisdom, understanding" (for MT *ʿôlām* in Gen. 21:33; Isa. 40:28; Jer. 6:16; 10:10; Hab. 3:6; Ps. 139:24; Eccl. 3:11);[6] **ʿa/olmâ,* "darkness, dark or hidden place" (Prov. 30:19, MT *ʿalmâ*).[7]

2. *Etymology.* The "communicative efficiency" of a language is hard to reconcile with the presence of too many homonyms.[8] In our case it is probably sufficient to identify two homonymous roots: *ʿlm* I, "be hidden," and *ʿlm* II, "be excited" (Arab. *ġalima*).[9] The hypothesis of a root *ʿlm* III (= Ugar. *ġlm,* "be[come] dark") is superfluous.[10] The semantic range of *ʿlm* I can easily accommodate both the notion of "hiding" and that of "being dark." In Ugaritic, too, identification of two analogously homonymous roots *ġlm* appears sufficient.

Apart from passages where Ugar. *ʿlm* probably corresponds to Heb. *ʿôlām* and Ugar. *ġlm(t)* to Heb. *ʿelem/ʿalmâ,* the dispute over whether Ugaritic has a noun *ġlmt,* "darkness," and/or a verb *ġlm,* "be dark," involves essentially just four texts.[11] Discussion of the three *ġlm* texts has not yet been decided in favor of *ġlm,* "be dark"; cogent arguments have been proposed for other etymologies.[12] Besides the *ġlm* problem, the texts also raise stichometric, lexical, and grammatical questions. The only real argument, the parallelism of *ġlmt* with *ẓlmt* ("darkness"),[13] does not necessarily mean that *ġlmt* and *ẓlmt* are synonyms (esp. since *ġ* may be an allophone of *ẓ*). The meaning "be hidden" is by no means ruled out.[14] The two other texts are even less clear. Indisputably, Sem. *ẓ* is sometimes represented by Ugar. *ġ.*[15] It remains an open question, however, whether **ġ/ẓlm* is an example of this alternation.[16]

A passage from a letter may be evidence for an Ugaritic verb **ʿlm.*[17] But this iso-

---

3. *KBL*², 1036a.
4. See R. Gordis, *JNES* 9 (1950) 319-21.
5. F. Hitzig, *Der Prediger Salomos. KEHAT* 7 (1947), in loc.; → VII, 420-21.
6. Thompson, 164-65.
7. Del Olmo Lete, 71.
8. J. Barr, *Comparative Philology and the Text of the OT* (1968), 134-51.
9. Thompson, 159-63.
10. *HAL,* II, 835, following Dahood, Pope, etc.
11. *KTU* 1.4, VII, 54 (= I.8, II, 7): *ġlmt;* 1.14, I, 19: *ġlm;* 1.16, I, 50: *ġlm;* and 2.14, 14: *yʿlm.*
12. Contra del Olmo Lete, 71-72. For a full bibliog. see ibid.
13. *KTU* 1.4, VII, 54-55 (= 1.8, II, 7-8).
14. J. C. de Moor, *Seasonal Pattern in the Ugaritic Myth of Baʿlu. AOAT* 16 (1971), 164, 172.
15. W. von Soden, "Kleine Beiträge zum Ugaritischen und Hebräischen," *Hebräische Wortforschung. FS W. Baumgartner. SVT* 16 (1967), 291-94 = idem, *Bibel und Alter Orient. BZAW* 162 (1985), 89-92.
16. Contra M. Dietrich and O. Loretz, *WO* 4 (1967/68) 308, 312-14.
17. *KTU* 2.14, 14. See J. L. Cunchillos, *UF* 12 (1980) 147, 151.

lated instance does not by itself demonstrate the existence of such a root;[18] we shall therefore ignore it here. The other texts cited by *HAL* under *ʿlm* I are irrelevant; they should be assigned to the particle *ʿlm (ʿl + -m),* "in addition, consequently."[19]

The root *ʿlm* I, "be hidden," is attested with certainty only in Hebrew. In this context we can leave open the question whether it is possible to identify a related root in South Semitic on the basis of the "opposite sense" theory (Arab. *ʿalama,* "denote"; *ʿalima,* "know, learn"; *ʿilm,* "knowledge"; *ʿalam/ʿalāma*[*t*], "mark, characteristic"; comparable forms and meanings in Old South Arabic and Ethiopic [Geʿez and several modern dialects]).[20]

Relics of this "contrary sense" would also be preserved in Hebrew if Hitzig, Thompson, and others are right in proposing nominal forms such as **ʿēlem,* "knowledge," or if Rosenthal is correct in his theory that the toponym *ʿalmôn* (Josh. 21:18; cf. *ʿālemet* in 1 Ch. 6:45[60]; *ʿalmōn diblāṯaymâ* in Nu. 33:46-47) corresponds to **ʿalamân,* "the two way sign."[21] This approach assumes that originally "knowledge" referred concretely to a vital familiarity with "way signs."[22]

The same uncertainty with respect to the etymology of the toponyms holds analogously with respect to such PNs as *ʿālemet* (1 Ch. 7:8; 8:36; 9:42) and *yaʿlām/yaʿᵃlām* (Gen. 36:5,14,18; 1 Ch. 1:35; Ps. 55:20[19] cj.).[23]

An etymological relationship between *ʿlm* I and *ʿôlām* is unlikely.[24] No less speculative is the connection between *ʿlm* I and II postulated by Gerleman.[25] Of course this observation does not preclude wordplays (possibly Prov. 30:19).[26]

II. Usage and Meaning.

1. *Semantic Field.* The verb *ʿālam* and the noun *taʿᵃlumâ* belong to the semantic field "hide."[27] Of the words belonging to this field, only the commonest verb (81 OT occurrences) → **סתר** *str* appears in parallel with *ʿlm* or in the immediate context: see esp. Job 28:21 (*ʿlm* niphal par. *str* niphal); also Nu. 5:13; Prov. 28:27-28 (association of ideas?); Ps. 10:1,11 (v. 1, *ʿlm* hiphil; v. 11, *str* hiphil + *pānîm*). Unlike *str* (hiphil + *pānîm,* almost always with God as subj.), *ʿlm* never appears with *pānîm* as object; con-

18. *WUS,* no. 2035: "know[?]."

19. *KTU* 1.43, 9; 1.105, 7, 16, 20, 14-15. See K. Aartun, *Die Partikeln des Ugaritischen. AOAT* 21/1 (1974), 11, 15; idem, *UF* 12 (1980) 2, 6.

20. See esp. L. Kopf, *VT* 8 (1958) 189-90 (no. 49) and 162 n. 2 (bibliog.).

21. See I.1 above; F. Rosenthal, *Knowledge Triumphant* (1970), 6-12. Cf. the somewhat different treatment by *HAL,* II, 836: *ʿalmôn* = "small way signs"; cf. J. J. Stamm, *Beiträge zur Hebräischen und altorientalischen Namenkunde. OBO* 30 (1980), 5-8.

22. Rosenthal; seconded by G. Krotkoff, *JAOS* 84 (1964) 170-71.

23. *GesTh,* III, 1035, interprets the latter name as meaning "the one whom God hides"; *KBL*[2], 389a, enters the name under *ʿlm* II; *HAL,* II, 421, leaves the etymology open.

24. E. Jenni, *TLOT,* II, 852; idem, *ZAW* 64 (1952) 199-200, contra the earlier scholars cited there; also contra Gerleman, 340-45; B. Kedar, *Biblische Semantik* (1981), 92; Thompson, 161.

25. Pp. 345-49; see already Jerome, cited by G. Brunet, *Essai sur l'Isaïe de l'histoire* (1975), 36, esp. nn. 5, 6, 8.

26. For other less persuasive possibilities see Ben-Reuven.

27. Balentine.

versely, *str* hiphil never appears with *ʿênayim* as object.[28] But *ʿlm* texts like Isa. 1:15 and Ps. 10:1 (see above) are practically identical in function and meaning.

In many passages *ʿlm* is virtually interchangeable with such words as → כחד *kḥd:* 1 K. 10:3, "nothing is hidden from the king," uses *ʿlm* niphal; the analogous statement in 2 S. 18:13 uses *str* hiphil. But *ʿlm* always has negative force ("prevent a person or thing from being perceived by others"); unlike other lexemes belonging to the semantic field, it cannot mean "find shelter." It is also not used to express the notion of physical concealment (except possibly in Job 6:16; see II.5 below).

When God is the subject, the following semantically related verbs are found in the same context: *ʿāmaḏ* + *berāḥôq* (Ps. 10:1); *šāḵaḥ* (Ps. 9:13,19[12,18]; 10:11-12; *ḥšh* hiphil (Isa. 57:11).[29]

2. *Cognitive Aspect.* Both *ʿālam* and *taʿalumâ* appear primarily "in contexts . . . having to do with knowing or not knowing."[30] This cognitive aspect appears in the idiomatic expression *ʿlm* hiphil + *ʿênayim,* which refers to physical sight only in Sir. 9:8 (and — with God as subj. — Isa. 1:15), as well as in *ʿlm* niphal *min* or *mēʿênê.* This aspect is also clear from the use of *ʿlm* as an antonym of *ngd* hiphil (1 K. 10:3 par. 2 Ch. 9:2); 2 K. 4:27; Isa. 57:11-12; cf. Job 11:6), *ydʿ* (Lev. 4:13-14; 5:3-4; Job 28:21,23; cf. Ps. 44:22[21]), and verbs of hearing (*šāmaʿ,* Isa. 1:15; Lam. 3:56; *ʾzn* niphal, Ps. 55:2[1]).

Especially complex is the language of Job 42:3: Job confesses that he has "hidden counsel" (*maʿlîm ʿēṣâ* [par. 38:2, *maḥšîḵ ʿēḏâ*]) by speaking (*ngd* hiphil) without "understanding" *(bîn)* about things beyond his comprehension *(belî ḏāʿaṯ; niplāʾōṯ mimmennî welōʾ ʾēḏāʿ).*

3. *Niphal.* Of the 16 occurrences of *ʿlm* in the niphal, 9 are constructed with *min* or *mēʿênê.* The object of the preposition is an individual or group, or "all living" (Job 28:21), from whom knowledge of a situation is temporarily or permanently "hidden" or "withdrawn." When we turn to the nature of what is hidden, we find unintentional transgressions that are "hidden" from the guilty "assembly" (Lev. 4:13) or the individual transgressor (Lev. 5:2,3,4), or the adultery of a woman, knowledge of which is "hidden" from her husband (Nu. 5:13; see below). Contrariwise, the answer to none of the riddles posed by the queen of Sheba was "hidden" from Solomon (1 K. 10:3 par. 2 Ch. 9:2). Wisdom is hidden from all who live, the work of God from humankind (Sir. 11:4). Forms of the niphal participle occur 7 times without *min:* Eccl. 12:14 ("every secret thing"); Nah. 3:11; Ps. 26:4; and 4 occurrences in the Dead Sea Scrolls.

Nah. 3:11a threatens Nineveh, the personified Assyrian capital: "You also [like Thebes in vv. 8-10] will be drunken and out of your senses *(tehî naʿalāmâ).*" Drunkenness and its consequences are a very common "collective punishment" in the prophets (e.g., Isa. 19:14; 28:7; Jer. 51:7,39,57; Ob. 16). Here in Nahum the niphal of *ʿlm* cannot

28. On *str* with God as subject see ibid.; on *str* and *ʿênayim* see ibid., 13.
29. Perlitt, 369-70.
30. Jenni, *ZAW* 64 (1952) 199 n. 3.

mean "be despised," as the LXX translates. The cognitive nuances of the word (see II.2 above) suggest that it refers here to a lowered level of consciousness, which will manifest itself as helplessness in the face of the enemy (v. 11b). There is no need to emend the text.[31]

Uniquely in the OT, Ps. 26:4 uses *na'ᵃlāmîm* to refer to a group of people from whom the psalmist, avowing his innocence, wishes to dissociate himself; they are "those who conceal themselves, i.e. insidiously, craftily,"[32] sinister figures who act in secret, avoiding the light of day. Since the negative qualification in vv. 4-5 appears in parallel with such general terms as *mᵉṯê šāw'*, *mᵉrē'îm,* and *rᵉšā'îm,* a more precise definition is impossible. The Dead Sea Scrolls frequently use the language of Ps. 26 to refer to enemies of the community or of the Teacher of Righteousness (1QH 3:28; 4:13; 7:34 [*sôḏ ma'ᵃlāmîm* par. *'ᵃḏaṯ šāw*]).[33]

Only in these special cases is a person (or a personified city) the subject of *'lm* niphal. It is therefore unlikely that in Nu. 5:13 the lover of a woman suspected of adultery should "remain concealed from the eyes of her own husband,"[34] or that the masc. form *wᵉne'lam* should be emended (following Sam^{MSS}) to the fem. *wᵉne'elmâ* (par. *wᵉnistᵉrâ,* with the woman under suspicion as subject.[35] The latter would be the easier reading. As in Lev. 5:2-4 (cf. 4:13), the form *wᵉne'lam* syntactically has an impersonal subject (NRSV "it is hidden"); semantically, the subject is the act of adultery.

4. *Hiphil.* Poetic texts use the hiphil of *'lm* with reference to God absolutely in the sense of "hide oneself" (Ps. 10:1; Isa. 57:11 LXX; see below). Much more frequent is the idiomatic expression *'lm* hiphil + *'ênayim,* "hide one's eyes," i.e., "avert one's eyes, look away, pay no attention to, close one's eyes to" (Lev. 20:4); *'yn* appears usually with a suffix, e.g., "I hide my eyes." Examples include Lev. 20:4; Ezk. 22:26; Sir. 9:8 (all three with *min* + the personal or impersonal obj. from which the eyes are hidden); Prov. 28:27; 1 S. 12:3 (see below); Isa. 1:15 (with God as subj.). In Lam. 3:56 the verb is used with the ear *('oznᵉḵā)* as object, with reference to the poet's prayer for help. There are three other occurrences of the hiphil: 2 K. 4:27 (see III.1 below); Job 42:3 (Job "hides/darkens" God's *'ēṣâ*); Sir. 37:10 ("Hide your plan [*sôḏ*] from those who are jealous of you").

In Isa. 57:11 the reading *ûma'lîm,* which most likely lies behind LXX *paroró* (and Vulg. *quasi non videns*), is clearly the more difficult reading in comparison to the MT, which has been assimilated to Isa. 42:14 (even though MT is supported by 1QIs^a, 4QIs^d, Syr., and Targ.).[36] Ps. 10:1 confirms the absolute use of *'lm* hiphil (without *'ênayim*).

In a notarial proceeding to assert his innocence (1 S. 12:3-5), Samuel asks (among

---

31. As also noted by *HAL,* II, 834.
32. Ibid.
33. See *DJD,* I, 35, 1, 8.
34. M. Noth, *Numeri. ATD* 7 (1966), in loc. (not in Eng. trans.).
35. Contra Wagner, → X, 365.
36. D. Barthélemy, *Critique textuelle de l'AT. OBO* 50/2 (1986), 414.

other things): "From whose hand have I taken a bribe *(kōp̄er)* to hide [NRSV 'blind'] my eyes with it *(weʾaʿlîm ʿênay bô)?*" (v. 3b). The formulation of the question implies the possibility that Samuel allowed himself to be bribed to side with the guilty party when rendering judgment (Ex. 23:8 [cf. Dt. 16:19b]: "You shall take no bribe [*šōḥad̲*], for a bribe blinds the clear-sighted [*yeʿawwēr piqḥîm*]"). In place of the MT, the LXX reads *kaí hypódēma; apokríthēte kat' emoú,* probably representing Heb. *wenaʿalayim ʿanû b̲î.* With its highly unusual construction (only here is *ʿlm* hiphil + *ʿênayim* constructed with instrumental *be*), the MT is the more difficult reading.[37] The LXX has to repeat unnecessarily *ʿanû b̲î* from the beginning of the verse. The "inverted quotation"[38] in Sir. 46:19 only confirms the Hebrew text represented by the LXX; it is not, however, an independent witness against the MT. Furthermore, the *naʿalāmîm* of Ps. 26:4 (see II.3 above) are people "whose right hands are full of bribes *(šōḥad̲)*" (v. 10); in Lev. 20:4, too, *ʿlm* hiphil + *ʿênayim* describes judicial partisanship.

5. *Hithpael.* The usage of *ʿlm* hithpael is uniform to the point of being formulaic. Most of the ten occurrences are in negated verbal clauses (directives not to "ignore" an individual or a stray animal belonging to "your brother," Dt. 22:1-4). Other occurrences, frequently constructed with *min,* are in semantically negative contexts (CD 8:6; Job 6:16; see below). To hide from someone means to ignore that person, even though one clearly "sees" the need for help *(rāʾâ:* Dt. 22:1,4 par. 11QT 64:13-14; Isa. 58:7; see III.2 below). In Ps. 55:2(1) God is the subject: he is called on not to ignore the supplication of the psalmist.

Job 6:15-17 likens Job's untrustworthy friends to wadis that are full of water in winter but dry up in summer. V. 16 (*ʿlm* hithpael) speaks of "snow that 'hides itself,' 'vanishes away' upon the water,"[39] representing metaphorically Job's "companions" (v. 15) who desert him.

In several passages *ʿlm* hiphil + *ʿênayim* and *ʿlm* hithpael *(min)* are practically synonymous: cf. Prov. 28:27 (hiphil) with Isa. 58:7 (hithpael); Isa. 1:15 and Lam. 3:56 (hiphil, with *ʾōzen* as obj.) with Ps. 55:1(1) (hithpael). The last three occurrences have God as subject.

III. Theological Usage.

1. *Hiddenness of God.* While more than half the occurrences of *sāt̲ar* refer to God, this is true of just 7 of the 39 occurrences of *ʿlm.*[40] Such usage does not occur at all in the Dead Sea Scrolls.

In two prophetic texts God describes himself as "hiding himself." In Isa. 57:11 LXX (see II.4 above), he says that the reason some Israelites do not fear him but turn to idol-

---

37. Contra → IX, 466, as well as H. J. Stoebe, *Das erste Buch Samuelis. KAT* VIII/1 (1973), in loc.; P. K. McCarter, *I Samuel. AB* 8 (1980), in loc.; B. Janowski, *Suhne als Heilsgeschehen. WMANT* 55 (1982), 167-68, with bibliog.

38. P. C. Beentjes, *Bibl* 63 (1982) 506-7.

39. F. Horst, *Hiob. BK* XVI/1 (1968), in loc.

40. Balentine, 2-14. See I.1 above.

atry is that he has kept silent and hidden himself. In Isa. 1:15 he hides his eyes from those who think they can make prayers to him even though their hands are full of blood. In Ps. 10:1 the psalmist in turn asks in his lament why God hides himself and stands far off, reversing the correlation of desert and fortune (passim). The supplicant beseeches God not to hide from his prayer (Ps. 55:2[1], *ʿlm* hithpael; Lam. 3:56, *ʿlm* hiphil + *ʾōzen*), obviously convinced that it is possible to pray even when God is hidden, that God is not totally absent. Finally, the prophet Elisha is forced to confess that Yahweh has left him in the dark concerning the reasons for the Shunammite woman's distress (2 K. 4:27). With reference to the existence of human misery, Sirach declares objectively that God's works are concealed from humankind (Sir. 11:4).[41] This statement resembles some of the things Ecclesiastes says in different language (e.g., 3:11; 8:16-17; 11:5) and is probably related also to the idea of God's "hidden wisdom" (Job 28).[42]

Job 28 comprises three sections: vv. 1-11,12-22,23-28.[43] Sections one and two culminate in antithetical *ʿlm* statements: v. 11 says that humans are able to bring to light the *taʿalumôṯ* of the earth, while v. 21 states that wisdom remains hidden (*ʿlm* niphal par. *str* niphal) from humankind — indeed, from all things living. Vv. 23-28, however, declare that as creator God "understands *(hēḇîn)* the way to it, and he knows *(yāḏaʿ)* its place" (v. 23). God can therefore "tell you the secrets of wisdom" (*weyaggeḏ-lekā taʿalumôṯ hoḵmâ,* 11:6). Job's confession (42:3) may allude to 28:23: *bîn* (qal/hiphil) and *yāḏaʿ* are characteristic of God, but forsake the unaided human being. This anthropological observation suggests other texts that use *ʿlm* to describe the limitations of human knowledge. There are "hidden" sins (Lev. 4:13; 5:2-4; Ps. 90:8 *ʿalumēnû* par. Ps. 19:13[12] *nistārôṯ*), i.e., sins unknown to those who commit them; indeed, all kinds of human deeds are hidden, "whether good or evil" (Eccl. 12:14). And it is always true that "God knows the secrets of the heart" (*hûʾ yōḏēaʿ taʿalumôṯ lēḇ,* Ps. 44:22[21]).

2. *Refusal to Help.* The hithpael of *ʿlm* (in Prov. 28:27 the hiphil + *ʿênayim*) is used in paraenetic contexts to warn against refusing to help those in need. In Dt. 22:1-4 (par. 11QT 64:13ff.; cf. Ex. 23:4-5) the text moves from a strayed animal or a lost garment to anything at all that is lost. The emphasis is on the very concrete "neighbor" whose living is imperiled: "You may not withhold your help" (v. 3b). Isa. 58:7 and Sir. 4:2 (cf. Prov. 28:27) then call to mind the socially powerless, from whom one must not hide oneself, for they are one's own flesh (*ûmibbeśāreḵā;* NRSV "next of kin"). According to Sir. 38:16, the requirement to help extends even to the dead and dying. Finally, in CD 8:6 — echoing Isa. 58:7 — the "princes of Judah" are charged with turning their backs on their blood relations. These texts, appearing in a wide variety of literary settings and dating from many different eras, bear witness to a powerful ethic of readiness to help one's neighbor.

---

41. M. Hengel, *Judaism and Hellenism,* 2 vols. (Eng. trans. 1974), I, 147, and II, 94 n. 254.
42. See P. S. Fiddes, "The Hiddenness of Wisdom in the OT and Later Judaism" (diss., Oxford, 1976) (not available to me).
43. J. Krašovec, *Antithetic Structure in Biblical Hebrew Poetry. SVT* 35 (1984), 115-19.

IV. LXX. The LXX uses a wide variety of translations, for the most part appropriate to the contextual meaning. For the niphal, *lantháneín* is used 5 times, *kryptós* once (Sir. 11:4), *parorán* passive twice, and *hyperorán* passive (Nah. 3:11), *paranomeín* (Ps. 26:4), and *parérchesthai* (2 Ch. 9:2) once each. The idiom *'lm* hiphil + *'ênayim* is rendered 3 times by *apostréphein* and once by *parakalýptein* (each time with the obj. *ophthalmós* in the acc.); in Lev. 20:4 we find the rather bombastic *hyperópsei hyperídōsin toís ophthalmoís autṓn.* Elsewhere the hiphil is represented 3 times by *krýptein* and once each by *apokrypteín* (2 K. 4:27), *hyperorán* (Ps. 10:1), and *parorán* (Isa. 57:11). The hithpael is rendered 6 times by *hyperorán;* only in Sir. 4:4 do we find *apostréphein tó prósōpon.* Job 6:16 is translated very freely.[44]

For *ta'alumâ/ôt,* the LXX uses *tá krýphia* (Ps. 44:22[21]) and *dýnamis* (Job 11:6; 28:11).[45] In Ps. 90:8 the LXX (*ho ain hēmṓn*) has clearly derived the unique *'lmnw* from *'ôlām.*

Locher

44. For further details, including a discussion of passages where the LXX appears to have confused *m'l* with *'lm,* see P. Walters, *The Text of the Septuagint* (1973), 262-64.

45. See H. Heater, *A Septuagint Translation Technique in the Book of Job. CBQMS* 11 (1982), 87-88 (§71).

עַלְמָה *'almâ;* עֶלֶם *'elem*

I. Semitic Equivalents: 1. Distribution; 2. Meaning; 3. Etymology. II. OT: 1. Occurrences and Usage; 2. Ancient Versions. III. Semantic and Literary Associations: 1. Plural; 2. Singular. IV. Isa. 7:14 in the NT.

'almâ. J. M. Asurmendi, *La guerra Siro-Ephraimita. Institución San Jerónimo* 13 (1982); R. Bartelmus, "Jes 7,1-17 und das Stilprinzip des Kontrastes," *ZAW* 96 (1984) 50-66; W. Berg, "Die Identität der 'jungen Frau' in Jes 7,14.16," *BN* 13 (1980) 7-13; R. G. Bratcher, "A Study of Isaiah 7:14," *BT* 9 (1958) 97-126; G. Brunet, *Essai sur l'Isaïe de l'histoire* (1975); D. Buzy, "Les machals numériques de la sangsue et de l''almah," *RB* 42 (1933) 5-13; E. W. Conrad, "The Annunciation of Birth and the Birth of the Messiah," *CBQ* 47 (1985) 656-63; J. Coppens, "L'interprétation d'Is VII,14 à la lumière des études les plus récentes," *Lex tua veritas. FS H. Junker* (1961), 31-45; idem, "La mère du Sauveur à la lumière de la théologie vétérotestamentaire," *ETL* 31 (1955) 7-20; idem, "La prophétie de la 'Almah," *ETL* 28 (1952) 648-78; G. Delling, "παρθένος," *TDNT* V, 826-37; L. Dequeker, "Isaïe vii 14," *VT* 12 (1962) 331-35; C. Dohmen, "Verstockungsvollzug und prophetische Legitimation," *BN* 31 (1986) 37-56; A. M. Dubarle, "La conception virginale et la citation d'Is. VII,14 dans l'évangile de Matthieu," *RB* 85 (1978) 362-80; J. A. Fitzmyer, "παρθένος," *EDNT* III, 39-40; G. Fohrer, "Zu Jes 7,14 im Zusammenhang von Jes. 7,10-22," *ZAW* 68 (1956) 54-56; G. Gerleman, "Die sperrende Grenze," *ZAW* 91 (1979)

I. Semitic Equivalents.

1. *Distribution.* Many Semitic languages have equivalents to the Hebrew fem. noun *ʿalmâ* and its masc. equivalent *ʿelem.* Apart from the alternation between ʿ and *ǵ* as the first consonant in the various languages, which can be explained by the historical de-

---

338-49; H. Gese, "Natus ex virgine," *Probleme biblischer Theologie. FS G. von Rad* (1971), 73-89; M. Görg, "Hiskija als Immanuel," *BN* 22 (1983) 107-25; C. H. Gordon, "ʿAlmah in Isaiah 7:14," *JBR* 21 (1953) 106; N. K. Gottwald, "Immanuel as the Prophet's Son," *VT* 8 (1958) 36-47; H. Gross, "Die Verheissung des Emmanuel (Is 7,14)," *BiKi* 15 (1960) 102-4; H. Haag, "Jes 7,14 als alttestamentliche Grundstelle der Lehre von der Viriginitas Mariae," *Das Buch des Bundes* (1980), 180-86; F. Hahn, *Titles of Jesus in Christology* (Eng. trans. 1969), 258ff., 288ff.; E. Hammershaimb, "The Immanuel Sign," *ST* 3 (1949) 124-42; P. Höffken, "Notizen zum Textcharakter von Jesaja 7,1-17," *TZ* 36 (1980) 321-37; F. D. Hubmann, "Randbemerkungen zu Jes 7,1-17," *BN* 26 (1985) 27-46; H. Irsigler, "Zeichen und Bezeichnetes in Jes 7,1-17," *BN* 29 (1985) 75-114; R. Kilian, "Die Geburt des Immanuel aus der Jungfrau Jes 7,14," in K. S. Frank et al., *Zum Thema Jungfrauengeburt* (1970), 9-35; idem, *Jesaja 1–39. EdF* 200 (1983); idem, "Prolegomena zur Auslegung der Immanuelverheissung," *Wort, Lied und Gottesspruch. FS J. Ziegler. FzB* 2 (1972), 207-15; idem, *Die Verheissung Immanuels Jes 7,14. SBS* 35 (1968); L. Köhler, "Zum Verständnis von Jesaja 7,14," *ZAW* 67 (1955) 48-50; H. Kruse, "Alma Redemptoris Mater," *TTZ* 74 (1965) 15-36; C. Lattey, "The Term ʿAlmah in Is. 7:14," *CBQ* 9 (1947) 89-95; E. R. Lacheman, "Apropos of Isaiah 7:14," *JBR* 22 (1954) 42; H. Lenhard, "'Jungfrau' oder 'junge Frau' in Jesaja 7,14?" *Theologische Beiträge* 7 (1976) 264-67; T. Lescow, "Das Geburtsmotiv in den messianischen Weissagungen bei Jesaja und Micha," *ZAW* 79 (1967) 172-207; idem, "Jesajas Denkschrift aus der Zeit des syrisch-ephraimitischen Krieges," *ZAW* 85 (1973) 315-31; J. Lindblom, *A Study on the Immanuel Section in Isaiah* (1957); J. A. MacCulloch, "Virgin Birth," *ERE,* XII, 623-26; E. C. B. MacLaurin, "The Canaanite Background of the Doctrine of the Virgin Mary," *Religious Traditions* 3 (1980) 1-11; W. McKane, "The Interpretation of Isaiah VII 14-25," *VT* 17 (1967) 208-19; H.-P. Müller, "Glauben und Bleiben," in *Studies on Prophecy. SVT* 26 (1974), 25-54; A. E. Myers, "The Use of *Almah* in the OT," *LQ* 7 (1955) 137-40; G. del Olmo Lete, "Nota sobre Prov 30,19 *(w^{e}derek geber b^{e}ʿalmâ),*" *Bibl* 67 (1986) 68-74; J. Prado, "La Madre del Emmanuel," *Sefarad* 2 (1961) 85-114; M. Rehm, *Der königliche Messias im Licht der Immanuel-Weissagungen des Buches Jesaja. Eichstätter Studien* N.S. 1 (1968); idem, "Das Wort *ʿalmâ* in Is 7,14," *BZ* 8 (1964) 89-101; L. Reinke, *Die Weissagung von der Jungfrau und vom Immanuel Jes 7,14-16* (1848); L. G. Rignell, "Das Immanuelszeichen," *ST* 11 (1957) 99-119; H. Ringgren, *The Messiah in the OT. SBT* 1/18 (1956); C. Schedl, "Textkritische Bemerkungen zu den Synchronismen der Könige von Israel und Juda," *VT* 12 (1962) 88-119; J. Schreiner, "Zur Textgestalt von Jes 6 und 7,1-17," *BZ* 22 (1978) 92-97; A. Schulz, *"ʿAlmâ," BZ* 23 (1935/36) 229-41; K. Seybold, *Das davidische Königtum im Zeugnis der Propheten. FRLANT* 107 (1972); J. J. Stamm, "Die Immanuel Perikope," *TZ* 30 (1974) 11-22; idem, "Die Immanuel-Perikope im Lichte neuerer Veröffentlichungen," *ZDMG Sup 1* (1969), 281-90; idem, "Die Immanuel-Weissagung," *VT* 4 (1954) 20-33; idem, "Die Immanuel-Weissagung und die Eschatologie des Jesaja," *TZ* 16 (1960) 439-55; idem, "Neuere Arbeiten zum Immanuel-Problem," *ZAW* 68 (1956) 46-53; idem, "La prophétie d'Emmanuel," *RHPR* 23 (1943) 1-26; O. H. Steck, "Beiträge zum Verständnis von Jesaja 7,10-17 und 8,1-4," *TZ* 29 (1973) 161-78 = his *Wahrnehmungen Gottes im AT. ThB* 70 (1982), 187-203; J. E. Steinmüller, "Etymology and Biblical Usage of *ʿAlmah,*" *CBQ* 2 (1940) 28-43; H. Strauss, *Messianisch ohne Messias. EH* XXIII/232 (1984); J. A. Thompson, "The Root *ʿ-L-M* in Semitic Languages and Some Proposed New Translations in Ugaritic and Hebrew," *Tribute to A. Vööbus* (1977), 159-66; M. E. W. Thompson, "Isaiah's Sign of Immanuel," *ExpT* 95 (1983/84) 67-71; idem, *Situation and Theology* (1982); R. Tournay, "L'Emmanuel et sa Vierge-Mère,"

velopment of Semitic, the feminine form of the noun is remarkably more common in Hebrew than the masculine form (see II.1 below). To date, no clear parallels to the noun under discussion have been discovered in East Semitic. The majority of occurrences are in West Semitic, but some occurrences are attested in South Semitic as well.

In Ugaritic the masc. noun *ǵlm* occurs many times and the fem. *ǵlmt* a few.[1] For Canaanite, besides the occurrences in Biblical Hebrew (see II.1 below), the fem. *'lmt* occurs only twice, in Phoenician.[2] The various Aramaic dialects offer a richer source of material. Unique to Aramaic is the feature that, with few exceptions (3 occurrences of masc. *'lm* in a Palmyrene-Greek tax tariff dated 4 April 137 B.C.E. and one occurrence of Palmyrene fem. *'lmt*),[3] all occurrences of both the masculine and feminine are *quṭil* diminutives.[4] This phenomenon may be explained by the semantic development of the noun (see I.2 below). In Old Aramaic, masc. *'lym* occurs twice: once in an inscription on a 9th-century statue from Tell Fekherīye, and once in the Sefire inscriptions,[5] dating from the mid-8th century; the section in which this latter occurrence appears may be dependent on the Tell Fekherīye inscription. Masculine and feminine occurrences — the former more frequent than the latter — are also found in Imperial Aramaic (esp. in the Elephantine texts), Nabatean, Palmyrene, Punic, Syriac, and Christian Palestinian Aramaic.[6]

In South Semitic, equivalents of the noun are found in North Arabic as well as Old South Arabic;[7] these occurrences fall entirely within the semantic range of contemporary (the OSA inscriptions begin in the 8th century B.C.E.) Aramaic occurrences.[8] South Semitic nevertheless displays a wide range of meanings, reflected in numerous nominal and verbal derivatives.

The earliest occurrences are restricted to nominal forms. Even so, however, the noun is very rare except in Ugaritic; it is reasonable to suppose that the numerous occurrences in later dialects, along with the rather large number of derived forms, are due to a semantic development progressing from the specific to the general.

Revue Thomiste 55 (1955) 249-58; M. de Tuya, "¿La profecia de la 'Almah (Is. 7,14), un caso de 'tipologia redaccional'?" *Studium* 24 (1984) 231-67; B. Vawter, "The Ugaritic Use of *ǴLMT*," *CBQ* 14 (1952) 319-22; J. Vermeylen, *Du Prophète Isaïe à l'Apocalyptique* (1977/78); W. Werner, "Vom Prophetenwort zur Prophetentheologie," *BZ* 29 (1985) 1-30; H. M. Wolf, "A Solution to the Immanuel Prophecy in Isaiah 7:14–8:22," *JBL* 91 (1972) 449-56; H. W. Wolff, *Frieden ohne Ende. BSt* 35 (1962).

1. *WUS*, no. 2150; *UT*, no. 1969.
2. *KAI* 24.8; 37B.9.
3. For the former see *CIS*, II, 3913, 4, 5, 86; for the latter, 4540, 4.
4. Beyer, 437; R. Degen, *Altaramäische Grammatik* (1969), 47.
5. See A. Abou-Assaf, P. Bordreuil, and A. R. Millard, *La Statue de Tell Fekherye* (1982), Aramaic l. 21; *KAI* 222A.21-22.
6. For Elephantine see *AP*, index s.v. No inscriptions in Punic, but see M. Sznycer, *Les passages puniques en transcription latine dans le "Poenulus" de Plaute* (1967), 128; P. Schroeder, *Die phönizische Sprache* (1869), 174. For Syriac see *CSD*, 414. For Christian Palestinian Aramaic see F. Schulthess, *Lexicon Syropalaestinum* (1903), 147.
7. For the former see Wehr, 682; for the latter, Conti-Rossini, 216; Biella, 395.
8. On OSA inscriptions see M. Höfner, *Semitiskik. HO* III/2-3, 315. On the Aramaic see above.

2. *Meaning.* Semantic analysis here begins with Ugaritic, which clearly has the earliest occurrences. Lexically, a wide range in meanings is usually posited for Ugar. *ǵlm/ ǵlmt:* "youth, child, male offspring, servant, messenger, girl, maid, etc."[9] The vast majority of the occurrences of *ǵlm* refer to messengers or servants of the gods. The sons of Krt are likewise called *ǵlm,* and Krt himself is given the epithet *ǵlm il.* This usage suggests a basic meaning that can be represented by the notion of "representation" (see I.3 below).

The paucity of occurrences of the fem. form *ǵlmt* makes it impossible to determine well-defined areas of usage. Of the occurrences of *ǵlmt* cited by Whitaker,[10] only three can be interpreted with certainty as the fem. form of *ǵlm.* In these three texts *ǵlmt* is the name of a goddess.[11] The phrase *bn ǵlmt* refers twice to messengers of Baal.[12] This expression is no longer interpreted as meaning "sons of a maiden"; because of the par. *bn ẓlmt,* it is connected with *ẓlmt,* "darkness," or else with the divine name just cited.[13]

The formal similarity between Isa. 7:14 *(hinnēh hā'almâ hārâ wᵉyōleḏeṯ bēn)* and *KTU* 1.24, 7 *(hl ǵlmt tld bn)* has engendered many attempts to establish a connection between the two texts,[14] but the similarity does not extend beyond the use of the same form in a birth oracle. In interpreting the form *ǵlmt,* we note that the text in question deals with the marriage of the Sumerian and Hurrian moon goddess Nkl to the West Semitic moon god Yrḫ. The context suggests that *ǵlmt* here marks the ethnic difference of the woman, not her juridical or physical status. This theory is confirmed by the two other Ugaritic occurrences of *ǵlmt,* which are found in the so-called Krt Epic and refer to Ḥry, the daughter of the king of Udm, whom Krt demands as tribute after the siege of the city. The few occurrences of the fem. *ǵlmt* in Ugaritic agree semantically at least on the point that the term always refers to a woman of alien ethnicity who has entered into a relationship with a man of different origins.

In the curse formulas of the Tell Fekherīye and Sefire inscriptions (see I.1 above), we find the word *'lym,* which comports well with the semantic realm of Ugar. *ǵlm,* referring to sons or descendants: "a hundred women shall suckle an infant, but he shall not have his fill." Since the texts refers specifically to an "infant," the use of the diminutive is quite natural (see I.1 above). The Kilamuwa inscription describes the situation before Kilamuwa came to power: "one gave an *'lmt* for a sheep and a *gbr* for a garment."[15] The text may be using fem. *'lmt* in the sense of Ugar. *ǵlmt,* "ethnically alien woman." We find *'lmh* once more in the Aramaic inscription from Deir 'Allā (ca. 750-650 B.C.E.); the context is so fragmentary that it is impossible to determine the exact

9. *WUS,* no. 2150; *UT,* no. 1969.

10. P. 515.

11. *KTU* 1.41, 25 (+ duplicate); 1.39, 19; cf. J.-M. Tarragon, *Le culte à Ugarit d'après les textes de la pratique en cunéiformes alphabétiques. CahRB* 19 (1980) 166.

12. *KTU* 1.4, VII, 54; 1.8, II, II, 7.

13. Contra Aistleitner, see W. C. Kaiser Jr., "The Ugaritic Pantheon" (diss., Brandeis, 1973).

14. Vawter; A. van Selms, *Marriage and Family Life in Ugaritic Literature* (1954), 108ff.; A. S. Schoors, *RSP,* I, 46-49, no. 36.

15. *KAI* 24.8.

meaning.[16] From the 6th century B.C.E. onward, the nouns under discussion appear with increasing frequency in various Semitic languages, being used in a quite general and unnuanced sense for "boy, girl, slave, handmaid, etc." One text from the 4th or 3rd century B.C.E. appears to use *'lmt* in the sense of "female cultic servants."[17]

3. *Etymology.* To date, no generally satisfactory etymology for Heb. *'almâ* has been proposed.[18] Attempts at an explanation have either focused on semantic differentiation within the broad realm of Semitic texts using the root → עלם *'lm* or sought to determine a basic meaning from observed Hebrew usage.[19] The uncertainty is especially clear when studies focusing on Hebrew cite Ugar. *ǵlm* in support of the meaning "young woman," while studies focusing on Ugaritic cite Heb. *'almâ* in support of the same meaning.

Gerleman's proposed etymology cannot be accepted, because he examines only the OT occurrences of the root *'lm.* He concludes: "The noun עַלְמָה/עֶלֶם derives from the same root as עולם and falls likewise in the semantic domain of 'barring'; it does not mean 'young man/young woman,' but 'ignorant, uninitiated.'"[20] The other Semitic occurrences of the noun under discussion, cited above, show that this conclusion makes no sense.

If we are to pursue the etymology of *'almâ* afresh, we must take particular account of the characteristics listed above (age; the relationship between occurrences of the verb and occurrences of the noun, as well as between occurrences of the masc. and of the fem.). We must therefore take as our point of departure the Ugaritic occurrences of the masc. noun *ǵlm,* the verb being unattested in Ugaritic.[21] In our search for potential roots, the first problem is the Ugaritic consonant *ǵ.*[22] The semantics of the Ugaritic occurrences just outlined suggests considering a derivation of the Ugaritic noun *ǵlm* from Akk. *ṣalmu,* "statue, image."[23] First, no clear equivalent of Sem. *ṣlm,* "statue," has been found to date in Ugaritic; second, in Akkadian (and other Semitic languages) we find a metaphorical use of *ṣlm* that coincides to some extent with the usage of the Ugaritic nouns *ǵlm/ǵlmt.* Since the concept of an image necessarily involves its being an image of something or standing for something, it touches inherently on the notion of "representation." The use of Akk. *ṣalmu* in this sense is well attested: an incantation priest is

16. See H.-P. Müller, *ZAW* 94 (1982), 214-44, esp. 231-32.

17. *KAI* 37B.9.

18. See *HAL,* II, 835-36.

19. For the former see, e.g., J. Thompson, Steinmueller, Rehm; for the latter, e.g., Schulz, Rehm, Gerleman.

20. P. 349.

21. Against *ǵlm,* "be excited, rage" (*WUS,* no. 2149), see, e.g., Dietrich and Loretz, "Der Prolog des KRT-Epos," *Wort und Geschichte. FS. K. Elliger. AOAT* 18 (1973), 34; A. Caquot, M. Sznycer, and A. Herdner, *Textes Ougaritiques,* I (1974), 555 n. x; J. J. Scullion, *UF* 4 (1972) 115.

22. Dietrich and Loretz, *WO* 4 (1967/68) 299-315; S. Moscati et al., *Intro. to the Comparative Grammar of the Semitic Languages. PLO* 6 (^{3}1980), esp. §§8.44–8.49.

23. See I.2 above; → צלם *ṣelem.*

the *ṣalam Marduk;* the king is the "image" or representative of the deity; children are the "images" of their parents.[24] This etymology is also supported by the observation that to date no explicit terminology for "image" has been found in Ugaritic, so that it is reasonable to suppose that Ugaritic borrowed and then lexicalized a specialized metaphorical use of Akk. *ṣalmu.*

Further analysis of particular cases must determine whether all occurrences of corresponding equivalents in other Semitic languages derive from this borrowing — for Biblical Hebrew, the observed usage makes this a reasonable supposition (see III below) — or whether we are dealing with homonymous roots,[25] or whether related phonemes gave rise to semantic overlappings (cf., e.g., *ḥlm,* "be strong, mature"[26]). The proposed etymology based on a phonetic shift from *ṣ* to *ǵ* also needs further study, but the possibility of transmission through Hurrian makes it a live possibility (cf. Hurr. *zalmi*).[27]

Dohmen

This etymology requires some kind of borrowing, for, as Aram. *ṣᵉlēm* shows, Akk. *ṣalmu* reflects Proto-Sem. *ṣ,* which should appear as *ṣ* in Ugaritic. The conventional etymology treats *'elem* (and fem. *'almâ*) as a primary noun related to Ugar. *ǵlm,* "young man, servant, messenger," OSA *ǵlm,* "child, boy," Arab. *ǵulām,* "young man, slave," and Aram. *'lym,* "child, servant, slave" (fem. "young girl").[28] A semantic development "young man" > "servant" is natural (cf. → נער *na'ar*).

Ringgren

II. OT.

1. *Occurrences and Usage.* The noun *'almâ* occurs 9 times in the OT (4 times sg., 5 times pl.). Two instances of the plural involve the difficult expression *'al-'ᵃlāmôṯ* (Ps. 46:1[superscription]; 1 Ch. 15:20; see III.1 below). The meaning of the other plural occurrences (Ps. 68:26[25]; Cant. 1:3; 6:8) cannot be defined precisely (see III.1 below). All 4 occurrences of the singular (Gen. 24:43; Ex. 2:8; Isa. 7:14; Prov. 30:19), however, appear to belong to the same historical or literary context (see III.2 below) and must be understood in the light of Isa. 7:14.

The masc. form *'elem* appears only twice in the OT; the divergence from the ratio of masculine to feminine in other Semitic languages provides food for thought. But since both occurrences (1 S. 17:56; 20:22) are in the Court History of David,[29] it is worth considering whether we may be dealing here with a usage characteristic of a specific

---

24. *AHw,* III, 1079; *CAD,* XVI, 78-85.
25. → עלם *'lm.*
26. *HAL,* I, 320; Beyer, 508.
27. See W. von Soden, *Hebräische Wortforschung. SVT* 16 (1967), 291-94; E. Laroche, *Glossaire de la langue Hourrite* (1980), s.v.
28. For Old South Arabic see Biella, 395; for Aramaic, *DNSI,* II, 862.
29. On the dubious conjectural emendation of *'im* to *'elem* in 1 S. 16:12 (*HAL,* II, 835), see Stoebe, *Das erste Buch Samuelis. KAT* VIII/1 (1973), 302.

region or textual stratum. However that may be, it is noteworthy that in both texts the individual referred to by *'elem* is also called a *na'ar* in the immediate context (1 S. 17:55; 20:21).

2. *Ancient Versions.* The LXX is inconsistent in translating *'almâ.* Twice (Gen. 24:43; Isa. 7:14) it uses *párthenos,* elsewhere *neánis.* Elsewhere the LXX uses the former primarily to represent → בתולה *bᵉṯûlâ,* the latter to represent *naʿᵃrâ* (→ נער *na'ar*). Jerome follows this precedent, using *virgo* in Isa. 7:14 and Gen. 24:43, *puella* or *adolescentula* elsewhere. By contrast, Aquila, Symmachus, and Theodotion all use *neánias* is Isa. 7:14, with the result that early Christian literature already contains references to *neánias* as meaning "virgin," although the translation here may represent a deliberate attempt to preclude a christological interpretation of the text.[30] The Syr. similarly uses *btwlt'* in Isa. 7:14 instead of *'lymt',* which is the usual translation of *'almâ* and derives from the same root. It is unlikely that the LXX tried to import the concept of a virgin birth, a familiar idea in many religious traditions, into Isa. 7:14.[31] It is also possible that the unusual translation of the LXX is an attempt to accommodate the meaning of the text as altered by both the redaction and the reception of the original prophetic oracle (see III.2 and IV below).

III. Semantic and Literary Associations. A survey of the OT *'almâ* texts shows that, despite their small number, there is a real difference between the use of the singular and the use of the plural: the occurrences of the plural all stand in isolation, whereas the occurrences of the singular stand in a kind of mutual relationship.

1. *Plural.* Cant. 6:8 occupies a special place among the texts using the plural: the triad of *mᵉlāḵôṯ, pîlagšîm,* and *ʿᵃlāmôṯ* makes clear that the term *'almāh* has a special semantic force here; otherwise the juxtaposition of the three words would make little sense. Rehm's theory that the passage speaks of female slaves together with queens and concubines is dubious; the context makes it more likely that the triad expresses the distinct legal status of the various women belonging to the royal harem.[32] In this interpretation the text speaks of wives, concubines, and probably a group of foreign women (princesses?), whom diplomatic relationships brought into every ancient Near Eastern king's harem.[33] The OT itself clearly speaks of such a group in connection with King Solomon (1 K. 11, but using the term *nāšîm*). It is noteworthy that the *ʿᵃlāmôṯ* are more numerous than the other two groups ("without number"). The second text in the Song of Solomon is less eloquent: 1:3b speaks of *ʿᵃlāmôṯ* ("therefore the *ʿᵃlāmôṯ* love you"). It is impossible to decide with certainty whether the word refers to a particular group of women or simply to "anonymous intermediary figures" representing a "literary commonplace."[34] It is hardly possi-

---

30. Rehm, *Messias,* 54.
31. Delling, 827-31, 833.
32. "'almâ," 92.
33. W. Röllig, *RLA,* IV, 282-87.
34. G. Gerleman, *Ruth-Das Hohelied. BK* XVIII (²1981), 97.

ble to determine in each individual case the precise meaning conveyed by *'almâ*. This holds true also in Ps. 68:26(25), which speaks of *'ªlāmôṯ tôp̄ēp̄ôṯ*. This text may use *'almâ* in the sense of "girls," but it is also possible that the term refers to foreign women.[35]

The much-debated problem of the expression *'al-'ªlāmôṯ* (Ps. 46:1[superscription]; 1 Ch. 15:20[36]) may also belong in this context. Taken as referring to a style of musical performance, the *'almûṯ* of Ps. 9:1(superscription) (many mss.: *'al-mûṯ;* LXX *hypér tṓn kryphíōn*) and the *'al-mûṯ* of Ps. 48:15(14) are often included here and emended by the addition of *'al* to read *'al-'ªlāmôṯ.*[37]

2. *Singular.* When we examine the occurrences of *'almâ* in the singular, we note two phenomena: we appear to be dealing with a term that is highly specialized semantically, but the individual texts do not use the term in such a way as to make its specialized nature clear. In any case it seems advisable to treat Isa. 7:14 as primary in the series of *'almâ* texts, since there the term serves clearly as the focus of the passage, an observation confirmed by the variety of translations found in the versions (see II.2 above).

With respect to the semantic definition of *'almâ,* Isa. 7:14 presents great difficulties, because the exegesis of v. 14 depends critically on the analysis and interpretation of the chapter as a whole. There is consequently a wide range of theories concerning identification of *'almâ.* She has been identified — in part on the basis of very different analyses — as the wife of Ahaz (i.e., the queen), the wife of Isaiah, the "prophetess" mentioned in 8:3, an anonymous lady of the court, or even a female hierodule. Some have even proposed a collective interpretation, seeing the *'almâ* as representing women in general. Finally, it has been suggested that the word conveys a symbolic allusion to the daughter (of) Zion.[38] Dependent on the answer is then the much-debated question whether Isa. 7 promises salvation or disaster.

If we attempt to define the literary nature of the chapter more precisely,[39] traditio-historical analysis reveals behind the 3rd-person narrative account (literarily the final stage) a prophetic oracle culminating in the promise of a sign together with the motivation for the promise. In form and content, the passage is a threat against Ahaz. The putative basic meaning of *'almâ* established above ("alien woman") makes the nature of the threat particularly clear: if a non-Israelite is expecting a child by King Ahaz and is to give it the programmatic name Immanuel, the oracle is directed primarily against Ahaz, since the "we" of the name refers in the first instance to the woman and her child. For the Davidic dynasty, this spells continuity and discontinuity at the same

35. But cf. the female cultic servants in *KAI* 37, mentioned above.

36. *BHS* proposes *'ēlāmîṯ*.

37. See H. Gunkel and J. Begrich, *Intro. to Psalms* (Eng. trans. 1997), 350; S. Jellicoe, *JTS* 49 (1949) 52-53; W. Rudolph, *Chronikbücher. HAT* I/21 (1955), 118; S. Mowinckel, *The Psalms in Israel's Worship,* 2 vols. (Eng. trans. 1962), II, 215-17; L. Delekat, *ZAW* 76 (1964) 292; H.-J. Kraus, *Psalms 1–59* (Eng. trans. 1988), 31.

38. For details see Kilian, *Jesaja,* 15-21.

39. Dohmen, "Verstockungsvollzug."

time. The dynasty will not continue linearly but will be given a new beginning by God (cf. also the later interpretation of 11:1). This conclusion is confirmed by the juxtaposed and related statements of the motivation in 7:16 and 17.

The evolution of the present narrative account in Isa. 7 and its continuation in the same chapter in themselves show that there was ongoing and growing interest in the oracle at the heart of the chapter. Not the least grounds for this interest may have been the relationship of Ahaz's successor to the prophet Isaiah. Largely positive experiences with King Hezekiah could well have impelled a new reading and interpretation of the threat in 7:14. In the course of this reinterpretation of the prophetic oracle, the sign described in v. 14 becomes a symbol, and Immanuel becomes a savior figure expected in the future.[40] In the postexilic period Isa. 7:14 was interpreted messianically in this sense.[41]

In Prov. 30:19 *'almâ* appears in the context of a four-part numerical proverb (vv. 18-19) based on the catchword *dereḵ;* the final phrase is *dereḵ geḇer bᵉ'almâ.* Many interpretations of the expression have been proposed.[42] The word *'almâ* here is either understood very generally as meaning "woman," so that the phrase refers simply to the relationship between the sexes; or it is derived from a different root and interpreted as meaning "darkness," so that the phrase refers to the "way of a man in the dark."[43] Since these meanings make little sense in a numerical proverb dealing with wonderful things (v. 18), it is worth considering the possibility that the phrase criticizes the same situation that lies behind Isa. 7:14: it asks how a prominent person (→ גבר *geḇer*) can get involved with an alien woman (*'almâ*). We may note that the Kilamuwa inscription also uses the words *'lmt* and *gbr* in conjunction.

Both Ex. 2:8 and Gen. 24:43 use *'almâ* in a narrative; in neither instance does the immediate context provide further details that might bear on a special meaning of the word. It is worth noting, however, that both texts refer to Israelite women living abroad: the first to Moses' sister in Egypt, the second to Rebekah in Mesopotamia, Abraham's homeland. Since both texts can be assigned to JE, writing in the time of Manasseh, we may ask whether the use of the term *'almâ* is tendentious. In both passages JE has attempted to strip the term *'almâ* of its connotation of "alien" and shift its meaning in the direction of "foreign." Thus both texts are associated with the reception of Isa. 7:14 within the OT. Since Gen. 24 goes on to address the theme of "marrying alien women" (vv. 3,37), its connection with Isa. 7:14 is more direct, as the ancient versions appear to have recognized, using a different word than usual to translate *'almâ* in both Gen. 24:43 and Isa. 7:14 (see II.2 above).

IV. Isa. 7:14 in the NT. Only in Mt. 1:23 does the NT quote Isa. 7:14. The difference between the names — Immanuel and Jesus — is striking, as is the awkward and incongruous juxtaposition of the story of the virgin birth (vv. 18ff.) with a genealogy tracing Jesus' ancestry back to Joseph (vv. 1ff.). Here the Gospel of Matthew rejects

40. Ibid., 49-50 n. 48, 55.
41. Kilian, *Jesaja,* 10; W. Werner, *Eschatologische Texte in Jesaja 1–39. FzB* 46 (1982), 197.
42. See esp. the summary in del Olmo Lete.
43. But see *GesTh,* II, 1037: "It refers to clandestine thefts."

both Jewish expectations of a Davidic messiah and pagan expectations of an individual born of a virgin.

The NT taking up of Isa. 7:14, consequently, is not a piece of theologizing inspired by the LXX translation of the verse; on the contrary, it stands solidly in the tradition of the uses made of this verse within the OT itself, which lead up to a messianic interpretation.

Dohmen

עָלַץ *'ālaṣ* → עָלַז *'ālaz*

עַם *'am*

I. Etymology; Ancient Near East: 1. Etymology; 2. Eblaite and Akkadian; 3. Ugaritic; 4. Amorite; 5. Akkadian Texts of the 1st Millennium; 6. Phoenician and Punic; 7. Ammonite and Moabite; 8. North Arabian; 9. South Arabian; 10. Classical Arabic; 11. Aramaic; 12. Summary. II. Individual Sense: 1. Proper Names; 2. Burial Formula; 3. Banishment Formula; 4. Covenant Formula. III. Collective Sense: 1. Assembly of the Israelites; 2. The People of the Land in Judah; 3. The Postexilic Assembly; 4. The People as a Whole; 5. Warriors; 6. The People of God; 7. Foreign Peoples. IV. Dead Sea Scrolls.

'am. B. Alfrink, "L'expression נֶאֱסַף אֶל־עַמָּיו," *OTS* 5 (1948) 118-31; F. I. Andersen, "Israelite Kinship Terminology and Social Structure," *BT* 20 (1969) 29-39; G. W. Anderson, "Israel: Amphictyony: *'am, ḳāhāl, 'ēḏāh,*" *Translating and Understanding the OT. FS H. G. May* (1970), 135-51; E. Auerbach, *"'Am hā'āreṣ," Proceedings of the First World Congress of Jewish Studies* (1952), 362-66; A. J. Brawer, *"'Am hā'āreṣ kip^ešûṭô bammiqrā'," BethM* 15 (1969/70) 202-6; N. A. Dahl, *Das Volk Gottes* (1941, [2]1963); M. Dahood, "Hebrew-Ugaritic Lexicography VII," *Bibl* 50 (1969) 227-56, esp. 249-50; S. Daiches, "The Meaning of עם הארץ in the OT," *JTS* 30 (1929) 245-49; R. Deutsch, "The Biblical Concept of the 'People of God,'" *South East Asia Journal of Theology* 13/2 (1972) 4-13; A. K. Fenz, "Volk Gottes im AT," *BiLe* 38 (1964) 163-90; G. Fohrer, "Der Vertrag zwischen König und Volk in Israel," *ZAW* 71 (1959) 1-22; I. J. Gelb, *Computer-Aided Analysis of Amorite. AS* 21 (1980), 92-95, 260-64; E. Gillischewski, "Der Ausdruck עַם הָאָרֶץ im AT," *ZAW* 40 (1922) 137-42; M. D. Goldman, "Concerning the Meaning of *'am,*" *ABR* 3 (1953) 51; R. M. Good, *The Sheep of the Pasture. HSM* 29 (1983); R. Gordis, "Sectional Rivalry in the Kingdom of Judah," *JQR* 25 (1934/35) 237-59; G. B. Gray, "Ammi, Names with," *EncBib,* I (1899), 138-40; M. Greenberg and A. Oppenheimer, "Am ha-areẓ," *EncJud,* II, 833-36; D. R. Hillers, "*Bĕrît 'ām,* 'Emancipation of the People,'" *JBL* 97 (1978) 175-82; A. R. Hulst, "גּוֹי/עַם *'am/gôy* people," *TLOT,* II, 896-919; Ihromi, "Die Königmutter und der *'amm ha'arez* im Reich Juda," *VT* 24 (1974) 421-29; T. Ishida, "'The People of the Land' and the Political Crises in Judah," *AJBI* 1 (1975) 23-38; E. Janssen, *Das Gottesvolk und seine Geschichte* (1971); T. W. Juynboll, "Über die Bedeutung des Wortes *'amm,*" *Orientalische Studien. FS T. Nöldeke,* 2 vols. (1906), I, 353-56; A. Koschel, "'Volk Gottes' in der deuter-

I. Etymology; Ancient Near East.

1. *Etymology.* The noun *'am(m),* characterized by the root vowel *a* and a doubled second consonant, occurs more than 1,950 times in the Hebrew OT; there are 15 addi-

---

onomistischen Paränese" (Lizentiat Arbeit, Münster, 1969); M. Krenkel, "Das Verwandschaftswort עם," *ZAW* 8 (1888) 280-84; C. Levin, *Der Sturz der Königin Atalya. SBS* 105 (1982); J. Lewy, "The Old West Semitic Sun-God Ḥammu," *HUCA* 18 (1944) 429-88; N. Lohfink, "Beobachtungen zur Geschichte des Ausdrucks עם יהוה," *Probleme biblischer Theologie. FS G. von Rad* (1971), 275-305; D. D. Luckenbill, "The Name Hammurabi," *JAOS* 37 (1917) 250-53; J. Maier, "Zum Gottesvolk und Gemeinschaftsbegriff in den Schriften vom Toten Meer" (diss., Vienna, 1958); H. G. May, "'This People' and 'This Nation' in Haggai," *VT* 18 (1968) 190-97; J. McKenzie, "The 'People of the Land' in the OT," *Akten des 24. Internationalen Orientalisten-Kongresses, München 1957* (1959), 206-8; T. N. D. Mettinger, *King and Messiah. CB* 8 (1976), 107-30; R. Meyer, "Der *'Am hā-'Āreṣ,*" *Jud* 3 (1947) 169-99; J. Muilenburg, "Abraham and the Nations," *Int* 19 (1965) 387-98; E. W. Nicholson, "The Meaning of the Expression עם הארץ in the OT," *JSS* 10 (1965) 59-66; M. Noth, *IPN,* 76-79; A. Oppenheimer, *The 'Am ha-Aretz. ALGHJ* 8 (Eng. trans. 1977); A. Passoni dell'Acqua, "Precisazione sul valore di δῆμος nella versione dei LXX," *RivB* 30 (1982) 197-214; idem, "La versione dei LXX e i papiri," *Proceedings of the 16th International Congress of Papyrology* (1981), 621-32, esp. 623-25; L. B. Paton, "'Amm, 'Ammi," *ERE*², I (1925), 386-89; M. H. Pope, "'Am Ha'arez," *IDB,* I, 106-7; N. W. Porteous, "Volk und Gottesvolk im AT," *Theologische Aufsätze. FS K. Barth* (1936), 146-63; J. D. Prince, "The Name Hammurabi," *JBL* 29 (1910) 21-23; G. von Rad, *Das Gottesvolk im Deuteronomium. BWANT* 47 (1929); H. Reviv, *The Elders in Ancient Israel* (1983) (Heb.); G. Rinaldi, "Populi e paesi nei Salmi," *BietOr* 17 (1975) 97-111; L. Rost, "Die Bezeichnungen für Land und Volk im AT," *FS O. Procksch* (1934), 125-48 = his *Das kleine Credo und andere Studien zum AT* (1965), 76-101; W. Rudolph, "Die Einheitlichkeit der Erzählung vom Sturz der Atalja (2 Kön 11)," *FS A. Bertholet* (1950), 473-78; H. Schmid, "Die Gestalt Abrahams und das Volk des Landes," *Jud* 36 (1980) 73-87; N. Slouch, "Representative Government among the Hebrews and Phoenicians," *JQR* 4 (1913/14) 303-10; M. S. Smith, "*Běrît 'am/Běrît 'ôlām:* A New Proposal for the Crux of Isa 42:6," *JBL* 100 (1981) 241-43; J. A. Soggin, "Der judäische *'am-ha'areṣ* und das Königtum in Juda," *VT* 13 (1963) 187-95; E. A. Speiser, "'People' and 'Nation' of Israel," *JBL* 79 (1960) 157-63; repr. in J. J. Finkelstein and M. Greenberg, eds., *Oriental and Biblical Studies* (1967), 160-70; J. J. Stamm, "*Berît 'am* bei Deuterojesaja," *Probleme biblischer Theologie. FS G. von Rad* (1971), 510-24; idem, "Ursprung des Namens der Ammoniter," *AcOr* 17 (1949) 379-82; M. Sulzberger, *The Am-ha-aretz* (²1910); M. Sznycer, "'L'assemblée du peuple' dans les cités puniques d'après les témoignages épigraphiques," *Sem* 25 (1975) 47-68; H. Tadmor, "'The People' and the Kingship in Ancient Israel," *Cahiers d'histoire mondiale* 11 (1968) 46-68; S. Talmon, "The Judean *'am hā'āreṣ* in Historical Perspective," *Proceedings of the Fourth World Congress of Jewish Studies,* I (1967), 71-76; C. C. Torrey, "'Amm," *Jewish Encyclopedia,* I (1901), 521; R. de Vaux, "Le sens de l'expression 'peuple du pays' dans l'AT et le rôle politique du people en Israël," *RA* 58 (1964) 167-72; C. Virolleaud, "Sur le nom de Hammurabi," *JA* 248 (1955) 133-34; idem, "Le vrai nom de Hammurabi," *GLECS* 7 (1955) 1; O. Weber, "Der Name Hammurabi in einer südarabischen Inschrift," *OLZ* 10 (1907) 146-49; H. M. Weil, "*'Ammî* 'compatriote, consanguin'," *Revue des études sémitiques et Babyloniaca* 1941/45, 87-88; J. P. Weinberg, "Der *'am hā'āreṣ* des 6.-4. Jh. v.u.Z.," *Klio* 56 (1974) 325-35; J. Wellhausen, "Die Ehe bei den Arabern," *NGWG* 49 (1983) 431-81; J. A. Wilson, "The Assembly of a Phoenician City," *JNES* 4 (1945) 245; C. U. Wolf, "Traces of Primitive Democracy in Ancient Israel," *JNES* 6 (1947) 98-108; E. Würthwein, *Der 'amm ha'arez im AT. BWANT* 66 (1936).

tional occurrences in personal names. There are 15 occurrences of Aram. *'am(m),* whose second consonant reduplicates in the pl. *'am^{e}mayyā'.*

The noun designates an agnate relationship. It is part of the basic vocabulary of the West Semitic languages (except for Ethiopic) and appears to be linked etymologically with the prep. *'im(m)/'am(m),* which denotes propinquity: "with."

2. *Eblaite and Akkadian.* Despite the identification proposed by Dahood,[1] *'am(m)* is not attested to date in the Ebla texts, although the PN *A-mu* might come under consideration.

The word is also unknown in Akkadian, where the verb *ḫamāmu,* "amass," and its derivatives reflect the same root as Arab. *ḫamma,* "sweep together." This root is also reflected in the Mari word *ḫimmu,* which denotes a "list" of persons and is the masculine equivalent of *ḫimmatu.*[2] Contrary to *AHw,*[3] Akk. *ummānu/ummannu,* "multitude, army," is not connected with the word *'am(m);* it is the equivalent of Heb. *hāmôn,* derived from → המה *hāmâ.*

3. *Ugaritic.* Neither does the word *'am(m)* appear in the vocabulary stock of Ugaritic, which does, however, include the prep. *'im(m),* "with." Three texts merit special attention. The first reads *'mmym,* which can be analyzed as *'m mym* and must be identified with Akk. *ḫa-am-me me-e* of the major lexical series *ḪAR-ra = ḫubullu* XIV.[4] This word, which may mean "jellyfish, sea nettle," serves in Ugaritic as an epithet of the mother of Gupan and Ugar.[5] The element *'m* is connected with Akk. *$^{(\acute{u})}$ḫammmu/ammu(m),* a kind of seaweed.[6] The second text contains the word *'mdtn,* usually analyzed as *'m dtn,* "with Ditanu."[7] This interpretation is confirmed by ll. 13-14, where Ditanu is the subject of the verb *'ny,* "answer." The third passage contains the repeated phrase *ztr 'mh/'mk/'my.*[8] The expression *ztr 'm* here parallels *skn il ib,* "stele of the ancestral god," so that we may suggest the meaning "eponymous ancestor" for *'m,* a meaning that the word has in the Amorite onomasticon. Many interpretations have been proposed for the word *ztr;* if we add the meaning "urn," suggested by association with Old Akk. ^{dug}*zitūrum,*[9] we may translate *ztr 'm* as "urn of the eponymous ancestor," the focus of a family cult. This would be the only instance of the noun *'am(m)* in Ugaritic. But since it is associated with the word *ztr,* otherwise unattested in Ugaritic, it is reasonable to suggest that *ztr 'm* is not a native Ugaritic expression but a borrowing from the Amorite terminology of the funerary cult. The element *'am(m)* is quite com-

---

1. *Congress Volume, Göttingen 1971. SVT* 29 (1978), 87.
2. See *ARM,* XIV, 70, vo. 5′; *AHw,* I, 346.
3. P. 1413.
4. See *KTU* 1.4, VII, [55] = 1.8, II, 8. On the Akkadian see *MSL* VIII/2, 38, 345.
5. See *AHw,* I, 318a; E. Lipiński, *BiOr* 38 (1981), 385.
6. *AHw,* I, 317b.
7. *KTU* 1.123, 2.11.
8. *KTU* 1.17, I, 27. [45]; II, [1]. 17.
9. *AHw,* III, 1534a.

mon in the Amorite onomasticon; the fifteen Ugaritic proper names using *'am(m),* including the two royal names *'ammištamru* and *'ammurapi,*[10] belong to the same onomastic tradition.

4. *Amorite.* The element *'am(m)* is very common in the Amorite onomasticon, entering into the formation of more than two hundred proper names.[11] Names like *'ammu-'il* and *'ilî-/'ila-'ammu* show that it is a theophorous element. At the same time, however, it indicates kinship, because it is used in the series of names that appear to express grief over the death of a family member, such as *'ayya-'ammuhū,* "Where is his *'am(m)?*" i.e., the *'am(m)* of the child. This observation is confirmed by the total absence of names in which the terms *'am(m)* and "father" or "brother" occur together. There is, however, a name *'ammu-ḫālum,* with the unlikely interpretation "the paternal uncle is the maternal uncle" based on the meaning of Arab. *'amm* and *ḫāl.* The royal name *'ammî-ditāna,* in which the tribal appellative "Ditanu" appears in the genitive of the diptotic declension of nouns in *-ānu,*[12] appears to presuppose that the Babylonian king, the only individual known to bear this name, claimed the status of *'am(m)* of the royal house. This role would suggest that *'am(m)* denotes the tribal eponym. Among the Amorites, this founder was not only "like a god" *('ammuš kī 'il),* enjoying the privilege of a cult at the site where his remains were interred, but could even be identified with one of the higher deities of the pantheon, as is exemplified by such names as *'ammî-haddu, 'ammî-'anat, 'ammî-dagān,* and *'ammu-'el.* The Ugaritic names using *'am(m)* follow Amorite onomastic practice; many biblical names go back to this same source.

Outside the onomasticon, which is also attested in the Egyptian Execration Texts, the noun *'ammu* appears in the Old Babylonian Hymn to Ishtar, in which the god Anu is called *ḫa-mu-uš,* literally "the head of their clan."[13] It apparently appears also in the Code of Hammurabi, in one of the titles claimed by Hammurabi: *mušēpī kinātim mušēšer ḫammi,* "Revealer of truths, guide of the head of the clan."[14] This title signifies that he applied and put into effect the true principles promulgated by the king. It would seem, therefore, that the earliest known meaning of *'am(m)* is "head" or "founder" of a clan, i.e., the eponym or common ancestor of a tribe or family.

5. *Akkadian Texts of the 1st Millennium.* Out of this meaning grew the double meaning, both collective and individual, of the word *'am(m)* in the 1st millennium. It can denote all the descendants of a common ancestor or the agnate as an individual, just as → אדם *'āḏām* can mean both "humankind" and "human individual." That the collective sense of *'am(m)* was known in Mesopotamia is shown by a list explaining non-Akkadian names, which glosses Hammurabi as *kimtum rapaštum,* "extended family,"

---

10. *PNU,* 109.
11. Gelb; *APNM,* 196-98.
12. E. Lipiński, *Studies in Bible and the Ancient Near East. FS S. E. Loewenstamm,* 2 vols. (1978), II, 91-94.
13. *AHw,* II, 317b; *CAD,* VI, 69.
14. CH, IV, 54; cf. J. Nougayrol, *RA* 45 (1951) 75, 10.

and Ammiṣaduqa as *kimtum kittum,* "legitimate family."[15] These explanations show that Babylonian scholars of the 1st millennium interpreted the element *'ammu* in the sense of "family." This interpretation also accounts for the identification *'am-mu* = *zeru,* "descendants," found in a synonym list.[16]

6. *Phoenician and Punic.* The term *'am(m)* is common in Phoenician and Punic, where it generally serves to designate the populace of a city or town, i.e., the assembly of the citizens of a municipality. This "municipal" meaning of the word *'am(m)* is attested as early as the 8th century in the Karatepe inscriptions, where it designates the inhabitants of the city without any institutional or familial connotations.[17] This is no longer true, however, of the expression *'m 'rṣ z* in the Yeḥawmilk inscription of the 5th century. Here the king requests the Mistress of Byblos "to bestow her favor in the eyes of the gods and in the eyes of the 'people of this land' together with the favor of the 'people of this land.'"[18] The *'m 'rṣ z* — an expression comparable to the biblical *'am hā'āreṣ* — must refer to a corporate body whose opinion meant every bit as much as that of the gods, as expressed by the proverb *Vox populi, vox Dei.*

This institutional sense of the word *'am(m)* appears even more clearly in the later inscriptions, where it is further qualified by the name of the municipality in question: *'m ṣdn,* "people of Sidon";[19] *'m ṣr,* "people of Tyre";[20] *'m lpṭ,* "people of Lapethos";[21] *'m gwl,* "people of Gaulos";[22] *'m byt'n,* "people of Bitia";[23] *'m lkš,* "people of Lixus";[24] *'m 'lpqy,* "people of Leptis (Magna)";[25] *'m ršmlqrt,* "people of Cape Melqart";[26] *'m 'gdr,* "people of Cadiz";[27] *'m šmš,* "people of Heliopolis(?)";[28] *'m qrtḥdšt,* "people of Carthage."[29] In addition, in a bilingual inscription from Leptis Magna, Neo-Pun. *bn' 'm,* "sons of the people," corresponds to Lat. *cives,* while *'rṣ* is the equivalent of *patria.*[30]

A different collective sense of the word *'am(m)* appears in the great Maktar Inscription, in which *'m' yšb 'dmt,* "its people dwelling in the region," is subordinate to the *mzrḥ* (probably "college" or "corporation"), since the pronominal suffix of *'m'* refers to it.[31] Here *'m* appears to refer to "people" dependent on the *mzrḥ* but dwelling in the

15. H. Rawlinson, *The Cuneiform Inscriptions of Western Asia,* V (1884), pl. 44, I, 21-22.
16. *malku* = *šarru,* I, 158; *CAD,* I/2, 77.
17. *KAI* 26A.III.7.
18. *KAI* 10.10-11.
19. *KAI* 60.1.
20. *KAI* 18.5-6; 19.8.
21. *KAI* 43.5.
22. *KAI* 62.1, 8.
23. *KAI* 173.1.
24. *KAI* 170.3.
25. *KAI* 126.7.
26. *CIS,* I, 3707, 4-5.
27. *KAI* 71.3.
28. *KAI* 51. vo. 4.
29. *CIS* 269, 5; 270, 3; 271, 4; 290, 6-7; 291, 5-6; 4908, 5; 4909, 5; cf. 272, 5.
30. *KAI* 126.4-6.
31. *KAI* 145.3; see M. Sznycer, *Sem* 22 (1972) 36-39.

countryside *('dmt),* like those in 1 K. 19:21 and 2 K. 4:41. Instead, the legend *'m mḥnt* of Siculo-Punic coins means "people of the military camp," so that here *'amm* denotes the army, an additional collective usage well attested in the Bible.

These collective senses of *'am(m)* stand in contrast to the handful of personal names formed with *'m.*[32] Apart from the hypocoristica *'m, 'm',* and *'[m]y,* the only certain PNs are *'l'm* (cf. Heb. *'elî'ām*), *'myl* (cf. Heb. *'ammî'ēl*), *'myyḥn* (probably to be interpreted as *'ammîyēḥan*), and *'mskr.*[33] This last is also found in Neo-Assyr. *am-maš-ki-ri,* "the *'am(m)* is the one who gives the name" (*maskîr;* cf. Isa. 49:1).[34] Since the name is typically Phoenician-Punic *(skr* for *zkr),* we can be almost certain that in Phoenician-Punic the word *'am(m)* could be used as an individual noun, in the sense of "eponymous ancestor."

Neither the prep. *'im* nor a fem. subst. *'mt* meaning "people, society, congregation" is attested in Phoenician-Punic.[35] The forms *b'mt* ("after the manner of") and *'l'mt* (probably "vestibule"; cf. Heb. *'ûlām*) belong elsewhere.[36]

7. *Ammonite and Moabite.* In Ammonite, *'m* has been found only in the PN *'mndb,* which appears in Neo-Assyrian as *am-mi-na-ad-bi,*[37] as well as in the name Ammon *('mn)* itself, which is a hypocoristicon formed from the root *'amm-* by the addition of *-ān* > *-ōn.* It is common in Amorite names, especially at Mari.[38] In Moabite, *'m* appears twice in the Mesha Inscription, where it refers to the inhabitants of a town.[39]

8. *North Arabian.* North Arabian inscriptions include several proper names using *'m;* to these should be added the masc. names *'mw* in Nabatean and *'mt* in Palmyrene.[40] The generic name *'m* is unquestionably a familial noun denoting a male agnate. In two Nabatean inscriptions, *'m* clearly means "great-grandfather," a concretization of the Amorite meaning "eponymous ancestor."[41] This same meaning appears in a Safatic inscription, whose author lists four persons, each of whom he calls "his *'mt* [fem. of *'m*]," probably female ancestors.[42] An *'m* would thus be a male agnate. The collective meaning of *'m,* "people," common in Nabatean, may also be attested in a Safaitic inscription.[43] Safaitic also uses the prep. *'m.*[44]

---

32. Benz, 379.
33. See, respectively, *CIS,* I, 147, 6; 4911, 4; 5165, 4-5; 3303, 4.
34. *APN,* 22a.
35. *DNSI,* II, 864-69.
36. For the former see *CIS,* I, 263, 3-4; for the latter, *KAI* 145.2.
37. See K. P. Jackson, *The Ammonite Language of the Iron Age. HSM* 27 (1983), 97; *APN,* 22.
38. *ARM,* XVI/1, 98-99; cf. V. Sasson, *RA* 66 (1972), 179.
39. *KAI* 181.11, 24.
40. See, respectively, G. L. Harding, *An Index and Concordance of Pre-Islamic Arabian Names and Inscriptions* (1971), 434ff.; *Syr* 45 (1968), 6; *PNPI,* 45a and 106b.
41. *CIS,* II, 182, 2; 354, 2.
42. *IM* 49217; G. G. Harding, *Sumer* 6 (1950), 124, 5ff.
43. For Nabatean see *DNSI,* II, 865; for Safaitic, W. G. Oxtoby, *Some Inscriptions of the Safaitic Bedouin* (1968), 101.
44. *CIS,* V, 4417 and 4443.

9. *South Arabian.* The element *ʿm* also appears in Old South Arabian names.[45] In the area of Qataban, however, it can also refer to the moon god ʿAmm.[46] Although *ʿm* is usually translated "paternal uncle,"[47] the pl. *ʾʿmm* refers to agnates in general; the same is true for Sabaic and Minaean.[48] The sg. *ʿm* appears occasionally to mean "clan" or "people." The name of the god ʿAmm is to be interpreted as meaning that he is a "parental" god, even an "eponymous ancestor."

Sabaic has a verb *hʿmm* derived from the collective noun *ʿm,* "people"; it means "collect." Two related nouns are *tʿmm,* "publicity, publication," and *ʿmt,* "rabble."[49] The prep. *ʿm* also appears in Old South Arabic.

10. *Classical Arabic.* Arabic uses the words *ʿamm* and *ʿamma* in the sense of paternal "uncle" and "aunt," but more for a paternal agnate in the widest sense.[50] The collective meaning of *ʿamm* is also found and is probably preserved in the phrase *banū ʿamm.*[51] The denominative verb *ʿamma* is used with the meaning "be general."[52] A connection between derivatives of the root *ʿamm* and *ʿāma* (*ʿym*), "become unaccustomed," or the particle *ʿamma/ʿammā* < *ʿan-mā* is out of the question.[53]

11. *Aramaic.* The noun *ʿam(m),* emph. pl. *ʿammayyāʾ, ʿammᵉmayyāʾ,* or *ʿammᵉmêʾ,* appears in Old Aramaic, Imperial Aramaic,[54] Jewish Aramaic, Nabatean, Syriac, and Mandaic with the meaning "people"; it occasionally has the nuance of "multitude," "congregation," "sect," or "rabble." The earliest text in which it is used is the Deir ʿAlla plaster inscription.[55] Occurrences of *ʿm* in Nabatean with the meaning "great-grandfather" are dependent on North Arabian influence.[56] Syr. *ʿammᵉṯāʾ* means "paternal aunt"; the masc. form *ʿamm* appears in many Aramaic proper names of the 1st millennium;[57] in this context it can be a theophorous element, but it can also refer to a relative. Thus the meaning of *ʿam(m)* in Aramaic proper names appears to resemble Amorite and Nabatean usage.

12. *Summary.* In summary, we can say that the West Semitic word *ʿamm* refers to agnates, both individually and collectively. The individual sense can take on a specific meaning, denoting an eponymous ancestor, a great-grandfather, or, in a later stage of

---

45. G. L. Harding, 434ff.
46. *WM,* I/1, 494-95.
47. Biella, 371.
48. For Sabean see *CIS,* IV, 37, 6; *RÉS* 4018, 2; for Minaean, *RÉS* 2771, 8; 3017, 2.
49. A. F. L. Beeston et al., *Sabaic Dictionary* (1982), 16-17.
50. Wellhausen, 480-81.
51. Good, 37-41.
52. Wehr, 640.
53. E. Lipiński, *BiOr* 43 (1986), 182.
54. *DNSI,* II, 865.
55. Combination I, 4(6).
56. *DNSI,* II, 865.
57. See Brockelmann, *LexSyr,* 252; R. Zadok, *On West Semites in Babylonia* (^{2}1978), 55-56.

development, a paternal uncle, or even (in modern Arabic) a father-in-law. The collective sense includes the totality of agnates, a clan, but also the people as a whole, a multitude, or a religious assembly. The biblical usage of *'am* appropriates this double meaning without any difficulty.

II. Individual Sense.

1. *Proper Names.* In Biblical Hebrew the individual sense of *'am* is attested primarily in proper names. Some of these names reflect a very ancient tradition, going back to a prebiblical use of the word. This is particularly true of *'ᵉlî'ām* (2 S. 11:3; 23:34), *'ammî'ēl* (Nu. 13:12; 2 S. 9:4-5; 17:27; 1 Ch. 3:5; 26:5), and *yiṯrᵉ'ām* (2 S. 3:5; 1 Ch. 3:3), all of which appear as Amorite personal names, as well as *'ammôn,* the eponymous ancestor of the Ammonites. The name *'ammînāḏāḇ* (Ex. 6:23; Nu. 1:7; 2:3; 7:12,17; 10:14; Ruth 4:19-20; 1 Ch. 2:10; 6:7[Eng. v. 22]; 15:10-11; also to be read in Cant. 6:12) was borne by two Ammonite kings.[58] Here the element *'ammî* is the subject, as well as in *'ammîhûḏ* (Nu. 1:10; 2:18; 7:48,53; 10:22; 34:20,28; 1 Ch. 7:26; 9:4), in the Aramaic name *'ammîzāḇāḏ* (1 Ch. 27:6), in the North Arabian name *'ᵃnî'ām* (1 Ch. 7:19), as well as in *yᵉqam'ām* (1 Ch. 23:19; 24:23; cf. the toponym *yoqmᵉ'ām*), *yāroḇ'ām,* and *rᵉḥaḇᵉ'ām.*[59] It is the predicate in *'ammîḥûr* (2 S. 13:37 *K*), a theophorous name with Horus, and in *'ammîšadday* (Nu. 1:12; 2:25; 7:66,71; 10:25). There are also the toponyms *yoqmᵉ'ām* (1 K. 4:12; 1 Ch. 6:53[68]); *yoqnᵉ'ām* (Josh. 12:22; 19:11; 21:34), *yoqdᵉ'ām* (Josh. 15:56), which should possibly be emended to *yoqrᵉ'ām* (1 Ch. 2:44); and perhaps also *yiḇlᵉ'ām* (Josh. 17:11; Jgs. 1:27; 2 K. 9:27; cf. 1 Ch. 6:55[70]). Two of these toponyms appear also as Amorite PNs: *yaqun-'ammu* and *'ammu-yaqar.*[60]

The relatively frequent correlations with Amorite onomastica can indicate that *'amm* in most PNs originally had the meaning "eponymous ancestor" or "paterfamilias." The popular etymology in Gen. 19:37f. attests similar meaning. Here the name Moab is explained with the help of *me'āḇ,* "came forth from their father"; *ben-'ammî* must then mean "son of my clan-father" or "family father." Accordingly, the Hebrew PN with the element *'amm* can reflect an ancestral cult, vestiges of which would obviously be nuanced when transmitted in the biblical texts.

2. *Burial Formula.* Nevertheless, the written language of the biblical period has preserved the individual usage of *'am* in a few expressions, especially the burial formula *ne'ᵉsap̱ 'el-'ammāyw* (Gen. 25:8,17; 35:29,33; Nu. 20:24; 27:13; 31:2; Dt. 32:50 [twice]). It is a euphemism for "die," meaning literally "be gathered to his ancestors." Other texts express the same notion with the verb *ne'ᵉsap* (Nu. 20:26; Isa. 57:1; Hos. 4:3; Sir. 8:7; 40:28; cf. Ezk. 34:29) — a usage already attested at Ugarit[61] — or connect it with other adverbial phrases such as *ne'ᵉsap̱ 'el-'ᵃḇôṯāyw,* "be gathered to his fathers"

---

58. See *IPN,* 193; Jackson, *Ammonite Language,* 97.
59. See *IPN,* 146; on the North Arabic name see Harding, *Index,* 80, 145.
60. For the former see *TCL,* I, 238, 42; for the latter, *ARM,* XVI/1, 101.
61. *KTU* 1.14, I, 18.

(Jgs. 2:10; cf. 2 K. 22:20; 2 Ch. 34:28);[62] or *ne'ᵉsap 'el-qiḇrōṯeyḵā,* "be gathered to your tombs" (2 K. 22:20; 2 Ch. 34:28). The pl. *'el-'ammāyw* is therefore no standing element of the idiom. The LXX simply translates it as *laós* (Gen. 25:8; 49:29,33; Nu. 20:24; 27:13; 31:2; Dt. 32:50) or *génos* (Gen. 25:17; 35:29). Targ. Onqelos retains the pl. *'ammêh,* but this is only a mechanical borrowing of the Hebrew term. Taking into account the idiom *'āsap/ne'ᵉsap 'el-'ᵃḇôṯāyw* (Jgs. 2:10; 2 K. 22:20; 2 Ch. 34:28) and the meaning of *'am* in onomastics, we may conclude that here *'ammîm* refers to departed progenitors, to forefathers in the widest sense of the word. Above and beyond its use as a periphrastic euphemism for "die," the idiom may embody a concealed allusion to a cult of departed ancestors celebrated at their tombs (2 K. 22:20; 2 Ch. 34:28).

3. *Banishment Formula.* The individual usage of *'am* occurs also in the penalty formula *niḵrᵉṯâ hannepeš hāhî' mē'ammeyhā.* With a few variants (Ex. 12:15,19; Nu. 19:20), it appears in 30 OT texts: Gen. 17:14; Ex. 12:15,19; 30:33,38; 31:14; Lev. 7:20,21,25,27; 17:4,9,10,14; 18:29; 19:8; 20:3,5,6,17,18; 23:29,30; Nu. 9:13; 15:30, 31; 19:13,20; Ezk. 14:8,9. It clearly refers to exclusion from the community, without going into detail about the modalities.[63] The double formulation of the punishment in Ex. 31:14 appears to indicate that this excommunication has replaced the death penalty, which was prescribed originally for breaking the sabbath (Ex. 31:14a; Nu. 15:32-36). With the passage of time, the use of the pl. *'ammîm* ceased to be clear; later texts therefore replaced it with *yiśrā'ēl* (Ex. 12:15), *'ēḏâ* (Ex. 12:19), or *qāhāl* (Nu. 19:20), or changed the formula slightly to *hiḵrîṯ . . . miqqereḇ 'ammāh/'ammô* (Lev. 17:10; 20:3,6), *niḵraṯ miqqereḇ hammaḥᵃneh* (CD 20:26), *niḵraṯ mittôḵ kol bᵉnê 'ôr* (1QS 2:16), or *mittôḵ 'ᵃmāmēh* (11QT 27:7-8). At first glance, the pl. *'ammîm* of the original idiom can refer only to the members of the clan or tribe, both living and dead, since such excommunication was intended to exclude the banished individual from the family tomb. It is likely, however, that the real purpose of the punishment was exclusion from the cult of the dead, since the formula uses the term *nepeš,* possibly to be understood in the sense of *nepeš mēṯ.* Under this interpretation, the pl. *'ammîm* would have exactly the same meaning as in the burial formula *ne'ᵉsap 'el-'ammāyw,* to which the banishment formula stands in contrast.

4. *Covenant Formula.* It is possible that the individual sense of *'am* was also present in the covenant formula: "I will be God for you, and you will be *'am* for me" (Lev. 26:12; cf. Ex. 6:7; Dt. 26:17-18; 29:12[13]; Jer. 7:23; 11:4; 24:7; 30:22; 31:1,33; 32:38; Ezk. 11:20; 14:11; 36:28; 37:23,27; Zec. 8:8; 11QT 59:13). This statement uses the ancient word pair "God" and "ancestor" that appears in the Amorite PNs *'ammuš-kī-'il* ("his ancestor is like God") and *'ilī/'ila-'ammu* ("the ancestor is [my] God") as well as Ruth 1:16: "Your ancestor will be my ancestor, and your God will be my God." The words of the covenant thus conjure up a mutual relationship that practically re-

62. → I, 10.
63. → VII, 347-49.

quires interpreting the word *'am* in the sense of "agnate," since the specific meaning "progenitor" is impossible. Yahweh and Israel would be understood henceforth as a kind of family, with Yahweh in its midst: "I shall walk in your midst" (Lev. 26:12). The word *'am* was undoubtedly understood later in the sense of "my people," but Lev. 26:12 speaks only of an *'am,* with no suffix, which makes sense only with the meaning "agnate" or "blood relative," as a newly established kinship relationship. Later a more precise definition claimed the day, based on the relationship traditionally established between the covenant formula and the expression *'am yhwh* (1 S. 2:24; 2 S. 1:12; 6:21; 2 K. 9:6; cf. *'am *ᵉ*lōhîm* in 2 S. 14:13), a construct phrase expressing the relationship between Israel and God, which gave rise to the use of the suffix "my people" (1 K. 14:7; 16:2; etc.), "your people" (Hab. 3:13; Ps. 3:9[8]; 79:13; etc.), "his people" (Ps. 29:11; 78:71; etc.). It is likely, however, that originally the expression did not refer to the Israel that settled west of the Jordan toward the end of the 13th century, but to the "clan" or "tribe" of Yahweh dwelling in Edom.[64] The notion of kinship was undoubtedly present at the outset, but the word had a collective sense, just as in the expression *'am k*ᵉ*mōš* (Nu. 21:29).

The complete covenant formula — for the most part already reinterpreted collectively — appears first in Ex. 6:7 in connection with the commissioning of Moses; it appears subsequently in contexts emphasizing obedience to the law as a condition of the covenant (Lev. 26:12 [H]; Dt. 26:17-18; 29:12-13(13-14); Jer. 7:23; 11:4), as a consequence of a new heart (Jer. 24:7; 31:33; Ezk. 11:20), as a consequence of purification (Ezk. 14:11; 37:23), and in the context of a general restoration of Israel (Jer. 30:22; 31:1; 32:38; Ezk. 36:28; 37:27; Zec. 8:8). Other texts may be read as alluding to the formula, e.g., Jer. 13:11 ("in order that they might be my people"), Isa. 40:1 (when one can speak of "my people" and "your God," the covenant is still in force; on "comfort," cf. 49:13; 52:9), 51:16 (". . . saying to Zion, 'You are my people' "), 51:22 ("your God, who pleads the cause of his people"), and 63:8 ("surely they are my people . . . he became their savior").

In Jgs. 5:11,13, the expression *'am yhwh* seems to mean "army of Yahweh" (see III.5 below), but this is clearly a specialized meaning here. Elsewhere the complete expression and the suffixed forms appear in contexts dealing with the intimate bond between Yahweh and his people ("clan, kindred"). The expression is especially common in prophetic language and in the Psalms; it is not found in the laws or wisdom literature. According to Lohfink, it belongs "primarily to the situation of dialogue between Yahweh and Israel, less to the situation of objective speaking about Israel."[65]

The relationship between Yahweh and his people can find negative or positive expression, depending on whether it provokes his intervention to punish or to help. Yahweh is angry with his people (Isa. 5:25; 47:6; Ps. 106:40), "sells" them (Ps.

---

64. See R. Giveon, *Les bédouins Shosou* (1971), 26-28, 75; contra L. E. Stager, *ErIsr* 18 (1985) 56-64.

65. P. 280.

44:13[12]), makes them suffer hard things (Ps. 60:5[3]), gives them to the sword (Ps. 78:62), requites their wickedness (Jer. 7:12). But he also observes the misery of his people (Ex. 3:7) and delivers them out of Egypt (1 K. 8:16; Ps. 105:43; Dnl. 9:15; cf. Ps. 77:16[15][*gāʾal*]), binds up their wounds (Isa. 30:26), goes forth to save his people (Hab. 3:13), restores their fortunes (*šûḇ šᵉḇûṯ,* Jer. 30:3; Hos. 6:11; Ps. 53:7[6]). He gives blessings, help, peace, and strength (Dt. 26:15; Ps. 3:9[8]; 28:9; 29:11); he makes known his power and sends redemption (Ps. 111:6,9). The people are his flock, which he pastures (Ps. 79:13; 100:3; cf. 77:21[20]; 78:52); he takes special care of the powerless among his people (Isa. 10:2; 14:32). He is a refuge for his people (Joel 4:16[3:16]). He sets princes or kings over his people (1 S. 9:16; 13:14; 15:1; 2 S. 6:21; 7:8; 1 K. 14:7; 16:2; 2 K. 9:6). He speaks to his people and admonishes them (Ps. 50:7; 81:9[8]; cf. 78:1). He laments that his people do not understand (Isa. 1:3; here the familial aspect surfaces: rebellious, degenerate children). He asks in desperation, "What can I do with my sinful people?" (Jer. 9:6[7]) or reproachfully, "O my people, what have I done to you?" (Mic. 6:3). Particularly impressive is the concentration of occurrences in Solomon's prayer at the dedication of the temple (1 K. 8:23-52). The entire dedication ceremony is represented as involving God's people: the people possess the land as God's gift (vv. 36,51), are obligated to fear God (v. 43), and expect that God will hear their prayers (vv. 30,38,52) and forgive their sins (vv. 34,36,50).

This notion plays a special role in the thought of Hosea. He calls his son Lo-ammi, because Israel is no longer God's people (1:9). Later, however, Yahweh takes back his people, and we hear again the words *ʿammî* and *ʾᵉlōhay* (2:25[23]).

Isa. 2:6 is a special case: *kî nāṭaštâ ʿammᵉḵā bêṯ yaʿᵃqōḇ*. In the context of vv. 6-22, an apostrophe to the house of Jacob would be unique (v. 9c is either parenthetical or corrupt). The LXX reads: "He has rejected his people, the house of Jacob," which may make the best sense. The Targ. reads "your strength" (*ʿuzzᵉḵā),* i.e., God. In discussing Hos. 4:4, Nyberg has pointed out the possibility of taking *ʿam,* "relative," as a reference to the deity, an interpretation that would also be possible here.[66] Saadiah interprets *ʿam* as "national character"; Wiklander has a similar reading: "the congregation of those who worship Yahweh."[67] The change of person, however, remains difficult, and it is probably impossible to reach a totally satisfying solution.

Lipiński

It should be noted that outside Israel the concept of a "people" is totally absent from the ancient Near East. Groups of human beings are distinguished by their dwelling places, geographical regions, and social classes, as well as by their various languages, a distinction that sometimes results in different groupings.[68]

Von Soden

---

66. H. S. Nyberg, *Studien zum Hoseabuche. UUÅ* 1935:6, 27-28.

67. B. Wiklander, *Prophecy as Literature: A Text-Linguistic and Rhetorical Approach to Isaiah 2–4. CB* 22 (1984), 71-72.

68. See W. von Soden, *The Ancient Orient* (Eng. trans. 1994), 13-14.

III. Collective Sense. The semantic content of the word *'am* developed primarily in an urban milieu, taking on a variety of collective nuances in which the notion of kinship among members of a clan or with the tribal "totem" was lost. This connotation vanished from common usage at the time when *'am* came to be used in synonymous parallelism with → גּוֹי *gôy* (Dt. 4:6; Ezk. 36:15; Ps. 96:3,10; 106:34-35) and → לְאֹם *le'ōm* (Gen. 27:29; Isa. 17:12; Jer. 51:58; Hab. 2:13; Ps. 47:4[3]; 57:10[9]; 67:5[4]; 108:4[3]; Prov. 24:24) without any detectable special nuance. Instead, the term *'am* frequently suggests the notion of totality, of the people as a whole, like Arab. *'āmma.* It is used in connection with political, civil, and religious institutions: levy of troops, popular assembly, populace, congregation of the faithful, and religious community.

1. *Assembly of the Israelites.* As in Phoenician and Punic, *'am* can refer to the totality of an urban population enjoying full civil rights (Ruth 4:4,9), e.g., the people of Jerusalem (2 Ch. 32:18). When they meet to make decisions, they constitute the popular assembly, called simply *hā'ām* or *kol-hā'ām.* In Jgs. 10:18, e.g., *'am* refers to the assembly of the inhabitants of Gilead, who appoint Jephthah commander (11:11) and whose elders (→ זָקֵן *zāqēn*) act as their authorized representatives (11:5-11). The situation is similar in 1 S. 10:17,22-24, where the *'am* assembled at Mizpah determines to elevate Saul to the kingship. In both cases the *'am* is a tribal assembly, of Gilead and Benjamin respectively. A more inclusive assembly appears in 1 K. 12. The *'am* at Shechem comprises the northern tribes, i.e., Israel; the elders take counsel with Rehoboam as delegates of the people. When an author wants to underscore the fact that a decision is reached by the whole assembly, the expression *kol-hā'ām,* "all the people," is used (1 K. 20:8, where the full assembly of the people of Samaria with all the elders serving as its spokespersons intervenes with the king). The expression "all Israel" refers only to the northern kingdom, since Judah never belonged to Israel in the strict sense of the word. For example, Omri is acclaimed king by "all Israel" (1 K. 16:16); then, however, the *'am* of Israel was divided (v. 21) and civil war ensued.

2. *The People of the Land of Judah.* In Judah the popular assembly of all citizens — during the monarchy, distinct from the inhabitants of Jerusalem — bore the special designation *'am hā'āreṣ,* literally "people of the land" (cf. 2 K. 14:21 with 2 K. 23:30). This *'am hā'āreṣ* can be compared to the *'m 'rṣ z* in the inscription of Yehawmilk, king of Byblos (see I.6 above). It is distinguished from or contrasted with the king or prince (2 K. 16:15; Ezk. 7:27; 45:22; Dnl. 9:6), the king and his ministers (Jer. 37:2), and the notables, priests, and prophets (Jer. 1:18; 34:19; 44:21; Ezk. 22:24-29). It is also distinct from the population of the royal city of Jerusalem (2 K. 11:20; cf. Jer. 25:2), which comprised primarily functionaries, mercenaries and their families, court personnel, and temple servants. As a consequence, the *'am hā'āreṣ* consisted essentially of the people inhabiting the province. Nevertheless, it acclaimed Joash (2 K. 11:14,18; 2 Ch. 23:13) and subsequently Josiah (2 K. 21:14; 2 Ch. 33:25) as king. It also decided to destroy the temple of Baal and to execute both Mattan the priest of Baal and Queen Athaliah (2 K. 11:18,20; 2 Ch. 23:17,21), thus functioning as defender of autochthonous Judahite traditions against foreign influences associated with the entourage of Athaliah.

After the exile, this notion of an autochthonous native people comprising the inhabitants of the province was adopted by the exiles who returned from Babylonia. "The poorest of the *'am hā'āreṣ,*" who had remained in Judah (2 K. 24:14) and intermarried with non-Jews (cf. Neh. 13:23), the revenants looked on as people who neither knew nor obeyed the law, hindered observance of the sabbath, and interfered with the work of national and religious restoration (Ezr. 9:1-2,11; 10:2,11; Neh. 10:29,31-32). On the basis of this notion, the term *'am hā'āreṣ* was applied to the Samaritans (Ezr. 4:4), then to the non-Jewish inhabitants of Palestine (Ezr. 3:3; 9:1; Neh. 9:30; Gen. 23:12-13; Nu. 14:9), and finally to natives in general, e.g., the Egyptians in Egypt (Gen. 42:6). This pejorative sense of *'am hā'āreṣ* continued in Mishnaic Hebrew usage. As in Ezr. 9:1-2,11; 10:2,11; Neh. 10:29,31-32, the term referred to Jews who do not know the law and hence are suspected of not observing the ritual regulations and not offering in the temple tithes of the fruits of the field. The Mishnah tractate *Demai* therefore regulates the use of products bought from the *'am hā'āreṣ.* The term was often used to designate an individual, another sign of the ambivalence of the word *'am.* Hence the pl. *'ammê hā'āreṣ* or *hā'ᵃrāṣôṯ,* "people of the land," appears in postexilic (Ezr. 3:3; 9:1-2,11; 10:2,11; Neh. 10:29,31-32[28,30-31]) and even Talmudic Hebrew (Bab. *Šab.* 63a; *Ḥul.* 92a).

3. *The Postexilic Assembly.* In the postexilic period, the term *'am* also continued to denote the popular assembly, which played an active role in postexilic Jerusalem, e.g., in Neh. 8, at the hour of birth of Judaism. Even when the text uses the term → קהל *qāhāl* (vv. 2,17), the expression *kol-hā'ām* predominates (vv. 1,3,5,9,11,12); the elders are even described as *rā'šê hā'āḇôṯ lᵉḵol-hā'ām,* "heads of the households of all the people" (v. 13). In the Maccabean period, when Judah was again largely independent, a great popular assembly decides to bestow on Simon and his descendants the hereditary authority of ethnarch, high priest, and commander of the Jewish nation (1 Mc. 13:42; 14:46-47).

The Greek terms used merely mimic the terminology of the Hebrew original. The assembly is quite simply *ho laós* (1 Mc. 13:42) and *pás ho laós* (14:46). At first glance the use of the word *laós,* which the LXX employs in the special sense of "Jewish people," is startling. Greek uses a different word, *dḗmos,* to refer to the assembly of all free citizens; in 8:29; 14:20; 15:17 it refers to the assembly of the Jewish people. But these last texts are taken from official documents, composed originally in Greek and using the terminology of institutions belonging to the Hellenistic world. By contrast, 13:42 and 14:46 reflect Hebrew usage, rendering *hā'ām* almost automatically as *ho laós.* In reality, *(pás) ho laós* and *ho dḗmos* are different terms for the same popular assembly in the period of the Maccabees.

4. *The People as a Whole.* The word *'am* was used in a still broader sense, without any institutional connotations and even more inclusively than in the postexilic usage of *'am hā'āreṣ.* The word can mean a chance gathering, a multitude (Dt. 13:10[9]: *kol-hā'ām,* "everybody"), or the laity *(hā'ām)* in contrast to the priests (Dt. 18:3; Isa. 24:2; Jer. 26:7; 28:5; Neh. 10:35). Elsewhere *'am* refers to the people in the vicinity of a

prophet (1 K. 19:21) or the people in general (2 K. 4:41). The subjects of a king are called his *ʿam* (Ex. 1:22; 7:29; 8:4; etc. [of Pharaoh]; 1 Ch. 18:14 [of David]; 2 Ch. 21:14 [of Joram]; 33:10 [of Manasseh]; in 1 K. 20:42; 22:4; Ezk. 30:11, the sense of "military host" may also be present). Often (but not always; cf. Ex. 3:21; 5:22) the expression *hāʿām hazzeh* has pejorative overtones (Isa. 6:9; 8:6,11; 28:11; 29:1; etc.). Only the context permits a semantic definition. By a still broader extension of meaning, the word *ʿam* can refer to an animal population (Ps. 74:14; Prov. 30:25-26). In this usage all sense of kinship has vanished.

5. *Warriors.* Another ancient meaning of *ʿam* is "troops"; it derives from the obligation to provide armed assistance that an agnate relationship imposed upon members of a clan or tribe assumed to be descended from a common ancestor. In certain instances no trace remains of this reference to familial ties, although the word *ʿam* without further specification can refer to the army or general levy (Nu. 20:20; 21:33; 1 S. 14:28ff.; etc.). We sometimes find the expression *ʿam hammilḥāmâ,* "fighting men" (Josh. 8:1,3; 10:7; 11:7). Earlier, in the time of the "wars of Yahweh" (Nu. 21:14; 1 S. 18:17; 25:28; Sir. 46:3), the army was called *ʿam yhwh,* "the people of Yahweh" (Jgs. 5:13), an expression that suggests kinship with God. During the period of the monarchy, especially at its outset, this popular host was clearly distinct from the mercenaries, who were "servants" of the king (2 S. 11:11). The expressions *ʿam yᵉhûḏâ* and *ʿam yiśrāʾēl* in 2 S. 19:41 probably refer to this host, while *ʿam kᵉnaʿan* in Zeph. 1:11 means "people" in general. The people in arms could identify itself with the freemen's assembly, for in 1 K. 16:15-16 we see it proclaiming Omri king. During Sennacherib's siege of Jerusalem, it was once again the popular levy that kept watch on the walls (2 K. 18:26; Isa. 36:11). In Gen. 32:8(7), 33:15, and 35:6, too, *ʿam* probably refers to men in arms; here, however, the word does not mean "army" in the strict sense.

6. *The People of God.* The cultic and religious assembly of Yahweh's faithful is frequently called the "people of Yahweh" (Nu. 11:29, *ʿam yhwh*), the "people of God" (Jgs. 20:2, *ʿam ʾᵉlōhîm*), or simply "the people" *(hāʿām).* The ancient agnatic connotations of the word had probably vanished, while the notion of religious and cultic dependence and ties won the upper hand (we even find the "people of the calf" in Hos. 10:5). In this sense texts often speak of "my/your/his people" (Ex. 3:7; 5:1; 18:1; Dt. 32:9; etc.), with the suffix referring to Yahweh in each case (see II.4 above). Sometimes the text also speaks of the *ʿam qāḏôš,* "holy people" (Dt. 7:6; 14:2,21; 26:19; 28:9; cf. Isa. 62:12, *ʿam-haqqōḏeš*); this phrase does not express an inherent attribute, but kinship with Yahweh.[69] Other expressions are *ʿam sᵉgullâ* (→ סגלה) *mikkol-hāʿammîm,* God's "own people among all the peoples" (Dt. 7:6; 14:2; cf. 26:18), and *ʿam naḥᵃlâ* (→ נחל *nāḥal*), God's "hereditary people" (Dt. 4:20; cf. 9:29; 1 K. 8:51; 2 Ch. 6:27). The Greek translation often uses *laós* for *ʿam* in this sense. The LXX

69. → קדשׁ *qdš;* see Hulst, 907.

breathed new life into this ancient Greek word by associating it emphatically with the chosen people in contrast to the *éthnē,* the "gentiles" or "heathen."

7. *Foreign Peoples.* Finally, *'am* can refer to a foreign nation like Cush (Isa. 18:2) or Egypt (30:5); in the plural *('ammîm),* it can mean the foreign nations in contrast to Israel (2:3; 8:9; 12:4; etc.), a meaning found also in the expressions *'ammê hā'āreṣ* (Est. 8:17) and *'ammê hā'ᵃrāṣōṯ* (Neh. 9:30). This usage appears frequently in the Essene literature, where *'ammê hā'ᵃrāṣôṯ* (1QM 10:9; 1QH 4:26), *kōl hā'ammîm* (1QpHab 3:6,11,13; 6:7; 8:5), and *(hā)'ammîm* (CD 8:10; etc.) refer to the gentile nations.

IV. Dead Sea Scrolls. The Essene writings put special emphasis on the holiness of the chosen people by identifying them with the righteous, the "sons of light." The chapter of the War Scroll describing the standards specifies that the words *'am 'ēl,* "people of God," are to be written upon the great banner that will go "at the head of all the people," i.e., the army (1QM 3:13; cf. 1:5). This military connotation of *'am* appears not only in the War Scroll but also in the Temple Scroll (58:5,10,11,16; 61:13). The holiness of the *'am* is expressed in 11QT 48:7,10 by the phrase *'am qāḏôš,* taken from Dt. 7:6; 14:2. Elsewhere the same purpose is served by *'am qôḏeš* (1QM 12:1; 14:12; cf. also Dnl. 8:24), *'am qᵉḏôšîm,* "people of the saints" (1QM 12:8; cf. again Dnl. 8:24), or *'am qᵉḏôšêḵâ,* "people of your saints" (1QH 11:11-12). Although the latter expression also admits the reading *'im qᵉḏôšêḵâ,* "with your saints" (cf. 1QM 12:4), the sentence structure makes it more likely that we have here a variant of *'ᵃḏaṯ qᵉḏôšêḵâ,* "congregation of your saints" (1QM 12:7; 1QH fr. 5:3), and *ṣᵉḇā' qᵉḏôšêḵâ,* "army of your saints" (1QH 10:35).

Apart from this emphasis on the holiness of the true people of God, the usage of *'am* in the Dead Sea Scrolls hardly differs from OT usage. It can mean the cultic assembly (11QT 32:6; 35:12,14; cf. 51:11), it can sometimes denote the laity as distinct from the priests (15:17), but it can also be used in a very general sense. Thus *'am haqqāhāl* (18:7; 26:7,9) means "the members of the assembly," and *kōl hā'ām* can simply stand for "everyone." It is interesting that *kol-gôy ûmamlāḵâ* (2 Ch. 32:15) becomes *kôl gôy wᵉ'am* in 11QT 58:3; furthermore, 11QtgJob 34:29 uses *'am* to represent both *gôy* (Job 34:29) and *'āḏām* (36:28). In CD 1:21 *rîḇ 'am* probably means "strife" (cf. 2 S. 22:44 = Ps. 18:44[43]). The Essenes and their contemporaries in Judea thus apparently did not attribute particular theological significance to the word *'am,* unlike the LXX translators, who assigned a specific value to the terms *laós* and *éthnos.*

Lipiński

עִם *'im* → אֵת *'eṯ*

עָמַד ʿāmaḏ; עֹמֶד ʿōmeḏ; עֶמְדָּה ʿemdâ; מַעֲמָד maʿamāḏ; מָעֳמָד moʿomāḏ

I. 1. Etymology; 2. Occurrences. II. Verb: 1. Qal; 2. Hiphil. III. Nouns. IV. 1. LXX; 2. Dead Sea Scrolls.

I. 1. *Etymology.* Etymologically, Heb. *ʿāmaḏ,* "approach, stand," corresponds to Akk. *emēdu,* "lean on, lay upon,"[1] and Arab. *ʿamada,* "support, intend"; but this relationship contributes nothing to our understanding of Hebrew usage. The root is not found in Ugaritic; Aramaic and Phoenician attest only *ʿāmmûḏ/ʿmd,* "pillar." The only occurrence of the verb in Aramaic, Ahiqar 160, is uncertain;[2] Aramaic uses *qûm* instead.

2. *Occurrences.* The 435 occurrences of the verb in the qal are distributed quite evenly through the whole OT; the 85 occurrences of the hiphil appear predominantly in late texts (the Chronicler's History and Daniel). The hophal occurs twice. Besides → **עמוד** *ʿammûḏ,* "pillar," there are four nominal derivatives: *ʿōmeḏ,* "standing, place" (9 times in Daniel, Nehemiah, and 2 Chronicles); *ʿemdāh,* "place for stopping" (Mic. 1:11); *maʿamāḏ,* "attendance, function" (5 occurrences); and *moʿomāḏ,* "foothold" (Ps. 69:3[2]).

II. Verb.

1. *Qal.* The verb *ʿāmaḏ* is in common use with the basic meaning "approach, place oneself," or (primarily as a ptcp.) simply "stand." Any theological overtones derive from the context.

a. *Approach.* We find *ʿāmaḏ* with the meaning "approach, go and stand" in a variety of contexts. Moses comes before Pharaoh (Ex. 9:10); the Israelites go to the entrance of the tent of meeting and offer incense (Nu. 16:18); the angel of Yahweh takes a stand in a narrow path to block Balaam's way (Nu. 22:24,26); Jotham goes and stands on Mt. Gerizim to tell his fable (Jgs. 9:7); David runs and stands over Goliath (1 S. 17:51); Saul says to the Amalekite, "Come, stand over me and kill me" (2 S. 1:9-10); Absalom positions himself by the road into the city gate (2 S. 15:2); a member of a company of

---

ʿāmaḏ. S. Amsler, "**עמד** *ʿmd* to stand," *TLOT,* II, 921-24; D. R. Ap-Thomas, "Notes on Some Terms Relating to Prayer," *VT* 6 (1956) 225-41; P. A. H. de Boer, "**בבריתם עמד זרעם**: Sirach xliv 12a," *Hebräische Wortforschung. FS W. Baumgartner. SVT* 16 (1967), 25-29; B. Gemser, "The *rîb-* or Controversy-Pattern in Hebrew Mentality," *Wisdom in Israel and in the Ancient Near East. FS H. H. Rowley. SVT* 3 (1955), 120-37; W. Grundmann, "Stehen und Fallen im qumrānischen und neutestamentlichen Schrifttum," *Qumrān-Probleme,* ed. H. Bardtke (1963), 147-66; J. F. A. Sawyer, "Hebrew Words for the Resurrection of the Dead," *VT* 23 (1973) 218-34, esp. 222-23.

1. *AHw,* I, 211.
2. P. Grelot, *RB* 68 (1961) 190.

prophets goes to stand beside the road to wait for the king (1 K. 20:38); Jehoshaphat comes forward and cries out, "Listen to me" (2 Ch. 20:20); Jeremiah goes and stands in the gate of the temple to deliver his temple sermon (Jer. 7:2; 26:2; cf. 19:14).

In military contexts, *ʿāmaḏ* means "take a position, form up" (1 S. 17:3; 2 S. 2:25; 2 K. 3:21; 11:11). In Neh. 12:40 the verb refers to the appearance of festal choruses in the temple.

b. *With Statement of Purpose.* Sometimes people approach for a particular purpose. The inhabitants of Aroer are to stand by the road and watch to find out what has happened (Jer. 48:19). Using similar language, Jeremiah exhorts his listeners to stand at the crossroads to ask for the ancient paths, i.e., to learn from history (Jer. 6:16). People stand to pray: Naaman expects Elisha to come out and stand before him and call on the name of Yahweh (2 K. 5:11). Jehoshaphat appears in the *qāhāl* in the temple to pray to Yahweh (2 Ch. 20:5). Yahweh says to Jeremiah: "Even were Moses and Samuel to come and stand before my face, my heart would not turn toward this people" (Jer. 15:1). Here the purpose is intercession, as also in Jer. 18:20: "Remember how I stood before you to speak good for them," and perhaps also Gen. 19:27, if it refers to 18:22-23: Abraham stands *(ʿōmēḏ)* before Yahweh, then comes closer *(ngš)* and intercedes.

c. *In Court.* We often find *ʿāmaḏ* in the context of judicial proceedings. In a controversy, according to Ezk. 44:24, the priests are to "stand" to judge *(šāpaṭ);* here *ʿāmaḏ* can hardly mean "stand," but must mean simply "act as judges."[3] So also of Yahweh: "He stands ready *(niṣṣāḇ)* to give justice *(rîḇ),* he stands present *(ʿōmēḏ)* to judge *(dîn)* his people [MT 'the peoples']" (Isa. 3:13). Since judges normally sit (*yāšaḇ,* Ex. 18:13; Isa. 16:5; Joel 4:12[Eng. 3:12]; Ps. 9:5,8-9[4,7-8]; Prov. 20:8; Dnl. 7:9), Boecker assumes that here Yahweh functions as plaintiff.[4] But the verb *dîn* is hardly appropriate for the plaintiff, unless Yahweh is here both plaintiff and judge. It is better to follow Gemser in assuming that the judge rises to pronounce judgment (cf. Ps. 76:9-10[8-9], where *qûm lammišpāṭ* parallels *hišmîaʿ dîn*).[5] Wildberger believes that those hearing the case were seated but rose to speak (cf. Ps. 82:1, *niṣṣāḇ* par. *šāpaṭ*).[6] We may note that Akkadian, too, uses both *ašābu,* "sit," and *izuzzu,* "stand," with reference to judges.

Much more often the text says that the parties come or stand before the judge. The people stand before Moses through the entire day while he "judges" *(šāpaṭ)* them (Ex. 18:13). The daughters of Zelophehad come and stand before Moses and Eleazar to request a judgment (cf. v. 21). In cases involving the law of asylum, the slayer is to come and stand before the congregation (*lip̱nê hāʿēḏâ,* Nu. 35:12; cf. Josh. 20:4,6,9). When there is false testimony in court, both parties shall appear before Yahweh, the priests, and the judges (Dt. 19:17). The accuser *(śāṭān)* also "stands" or "takes his place" at the right

3. So Gemser, 123; NRSV; contra G. R. Driver, *Bibl* 35 (1954) 310; W. Zimmerli, *Ezekiel 2. Herm* (Eng. trans. 1983), 450.

4. *Redeformen des Rechtsleben im AT. WMANT* 14 ([2]1970), 85.

5. P. 123.

6. Wildberger, *Isaiah 1–12* (Eng. trans. 1991), 141. See also L. Köhler, *Hebrew Man* (Eng. trans. 1956), 132.

hand of the accused "to accuse him" (Zec. 3:1; cf. also Ps. 109:6). According to Gemser, the accused also stand (Ps. 76:8[7]; 130:3; Jer. 49:19; 1 S. 6:20), but here *ʿāmad* could also be taken to mean "be vindicated."[7] The verb *qûm* is used of witnesses (Dt. 19:15-16; Ps. 27:12; 35:11), while *ʿāmad* is used of Yahweh as advocate (Ps. 109:31).

Deutero-Isaiah borrows the language of the court. In the third Servant Song, we read: "Who will venture to contend *(rîb)* with me? Let us stand up together *(naʿamdâ yāḥad)*" (Isa. 50:8). In a similar vein, those who make idols are to come and stand before Yahweh to be put to shame (Isa. 44:11, though here a legal action is not involved).[8]

d. *Stand Up.* In other cases *ʿāmad* means "stand up, rise." Ezekiel is commanded: "Stand up on your feet, and I will speak with you" (Ezk. 2:1; cf. Dnl. 10:11). All the people stand up when Ezra opens the book of the law (Neh. 8:5). The people stand on opposite sides of the ark while Joshua writes down the law and probably also afterward while he reads it (Josh. 8:33-34). At the dedication of the temple, Solomon rises *(qûm)* after kneeling before the altar, comes forward (NRSV "stood"; *ʿāmad*), and pronounces the blessing over the people (1 K. 8:54-55). Dnl. 12:13 even uses *ʿāmad* to refer to the resurrection (cf. Isa. 26:19, *qûm*).

e. *Enter.* In 2 K. 23:3 *ʿāmad babbᵉrîṯ* means "enter into the covenant" (Dt. 29:11 uses *ʿāḇar* in a similar context) or "stand by the covenant" (Sir. 44:12).[9] In Jer. 23:18,22, *ʿāmad bᵉsôḏ yhwh* means "stand in the council of Yahweh" or, more likely, have access to the heavenly council — which is precisely what the false prophets do not have. The text of Eccl. 8:3 is difficult. "Do not enter into an unpleasant [i.e., dangerous] matter" has been proposed.[10] Lauha suggests rebellion against the king, and Zimmerli thinks in terms of legal proceedings;[11] the EÜ interprets the clause to mean "Do not adhere obstinately to something that threatens to end in disaster." Ps. 1:1 is clearer: "Happy is the man . . . who does not take the path of sinners," i.e., does not consort with sinners.

f. *Come into Being.* A unique usage is found in Est. 4:14: if Esther fails to speak, deliverance will "arise" for the Jews from another quarter *(māqôm ʾaḥēr),* i.e., from God. Hos. 13:13 compares Israel to a child that does not "present himself" (i.e., is not born) at the proper time. Ps. 33:9 also has to do with "coming into being": "He spoke, and it came to be *(wayyehî);* he commanded, and it stood firm," i.e., it (the universe) came into existence (in Isa. 66:22 the context is similar but the meaning is different; see below). Isa. 48:13 may also deal with the creation of the universe: "My hand laid the foundation of the earth, and my right hand spread out the heavens; I summon them, and they stand in existence forever." According to Westermann, in the beginning God called heaven and earth into being.[12] It is also possible, however, that God summons heaven and earth and they stand at attention, ready to serve.

---

7. P. 123.
8. Westermann, *Isaiah 40–66. OTL* (Eng. trans. 1969), 148-49.
9. De Boer.
10. *HAL,* II, 840; also Lauha, *Kohelet. BK* XIX (1978), 146.
11. *Sprüche-Prediger. ATD* 16/1 (^{3}1962), 213.
12. *Isaiah 40–66,* 201.

g. *With min.* With *min, 'āmad* means "stand apart from, cease." A woman "ceases bearing," i.e., becomes infertile (Gen. 29:35; 30:9). When Jonah is thrown into the sea, it ceases from its raging (Jon. 1:15). The verb is used absolutely in 2 K. 13:18: the king strikes three times and stops.

The expression *'āmad mērāḥōq* means "stand at a distance." It is used of the people who witnessed the theophany at Sinai (Ex. 20:18,21) and of the sons of the prophets who followed Elijah and Elisha but stood at some distance from them (2 K. 2:7). Isa. 59:14 says that righteousness stands at a distance; the parallel stich says that justice turns back *(hussag 'āḥôr).* In Ps. 10:1 Yahweh stands far off and hides himself from the psalmist's distress, i.e., does not intervene and appears to have no interest in the psalmist. In Ps. 38:12 it is the psalmist's friends and companions who stand aloof, breaking the ties of normal community and heightening the psalmist's affliction.

h. *Stand.* Sometimes *'āmad* means simply "stand." Abraham's servant stands by the camels (Gen. 24:30; cf. v. 31). God says to Moses: "The place on which you are standing is holy ground" (Ex. 3:5). The pillar of cloud stands (or takes its place) in front of the tent of meeting (Ex. 14:19; 33:10; Nu. 12:5; 14:14; Dt. 31:15). It is even possible to say that a town "stands" on its *tēl* (Josh. 11:13; possibly, though, the reference is to towns left "standing" because the Israelites had not destroyed them) or that the people "stand" (i.e., live) in Goshen (Ex. 8:18[22]). This meaning is particularly common in visions and dreams. Pharaoh sees the cows "standing" on the bank of the Nile (Gen. 41:3); Joshua sees the commander of Yahweh's army standing before him (Josh. 5:13). Micaiah ben Imlah sees all the host of heaven standing around *('al)* Yahweh (1 K. 22:19). In Isa. 6:2 the seraphs in Isaiah's vision stand *mimma'al l^eyhwh,* which does not necessarily mean that they stand (protectively) over him; as in Ex. 18:13 *('al)* and Jer. 36:21 *(mē'al),* the idiom describes people standing around someone who is seated. There may also be an echo of *'āmad 'al* in the sense of "attend" (cf. Gen. 18:8). The living creatures in Ezekiel's call vision stand similarly (Ezk. 1:21,24; cf. 10:17,19); even the glory of Yahweh stands (Ezk. 3:23; cf. 10:18). In the Ezekiel texts the meaning fluctuates between "stand," "stand still," and "remain standing." In Ezk. 40:3 a man with a measuring reed stands before the prophet (cf. 43:6).

Standing can have a variety of connotations. The psalmist stands on level ground (*mîšôr,* Ps. 26:12), i.e., stands secure. Pilgrims stand within the gates of Jerusalem (Ps. 122:2: they have entered or are already standing there). The king "stands by the pillar" to receive the homage of the people (2 K. 11:14); he comes to the pillar to make a covenant with Yahweh (2 K. 23:3). A sentinel stands on a tower and reports what he sees (2 K. 9:17). The prophet stands (or takes up his post, par. *yṣb* hithpael) on his watchtower to see what Yahweh will say to him (Hab. 2:1). Whether this language describes a cult prophet who is literally looking for a sign from Yahweh or refers to a subjective experience is debated.[13] Isa. 21:8 probably refers to a dreamlike vision:[14] the seer

---

13. See Rudolph, *Micha-Nahum-Habakuk-Zephanja. KAT* XIII/3 (1975), in loc.
14. Kaiser, *Isaiah 13–39. OTL* (Eng. trans. 1974), 126-27, with bibliog.

(reading *hārō'eh* for *'aryēh*) stands on his watchtower *(miṣpeh,* par. *nṣb* niphal with *mišmereṯ)* and experiences the destruction of Babylon.

i. *With Statement of Purpose.* The texts that state the purpose of (going and) standing constitute a special group. Jeroboam stands by the altar to offer incense *(lᵉhaqṭîr,* 1 K. 13:1). Goliath advances to speak to the ranks of Israel (1 S. 17:8). Jehoshaphat comes forward to address the people (2 Ch. 20:20). The shoot from the root of Jesse will stand as a signal to the people (Isa. 11:10). The future ruler will stand (or come forth) and feed his flock (Mic. 5:3[4]; cf. Isa. 61:5). Yahweh appears and shakes *(mdd)* the earth (Hab. 3:6, theophany).[15] These texts give the impression that *'āmaḏ,* like *qûm,* serves merely to introduce the particular action.

j. *Serve.* In many cases to "stand before" a person has a purely locative sense (e.g., Dt. 4:10; 1 K. 1:28; 19:11; Jer. 36:21). Often, however, it means "stand respectfully before," "stand in service of." In this sense Joseph stands before Pharaoh (Gen. 41:46), Joshua stands before Moses (Dt. 1:38), David enters Saul's service (1 S. 16:21-22), Abishag the Shunammite waits on the aging David (1 K. 1:2). The queen of Sheba praises the *ᶜᵃḇāḏîm* of Solomon, who attend him and hear his wisdom (1 K. 10:8); here, however, the sense may be locative: they stay close to him and have the opportunity to listen to him (cf. Yahweh's heavenly court; see h above).

Ancient Near Eastern art frequently depicts servants standing before their master or ruler.[16] Their position clearly reflects the notion that they are ready to fulfill their master's every wish.

k. *Priestly Service.* Quite similar is the use of *'āmaḏ* for priestly service. Dt. 10:8 defines the duties of the priests from the tribe of Levi as "carrying the ark, standing before Yahweh, ministering *(šrt)* to him, and blessing in his name." Ezk. 44:15 similarly links *'āmaḏ lipnê* with *šrt;* it also includes sacrificial duties. In 1 K. 8:11 "stand to minister *(šrt)*" describes priestly service. Jgs. 20:28 records that Phinehas "stood before *('al)* the ark," i.e., ministered; the Israelites turned to him when they wanted to inquire of Yahweh. In Neh. 12:44 *'āmaḏ* by itself means "minister" (Neh. 12:44); the same is true in 1 Ch. 6:18, where vv. 16-17 show clearly that the reference is to priestly service.

The prophetic office can also be described as "standing before Yahweh" (1 K. 17:1; 18:15; 2 K. 3:14; 5:16). The wording shows that this expression does not refer to standing as a bodily posture (conceivable in the case of priests) but to service in the general sense ("God, before whom I stand"). Jer. 15:19 uses "stand before me" in parallel with "serve as my mouth"; the purpose of this service is proclamation of God's word. The statement about the Rechabites in Jer. 35:19 must also be interpreted in this general sense: a descendant of Jonadab will always stand before Yahweh.

l. *Worship.* The cultic congregation stands before Yahweh when it worships. When Aaron offered his first sacrifice, Lev. 9:5 says that the congregation *('ēḏâ)* drew near *(qārab)* and stood before Yahweh. In the same sense Jer. 7:10 says: "You come *(bô')* and stand before me in this house." Further, 2 Ch. 20:13 recounts how all Judah stood

15. See Rudolph, *KAT,* in loc.
16. See *ANEP,* nos. 460, 463, 515.

before Yahweh when Jehoshaphat recited his prayer (but cf. v. 5, which says that he stood in the *qāhāl*). The servants *(ʿa̱bāḏîm)* of Yahweh "who stand in the house of Yahweh" (Ps. 134:1; 135:2) probably represent the cultic congregation. But this language hardly supports the conclusion that *ʿāmaḏ* denotes the common posture of prayer, for *ʿāmaḏ* means both "stand" and "approach." Neh. 9:2-3 must be translated: "They came forward *(ʿāmaḏ)* and confessed their sins. . . . They stood up *(qûm)* in their places *(ʿōmeḏ)* and read from the book of the law. . . . Then they made confession and prostrated themselves *(hištaḥᵃwâ)* before Yahweh." As Ap-Thomas notes, if *ʿāmaḏ* is translated "stand," the text is self-contradictory.[17] There were clearly portions of the liturgy during which the people stood and other portions during which they kneeled or prostrated themselves. We read in 1 K. 8:22, for example, that Solomon approached the altar and prayed there. After praying, he arose *(qûm)* from his knees *(kāraʿ ʿal-birkāyw),* approached (or stationed himself: *ʿāmaḏ*), and pronounced the blessing (vv. 54-55; cf. 2 Ch. 6:12-13).

m. *Stand Firm.* The expression *ʿāmaḏ lipnê* means "stand firm, withstand." The magicians of the Egyptians could not withstand Moses (Ex. 9:11). Joshua is not to fear the five kings, for not one of them will be able to withstand him (*bᵉpāneyḵā,* Josh. 10:8; also in the context of the holy war: 21:44; 23:9). When Yahweh was angry, the Israelites were not able to withstand their enemies (Jgs. 2:14; cf. also 2 K. 10:4). Other examples of standing firm in battle include Ezk. 13:5; Am. 2:15; and (more generally) Eccl. 4:12: "Although one might prevail over another, two will withstand one." Prov. 27:4 asks, "Who is able to withstand jealousy?"

This usage is also extended to religious contexts. Yahweh says to Jeremiah: "Who is like me . . . and who is the shepherd who can withstand me?" (Jer. 49:19; 50:44). The men of Beth-shemesh say: "Who can withstand Yahweh, this holy God?" (1 S. 6:20). Nahum says: "Who can withstand his indignation?" (Nah. 1:6, par. *qûm;* cf. Ps. 76:8[7]). According to Ps. 147:17, no one can withstand his cold (or: before him the waters congeal). Even when used by itself, *ʿāmaḏ* can have this meaning: "If you, Yah, should mark iniquities, who could survive?" (Ps. 130:3); "Who can endure (*kwl* pilpel) the day of his coming, and who can survive when he appears?" (Mal. 3:2); "Can your heart [courage] endure . . . when I shall deal with you?" (Ezk. 22:14).

n. *Stop.* With various nuances, *ʿāmaḏ* can mean "stand still, stop, stay." All the people passing by stopped when they saw Amasa wallowing in his blood (2 S. 20:12). The cart carrying the ark stopped in a field (1 S. 6:14). The water of Jordan stopped flowing while the Israelites crossed the river (Josh. 3:13,16). The sun stood still and the moon stopped *(dmm)* until the Israelites carried the day at Gibeon (Josh. 10:13; v. 12 uses *dmm* for both). Similarly, Hab. 3:11 says that the moon stood still at the appearance of Yahweh in a theophany (the text is corrupt: *šemeš* has no verb). The fugitives stop exhausted in the shadow of Heshbon (Jer. 48:45). Jeremiah warns about the attack of the foe from the north: "Flee for safety *(ʿûz),* do not stand still" (Jer. 4:6). After victory at Gibeon, Joshua exhorts the Israelites: "Do not stay there, pursue your enemies" (Josh.

---

17. P. 225.

10:19; cf. 2 S. 2:28: the people stop and do not pursue). In Nineveh they cry out, "Halt! Halt!" but no one turns back from flight (Nah. 2:9[8]; cf. also Jer. 51:50). But when Joseph requests his father, "Come down to me, *'al-taʿᵃmōḏ,*" the most likely meaning is "do not delay, come at once" (Gen. 45:9).

Stopping can also imply waiting. Moses tells the lepers to wait while he inquires of Yahweh (Nu. 9:8). Moses is to wait while Yahweh tells him the commandments (Dt. 5:31). Saul is to wait with Samuel so that Samuel can inform him about everything (1 S. 9:27). Simple "staying" is the sense of Ex. 9:28: the Israelites will not have to stay in Egypt any longer. Cf. Hag. 2:5: "My spirit abides among you" (*ʿōmeḏeṯ* may also go with the preceding *dāḇār:* "my word [covenant?] endures").

Another nuance is "last, endure." The fear (*yir'aṯ* [or read *'imraṯ,* "word"] of Yahweh endures forever (Ps. 19:10[9]), as do his counsel (33:11), his righteousness (111:3; 112:3,9), and his praise (111:10). Heaven and earth perish *('āḇaḏ),* but God endures forever (102:27). By contrast, Eccl. 1:4 says that generations come and go, but the earth remains forever. According to Isa. 66:22, Israel will endure just as the new heavens and the new earth will endure. The meaning "be left" is also possible: "There is no strength left in me," says Daniel (Dnl. 10:17). Qohelet asserts that with all his greatness, he retained his wisdom (Eccl. 2:9).

A deed of purchase "remains permanently in effect" as a legal document (Jer. 32:14); the flavor of wine remains unchanged (Jer. 48:11; antonym → מור *mwr*); a victim of a beating survives for a time (Ex. 21:21); leprosy is checked (Lev. 13:5,23,28,37); a man persists in his refusal to enter into a levirate marriage (Dt. 25:8); Israel continues unchanged in its sin (Hos. 10:9).

2. *Hiphil.* In the case of the hiphil, the concentration of its occurrences in late texts is striking (the Chronicler's History, Esther, Daniel, Ecclesiastes). All the occurrences are causatives within the semantic field of the qal.

Thus *heʿᵉmîḏ* means "set, place." The Philistines place Samson between two pillars (Jgs. 16:25); Ezekiel is to set a pot on the fire (Ezk. 24:11). God sets the psalmist on the heights *(bāmôṯ),* implying either security or victory (Ps. 18:34[33] = 2 S. 22:34; Ps. 30:8[7] is similar if we may read *heʿᵉmaḏtanî bᵉharᵉrê ʿōz,* "You established me on strong [= protecting] mountains"). Or God sets the psalmist's feet in a broad place, i.e., gives him living space (Ps. 31:9[8]). Having created sun, moon, and stars, God "establishes" them and gives them a law *(ḥōq)* that they may not transgress (Ps. 148:6). Guards are posted to watch the gates (2 Ch. 23:19; Neh. 13:19; *mišmar,* Neh. 4:3[9]). Isaiah is to post a lookout (Isa. 21:6; see II.1.h above).

The people are arranged by ancestral houses (2 Ch. 25:5; Neh. 4:7[13]; cf. 2 Ch. 23:10). Nehemiah appoints festal choruses (*tôḏôṯ,* Neh. 12:31). An army is assembled, i.e., mobilized (Dnl. 11:13). Manasseh sets up asherim and idols (2 Ch. 33:19), as Amaziah sets up images of the gods (2 Ch. 25:14).

People are appointed to certain assignments and functions. Jeroboam appoints *bāmôṯ* priests to serve at Bethel (1 K. 12:32). Rehoboam appoints Abijah as chief prince among his brothers (2 Ch. 11:22). Esther has courtiers assigned to her service by the king (Est. 4:5). Ezra appoints the Levites to oversee the rebuilding of the temple

(Ezr. 3:8). Nehemiah is accused of having appointed prophets (Neh. 6:7). Cf. also Nu. 3:6: "Let the tribe of Levi come before Aaron to assist him."

Corresponding to the expression *ʿāmaḏ babbᵉrîṯ,* 2 Ch. 34:32 uses the hiphil to mean "cause to enter into the covenant." To the qal "stand up" there corresponds the hiphil "set someone on their feet" (Ezk. 2:2; 3:24; cf. Daniel, whom God rouses from his trance and sets on his *ʿōmeḏ,* Dnl. 8:18). In Ps. 107:25, the hiphil appears to mean "call into being": God raises a stormy wind through his word.

When *ʿāmaḏ* means "survive, endure," *heʿᵉmîḏ* means "spare, establish," or the like. Thus God says to Moses, "I have let you live to show my power" (Ex. 9:16). A Deuteronomistic commentator says in 1 K. 15:4 that for David's sake God set up *(hēqîm)* his son Jeroboam and established Jerusalem. The Chronicler has the queen of Sheba say to Solomon that God will establish Israel through him (2 Ch. 9:8). Yahweh likewise promises to confirm Solomon in his house and his kingdom and establish his throne (1 Ch. 17:14). A wisdom maxim states that by justice a king gives stability to his land (Prov. 29:4).

With *bᵉrîṯ* as object, *heʿᵉmîḏ* means "establish, confirm" (Ps. 105:10). A vision is "fulfilled" (Dnl. 11:14). The hiphil of *ʿmd* is also used for the rebuilding of the temple (2 Ch. 24:13; Ezr. 2:68; 9:9). With *pānîm* as object, the hiphil means "fix one's gaze": the man of God stares straight ahead (2 K. 8:11). Other expressions include: lay an obligation on oneself (Neh. 10:33[32]); allocate land (2 Ch. 33:8); with *lᵉ,* "decide to do something" (2 Ch. 30:5). Uncertain is 2 Ch. 18:34, where the hophal should probably be read (with 1 K. 22:35): the king stood upright in his chariot. The second occurrence of the hophal is in Lev. 16:10: the scapegoat is presented alive before God (cf. Lev. 14:11, hiphil).

III. Nouns. Of the nouns, only *ʿemdâ* and *maʿᵃmāḏ/moʿᵒmāḏ* appear in early texts. The only occurrence of *ʿemdâ* is in Mic. 1:11, where the text is almost certainly corrupt. A lament over the devastation of the hill country of Judah, full of wordplays, includes a passage that says literally: "He shall remove his place for stopping from you." None of the proposed emendations is convincing. Ps. 69:3(2) uses *moʿᵒmāḏ* in a description of the psalmist's affliction: "I sink in deep mire, where there is no foothold [i.e., place to stand]." The noun *maʿᵃmāḏ* appears in the story of the queen of Sheba, who saw the "attendance" (see II.1.j above) of Solomon's servants (1 K. 10:5; 2 Ch. 9:4), and in Isa. 22:19, where God threatens to thrust Shebna from his office *(maṣṣāḇ)* and drive him from his "post."[18] The same word appears also in 1 Ch. 23:28 and 2 Ch. 35:15 referring to the position or function of the Levites and temple singers.

The noun *ʿōmeḏ* occurs only in the Chronicler's History and Daniel. It denotes the place where someone stands (Dnl. 8:17; 10:11; cf. 8:18: "he set me up [*ʿmd* hiphil] on my [standing] place"), specifically in liturgical contexts the place where one performs one's function (Neh. 8:7; 9:3; 13:11; 2 Ch. 30:16; 35:10; cf. also 34:31: "the king took his place").

---

18. On the text see *BHS*.

IV. 1. *LXX.* The LXX usually uses *histánai* and its compounds (e.g., *paristánai, anistánai, ephistánai, anthistánai*) to translate *'āmaḏ;* sometimes it uses *ménein* or *diaménein*.

2. *Dead Sea Scrolls.* When we turn to the Dead Sea Scrolls, we note that the Temple Scroll stays totally within the framework of OT usage. One comes before priests and judges (61:8); priests "stand" and minister (56:9; 60:11,14). The text also speaks of standing pillars (35:10). In the War Scroll *'āmaḏ* often means "get into formation, take one's position in the battle line" (1QM 6:1,4,8,10; 7:18; 8:4,6; 9:4; 16:4,6,12); *ma'ᵃmāḏ* denotes the position of the individual (2:3; 6:1,4; 8:6; esp. with *hiṯyaṣṣēḇ,* 8:3,17; 16:5; 17:11; cf. 1QSª 1:22 with reference to the Levites). We read also that the high priest and/or the priests "come forward" to deliver a speech or recite a prayer (10:2; 15:4; 16:13; 18:5).

Elsewhere, possibly through the influence of military usage, *ma'ᵃmāḏ* denotes the hierarchical position of each member of the community: "Everyone in Israel is to have a *ma'ᵃmāḏ* [position, function]" (1QS 2:22); no one is to be "lowly or high" on account of this position, for all constitute a community of truth, humility, and love (2:23). CD 20:5 says that an offender is to be punished until he can take his place once more among the men of perfect holiness. Cf. also 1QH 3:21: "take one's position among the host of the saints," i.e., take one's place in the eschatological community.

In several texts *'āmaḏ* has the meaning "arise, appear." The wicked priest was named with the name of truth "at the beginning of his appearance [or: 'office']" (1QpHab 8:9). This meaning is especially common in the Damascus Document. A man of scorn arose (CD 1:14); famous men *(qᵉrî'ê haššēm)* will arise at the end of days (5:5). There arose Moses and Aaron through the prince of light, but Belial caused adversaries to arise (*hēqîm,* 5:17-18). "Shifters of boundaries" arose and led Israel astray (5:20). Noteworthy is the expression "until the teacher of righteousness/messiah appears" (6:10 par. 12:23; 20:1). Cf. also 4QFlor (4Q174) 1:11: the branch of David will arise with the interpreter of the law; and 4QTest (4Q175) 24: an accursed man of Belial will arise to be a net and snare for the people.

Just as the OT speaks of coming before the court, the novice entering the order comes before "the many" to be questioned (1QS 6:15; cf. CD 15:11: "come before the *mᵉḇaqqēr*").

The verb *'āmaḏ* undergoes a special semantic development in the *Hodayot,* which speak of "standing before God" in a sense that implies both service and endurance. "Those in harmony with you will stand *('md)* before you forever; those who walk on the path of your heart will be established *(kwn)* eternally" (1QH 4:21-22). The singer has stumbled and fallen, but God has raised him up and now he stands before God. "By the secret of your wonders you have strengthened my position *('mdy)*" (4:28). "In your justice you have established (*'md* hiphil) me in your covenant" (7:19). God purifies and forgives the children of truth, to make them stand in his presence (7:31). Now the singer can say: "My foot remains on the right path" (2:29), but only through the grace of God: "It is through your grace that I subsist" (2:25; cf. 2:22: "My *ma'ᵃmāḏ* comes from you"); and, "How can I be strong *(ḥzq* hithpael) if you do not make me stand *('md* hiphil)?" (10:6; cf. 1QH fr. 3:6). Through God's strength and compassion, the singer's spirit can "keep firmly in place in the face of distress" (4:36).[19]

Ringgren

---

19. On the whole topic see Grundmann.

עַמּוּד *ʿammûḏ*

I. General. II. Ancient Near East. III. Architectural Use. IV. The Two Bronze Pillars of the Temple. V. The Pillar of Fire and of Cloud. VI. Metaphorical Usage. VII. LXX and Dead Sea Scrolls.

I. General. The noun *ʿammûḏ,* derived from the verb → עמד *ʿāmaḏ,* "stand," occurs approximately 110 times in the OT, referring primarily to pillars or beams supporting roof structures. In this context the word appears frequently in connection with the building of the tent of meeting and the temple. Never, however, does it denote the "piles of stones" *(maṣṣēḇôṯ)* that served as boundary markers and landmarks of religious significance, often being objects of worship. The most important theological use of *ʿammûḏ* occurs in the exodus narratives where it frequently signifies God's presence in a pillar of fire and cloud. Metaphorically, the word refers to the foundations of heaven and earth.

ʿammûḏ. W. F. Albright, "Two Cressets from Marisa and the Pillars of Jachin and Boaz," *BASOR* 85 (1942) 18-27; T. A. Busink, *Der Tempel von Jerusalem. SFS* 3 (1970), 299-321; E. Cassin, *La splendeur divine* (1968); M. Dahood, "Hebrew-Ugaritic Lexicography VII," *Bibl* 50 (1969) 337-56, esp. 350; M. Görg, "Zur Dekoration der Tempelsäulen," *BN* 13 (1980) 17-21, esp. 20-21; S. Grill, *Die Gewittertheophanie im AT* ([2]1943); J. Jeremias, *Theophanie. WMANT* 10 ([2]1977); W. Kornfeld, "Der Symbolismus der Tempelsäulen," *ZAW* 74 (1962) 50-57; T. W. Mann, "The Pillar of Cloud in the Reed Sea Narratives," *JBL* 90 (1971) 15-30; H. G. May, "The Two Pillars before the Temple of Solomon," *BASOR* 88 (1942) 19-27; G. E. Mendenhall, *The Tenth Generation* (1973), 32-66; M. Noth, *Könige 1. BK* IX/1 (1968), 141-67; J. Ouellette, "Le vestibule du Temple de Salomon," *RB* 76 (1969) 365-78; W. J. Phythian-Adams, *The People and the Presence* (1942); R. B. Y. Scott, "The Pillars of Jachin and Boaz," *JBL* 58 (1939) 143-49; S. Talmon, "An Apparently Redundant MT Reading, Jeremiah 1:18," *Textus* 8 (1973) 160-63; H. Weippert, "Säule," *BRL*[2], 259-60; S. Yeivin, "Jachin and Boaz," *PEQ* 91 (1959) 6-22. → עָנָן *ʿānān.*

II. Ancient Near East. All the ancient Near Eastern occurrences of *ʿmwd* outside the OT refer to pillars, usually associated with permanent structures such as porticos or temples. Of particular interest are its occurrences in the Imperial Aramaic Elephantine papyri. In one text,[1] dating from 408 B.C.E., the Jewish priest Jedoniah and his companions complain to Bagohi, the Persian governor of Judah, that the Egyptians, instigated by the governor in Egypt, have destroyed the Elephantine temple, including its "pillars of stone" *(wʿmwdyʾ zy ʾbn)*.

The Phoenician Yehawmilk stela (ca. 500-400 B.C.E.) was erected at the dedication of a portico *(ʿmd)*.[2] A Latin–Neo-Punic bilingual from North Africa (53 B.C.E.) mentions a master architect who "had the pillars covered," i.e., probably supervised construction of a roof over a commercial arcade or the like.[3] The word also occurs in Palmyrene.[4]

III. Architectural Use. On the one hand, the noun *ʿammûḏ* appears frequently in connection with descriptions of the tent of meeting: in the construction directives (Ex. 25:1–27:19) and in the accounts of its construction (35:1–38:31), its inspection by Moses (39:32-43), and its assembly (ch. 40). Four "poles" (NRSV "pillars") of acacia wood overlaid with gold and resting on silver bases supported the curtain separating the holy place from the most holy place (Ex. 26:32; 36:36). In similar fashion, a screen of poles of acacia wood overlaid with gold separated the outer court of the tent from the holy place (Ex. 26:37; 36:38; cf. 11QT 10:11?). The walls enclosing the court, with the gate to the court and its hangings, were supported by poles of acacia wood overlaid with silver (Ex. 27:9-19; 38:9-20 passim). The costliness of the metal overlaying the *ʿammûḏîm* rose with increasing proximity to the most holy place. During the desert period the Levitical house of Merari was responsible for the poles and their bases (Nu. 3:33-37; 4:29-33). The translation "pole" is also appropriate in Cant. 3:10, where Solomon makes himself a palanquin of Lebanese cedar with silver poles *(ʿammûḏîm kesep̱)*.

On the other hand, *ʿammûḏ* is best translated "pillar" when it bears the weight of a permanent structure. Solomon's great building projects are particularly famous for such pillars: the House of the Forest of Lebanon, consisting of two-story chambers supported by rows of pillars (1 K. 7:2-3), and the portico (7:6). The story of Samson clearly reveals the bearing function of the pillars in a Philistine temple: according to Jgs. 16:25,26,29, Samson brought down the bearing central pillars *(ʾ^{a}šer habbayiṯ nāḵôn ʿ^{a}lêhem)* of the temple. Weippert discusses the archaeological evidence.

IV. The Two Bronze Pillars of the Temple. The most famous pillars in the OT are also the most difficult to interpret: the two bronze pillars at the entrance to the temple. The southern pillar was named Jachin (from *yāḵîn,* "he will establish"), the northern

1. *AP* 30:9; cf. the copy, 31:8.
2. *KAI* 10.6.
3. *KAI* 124.1.
4. *DNSI,* II, 869-70.

Boaz (from *bōʿaz,* "in him is strength" [?]) (1 K. 7:15-22 = 2 Ch. 3:15-17; 1 K. 7:40-42 = 2 Ch. 4:12-13).[5] Whether they were freestanding, with no architectural function, or (despite the description in 1 K. 7) did in fact support the roof of the vestibule is disputed.[6] Also in question is their religious or possibly dynastic significance. They were so important to the cultic community that their destruction was prophesied (Jer. 27:16) and described (2 K. 25:13-17; Jer. 52:17-23).

The most likely hypothesis (ultimately not demonstrable) is that the function of the temple pillars resided essentially in their names.[7] This hypothesis suggests two major interpretations, one theological, the other dynastic. On the one hand, the names of the two bronze pillars may enshrine a reference to the temple as the house of the mighty God of Israel[8] and at the same time a reminder to the people that their community was established by Yahweh and that its existence rested on his might. On the other hand, standing at the entrance to the royal chapel, the pillars could define the relationship between Yahweh and the house of David. The roots of their names appear in the psalms referring to the royal house (e.g., Ps. 89:5[4]: "I will establish [*'āḵîn*] your house forever"). It is also conceivable that the names are artificial constructs composed of initial letters. For example, Ps. 89 contains all the elements of a possible dynastic oracle such as *yāḵîn kissē' ne'ᵉmān bānâ ʿaḏ-ʿôlām zeraʿ-dāwīḏ,* the initial letters of which spell out the names *ykn* and *bʿz.*[9] The oracle is not extant in this form, but cf. 2 S. 5:12 and 7:12 (= 1 Ch. 17:11).

Freedman — Willoughby

Other interpretations based on archaeological evidence have been proposed. The pillars may have been:

a. *maṣṣebahs* like those of the temple at Shechem;[10]
b. *asherahs,* on account of their botanical capitals;[11]
c. comparable to the phallic symbols at the entrances of many temples;[12]
d. comparable to Egyptian obelisks;
e. oversized lampstands or stands for incense burners, recalling the pillar of cloud and fire at the exodus;[13]
f. symbols of permanence, like the Egyptian *djed* pillars;[14]
g. symbols of majesty, sovereignty, divine omnipotence, or God's presence;[15]

---

5. → כון *kwn;* → עזז *ʿzz.*
6. For a summary of the debate see V. Fritz, *Tempel und Zelt. WMANT* 47 (1977), 14-15.
7. Scott, Noth, et al.
8. Vincent, Busink, 312: "Yahweh will protect this house."
9. Scott, Albright.
10. Benzinger; E. Sellin, *ZDPV* 51 (1928) 119-23.
11. Möhlenbrink.
12. B. D. Eerdmans.
13. Albright, May.
14. Kornfeld.
15. See, respectively, Yeivin, Andrae, Vincent.

h. standards identifying the temple as the house of Yahweh, originally of pagan provenance and therefore found only in the Solomonic temple and not later[16] (but cf. Ezk. 40:49; 42:6).

Fabry

The new temple envisioned by Ezekiel as the centerpiece of Israel's renewal and restoration is also to be provided with pillars (albeit without names) in its vestibule (Ezk. 40:49; 42:6). The text gives no details on the function of these pillars in the description of the building.

It is unclear whether these pillars Jachin and Boaz are meant when we are told that the king stood "beside/on the pillar" *(ʿal-hāʿammûḏ)* on important occasions. Joash was proclaimed king by the priest Jehoiada while standing "by the pillar [or: 'on the podium'],[17] according to custom" (2 K. 11:14 = 2 Ch. 23:13). This clear reference to a "specific" place for the king to stand *ʿal-hāʿāmmûḏ* on special occasions — if it is in fact intended to convey specific information, as the appended *kammišpāṭ* would suggest — has been subject to a wide variety of interpretations. As a parallel, de Vaux cites a Ras Shamra stela depicting the king on a socle before the image of a god.[18] Noting Pharaoh's special place in the temple, von Rad suggests a podium.[19] The elevation of the king was less important than the delimiting of the location, which was considered cultically pure.[20]

V. The Pillar of Fire and of Cloud. The pillar of fire *(ʿammûḏ ʾēš)* and the pillar of cloud *(ʿammûḏ ʿānān)*[21] are theophanic concepts used by specific sources in the exodus and desert narratives to represent the presence of Yahweh. In J it is Yahweh himself who frees and assists the Israelites during their desert wanderings; in E it is the *malʾaḵ ʾᵉlōhîm;* in Deuteronomy and P it is the cloud that signals God's presence. Only the J redactor of Hezekiah's period[22] speaks of a pillar of cloud *(ʿammûḏ ʿānān)* and a pillar of fire *(ʿammûḏ ʾēš)* (Ex. 13:21-22; 14:19-24; cf. Nu. 9:15-22; also Dt. 1:33; 31:15; Ps. 78:14; 105:39), which guide the Israelites by day and night on their journey to the Sea of Reeds[23] (cf. Nu. 14:14). According to Mendenhall, the pillars are visible media through which the deity is perceptible to human beings. The form of the pillar is described by the word *ʿānān,* a cloudlike covering enveloping and concealing the deity; at night the fiery radiance of Yahweh shines forth. Although Ex. 14:19 apparently shows that the pillar of cloud and fire is the same manifestation of Yahweh as the *malʾaḵ hāʾᵉlōhîm,* since both perform the same function, the Hebrew text is a conflation of dif-

16. Busink, 317.
17. G. Widengren, *JSS* 2 (1957) 9-10.
18. R. de Vaux, *AncIsr,* I, 102-3; cf. *Syr* 14 (1933) pl. 16; *ANEP,* no. 490.
19. G. von Rad, "Royal Ritual in Judah," *Problem of the Hexateuch and Other Essays* (Eng. trans. 1966)), 224; cf. also E. Würthwein, *Die Büchern der Könige. ATD* 11/2 (1984), 351, 452.
20. M. Metzger, *Congress Volume, Uppsala 1971. SVT* 22 (1972), 165-66.
21. → ענן *ʿānān.*
22. P. Weimar, *Die Meerwundererzahlung. ÄAT* 9 (1985), 272.
23. → ים *yām;* → סוף *sûp̱.*

ferent sources. Ex. 14:24 contains a construct that diverges from the other texts. The pillar of cloud and the pillar of fire usually appear as two distinct phenomena; here, however, the theophany is manifest in a single form *(bᵉʿammûḏ ʾēš wᵉʿānān).* Mendenhall has theorized that *ʿānān* is equivalent to Akk. *melammū,* a "mask" of the deity.[24]

Outside the exodus narrative, the ancient sources of the Pentateuch also speak of a pillar of cloud as a sign of God's presence. When the tent of meeting was set up for worship outside the camp, Yahweh descended in a pillar of cloud and stood at the entrance to the tent. He remained veiled in his cloud when he approached the Israelites, but with Moses he spoke "face to face" (Ex. 33:9-11).

VI. Metaphorical Usage. Except for Jgs. 20:40, where *ʿammûḏ* describes a smoke signal as a "pillar of smoke," the other texts use *ʿammûḏ* metaphorically. God strengthens Jeremiah by making him a "fortified city and an iron pillar" *(lᵉʿîr miḇṣār ûlᵉʿammûḏ barzel),* mighty and indestructible in the face of opposition (Jer. 1:18). In Cant. 5:10-16 the bride uses a series of metaphors to describe her beloved. His legs are like "alabaster pillars, set on bases of gold" (*ʿammûḏê šēš mᵉyussāḏîm ʿal-ʾaḏnê-pāz,* v. 15).

Two texts refer to the pillars of the earth (Ps. 75:4[3]; Job 9:6), one to the pillars of heaven (Job 26:11). The earth was generally thought to rest on pillars or columns (1 S. 2:8, *māṣûq;* Ps. 18:8[7], *môsāḏ;* 104:5, *māḵôn;* Job 38:4-6, *yᵉsôḏ*), held up by God and shaken by God when angry. In the OT view, the cosmos was structured on the basis of fixed principles (Ezk. 40:3–43:17; Zec. 1:16) and laid out by God with a measuring line (Isa. 34:11; Jer. 31:39); the new temple was his earthly dwelling place, built to the same standard. The heavens were likewise thought to be held up by pillars in the form of mountains. Prov. 9:1 speaks of the house of wisdom, supported by seven pillars, analogous to the four pillars supporting the heavens in Egyptian cosmology. With its sacral and literary connotations, the number seven implies fullness and perfection; it probably does not reflect architectural prototypes.[25]

Freedman — Willoughby

VII. LXX and Dead Sea Scrolls. The LXX consistently uses *stýlos* to translate *ʿammûḏ;* it uses the same word to represent the less common *qereš,* "wooden frames, beams," in the account of the construction of the desert sanctuary (Ex. 26 and 36) (reflecting the technical ignorance of the translator?).[26] For the pillar of cloud we always find *stýlos (tḗs) nephélēs;* for the pillar of fire, *stýlos (toú) pyrós.* It is worth noting that *stýlos* also translates *ʿammûḏ* in the royal ritual (2 K. 11:14; 23:3), a translation that makes interpretations along the lines of "podium" less likely. Only four texts use *kíōn,* perhaps out of reverence for the cosmic mythological motifs it suggests (Jgs. 16:25ff.).

---

24. → ענן *ʿānān.*
25. Contra G. W. Ahlström, "The House of Wisdom," *SEÅ* 44 (1979) 74-76.
26. U. Wilckens, *TDNT,* VII, 733 n. 8.

Rabbinic literature continued to use *ʿammûḏ* metaphorically: the devout are pillars, one who teaches *tôrāh* is a pillar, Abraham was a pillar of the world, etc.[27] At Qumran, however, the range of usage of the word is surprisingly narrow. In almost all of its 16 occurrences, *ʿammûḏ* means a pillar as an architectural component of a building in the temple complex (11QT 10:11), a stair tower with a central column (30:9; 31:9), a slaughterhouse for sacrificial animals (12 columns with supporting beams north of the altar of burnt offering, 34:2,3,15), a peristyle west of the sanctuary with freestanding pillars (35:10), a colonnaded pergola on the roof as a site for huts (42:11).[28] Whether *ʿammûḏ haššēnî* in the cryptographic fragment 4Q186 fr. 1 2:6; fr. 2 1:7 is related to the *ʿammûḏê šāmayim* of Job 26:11 (cf. 1 Enoch 18:3) is quite uncertain; if so, it belongs to the realm of cosmological metaphor.

The Copper Scroll uses *ʿammûḏ* in the same way (3Q15 4:1; 11:3). In 6:1 we find the toponym *mʿrt hʿmwd,* "Cave of the Pillars," a cave linking two larger caves in the rocky declivity between Jericho and Qumran.

In 1QM 5:10, finally, the fluting of a column is taken as a model for the decoration of the hafts of the lances carried by the Essene warriors.

Fabry

---

27. For citations see Wilckens, 734.
28. → סכך *sāḵaḵ*.

עָמִית ʿāmîṯ

I. 1. Etymology; 2. Occurrences; 3. Meaning; 4. LXX. II. Social Solidarity as a Religious Value: 1. Related Words; 2. Leviticus; 3. Zec. 13:7; 4. Dead Sea Scrolls.

I. 1. *Etymology.* The noun *ʿāmîṯ* derives either from *ʿm* or from an otherwise unattested root *ʿmh,* related to the root *ʿmm,* "join with."[1] Outside the OT, it appears also in Middle Hebrew, Jewish Aramaic, Arabic, and Old South Arabic.[2] "The ending *-îṯ* became an independent afformative, used to form abstract nouns."[3] Grammatically, therefore, *ʿāmîṯ* is an abstract noun.

---

1. For the first derivation see J. Wellhausen, *Die kleinen Propheten* (⁴1963), 195. For the second, see *GesB,* 600-601; *HAL,* II, 845.
2. W. W. Müller, *ZAW* 75 (1963) 304-16, esp. 312.
3. J. Körner, *Hebräische Studiengrammatik* (1983), 106; cf. *GK,* §86k-l.

2. *Occurrences.* The noun occurs 12 times in the OT: 11 times in Leviticus and in Zec. 13:7. It occurs twice in the Dead Sea Scrolls (1QS 6:26; CD 19:8); CD 19:7-9 quotes Zec. 13:7 word for word. It appears only in the singular, and always with a suffix: *ʿ^{a}mîṯî* (Zec. 13:7 = CD 19:8), *ʿ^{a}mîṯ^{e}ḵā* (Lev. 18:20; 19:15,17; 25:14[twice],15), *ʿ^{a}mîṯô* (Lev. 5:21[Eng. 6:2][twice]; 19:11; 24:19; 25:17; 1QS 6:26).

3. *Meaning.* The basic meaning of *ʿāmîṯ* is as disputed as its grammatical analysis is secure. Wellhausen says that our word "originally meant 'relationship,' 'kinship,' then a relative or kinsman."[4] The others, who postulate a basic meaning "community" or the like, differ as to whether they take the abstract noun as exhibiting the original meaning, believing that the concrete meaning "kinsman" is a secondary development through omission of the noun *geḇer* — abstract for concrete — or argue for the concrete meaning, totally rejecting the idea of an abstract noun.[5]

The phrase *geḇer ʿ^{a}mîṯî* (Zec. 13:7) plays a key role in the discussion. Some have argued that this phrase is syntactically unique: a noun in apposition to a construct.[6] As a consequence, it could be translated "the man who is my associate."[7] Others analyze the combination as a construct phrase, to be translated "the man of my community."[8] Those who espouse this view must then assume that the word underwent a secondary personification in all the Leviticus texts.[9] Finally, we must not overlook that the etymology of *ʿāmîṯ* is "obscure" and that its specific meaning "can no longer be determined with certainty."[10]

4. *LXX.* In all the Leviticus texts the LXX uses *ho plēsíon,* "the neighbor," to translate *ʿāmîṯ*. In Zec. 13:7 it translates: *ho anḗr polítēs mou.*

II. Social Solidarity as a Religious Value.

1. *Related Words.* Apart from Zec. 13:7, *ʿāmîṯ* occurs only in prose; therefore it does not appear in parallelism with any true synonyms. The noun → רֵעַ *rēaʿ*, however, does appear occasionally as a closely related term. In Lev. 19 one could almost speak of a regular alternation between the two words: *ʿāmîṯ* appears in vv. 11,15,17, *rēaʿ* in vv. 13,16,18, with no observable difference in meaning. Lev. 18:20 speaks of adultery with "the wife of your *ʿāmîṯ*"; in 20:10 the adultery is with "the wife of his *rēaʿ*." In 1QS 6:26, too, *ʿāmîṯ* and *rēaʿ* are very close in meaning.

---

4. Wellhausen, *Kleinen Propheten,* 195.

5. Advocates for the former range from C. von Orelli, *Minor Prophets* (Eng. trans. n.d.), 370; to, most recently, *HAL,* II, 845. For the latter see *GesB,* 600. On the abstract for concrete usage see E. König, *Stilistik, Rhetorik, Poetik* (1900), 66.

6. *GK,* §130e.

7. *GesB,* 600.

8. F. Hitzig, *Die zwölf kleinen Propheten. KEHAT* (^{2}1852), 379; most recently K. Elliger, *Das Buch der zwölf kleinen Propheten. ATD* 25 (^{7}1975), 174; W. Rudolph, *Haggai-Sacharja 1–8-Sacharja 9–14-Maleachi. KAT* XIII/4 (1976), 212; H. Bardtke, *Die Handschriften funde am Toten Meer* (1958), 273.

9. Elliger, *Leviticus. HAT* I/4 (1966), 241 n. 19.

10. M. Noth, *Leviticus. OTL* (Eng. trans. ^{2}1977), 48-49.

Other terms can express the same meaning as *ʿāmîṯ:* Lev. 19:17 and 25:14 use *ʾāḥ,* "brother," side by side with the synonymous *ʿāmîṯ;*[11] Lev. 19:18, finally, uses *b^enê ʿamm^eḵā,* "your kin." These related terms call our attention to what the whole group has in common: an *ʿāmîṯ* is a member of the people of Israel with whom one has a special relationship like that between two brothers, shaped by a common faith in Yahweh. Elliger's definition — an *ʿāmîṯ* is "a member of the national community whose lord is Yahweh" — catches the essence.[12] The best translation, therefore, is not "kinsman" but "member of the national community, fellow citizen."[13]

2. *Leviticus.* The word *ʿāmîṯ* is closely associated with the Holiness Code (Lev. 17–26). Only the two occurrences in Lev. 5:21(6:2) are outside this section. They belong to a passage (vv. 20-26[6:1-7]) that Elliger has shown to be the latest of several addenda to Lev. 4:1–5:13;[14] this dating raises the possibility of explaining the use of the word in Lev. 5 as being due to the influence of the Holiness Code on P. In any case, the Holiness Code is earlier than Deutero-Zechariah, so that these occurrences of *ʿāmîṯ* are the earliest in the OT.

All the passages deal with proper conduct toward a fellow citizen. When buying or selling, do not exert undue pressure (Lev. 25:14,15,17). Do not steal from, deceive, or lie to a fellow citizen (19:11), render an unjust judgment against him (19:15), hate him (19:17), do him bodily harm (24:19), or have sexual relations with his wife (18:20). Judge him with justice (19:15) and reprove him (19:17). That the two positive commandments in Lev. 19 are traditio-historically secondary is clear from the preponderance of negative formulations.[15] The prohibitions are therefore the original laws. These rules of conduct are all religiously motivated (cf. 19:11-14,16,18; 25:17): every admonition to act so as to benefit society and promote the well-being of a fellow citizen is based on respect for the "I" who is Yahweh. This holds true even of the prohibition against invading another's marriage, which is grounded in the defilement of the adulterer (18:20), excluding him "from participating in the cult, i.e., from intercourse with God and participation in . . . its benefits."[16] One's fellow citizen is an equal member of God's community and therefore has a claim to help and protection, even against secret hostile thoughts and feelings.[17]

Finally, the strict law of talion emerges from this comprehensive protection from any kind of injury at the hands of a fellow citizen. That Lev. 24:15b-22 is a distinct block of traditional material can be seen from its different form: not prohibition and admonition, but statements resembling casuistic law, like v. 19: "Anyone who maims a fellow citizen shall suffer the same injury in return."[18] That this law, too, is based on re-

---

11. Elliger, *HAT* I/4, 345.
12. P. 258.
13. Elliger, *HAT* I/4, 241; Hulst, *TLOT,* II, 902.
14. Pp. 65-66.
15. Elliger, *HAT* I/4, 248.
16. Ibid., 240.
17. Ibid., 258, 259.
18. Ibid., 331.

ligious principle is clear, whether one thinks of the holiness of the community or the sanctity of life.[19] Since this section incorporates inherited earlier material,[20] it is likely that our word, too, derives from an early legal tradition.

This religious foundation is also exhibited in Lev. 5:21(6:2): deceiving a fellow citizen is understood as a "trespass against Yahweh"; the guilty party must, among other things, offer an *ʾāšām* to Yahweh.

3. *Zec. 13:7.* Zec. 13:7 is an oracular threat placed in the mouth of Yahweh, who calls on his sword to awaken against "my shepherd" *(rōʿî)* and against "the man of my community" *(geḇer ʿᵃmîṯî).* The interpretation of this phrase (like that of the entire section) is debated, as the proposed translations show: "my associate," "the man who is my companion," "the man who is closest to me."[21] Elliger asks whether the translation should not really be "kindred" rather than "community," pointing out that the text does not use *ʾîš* but *geḇer,* a word "from the domain of elevated language, not rarely emphasizing strength and heroism."[22] This observation supports the conclusion that both terms refer to a messianic figure. If so, this passage would be predicting the "fiasco" of the messiah as a consequence of the gravity of the people's sin.[23] Otzen takes a different approach, finding in v. 7 "a concealed reference to the cultic suffering of the king," through which on the one hand the events of the year 587 are "described succinctly" and on the other "events to come" (vv. 8-9) are delineated in the form of "an interpretation of 587."[24] Wellhausen suggests the high priest.[25]

4. *Dead Sea Scrolls.* With respect to our word, OT usage continues to dominate in the Dead Sea Scrolls. It appears in conjunction with *rēaʿ* and in the context of a "penal code" (1QS 6:26).[26] Unfortunately the text is fragmentary, so that proposed interpretations must be tentative, although the context is clear: whoever transgresses against his neighbor is excluded from the community for a limited time (6:24-27). This regulation uses the expression *yswd ʿmytw,* which Maier translates "the 'foundation' (?) of his associate." Lohse and Molin translate the words more adequately as the "the basis of his association" (Bardtke and Wernberg-Møller read *yswr ʿmytw,* "the 'correction' of his comrades"), interpreting the passage to mean that the offense against the transgressor's

19. Noth, *Leviticus,* 180-81; Elliger, *HAT* I/4, 335.
20. Noth, *Leviticus,* 180.
21. For the first see Rudolph, *KAT* XIII/4, 212; also NRSV. For the second, F. Horst, *Die zwölf kleinen Propheten. HAT* I/14 (1954), 252; already proposed by Wellhausen, *Kleinen Propheten,* 49. For the third, *Zürcher Bibel;* cf. NIV; for CD 19:8 see J. Maier, *Die Texte vom Toten Meer,* 2 vols. (1960), I, 67; E. Lohse, *Die Texte aus Qumran* (1964), 101.
22. *ATD* 25^7, 175-76.
23. Rudolph, *KAT* XIII/4, 213-14.
24. B. Otzen, *Studien über Deuterosacharja. AcThD* 6 (1964), 193-94.
25. Wellhausen, *Kleinen Propheten,* 195. See also I. Willi-Plein, *Prophetie am Ende: Untersuchungen zu Sacharja 9–14. BBB* 42 (1974), 77.
26. Maier, *Texte,* II, 27.

neighbor is punished so severely because it destroys the basis of God's community, imperiling its common life.

CD 19:8 cites Zec. 13:7 in connection with the coming visitation with its eschatological judgment, which will strike all who have scorned the commandments and statutes. In this visitation, what was predicted in Zec. 13:7 will come to pass.

Zobel

עָמָל *ʿāmāl;* עָמַל *ʿāmal;* עָמֵל *ʿāmēl*

I. Etymology. II. OT: 1. Statistics, LXX, General; 2. "Work"; 3. Individual Laments; 4. Wisdom Literature; 5. Ecclesiastes. III. Late Hebrew.

I. Etymology. The root *ʿml* is represented in most Semitic languages; it is especially common in their late dialects. The basic meaning of the root is presumably "be(come) tired"; around this basic meaning cluster a series of semantically related meanings: on the one hand, *ʿml* denotes what makes people tired, i.e., "work" (verb and noun); on the other, it refers to the condition of someone who is exhausted, i.e., "trouble," "misery," and "ruin." Finally, it can denote the positive result of toil: "earning." Despite the wide range of nuances, one can hardly speak of semantic development. It is more appropriate to understand the variety as an expression of the "global thinking" of the ancient Semites. When the Semites express a concept, all its aspects resonate, although in a given context one particular nuance will be in the foreground. The concept of "being tired" includes all the aspects listed above: work is exhausting, as are misery and affliction; but toil can bring gain.[1] The root → יגע *yāgaʿ* has similar nuances.

In Akkadian the root appears only in the common subst. *nēmelu,* "gain."[2] Arabic has the verb *ʿamila,* "work," and the noun *ʿamal,* "work"; in Ethiopic we find *māʿbal,* "tool."[3] In Old Aramaic the verb occurs on the Barrakib stele, probably with the meaning "take pains";[4] in the Sefire inscriptions the noun appears in a curse formula in the

---

ʿāmāl. G. Bertram, "Hebräischer und griechischer Qohelet," *ZAW* 64 (1952) 26-49; R. Braun, *Kohelet und die frühhellenistische Popularphilosophie. BZAW* 130 (1973); I. Engnell, "Work in the OT," *SEÅ* 26 (1961) 5-12; G. Fohrer, "Twofold Aspects of Hebrew Words," *Words and Meanings. FS D. Winton Thomas* (1968), 95-103; H. L. Ginsberg, *Studies in Koheleth. Texts and Studies of the Jewish Theological Seminary of America* 17 (1950); idem, "Supplementary Studies in Koheleth," *PAAJR* 21 (1952) 35-62; J. Pedersen, *ILC;* G. von Rad, *Wisdom in Israel* (Eng. trans. 1972); H. H. Schmid, *Wesen und Geschichte der Weisheit. BZAW* 101 (1966); S. Schwertner, "עָמָל *ʿāmāl* toil," *TLOT,* II, 924-26.

1. *ILC,* I-II, 108-28; Fohrer, 101, 102.
2. *AHw,* II, 776.
3. Brockelmann, *VG,* I, 226.
4. See *DNSI,* II, 870-71; *KAI* 216.7-8.

phrase *kl mh ʿml,* "all possible afflictions."[5] In Imperial Aramaic a paronomasia occurs that appears also in the OT: *ʿml zy ʿmlt,* "the trouble you have caused me."[6]

The root appears again in later Palestinian Aramaic: in the Qumran fragments of the Testament of Levi,[7] the substantive has been lost in l. 1 (but cf. l. 3 of the Bodleian fragment),[8] but the verb is preserved in l. 2. Both words occur in lists of afflictions.[9] In synagogue inscriptions from northern Palestine (3rd-5th centuries C.E.), *ʿml* is clearly being used in a specialized technical sense when it denotes the donation of a private individual to the synagogue.[10] In Rabbinic Aramaic, the noun also means "rent" or "income,"[11] while the verb (as in Hebrew) means "work" (esp. "work at study of Torah"). In Syriac the usual meanings "toil" (noun) and "take pains" are commonly found in connection with ascetic exercises.[12]

II. OT.

1. *Statistics, LXX, General.* Forms of the root *ʿml* appear 75 times in the OT; 50 of these occurrences are in wisdom literature, especially Ecclesiastes (35). The root appears 14 times in the Psalms. The other occurrences are widely scattered. The noun *ʿāmāl* appears 55 times, the verb *ʿāmal* 11 times, and the adj. *ʿāmēl* 9 times. The PN *ʿāmāl* in 1 Ch. 7:35 corresponds to the Palmyrene name *ʿml',* which may mean "worker," and may also be related to the Edomite theophorous name *qwsʿml.*[13]

The LXX generally uses *móchthos, pónos,* or *kópos* to translate *ʿāmāl.*[14] It uses these same words to translate other Hebrew words as well, especially *yᵉgîaʿ.* In fact, → יגע *ygʿ* is the most important parallel to *ʿml;* like the latter, it has both negative ("toil") and positive ("gain") nuances.

The above statistical survey showed that *ʿml* belongs to the specialized vocabulary of wisdom literature and is therefore typical of the later linguistic stratum of the OT. Nevertheless, the noun *ʿāmāl,* "affliction," appears frequently in individual psalms of lament. The six occurrences in the prophets are more or less influenced by these psalms. Analysis reveals clear differences between the semantic fields of the root *ʿml* in the different literary groups, although no semantic development is discernible.

2. *"Work."* Except in Ecclesiastes (see II.5 below), the OT rarely uses the root with the neutral meaning "work." In Jgs. 5:26 Jael grasps the *halmûṯ ʿᵃmēlîm* ("work-

5. *KAI* 222A.26.
6. *AP* 40:2.
7. *DJD,* I, 21.[1-]2.
8. R. H. Charles, *The Greek Versions of the Testaments of the Twelve Patriarchs* (1908), 246.
9. Cf. *APOT,* II, 364.
10. J. A. Fitzmyer and D. J. Harrington, *A Manual of Palestinian Aramaic Texts. BietOr* 34 (1978), texts A26.10; A27.3-4; A28.2-3; A39.3.
11. Levy, *WTM,* s.v.
12. *CSD,* 417.
13. For the former see *PNPI,* 106; for the latter, T. C. Vriezen, *OTS* 14 (1965) 330-31.
14. Bertram, 35-47.

men's mallet"), normally used by workers. In Prov. 16:26 we find a "macabre joke"[15] whose translation runs something like: "The hunger of the worker *(ʿāmēl)* works *(ʿām^elâ)* for him"; in other words, even if he does not enjoy his work, at least his need for the basic necessities of life impels him to work. The passage uses both words in a neutral sense, but we may perceive a subtext: do not envy the worker, for his work is agonizing and the work that hunger accomplishes "for him" only aggravates his suffering.[16]

The verb appears without negative connotations in Jon. 4:10, where Yahweh says to Jonah, "You are concerned about the castor bean bush, for which you did not work *(ʿāmaltā)* to make it grow," and in Ps. 127:1, which says that the workers work *(ʿām^elû)* in vain if Yahweh does not build the house.

3. *Individual Laments.* The Psalms and Prophets (with the exception of the texts just discussed) use only the noun *ʿāmāl;* here it clearly means "drudgery," "affliction," and "mischief." A striking exception is Ps. 105:44 (see III below). It appears in parallel with *ʿ^onî, ḥāmās, šeqer, mirmâ, tōḵ, kaʿas,* and especially *ʾāwen,* which clearly define its semantic field. In these texts it refers primarily to the afflictions people impose on others. It is associated most frequently with *ʾāwen,* "iniquity." Typical is the proverbial expression "conceive *ʿāmāl* and give birth to *ʾāwen*" (Isa. 59:4; Job 15:35; in Ps. 7:15[Eng. v. 14] *šeqer* ["lies"] is added as well).[17]

We also find the combination of *ʿāmāl* and *ʾāwen* in other individual laments, which contrast the wicked *(rāšāʿ)* with the righteous *(ṣaddîq).* Ps. 55 says that the city is under the sway of the wicked; "*ʾāwen* and *ʿāmāl* are in its midst" (v. 11[10]; v. 12[11] adds *hawwôṯ, tōḵ,* and *mirmâ,* while v. 10[9] mentions *ḥāmās* and *rîḇ*). Here the offense is social oppression; similar terminology appears in prophetic indictments of social iniquity: in Hab. 1:3 — in a text composed totally in the form of an individual lament — and in Isa. 10:1, an imprecation of woe that must be read in the context of the lament in Ps. 94:20 and probably refers to the wicked ruler who perverts the law to oppress the weak and righteous.

The meaning "affliction" or "mischief" is obvious in these passages, where the context is the genre of individual lament. Other texts say that the wicked has *ʿāmāl w^eʾāwen* under his tongue (Ps. 10:7) and that his lips speak *ʿāmāl* (Ps. 140:10[9]). This terminology may come from wisdom instruction; Prov. 24:2 cautions against "the wicked" (v. 1) whose minds devise violence and whose lips talk of *ʿāmāl.* This wisdom tradition is probably also the source of the notion of retribution: *ʿāmāl* will be inflicted on those who practice it (Ps. 140:10[9]); "their *ʿāmāl* returns upon their own heads, and on their own heads their violence *(ḥāmās)* descends" (Ps. 7:17[16]); cf. also Job 4:8: "Those who plow *ʾāwen* and sow *ʿāmāl* reap the same," and Job 20:22: the wicked (v. 5) are struck by the "hand of disaster" (*yaḏ ʿāmāl* [reading *ʿāmāl* instead of

---

15. Plöger, *Sprüche Salomos. BK* XVII (1984), 195.
16. Engnell, 10; W. McKane, *Proverbs. OTL* (1970), 490-91.
17. → I, 142.

'āmēl]).[18] Conversely, it is a stumbling block for the sufferer when the wicked are not afflicted with *'ᵃmal 'ᵉnôš,* "human misery" (Ps. 73:5).

In the individual laments, we find the prayer that Yahweh will look on *(rā'â)* the affliction *('ᵒnî)* and trouble *('āmāl)* of the psalmist (Ps. 25:18), i.e., to provide aid against the psalmist's foes (v. 19). This prayer emerges from the conviction that Yahweh at all times sees *(rā'â)* the *'āmāl wāḵa'as* ("trouble and grief") of the righteous and extirpates the wicked (Ps. 10:14). According to Hab. 1:13, Yahweh's eyes are too pure to behold *(rā'â)* evil *(rā')* and to look on (*nbṭ* hiphil) wrongdoing *('āmāl);* when he sees them, he must intervene (cf. v. 3). If the older translations are correct, the Balaam oracle in Nu. 23:21 says the same thing: "He [Yahweh] cannot behold (*nbṭ* hiphil) *'āwen* in Jacob and cannot see *(rā'â) 'āmāl* in Israel."

This characteristic use of the verb *rā'â* with *'āmāl* appears also in Deuteronomistic texts: the Israelites cried out to Yahweh in Egypt, and he "heard our voice and saw *(rā'â)* our affliction *('onyēnû)* and our toil *('ᵃmālēnû)*" (Dt. 26:7). According to Jgs. 10:16, after the Israelites put away the foreign gods, Yahweh could no longer bear to see their affliction *('āmāl).* Here and in Ps. 107:12 *'āmāl* means not so much the afflictions brought on Israel by others as God's punishment of his people. This psalm bears the clear marks of Deuteronomistic influence; in the Deuteronomistic tradition, *'āmāl* refers to God's chastisement of his people. Only rarely does the word denote God's punishment of an individual; such an idea may be suggested in Ps. 25:18 by the addition of "forgive all my sins." We also find *'āmāl* used for the sufferings of an individual chosen for a special mission: Joseph, who looks back after the birth of his sons on the *'āmāl* he has undergone (Gen. 41:51); the servant of Yahweh, who suffers *'āmāl* to atone for others (Isa. 53:11); and Jeremiah, who asks in his confessions why he was ever born, if he is to see only *'āmāl* (Jer. 20:18).

Only once is *'āmāl* used figuratively: in Ps. 73:16 the lamenting psalmist tries to understand his situation, but the attempt brings him only *'āmāl,* "spiritual anguish."

4. *Wisdom Literature.* In the wisdom tradition, a different nuance of *'ml* predominates: the affliction, or rather the misery, that is part of the fundamental human condition. Ps. 90, which bears the stamp of this tradition, describes the burdens of life: even if one attains a ripe old age, the "glory" of life is nothing but *'āmāl wā'āwen* (v. 10). Job expresses the same idea when he says that life is slavery and nights of *'āmāl* are the human lot (Job 7:3). Eliphaz asserts that human beings are born *lᵉ'āmāl* (Job 5:7; possibly the text should be emended to read "human beings bring forth misery").[19]

Since human life is burdened by misery, it is possible to try to escape from this reality: one can drink to forget the *'āmāl* of life (Prov. 31:7). Or one can stretch forth one's hands to God — then *'āmāl* vanishes like water flowing away (as Zophar urges, Job 11:16). For Job himself, these evasions will not work: his friends are merely *'āmāl-*

18. Fohrer, *Hiob. KAT* XVI (1963), 326.

19. Fohrer, *KAT* XVI, 132; Horst, *Hiob. BK* XVI/1 (1968), 62, 81; for a different view see von Rad, 130.

comforters (16:2)! He knows that *ʿāmāl* has been his fate since birth (Job 3:10); he can only ask why God lets the one in misery *(ʿāmēl)* see the light of day (3:10; cf. Jer. 20:18).

5. *Ecclesiastes.* Ecclesiastes takes a critical stance toward traditional wisdom; not by accident, it understands the word *ʿāmāl* in a different sense than Proverbs and Job. In its reflections on the meaning of human life, there are 35 occurrences of words derived from the root *ʿml* (22 of the noun *ʿāmāl,* 8 of the verb, 5 of the adj. *ʿāmēl*). Ecclesiastes employs paronomasia frequently: *kol-ʿᵃmālô šeyyaᵃmōl* (1:3); *kol-ʿᵃmālô . . . šehûʾ ʿāmēl* (2:22; cf. 2:11,18,20,21; 5:17[18]; 9:9).

If the author does not associate *ʿml* with "the misery of the human condition," it is because he needs to emphasize other nuances of the word to elucidate his notions concerning human life. For him *ʿāmāl* denotes the ceaseless toil that characterizes human existence. Here he comes close to the neutral meaning of *ʿāmal,* "work," and *ʿāmēl,* "worker" (see II.2 above). But for him the words have an undertone of frustration, suggesting "toilsome labor" or, better, the unending human striving that he can only consider vanity. For him labor and industry are without purpose because they are without meaning; they cannot make life — or even the quality of life — secure. Nevertheless, human beings should enjoy the fruits of their labor and industry while they are alive. Thus *ʿml* occupies a central place in the intellectual world of the author, as he tries to come to terms with the unfolding of human life.[20]

When the author wants to say that work is meaningless and purposeless, he often combines *ʿāmāl* with his characteristic word *yiṯrôn,* "gain,"[21] in the form of a rhetorical question: "What do people gain from all the toil *(ʿᵃmālô)* with which they toil *(yaʿᵃmōl)* under the sun?" (1:3; cf. also 3:9; 5:14-15).

This view is expounded quite straightforwardly in the long section on the futility of human existence (1:12–2:26). It is true that pleasure may be gratifying, but then "I considered all that my hands had done and the toil I had spent *(beʿāmāl šeʿāmaltî)* in doing it *(laʿᵃśôṯ),* and again, all was vanity and a chasing after wind, and there was no gain *(yiṯrôn)* under the sun" (2:11; cf. 4:4). The maxim "Better is a handful with quiet than two handfuls with toil *(ʿāmāl)*" (4:6) expresses the same idea.

A special case is the situation of the solitary individual (4:7-12), for whom toil is especially meaningless because he has no heir. Nevertheless, "there is no end to all his toil *(ʿᵃmālô),* and his eyes are never satisfied with his riches." Under such circumstances, one can truly ask, "For whom am I toiling *(ʿāmēl)*?" Then it is indeed better for two to be together; they can help each other and together "receive a good reward for their toil *(baʿᵃmālām).*"

But even someone with an heir has problems, which the author expounds in a short passage in which he plays with the root *ʿml* ten times (2:18-23): "I hated all my toil in which I had toiled under the sun *(ʾeṯ-kol-ʿᵃmālî šeʾᵃnî ʿāmēl taḥaṯ haššemeš),* seeing

---

20. On the corresponding terminology of Hellenistic popular philosophy, see Braun, 48-49.
21. → יתר *ytr.*

that I must leave it to one who comes after me. Who knows whether he will be wise or foolish?" That is precisely the problem: all this toil will have been in vain if the heir cannot administer the estate wisely. At the end of this exposition, the author can only sigh, "What does a mortal get from all his toil *(beḵol-ʿamālô)* and the strain with which he toils *(šehûʾ ʿāmēl)* under the sun?" (v. 22).

This negative verdict on toil is based on the conviction that despite all wisdom, no one can "discover the meaning of what is done on earth"[22] — the more so when it is the work of God *(maʿaśēh ʾelōhîm)*: "However much one may toil *(yaʿamōl)* in seeking, no one will find it out" (8:17).

Faced with this meaninglessness, people should simply give up. But this is not the author's view. Even though toil may be meaningless, one can at least enjoy it! The fruits of toil are God's good gift. Many sense a certain inconsistency here.[23] But in these words we hear a kind of resignation to God's will that finally allows the author to abandon his attempts to "fathom the work of God." This fundamental attitude helps the author achieve an openness to the world and to life that finds expression in several statements where *ʿāmāl* is coupled characteristically with the word *ḥēleq* ("portion, lot"). Just before 2:11, which speaks of the meaningless toil of life (see above), the king recounts his many activities, ending v. 10 with the confession that he had denied his heart no pleasure, "for my heart found pleasure in all my toil *(mikkol-ʿamālî)*, and that was my portion [*ḥelqî;* NRSV 'reward'] for all my toil." What is most fitting is "to eat and drink and find enjoyment in all the toil with which one toils *(beḵol-ʿamālô šeyyaʿamōl)* under the sun all the days of the life God gives one; for this is one's lot *(ḥelqô)*" (5:17[18]). The rich man can "eat" of his wealth and accept his lot *(ḥelqô)* and find enjoyment in his toil *(baʿamālô)* — "this too is the gift of God" (v. 18[19]; similar sentiments in 2:24; 3:13; 8:15).[24]

But the author counters these lighthearted remarks with a statement intended to make the point that carefree eating and drinking may bring pleasure but also have a darker side, the insatiable craving for life: "All human toil *(kol-ʿamal hāʾāḏām)* is for the mouth, yet the appetite is not appeased" (6:7). The same bitter note is heard in a final piece of advice: eat and drink with pleasure, anoint your body and wear white garments, enjoy life with the wife you love, "for that is your portion in life *(ḥelqeḵā baḥayyîm)* and in your toil at which you toil *(ûḇaʿamāleḵā ʾašer-ʾattāh ʿāmēl)* under the sun" — do all this, for only one thing is certain for you: death (9:7-10).

III. Late Hebrew. In an OT passage from the same late period as Ecclesiastes the word *ʿāmāl* clearly means "earning," i.e., what is earned through toilsome labor (see I above): Ps. 105:44, which describes the occupation of the promised land: "They took possession of the earning of the nations *(ʿamal leʾummîm)*." Ginsberg has attempted to impose this same meaning on *ʿāmāl* throughout Ecclesiastes (with a few exceptions).[25]

---

22. Zimmerli, *Prediger. ATD* 16/1 (³1962), 218.
23. Schmid, 193-94.
24. On the whole subject see von Rad, 229-37.
25. Ginsberg, *Studies,* 1ff.; idem, "Supplementary Studies," 35-39.

In some passages this nuance may well be present, but to translate the word consistently as "earning" appears forced.[26]

In Postbiblical Hebrew the meaning "earning" is clearly present. In 1QS 9:22, we read that the righteous members of the community should leave "wealth and the earning of hands" *(hwn wʿml kpym)* to the unrighteous. Elsewhere in the Dead Sea Scrolls, *ʿāmāl* has its customary sense of "toil" (8 times, many of which cite biblical texts). In Rabbinic Hebrew the verb in particular is used in the neutral sense of "work diligently" (often studying the Torah). The noun more often has the biblical meaning "toil," but can also mean "property."[27]

Otzen

26. Galling (*Der Prediger. HAT* I/18 [[2]1969]) argues successfully for this meaning in 2:18-19; cf. also Zimmerli, *ATD* 16/1[3], 157-58.
27. Levy, *WTM,* s.v.

עֵמֶק *ʿēmeq;* עָמַק *ʿāmaq;* עֹמֶק *ʿōmeq;* עָמֹק/עָמֵק *ʿāmēq/ʿāmōq;* מַעֲמַקִּים *maʿᵃmaqqîm*

I. Cognates. II. OT: 1. Occurrences; 2. Verb; 3. *ʿēmeq;* 4. *ʿōmeq* and *ʿāmēq/ʿāmōq;* 5. *maʿᵃmaqqîm.* III. 1. Jewish Aramaic; 2. Dead Sea Scrolls; 3. LXX.

I. Cognates. Forms of the root *ʿmq* appear in almost all Semitic languages; its various meanings are not derivable from one another.

Most of the occurrences involve the concept of depth in the literal or transferred sense. As early as Old Akkadian,[1] *emēqu(m)* I means "be wise" and is used of deities

ʿēmeq. A. Bongini, "Ricerche sul lessico geografico del semitico nord-occidentale," *AION* 19 (1969) 181-90, esp. 188-90; M. Dahood, "The Value of Ugaritic for Textual Criticism," *Bibl* 40 (1959) 160-70, esp. 166-67; E. C. Dell'Oca, "El Valle de Josafat: ¿nombre simbólico o topográfico?" *Revista Biblical Raf. Calzada* 28 (1966) 169ff.; G. R. Driver, "Difficult Words in the Hebrew Prophets," *Studies in OT Prophecy. FS T. H. Robinson* (1950), 52-72; J. C. Greenfield, "Ugaritic Lexicographical Notes," *JCS* 21 (1967) 89-93, esp. 89; W. Herrmann, "Philological hebraica," *ThV* 8 (1977) 35-44; A. Jirku, *Eine Renaissance des Hebräischen. FuF* 32 (1958), 211-12; L. Krinetzki, "'Tal' und 'Ebene' im AT," *BZ* 5 (1961) 204-20; H.-D. Neef, "Die Ebene Achor — das 'Tor der Hoffnung,'" *ZDPV* 100 (1984) 91-107; J. Reider, "Etymological Studies in Biblical Hebrew," *VT* 2 (1952) 113-30; K.-D. Schunck, "Bemerkungen zur Ortsliste von Benjamin," *ZDPV* 78 (1962) 143-58; A. Schwarzenbach, *Die geographische Terminologie im Hebräischen des ATs* (1954); A. A. Wieder, "Ugaritic-Hebrew Lexicographical Notes," *JBL* 84 (1965) 160-64, esp. 162-63; H. W. Wolff, "Die Ebene Achor," *ZDPV* 70 (1954) 76-81.

1. *AHw,* I, 213, 215.

and mortals; in Babylonia similarly the adj. *emqu(m)* means "wise, clever" (the king, an artisan). This figurative meaning continues in Jewish Aramaic and in the Dead Sea Scrolls (see III below). The literal physical meaning of *ʿmq,* "(broad) valley," is as common in Semitic languages outside the Bible as in the OT itself.[2] It appears in Ugaritic ("valley, lowland") and Phoenician (Karatepe inscription, *ʿmq ʾdn,* "Plain of Adana"; Maktar inscription, *yrd bʿmq*).[3] It is common as a geographical term in the Amarna letters and at Mari.[4] In Old Aramaic a verb in the haphel is derived from the root *ʿmq* (Zakir inscription, *whʿmqw ḥrṣ,* "they dug a ditch").[5]

In Ugaritic as well as in Middle Assyrian and Neo-Assyrian there is a homonymous root *ʿmq* II: Ugar. *ʿmq* means "able, strong";[6] Assyr. *emūqu(m)* means "strength, power, violence";[7] *emūqa(mma)* and *emūqattam* mean "violent,"[8] and may be cited in interpreting such texts as Jer. 47:5 and Job 39:21.[9]

II. OT.

1. *Occurrences.* There are 100 occurrences of the root *ʿmq* in the OT, distributed as follows: the verb occurs once in the qal ("be deep [inscrutable]") and 8 times in the hiphil ("make deep," both literally and figuratively); *ʿēmeq,* "valley," occurs 65 times; *ʿōmeq,* "depth," occurs twice; the adj. "deep" in the forms *ʿāmēq* (Aram. *ʿammîq*) and *ʿāmōq* occurs 19 times. The derived noun *maʿamaqqîm,* "depths," occurs 5 times.

2. *Verb.* While the qal of the verb *ʿmq* is associated with the abstract sphere (Ps. 92:6[Eng. v. 5]: "How great are your works, O Yahweh! Your thoughts are very deep!"), the hiphil denotes active "going deep": digging in out of fear of the enemy (Jer. 49:8,30), making a pitfall (Hos. 5:2), or constructing a fire pit (Isa. 30:33). Isa. 7:11 can also be cited here ("Ask a sign of Yahweh; make it as deep as Sheol or as high as heaven!"). The verb is also used adverbially in a metaphorical sense: "they hid a plan too deep for Yahweh" (29:15); "They have deeply betrayed" (31:6); "They have deeply corrupted themselves" (Hos. 9:9).

3. *ʿēmeq.* The noun *ʿēmeq,* "valley," is a geographical term used in a variety of combinations: (a) with names of towns; (b) with other proper nouns; (c) in historical contexts that make a topographical identification possible; (d) as a descriptive term characterizing a geographical region. (e) In some cases important theological statements are associated with specific valleys. (f) The number of terms besides *ʿēmeq* that refer to

---

2. *HAL,* II, 847.

3. For Ugaritic see *WUS,* no. 2050; *UT,* no. 1873. On Karatepe see *KAI* 26.I.4; II.8-9, 14, 15. For Maktar see *KAI* 145.8.

4. For Amarna see EA 1112, 1571; see M. Noth, *ABLAK,* II, 60. For Mari see *ABLAK,* II, 269.

5. *KAI* 202A.10.

6. *WUS,* no. 2050; *UT,* no. 1874.

7. *AHw,* I, 216.

8. *AHw,* I, 215.

9. M. Noth, *Das Buch Josua. HAT* I/7 (²1953), 111; J. Simons (*GTTOT,* §327) says much the same; Schunck (153-58) identifies it with a dispersed settlement north and south of Wadi el-Qelṭ.

valleys, depressions, and plains makes it necessary to define these terms more precisely. (g) Finally, we shall discuss the texts that use *ʿmq* II.

a. *With Names of Towns.* The association of *ʿēmeq* with the name of a town (usually in a const. phrase) makes it possible to identify the following valleys: *ʿēmeq ʾayyālôn* (Josh. 10:12), *ʿēmeq ʾᵃšer lᵉbêṯ-rᵉḥôḇ* (Jgs. 18:28), the *ʿēmeq* of *bêṯ šemeš* (1 S. 6:13), *ʿēmeq bᵉgiḇʿôn* (Isa. 28:21), *ʿēmeq ḥeḇrôn* (Gen. 37:14), *ʿēmeq yizrᵉʿeʾl* (Josh. 17:16; Jgs. 6:33 [7:1,8,12]; 1 S. 31:7 par. 1 Ch. 10:7; Hos. 1:5), and *ʿēmeq sukkôṯ* (Ps. 60:8[6] = 108:8[7]). The location of *ʿēmeq qᵉṣîṣ* (Josh. 18:21) in Benjamin cannot be identified with certainty ("about עמק קציץ [which the context indicates must be the name of a town, despite its form] . . . we know nothing").[10] The toponym *bêṯ hāʿēmeq* (Josh. 19:27) presents the elements in reverse order. The name of this village in Asher may survive in the name of the modern village of *ʿamqa.*[11]

In Cant. 2:1 *ʿēmeq* parallels *haššārôn,* probably referring to the whole region.

b. *With Other Proper Nouns.* Identification of the valleys associated with proper nouns poses greater problems.

ʿēmeq hāʾēlâ (1 S. 17:2,19; 21:10). This is the site of the battle between Saul and the Philistines in the course of which David slew Goliath; the mention of the towns of Socoh and Azekah in 17:1 enables us to locate it on the western edge of the Judean hill country.

ʿēmeq habbāḵāʾ (Ps. 84:7[6]). Simons calls identification with Wadi el-Mes, which runs northwest from the Jaffa Gate, "highly hypothetical,"[12] but it would be appropriate in a "pilgrim hymn before the gates of the sanctuary." Reference to *bāḵāʾ* trees, which are mentioned also in 2 S. 5:23-24 par. 1 Ch. 14:14 and may have stood in the Valley of Rephaim (see below), provides no useful information.

ʿēmeq hammeleḵ (Gen. 14:17; 2 S. 18:18). Both the legendary tradition of Gen. 14 and the trustworthy Court History of David mention the "King's Valley," in the immediate vicinity of Jerusalem;[13] we should most likely look for it to the north rather than accepting the later tradition that associated it with the Valley of Kidron.[14] The phrase *ʿēmeq šāwēh* (Gen. 14:17) is best explained as the addition of *ʿēmeq* as a gloss to *šāwēh;* the combination was misinterpreted as a synonym of *ʿēmeq hammeleḵ.*

ʿēmeq ʿāḵôr (Josh. 7:24,26; 15:7; Isa. 65:10; Hos. 2:17[15]). The Valley of Achor, the site of the stoning of Achan immediately after the unsuccessful attack on Ai (Josh. 7:24,26), is also a point on the boundary between Judah and Benjamin (Josh. 15:7). Citing Hos. 2:17(15), which calls the Valley of Achor a gateway ("door of hope") to the promised land, Simons (and more recently Neef) supports the identification of this valley with the lowlands along the Wadi en-Nuweʿime north of Jericho. Wolff was the first

---

10. *GesB,* 97; J. Simons (*GTTOT,* §332) also mentions Tell Mimas as a further attempt at archaeological identification.
11. *GTTOT,* §760.
12. Josephus *Ant.* 7.10.2 §243.
13. *GTTOT,* §364.
14. *GTTOT,* §469.

to propose this identification,[15] which he defends in his commentary on Hosea against various objections. Noth argues for a different location.[16]

ʿēmeq rᵉpāʾîm (Josh. 15:8; 18:16; 2 S. 5:18,22 par. 1 Ch. 14:9-13; 2 S. 23:13 par. 1 Ch. 11:15; Isa. 17:5). This valley, named for "an important tribe belonging to the indigenous population of Palestine,"[17] is mentioned as a point on the boundary between Judah and Benjamin (Josh. 15:8; 18:16 [secondary according to Noth]).[18] It is best known as the site of military conflicts between David (2 S. 5:18,22 par. 1 Ch. 14:9,13) or his chiefs (2 S. 23:13 par. 1 Ch. 11:15) and the Philistines; it must therefore be close to Jerusalem. Its identification with "the beqʿah sw. of Jerusalem" is correct.[19]

ʿēmeq haśśiddîm (Gen. 14:3,8,10). Wellhausen and Westermann emend *śiddîm* to *šēḏîm* ("Valley of Demons"). If we do not accept this emendation, the site — described as a battlefield — must be near the Dead Sea (as the gloss in v. 3 suggests); it cannot, however, be the territory of the Dead Sea itself. This location is also supported by the mention of the town *ḥaṣᵉṣōn tāmār* in v. 7; it was located southwest of the Dead Sea's southern shore. "One has the impression that 'the plain of the Siddim' was the local designation of a relatively small section of the Jordan Valley, close to the Dead Sea and to the Jordan."[20]

c. *Historical Contexts.* The valleys where Nu. 14:25 says the Amalekites and Canaanites dwell (or will continue to dwell) are the same regions mentioned later (Jgs. 1:19,34) in accounts of the occupation of the promised land by Judah and Dan (cf. also Nu. 13:29). The *ʿēmeq* near Ai mentioned in Josh. 8:13 is identified by Noth with a village a mile and a half southeast of Ai, modern *kufr nāta;*[21] *BHS* emends *ʿēmeq* to *ʿam* (Josh. 8:3, *wᵉḵol-ʿam hammilḥāmâ*).[22] In the descriptions of the boundaries of Reuben and Gad in Josh. 13:19,27, *ʿēmeq* clearly refers to the valley of the Jordan.[23] The same is probably true of the *ʿēmeq* in Jer. 48:8, where the eastern edge of the rift valley is described as Moabite territory.[24] The description of the battle between Deborah and Siserah in Jgs. 4:12-16 shows that the *ʿēmeq* in 5:15 is the valley of the Kishon.

The prophets' words of admonition and comfort to Jerusalem frequently mention the valleys surrounding the city, in some cases using the word *ʿēmeq.* Isa. 22:1 speaks of the *gêʾ ḥizzāyôn,* probably identical with the Valley of Hinnom; v. 7 describes it as filled with chariots and cavalry. According to Jer. 31:40, the valley rendered unclean by dead bodies and ashes (probably once again the Valley of Hinnom, named in Jer. 19:6) will once again be sacred to Yahweh.

---

15. Wolff, 76-79.
16. *HAT* I/7², in loc.
17. *GesB,* 770.
18. *HAT* I/7², in loc.
19. *GTTOT,* §758.
20. *GTTOT,* §413.
21. Noth, *HAT* I/7², in loc.
22. Cf. Schwarzenbach, 34.
23. Noth, *HAT* I/7², 80; *GTTOT,* §137.
24. W. Rudolph, *Jeremia. HAT* I/12 (³1958), in loc.

d. *Descriptive Terminology.* Ps. 65:14(13) sings the praises of *ʿᵃmāqîm* as areas suitable for agriculture and raising flocks. Therefore Job 39:10 can ask rhetorically whether "the wild ox will harrow the valleys after you." David's officers in charge of the royal herds *baššārôn* and *bāʿᵃmāqîm* are mentioned in 1 Ch. 27:29. When the Jordan overflows its banks during the rainy season, "it puts to flight [?] all the valleys to the east and to the west" (1 Ch. 12:16[15]).

e. *Theological Contexts.* We also find *ʿēmeq* in theological contexts. During Ahab's Aramean wars, the view of the Arameans is reported: "Yahweh is a god of the hills but he is not a god of the valleys" (1 K. 20:28); they therefore conclude that they should fight their next battle with Ahab in the valley of Aphek. The mention of the *ʿēmeq rᵉpāʾîm* in an oracle against Damascus (Isa. 17:5) is symbolic: "It shall be as when one gleans the ears of grain in the Valley of Rephaim" — nothing will be left (cf. also the image of the olive harvest in v. 6). Mic. 1:3-4 describes a theophany: the mountains will melt (v. 4aαb) and the valleys will burst open (v. 4aβ); the characteristic features of each will be annihilated. The story of the legendary victory of Jehoshaphat, king of Judah, is set in the *ʿēmeq bᵉrāḵâ* (2 Ch. 20:26). Galling believes that this is an etiological legend connected with Wadi Berekut, located between Bethlehem and Hebron, west of Tekoa.[25] The prophet Joel may have borrowed this tradition when he located the eschatological judgment on the nations in the *ʿēmeq yᵉhôšāpāṭ* (Joel 4:2,12[3:2,12]); for this reason he also called it the *ʿēmeq ḥārûṣ*, "valley of decision" (v. 14; identified with the former by the Targ.), if we are not in fact dealing with the symbolic name "Yahweh judges."[26]

f. *Related Terms.* The OT uses a variety of words for "valleys, depressions, and plains":[27] *biqʿâ, gayʾ, mîšôr,* → נחל *naḥal, ʿēmeq, šāwēh.* Twice we find *ʿēmeq* in parallel with *mîšôr* (Jer. 21:13 [see 3.g below]; 48:8); in Jer. 31:40 it appears in conjunction with the *naḥal qiḏrôn* and in Isa. 22:7 with *gêʾ ḥizzāyôn* (v. 1); it is used three times in connection with the Plain of Sharon (Isa. 65:10; Cant. 2:1; 1 Ch. 27:29). Mic. 1:4 uses *ʿēmeq* as an antonym of → הר *har.*

Although the terms just listed have their own specific meanings, they may overlap. Schwarzenbach defines the meanings thus: a *naḥal* is a "winter watercourse"; *gayʾ* denotes a "sharply defined valley, which can be very narrow or very broad," but in any case is flanked by two ranges of mountains or hills.[28] The noun *ʿēmeq* "denotes a 'lowland' with visible boundaries, providing space for dwellings, fields, and pastures . . . as well as appearing suitable for military maneuvers,"[29] as confirmed by Gen. 14:3,8,10; Josh. 10:12; Jgs. 6:33; 1 S. 17:2,19; 2 S. 5:18,22; Isa. 28:21; Joel 4:2,12(3:2,12); 2 Ch. 20:26. A *biqʿâ* is a "broad valley . . . in contrast to uplands";

25. K. Galling, *Die Bücher der Chronik, Esra, Nehemia. ATD* 12 (1954), 128; cf. *GTTOT,* §995.

26. Krinetzki, 215-16.

27. Schwarzenbach, 30.

28. Ibid., 37ff.

29. Ibid., 33.

mîšôr denotes a plateau.[30] Besides *ʿēmeq,* only *gay'* and *naḥal* appear in combination with proper names.

g. *ʿmq II.* In some texts the translation reflects the homonymous root *ʿmq* II.[31] The MT of Jer. 47:5, in the context of an oracle against the Philistines, would be translated: "Baldness has come upon Gaza, Ashkelon is silenced, the remnant of their valleys — how long will you mourn?" Citing Josh. 11:21-22, *BHS* conjectures emending the text to "the remnant of the Anakim." G. R. Driver and others, however, find here an instance of *ʿmq* II and translate: "O remnant of their strength."[32] The same holds true in Job 39:21, in the description of a horse, where *ʿēmeq* parallels *kōaḥ:* "It paws violently and neighs, mightily it goes forth to meet the battle line."[33] Schwarzenbach identifies two additional texts where he believes a translation based on *ʿmq* II yields better sense.[34] In Jer. 21:13 he translates: "You, reigning with power *(ʿēmeq),* O stronghold *(ṣûr)* of righteousness *(mîšôr)*"; in their context these are words of bitter irony. In Jer. 49:4, while the *ʿᵃmāqîm* in the oracle against the Ammonites can be understood as valleys of the Jabbok and its tributaries, Schwarzenbach translates (accepting the emendation of the MT in *BHS*): "Why do you boast in your strength?" The NRSV follows this interpretation in Job 39:21 and Jer. 49:4.

4. *ʿōmeq and ʿāmēq/ʿāmōq.* Only rarely do the noun *ʿōmeq* and the adj. *ʿāmēq/ʿāmōq* denote something physically "deep." Ezk. 23:32 describes the cup of Yahweh's wrath as "deep and wide" *(hāʿᵃmuqqâ wᵉhārᵉḥāḇâ).* In the regulations governing leprosy in Lev. 13, the affected area of the skin is described as *ʿāmōq mēʿôr bᵉśārô, ʿāmōq min-hāʿôr,* or the like (vv. 4,5,25,30-32,34). Depth is often figurative: "The mouth of a strange woman is a deep pit" (Prov. 22:14; 23:27); rather more vague is the statement that "the words of the mouth" or "the purposes of the human mind" are "deep water" (18:4; 20:5: unfathomable, possibly also dangerous). The adj. *ʿāmōq* also describes the inaccessibility of the netherworld (Job 11:8; 12:22; cf. Prov. 9:18, *ʿimqê šᵉ'ôl*). Thus the adjective also takes on the sense of "impenetrable" (Ps. 92:6[5]; see 2 above), describing both the mysteries of the world (Eccl. 7:24; Dnl. 2:22 [Aram. *mᵉsattᵉrāṯā'* par. *ʿammîqāṯā'*]) and the inner life of human beings (Ps. 64:7[6]; Prov. 25:3). An incomprehensible foreign language (Isa. 33:19: Assyrian; Ezk. 3:5,6: Babylonian) is described as *ʿāmēq,* "deep," *kāḇēḏ,* "heavy,"[35] or *nilʿag,* "barbarous"; one cannot understand what one hears.

5. *maʿᵃmaqqîm.* The pl. *maʿᵃmaqqîm* stands concretely for the depths of the sea, into which the riches of Tyre vanish like a sunken ship (Ezk. 27:34), or the deep sea, which Yahweh dries up so that the redeemed may cross over (Isa. 51:10). The speaker of Ps.

30. Ibid., 38-39.
31. Not certain according to *HAL,* II, 848-49.
32. P. 61.
33. Herrmann, 39, shifting the *athnach;* see also Reider, 129.
34. P. 35.
35. → כבד *kāḇēḏ.*

69 says figuratively that he has come into deep waters that threaten to drown him (v. 3[2]) and prays that God will deliver him from these deep waters (v. 15[14]). The psalmist cries "out of the depths" in Ps. 130:1; this can certainly mean "out of deep affliction," but there are probably overtones of the waters of the netherworld.

III. 1. *Jewish Aramaic.* In Jewish Aramaic the root *ʿmq* exhibits the same literal and figurative meanings as in Biblical Hebrew.[36] For example, *ʿûmᵉqāʾ* means both the "depths" of a house (a kind of cellar)[37] and depth of knowledge: "Follow R. Nathan, for he was a judge and plumbed the depths of the law."[38] The adj. *ʿāmîq/ʿammîq* means "deep, impenetrable, profound."[39] *ʿēmeq* appears as a toponym.[40]

2. *Dead Sea Scrolls.* The Dead Sea Scrolls speak of the holy angels "whose ears are opened to perceive unfathomable things" (1QM 10:11). The Copper Scrolls mention the Valley of Achor as a hiding place for treasure (3Q15 1:1; 46; cf. 4QpHos[b] 1:1; see II.3.b above). Allegro identifies this location with the lowland called *buqēiʿa* on the northwest shore of the Dead Sea; but the site near Jericho is also possible, because there, too, according to the text of the scroll, there is a hiding place for treasures. In the former case, we may be dealing with a pseudonymous designation of the site near Khirbet Mird.[41] The phrase *ʿmqy bwr,* "'valleys' of the well" or "'depths' of the well" is unique (4Q184 1:6).

3. *LXX.* The LXX translation of the geographical term *ʿēmeq* varies widely.[42] The word used most often (39 times) is *koilás,* especially in the Pentateuch, Samuel, and the Book of the Twelve. The translation *pháranx* (7 times) is found in Isaiah and sometimes in Joshua, which also transliterates: *Emekachōr* (7:26), *Emekraphaim* (18:16), *Amek(k)asis* (18:21). The translation of Chronicles uses *aúlōn* for *ʿēmeq.* Elsewhere we find *pedíon* (4 times), *aúlax* (Job 39:10), and *koílos* (Joel 4:14[3:14]).

Beyse

---

36. *WTM,* III, 664-65.
37. Bab. *B. Bathra* 63a.
38. Bab. *B. Mez.* 117b.
39. See the discussion of Dnl. 2:22 above.
40. Jer. *Sheb.* 10.38; cf. Mish. *Kel.* 26.1; Bab. *Taan.* 21a.
41. J. M. Allegro, *DJD,* V, 75ff.
42. Schwarzenbach, 34.

עֵנָב *'ēnāḇ;* אֶשְׁכּוֹל *'eškôl;* צִמּוּקִים *ṣimmûqîm*

I. History of Viticulture. II. Etymology. III. OT: 1. Occurrences; 2. Yahweh as Vintner; 3. "Blood of Grapes." IV. LXX; Dead Sea Scrolls.

I. History of Viticulture. The earliest reference to viticulture in the region of Syria (TM 75 G 1847 from Ebla, 2500/2400 B.C.E.) speaks of 3 *mi-at la-a GEŠTIN,* "300 casks of wine."[1] When the Hurrians invaded, Hittite strategy called for the wine grapes of Gašaša to be harvested and brought into the citadel.[2] Besides being made into wine, grapes were a central part of the diet (juice, honey, raisin cakes, fresh fruit). Canaan was the site of viticulture from time immemorial;[3] in Biblical Hebrew 32 lexemes are associated with it.[4] We do not know what kinds of grapes were grown in the biblical period; the syntagm "blood of the grape" and Isa. 63:2; Prov. 23:31; Mt. 26:27-28; Rev. 14:19-20 suggest dark blue varieties.[5]

Depending on geographical location and weather, grapes were harvested from August through October; they were collected in baskets (Jer. 6:9), then set out to dry in the sun or pressed immediately by foot *(dāraḵ)* or under weights *(gaṯ,* → יקב *yeqeḇ, pûrâ).* Grape juice *(mišâ, 'āsîs, dam 'ᵃnāḇîm)* or must (→ תירוש *tîrôš*) ferments quickly. Wine was drunk at meals and was used in the cult.

Together with bread and olives (or olive oil), grapes constituted a major element of the diet. They were eaten even before they were ripe (*bōser,* "sour grapes," Jer. 31:29; Ezk. 18:2; Job 15:33), although such grapes proverbially set the teeth on edge. More mature grapes (*bōser gōmēl,* Isa. 18:5) were considered delicacies.

Part of the harvest was marketed as table grapes and part was dried to make raisins *(ṣimmûq).* Raisin cakes were popular (1 S. 25:18; 30:12; 2 S. 16:1; 1 Ch. 12:41([Eng. v. 40]); a raisin cake (*'ᵃšîšâ,* 2 S. 6:19; Cant. 2:5) served as a cultic offering (Hos. 3:1). The vine prevented (*ḥāmas,* "suppressed," Job 15:33; Lam. 2:6[6]) the complete ripening of the immature grapes or made them shrivel (*bᵉ'ušîm,* Isa. 5:2,4). The doublet "vine

---

'ēnāḇ. L. Anderlind, "Die Rebe in Syrien, insbesondere Palästina," *ZDPV* 11 (1888) 160-77; A. Charbel, "Come tradurre *'eškôl hak-kôfer* (Cant 1,14)?" *BeO* 20 (1978) 61-64; J. Döller, "Der Wein in Bibel und Talmud," *Bibl* 4 (1923) 143-67, 267-99; K. Galling, "Wein und Weinbereitung," *BRL*², 361-63; M. Kochavi, "Khirbet Rabûd = Debir," *Tel Aviv Journal* 1 (1974) 2-33; G. del Olmo Lete, *Interpretación de la mitología cananea* (1984); idem, *Mitos y leyendas de Canaán según la tradición de Ugarit* (1981); O. Rössler, "Ghain im Ugaritischen," *ZA* 54 (1961) 158-72; A. van Selms, "The Etymology of *Yayin,* 'Wine,'" *JNSL* 3 (1974) 76-84. → גפן *gepen;* → יין *yayin;* → כרם *kerem.*

1. G. Pettinato, 160.
2. Maşat 75/104, ll. 8-12.
3. → III, 53-55; VI, 60-61.
4. Van Selms, 76-77.
5. Döller, 151-52.
6. → IV, 480.

and fig tree" or "grapes and figs" characterized the ideal of a rich agricultural region from the 8th century onward.[7] Areas devoid of grapes and figs were devalued, belonging to the period of the wilderness (Nu. 20:5).

Grapes were integrated into the cult of the Jerusalem temple by the offering of the firstfruits of wine (Nu. 18:12-13; Dt. 18:4). The people living near Jerusalem offered fresh grapes (Dt. 26:2); those living farther away probably offered dried grapes. Grapes were subject to the tithe (Dt. 12:17-18; 14:22-26), the Levitical tithe (Dt. 14:28; 26:12), the assessment to support the priests (Nu. 18:11-19), the regulations governing the corners of fields,[8] the fallow seventh year (Ex. 23:10-11; in Lev. 25:5, the sabbath year), and the Jubilee Year (Lev. 25:11).

The law requiring the owner to leave the gleanings of the vineyard for the poor (Dt. 24:21; Lev. 19:10)[9] applied to grapes that had been missed during the harvest or left behind because they were not ripe. Depictions of grapes served to decorate the entrance to the most holy place,[10] synagogues, and coins.

II. Etymology. Terms relating to viticulture exhibit remarkable variations of meaning in the individual Semitic languages. Ugar. *gpn,* cognate to Heb. *gepen,* "vine,"[11] means "grapevine" and "vineyard"; an Arabic cognate to Heb. → כרם *kerem,* "vineyard," refers to its product, "wine"; OSA *w/yyn* means both "grape" and "vineyard."[12] The word *inbu(m),* "fruit," found already in Old Akkadian, is associated with human sexuality, referring to both "masculine potency" and "feminine attraction"; it also has the resultative meaning "child." Ishtar bears the epithet *bēlet inbi.* The meaning "grape" is unattested.[13] In the Mari texts the root occurs in proper names.[14]

Ugar. *ǵnb(m),* "grapes,"[15] appears in a prayer of Danel,[16] the Aqhat Epic, and a hymn in Shahar and Shalim.[17] In Old South Arabic inscriptions, we find *'nb,* "vineyards," paired with *'brt,* "meadows."[18] Arab. *'inab* means "grape."[19] The Phoenician PN *'nbtb'l* may suggest a role of grapes in the cult of Baal.[20]

In the Aramaic language family, *'nb* appears on an ostracon with the meaning "grapes"; in Egyptian Aramaic it probably means "harvest, fruit," as does Mand. *'nba,*

---

7. → III, 59-60.
8. → פאה *pē'â.*
9. → עלל *'ll.*
10. Mish. *Mid.* 3.8.
11. → III, 55-56.
12. Biella, 127, 131.
13. *AHw,* I, 381.
14. C. G. Rasmussen, 259-60; cf. *HAL,* II, 851; see also III.1 below.
15. *UT,* no. 1976; *WUS,* no. 2159.
16. *KTU* 1.19, I, 38-48.
17. *KTU* 1.23, 26.
18. Biella, 373.
19. Wehr, 647.
20. *CIS,* I, 5893, 4; Benz, 381: "unexplained."

"fruit, grapes, trees."[21] Jewish Aram. *ʿēnāḇ* or *ʿinbāʾ*, with the fem. form *ʿēnabtāʾ*, "grape,"[22] Sam. *ēnåb*, and Syr. *ʿenbᵉṯā* are closer to Hebrew usage; Jewish Aram. *ʿᵉnaḇtāʾ* means "berry, grain." Heb. *ʿēnāḇ* denotes the sweet, mature grape in contrast to the table grape *(ʾeškôl);* the plural refers collectively to "grapes" (albeit always sg. in the LXX). The noun *ʾeškôl* denotes the "clusters" borne by the grapevine (Cant. 7:9) and other plants (Cant. 1:14; 7:8). Nu. 13:23 combines the two terms: "a cluster of grapes."

III. OT.

1. *Occurrences.* The noun *ʿēnāḇ* appears 19 times in the Hebrew OT and twice in the Hebrew fragments of Sirach.

The grape symbolism in Nu. 13:17-24 paints Canaan as a rich agricultural land. As proof, the spies bring back pomegranates, figs, and from Wadi Eshkol, the "valley of grapes," a firstfruits cluster of grapes on a pole carried by two bearers.[23] Josh. 11:21 and 15:50 mention a village of the Anakim called *ʿᵃnāḇ* (LXX *Anabōth!*) (identified with Khirbet ʿAnab es-Seghira, near Rabud), suggesting "grapes" or "grain" (Jewish Aram. *ʿᵉnaḇtāʾ*). In a dream Pharaoh's cupbearer uses his hand to press juice out of grapes over Pharaoh's cup (Gen. 40:10-11). Hos. 3:1 mentions grapes in raisin cakes in connection with the syncretistic cult of the northern kingdom.

The use of grapes in the cult was regulated by specific ordinances. Lev. 25:5 (H) prohibits harvesting grapes from unpruned vines during the sabbatical year. The nazirite oath in Nu. 6:2-4 prohibits alcoholic beverages in general as well as all grape products, from the skins to the seeds. An ancient law (Dt. 23:25[24]) allows travelers to eat their fill of grapes in a vineyard. Neh. 13:15 chastises farmers around Jerusalem for treading winepresses and bringing produce to the city on the sabbath.

2. *Yahweh as Vintner.* Yahweh's testing of the conduct of the nations is presented under the image of a vintner inspecting his grapes. According to Dt. 32:32, the grapes of Israel's enemies are descended from the poisonous grapes on the vinestock of Sodom; CD 8:8 and 19:22 interpret this image allegorically as referring to the sinful way of the wicked. The Song of the Vineyard (Isa. 5) asserts that Yahweh expected sweet grapes but only shriveled grapes appeared. In a prophetical oracle of judgment (Jer. 8:13), Yahweh looks in vain for fruit from his grapevine/fig tree Israel; among the people of the wilderness generation, however, he found both kinds of fruit (Hos. 9:10). The postexilic (Deuteronomistic?) oracle of deliverance in Am. 9:13 promises paradisaical fertility: grain and grapes grow up and ripen in an instant.

3. *"Blood of Grapes."* The fixed syntagm *dam ʿᵃnāḇîm*, "blood of grapes," occurs three times (cf. 1 Mc. 6:34); it refers to red grape juice (like Ugar. *dm ʿṣm*, "grape

---

21. For the ostracon see Nisa 16.1; for Egyptian Aramaic, *AP,* 81:1; *DNSI,* II, 874.
22. *ANH,* 316-17.
23. See the accounts of large grapes from Hebron in Anderlind, 174.

juice"). Gen. 49:11, in the Blessing of Jacob, describes Judah or the messianic warrior king (David) as washing his garments in wine, his robe in the blood of grapes; he wallows in Judah's eschatological endowments. Dt. 32:14 lists the agricultural products of Canaan, including fermented grape juice, as signs of abundance. A hymn in Sir. 39:26 (ms. B) speaks of similar things as the elementary necessities of human life. Sir. 51:15(16) describes the poet's progress in wisdom as the progression from blossoms to ripe grapes (11QPs[a] XXII; ms. B has a different text).

IV. LXX; Dead Sea Scrolls. The LXX consistently uses the sg. *staphylḗ* (usually pl. in classical Greek) to translate Heb. *ʿēnāḇ;* only in Hos. 3:1 does it use the interpretive translation *staphís,* "raisin." The Heb. sg. *ʾeškôl* is represented by Gk. *bótrys,* "grape," the Heb. plural by the corresponding Gk. plural.

There is only one occurrence of *ʿnb* in the Dead Sea Scrolls (11QT 21:7), in the ritual of the vintage festival. The celebrating priests are to eschew unripe grapes *(ʿnb pr*[*y*] *b*[*w*]*sr)* from the vines *(gpnym).*

Angerstorfer

עָנַג *ʿānaḡ;* עֹנֶג *ʿōneḡ;* עָנֹג *ʿānōḡ;* תַּעֲנוּג *taʿanûḡ*

I. Etymology. II. Occurrences. III. Verb: 1. Pual; 2. Hithpael. IV. Nouns: 1. *ʿōneḡ;* 2. *ʿānōḡ;* 3. *taʿanûḡ.* V. LXX. VI. Dead Sea Scrolls.

I. Etymology. Biblical Heb. *ʿng* corresponds to Arab. *ǵnǧ:* the verb *ǵaniǧa* I and V means "adorn oneself, flirt" (II occasionally also "pamper, be ingratiating"); the nouns *ǵunǧ* and *uǵnūǧa* refer to the "sexually inviting demeanor" of a woman; a coquettish woman is called *ǵaniǧa, maǵnūǧa,* etc.[1] Cf. also Eth. *ʾaʿnūg* (pl.), "ring (for the ear or nose)," and the rare Tigrē word *ʿanig,* "beautiful" (fem. only).[2]

The functions of this root in Biblical Hebrew are continued in the Dead Sea Scrolls (see VI below), in Samaritan,[3] and in Middle Hebrew (verb: qal, "be soft, compliant"; piel, "make soft, delicate"; hithpael, "enjoy oneself"; nouns: *ʿōneḡ, ʿinnûḡ,* and *taʿanûḡ,* "pleasure, enjoyment, delight"); in Rabbinic Aramaic, the pael of the verb means "make the skin soft" (by anointing, bathing, etc.).[4]

II. Occurrences. The verb *ʿānaḡ* occurs 10 times in the OT: once in the pual, "be delicate" (Jer. 6:2), and 9 times in the hithpael, "take pleasure in," occasionally also "pamper," "make fun of" (4 times in Trito-Isaiah, twice each in Job and Psalms, once in

1. Lane, I/6, 2299c-2300a; Dozy, II, 228b.
2. For the former see *LexLingAeth,* 993; for the latter, *WbTigr,* 475a.
3. *LOT,* II, 556a.
4. Jastrow, 1092a.

Deuteronomy). The noun *ʿōneg*, "pleasure," occurs twice (Isa. 13:22; 58:13), *ʿānōg*, "delicate," 3 times (Dt. 28:54,56; Isa. 47:1), and *taʿᵃnûg*, "pleasure, delight," 5 times (sg. only in Prov. 19:10; pl.: Mic. 1:16; 2:9; Cant. 7:7; Eccl. 2:8).

III. Verb.

1. *Pual.* The theological significance of the only OT occurrence of the pual of *ʿānag* (Jer. 6:2) is hard to determine. The MT has Yahweh say (with reference to the foe from the north): "I shall destroy daughter Zion, beautiful and delicate" *(hannāwâ wᵉhammᵉʿuggānâ dāmîṯî baṯ-ṣîyôn).* The description of Zion as a pampered woman living a life of luxury is reinforced by Dt. 28:56 and Isa. 47:1 (daughter Babylon!). If, however, we accept the emendation *hᵃlinwēh maʿᵃnāg dāmᵉṯâ,* the text asks whether Zion "is like a lovely pasture"; cf. the statements about delighting in the prosperity of the land in Isa. 55:2 and Ps. 37:11.[5] But the noun *maʿᵃnāg* is otherwise unattested.

2. *Hithpael.* The 9 occurrences of *ʿānag* in the hithpael point in several directions. One text speaks of a "pampered" woman (Dt. 28:56; see IV.2 below); another presents the image of a child "nursing happily" from the consoling breast of Jerusalem (Isa. 66:11). The leaders of Israel are asked ironically whom they intend to "make fun of" (*ʿal-mî tiṯʿannāḡû,* Isa. 57:4).

In the remaining 6 occurrences, the hithpael has the meaning "delight oneself." Twice it is the land that is the source of delight: Ps. 37, a didactic psalm, asserts that the poor *(ʿᵃnāwîm)* shall inherit the land "and delight themselves in abundant prosperity" (v. 11); and Deutero-Isaiah says in an oracle of Yahweh: "If you listen to me, you will eat what is good and delight yourselves in rich food" (Isa. 55:2).

But delight in the prosperity of the land is linked indissolubly with delight in Yahweh. Those who delight in Yahweh receive from him the desires of their hearts (Ps. 37:4); those who observe Yahweh's sabbath will take delight in Yahweh and feast on the land (Isa. 58:14). Thus Eliphaz can declare in his third answer to Job that Job — if he returns to the Almighty *(šadday)* — will delight himself in *šadday* (Job 22:26); and Job, for his part, says that the wicked cannot possibly delight in *šadday* (27:10). Gordis believes that in Job 22:26 and similar passages (he lists Isa. 57:4; Ps. 37:4; Job 27:10) the hithpael of *ʿnq* has the meaning "request, desire."[6] This suggestion is noteworthy, but his reference to Arab. *naǧaʿa* VIII (metathesis) is not without its problems; neither is his appeal to Saadia's interpretation *(dalla),* for *dalla/yadillu* (like *ǵnǧ;* see I above) means "flirt" (I and V) and "pamper" (V), but never "request."

IV. Nouns.

1. *ʿōneg.* The noun *ʿōneg* occurs twice; it means "sensual pleasure." On the one hand, an oracle on the fate of Babylon describes in macabre terms how jackals now

---

5. Proposed by W. Rudolph, *Jeremia. HAT* I/12 (³1968), 42; cf. *BHS* and NRSV. See III.2 below.

6. R. Gordis, *Book of Job* (1978), 250-51.

take refuge "in the palaces of pleasure" (*behêkelê ʿōneg,* Isa. 13:22), i.e., "in the chambers in which one would have heard the echoes of the sounds of joyful pleasure at an earlier time."[7] On the other hand, perfect delight (both mental and physical) is the essence of Israel's proper observance of Yahweh's sabbath (Isa. 58:13).

2. *ʿānōg.* The word *ʿānōg,* which functions as an adjective, occurs only in Deutero-Isaiah (47:1) and the Deuteronomistic strata of Deuteronomy (28:54,56).[8] In a taunt song over Babylon, Deutero-Isaiah declares that daughter Babylon will no longer be called "tender and pampered" *(rakkâ waʿanuggâ).* In similar terms Deuteronomy 28 describes retrospectively the afflictions of the exile: in that accursed time, a man who was once "refined" *(rak)* and "pampered" *(ʿānōg)* is forced to eat his own son (v. 54); a woman was formerly so "refined" *(rakkâ)* and "pampered" *(ʿanuggâ)* that she would not have ventured to set the sole of her foot on the ground "out of pampering and refinement" (*mēhitʿannēg ûmērōk,*[9] v. 56).

3. *taʿanûg.* The only occurrence of the noun *taʿanûg* in the singular describes a life of ease and pleasure: "It is not fitting for a fool to live in luxury" (Prov. 19:10). Some scholars, including G. R. Driver and D. Winton Thomas, interpret *taʿanûg* here as "governance" or "supervision," after the analogy of the second hemistich,[10] but this interpretation is open to objections. The proposed meanings are not found elsewhere; indeed, the second hemistich appears to represent an intensification.[11]

Micah also speaks of sensual pleasure,[12] saying to daughter Zion: "The children of your delight" *(benê taʿanûgāyik)* must now go into exile (1:16); and the women of the people will be driven "from their pleasant houses" *(mibbêt taʿanûgeyhā)* by the new rulers (2:9).

Qohelet's description of his approach to life speaks even more clearly of la dolce vita: riches, wine, song, and "the delights of the sons of man" *(taʿanûgōt benê hāʾādām):* concubines without number (Eccl. 2:8).[13] The poem of admiration in Cant. 7:7-10a extols feminine beauty in similar terms: the subject is a "maiden of delight" *(bat taʿanûgîm).*[14]

V. LXX. The LXX generally uses *en/kata/tryphán* to translate the hithpael of *ʿānag, trypherós* to translate *ʿōneg* and *ʿānōg,* and *tryphḗ* to translate *taʿanûg.*

---

7. H. Wildberger, *Isaiah 13–27* (Eng. trans. 1997), 32.
8. H. D. Preuss, *Deuteronomium. EdF* 164 (1982), 59, 157.
9. → רכך *rākak.*
10. Driver, "Problems in the Hebrew Text of Job," *Wisdom in Israel and in the Ancient Near East. FS H. H. Rowley. SVT* 3 (1955), 84; D. Winton Thomas, *VT* 15 (1965) 271-79.
11. O. Plöger, *Sprüche Salomos. BK* XVII (1984), 222.
12. On the question of authorship see H. W. Wolff, *Micah* (Eng. trans. 1990), 64.
13. On *šiddâ* see H. W. Hertzberg, *Der Prediger. KAT* XVII/4-5 (1963), 80.
14. On the text see IX, 469.

VI. Dead Sea Scrolls. Interpreting Ps. 37:11, 4QpPs[a] (4Q171) 2:8-11 says: "Its interpretation refers to the community of the poor [i.e., all Jews; cf. 1QpHab 8:1; 12:4; 4QpNah (4Q169) 3:4], who have taken upon themselves the time of fasting, who will be delivered from all the snares of Belial; afterward they will delight in [. . .] of the land and will enjoy all the pleasure of the flesh *(whtdšnw bkwl tʿnwg bśr).*" In similar fashion, interpreting Ps. 37:21-22, 3:11 says that the community of the poor "will possess the holy mountain of Isra[el and] and delight [in] its sanctuary *(. . . [wb]qwdšw ytʿngw).*" Speaking of the daily prayers, 4Q503 24, 5:5 mentions the election of the people of God "for a festival of rest and delight" *(lmw[ʿd] mnwḥ wtʿnwg).* Two other occurrences of *taʿ[a]nûg* are uncertain (1QH[f] 22:3; 1QS[b] 4:2). It is possible that the latter text mentions "the deli[ghts of the sons of man]" (*tʿnwg*[*wt bny ʾdm*]), recalling Eccl. 2:8.

Kronholm

עָנָה *ʿānâ* I; מַעֲנֶה *maʿ[a]neh;* עִנְיָן *ʿinyān;* עֹנָה *ʿōnâ*

I. 1. Root; 2. LXX. II. OT: 1. Negotiations and Disputes; 2. Trials; 3. Prophecy; 4. Cult; 5. Miscellaneous; 6. Yahweh as Subject; 7. Niphal and Hiphil; 8. *ʿnh* III; 9. *ʿnh* IV. III. Derivatives: 1. *maʿ[a]neh;* 2. *maʿ[a]nâ;* 3. Proper Names; 4. *maʿ[a]neh,* "Purpose"; 5. *maʿan;* 6. *yaʿan;* 7. *ʿinyān;* 8. *ʿōnâ;* 9. *ʿēṯ.* IV. Deuterocanonical Books. V. Dead Sea Scrolls.

I. 1. *Root.* Lexicons commonly distinguish four homonymous roots *ʿnh.*[1] That this distinction is not unquestioned is noted by *HAL,*[2] with the comment that *ʿnh* IV, "sing," cannot always be differentiated clearly from *ʿnh* I, "answer." Mandelkern also combines *ʿnh* I and IV, and brings *ʿnh* III, "exert oneself," in part together with *ʿnh* I and *ʿnh* II, "be afflicted."[3] Birkeland traces *ʿnh* I and II to a common root.[4] Bammel follows Birkeland, with the unconvincing argument that *ʿānî* denotes the situation of answering as well as the willingness to answer, while the longer form denotes inferior status with

---

ʿānâ. C. Barth, "Die Antwort Israels," *Probleme biblischer Theologie. FS G. von Rad* (1971), 44-56; H. J. Boecker, *Redeformen des Rechtslebens im AT. WMANT* 14 (1964); F. Büchsel, "ἀποκρίνω," *TDNT,* III, 944-45; L. Delekat, "Zum hebräischen Wörterbuch," *VT* 14 (1964) 7-66, esp. 37-43; B. Glazier-McDonald, "*ʿēr wĕʿōnēh* — Another Look," *JBL* 105 (1986) 295-98; P. Joüon, "'Respondit et dixit,'" *Bibl* 13 (1932) 309-14; C. J. Labuschagne, "**ענה** *ʿnh* I to answer," *TLOT,* II, 926-30; B. O. Long, "Two Question and Answer Schemata in the Prophets," *JBL* 90 (1971) 129-39.

1. *GesB,* 603-5; *HAL,* II, 851-54; cf. Lisowsky, 1094-98.
2. P. 854.
3. *Concordantiae,* 899-904.
4. H. Birkeland, *ʿānî and ʿānāw in den Psalmen* (1933), 10-11.

respect to the person demanding an answer.[5] Kutsch has argued against this theory, maintaining that *'nh* III diverged from *'nh* II at a relatively late date, while *'nh* IV might have coincided originally with *'nh* I.[6]

Delekat argues that *'nh* IV is an independent root, whereas *'nh* III is an Aramaic loanword; its original meaning, "be concerned with, intend, mean, refer to," remained current in Hebrew, as evidenced by *l^ema'an,* "with respect to," and *ya'an,* "on account of." This meaning, he claims, is also present whenever *'nh* I appears in early texts without a preceding statement or question. In such contexts, *'nh* has an implied accusative of the subject and means "refer to what has just been mentioned." Only in late texts did *'nh* without a preceding statement or question come to be used in the sense of "commence." Therefore *'nh* I and III are identical. Citing Akk. *enûm,* "change the terms of an agreement," transitively "displace," and Egyp. *'n(n),* "turn back, turn toward, turn away," Delekat defines the original meaning of *'nh* as "turn."[7] Now it is the formal attribute of the forms assigned to *'nh* II not to have an implicit or explicit object, personal or impersonal. But probably the qal should be read only in Isa. 31:4 and 25:5 (although it is preferable to follow *BHS* in reading the latter as a niphal).[8] Especially in Isa. 31:4, the use of *'nh* I, "answer," in the sense of "be responsive, accommodating," is so appropriate that the hypothesis of a separate root appears unnecessary. Thus all the senses of *'nh* except for *'nh* IV can be assigned to a root with the basic meaning "turn."[9]

Delekat's contention appears plausible with respect to the relationship between *'nh* I and III. He can hardly claim success, however, in demonstrating the identity of *'nh* I and II, since his argument rests on extremely limited textual evidence and assumes a very restricted meaning of *'nh* in the sense of "be responsive." In the light of his passion for finding identity, it is surprising that he wants to consider *'nh* IV a distinct root.

Labuschagne points out that Arab. *ǵannā,* "sing," might support the existence of a separate root *'nh* IV.[10] But the absence of a corresponding root **ǵny* in Ugaritic, while Ugar. *'ny* (related to Heb. *'nh* I), "answer," may also mean "sing," may occasion second thoughts. The Ugaritic evidence suggests the identity of *'nh* I and IV.[11] We shall accordingly assume the identity of *'nh* I, III, and IV.

The root *'nh* I, "answer," appears in Ugaritic as *'ny.*[12] There we find several word pairs that illuminate the links between Ugaritic and Hebrew literature. Examples include *'ny* and *šm'*[13] (cf. Gen. 23:5-6; Isa. 65:12,24; Jon. 2:3; Job 35:12-13; Prov. 15:28-29), *'ny* and *ṯb*[14] (cf. *šwb* in Jgs. 5:29; Hos. 7:10; Hab. 2:1-2; Job 13:22; 20:2-3; 32:14-

5. E. Bammel, *TDNT,* VI, 888.
6. E. Kutsch, *ZTK* 61 (1964) 197.
7. Pp. 38-39.
8. See also H. Wildberger, *Isaiah 13–27* (Eng. trans. 1977), 516.
9. Delekat, 42-43.
10. *TLOT,* II, 926-27.
11. But see also J. Barr, *Comparative Philology and the Text of the OT* (1968), 127.
12. *UT,* no. 1883; *WUS,* no. 2060; D. Pardee, *UF* 7 (1975) 363; idem, *UF* 8 (1976) 261.
13. M. Dahood, *RSP,* I, 300, no. 437.
14. *RSP,* I, 300-301, no. 438.

15; 40:2,4; Prov. 15:1),[15] and *šm'* and *'ny*[16] (cf. Jer. 7:13,27; 35:17; Job 20:3; 31:35; Ps. 55:20[Eng. v. 19]; also possibly Gen. 16:11[17]).

In the texts from Deir 'Allā, we find *'nyh* (1:13); the same form occurs in Old Aramaic, Egyptian Aramaic, Palmyrene, Jewish Aramaic, Samaritan, Christian Palestinian, Syriac, and Mandaic.[18] Egyptian has *'n(n),* "turn (intransitive); turn toward, turn away from (transitive)"; Akk. has *enû(m),* "turn, change."[19]

The root *'nh* II, "exert oneself," is found in Hebrew only in Ecclesiastes. It appears in Syriac as *'ᵉnā',* "exert oneself for," pass. ptcp. *'ᵉnē',* "busy";[20] in Christian Palestinian, we find the ptcp. *'nyn,* "busy people, laboring people";[21] Arabic has *'anā,* "concern, disquiet, seriously engage"; and *'aniya,* "be concerned, be worried, take pains";[22] in Old South Arabic we find *'ny,* "take pains, struggle with."[23]

The root *'nh* IV, "sing," appears in Middle Hebrew as *'innûy,* in Jewish Aramaic as *'innûyā,* "lament," and in Syriac with the meaning "sing (antiphonally)" for the pael and "lead a song, sing" for the aphel; it has a similar meaning in the Deir 'Allā texts (1:10).[24] Its Arabic equivalent is *ġny* II, "sing."[25]

We must agree with Labuschagne that the original sense of *'nh* was "turn (one's face or eyes)."[26] This developed into a basic meaning "react, respond," the basis for *'nh* I and II (and probably also IV) and their derivatives.

2. *LXX.* The LXX uses *apokrínomai* to translate *'ānâ.* The combination of *apokrínesthai* with *légein, eipeín,* etc., represents a genuine Semitism. In three texts *'ānâ* is translated with *antapokrínomai.*[27]

II. OT.

1. *Negotiations and Disputes.* The root *'nh* I occurs 316 times in the OT. The Aramaic verb appears 30 times in Daniel, always in combination with → אמר *'āmar.* In Hebrew, *'ānâ* + *'āmar* appears 142 times; in some 100 of these occurrences, it is a discourse formula in dialogue. There are 6 occurrences of the combination *'ānâ* + *dibber* (Gen. 34:13; Josh. 22:21; 1 K. 12:7; 2 K. 1:10,11,12).[28] This evidence shows that *'ānâ*

15. See also Y. Avishur, *Stylistic Studies of Word-Pairs in Biblical and Ancient Semitic Literatures. AOAT* 210 (1984), 396, 664.
16. Dahood, *RSP,* I, 363, no. 570.
17. If we accept the reading of M. Dahood, *Bibl* 49 (1968) 87-88.
18. On Deir 'Allā see *ATDA,* 212; on Palmyrene, *DNSI,* II, 875-76; on Mandaic, *MdD,* 24a.
19. See *WbÄS,* I, 188-89; *AHw,* I, 220-21; *CAD,* IV, 173-77.
20. *LexSyr,* 534a.
21. Schulthess, *Lex. Syropal.* (1903), 149b.
22. Wehr, 650.
23. Conti Rossini, 210a; Müller, 81; cf. Biella, 374: "sense doubtful."
24. *ATDA,* 202.
25. On the whole subject of etymology see *HAL,* II, 851-54; on Ugaritic, see J. C. de Moor, *The Seasonal Pattern in the Ugaritic Myth of Ba'lu. AOAT* 16 (1971), 93.
26. *TLOT,* II, 927.
27. Büchsel, 946-47.
28. *TLOT,* II, 928.

in the sense of "react" needs additional qualification when the reaction is verbal. When the combination of *'ānâ* with *'āmar* or *dibber* was understood as a hendiadys, *'ānâ* could also be used without more precise qualification. In many instances *'āmar* appears by itself in dialogue.[29]

The basic meaning "react, respond" points in the first instance to the realm of negotiations and disputes, e.g., Gen. 18:27; 23:5,10,14; Ex. 4:1; Nu. 11:28; Dt. 1:14,41; Josh. 1:16; Jgs. 8:8; 1 S. 1:15; Isa. 14:32; Am. 7:14; Mic. 6:5; Ps. 119:42; Job 3:2; 4:1; 6:1; 8:1; 9:1; 32:1,6,12,15,16,20; 1 Ch. 12:18; 2 Ch. 10:13. It is noteworthy that in all cases the language appears elevated. The combination of *'ānâ* and *'āmar* in particular, which should translated "he responded and said, he responded by saying," suggests a stereotyped dialogue formula. In most cases the context is also out of the ordinary.

In Job 20:3 Zophar's *rûaḥ* is the subject of *'ānâ:* "A spirit from my understanding makes me answer";[30] also possible is the translation "answers me" (NRSV). In Prov. 15:28 the subject is the heart of the *ṣaddîq.*[31] From such texts it is no long distance to Prov. 1:28, where Lady Wisdom appears as the subject of *'ānâ.*[32]

Prov. 26:4-5 merits special mention: "Do not answer a fool according to his folly, lest you become like him. Answer a fool according to his folly, lest he become wise in his own eyes." These seemingly contradictory maxims are probably meant as advice for different situations: silence is advisable for the wise who cannot reach an understanding with a fool on the fool's own terms, correction when the fool claims equal status with the wise.[33]

In Gen. 30:33 the subject of *'ānâ* is *ṣeḏāqâ.* In his dispute with Laban over his wages as a shepherd, Jacob appeals to his "cooperativeness"[34] (NRSV "honesty"), which will speak for him like an advocate in a dispute.

In Gen. 34:13 *'ānâ* is done deceitfully *(bᵉmirmâ),* thus serving as a means of deception in negotiations.

Ex. 19:8 states that the people "as one" *(yaḥdāw)* responded positively to the words of Yahweh set forth by Moses (cf. Ex. 24:3, *qôl 'eḥāḏ*). In the context of legislation governing war, Dt. 20:11 contains the statement that a city under attack "answers peace" *(šālôm ta'ᵃneh)*[35] during capitulation negotiations, after terms of peace have been offered (v. 10). Here *šālôm 'ānâ* means submission to the demand for capitulation that promotes the *šālôm* of Israel, the *pax israelitica.*[36]

Satan is the subject of *'ānâ* in the context of a dispute within the assembly of

---

29. Long; Labuschagne, *TLOT,* II, 929.
30. G. Fohrer, *Das Buch Hiob. KAT* XVI (1963), 325.
31. See *BHS.*
32. See B. Lang, *Frau Weisheit* (1975), 46-47.
33. O. Plöger, *Sprüche Salomos. BK* XVII (1984), 310.
34. K. Koch, *ZEE* 5 (1961) 72-90.
35. Delekat, 38: "If the city . . . responds to you peacefully."
36. H. H. Schmid, *Šālôm, "Frieden," im alten Orient und Alten Testament. SBS* 51 (1971), 60.

Yahweh's court (Job 1:7,9; 2:2,4).[37] In Job 5:1 a heavenly being is probably the subject.[38]

2. *Trials.* The specialized use of *ʿānâ* as a technical term of forensic language probably derives from its use in the context of negotiations and disputes, for the verbal response expressed by *ʿānâ* can be evoked by an experience, a perception, or an event.[39]

In Ex. 23:2 *ʿānâ* refers to statements of a witness, as it does in the Decalogue (Ex. 20:16; Dt. 5:20).[40] The difference in formulation should be noted. While Ex. 23:2 uses *ʿānâ* with *ʿal-rîḇ* (which Noth translates "against a legal adversary," whereas I would prefer "in a lawsuit"),[41] Ex. 20:16 and Dt. 5:20 use it with *bᵉrēʿᵃḵā,* "against your neighbor."[42] The Decalogue texts also use different words to qualify *ʿēḏ:* Ex. 20:16 speaks of *ʿēḏ šāqer,* a "lying witness"; Dt. 5:20 speaks of *ʿēḏ šāwʾ,* a "worthless witness." By using this divergent formulation, Dt. 5:20 echoes Dt. 5:11 (= Ex. 20:7), thus including the oath frequently associated with statements of a witness.[43]

Nu. 35:30 prohibits executing a murderer on the evidence of a single witness. Dt. 19:16-19 requires that a witness who accuses someone of a breach of the peace and is found to be lying shall suffer the fate intended for the accused.

We also find *ʿānâ* used as a technical term in Dt. 21:7; 25:9; 31:21 (subj.: *šîrâ,* "song");[44] Josh. 7:20 (confession of guilt by the accused); Jgs. 20:4; 1 S. 12:3; 14:39 (in the sense of "denounce"); 2 S. 1:16 (subj.: *peh,* "mouth"); 1 K. 3:27 (judge's decision); Isa. 3:9 (subj.: *hakkāraṯ pᵉnêhem*); 59:12 (subj.: *ḥaṭṭāʾṯēnû*);[45] Jer. 14:7 (subj.: *ʿᵃwōnênû*); Hos. 5:5 (*ʿānâ bᵉ* denotes the incriminating evidence of a witness confronting the guilty party; Israel's pride is the final witness for the prosecution);[46] 7:10 (a gloss based on 5:5a); Mic. 6:3 (because of the forensic context, the translation should reflect the concrete juridical meaning: "testify against me");[47] Hab. 2:11 (subj.: *kāp̄îs mēʿēṣ,* "rafters from the timberwork"; since *zāʿaq/ṣāʿaq* is not a term of formal forensic language[48] but rather denotes an appeal of a victim without resources for legal protection, *ʿānâ* in parallel must mean "join in the hue and cry"; the walls and timberwork of the palaces cry to Yahweh for help, because no one comes forward to function as plain-

---

37. See F. J. Stendebach, *BiKi* 30 (1975) 2-7.
38. Fohrer, *KAT* XVI, 146.
39. *TLOT,* II, 929-30.
40. See M. Noth, *Exodus. OTL* (Eng. trans. 1962), 188-89; H. J. Stoebe, *WuD* 3 (1952) 108-26.
41. *Exodus. ATD* 5 (²1961), 138 (not in Eng. trans.); cf. Zorell, *LexHebAram* (²1962), 770; NRSV.
42. Boecker, 103.
43. H. Schüngel-Straumann, *Der Dekalog-Gottes Gebote? SBS* 67 (²1980), 66; for a different interpretation see F.-L. Hossfeld, *Der Dekalog. OBO* 45 (1982), 78; → עוד *ʿwd* II.1.b.
44. → עוד *ʿwd.*
45. See *BHS.*
46. H. W. Wolff, *Hosea. Herm* (Eng. trans. 1974), 100.
47. Boecker, 103.
48. → IV, 115ff.

tiff before the court[49]); Mal. 2:12 (*'ōneh* = "advocate," contra Hartmann,[50] who interprets *'ōneh* as the piel ptcp. of *'nh* II, synonymous with *m^e'anneh,* "oppressor"); Job 9:3,14,15,32; 13:22; 14:15; 40:2-3,5; 42:1 (*'ānâ* as the response of a legal adversary); 15:6 (subj.: Job's lips); 16:8 (subj.: Job's *kaḥaš,* "leanness"[51]).

Wisdom literature also warns against giving false witness. Prov. 25:18 compares the *'ōneh 'ēḏ šāqer* to a war club, a sword, and an arrow.

In Isa. 50:2 Yahweh asks: "Why was no one there when I came? Why did no one answer (*'ên 'ôneh)* when I called?" The oracle in 50:1-3 stands in a group of judgment discourses in which Yahweh and Israel confront each other, with Yahweh as the accused. V. 2a reflects the silence of the accuser. It is significant to observe in this context that when a person is the subject of *'ānâ,* it is not that person but Yahweh who "calls" *(qārā'),* taking the initiative (cf. also Isa. 65:12; Jer. 7:13; 35:17; Job 14:15; Mic. 6:3). Here the human response is preceded by a challenge spoken by Yahweh.

Here I also note the two occurrences of *'ānâ* in the sense of "bear witness on behalf of" in the ostraca from Yavneh-yam.[52]

3. *Prophecy.* In Gen. 40:18 and 41:16, *'ānâ* appears in the context of dream interpretation (cf. Jgs. 7:14). Thus it can also introduce a prophet's words (as in 2 K. 1:10,12). In Jer. 11:5 it introduces the prophet's answer to a word from Yahweh; and in Hag. 2:14 it introduces a prophetic adaptation of a priestly *tôrâ.*

Isa. 65:12 suggests a prophetic context: "I called, but you did not answer." Here the verbal transaction between Yahweh and Israel, mediated by a prophet, is understood as a dialogue, albeit a dialogue in which Israel refuses to participate. Westermann finds here a similarity to Deuteronomistic language, but there is no evidence for this theory (cf. also Isa. 66:4; Jer. 7:13,27; 35:17; the Jeremiah texts belong to stratum D; there are no parallels in Deuteronomic or Deuteronomistic literature).[53]

This brings us to Hos. 2:17(15), where the basic meaning "respond" suggests the translation "follow willingly." The construction is pregnant: the meaning of the passage requires that a verb of motion be supplied.[54] The object of Yahweh's wooing — Israel — does what the appeal expects: she is once again ready for a marital relationship.[55]

With reference to Isa. 65:12 and Hos. 2:17(15), we can make the fundamental observation that communication is realized in Israel's response to Yahweh's appeal, me-

---

49. J. Jeremias, *Kultprophetie und Gerichtsverkündigung in der späten Königszeit Israel. WMANT* 35 (1970), 72.

50. B. Hartmann, *Hebräische Wortforschung. FS W. Baumgartner. SVT* 16 (1967), 104-5.

51. G. Fohrer, *KAT* XVI, 280.

52. *KAI* 200.10-11.

53. Westermann, *Isaiah 40–66. OTL* (Eng. trans. 1969), 405. See W. Thiel, *Die deuteronomistische Redaktion von Jeremia 1–25. WMANT* 41 (1973), 113.

54. *GK,* §119ee-gg.

55. Wolff, *Hosea,* 31, 43; Labuschagne (928) understands *'ānâ* as referring to the "willing response" of the bride in the sexual sense.

diated by a prophet. By contrast, silence means a deliberate termination of the personal relationship.[56]

In Zechariah *'ānâ* occurs more frequently, albeit only in the vision cycle (1:10, 11,12; 4:4,5,6,11,12; 6:4,5) and the vision (not a part of this cycle) of the investiture of Joshua (3:4). In these passages, however, *'ānâ* does not perform an authentically prophetic function; it is occasioned by the dialogic style of the visions.

In this context one may note the occurrence of two question-answer schemata. The first appears in such passages as Jer. 22:8-9; Dt. 29:23-27(24-28); 1 K. 9:8-9 and comprises the following elements: (1) identification of the interrogator; (2) citation of the question; (3) citation of the answer. This schema derives from Assyrian treaties and historiography. The answer is introduced not by *'ānâ* but by *'āmar.* The second schema appears in Jer. 5:19; 13:12-14; 15:1-4; 16:10-13; 23:33; Ezk. 21:12; 37:18-19 and is always found in words spoken by Yahweh to a prophet. The answer is introduced by *'āmar* or *dibber.* The setting is a situation in which a prophet responds to a question about divine messages.[57] The observation that *'ānâ* does not appear in either schema shows that *'ānâ* is not rooted inherently in a prophetic context.

Malamat notes the term *āpilum/aplûm,* "the one who answers," in the Mari texts and connects it with 1 S. 7:9; 9:17; 28:6,15; 1 K. 18:26,37; Jer. 23:33-40; 33:3; Mic. 3:7; Hab. 2:2.[58] There is a crucial difference, however: in the OT texts it is not a prophet but Yahweh who is the subject of *'ānāh.* The same is true in another text, where Be'elšamayn is the subject making the answer, albeit through the agency of seers and soothsayers, and in the Edomite name *qws'nl* on a 7th-century seal from Ezion-geber: *qws 'ānā lî,* "[The deity] Qaus answered me."[59] The "answering" of a prophet is attested in Mic. 6:5. Mal. 2:12 is obscure and is better left out of the discussion.

4. *Cult.* The verb *'ānâ* appears to be rooted more firmly in cultic contexts. The "short confession of faith" in Dt. 26:5-9 is introduced by *w^e'ānîṯā* (+ *'mr*). In Dt. 27:14 the declaration of the curse by the Levites is introduced by *w^e'ānû* (+ *'mr*), as is the response of the people in v. 15. Since neither Dt. 26:5 nor 27:14 is preceded by any words requiring an answer, in these texts *'ānâ* is best translated "speak up," i.e., respond verbally in a particular (cultic) situation (cf. also Ezr. 10:2; 2 Ch. 29:31; 34:15).[60] In 1 S. 1:17 *'ānâ* introduces a priestly oracle of favor; in 1 S. 21:5-6 it occurs in the context of a priestly *tôrâ,* giving David's response.

A cultic context is suggested also by 1 K. 18:21, which states that the people did not respond to Elijah's question demanding a decision for either Yahweh or Baal (*lō'-'ānû;* cf. 1 K. 18:24; Jer. 44:15,20; Ezr. 10:12; Neh. 8:6). A priestly *tôrâ* is the

---

56. → I, 331-32.

57. Long.

58. A. Malamat, *Volume du Congrès, Genève 1965. SVT* 15 (1966), 211-13. See *AHw,* I, 58; *CAD,* I/2, 170.

59. For the former see *KAI* 202.11-12 = *ANET*², 501; for the latter, N. Glueck, *BASOR* 73 (1938) 13 n. 45.

60. See Joüon.

subject of Hag. 2:12-13; in each case, the answer of the priests is introduced by *ʿānâ* (see 6 below).

With respect to Dt. 27:15; 1 K. 18:21; Ezr. 10:12; Neh. 8:6, as well as Ex. 19:8; 24:3; Nu. 32:31; Josh. 1:16; 24:16 (see II.1 below), Barth observes that in each case *ʿānâ* has the meaning of a real, dialogic answer, that it always refers directly to a preceding question addressed to Israel from a particular side and evoking the answer.[61] In dialogue between Yahweh and Israel, "the figure of a human leader regularly appears as a mediator"; except in Ex. 19:8, the mediation is always "from above to below."[62] Israel's answer always involves a "declaration of readiness." "As the site of such declarations, . . . a liturgical act is identifiable in every text."[63] All the passages derive from Deuteronomic/Deuteronomistic theology or exhibit its influence. "Talk of 'Israel's answer' appears in a particular stratum of the tradition, and is therefore to be interpreted from the perspective of the historical and theological postulates of that stratum."[64]

5. *Miscellaneous.* Apart from the contexts just examined, it remains true that *ʿānâ* appears without exception in elevated language or exalted contexts (Jgs. 5:29; 1 S. 9:8,12,19; Prov. 18:23; Ruth 2:6,11; Cant. 2:10).

We find *ʿānâ* in military contexts in Jgs. 18:14; 1 S. 4:17; 14:21,28; 26:6,14; 30:22; 2 S. 15:21; 20:20; 2 K. 1:11; Isa. 21:9. It appears in the milieu of the court in 1 S. 16:18; 20:10,28,32; 22:9,14; 26:22; 29:9; 2 S. 4:9; 13:32; 14:18-19; 19:22(21); 1 K. 1:28,36,43; 13:6; 2 K. 3:11; 7:2,13,19; Isa. 14:10 (in the netherworld); Est. 5:7; 7:3.

In 2 K. 4:29 *ʿānâ* appears in a command not to return a greeting: Elisha orders his servant not to answer a greeting while he is on his way — probably so as not to lose time.

Jgs. 19:28 says of a dead woman: *ʾên ʿōneh,* probably best translated "she did not respond" (cf. 1 S. 4:20). Lack of response is also described in Job 19:16 and Cant. 5:6. Gen. 45:3 says that Joseph's brothers could not respond when he revealed his identity to them.

In Eccl. 10:19 money *(kesep)* is the subject of *ʿānâ,* which probably here means "provide for, pay for" (cf. Akk. *apālu*).[65] Labuschagne, however, interprets *yaʿᵃneh* as a hiphil and translates: "Money lets everyone react willingly."[66]

6. *Yahweh as Subject.* In many passages where Yahweh is the subject of *ʿānāh,* the response is nonverbal; Labuschagne appears to give too much weight to this observation when he includes Gen. 41:16 in this category (cf. Dt. 20:11; 1 S. 20:10; 1 K. 12:13; 2 Ch. 10:13).[67]

61. Barth, 48-49.
62. Barth, 50-51.
63. Barth, 53.
64. Barth, 55.
65. See O. Loretz, *Qohelet und der Alte Orient* (1964), 266 n. 228; *AHw,* I, 56.
66. *TLOT,* II, 927. See also R. B. Salters, *ZAW* 89 (1977) 425.
67. *TLOT,* II, 929.

Gen. 35:3 (E) applies the epithet *ʿōneh* to the El of Bethel. In the context of dream interpretation, Gen. 41:16 (E) says that Elohim, not Joseph, will give the answer.[68] In Ex. 19:19 (E), Elohim answers Moses in thunder *(b^e^qôl);* presumably this description reflects oracular practice.[69] In 1 S. 7:9 Samuel cries out to Yahweh, who answers him, i.e., grants his request (cf. 1 S. 8:18; 22:12). We find *ʿānâ* used as a technical term in oracular practice in 1 S. 14:37; 23:4; 28:6,15; 2 S. 22:36; cf. 1 S. 9:17. The focus of 1 K. 18:24ff. is the question which deity — Yahweh or Baal — will respond with fire to sacrifice and prayer (vv. 24,26,29,37; cf. 1 Ch. 21:26,28).

It would probably not be wrong to see oracular practice at the root of all the passages in which God is the subject of *ʿānâ,* even though the oracular background is often faint (Isa. 30:19; 41:17; 49:8; 58:9; 65:24; Jer. 23:35,37; 33:3; 42:4; Hos. 14:9[8] [here the LXX reads *ʿnh* II];[70] Joel 2:19; Mic. 3:4; Hab. 2:2; Zec. 1:13; 10:6;[71] 13:9). Hos. 2:23-24(21-22) deserves special note: "It will come to pass on that day that I will answer[72] — oracle of Yahweh — I will answer the heavens, and they shall answer the earth; and the earth shall answer the grain, the wine, and the oil, and they shall answer Jezreel." The presupposed prayer of Jezreel is not heard directly by Yahweh; it is transmitted through a chain of intermediaries. The sequence exhibits the influence of didactic motifs from the wisdom tradition of natural history.[73] The form of the chain locution may go back to ancient magical formulas, but the magical element is transcended in Hosea by the emphasis on Yahweh as the ultimate source of all fertility.

Jacob, however, sees behind the repeated use of *ʿānâ* in Hos. 2:23-24(21-22) a scarcely veiled reference to the goddess ʿAnat.[74] The people of Elephantine, he claims, concluded from this passage that ʿAnat and Yahweh were a divine dyad. Guillaume interprets *ʿnh* in Hos. 2:23-24(21-22) not as "answer" but — on the basis of Arabic — as "flow," hiphil "cause to flow, make fruitful, produce."[75]

We find *ʿānâ* with Yahweh as subject most often in the Psalms, especially prayers of an individual and their corresponding thanksgivings. These hymns reveal a cultic divine tribunal, in the context of which *ʿānâ* denotes the oracle that vouchsafes the psalmist vindication and deliverance.[76] Specific instances are: Ps. 3:5(4); 4:2(1); 13:4(3); 17:6; 18:42(41); 20:2,7,10(1,6,9); 22:3,22(2,21) (retaining the MT;[77] the present/future translation of Fuchs must be rejected, along with his denial that the institu-

---

68. See *BHS.*

69. H. Schmid, *Mose: Überlieferung und Geschichte. BZAW* 110 (1968), 58.

70. Wolff, *Hosea,* 233.

71. See *BHS.*

72. See *BHS.*

73. Wolff, *Hosea,* 53-54.

74. E. Jacob, *UF* 11 (1979) 404.

75. A. Guillaume, *JTS* 15 (1964) 57.

76. J. Begrich, *GSAT,* ed. W. Zimmerli. *ThB* 21 (1964), 217-31; W. Beyerlin, *Die Rettung der Bedrängten in den Feindpsalmen. FRLANT* 99 (1970), 140-42; H. Madl, "Die Gottesbefragung mit dem Verb *šāʾal,*" *Bausteine biblischer Theologie. FS G. Botterweck. BBB* 50 (1977), 37-70.

77. H.-J. Kraus, *Psalms 1–59* (Eng. trans. 1988), 292; R. Kilian, *BZ* 12 (1968), 173.

tion of the oracle of salvation existed);[78] 27:7; 34:5(4); 38:16(15); 55:3(2) (the text of v. 20[19] is corrupt; *ya'anēm* must be emended);[79] 60:7(5);[80] 65:6(5); 69:14,17, 18(13,16,17); 81:8(7); 86:1,7; 91:15; 99:6,8; 102:3(2); 108:7(6) (cf. 60:7[5]); 118:5,21;[81] 119:26,145; 120:1; 138:3; 143:1,7; cf. Jon. 2:3; Job 12:4; 30:20; 35:12.

In God's response when his worshipers call (→ קרא *qārā'*), cry out (→ זעק *zā'aq*), and make inquiry (→ דרש *dāraš;* שׁאל *šā'al*), we see revealed the profoundly dialogical nature of the relationship between God and human beings in the OT;[82] Yahweh intervenes on behalf of his worshipers, helping and delivering them. Metaphorically, *'ānâ* belongs to the semantic domain of *yš'*.[83] This conclusion is supported by the use of *yš'* in parallel with *'nh* in 2 S. 22:42 = Ps. 18:42(41); Isa. 46:7; Ps. 20:10(9); 22:22(21); 60:7(5) = 108:7(6).

When Kraus argues against the "dialogical principle" on account of its potential for misunderstanding, as though God and human beings faced each other on the same plane as equal partners and a "dialogical principle" could plumb the mystery of their correspondence,[84] he is being overly cautious. Even from the depths (Ps. 130:1) and from great distance (Ps. 8:5[4]), genuine dialogue with God is possible.

Prayers from Mesopotamia likewise anticipate the deity's answer in the form of an "oracle of salvation": "At your exalted command, which is immutable, upon your sure affirmation, which cannot be abrogated, may I your servant live and regain my health."[85]

Job 9:16 brings us to the realm of the lawsuit between a human being and God.[86] Here too it holds true that in its forensic usage *'ānâ* denotes "all the legal evidence advanced by the parties . . . to the suit, their testimony, objections, rejoinders, and denials."[87] Fohrer actually translates *qārā'* as "summon" and *'ānâ* as "take the stand";[88] cf. Job 23:5; 31:35;[89] 33:13; 38:1; 40:1,6 (both verses are glosses that should be deleted).[90] This forensic transaction, too, makes sense only against the background of the dialogical relationship between Job and Yahweh (cf. also Ruth 1:21).

In most cases where Yahweh appears as the subject of *'ānâ,* God "responds" to human initiative. Only six texts speak of Yahweh himself as taking the initiative.

---

78. O. Fuchs, *Die Klage als Gebet* (1982), 110, 178-83, 319-20.
79. F. Delitzsch, *Psalms. KD* (Eng. trans., repr. 1954), II, 162-63; Kraus, *Psalms 1–59,* 519.
80. See *BHS.*
81. E. Kutsch, *ZTK* 61 (1964) 197.
82. F. J. Stendebach, "Theologische Anthropologie des Jahwisten" (diss., Bonn, 1970), 339-41.
83. → VI, 445-46.
84. *Theology of the Psalms* (Eng. trans. 1986), 11-12.
85. *SAHG,* 347.
86. See *BHS.*
87. F. Horst, *Hiob. BK* XVI/1 (1968), 148; citing the language of prayer in the Psalms, Horst nevertheless expresses uncertainty whether in Job 9:16 *qārā'* and *'ānâ* are still in the forensic domain.
88. G. Fohrer, *KAT* XVI, 195, 199, 207-8.
89. Ibid., 443.
90. Ibid., 494.

7. *Niphal and Hiphil.* The total absence of the qal of *'ānâ* from Ezekiel is striking. Instead we find the niphal used twice in the reflexive sense of "condescend to answer," with Yahweh as subject (Ezk. 14:4,7; according to Zimmerli, v. 4 should be emended to *na'ᵃnîṯî lô ḇî* on the basis of v. 7).[91] In v. 7bβ Yahweh declares: "I, Yahweh, will find it within myself to answer him." The niphal probably suggests a conscious independence on the part of Ezekiel's language, expressing the notion of an almost passive "letting oneself be pressed to answer."

The niphal appears also in Job 11:2 (dispute) and 19:7 (lawsuit), as well as Prov. 21:13, in the sense of "receive an answer." The hiphil occurs in Job 32:17[92] and Prov. 29:19 with the meaning "acquiesce."

The Aramaic occurrences of *'nh* in the peal contribute nothing new to the picture so far drawn (Dnl. 2:5;[93] 2:7,8,10,15,20,26,27,47; 3:9,14,16,19,24,25,26,28; 4:16,27[19, 30]; 5:7,10,13,17; 6:13,14,17,21[12,13,16,20]; 7:2[94]).

8. *'nh III.* The only occurrences of *'nh* III, "exert oneself," are in Eccl. 1:13 and 3:10. Both passages refer to the "business" (*'inyān;* see below) God has given human beings to labor at — an expression of the skeptical realism typical of Qohelet.[95]

Eccl. 5:19(20) uses the hiphil with God as subject:[96] the true gift of God is that one need not brood so much over the days of one's life, because God keeps one occupied with the joy of one's heart. "When one is happy, the thought of death — which is what Qohelet is trying to remind his readers of — retreats into the background and becomes rare."[97]

9. *'nh IV.* Ex. 15:21 uses *'nh* for Miriam's response to Israel's deliverance at the sea; in this context it means "sing" (*'nh* IV). Here we see that the first human reaction to an act of God is a hymn, which follows immediately in classic form. In such "victory hymns," one of the women began the singing to greet the returning warriors; the hymn was then taken up and repeated by the chorus of other women (1 S. 18:7; 21:12[11]; 29:5).

The qal of *'nh* IV occurs also in Nu. 21:17; Isa. 13:22 (subj.: *'îyîm,* "jackals"; Jenni derives the verb from *'wn,* "dwell"[98]); Jer. 25:30 (subj.: Yahweh); 51:14; Ps. 119:172; 147:7; Ezr. 3:11.

Ex. 32:18 is difficult. The inf. of *'nh* occurs three times, twice in the qal and once in the piel: "It is not the sound of victory songs (*'ᵃnôṯ gᵉḇûrâ*) and not the sound of

---

91. W. Zimmerli, *Ezekiel 1. Herm* (Eng. trans. 1983), 300-301.
92. But see *BHS;* Fohrer, *KAT* XVI, 449.
93. See *BHS.*
94. See *BHS.*
95. F. J. Stendebach, *Glaube bringt Freude* (1983), 88-109.
96. See *BHS.*
97. N. Lohfink, *Kohelet. NEB* (1980), 46.
98. *HP,* 291; cf. *GesB,* 572; see the reservations of Barr, *Comparative Philology,* 243, 250; see also I. Eitan, *HUCA* 12/13 (1937/38) 61.

defeat songs (*ʿ^a^nôṯ ḥ^a^lûšâ*), but the sound of singing (*ʿannôṯ*) that I hear." It is likely that something has dropped out of the third stich.[99] There is no foundation for the proposal to read *tannôṯ* (piel of *tnh,* "extol") instead of *ʿannôṯ.*[100] The root *ʿnh* IV is identical with *ʿnh* I and emphasizes the antiphonal or responsive character of singing; the piel might denote a special mode of performance, in which a song was sung responsively to accompany a round dance (Ex. 32:19).[101] Instead of *ʿannôṯ,* Edelmann proposes reading *ʿ^a^nāṯ,* the name of the Canaanite goddess who with all that she represents is contrasted with whatever might have sounded like the noise of a victory or defeat; this theory is out of the question.[102] Mittmann proposes identifying the word omitted after *ʿannôṯ* in v. 18 with the *m^e^ḥōlôṯ* ("round dances") of v. 19.[103]

The piel is also found in Isa. 27:2 and Ps. 88:1(superscription).[104] Seybold reads instead the piel of *ʿnh* II: "for humiliation."[105] Glueck sees the word as a technical musical term referring to "responsive, antiphonal performance."[106]

III. Derivatives.

1. *maʿ^a^neh.* The noun *maʿ^a^neh,* "answer,"[107] is also found in Middle Hebrew. Ugaritic has *mʿn;*[108] Akk. *maʾna* is uncertain.[109] The noun's OT occurrences are limited almost exclusively to wisdom literature. Prov. 15:1 states that a soft answer turns away wrath.[110] Prov. 15:23 says that there is joy in making an apt answer. "The answer that averts wrath [as in v. 1] also fills the one who makes it with joy."[111] Prov. 16:1 teaches: "The plans of the heart belong to mortals, but the answer of the tongue is from Yahweh." Finding the words that best express plans is "looked upon as a talent not possessed by everyone, which must therefore be the gift of Yahweh."[112]

Job 32:3 and 5 say that Job's friends could no longer find an answer to his words.

---

99. Noth, *Exodus. OTL,* 249.

100. J. Morgenstern, *HUCA* 19 (1945/46) 492; *KBL*², 1034.

101. J. M. Sasson, "The Worship of the Golden Calf," *Orient and Occident. FS C. H. Gordon. AOAT* 22 (1973), 157; for a different view, see W. F. Albright, *Yahweh and the Gods of Canaan* (1968), 19 n. 53.

102. Contra R. Edelmann, *VT* 16 (1966) 355, see R. N. Whybray, *VT* 17 (1967), 122, 243; for a different view see F. I. Andersen, *VT* 16 (1966) 108-12.

103. S. Mittmann, *BN* 13 (1980) 43.

104. See *HP,* 219-20; Sasson, *AOAT* 22 (1973), 157; Kraus, *Psalms 60–150* (Eng. trans. 1989), 190.

105. K. Seybold, *Das Gebet des Kranken im Alten Testament. BWANT* 99 (1973), 113-14, citing E. A. Leslie, *The Psalms Translated and Interpreted in the Light of Hebrew Life and Worship* (1949), 397.

106. I. J. Glueck, *OTWSA* 6 (1963) 35-36.

107. *BLe,* 491n.

108. *UT,* no. 1883.

109. Cf. *AHw,* II, 601; *HAL,* II, 614-15.

110. W. Bühlmann, *Vom rechten Reden und Schweigen. OBO* 12 (1976), 75ff.

111. Plöger, *BK* XVII, 183; cf. Bühlmann, 261ff.

112. Plöger, *BK* XVII, 189; cf. Bühlmann, 322ff.

Mic. 3:7 speaks of God's answer, which is not imparted to the seers and diviners. This text obviously reflects oracular practice.[113]

Barth points out that — in contrast to OT usage — *m'n* is used in Ugaritic to denote a liturgical response.[114]

2. *ma'ᵃnâ.* The noun *ma'ᵃnâ* means "plow path."[115] The word may appear in Ugaritic as *'nt,* "furrow."[116] It refers to the path at the end of which a plow is turned and occurs only twice in the OT: 1 S. 14:14 and Ps. 129:3.[117]

3. *Proper Names.* The root *'nh* serves as a verbal element in several proper names: (1) *ya'nay* or *ya'ᵃnâ,* a hypocoristicon meaning "may (God) answer" or "(God) answered" (1 Ch. 5:12).[118] (2) *'unnî, K 'unnô* (1 Ch. 15:18,20; Neh. 12:9). The meaning is uncertain; it is either a hypocoristic form of the phrase name *'ᵃnāyâ* or *'ᵃnanyâ,* "Yahweh has answered," or a descriptive name meaning "the answered one" (like Akk. *Šūzubu,* "the saved one," related to *ᵈNergal ušēzib*).[119] (3) *'unnā* (cf. 1 Ch. 15:18,20; Neh. 12:9) is the eponym of a Levitical family.[120] (4) *'ᵃnānî* (1 Ch. 3:24) appears in Egyptian Aramaic as *'nny* and in Babylonian Aramaic as *'anānī.*[121] The name is a shortened form of *'ᵃnānyâ*[122] and means "He (Yahweh) has answered me." (5) *'ᵃnāyâ* (Neh. 8:4;[123] 10:23[22]).[124] This name, which is also attested epigraphically, is analogous to the form *'n'l* (Bab. Aram. *'anā'ēl*).[125] (6) *'ᵃnānᵉyâ* (Neh. 3:23) appears as *Ananía(s)* in the LXX; cf. Egyp. Aram. *'nnyh.*[126] It means "Yahweh has answered me" or "Yahweh revealed himself."[127] All these personal names have theological force. Naturally we often hear in them "tones familiar from Israelite laments."[128]

---

113. Barth, 47.

114. Ibid., 48; *UT,* no. 1883.

115. *BLe,* 492p.

116. J. Gray, *Legacy of Canaan. SVT* 5 (²1965), 71 n. 3.

117. *HAL,* II, 615; Delekat, 38-39; G. Dalman, *AuS,* II², 171-72. On both texts see *BHS.*

118. *IPN,* 27 n. 1, 28, 198; *HAL,* II, 471.

119. *IPN,* 39, 185; *AN,* 112.

120. *DJD,* II, 10, I, 3, p. 91.

121. See P. Grelot, *Documents araméens d'Egypte* (1972), 465-66; M. D. Coogan, *West Semitic Personal Names in the Murašû Documents. HSM* 7 (1976), 32, 80.

122. J. J. Stamm, "Hebräische Ersatznamen," *Studies in Honor of B. Landsberger* (1965), 414 n. 6; repr. in *Beiträge zur hebräische und altorientalischen Namenkunde. OBO* 30 (1980), 60 n. 6; for a different view see *IPN,* 184-85.

123. See *BHS.*

124. *IPN,* 185.

125. See *LidzEph,* II, 196-97; W. F. Albright, *BASOR* 149 (1958) 33, l. 1; Coogan, *West Semitic Personal Names,* 32, 80.

126. P. Grelot, *Documents,* 466.

127. For the former see J. J. Stamm, *OBO* 30, 60 n. 6; for the latter, *IPN,* 184, citing Arab. *'anna,* "appear."

128. *IPN,* 198.

Whether the name of the goddess ʿAnat is connected with *ʿnh* in the sense of "be sexually responsive" must remain an open question.[129] Kapelrud connects the name with *ʿnh* IV, "sing," also "lament."[130]

4. *maʿᵃneh, "Purpose."* The noun *maʿᵃneh* with the meaning "purpose" derives from *ʿnh* III;[131] cf. Arab. *maʿnā,* "meaning." It occurs in Prov. 16:4: "Yahweh has made everything for its purpose."[132]

5. *maʿan.* The particle *maʿan* derives from *ʿnh* III by way of *maʿᵃneh;* it is found also in Egyptian Aramaic.[133] It is always combined with the prep. *lᵉ* to mean "with respect to, for the sake of, on account of."[134]

6. *yaʿan.* The particle *yaʿan,* "on account of, because," derives from *ʿnh* III; cf. Arab. *ʿanā,* "intend, plan." It was originally a substantive meaning "occupation, plan," and developed into a preposition.[135] Mulder locates the *Sitz im Leben* of the particle in the motivations of prophetic oracles of weal and woe.[136] Labuschagne differs, seeing in *yaʿan* an original jussive introducing the indictment, which became a fossilized verbal form.[137]

7. *ʿinyān.* The noun *ʿinyān,* "business," deriving from *ʿnh* III,[138] is an Aramaic loanword. It appears also in Middle Hebrew and Jewish Aramaic as *ʿinyānāʾ,* in Samaritan[139] and Christian Palestinian as *ʿnyn,* and in Syriac as *ʿenyānāʾ,* "affair, concern." It occurs only in Ecclesiastes, always with negatively skeptical connotations. It refers to everything with which human beings "busy themselves" (*ʿnh* III) as ordained by God (1:13; 3:10), their gathering and heaping, which is all vanity[140] (2:26), their activities (5:2[3]; 8:16), which bring only pain and vexation and are *hebel* (2:23). The negative connotations are reinforced by the phrase *ʿinyān raʿ* in 1:13,[141] 4:8 (striving after riches is "an unhappy business" and *hebel*), and 5:13(14) (riches are lost "in a bad venture").

---

129. Labuschagne, 927, with reference to Hos. 2:17 and Ex. 21:10.
130. A. S. Kapelrud, *The Violent Goddess* (1969), 28; disputed by J. C. de Moor, *UF* 1 (1969) 224.
131. *BLe,* 491n.
132. Plöger, *BK* XVII, 187, 190.
133. See *BLe,* 492o; *DNSI,* II, 260-71.
134. *HAL,* II, 614; H. A. Brongers, *OTS* 18 (1973) 84-96.
135. *BLe,* 635b; *HAL,* II, 421.
136. M. J. Mulder, *OTS* 18 (1973) 49-83; cf. D. E. Gowan, *VT* 21 (1971) 178-84.
137. *TLOT,* II, 930.
138. *BLe,* 500o; Wagner, 92, no. 222.
139. *LOT,* II, 479, 499.
140. → הבל *hebel.*
141. *GK,* §128w; see above.

8. *ʿōnâ.* Whether *ʿōnâ* derives from *ʿnh* II, *ʿnh* III, or *ʿēṯ* ("time") is disputed. In Middle Hebrew the noun has the meaning "specific time"; Jewish Aram. *ʿunᵉṯāʾ/ʿonᵉtāʾ* means "time, hour," in metaphorical usage "time of marital duty, cohabitation."[142] In 1QapGen 2:10 we find *ʿntʾ,* probably with the same meaning.[143]

The only OT occurrence is in Ex. 21:10, in the context of legislation governing slaves: "If he takes another wife to himself, he shall not diminish the food, clothing, or *ʿōnâ* of her [sc. the Israelite slave taken as the first wife]."[144] This laws treats the sexual satisfaction of the female slave as a fundamental right.[145] Paul disputes this interpretation, citing Mesopotamian legal texts that list the elements of a wife's maintenance as food (Akk. *eprum*), oil *(piššatum),* and clothing *(lubuš/lubultum): ʿōnâ* is therefore to be interpreted as the equivalent of *piššatum.*[146] Nowhere in any legal text of the ancient Near East does he find any mention of "marital rights." There are linguistic reasons to doubt this interpretation of *ʿōnâ,* but a theory proposed by von Soden merits consideration.[147] He maintains that there is no root *ʿnī* or *ʿûn* used in texts dealing with sexual intercourse. Neither is it usual in the ancient Near East for laws to regulate what women a free man may have intercourse with outside his marriage. But the woman needs a place to live. Now the verb *ʿûn,* "live, dwell," is not attested with certainty in the OT, which uses the nominal derivative *māʿôn,* "habitation," only for accommodations for animals and the house of God — in the sense of a permanent dwelling place. According to von Soden, *ʿu/ônâ* is a rare and probably archaic word for a temporary dwelling. In my opinion this interpretation is highly likely. If so, *ʿônâ* derives not from the root *ʿnh* but from *ʿûn.*[148]

9. *ʿēṯ.* The occasional proposal to derive → עת *ʿēṯ,* "time," from *ʿnh* cannot be sustained.[149]

IV. Deuterocanonical Books. In the deuterocanonical books *apokrínesthai* occurs in everyday usage, albeit in literarily elevated texts (Tob. 2:3 S; 2:14; 5:1; 5:3; 5:10 S; 6:14 S). It appears in political contexts in Jdt. 6:16; 1 Mc. 2:17,19,36; 10:55; 13:8,35; 15:33,36. It appears in a forensic context in 2 Mc. 4:47, in the sense of "condemn" (cf. 2 Mc. 7:8). In 1 Mc. 4:46 *apokrínesthai* refers to prophetic guidance (cf. 2 Mc. 15:14). Sir. 4:8 exhorts the reader to respond to the greeting of the poor; 5:12, to answer a

---

142. Levy, *WTM,* III, 627-28; Dalman, *ANH,* 318.

143. J. A. Fitzmyer, *Genesis Apocryphon of Qumran Cave I. BietOr* 18A (²1971), 87.

144. H. Cazelles, *Études sur le Code de l'Alliance* (1946), 49, citing Hos. 2:17(15); 10:10 *Q.*

145. Boecker, 138-39.

146. S. M. Paul, *Studies in the Book of the Covenant in the Light of Biblical and Cuneiform Law. SVT* 18 (1970), 57-61.

147. W. von Soden, *UF* 13 (1981) 159-60; repr. in *Bibel und alter Orient. BZAW* 162 (1985), 198-99.

148. See also North, *VT* 5 (1955) 205-6; E. Oren, *Tarbiz* 33 (1953/54) 317; I. Cardellini, *Die biblischen "Sklaven"-Gesetze im Lichte des keilschriftlichen Sklavenrechts. BBB* 55 (1981), 255-56.

149. Contra J. Muilenburg, *HTR* 54 (1961) 234.

neighbor only when one knows what to say; 11:8, not to answer before listening; cf. 33:4 G, which should, however, be corrected by reference to the Hebrew text.[150] The noun *apókrisis* occurs in Sir. 5:11; 8:9; 20:6.

V. Dead Sea Scrolls. The Dead Sea Scrolls often use *ʿnh* in cultic contexts — e.g., 1QS 2:5,18 in connection with ritual cursing; 1QM 13:2; 14:4; 18:6 in the context of blessing *(brk)* and cursing; 1QM 15:7 and 16:15 in the context of ritual exhortation before battle. We find *ʿnh* in juridical contexts in CD 9:7; 13:18; 11QT 61:8 with reference to Dt. 19:15-21 and in 11QT 63:5 with reference to Dt. 21:1-9. In the political sphere 11QT 62:7 uses *ʿnh* with reference to Dt. 20:10-18. God is the subject of *ʿnh* in 1QH 4:18 (*ʿnh lᵉ* instead of *ʿnh* with the accusative reflects Aramaic influence[151]); 11QT 59:6 (cf. Dt. 28; the context is a mosaic of biblical motifs[152]).

The noun *maʿᵃneh* appears in 1QH 2:7; 7:11,13; 11:34; 16:6; 17:17 — all in a construct phrase with *lāšôn,* "tongue." These texts are probably dependent on Prov. 16:1, but the expression "from Yahweh" has turned "spoken by the tongue" into inspired speech or "speaking in tongues," especially in 1QH 11:34; 17:17.[153]

Stendebach

150. J. Sauer, "Jesus Sirach," *JSHRZ* III/5, 585.
151. *TLOT,* II, 930.
152. J. Maier, *Temple Scroll. JSOTSup* 34 (Eng. trans. 1985), 128.
153. Barth, 47; Labuschagne, 930.

עָנָה II *ʿānâ;* עֲנָוָה *ʿᵃnāwâ;* עֱנוּת *ʿᵉnûṯ;* עֹנָה *ʿōnâ;* תַּעֲנִית *taʿᵃnîṯ;* עָנִי *ʿānî;* עָנָו *ʿānāw*

I. Occurrences and Distribution: 1. OT; 2. Ancient Near East; 3. Statistics; 4. Lexical Fields; 5. Genres; 6. LXX; 7. Dead Sea Scrolls. II. Verb: 1. Piel; 2. Hiphil and Hithpael; 3. Qal and Niphal. III. Nouns: 1. *ʿᵒnî;* 2. Other Nouns. IV. Adjective: 1. Forms; 2. Outside the Psalms; 3. Psalms; 4. Excursus: Poverty. V. Theology of the Oppressed: 1. Assumptions; 2. Individuals and Marginal Groups; 3. The Whole Community; 4. Liberation. VI. Broader Horizons: 1. Hellenism; 2. Judaism; 3. Christianity.

ʿānâ II. K. Aartun, "Hebräisch *ʿānī* und *ʿānāw,*" *BiOr* 28 (1971) 125-26; W. W. Graf Baudissin, "Die alttestamentliche Religion und die Armen," *Preussische Jahrbücher* 149 (1912) 193-231; H. Birkeland, *ʿānî und ʿānāw in den Psalmen* (1933); H. A. Brongers, "Fasting in Israel in Biblical and Postbiblical Times," *OTS* 20 (1977) 1-21; A. Causse, *Les "pauvres" d'Israel*

I. Occurrences and Distribution.

1. *OT.* Is there in fact an independent root *ʿānâ* II? Delekat denies its existence emphatically, assigning all Hebrew lexemes with the consonant sequence *ʿ-n-h* to "a root with the basic meaning 'turn toward.'"[1] There are several arguments against this single-root theory: (a) the marked semantic differences among the lexemes based on *ʿ-n-h;* (b) the concentration of occurrences of words assigned to *ʿānâ* II in specific literary genres; (c) the possibility of separate historical development of the roots; (d) the evidence of comparative linguistics (see I.2 below). Of course semantic similarities appear in individual texts and misunderstandings in the course of transmission have led occasionally to the confusion of roots, as is always the case with homonymous roots. But the vast majority of the words traditionally assigned to *ʿānâ* II can defend their claim to etymological independence (see I.4 below). The argument based on genre (b) plays a special role in the discussion to follow. The possibility that *ʿānâ* II derives from an original *ʿnw* in contrast to *ʿānâ* I < *ʿny* is a strong (albeit not certain) argument for distinguishing the roots.[2] Brockelmann establishes the early pre-Israelite coalescence of the two roots.[3]

The root *ʿānâ* III, "be troubled about, keep someone busy,"[4] possibly attested in Eccl. 1:13; 3:10; 5:19(Eng. v. 20), might be simply a semantic variant of *ʿānâ* I or II.[5]

(1922); J. S. Croatto, "Liberar a los pobres," in Croatto et al., *Los pobres* (1978), 15-28; L. Delekat, "Zum hebräischen Wörterbuch," *VT* 14 (1964) 7-66, esp. 35-49; T. Donald, "The Semantic Field of Rich and Poor in the Wisdom Literature of Hebrew and Accadian," *OrAnt* 3 (1964) 27-41; A. Gelin, *The Poor of Yahweh* (Eng. trans. 1964); G. Gutiérrez, *The Power of the Poor in History* (Eng. trans. 1983); T. D. Hanks, *God So Loved the Third World* (1983); H.-P. Hasenfratz, *Die toten Lebenden. BZRGG* 24 (1982); J. Jocz, "God's 'Poor' People," *Jud* 28 (1972) 7-29; D. C. Jones, "Who Are the Poor?" *Evangelical Review of Theology* 2 (1978) 215-26; Y. I. Kim, "The Vocabulary of Oppression in the OT" (diss., Drew, 1981); H. G. Kippenberg, *Religion und Klassenbildung im antiken Judäa. SUNT* 14 (1978); K. Koch, "Die Entstehung der sozialen Kritik bei den Propheten," *FS G. von Rad* (1971), 236-57; A. Kuschke, "Arm und reich im AT," *ZAW* 57 (1939) 31-57; E. Kutsch, "עֲנָוָה ('Demut')" (Habil., Mainz, 1960); idem, "Deus humiliat et exaltat," *ZTK* 61 (1964) 193-220; idem, "'Trauerbräuche' und 'Selbsminderungsriten' im AT," in K. Lüthi et al., *Drei Wiener Antrittsreden. ThS* 78 (1965), 25-42; S. Łach, "Die Termini ʿAni und ʿAnaw in den Psalmen," *AcBibCrac* 1972 (1974) 42-64; E. Lákatos, "Un pueblo hacía la madurez," *RevBibl* 32 (1970) 227-32; J. M. Liaño, "Los pobres en el AT," *EstBib* 25 (1966) 117-67; N. Lohfink, "'Gewalt' als Thema alttestamentlicher Forschung," in E. Haag et al., eds., *Gewalt und Gewaltlosigkeit im AT. QD* 96 (1983), 15-50; D. Michel, "Armut. II, AT," *TRE,* IV (1979), 72-76; P. D. Miscall, "The Concept of Poor in the OT," *HTR* 75 (1972) 600-612; J. van der Ploeg, "Les pauvres d'Israel et leur piété," *OTS* 7 (1950) 236-70; J. Pons, *L'oppression dans l'AT* (1981); A. Rahlfs, עָנִי *und* עָנָו *in den Psalmen* (1892); C. Schultz, "*ʿānî* and *ʿānāw* in Psalmen" (diss., Brandeis, 1973); M. Schwantes, *Das Recht der Armen. BBET* 4 (1977); J. Sobrino, "Die 'Lehrautorität' des Volkes Gottes in Lateinamerika," *Conc* 21 (1985) 269-74; E. Tamez, *Bible of the Oppressed* (Eng. trans. 1982). For further bibliog. → אביון *'eḇyôn;* → דל *dal.*

1. P. 42.
2. *GK,* §75b, etc.
3. *VG,* I, §271.
4. *HAL,* II, 854.
5. Delekat, 38.

Analogous nuances are found in Arabic (*ʿanā* < *ʿanaya,* "disturb, interest, worry, etc.") and Syriac.[6]

The lexicons also list a root *ʿānâ* IV, "sing."[7] It is clearly related closely to *ʿānâ* I (1 S. 18:7; 21:12[11]; 29:5; Ps. 119:172; 147:7; Nu. 21:17; Ex. 15:21; Ezr. 3:11), but its existence as a separate root is supported above all by Arab. *ǵny* II.[8] For a more extensive etymological discussion → עָנָה *ʿānâ* I.

2. *Ancient Near East.* Both *ʿānâ* I and *ʿānâ* II occur in the immediate geographical environment of Israel in the OT period, but in different linguistic zones. Ugaritic clearly employs *ʿny,* "answer," in various stems and with a nominal derivative.[9] Whether *ʿnw* is also found remains disputed.[10] Moab. *ʿnw* appears in the Mesha inscription ("Omri was king of Israel, and he oppressed Moab for a long time. . . . And his son succeeded him. And he said, 'I will oppress Moab'").[11] Alongside this text we can probably place another with three instances of the piel of Phoen. *ʿnh* II, "subjugate."[12] Conversely, contemporary instances of *ʿnh* I, "answer, testify," in the region of Canaan and Syria are very rare.[13] The existence of the semantic variant "(cause to) triumph" identified by Dahood (Ps. 20:7[6]; 60:7[5]; 89:23[22]; 118:21; etc.) must be demonstrated for each occurrence.[14] Moabite "oppress" and Phoenician "subjugate" are two sides of the same coin; the former at least is also common in political contexts of the OT.

The Arabic verb *ʿanā,* "be humble," occurs in both the northern and southern regions.[15] From the same root we also find *ʿanwa,* "violence," and *ʿānī,* "submissive, captive."

The various Aramaic dialects use words containing the radicals *ʿ-n-h* with the meaning "answer" as well as "humiliate, torment." The latter usage (e.g., *ʾš ʿnh,* "a humble man")[16] suggests a root *ʿnh* II. Brockelmann cites *ʿᵉnâ* I, "answer," and *ʿᵉnâ* III ethpael, "he humbled himself."[17] In Biblical Aramaic the root appears only in Dnl. 4:24(27): *miḥan ʿᵃnāyin,* "have mercy on the oppressed."

Akkadian and the non-Semitic languages of the ancient Near East provide no clear

---

6. See Wehr, 650; Brockelmann, *LexSyr,* 534a.
7. *HAL,* II, 854; *LexHebAram,* 613; *GesB,* 627; *BDB,* 777.
8. Wehr, 686.
9. *WUS,* nos. 2060, 2060a.
10. See *KTU* 1.2, I, 26, 28, 35; 1.16, VI, 58; A. van Selms, *UF* 2 (1970) 259-60, contra *HAL,* II, 853.
11. *KAI* 181.5, 6.
12. *KAI* 26A.I.18-20; see J. Friedrich, *Phönizisch-punische Grammatik. AnOr* 32 (1951), §174.
13. *KAI* 200.10, 11.
14. M. Dahood, *Psalms I: 1–50. AB* 16 (1966), 116, 118; idem, *Psalms III: 101–150. AB* 17A (1970), 243.
15. Wehr, 650; Biella, 383.
16. *KAI* 202A.2; commentary: *KAI,* II, 206. See also Jastrow, 1092ff.
17. *LexSyr,* 533-34.

evidence of a root *'ānâ* I or II. Akkadian uses a series of etymologically unrelated words to illuminate the conceptual realm, e.g., *dalālu* I, "be wretched," D stem "oppress"; *dallu,* "wretched"; *šukēnu,* "prostrate oneself"; *muškēnu,* "court dependent, poor person."[18]

The conclusion: *'ānâ* II may be considered an independent root.

3. *Statistics.* Because the boundaries are somewhat ill defined, it is easy for identifications of the root to differ. Lisowsky lists 79 individual verb forms, 45 noun forms, and 96 adjective forms deriving from *'ānâ* II. Mandelkern lists 78, 45 (plus 8 instances of *'inyān,* "business," and 2 of *ma'ᵃnâ,* "plow path"), and 94; Even-Shoshan 80, 45, and 96. Like Lisowsky, Martin-Achard adheres closely to the MT, listing 79, 44, and 96 occurrences.[19] Proper names are unlikely to derive from *'ānâ* II (but cf. *'ᵃnâ,* Gen. 36 passim;[20] *'unnî,* 1 Ch. 15:18,20; Neh. 12:9). I take Lisowsky's data as my point of departure and reserve for later discussion possible subtractions (e.g., Zec. 11:7,11) and additions (Eccl. 10:19: "Money conquers all";[21] Hos. 2:17[15]: the woman follows the man submissively[22]). The data are displayed in the table on p. 234.

Joshua is the only substantial book in which *'ānâ* II does not occur, but the root is rare in the Former Prophets. Of the 18 occurrences in these books, 15 are verbs (12 piel forms); there are almost no occurrences of nouns or adjectives (only *'ᵒnî* in 1 S. 1:11 and 2 K. 14:26 and *'ānî* in 2 S. 22:28; both Samuel texts are psalms). The lexical group is also infrequent in the Chronicler's History: the piel does not occur, and the two instances of the verb are a literal quotation of 1 K. 8:35 in 2 Ch. 6:26 and a technical term for fasting in Ezr. 8:21; there is no parallel to 1 K. 2:26, because the Chronicler presents Solomon's accession very differently. The 3 occurrences of nouns (Ezr. 9:5; Neh. 9:9; 1 Ch. 22:14) appear in a penitential rite and a fixed Davidic tradition. It is noteworthy that the historical tradition as a whole does not use *'ānâ* II for Israel's many afflictions; Jeremiah (one occurrence of *'ānî* in an ethical/juridical context [Jer. 22:6]) and Daniel (hithpael of the verb in 10:12, an apocalyptic wisdom text, and an Aramaic word in 4:24[27]) scarcely count.

By contrast, a few literary units exhibit a concentration of words deriving from *'ānâ* II. Derivatives of the root occur 45 times in the Pentateuch (some 20 percent of the total), including 24 occurrences of the piel. The prophetic books concentrate their use in the two adjectives (30 times, esp. frequent in Isaiah [16]; also Zechariah [4], Amos and Zephaniah [2 each], and Habakkuk [1]); there are 48 occurrences of the root altogether, some 22 percent of the total. Jeremiah ignores the root almost totally. The Writings make the heaviest use of *'ānâ* II; these books — excluding Ezra, Nehemiah, Chronicles, and Daniel — use the verb and its derivatives 101 times (about 46 percent of the total). Especially frequent are the adjs. *'ānî* and *'ānāw* (55 times) and the noun *'ᵒnî* (22

---

18. For citations see *AHw,* s.v.; cf. *BWL,* 18 n. 1.
19. R. Martin-Achard, *TLOT,* II, 931.
20. M. Weippert, "Edom" (Habil., Tübingen, 1971), 245.
21. Delekat, 41.
22. H. W. Wolff, *Hosea. Herm* (Eng. trans. 1974), 31, 43; *HAL,* II, 852: *'ānâ* I, no. 3a.

times). When we look for the "home" of ʿ*ānâ* II, therefore, we must pay particular attention to the genres appearing in Psalms, Job, Proverbs, and the Five Scrolls.

4. *Lexical Fields.* The words associated with the root ʿ*ānâ* II belong to a negatively charged domain of knowledge and experience. It is impossible to identify a neutral basic meaning. Positive valuation is present only when the detrimental force is surmounted or placed temporarily in the service of something beneficial. The nouns and adjectives refer to situations inimical to human life. The basic experience appears to be "affliction" in its various forms. Synonyms depict it as "hardship, torment, pain, despair" (see III below). "Days of affliction" (Job 30:16,27) are evil times, diametrically opposed to well-being (Job 29; cf. "now" in 30:1,9,16); they are life-destroying. The adjectives always describe people in "oppressed, constrained, fatal" situations. The verb usually expresses the notion that someone is depreciating or threatening the life of another or temporarily embracing such a fate. The afflicted (Prov. 31:5, b^{e}*nê* ʿ^{o}*nî*) are almost beyond help. "Give strong drink to one who is perishing, wine to one in bitter

	Qal/Niphal	Piel/Pual	Hiphil/Hithpael	ʿ^{o}*nî*	Other nouns	ʿ*ānî*/ʿ*ānāw*
Gen		4	1	4		
Ex	1	5		3	1	1
Lev		5				2
Nu		4				1
Dt		7		2		4
Total	1	25	1	9	1	8
Jgs		5				
S		5		1		1
K		2	3	1		
Total		12	3	2		1
Isa	3	5	1	1		16
Jer						1
Ezk		2				4
Minor	2	3			1	9
Total	5	10	1	1	1	30
Ps	2	10	2	10	3	38
Job		2		6		7
Prov				1	3	9
Cant		2		5		1
Dnl			1			
Ezr			1	1	1	
Ch			1	1		
Total	2	14	5	24	7	55

distress; let him drink and forget his poverty *(rîš)* and remember his misery (→ עמל *ʿāmāl)* no more" (Prov. 31:6-7). Thus the semantic content of our lexical group reflects fear and a sense of impending death; it is set against the experience of security, happiness, strength, and superiority. Together with many other lexical groups of similar content, this group arises from the darkness of human experience, the shadow side of life.[23]

5. *Genres.* The focal usage of this lexical group becomes even clearer when we examine the genres that use these words and thus the concrete situations the words reflect. Most numerous and important are liturgical texts and observances. Affliction and its causes are described vividly in the Psalms, Lamentations, and Job, as well as in scattered prayers (1 S. 1:11; cf. Dt. 26:7). This has long been recognized (see the studies of *ʿānî,* esp. in the Psalms). It is less well known that extensive blocks of text, especially in the prophets and wisdom literature, are liturgical in origin. This is immediately clear in the case of Deutero-Isaiah: *ʿānî* appears in words of comfort to Israel (Isa. 41:17; 49:13; 51:21; 54:11; cf. 61:1) that were preserved and transmitted in the cultic congregation. The same is true of the divine utterances in Isa. 66:2; Zeph. 3:12; Zec. 7:10; etc., as well as more paraenetic passages (e.g., Isa. 58:7; 66:2; Ezk. 18:12,17; 22:29; etc.) that are in part cultic and exhibit affinities in vocabulary and intention to legal and wisdom texts. These are the two other major sorts of text. Laws and admonitions forbid abusing the afflicted. The paraenetic style (Ex. 22:20ff.[21ff.]; Lev. 19:9-10)[24] or liturgical background (Job 24:1ff.; 29:1ff.; 34:17ff.; 36:5ff.) of these texts are conspicuous. The verb, especially in the piel, describes the origin of the affliction. The act of affliction or oppression is reprehensible (Ex. 22:21-22[22-23]; Prov. 22:22); the condition must be overcome (Job 36:8ff.; Jer. 22:16). Didactic narratives describe the ethical and juridical situation (Gen. 16:4-12; Ex. 1:6-14). Prophetic indictments also depict oppression and injustice (Am. 2:6-7; 8:4-6). Thus we can recognize a common thread: the various literary genres describing and reflecting the religiously significant affliction of an individual or the people use — along with other expressions — words derived from *ʿānâ* II.

6. *LXX.* The LXX picks up the Hebrew terminology on a broad front and with a variety of nuances.[25] The ambiguity of the Hebrew root leads to discrepant interpretations, e.g., Ruth 1:21; Hos. 2:17(16); 5:5; 7:10; 14:9(8); Mal. 2:12, where Greek terminology of abasement represents MT *ʿānâ* I. Conversely, expressions denoting speaking or answering may replace the terminology of oppression or affliction (e.g., Isa. 60:14, where the LXX simply has two ptcps. following *bᵉnê;* Ps. 22:25[24], where *déēsis* represents Heb. *ʿᵉnûṯ*). In most cases, however, the Greek translation agrees with the two distinct roots of the Hebrew text.

---

23. → כאב *k'b;* → מות *mûṯ.*
24. J. Halbe, *Das Privilegrecht Jahwes. FRLANT* 114 (1975), 426ff., 451ff.
25. W. Grundmann, *TDNT,* VIII, 6.

Despite the variety — the LXX (including Sirach) uses 36 words to represent 13 Hebrew terms (including the six verbal stems) — we can observe a preference for certain expressions. Most of the translations involve *tapeinoún/tapeinós/tapeínōsis,* "(make) low" (Gen. 15:13; Lev. 16:29,31; Dt. 21:14[13]; Jgs. 16:5-6; Ps. 82:3; Isa. 14:32; Gen. 16:11; Dt. 26:7);[26] *ptōchós/ptōcheía,* "poor, poverty" (Lev. 19:10; Ps. 10:2,9; Job 30:27; Isa. 48:10);[27] *pénesthai/pénēs/penechrós/penía,* "needy" (Dt. 24:12[11]; Ps. 10:12; Prov. 31:20; Eccl. 6:8; Ex. 22:24[25]; Job 36:8), synonymous with *ptōchós* (cf. "penury"); *praǘs/praǘtēs,* "meek(ness)" (Zeph. 3:2; Zec. 9:9; Isa. 26:6; Ps. 45:5[4]); or *kakoún/kakía/kákōsis/kakoucheín,* "(do) evil" (Gen. 16:6; Dt. 8:2-3; Ex. 22:22[23]; Isa. 53:4; 1 K. 2:26). Statements concerning affliction and abasement, some of which are meant in a positive sense *(praǘs!),* must be interpreted in the light of the contemporary social order (see VI.1 below).

7. *Dead Sea Scrolls.* The lexical group plays an important role in postcanonical writings, especially the Dead Sea Scrolls. The members of the sect understood themselves as the poor, the devout, the elect.[28] In 4QpPs 37:2,8-9, *'ᵃnāwîm* "refers to the congregation of the poor" = *'ᵃdaṯ hā'eḇyônîm.*[29] Frequently, therefore, they call themselves *'ānî* or *'ānāw.* Kuhn lists 18 passages,[30] of which 7 are in the *Hodayot* (1QH 1:36; 2:34; 5:13,14,21; 14:3; 18:14). The verb appears 6 times (1QpHab 9:10: God disgraces the wicked priest; 1QM 12:14: the oppressors of Israel) and *'ᵃnāwāh* 9 times, primarily in the Manual of Discipline (1QS 2:24; 3:8; 4:3; 5:3,25; 9:22; 11:11; 1QH 17:22: "a proper self-assessment before human beings and God"). "Let no one be lower than his rank or raise himself from the place of his lot. For all must conduct themselves toward their neighbors as a single community of truth *(yaḥaḏ 'ᵉmeṯ),* with humble goodness *('anwaṯ ṭôḇ),* loving compassion *('ahᵃḇaṯ ḥeseḏ),* and upright purpose *(maḥᵃšeḇeṯ ṣeḏeq)*" (1QS 2:23ff.;[31] cf. 1QS 4:2-6; 5:23-25; 10:24–11:2). "An upright spirit" *(rûaḥ yōšer),* "humility" *('ᵃnāwâ),* and "submissiveness" *('anwaṯ nepeš)* to all the laws of God effect reconciliation and purification (1QS 3:8). The noun *ta'ᵃnîṯ* clearly occurs in 4QpPs [4Q171] 37:2,10 and CD 6:19 in the sense of "fasting" (cf. the use of the verb in this sense ["fast on the Day of Atonement"] in 11QT 25:12; 27:7); finally, the verb also appears with the meaning "overpower" (66:3,11). Concordances give equivalents to *'ānâ* II in the Greek Apocrypha and Pseudepigrapha.[32] Except in Maccabees and Sirach, these documents make little use of the lexical group.

---

26. W. Grundmann, *TDNT,* VIII, 1-26.
27. E. Bammel, *TDNT,* VI, 888-915.
28. J. Maier, *Die Texte vom Toten Meer,* 2 vols. (1960), II, 83-87.
29. E. Lohse, *Die Texte aus Qumran* (1981), 272-73.
30. Kuhn, 167 n. 4: "A clear differentiation . . . is hardly possible."
31. Following Maier, *Texte,* I, 24.
32. E. Hatch and H. A. Redpath, *Concordance to the Septuagint,* 3 vols. in 2 (1897, repr. 1983); C. A. Wahl, *Clavis Librorum Veteris Testamenti Apocryphorum Philologica* (1853, repr. 1972).

II. Verb.

1. *Piel.* The piel is the commonest stem of the verb; its 54 occurrences are relatively evenly distributed.[33] Physical or psychic force is used to alter the status of someone for the worse. A person who "oppresses, violates, abases, humiliates" is using power contrary to the demands of justice.

a. *Juridical Usage.* The use of the piel in juridical texts is sharply defined. Because the slave Hagar has done wrong (*ḥāmās,* "impairment," Gen. 16:5) to her mistress Sarai, Sarai receives permission to punish her (v. 6a), i.e., to interfere with her status as concubine and vicarious mother. Sarai "degrades" her (*watteʿʿannehā,* v. 6b; LXX [moralizing]: *ekákōsin autḗn*). The angel commands Hagar to accept this degradation (*hiṯʿannî,* "submit," v. 9; LXX *apostráphēti*). The marriage contract agreed to by Laban and Jacob contains a clause stipulating that the bridegroom must not "slight" Laban's daughters in favor of other wives (Gen. 31:50)

When *ʿānâ* II must be translated "violate," the central idea is not the use of brute force but rather civil defamation and its concomitant loss of status. This is illustrated most clearly by 2 S. 13:11ff., where Amnon forces Tamar to have intercourse with him. She objects to the destruction of her being — it is an outrage (*neḇālâ,* v. 12), a disgrace (*ḥerpâ,* v. 13). Other texts point in the same direction: Gen. 34:2; Dt. 21:14 (change of status through intercourse); 22:24,29 (the man is punished because he has violated a legal asset [cf. 11QT 66:3,11]); Jgs. 19:24; 20:5; Lam. 5:11 (rape as an offense against the person); in Dt. 22,24,29, the degradation is presumed but is not mentioned explicitly. Only in the late text Ezk. 22:10-11 does the piel of *ʿānâ* II mean simply "have intercourse" (Zimmerli translates "abuse";[34] possibly the etymological source of *ʿōnâ* in Ex. 21:10).

The juridical nature of the verb is also apparent in texts that speak of "degrading" the underprivileged: Ex. 22:21-22(22-23); cf. Ps. 94:5-6; Ezk. 22:7-12 (a catalog of vices: v. 7, exploitation of the weak; vv. 8-12, cultic offenses). In Jgs. 16:5,6, the repeated "bind and subdue" signifies not only loss of strength but loss of status; v. 19 says in conclusion: "Thus she began to rob him of his strength" (or [niphal inf.]: "Thus he began to be abased, to lose his status"; cf. LXX^{A} *tapeinoústhai*). A process of personal and social disintegration begins that can end only in death (vv. 28-30; at the same time, rehabilitation through revenge).[35]

The juridical concept can also be applied to the people as a whole; examples includes Dt. 8:2-3,16 and Ex. 1:11-12. The Deuteronomist describes Yahweh himself as temporarily repudiating Israel's elect status (cf. also Isa. 64:11; Nah. 1:12; and the theological explanation in Lam. 3:31-33; Job 37:23). Hunger (Dt. 8:3) is not part of the covenant design; it is a test of faith, a temptation (vv. 2,16). In Ex. 1:11-12 it is the Egyptians who grossly violate the rights of their Israelite neighbors by enslaving them (cf. v. 14, "brutal forced labor"; similarly Dt. 26:6; Gen. 15:13; cf. Nu. 24:24; 2 S.

---

33. E. Jenni (*HP,* 288) mentions 57 occurrences, without evidence.
34. W. Zimmerli, *Ezekiel 1. Herm* (Eng. trans. 1979), 453.
35. Hasenfratz, 70-80: social death in anomie.

7:10; 1 K. 11:39; 2 K. 17:20; Ps. 89:23[22]). Two texts use the participle to denote the oppressors (Isa. 60:14; Zeph. 3:19).

b. *Liturgical Usage.* The liturgical usage of the verb is closely connected with its juridical usage. The point at issue is the transgression of norms, even when Yahweh is the subject. Because affliction is contrary to the divine order, it can be cultically alleviated. Only God can guarantee *ṣeḏāqâ,* "justice"[36] (cf. Ps. 82). Therefore individuals lament their degraded circumstances (Ps. 90:15; 102:24[23]: "He has broken my strength in midcourse," i.e., "He has made me incapable of living" through sickness [vv. 4-6(3-5)], enemies [v. 8(7)], and social death;[37] Ps. 119:75). Communal lament, too, springs from the experience of degraded life (Ps. 90:15; 94:5); assurance of a favorable hearing is the cultic response (Zeph. 3:19; Ps. 89:23[22]). Some texts are obscure: Ps. 88:8b(7b), ". . . waves, you overwhelm [me]?"; Job 30:11, ". . . bowstring, and afflicts me?"; Ps. 105:18, "afflict with fetters?"

Degradation need not always be inflicted from without: voluntary self-degradation is also possible.[38] The supplicant bows down in the dust, fasts, demonstrates his worthlessness. Alongside other expressions of self-degradation, the expression *'innâ 'eṯ-nepeš,* "humble oneself," has become an OT idiom (Lev. 16:29,31; 23:27,32; Nu. 29:7; 30:14[13]; Isa. 58:3,5; Ps. 35:13).

The rare instances of the pual fit the same picture. Lev. 23:29 refers to fasting; Isa. 53:4 and Ps. 119:71 are cultic in nature. The sufferings of the servant of Yahweh reflect communal theology (*nāgûa', mukkēh, mᵉḥōlāl,* Isa. 53:4-5). Finally, Ps. 132:1 either draws on the fasting idiom or reflects a separate tradition of "David's abasement" (cf. 1 Ch. 22:14).

The juridical and cultic usages of *'ānâ* II piel and pual are so interwoven that it is impossible to assign priority to one or the other.

2. *Hiphil and Hithpael.* The usage of the hiphil and hithpael is most compatible with that of the transitive piel. I have already discussed the hithpael in Gen. 16:9 (acceptance of degradation). The banishment of Abiathar also belongs here (1 K. 2:26-27): he is spared for the time being because he shared David's low position on the social ladder. The cultic sense of the hithpael is manifest in Ezr. 8:21 and Dnl. 10:12; Ps. 107:17 can be interpreted either passively (most comms.) or reflexively: "Because of their iniquities they were exposed to deadly peril" (v. 19, *ṣar*) — sickness and starvation (cf. v. 18).

The hiphil in 1 K. 8:35 par. 2 Ch. 6:26 is synonymous with the piel (cf. LXX; or is this *'ānâ* I?). In Isa. 25:1-5, a hymn of praise, one of the themes is Yahweh's help for the poor (v. 4), echoed by his humiliation of the enemy (v. 5). The vocalization of the hiphil *ya'ᵃneh* follows the parallel hiphil *taḵnîa'* (the Syr. has a niphal; cf. also the hiphils in vv. 11-12); the meaning is that of the piel. The text of Ps. 55:20(19) is corrupt.[39] The two verbs were originally probably "hear and answer (*'ānâ* I)." The imme-

36. → צדק *ṣdq.*
37. Hasenfratz, 70ff.
38. See Kutsch.
39. H.-J. Kraus, *Psalms 1–59* (Eng. trans. 1988), 519.

diate context requires that proper names be supplied from Gen. 36:3,5; the extended context should probably be reconstructed as a lament, a declaration of trust, and a curse (vv. 18-20[17-19]).

3. *Qal and Niphal.* The few instances of the qal and niphal appear also to refer to the mental state of those who have been abased. Social degradation has its psychic consequences: "I have sunk very *(mᵉ'ōḏ)* low" (Ps. 116:10 qal, LXX pass.; 119:107 niphal). To utter these words in prayer is to accept that one is "down," acknowledging and lamenting one's sins (Ps. 119:67 qal; LXX pass.); cf. v. 71 ("It is good for me . . .") and v. 75. Various afflictions are referred to in vv. 19,25,50,92,95; expressions of lowliness appear in vv.125,141,176, etc.; contrast the "insolent" (*zēḏîm:* vv. 21,51,78,85, etc.). A sufferer is *nepeš na'ᵃnâ,* "an abased soul" (Isa. 58:10; cf. 53:7), corresponding to *'ānî* in 58:7.

The juridico-cultic notion of deterioration also casts light on secular contexts. A young lion is not daunted (Isa. 31:4). In Zec. 10:2 Israel is described metaphorically as straying and "disintegrating" (qal)[40] like sheep, i.e., losing its status as a nation. Pharaoh must give up his arrogant sovereignty over the Israelites (Ex. 10:3 niphal).

The verb appears most commonly in the piel, conveying the cultic and juridical sense of degrading someone from his or her divinely ordained status. The other verbal stems are explainable on the basis of this usage.

III. Nouns.

1. *'ᵒnî.* The commonest noun is *'ᵒnî;* its occurrences are concentrated in liturgical wisdom texts and cultic contexts. It has a narrow semantic range: "misery" that cries to heaven.

There are a few possible exceptions. A tradition concerning David turns up in the Chronicler's special material (cf. 1 K. 2:26; Ps. 132:1; 1 S. 18:23): "with great pains" *(bᵉ + 'ᵒnî)* David provided the materials for building the temple (1 Ch. 22:14). Surely this refers to the perilous times before the *pax Salomonica* (cf. 1 Ch. 22:8,18).[41] But do we have here a theological reevaluation of David's "underground" period (1 K. 2:26)? This is most unlikely, for the only other occurrence of *'ānâ* II in Chronicles is in Solomon's prayer at the dedication of the temple (2 Ch. 6:26 [= 1 K. 8:35]); in fact, the Chronicler does not deal at all with the lexical field of misery, oppression, poverty, etc.[42] (Only in Ezra/Nehemiah do we find an isolated liturgical *'ᵒnî* in Neh. 9:9 and the hapax legomenon *ta'ᵃnîṯ* in Ezr. 9:5.) The most immediate interpretation of 1 Ch. 22:14, therefore, is personal. Secondarily, *'ᵒnî* is here a background setting for the golden age of Solomon (v. 9).[43] Gen. 31:42, too, refers to everyday "toil and labor"

---

40. Rudolph, *Haggai-Sacharja 1–8-Sacharja 9–14-Maleachi. KAT* XIII/4 (1976), 190.

41. P. Welten, *Geschichte und Geschichtsdarstellung in der Chronikbüchern. WMANT* 42 (1973), 49-50.

42. J. P. Weinberg, *ZAW* 98 (1986) 89-90: the Chronicler suppresses the problem of marginal groups.

43. J. D. Newsome, "Toward a New Understanding of the Chronicler and His Purposes," *JBL* 94 (1975) 201-17; S. Japhet, "Conquest and Settlement in Chronicles," *JBL* 98 (1979) 205-18.

(*ʿᵒnî* and *yᵉgîaʿ kap),* albeit "seen by God"! The "bread of affliction" in Dt. 16:3 may also belong here, with a possible wordplay on *leḥem ʾônîm,* "bread of mourners" (Hos. 9:4). The *maṣṣôṯ* are not so referred to elsewhere; but cf. Ps. 127:2, "bread of anxious care"; 1 K. 22:27 par. 2 Ch. 18:26, "prison bread"; Prov. 20:17; 23:3, "bread of deceit"; Ezk. 24:17,22 (cj. *leḥem ʾᵃḇēlîm*), "bread of mourners"; Ps. 80:6(5), "bread of tears"; etc. A secular usage (secondary?) of *ʿᵒnî* can be discerned.

But the great majority of texts speak of a plight demanding Yahweh's intervention. A characteristic idiom is "God saw the misery of . . ." (Gen. 29:32; 31:42; Ex. 3:7; 4:31; Dt. 26:7; 1 S. 1:11; 2 K. 14:26; Ps. 9:14[13]; 25:18; 31:8[7]; 119:153; Job 10:15; Lam. 1:9; Neh. 9:9); alternative verbs: hear (Gen. 16:11), remember (Lam. 3:19). This idiom is especially common in prayers of individuals, where it appears with the 1st-person suffix, "my misery" (Gen. 29:32; 31:42; 41:52; 1 S. 1:11; Ps. 9:14[13]; 25:18; 31:8[7]; 119:50,92,153; Job 10:15; Lam. 1:9; 3:19; cf. 1 Ch. 22:14). In collective prayers we find the corresponding "our misery" (Dt. 26:7; Ps. 44:25[24]; "the misery of our fathers," Neh. 9:9) and in cultic promises or divine discourse "your/his/her/their misery" (Gen. 16:11; Ex. 3:7; "you" [pl.], Ex. 3:17; in a lament describing misery, Lam. 1:7). Narrative references to the misery of others emphasize this existential, cultic usage (Ex. 4:31; Job 36:15; 2 K. 14:26). The plight is always personal. As a rule, it is expressed in a lament, petition, expression of trust, or thanksgiving addressed to Yahweh; *ʿᵒnî* is always misery that affects God. Once Yahweh is reproached harshly: "You have ignored our misery" (Ps. 44:25[24]).

In the nature of the case, such misery is never concrete. Cultic usage comprehends a broad spectrum of threats, perils, and fears brought before Yahweh by an individual or the community. These are defined by the synonyms appearing in the immediate context of expressions of *ʿᵒnî: ʿāmāl,* "hardship" (Gen. 41:51; Dt. 26:7; Ps. 25:18; Prov. 31:7); *laḥaṣ,* "oppression" (Dt. 26:7; Ps. 44:25[24]; Job 36:15); *ḥōšeḵ,* "darkness" (Ps. 107:10; Lam. 3:1-2); *ṣᵉʿāqâ,* "cry" (Ex. 3:7); *zᵉʿāqâ* (Neh. 9:9); *mārûḏ,* "homelessness" (Lam. 1:7; 3:19); *yāḡîaʿ,* "labor" (Gen. 31:42); *maḵʾōḇ,* "suffering" (Ex. 3:7); *ḥaṭṭāʾṯ,* "sin" (Ps. 25:18); *ṣārôṯ,* "adversities" (Ps. 31:8[7]); *ʿᵃḇōḏâ,* "servitude" (Lam. 1:3); *rēš,* "poverty" (Prov. 31:7); cf. the extended descriptions of misery in Lam. 3:1-21; Ps. 31:8-13(7-12); 44:10-17,25(9-16,24); 88:4-10(3-9), and the summaries in 2 K. 14:26; Dt. 26:7; Job 10:15; Neh. 9:9. A specialized conception views misery as a (magical or cultic?) binding or restraining force (Ps. 88:9-10[8-9]; 107:10 [obviating the emendation *kᵉḇālîm,* "fetters"?]; Job 36:8).

Misery can occur in the setting of a family or nation. Childlessness threatens the very essence of a woman's life; *ʿᵒnî* therefore appears in petitions and vows (1 S. 1:11) and in thanksgivings at the birth or naming of a child (Gen. 29:32; 41:52; cf. also Gen. 16:11). In the laments of an individual it is easy to recognize the typical afflictions of persecution by enemies and suffering occasioned by God's anger or punishment (Ps. 9:14[13]; 25:18; 31:8[7]; 88:10[9]; 107:10,14; 119:50,92,153; Job 10:15; 30:16,27; 36:8,15,21; Prov. 31:5; Lam. 3:1,19; 1 Ch. 22:14). Only one text explicitly mentions the economic exploitation of an individual (Gen. 31:42: Laban's exploitation of Jacob).

The focus, then, is not on the cause, termination, or purpose of misery. The noun refers to a burden of suffering that affects Yahweh, always with social implications. The same holds true for Israel. The parade example is the oppression of Jacob's descendants by the Egyptians (Ex. 1:6-14). Hard labor as slaves is intended to destroy them. This situation is formalized as *ʿonî* (Ex. 3:7,17; 4:31; Dt. 26:7; Neh. 9:9). Later crises affecting Israel appear in the same light (2 K. 14:26), especially the Babylonian catastrophe (Ps. 44:25[24]; Lam. 1:3,7,9). Isa. 48:10 uses the image of a "furnace of misery" *(kûr ʿonî)* to summarize the experience of Israel's history; the same metaphor, without *ʿonî,* appears in Dt. 4:20; 1 K. 8:51; Jer. 11:4. As a whole, the usage of *ʿonî* is concentrated clearly in religious and cultic life. Two test examples prove the point: The few texts where *ʿonî* appears without a suffix or attributive genitive (Isa. 48:10; Ps. 88:10[9]; 107:10,41; Job 30:16,27; 36:8,21; Prov. 31:5; Lam. 1:3) grow out of religious experience and are associated more or less directly with cultic language. And putative secular usage (Gen. 31:42; Dt. 16:3; Job 30:16,27; 36:21; Prov. 31:5; 1 Ch. 22:14) may derive from cultic notions.

2. *Other Nouns.* The noun *ʿᵃnāwâ* or *ʿanwâ* (the latter form occurs only in Ps. 18:36[35] and 45:5; the difference, assumed by the MT, has no semantic significance[44]) refers to a human quality or a social condition. This quality can be sought, like *ṣᵉḏāqâ,* "righteousness," or *ḥoḵmâ,* "wisdom": *baqqᵉšû ʿᵃnāwâ,* "seek humility," Zeph. 2:3 exhorts. Similar prophetic admonitions urge the hearer to seek what is good, to seek Yahweh (Am. 5:14-15; Zeph. 2:3; cf. Ps. 27:8; 105:4). The quest for the outlook that leads to true life also informs the thinking of wisdom (Prov. 15:14; 21:21; etc.). It would be wrong to think of *ʿᵃnāwâ* as an exclusively psychological or ethical attitude. It has practical consequences for the conduct of life and the role one plays. Wisdom and the cult are the spheres from which the concept of *ʿᵃnāwâ* emerges. Prov. 15:33 and 18:12 contain the saying "Before honor, humility." Honor *(kāḇôḏ)* is the polar concept (cf. 29:23). Parallel statements contrast pride and fall (16:18; 18:12a). In other words, *ʿᵃnāwâ* is the human quality that makes it possible to live in harmony with the world.[45] According to 22:4, *ʿᵃnāwâ* is the wellspring of everything: fear of God (the copula "and" is a modern invention), riches, honor, life.[46] The virtue of *ʿᵃnāwâ* is acknowledgment of one's proper status, not hypocritical false modesty.[47]

Synonyms derive from the roots → שׁפל *špl,* "be low" (Isa. 2:9-11; 13:11; 25:11-12; 26:5; 29:4; Prov. 16:19; 29:13) and → דל *dal,* "low."

Two passages are difficult. Ps. 18:36(35) speaks of Yahweh's *ʿᵃnāwâ* (2 S. 22:36 has the qal inf. of *ʿānâ* I, "your answering"; LXX *hypakoḗ* or *paideía*). In Ps. 45:5(4) "humility" seems out of place with "righteousness" or "victory." Later redaction introduced the notion of "self-restraint." Nothing is gained by postulating *ʿānâ* III, "be concerned for" or "exult."[48] We must instead reckon with a late theology of humility that imputes to God and the messiah a humble solidarity with the suffering people (cf. Zec. 9:9).

---

44. *HAL,* II, 855; G. Schmuttermayr, *Psalm 18 und 2 Samuel 22. SANT* 25 (1971), 148-53.
45. H. D. Preuss, M. Awerbuch, and S. Rehrl, "Demut," *TRE,* VIII, 459-68.
46. On the rabbinic debate over the value of humility, see St.-B., I, 189-94, 789.
47. Cf. the Qumran Manual of Discipline (I.7 above).
48. Dahood, *Psalms I: 1–50. AB* 16 (1966), in loc.

The two nouns *ʿenûṯ* (Ps. 22:25[24]) and *taʿanîṯ* (Ezr. 9:5) are totally different. Late redaction understood the meaning of the former to be "lowliness"; the original text probably read "cry," "prayer," or "groaning."[49] The hapax legomenon in Ezr. 9:5 is a technical term: "penitential rites" must be ended when the worshiper moves on to adoration and supplication (kneeling, outstretched hands, prayer, vv. 5-6). The rites referred to by *taʿanîṯ* are not described.[50]

IV. Adjective.

1. *Forms.* The semantics of the adjective are difficult, because several forms coexist. Is there a difference in meaning between *ʿānî* and *ʿānāw?*[51] We may note the following data: in the MT *ʿānî* appears in both the singular (57 occurrences) and the plural (19 occurrences). Even if some instances of the singular refer to collective entities, the singular predominates: an individual is characterized as *ʿānî.* In the case of *ʿānāw,* there are 19 instances of the plural and only 1 of the singular, and that (Nu. 12:3) appears to be represented by *ʿānî* in the Samaritan version.[52] The problem, therefore, involves the plurals almost exclusively. Was *ʿanāwîm* the original plural of *ʿānî?*[53] If so, *ʿanîyîm* is a scribal error or an artificial formation used secondarily to convey a semantic distinction. Most scholars believe that the pls. *ʿanîyîm* and *ʿanāwîm* always existed side by side, even though they were often confused. The Masoretes occasionally prefer a *y*-form to a *w*-form (*Q:* Isa. 32:7; Am. 8:4; Ps. 9:19[18]; Job 24:4) or a *w*-form to a *y*-form (Ps. 9:13[12]; 10:12; Prov. 3:34; 14:21; 16:19; possibly random scribal variation; cf. the lack of uniformity in Ps. 9/10). We can possibly discern a conscious development in which *ʿanîyîm* = "poor" and *ʿanāwîm* = "humble, devout," but the distinction should not be pressed.[54]

2. *Outside the Psalms.* a. *Juridical Texts.* Leaving the Psalms aside, I shall sketch the areas with which *ʿānî* is naturally associated. As in the case of the verb, the juridical sphere is of special importance. Persons deprived of certain natural rights, who experience a perceptible diminution of their quality of life, are called *ʿanîyîm.* Legal offenses against them are associated with the laws governing loans and credit. A collection of parenetically formulated precepts protecting marginal groups (Ex. 22:20-26[21-27]) includes a prohibition against exacting interest from an *ʿammî heʿānî,* an "impoverished member of your clan" (v. 24[25]). The following verse deals with a pledge taken from a neighbor *(rēaʿ).* Both *ʿam* and *rēaʿ* refer to a consanguineous neighbor, originally a "father's brother."[55] This individual is further defined by an attributive adjec-

---

49. Cf. LXX; H. Gunkel, *Die Psalmen. HKAT* II/2 (^{4}1929), 97: "to answer."
50. Cf. Qumran, I.7 above.
51. As asserted by Birkeland, Causse, Gelin, and others.
52. *HAL,* II, 855.
53. Delekat, Rudolph.
54. See the cautions articulated by Martin-Achard, *TLOT,* II, 932-33; Grundmann, *TDNT,* VIII, 6.
55. →עם *ʿam;* cf. *HAL,* II, 837, citing A. R. Hulst, *TLOT,* II, 896.

tive: *heʿānî,* someone living in reduced economic circumstances, dependent, in danger of losing the necessities of life (cf. Lev. 25:25-38; Dt. 23:20-21[19-20]; 24:6,10-13,17; Ezk. 18:7-8,16-17; also Am. 2:8; Job 24:9; Ezk. 22:12; Prov. 19:17; 22:7; 27:13). Such individuals are granted special protection when they take out a loan or pawn their possessions. The prohibitions are grounded in a direct, personal responsibility toward the "poor," the "economically disadvantaged" (Lev. 19:10; 23:22). "Your hand shall be open to your poor and needy brother" (Dt. 15:11). Here too the adjs. *ʿānî* and *'eḇyôn* further qualify the critical term of relationship *'āḥîḵā,* "your brother," which plays a major role as an equivalent to *rēaʿ* and *ʿam* (Lev. 19:17; 25:25; Dt. 23:20; cf. the precise terminology of Dt. 24:14-15, *śāḵîr ʿānî wᵉ'eḇyôn mē'aḥeyḵā 'ô miggērᵉḵā,* a laborer who is poor and needy and is a member of your tribe or a resident alien). Day laborers are economically disadvantaged. But why the double terminology "poor and needy"? Are we dealing with liturgical language (see 3 below)? Since Rahlfs's study, it has been clear that these terms refer to an Israelite dependent on society for protection and support, an individual who is unemployed or on welfare (see the charitable provisions in Ex. 23:11; Lev. 19:9-10; 23:22; Dt. 24:19-22), who has come down in the world.

b. *Wisdom.* A second focal point of the adj. *ʿānî* is the language and intellectual world of wisdom. Here we find the prohibition: "Do not rob the poor (→ דל *dal*) because they are poor, or crush the lowly *(ʿānî)* in court, for Yahweh pleads their cause" (Prov. 22:22-23).[56] Similarly in the instructions to Lemuel: "Defend the rights of the poor and needy" (Prov. 31:9). The call to intervene on behalf of the economically disadvantaged is heard in catalogs of virtues and in confessions of faith. The ideal housewife "opens her hand to the poor *(ʿānî)* and reaches out her hands to the needy *('eḇyôn)*" (Prov. 31:20). Job describes his exemplary life: "I delivered the poor *(ʿānî)* who cried and the orphan *(yāṯôm)* who had no helper; the blessing of the wretched *('ōḇēḏ)* came upon me, and I caused the heart of the widow *('almānâ)* to sing for joy" (Job 29:12-13). These groups are similar to those mentioned in the legal texts; vv. 15-16 go on to include the blind, the lame, the needy *('eḇyônîm),* and strangers *(lō'-yāḏaʿtî).* Malfeasance is exposed: Job 24 castigates the conduct of the wicked: "They drive away the donkey of the orphan and take the widow's ox for a pledge; they thrust the needy *('eḇyônîm)* off the road; the poor of the land *(ʿᵃnîyê-'āreṣ)* all hide themselves. . . . They snatch the orphan child from the breast and take a pledge from the poor *(ʿānî)*. . . . At daybreak the murderer goes forth to kill the poor and needy *(ʿānî wᵉ'eḇyôn)*" (Job 24:3-4,9,14).[57] Prov. 30:11-14 is a kind of curse on the proud and godless "generation" *(dôr)* that disdains all norms, seeking to devour the "poor" *(ʿᵃnîyîm)* and the "needy" *('eḇyônîm)* (v. 14; the climax of their transgressions?). Contrariwise, the wise repeatedly pronounce blessings on those who acknowledge that they are bound by the rules of neighborly conduct. Prov. 3:33-35 says: "Yahweh . . . blesses the abode of the righteous *(ṣaddîqîm)* . . . to the wretched *(ʿᵃnîyîm)* he shows favor . . . the wise *(ḥᵃḵāmîm)* will inherit honor" (cf. 14:21; 16:19). According to Elihu, God himself

56. Cf. Amen-em-ope iv.4-5 (*ANET,* 422a).
57. G. Fohrer, *Das Buch Hiob. KAT* XVI (1963), 367ff.

is absolutely just and impartial (Job 34:19), so that he hears the cry of the afflicted (*dal* and *ʿᵃnîyîm*, 34:28; cf. 36:6). Indeed, he goes so far as to argue that God uses the affliction of the poor for positive ends (36:15). Prov. 15:15 and Eccl. 6:8 reflect on the fate of the poor, both with stoic objectivity.

As a result, we can see in these wisdom texts the system of societal norms that supports and integrates marginal groups. The socialization process inculcates these norms, bringing them constantly to mind through various forms of exhortation and admonition. The *ʿānî* is never an isolated individual but a representative of a social stratum; by law and custom, such a person has a claim on divine and human help.[58] The *ʿᵃnîyîm* and *ʿᵃnāwîm* are synonymous with the economically and socially deprived and vulnerable; they are identical with the *dallîm, ʾeḇyônîm,* and *rāšîm.*[59]

c. *Prophets.* Can the usage of juridical texts and wisdom literature explain the other occurrences, especially in the prophets? In fact, many prophetic oracles reflect the charitable norms of the laws and wisdom instruction. Amos's championship of the disadvantaged is well known (Am. 2:6ff.; 4:1; 5:11-12). In 2:7 and 8:4 *(K)* he uses the terms *ʿᵃnāwîm* and *ʿanwê-ʾāreṣ* (elsewhere *ʾeḇyônîm, ṣaddîq, dallîm*). His vocabulary recalls legal and wisdom language (on Am. 2:7 cf. Ex. 23:2; Lev. 19:15; Job 24:4; Prov. 22:22; on Am. 8:4 cf. Ex. 22:21-23[22-24]; Job 24:4,14; Prov. 30:14; clan wisdom? cultic norms?).[60] Zec. 7:9-10 is even clearer: "Render true judgments, show kindness and mercy to one another; do not oppress the widow, the orphan, the alien, or the poor; and do not devise evil in your hearts against one another." The obligation to champion the weak, the admonition not to abuse one's own power, and the reference to marginal groups fit with wisdom and law.

Delineations of transgressions reveal the same picture (Isa. 3:14-15; 10:2; Jer. 22:16; Ezk. 16:49; 18:12,17; 22:29). Without reference to fundamental norms, such charges are inconceivable; Isa. 10:1 speaks of written statutes. At times prophetic discourse shifts to exhortation (Isa. 58:7; Zeph. 2:3), description of the future (Isa. 32:7), or eschatological hymnody (Isa. 26:6). The *ʿᵃnāwîm* always enjoy Yahweh's special protection (Isa. 11:4; 14:32; 26:6; 29:19; 32:7; 41:17; 49:13; 61:1; Zeph. 3:12; Zec. 9:9). In the salvation and consolation oracles of the prophetic books we hear the voice of the cultic tradition (see IV.3 below).

The rare feminine forms of the adj. *ʿānî* are significant. Applied attributively to personified cities (Isa. 10:30; 51:21; 54:11), they describe a captured, destroyed, desecrated city (in 10:30 the context also permits the translation "answered" [NRSV], representing the fem. sg. impf. of *ʿānâ* I). The image is that of a disgraced woman (see II.1.a above). With *ʿᵃnîyâ* we find such terms as "forsaken" (54:6), "barren" (54:1), "hated" (60:15), and "desolate" (54:1; 62:4).

The prophetic books appear to reflect an incipient differentiation of *ʿᵃnîyîm* and *ʿᵃnāwîm.* Both contextual analysis and the Masoretic textual tradition support the dis-

---

58. Schwantes.

59. → דל *dal;* → אביון *ʾeḇyôn;* → רוש *rwš.*

60. H. W. Wolff, *Amos the Prophet* (Eng. trans. 1973), 70-73.

tinction. The two plural forms appear side by side: *ʿaniyîm* (Isa. 3:15; 10:2; 14:32; 58:7; in Isa. 32:7 and Am. 9:4, MT has *Q ʿaniyîm;* in Prov. 3:34; 14:21; 16:19 MT *Q* = *ʿanāwîm*) and *ʿanāwîm* (Isa. 11:4; 29:19; 32:7 *K;* 61:1; Am. 2:7; 8:4 *K;* Zeph. 2:3). There appears to be a slight preponderance of *ʿanāwîm* in Isaiah and Zephaniah, reinforced by the aim of the texts (cf. also Proverbs; in contrast, *ʿaniyîm* appears more often in stereotyped contexts: Isa. 3:14; 10:2; 58:7). We also find the fixed phrases *ʿaniyê ʿammî* (Isa. 10:2; 14:32; cf. 49:13; Ps. 72:4) and *ʿanwê (hā)ʾāreṣ* (Isa. 11:4; Am. 8:4; Zeph. 2:3; cf. Ps. 76:10[9]; Job 24:4). There is particular emphasis on collective entities. Of the 28 relevant occurrences from Isa. 3:14 to Zec. 9:9, 18 refer to human groups — the people of Israel, the city of Jerusalem, population strata, an exclusive society — and only 10 to a needy individual (Isa. 3:14; 66:2; Jer. 22:16; Ezk. 16:49; 18:12,17; 22:29; Hab. 3:14; Zec. 7:10; 9:9, exhibiting a marked affinity to the texts establishing norms).

Parallel to the collective emphasis, however, we can also observe an individualization of the term. Many plurals clearly refer to a group made up of individuals; cf. Isa. 61:1: "to bring good news to the oppressed, to bind up the brokenhearted"; Isa. 3:15: "They grind the face of the poor." The phrase *ʿaniyê ʿam* should also be interpreted as referring to a collection of individuals: "They write statutes . . . to rob the poor of my people of their right" (Isa. 10:1-2). The pl. *ʿaniyîm /ʿanāwîm* resolves a group into its components in a way that the traditional appellative "Israel" cannot. The addition of an attributive expression (cf. *śāḵîr ʿānî,* Dt. 24:14; *ʿammî heʿānî,* Ex. 22:24[25]) turns the adj. *ʿānî* into a substantive and a technical sociological term: the poor of the people of Israel, of the (whole) land! Here we find the beginnings of a class concept (cf. Isa. 32:7; Am. 8:4).

3. *Psalms.* The largest concentration of *ʿānâ* II and its derivatives is in the Psalms. The two adjectives account for 38 of the 65 occurrences of the root.

a. *Singular.* When we examine the 24 occurrences of the sg. *ʿānî* and *ʿānāw,* we recognize the situation of the individual supplicant. The connection with the norms laid down by laws and literature is sometimes quite clear. The psalmist uses *ʿānî* and certain synonyms to describe himself: "This poor soul cries" (Ps. 34:7[6]); "I am wretched and in pain *(kôʾēḇ)*" (69:30[29]); "I am lonely *(yāḥîḏ)* and afflicted" (25:16); "I am poor and needy *(ʾeḇyôn)*" (40:18[17]; 70:6[5]; 86:1; 109:22; cf. 35:10; 37:14; 74:21; 109:16; never pl.). The mortal affliction of the psalmist is evident, wrapped in the mantle of liturgical conceptuality and cultic ritual, as he describes his distress. The adj. *ʿānî* and its synonyms is a general signal for personal affliction (see III.2 above) in all its manifestations. "Poor and needy" is an important formula, used also outside the Psalms (Dt. 24:14; Jer. 22:16; Ezk. 18:12; 22:29; Job 24:14; Prov. 21:9). It expresses a claim and plays a special role in supplicatory ritual.[61] The "patient" lays claim to his rights as a poor individual.[62] He assigns himself to the category of those with a right to

61. E. S. Gerstenberger, *Der bittende Mensch. WMANT* 51 (1980), 134ff.
62. Schwantes.

help on the part of the tutelary deity (cf. the formulas avowing innocence and confessing sin, such as Ps. 51:6[4] and 26:1a,11a).[63]

Of the remaining occurrences of the singular, two are textually uncertain: Ps. 14:6, on account of the divergent parallel tradition in Ps. 53:6(5) and the obscure meaning of the passage,[64] and Ps. 68:11(10) (*ʿānî* in parallel with *ḥayyâ,* "flock"; possibly read cj. *ʿam,* "people"). However that may be, the final redactions speak of "plans of the poor" (14:6) and food "for the poor" (68:11[10]), i.e., "the people" in the wilderness.[65]

Finally, there are texts in which the *ʿānî* is affected by certain actions on the part of others or appears as a reactive supplicant. Enemies persecute the poor psalmist, seeking to kill him (Ps. 10:2,9; 37:14; 109:16; does *ḥtp* in 10:9 refer to abduction? [cf. Jgs. 21:21]; more likely it is a metaphor that projects fear, drawn from the language of hunting[66]). God or the king, the maintainer of order, delivers the poor supplicant from his affliction (Ps. 35:10; 72:12) by rendering a just verdict (82:3; 140:13[12]; cf. 72:2,4). Ps. 34:7(6); 74:21; 102:1 (cf. 9:13[12]; 12:6[5]; 22:25[24]) mention the prayer of the *ʿānî,* his cry for help, and his hymn of praise. All in all, the *ʿānî* is at the mercy of powerful enemies and forces at work in society. He turns to his God, asserts his desperate situation, appeals to God for vindication, trusts in God's judicial intervention, rejoices at his deliverance. All this takes place in the setting of a supplicatory liturgy for the *ʿānî* (see above).

b. *Plural.* The plural of the adjective can refer to the sum of individual fortunes as well as to a group, a class, or the people as a whole. Neh. 5 vividly describes a catalog of afflictions. Many are suffering under the adverse economic and political situation, each experiencing a particular hardship: the need to mortgage property (v. 3) or borrow (v. 4), enslavement for debt (v. 5). Bands of people living in marginal circumstances are mentioned in 1 S. 22:2 and Jgs. 11:3. Ps. 12 should be read in the same light: the affliction of individuals (v. 6[5]; cf. v. 3[2]) accumulates before Yahweh and moves him to intervene. The summarizing *kol* in Ps. 76:10(9) (cf. Zeph. 2:3) gives voice to the fate of individuals. The mention of "establishing judgment" on behalf of the oppressed is rooted in the notion of justice for the individual (see above); it is then extended to groups (Ps. 12:6[5]; 76:10[9]). The use of plural and singular forms side by side in the same psalm text (10:2,9,12,17; 22:25,27[24,26]; 25:9,16; 34:3,7[2,6]; 37:11,14; 69:30,33[29,32]; 72:2,4,12; 74:19,21; 109:16,22) demonstrates not only the potential collective meaning of singulars but also the microstructure of the collective.

In many cases, however, a preponderant sense of the group is clearly present, whether the "poor" are identified with "all Israel" (Ps. 72:2; 74:19; 147:6; 149:4; cf. Isa. 49:13) or represent a particular group, category, or stratum within Israel. Then they are contrasted with the "violent," the "wicked," "transgressors," "sinners," etc. How do such collective concepts enter into cultic usage?

---

63. E. S. Gerstenberger, *TRE,* XIII, 386-88.

64. See the comms.

65. H. Gunkel, *HKAT* II/2[4], 289; cf. Kraus, *Psalms 60–150* (Eng. trans. 1989), 44, 46, 52.

66. For the former see A. Alt, *KlS,* I, 333-40; for the latter, O. Keel, *Feinde und Gottesleugner. SBM* 7 (1969).

The phrase ʿᵃnîyê or ʿanwê-ʿam clearly denotes a group (Ps. 72:4; Isa. 10:2; 14:32). References to the exploited and persecuted poor are concentrated in Ps. 9/10; 25; 34; 37; 69; 72; 109. The acrostic Ps. 9/10 (Ps. 25, 34, and 37 are also examples of this late form) furnishes the clearest example. This psalm contains elements of an individual thanksgiving and lament, but it universalizes the description of distress and the violence of the oppressors (esp. 10:3ff.). The shift from the catalog of individual victims of these machinations — the sorely pressed and delivered "I" (9:2ff.[1ff.]), the oppressed (*daḵ,* 9:10[9]; 10:18), the helpless (? *ḥêlᵉḵâ,*[67] 10:8,14), the orphan (*yāṯôm,* 10:14,18), the poor (*ʿānî,* 10:2,9) — to the plural referring to the persecuted and exploited (*ʿᵃnāwîm/ʿᵃnîyîm,* 9:13,19[12,18]; 10:12,17) provides the interpretive key. Those who used this psalm obviously thought of themselves as poor wretches, marginalized by the power elite, impoverished and déclassé — cf. the image of the lion (10:9) and the description of the blasphemous brutality of those in power (10:3ff.). These *ʿᵃnāwîm* constituted a cultic community, for they addressed Yahweh collectively (10:17-18); the acrostic form does not argue the contrary.[68] The traditions of the poor and afflicted individual and the divine helper have been assimilated. There is a similar polarization in Ps. 34 and 37.[69] Such a group is conceivable only in the context of exilic/postexilic community development. Ps. 25 is a communal confession of sin. Ps. 69 and 109 have been subjected to redaction. Ps. 72 bears a messianic stamp: the oppressor is external (vv. 4,11), but the rift also divides Israel (vv. 4 [*ʿᵃnîyê-ʿam*],12-14).

Did this development lead to a new meaning for *ʿᵃnāwîm,* "humble"? Did it become a self-description? We can only speculate. Our word appears occasionally in parallel with "brokenhearted" (Ps. 109:16,22; 147:3; cf. Isa. 61:1; 66:2). The physical affliction of the psalmist also has a psychic aspect (cf. the stereotyped descriptions of affliction in Ps. 22:7-19[6-18]; 38:4-9[3-8]; 55:5-6[4-5]; 69:4; etc.). The contrition and inner torment of the psalmist are also emphasized as being pleasing to God (51:19[17]). This language does not imply a particular spiritualization of affliction. The condition described by *ʿānî* involves the total person. The group or community used the plural in the cult to describe their condition; they did not employ it as a self-designation, preferring instead such terms as *ṣaddîqîm,* "the righteous" (1:5-6; 34:16[15]; 37:17,29,39; 69:29[28]; 97:12; 125:3; 146:8), *ḥᵃsîḏîm,* "the faithful" (30:5[4]; 31:24[23]; 52:11[9]; 79:2; 85:9[8]; 89:20[19]; 97:10; 116:15; 148:14; 149:1,5,9), *yirʾê yhwh,* "those who fear Yahweh" (15:4; 22:24[23]; 33:18; 103:17; 115:11; 118:4), *yišrê-lēḇ,* "the upright" (7:11[10]; 11:2; 32:11; 36:11[10]; 64:11[10]; 94:15; 97:11), and *yišrê-ḏāreḵ,* "those whose way is upright" (37:14). The consonantal text uses *ʿᵃnāwîm* (10 times) more of-

---

67. → III, 205-6.

68. Contra S. Mowinckel, *The Psalms in Israel's Worship,* 2 vols. (Eng. trans. 1962), II, 111ff. ("never ritually used," 114); H. Gunkel and J. Begrich, *Intro. to Psalms* (Eng. trans. 1998), 294: "superficial adornment"; cf. E. Gerstenberger, *Psalms, Part I. FOTL* XIV (1988), 72-76 (on Ps. 9/10).

69. P. A. Munch, *ZAW* 55 (1937) 36-46; Gunkel and Begrich, 150: "The pious belong to the lower classes. The rich and the powerful stand over against them." O. Michel, *TRE,* IV, 75: "a group . . . that has separated from the rest of the people."

ten than *ʿᵃnîyîm* (6 times). There are 2 occurrences of *ʿᵃnāwîm* as a *Q* reading (9:13[12]; 10:12; cf. 12:6[5]) and one of *ʿᵃnîyîm* (9:19[18]; cf. 10:17). There does appear to be one bit of evidence for an idealization of humility: Nu. 12:3 describes the exemplary figure of Moses as *ʿānāw* (sg. and superlative) — the only instance of concrete historical usage! Here modesty is a virtue.[70] It is of interest that one text uses the phrase *ʾš ʿnh,* "a humble man," as a royal predicate, possibly of cultic significance.[71]

4. *Excursus: Poverty.* This word group, especially the adjectives, has occasioned numerous studies of Israel's sociological history.[72] Many of these have espoused some form of the theory that over the course of centuries in Israel the socioeconomic concept of poverty developed into an ideal of spiritual poverty before God and humility toward God. Sociologically, this theory holds that at the end of this development the *ʿᵃnāwîm* represented a movement or group embracing poverty, an outgrowth of the suffering and oppression experienced during the exile: "Israel became *ʿanaw* through the exile"; in any case, "there came into being in Israel a party that voluntarily realized that transformation in its own life."[73]

The history of poverty in Israel is part of its sociological development. The latter is not easy to trace. Using the sources with caution (does the OT include texts composed by the "poor"?), taking into account the realities of life in the ancient world, and avoiding modern thought categories, we can sketch various stages in the history of the poor.[74]

Individual poverty and misery were unknown in the early family structure of Israel. Production and provision of life's necessities were functions of the community. If anyone suffered, the group also suffered, even in cases of sickness or accident. The early individual laments do not mention poverty; it does not appear until the socioeconomic system became more complex. Aggregations of latifundia, urbanization, introduction of a money economy, administrative centralization, all of which undermined rural family businesses as well as the social structure based on families and villages, were necessary conditions for the appearance of the "poor." Laws, prophetical writings, and psalms document a centuries-long struggle against poverty. It began during the early monarchy (1 S. 22:2, without *ʿānâ* II; possibly Deuteronomistic language) and lasted into the late OT period (Lev. 25; Neh. 5; Job 24:2-9). Economic politics and the tax system of the Persian Empire hastened the dissolution of familial associations and the growth of a proletariat.[75]

In the midst of these changing social structures, with the end of political independence there came into being Jewish communities held together by a common tradition,

70. Cf. I.7 above and VI.2 below.
71. *KAI* 202A.2.
72. See the bibliog.
73. Rahlfs, 84, 85; → אביון *ʾeḇyôn;* → דל *dal.*
74. On methodology see G. Hamel, "Poverty and Charity in Roman Palestine" (diss., Santa Cruz, 1983); W. Thiel, *Die soziale Entwicklung Israels in vorstaatlicher Zeit* (^{2}1985), esp. 150ff.
75. Kippenberg.

by temple and torah. The lexical group associated with *ʿānâ* II probably did not attain its documented meaning until after the exile; most texts appear not to antedate the 6th century. The "misery" of the Israelites was caused by external and internal oppression and exploitation, both political and social. These communities could draw on the tradition that "Yahweh helps the poor" dating from the period of the monarchy, understanding themselves as the true Israel (collective consciousness) while repudiating the Babylonian and Persian oppressors and their domestic collaborators (particularist consciousness).

We have no precise information about the extent of poverty in Israel. Natural catastrophes and wars aggravated social grievances; political or economic good fortune created periods of temporary prosperity. The population as a whole, however, became increasingly impoverished. As had been true for ages, those who had lost their familial support were the most vulnerable: widows, orphans, aliens (Ex. 22:21ff.[22ff.]; Dt. 24:19-21; Job 24:3), the blind, the lame, and others with physical defects (Lev. 19:14; Ps. 146:8), prisoners (Ps. 68:7[6]; 69:34[33]; Job 36:8), smallholders (1 K. 21:1-13), debtors (1 S. 22:2), and laborers (Lev. 19:13; Dt. 24:14). At the same time, the ancient tradition of familial and tribal unity associated with the religion of Yahweh encouraged solidarity with the innocent poor. Which groups of persons slipped through the safety net at what point is difficult to determine, but there is evidence that it happened (1 K. 17:12; Jgs. 11:7; Gen. 37:18-28).

V. Theology of the Oppressed.

1. *Assumptions.* How did a theology of the poor come into being in Israel? Several factors contributed: (a) In the domain of family religion, the personal tutelary deity of the family was responsible for the well-being of the devotees.[76] (b) As centralized states developed, the king (at least in theory) as representative of the deity took responsibility for public welfare; this was the case in Israel (Ps. 72). The reform laws of Sumerian and Akkadian rulers from Urukagina of Lagash to Hammurabi of Babylon bear eloquent witness to this responsibility.[77] (c) In Israel, in the incipient theocracy of the exilic and postexilic period, Yahweh championed the cause of the poor. "Father of orphans and protector of widows" is one of God's titles, reflecting the ancient familial ideology (Ps. 68:6[5]; cf. Dt. 10:17-19; Lam. 5:1-3; Isa. 63:8,16; 64:7[8]). (d) Priests, Levites, scribes, and community leaders inculcated the theology of the mighty God who showed mercy to each individual and in particular championed the cause of the poor on the principle of familial solidarity. Many of the spiritual leaders of the early Jewish community were so close to the people and economically underprivileged that a genuine theology of the poor came into being. The sufferings of the people of Israel, especially the impoverished rural population, were incorporated into the liturgical texts of the prophetic corpora and the Psalter.

---

76. H. Vorlander, *Mein Gott. AOAT* 23 (1975); R. Albertz, *Persönliche Frömmigkeit und offizielle Religion* (1978).

77. *Rechts- und Wirtschaftsurkunden: Historisch-chronologische Texte. TUAT* I/1 (1985).

2. *Individuals and Marginal Groups.* Yahweh preferentially cares for the needy individuals and marginal groups. Why? The ancient laments associated with the extended family were incorporated into the religion of Yahweh and the larger social unit. God's solidarity was extended to the sick (Ps. 38), the innocent victim of persecution (Ps. 7; 17; 26), sinners (Ps. 51), and the *'ānî,* the economically destitute (Ps. 9/10; 37). Yahweh, God of the poor — this is a heritage from familial religion in a new, extended social setting. The impoverished individual appears as a new type of person in need of help. Deuteronomy speaks of orphans, widows, and aliens (as well as the Levites!) (Dt. 10:18; 14:29; 16:11,14; 26:12-13; 27:19). In Dt. 24:10-15 the *'ānî* and *śāḵîr,* the new categories of the underprivileged, are listed before the traditional categories (24:17-21) and are equated with them. Ps. 82:3-4 names three pairs of people seeking justice: *daḵ* (cj. for *dal*) *wᵉyāṯôm,* "the weak and the orphan"; *'ānî wārāš,* "the lowly and destitute"; and *dal wᵉ'eḇyôn,* "the weak and the needy," thus including the *'ᵃnîyîm* in the list (cf. Zec. 7:10; Isa. 58:6-7,10). In the late psalms primary emphasis is on the *'ᵃnāwîm* (Ps. 9/10; 25; 34; 37; 119).

Yahweh is also the God of the economically vulnerable; by virtue of ancient familial tradition, he stands in solidarity with them as a trustworthy helper and a proven savior. He hears the laments and the prayers of his own; to him expressions of trust and praise are addressed. "You do not forget the oppressed" (Ps. 10:12). "Good and upright is Yahweh; therefore he instructs sinners in the way. He leads the humble in what is right, and teaches the humble his way" (25:8-9). "My soul makes its boast in Yahweh; let the humble hear and be glad" (34:3[2]; cf. 22:27[26]; 69:33). Enemies, however, sometimes prevail (Ps. 9/10) — "brothers" from the supplicant's own people (Isa. 66:5).

3. *The Whole Community.* All Israel — or more precisely the postexilic temple community and the local communities of Palestine or in exile — could think of themselves as *'ᵃnāwîm* (Isa. 14:32; 26:1-6; 41:17; 49:13; 61:1-7; Zeph. 2:3; Ps. 18:28[27]; 69:31-34[30-33]; 72:2; 74:18-23; 147:3-6; 149:4). How does the theological language change when these communities become exclusive? Just as the theology of marginal groups draws on familial traditions, so the "all Israel" theology of the poor emerges from traditions of the monarchy and a universalistic ideology. Universal symbols are necessary, the traditions of Zion and David, myths of a world mountain and battle with chaos (Ps. 72; 76; Isa. 25:1-5; 29:17-21; 61:1-9). The danger of jumping from wretchedness to a halo of triumphalism is greater than in the case of a smaller group. The enemy city is trampled by the poor (Isa. 26:6). The needy remnant of Israel will live in renewed glory, but God will kill the Philistines (14:30,32). Upon liberation, the depression of those who suffered turns into a hymn of victory (49:13). At the same time, however, the sufferings of the whole exilic and postexilic community bring new recognition (52:13–53:12): in the figure of the moribund servant (*'ānâ* II in vv. 4,7), contrary to all outward appearances, inchoate life is already present.

4. *Liberation.* This is in fact the goal of all laments and supplications on the part of the afflicted: may Yahweh vanquish their suffering and establish the full, intact potentiality of life. The sufferer hopes for the restoration of health and social status (Ps. 35:10;

40:18[17]; 69:30[29]). Marginal groups are to be sustained. "Indeed, there should be no poor among you" (Dt. 15:4). But since there are, it is the duty of society as a whole to rehabilitate them (Dt. 15:7-8,11; Lev. 25:25ff.). To overcome affliction means to destroy the hostile powers that cause misery. God's righteousness and power succeed, now and in the future, in bringing about this miracle, which is appropriately celebrated in hymns (cf. the rejoicing of the afflicted in Ps. 22:27[26]; 34:3[2]; 69:33[32]). This is the beginning of true life, peace, and salvation for the afflicted. From this perspective, affliction is preliminary, perhaps a trial by fire for the kingdom of righteousness. Thus *ʿānî* and *ʿonî* take on eschatological overtones (Zeph. 3:11-13; Isa. 61:1ff.). Reflective wisdom can already say: "He delivers the afflicted by their affliction, and opens their ear by adversity" (Job 36:15; cf. 33:14-22). For the early Jewish community, suffering becomes a passage to salvation (Isa. 52:13–53:12). The *ʿanāwîm* acquire special significance. Yahweh stands in solidarity with them (Isa. 41:17; 66:2; Ps. 18:28[27]; 22:25[24]; etc.). They are his possession (Isa. 49:13; Ps. 72:1-2), his "mediators" (Isa. 53:4-5; 62:1-5; Ps. 41:2[1]; Prov. 17:5). This identification continues in full force in Mt. 25:34-40.

VI. Broader Horizons. The "theology of the poor" has continued to be influential down to the present day. The OT never glorified or trivialized poverty. It had to be suffered through, and became a reference point for theological thought and language.

1. *Hellenism.* During the 3rd century B.C.E., Greek-speaking Jewish communities came into existence. By using terms like *tapeinós* to translate *ʿānâ* II (see I.6 above), did they promote an introverted spiritualization of poverty? Hellenistic social conditions were no paradise.[78] An aristocratic social structure, deification of the king, the economic system (including taxation), and extravagant expenditures on arms and military operations could only aggravate the wretchedness of broad strata of the populace. The Hellenephone Jewish communities shared to some extent in the prosperity of the upper classes, but had to suffer the fate of an oppressed minority; they lived in the tradition of the OT. The tension inherent in such an existence is especially notable in the life and work of Philo of Alexandria and Flavius Josephus. The language of affliction and poverty therefore was not abstractly spiritualized.[79] In the Greek Apocrypha and Pseudepigrapha (e.g., Sirach), oppression, lowliness, and poverty play an important role (Sir. 3:17-25; 4:1-10; 7:4-7; 13:18-20; 35:14-21; etc.); the apocalypses project tribulation and deliverance into the eschaton (see 2 below).

2. *Judaism.* We likewise find the theme of affliction and oppression in the Hebrew and Aramaic tradition. The original Hebrew text of Sirach may be cited as an example (cf. Pss. Sol. 5; 10). The Zadokite Fragment (8:13) quotes Isa. 10:2.[80] In 1 Enoch the

78. M. Hengel, *Judaism and Hellenism,* 2 vols. in 1 (Eng. trans. 1974, repr. 1981); Kippenberg, 78ff.
79. W. Grundmann, *TDNT,* VIII, 1ff.
80. Charles, *APOT,* II, 814.

spirits of the giants torment the world (15:11) as the princes of the eschatological age do the righteous (46:8; 53:7). The paradise to come is marked by the absence of all torment and distress for the righteous (20:6; 4 Ezra 7:114) and suppression of the evil powers (1 Enoch 48:8,10; 50:2; 62:4-5,10; 91:12).

Apocalyptic literature uses oppression as an eschatological commonplace. "Woe to you mighty, who oppress the righteous with violence. The day of your destruction is coming" (1 Enoch 96:8). The Testaments of the Twelve Patriarchs, which stands closer to the wisdom tradition, promotes "lowliness of heart" (T. Reub. 6:10). Issachar is a model of modesty and simplicity; he sympathizes with the "poor and weak" (T. Iss. 4:1–5:3, esp. 5:2; 6:5). Sympathy is the motto of Zebulun (T. Zeb. 5:1ff.). A personal attitude of modesty and lowliness is also urged by Pirqe Abot (1:3; 4:4,12; 6:6; etc.). Generosity to the poor goes without saying (1:5). The members of the Qumran sect were instructed along the same lines (1QS 2:24; 4:3; 5:3,25; 9:22; 10:26). The poor and lowly are identified with the devout, the righteous, the elect (1QH 2:13,32,34; 3:25; 5:13-22 [six relevant words and phrases, including *ʿānî* and *ʿᵃnāwîm*]; 14:3; 18:14-15; 1QM 11:9; 13:14; 14:5-11). Violent, colorful images describe the apostate antagonists and authorities (the orthodox Jews?).

To sum up: in the different streams of OT tradition about the "poor, lowly, oppressed," various nuances of our lexical family evolve in various places. Included are texts referring to the psychic and personal qualities, characteristics, and attitudes. But there is no observable "development" in the direction of spiritualization.

3. *Christianity.* The tradition continues in the NT, taking on new accents. Jesus understands his mission as being primarily to the humble (Lk. 5:31-32; Mt. 19:14). They are awaiting their physician and redeemer; they are more inclined and able to accept the gospel of the kingdom of God than are the wealthy and the orthodox, the teachers of the law and the politicians. For Paul, too — by virtue of theological reasoning as well as the realities of the Christian community — the priority of the lowly was clear (1 Cor. 1:26-28).

The OT heritage has descended through subsequent ages, primitive Christianity, the Middle Ages, and the dawn of the industrial age, down to the present with its controversies over capitalism, imperialism, the social state, and the impoverishment of the "third and fourth worlds" in the Latin American church.[81]

Gerstenberger

81. On the Middle Ages see M. Mollat, *Die Armen im Mittelalter* (1984); the history of the monastic orders. On the industrial age see C. Jantke and D. Hilger, ed., *Die Eigentumslosen* (1965); K. Marx and F. Engels. On the present see Croatto, Gutiérrez, Hanks, Schwantes, Tamez, Lohfink.

עָנָן *'ānān*

I. Occurrences and Distribution: 1. Etymology; Ancient Near East; 2. OT Occurrences. II. Meaning and Usage: 1. Meteorological Phenomenon; 2. Metaphorical Usage; 3. LXX and Dead Sea Scrolls.

I. Occurrences and Distribution.

1. *Etymology; Ancient Near East.* The noun *'ānān,* "cloud," occurs 87 times in the OT; in addition, there is a hapax legomenon, Aram. *'ᵃnān* (Dnl. 7:13), and a collective noun *'ᵃnānâ* (Job 3:5). The PN *'ānān* (Neh. 10:27[Eng. v. 26]) also belongs under this heading.[1] The word is probably a primary noun, for the verb *'ānan* piel, found only in Gen. 9:14, has the meaning "cause clouds to gather" *(figura etymologica)* and is clearly denominative. Whether the polel form, meaning "interpret signs, divine," derives from this verb or from a homographic lexeme is uncertain, but the latter assumption is more likely.[2]

The noun is rare outside Hebrew, occurring predominantly in later languages: in Jewish Aramaic, Syriac, Mandaic, and Arabic *('anān),* the meaning "cloud" is clearly attested.[3] A noun *'nn* occurs 6 times in Ugaritic texts and should probably be supplied in *KTU* 1.2, I, 18. In *KTU* 1.2, I, 34-35, *b'l w'nnh* is generally translated "Baal and his servants [messengers]." In *KTU* 1.4, IV, 59, we find *'nn 'ṯrt,* said to mean "a servant of Asherah"; similarly *'nn ilm,* "servant of the gods."[4] Two other occurrences are damaged.[5] The meaning of the Ugaritic texts is unclear. Most scholars interpret *'nn* as "servant" or "messenger," deriving the Ugaritic word from a root distinct from biblical *'nn.* In all the legible texts, it is associated with deities. It is therefore reasonable to accept

---

'ānān. É. Cassin, *La splendeur divine* (1968); S. Grill, *Die Gewittertheophanie im AT. Heiligenkreuzer Studien* 1 (1931); B. Holmberg, "Herren och molnet i Gamla testamentet," *SEÅ* 48 (1983) 31-47; E. Jenni, "עָנָן *'ānān* cloud," *TLOT,* II, 937-39; J. Jeremias, *Theophanie. WMANT* 10 (²1977); L. Kopf, "Arabische Etymologien und Parallelen zum Bibelwörterbuch," *VT* 8 (1958) 161-215; J. Luzarraga, *Las tradiciones de la nube en la Biblia y en el Judaismo primitivo. AnBibl* 54 (1973), esp. 15-41; T. W. Mann, "The Pillar of Cloud in the Reed Sea Narrative," *JBL* 90 (1971) 15-30; E. Manning, "La nuée dans l'Écriture," *BVC* 54 (1963) 51-64; G. E. Mendenhall, *The Tenth Generation* (1973), esp. 32-66; A. Oepke, "νεφέλη," *TDNT,* IV, 902-10; W. J. Phythian-Adams, *The People and the Presence* (1942); G. von Rad, "The Tent and the Ark," *Problem of the Hexateuch and Other Essays* (Eng. trans. 1966), 103-24; P. Reymond, *L'eau, sa vie et sa signification dans l'AT. SVT* 6 (1958); L. Sabourin, "The Biblical Cloud," *BTB* 4 (1974) 290-312; R. B. Y. Scott, "Behold, He Cometh with Clouds," *NTS* 5 (1958/59) 127-32; idem, "Meteorological Phenomena and Terminology in the OT," *ZAW* 64 (1952) 11-25; L. I. J. Stadelmann, *The Hebrew Conception of the World. AnBibl* 39 (1970), esp. 97ff.; E. F. Sutcliffe, "The Clouds as Water-Carriers in Hebrew Thought," *VT* 3 (1953) 99-103.

1. *PNPI,* 106, contra *IPN* 38, 184; Benz, 382.
2. For the former see *HAL,* II, 857; cf. Jenni, 937. On the discussion see Kopf, 190.
3. See *LexSyr,* 533; *MdD,* 24; Wehr, 647.
4. *KTU* 1.3, IV, 32; 1.4, VIII, 15.
5. *KTU* 1.10, II, 33 and 2.8, 4.

Mendenhall's theory that *ʿnn* as a "cloud" or "veil" of a god is the Semitic equivalent of Akk. *melammū.*

Freedman — Willoughby

2. *OT Occurrences.* The 87 OT occurrences are distributed as follows: 51 in the Pentateuch (4 in Gen. 9; 20 in Exodus [5 in Ex. 40]; 2 in Leviticus; 20 in Numbers [Nu. 9–10, with 14 occurrences, has the densest "cloud concentration" in the OT]; 5 in Deuteronomy); 2 in the Deuteronomistic History; 4 in the Chronicler's History; 2 in Hosea; 1 each in Isaiah, Deutero-Isaiah, Jeremiah, Joel, Nahum, and Zephaniah; 11 in Ezekiel; 4 in Psalms; 6 in Job; 1 in Lamentations. It is hard to assign the word to the individual sources of the Pentateuch, but this distribution — as regards the meteorological phenomenon — is not significant. Only in accounts of theophanies do we find marked divergences specific to particular sources.[6] In describing a theophany J and E prefer direct (J) or indirect (E) confrontation with the deity; JE, D, and P, however, frequently employ the cloud motif in this genre.

Fabry

II. Meaning and Usage.

1. *Meteorological Phenomenon.* The occurrences are concentrated chiefly in metaphorical usage, more precisely in descriptions of theophanies; clouds as a meteorological or atmospheric phenomenon receive little attention (Gen. 9:13-16; Isa. 44:22; Job 3:5; 7:9; etc.). Only once does *ʿānān* refer to a cloud of incense (Ezk. 8:11), a usage from which the metaphor of a cloud as a sign of God's presence in the sanctuary probably evolved (Lev. 16:13).[7]

Freedman — Willoughby

Besides *ʿānān,* the lexical field "cloud" includes the less common → עָב *ʿāḇ,* "cloudbank," → שחק *šaḥaq,* "cloud (of dust)," as well as → ערפל *ʿ^a^rāp̄el,* "thick clouds, darkness," *qîṭôr,* "smoke," *nāśîʾ,* "vapor," *ḥāzîz,* "thundercloud," etc.[8] In arid Palestine clouds were important as bringers of rain.[9]

Fabry

2. *Metaphorical Usage.* The OT uses clouds chiefly in similes and metaphors, in three ways: (a) to represent impermanence; (b) to represent opacity; and (c) on account of their association with storms and elemental violence, to represent a theophany.

a. *Impermanence.* Hos. 6:4 compares Ephraim's love of God to a morning cloud, and to the dew, which vanishes quickly. Because of its sins, Ephraim is like the morning mist or the dew that goes away early (Hos. 13:3). Since Ephraim's love is not constant, Ephraim itself will not endure.

---

6. See II.2 below.
7. See further discussion below.
8. See Scott, Reymond, Luzarraga, Jenni.
9. See Scott, Sutcliffe; also → מטר *māṭār,* esp. VIII, 254-57.

b. *Opacity.* Ezekiel uses the opacity of clouds as an image to describe Gog's overwhelming invasion of Israel. Gog will advance "like a cloud covering the land" (Ezk. 38:9,16). The whole land will be devoured by a cloud from which there is no escape. In Lamentations the poet describes separation from God: "You have wrapped yourself with a cloud so that no prayer can pass through" (3:44). The opacity of clouds or the impenetrability of the morning mist is used to describe the total inaccessibility of the deity.

c. *Theophany.* The association of clouds with storms, tempests, and the powerful forces of nature is used by the prophets when they want to describe God's anger against his enemies (Zeph. 1:15 = Joel 2:2; Nah. 1:3; Ezk. 30:3,18; 32:7; 34:12). God's appearance on the "day of Yahweh"[10] is depicted by thick clouds and darkness *(ḥōšeḵ);* ruin and destruction will reign. Storm clouds provided the prophets an impressive image for describing the devastating anger of God toward his enemies. This use of *ʿānān* is rooted in the ancient tradition of describing God as wrapped in a cloak of clouds or light (Ps. 104:2).

Quite independently of what source stratum they belong to, all the theophany descriptions with *ʿānān* are associated with the exodus and wilderness tradition. While J sees Yahweh himself at work in the act of deliverance, and E the *mal'aḵ hā'ᵉlōhîm,* the JE material[11] uses *ʿammûḏ ʿānān,* "pillar of cloud," together with *ʿammûḏ 'ēš,* "pillar of fire," to describe how God appears to the Israelites (Ex. 13:21-22; 14:19,24; Nu. 12:5; Neh. 9:12,19; Nu. 14:14). The pillar of cloud by day and the pillar of fire by night lead the Israelites and protect them from the Egyptians. The Deuteronomist speaks instead only of the "cloud" (Ex. 14:20), darkness, and fire (Nu. 9:15,22; Dt. 1:33); P once again understands Yahweh and his *kāḇôḏ* as the effectual agent, but combines *kāḇôḏ,* "glory," with *ʿānān:* God's glory is in the cloud (Ex. 16:10; cf. Ezk. 10:3-4; 1 K. 8:10-11 = 2 Ch. 5:13-14).

According to Ex. 33:9-10, too, Yahweh is present only in the "pillar of cloud" in the tent of meeting. The cloud indicates God's presence while at the same time concealing God's radiance (= *kāḇôḏ* in P). God appears veiled within the cloud to Moses on Mt. Sinai to present him with the law (Ex. 19:9,16; 24:15-18; 34:5; cf. Dt. 5:22, where we also find *'ēš*). The *ʿānān* also veils God when God descends to speak with Moses (Nu. 11:25) and with Aaron and Miriam (Nu. 12:5; Ps. 99:7). It reveals God's presence in the tent of meeting (Ex. 40:34,38; Nu. 9:15-22; 17:7[16:42]; Dt. 31:15) and in the temple at its dedication (1 K. 8:10-11 = 2 Ch. 5:13-14).

Thus "cloud" and "fire" symbolize God's being and presence, while at the same time concealing God's nature. By contrast, the *mal'aḵ yhwh,* "angel of Yahweh," is an emissary endowed with divine authority.[12] The long argument between Moses and Yahweh over who will accompany the Israelites on their journey through the wilderness and if necessary into the promised land makes the difference clear. Yahweh says

---

10. → יום *yôm.*
11. P. Weimar, *Die Meerwundererzählung. ÄAT* 9 (1985), 272.
12. → מלאך *mal'āḵ.*

that he will send his messenger (*mal'āḵ,* Ex. 23:20,23; 32:34), but Moses insists that Yahweh come in person (33:12–34:9). Veiled in a cloud, God actually leaves the traditional abode on Mt. Sinai to go with Israel.

In Ex. 14:19 redaction has effaced the distinction between God hidden in the pillar of cloud (JE) and God's messenger: "The angel of God *(mal'aḵ hā'ᵉlōhîm)* who was going before the Israelite army arose and went behind them" (v. 19a); the pillar of cloud *(ʿammûḏ heʿānān)* executes the same movement (v. 19b). The angel of God and the pillar of cloud are two different modes of treating the same event, even when the descriptions do not match. The *ʿānān* mediates Yahweh's presence, whereas the angel acts as Yahweh's agent; the "cloud" shows that Yahweh is present in person; the messenger indicates that Yahweh, present somewhere else, is represented by his agent.

Freedman — Willoughby

Mendenhall suggests that *ʿānān* is an earlier theophanic term than *mal'āḵ*. This theory may be correct; but it is not supported by current German pentateuchal criticism, which concludes that *mal'āḵ* is specific to the earlier E, in contrast to the pillar of cloud of the later JE and the cloud of the Deuteronomist. It is possible for later strata to contain earlier traditions.

Fabry

Moses spoke with Yahweh "face to face" (Nu. 14:14; Ex. 33:11). In these passages Yahweh removed the concealing cloud, which actually represents an element protecting the partner in dialogue with God: when Moses came down from Sinai, his face reflected the radiance of the *kᵉḇôḏ yhwh* (Ex. 34:29-35). All the Israelites were allowed to see the cloud and the fire, but only Moses was allowed to look on Yahweh without his "veil."

The *kāḇôḏ* is in the cloud (Ex. 16:10; 1 K. 8:10-11; Ezk. 10:3-4) that floats around and above the cover of the ark in the most holy place of the tent of meeting (Lev. 16:2).

In Ezekiel's vision of God's appearance (Ezk. 1:4,28), the figure of God can be seen as a human form within a fiery cloud (v. 4). In short, OT theophanic terminology is not invariant. What can be seen is described as a "pillar of fire" or "pillar of cloud" (often depending on whether it is day or night), sometimes simply as a "cloud" (the omission of "pillar" [→ עמוד *ʿammûḏ*] being apparently unimportant) or a "pillar of cloud and fire" (Ex. 14:24). Mendenhall suggests a religio-historical connection between *ʿānān* and Akk. *melammu,* the "awe-inspiring radiance" masking the deity, and between *'ēš* and Akk. *puluḫtu,* the "fearsomeness" in which the deity is clothed when appearing to mortals.[13] Mendenhall states: "These theophanies become reality in human experience and in the corresponding human reaction to them" (see the eschatological texts Dnl. 7:13-14 and Isa. 4:5).

Freedman — Willoughby

13. See *AHw,* II, 643, 878-79.

III. LXX and Dead Sea Scrolls. The LXX consistently uses *nephélē* or *néphos* to translate *'ānān* and *'āḇ,*[14] more rarely *skótos* (Ex. 14:20) or *gnóphos* (Dt. 4:11; Isa. 44:22).

In the Dead Sea Scrolls 3 occurrences of *'ānān* have been identified. The messenger concept appears in 1QM 12:9, "Our cavalry are like clouds."[15] The other occurrences (4QDibHam[a] 6:10 and 4QDibHam[c] 126:2) recall the presence of God in the cloud and pillar of fire (Ex. 14:24).

Fabry

14. → X, 375; cf. Oepke, *TDNT,* IV, 902.
15. See the discussion → X, 375-76.

עָפָר *'āpār;* עפר *'pr;* אֵפֶר *'ēper*

I. 1. Etymology; 2. Occurrences; 3. LXX. II. General Usage: 1. Loose Earth, Dirt; 2. Soil, Ground; 3. Dust; 4. Ashes; 5. Plaster, Debris. III. Figurative Usage: 1. Multitude; 2. Worthlessness; 3. Devastation; 4. Humiliation; 5. *'ēper.* IV. Religious Significance: 1. God Casts Down and Raises Up; 2. Rites of Abasement and Self-Abasement; 3. Self-Abasement Formulas; 4. Return to Dust; 5. The Grave and the Netherworld. V. Dead Sea Scrolls.

I. 1. *Etymology.* The root *'pr* appears as a common Semitic nominal stem meaning "loose earth, dust."[1] Besides Hebrew, it is found in Akkadian,[2] Ugaritic, Arabic, Ara-

'āpār. S. Abir, "Das Erdreich als Schöpfungselement in den Mythen der Urgeschichte," *Jud* 35 (1979) 23-27, 125-30; G. W. Coats, "Self-Abasement and Insult Formulas," *JBL* 89 (1970) 14-26; M. Dahood, "Hebrew-Ugaritic Lexicography VII," *Bibl* 50 (1969) 352; P. Fronzaroli, *Studi sul lessico comune semitico. AANLR* VIII/23 (1968), 271, 287, 298; A. Guillaume, "A Note on Numbers xxiii 10," *VT* 12 (1962) 335-37; J. Heller, "Noch zu Ophra, Ephron und Ephraim," *VT* 12 (1962) 339-41; J. Hempel, *Gott und Mensch im AT. BWANT* 38 ([2]1936); E. Kutsch, *"Trauerbräuche" und "Selbstminderungsriten" im AT. ThS* 78 (1965); E. Y. Kutscher, "עֵפֶר," *Leš* 27/28 (1964) 183-88; C. Rabin, "Etymological Notes," *Tarbiz* 33 (1963/64) 109-17; A. F. Rainey, "Dust and Ashes," *Tel Aviv Journal* 1 (1974) 77-83; N. H. Ridderbos, "עָפָר als Staub des Totenortes," *OTS* 5 (1948) 174-78; W. H. Schmidt, *Die Schöpfungsgeschichte der Priesterschrift. WMANT* 17 ([2]1967), 197-99, 214-18; A. Schwarzenbach, *Die geographische Terminologie im Hebräischen des ATs* (1954), 123-29; R. Smend, "Asche," *BHHW,* I, 136; K. L. Tallqvist, *Sumerisch-akkadische Namen der Totenwelt. StOr* V/4 (1934); L. Wächter, *Der Tod im AT. AzT* II/8 (1967), 48-52, 97-106, 161; idem, "Unterweltsvorstellung und Unterweltsnamen in Babylonien, Israel und Ugarit," *MIO* 15 (1969) 327-36; G. Wanke, "עָפָר *'āpār* dust," *TLOT,* II, 939-41.

1. Fronzaroli, 271, 287, 298.
2. W. von Soden, *ZA* 76 (1986) 155.

maic, and Syriac. From this stem Hebrew forms the noun ʿāp̄ār and its verbal derivative ʿpr piel, "throw dirt."

The noun ʾēp̄er, which resembles ʿāp̄ār phonologically, partially corresponds to it semantically. It is found only in Hebrew, Jewish Aramaic, and Ethiopic.[3] Until recently, ʾēp̄er was translated as "ashes." Barth defined it as synonymous with ʿāp̄ār, with the original meaning "dust"; Zimmern explained it as a loanword from Akk. epru.[4] This explanation appeared to solve the problem, especially since the linguistic development of epru from ʿpr in Akkadian is easy to explain.[5] Schwarzenbach and Rainey take other approaches. Schwarzenbach does not dispute Zimmern's theory, but seeks to demonstrate a semantic distinction between ʿāp̄ār and ʾēp̄er on the evidence of differing lexical fields, returning to the traditional translation "dust" for ʾēp̄er.[6] Rainey maintains that the etymology of ʾēp̄er is still a riddle.[7] The word, he claims, refers to the ashes found in all settled sites, which were mixed with clay or dirt to reinforce streets. This theory by no means refutes Zimmern's etymology.

2. *Occurrences.* There are 110 occurrences of ʿāp̄ār in the OT, only 2 of which (Job 28:6; Prov. 8:26) are in the plural. Its frequency varies greatly in the different books: 26 occurrences in Job, 13 in Psalms, 15 in Isaiah, none at all in Jeremiah. The verb ʿpr piel appears only in 2 S. 16:13.

There are 22 occurrences of ʾēp̄er, mostly in relatively late texts (Job, Esther, Trito-Isaiah, Ezekiel). The only preexilic texts are 2 S. 13:19, Jer. 6:26, and possibly Gen. 18:27.

3. *LXX.* The most common translations in the LXX are gḗ (43 times) and choús (41 times). Nine times the LXX uses chṓma (which like choús has the basic meaning "heaped-up earth") and 4 times édaphos, "soil."

Dt. 9:21 twice translates ʿāp̄ār with koniortós, "(cloud of) dust," which elsewhere represents ʾāḇāq. In promises of increase, the translations ámmos, "sand" (3 times), and spérma (Nu. 23:10) are striking. Job 14:8 uses the translation pétra, "stone"; in Job 30:6, however, petrṓn represents kēp̄îm and ʿāp̄ār is untranslated. The same is true in Job 4:19: pēlós, "clay," does not stand directly for ʿāp̄ār. Nu. 19:17 deals with ashes, and therefore the translation spodía is used.

The variation in translation is based only in part on perceived semantic differences (when ʿāp̄ār refers to plaster or rubbish, choús is always used); in part the choice of word depends on the personal preference of the group of translators. In Job the LXX prefers gḗ (17 times), as in Isaiah; in Psalms choús predominates (10 times).

The translation of ʾēp̄er is uniform: spodós, "ashes"; only Nu. 19:10 uses the synon-

---

3. Leslau, *Contributions,* 11.

4. J. Barth, *Etymologische Studien,* 20-21; H. Zimmern, *Akkadische Fremdwörter* (²1917), 43; *AHw,* I, 222-23; *CAD,* IV, 184, 190, 246.

5. Heller, 339.

6. P. 128.

7. P. 81.

ymous *spodía,* since *spodós* appears already in the preceding clause. Job 2:8 is an apparent exception, with *kopría,* "dung heap." But the LXX reflects a different textual tradition: according to the MT, Job sits at home among the *ʾēp̱er,* whereas according to the LXX he sits outside the city on a dung heap.

II. General Usage. Starting from the basic meaning "loose earth, dirt, dust," *ʿāp̱ār* developed a range of meanings, extending on the one hand as far as "ground" and on the other as far as "ashes."

1. *Loose Earth, Dirt.* The Philistines fill the wells with loose earth *(ʿāp̱ār)* to make them unusable (Gen. 26:15). The blood spilled when animals or birds are slaughtered is to be covered with earth (Lev. 17:13). The Chaldeans heap up earth to capture fortresses (Hab. 1:10). Shimei throws stones and flings clods of earth *(ʿippar beʿāp̱ār)* at David (2 S. 16:13). Ezk. 24:7 vividly describes Jerusalem's bloodguilt: the blood she shed was poured on bare rock rather than on the ground *(ʿal- hāʾāreṣ),* where it could be covered with earth *(leḵassôṯ ʿālāyw ʿāp̱ār,* Ezk. 24:7). By contrast, Job 16:18 reads: "O earth *(ʾereṣ),* do not cover my blood." The same notion appears in Isa. 26:21. Thus meanings of *ʿāp̱ār* and *ʾereṣ* intersect.[8] The same holds true for *ʾaḏāmâ.*[9] Gen. 2:7 — God "formed man from earth *(ʿāp̱ār),* from the ground *(min-hāʾaḏāmâ)*" — distinguishes loose earth (*ʿāp̱ār*) from the ground *(ʾaḏāmâ).* In Gen. 3:19, however, the statements about returning to the *ʾaḏāmâ* from which the man was taken and returning to dust are placed in parallel. Even if there is a traditio-historical explanation for the difference,[10] these two passages nevertheless reveal that the meanings of *ʿāp̱ār* and *ʾaḏāmâ* also intersect. For this reason, too, the "dust" sprinkled on the head in rituals of (self-)abasement (see IV.2 below) can be called *ʿāp̱ār* or *ʾēp̱er* as well as *ʾaḏāmâ.*

2. *Soil, Ground.* In Job 5:6 "ground, soil" is the meaning of both *ʿāp̱ār* and *ʾaḏāmâ* in the parallel statement: "Misery does not come from the soil *(mēʿāp̱ār*], nor does trouble sprout from the ground *(ûmēʾaḏāmâ).*" In Job 14:8 and Isa. 34:7, *ʾereṣ* and *ʿāp̱ār* are used synonymously side by side. In Isa. 34:9, too, *ʿāp̱ār* means "soil." Snakes are called "ground creepers" — *zōḥalê ʿāp̱ār* in Dt. 32:24, *zōḥalê ʾereṣ* in Mic. 7:17. Iron is taken out of the ground (*ʿāp̱ār,* Job 28:2); torrents of rain can wash away the topsoil of the land (Job 14:19). Isa. 2:19 assumes more permanent features: "They will enter caves of the rocks and caves of the ground *(meḥillôṯ ʿāp̱ār)* from the terror of Yahweh" (cf. v. 10). Job 30:6 also mentions holes in the ground *(ḥōrê ʿāp̱ār),* and 38:38 speaks of the ground's baking solid *(beṣeqeṯ ʿāp̱ār lammûṣāq).*

Finally, as a further development of the meaning "ground," *ʿāp̱ār* could refer to the earth in the comprehensive sense. Job 41:25(Eng. v. 33) says of the crocodile: "On earth it has no equal" *(ʾên-ʿal-ʿāp̱ār mošlô).* This may also be the meaning in 19:25.

---

8. → ארץ *ʾereṣ,* II.2.
9. → אדמה *ʾaḏāmâ,* II.2.a; III.2.a.
10. C. Westermann, *Genesis 1–11* (Eng. trans. 1984), 204-5; Schmidt, 216.

3. *Dust.* In a number of texts (e.g., Gen. 2:7; 3:19), it is possible to waver between the translations "earth" and "dust" for *'āp̱ār.* The situation in Dt. 28:24, however, is clear: "Yahweh will change the rain of your land into powder *('āḇāq)* and dust *('āp̱ār).*" The word for the fine dust stirred up by horses and pedestrians and carried off by the wind, *'āḇāq* (also Isa. 5:24; 29:5; Ezk. 26:10; Nah. 1:3; soot: Ex. 9:9), is here conjoined with *'āp̱ār.*

Dust *('āp̱ār)* is raised by threshing (2 K. 13:7); it lies on the floor of dwellings (Nu. 5:17) and sticks to people's feet (Isa. 49:23). Aaron strikes the dust of the earth *('ᵃpar hā'āreṣ)* with his staff and the dust turns into gnats (Ex. 8:12-13[16-17]). The ostrich leaves its eggs on the ground *(ta'ᵃzōḇ lā'āreṣ)* to be warmed in the dust *('al-'āp̱ār)* (Job 39:14). The snake eats or licks dust (Gen. 3:14; Isa. 65:25; Mic. 7:17). The use of *'āp̱ār* in the sense of dust is common in figurative expressions (see III below) and self-abasement formulas (see IV.3 below).

4. *Ashes.* a. *'āp̱ār.* Now and again, *'āp̱ār* can denote ashes or dust mixed with ashes. The latter usage occurs in Dt. 9:21: the image of a calf made by the Israelites is burned, crushed, and ground until it is reduced to dust *(daq lᵉ'āp̱ār).* A similar process is described in 2 K. 23:4,6 (also vv. 12,15, without mention of burning: altars are the objects destroyed). Solid metal images could not have been ground to dust, much less burned. This was possible, however, in the case of images with a wooden core overlaid with gold or silver; the production of such images is described in polemics against idolatry (Isa. 40:19-20; 41:6-7; 44:9-20; etc.). When such an image is burned, the *'āp̱ār* includes a substantial component of ashes.

The pure ashes of the red heifer used in the preparation of water for purification are the subject of Nu. 19:17.

b. *'ēp̱er.* The same ashes are called *'ēp̱er* in Nu. 19:9-10. This is the domain where the meanings of *'āp̱ār* and *'ēp̱er* coincide. The range of meanings of *'ēp̱er* is narrower than that of *'āp̱ār; 'ēp̱er* always denotes loose dust or ashes. The translation "ashes," traditional since the LXX, limits the range of meanings. Nu. 19:9-10 provides the only clear basis for this translation, which is probably also correct in Ps. 147:16: "He gives snow like wool, he scatters frost like ashes *(kā'ēp̱er).*" The situation differs in 2 S. 13:19: since Tamar has been ejected from house and home when she puts *'ēp̱er* on her head, the word can only refer to dust.

5. *Plaster, Rubble.* Starting from the meaning "loose earth," *'āp̱ār* can also take on the meaning "plaster" or "rubble." A house infected with "leprosy" is scraped down and the plaster *('āp̱ār)* is dumped in an unclean place (Lev. 14:41,45); new plaster is used when the house is repaired (14:42). In 1 K. 18:38, too, *'āp̱ār* probably refers to plaster: fire consumes the burnt offering, the wood, the stones, and the *'āp̱ār* of the Carmel sanctuary.[11] The rubble of destroyed cities is mentioned in 1 K. 20:10; Ps. 102:15(14); Neh. 3:34; 4:4(10). The same meaning is probably found in Ezk. 26:4,12:

---

11. Schwarzenbach, 125.

the oracles against Tyre speak of demolishing walls and towers (v. 4) or walls and houses (v. 12), and then of the *ʿāpār* that is swept (vv. 4-5) or cast into the sea along with stones and timber (v. 12).

III. Figurative Usage.

1. *Multitude.* Like *ḥôl,* "sand," *ʿāpār* is used in some passages to suggest an incalculable multitude. This usage appears in promises of multiplication of descendants (Gen. 13:16; 28:14). Israel is as numerous as the dust of the earth, says Solomon in 2 Ch. 1:9.

The meaning of Nu. 23:10 ("Who can count the dust of Jacob?") is disputed. The ancient versions do not paint a uniform picture, and the proposed emendations are not helpful. Rabin and Guillaume attempt to interpret the text as it stands with the aid of Arabic, Rabin by connecting *ʿāpār* with Arab. *ǵafir(â),* "multitude," Guillaume by citing Arab. *ʿifr,* "warrior": "Who can count the warriors of Jacob?"[12] Heavy reliance on Arabic "parallels" is problematic.

Ps. 78:27 shows how close *ʿāpār* can come in meaning to *ḥôl:* "He rained flesh on them like dust *(keʿāpār),* winged birds like the sand of the sea *(keḥôl yammîm).*" Isa. 40:12 probably also refers to a multitude: "Who has enclosed the dust of the earth *(ʿapar hāʾāreṣ)* in a measure?"

2. *Worthlessness.* The notion of worthlessness appears in passages that choose *ʿāpār* as a parallel for "dirt" or "dung." Examples are Zec. 9:3, "Tyre has . . . heaped up silver like dust and gold like the dirt of the streets *(keṭîṭ ḥûṣôṯ)*"; and Job 27:16, "though they heap up silver like dust and pile up clothing like clay *(kaḥōmer).*" Zeph. 1:17b uses *ʿāpār* in parallel with *gelālîm,* "dung"; Ps. 18:43(42) (= 2 S. 22:43) in parallel with *ṭîṭ ḥûṣôṯ,* "dirt of the streets."

3. *Devastation.* The last examples appear in contexts describing total devastation. The same is true of 2 K. 13:7, which records that the king of Aram made the Israelites like the dust at threshing *(ʿāpār lāḏûš),* and Isa. 41:2, which says of Cyrus: "His sword makes them like dust *(keʿāpār*], like driven stubble *(keqaš niddap)* his bow." Quite similar are texts like Isa. 25:12 and 26:5, which threaten a city with destruction and devastation "even to the dust" *(ʿaḏ-ʿāpār).*

4. *Humiliation.* When referring to human individuals, such idioms express humiliation and abasement. Ps. 7:6(5): "Then let my enemy . . . trample my life to the ground *(lāʾāreṣ)* and lay my soul in the dust *(leʿāpār yaškēn).*" Ps. 119:25: "My soul clings to the dust" (cf. Ps. 44:26[25]). Job 30:19: "He has cast me into the mire *(laḥōmer*], and I have become like dust and ashes *(ʿāpār wāʾēper).*"

"Licking the dust" of someone's feet is a sign of total submission. Isa. 49:23 promises exiled Israel that kings and princesses "with their faces to the ground will bow down to you and lick the dust of your feet" (cf. Ps. 72:9; Mic. 7:17).

---

12. Rabin, 114; Guillaume, 336-37.

5. *'ēper.* For this group of meanings, analogous texts use *'ēper* instead of *'āpār.* Worthlessness and futility are the point of the saying in Isa. 44:20: "He who herds ashes *(rō'eh 'ēper)* has been led astray by a deluded heart." This idiom is comparable to "herding wind" (*r'h rûaḥ,* Hos. 12:2[1]). "Proverbs of ashes" or "proverbs of dust" (*mišlê 'ēper,* Job 13:12) are spoken into the wind, without value or endurance.

Total destruction is the aim of the oracle against the king of Tyre in Ezk. 28:18: "I turned you into dust on the earth *(le'ēper 'al-hā'āreṣ).*" The same is true in Mal. 3:21(4:3): "You shall tread down the wicked, for they will be dust under the soles of your feet *('ēper taḥaṯ kappôṯ raglêḵem).*" The same idiom is also found in Akkadian.[13] In Job 30:19 utter abasement is expressed by *'āpār wā'ēper* (see above). In Lam. 3:16, in the context of other expressions of abasement, we find, "He made me cower in the dust" *(hikpîšanî bā'ēper).* Comparable is Ps. 102:10(9): "For I eat ashes like bread." There are very close parallels from Babylonia, where "eat dust" is tantamount to "be vanquished."[14]

IV. Religious Significance.

1. *God Casts Down and Raises Up.* When *'āpār* is used figuratively, a religious component is often present. It can be a human enemy who casts down into the dust, who destroys and abases, but it can also be God (Isa. 25:12; 26:5; Ezk. 26:4,12; Zeph. 1:17b; etc.). This is especially frequent in the case of self-descriptions by supplicants (Ps. 119:25; Job 30:19; etc.). But God, who casts down into the dust, can also raise the abased individual from the dust (1 S. 2:8; 1 K. 16:2; Ps. 113:7; Isa. 61:3, *pe'ēr taḥaṯ 'ēper,* "a garland instead of ashes"). Through the mouth of a prophet, God addresses Jerusalem (Isa. 52:2): "Shake off your dust" *(hiṯna'arî mē'āpār).* Contrariwise, the prophet bids Babylon: "Come down and sit in the dust, virgin daughter Babylon! Sit on the ground without a throne, daughter Chaldea!" (47:1).

2. *Rites of Abasement and Self-Abasement.* This usage reflects rites of abasement and self-abasement common in Israel and the ancient Near East.[15] An Ugaritic myth describes El's reaction to the news of Baal's death: he descends from his throne and sits upon the ground, "he strews ashes *('mr)* of mourning upon his head, dust *('pr)* in which he rolls upon his pate."[16] The response to occasions of grief or serious disaster, whether experienced or anticipated, was to tear one's garments, put on a mourning garment (sackcloth, *śaq*), fast, put dust on one's head, sit on the ground, and roll in the dust. When the attack on Ai failed, Joshua and the elders of Israel tore their clothes, fell to the ground on their faces, and "put dust on their heads" (Josh. 7:6). Messengers bearing news of a defeat (1 S. 4:12; 2 S. 1:2) come with torn clothes and earth *('adāmâ)* on their heads. Hushai appears before King David in the same attire following the revolt of Absalom (2 S. 15:32). Other texts that mention putting dust on one's head include 2 S.

13. *AHw,* I, 223; *CAD,* IV, 186-87.
14. *AHw,* I, 223; *CAD,* IV, 186.
15. Kutsch, 26-35.
16. *KTU* 1.5, VI, 11ff. See *WUS,* nos. 295, 2227.

13:19 *(ʾēper);* Ezk. 27:30 *(ʿāpār);* Lam. 2:10 *(ʿāpār);* Neh. 9:1 *(ʾ^{a}dāmâ);* cf. also 1 Mc. 4:39; 11:71; 3 Mc. 1:18; Jdt. 4:15; 9:1; Rev. 18:19. Lam. 2:10 lists sitting on the ground, dust on the head, putting on sackcloth *(śaq),* and bowing the head to the ground.

When Job's friends see him sitting in the dust in his misery (Job 2:8), they tear their robes and throw dust *(ʿāpār)* in the air on their heads (v. 12). Two rites are combined here: the abasement rite of "dust on the head" and the rite of forcing back upon its bearer (cf. Ex. 9:8,10).[17]

Mordecai (Est. 4:1) "tore his clothes and put on sackcloth and ashes." V. 3 goes on to say: "Sackcloth and ashes were handed out to the multitude." Does this mean that a supply of ashes or dust was kept for occasions of general distress, to lend greater force to prayers through a communal ritual of rolling in dust or ashes? Mic. 1:10 speaks of rolling in *ʿāpār,* Jer. 6:26 of rolling in *ʾēper* (par. putting on sackcloth); the ritual is alluded to in Jer. 25:35 and Ezk. 27:30 (par. *ʿāpār* on the head). Isa. 58:5; Jon. 3:6; and Dnl. 9:3 also mention sackcloth and ashes as a sign of self-abasement.

Rites of self-abasement are also met with in the secular realm (elsewhere in the ancient Near East as well).[18] They were performed in the hope of being spared affliction (1 K. 20:31ff.).

The hope to be spared is the goal above all in the religious realm. Through these rituals, the worshiper submits humbly to God and implores God's mercy (Lam. 3:29: "Let him put his mouth in the dust — there may yet be hope").

3. *Self-Abasement Formulas.* Such humble submission to God also finds verbal expression in words of self-abasement.[19] When Job submits to God (Job 42:6), he declares that he recants and repents in dust and ashes. In addressing God, Abraham refers to himself as dust and ashes (Gen. 18:27).

Job's lament (Job 16:15), "I have sewed sackcloth upon my skin and have laid my horn in the dust *(w^{e}ʿōlaltî be͟ʿāpār qarnî),*" contains a double expression of abasement: his mourning garment is never removed from his body, and he is profoundly humiliated. "Raising one's horn," an image of pride borrowed from the bull (1 S. 2:1; Ps. 75:5-6,11[4-5,10]), has turned into its opposite for Job, a metamorphosis further underlined by the word "dust."[20]

Ps. 103:14 emphasizes that we mortals are simply dust; Job 4:19 calls human beings "dwellers in houses of clay, whose foundation is in the dust," an allusion to the physical composition and frailty of the human body.

The same point can be expressed by other images, above all that of withering grass (Isa. 40:8; 51:12; Ps. 90:5-6; 103:15-16) or a shadow (Ps. 102:12[11]; 144:4; Job 8:9; 14:2; 1 Ch. 29:15; etc.).[21] Such expressions emphasizing the transitoriness of human

---

17. G. Fohrer, *Das Buch Hiob. KAT* XVI (1963), 104, 106.
18. Kutsch, 30.
19. Coats.
20. Fohrer, *KAT* XVI, 289.
21. See Wächter, *Tod,* 98-106. On "withering grass" → חָצִיר *ḥāṣîr;* on "shadow" → צֵל *ṣēl.*

life serve to incline God to be merciful but at the same time to glorify God's imperishable greatness.

4. *Return to Dust.* The saying "For you are dust and to dust you shall return" *(kî-'āpār 'attâ wᵉ'el-'āpār tāšûḇ),* originally independent,[22] has been attached to the sentence pronounced on the man in Gen. 3:19. It emphasizes impressively the transitoriness of human life. "Return to dust" is also mentioned in Ps. 90:3 (with *dakkā'*); 104:29; 146:4 (with *'ᵃḏāmâ*); Job 10:9; 34:14-15; Eccl. 3:20; 12:7 (with *'ereṣ*). The notion of the breath of life, which God has given (Gen. 2:7) and can take away (Ps. 104:29; 146:4; Job 34:14-15; Eccl. 12:7), is therewith connected. According to Eccl. 3:18-21, humans and animals suffer the same fate: they are made of dust and must return to dust (v. 20). The author questions whether the breath of human goes upward (to God) and that of animals downward to the earth *('ereṣ),* i.e., the netherworld. As to the breath, this question is answered positively in Eccl. 12:7: the dust returns to the earth, the breath *(rûaḥ)* to God who gave it.

The statement that humans are dust and will return to dust is probably associated with the burial rites of ancient Palestine. The dead were not buried in arable land; mountain caves were used for bench tombs, in which the decay of the remains into dust could be observed in the course of new burials.

5. *The Grave and the Netherworld.* Therefore the dead can be equated with dust (Ps. 30:10[9]), the departed are called "dwellers in the dust" (*šōḵᵉnê 'āpār,* Isa. 26:19), the expression "dust of death" is used (Ps. 22:16[15]), and the dying can be described as lying down in the dust (Job 7:21; 20:11; 21:26). Of course this language refers to the tomb, but the notion of the netherworld probably also played a role in many cases.[23]

In Ps. 30:10(9) the parallel to "Will the dust praise you? Will it tell of your faithfulness?" is "What profit is there in my blood, if I go down to the Pit?"[24] The words "go down to the Pit," in the OT usually *yrd bôr*[25] (Isa. 38:18; Ezk. 26:20; 31:14,16; 32:18,24,25,29-30; Ps. 28:1; 30:4[3]; 88:5[4]; 143:7; Prov. 1:12), refer to a journey to the netherworld. In Ps. 22:30(29) "go down to the dust" *(yrd 'āpār)* has the same meaning. Job 17:16 uses "go down to the netherworld *(šᵉ'ôl)*" in parallel with "descend into the dust." In Isa. 26:19 the context suggests that "dwellers in the dust" are the inhabitants of the netherworld; this interpretation is supported by the use of the word *rᵉpā'îm,* "shades," in the same verse. The "land of dust" (*'aḏmaṯ 'āpār,* Dnl. 12:2) from which many who sleep will awake is the netherworld: the Akkadian expression *bît epri* is the exact equivalent.[26] "Dust" could be an appropriate term for both the tomb and the neth-

---

22. Schmidt, 216-17; W. Schottroff, *Der alttestamentliche Fluchspruch. WMANT* 30 (1969), 153; Westermann, *Genesis 1–11,* 263-67.

23. → שאול *šᵉ'ôl;* see Tallqvist; Ridderbos, 174-78; Wächter, *Tod,* 48-52; idem, "Unterweltsvorstellung," 329-34.

24. → שחת *šaḥaṯ.*

25. → באר *bᵉ'ēr* III.

26. Tallqvist, 37; *AHw,* I, 223.

erworld because the netherworld, a great open space in the bowels of the earth, was thought to be as dusty as a tomb.

V. Dead Sea Scrolls. The Dead Sea Scrolls, especially the *Hodayot,* contain a wealth of terms of self-abasement (cf. Job). Among these, expressions using *ʿāpār* occupy a significant place. Mortals are dust (1QH 15:21), creatures of dust (18:31), piles of dust (12:25), creatures of dust and clay (11:3; 18:12), created (3:21) or formed (1QS 11:21) from dust, structures of dust shaped with water (1QH 13:15), taken from dust and formed from clay (12:24). They are formed of clay and their desire is for dust (1QS 11:22); they are dust and ashes (1QH 10:5), having ears (18:4,27) and hearts (18:24) of dust.

The expression "return to dust" is common (1QH 10:4,12; 12:26-27,31).[27]

God can raise up out of the dust (1QM 14:14). Into the hand of the poor — those bowed into the dust — are delivered the enemies of all nationalities (1QM 11:13). The sons of light who "lie in the dust," i.e., suffer oppression, will raise a banner (1QH 6:34) and be raised from the dust (11:12).

By contrast, secular usage of *ʿāpār* recedes into the background. In 1QH 5:27 slanderers are called "creepers in the dust" *(zôḥᵃlê ʿāpār)* (cf. Dt. 32:24), in conjunctions with other allusions to snakes. In CD 11:10-11 and 12:15-16, *ʿāpār* means "loose earth." In 1QH 3:13-14 the *yôšᵉḇê ʿāpār,* "inhabitants of the dust," are contrasted to those who travel on the sea; here *ʿāpār* is equivalent to "dry land."

11QT 53:6 requires that blood spilled when animals are slaughtered be covered with *ʿāpār* (cf. Lev. 17:13).

Wächter

---

27. H. J. Fabry, *Die Wurzel šûb in den Qumran Literatur. BBB* 46 (1975), 110-20.

עֵץ *ʿēṣ*

I. Ancient Near East: 1. Egypt; 2. Mesopotamia. II. 1. Etymology and Meaning; 2. Occurrences; 3. Lexical Field. III. Secular Usage: 1. Tree, Trees; 2. Wood; 3. Fruit Trees. IV. Religious Usage: 1. Sacred Trees; 2. Tree of Life; 3. Tree of the Knowledge of Good and Evil. V. Metaphorical Usage: 1. Tree; 2. Wood; 3. Related Metaphors. VI. Dead Sea Scrolls.

ʿēṣ. L. Alonso-Schökel, *Das AT als literarisches Kunstwerk* (1971); P. J. Becker, "Wurzel und Wurzelspross," *BZ* 20 (1976) 22-44; M. Dahood, "Accusative *ʿēṣâ,* 'Wood,' in Isaiah 30,1b," *Bibl* 50 (1969) 57-58; I. Engnell, "'Knowledge' and 'Life' in the Creation Story," in *Wisdom in Israel and in the Ancient Near East. FS H. H. Rowley. SVT* 3 (1955), 103-19; idem, "'Planted by the

I. Ancient Near East.

1. *Egypt.* Egyp. *ḫt* means both "tree" and "wood." Wood is scarce in Egypt; it is therefore no wonder that trees, as providers of shade and fruit, played a role in religious ideas. The grounds of every temple and palace included a garden.

There were sacred trees in many nomes (persea, holly, acacia, sycamore, tamarisk); they did not play a major role in the public cult, but belonged to the realm of popular faith, usually as the abode of deities. For example, Hathor was "Lady of the Southern Sycamore"; Nut was often represented as a tree goddess.

As early as the Pyramid Texts, we find the notion of two sycamores on the eastern border of the heavens, between which the sun rises.[1] There is also mention of a single sycamore "on which the gods rest" or "which shelters the god."[2] The Book of the Dead speaks of a sycamore in the west that gives the departed breath and life.[3] Drawings depict a tree goddess holding out water and fruit to the dead. Shade and refuge are also emphasized in this context.

Another sacred tree was the *ished* (hardly a persea). Such a tree "broke open" near Re at Heliopolis "in the night of the war against the rebels."[4] On the leaves of a *ished* tree, Thoth and Seshat wrote the names and years of the king, a kind of augury.[5]

In the Tale of Two Brothers, trees contribute to the preservation of imperishable life. The heart of the younger brother is hidden in a cedar; when he returns to Egypt as an ox, two persea trees grow out of the drops of his blood. When they are cut down to

---

Streams of Water,'" *Studia Orientalia Ioanni Pedersen* (1953), 85-96; idem, *Studies in Divine Kingship in the Ancient Near East* (1943); K. Galling, "Der Weg der Phöniker nach Tarsis in literarischer und archäologischer Sicht," *ZDPV* 88 (1972) 1-18; H. Genge, "Zum 'Lebensbaum' in den Keilschriftkulturen," *AcOr* 33 (1971) 321-34; F. F. Hvidberg, "The Canaanitic Background of Gen. I–III," *VT* 10 (1960) 285-94; E. O. James, *The Tree of Life* (1966); K. Jaroš, "Die Motive der heiligen Bäume und der Schlange in Gen 2–3," *ZAW* 92 (1980) 204-15; idem, *Die Stellung des Elohisten zur kanaanäischen Religion. OBO* 4 (1974); Y. Kahaner, "The Metaphors of the Vine and the Olive Tree," *Dor leDor* 2 (1973/74) 15-20; A. Kapelrud, *Joel Studies* (1948), 26ff.; O. Keel, *Symbolism of the Biblical World* (Eng. trans. 1978); B. Lang, *Kein Aufstand in Jerusalem* (1978); E. Lipiński, "'Garden of Abundance, Image of Lebanon,'" *ZAW* 85 (1973) 358-59; F. Lundgreen, *Die Benutzung der Pflanzenwelt in der alttestamentlichen Religion. BZAW* 14 (1908); M. J. Mulder, "Bedeutet **עצים** in 1 Reg 5, 13 'Pflanze'?" *ZAW* 94 (1982) 410-12; K. Nielsen, *For et træ ere der håb* (1985); M. B. Rowton, "The Woodlands of Ancient Western Asia," *JNES* 26 (1967) 261-77; A. E. Rüthy, *Die Pflanze und ihre Teile im biblisch-hebräischen Sprachgebrauch* (1942); K. Seybold, "Bildmotive in den Visionen des Propheten Sacharja," *Studies on Prophecy. SVT* 26 (1974), 92-110; F. Stolz, "Die Bäume des Gottesgartens auf dem Libanon," *ZAW* 84 (1972) 141-56; C. Westermann, *The Parables of Jesus in the Light of the OT* (Eng. trans. 1990); G. Widengren, *The King and the Tree of Life in Ancient Near Eastern Religion. UUÅ* 1951:4; U. Winter, "Der stilisierte Baum," *BiKi* 41 (1986) 171-77; G. R. H. Wright, "The Mythology of Pre-Israelite Shechem," *VT* 20 (1970) 75-82; M. Zohary, *Plants of the Bible* (1982; with bibliog.).

1. *Pyr.,* 1433; Book of the Dead 109.
2. *Pyr.,* 916, 1485.
3. Book of the Dead 59.
4. Book of the Dead 17; *Urk.,* V, 50; Ritual of Amon, 25, 1.
5. *RÄR,* 84.

make furniture, a chip impregnates his wife, who gives birth to a new king.[6] Cf. the *'š* tree (hardly a cedar) that bestows life as it surrounds the coffin of Osiris.

Well known but unique is the passage in the Wisdom of Amenemope that compares the impassioned individual to a withered tree, the "silent" individual to a green tree.[7]

A fruit tree is called a "tree of life" *(ḫt n 'nḫ).*[8] The Turin Papyrus compares lovers to a fig tree and a small sycamore.[9] More extensive discussion of Egyptian tree worship can be found elsewhere.[10]

2. *Mesopotamia.* Both Sum. *giš* and Akk. *iṣu* mean "tree" as well as "wood." The only native trees were the Euphrates poplar and the tamarisk,[11] but texts name many others: fruit trees, date palms, cedars, etc. There is frequent mention of the felling and planting of trees.[12] We know of expeditions to bring cedarwood from Lebanon.

The *kiškanū* tree appears to be ideologically important: "In Eridu there is a black *kiškanū* tree; it was created in a pure place. Its appearance is like lapis lazuli; it spreads over Apsū."[13] The context speaks of the mouth of the two rivers; we are therefore dealing with cosmic symbolism in the temple.[14]

Sumerian royal hymns liken the king to a tree: "Scion of a cedar, a forest of cypresses am I, a box tree with sweet luxuriance am I"; "A thick *mes* tree . . . with radiating outstretched branches am I, the refuge of Sumer, its sweet shade am I."[15] The tree is an image of shade and refuge; there is no suggestion that the king is a "tree of life."[16] Several bilingual hymns describe the word of Enlil as a gale that uproots even great *mēsu* trees.[17] In one fable the tamarisk contends with the palm over which is greater.[18]

The so-called tree of life in pictorial representations is a stylized palm being manipulated in some way by flanking figures (hardly artificial fertilization), obviously a symbol of life. The expression "tree of life" does not occur in Akkadian,[19] although we do find "plant of life," "water of life," and "food of life."

Ringgren

---

6. *RAO,* 34.

7. *ANET,* 422.

8. Mythologically bestowing life: *Pyr.,* 1216; made by Amon: Hymn to Amon, 1, 7.

9. *Lit. Äg,* 312; see H. Grapow, *Bildliche Ausdrücke,* 105; cf. 46, 101.

10. *LexÄg,* I, 655-60; *RÄR,* 82-87; M. L. Buhl, *JNES* 6 (1947) 80-97; E. Hermsen, *Lebensbaumsymbolik im alten Ägypten. Arbeitsmaterialien zur Religionsgeschichte* 5 (1981).

11. Meissner, *BuA,* I, 211.

12. For citations, see *CAD,* VII, 215-16.

13. *CT,* XVI, 46, 183ff.; Widengren, 5-6.

14. See Widengren, 9, on the restoration of the *kiškanū* tree.

15. W. H. P. Römer, *Sumerische Königshymnen der Isin-Zeit* (1965), 53, 52, respectively; cf. also 30: "a proud cedar . . . possessed of power."

16. Widengren, 42.

17. G. Q. Reisner, *Sumerisch-babylonische Hymnen* (1856), 4, 34-35; cf. L. Dürr, *MVAG* 42ff. (1938) 13, 15, 20-21.

18. *BWL,* 151-64; the conclusion is unfortunately lost.

19. Å. Sjöberg, "Eve and the Chameleon," *In the Shelter of Elyon. FS G. W. Ahlström. JSOTSup* 31 (1984) 219ff.

II. 1. *Etymology and Meaning.* In Hebrew the biliteral root *'ēṣ* means both "tree(s)" and "wood."[20] The same root appears with the full range of meanings in the following Semitic languages: Akk. *iṣu/iṣṣu;* Ugar. *'ṣ;* Eth. *'ĕḍ.*[21] In Biblical Aramaic the meaning of the root has been narrowed: *'ā'* (in Old Aramaic texts *'q*)[22] means only "wood" (Dnl. 5:4,23) or "timber" (Ezr. 5:8; 6:4,11), while "tree" is represented by *'îlān* (Dnl. 4:7,8,11,17,20,23[10,11,14,20,23,26]). In the Targs. *'ēṣ* is replaced by *'îlān* ("tree") and *qêsā'* ("wood").[23] In Middle Hebrew both *'ēṣ* and *qîsā'* occur, each with the full range of meanings ("tree" and "wood"); *'îlān* occurs only with the meaning "tree."[24] The root *'ēṣ* has disappeared from Syriac, being replaced in the meaning "wood" by *qîsā'* and in the meaning "tree" by *'îlānā'.*[25] The root *'ēṣ* also appears in Punic.[26] It occurs twice; in both passages it means "wood."[27] In Old South Arabic we find the root *'ḍ* with the meaning "wood."[28] In North Arabic *'iḍa, 'iḍat,* and *'iḍḍ* mean "thorny trees and bushes,"[29] while "tree" in general is represented by *ġaḍan* or *šaǧar,* "wood," by *ḥašab.*

The form *'ēṣâ* in Jer. 6:6 has been identified as a fem. form of *'ēṣ;* more likely, however, it should be read as *'ēṣ* with the 3rd person fem. sg. suffix.[30] Dahood explains *'ēṣâ* in Isa. 30:1 as the acc. of *'ēṣ,* but his argument is not convincing.[31]

2. *Occurrences.* The root *'ēṣ* occurs 330 times in the OT; its distribution is relatively uniform, although a concentration can be observed in exilic texts.

3. *Lexical Field.* In the OT the lexical field "tree" is highly differentiated by specific botanical terms: *'erez,* "cedar"; *b^erôš,* "cypress"; → גפן *gepen,* "grapevine"; → זית *zayiṯ,* "olive"; *rimmôn,* "pomegranate"; *šiṭṭâ,* "acacia"; *t^e'ēnâ,* "fig"; *tāmār,* "date palm." Here we should also mention the word group *'ayil, 'ēlâ, 'allâ, 'ēlôn, 'allôn,* used indefinitely to refer to a "large tree" but especially an "oak."[32] The lexical field also includes words denoting parts of a tree, e.g., *gēza',* "rootstock"; *ḥōṭer,* "branch"; → נצר *nēṣer* and *ṣemaḥ,* "shoot"; *šōreš,* "root";[33] as well as various forms of growth, e.g., → גן *gan,* "garden"; → יער *ya'ar,* "forest"; → כרם *kerem,* "vineyard." See also the lexical field → יער *ya'ar,* "forest."

---

20. *HAL,* II, 863-64; Rüthy, 10-11, 41-42.
21. *AHw,* I, 390-91; *UT,* no. 1903; *WUS,* no. 2078-79; *LexLingAeth,* 1025-26.
22. S. Segert, *Altaramäische Grammatik* (1975), 3.2.6.
23. *KBL*², 1053a, 1049; Levy, *ChW,* I, 33; II, 359.
24. Levy, *WTM,* I, 65; III, 67; IV, 298.
25. *NBSS,* 144-45; *KBL*², 1053a.
26. *DNSI,* II, 879-80.
27. *CIS,* I, 346, 3; A. M. Bisi, *OrAnt* 9 (1970) 249-58; Rüthy, 41.
28. Biella, 378.
29. Rüthy, 41; *NBSS,* 144-45.
30. For the former see *KBL*², 272; for the latter, *HAL,* II, 863, 867.
31. Dahood. Cf. *HAL,* II, 863, 867.
32. *HAL,* s.v.
33. Rüthy.

III. Secular Usage.

1. *Tree, Trees.* The noun *'ēṣ* can denote both an individual tree, in whose shade one can rest (Gen. 18:4,8), and an indefinite number, as in "the trees of the field" (Ex. 9:25; 10:5; Lev. 26:4; Jer. 7:20). The pl. form *'ēṣîm* does not differ greatly in usage from the collective *'ēṣ* (e.g., Ps. 96:12; 104:16; Isa. 55:12; Joel 1:12). It can denote various kinds of trees (1 K. 5:13; Isa. 44:13-14) or simply several trees (e.g., Jgs. 9:8ff.; Ezk. 17:24; 31:4ff.).

2. *Wood.* Different kinds of trees were used for different purposes. Some trees provided timber for construction; others, such as fruit trees, were valued for the food they yielded (Dt. 20:19-20). The best wood for construction is cedar and cypress. Of course the dwelling place of God must be made of cedar, as 2 S. 7:7 implies: Yahweh never demanded a "house of cedar." To build the temple, Solomon imported cedars and cypresses from → לבנון *l^e^b̲ānôn,* where the Sidonians cut the trees (1 K. 5:22,24; 6:10,34; etc.). Part of Solomon's palace was called the House of the Forest of Lebanon (1 K. 7:2); the name indicates the source of the cedar. Nebuchadnezzar imported cedars of Lebanon to build the temple of Marduk; see also the accounts of the building of temples and palaces by Ashurbanipal II and Esarhaddon.[34] These cedars were also used to build the temple of Baal.[35] In Egypt cedars of Lebanon were also used in shipbuilding (cf. Ezk. 27:5).[36]

In the traditions of the wilderness sanctuary, acacias *(šiṭṭîm)* play the central role as structural timber (Ex. 25:5,10,13,23,28; 26:15,26,32,37; etc.). Other kinds of trees could also be used: sycamore (*šiqmâ,* Isa. 9:9[Eng. v. 10]); olive (*'^a^ṣê-šāmen,* 1 K. 6:23,31ff.); *'^a^ṣê 'almuggîm,* not sandalwood, as is often claimed[37] (1 K. 10:11-12; 2 Ch. 2:7[8]; 9:10-11); *'^a^ṣê-g̲ōp̲er,* pine (Gen. 6:14).

The difficulties involved in felling large trees are clear from Sennacherib's boasting (Isa. 37:24) and Solomon's singling out the Sidonians as expert cutters of timber (1 K. 5:20[6]).[38] The building material is often called simply *'ēṣ* or *'ēṣîm* (e.g., Lev. 14:45; 1 S. 6:14; 2 K. 12:13; Hag. 1:8).

Wood was used as a material for all kinds of objects. A gallows could simply be called *'ēṣ* (Gen. 40:19; Dt. 21:22-23; Est. 2:23; etc.).[39] Various implements were fashioned out of wood (Lev. 11:32; 15:12; Nu. 31:20; 35:18; etc.); in an ironic description of an idolater, Isa. 44:13ff. depicts the carpenter *(ḥārāš 'ēṣîm)* as a skilled and careful artisan, whose craft requires fine tools (see also 2 S. 5:11; 2 K. 12:12[11]; 1 Ch. 14:1).[40]

Wood also served as firewood, both for sacrifice and for everyday cooking (Gen.

---

34. For Nebuchadnezzar see *ANET,* 307; *AOT,* 365. For the others see *ANET,* 275-76, 291.
35. *KTU* 1.4, V, 10ff.
36. *ANET,* 252, 254; see also 27b, 240b, 243.
37. *BRL*², 12.
38. Rowton, 275; *AuS,* VII, 32-45; → יער *ya'ar.*
39. On execution by "hanging on a tree," see VI below.
40. *AuS,* VII, 42f.; *BRL*², 147ff., 356ff.

22:7,9; Lev. 1:8; 3:5; 1 K. 18:23,33-34; etc.). Firewood could either be gathered (1 K. 17:10,12; Nu. 15:32) — usually by poor people — or chopped. Since felling trees is hard work, Josh. 9:21ff. imposes it on the Gibeonites, i.e., aliens.

3. *Fruit Trees.* The text speaks occasionally of felling trees in general rather than specific species (e.g., Dt. 19:5; Ps. 74:5; 2 Ch. 2:15[16]; see also Isa. 10:19); Dt. 20:20 speaks only of trees that do not produce food. Without further definition, the OT often speaks of the "trees of the field" (Gen. 23:17; Ex. 9:25; Isa. 55:12; Ezk. 17:24), but it is often clear from the context that the reference is to fruit trees (e.g., Lev. 26:4; Dt. 20:19; Jer. 7:20; Joel 1:12,19; Ezk. 34:27). In several passages the nature of the trees called simply *'ēṣîm* is unknown (Jgs. 9:8ff.; 1 K. 5:13[4:33]; 2 K. 6:4; Isa. 7:2; 44:23; Ezk. 21:3[20:47]; 31:5ff.; Cant. 2:3; Eccl. 2:6; Ps. 96:12; 104:16; 1 Ch. 16:33; etc.); in others the context suggests fruit trees (Ex. 10:15; Lev. 26:20; Nu. 13:20; Dt. 28:42; 2 K. 3:19,25; Joel 2:22; Ps. 105:33; etc.).

The most important fruit trees of Palestine are the olive (→ זית *zayiṯ*), the (grape) vine (→ גפן *gep̱en*), the fig *(t^e'ēnâ),* and the pomegranate (*rimmôn,* Dt. 8:8; cf. Dt. 6:11; Nu. 20:5). Jotham's fable (Jgs. 9:8ff.) describes the olive as the natural king of trees. In second and third place follow the fig and the vine. These two fruit trees were often planted together, and therefore the OT often mentions them together (e.g., 1 K. 5:5[4:25]; 2 K. 18:31; Mic. 4:4). The fruit of the fig tree could be eaten fresh (Isa. 28:4) or used in cakes (1 S. 25:18; 30:12). The vine, primarily a source of wine, requires much more care than the olive or fig. "The olive tree is like a bedouin woman *(bedawīye)* who knows how to take care of herself, while the fig tree like a peasant woman *(fellāḥa)* and above all the vine like a lady *(sitt)* demand quite different attention."[41] Therefore vines and vineyards play a much greater role in OT imagery than the other fruit trees, concerning which there is less to say (→ כרם *kerem*).

Because fruit trees were vital to the Israelites, they understood the fertility of the trees as a sign of God's favor. Absent this favor, thorns and thistles take over the vineyard (Isa. 5:6; 7:23; 27:4; 32:13); conversely, the desert becomes fertile when Yahweh's punishment is past (32:15; 29:17; see also the description of the future in Ezk. 47:12).

The pomegranate was also among the prized varieties of fruit tree. It appears not only in descriptions of Israel's fertility (Nu. 13:23; 20:5; Hag. 2:19; see also Joel 1:12) but also in the decoration of the wilderness sanctuary and the temple (e.g., Ex. 28:33-34; 39:24ff.; 1 K. 7:18,20,42; 2 Ch. 3:16; Jer. 52:22-23). The symbolic function of this tree is also evident in the Song of Songs (4:3,13; 6:7,11; 7:13[12]; 8:2).

In the OT the date palm *(tāmār)* is also a symbol of fertility, as in the description of Jericho as a city of palms (Dt. 34:3; Jgs. 1:16; 3:13; 2 Ch. 28:15) and the description of Elim, where there were twelve springs of water and seventy palm trees (Ex.

---

41. *AuS,* IV, 173.

15:27; Nu. 33:9). The trees growing in paradise are described quite naturally as trees from which one can (but not necessarily may) eat (Gen. 2:9,16; 3:1-2; cf. Ezk. 47:7). In Gen. 1, also, the trees that were created should probably be thought of as fruit trees (Gen. 1:11,12,29). That attractive, fertile gardens had aesthetic value in Israel as well as in Mesopotamia and Egypt can be seen from descriptions in the Song of Songs, the traditions concerning the garden of Eden (Gen. 2–3) and the royal garden in Eccl. 2:5-6.[42]

IV. Religious Usage.

1. *Sacred Trees.* Trees signal the presence of the holy.[43] This was true in ancient Canaan, and several passages in the OT mention sacred trees. The oak of Moreh clearly belonged to the cultic center at Shechem, where Abram built an altar after the revelation of Yahweh (Gen. 12:6-7). The name of the oak, *'ēlôn môreh,* suggests that it functioned as an oracular tree (Hos. 4:12). According to Gen. 35:4, the foreign gods were buried under a tree at Shechem; in Josh. 24:26 Joshua sets up a large stone of witness under an oak near the sanctuary of Yahweh. The function of both emphasizes the religious significance of trees. At Beer-sheba Abraham planted a tamarisk *('ēšel)* and called there on the name of Yahweh (Gen. 21:33). Abram built an altar in the grove of Mamre, near Hebron (Gen. 13:18), and the angel of the Lord came and sat under the oak at Ophrah (Jgs. 6:11). Gen. 35:8 records a burial under an oak near Bethel. Saul and his sons were buried under the tamarisk in Jabesh (1 S. 31:13).

The significance of sacred trees for the Israelites can also be seen from descriptions of the temple. The sacred tree represents one of the most widespread motifs of ancient Near Eastern pictorial art.[44] The two pillars Jachin and Boaz in front of the vestibule of the temple (1 K. 7:15-22) were doubtless stylized trees.[45] The multitude of decorations employing motifs from the plant kingdom (trees, fruit, flowers, leaves) underline the close association between vegetation and the holy (→ מנורה *m*^{e}*nôrâ*). Where a sacred tree grows, there is life. The many instances of sacred oaks suggest that this tree had a particular association with cultic sites (Gen. 13:18; Jgs. 6:19; 1 K. 13:14; 1 Ch. 10:12).[46]

That trees played a role not only in the Canaanite cult of Baal but also in the cult of Yahweh is reflected in vehement prophetic and Deuteronomistic polemic. This cult was clearly widespread and popular in groves and under green trees (Hos. 4:12-13; Isa. 57:5; Jer. 2:20,27; 3:6,9,13; 17:2; Ezk. 6:13; 20:28,32; Hab. 2:19).[47] The sexual fertility rites that were part of this cult were condemned as apostasy from Yahweh, the bestower of life. In the prohibition of Dt. 16:21, "You shall not set up any *'*^{a}*šērâ kol-'ēṣ*

---

42. On the "tree of the knowledge of good and evil," see J. P. Floss, *BN* 19 (1982) 59-120, esp. 100ff.

43. Jaroš, 231.

44. *BRL*^{2}, 34-35.

45. James, 37; Lundgreen, 33-43.

46. Lundgreen, 24.

47. W. L. Holladay, *VT* 11 (1961) 170-76.

beside the altar of Yahweh," the verb → נטע *nāṭaʿ* suggests a living tree; but this verb can also be used figuratively. Dt. 12:2-3 demands the demolition of all sacred sites where the previous inhabitants worshiped their gods (e.g., under green trees) and the burning of their *asherim* (cf. 1 K. 14:23; 2 K. 17:10; 2 Ch. 28:4). According to 2 K. 16:4, Ahaz offered sacrifice and incense on the high places, on the hills, and under every green tree. As part of his cultic reform, his son Hezekiah removed the high places *(bāmôṯ;* → במה *bāmâ),* broke down the pillars *(maṣṣēḇôṯ;* → מצבה *māṣṣēḇâ),* cut down the *asherah (*→ אשרה *ʾašērâ),* and broke to pieces the bronze serpent *(neḥaš hannᵉḥōšeṯ;* → נחש *nāḥāš;* → נחשת *nᵉḥōšeṯ)* that Moses had made (2 K. 18:4; cf. Josiah in 2 K. 23:4ff.). Gideon pulled down the altar of Baal, cut down the *asherah,* built a new altar to Yahweh, and used the wood of the *asherah* for firewood (Jgs. 6:25ff.), thus manifesting his conversion from the Baal religion of Canaan to the religion of Yahweh.

The ideology of the cult also included the notion of a close association between tree and king.[48] This notion finds its way into the OT above all in the use of tree metaphors in texts that speak of the king or messiah (see below). Because *ʿēṣ* can mean both "tree" and "wood," it is often hard to decide whether the cultic object is a living tree or, for example, a pole-shaped wooden object, possibly a stylized tree.

The OT frequently mentions cultic objects made of wood. In a great admonitory address, Moses predicts that in the promised land Israel will serve idols that are the work of human hands, wood and stone, which cannot hear, eat, or smell (Dt. 4:28; cf. Dt. 28:36,64 [cf. 11QT 59:3]; Dt. 29:16[17]; 2 K. 19:18 par. Isa. 37:19; Isa. 44:19; Jer. 10:3). That not just a tree but also wood in general could symbolize and bestow life is shown by the use of wood as a medicament. A piece of wood transformed the undrinkable water of Marah into sweet water (Ex. 15:25). Cedarwood can cleanse a leper and a leprous house (Lev. 14:4,6,49,51-52; cf. Nu. 19:6).

2. *Tree of Life.* The best-known trees in the OT are the two trees in the garden of Eden. The tree of life *(ʿēṣ haḥayyîm)* is mentioned in this connection only in Gen. 2:9; 3:22,24, i.e., in the introduction and at the conclusion of the paradise narrative. This fact enables Westermann to conclude with assurance that the original narrative dealt only with a single tree, the tree in the midst of the garden (3:3), the forbidden tree (3:11).[49] The narrative was later expanded to include the familiar motif of the desire for everlasting youth, i.e., eternal life (cf. similar notions concerning the plant of life in the Gilgamesh Epic).[50] The combination of the two motifs is explained by the fact that wisdom (the tree of knowledge) and eternal life (the tree of life) are the two attributes peculiar to the deity. The author's theological purpose is to underline the difference between God and mortals by introducing the secondary theme of the tree of life. The two different themes have produced a

---

48. Engnell, Widengren.
49. C. Westermann, *Genesis 1–11* (Eng. trans. 1984), 212-14, following Budde.
50. Gilg. XI, 266ff.

single story, whose conclusion is that mortals have attained knowledge of good and evil, but eternal life belongs to God. The notions surrounding the tree of life are related to those surrounding sacred trees. Behind the description of the garden of God, scholars (not least the Scandinavians) see the Canaanite grove with its sacred trees and springs.[51] The purpose of the Canaanite tree cult was to create life. In this context, Gen. 2–3 can be viewed as a narrative polemic. Its message resembles that of the prophet Hosea: the human search for eternal life results not in life but in death.

The book of Proverbs uses the tree of life metaphorically (see below). For later notions of the tree of life, see T. Lev. 18:10-11; 4 Ezra 8:52; Pss. Sol. 14:3; Rev. 2:7; 22:1ff.

3. *Tree of the Knowledge of Good and Evil.* While the tree of life has many religio-historical parallels, we know the tree of the knowledge of good and evil *(ʿēṣ haddaʿaṯ ṭôḇ wārāʿ)* only from Gen. 2:9,17. According to Westermann, only the term "tree of life" is a traditional expression.[52] The author coined the name of the other tree from the narrative (3:5b). The knowledge of good and evil can be understood in various ways: (a) the totality of knowledge, i.e., divine omniscience; (b) the capacity to make ethical decisions — perhaps interpreted in a more functional or utilitarian sense: helpful vs. harmful — that makes human beings autonomous; (c) sexual knowledge and experience.[53] Gunkel and above all Engnell have emphasized sexuality as a central motif of Gen. 3, interpreting knowledge as knowledge of the difference between the sexes, through which human beings attain maturity.[54] According to Engnell, the verb "know" must also be interpreted sexually in this context. By eating of the tree of knowledge, humans acquire the ability to create new life, thus becoming like God. Banishment from paradise was necessary because by eating of both trees they would have attained both individual and collective immortality. This interpretation is supported by sexual allusions in the text: in Canaanite religion the serpent functions as a sexual symbol; eating the fruit makes the humans recognize that they are naked; the fig leaves with which they cover their loins are probably to be understood as aphrodisiacs; the curse on the woman strains her pregnancy and her relationship with the man.

The conclusion of this interpretation is that Gen. 3 expresses not an antisexual message in general — such a notion would be alien to the OT — but anti-Canaanite polemic. The sexual cult through which people try to (pro)create like gods brings only a curse and death. It must not be forgotten, however, that Gen. 3 also marks the beginning of civilized life, the life of the entire human race. Civilization does not arise until after a "fall," in which humanity has stolen something divine.

---

51. Hvidberg, 285-94.
52. *BK* I/1, 290.
53. → ידע *yāḏaʿ*.
54. Engnell, "Knowledge."

V. Metaphorical Usage.

1. *Tree.* Like water, *'ēṣ* is ambivalent as a metaphor.[55] Positively, it characterizes the devout: "They are like trees planted by streams of water, which yield their fruit in its season" (Ps. 1:3; cf. Jer. 17:8); similarly the promise in Isa. 65:22: "For like the days of a tree shall the days of my people be." The opponents of the prophet Jeremiah took counsel against him and said: "Let us destroy the tree in its prime" (Jer. 11:19). In the Song of Songs we read: "As an apple tree *(tappûaḥ)* among the trees of the wood, so is my beloved among young men" (2:3); in a similar vein, the young bride is likened to all kinds of wood used as incense (4:14).

In the great figurative discourse Ezk. 31, where Pharaoh is compared to a cedar *('erez)* of Lebanon,[56] the cedar stands among the trees of the field and is envied by all the trees in the garden of God (vv. 4,5,9), "for no tree in the garden of God was like it in beauty" (v. 8). But pride comes before a fall. Not only the proud cedar but the other tall trees as well must go down among the dead (vv. 14ff.). See also Ezk. 17:24: "All the trees of the field shall know that I Yahweh bring low the high tree and make high the low tree, dry up the green tree and make the dry tree flourish." In Ezk. 21:3(20:47), too, the image of the destruction of trees describes God's judgment on humans: Yahweh's fire will devour all trees, both green and dry.

The discourses in Ezk. 31, 17, and 21 refer to political situations. So does the fable of Jotham in Jgs. 9:8ff., where the inhabitants of Shechem, who made Abimelech king, are compared to trees that want to have a bramble *('āṭāḏ)* as king. The description shows that the bramble is considered the least among the trees, while the olive tree is the natural king.[57] After the olive come the fig and the vine, other fruit trees. When the trees choose the bramble as king, they must take refuge in its shade: "if not, let fire come out of the bramble and devour the cedars of Lebanon" (v. 15).

Job 19:10 speaks of the destruction of a tree: Job laments that God has uprooted his hope like a tree. Isa. 10:17-19 uses the image of a forest fire to describe the punishment of the arrogant king of Assyria. The glory of the king's forests and gardens will be destroyed, and "the remnant of the trees in his forest can be counted even by a child." In Isa. 56:3 a dry tree serves as an appropriate metaphor for a eunuch. In Isa. 7:2 the image of trees in a forest shaking before the wind describes the fear of Rezin and Pekah shared by the king and the people.

The phrase *'ēṣ-haḥayyîm* appears in Proverbs, but only as a metaphor (3:18; 11:30; 13:12; 15:4). In 3:18 wisdom is characterized as a tree of life; in 11:30, the fruit of righteousness; in 13:12, desire fulfilled; and in 15:4, a gentle tongue. It is hard to say what the metaphor is meant to convey — probably just that these four things are beneficial to life.

---

55. Alonso-Schökel, 329-30.

56. On the Lebanon cedar as a "cosmic tree," → VII, 454; Zimmerli, *Ezekiel 2* (Eng. trans. 1983), 146-47.

57. → IV, 61.

2. *Wood.* Not only trees but also wood appears in the figurative language of the OT. Lam. 4:8 compares the dry skin of the inhabitants of Jerusalem to wood. Jer. 10:8 brands all idolatry as wood — i.e., dead. Ezekiel's verdict on the inhabitants of Jerusalem is equally negative. As *ʿēṣ-haggep̄en,* they thought themselves better than any tree *(ʿēṣ).* They are not so, however, for from their wood *(ʿēṣ)* it is impossible to make even a peg — it will be cast on the fire (Ezk. 15:2ff.). The text plays quite artfully on the ambiguity *ʿēṣ* = "tree"/"wood." In consequence of Jer. 5:14, Yahweh will make his words in the prophet's mouth "a fire, and this people wood, and it will devour them." Zec. 12:6 describes God as making the clans of Judah a blazing pot on a pile of wood, so that "they shall devour to the right and to the left all the surrounding peoples." A similar image in Ezk. 24:10 proclaims the destruction of Jerusalem. In Ps. 74:5 the destruction of the sanctuary is likened to chopping wood. Jer. 46:22 describes the enemies of Egypt as those who fell trees. The two sticks with the names of Joseph and Judah in Ezk. 37:16ff. should probably also be understood metaphorically.

The connotations of the word "tree" are fundamentally associated with life, even when the text deals with the destruction of trees. "Wood" is associated with something dead. Nevertheless, figurative language does not always view vigorous trees in a positive light. In Ezk. 31, for example, the luxuriance of the trees is condemned as arrogance, justifying their destruction. Figurative language often associates *ʿēṣ* with the proclamation of judgment, involving the destruction of trees or wood by fire.

3. *Related Metaphors.* A survey of metaphorical usage cannot be limited to analyzing the occurrences of *ʿēṣ.* Trees as such play a large role in the OT, but often implicitly under the names of particular species (cedar, cypress, oak, vine, olive, fig, date palm, etc.) or through some related term (forest, Lebanon, vineyard, root, shoot, etc.). This is especially the case in the book of Isaiah. If we limit our attention to chs. 1–39, where a remarkable number of tree metaphors appear,[58] we observe that the word *ʿēṣ* appears as a metaphor only in 7:2 and 10:19. All other texts using tree metaphors — primarily 1:29-31; 2:12-17; 4:2-6; 5:1-7; 6:12-13; 9:7-20(8-21); 10:16-19; 10:33–11:10; 14:4b-20; 27:2-6; 32:15-20; 37:22b-32 — employ the name of the tree: oak, linden, vine, thorns and thistles, mulberry, cedar, cypress, or some other work that makes it clear that trees are involved: garden, vineyard, holy seed, fruit, the lofty and proud (in Lebanon), branch, stick, scion, shoot, stump, root, Lebanon, forest.[59] We note that trees valued for their timber are used metaphorically as well as fruit trees. Many texts clearly reflect Canaanite notions associated with sacred trees (e.g., 1:29-31). The figurative discourses in Isa. 1–39 often speak of destroying trees, either by cutting or by burning. The reason for their destruction emerges more or less directly from the description of the trees:

58. See esp. Nielsen.

59. On scion → חֹטֶר *ḥōṭer;* on shoot → נֵצֶר *nēṣer,* → צֶמַח *ṣemaḥ;* on forest → יַעַר *yaʿar.*

because of their arrogance — trust in their own strength and their own resources — the trees are cut down or devoured by fire. These figurative discourses enable us to see how Isaiah and his disciples interpreted the political situation of their age. Both the enemy and their own people are condemned for their arrogant pride, and pride comes before a fall (cf. the theory of Stolz that a Lebanon myth lies behind the OT notions associated with cutting down a tree). But Isaiah also points to the positive potential of trees. A tree that has been cut down can sprout again and put forth branches. The destruction of the enemy is total (e.g., 14:19), but for Israel there is still hope (e.g., 6:12-13; 10:33–11:10).

Like all good images, the tree metaphors in Isa. 1–39 stir the audience to participate actively in interpreting the image. Thus the audience, if the metaphor is successful, embraces the ideas of the speaker. Isaiah's audience learns to see the situation of the people through the tree imagery, understanding on the one hand why Yahweh's judgment is necessary and justified and on the other that hope for the future is not foreclosed. The image of the felled tree that puts forth new branches points to the central theme of Isa. 1–39: judgment and salvation go hand in hand. The image establishes their necessary connection in the history of Israel, for both are planned by Yahweh. Arrogance must be punished, but, after the proud king has been cut down, a new king will come, the scion that springs from the tribe of Jesse. A tree can also serve as a metaphor for the messianic notions associated with the coming ruler (e.g., Isa. 11:1,10; 4:2; 53:2; Jer. 23:5; 33:15).[60]

Because figurative language is particularly open to reinterpretation, the tree metaphors in Isa. 1–39 were reinterpreted frequently, becoming themselves the root of new branches. For example, Isa. 27:2-6 is dependent on 5:1-7; and Nebuchadnezzar's dream of the great world tree that is cut down (Dnl. 4) has been influenced by the earlier texts. The many parables of Jesus in the NT and the figurative discourses in the Pseudepigrapha (e.g., 2 Apoc. Bar. 36–37) must also be considered new branches from the same trunk.

VI. Dead Sea Scrolls. The word *ʿēṣ* occurs 35 times in the Dead Sea Scrolls (e.g., 1QpHab 10:1; 13:2; 1QH 2:26; 3:29; 8:5,6,9,12,22,25; 1Q35 2:2; 4QpNah 1:8; CD 11:19; 12:15). The meanings "tree" and "wood" are both found; see, e.g., 1QpHab 10:1 and CD 11:19, where *ʿēṣ* means timber, and 1QH 3:29 and CD 12:15, where trees are mentioned. In 1QpHab 13:2 *ʿēṣ* stands for idols. Metaphorical usage of *ʿēṣ* appears in 1QH 8:4ff. This psalm compares the community to a tree that drinks the water of life. Those who are not members of the community are described as trees, but they drink only ordinary water. In addition to *ʿēṣ,* we find the names of specific species and words that designate parts of trees.

K. Nielsen

60. See Engnell and Widengren for the religio-historical background of these notions.

The semantic domain of *ʿēṣ* thus corresponds essentially to that in the OT. But there are many texts of such weight that they deserve individual mention. For example, regulations in the Temple Scroll decree the use of cedar in the area of the temple gates (11QT 41:16) and walls (42:4). The court of the priests contained a wooden structure, not further identifiable (38:7). According to 49:3,15, wood was subject to certain rites of purification. If Yadin's reconstruction is correct, the Temple Scroll recognized a "wood offering" (*qorbān hāʿēṣîm,* 43:4). The polemic of Deuteronomy against idols (see above) is taken up by 11QT 59:3: Israel will serve other gods, the work of human hands, of wood and stone, silver and gold.

Of extraordinary potential are the five occurrences referring to the punishment of being "hanged on a tree" (*tālâ ʿal-hāʿēṣ,* 11QT 64:8,9,10,11,12). A directive in Dt. 21:22-23 requires that the corpse of a person executed not remain all night upon the tree (cf. the discharge of this duty in Josh. 8:29; 10:26; similarly 2 S. 4:12). "Hanging on a tree," therefore, was done to someone already executed: it was a demonstration, not an execution. In contrast to this Jewish practice, the Temple Scroll appears to refer to "crucifixion" (provided for in cases of high treason) of living criminals. They are to be hanged on a tree to die (64:7-8,10-11). In l. 9, by contrast, the regulation is unclear, since here the criminal is to be killed *and* hanged on a tree. This language raises the question whether the Qumran community was thinking of a practice like Roman crucifixion. Such an interpretation is supported by 1QpNah 1:8, which speaks of being hanged on a tree alive *(ḥay).*[61]

Another passage that has occasioned substantial discussion is 11QPsª 28:6 (= Ps. 151). Here the Qumran text is longer than the LXX, ascribing to David these words in v. 3: "The mountains do not bear witness to him [?; sc. God] nor do the hills proclaim, but the trees shall praise his [?] words and the sheep his [?] deeds." Since this verse is preceded by the making of musical instruments (v. 2), it is not hard to see in the combination the bucolic Orphic motif of trees and animals praising God. The intrusion of this Hellenistic motif led the LXX to purge the offending words and the Masoretes to reject the entire psalm.[62]

Fabry

61. See the discussion in J. Maier, *The Temple Scroll. JSOTSup* 34 (Eng. trans. 1985), 132-34, with bibliog.; → תלה *tālâ.*

62. J. A. Sanders, *DJD,* IV (1965), 58-64; F. M. Cross, *BASOR* 231 (1978) 69-71; S. Smith, *ZAW* 93 (1981) 247-53; H. J. Fabry, "11Q PSª und die Kanonizität des Psalters," *Freude an der Weisung des Herrn. FS H. Gross* (1986), 45-67.

עָצַב *ʿāṣaḇ;* עֶצֶב*; ʿeṣeḇ;* עֹצֶב *ʿōṣeḇ;* עָצֵב *ʿāṣeḇ;* עִצָּבוֹן *ʿiṣṣāḇôn;* עַצֶּבֶת *ʿaṣṣeḇeṯ;* מַעֲצֵבָה *maʿaṣēḇâ*

I. Etymology. II. Occurrences. III. Meaning: 1. Verb; 2. Nouns; 3. Gen. 3:16. IV. LXX.

I. Etymology. The root *ʿṣb* is not very common in Semitic languages. In addition to Hebrew, it occurs in Arabic, Aramaic, Postbiblical Hebrew, Ethiopic, and (albeit rarely) in the Targums. In Biblical Hebrew the verb is semantically fixed, with one possible exception. The substantives are more variable. This divergent usage could be due to differing meanings of the same root or to distinct roots. Arabic supports the latter theory. Alongside *ʿṣb* I, "grieved" (cf. Arab. *ġaḍiba,* "be angry"), Driver postulates an *ʿṣb* II, "reviled, upbraided, cut off," on the basis of Arab. *ʿḍb,* "cut," metaphorically "cut with words," as well as an *ʿṣb* III, "toil."[1] None of the senses of the Hebrew verb supports the latter, but some of the nouns appear to require it. Eth. *ʿaṣ(a)ba,* "be difficult, be in difficulties," would be related to *ʿṣb* III, if in fact a third root is reflected in Biblical Hebrew.[2]

II. Occurrences. The verb *ʿāṣaḇ* occurs 15 times (+ a conjectural emendation in 2 S. 13:21).[3] The occurrences are distributed among J, E (Gen. 6:6; 34:7; 45:5), the Deuteronomistic History (1 S. 20:3,34; 2 S. 19:3; 1 K. 1:6 [but cf. the proposed reading *ʿaṣārô*[4]]), the Prophets (Isa. 54:6; 63:10), Psalms (Ps. 56:6[Eng. v. 5]; 78:40), wisdom (Eccl. 10:9), and the Chronicler's History (1 Ch. 4:10; Neh. 8:10-11).

The qal appears 4 times, the niphal 7, the piel twice, the hiphil once, and the hithpael twice. The tendency to prefer reflexive forms may be due to the verb's introspective, personal, and emotional semantic content.

Except in the special cases of Gen. 3:16,17, and 5:19 (all J), the substantives do not appear in the Pentateuch or in Deuteronomic texts, but are found primarily in poetic texts: 6 times in Proverbs (5:10; 10:10,22; 14:23; 15:1,13), 4 times in Psalms (16:4; 127:2 [Dahood derives this occurrence from *ʿṣb* I and translates "bread of idols"];[5] 139:24 [Dahood treats it like 127:2];[6] 147:3), possibly once in Job (7:15, if MT *ʿṣmwty* is emended to *ʿṣbwty*), and 3 times in the Prophets (Isa. 14:3; 50:11; 58:3).[7] The only other occurrence is in 1 Ch. 4:9 (*ʿōṣeḇ* in a strained wordplay on the name Jabez in etymological anticipation of the verb *ʿṣb* in the following verse).

ʿāṣaḇ. M. Greenberg, "Labor in the Bible and Apocrypha," *EncJud,* X, 1320-22; J. Scharbert, *Der Schmerz im AT. BBB* 8 (1955); C. U. Wolf, "Labor," *IDB,* III, 51-52.

1. *JBL* 55 (1936), 115-17.
2. See Scharbert, 27ff., 31; *WbTigr,* 491a; *LexLingAeth,* 1019-20.
3. P. K. McCarter, *II Samuel. AB* 9 (1984), 314, 319-20.
4. J. Gray, *I and II Kings. OTL* (²1970), 78 note f.
5. M. Dahood, *Psalms III: 101–150. AB* 17A (1970), 273.
6. Ibid., 292.
7. On Jer. 11:19 see R. Houberg, *VT* 25 (1975) 676-77.

The form *ʿeṣeb̲* appears most frequently (6 times), followed by *ʿaṣṣeb̲et̲* (5 times, always either in construct or with a suffix), *ʿōṣeb̲* (3 times), *ʿiṣṣāb̲ôn* (3 times), *ʿāṣēb̲* (once; preferable to *ʿaṣṣāb̲* as the sg. of a word found only in the pl. [Isa. 58:3]) and *maʿaṣēb̲â* (once).

III. Meaning.

1. *Verb.* As a verb, *ʿṣb* indicates a state of mental or emotional distress. The serious inward agitation denoted by the word can be defined more precisely by noting the terms with which it is used. It is associated with *lēb̲,* "heart" (Gen. 6:6), the essential self of an individual, as well as with *rûaḥ,* "spirit" (Isa. 54:6; 63:10), the soul or spirit of a person. The serious aspect of the verb's meaning appears where it is used in contrast to great "joy" (Neh. 8:10: rejoicing accompanying worship and sacrifice on a day holy to the Lord) or well-being and peace (Neh. 8:11) as well as blessing and prosperity (1 Ch. 4:10). Finally, the verb's emotional aspect is clear from its use in parallel with words for vexation (*ḥrh,* Gen. 34:7; 45:5; 1 S. 20:34), rebellion (*mrh,* Isa. 63:10; Ps. 78:40), sorrow (*nḥm,* Gen. 6:6), and mourning (*ʾbl,* 2 S. 19:3[2]).

Both human beings and God (Gen. 6:6; Ps. 78:40) can suffer the distress denoted by *ʿṣb.* It can be due to self-reproach for a mistake or failure (Gen. 6:6; 45:5) or be grounded in the acts of others (e.g., Ps. 56:6[5]; 78:40). Or it can grow out of awareness of a situation before which one stands helpless (e.g., 1 S. 20:3).

The only exception to this specific semantic domain of "mental suffering" is Eccl. 10:9, where it refers to a physical condition. Here the verb denotes an injury caused by rock fragments; it refers more to lacerations than to the accompanying pain. In this text, therefore, *ʿṣb* should be assigned to *ʿṣb* II.

2. *Nouns.* The occurrences of the nouns fall into two groups: in the first, the noun clearly derives from the verb *ʿṣb* and refers to emotional or mental suffering (Prov. 10:10; 15:1,13; Job 9:28; Isa. 50:11; Ps. 139:24). Some texts use the auxiliary vocabulary that signals the nuances of *ʿṣb:* "anger" (Prov. 15:1), "heart" and "spirit" (15:13). Texts without such indicators contain sufficient contextual references to distress. Ps. 16:4 may belong to this group, although its association with the verb *rbh* recalls the first clause of Gen. 3:16, where the issue, however, is not mental suffering.[8]

The second group involves the concept of physical work (Gen. 3:16,17; 5:29; Isa. 14:3; 58:3; Ps. 127:2; Prov. 5:10; 10:22; 14:23). It is possible that these occurrences reflect a derivation of the term from a different root. Nevertheless, a connection between the nouns "anguish" and "work" is possible when we observe the semantic nuances of the biblical vocabulary associated with physical labor (→ יגע *ygʿ,* → עשׂה *ʿśh,* → עבד *ʿbd,* → עמל *ʿml,* → פעל *pʿl*).

In general the OT views positively the work involved in producing food and satisfying other human needs.[9] God worked in the act of creation and continues to do so. Hu-

8. See III.3 below.
9. Greenberg, 1320; Wolf, 252.

man labor, too, is considered honorable; in the sabbath commandment, the Decalogue includes the complementary notion that six days of work are required (Ex. 20:9-11). But the actual experience of Palestinian peasants showed that sometimes even the most vigorous labor was in vain. The highlands of Palestine were ecologically relatively unproductive; the possibility of failure despite all human efforts was always present.[10] Inevitably, work was sometimes accompanied inevitably by disappointments. The mental anguish expressed by *'ṣb* would therefore be an appropriate aspect of the various nouns meaning "work" derived from this root. The two related texts, Gen. 3:17 and 5:29, suggest that productive work could take on the character of extremely arduous labor and result in psychological malaise due to the uncertainty of its results; this malaise required "comfort." In this sense *'ṣb* differs from → לאה *l'h,* which appears to emphasize the physical fatigue resulting from hard work.

3. *Gen. 3:16.* Gen. 3:16 represents a special case in our understanding of *'iṣṣāḇôn* and *'eṣeḇ*. The traditional translations render both terms with words for physical pain. Since *'ṣb* II refers more to mental than to physical pain, however, this traditional interpretation must be called into question. That the two other occurrences of *'iṣṣāḇôn* (3:17; 5:29) refer explicitly to physical labor suggests that here too physical labor is mandated for the woman. Moreover, the first verb *(rbh)* of this verse has two objects, *'iṣṣāḇôn* and *hērôn,* "conception" or "pregnancy." In the nuanced biblical lexical field of pregnancy and birth (→ הרה *hārâ*), the latter does not refer to the actual process of childbirth. Since neither conception nor pregnancy is painful, the *'iṣṣāḇôn* connected with pregnancy cannot mean "pain." The first part of v. 16 therefore says that God will increase the number of the woman's pregnancies and also the amount of hard work she has to do, for in ancient agricultural society women performed a high percentage of the necessary tasks.[11] The second clause of v. 16 deals with the theme of "having children"; it does not necessarily refer to the process of childbirth itself, for → ילד *yālaḏ* can mean simply "have" or "produce" children and is used of both men and women. Having many children was a desirable and fundamental aspect of the labor-intensive agricultural society, albeit not without difficulties: parenting had its own special "pain." Thus the meaning of *'eṣeḇ* in this text is ambiguous: it can mean "labor" and "work" and intensify that statement of the preceding clause; it can refer to the psychological stress of family life; or it can mean both. But it does not mean physical pain.

IV. LXX. The LXX translated the occurrences totally differently, revealing the difficulty of distinguishing between *'ṣb* I and *'ṣb* II. The equivalent is probably *lypḗ, lypeín,* etc., but we also find *tapeinoún, asthéneia,* etc.

C. Meyers

---

10. D. C. Hopkins, *The Highlands of Canaan. SWBA* 3 (1985).

11. C. Meyers, "Gender Roles and Genesis 3:16 Revisited," *The Word of the Lord Shall Go Forth. FS D. N. Freedman* (1983), 337-54.

*עָצָב *ʿāṣāḇ

I. Occurrences and Etymology. II. Meaning. III. Prophetic Indictments. IV. Polemics against Idolatry. V. LXX. VI. Dead Sea Scrolls.

I. Occurrences and Etymology. The noun *ʿāṣāḇ occurs 19 times in the OT. It appears almost exclusively in the plural (1 S. 31:9 = 1 Ch. 10:9; 2 S. 5:21; Isa. 10:11; 46:1; Jer. 50:2; Hos. 4:17; 8:4; 13:2; 14:9[Eng. v. 8]; Mic. 1:7; Zec. 13:2; Ps. 106:36,38; 115:4; 135:15; 2 Ch. 24:18). Only twice does the singular occur: Isa. 48:5 (MT) and probably also Ps. 139:24;[1] its unusual vocalization — *ʿōṣeḇ* instead of *ʿāṣāḇ* — is obviously intended to recall *bōšeṯ* and qualify the term.[2]

Few modern commentators have accepted the conjectural emendations that find this noun in Isa. 2:8,[3] Hos. 10:6,[4] and Mic. 5:13.[5] Hardly convincing is Wellhausen's proposal to connect the fem. pl. *ʿaṣṣāḇôṯ* in Ps. 16:4 with *ʿāṣāḇ instead of *ʿaṣṣeḇeṯ,* "pain, torment, grief."[6]

The noun *ʿāṣāḇ* is usually derived from the verb *ʿṣb* I, "plait, make, form,"[7] found twice in the OT. In Job 10:8 (piel), in parallel with *ʿāśâ,* it refers to God's act of creation. In Jer. 44:19 (hiphil) the women who have taken refuge in Egypt justify their making *(ʿāśâ)* cakes to offer to the queen of heaven "marked with her image." It is true that the LXX and Syr. omit *l^eha^{ʿa}ṣiḇâ,* but probably only because they no longer understood the meaning of the word (cf. Vulg. *ad colendum eam,* "to honor her").

II. Meaning. Jer. 44:19 points to the meaning of *^{ʿa}ṣabbîm;* the noun belongs to the idol terminology of the OT. Without reference to the different ways they are made, it serves as a comprehensive term for images of alien gods (2 S. 5:21; Isa. 46:1; Jer. 50:2).[8] Since the OT does not distinguish alien deities from their images, *^{ʿa}ṣabbîm* can also stand for the gods themselves (1 S. 31:9 = 1 Ch. 10:9; Ps. 106:38; 2 Ch. 24:18).[9]

ʿāṣāḇ. K.-H. Bernhardt, *Gott und Bild. ThArb* 2 (1956); C. Dohmen, *Das Bilderverbot. BBB* 62 (²1987); O. Eissfeldt, "Gott und Götzen im AT," *TSK* 103 (1931) 151-60 = *KlSchr,* I (1962), 266-73; J. Hahn, *Das "Goldene Kalb." EH Theologie* 154 (1981); C. R. North, "The Essence of Idolatry," *Von Ugarit nach Qumran. FS O. Eissfeldt. BZAW* 77 (²1961), 151-60; H. D. Preuss, *Verspottung fremder Religionen im AT. BWANT* 92 (1971); J. Scharbert, *Der Schmerz im AT. BBB* 8 (1955), 27-32; S. Schroer, *In Israel gab es Bilder. OBO* 74 (1987); → מסכה *massēḵâ.*

1. E. Würthwein, *VT* 7 (1957) 173-74 = *Wort und Existenz* (1970), 187-88.
2. North, 154.
3. B. Duhm, *Das Buch Jesaia. HKAT* III/1 (⁴1922), 18.
4. J. Wellhausen, *Die kleinen Propheten* (⁴1963), 125.
5. W. Nowack, *Die kleinen Propheten. HKAT* III/4 (³1922), 226.
6. *Skizzen und Vorarbeiten* 6 (1899) 168.
7. *GesB,* 609; *HAL,* II, 864-65.
8. Dohmen, 259.
9. W. Rudolph, *Hosea. KAT* XIII/1 (1966), 114.

Thus the term embodies negatively, as it were, the two characteristics of Yahwism that distinguish Israel profoundly from its neighbors: Yahweh's demand for exclusivity and the absence of images from worship of Yahweh. Therefore *ʿaṣabbîm* is used where the relationship of Israel to the world around it is at issue. The term appears both in prophetic indictments charging Israel with unfaithfulness to Yahweh (Hos. 4:17; 8:4; 13:2; 14:9[8]; Mic. 1:7; cf. Zec. 13:2; Ps. 106:36) and in pejoratives applied to alien gods in polemics against idols (Isa. 10:11; 46:1; 48:5; Jer. 50:2; Ps. 115:4; 135:15). In the setting of prophetic indictments, homonymity with the root → **עצב** *ʿṣb* II, "grieve, sadden," probably already lent the word negative overtones.[10]

Only the occurrence in Ps. 139 stands by itself. V. 24 contrasts the way of the *ʿāṣāḇ* (cj. for MT *ʿōseb;* see I above) with "the everlasting way." The psalmist prays to God to try to discover any trace of idolatry "in him" and guide him in the right way.[11]

III. Prophetic Indictments. The earliest datable occurrences are in the indictments of Hosea. The date of Ps. 139 can hardly be determined.[12] 2 S. 5:21 is secondary.[13] It is probably a contrastive allusion to 1 S. 4:11, the loss of the ark.[14] Since the LXX and 1 Ch. 14:12 read *ʾelōhîm* at this point, it is arguable that *ʿaṣabbîm* itself is a later addition to the text.[15] 1 S. 31:9 also does not fit seamlessly into its context. What is the point of exhibiting publicly a decapitated corpse in which no one could recognize Saul? It appears that a short notice concerning the exhibition of Saul (and his sons? cf. v. 12) has been expanded to reflect 1 S. 17:51,54, to contrast one last time the fate of Saul and the triumph of David.[16]

Returning to Hosea, we note that 13:2 describes the calf image of Bethel as a "cast image . . . after the model of idols."[17] This image was conceived of originally as a theriomorphic pedestal on which Yahweh was enthroned invisibly; it therefore escaped the notice of Elijah and Amos. Now Hosea sees it as a representation of Yahweh: "the representation has taken the place of the subject represented."[18] "People are kissing calves!" (13:2b).[19] The pl. "calves" suggests that here, as in 8:4b, Hosea is thinking of copies of the calf image in the form of statuettes or plaques, intended for public and private use.[20]

---

10. North, 154; H. W. Wolff, *Hosea. Herm* (Eng. trans. 1974), 139; Dohmen, 259; cf. Rudolph, *KAT* XIII/1, 114-15; disputed by B. Lang, *TQ* 166 (1986) 137.
11. H. Ringgren, *The Faith of the Psalmists* (1963), 56.
12. H.-J. Kraus, *Psalms 60–150* (Eng. trans. 1989), 513.
13. T. Veijola, *Die ewige Dynastie. AnAcScFen* B 193 (1975), 97-98.
14. → VIII, 433.
15. W. Rudolph, *Chronikbücher. HAT* I/21 (1955), 114; North, 154; otherwise J. W. Rothstein and J. Hänel, *Kommentar zum ersten Buch der Chronik. KAT* XVIII/2 (1977), 267, 270; cf. T. Willi, *Die Chronik als Auslegung. FRLANT* 106 (1972), 153.
16. → VIII, 433; see also F. Stolz, *Das erste und zweite Buch Samuel. ZBK* 9 (1981), 183.
17. Cj. *BHS.*
18. H. Utzschneider, *Hosea. OBO* 31 (1980), 102.
19. → **עגל** *ʿēgel.*
20. J. Jeremias, *Der Prophet Hosea. ATD* 24/1 (1983), 162.

At the same time, Hosea defines the calf image cult as worship of alien gods. "Since Israel's neighbors worship their gods in images, the creation of any image means taking over foreign examples, and so a measure of assimilation to their understanding of God."[21] This holds true especially for the calf image, which was a symbol of Baal in the Canaanite world surrounding Israel. It is debated, however, whether Hosea presupposes the second commandment, which attacks images per se — as some commentators maintain — or, by revealing the ambivalence of images for the first time, lays the foundation for the second commandment.[22] In any case, the choice of the term *'aṣabbîm* shows that the focus is on Yahweh's demand for exclusivity.[23] But does the terse, briefly stated criticism by the prophet suffice without the substantial presupposition of the second commandment, if the indictment has the function of enabling the audience to "affirm"[24] the prophet's radical announcement of disaster?

We should probably interpret 14:9(8) in the light of 13:2 and 8:4b-5. In 4:17, however, the prophet appears to have his eyes rather on the cult of high places.[25] Hosea's attack finds a powerful echo in the secondary passage Mic. 1:7a.

In the postexilic period, Hosea's indictment turns into a confession of personal guilt (Ps. 106:36,38) and therefore of hope in God (Zec. 13:2).

IV. Polemics against Idolatry. In parallel with its use in prophetic indictments, *'aṣabbîm* becomes a polemical pejorative for alien gods.[26] The identification of the deity with its image — which hardly reflects the self-understanding of Israel's neighbors[27] — means that the gods are judged by the standard of their images. They are "silver and gold, the work of human hands" (Ps. 115:4; 135:15), dead matter (*gillûlîm,* Jer. 50:2), "nothings" (*'elîlîm,* Isa. 10:11). These texts, strictly speaking, do not contest the existence of these gods. It is not their existence but their efficacy that is denied.[28] Though they have mouth, eyes, ears, nose, hands, and feet, they are unable to speak, see, hear, smell, feel, walk (Ps. 115:5-7; 135:6-17). Over against them stands Yahweh, transcendent in heaven, distinct from the entire created order and omnipotent (115:3; 135:6). Unlike the alien gods, he has demonstrated his power through the fulfillment of his word (Isa. 48:5). The likely starting point for these polemics (late as a group) is the preaching of Deutero-Isaiah. For one moment, the prophet distinguishes between deity and image, but only to insist all the more on the impotence of the gods and their dependence on their images (46:1-2). After the downfall of Bel and Nebo in the political catastrophe of Babylon, their images are carted off by their worshipers.

---

21. W. H. Schmidt, *Faith of the OT* (Eng. trans. 1983), 79.
22. Dohmen, 259-60.
23. Jeremias, *ATD* 24/1, 162.
24. H. W. Wolff.
25. Jeremias, *ATD* 24/1, 72.
26. Eissfeldt.
27. Preuss, 42ff.; A. H. J. Gunneweg, "Bildlosigkeit Gottes im Alten Israel," *Henoch* 6 (1984), 259ff.; Schmidt, *Faith,* 81-82.
28. Schmidt, *Faith,* 278-79.

The gods cannot save their own images; they are a burden to their worshipers and must go into captivity along with their images. Unlike Yahweh, who, far from having to be carried, carries his people and will save them (46:3-4), the chief gods of Babylon are tied to their images and the political fate of their people.[29]

Is there a connection between Hosea's use of *ʿᵃṣabbîm* and its appearance in the context of polemic against idols? Perhaps Hosea anticipates the latter ridicule of alien gods: "They are all the work of human hands" (Hos. 13:2; cf. 8:6a; 14:4a[3a]). The date of these passages is disputed.[30] In any case, Hosea contrasts the "calves" characterized as idols to Yahweh, the living God (cf. Rom. 1:22ff.). Besides him there is no savior (Hos. 13:4) — the criterion by which later writers judge alien gods (Isa. 43:11).

V. LXX. The LXX translates **ʿāṣāḇ* with *eídōlon.* In just three passages (Isa. 46:1; Ps. 106:36,38) it uses the nominalized adj. *glyptós,* the regular translation of *pesel/*pāsîl.*

VI. Dead Sea Scrolls. In the Dead Sea Scrolls the only certain occurrence of *ʿṣb* I is in 1QpHab 13:3; to the extent that the surviving text can be read, 2Q23 1:8 and 4Q509 16:2 use *ʿṣb* II. The entire lexical field of idolatry *(pesel, massēḵâ, yeṣer, ʾᵉlîlîm, ʿēṣ, ʾeḇen)* used in Hab. 2:18-19 is incorporated here and concentrated in the term *ʿᵃṣabbîm:* "On the day of judgment, God will obliterate all those who worship idols, all the wicked, from the earth."

Graupner

29. C. Westermann, *Isaiah 40–66. OTL* (Eng. trans. 1969), 180-81.
30. Jeremias, *ATD* 24/1, 108, 169ff.; Dohmen, 148 n. 243, 151 n. 249.

עָצֵל *ʿāṣēl*

I. Etymology. II. 1. Distribution; 2. Textual Problems; 3. Lexical Field; 4. LXX. III. OT Usage: 1. Jgs. 18:9; 2. Wisdom Literature.

I. Etymology. In Akkadian we find *eṣēlu,* "cripple," and *eṣlu,* "heavy of movement."[1] The root does not occur in Ugaritic. Related are Syr. *ʿᵉṭēl, ʿaṭlāʾ,* "deaf, numb,

ʿāṣēl. A. Barucq, *Le Livre des Proverbes. SB* (1964), 77ff., 155ff.; J. T. Draper, *Proverbs* (1977), 58-65.

1. For the former see *AHw,* I, 251; *CAD,* IV, 341. For the latter, *CAD,* IV, 350.

willful, stupid," ʿaṭlûṯāʾ, "willfulness, stupidity"; Middle Heb. ʿāṣēl, "negligent," ʿaṣlûṯ, "sloth," ʿaṣlān, "slothful"; Jewish Aram. ʿaṭlāʾ, "lazy," ʿaṭlûṭāʾ, "laziness"; and Arab. ʿaṭila, "be uncovered, not work"; cf. ʿaṣala, "twist," ʿaṣila, "be hidden."

II. 1. *Distribution.* Except for one occurrence of the verb in Jgs. 18:9, the use of the root *ʿṣl* is limited to wisdom literature (Proverbs plus one occurrence in Ecclesiastes). The verbal adj. *ʿāṣēl* occurs 15 times. It is usually used as a noun; it appears as an adjective in Prov. 24:30. The derivatives *ʿaṣlûṯ* (31:7) and *ʿaṣlâ* (19:15) as well as the unusual dual in Eccl. 10:18 should be noted.

2. *Textual Problems.* If we follow Fichtner in Prov. 13:4, *nap̱šô* should be deleted (cf. the ancient versions).[2] In this case *ʿāṣēl* is the subject and the verb should be emended to *miṯʾawweh.* If we accept the *lectio difficilior,* the suffix in *nap̱šô* requires explanation. An archaic nominative ending is one solution.[3] We should not reject out of hand the possibility of an erroneous carryover from v. 3a.[4]

In Prov. 15:19b the reading *ḥārûṣîm* instead of *y^e^šārîm* has been proposed on the basis of the LXX *(tṓn andreíōn);* cf. the parallel in 13:4.[5] Since *ʿāṣēl* conveys a derogatory sense and is closely related to *rāšāʿ,* however, *y^e^šārîm* may be intended as an antithesis.

In Eccl. 10:18 the dual *baʿ^a^ṣaltayim* serves to "reinforce the concept."[6]

3. *Lexical Field.* The meaning "lazy, laziness" — according to Lauha,[7] "a central topic of wisdom literature" — is assured by the context, but attempts at a more precise definition show that the semantic field is wide-ranging and cannot be defined exhaustively by contrast with *ḥārûṣ* (Prov. 13:4). Unreliability (10:26 [cf. 13:7;[8] 25:13]; 20:4), negligence to the point of fraud (*r^e^mîyâ,* 19:15; cf. 10:4; 12:24), even stupidity (*ḥ^a^sar-lēḇ,* 24:30) bring the term into the domain of the treacherous (*bōg^e^ḏîm,* 13:2), who are inclined to violence, as — continuing to follow the trail of the lexical fields — an affinity for the *rāšāʿ* with all the associated wickedness shows, so that the life of the *ʿāṣēl* is at risk (21:25). All in all, the word conveys a strongly pejorative sense: it is not simply a superficially derogatory term for an idler, but a concentrated expression denoting someone who, through laziness, both endangers his own well-being, indeed his very life and existence, and exerts a baneful influence on society: "as to the social aspect of the vice of laziness, a lazy person is a repugnant creature."[9] No theological arguments or allusions appear in the immediate context.

---

2. *BHS.*
3. *GK,* §90.
4. M. Lambert, *Traité de grammaire hébraïque* (1938), 143 n. 1.
5. *BHS;* comms. by C. H. Toy, *ICC* (1899); B. Gemser, *HAT* I/16 (²1963); W. McKane, *OTL* (1970).
6. A. Lauha, *Kohelet. BK* XIX (1978), 196; cf. H. W. Hertzberg, *Der Prediger. KAT* XVII/4-5 (1963), 194; on the entire verse see M. Dahood, *JQR* 62 (1971/72) 84-87.
7. *BK* XIX, 197.
8. Oesterley, *Book of Proverbs* (1929), 103.
9. Barucq, 78.

4. *LXX.* The LXX has ten occurrences of *oknērós* and one of *oknēría.* Twice *aergós* is used. In the text used by the translators, *ʿāṣēl* may have appeared in 19:15b instead of 19:15a. The remaining equivalents (10:26; 19:24; 24:34) are not direct translations but stay within the domain of the pejorative lexical field.

The word does not occur in Sirach or the Dead Sea Scrolls.

III. OT Usage.

1. *Jgs. 18:9.* The only occurrence outside wisdom literature (Jgs. 18:9) appears not to convey a derogatory sense. In the context of the narrative in which the Danites' spies encourage them to attack the prosperous and untroubled city of Laish, the niphal of *ʿṣl* is used. The preceding *ḥšh* (even if the text of the clause is in doubt,[10] the verbal root is not) makes it hard to perceive any morally derogatory nuance in *ʿṣl:* it simply means "do not hesitate, do not delay."

2. *Wisdom Literature.* Within the framework of usage in wisdom literature, several connotational foci can be identified:

a. The lazy strive after a false goal. It is significant that there is an element of dynamic craving in the conduct of an *ʿāṣēl.* This element is documented in the use of *ʾwh* hithpael or *taʾᵃwâ* (Prov. 13:4; 21:25) and *nep̱eš* (in parallel and in the same context: 13:2-4; 19:15); the use of *nep̱eš* generally emphasizes "appetite."[11] The goal of this craving is attained on the road of life.[12] The wise, correct way (7:25; 21:16; 23:19) is contrasted frequently with its opposite (2:12; 22:5); a frequent parallel is *ʾōraḥ,* "path" (15:19). The two ways of life stand in sharp contrast: the right way is simple (15:19) and leads to increased vitality (19:16; 22:5); the wrong way leads to a diminished life (22:5a: "thorns and snares are in the way of the perverse"). Prov. 15:19 ("the way of the lazy is overgrown with thorns") associates such diminution of life with the lazy, who always find "impediments and pretexts to excuse their indolence,"[13] thus implying that ethical misconduct and genuine laziness — not just lethargy[14] — are closely related. This is underlined by 21:25: how are we to understand the statement that "the craving *(taʾᵃwâ)* of a lazy person is fatal (*mûṯ* hiphil)"?

The noun *taʾᵃwâ* denotes more than a "desire for peace and quiet."[15] When it is associated with negative entities (rebelliousness: 18:1; profit: 19:22; the wicked: 21:26), it brings calamity. In the extreme case, the diminution of life can be fatal (21:25). The book of Proverbs promises death primarily to the wicked (*rāšāʿ;* cf. also 14:32) and their like (including, e.g., the *ʿāṣēl*). Deliverance from death is effected not by riches (11:4; 21:6) but by righteousness (*ṣᵉḏāqâ,* 10:2; 11:19; 12:28), discipline as understood by the wisdom school (19:18; 23:13; 15:10; 5:23), and above all by discernment

10. Comms. by W. Zapletal, *EHAT* VII/1 (1973), 266; G. F. Moore, *ICC* (1910), 393.
11. McKane, *Proverbs,* 457.
12. On *dereḵ* as "way of life, conduct of life" → III, 286-88.
13. Ringgren, *Sprüche. ATD* 16/1 (³1980), 65.
14. McKane, *Proverbs,* 530.
15. Gemser, *HAT* I/16², 81.

as taught by the wise (13:14; cf. 10:21). If the terminological links guide our interpretation correctly, the reason why the lazy stand in risk of their lives is not so much that they simply refuse to labor (NRSV) but that they do not vigorously endeavor to achieve the opposite of wrong, under the spell of which laziness brings the individual. In this case it is not enough to speak simply of an unfulfilled life.[16] Therefore the question of what an *ʿāṣēl* neglects becomes urgent.

b. First, we note that the *ʿāṣēl* gives reasons that appear convincing but are in fact nearly incredible[17] why he cannot undertake any meaningful action: lions are abroad, and he would be killed outdoors in the streets (Prov. 22:13; 26:13; → **רצח** *rṣḥ* denotes killing in the strict sense of homicide). While the street or the outdoors *(rᵉḥōḇ, ḥûṣ)* is the domain where people must prove themselves to show that they can support a family (24:27) and where Wisdom practically forces people to take notice of her (1:20), it is also the perilous terrain where a seductive woman can practice her wiles (7:12; cf. 5:16). In 22:13 and 26:13, this pejorative aspect of "street" appears clearly to play a role, so as to lend more "conviction" to the argument used by the *ʿāṣēl* to justify inaction.

When an *ʿāṣēl* has evaded working outdoors, he devotes himself to unproductive repose.[18] As a door turns on its hinges, he turns in his bed, not thinking for a moment about leaving his bedroom (26:14). While this text does not require us to picture the lounging *ʿāṣēl* as asleep, 19:15 clearly does. This sleep of the *ʿāṣēl* is like an unconscious "deep sleep" (*tardēmâ;* Gemser's interpretation as "apathy and lethargy" is unnecessary).[19] This leads to a slothful inertia that can be criticized only by sarcastic ridicule: when such a lazybones buries his hand in his food bowl, he is too indolent to remove it or bring it to his mouth (19:24; 26:15).

The *ʿāṣēl* is in danger of losing his possessions and failing to provide for his own nourishment. But it would be wrong to conclude from this observation that working in the fields is the particular criterion of diligence.[20] The point is rather that making provision for food is a vital concern. That "climate, location, and the memory of nomadic life" provided the impetus here appears highly dubious.[21] Failure to provide for food is irrevocable, as experience shows. Therefore many proverbs attack the love of sleep, for it gives birth to poverty (20:13; cf. 24:33). The grain must be harvested at the right moment (10:5). The *ʿāṣēl* could observe this fact in the animal kingdom and learn from the example. He should go to the ant (6:6). The advice is not meant as a subtle parable;[22] it presents a straightforward didactic analogy: among the ants, the *ʿāṣēl* will find a "people" without administrative officials (6:7); neverthe-

---

16. McKane, *Proverbs,* 550.
17. Ringgren, *ATD* 16³, 87: "preposterous excuse"; McKane, *Proverbs,* 569.
18. Draper, 61.
19. *HAT* I/16², 77.
20. As maintained by Gemser, *HAT* I/16², 39; Ringgren, *ATD* 16³, 31-32.
21. Contra Gemser, *HAT* I/16², 39; Lamparter, *Das Buch der Weisheit: Prediger und Sprüche. BAT* XVI (1955), 271.
22. As claimed by McKane, *Proverbs,* 324.

less, in the summer they gather the food they need (6:8). The accent is more on diligent preparedness than on "the ceaseless activity that is especially characteristic of the ant."[23] Instead, the *ʿāṣēl* lies abed and sleeps (6:9), and poverty is suddenly at hand (6:10-11). That poverty is not "fated" — not even for the *ʿāṣēl* (Prov. 24:30-34; Eccl. 10:18) — but is to a large extent the individual's own fault is emphasized by a variety of proverbs. Laziness has its deeper roots in a failure to heed conventional wisdom and discipline: "Poverty and disgrace await one who ignores discipline" (Prov. 13:18a). The remedy is diligence (e.g., 12:27; 21:5), evidenced especially in honest labor (28:19). But how can someone harvest grain in summer if, like the *ʿāṣēl,* he does not plow in the spring? Naturally when harvest comes there is nothing to be found (20:4).

c. The conduct or "lifestyle" of an *ʿāṣēl* can be assessed from two viewpoints: from the perspective of ethical expectations and on the basis of the fundamental order reflected in wisdom instruction. Manifestations of want cry out for such assessment. As we have already seen, the *ʿāṣēl* is characterized by appetite, craving, and vitality (*nep̱eš* in Prov. 13:4; 19:15; the use of *nep̱eš* is an argument for viewing 13:2-4 as a redactional unit[24]). Slackness to the point of deceit is contrasted with diligence: it results in poverty: "A slack *(rᵉmîyâ)* hand causes poverty, but the hand of the diligent *(ḥārûṣ)* makes rich" (10:4; cf. 12:24). The close association of *nep̱eš, rᵉmîyâ, ḥāmās,* and *ʿāṣēl* (6:6) as well as the connection with *rāšāʿ* (21:24-29) shows that being *ʿāṣēl* is not value neutral. Neither does one become *ʿāṣēl* as a result of the correlation of desert and fortune. An *ʿāṣēl* is simply a person who lets himself drift, refusing to observe his fundamental obligation to provide for the necessities of life, devoting himself instead to irresponsible indolence. Therefore his unreliability is an obstacle to the functioning of society (10:26).

Common sense *(lēḇ)* should prevent such destructive tendencies; a normal measure of intelligence *(ḥkm)* should point the right way. Therefore the *ʿāṣēl* is sent to the ant, where he can observe the necessary foresight and learn the right lesson (6:6). But the *ʿāṣēl* is like an *ʾāḏām ḥᵃsar-lēḇ* (24:30). Derisively, 26:16 chides the *ʿāṣēl:* "The lazy person thinks himself wiser than seven who can answer discreetly." The *ʿāṣēl* does not make a critical assessment of himself; his smugness prevents him from reshaping his life, and he is alienated from the counsels commended by wisdom.[25]

Reiterer

---

23. O. Plöger, *Sprüche Salomos. BK* XVII (1984), 6.
24. Ibid., 158.
25. McKane, *Proverbs,* 601; Ringgren, *ATD* 16^3, 105: "That is ultimate stupidity." On "smugness" see J. van der Ploeg, *Spreuken. BOT* VIII (1952), 90; R. N. Whybray, *Proverbs. CBC* (1972), 153.

עָצַם *ʿāṣam;* עָצוּם *ʿāṣûm;* עֹצֶם *ʿōṣem;* עָצְמָה *ʿoṣmâ;* תַּעֲצֻמוֹת *taʿaṣumôṯ*

I. General: 1. Scope; 2. Other Semitic Languages; 3. LXX; 4. Dead Sea Scrolls. II. Usage and Meaning: 1. *ʿāṣûm;* 2. Verb; 3. Other Nouns; 4. God. III. Theological Contexts: 1. God as Giver of Increase and Power; 2. Human Power against God; 3. The Promises to the Patriarchs; 4. The Increase of Israel in Egypt; 5. The Nations of Canaan; 6. The Assault of the Nations; 7. Deutero-Isaiah; 8. The Pilgrimage of the Nations; 9. The Cultic Community of Israel; 10. Daniel; 11. Sins.

I. General.

1. *Scope.* Despite the assumed common root, this article does not discuss → עצם *ʿeṣem,* "bone," and its associated words, *ʿṣm* III, "close (eyes)," or **aṣmâ,* "great event; misfortune, suffering, torment," which Driver postulates in Ps. 22:18(Eng. v. 17); 53:6(5); Job 4:14; 7:15.[1]

2. *Other Semitic Languages.* The root *ʿṣm* probably derives from Proto-Sem. *ʿẓm.* Words based on this root meaning "numerous, mighty," occur in Ugaritic, Phoenician, Arabic, and Ethiopic. In the Deir ʿAllā inscriptions (I, 8-9), we find *ḥšk wʾl ngh ʿṭm wʾl smrky.* Hoftijzer cautiously interprets *ʾl ngh ʿṭm* as "powerful absence of light"; his syntactic analysis, however, and the presence of our root have rightly been disputed.[2] A clearly "Semitic" *ʿdmm* oil resists interpretation.[3]

3. *LXX.* The LXX does not have a fixed translation for this group of words, clearly not perceiving them as conveying a meaning that could be conveyed by concordant treatment. There is likewise no specific echo of the Hebrew word group in the NT.

4. *Dead Sea Scrolls.* Occurrences in the Dead Sea Scrolls: *ʿṣm:* 1QH 6:31; 1QH fr. 52:1; *ʿṣwm:* 1QM 11:5; 4Q184 1:14.

ʿāṣam. Y. Avishur, *Stylistic Studies of Word-Pairs in Biblical and Ancient Semitic Literatures. AOAT* 210 (1984), 399; R. Giveon, "A Ramesside 'Semitic' Letter," *RSO* 37 (1962) 167-73; M. D. Goldman, "Lexical Notes on Exegesis," *ABR* 4 (1954/55) 87-90, esp. 89-90; W. Gross, *Bileam. SANT* 38 (1974), 258-60; H. W. Hertzberg, "Die 'Abtrünnigen' und die 'Vielen,'" *Verbannung und Heimkehr. FS W. Rudolph* (1961), 97-108, esp. 104-5; N. Lohfink, "Zum 'kleinen geschichtlichen Credo' Dtn 26,5-9," *TP* 46 (1971) 19-39, esp. 28-29, 31; J. L. Palache, *Semantic Notes on the Hebrew Lexicon* (Eng. trans. 1959), 18; P. Weimar, *Untersuchungen zur priesterschriftlichen Exodusgeschichte. FzB* 9 (1973), esp. 25-36.

1. G. R. Driver, *ExpT* 57 (1945/46) 193, 249; idem, *WO* 1 (1947-1952), 411-12; rejected by A. R. Johnson, *The Vitality of the Individual in the Thought of Ancient Israel* (1964), 8.

2. J. Hoftijzer, *ATDA,* 197. Cf. J. Naveh, *IEJ* 29 (1979) 136; J. C. Greenfield, *JSS* 25 (1980) 251; H. and M. Weippert, *ZDPV* 98 (1982) 93.

3. Cf. Rossi-Pleyte, *Papyrus Turin,* II, 8; Giveon.

II. Usage and Meaning.

1. *'āṣûm.* The adj. *'āṣûm* occurs 31 times in the OT (counting Ps. 10:10 but not Isa. 41:21 or Job 7:15) and once in Sirach. There are 12 occurrences in the historical books and the Pentateuch, 11 in the Prophets (esp. Isaiah and Joel), 3 in the Psalms, 4 in wisdom literature, and 2 in Daniel. Of the total, 18 are in poetry and 14 in prose; of the latter, at least 6 appear in Deuteronomistic rhetorical prose, with its propensity for parallelisms and series. The earliest texts are Ex. 1:9 (J); Am. 5:12; Isa. 8:7; the latest are Dnl. 8:24; 11:25; Sir. 16:5. The majority appear to be exilic or postexilic. There is no obvious concentration in a specific period or genre.

In Isa. 41:21 *'ᵃṣumôṯ* refers to forensic proofs; it is reasonable to assume a connection with *'āṣûm* (cf. the discussion below of *'ṣm* in Ps. 69:5[4]). This is clearly a specialized meaning, however, so that it is better not included here. It is less clear whether an already independent specialized meaning should also be postulated in Ps. 10:10, and certainly not what that meaning might be. It is pointless to be tempted into conjectural emendation in this verse, which presents other difficulties as well. In any case, it witnesses to the Masoretic interpretation of the text, in which the *Q* reading of *ḥlk'ym* finds a military metaphor ("army of the weak"). I forgo including the totally conjectural *mē'ᵃṣumôṯāy,* "than these my defensive arguments," in Job 7:15.[4]

Association with certain words is significant. In 21 instances *'āṣûm* appears attributively or predicatively with *'am* or *gôy* (in the sense of "nation" or "army"). Five additional occurrences deal with the same subject without using either word, although *'am* or *gôy* generally appears in the context (Isa. 8:7; 53:12; Joel 2:11; Dnl. 8:24; 11:25). In only five texts does *'āṣûm* modify other entities: Nu. 32:1 (cattle); Am. 5:12 (sins); Ps. 10:10 (snares, pits?); Prov. 7:26 (victims of the strange woman); 18:18 (contenders at law); Sir. 16:5 (striking tales of God's wrath). In short, *'āṣûm* belongs primarily to the lexical environment of *'am* and *gôy.*

This focused usage also explains the prevailing appearance of the word in serial and parallel constructions with *raḇ* (16 times) and *gāḏôl* (8 times). In 5 additional cases *raḇ* occurs in the immediate context, and in 2 *gāḏôl.* Only 8 occurrences involve neither *raḇ* nor *gāḏôl* (Nu. 22:6; Isa. 60:22; Joel 1:6; Mic. 4:7; Ps. 10:10; Prov. 18:18; 30:16; Dnl. 8:24). Both adjectives were identified with the words *'am* and *gôy* even before they became associated with *'āṣûm: gôy gāḏôl* and *'am raḇ* are common phrases. Only occasionally is *'āṣûm* added for emphasis. Therefore when it does occur it appears in second place, with just two exceptions: *'āṣûm* + *raḇ* in Dt. 9:14 and *mê hannāhār hā'ᵃṣûmîm wᵉhārabbîm* in Isa. 8:7. A special case is the compound series in Dt. 26:5: *gôy* + *'āṣûm* + *raḇ* (see III.4 below). The emphatic nature of *'āṣûm* appears clearly in texts that use the shorter expression (just *raḇ* or *gāḏôl*) and then repeat it with the addition of *'āṣûm* (Dt. 4:38 [see vv. 6,7,8]; 7:1 [see earlier in the same verse]; Mic. 4:3 [see vv. 2,13; 5:6,7]; Dnl. 11:25 [see in the same verse]).[5]

In some cases an earlier version of the text without *'āṣûm* has been emphasized by

4. J. Reider, *VT* 2 (1952) 126.
5. On the interpretation of this stylistic technique, see Avishur, 125.

the addition of the word in the new text: Gen. 18:18 (cf. 12:2); Nu. 14:12 (cf. Ex. 32:10); Joel 2:2 (cf. Isa. 13:4); Mic. 4:3 (cf. Isa. 2:4). The series *rb* + *'ẓm* may also be found in Ugaritic: *biku rabbu 'aẓumu,* "a large vial."[6] Emphatic use of *'āṣûm* is also present (esp. in late texts) when other expressions paraphrase or substitute for the nouns *'am* and *gôy.* In a few cases *'āṣûm* alone modifies *'am* (Nu. 22:6; Joel 2:5) or *gôy* (Isa. 60:22; Mic. 4:7).

On the periphery of this picture we find some additional words and motifs used in parallel or close association. They too belong to the domain of *'am* and *gôy, gādôl* and *rab.* These include the physical stature and irresistible strength of the Anakim and the fortification of the Canaanite cities (Dt. 9:1), the word *'elep* (Isa. 60:22 — a countless number, but perhaps as a military term?), *'ên mispār* (Joel 1:6), *šᵉ'ērîṯ* (Mic. 4:7 — division of an army, with military connotations), the inhabitants of many cities (Zec. 8:20,22), *qāhāl* (Ps. 35:18), *meleḵ* (Ps. 135:10; Prov. 30:26-27). Even the lions' teeth in Joel 1:6 and the word *'āz* in Prov. 30:25 (with v. 26) have military associations.

The metaphors in which *'āṣûm* appears stay in this same domain. Isa. 8:7 uses the image of the water of a river overflowing its banks. The Joel passages have to do with an army of locusts covering the whole land (the expression *kissâ 'eṯ-'ên hā'āreṣ* associated with Nu. 22:6 may also suggest locust imagery;[7] in Prov. 30:26 the theme of locusts appears in the following verse). Joel 2:2 (continued by v. 5) speaks of the dawn, Mic. 4:6-7 of a flock scattered over the land. What all these passages have in common is an image of the earth as a broad surface over which extends something mobile, new, altering, numerous, often frightening.

It may be possible to define the associational sphere of *'āṣûm* more precisely. The word occurs 21 times in conjunction with hostility and conflict (Ex. 1:9; Nu. 22:6; Dt. 4:38; 7:1; 9:1; 11:23; 26:5; Josh. 23:9; Isa. 8:7; 53:12; Joel 1:6; 2:2,5,11; Mic. 4:3; Ps. 10:10; 135:10; Prov. 7:26; 18:18; Dnl. 8:24; 11:25). Seven additional passages are at least related to this theme (Nu. 14:12; Dt. 9:14; Isa. 60:22 [alluding to the Dtr texts concerning conquest of the land]; Am. 5:12; Mic. 4:7; Ps. 35:18 [surrounding verses]; Sir. 16:5 [introducing tales of God's wrath]). There are only four occurrences outside this connotative sphere (Gen. 18:18; Nu. 32:1; Zec. 8:22; Prov. 30:26).

Connected with the sphere of conflict is the frequent use of *min* following *'āṣûm.* In Ex. 1:9 and Nu. 22:6 this construction should probably be translated "too numerous/mighty for"; in Nu. 14:12 and Dt. 9:14 it clearly means "more numerous/mighty than." In the remaining passages (Dt. 4:38; 7:1; 9:1; 11:23), the decision is more difficult, but "more numerous/mighty than" is likely (note esp. the context of 7:1). The construction in this situation has been called a "superiority formula."[8]

The relatively rare contrastive expressions denote smallness in size and number, insignificance, weakness (Dt. 7:7, *mᵉ'aṭ* [cf. 7:1]; 26:5, *mᵉṯê mᵉ'aṭ;* Isa. 8:6-7, *hōlᵉḵîm*

---

6. *KTU* 1.3, I, 12. See E. Lipiński, *UF* 2 (1970) 77, 81; M. Dahood, *RSP,* I, II, 516; rejected by J. C. de Moor and P. van der Lugt, *BiOr* 31 (1974) 6 n. 11.

7. See the discussion in Gross, 95-96.

8. Weimar, 33.

le'aṭ; 60:22, *qāṭôn, ṣāʿîr;* Mic. 4:6-7, lameness, distance, rejection). The expression *'ên mispār* in Joel 1:6 could be taken as a quasi-definition of *ʿāṣûm.* There is probably an elative or superlative element inherent in the word *ʿāṣûm* — but (as in the case of the verb) this element can be reinforced further by *me'ōḏ* (Nu. 32:1; Dnl. 11:25; cf. Joel 2:11).

The meaning of *ʿāṣûm* oscillates between "numerous, many" and "mighty, powerful." On the one hand, Nu. 22:6 and 32:1 clearly require the translation "numerous." In Ex. 1:9; Dt. 26:5; Isa. 60:22; Joel 2:2,5,11; Zec. 8:22 (cf. v. 20: "inhabitants of many cities"); Ps. 35:18, individual elements in the context at least suggest that the numerical aspect is primary. Overtones of this aspect can be heard in all occurrences, so that there is no really clear instance of the idea of pure might and power apart from any numerical aspect. On the other hand, contextual elements in Dt. 7:1; 9:1 (and consequently also in the associated texts 4:38; 11:23; Josh. 23:9); Isa. 8:7 (cf. the contrastive language of v. 6); 53:12 (note the reference to the introductory 52:13); Am. 5:12 (cf. v. 9); Ps. 10:10; 135:10 indicate that here the aspect of power and might is primary. In other passages it is very difficult to decide; there is a similar semantic oscillation in the case of *raḇ,* so that the use of *ʿāṣûm* and *raḇ* in parallel does not imply the numerical sense of *ʿāṣûm* (cf. Josh. 17:17, *ʿam raḇ* par. *kōaḥ gāḏôl*). One must remember that in segmentary societies the power and prestige of a family were defined by the number of its members and their cattle, and that in pretechnological warfare military power depended primarily on the number of warriors. There was therefore no reason to separate the two aspects linguistically. The semantic oscillation that causes problems for us is due to the language of translation and its sociocultural presuppositions. Even the notion that the nominal pl. *ʿaṣûmîm* should always be translated "mighty (persons, rulers)" turns out to be wrong. It identifies correctly the primary aspect in Prov. 18:18 and Dnl. 8:24, and probably also in Isa. 53:12,[9] but is by no means certain in Prov. 7:26. The aspect of numerical multitude, present to a greater or lesser degree, probably does not refer to numbers that can be counted on the fingers of a hand but to quantities that are hard to count, going into the hundreds, thousands, and beyond.

If the basic meaning of *ʿāṣûm* is "multiplicity,"[10] then more precise analysis is needed. In 17 cases *ʿāṣûm* qualifies a singular entity, within which the multiplicity must be asserted. This involves no problems in the case of the collectives *ʿam* and *gôy.* The same is true of other words. When the referent is plural, as in *gôyim ʿaṣûmîm,* the meaning must be "many" nations (which together as a multitude of nations would be "mighty") *or* "populous nations," each of which would then be "mighty" individually. Because *ʿāṣûm* can already qualify a sg. "nation," the second alternative is preferable (Dt. 4:38; 7:1; 9:1; 11:23; Josh. 23:9; Mic. 4:3; Zec. 8:22; similarly Isa. 53:12; Dnl. 8:24). In Dt. 7:1 the seven nations named explicitly, despite their symbolic character, are probably too few in number to suggest "many." The aspect of the size of each individual nation becomes thematic in v. 7. There are only two *ʿaṣûmîm* in Prov. 18:18. If

9. Contra Herzberg, 104-5.
10. Contra Palache.

the idea of multiplicity is involved, it can only be because having many family members or adherents makes the contenders mighty. Ps. 135:10 is similar: each of the kings has a great nation behind him. The question remains open in Prov. 7:26 and the metaphorical occurrences in Am. 5:12 and Sir. 16:5. It is impossible to cite a counterexample, where *ʿāṣûm,* appearing with an entity in the plural, is shown by the context to be qualifying this plurality rather than distributively each individual instance of the multitude.

Ps. 135:10 borrows the Deuteronomistic topos of the mighty nations of Canaan, although it does not speak simply of the "nations." Vv. 17-20 of the following psalm even apply the same topos to the kings alone, clearly in the sense of their power and might. Ps. 135:10 stands somewhere in the middle. Here the meaning of *ʿāṣûm* depends on the precise sense of *raḇ,* which here takes the place of the traditional *gāḏôl.* The texts would seem at first glance to speak of "many nations." To the two classic Transjordanian kings of Dt. 2–3 and Ps. 136:19-20 are added all the *maml^eḵôṯ* of Canaan. Nevertheless, *gôyim rabbîm* probably does not mean "many nations (of Canaan)." In the parallelism of *gôy* and *meleḵ, gôy* refers to the subjects rather than the sovereign.[11] Perhaps that is why *raḇ* had to replace *gāḏôl* here. The latter could probably be linked with *gôy* only when the word was not paired with a word referring to the sovereign but included the sovereign. In Ps. 135:10, therefore, the *rabbîm* with *gôyim* qualifies each individual nation; to be consistent, the *ʿ^aṣûmîm* with *m^elāḵîm* must qualify the individual kings. The translation should read: "populous nations . . . mighty kings," with the might of the kings deriving from the great number of the nations they reign over.

2. *Verb.* There are 17 occurrences of *ʿṣm* (including Jer. 30:14 and Ps. 69:5[4], but excluding the piel in Jer. 50:17 and the conjectural occurrence in Dnl. 11:4), 16 in the qal and one in the hiphil. It appears 3 times in Genesis and Exodus, but nowhere else in the Pentateuch and the historical books. It appears 5 times in the Prophets, but only in Isaiah and Jeremiah — always in authentic texts. It is thus totally absent from the Deuteronomistic corpus. It appears 6 times in the Psalter and 3 times in Daniel. There are no occurrences in wisdom literature. Eleven occurrences are in poetic texts (Prophets and Psalms), 6 in prose (Genesis, Exodus, Daniel). Seven occurrences date from the period of the monarchy. Of these, Gen. 26:16 (J) could derive from a prior oral Isaac tradition; Jer. 15:8 bears witness to the events of 597 or 587. The majority of the postexilic occurrences are late. The occurrences in the Psalter are mostly in psalms of an anthological nature (40:6,13[5,12]; 69:5[4]; 105:24).

Jer. 30:14b should not be deleted, even though it is identical with v. 15b.[12] The piel of *ʿṣm* in Jer. 50:17 is a denominative from *ʿeṣem,* "bone."[13] In Ps. 69:5(4) we may be dealing with a specialized meaning: "make oneself strong in a lawsuit = bring suit

11. W. L. Moran, "A Kingdom of Priests," *FS M. J. Gruenthaner* (1962), 7-20.
12. N. Lohfink, "Der junge Jeremia als Propagandist und Poet," in *Le livre de Jérémie. BETL* 54 (1981), 351-68.
13. *HP,* 267.

against";[14] cf. *ʿᵃṣûmôṯ* in Isa. 41:21 (see above) and Middle Heb. *ʿṣm* hithpael, "engage in a lawsuit." Since the meanings here have not yet really drifted apart, I include this text. The conjectural *keʿoṣmô* in Dnl. 11:4 should be rejected as a harmonizing assimilation to 8:8.[15]

In sharp contrast to the usage of *ʿāṣûm,* only in Ex. 1:20 and Ps. 105:24 (both times in connection with Israel's becoming a nation in Egypt) is the subject of the situation expressed by *ʿṣm* designated by the word *ʿam.* The word *gôy* is never used. Indeed, Dnl. 11:23 says of Antiochus IV: *weʿāṣam bimʿaṭ-gôy,* "he became mighty even though his supporters were few." In three passages, however, the subject is equivalent to *ʿam/gôy:* Ex. 1:7 (Israelites); Isa. 31:1 (horsemen/chariots of an army); Jer. 15:8 (the widows of the people of Yahweh — an ironic allusion to the promise of many descendants). In three other passages, individuals must be viewed as representatives of their clans or kingdoms: Gen. 26:16 (Isaac), Dnl. 8:8 (Alexander the Great), and Dnl. 11:23 (Antiochus IV). Finally, Dnl. 8:24 must be included (the "power" of Antiochus IV as the subj. of *ʿṣm*). This accounts for 9 out of 17 occurrences. Somewhat similar are Ps. 38:20(19) and 69:5(4), which make statements about the psalmist's enemies: they can hardly be meant as individuals, but they can as representatives of clans. The 6 remaining texts are metaphorical; the subject of the verb is the sins of Israel or the psalmist (Jer. 5:6; 30:14-15; Ps. 40:13[12]), God's wondrous deeds (Ps. 40:6[5]), or the sum of God's thoughts (Ps. 139:17). Although usage of the verb fundamentally resembles that of *ʿāṣûm,* we find less association with particular words and a greater tendency toward metaphor.

Corresponding to the absence of *gôy* as subject is the fact that *gdl* appears only once in a series (Dnl. 8:8, where *gdl* introduces the series). Appearance in series with *rbb, rbh,* or *raḇ,* however, is common (Ex. 1:7,20; Isa. 31:1; Jer. 5:6; 30:14-15 [twice]; Ps. 40:6[5]; 69:5[4] with *rb* before *ʿṣm;* Ps. 38:20[19]; 139:17-18 with *ʿṣm* before *rb:* a total of 10 occurrences). In addition, *gdl* and *rb* appear in Gen. 26:13-14, a proleptic explanation of v. 16. In Ps. 139:18 we find something like a definition of *ʿṣm:* "They are more than the sand" (cf. also Jer. 15:8, "the sand of the seas"). Cf. also Ex. 1:17; Ps. 40:13(12); 105:24; 139:17; Dnl. 8:24. The clearest parallel is probably the phrase *ʾên mispār* in Ps. 40:13(12). As opposites we find in Ps. 38:12(11) (cf. v. 20[19]) and 69:9-13(8-12) (cf. v. 5) the social isolation of the psalmist, and in Dnl. 8:7 (cf. v. 8) the impotence of an opponent.

The verb, too, is usually associated with enmity, conflict, etc. In 10 occurrences this hostility is found in the immediate context (Gen. 26:16; Ex. 1:20; Isa. 31:1; Jer. 15:8; Ps. 38:20[19]; 69:5[4]; 105:24; Dnl. 8:8,24; 11:23); in 4 it appears at least in the extended context (Ex. 1:7; Jer. 5:6; 30:14-15). Construction with *min,* common with *ʿāṣûm,* appears in Gen. 26:16; Jer. 15:8; Ps. 40:6,13(5,12); 105:24.

Again the meaning oscillates between "be numerous" and "be mighty." Gen. 26:12-16 shows clearly how under fractionated circumstances both aspects go together. In the

---

14. Goldman.

15. First proposed by H. Graetz, *MGWJ* 20 (1871) 142.

case of the verb (in contrast to *ʿāṣûm*), however, especially in later texts, the aspect of multiplicity clearly becomes secondary to that of might and power. A total dissociation of the aspect of "might" from that of great numbers appears in Dnl. 11:23 ("despite the small size of his party"). In Isa. 31:1, on the contrary, the point is precisely the great multitude of the Egyptian cavalry — for the context promises their defeat. Comparison to the hairs of the psalmist's head in Ps. 40:13(12) and 69:5(4) likewise admits only a numerical sense.

Again the question of the actual subject of the expression of multiplicity arises when that entity appears in the plural: is it the plurality itself or distributively the individual member of the plurality? Once again, multiplicity can be predicated of a singular entity (Gen. 26:16; Ex. 1:20; Ps. 105:24). In the case of the psalmist's enemies in Ps. 38:20(19); 69:5(4) (cf. Prov. 18:18) and of the sins described in Jer. 5:6; 30:14-15; Ps. 40:13(12) (cf. Am. 5:12), the verb should possibly be interpreted distributively. But a text like Ex. 1:7 ("Israelites" as subj.) shows that a different perspective can make its appearance in the case of the verb. The plural subject is perceived as a collective and thus as a totality can become the entity of which multiplicity and might are predicted. This is clearly true in Isa. 31:1; Jer. 15:8; Ps. 40:6(5); 139:17 as well.

3. *Other Nouns.* If Isa. 11:15 and Ps. 139:15 are not counted, the noun *ʿōṣem* appears twice (Dt. 8:17; Job 30:21); if Sir. 38:18 is not counted and Isa. 40:29 is counted, the noun *ʿoṣmâ* (overlooked by *KBL*³) appears 5 times (Isa. 40:29; 47:9; Nah. 3:9; Sir. 41:2; 46:9). In Ps. 68:36(35) the word *taʿᵃṣûmôṯ* appears as a hapax legomenon parallel to *ʿōz,* with the meaning "power." Ps. 68 could be very ancient. Nah. 3:9 is certainly preexilic. Dt. 8:17 (the only occurrence in prose) belongs to a late Deuteronomistic stratum.

None of the ancient versions supports the interpretation of the hapax legomenon *baʿyām* in Isa. 11:15 as a corruption of *bᵉʿōṣem.*[16] The LXX and other ancient versions support the reading *ʿoṣmâ* in Isa. 40:29.[17] In Nah. 3:9 it is unlikely that the Masoretes "carelessly"[18] omitted the *mappiq;* this is therefore an occurrence of *ʿoṣmâ,* not *ʿōṣem;* the ancient versions added the personal pronoun that the sense requires. In Ps. 139:15 *ʿōṣmî* is the original reading, not the *ʿṣby* of 11QPsᵃ; but the word in question is *ʿōṣem* II, "body," related to *ʿeṣem,* "bone" (cf. "soul" in v. 14). In Sir. 38:18, B reads *ybnh ʿṣbh,* "brings tribulation"; LXX *kámpsei ischýn* might reflect *yᵉʿannēh ʿoṣmâ,*[19] but this is not certain.

The word *ʿōṣem* exists only in the bound phrase *ʿōṣem yāḏ* (Dt. 8:17; Job 30:21); in both its occurrences it clearly means "power, might." The phrase may already be found in Ugaritic,[20] but the one occurrence of *ʿẓm yd* could be vocalized as meaning either "might of hand" or "forearm bone."

---

16. First proposed by Luzatto; cf. Delitzsch, *Isaiah. KD* I, 292.
17. K. Elliger, *Deutero-Jesaja. BK* XI/1 (1978), 93-94.
18. W. Rudolph, *Micha-Nahum-Habakuk-Zephanja. KAT* XIII/3 (1975), in loc.
19. N. Peters, *Das Buch Jesus Sirach. EHAT* 25 (1913), in loc.
20. *KTU* 1.12, I, 24.

The meaning of the more freely used *'oṣmâ* oscillates between the two now familiar possibilities. Isa. 47:9 clearly has to do with numerical multiplicity, and probably Nah. 3:9 as well; Isa. 40:29; Sir. 41:2; 46:9 more likely deal with "power, might." In Isa. 40:29 (opposite *'ên 'ônîm*), the reference may even be to the power of wealth, an interpretation supported by the Targum. The problem of a plural referent appears only in Isa. 47:9, where the context sheds no light.

Of the familiar parallel roots, *gdl* does not appear, but *rb* does: Dt. 8:17 (cf. v. 13); Isa. 40:29 (as a verb); 47:9 (*rōḇ* — cf. the similar expression in v. 12 with *rōḇ* but not *'oṣmâ*). New parallels include *kōaḥ* (Dt. 8:17, with *kōaḥ* then appearing by itself in v. 18; Isa. 40:29, where *kōaḥ* is a key word in the context; Job 30:21, where the *'ōṣem yāḏ* of the divine enemy is an augmentation of the *kōaḥ yāḏ* of the human enemy in v. 2), *'ên qēṣeh* (Nah. 3:9), and *'ōz* (Ps. 68:36[35]). In the context of Isa. 40:29, the image of eagle wings (v. 31) deserves mention. In 4 of the 8 occurrences, the theme of conflict and war is sounded: Isa. 47:9; Nah. 3:9; Job 30:21; Sir. 46:9 (on the warlike overtones of *drk 'al bāmôṯê 'ereṣ,* cf. Dt. 33:29; Mic. 1:3).

4. *God.* In secular usage the word group refers to individuals as well as nations, armies, and other collectives; unlike other words for power and might, however, it never appears in a direct statement concerning God. The texts that come closest are Ps. 40:6(5) (verb: Yahweh's wondrous deeds are myriad), Ps. 139:17 (verb: the great sum of El's thoughts), Job 30:21-22 (*'ōṣem:* the might of Eloah's hand lifts Job into the gale to destroy him), and possibly Sir. 16:15 (*'āṣûm:* many/mighty evidences of Yahweh's wrath recorded in the Bible). But all these passages use the word in question indirectly; never is the root associated directly with God. The word group must have had a connotation that made such association impossible. Was the semantic element of "multiplicity" so dominant that it appeared irreconcilable with the one and only God of Israel, who did not belong to any divine family constellation? Was the connotation of conflict and struggle so indicative of an open, unresolved situation that Yahweh could not be conceived in such a setting? That the word group is never used of God should not, however, lead us to conclude that its meaning was fundamentally negative. The error of such a conclusion is demonstrated by its use in connection with God's gracious acts in history on behalf of human beings.

III. Theological Contexts.

1. *God as Giver of Increase and Power.* Independently of the special theological topoi concerning Israel, the word group appears to be available to represent the beneficent intervention of the deity in history on behalf of human beings. Isaac's power, achieved by increase of possessions, cattle, and household (Gen. 26:13-14, anticipating v. 26), is ascribed to God's abundant *(m^e'ōḏ)* blessing (v. 12). In the hymnic conclusion of Ps. 68 (possibly very early and, if so, northern in origin), the kingdoms/kings of the earth/land (v. 33[32]) praise Yahweh as the "El of Israel," who "gives power and strength *('ōz w^eṯa$^{'a}$ṣûmôṯ)* to his people [or 'the people,' i.e., humankind]" (v. 36[35]). Yahweh is also in the background when Dnl. 8:24 says that Antiochus IV will grow strong in power, "but not with his [own] power." In some occurrences in the books of

Isaiah and Sirach, too, the use of the word group can hardly be ascribed solely to the influence of classical texts recounting the sacred history of Israel, even when (as in Isa. 60:22 and Sir. 46:9) the context includes elements associated with such texts. In Isa. 40:27-31 the prophet reminds the disheartened Jacob-Israel of the exile of what it has long known (v. 28): Yahweh gives power *(ʿoṣmâ)* to the faint (v. 29). He can and — the point of the entire passage — he will. In Isa. 60, the central chapter of Trito-Isaiah, the description of Yahweh's eschatological transformation of Zion ends with the statement: "The least of them shall become a 'thousand,' and the smallest one a *gôy ʿāṣûm*" (v. 22). In Sirach's "Hymn Honoring Ancestors," it is said of Caleb — without any basis in the Hexateuch — that Yahweh gave him *ʿoṣmâ* and stood by him in his old age (Sir. 46:9). Therefore, it was probably an open linguistic possibility to say that the deity makes someone favored *ʿāṣûm*.

2. *Human Power against God.* At the same time, it appears to have been possible — likewise anticipating the salvation-history theology of Israel — to use the word group to describe those who unfold their own human power against the deity or the faithful. We are still within the framework of normal secular usage when a lament describes the psalmist's enemies as *ʿaṣûmîm* (Ps. 10:10; 38:20[19]; 69:5[4]). But the psalmist thinks of himself as being on the side of his God, and so the overall context brands the power unfolded by the psalmist's enemies as ungodly. On a national scale, the same constellation appears in an oracle of Isaiah against Israel for allying itself with Egypt (Isa. 31:1, with reference to the multitudes of Egyptian cavalry), in an oracle of Nahum against Nineveh (Nah. 3:9, with reference to Cush and Egypt as the great human reservoir supplying troops for Assyria), and in Deutero-Isaiah's ironic lament for fallen Babylon (Isa. 47:9, with reference to the multitude of Babylon's magical texts, which it thought guarantees its security). Dt. 8:17 must also be included here: the warning to Israel not to ascribe the wealth it will acquire to the "might" of its own hand, when in fact the wealth comes from Yahweh. Although these prophetic and Deuteronomistic occurrences appear in texts that deal with sacred history, they probably point to the preexisting lexical possibility of using our word group for an ungodly unfolding of power.

3. *The Promises to the Patriarchs.* Against the broader background of the general use of this word group in theological contexts, the occurrences related directly to sacral history take on a sharper outline. First, a negative observation often not recognized in the literature: the word group does not belong to the genuine vocabulary of the promises to the patriarchs. In the pentateuchal texts recording the promises, only in Gen. 18:18 do we find the expression *gôy gāḏôl weʿāṣûm,* which expands the phrase *gôy gāḏôl* of 12:2 (cf. also 17:20; 21:18; 46:3). Whether 18:18-19 belongs to the source stratum of chs. 18–19 (J) is both affirmed and disputed. If the text is late, one might theorize that the expression *gôy gāḏôl weʿāṣûm,* which Deuteronomistic usage had made formulaic in a different context, has here been introduced secondarily into the topos of the promises to the patriarchs. Similarly, the verb *ʿṣm* in Jer. 15:8 and the noun *ʿāṣûm* in Isa. 60:22 appear in late and very tenuous allusions to the promises to the patriarchs.

4. *The Increase of Israel in Egypt.* A topos of sacred history to which the word group genuinely belongs is the increase of Israel in Egypt to become a populous nation. The occurrences at the beginning of Exodus belong to several pentateuchal strata — both the early sources (1:9,20) and P^G (v. 7). Either *rbh* or *rab̠* always precedes; the subject is *ʿam* or *b^enê yiśrā'ēl.* In the early sources, the statement asserts that the Israel became too numerous for the Egyptians (v. 9, *ʿāṣûm min*), explaining why Egypt oppressed Israel. This oppression impels the events of the exodus narrative. The situation is identical in P^G; but the construction with *min* is absent, because P^G has introduced the key word *ʿṣm* into a declaration, crucial to the construction of the work as a whole, recording the fulfillment of the blessing on creation (Gen. 1:28) and the blessing following the covenant with Noah (Gen. 9:7) (verbs: *prh, šrš, rbh, ml'*). Israel is the exemplary nation in whom that which was set in motion with the creation of humankind is now fulfilled — with one outstanding exception: conquest *(kbš)* of the earth. For Israel, concretely, this means taking possession of its own land. This cannot happen in the land of Egypt. In a manner typical of P, this new inclusion of *ʿṣm* and its association with the *rbh* of creation blessing sets in motion the events of the exodus, beginning with oppression in Egypt: a reference back to the dynamics already established at creation. The declaration that this final unfinished element of the creation blessing has been fulfilled will not appear until Josh. 18:1.[21]

The widespread theory that the combination of *rbh* and *ʿṣm* in Ex. 1:7 does not belong to P^G but was introduced by a redactor or compiler of the Pentateuch, on the grounds that *ʿṣm* does not appear in Gen. 1:28, is unfounded. It fails to recognize the literary technique of P^G, found elsewhere as well, which incorporates linguistic signals from the early sources at a point characteristic of them.[22]

But even before P^G used this technique to link the exodus with creation, the topos of Israel's increase in Egypt was already illuminating other textual complexes, including occurrences of the root *ʿṣm.* In the story of Balaam, the Moabite king Balak feels threatened by Israel, which "has come out of Egypt, spread over the face of the earth, and settled next to me" (Nu. 22:5). This nation is "too *ʿāṣûm* for me" (v. 6). Therefore he calls on Balaam to curse this nation. Like the statement describing the increase of Israel in Egypt, this statement sets in motion the events of the narrative it begins. The reader is to recognize the associations in Balak's words and even at this point imagine how the unsuspecting Balak will cross swords with Yahweh. The use of *ʿāṣûm* in Nu. 22:6 thus presupposes that not only the author but also the expected readership is familiar with an exodus narrative like that in the early pentateuchal sources — whether through oral or written tradition, or because the Balaam story struck the reader at once as part of a literary complex beginning with Ex. 1.

It is likely that a proto-Dtn JE redaction (at the earliest) introduced into the story of the golden calf the scene of Moses' intercession (Ex. 32:7-14). Yahweh informs Moses

21. N. Lohfink, "Die Priesterschrift und die Geschichte," *Congress Volume, Göttingen 1977. SVT* 29 (1978), 218-20.

22. For a more detailed refutation of this assessment, see Weimar, 25-26.

of his intention to destroy this nation and begin all over by making of Moses a *gôy gāḏôl* (v. 10). This verse clearly echoes the promise to Abraham in Gen. 12:2: Moses is to be a new Abraham. Nu. 14:11-20, an intercession scene inserted soon after into the story of the spies (and incorporating even later expansions), is dependent on the scene in Ex. 32, but introduces fresh nuances, including Yahweh's new words to Moses: "I will make of you a *gôy gāḏôl wᵉʿāṣûm mimmennû*" (v. 12). Here *gāḏôl* comes from Ex. 32:10, the prototype, but the expansion derives from Ex. 1; its purpose is to bring the intended new Mosaic nation into an exodus situation with respect to Israel analogous to that of Israel with respect to Egypt in Ex. 1. This explains why Yahweh's act of destruction is conceived as a plague (14:12a) — it is analogous to the Egyptian plagues. Thus the introduction of *ʿāṣûm* directs attention not to Abraham but to the exodus story. While the root *rb* always precedes the root *ʿṣm* in Ex. 1, the dependence on 32:10 now includes the root *gdl* in this complex.

This presumably established the pattern for the formulation of the increase in Egypt that appears in the Deuteronomic "short historical credo": "There [in Egypt] he [my ancestor] became *lᵉgôy gāḏôl ʿāṣûm wārāḇ*" (Dt. 26:5). The prototype Nu. 20:15-16 did not include the motif of increase in Egypt.[23] It is obvious that certain language was incorporated from Ex. 1. The total formulation, however, is new and is repeated in this exact form nowhere else in the OT. The threefold qualification of *gôy* is forced by the poetic form of the credo in Dt. 26, for it is a kind of metrical variant of the first clause *'ᵃrammî 'ōḇēḏ 'āḇî* with its three accents.[24] If Gen. 18:18 was not present in the then extant form of the Tetrateuch, the Deuteronomic author of the credo used as his prototype the formulation in Nu. 14:12 (missing the connection with the increase in Egypt), adding *raḇ,* the original parallel to *ʿāṣûm* in Ex. 1:9, as a third attribute. In a three-stress unit, metrical considerations probably helped account for its final position. Dt. 26:5 contains the *only* Deuteronomic/pre-Deuteronomistic occurrence of *ʿāṣûm;* there can be no thought of a "Deuteronomic stereotype" here.

In turn, the formulation in Dt. 26:5 presumably provided the basis for the highly unusual variant of God's words to Moses in the intercession narrative as formulated by the (probably Josianic) author of the earliest recension of the Deuteronomistic History in Dt. 9:11-14,25-29: "I will make of you a *gôy ʿāṣûm wārāḇ mimmennû*" (v. 14). Both prototypes in Ex. 32 and Nu. 14 as well as Dt. 26:5 had *gāḏôl;* the LXX prototype also added it promptly to Dt. 9:14. The word *rāḇ* came first in Ex. 1:9, which is also its normal place in combination with *ʿāṣûm.* One possible explanation of the word order in Dt. 9:14 is that Dtr I recalled and consciously adopted the formulation of 26:5, simultaneously eliminating the first element *gāḏôl* in order by means of this null statement to banish from the context any association with the promise of increase to the patriarchs. The latter purpose appears to make itself felt elsewhere in the same context: when the patriarchs are mentioned in Moses' prayer of intercession (9:27), the promise that the patriarchs would become a nation, pres-

23. Lohfink, 25-28.
24. Ibid., 24-25.

ent in the prototype in Ex. 32:13, is likewise omitted. The motivation for this omission cannot be pursued here.

Otherwise the root *ʿṣm* plays no further role in Deuteronomic and Deuteronomistic literature in connection with the increase of Israel in Egypt. In other literary domains as well, the topos with this root seldom appears. The postexilic texts Isa. 60:22 and Mic. 4:7 may allude to it faintly. Ps. 105, an historical psalm that presupposes the Pentateuch, contains the motif (v. 24). Here we find the only occurrence of the hiphil of *ʿṣm:* more directly than in the early texts, Yahweh is presented as the agent of Israel's increase.

5. *The Nations of Canaan.* In some late Deuteronomistic redactional strata, however, the word *ʿāṣûm* enters the stock of Deuteronomistic clichés in a totally different context. It builds on the use of the word group for the autonomous might of the enemies of the deity and the psalmist. The most extensive text of "DtrN" (shown to be present in Joshua and Judges by Smend and probably also found in Deuteronomy)[25] is Josh. 23:1-16. Its theme is the "nations" (*gôyim,* vv. 3,4,7,9,12,13) destroyed (or not yet destroyed) by Israel during the conquest. The future role of the nations with respect to Israel is determined by Israel's faithful adherence to the Torah. After an initial rhetorical arc, vv. 9-10 begin afresh: Israel has experienced its ability to destroy more powerful nations, and in the future it may be in a position to do so again. In v. 9 the expression *gôyim g^e^ḏōlîm wa^ca^ṣûmîm* appears as the object of *yrš* hiphil; it is by no means a stereotyped cliché (like the nations "left here" in the same text). Later Dt. 7:1; 9:1; 11:23 seize on the expression as a kind of catchword, always in conjunction with *yrš* qal or hiphil and other verbs meaning "destroy." These passages belong to a stratum of Deuteronomy that takes a critical position with regard to the nomistic theology of DtrN.[26] Here the expression is always a new addition to the existing text: for 7:1-5, cf. Ex. 23:23-24 and 34:11; for 9:1-2, cf. Nu. 13:28,31 and Dt. 1:28; for 11:23-25, cf. Dt. 1:7-8 and Josh. 1:3-5. The central argument against the nomistic theology of DtrN appears in 9:1-5: it is not on account of any inherent "righteousness" on the part of Israel that Yahweh destroyed the more powerful enemy nations for Israel's benefit. Within the total argument, the motif of the nations' superiority serves to glorify the miraculous nature of Yahweh's aid, vouchsafed quite unmerited by Israel.[27]

Without the root *ʿṣm,* the same stratum also mentions these *gôyim* in Dt. 7:1,17,22; 8:20; 9:4-5; 11:23. Dt. 7:1 designates them as the seven nations of the early list of nations. In 7:17-24 in particular, we find a call to trust in Yahweh's help. The miraculous character of the destruction of the nations is likewise the subject of 4:38, a text belonging to an even later stratum, where the expression appears to be used formulaically in a thoroughly appropriate context. Outside Deuteronomistic literature, a variant of the

---

25. R. Smend, "Das Gesetz und die Volker," *Probleme biblischer Theologie. FS G. von Rad* (1971), 494-509; N. Lohfink, "Kerygmata des Deuteronomistische Geschichtswerks," *Die Botschaft und die Boten. FS H. W. Wolff* (1981), 87-100.

26. See Lohfink, "Kerygmata," 99-100.

27. G. Braulik, *ZTK* 79 (1982) 127-60.

formula *(raḇ* instead of *gāḏôl)* appears in Ps. 135:10, in a summary of the conquest based on the accounts in Deuteronomy and Joshua (on the introduction of the nations' kings, cf. Dt. 7:24).

6. *The Assault of the Nations.* Independently of this use of *ʿāṣûm* for the hostile nations of Canaan, doomed to destruction, and at a much earlier date,[28] Isa. 8:7 (authentic) in Isaiah's "memoir" uses the image of *mê hannāhār hāʿ^{a}ṣûmîm w^{e}hārabbîm,* overflowing the river's banks and inundating even Judah, to depict the oppressive might of Assyria. This is Judah's punishment for refusing "the water of Shiloah that flow gently." Judah wanted a role on the world stage — now its life is at stake! But in the canonical text, at least, v. 8b (authenticity disputed) describes Yahweh as imposing a limit on the catastrophe (the enormous protective bird is Yahweh!). This limit is reinforced by the ironic "challenge" addressed to the nations of the world in vv. 9-10 (authenticity likewise disputed). On this image and its use cf. Isa. 17:12-14. The concrete situation is presented in terms of the motif of the nations' assault on Zion and its termination by Yahweh.

This motif connects this constellation of material with that of the book of Joel, where *ʿāṣûm* appears frequently: in the earlier description of the invading army of locusts (1:6) and in ch. 2, where everything is presented in terms of the eschatological assault of the nations (2:2,5,11 — at the beginning, in the middle, and at the end of an overall palindromic structure). In Joel the interpretive element of the "day of Yahweh" is added and the military aspect is strongly emphasized. At the end of the book we find once more an ironic challenge to eschatological battle (4:9-14[3:9-14]).

7. *Deutero-Isaiah.* In Deutero-Isaiah an exhausted and powerless Israel has ceased to believe that Yahweh can once more give it *ʿoṣmâ* (Isa. 40:29; see III.1 above). Conversely, the *ʿoṣmâ* of magic cannot help Babylon, the oppressor (47:9; see III.2 above). Yahweh will deliver his "servant" from death. The total commitment of Yahweh to his servant after his death and humiliation culminates in 53:12 in the image of dividing the spoil after a great battle. Among the *rabbîm,* Yahweh gives his servant a share of the spoil; with the *ʿ^{a}ṣûmîm* he divides the spoil. The word *rabbîm* is a key word in the framework of 52:13–53:12 (52:14,15; 53:11,12 [twice]). Isa. 52:15 points to the *gôyim rabbîm* and their kings, the great nations of the world, which have oppressed Yahweh's servant (in the definitive text: Israel). Formerly they were appalled to behold the terrible appearance of Israel (52:14). Then, however, the servant bore their sins (53:12) and made them "righteous" (53:12). Their reaction is total astonishment (52:15). But the servant is translated to the sphere formerly characteristic of the other nations and kings: the sphere of victory and dividing the spoil (53:12). The sphere of might, denoted by the word *ʿāṣûm,* is now Israel's very own domain. Is this purely an image representing the exaltation of the delivered servant? Or is Israel really to take its place in the midst of the great nations? If so, after recognizing and accepting the truth of his-

28. Contra Wildberger, *Isaiah 1–12* (Eng. trans. 1991), 341-42.

tory, they would not cease to be great and powerful. This would be a conception similar to that presented by the image of the pilgrimage of the nations.

Hertzberg points out that, even if the servant in the fourth "Servant Song" is interpreted as an individual and the speakers of Isa. 53:1-11a are interpreted not as the nations and kings of the world but as Israel, the *rabbîm* and *ʿaṣûmîm* of the framework are clearly these nations.[29]

8. *The Pilgrimage of the Nations.* In Isa. 2:2-5 (= Mic. 4:1-4), the classical text describing the pilgrimage of the nations, *ʿāṣûm* appears in the Micah version (4:3; no earlier than postexilic, no matter how one may think the text originated): from Zion, after the nations have assembled there, Yahweh "shall judge between *ʿammîm rabbîm* and shall arbitrate between *gôyim ʿaṣûmîm* — even those far away." Possibly — but only possibly — this passage echoes the Deuteronomistic terminology for the destroyed nations of Canaan (Dt. 7:1; 9:1), suggesting how the end of history differs from the beginning of history. But the purpose may also have been to point to recall Isa. 53:12 by the expansion of the text.

Comparison of Mic. 4 with Isa. 2 shows that in Isaiah *gôy* is the leading word, with *ʿam* appearing in parallel; in Micah the situation is reversed. That the Isaiah pattern is the original is shown by the formulation of Isa. 2:4b (retained in Micah), where the expression *gôy ʾel-gôy* uses only the leading word. In Micah redaction has included *ʿammîm (rabbîm)* in a more comprehensive text, thus making it the leading word in this oracle (cf. Mic. 4:5; 5:6,7). In the original oracle, there was no modifier of *gôyim* (cf. Isa. 2:2,4), while in each parallel stich *ʿammîm* was modified by *rabbîm.* The Micah redaction used two different approaches to solve the problem of balance that arose when its operation changed the order of terms. In Mic. 4:1-2 it left *ʿammîm* unmodified and associated *rabbîm* with *gôyim,* now in second position. In 4:3, however, *ʿammîm* in initial position retained *rabbîm,* and so an attributive had to be added to *gôyim* in second position. Thus *ʿaṣûmîm* was introduced here. That the prophecy encompasses all the nations of the world was underlined by the further addition of *ʿaḏ-rāḥôq.*

The concluding text of Proto-Zechariah (Zec. 8:20-23; cf. the previous 2:15) takes up the theme of the pilgrimage of the nations; vv. 20-21 are probably authentic. As in Isa. 2 = Mic. 4, nations *(ʿammîm)* and the inhabitants of many cities *(ʿārîm rabbôṯ)* address each other, calling for a pilgrimage to Jerusalem — in this case to appease the anger of Yahweh and to make inquiry of the oracle of Yahweh of hosts. In Zec. 8:22 a chiastic addition resumes and clarifies the theme: the text deals with *ʿammîm rabbîm wᵉgôyim ʿaṣûmîm.* Here we may see an actual literary cross-reference to the oracle of Mic. 4:1-4, already part of the prophetic canon.

9. *The Cultic Community of Israel.* The use of *ʿam ʿāṣûm* in Ps. 35:18, a vow of thanksgiving, is clearly unique: it denotes the cultic community before which the lamenting psalmist will give thanks for deliverance. It is preceded in the parallelism by

29. Pp. 102-6.

qāhāl rāḇ, to which we may compare Ps. 22:26(25) (likewise a vow of thanksgiving; par. "those who fear him"; cf. already 22:23[22]) and 40:10(9). In Ps. 22:25,27(24,26); 35:10, the "poor" play a role in the context. All three texts are probably late. Was *ʿam ʿāṣûm* a common designation of the cultic community, which only by chance is not attested elsewhere? Or are we dealing here with a new formulation dating from a late period that was no longer secure linguistically? Ps. 35 is also unusual in another respect: it divides the vow of thanksgiving and places it at the end of each of its three sections (vv. 9-10,18,27-28). Recognizing this, we can observe a wordplay between *kol ʿaṣmôṯay,* "my whole body" (v. 10, par. to *napšî* in v. 9), and *ʿam ʿāṣûm* in v. 18. This by itself may explain the choice of words (cf. the similar wordplay in Ps. 135:15,17). Of course the worshiper is meant above all to hear echoes of the texts recalling how Israel grew numerous and mighty in Egypt and then became a *qāhāl* at Sinai.

10. *Daniel.* Dnl. 8–12 uses our word group to describe especially mighty kings or armies. Such might is always the gift of God, who also determines whether it succeeds or fails. The distribution of the verb and *ʿāṣûm* is linguistically interesting: the verb is used of Alexander the Great and Antiochus IV (8:8,24; 11:23), while *ʿāṣûm* represents the enemies of Antiochus IV (8:24; 11:25).

11. *Sins.* Amos used *ʿāṣûm* metaphorically for the social sins of the northern kingdom: *yāḏaʿtî rabbîm piš ʿêḵem waʿᵃṣūmîm ḥaṭṭōʾṯêḵem* (Am. 5:12). The text goes on to speak of sins in the gate, i.e., in the administration of justice. Sins surround the sinful upper class like a superior hostile army.

During the last years of Josiah, when Jeremiah propagandistically legitimated Josiah's expansion to the north and in the process formulated the core of Jer. 30–31,[30] in his retrospective summary of the disastrous history of the north, he cited the obviously familiar words of Amos in a clause forcibly repeated at the conclusion of a strophe: *ʿal rōḇ ʿᵃwōnēḵ ʿāṣᵉmû ḥaṭṭōʾṯāyiḵ (ʿāśîṯî ʾēlleh lāḵ)* (30:14-15). Under Jehoiakim, Jeremiah himself became a prophet of disaster in Judah; in 5:6 he turned the words of Amos against Jerusalem: *rabbû piš ʿêhem ʿāṣᵉmû mᵉšūḇôṯêhem.* That he was adapting his earlier oracle against the north is shown by the catchword *nkh* hiphil (cf. 30:12,14 with 5:6). That he was still drawing on Amos is shown by the catchwords *mišpāṭ, dal,* and *pešaʿ* (cf. Am. 5:7,11,12 with Jer. 5:4,6). New here is the charge of obduracy in wickedness, an obduracy that is underlined by the fact that ancient prophet oracles, pronounced in a bygone era, must be repeated.

When the final redactor of Ps. 40 (postexilic) wanted in v. 13(12) to forge a link between the two existing sections of the psalm, he drew on both v. 6(5) (*rabbôṯ ʿāśîṯā . . . niplᵉʾōṯeyḵā . . . ʿāṣᵉmû missappēr*) and, instigated by the root *ʿṣm,* the prophetic motif of multitudinous and mighty sins: *ʿᵃwōnōṯay . . . ʿāṣᵉmû miśśaʿᵃrôṯ rōʾšî.*[31]

Lohfink

30. N. Lohfink, *Le livre de Jérémie. BETL* 54 (1981), 351-68.
31. G. Braulik, *Psalm 40 und der Gottesknecht. FzB* 18 (1975), 232-33.

עֶצֶם ʿeṣem; עֹצֶם ʿōṣem

I. Ancient Near East. II. Etymology, Occurrences, and Meaning: 1. Etymology; 2. Occurrences and Meaning. III. Usage: 1. Secular Literal; 2. Secular Metaphorical; 3. Religious and Cultic; 4. Theological. IV. Extrabiblical Usage: 1. Dead Sea Scrolls; 2. Postbiblical Aramaic; 3. LXX.

I. Ancient Near East.[1] The noun *ʿeṣem,* "bone, skeleton," is common to all branches of Semitic. Akk. *eṣemtu(m)* means "bone(s)" (broken, inflamed, etc.) or "skeletons of the dead"; *eṣem/nṣēru,* with the basic meaning spine, can refer to the line on a horse's back or the keel of a ship.[2] The Ugaritic Epic of Aqhat recounts how Danel, searching for the remains of his missing son, wonders whether "scraps of flesh" *(ʿšmt)* or "bones" *(ʿẓm)* might be found in the entrails of eagles that could have carried him off.[3] Several Phoenician and Punic inscriptions on sarcophagi describe the contents ("the bones of . . .") or warn potential grave robbers: "You shall not open this resting place above me to disturb my bones" (inscription of the son of Šipiṭbaʿal III, ca. 300 B.C.E.).[4] A Hebrew inscription found in the village of Silwan may be cited in this context: "This is the [tomb of . . .] YHW, the steward of the house. There is no silver and gold here, [for] only [his bones] and the bones of his female slave are with him. Cursed be the person who opens this."[5]

There is an interesting occurrence in the "Ramesside 'Semitic' Letter," a model letter for an Egyptian apprentice scribe fluent in Semitic; this letter contains a list of goods, and among other pharmaceutical salves and oils it mentions "*ʿdmm* oil."[6]

ʿeṣem. K. Bornhäuser, *Die Gebeine der Toten. BFCT* 26/3 (1921); L. Delekat, "Zum hebräischen Wörterbuch," *VT* 14 (1964) 7-67 (*ʿæṣem:* 49-52); R. Giveon, "A Ramesside 'Semitic' Letter," *RSO* 32 (1962) 162-73; O. Keel, *Symbolism of the Biblical World* (Eng. trans. 1978); L. Köhler, *Hebrew Man* (Eng. trans. 1956); J. Pedersen, *ILC,* I-II, 172ff., 267ff.; W. Reiser, "Die Verwandschaftsformel in Gen 2,23," *TZ* 16 (1960) 1-4; J. Scharbert, *Der Schmerz im AT. BBB* 8 (1955), 91-97; W. H. Schmidt, "Anthropologische Begriffe im AT," *EvT* 24 (1964) 374-88; G. Stemberger, *Der Leib der Auferstehung. AnBibl* 56 (1972); L. Wächter, *Der Tod im AT. AzT* II/8 (1967), 171-80; H. W. Wolff, *Anthropology of the OT* (Eng. trans. 1974).

1. Additional extrabiblical usage is discussed in IV below.

2. *AHw,* I, 251.

3. *WUS,* no. 2082; *UT,* no. 1814; *KTU* 1.19, III, 5, 11, 19, 25, 34, 39.

4. For Phoenician see *KAI* 9A; for Punic, *RES,* 593, 892, 906, 937, 949, 950, 951; cf. *DNSI,* II, 880. For Šipṭibaʿal see *KAI* 9A.5.

5. *KAI* 191; Keel, fig. 73. Translation based on *KAI,* II, 189; and Keel, 67.

6. Giveon, 167, 171; cf. H. Grapow, *Wörterbuch der ägyptischen Drogennamen* (1959), 449-50.

II. Etymology, Occurrences, and Meaning.

1. *Etymology.* Although the noun *'eṣem* and the verb *'ṣm* exhibit the same consonants, current Semitic linguistics does not derive the noun from the verb but calls *'eṣem* a "primary noun."[7]

2. *Occurrences and Meaning.* There are 123 occurrences of *'eṣem* in the OT; the basic meaning may be defined as "bone(s)." The noun can denote the entire skeleton as well as individual bones; from the latter usage derives the meaning "limbs" (see above). Besides the physical sense (Gen. 50:25; 2 S. 21:12-13: human bones placed in a tomb; Ezk. 24:4-5: animal bones cooked in a stew), we find poetic usage in the figurative language of the Psalms and wisdom aphorisms.[8] Since bones are "man's most durable part — his core, so to speak," *'eṣem* takes on the meaning "self," as in the formula *b*ᵉ*'eṣem hayyôm hazzeh,* "on the very day" (Gen. 7:13; etc.).[9]

It is noteworthy that the noun has two plural forms: masc. *'*ᵃ*ṣāmîm* and fem. *'*ᵃ*ṣāmôṯ.* Delekat interprets the situation by identifying the masc. form with the meaning "limbs," while the fem. should be translated "bones (collectively), frame." This is clearly true for a portion of the texts he cites (e.g., Jgs. 19:29; Ezk. 24:4-5; Job 2:5; 40:18; Eccl. 11:5; cf. Ps. 139:15), but "the general difference remains uncertain."[10] According to Michel, the masc. pl. denotes bones in a collective sense, while the fem. pl. refers to the individual bones.[11]

III. Usage. The usage of *'eṣem* in the OT is very complex and can hardly be divided into a secular realm and a religious or theological realm. Although the boundaries are fluid, my presentation will use the following categories: (1) secular literal, (2) secular metaphorical, (3) religious and cultic, (4) theological.

1. *Secular Literal.* Job 40:18 describes the enormous body of the hippopotamus with the words "his limbs are [like] iron tubes." In Ezekiel's vision of a pot on a fire, the prophet sees the flesh and bones of a slaughtered animal cooking (vv. 4-5); the bones finally char because the broth has been poured off and the pot has become red hot (v. 10).

If burial of the dead is thought of in the first instance as nothing more than manual labor, then the appearance of *'eṣem* in the context can be taken as "secular usage." Gen. 50:25; Ex. 13:19; Josh. 24:32 have to do with the bones of Joseph, who died in Egypt; they are to find their final resting place in the "promised land," at Shechem. In 1 S. 31:13 (→ גויה *g*ᵉ*viyyâ* in v. 12 parallels *'eṣem* in v. 13)[12] and 2 S. 21:12-14 par. 1 Ch.

---

7. *BLe,* 456; cf. *HAL,* II, 869. Contra *GesTh,* II, 1058: "*bone,* so called from its hardness and strength, compare the root no. 2," which it translates "be strong."

8. See III.2-4 below.

9. Quotation from Keel, 66; similarly W. Eichrodt, *Theology of the OT,* 2 vols. (Eng. trans. 1961-67), II, 146. See III.1 below.

10. *HAL,* II, 869.

11. D. Michel, *Grundlegung einer hebräischen Syntax,* I (1977), 49-50.

12. → II, 436.

10:12 are described the ceremonies surrounding the burial with full honors of Saul and his son Jonathan, slain in battle with the Philistines. Ezk. 32:27, too, deals with the burial of warriors: their shields[13] are laid on their bones and their swords under their heads. Am. 6:10 describes how the *ʿaṣāmîm* — here probably "corpses"[14] — are removed from a house destroyed in the tumult of battle. According to Jgs. 19:29, in a gruesome symbolic action a corpse is cut in pieces "limb by limb" *(laʿaṣāmeyhā)* as a call for vengeance following an outrageous crime.

On the basis of bones recovered by archaeologists from Palestinian tombs, Köhler attempts to determine the approximate height of a typical Hebrew, which he gives as approximately 65-67 inches.[15]

All other occurrences of *ʿeṣem* in the sense of "bones of the dead, corpse" appear in the context of transgressions of ethical or cultic norms and therefore belong to the "religious and cultic use" of the word.[16]

The words for the fundamental constituents of the human body, → בשׂר *bāśār* and *ʿeṣem* (cf. Job 2:5), are used in the "kinship formula" *ʿaṣmî ûḇeśārî ʾattâ/ʾattem,* which emphasizes the close relationship between individuals (Gen. 29:14; 2 S. 19:14 [Eng. v. 13]) or groups (Jgs. 9:2; 2 S. 5:1 [par. 1 Ch. 11:1]; 19:13).[17] In Gen. 2:23 this formula, "physically graphic,"[18] describes the relationship between man and woman.

Next we find *ʿeṣem* in a secular sense in the formula *beʿeṣem hayyôm hazzeh,* "on this very day," used as an expression of time in Gen. 7:13 (deluge); 17:23,26 (circumcision of Abraham and Ishmael); Ex. 12:17,41,51; Lev. 23:14,21,28-30; Josh. 5:11 (Passover and other feasts); Dt. 32:48 (Blessing of Moses); Josh. 10:27 (battle at Gibeon); Ezk. 2:3 (Ezekiel's call); 24:2 (beginning of the conquest of Jerusalem); 40:1 (vision of the new temple). Very similar is the idiom stating that someone dies "in full prosperity" (*beʿeṣem tummô,* Job 21:23). Alongside this formula we may place the expression in Ex. 24:10 that says that, when God appeared to Moses and the elders, "under his feet there was something like a pavement of sapphire stones, like the very heaven for clearness" (NRSV; MT *ûḵeʿeṣem haššāmayin lāṭōhar*). This usage survives in Modern Hebrew, e.g., *beʿeṣem,* "actually"; *yôm hāʿaṣmāʾût,* "Independence Day."

2. *Secular Metaphorical.* Secular usage can also be metaphorical. Wisdom aphorisms use *ʿeṣem* in parallel with another part of the body as a synonym for the whole person. An example is Prov. 3:7-8 ("Do not be wise in your own eyes; fear Yahweh and turn away from evil. It will be a healing for your strength [lit. 'flesh'][19] and a refresh-

13. W. Zimmerli, *Ezekiel 2. Herm* (Eng. trans. 1983), in loc.
14. Delekat, 51.
15. P. 12.
16. See III.3 below.
17. Reiser.
18. Reiser, 3.
19. See *BHK* and B. Gemser, *Sprüche Salomos. HAT* I/16 (1963), 26.

ment for your bones"); similar are 15:30 ("Shining eyes rejoice the heart [→ לב *lēḇ*], good news refreshes the bones") and 16:24 ("Pleasant words are like a honeycomb, sweetness to the soul [→ נפש *nepeš*] and refreshment to the bones"). Qualities or situations that bring misfortune are twice likened to "bone rot" *(rāqāḇ + 'eṣem):* passion (*qin'â,* Prov. 14:30) and a wife who brings shame (*m^eḇîšâ,* 12:4; → קנא *qn';* → בוש *bôš*). Also reminiscent of wisdom is the observation of Job 20:11 that even limbs filled with youthful vigor will one day lie down in the dust. Similar metaphors and parallels appear in the Psalms and Job, but there as laments addressed to God they have theological relevance (see III.3 above).

3. *Religious and Cultic.* Human and animal bones also have a religious and cultic dimension. This is clear from the directive in Ex. 12:46 and Nu. 9:12 "not to break the bones" of the Passover lamb. A better translation would be "divide," for "an undivided company" is to share "an undivided animal" when the Passover meal is celebrated, as Ex. 12:4 requires — in other words, the sacrificial animal is not to be divided before the feast.

Very important is the cultic uncleanness caused by contact with human bones, a corpse, or a tomb; this state lasts a week and must be expunged by special purification rites (Nu. 19:16,18; cf. Ezk. 39:15: collecting and burying the bones of the dead lying unburied on the battlefield after the final battle makes the land clean once more). Prophets therefore often use it to prophesy disaster (1 K. 13:2; cf. 2 K. 23:14,16,20 par. 2 Ch. 34:5); to escape this disaster, the local counterpart of the man of God from Judah, living in Bethel, asks to be buried in the latter's tomb (1 K. 13:31; cf. 2 K. 23:18). By contrast, a legendary story in 2 K. 13:21 tells how contact with the burial place of Elisha restores a dead man to life. On the other side stands respectful and careful burial of the bones of those who have died (1 S. 31:13; 2 S. 21:12ff.); to refuse such treatment is a great wrong (Am. 2:1) or a punishment (Jer. 8:1; cf. 2 K. 23:14ff.,20; Ezk. 6:5).

It is clearly very important for bones in a tomb to rest intact and undisturbed; "this reflects . . . a concern to preserve personal identity and association with one's clan even after death."[20] For a human skeleton to be torn apart by a lion (Isa. 38:13) or to dry out in the sun and disintegrate (2 S. 21:10) is therefore a terrible disaster.[21] This view may also explain the warning in mortuary inscriptions against unauthorized opening of the tomb: the fear of desecration is greater than the fear of robbery (see I above).

The bones of the dead, totally desiccated but all still in place, play a role in the powerful vision of Ezk. 37:1-10: at Yahweh's command, they come together again, are clothed with flesh, sinews, and skin, and arise once more as living human beings, interpreted in vv. 11-14 as the resurrected nation of Israel. Bornhäuser points to the belief in the NT period that the presence of all the bones, undamaged and intact, is

---

20. Stemberger, 60 n. 19; similarly Bornhäuser, 21-22; in the opposite case, Wächter, 171ff., speaks of an "aggravated form of death."

21. See Bornhäuser, 10-11.

necessary for bodily resurrection — except in the case where God's power restores the remains of a mutilated martyr to new bodily life.[22] In addition, Ezk. 37:1ff. describes the bones in their anatomical context with sinews, flesh, and skin (cf. Job 10:11). Their formation in the womb appears a divine miracle to the wisdom teacher in Eccl. 11:5; they are already known to Yahweh before birth (Ps. 139:15: here *ʿōṣem*).

4. *Theological.* As part of the body (often in parallel with other parts of the body) or as a synecdoche for the body, the bones play a prominent role in the language of OT laments; their desolate condition signalizes physical and psychological collapse.[23] This is quite clear in Jer. 23:9: "My heart [→ לב *lēḇ*] is crushed within me, all my limbs shake." The combination of *bāśār* and *ʿeṣem* used in the "kinship formula" returns in descriptions of total deterioration: Ps. 38:4(3) (cf. 102:6[5]); Job 33:21; Lam. 3:4 (see III.1 above). The outward skin *(ʿôr)* is also involved in this process of decay (Job 19:20; 30:30; Lam. 4:8). The bones or limbs are the foundation of the body and are therefore synonymous with the person of the speaker;[24] their sympathetic involvement is profound: Isa. 38:13 (three images in vv. 12-13 express the same thing); Hab. 3:16 ("bone rot," *rāqāḇ baʿᵃṣāmay;* cf. Prov. 12:4; 14:30); Ps. 6:3(2); 22:15(14); 31:11(10) (in parallel with *ḥayyîm;* → חיה *ḥāyâ*); 32:3 (cf. Jer. 20:9); Ps. 42:11(10); 102:4(3); Job 4:14; 21:24; 30:17; 33:19; Lam. 1:13.

Alongside the description of affliction we find a supplication for healing (Ps. 51:10[8] — here *ʿᵃṣāmôṯ* stands eloquently alongside the acc. of the personal pronoun as a synonym) or a call to praise God (Ps. 35:10). Ps. 34:21(20) expresses the psalmist's confidence that his bones will be preserved and not broken (cf. Isa. 38:13; also III.3 above); in Isa. 58:11 and 66:14 an oracle promises strong and vigorous bones.

Nu. 24:8 and Mic. 3:2,3 bring us into the realm of politics and economics: in the former the seer Balaam prophesies that Jacob-Israel will crush the bones of his foes; in the latter the greedy rich, who "tear the flesh off the bones" of the people, are threatened with retaliatory punishment.

Three passages containing the noun *ʿeṣem* are difficult to interpret and translate: (1) Lam. 4:7 bemoans the young men of Jerusalem: "Their *ʿeṣem* was more ruddy than pearls." Kraus translates *ʿeṣem* as "bodies";[25] *BHK* suggests the conjectural emendation *ʾāḏam ʿôrām* or *ʾāḏᵉmâ śᵉpāṯām; GesB* proposes the reading *ʾāḏᵉmû mēʿᵃṣê pᵉnînîm,* "more than branches of coral."[26] (2) According to Schmidt and Kraus, Ps. 109:18 is part of an indictment against the psalmist, charging him with "employing black arts";[27] his curse is reputed to have soaked "into the body [→ קרב *qereḇ*] like

---

22. Pp. 26ff.
23. Scharbert, 91-92.
24. See Delekat and II.2 above.
25. H.-J. Kraus, *Threni. BK* XX (1956), 70; also NRSV.
26. *GesB,* 611.
27. H. Schmidt, *Die Psalmen. HAT* I/15 (1934), 201; H.-J. Kraus, *Psalms 60–150* (Eng. trans. 1989), in loc.

water, like oil into the bones"[28] of a sick individual. Gunkel sees the psalmist as pronouncing these curses upon his false accusers.[29] (3) The interpretation and translation of Ps. 141:7 are also very uncertain;[30] the verse may describe the destruction of the wicked (reading *ʿaṣmêhem*)[31] by an earthquake (cf. Nu. 16:32-33).

IV. Extrabiblical Usage.

1. *Dead Sea Scrolls.* The use of *ʿeṣem* in the Dead Sea Scrolls always has theological relevance. We encounter expressions that recall OT usage: lions dismember bones (1QH 5:7; cf. Isa. 38:13); bones fall asunder (1QH 7:4; cf. Ps. 22:15[14]; 32:3); there is fire in the speaker's bones (1QH 8:30; cf. Jer. 20:9); anxious thoughts penetrate the heart and bones (1QH 11:21; cf. Jer. 20:9; 23:9). Ps. 109:18 is brought to mind by 1QH 5:35: "My bread turned into a quarrel . . . and it entered my bones."

The Qumran fragment 1Q34 is a collection of liturgical prayers;[32] in the context of the righteous *(ṣaddîq)* and the wicked *(rāšāʿ),* 3:1,3 says that *bʿṣmwtm ḥrph lkl bśr,* "in their bones is a disgrace for all flesh." Here *ʿeṣem* is clearly to be understood in the personal sense as "being" or "nature." But the fragmentary state of the text makes a precise interpretation difficult. The four occurrences in the Temple Scrolls also stand entirely within the OT tradition (cf. 11QT 50:5; 51:4 with Nu. 19).

2. *Postbiblical Aramaic.* The double sense of *ʿeṣem* is still found in Postbiblical Aramaic.[33] In some texts the meaning is "bone(s)" (e.g., Jer. *Abod. Zar.* II 40d: "It is permitted on the sabbath to raise [= restore to its original position] a headbone *(ʿṣm šl rʾš)* [that has been dislocated]"), in others, "being, self" (e.g., *Sifre Debarim* §9, reporting Moses as saying to Israel: "I did not tell you this of my own accord" *(lôʾ mēʿaṣmî ʾanî ʾōmar lāḵem).*

3. *LXX.* The LXX uses *ostéon/ostoún* to translate *ʿeṣem.* There are also isolated occurrences of other words, e.g., *sṓma, krátos, eídos,* etc. The same is true for *ʿōṣem.*

Beyse

---

28. NRSV; EÜ: "limbs"; Schmidt: "like anointing oil into the pores of the skin."
29. H. Gunkel, *Die Psalmen. HKAT* II/2 (^{4}1926), 475ff.
30. Kraus, *Psalms 60–150,* 526, 528.
31. See *BHK.*
32. D. Barthélemy, *DJD,* I, 153.
33. *WTM,* III, 679.

עָצַר *ʿāṣar;* **עֶצֶר** *ʿeṣer;* **עֹצֶר** *ʿōṣer;* **עֲצֶרֶת** *ʿᵃṣereṯ;* **עֲצָרָה** *ʿᵃṣārâ;* **מַעְצוֹר** *maʿṣôr;* **מַעְצָר** *maʿṣār*

I. Etymology. II. Verb: 1. Meaning; 2. Problems. III. Nouns: 1. *ʿeṣer;* 2. *ʿōṣer;* 3. *ʿᵃṣereṯ* and *ʿᵃṣārâ;* 4. *maʿṣôr;* 5. *maʿṣār.* IV. 1. LXX; 2. Dead Sea Scrolls.

I. Etymology. Heb. *ʿāṣar* reflects the root **ʿṣr,* which is also found in other Semitic languages: Arab. *ʿaṣara,* "press out, squeeze out"; *ʿaṣr,* "act of pressing out, time, period";[1] *ʿaṣar,* "refuge";[2] Eth. *ʿaṣara* and Jewish Aram. *ʿᵃṣar,* "press out"; *ʿaṣrā,* "winepress, cask"; Syr. *ʿṣr,* "tread out (grapes or olives), press out," etc.; Mand. *ʿṣr,* "wring out";[3] possibly also Old Can. *ha-zi-ri,* "be held back."[4] The possibility of connecting *ʿeṣer* in Jgs. 18:7 with Arab. *ǵaḏara* and *ʿōṣer* in Prov. 30:16 with Arab. *ʿaṭara* is discussed below. It is unclear whether Ugar. *ǵṣr* belongs with Sem. **ʿṣr* or with *ǵḏr.*[5] Akk. *eṣēru* is unrelated.[6]

ʿāṣar. S. Ahituv, "*ʿaṣeret,*" *EMiqr,* VI (1971), 335-36; G. W. Ahlström, "Notes to Isaiah 53:8f.," *BZ* 13 (1969) 95-98; A. Ahuvyah, "*ʿāṣûr wĕʿāzûb bĕyiśrāʾēl,*" *Leš* 30 (1965/66) 175-78; idem, "Again Concerning '*ʿāṣûr wĕʿāzûb*'," *Leš* 31 (1966/67) 160; idem (unsigned article), "Again Concerning '*ʿāṣûr wĕʿāzûb*'," *Leš* 33 (1968/69) 70-71; P. J. Calderone, "Supplementary Notes on *HDL*-II," *CBQ* 24 (1962) 412-19; L. Delekat, *Asylie und Schutzorakel am Zionheiligtum* (1967), esp. 320-41; G. R. Driver, "Isaiah 52:13–53:12," *In Memoriam P. Kahle. BZAW* 103 (1968), 90-105; I. Efros, "Textual Notes on the Hebrew Bible," *JAOS* 45 (1925) 152-54; A. Guillaume, "Hebrew and Aramaic Lexicography," *Abr-Nahrain* 1 (1961) 3-35; idem, "The Root און in Hebrew," *JTS* 34 (1933) 62-64; M. Held, "The *YQTL-QTL (QTL-YQTL)* Sequence of Identical Verbs in Biblical Hebrew and Ugaritic," *Studies and Essays in Honor of A. A. Neuman* (1962), 281-90, esp. 283 n. 8; P. Joüon, "Notes de lexicographie hébraïque," *MUSJ* 4 (1910) 1-18; R. Kasher, "Again on '*ʿāṣûr wĕʿāzûb,*'" *Leš* 31 (1966/67) 240; E. Kutsch, "מִקְרָא," *ZAW* 65 (1953) 247-53; idem, "Die Wurzel עצר im Hebräischen," *VT* 2 (1952) 57-69; E. Y. Kutscher, "Concerning *ʿāṣûr wĕʿāzûb,*" *Leš* 31 (1966/67) 80; J. Lewy, "Lexicographical Notes III," *HUCA* 12/13 (1937/38) 99-101; E. Lohse, "πεντηκοστή," *TDNT,* VI, 44-53, esp. 49; P. P. Saydon, "The Meaning of the Expression וְעָזוּב עָצוּר," *VT* 2 (1952) 371-74; H. Seebass, "Tradition und Interpretations bei Jehu ben Chanani und Ahia von Silo," *VT* 25 (1975) 175-90; J. A. Soggin, "Tod und Auferstehung des leidenden Gottesknechtes," *ZAW* 87 (1975) 345-55; D. Winton Thomas, "A Consideration of Isaiah LIII in the Light of Recent Textual and Philological Study," *ETL* 44 (1968) 79-86; idem, "Textual and Philological Notes on Some Passages in the Book of Proverbs," *Wisdom in Ancient Israel and in the Ancient Near East. FS H. H. Rowley. SVT* 3 (1955), 280-92; I. N. Vinnikov, "L'énigme de '*ʿāṣûr* et *ʿāzûb,*'" *Hommages à André Dupont-Sommer* (1971), 343-45; A. S. Yahuda, "Über *ʿāṣûr wĕʿāzûb* und *ʿēr wĕʿōneh* im AT," *ZA* 16 (1902) 240-61; H. Yalon, "The Plain Meaning of Some Biblical Verses," *BethM* 11/4 (1966) 17-20.

1. Wehr, 616.
2. Yahuda, 243-49.
3. *MdD,* 33.
4. EA 138:130; *DNSI,* II, 881.
5. For the former see *WUS,* no. 2163; *CML*², 155; Calderone, 413 n. 10; *HAL,* II, 870. For the latter, *UT,* no. 1982.
6. *AHw,* I, 252.

II. Verb. The basic meaning of *ʿāṣar* is "hold back." The root occurs 46 times: 36 times in the qal, 10 in the niphal.

1. *Meaning.* Five semantic fields can be distinguished:

a. The basic and best-attested meaning is "hold back, retain, limit, detain": Samson's parents detain an angel (Jgs. 13:15-16, in both instances with dir. obj.); rain threatens to stop or impede Ahab (1 K. 18:44, dir. obj.; but cf. LXX [rain "comes upon" him]).[7] People "hold back" their words, i.e., refrain from speaking (Job 4:2; 29:9, *bᵉ* + obj.). God withholds the waters (Job 12:15). Women are kept away from David and his men (1 S. 21:6[Eng. v. 5], pass. ptcp.). David is "kept away" (i.e., hidden) from Saul in Ziklag (1 Ch. 12:1). The Shunammite woman orders her servant not to detain her on her way to Elisha (2 K. 4:24, *lᵉ* + obj.).

The use of the niphal also belongs here. Plagues are "stopped": after Korah's revolt (Nu. 17:13,15[16:48,50]), after the sin with Baal of Peor (Nu. 25:8; Ps. 106:30), and after David's census (2 S. 24:21,25; 1 Ch. 21:22).

b. The verb can also mean "close, shut up." God "closes" a woman's womb so that she cannot bear children (Gen. 16:2, suff. as dir. obj.; 20:18, *bᵉʿaḏ* + obj.; Isa. 66:9, no obj.; cf. Prov. 30:16). The niphal appears in the same context in Sir. 42:10. God also "shuts up" the heavens so that no rain can fall (Dt. 11:17; 2 Ch. 7:13; 1 K. 8:35 par. 2 Ch. 6:26 niphal). Cf. Sir. 48:3. God's word was "shut up" (pass. ptcp. *ʿāṣûr*) within Jeremiah like a blazing fire (Jer. 20:9); *ʿāṣûr* (with the preceding *wᵉhāyâ*) appears to refer to *dāḇār* in v. 8, but it is also possible that it refers to *ʾēš*;[8] it is doubtful that it refers to God or *šᵉmô*. Emendation to *ʿeṣer, ʿōṣer,* or *ʿaṣurâ* is unnecessary.[9]

c. The verb appears 3 times with the meaning "confine, imprison." The Assyrian king imprisoned Hoshea for taking part in a conspiracy (2 K. 17:4); Jeremiah was confined in the court of the guard (Jer. 33:1; 39:15).

d. In one instance the verb means "rule." Saul is to "rein in" the people, i.e., rule over them (1 S. 9:17; LXX *árxei*).[10]

e. The expression *ʿṣr kōaḥ* means "have strength" (Dnl. 10:8,16; 11:6; 2 Ch. 13:20; 22:9) and, more idiomatically, "be able to" (1 Ch. 29:14; 2 Ch. 2:5). The same meaning is present in 2 Ch. 14:10(11) without *kōaḥ:* Asa prays, "let no mortal prevail against you" *(ʾal-yaʿṣōr ʿimmᵉḵā ʾᵉnôš).* The sense requires that *kōaḥ* be supplied.[11] The situation in 2 Ch. 20:37 is similar: the ships of Jehoshaphat and Ahaziah were destroyed in Ezion-geber, "and they were not able to go to Tarshish" (*wᵉlōʾ ʿāṣᵉrû lāleḵeṯ,* + inf.). Here too *kōaḥ* has been omitted.

2. *Problems.* Some occurrences of the verb *ʿāṣar* are hard to interpret:

a. The qal pass. ptcp. in the alliterative expression *ʿāṣûr wᵉʿāzûḇ* presents great diffi-

---

7. See also Delekat, 326.
8. See *GK,* §132d.
9. Contra Delekat; Kutsch; W. Rudolph, *Jeremia. HAT* I/12 (1958).
10. See H. Seebass, *ZAW* 78 (1966) 174; in "Tradition" he interprets the text differently.
11. Contra Joüon, 11.

culties.[12] The idiom appears 3 times in connection with a curse on the royal house of northern Israel (Jeroboam, 1 K. 14:10; Ahab, 1 K. 21:21; 2 K. 9:8). It appears also in Dt. 32:36, which speaks of God's intervention on behalf of his people when they have lost their power and neither *ʿāṣûr* nor *ʿāzûḇ* remains. In 2 K. 14:26 we read that God saved his people when "there was neither *ʿāṣûr* nor *ʿāzûḇ* and there was no one to help Israel."

The following attempts have been made to explain this idiomatic dyad (understood as an opposition).

1. Those who are unclean, under a taboo and excluded from the cult, vs. those who are not unclean and are therefore not excluded.[13]
2. Those who stay at home (on account of illness, old age, etc.) vs. those who can leave.[14]
3. Slaves vs. free citizens.[15]
4. Those under the protection of a tribe or clan vs. those who lack such protection.[16]
5. Minors under the authority of their parents vs. those who are of age.[17]
6. Married vs. single.[18]
7. Those liable for military service vs. those exempt.[19]

Other interpretations understand the components of the idiom as synonyms:

8. The upper or ruling class of Israel.[20]
9. Flocks remaining near the village and kept in a secluded pasture.[21]
10. The helpless and worthless.[22]
11. The oppressed and the helpless.[23]
12. Increasing and enduring power or dominion.[24]
13. Warriors and military victors.[25]

---

12. See Brongers, *OTS* 15 (1965) 111.
13. W. Robertson Smith, *Religion of the Semites* (repr. ²1956), 456; cf. S. R. Driver, *Deuteronomy. ICC* (³1902), 376.
14. Oettli, cited by Driver, *Deuteronomy,* 376.
15. *BDB,* 737b.
16. Yahuda, Driver, Delekat, NEB.
17. Kutsch; Willi, *Beiträge zur alttestamentlichen Theologie. FS W. Zimmerli* (1977), 540.
18. Keil and others, cited by Driver, 376.
19. Seebass, 182-83.
20. Efros, Held.
21. Vinnikov.
22. Saydon.
23. Joüon, 9-12.
24. Yalon, 18ff.
25. Ahuvyah.

This last interpretation appears more cogent than the others, since it is better supported by the text.[26]

b. Two other occurrences of the pass. ptcp. *ʿāṣûr,* both of which are similar, are also obscure: (1) Jeremiah cannot go to the temple to read from his scroll (Jer. 36:5). This is understood to mean that he is prevented from going to the temple by ritual uncleanness (cf. 1 S. 21:6), that he is under arrest or under guard (LXX; cf. Jer. 33:1; 39:15; but 36:19,26 do not support this solution), that he is in protective custody,[27] that he is forced to stay at home because of public pressure or threats,[28] or because he has gone into hiding (cf. 1 Ch. 12:1). The last explanation is probably the best. (2) The occurrence of *ʿāṣûr* in Neh. 6:10 should possibly be interpreted in the same way, though some think that Shemaiah was deterred by ritual uncleanness, prophetic ecstasy, confinement,[29] or an emergency.

c. Doeg was "detained [niphal] before Yahweh" at Nob when David was there with his men (1 S. 21:8[7]). The attempts made to interpret this statement — Doeg had received an oracle in a dream, was practicing ascesis, fulfilling a vow, seeking asylum,[30] or taking refuge in the sanctuary — are unconvincing. It is more likely that he was kept away from the sanctuary on account of uncleanness or similar reasons.[31]

III. Nouns. Six nouns, with a total of 17 occurrences, derive from the verb.

1. *ʿeṣer.* It is difficult to determine the meaning of this noun, because it occurs only once (Jgs. 18:7), in the expression *yôrēš ʿeṣer.* The best interpretation is that it means "dominion, power" (cf. 1 S. 9:17); *yôrēš ʿeṣer* is thus a person who "seizes power." Alternatively, Delekat suggests that it is someone who "possesses rights to protection."[32] Calderone connects *ʿeṣer* with Arab. *ǵaḍara,* "be luxuriant," and *ǵaḍr,* "fertile soil," so that *yôrēš ʿeṣer* means "land possessing fertile soil."[33] Guillaume connects it with the same Arabic verb, but translates the expression as "possess wealth."[34]

2. *ʿōṣer.* In Ps. 107:39 *ʿōṣer* means something like "oppression" (note the context: *rāʿâ,* "trouble"; *yāḡôn,* "sorrow"). In Prov. 30:16 the best translation of *ʿōṣer rāḥam* is "barrenness" (lit. "closure of the womb"). Winton Thomas connects it with Arab. *ʿaẓara,* "be disgusted by something," but also "drink too much."[35] Interpreting *rāḥam* as "vulture," he arrives at the translation "greediness of a vulture" from *ʿōṣer rāḥam.*

---

26. Other conclusions are reached by Driver, *Deuteronomy,* 376; Yahuda, 240-43; Kutsch, 60-65; J. Gray, *I and II Kings. OTL* (²1970), 337-38; *HAL,* II, 871; → עזב *ʿāzaḇ.*
27. Delekat.
28. Joüon, 10.
29. Kutsch, 59-60.
30. Yahuda.
31. Kutsch, 65ff.
32. P. 338; similarly Yahuda, 249.
33. Pp. 413-14.
34. P. 30.
35. "Textual and Philological Notes," 290.

Yalon suggests "growth or increase of (sexual?) desire" (cf. LXX *érōs gynaikós*).[36] In Isa. 53:8 *ʿōṣer* is harder to understand; the following meanings have been proposed: imprisonment, custody, arrest; oppression; impediment; strength; delay; dismissal (in the legal sense); power or authority; legal (or other) protection.

3. *ʿᵃṣereṯ/ʿᵃṣārâ*. The meaning of the nouns *ʿᵃṣereṯ* and *ʿᵃṣārâ* is likewise disputed. The former denotes (a) a ritual performed on the eighth day of the Feast of Booths (Lev. 23:36; Nu. 29:35; Neh. 8:18); (b) a ritual performed on the eighth day of the dedication of Solomon's temple, analogous to the ritual on the eighth day of the Feast of Booths (2 Ch. 7:9); and (c) a ritual performed on the seventh day of the Feast of Unleavened Bread (Dt. 16:8).

The noun *ʿᵃṣārâ* denotes (a) ritual observances or ceremonies in general (Isa. 1:13; the context includes *ḥōḏeš, šabbaṯ, miqrāʾ,* and *môʿᵃḏîm*), (b) ad hoc observances requesting God's help, accompanied by fasting and lamentation (Joel 1:14; 2:15), and (c) a feast in honor of Baal (2 K. 10:20). The pl. *ʿaṣṣᵉrōṯêḵem* in Am. 5:21 denotes ritual observances or ceremonies in general (par. *ḥaggîm*). The form *ʿᵃṣereṯ* in Jer. 9:1(2) is a construct and means "group" or "band."

The current interpretation is that (a) these nouns mean "gathering, festival assembly."[37] Taking into consideration other occurrences of this root, we may also think of an "association (of individuals)," a "meeting."[38] This interpretation is supported by Jer. 9:1(2) and assemblies in the contexts of 2 K. 10:20-21; Joel 1:14; 2:15-16. (b) Frequently the nouns are interpreted as referring to "rest from labor," usually associated with festal observances. This usage led to the meaning "celebrate a festival." Later still, the nouns came to refer to the group celebrating the festival, e.g., "band" (Jer. 9:1[2]).[39] This explanation is supported by the basic meaning of *ʿṣr* and the prohibition of work (Lev. 23:36; Nu. 29:35; Dt. 16:8). In 1 S. 21:8, therefore, the words *neʿṣār lip̄nê yhwh* could describe Doeg as someone celebrating a festival. (c) Another interpretation starts from the assumption that the nouns originally denoted the concluding ceremony of a festival. From this basic meaning developed the sense "festal observance or assembly," then simply "assembly." This theory is supported by the basic meaning of the root and the use of *ʿᵃṣereṯ* for the ritual observed on the last day of festivals lasting several days (see above). Less likely interpretations include (d) "conclusion of a celebration" in the sanctuary, (e) "state of ritual cleanness" (cf. 1 S. 21:6), and (f) "kinship meal."[40]

The purpose of the *ʿᵃṣereṯ/ʿᵃṣārâ* depends on when the festival or observance was initiated. Joel 2:15 casts some light on such a festival. The prophetic summons, "Blow the trumpet in Zion, sanctify a fast, call an *ʿᵃṣārâ*," corresponds to the festival sequence of New Year's Day (Lev. 23:24), the Day of Atonement (v. 27), and the eighth day of the Feast of Booths (v. 36). Since the reason for Joel's *ʿᵃṣārâ* was a plea for rain, it is

---

36. Pp. 18-19.
37. Ahituv; M. Haran, *Temples and Temple-Service in Ancient Israel* (1978), 296-97 n. 14.
38. Seebass, 182.
39. Kutsch, 65ff.
40. Yahuda, 249 n. 1.

likely that the three fall festivals had a similar function.[41] It is probably no accident that in synagogue worship a special prayer for rain is pronounced on the eighth day of the Feast of Booths.

4. *ma'ṣôr.* The noun *ma'ṣôr,* "hindrance," occurs only in 1 S. 14:6: "Nothing can hinder Yahweh from saving" *('yn lyhwh m'ṣwr).*

5. *ma'ṣār.* The noun *ma'ṣār,* "control, restraint," occurs only in Prov. 25:28: "Like a city breached, without walls, is one who lacks self-control."

IV. 1. *LXX.* The LXX uses 23 different verbs and verb + substantive combinations to render the 46 occurrences of *'āṣar.* Most frequent is *synéchein* (12 times, also translating *ma'ṣôr*), followed by *échein* (3 times), *katischýein* (2 times, plus 2 times for *'āṣar kōaḥ*), and *synkleíein* (3 times, for *'āṣar* referring to barrenness).

2. *Dead Sea Scrolls.* The usage of *'āṣar* in the Dead Sea Scrolls follows that already observed in the Bible. It is used in three general senses: (a) "hold back" (the "drink of knowledge," *mšqh d't,* 1QH 4:11; "protection," *m'wz,* 8:24; "incurable pain that does not stop," *l'yn 'ṣwr,* 8:28), (b) "shut, close" (the heavens and subterranean waters, 1Q22 2:10; "enclosed" fire, 1QH 8:30, echoing Jer. 20:9), and (c) with *kōaḥ,* "have power, be able to" (with an inf.: *lhtyšb,* 1QH 10:11; *ld't,* 1QH fr. 10:3; also *ld't* without *kwḥ,* 1QH fr. 1:4; cf. 1QH 10:12). See also 11:35 (fr.). The restoration of *'aṣeret* is dealt with in 11QT 17:16; 29:10.

Wright — Milgrom

41. Knohl, private communication.

עקב *'qb;* עָקֵב *'āqēḇ;* עֵקֶב *'ēqeḇ;* עָקֹב *'āqōḇ*

I. 1. Occurrences; 2. Meaning, LXX. II. Theological Relevance: 1. Figurative Usage; 2. Anthropology; 3. Yahweh.

I. 1. *Occurrences.* As a rule, lexicographers assume two roots *'qb: 'qb* I, a denominative from *'āqēḇ,* "heel," and *'qb* II, "preserve, protect," attested in such languages as

'qb. P. R. Ackroyd, "Hosea and Jacob," *VT* 13 (1963) 245-59; R. B. Coote, "Hosea XII," *VT* 21 (1971) 389-402; H.-D. Neef, "Die Heilstraditionen Israels in der Verkündigung des Propheten Hosea" (diss., Tübingen, 1984); → VI, 185ff.

Old South Arabic, Amorite, and Ethiopic. The latter occurs in Hebrew only in the PNs *ya'ᵃqōḇ, ya'ᵃqōḇâ,* and *'aqqûḇ,* unless, following Dietrich and Loretz, one assumes a meaning "follow directly after, be near," a sense found in Ugaritic, Amorite, and Phoenician.[1] On the basis of Bab. *Sanh.* 109b, Prijs deduces a talmudic *'qb,* "turn toward, start off toward."[2]

The root *'qb* I occurs 5 times in the OT: the qal in Gen. 27:36; Jer. 9:3(Eng. v. 4) (twice); Hos. 12:4(3); the piel in Job 37:4. If we follow *BHS* in emending *'ᵃqēḇay* to *'ōqᵉḇay* in Ps. 49:6(5), the qal occurs 5 times (see below). The root is attested in Ugaritic in the form *m'qbk,* "the one who defrauds you" or "the one who holds you back."[3]

The noun *'āqēḇ,* "heel," from which the verb derives, occurs 14 times in Hebrew (13 if we do not count Ps. 49:6[5]; see above): 5 (or 4) times in the Psalms, 4 times in Genesis, and once each in Joshua, Judges, Jeremiah, Song of Songs, and Job. It appears also in Ugaritic, as well as Akkadian, Arabic, Syriac, Tigre, and Aramaic.[4] It occurs 3 times in Sirach (10:16; 13:25; 16:3) and once in the Dead Sea Scrolls (1QH 5:24).

The noun *'ēqeḇ,* "reward," is to be understood as an extension of *'āqēḇ;* it is found in Arabic[5] and occurs 4 times in Hebrew, albeit more often as a conjunction.

Finally, the noun *'āqōḇ* occurs 3 times in Hebrew (Isa. 40:4; Jer. 9:3[4]; Hos. 6:8) as well as in Sir. 36:25; the noun *'oqbâ* appears in 2 K. 10:19.

2. *Meaning, LXX.* Clear as it is that all these words are connected with a root *'qb,* their actual meaning is often unclear. Ackroyd's statement that "the exact meaning of the group of words from the root *'qb* is not easy to determine" is still true.[6] This is immediately clear when we address the various meanings of the noun *'āqēḇ*. Arab. *'aqib* means "heel of the foot"; this meaning is also found in Gen. 3:15 and 25:26, where it refers respectively to the human heel, which is the serpent's target, and Esau's heel, which Jacob grips. In the genitive phrase *'iqqᵉḇê-sûs* (Gen. 49:17; Jgs. 5:22), our word could mean "[horse's] hoof."[7] That makes sense in Jgs. 5, where the reference is to the noise made by horses' hooves as they gallop away.[8] But this meaning does not really fit Gen. 49:17, which describes a snake biting a horse's "fetlock."[9] In Jer. 13:22 the clause "your skirts are lifted up" parallels "*'ᵃqēḇāyiḵ* are laid bare," which may be analyzed as

---

1. M. Dietrich and O. Loretz, *BiOr* 23 (1966) 127-33, esp. 131. For Ugaritic see *KTU* 4, 645, 1, contra *HAL,* II, 872: "be rough, hilly." For Phoenician see *KAI* 37B.1: "continuation," or the like.

2. L. Prijs, *ZDMG* 120 (1970) 22-23.

3. *KTU* 1.18, I, 19; *WUS,* no. 2086.

4. On Ugaritic see *KTU* 1.17, VI, 20, 23; on Aramaic, *KAI* 223.11 (p. 285): " 'at the heel' as a metaphor for 'at once.' "

5. On Hatra 3, 2, see *DNSI,* II, 882.

6. P. 249.

7. *HAL,* II, 873.

8. Hertzberg, *Die Bücher Josua, Richter, Ruth. ATD* 9 (⁴1969), 181.

9. Westermann, *Genesis 37–50* (Eng. trans. 1986), 218; contra Rin, *BZ* 11 (1967) 190 ("tendons").

a dual with a pronominal suffix and interpreted as a euphemism for "backside" or the pudenda.

In these passages the LXX uses *ptérna,* which represents *'āqēḇ* in 8 texts. These include Cant. 1:8, where *'iqḇê haṣṣō'n* means "tracks of the flock." This meaning is also found in Ugar. *'qbt ṯr:* Aqhat wants to follow the "tracks of the bull."[10] The "footsteps" of Yahweh's anointed (Ps. 89:52[51]) the LXX translates with *antállagma* and the "footprints" of Yahweh (Ps. 77:20[19]) with *íchnē.* Finally, *'ᵃqēḇām* must be read in Gen. 49:19, which could mean "their rear guard" but can also be translated quite literally: "He [Gad] pursues [the raiders] at their heels" (LXX *katá pódas*).[11] Josh. 8:13 speaks of the "heel of the camp," meaning "ambush" or, more likely, "rear guard," because v. 12 uses *'ōrēḇ* for the ambush (the verse is lacking in the LXX).[12] Sir. 16:3 uses our word to mean the "end of life."

Also associated with this meaning is the noun *'oqbâ,* "fraud, deceit" (2 K. 10:19; LXX *pternismós,* the trans. used also for *'āqēḇ* in Ps. 41:10[9]).

This is clearly one of the primary meanings of the root *'qb* I. For Gen. 27:36 provides a popular etymology for the name "Jacob": Esau charges that Jacob has "defrauded" him twice (Gen. 25; 27). This is also the meaning of Hos. 12:4(3), except that there the fraud is advanced to the womb; Coote therefore proposes the translation "seize."[13] Finally, in Jer. 9:3 the words *kol-'āḥ 'āqôḇ ya'qōḇ,* "every brother is a defrauder," play on the name "Jacob"; Rudolph therefore translates: "Every brother defrauds like Jacob."[14] The LXX always translates our verb with *pternízō.*

The question how the meaning "ambush, defraud" developed from the meaning "heel" can be answered to a certain extent: the verb actually meant "sneak close behind someone"; this led to the meaning "deceive, defraud."[15] Jirku accepts this meaning also for Ugar. *m'qbk:* "Anyone who defrauds you shall be thrashed."[16] Aistleitner, however, assigns the meaning "hold back, restrain" to the word.[17] This corresponds to the meaning of *yeʿaqqeḇēm* in Job 37:4: "He [Yahweh] does not restrain them [the lightning bolts],"[18] which the LXX translates precisely with *antallássō.* We must presume that this meaning derives from some such expression as "hold by the heels."

---

10. *KTU* 1.17, VI, 23; *WUS,* no. 2086. C. H. Gordon, *UT,* no. 1907: "'tendon(s) of a bull' [for making a bowstring]"; Gordon interprets *'qbm dlbnn* in *KTU* 1.17, VI, 20-21 in the same way (according to *KTU,* the reading is no longer tenable). *WUS,* no. 2087: "'qb II: black eagle, sea eagle."

11. Westermann, *Genesis 37–50,* 218. See H.-J. Zobel, *Stammesspruch und Geschichte. BZAW* 95 (1965), 5, 19.

12. For the former see Noth, *Das Buch Josua. HAT* I/7 (³1971), 51; see also Hertzberg, *ATD* 9⁴, 57. For the latter, *HAL,* II, 873.

13. P. 392; for yet another translation see Neef, 26.

14. *Jeremia. HAT* I/12 (³1968), 64.

15. Cf. *GesB,* 612-13.

16. A. Jirku, *Kanaanäische Mythen und Epen aus Ras Schamra-Ugarit* (1962), 125. See *KTU* 1.18, I, 19.

17. *WUS,* no. 2086.

18. Contra L. I. J. Stadelmann, *Hebrew Conception of the World. AnBibl* 39 (1970), 111 n. 591.

In Isa. 40:4 *ʿāqōḇ* means "rough places" (LXX *tá skoliá*) in contrast to "plain" *(mîšôr)*.[19] This meaning is hard to associate with "heel." The same is true of *ʿeqeḇ*, "reward" (possibly "what follows after" = consequence), which the LXX translates with *geneá* in Prov. 22:4 and *antapódosis* in Ps. 19:12(11).

In four passages (Josh. 8:13; Jer. 17:9; Hos. 6:8; Job 18:9), the LXX uses a totally different translation or the corresponding section of the text is absent.

II. Theological Relevance.

1. *Figurative Usage.* The theological relevance of the root *ʿqb* may be observed first in figurative idioms that are part of the religious language of Israel. All the texts have to do with the human heel. When Bildad says that people are thrust into the net by their own feet and that a trap *(paḥ)* seizes them by the heel and a snare lays hold of them (Job 18:8-9), he is employing imagery from the use of snares in hunting to describe the self-entrapment of the wicked.[20] In Ps. 56:7(6) the psalmist laments that his enemies are conspiring together, lurking, and watching *(šmr)* his heels; this language may also reflect hunting imagery: the hunter following the track of the prey.[21] But this interpretation is not definite; the figurative language may express attentive observation of the devout, to seize every possible chance to accomplish his downfall. The figure of speech voices the psalmist's anxiety, distress, and fear. The same note is probably heard in Ps. 49:6(5): "The iniquity of my heels surrounds me."[22] Finally, Ps. 41:10(9) says that the former friend of the psalmist has become an enemy and "now makes his heel great against me." The appearance of practically the same words in 1QH 5:24 argues against the almost universal attempts to emend the MT, even though in the final analysis it is impossible to determine the precise meaning of what is clearly an idiom: "turn away, deceive (?), lift the heel (= foot), i.e. tread."[23]

It is no longer possible to say exactly what Hos. 6:8 means when it calls Gilead a "city of evildoers" and says in parallel *ʿ*ᵃ*qubbâ middām,* translated by Jeremias as "full of bloody footprints" and by Rudolph as "full of bloody tracks," while others emend the text.[24] However the text is rendered, what is clear is that "Gilead" refers not to the region but to the city of the same name, whose inhabitants are called evildoers. The nature of their wickedness is unclear because, as is common in Hosea, we are dealing with an historical allusion. Whether *ʿ*ᵃ*qubbâ* alludes to an otherwise unknown Jacob tradition, as proposed by Nielsen and Coote, can hardly be decided.[25] We may also note Wellhausen's reference to Gesenius, who in his *Thesaurus* cites *ʿqybt yyn,* "polluted by wine."[26]

---

19. *HAL.*
20. See Dalman, *AuS,* VI, 320-21, 323-24.
21. Kraus, *Psalms 1–59* (Eng. trans. 1988), 526.
22. But see *BHS* and the comms.
23. Maier, *Die Texte vom Toten Meer,* 2 vols. (1960), II, 87.
24. J. Jeremias, *Das Prophet Hosea. ATD* 24/1 (1983), 89; W. Rudolph, *Hosea. KAT* XIII/1 (1966), 141.
25. E. Nielsen, *Shechem* (1955), 291; Coote, 393.
26. J. Wellhausen, *Die kleinen Propheten* (⁴1963), 117.

With its etiological explanation of the elemental enmity between the serpent and the human race, Gen. 3:15 brings us into the realm of OT anthropology. As in 49:17, the text alludes to the cunning or treachery of the serpent, presupposing that it attacks from behind.[27] But the human heart is described in the very same terms. If the text is not emended, Jer. 17:9 speaks of the cunning or craftiness of the heart (cf. Sir. 36:25[20]: "A perverse heart will cause grief"; contrast the good heart in 13:25).[28] This language expresses the "unfathomable contradictions of the human condition";[29] it also addresses the problem of theodicy by insisting that no one can look into the heart of another. An explanatory gloss in 2 K. 10:19 connects Jehu's summons to the great Baal sacrifice with the king's cunning.[30]

Finally, Hosea's inclusion and interpretation of the Jacob tradition (Hos. 12:4[3]) is as an accusatory reference to Israel's offenses; it cites the "defraud" etiology already connected with the name "Jacob" in Gen. 27:36 (in contrast to 25:26) and associates it with the people of the northern kingdom, implying that they are the direct heirs of Jacob with respect to cunning and deceit as well.[31] The same idea is conveyed by Jer. 9:1-4(2-5), an invective castigating faithlessness, deceit, and slander: v. 3(4) charges that brother deceives brother.

Ps. 89:52(51) speaks of the taunting of Yahweh's anointed, probably by the king, by the enemies of Yahweh; Jer. 13:22 describes the humiliation of Jerusalem by "laying bare her backside" (cf. 2 S. 10:4).

Finally, the mention of the rich reward the psalmist receives for keeping the commandments (Ps. 19:12[11]; also 119:33) brings us to the correlation of desert and fortune, a central concept of wisdom thought. This "reward for humility and fear of God is riches and honor and life" (Prov. 22:4) and endures forever (*l*^{e}*'ôlām 'ēqeḇ,* Ps. 119:112). If Sir. 10:16 can be read as *'qb g'ym,* "footsteps of the proud,"[32] this text too expresses God's retributive justice, for God "blots out the footsteps of the proud and cuts off their root to the ground."

3. *Yahweh.* Only three texts associate *'qb* directly with an act of Yahweh; each time it is something different. Isa. 40:4 announces that the "uneven ground" will become level, that Israel's period of exile may come to an end. Here *'āqōḇ* is an "image for rough, hilly terrain."[33] Although v. 3 is addressed to the people and v. 4 is formulated in neutral terms, it is clear that Yahweh himself is at work: the passage deals with the "way of Yahweh" (v. 3) and the revelation of the "glory of Yahweh" (v. 5).[34]

---

27. Westermann, *Genesis 1–11* (Eng. trans. 1984), 259-60.

28. For "cunning" see A. Weiser, *Jeremia. ATD* 20/21 (^{6}1969), 143. For "craftiness," W. Rudolph, *Jeremia. HAT* I/12 (^{3}1968), 114.

29. Weiser, *ATD* 20/21^{6}, 146.

30. Würthwein, *Die Bücher der Könige. ATD* 11/2 (1984), 340 n. 2; Hentschel, *1 Könige. NEB* 12 (1984), 48.

31. See esp. Coote, 392-93.

32. Sauer, "Jesus Sirach," *JSHRZ* III/5, 529.

33. K. Elliger, *Deutero-Jesaja. BK* XI/1 (1978), 19.

34. See R. Kilian, "'Baut eine Strasse für unseren Gott!'" *Künder des Wortes. FS J. Schreiner* (1982), 53-60.

Here one can only aver that Yahweh can transform nature because he is its creator, on the grounds that elsewhere as well Deutero-Isaiah stresses that Yahweh is God the creator; this point is made more directly in the other two passages. Job 37:4 is embedded in a description of meteorological phenomena such as thunder (vv. 2,4,5), lightning (vv. 3,4), snow, and rain (v. 6). It is Yahweh who "does not restrain the lightnings when his voice is heard" (v. 4). He is the Lord of nature. And Ps. 77:11-21(10-20) speaks of the wonderful "hand of the Most High," whose power is revealed in the redemption of his people (v. 11[10]) as well as in floods, thunder, and lightning, accompanied by earthquakes (vv. 17-19[16-18]). The psalm continues with a confessional affirmation: "Your way was through the sea, . . . yet your footprints were unseen" (v. 20[19]), which introduces the leading of the people by the hand of Moses and Aaron (v. 21[20]). Just as the Most High God was present invisibly during the exodus of the people and its accompanying meteorological phenomena, so is God present again and again — giving the psalmist the faith to see nothing and yet to believe.

Zobel

עָקַר *ʿāqar;* עָקָר *ʿāqār;* עֵקֶר *ʿēqer;* עִקָּר *ʿiqqār*

I. Etymology and Distribution. II. Meaning: 1. Verb; 2. Adjective; 3. Nouns. III. LXX and Dead Sea Scrolls.

I. Etymology and Distribution. The search for the etymon encounters many difficulties because the morpheme is distributed among several lexemes, all of which occur only a few times. The semantic specifications of the individual lexemes diverge substantially. The verb *ʿāqar* clearly denotes a destructive action: "tear out by the roots" (Eccl. 3:2, qal), "become uprooted" (Zeph. 2:4, niphal).[1] This meaning links without any semantic problems with the noun *ʿiqqār,* "root" (Job 30:3 cj.; Sir. 37:17), the PN *ʿēqer* (1 Ch. 2:27), and the occurrences in Late Hebrew.[2] If the uncertain Can. noun *ʿqrt,* "granary,"[3] documents a semantic relationship leading from "tear out" to "harvest," then the latter semantic sector has at least temporal priority.

The noun *ʿēqer,* "offspring," which occurs frequently in the Sefire inscriptions, can be traced back to the 8th century; it may be connected with the adj. *ʿāqār,* "barren, without offspring" (ancient in the biblical material) via antithetical development within

---

ʿāqar. L. W. Batten, "David's Destruction of the Syrian Chariots," *ZAW* 28 (1908) 188-92; S. Gevirtz, "Simeon and Levi in 'The Blessing of Jacob' (Gen. 49:5-7)," *HUCA* 52 (1981) 93-128, esp. 110-11; W. Krebs, "'. . . sie haben Stiere gelähmt' (Gen 49,6)," *ZAW* 78 (1966) 359-61.

1. *HAL,* II, 874; *GesB,* 613-14.
2. *WTM,* III, 688.
3. *DNSI,* II, 883; *KAI* 26A.I.6; see M. Dahood, *Bibl* 47 (1966) 270.

the root, with the complex view of progeniture among the Semites making it possible to establish linguistic identification of "root" and "offspring."

Whether the verb *'iqqēr* (piel), "hamstring," found already in J, should be assigned to the root under discussion is hard to judge, since the only apparent semantic element they have in common is destructive activity. Even that is true only with certain restrictions, since all its occurrences — and especially the occurrences of the Arabic cognate[4] — appear to be connected with ban and sacrifice, where the relationship between positive and negative shifts.

Other extrabiblical occurrences of *'qr* are concentrated in postbiblical languages: Christian Palestinian, Syriac, Mandaic, and various Arabic dialects; but cf. Akk. *uqquru,* "handicapped person."[5]

II. Meaning.

1. *Verb.* The verb *'āqar* is found in the qal, niphal, and piel, with differing semantics.

a. *Qal.* The meaning of the qal is defined consistently as "tear up by the roots, weed."[6] In the Phoenician Karatepe inscription (ca. 720 B.C.E.), however, King Azitawadda declares that he filled the *'qrt* ("granary"?) of P'R.[7] This usage and the antithetical parallelism of the only biblical occurrence (Eccl. 3:2) suggest that the translation "reap" is preferable.[8] For Ecclesiastes, there is a time for everything: to be born and to die, to plant (→ נטע *nāṭa'*) and to reap.

b. *Niphal.* The only occurrence of the niphal is Zeph. 2:4 (secondary?) (the ethpael is found in Dnl. 7:8), in a threat that uses wordplay: "Gaza shall be deserted, Ashkelon become a desolation; Ashdod's people shall be driven out in broad daylight, and Ekron shall be plowed up *('eqrôn tē'āqēr).*" The meaning of the threat is clear from the anti-Philistine oracles of other prophets (cf. Am. 1:7-8; Ezk. 25:16; etc.) and the use in parallel of the verbs *'zb,* "be left desolate," *grš,* "be driven out," and *šmm,* "become a desert," even if the paronomasia hides the specific nuance of *'qr.*

c. *Piel.* The piel *'iqqēr* refers to the practice of severing the tendons of the hind legs of certain animals so that they cannot move. In the ancient period, the Israelites clearly did this to the teams of captured chariots to make them unusable in case the tide of battle turned (Josh. 11:6,9, the horses [*sûsîm*] of the northern kings).[9] This action probably involved more than military tactics, however, since David hamstringed the chariot horses *(reḵeḇ)* of the Moabites even though he could have incorporated them into his own chariot corps (2 S. 8:4; 1 Ch. 18:4). It probably reflects an ancient provision of the ban (→ חרם *ḥāram;* note the par. verbs *hrg,* "slay," *śrp,* "set on fire," and *nkh* hiphil, "smite"). Thus hamstringing an animal was clearly a mandatory sacrificial ritual and had no place outside that context. To mutilate animals in this fashion "capriciously"

---

4. See Krebs.
5. See *HAL,* II, 874; Lane, I/5, 2107ff.; *AHw,* III, 1427a.
6. *HAL.*
7. *KAI* 26A.I.6.
8. Lohfink, *Kohelet. NEB* (1993).
9. See Krebs.

(b^e^rāṣôn) was considered utterly reprehensible (Gen. 49:6; is the sequence "kill men — hamstring oxen" climax or anticlimax?).

2. *Adjective.* The adj. *'āqār* occurs only in the Bible, where it means "barren." This meaning is contextually assured by the synonyms *šômēmâ,* "desolated," *'almānâ,* "widow," and *m^e^šakkēlâ,* "miscarrying," as well as *'umlal,* "wither," "be childless." This is contrasted with the following antonyms: *hārâ,* "conceive," *ḥîl,* "have labor pains," *pāṯaḥ reḥem,* "open the womb," and *yālaḏ,* "bear." The social position of a childless woman is revealed by the fact that she is "despised" *(śānē',* qal pass. ptcp.) and counted among the poor and lowly *(dal)* and the helpless *('eḇyôn).* In contrast stands the woman who is "rich in children" *(rabbaṯ bānîm),* the "joyful mother" *('ēm ś^e^mēḥâ),* the woman who is blessed *(bārûḵ).*

J records the barrenness of the matriarchs Sarai (Gen. 11:30), Rebekah (25:21), and Rachel (29:31) in order to emphasize the contrasting motif: God's promise of many offspring. It was probably Deuteronomistic theology that elaborated the prediction of Samson's birth to predict the birth of a nazirite (Jgs. 13:2-3). His mother is *'^a^qārâ* and receives a private oracle foretelling the significance of the promised son. For a late Deuteronomistic writer, it was a common article of faith that in the future there would no longer be an *'^a^qārâ* in Israel (Ex. 23:26; late framework of the Covenant Code). This voice even frames the striking statement that Israel is the most blessed of peoples: among them and their livestock (secondary?) none will be barren, male (*'āqār,* masc.!) or female (Dt. 7:14). This formulation was probably chosen less for reasons of assonance[10] than to emphasize universal fertility (cf. the bombastic promise of increase in v. 13). It is probable that in every era the Israelites (drawing intentionally on Canaanite fertility ideology) extolled Yahweh for transforming barrenness, the greatest disgrace that could befall a woman (Isa. 54:1; Ps. 113:9), into its opposite: the honor of bearing many children (cf. the Song of Hannah and its continued influence in Lk. 1:46ff.).

The interpretation of Job 24:21 is difficult. The wicked harm the childless woman and do no good to the widow. Here a postexilic sage is probably castigating the antisocial conduct of the times. In the light of the parallelism exhibited by the verse, the substantial restructuring of the text proposed by Fohrer should be rejected.[11]

3. *Nouns.* The noun *'iqqār* in Biblical Hebrew is very marginal: it is a conjectural emendation in Job 30:3 (people who gnaw the grass and its "roots"); it is used figuratively in Sir. 37:17 (the heart [→ לב *lēḇ*] is the root of all human conduct). In Nebuchadnezzar's dream of the tall tree, *'iqqār* refers to the "rootstock" that is preserved in spite of all humiliations (Dnl. 4:12,20,23[15,23,26]). Nebuchadnezzar will remain king if he acknowledges God (v. 23[26]).

The noun *'ēqer* occurs only once in the OT, in Lev. 25:47. In this late passage in the

---

10. P. P. Saydon, *Bibl* 36 (1955) 39.
11. G. Fohrer, *Das Buch Hiob. KAT* XVI (1963), 368.

Holiness Code, it is a general term for the descendants of a family. Here it embodies the meaning already richly attested (20 times) in the Sefire inscriptions of the 8th century B.C.E., where *ʿqr* refers quite generally to the descendants of both parties to the treaty. These descendants are included in the treaty; they must keep it and abide by its provisions; if they break it, they are threatened with the appropriate punishment.

III. LXX and Dead Sea Scrolls. The LXX translates the qal of the verb with *ektíllein,* the niphal with *ekrízoun,* and the piel with *neurokopeín;*[12] only in 2 S. 8:4 does it use *paralýein* for the piel, on account of the difficult obj. *reḵeḇ*. The adjective is represented almost uniformly by *steíros/steíra, ʿēqer* by *genetḗ,* and *ʿiqqār* by *phyḗ*.

Two occurrences of the root have been identified in the Dead Sea Scrolls. In 4Q179 2:7, with an allusion to Lam. 1, destroyed Jerusalem is compared to a barren and embittered (*mrr;* par. "sad" [*ʾbl*] and "bereft" [*škl*]) woman. In 4Q509 283:1 the context is fragmentary.

Fabry

12. For extrabiblical usage see Krebs.

עקשׁ *ʿqš;* עִקֵּשׁ *ʿiqqēš;* עִקְּשׁוּת *ʿiqqᵉšûṯ;* מַעֲקַשִּׁים *maʿᵃqaššîm*

I. Etymology. II. Occurrences and Usage. III. LXX and Vulgate.

I. Etymology. There is scant evidence of the root in other Semitic languages. A connection with Mand. *ʿqisa* is dubious if *ʿqisa* is derived from the root *qss.*[1] The emphatic sibilant casts doubt on a relationship with Arab. *ʿaqaṣa.*[2] Also uncertain is a relationship with Egyp. *ʿa-ga-ś(a)* and *ʿa-ga-ś-u,*[3] as well as with Syriac parallels.

II. Occurrences and Usage. The verb *ʿqš,* "twist, pervert," occurs 5 times in the OT: once in the niphal (Prov. 28:18), 3 times in the piel (Mic. 3:9; Isa. 59:8; Prov. 10:9), and once in the hiphil (Job 9:20). The adj. *ʿiqqēš,* "crooked, perverse, dishonest" occurs 11

ʿqš. W. Brueggemann, "A Neglected Sapiential Word Pair," *ZAW* 89 (1977) 234-58; M. Dahood, "Hebrew-Ugaritic Lexicography VII," *Bibl* 50 (1969) 353-54; F. Nötscher, *Gotteswege und Menschenwege in der Bibel und in Qumran. BBB* 15 (1958), 55-56.

1. Cf. *HAL,* II, 875; *MdD,* 356b.
2. *HAL,* II, 875.
3. Helck, *Die Beziehungen Ägyptens zu Vorderasien im 3. und 2. Jahrtausend v. Chr.* ([2]1971), 510.

times (Dt. 32:5; Ps. 101:4; 18:27[Eng. v. 26] = 2 S. 22:27; Prov. 2:15; 8:8; 11:20; 17:20; 19:1; 22:5; 28:6), the subst. *ʿiqqᵉšûṯ* twice (Prov. 4:24; 6:12), and *maʿᵃqaššîm* once (Isa. 42:16). All the occurrences are in poetical texts; most are in Proverbs.

The concrete meaning can be seen in *maʿᵃqaššîm,* "rough terrain," with its antonym *mîšôr,* "level ground, plain" (Isa. 42:6, in a description of the way for the returnees). The verb, the adjective, and the noun *ʿiqqᵉšûṯ* are used only figuratively, e.g., the piel of *ʿqš* in Mic. 3:9, where the concrete image is still recognizable. The antonym in Mic. 3:9 is *yᵉšārâ,* a word from the same root as *mîšôr* in Isa. 42:6; "make crooked everything straight" means "pervert all equity" — cf. the par. "abhor *(tʿb)* justice *(mišpāṭ).*" As in these passages, we regularly find in the immediate or extended context of *ʿqš/ʿiqqēš* certain typical concepts closely associated with the word: the image straight vs. crooked, the motif of the "way" (always metaphorical except in Isa. 42:6), and specific parallel or contrastive terms. For example, Isa. 59:8 exhibits a chiastic structure using the "way" motif in parallel with *ʾên mišpāṭ* (cf. Mic. 3:9). Dt. 32:5-6 (where none of the typical terminology appears with *ʿiqqēš* in v. 5) contrasts with v. 4, where *dereḵ* appears together with the figurative antonym *yāšār* and the semantically related *tāmîm, mišpāṭ,* and *ṣaddîq.*

In Proverbs (and Psalms) we find an increasing tendency to use *ʿiqqēš* and *ʿiqqᵉšûṯ* absolutely. In Prov. 10:9 the concrete image is still present behind the metaphor; and in 2:15; 28:6,18 (and to some extent in 22:5), *ʿqš* and *ʿiqqēš* are still associated with the motif of the way in some element of the idea presented; in 17:20; 8:8 and 4:24; 6:12 (both *ʿiqqᵉšûṯ*), however, abstract usage appears. In other words, when the imagery is concrete, misconduct is represented "in an immediately perspicuous metaphor as a crooked, perverse, or winding way."[4] Finally, this moralistic description of a corrupt life becomes spiritualized, and *ʿiqqēš* becomes an ethical term meaning "wrong, dishonest, culpable," sometimes used absolutely (Prov. 8:8; 22:5; also Dt. 32:5; 2 S. 22:27 = Ps. 18:27[26]), sometimes qualified in a construct phrase (with "heart" in Prov. 11:20; 17:20; with "his lips" in Prov. 19:1; in Ps. 101:4 as an adj. modifying "heart" [→ לב *lēḇ*]).

The most important antonym in Proverbs is *tām.* The two terms can be called a sapiential word pair; they appear together in Prov. 10:9; 11:20; 19:1; 28:6,18 — all texts from the earlier section of Proverbs.

a. Three words are used as parallels a single time: *nᵉlôzîm* (*lwz* niphal), "devious" (Prov. 2:15); *raʿ,* "evil" (Ps. 101:4); *nip̄tāl* (in a word pair), "deceitful" (Prov. 8:8).

b. In defining who is *ʿiqqēš,* two individuals or groups may be contrasted (pl., Prov. 11:20; sg., 17:20; 10:9; 28:6,18); or the distinction may represent a choice placed before a single individual (4:24; cf. Ps. 101:4).

c. The MT vocalization of *drkym* as a dual in Prov. 28:6,18 should be rejected; for, although two different ways are contrasted in the two cola, the second colon does not present a choice between two ways (there is no element of choice implied by *ʿqš;* such an element would have to be a later development of totally abstract usage).

---

4. Nötscher.

d. In Job 9:20 the verb should probably be read as a hiphil; it is otherwise treated as a hybrid form or a piel.[5] "Parallel to רשׁע hiphil, . . . only the hiphil *treat as perverse* fully brings out the paradox" ("my own mouth would condemn me and prove me perverse, even were I blameless").[6]

e. In Prov. 2:15 *ʿiqqᵉšîm* may qualify *ʾorḥōṯêhem* despite the difference in gender; alternatively, *ʿiqqᵉšîm* may qualify the subject of the context, with *bᵉ* being supplied before *ʾorḥōṯêhem* by analogy with the second colon.[7] Another possibility is to read *mᵉʿaqqᵉšîm.*[8]

In some instances the context describes concretely what is judged *ʿqš/ʿiqqēš*. In Mic. 3:9 "make crooked everything straight" (par. "abhor justice") means to "build Zion with blood and Jerusalem with wrong" (v. 10; v. 11: judgment for a bribe, instruction for a price, prophetic oracles for pay). According to Isa. 59:8, there is no justice in the paths that the people have perverted; in particular, those who walk in them know no peace. In Ps. 101 (v. 4, "perverseness of heart shall be far from me"), the king undertakes specific obligations in the immediate context (vv. 3,5ff.). When there is nothing twisted or crooked in the words of one's mouth, they are righteous (Prov. 8:8). Here *ʿiqqᵉšûṯ peh* ("perverseness of the mouth") means false or deceitful speech. In Proverbs *ʿiqqēš* is generally not elaborated on, however; sapiential language uses it as a technical term for a certain type of conduct, the consequences of which are often described: one who follows crooked ways will fall into the pit (Prov. 28:18), will be found out (10:9), or will come upon thorns and snares (22:5). Crooked hearts are an abomination to Yahweh (11:2) and do not prosper (17:20).

Exegetes differ in their appraisal of the theological context. Nötscher (esp. with respect to Isa. 59:7-8) emphasizes that morally crooked paths are roads to perdition. Those who follow them are lost. The crooked way leads to a bad end and becomes its own fate. Kraus (with reference to Ps. 101:4) gives the following definition: "עקשׁ denotes the wrong direction of the innermost being."[9] He cites the principle of analogy: those who despise Yahweh or Yahweh's statutes exclude themselves from the domain of salvation.[10]

The word pair *tm/ʿqš* makes a general statement as to how one lives one's life.[11] The adj. *ʿiqqēš* means "twisted, perverse" (implying an act, unlike *tm*) and insists on the notion of departing from a straight path (that serves as a guide) to follow a path that leads astray. In contrast to *tm* (integrity and solidarity with the community; → תמם *tmm*), *ʿiqqēš* means deviation, ignominy (Prov. 10:9), and isolation (28:18). The *ʿiqqēš* separates from the community and goes a different way. The pair *tm/ʿqš* can have the same meaning in the context of royal traditions (Ps. 101:2-4) (whether or not the king works for the benefit of the community).

---

5. See *BHK*³; Horst, *Hiob. BK* XVI/1 (³1968), 140.
6. *HP,* 236; *GK,* §53n; M. Lambert, *REJ* 50 (1905) 262.
7. Dahood.
8. *BHS.*
9. *Psalms 60–150* (Eng. trans. 1989), 279.
10. Idem, *Psalms 1–59* (Eng. trans. 1988), 263.
11. Brueggemann.

Some occurrences of *ʿāšaq* and *ʿōšeq* derive from *ʿqš* by metathesis and should be translated accordingly (for *ʿōšeq* some exegetes read an otherwise unattested *ʿōqeš* or, better, *ʿiqqēš*). Such metathesis is recognized in Hos. 12:8(7) and Isa. 30:12, sometimes in Isa. 59:13, and generally in Ps. 73:8. But this reading must be supported in each instance by the meaning required by the context.

III. LXX and Vulgate. The LXX renders the verb 3 times with *diastréphein* ("pervert," Mic. 3:9; Isa. 59:8; Prov. 10:9) and twice with *skoliós* ("twisted, bent, perverse, deceitful," Prov. 28:18; Job 9:20). The predominant translation of the adjective is *skoliós* (Dt. 32:5; Isa. 42:16; Prov. 2:15; 4:24; 22:5). Seven other words are used once. The most common translations in the Vulg. are *pervertere/perversus* and *pravus* ("twisted, perverse, improper, evil").

The word has not been found in the Dead Sea Scrolls.

Warmuth

עָרַב I *ʿārab̲* I; עֲרֻבָּה *ʿarubbâ;* עֵרָבוֹן *ʿērāb̲ôn;* עָרֵב *ʿārēb̲;* תַּעֲרוּבָה *taʿarûb̲â*

I. Usage: 1. Verb; 2. Nouns. II. Pledge and Surety.

ʿārab̲ I. A. Abeles, "Der Bürge nach biblischem Recht," *MGWJ* 66 (1922) 279-94; 67 (1923) 35-53; idem, "Bürge und Bürgschaft nach talmudischem Recht," *MGWJ* 67 (1923) 122-30, 170-86, 254-57; J. Behm, "ἀρραβών," *TDNT,* I, 475; Z. Ben-Hayyim, "השורה ערב," *Leš* 44 (1979/80) 85-99; idem, ed., "השורה ערב," *Leš* 46 (1981/82) 165-267; idem, "נתון בערבים," *Leš* 45 (1980/81) 307-10; G. Boström, *Proverbiastudien* (1935), esp. 54-57; E. M. Cassin, "La caution à Nuzi," *RA* 34 (1937) 154-68; M. Cohen, "À propos de 'gage, caution' dans les langues sémitiques," *GLECS* 8 (1957-60) 13-16; É. Cuq, *Études sur le droit babylonien, les lois assyriennes et les lois hittites* (1929), esp. 310-38; M. Dietrich, O. Loretz, and J. Sanmartín, "Keilalphabetische Bürgschaftsdokumente aus Ugarit," *UF* 6 (1974) 466-67; H. Donner, "Bemerkungen zum Verständnis zweier aramäischer Briefe aus Hermopolis," in H. Goedicke, ed., *Near Eastern Studies in Honor of W. F. Albright* (1971), 75-85, esp. 76-83; G. R. Driver and J. C. Miles, *The Assyrian Laws* (1935), 271-90; idem, *The Babylonian Laws,* I (1952), 208-21; II (1955), 204-9, 229; M. Elon, "Pledge," *EncJud,* XIII, 636-44; idem, "Suretyship," *EncJud,* XV, 524-29; Z. W. Falk, "Zum jüdischen Bürgschaftsrecht," *RIDA* 3/10 (1963), 43-54; R. Haase, *Einführung in das Studium keilschriftlicher Rechtsquellen* (1965), 106-11; P. Koschaker, *Babylonisch-assyrisches Bürgschaftsrecht* (1911); M. Liverani, "Due documenti ugaritici con garanzia di presenza," *Ugaritica* 6 (1969) 375-78; É. Masson, *Recherches sur les plus anciens emprunts sémitiques en grec* (1967), 30-31; H. Petschow, "Ein neubabylonischer Bürgschaftsregress gegen einen Nachlass," *Tijdschrift voor Rechtsgeschiedenis* 19 (1951) 25-27; idem, *Neubabylonisches Pfandrecht. ASAW* 48/1 (1956); idem, "Zum neubabylonischen Bürgschaftsrecht," *ZA* 53 (1959) 241-47; B. Porten and J. C. Greenfield, "The Guarantor at Elephantine-Syene," *JAOS* 89 (1969) 153-57; E. Pritsch, "Zur juristischen Bedeutung der *šubanti*-Formel," *Alttestamentliche Studien. FS F. Nötscher. BBB* 1 (1950), 172-88; M. San Nicolò, "Bürgschaft," *RLA,* II, 77-80; idem, *Zur Nachbürgschaft in den Keilschrifturkunden und in gräko-ägyptischen Papyri. SBAW* 6 (1937); É. Szlechter, "Le cautionnement à Larsa," *Revue*

I. Usage.

1. *Verb.* The use of the verb *'ārab̲* to mean "stand surety" goes back at least to the 2nd millennium B.C.E. In the Alalakh texts *ana qātāti*/ŠU.DU$_8$.A *ana* PN *īrub* or *aššum* PN ŠU.DU$_8$.A *īrub* means "stand surety for someone."[1] The subject of the verb *erēbu* (*'rb*), which means literally "enter," is the person — slave, wife, or son — who serves as the pledge. All law codes of the ancient Near East down to the Neo-Babylonian era bear witness to the use of personal surety, predominantly antichretic, i.e., the creditor is indemnified through the labor of the person pledged as surety. The practice of personal surety is also found in the OT (Lev. 25:39,47; Dt. 15:2,12; Neh. 5:2,5-7). The verb used in this context is *'rb,* at least in Neh. 5:2 (emended) and Ps. 119:121b-122, where the psalmist prays to God: "Do not deliver me to my creditors; give your servant as a pledge (*'ᵃrōb̲*) to some good man (*lᵉṭôb̲*), lest the proud distrain me." The subject of *'rb* is no longer the person given in pledge, as at Alalakh, but the one who pledges the surety. The development leading to this usage may already be observed in Ugaritic texts,[2] where the syntagm *'rb b* PN means "guarantee," "pledge oneself on someone's behalf"; the prep. *b* expresses the idea of equivalence. The verb in Ugaritic does not yet have a direct object, as it will in Ps. 119:122. In Prov. 17:18 the direct object of the ptcp. *'ōrēb̲* is *'ᵃrubbâ,* "pledge," without further specification; in Neh. 5:3 it is the fields, vineyards, and houses mortgaged to raise money. The same construction occurs in v. 2, where *'ōrᵉb̲îm* should be read instead of *rabbîm,* so that the sons and daughters pledged as surety are the direct object of *'rb.* Jer. 30:21 uses the giving of surety figuratively: "Who has given his heart in pledge in order to approach me?" It was believed that to approach God without being called is to risk one's life. A clause in a Nabatean contract from Naḥal Ḥever reads: *w'rbt wḥšbt bty wmnyt ly bpg'wn hw,* "and I have pledged (*'rbt*) my house, and you have appraised (*ḥšbt*) (it), and you have credited (it) to me in this agreement."[3] This statement should be compared to Dnl. 4:32(Eng. v. 35), where *ḥšb* parallels *mḥ' byd,* "strike one's hand," a symbolic gesture on the part of the guarantor, who promises to the creditor to fulfill the terms of a contract if the principal debtor does not: "All the inhabitants of the earth are accounted as nothing . . . and there is no one who strikes his hand." In other words, the inhabitants of the earth are left to God's mercy, as debtors for whom no one can stand surety.

Instead of the Ugaritic syntagm *'rb b* PN, Hebrew uses the formula *'rb l* PN (Prov. 6:1; cf. Sir. 29:14) to express the same basic idea, "stand surety for someone." A different idiom uses *'rb* with the accusative of the person on behalf of whom one stands

---

historique de droit français et étranger (1958), 1-39; A. Verger, *Ricerche giuridiche sui papiri aramaici di Elefantina* (1965), 137-40; H. M. Weil, "Le cautionnement talmudique comparé aux institutions correspondantes de l'ancien Orient," *AHDO* 3 (1948) 167-208; idem, "Exégèse de Jérémie 23,33-40 et de Job 34,28-33," *RHR* 118 (1938) 201-8; idem, "Gage et cautionnement dans la Bible," *AHDO* 2 (1938) 171-241.

1. For the former see D. J. Wiseman, *Alalakh Tablets* (1953), 82:11-13; 84:4-5. For the latter, 83:56.

2. *KTU* 3.3, 2; 3.7, 1; 3.8, 6.

3. A 11; J. Starcky, *RB* 61 (1954) 161-81.

surety: "O Lord, I am threatened with distraint; be my surety" (Isa. 38:14); "To stand surety for a stranger brings trouble" (Prov. 11:15; cf. 20:16; 27:13). The same construction appears in texts where the surety is meant figuratively, where it embodies the idea of making oneself a guarantor of someone's safety (Gen. 43:9; 44:32). Finally, we find *ʿrb* with the accusative of the secured debt: "Do not be one of those who become surety of debts" (Prov. 22:26). Sir. 8:13 uses *ʿrb* without any object, but it is clear that the text refers to simple surety for a third party.

The hithpael of *ʿrb* is used in 2 K. 18:23 = Isa. 36:8 in the sense of "wager" (cf. OSA *tʿrb,* "give pledges").[4]

2. *Nouns.* In Biblical Hebrew two nouns denote a pledge: *ʿērāb̲ôn* and *ʿᵃrubbâ.* The former appears in Gen. 38:17-18,20 and should also be read in Job 17:3: "Deposit my pledge *(ʿērᵉb̲ōnî)* in your presence." It appears often at Elephantine,[5] and is used in both Greek *(arrabṓn)* and Latin *(arr[h]abo),* where the vocalization and the reduplication of the *r* suggest that the word is borrowed from Phoenician rather than Hebrew or Aramaic. It does not appear, however, in the corpus of Phoenician and Punic inscriptions. The noun *ʿrbn* is found in Ugaritic, where it denotes the "guarantor."[6]

In Hebrew (Prov. 20:17) and Phoenician this meaning is conveyed by the subst. *ʿrb,* which can be read as the act. ptcp. *ʿōrēb̲* or, more likely, the nominalized verbal adj. *ʿārēb̲.*[7] The latter corresponds to the vocalization in Prov. 20:17, Talmudic Hebrew, and even Imperial Aramaic, as the orthography *ʿryb* of the word for "guarantor" at Saqqarah shows: *[ ]ḥ zk knm ʿryb hw,* "the aforementioned is guarantor in this manner."[8] The term *ʿrb* appears already in a letter from Hermopolis (ca. 500 B.C.E.), in the Saqqarah texts, and in the Aramaic contracts from Murabbaʿat and Naḥal Ḥever, where it always parallels the synonym *ʾḥry.*[9] This pair "surety and guarantor" appears already in Saqqarah document 29:6: *ʿrbyʾ wʾḥr[yʾ];* this expression should be compared particularly to *ʿrbʾ wʾḥryʾ* in Mur 32:4. The two terms appear in synonymous parallelism in Prov. 20:17, where we should probably read *ʾaḥᵃrāy millēʾ:* "A surety *(ʿārēb̲)* is deceitful bread for a person, and a guarantor *(ʾaḥᵃrāy)* fills the mouth with gravel." This image reflects the very common situation in which debt is incurred to feed one's family. After this text, we must wait until the sale contract Mur 30:5, 24, dating from 134 C.E., to find other occurrences of this Hebrew lexical pair: *kl šyš ly wšʾqnh ʾḥrym wʿrbym lmrq lpnk ʾt hmkr hzh,* "All that belongs to me and that I shall acquire is surety and guarantee to defend in your favor this sold parcel of land" (ll. 23-24; cf. Prov. 17:18). As we see, *ʿārēb̲* and *ʾaḥᵃrāy* can denote either the person who stands surety (cf. Prov. 20:17 and text B 11 from Naḥal Ḥever: *ʾnh ʾḥry ʿrb l[k],* "I am surety [and] guarantor

4. Cf. W. von Soden, *UF* 18 (1986) 341-42, who translates the verb instead as "get involved with."

5. *DNSI,* II, 884.

6. *KTU* 3.3, 1, 7.

7. *KAI* 60.6; cf. 119.7?

8. J. B. Segal, *Aramaic Texts from North Saqqarah* (1983), 21:5.

9. Saqqarah 21:5; 29:6; Mur 20:12; 26:1, 4; 28:1-2, 10; 32:4; Naḥal Ḥever B 11; C 11.

for [you]") or the property of the person in question (Mur 30, 23-24; contract C 11 from Naḥal Ḥever). It is probably this second meaning that we find in an Aramaic inscription from Babylon,[10] dated in the seventeenth year of Darius II (407 B.C.E.): *ʿrbʾ zy qdm kyšwš ʾt bytʾ*. . . "the security available to Ki-Shamash (consists) in *(itti)* the property. . . ." Finally, a Palmyrene inscription speaks of one who "would sell the security that (is deposited) for the tomb" (*yzbn ʿrbʾ zy qdm mʿrtʾ*).[11]

The second Hebrew word for "pledge" is *ʿᵃrubbâ.* It occurs only in 1 S. 17:18 and Prov. 17:18; but Old Assyr. *erub(b)ātu* with the meaning "pledge" appears as early as the 2nd millennium B.C.E. in the Kültepe texts, where it refers to mortgaged real estate, personal surety, or the tablet (with seal impressed) given to the creditor as security.[12] This term is not found subsequently in Akkadian. Its precise meaning in 1 S. 17:18 is obscure; in any case the text does not deal with surety in the legal sense.

The unique expression *bᵉnê hattaʿᵃrûb̲ôt̲* (2 K. 14:14 = 2 Ch. 25:24) is usually translated "hostages." This recalls OSA *tʿrb,* which means "warrant of good conduct,"[13] which is very close in meaning to the biblical expression.

The subst. *maʿᵃrāb̲,* used 9 times in Ezk. 27,[14] simply means "wares, cargo," and derives from the basic meaning *ʿrb,* "enter."[15]

II. Pledge and Surety. Hebrew terminology establishes a close connection between pledge and surety. Both practices served the purpose of protecting a creditor against a debtor's inability to pay. It is easy to understand that a creditor would seek to minimize his risks by refusing to make loans that were not secured by a mortgage or pledge.

A pledge is denoted by derivatives of the roots → חבל *ḥbl* and → עבט *ʿbṭ,* but *erub(b)ātu* > *ʿᵃrubbâ* (Prov. 17:18) and *ʿērāb̲ôn* (Gen. 38:17-18,20; Job 17:3) can have the same meaning; the various words appear to be synonyms. But *ʿrbn* in the Jewish Aramaic papyri from Egypt (like Gk. *arrabṓn* and Lat. *arr[h]abo*) can refer to pledged property that remained in the possession of the debtor and could be distrained by the creditor only if the debt was not paid before the designated due date. In Hebrew the verb *ʿāšaq* and the nouns *ʿōšeq* and *ʿošqâ* (1QIsᵃ 38:14) refer to this distraint of a pledge, which could be property or a person. At Elephantine the classic list of goods that could be pledged to guarantee repayment includes male and female slaves, bronze and iron objects, clothing, and grain.[16] No distinction was made between real property, goods and chattels, slaves, and even free individuals. In other words, the term *ʿrbn* also included the notion of a mortgage.

Neh. 5:3, where the Jews pledge *(ʿōrᵉb̲îm)* their fields, vineyards, and houses to buy grain, goes even further. Here more is involved than a hypothec, since the creditors

---

10. *CIS,* II, 65.
11. Published in *Berytus* 5 (1938) 133.
12. *CAD,* IV, 327; *AHw,* I, 248a.
13. Beeston, 19.
14. Cf. *AP,* 2:5.
15. E. Lipiński, *Studia Phoenicia,* III (1985), 216-17.
16. *BMAP,* 11:10; cf. *AP,* 10:9-10.

have already taken possession of the property (v. 5), so that Nehemiah demands its return (v. 11). The contractual pledge of real property denoted by *ʿrb* in v. 5 is clearly antichretic. The due date is presumed to be undefined, since the pledged property belongs in effect to "others." But the pledge is not treated as a kind of satisfaction, making the transaction tantamount to a sale with right of repurchase, the grain received by the mortgager representing the price. The requirement that the debt be repaid did not lapse with the transfer of the pledge; but it was more advantageous to the creditor not to set a due date, since he enjoyed usufruct of the pledge and did not have to press for repayment. The Nabatean contract A from Naḥal Ḥever provides no clue as to whether l. 11 refers to a hypothec or an antichretic mortgage.

Neh. 5:2, where *ʿōrᵉb̲îm* should be read, says that the Jews pledged their sons and daughters. In contrast to the narrative in 2 K. 4:1-7, where allowance may have been made for the tender age of the children, the personal surety described in Neh. 5:5 was established by the actual transfer of the individuals in question. The creditor was compensated by the usufruct and labor of the persons pledged. Ancient Near Eastern documents indicate that if a person given in pledge died, fell ill, or ran away, the debtor had to repay the debt immediately.[17]

If the pledged individual was not actually handed over, distraint of the person in the event the debtor was unable to pay could be suspended by surety (Isa. 38:14). Similarly, a borrower who was not in a position to provide sufficient pledges could obtain surety through a third party whose solvency was generally recognized. In the event of the failure of the principal debtor to meet his obligations at the due date or at the conclusion of a loan secured by a pledge, this third party "entered" *(ʿrb)* the lists on behalf of *(lᵉ/lip̲nê)* the insolvent debtor to discharge the liability. At the very outset of the agreement, the guarantor *(ʿārēb̲* or *ʾaḥᵃrāy wᵉʿārēb̲)* had to come forward with the symbolic gesture of "clapping" or "striking" the hand, in Hebrew *tāqaʿ kap̲* or *yād̲* (Prov. 6:1; 11:15; 17:18; 22:26; Job 17:3), in Aramaic *mᵉḥāʾ (bᵉ)yad̲* (Dnl. 4:32; Old Aramaic tablets in Brussels, O. 3658, 5; O. 3670, 3).

Surety is attested at a very early date in Mesopotamia; it is already denoted by the verb *ʿrb* at Ugarit. The law codes of the Bible do not mention it; but the early sapiential anthologies refer to it frequently (Prov. 11:15; 17:18; 20:16-17; 27:13), showing that this institution is not a late phenomenon in Palestine. Proverbs cautions those who stand surety for friends and above all for strangers (Prov. 6:1; 11:15; 20:16; 27:13). The guarantor should make every effort to be indemnified by constantly pressing the debtor to pay (6:3-5), because otherwise the guarantor would be subject to distraint (20:16; 22:26b,27; 27:13). In a later era Sirach esteems the practice of surety as an act of kindness (Sir. 29:14-20; cf. 8:13). He nevertheless cautions against standing surety beyond one's means (8:13; 29:20) and points out that debtors are not always grateful to their benefactors (29:15) and that surety has plunged many into ruin (29:17-18).

Lipiński

---

17. For example, *ARM* VIII, 31.

ערב II/III ʿrb II/III; עֵרֶב I ʿēreḇ I; עֵרֶב II ʿēreḇ II; עָרֹב ʿārōḇ; עָרֵב ʿārēḇ

I. Etymology and Distribution. II. Meaning: 1. The Verb ʿrb II; 2. The Noun ʿēreḇ II; 3. ʿēreḇ I; 4. ʿārōḇ; 5. ʿāraḇ III, ʿārēḇ. III. LXX and Dead Sea Scrolls.

I. Etymology and Distribution. The meanings of the verbal formatives ʿrb I-V in Hebrew are so different that they should not be traced to a single etymological root. In the case of ʿrb II, furthermore, we appear to be dealing with a late word concentrated primarily in the wisdom literature of the monarchic period and found outside the OT only in Aramaic (the two Egyptian Aramaic occurrences are uncertain), Syriac (*ʿᵉraḇ,* "mix"), and Mandaic ("mix, intermix, mingle").[1] The verb occurs almost exclusively in the hithpael with the meaning "have dealings with"; it does not come into common use until after the OT period in the Dead Sea Scrolls (13 occurrences) and in rabbinic literature.[2] From the same root derive the nominal formatives *ʿēreḇ* I, "mixed-weave fabric" (cf. Aram. *ʿarbāʾ*), and *ʿēreḇ* II, "rabble" (cf. Aram. *ʿirbûḇ, ʿêraḇrᵉḇîn*).[3]

The noun *ʿārōḇ,* "dog fly," is usually connected with this root,[4] but Akk. *urbattu,* "worm," in parallel with *tultu,* "worm," points in a different direction.[5]

The verb *ʿāraḇ* III, "be sweet," with its derived adj. *ʿārēḇ,* has etymological parallels only in South Semitic (Old South Arabic and Arabic dialects).[6]

II. Meaning.

1. *The Verb ʿrb II.* There are only 4 certain occurrences of the verb *ʿrb* II hithpael: Prov. 14:10; 20:19; Ezr. 9:2; Ps. 106:35. It has also been conjectured in Prov. 14:16; 24:21; 26:17.

In Prov. 14:16 the LXX *meígnytai* (= *miṯʿārēḇ*) casts doubt on the MT reading *ûḵᵉsîl miṯʿabbēr ûḇôṭēaḥ* in the second colon.[7] The first colon says: "The sage is cautious and turns away from evil"; as an antithesis, either reading makes sense: "The fool meddles and is gullible," or "The fool flares up [→ עבר *ʿāḇar* II] and feels secure."[8]

The text of 24:21 is highly corrupt: "Fear Yahweh, my son, and the king, *ʿim-šônîm ʾal-tiṯʿārāḇ.*" On the basis of the LXX, we should read *ʿal-šᵉnêhem tiṯʿabbār:* "Do not be disobedient to either" (*ʿbr* II).[9] Plöger retains *ʿrb* at the expense of an unusual inter-

---

ʿrb II/III. Z. Ben-Hayyim, "The Root *ʿRB,* Meaning and Parallels," *Leš* 44 (1979/80) 85-99; W. A. van der Weiden, "Radix hebraica ערב," *VD* 44 (1966) 97-104.

1. For Aramaic see *AP,* 2:5; Ahiqar 184; for Syriac, *LexSyr,* 546; for Mandaic, *MdD,* 35b.
2. *HAL,* II, 877; Levy, *WTM,* III, 691.
3. *WTM,* III, 693, 695-96.
4. *GesB,* 616; *HAL,* II, 879.
5. *AHw,* III, 1428; cf. *LexSyr,* 546.
6. Ben-Hayyim.
7. *HAL,* II, 877; → X, 426.
8. → II, 91; H. Ringgren, *Sprüche. ATD* 16/1 (1962), in loc.
9. *BHS;* → X, 426; B. Gemser, *Sprüche Salomos. HAT* XVI (1963), in loc.

pretation of *šônêhem:* "Do not associate with those who think differently than they [Yahweh and the king]."[10]

In 26:17, with a shift of the *athnach,* the MT reads *miṯʿabbēr ʿal-rîḇ lōʾ-lô,* "whoever loses his temper in a quarrel that does not concern him."[11] It may be emended on the basis of the Vulg. *impatiens commiscetur* (the verse is not in the LXX) to *miṯʿārēḇ,* "whoever meddles in a quarrel."[12] But the Targ. and Syr. support retaining the MT.

The meaning "mix" (with b^e or l^e) is secure and is represented accurately by LXX *(epi)meígnymi.* It is developed in two directions: association and adulteration. In the former case, confusion with *ʿbr* II is easily possible (see above). A slanderer is notorious for betraying secrets; therefore one should not "associate" with a gossip (Prov. 20:19; the context is characterized by a string of catchwords: *ʿrb* I, v. 16; *ʿrb* III, v. 17; *ʿrb* II, v. 19). Prov. 14:10 calls the heart (→ לב *lēḇ*) the inmost seat of the feelings and emotions; a stranger (the LXX moralizes: hybris) should not meddle in its joy.

The two late texts Ezr. 9:2 and Ps. 106:35 allude to the mixed marriages of the postexilic period. By mingling with the *gôyim,* the Israelites lost their morality (Ps. 106). Even more seriously, through this grave contamination they lost their identity, their "holy seed" (*zeraʿ haqqōḏeš,* Ezr. 9:2; cf. Isa. 6:13 [secondary]). This theological argumentation is based on the idea of Israel's privileged status (cf. Ex. 34:12,15-16), familiar to the people from late Deuteronomistic usage (Dt. 7:3; 20:16ff.) and the language of the prophets (e.g., Mal. 2:10-16), summarizing it in the prosaic verb *ʿrb.*

2. *The Noun ʿēreḇ II.* The noun *ʿēreḇ* II clearly refers to such an ethnically and morally contaminated group without theological identity. Ex. 12:38 (J) already uses *ʿēreḇ raḇ* for the mixed crowd of non-Israelites, described by Nu. 11:4 as "the rabble" *(hāʾsapsup̱),* that joined the Israelites during the exodus. Their denigration is clear: they are mentioned in the same breath as the livestock. This mongrel group in Egypt is also referred to in Jer. 25:20, a postexilic interpretive addition, where they are threatened with the cup of Yahweh's wrath. Jer. 50:37 (secondary) is a threat pronounced against the mongrel peoples of Babylon, auxiliaries of the Babylonian Empire[13] (relegated to a position after horses and chariots). According to Ezk. 30:5 (secondary), *ʿēreḇ* is a derogatory collective term that does not include people of Jewish descent, who are excepted as "sons of the land with which I made my covenant." If *ʿēreḇ* here alludes once more to Egypt, the people of Jewish descent might be the colony at Elephantine.

Neh. 13:3 completes the arc leading to the usage of the verb in Ezr. 9:2. In line with the post-Deuteronomistic decree that no "bastard" (*mamzēr,* "half-breed")[14] may be admitted to the → קהל *qāhāl* (Dt. 23:3-4[Eng. vv. 2-3]; Zec. 9:6 suggests that the term may refer to a person of mixed Israelite-Philistine blood), the *ʿēreḇ* was excluded from the postexilic community. Neh. 13:1 cites Dt. 23 only selectively, but probably has the whole decree in mind.

---

10. O. Plöger, *Sprüche Salomos. BK* XVII (1984), 264.
11. Ibid., 307.
12. NRSV; → X, 426.
13. W. Zimmerli, *Ezekiel 2. Herm* (Eng. trans. 1983), 129-30.
14. *HAL,* II, 595.

3. *ʿēreḇ I.* The noun *ʿēreḇ* I is a technical term of weaving. It may denote an item "woven" of linen or wool, either in the sense of a "mixed" fabric made with different kinds of yarn (as the etymology suggests) or in the sense of "warp and woof" (cf. the constant association with *šᵉṯî*) as a term for types of yarn.[15] There are 9 occurrences of *ʿēreḇ* I, all in the later expansions of the law governing leprosy (→ צרעת *ṣāraʿaṯ;* Lev. 13:48-59).

4. *ʿārōḇ.* The noun *ʿārōḇ,* "dog fly," with its Akkadian etymon probably has no connection with our root. It constitutes the fourth plague of Egypt (Ex. 8:17-27[21-31] [J]) and is mentioned only in that context (cf. the two later reminiscences in Ps. 78:45 and 105:31). Its precise zoological identification is uncertain. Bodenheimer suggests lice.[16]

5. *ʿāraḇ III, ʿārēḇ.* The verb *ʿāraḇ* III, "be sweet, please," occurs 6 times in the qal and once in the hiphil (Sir. 40:21); the adj. *ʿārēḇ,* "sweet, pleasant," occurs 3 times. Hos. 9:4 is disputed (see below). The things found pleasing are sacrifices, poetry, speech, lies, instruments, sleep, desires, and once Jerusalem, personified as a whore (Ezk. 16:37). These may be pleasing to God or to human beings. Something pleasant gives a sense of physical or psychological delight; this holds true for God as well, whose favor can be gained by means of things that are pleasing to him (e.g., sacrifices). As a technical cultic term,[17] *ʿrb* III is used in Jer. 6:20 (Dtr) and Mal. 3:4 to describe a sacrifice as being pleasing to God; it may therefore be compared with *rāṣôn* (→ רצה *rāṣâ;* Jer. 6:20). Because the people of Jerusalem do not give heed to the words of their Lord, he rejects their sacrifices and foretells instead destruction from the north (Jer. 6:16-26). Sacrifice will be pleasing once more to Yahweh only when Israel has been purified, as in the days of old (Mal. 3:4 [secondary]).

The textual emendation proposed in Hos. 9:4 (*BHS: wᵉlōʾ yaʿarᵉḵû-lô ziḇḥêhem* [from *ʿāraḵ,* "place in rows, arrange, compare"]) is not persuasive, since *ʿāraḵ* denotes the physical arrangement of the sacrificial offerings or wood (Gen. 22:9; Lev. 1:7,8,12; 24:8; Nu. 23:4), and is otherwise not found with *zeḇaḥ.* Hos. 9:4, by contrast, deals with the possibility or impossibility of offering any sacrifice in a foreign land. We must therefore posit a verb *ʿāraḇ* IV, "offer," "for the point is not whether the sacrifices are pleasing to Yahweh but the impossibility of offering any sacrifices in a foreign land."[18]

To excite God's pleasure was also the purpose of the author of Ps. 104:34 — in this case, not by offering sacrifice but by singing a hymn of praise. As in Jer. 6:20, the intent is to offer something to delight God in order that God may be favorably disposed (cf. Ps. 19:15[14] with *rāṣôn*).

In all periods, sleep *(šēnâ)* is felt to be especially sweet. It strengthens the body and is promoted by a prudent way of life (Prov. 3:24). Conversely, sweet, quiet sleep paints

15. See *HAL,* II, 878; Dalman, *AuS,* V, 104.

16. F. S. Bodenheimer, *Animal and Man in Bible Lands* (Eng. trans. 1960), 72-73.

17. G. Gerleman, *TLOT,* III, 1260-61.

18. Rudolph, *Hosea. KAT* XIII/1 (1966), 172, 176; with *HAL,* II, 877, et al., contra H. W. Wolff, *Hosea. Herm* (Eng. trans. 1974), 155.

a picture of a serene and carefree life (Jer. 31:26). The physical and psychological refreshment brought by sleep is associated with personal conduct, for those who do wrong cannot sleep (Prov. 4:16).

The verb *ʿāraḇ* III can express psychological as well as physical pleasure. Prov. 13:19 describes a realized desire as being sweet *(teʿerab)* to the soul.

In Ezk. 16:37 *ʿāraḇ* describes unfaithful Jerusalem, who has turned out to be a whore and fallen victim to her lovers. The emendation of *ʿāraḇt* to *ʿāgaḇt* (from *ʿāgaḇ*, "love, long for [*ʿal*] someone") is unjustified (cf. Ps. 104:34).[19]

The only occurrence of *ʿāraḇ* III hiphil is in Sir. 40:21, which says that flute and harp make a song *(šîr)* sweet (cf. 3Q6 1 and 11QPs[a] 22:14).

The NRSV twice translates the adj. *ʿārēḇ* as "sweet," which must be understood in a figurative sense. The bridegroom delights in the sweet voice of the bride (Cant. 2:14). Prov. 20:17 speaks of a sweetness that is deceptive: what is gained by lies may be very pleasing at first, but turns out ultimately to be deceitful. Sir. 6:5 describes pleasant speech as a mark of friendship: by it one gains friends.

III. LXX and Dead Sea Scrolls. The LXX uses the word group *meígnymi* and its compounds to translate *ʿrb* II; similarly it uses *epi/sym/míktos* for *ʿēreḇ* II. All the occurrences of *ʿēreḇ* I are represented by *krókē*, "yarn, cloth"; *ʿārōḇ* is rendered as *kynómuia*, "dog-fly." Both *ʿāraḇ* III and *ʿārēḇ* have a wide variety of translations: *hēdýnein/hēdýs/hēdéōs* (6 times), *ek/en/déchesthai, epimignýnai*, etc., once each.

There are 13 occurrences of *ʿrb* II in the Dead Sea Scrolls and 4 (?) of *ʿrb* III. The occurrences of *ʿrb* II in the disciplinary regulations of 1QS go back to the early period of the Essene movement at Qumran. It is a fundamental axiom that the property of the community must not be "confused" with the possessions of outsiders, postulants, novices, etc. (1QS 9:8; later elaborations include 9:8, followed by 6:17,22; 7:24). The Temple Scroll uses *ʿrb* II in cultic regulations. The functional structures within the temple precincts are to be so erected as to achieve maximal lucidity. There must be no way to "intermingle" the temple utensils (11QT 45:4), the sacrifices of the priests (35:12), and those of the people (37:11). The water with which the sacrificial animals are washed must finally be removed by a separate drain so that no one can touch it, since it is "mixed" with sacrificial blood (32:15). Finally, a theological statement is made in 1QH, a soteriological confession of faith, where the hymnodist appears to pray that the Spirit of God (?) may be "united" with his own spirit. The other occurrences of *ʿrb* II (1QS[b] 4:2; 4QOrd[b] [4Q513] fr. 10 2:3) and *ʿrb* III (4Q186 fr. 1 1:6; 4Q186 fr. 2 2:2) are in extremely fragmentary contexts.

CD 11:4, "No one must establish an *ʿērûḇ* [*ytʿrb*] voluntarily on the sabbath," may be an early attack on a practice later regulated by the tractate *ʿErubin*, "Mixtures, Combinations": a combination of courtyards and passageways to evade the law governing how far one may travel on the sabbath.

Fabry — Lamberty-Zielinski

---

19. Contra W. Zimmerli, *Ezekiel 1. Herm* (Eng. trans. 1979), 330, 347. Cf. *BHS*.

עֶרֶב ʿereḇ; עָרַב ʿāraḇ; מַעֲרָב maʿ*ᵃ*rāḇ

I. 1. Egyptian; 2. Akkadian. II. Etymology. III. 1. Extrabiblical Occurrences; 2. OT Occurrences. IV. 1. Chronological Usage; 2. Geographical Usage. V. Contexts: 1. Cult; 2. Creation; 3. Peril; 4. Deliverance. VI. LXX. VII. Dead Sea Scrolls.

I. 1. *Egyptian.* In Egyptian, evening is divided into *mšrw,* the time around sunset when there is still light, and *wḫꜣ/ḫꜣw,* the dark portion of the evening, when the stars are visible.[1]

Evening comes with the departure of the sun god, who visits the realm of the dead; it is marked by the cessation of all activity. By virtue of her sovereignty over the western desert, where the sun sets, Hathor becomes the Mistress of the Evening *(mšrw).*[2]

2. *Akkadian.* As the extrabiblical occurrences and some of the OT occurrences show, *ʿereḇ* derives from the root *ʿrb* with the meaning "enter."[3] In other words, when *ʿrb* is predicated of the sun, it is entering its dwelling place: it sets and evening begins. This sense is illustrated also by the Heb. verb *ʿāraḇ* V, "become evening" (Jgs. 19:9; Sir. 36:31), "come to an end" (Isa. 24:11), as well as Akk. *erēbu* and Ugar. *ʿrb* and *mʿrb.*[4]

The assumption of further etymological associations of *ʿrb* with *ʿrp* should be rejected; likewise derivation from Akk. *erēpu,* "become overcast, darken."[5] There is no apparent connection between *ʿereḇ* and *ʿᵃrāḇâ,* "desert."[6]

ʿereḇ. F. M. T. Böhl, "בין הערבים," *OLZ* 18 (1915) 321-24; G. B. Bruzzone, "'EREB nell'AT," *BibOr* 23 (1981) 65-70; G. Dalman, *AuS,* I/2 (1928), 620-30; K. Elliger, "Das Ende der 'Abendwölfe' Zeph 3,3 Hab 1,8," *FS A. Bertholet* (1950), 158-75; P. J. Heawood, "The Beginning of the Jewish Day," *JQR* 36 (1945/46) 393-401; B. Jongeling, "Jeux de mots en Sophonie III 1 et 3?" *VT* 21 (1971) 541-47; H. Lesêtre, "Soir," *DB,* V (1912), 1824-25; J. A. Loader, "The Concept of Darkness in the Hebrew Root *ʿrb/ʿrp,*" *De fructu oris sui. FS A. van Selms* (1971), 99-107; E. Mahler, "Die chronologische Bedeutung von ערבים und צהרים," *ZDMG* 68 (1914) 677-86; J. Nelis, "Abend," *BL*³ (1982), 5-6; S. J. Schwantes, "*ʿereḇ bōqer* of Dan 8,14 Re-examined," *AUSS* 16 (1978) 375-85; H. R. Stroes, "Does Day Begin in the Evening or Morning?" *VT* 16 (1966) 460-75; R. de Vaux, *AncIsr,* I, 180-83; W. A. van der Weiden, "Radix hebraica ערב," *VD* 44 (1966) 97-104; S. Zeitlin, "The Beginning of the Jewish Day During the Second Commonwealth," *JQR* 36 (1945/46) 403-14; J. Ziegler, "Die Hilfe Gottes 'am Morgen,'" *FS F. Nötscher. BBB* 1 (1950), 281-88.

1. E. Hornung, *LexÄg,* IV, 291-92; idem, *ZÄS* 86 (1961) 106-11; 87 (1962) 116-17, 119.
2. E. Hornung, "Licht und Finsternis in der Vorstellungswelt Altägytens," *StudGen* 18 (1965) 73-83.
3. For extrabiblical occurrences see III.1 below; for the OT see III.2.
4. See *GesB,* 615; *HAL,* II, 877; Loader, 99-100; *CAD,* IV, 269; *AHw,* I, 234; *WUS,* no. 2039.
5. Contra, respectively, Loader, 101-7; *CAD,* IV, 279-80.
6. Contra A. P. B. Breytenbach, "The Connection between the Concepts of Darkness and Drought as Well as Light and Vegetation," *FS A. van Selms* (1971), 2.

In Hebrew two nouns derive from *ʿrb* IV: (a) *maʿ^{a}rāḇ,* "setting (place of the sun)" (Isa. 43:5; 45:6; 59:19; Ps. 75:7[Eng. v. 6]; 103:12; 107:3), "west" (1 Ch. 7:28; 12:16[15]; 26:16,18,30; 2 Ch. 32:30; 33:14); and (b) *ʿereḇ,* denoting the evening (see III.2 below). In one text (Ps. 65:9[8]), *ʿereḇ* denotes the west. The segholate *ʿereḇ* represents a form of the root *ʿrb* found only in Hebrew, since in Old South Arabic, Syriac, Akkadian, and Ugaritic the word for "evening" does not derive from the root *ʿrb.*

III. 1. *Extrabiblical Occurrences.* In East Semitic the root *ʿrb* is represented by the verb *erēbu,* "sink," and the construct phrase *ereb šamši,* which means "sunset."[7]

In Northwest Semitic we find Ugar. *ʿrb,* "sunset," and *mʿrb,* "sinking."[8] Comparable are Aram. *mʿrb,* "sinking, west," and Syr. *ʿrb,* "sink," *mʿrb,* "west," and *mʿrby,* "western."[9]

In Old South Arabic the nouns *mʿrb/mʿrbyt,* "west," and *mʿrby,* "western," derive from *ʿrb* I.[10]

2. *OT Occurrences.* The 130 OT occurrences of *ʿereḇ* are found primarily in the Pentateuch (13 in Genesis, 13 in Exodus, 33 in Leviticus, 13 in Numbers, 5 in Deuteronomy) and the Deuteronomistic History (4 in Joshua, 4 in Judges, 3 in 1 Samuel, 3 in 2 Samuel, 2 in 1 Kings, 1 in 2 Kings). Occurrences are less common in the Prophets (1 in Isaiah, 1 in Jeremiah, 5 in Ezekiel, 2 in Zephaniah, 1 in Haggai, 1 in Zechariah), wisdom literature (2 in Job, 1 in Proverbs, 1 in Ecclesiastes), the Psalms (8), and apocalyptic literature (3 in Daniel). There are more occurrences in the Chronicler's History (3 in Ezra, 2 in 1 Chronicles, 5 in 2 Chronicles).

IV. 1. *Chronological Usage.* a. *Period of the Day.* The three terms → בקר *bōqer,* → צהרים *ṣoh^{o}rayim,* and *ʿereḇ* denote the three major periods of the day (cf. Ps. 55:18a[17a]). Our word means the close of the day (→ יום *yôm*), marked by sunset, as shown by the frequent combination of *ʿereḇ* with *bôʾ haššemeš* (Dt. 16:6; 23:12[11]; Josh. 8:29; 10:26-27; 2 Ch. 18:34; cf. Prov. 7:9).

As a term referring to the close of the day, *ʿereḇ* also denotes the end of work (Gen. 30:16; Jgs. 19:16; Ruth 2:17; Ps. 104:23; but cf. Eccl. 11:6), the time to draw water (Gen. 24:11) and to walk in the fields (Gen. 24:63; cf. Gen. 3:8) or to pitch camp for the night (2 S. 11:13; Zeph. 2:7), and the time to bring the bride to the bridegroom (Gen. 29:23). In this sense *ʿereḇ* can denote either a period of time or a point in time; the latter usage is apparent in the temporal expressions *l^{e}ʿēṯ ʿereḇ* (Gen. 8:11; 24:11; 2 S. 11:2), *ʿēṯ minḥaṯ ʿereḇ* (Dnl. 9:21; Ezr. 9:4-5), *ʿaḏ hāʿereḇ* (1 S. 20:5), *b^{e}ʿereḇ* (Gen. 19:1; 29:23; Ezk. 12:4,7), and *lipnôṯ ʿereḇ* (Gen. 24:63).

When *ʿereḇ* is used in combination with *bōqer,* the time span denoted by the pair can be either day or night. The phrase *mēʿereḇ ʿaḏ-bōqer* (Ex. 27:21; Lev. 24:3; Nu. 9:21;

7. *CAD,* IV, 258-59; *AHw,* I, 233-34.
8. *WUS,* no. 2093.
9. For Aramaic see *DNSI,* II, 671; *KAI* 215.13-14; Beyer, 664. For Syriac, *LexSyr,* 546-47.
10. Beeston, 18.

cf. Nu. 9:15), which appears in cultic contexts, refers to the entire night; the same period is expressed in Nu. 9:15 by *bā'ereḇ 'aḏ-bōqer* and in Est. 2:14 by *bā'ereḇ ûḇabbōqer.* Conversely, the phrase *min-(hab)bōqer 'aḏ-(hā)'ereḇ* (Ex. 18:13-14) or *mibbōqer lā'ereb* (Job 4:20) refers to the course of the entire day. This is also true of the phrases *'aḏ 'ereḇ bōqer* (Dnl. 8:14) and *mēhannešep w^e'aḏ hā'ereḇ* (1 S. 30:17; cf. Prov. 7:9).

Another use of the *'ereḇ-bōqer* pair refers not to a period of time but to distinct points in time associated with a common action and its consequences. In Gen. 49:27, for example, the parallelism of the two words suggests continual action.[11] The parallelism of *'ereḇ* and *bōqer* in Dt. 28:67 and Eccl. 11:6 is comparable: in the former it indicates that the state of dread is persistent; in the latter it describes unremitting activity. Ex. 16:6-7 assigns the knowledge of God's guidance to the evening and the vision of God's glory to the morning; here too the text does not refer to separate and distinct events — rather, *'ereḇ* and *bōqer* are used idiomatically for "soon."[12] The situation differs in Ex. 16:8-12, where the promise of meat in the evening and bread in the morning refers to two distinct events.[13]

b. *bên hā'arbayim.* The meaning of the temporal expression *bên hā'arbayim* (Ex. 12:6; 16:12; 29:39,41; 30:8; Lev. 23:5; Nu. 9:3,5,11; 28:4,8) is disputed. With the exception of Ex. 16:12, the phrase always appears in a cultic context (see IV.2 below); it seems to represent a dual (no pl. of *'ereḇ* is attested). But the only reason for interpreting the noun as a dual is the preceding prep. *bên;*[14] in fact, however, treatment of *bên* as a dual was based on the erroneous interpretation of *'arbayim* as a dual, whereas in reality it is an adverbial form.[15] Analysis of the cultic contexts of this formula shows that the reference is to a single evening, not two; this observation argues against the noun's being a dual. The phrase *bên hā'arbayim* can be understood as meaning "at twilight."[16]

Böhl theorized that in this formula *'ereḇ* means "setting" and that the phrase *bên hā'arbayim* refers to the settings of the sun and moon, and should therefore be understood as meaning "as long as the moon is in the sky"; the expression was transferred from the night of Passover to every night.[17] This theory is untenable.

The Samaritans and the Pharisees arrived at differing interpretations of *bên hā'arbayim* with reference to the sacrifice of the Passover lamb: the former understood the phrase to mean the time between sunset and total darkness (cf. Dt. 16:6); the latter understood it to mean the time between the sun's approaching the horizon and its setting.[18]

---

11. C. Westermann, *Genesis 37–50* (Eng. trans. 1986), 241.
12. B. S. Childs, *Exodus. OTL* (1974), 287.
13. Ibid.
14. T. Nöldeke, *ZA* 30 (1915) 168; JM, §91g.
15. Cf. *GK,* §88c; *BLe,* §63b′; Nelis, 6.
16. K. Elliger, *Leviticus. HAT* I/4 (1966), 302, 313; E. Zenger, *Das Buch Exodus* ([2]1982), 118, 164; Childs, *Exodus,* 179, 182, 272, 520-21.
17. Pp. 323-24.
18. Nelis, 6; Bruzzone, 65; Lesêtre, 1824.

c. *Verb.* The verb *ʿrb* IV also indicates time, as Jgs. 19:9 shows *(rāp̄â hayyôm laʿᵃrōḇ):* the waning *(rāp̄â)* of the day brings evening. The Isaiah apocalypse uses *ʿārab̲* figuratively in parallel with → גלה *gālâ* to describe the departure of all joy. The hiphil of *ʿārab̲* means "do in the evening"; 1 S. 17:16 uses it in parallel with *hiškîm,* "do in the morning." In Prov. 7:9 emendation of the MT on the basis of Jgs. 19:9 should be rejected, since the *lectio difficilior* of the MT makes sense.[19]

d. *Beginning of the Day.* The use of *ʿereḇ* in the story of creation (Gen. 1:5,8, 13,19,23,31) and in cultic texts (Ex. 12:18; Lev. 15:5-27; 23:32; Dnl. 8:4; cf. the religiously grounded law in Dt. 21:23) has occasioned the surmise that a day was reckoned from one evening to the next.[20] Even if this theory cannot be demonstrated for the P[G] creation account in Gen. 1 (see V.2 below), in cultic contexts the day begins with the preceding evening. This method of reckoning days is found from the postexilic period on, but even then it did not apply to secular chronology.[21]

2. *Geographical Usage.* As a designation for the geographical term "west," *ʿereḇ* appears only once, in Ps. 65:9(8); elsewhere the word for "west" is *maʿᵃrāḇ.* It makes its first appearance in Deutero-Isaiah (Isa. 43:5; 45:6) and Trito-Isaiah (59:19); it appears also in the Psalms (75:7[6]; 103:12; 107:3), the Chronicler's History (1 Ch. 7:28; 12:16[15]; 26:16,18,30; 2 Ch. 32:30; 33:14), and Daniel (8:5). In all its occurrences, it is a *mem*-locale formation based on *ʿārab̲,* "sink," denoting the place where the sun sets.

V. Contexts.

1. *Cult.* Evening plays a special role in the cult. The new day — including sabbaths and festivals — begins with evening. An origin of this chronological system in Israel's nomadic tradition is neither demonstrable nor credible;[22] neither can the creation tradition of Gen. 1 be cited as its basis (see V.2 below). It is preferable to stress (with Dt. 16:6) that the exodus from Egypt took place in the evening.

Neh. 13:19 attests to the beginning of the sabbath in the evening.[23] The duration of the Day of Atonement is defined as being *mēʿereḇ ʿaḏ-ʿereḇ* (Lev. 23:32), and the eating of unleavened bread begins in the evening and lasts until evening on the fourteenth day (Ex. 12:18). The gate of the inner court of the temple is to be opened on the sabbath and on the day of the new moon and is not to be shut until evening, i.e., at the end of the day (Ezk. 46:2).

In the context of Passover, several passages use the phrase *bên hāʿarbayim* to denote the time when the Passover lambs are slain (Ex. 12:6; cf. Dt. 16:4,6) and Passover is celebrated (Nu. 9:3,5,11; Lev. 23:5; cf. Josh. 5:10). Only in Dt. 16:6 do we find the explanation that this is the hour of the exodus from Egypt.

---

19. Contra *BHK/BHS.*
20. M. Noth, *ZDPV* 74 (1958) 138 n. 18; W. H. Schmidt, *WMANT* 17 (³1973), 68.
21. Zeitlin, 403-414.
22. Cf. U. Cassuto, *Comm. on the Book of Genesis,* I (Eng. trans. 1961), 29-30.
23. De Vaux, 181-82; Stroes, 464-65.

Apart from the context of Passover, a lamb is to be offered every morning and every evening (Ex. 29:39,41; Nu. 28:4,8), as well as a grain offering (Lev. 6:13[20]; 2 K. 16:15) and a burnt offering (Ezr. 3:3). From evening to morning, a lamp is to burn before Yahweh in the tent of meeting (Ex. 27:21; 30:8).

Evening marks the end of petitions and lamentations to Yahweh (Josh. 7:6; Jgs. 20:23; 21:2; 2 S. 1:12) as well as fasting (Jgs. 20:26; 2 S. 1:12). Vows are binding until evening (1 S. 14:24), and the sabbath ends at evening (Lev. 23:32). Evening fulfills an important function in the context of cultic cleanness, since uncleanness contracted in the course of the day lasts until evening (Lev. 11:24-25,27-28,31-32,39-40; 14:46; 15:5-7,8,10-11,16-19,21-23,27; 17:15; 22:6; Nu. 19:7-8,10,21-22) and cleanness begins in the evening (Lev. 17:15; Nu. 19:19; Dt. 23:12). This role of evening as the boundary between clean and unclean is connected with the cultic chronological system of the postexilic period, which counts each day as beginning with evening. The juridical day also ends at evening, as we can see from the removal of the body of an executed individual in the evening (Dt. 21:23; Josh. 8:29; 10:16-17; 11QT 64:11; cf. Mk. 15:42ff. par.; John 19:31).

The evening offering (Ex. 29:39; 30:8; Lev. 6:13[20]; Dt. 16:4; 2 K. 16:15; Ps. 141:2; Dnl. 9:21; Ezr. 3:3; 9:4-5; 1 Ch. 16:40; 23:30; 2 Ch. 2:3[4]; 13:11; 31:3) is a → **מנחה** *minḥâ* or an → **עלה** *'ōlâ*. The offering of the *minḥâ* took place at the ninth hour (3:00 p.m.), as is shown clearly in Ezr. 9:4-5, where the Peshitta replaces Heb. *minḥaṯ hā'ereḇ* with *ltš' š'ym.*[24] In the preexilic period there was an official grain offering *(minḥâ)* only in the evening (1 K. 18:29; 2 K. 16:15; cf. Ezr. 9:4), while the burnt offering took place in the morning.[25] In Lev. 6:13(20) there is a doubling of the still independent grain offering. As the sacrificial system developed, there came into being "a combination of burnt offering and grain offering in the morning with simultaneous replacement of the independent evening grain offering by a combination that included a burnt offering,"[26] as documented by Ex. 29:39 and Nu. 28:4, as well as the relevant texts in the Chronicler's History (1 Ch. 16:40; 2 Ch. 2:3[4]; 13:11; 31:3).

2. *Creation.* Many scholars claim that in the P^G creation story each day begins with evening.[27] That this is not the case can be seen from the correct translation of *wayᵉhî 'ereḇ* (Gen. 1:5,8,13,19,23,31), "and then evening came," so that in each case *'ereḇ* marks the conclusion of an act of creation.[28] On the first day, the process of creation begins with the creation of light, not with evening;[29] this also argues against reckoning the days as beginning with evening. Furthermore, the expression *wayᵉhî 'ereḇ* refers to

---

24. See *BHS.*

25. Elliger, *HAT,* I/4, 97.

26. Ibid.; W. Kornfeld, *Levitikus. NEB* (1983), 29.

27. For example, E. A. Speiser, *Genesis. AB* 1 (²1964), 5; W. H. Schmidt, *Die Schöpfungsgeschichte der Priesterschrift. WMANT* 17 (³1973), 68.

28. E. Zenger, *Gottes Bogen in den Wolken. SBS* 112 (1983), 68-69 n. 61, 185; de Vaux, 181; Bruzzone, 65.

29. De Vaux, 181; Schwantes, 385; Zenger, 68-69 n. 61.

the night that follows the day but does not explicitly mention night, since night already had negative connotations as the time of peril.[30]

These observations help explain the expression *('aḏ) 'ereḇ bōqer* in Dnl. 8:14, which does not refer to a day beginning with evening in a cultic context, but rather, influenced by the language of P^G in Gen. 1, denotes the entire day.[31]

3. *Peril.* In contrast to "God's help in the morning," evening marks the onslaught of menace and dread; in this context we observe that nowhere is God's help mentioned in connection with the evening offering.[32] This antithesis of evening and morning with their different connotations is especially clear in Ps. 30:6(5).

The menace of evening is clear when *'ereḇ* marks the onset of terror (Isa. 17:14) or the coming of death (1 K. 22:35; Ezk. 24:18; Ps. 90:6; 2 Ch. 18:34), bringing weeping (Ps. 30:6[5]) and lamentation (Ps. 55:18[17). Conversely, victorious battles last until evening (Ex. 17:12-13); if the day is not long enough, the sun must stand still to postpone evening (Josh. 10:12-13). Ps. 59:7,15(6,14) with its image of prowling dogs also associates negative connotations with *'ereḇ*. In the frequently cited texts Hab. 1:8 and Zeph. 3:3, *'ᵃrāḇâ,* "steppe," should be read instead of *'ereḇ*.[33]

The negative connotations of evening are linked to ancient mythological themes from the pre-Israelite period. "In the evening, the anonymous . . . foe assaults the city on the mountain of God; in the morning, the foe has vanished miraculously."[34] Isa. 17:12-14 in particular should be read in this light. In the background stands Shalem, the city god of Jerusalem, who is identified with sunset or the evening star.[35]

4. *Deliverance.* In contrast to the negative connotations of *'ereḇ,* four texts speak of *'ereḇ* as the time of deliverance. This is clearly the case in Ex. 16:6 and 16:12 (P^G). Similar to the latter is the feeding of Elijah in the morning and in the evening in 1 K. 17:6.

According to Zec. 14:6-7, which belongs to the last supplement to the book of Zechariah, the natural order will be abolished at the eschaton: the light of day will not vanish at evening time and the alternation of day and night will cease. In other words, the final state of salvation will be accomplished when there is still light at evening and "the primordial human fear of the darkness of night" is banished, so that the negative connotations so often associated with *'ereḇ* are overcome by the positive connotations of light.[36]

---

30. O. H. Steck, *Der Schöpfungsbericht der Priesterschrift. FRLANT* 115 (^{2}1981), 175; de Vaux, 181; Zenger, 68-69 n. 61.

31. Schwantes, 384-85.

32. → II, 226-28; Ziegler, 284.

33. Elliger; K. Seybold, *Satirische Prophetie. SBS* 120 (1985), 57 n. 11; idem, *Beiträge zur prophetischen Bildsprache in Israel und Assyrien. OBO* 64 (1985), 35; contra Jongeling, 545, et al.

34. E. Otto, *VT* 30 (1980) 321.

35. H. Gese, *Die Religionen Altsyriens, Altarabiens und der Mandäer. RM* 10/2 (1970), 80-81, 168-69; Otto, *VT* 30 (1980) 321; F. Stolz, *Strukturen und Figuren in Kult von Jerusalem. BZAW* 118 (1970), 181-85, 204-18.

36. W. Rudolph, *Haggai-Sacharja 1–8-Sacharja 9–13-Maleachi. KAT* XIII/4 (1976), 236; → אור *'ôr.*

VI. LXX. To translate *ʿereḇ,* the LXX uses the substs. *espéra* and *deilḗ,* the adj. *delinós,* and the adv. *opsé.* For the verb *ʿāraḇ* hiphil, we find *opsízein,* and for the phrase *ʿereḇ bōqer* (Dnl. 8:14), *nychthḗmeron.*

VII. Dead Sea Scrolls. The Dead Sea Scrolls use *ʿereḇ* primarily in cultic contexts. The Essenes are to repeat the precepts of God at the onset of evening and in the morning (1QS 10:10). The times of prayer referred to here are also mentioned in 1QM 14:14 and 1QH 12:5. The evening *minḥâ* appears in 11QT 17:7. In 4Q503 3:6 we read of a prayer of blessing on the evening of the fifth day of the month; cf. 4Q503 8:12; 10:18; 42-44:4; 64:1; 72:8(?); 76:1. The role of evening in the laws governing cleanness (Lev. 11, etc.) is adopted in 11QT 49:20; 50:4,12; 51:3.

Niehr

עֹרֵב *ʿōrēḇ*

I. Ancient Near East; Etymology. II. OT Usage. III. LXX.

I. Ancient Near East; Etymology. The Semitic languages do not distinguish between ravens and crows. The raven appears in the pre-Sargonic bird list; the Sumerian-Eblaite dictionary[1] cites *ḫa/ga-ri-bù,* Akk. *āribu/ēribu.* In the Gilgamesh Epic a raven signals the end of the deluge: it leaves the ark, eats, croaks, and does not return.[2] Late Babylonian texts mention a guard whose function it was to keep rooks away. In Late Babylonian astronomical texts, the Raven Star *(Corvus)* is the star of Adad; it is also an alias for Mars and Saturn.[3] The raven plays a religious role in omen texts;[4] its head is a

---

ʿōrēḇ. N. Avigad, "על תארים וסמלים בחותמות עבריים," *ErIsr* 15 (1981) 303-5; F. S. Bodenheimer, *Animal and Man in Bible Lands* (Eng. trans. 1960), 57; G. R. Driver, "Birds in the OT. I. Birds in Law," *PEQ* 87 (1955) 5-20; J. Feliks, "Rabe," *BHHW,* III, 1545; J. Göttsberger, "יָצוֹא וָשׁוֹב in Gn 8,7," *BZ* 6 (1908) 113-16; G. L. Harding, *An Index and Concordance of Pre-Islamic Arabian Names and Inscriptions. Near and Middle East Series* 8 (1971), 453; B. Kedar, *Biblische Semantik* (1981), 114; J. A. Loader, "The Concept of Darkness in the Hebrew Root *ʿrb/ʿrp,*" *De fructu oris sui. FS A. van Selms* (1971), 99-107; W. Richter, *Traditionsgeschichtliche Untersuchungen zum Richterbuch. BBB* 18 (1963); H. Rösel, "Studien zur Topographie der Kriege in den Büchern Josua und Richter," *ZDPV* 92 (1976) 10-46; A. Salonen, *Vögel und Vogelfang im alten Mesopotamien. AnAcScFen* 180 (1973), 124-31, 178-80; L. Störk, "Rabe," *LexÄg,* V, 74-75; E. Tichy, *Onomatopoetische Verbalbildungen des Griechischen. SAW* 409 (1983), 129-31, 168; F. V. Winnett and G. L. Harding, *Inscriptions from Fifty Safaitic Cairns. Near and Middle East Series* 9 (1978), index p. 599.

1. *MEE,* IV, no. 295.
2. Gilg. XI, 152ff.
3. *AHw,* I, 68a.
4. *CAD,* I/2, 265-66.

magical substance. The relationship with *ḫaḫḫūru* (fem. *ḫaḫḫurtu*), which appears in lexical lists[5] but not in omen texts, is unclear.

The lexeme **'rb* has not been found in Ugaritic, Phoenician, Punic, or Old South Arabic inscriptions; it does appear in Arab. *ġurāb* (pl. *ġirbān*)[6] and Ethiopic, e.g., Amhar. *k'urā,* with loss of the *-b.* In the Aramaic family it is found in Samaritan, Jewish Aramaic, Christian Palestinian, Syriac, and Mandaic. The Jewish Aramaic derivatives *'ôrbā'* and *'ûrbā'* (fem. *'ôraḇtā'*) still convey overtones of pagan magic.[7] An adj. *'ārbîṯ,* "like a raven," also appears.

In Safaitic the name of the bird is also used as a personal name (like Arab. *ġurāb*).[8] In Jgs. 7:25; 8:3 (Isa. 10:16; Ps. 83:12[Eng. v. 11]), *'ōrēḇ* is the name of a Midianite captain who (according to an Ephraimite tradition?) was captured by Gideon's band and killed at Raven Rock. The personal names are possibly derivatives of the toponyms.[9]

The Hebrew PN *'ōrēḇ* appears on a seal reading *l-'rb/nby,* with the picture of a bird.[10]

Loader assigns to Sem. *'rb* the meaning "enter," extending to a variety of domains and undergoing further semantic development in particular languages.[11] Within the semantic domain "set (the sun) > evening/darkness/west," the Akkadian and Hebrew participle might suggest an etymology "black(bird)." The Bab. expression *erēbu ṣalmu,* "black raven," then shows that this etymology was forgotten. More likely the word is onomatopoeic, like Gk. *kórax* and the denominative verb *krṓzō (< *krōg-ie),* "croak."[12]

II. OT Usage. There were four species of *Corvus* in Israel, the most common being the raven *(Corvus corax),* a carrion eater. The corpses of executed criminals were not buried but were left exposed to such scavengers. The words of Agur (Prov. 30:17) threaten those who do not honor their parents with this degrading fate. The raven nests on mountains or in wadis. In Cant. 5:11 the woman compares the color of her beloved's hair to the black plumage of a raven.

The rook *(Corvus frugilegus)* is distinguished by a white spot around its beak. The hooded crow *(Corvus coronae),* indigenous to the Jerusalem region, is an omnivore that nests in tall trees. The brown-necked raven or desert raven *(Corvus ruficollis)* lives in the Negeb.

The regulations governing purity (Dt. 14:14; Lev. 11:15 [P]) classify all kinds of ravens and crows as unclean. As carrion eaters, they are described by prophetic oracles

---

5. Salonen, 178ff.
6. Wehr, 668.
7. Bab. *Shab.* 67b.
8. Ryckmans, I, 176b; G. L. Harding, *Index,* 453; F. V. Winnett and G. L. Harding, *Inscriptions,* 599.
9. Richter, 208ff.; Rösel, 16, 20.
10. Avigad, 305, with pl. 57.3.
11. Pp. 99-100.
12. Tichy.

of judgment as living among ruins (Isa. 34:11; Zeph. 2:4 LXX and Vulg.) with sinister and demonic creatures.[13]

The greed of these notorious scavengers nevertheless establishes a close relationship with Yahweh. The young ravens serve as models for how Yahweh nourishes his creatures (cf. Lk. 12:24). Ps. 147:9 LXX interprets their croaking as pleas heard by Yahweh (cf. Job 38:41).

Unclean ravens bring food to the miracle-worker Elijah in the pre-Deuteronomistic narrative 1 K. 17:5b-7; the DtrP recension emphasizes in v. 4 that they do so explicitly at Yahweh's command.

Gen. 8:7 (J) has Noah send out a raven before sending out a dove three times — analogously to the three different birds in Gilg. X. As a "variant," the raven stands outside the framework of J's bird scene: its flying to and fro does not contribute anything to Noah's knowledge. The final redaction nevertheless kept the raven, to show that the earth was still inundated. Or is the necrophagous raven to render the terrain around the ark cultically clean for the altar (Gen. 8:20-21) by devouring the carrion?

III. LXX. The LXX consistently translates *ʿōrēḇ* with *kórax,* using the plural to render the collective in Ps. 147:9; Zeph. 2:14; Isa. 34:11.

Angerstorfer

---

13. H. Wildberger, *Jesaja 28–39. BK* X/3 (1982), 1347ff.

עֲרָבָה *ʿᵃrāḇâ* → מדבר *miḏbār*

עָרָה *ʿārâ;* מוֹרָה *môrâ;* מַעַר *maʿar;* עֶרְוָה *ʿerwâ;* עֶרְיָה *ʿeryâ*

I. Etymology. II. Occurrences. II. Usage: 1. Verb; 2. Noun (outside the P Tradition); 3. Holiness Code; 4. Ezekiel. IV. LXX. V. Dead Sea Scrolls.

ʿārâ. A. Alt, "The Origins of Israelite Law," *Essays on OT History and Religion* (Eng. trans. 1966), 79-132, esp. 115-16; F. W. Bassett, "Noah's Nakedness and the Curse of Canaan," *VT* 21 (1971) 232-37; S. R. Bigger, "The Family Laws of Lev 18 in Their Setting," *JBL* 98 (1979) 187-203; M. Dahood, "Hebrew-Ugaritic Lexicography VII," *Bibl* 50 (1969) 337-56, esp. 354; K. Elliger, "Das Gesetz Leviticus 18," *ZAW* 67 (1955) 1-25; J. Halbe, "Die Reihe der Inzestverbote Lev 18,7-18," *ZAW* 92 (1980) 60-88; F. L. Horton, "Form and Structure in Laws Relating to Women," *SBLSP* 1 (1973), 20-33, esp. 21-24; R. Kilian, *Literarkritische und*

I. Etymology. Akkadian has a root *erû(m)* V that means "be destitute" in the G stem and "lay bare" in the D stem.[1] From the same root is derived a subst. *ūru(m)* II meaning "nakedness, female genitals," as well as *erium,* "naked."[2]

In Northwest Semitic we find in Phoenician the derivative *ʿrh* (D stem) and in Aramaic *ʿry* I (D), "strip," and *ʿrh* III, "naked."[3] The existence of an Ugaritic root *ʿry* was long a matter of debate.[4] Collation of one text has now found a verb *ʿrw* used in parallel with *ʾbd,* "go to ruin," here to be translated "destroy."[5] A verb *ʿry,* "be destroyed, be laid bare," is also attested.[6]

II. Occurrences. Besides the verb *ʿārâ,* the root *ʿrh* occurs in the derivatives *môrâ, maʿar, ʿerwâ,* and *ʿeryâ.* The verb appears 14 times, with no noteworthy distributional features. The situation differs in the case of *ʿerwâ:* 37 of its 54 occurrences are in priestly material (30 in Leviticus, 7 in Ezekiel); the remaining 17 occurrences are distributed among the Pentateuch (5 in Genesis, 2 each in Exodus and Deuteronomy), the Deuteronomistic History (1 in 1 Samuel), the Prophets (1 in Isaiah, 1 in Hosea), and Lamentations (1).

Of the other derivatives, *maʿar* occurs once (Nah. 3:5),[7] *ʿeryâ* 6 times (4 times in Ezekiel), and *môrâ* 3 times (Jgs. 13:5; 16:17; 1 S. 1:11).

III. Usage.

1. *Verb.* The verb *ʿārâ* is used in two different ways. Analogously to extrabiblical usage, it appears in the piel (Isa. 3:17; 22:6; Hab. 3:13; Zeph. 2:14; Ps. 137:7) and hiphil (Lev. 20:18,19; Isa. 53:12) in the sense "lay bare" as well as in the hithpael (Lam. 4:21) in the sense "strip oneself bare." It also appears in the niphal (Isa. 32:15) and piel (Gen. 24:20; Ps. 141:8; 2 Ch. 24:11) in the sense "be poured out" and "pour out, empty." These two uses of *ʿārâ* as "lay bare" and "pour out" do not represent two distinct meanings; we are dealing instead with modifications of the root's basic meaning "be naked, empty" so as to mean "lay bear," "pour out, or "empty," depending on the object.

The use of *ʿārâ* in the sense "lay bare" has various connotations. For example, Yahweh will "lay bare" the forehead/temples of the haughty women of Jerusalem,

---

formgeschichtliche Untersuchung des Heiligkeitsgesetzes. BBB 19 (1963), esp. 25-26, 71-84; W. Kornfeld, *Studien zum Heiligkeitsgesetz (Lev 17–26)* (1952), esp. 89-134; A. Phillips, "Some Aspects of Family Law in Pre-Exilic Israel," *VT* 23 (1973) 349-61; H. Graf Reventlow, *Das Heiligkeitsgesetz formgeschichtlich untersucht. WMANT* 6 (1961), esp. 52-64; R. Yaron, "On Divorce in OT Times," *RIDA* 4 (1957) 117-28.

1. *AHw,* I, 247-48.
2. For the former see *AHw,* III, 1435; for the latter, I, 241ff.
3. For Phoenician see *KAI* 14.21; for Aramaic, *DNSI,* II, 887.
4. Cf. *WUS,* no. 2097; *UT,* no. 1920.
5. *KTU* 1.14, I, 6-8. See M. Dietrich and O. Loretz, *Wort und Geschichte. FS K. Elliger. AOAT* 18 (1973), 31-36, esp. 33; L. Badre et al., *Syr* 53 (1976) 95-125, esp. 96-97.
6. *KTU* 2.38, 25.
7. On 1 K. 7:36 see M. Noth, *Könige. BK* IX/1 (1968), 145; J. Gray, *I and II Kings. OTL* ([2]1970), 196.

meaning that he will shave their heads (Isa. 3:17).[8] The use of *'ārâ* piel to mean "shave" also lies behind the nominal derivative *môrâ,* "razor" (Jgs. 13:5; 16:17; 1 S. 1:11). Another text from Isaiah (22:6) uses the piel of *'ārâ* to say that Kir "bares" his shield, i.e., removes it from its sheath (cf. Hab. 3:9).

The hiphil of *'ārâ,* used in parallel with *gālâ,* has the same meaning in Lev. 20:18 (P). Here the object is the pudenda of a menstruating woman. Lev. 20:19 also forbids laying bare (*gālâ* piel) the nakedness of one's kin, for to do so is to lay bare (*'ārâ* hiphil) a blood relation. The hithpael of *'ārâ* appears in Lam. 4:21, which speaks of stripping oneself bare in a frenzy (cf. Gen. 9:21-22). In Ps. 37:35 *'ālâ* should be read for *'ārâ* hithpael (cf. LXX).

Like Ugar. *'rw,* the piel of *'ārâ* can be used in an extended sense to signify an act of destruction, as in Zeph. 2:14, Hab. 3:13, and Ps. 137:7.[9] In combination with *y^esôḏ,* the piel appears to be a technical term denoting systematic destruction; cf. *gālâ* niphal/piel in Ezk. 13:14; Mic. 1:6 with the same object, *y^esôḏ,* and with *môs^eḏôṯ* in Ps. 18:16(Eng. v. 15) = 2 S. 22:16.

In the sense of "pour out," *'ārâ* piel can be used both concretely to mean "empty a jar" (Gen. 24:20; 2 Ch. 24:11) and figuratively with *nep̄eš* as its object (Ps. 141:8) to mean "pour out a person's life." The latter formulation, with the hiphil instead of the piel, appears with the same meaning in Isa. 53:12: the servant of Yahweh poured out his life. That these passages treat *nep̄eš* as a kind of fluid is connected with the fact that, as the vital principle, the *nep̄eš* is associated with the blood (Gen. 9:4-5; Lev. 17:11; Dt. 12:23; cf. also Lam. 2:12; Job 30:16).[10] Isa. 32:15 uses the niphal of *'ārâ* figuratively to describe an outpouring of the spirit; we may note that here we do not yet find the established terminology of → שׁפך *šāp̄aḵ* or → יצק *yāṣaq* for the outpouring of the spirit.[11]

2. *Noun (outside the P Tradition).* a. *Cult.* The earliest occurrence of *'erwâ* is in the altar law of the Covenant Code, which prohibits going up by steps to the altar, lest the nakedness of the priest be exposed (*gālâ* niphal, Ex. 20:26). The precise nature of the prohibited action described by *gālâ 'erwâ* is disputed. According to Noth, the purpose is to prevent the introduction of sexual practices into the cult of Yahweh; Cazelles thinks that the action could have resulted in improprieties.[12] Conrad believes that the explanation in 20:26b is secondary: the prohibition of a stepped altar was aimed originally at the cult of a high god.[13] Ex. 28:42 responds to 20:26b by requiring that linen undergarments be made to cover the "naked flesh" *(b^eśar 'erwâ)* of the priest.

---

8. See H. Wildberger, *Isaiah 1–12* (Eng. trans. 1991), 149.

9. On Ugar. *'rw* see *KTU* 1.14, I, 6-8. On the text of Zeph. 2:14 see W. Rudolph, *Micha-Nahum-Habakuk-Zephanja. KAT* XIII/3 (1975), 278-79; K. Seybold, *Satirische Prophetie. SBS* 120 (1985), 53-54.

10. See H. W. Wolff, *Anthropology of the OT* (Eng. trans. 1974), 19; H. Seebass, → IX, 514.

11. H. Wildberger, *Jesaja 28–39. BK* X/3 (1982), 1277.

12. Noth, *Exodus. OTL* (Eng. trans. 1962), 177; H. Cazelles, *Études sur le Code de l'Alliance* (1946), 44.

13. D. Conrad, *Studien zum Altargesetz* (1968), 17-18, 53-57, 123. See also B. S. Childs, *Book of Exodus. OTL* (1974), 467.

b. *Family.* The story of Noah's curse and blessing (Gen. 9:18-29; a short independent story incorporated into JE) presupposes male garments similar to those implied by Ex. 20:26.[14] Noah's drunkenness led him to expose himself (*gālâ* hiphil; on the motif cf. Lam. 4:21; Hab. 2:15); Ham saw his nakedness *(ʿerwâ),* which Shem and Japheth covered with a wrap (*śimlâ,* vv. 22-23). Ham's offense did not consist in seeing the nakedness of his father or committing a sexual transgression,[15] but in his failure to cover his father so as to spare his father the disgrace of nakedness (cf. 2 S. 6:20; 10:4-5; Isa. 47:3).[16] A similar view of a son's duty to his drunken father appears in Ugaritic.[17]

The expression *rāʾâ ʾeṯ ʿerwâ* in Gen. 9:22 appears in the later text Lev. 20:17 in parallel with *gālâ ʿerwâ.* Whether Lev. 20 can be used to interpret the story in Gen. 9:22-23, suggesting that Ham had sexual intercourse with his father's wives, is highly dubious.[18] There is likewise nothing to support Gunkel's view that a later reader took such offense at Noah's son's action that he left it out.[19]

Another early occurrence of *ʿerwâ* is in 1 S. 20:30, in the context of the story of David's rise: Saul accuses Jonathan of having sought out David to his own disgrace and to the disgrace of his mother's nakedness. Here *ʿerwâ* refers to the womb, indicating that Jonathan has lived in disgrace from the beginning.

c. *Captivity.* Isa. 47:3 also uses *ʿerwâ* to express the disgrace of nakedness: Babylon is treated like a female prisoner, who as a token of her humiliation must raise her skirts and display her nakedness; the exposure of her shame *(ḥerpâ)* is mentioned in parallel.

The context of Isa. 20:4 is also captivity: an explanatory gloss[20] calls the leading away of the naked Egyptians as a disgrace for Egypt *(ʿerwaṯ miṣrayim).* Mic. 1:11, too, uses *ʿeryâ* in the context of captivity. The addition of *bōšeṯ* represents a later interpretation emphasizing the shame of nakedness. The word was not yet in the text translated by the LXX.[21]

d. *Adultery.* In Hos. 2:11(9) the husband takes from his divorced wife the wool and flax she would use to cover her nakedness. Ancient Near Eastern marriage law allowed a man to divorce an adulterous wife without support.[22]

Ezk. 16 describes Jerusalem as an adulterous wife: here it is Yahweh who covers the nakedness *(kāsâ ʿerwâ)* of the young maiden (v. 8). Other expressions in v. 8 *(pāras kānāp ʿal, nišbaʿ lᵉ, bôʾ biḇrîṯ ʾeṯ)* suggest the establishment of a marital relationship.[23]

---

14. P. Weimar, *Untersuchungen zur Redaktionsgeschichte des Pentateuch. BZAW* 146 (1977), 158-60.
15. As proposed by Bassett, 233-37.
16. J. Scharbert, *Genesis 1–11. NEB* (1983), 100.
17. *KTU* 1.17, I, 30, etc.; see O. Eissfeldt, *KlS,* IV, 265, 268-69; C. Westermann, *Genesis 1–11* (Eng. trans. 1984), 488.
18. Contra Bassett, 233ff.
19. H. Gunkel, *Genesis* (Eng. trans. 1997), 80.
20. H. Wildberger, *Isaiah 13–27* (Eng. trans. 1997), 285; *BHS.*
21. On the MT see H. W. Wolff, *Micah* (Eng. trans. 1990), 44; on emendation of *ʿeryâ* to *ʿîr,* see *BHS* and J. L. Mays, *Micah. OTL* (1976), 49 n. 1.
22. H. W. Wolff, *Hosea. Herm* (Eng. trans. 1974), 37.
23. G. Giesen, *Die Wurzel šbʿ, "schwören." BBB* 56 (1981), 332-34.

The adulterous wife has uncovered her nakedness (*gālâ ʿerwâ,* v. 36)), and therefore Yahweh will now uncover her nakedness to her lovers (v. 37). This motif of disgracing a woman also lies behind Nah. 3:5, which says nothing about adultery.[24] Lam. 1:8, too, should be read against the background of disgracing an adulterous wife: here conquered Jerusalem must expose her nakedness like a humiliated wife.

e. *Divorce.* The construct phrase *ʿerwaṯ dāḇār* refers to a circumstance that provides occasion for a man to give his wife a certificate of divorce (Dt. 24:1); its meaning is disputed. The expression appears first in 23:15(14) in the context of regulations governing the purity of the camp, where its antithesis is *qāḏôš.* If Yahweh sees any *ʿerwaṯ dāḇār,* he will turn away from the camp. In the context of purity ordinances, *ʿerwaṯ dāḇār* here must be interpreted as something offensive. Hence in 24:1 the phrase must also refer to something offensive, but in a different context. The *ʿerwaṯ dāḇār* is to be interpreted as "anything which the husband found distasteful in his wife other than her adultery";[25] it does not refer to adultery, which incurs capital punishment (22:22).

f. *Topography.* In Gen. 42:9,12, *ʿerwaṯ hāʾāreṣ* refers to the "nakedness of the land," i.e., land without military defenses, which spies can reconnoiter (cf. Job 26:6).[26]

g. *Figurative Usage.* In Ezr. 4:14 Aram. *ʿarwâ* denotes the disgrace of refusal of tribute that threatens the king.

3. *Holiness Code.* In the Holiness Code *ʿerwâ* appears in Lev. 18 and 20; in all its occurrences (except Lev. 20:17a), it is the obj. of *gālâ.* Of the 29 occurrences of *gālâ ʿerwâ,* 20 are formulated as prohibitions. In Ex. 20:26, its earliest occurrence, *gālâ ʿerwâ* means "uncover the nakedness"; in Lev. 18 and 20, it refers to "sexual activity of whatever kind."[27] Lev. 18:6-18 is a decalogue, constructed with the prohibitive *lôʾ tᵉgalleh ʿerwâ* with the addition of an enclitic personal pronoun or a substantive, forbidding all kinds of sexual intercourse with blood relatives. The use of the expression *gālâ ʿerwâ* must be considered a euphemism.[28] (The passage actually comprises eleven commandments. The original text may have been either a dodecalogue,[29] because a prohibition referring to a daughter has been omitted by homoioarcton between vv. 9 and 10,[30] or a decalogue, if v. 13 is secondary, since it deals with a mother's sister, who is not part of the extended family.[31])

The basic constituent of the series is *ʿerwaṯ . . . lōʾ ṯᵉgalleh* plus the designation of a female relative. The pure form of the prohibition is preserved in vv. 8a,12a,15a, and

---

24. See W. Rudolph, *Micha-Nahum-Habakuk-Zephanja. KAT* XIII/3 (1975), 178; J. Jeremias, *Kultprophetie und Gerichtsverkündigung in den späten Königszeit Israels. WMANT* 35 (1970), 36-37.
25. Phillips, 355; cf. Yaron, 127-28.
26. Horton, 22.
27. Elliger, 8.
28. W. Kornfeld, *Levitikus. NEB* (1983), 70.
29. Elliger, *Leviticus. HAT* I/4 (1966), 238; idem, "Gesetz," 2; Kornfeld, *Levitikus,* 70.
30. Elliger, *HAT* I/4, 234.
31. Elliger, *HAT* I/4, 239; disputed by Halbe, 60-88.
32. Elliger, *HAT* I/4, 231.

16a; motivations and repetitions of the prohibition have been added secondarily (vv. 7bβ,15bβ).[32] According to Alt, the *lō' tᵉgalleh* series is comparable to the list of capital offenses (Ex. 21:12,15,17), the list of accursed offenses (Dt. 27:15-26), and the decalogue (Ex. 20:2-17; Dt. 5:6-21).[33] Our list is distinguished from the first two by its prohibitive formulation, which states the laws as direct prohibitions. The purpose is to prevent chaotic sexual relations from causing the shared life of the extended family to degenerate.[34] Proposed datings vary from the premonarchic to the preexilic period.[35]

Aspects of Lev. 18:7-17 are incorporated and in part modified in Lev. 20:11,17, 18,19,20,21. The reason for the incorporation of these prohibitions may be deduced from the difference: Lev. 18 states prohibitions, Lev. 20 lays down punishments.[36] A further difference is that Lev. 20 deals with a narrower circle of relatives than Lev. 18, no longer encompassing four generations of the extended family.

4. *Ezekiel.* In Ezk. 22:10 the expression *'erwaṯ-'āḇ gālâ* is to be understood as meaning that violation of the father's wife uncovers the father's nakedness. We may compare this usage to Dt. 23:1(22:30), where *lāqaḥ 'ēšeṯ 'āḇ* and *gālâ kᵉnap̱ 'āḇ* appear in parallel; and Dt. 27:20, where *gālâ kᵉnap̱ 'āḇ* parallels *šāḵaḇ 'im-'ēšeṯ 'āḇ*. Lev. 18:8 and 20:11 may also be cited. The occurrence in Ezk. 23:18 is a secondary addition to the book of Ezekiel;[37] here the familiar formula *gālâ 'erwâ* of the Holiness Code is used in the sense of "act lasciviously." In addition, there are four occurrences in Ezekiel of the term *'eryâ* in combination with the subst. → עֵרוֹם *'ērôm* (16:7,22,39; 23:29). In contrast to *'erwâ, 'eryâ* refers in 16:7,22 to the nakedness of a newborn infant, and in 16:39 and 23:29 to the nakedness of a woman bereft of her lovers, who is naked as a newborn child.

IV. LXX. In priestly contexts (Holiness Code and Ezekiel), the LXX translates *'erwâ* with *aschēmosýnē;* an exception is Ezk. 16:37, where the repeated *'erwâ* of the MT is differentiated from *aischýnē* and *kakía.* Other Greek terms for *'erwâ* are *gýmnōsis* (Gen. 9:22-23), *tá íchnē* (Gen. 42:9,12), and *apokálypsis* (1 S. 20:30). The construct phrase *'erwaṯ dāḇār* is rendered as *aschēmosýnē prágmatos* in Dt. 23:15(14) and as *áschēmon prágma* in Dt. 24:1. Heb. *'eryâ* is translated with *aschḗmōn.* In translating the verb *'ārâ,* the LXX reflects its varying connotations, translating it with *apokalýptein* when it means "lay bare" (Lev. 20:18-19), *enkenoún* when it means "pour out, empty" (Gen. 24:20; Ps. 137:7; 2 Ch. 24:11), *tapeinoún* when it means "shave" (Isa. 3:17), and *paradidónai* (Isa. 53:12) or *antanalískein* (Ps. 141:8 = LXX 140:8) when it is used figuratively.

---

33. Pp. 311-17.

34. H. J. Boecker, *Law and the Administration of Justice in the OT and Ancient Near East* (Eng. trans. 1980), 202.

35. Premonarchic: Elliger, *HAT* I/4, 239, et al. Preexilic: Kilian, 169.

36. Elliger, *HAT* I/4, 265, 271-72.

37. Zimmerli, *Ezekiel 1. Herm* (Eng. trans. 1979), 487-88.

V. Dead Sea Scrolls. At Qumran, exposing one's nakedness is subject to punishment: if a man takes out his hand (euphemism?) from under his clothes so that his genitals can be seen, he is to be punished for thirty days (1QS 7:13-14). We hear an echo of the Holiness Code in CD 5:10-11: "If a brother's daughter uncovers the nakedness of her father's brother, she is [nevertheless] a blood relative, [and is therefore guilty of incest]," even though this is not the case in Lev. 18, where the situation is stated from the perspective of the brother (v. 9). The construct phrase *'erwaṯ dāḇār,* familiar from Dt. 23:15 and 24:1, appears in 1QM 7:7 and 10:1 as *'erwaṯ dāḇār ra',* in the sense of a disgraceful matter (cf. 11QT 58:17). In 1QM 7:7, as in Dt. 23:15, it appears in the context of regulations governing the camp. Semantically comparable is 1QH 1:22, where the hymnodist describes himself as the quintessence of shame *('erwâ).* We find a similar expression in 1QH 12:25, where the hymnodist calls himself a "wellspring of uncleanness and of vile disgrace *('erwâ).*" In 1QH 13:15 the same expression is used to describe the counsel of sinners as a "vile disgrace." Also comparable is *mišpaṭ 'erwâ* (CD 5:9), which means "law of incest"; the context cites Lev. 18.

Only in 4QM[a] (4Q491) frs. 1-3:8 is *'erwâ* to be understood as "nakedness."[38]

Niehr

38. M. Baillet, *DJD,* VII, 15.

עָרוֹם *'ārôm;* עֵירוֹם *'êrôm*

I. Ancient Near East: 1. Egypt; 2. Mesopotamia; 3. Syria and Canaan. II. 1. Etymology; 2. Occurrences. III. Contexts: 1. Poverty; 2. Defeat, Captivity, Grief; 3. Adultery; 4. Cult, Ecstasy; 5. Revelation; 6. Summary. IV. LXX. V. Dead Sea Scrolls.

'ārôm. P. Behrens, "Nacktheit," *LexÄg,* IV, 292-94; A. van den Born, "Nackt," *BL,* 1212; A. van der Flier, "Enkele opmerkingen over het paradijsverhaal (Gen. 2:4b–3:24)," *Nieuwe Theologische Studiën* 20 (1937) 306-15, esp. 306-11; G. Fohrer, "Kleidung," *BHHW,* II, 962-65; E. Haag, *Der Mensch am Anfang. TTS* 24 (1970), esp. 49-50, 58-59; C. Kuhl, "Neue Dokumente zum Verständnis von Hosea 2,4-15," *ZAW* 52 (1934) 102-9; H. Lesêtre, "Nudité," *DB,* IV, 1712-14; F. Pfister, "Nacktheit," *PW,* XVI/2, 1541-49; H. Ringgren, "Nacktheit," *BHHW,* II, 1277; J. M. Sasson, "*w*^{e}*lō' yitbōšāšû* (Gen 2, 25) and Its Implications," *Bibl* 66 (1985) 418-21; A. Waetzoldt, "Kleidung. A. Philologisch," *RLA,* VI (1980), 18-31; B. N. Wambacq, "'Or tous deux étaient nus, l'homme et sa femme, mais ils n'en avaient pas honte' (Gen 2,25)," *Mélanges bibliques en hommage à B. Rigaux* (1970), 547-56; U. Winter, *Frau und Göttin. OBO* 53 (1983), esp. 93-199, 272-76.

I. Ancient Near East.

1. *Egypt.* In Egypt nakedness represents in the first instance absence of status; children and dead enemies are therefore depicted naked.[1] The nakedness of child deities should be considered a secondary assimilation to the way children are depicted; it is meant to lend expression to their youthfulness in the context of rebirth symbolism.[2] Deities thought of as children are thus depicted naked, as well as those concerned with procreation.[3] Humans are depicted naked when engaged in physical labor; also naked are female servants, typified as "concubines."[4] Imported gods like Qodshu are also depicted naked; here nakedness was already associated with them in their country of origin; even Bes has non-Egyptian features.[5] In the rare instances where the king is depicted naked, we are dealing with an allusion to the creator god.[6]

2. *Mesopotamia.* In Mesopotamian eyes, clothing is "the second self of its wearers, whose power is transferred to their clothing."[7] This is especially clear in Ishtar's descent to the netherworld: with every article of clothing she removes, she loses power. The majority of the population probably possessed only a single garment, which they wore at all times. Clothing could be stripped from the body of a person guilty of misconduct or serving as a hostage.[8] At Nuzi an adulterous wife was punished by being stripped and led away naked (cf. Hos. 2:5[Eng. v. 3]).[9] In ancient Sumer the cult was performed by priests who were naked to emphasize their cultic purity.[10]

3. *Syria and Canaan.* Representing the territory of Canaan, an illuminating ivory carving from Megiddo[11] depicts two naked prisoners tied to a horse drawing a chariot. Iconographically, the figures of naked goddesses are especially important: in Syria as a tutelary intercessor and mediator (nakedness being a sign not of helplessness but of specifically feminine power),[12] in Ugarit as a fertility goddess.

II. 1. *Etymology.* The etymology of the Hebrew lexemes *ʿārôm/ʿêrôm* is disputed. Some scholars derive them from *ʿwr* II, which appears in the niphal in the OT (Hab.

---

1. E. Hornung, *Conception of God in Ancient Egypt: The One and the Many* (Eng. trans. 1982), 102.
2. Behrens.
3. For the former see Hornung, 121-22; for the latter, Behrens, 293.
4. W. Helck, *LexÄg,* I, 684-86.
5. Behrens, 293.
6. Hornung, *Der Eine und die Vielen* (^{3}1983), 165; Behrens, 293.
7. Waetzoldt, 18.
8. Waetzoldt, 24.
9. Waetzoldt, 25; *CAD,* IV, 320.
10. See the illustrations in L. Delaporte, *Musée du Louvre. Catalogue des cylindres, cachets et pierres gravées en style orientale* (1920), 13, no. I.110.
11. *BHHW,* II, 927-28.
12. Winter, 192-99, 280.

3:9) with the meaning "be made bare."[13] Others postulate a root *ʿrm* III, associated with Aram. *ʿᵃram,* "lay bare," but otherwise unattested in Hebrew.[14] The same holds true for the proposal to derive these lexemes from a root *ʿēr* (< **ʿauir*) with the suf. *-ôm.*[15] Others, however, argue for derivation from *ʿārâ* with the addition of *-ôm,* so that *ʿārôm* could be considered a *qāṭûl* formation.[16]

To elucidate further the etymology of *ʿārôm/ʿêrôm,* we may note other East Semitic and North Semitic words with related roots. In Akkadian, for example, we find the adj. *erû/erium* with the meaning "naked, destitute."[17] From Aramaic we may cite Old Aram. *ʿrh,* "naked, exposed," and Imperial Aram. *ʿrh,* "naked, exposed, without."[18] Ugaritic has the adj. *ʿry,* "naked," the subst. *ʿrm,* "nakedness," and the adv. *ʿrym.*[19] Phoenician uses the D stem of *ʿry,* "lay bare."[20] A subst. *ʿaryaṯ,* "nude," occurs in Syriac.[21]

2. *Occurrences.* The adj. *ʿārôm* occurs 15 times in the OT (once each in Genesis, the Dtr History, Hosea, Amos, Micah, and Ecclesiastes; 5 times in Job; 4 times in Isaiah) and the form *ʿêrôm* 5 times (3 times in Genesis, twice in Ezekiel). The subst. *ʿêrôm* occurs 5 times (once in Deuteronomy, 4 times in Ezekiel). There is also a subst. *maʿᵃrummîm* derived from *ʿêrôm* (2 Ch. 28:15; Sir. 48:18).

III. Contexts.

1. *Poverty.* Most of the OT occurrences of *ʿārôm* appear in the context of poverty and need.

a. *Creation.* The four occurrences of *ʿārôm/ʿêrôm* in Gen. 2:25; 3:7,10,11 give the terms a key place in the structure of J's creation account. Their use in these texts did not originate in the earlier story adapted by J; together with the story of the serpent, it represents J's unique contribution to this account.[22] The first section ends in Gen. 2:25 with the statement that the man and his wife were naked *(ʿārôm)* and were not ashamed. In the second section (3:1-7), the seduction of both by the serpent culminates in the knowledge that they are naked (*ʿêrôm:* v. 7). In the third section (3:9-23), J has introduced into the earlier story the theme of nakedness *(ʿêrôm)* (vv. 10,11) and Yahweh's provision of clothing for the man and his wife (v. 21).[23] This shows that

13. *GesB,* 573, 620.
14. *GesB,* 620.
15. *BLe,* §61c‴.
16. W. von Soden, *ZA* 41 (1933) 118 n. 1; *HAL,* II, 882; *BLe,* §61c‴; *NSS,* §27g, p. 42 n. 1.
17. *AHw,* I, 242; *CAD,* IV, 320-21.
18. For Old Aramaic see S. Segert, *Altaramäische Grammatik* (1975) 546. For Imperial Aramaic see *DNSI,* II, 887.
19. See, respectively, *WUS,* no. 2097; *UF* 12 (1980) 430; *KTU* 1.16, II, 29-30.
20. *DNSI,* II, 887.
21. Brockelmann, *LexSyr,* 548.
22. L. Ruppert, *BZ* 15 (1971) 192-94; P. Weimar, *Untersuchungen zur Redaktionsgeschichte des Pentateuch. BZAW* 146 (1977), 154-58.
23. Weimar, 156.

knowledge of nakedness is an important accent introduced by J. This knowledge of nakedness must be seen in relationship to the pre-J motif of the knowledge of good and evil (2:9,17; 3:5,22). This relationship is suggested by the verb *yāḏaʿ*, common to both motifs, as well as the shared feature of opening the eyes (3:5,7).

At the same time, however, the varying interpretations of this motif indicate the difficulty of achieving an adequate understanding. For example, Görg, borrowing a reflection of von Soden, finds in the primal history of J a veiled criticism of Solomon.[24] He interprets the serpent as a symbol of the goddess Renenutet, whose functions as "nurturer" and "keeper of the wardrobe" he connects with the sequence "eating of the tree" and "knowing nakedness."[25] "The author discredits faith that relies on this deity as the final source of support (food and clothing), threatening to lose from view any specific orientation toward Yahweh."[26] Similarly, Wambacq believes that the nakedness in the primal history is to be understood as signifying that the first humans were "poor creatures, needing protection and help."[27] The motif of nakedness in the primal history does not suggest any aspect of sexuality, which is nowhere associated with *ʿārôm/ʿêrôm.*[28] But 2:25 and 3:7 should call attention to the reciprocal aspect of nakedness in 3:7,10.[29]

In interpreting the motif of nakedness, we note that there is a wordplay in Gen. 3 between *ʿārûm* and *ʿārôm/ʿêrôm:* the serpent's craftiness *(ʿārûm)* leads to knowledge of nakedness *(ʿārôm/ʿêrôm)* on the part of the man and woman. In Gen. 2:25 *ʿārôm* precedes the mention of the serpent's craftiness *(ʿārûm)* in 3:1, while in 3:7,10-11 nakedness is denoted by *ʿêrôm.* Here we have a differentiated presentation of nakedness, since it is not yet qualified negatively in 2:25. The choice of *ʿêrôm* in 3:7,10-11 (cf. Dt. 28:48; Ezk. 16:7,22,39; 18:7,16; 23:29) makes clear the negative connotation of the motif of nakedness.

b. *Distraint.* Nakedness can also result from distraint of a garment. Ex. 22:25-26(26-27) protects against this possibility by forbidding a lender to keep a garment taken in pledge beyond sunset (cf. Dt. 24:12-13; Job 24:7),[30] placing the naked debtor under the protection of God's mercy.

Distraint is also addressed in Job 22:6, where "exact pledges" stands in parallel with "strip the naked of their clothing." Job is accused of both transgressions, which are among the reasons God has inflicted judgment on him. The charge in 22:6 is aggravated by saying that Job has taken the pledges "for no reason" and that it is the naked who have been stripped of their clothing; the latter expression means "exploit the weak."[31] There is a similar association of distraint and nakedness in Job 24:7-10.

---

24. M. Görg, *BN* 16 (1981) 42-59; W. von Soden, *WO* 7 (1973/74) 228-40.
25. Görg, 50-53.
26. Ibid., 53.
27. Pp. 551-52.
28. On nakedness as a sign of poverty, see also Haag, 49-50; W. H. Schmidt, *Die Schöpfungsgeschichte der Priesterschrift. WMANT* 17 (^{3}1973), 213.
29. Sasson.
30. See also *KAI* 200.
31. → VII, 461.

Distraint also provides the context for Eccl. 5:12-16. Here, in contrast to Job 1:21, the expression *šûḇ ʿārôm* does not refer to human death but to the departure of the debtor from the creditor, who has taken the debtor's clothing in pledge.[32]

c. *Clothing the Naked.* Isa. 58:7 demands the clothing of the naked, along with setting free slaves and captives, feeding the hungry, and sheltering the homeless poor (vv. 6-7). Comparable is the clothing of the naked captives in 2 Ch. 28:15; here they are called *maʿarummîm* (abstract for concrete).[33]

Ezk. 18:5-9 describes the righteous man: he oppresses no one, restores to the debtor his pledge, commits no robbery, gives his bread to the hungry, and covers the naked with a garment (v. 7; cf. v. 16). In harmony with this ideal, deuterocanonical literature includes clothing the naked and feeding the hungry among the works of mercy (Tob. 1:17; 4:16).

d. *Infants.* Nakedness is also a sign of poverty and vulnerability when the text speaks of a newborn infant emerging from the mother's womb (Job 1:21).[34] This fundamental human condition is extended to other situations to express human need and vulnerability. Hos. 2:5(3) says that the adulterous wife will be stripped naked (see III.3 below) and exposed as on the day of her birth, and turned into a desert so that she will die of thirst.

2. *Defeat, Captivity, Grief.* In the context of defeat, nakedness can symbolize captivity or grief. Am. 2:16 describes a warrior who flees naked on the day of Yahweh. In Mic. 1:8 the prophet reacts to God's judgment on Judah and Samaria by lamenting and wailing, by going barefoot and naked, to express his grief.[35] The mention of going barefoot shows that *ʿārôm* refers only to removal of one's outer garment, not total nakedness.[36] On going barefoot as a sign of grief, see also 2 S. 15:30; Ezk. 24:17,23.

This combination of going barefoot and naked appears also in Isa. 20:2-4, in the context of a prophetic symbolic act. Yahweh commands Isaiah to loose the *śaq* from his loins and remove the sandals from his feet. The meaning of *ʿārôm* in this text is indicated by the term *śaq,* which can refer to a wrap covering the whole body as well as a loincloth. Unlike Mic. 1:8, Isa. 20:2-4 does not describe a display of grief: the prophet's symbolic act anticipates deportation, since prisoners of war were deported naked (cf. Job 12:17,19; 2 Ch. 28:15). In addition, nakedness together with hunger, thirst, and poverty is a sign of oppression by the enemy (Dt. 28:48).

3. *Adultery.* Hos. 2:5(3) uses nakedness as a sign of repudiation following adultery: the prophet threatens to strip his adulterous wife naked as on the day of her birth. Since Ex. 21:10 (cf. Isa. 4:1) requires a man to provide clothing for a woman he takes in mar-

---

32. N. Lohfink, *Kohelet. NEB* (1980), 44-45; contra Wambacq, 550; and A. Lauha, *Kohelet. BK* XIX (1978), 111, who associate *šûḇ* with death.

33. Lesêtre, 1712.

34. N. C. Habel, in *Die Botschaft und die Boten. FS H. W. Wolff* (1981), 374-75.

35. Wambacq, 550.

36. W. Rudolph, *Micha-Nahum-Habakuk-Zephanja. KAT* XIII/3 (1975), 42 n. 20.

riage, Hos. 2:5(3) implies release from this obligation if divorce is occasioned by the woman.[37] The disgrace of being stripped as a punishment for adultery is mentioned several times in the OT (Jer. 13:26-27; Ezk. 16:36-37; 23:10,29; Nah. 3:5).

4. *Cult, Ecstasy.* The adj. *ʿārôm* does not appear in any cultic context. Several texts protect against cultic nudity (Ex. 20:26; 28:42-43; Lev. 6:3; Ezk. 44:18). David's dancing before the ark (2 S. 6:14) may suggest partial nudity in a cultic context.

Nakedness as an ecstatic phenomenon is mentioned in the story of Saul among the prophets (1 S. 19:18-24). Here, as in Job 22:6; 24:7,10; Isa. 20:2-4, we may ask whether the text refers to total nudity or merely removal of one's outer garments.[38] The ecstatic context makes the former likely, especially since the description recalls nakedness occasioned by ecstasy or drunkenness outside the cult (Gen. 9:21; Hab. 2:15; Lam. 4:21).

5. *Revelation.* Job 26:6 uses nakedness figuratively to describe the relationship between God and the netherworld: *ʿārôm š^{e}ʾôl negdô.* It is exposed to God's gaze, defenseless before God's eyes (cf. Job 12:22; Ps. 139:8,11-12; Prov. 15:11). Sir. 42:18 is similar: *maʿ^{a}rummîm* (cf. Dt. 28:48) describes the secrets of the abyss and of the human heart, which are known to Yahweh.

6. *Summary.* It is striking that — except in Gen. 2:25 — all occurrences of *ʿārôm/ʿêrôm* are in negative contexts, in which the nakedness denoted by *ʿārôm/ʿêrôm* is a sign of poverty, need, vulnerability, grief, captivity, or adultery. The words have no discernible sexual connotations; when nakedness appears in a sexual context (Dnl. 13; 2 S. 11:2), a different term is used.

IV. LXX. The LXX always translates *ʿārôm/ʿêrôm* with *gymnós;* the only exception is Sir. 42:18, where *maʿ^{a}rummîm* means "secrets," which the LXX translates with *panoúrgeuma.* The subst. *ʿêrôm* is translated by *gymnótēs* in Dt. 28:48, elsewhere by *gymnós.*

V. Dead Sea Scrolls. There are few occurrences of *ʿārôm* in the Dead Sea Scrolls. According to 1QS 7:12, whoever walks naked before his neighbor without needing to is punished for six months. In 4Q166 2:12, a *pesher* on Hos. 2:8-11(6-9), hunger and nakedness *(ʿêrôm)* are described as a punishment from God.

Niehr

37. Waetzoldt, 25; Kuhl, 105-7.
38. Lesêtre, 1713.

עָרַךְ *ʿārak̲;* עֵרֶךְ *ʿērek̲;* מַעֲרָכָה/מַעֲרֶכֶת *maʿ^a^rāk̲â/maʿ^a^rek̲et̲*

I. Etymology. II. Meaning: 1. Verb; 2. *ʿērek̲;* 3. *maʿ^a^rāk̲â/maʿ^a^rek̲et̲.* III. Dead Sea Scrolls; LXX.

I. Etymology. Outside Hebrew, the etymon is well attested in Arab. *ʿaraka,* "grind," *ʿarika,* "be valiant in battle," *ʿarka,* "battle, fight," etc.[1] Most of the nominal derivatives in Arabic have something to do with battle and war. In the other Semitic languages, we find few or no occurrences. Both important and disputed is Ugar. *ʿrkn.*[2] Another text reads *b ʾrbʿt ʿšrt bʿl ʿrkn;*[3] these words have to do with a temple, loaves of bread set out before the deity, or a warrior.[4] Also disputed is *ʿrk lb.*[5] Phoen. *ʿrkt* may mean "rank."[6]

II. Meaning. The verb occurs 75 times, the nouns 33 times. The basic meaning of *ʿārak̲* is "lay out, arrange, set in order."

1. *Verb.* As the basic meaning clearly shows, *šulḥān ʿārûk̲* (Isa. 21:5; 65:11; Ezk. 23:41; Ps. 23:5; 78:19; Prov. 2:9) does not mean a table *on* which things are laid out, but a table — originally a piece of leather[7] — that has been spread out. The arrangement of things *on* a table is expressed by the combination *ʿārak̲ ʿal* (Ex. 40:23). Therefore *ʿārak̲* is the appropriate verb to denote the spreading out of such a "table." Thus Ezk. 23:41 describes Israel as sitting on a couch and spreading out her table. When objects are laid out, they are arranged horizontally, e.g., wood on an altar (Gen. 22:9; 1 K. 18:33) or stalks of flax on a roof (Josh. 2:6). "Laying out" words (e.g., Job 32:14) refers to a distinct presentation of words in consistent order, a coherent argument. The expression *yaʿr^e^k̲ehā lî,* "Let him set it forth before me" (Isa. 44:7; par. to *higgîd̲,* "proclaim"), shows that the meaning resides in the demanded logical sequence of ideas. Thus the verb is used in forensic contexts to denote presentation of a legal case (Job 13:18; 23:4). Finally, the verb often refers to the formation of battle lines (Jgs. 20:22; 1 S. 17:8; 2 S. 10:8). The noun *maʿ^a^rāk̲â* accordingly means "battle line."

ʿārak̲. S. Abramson, "לח קר הערוך," *Leš* 36 (1971/72) 122-49; J. Milgrom, *Cult and Conscience. SJLA* 18 (1976), esp. 13ff., 44-54; E. A. Speiser, "Leviticus and the Critics," *Oriental and Biblical Studies* (1967), 123-42; F. Zorell, "Zur Vokalisation des Wortes עֶרְכְּךָ in Lev. 27 und anderwärts," *Bibl* 26 (1945) 112ff.

1. Wehr, 608.
2. *UT,* no. 1920a.
3. *KTU* 1.105, 4.
4. See, respectively, M. Dahood, *Bibl* 50 (1969) 355; H. Cazelles, *VT* 19 (1969) 504; L. R. Fisher, *RSP,* II, 142; cf. *HAL,* II, 884.
5. *KTU* 1.114, 29; on the discussion see *HAL,* II, 884.
6. *CIS* 132, 4; *DNSI,* II, 888.
7. *AuS,* VII, 126; Kraus, *Talmudische Archäologie,* I, 58-59.

Building on the meaning "set forth," the nominal form *'ēreḵ* takes on the meaning "layer, row, valuation." The notion of laying out *enumerated* objects leads to the more abstract sense of valuation ("reckon" < *"extend, reach"). This secondary meaning of "liken, compare" appears in such passages as Isa. 40:18; Ps. 40:6(Eng. v. 5); 89:7(6). But the translation "liken" does not capture the meaning exactly, as Isa. 40:18 with *d^emûṯ* indicates. A more precise and literal translation would be: "What likeness will you reckon to him?"

Ps. 40:6(5) ("none can compare with you") can be evaluated similarly. Buber's translation "none can be set beside you" is clearer; the point is not that God is incomparable but that mortals are incapable of understanding God adequately and setting forth all his acts. The question "Who can be compared to Yahweh?" (Ps. 89:7[6]) should also be interpreted in this sense: Yahweh is incomparable, for only Yahweh himself can set forth what he is or what he has done. The noun *'ēreḵ,* "valuation," derives accordingly from the meaning "reckon."[8] In Ps. 55:14(13) *'^enôš k^e'erkî,* "a person like me," is not an exception, *HAL* notwithstanding.[9] The translation of *BDB* is closer to the mark: "according to my valuation." The notion behind the expression is that of an absolute valuation on the part of the speaker, not comparison of one person with another. In other words, *'āraḵ* refers to the speaker's valuation of another person, not the equality of both in the eyes of a neutral observer.

The hiphil *he'^erîḵ* (2 K. 23:35; Lev. 27:8,12,14) is probably a denominative from *'ēreḵ*.

2. *'ēreḵ*. The meaning of *'ēreḵ* derives from the basic meaning "spread out, set forth" via the secondary meaning "reckon." In the administrative vocabulary of the kingdom, it meant "tax assessment" and its result, "assessed value, census" (2 K. 23:35; cf. 12:5, often emended to *'ēreḵ 'îš k^e'erkô*).[10] Although most of the occurrences of the term are in Priestly texts, it is not characteristically Priestly. Assessment of an individual's worth naturally did not say anything about the value of an individual per se, since biblical law considered life and money incommensurable.[11] It was simply an approximate measure of economic productivity based on age and sex, the "estimated value, i.e. the sum of money 'which measures the standard of a person according to the usual values.'"[12] The term never referred primarily to a pure market value. According to Lev. 27:3ff., an adult male had an equivalent value of 50 shekels, a woman 30, a male less than twenty years old 20, a girl 10, etc.

In the sense of "equivalent," the noun always appears with a fossilized 2nd person sg. suffix *(-kā),* even when the noun is otherwise determined (e.g., Lev. 27:2,12,23). This has misled some into treating the suffixed form as a relic in which the suffix was

---

8. → כ *k^e*; → דמה *dāmâ.*

9. *HAL,* II, 885, with discussion.

10. *BHS.*

11. M. Greenberg, "Some Postulates of Biblical Criminal Law," *FS Y. Kaufmann* (1960), 5-28.

12. *HAL,* II, 885, quoting K. Elliger, *Leviticus. HAT* I/4 (1966), 386-87.

no longer perceived as such.[13] For comparison, Speiser cites *bō'ᵃk̲â* (Gen. 10:19,30) and Akk. *mimma šumšu,* which later appears with its own suffix, e.g., *mimmu šunšuia.* But neither of the proposed parallels represents a truly analogous case of so weakened a suffix. It is difficult to offer a satisfactory explanation for the form *'erkᵉk̲ā.* Although today the grammatical category of an "interrupted construct" is often accepted (e.g., Lev. 26:42; Hab. 3:8), *'erkᵉk̲ā* as a suffixed noun is inappropriate to its context. The explanations given by Ehrlich (*'erkᵉk̲ā* is a pil'al) and Feigin (*-kā* represents an afformative *-k* of uncertain meaning) are grammatically problematic or unproductive. In Lev. 27:23, too, there are two occurrences of *'ērek̲* determined by both definite article and suffix.[14]

However one treats the problem of the *-kā* in *'erkᵉk̲ā,* the context makes its meaning clear. It refers to the "monetary equivalent"[15] of an object or person to be redeemed. In the case of persons, this redemption is obligatory (Lev. 27:2-8; Nu. 18:15) and the price is fixed. In the case of an animal, the price is variable, since the value of an animal varies with the market. The monetary equivalent of persons is relatively arbitrary; it is less the actual sum that is of interest than the valuation in relation to the individual groups and to animals. The Hittite law code values a sheep at one shekel, a bull at ten shekels.[16] At Nuzi the guilty party (committing an act of violence or refusing to abide by an oath) must make compensation defined by the value of certain animals in the relationship one bull = one ass = ten sheep = ten shekels.[17] (The example of Nuzi is esp. important, because it can explain the *'āšām* offering, the object of the "valuation" in Lev. 5:15ff.; see below.) In other words, the market value of animals is "assessed" for each case, whereas the sums of money established for persons do not appear to represent any actual economic value. Such an estimate is intended to emphasize the importance of an individual's offering; it does not reflect any market conditions, nor does it define an ultimate value.[18]

Speiser connects the formula *bên ṭôb̲ ûb̲ên rā'* in Lev. 27:12 with the Nuzi texts describing an exchange of fields, which state that the agreement cannot be altered: *šumma eqlu mād lā inakkis šumma ṣeḫer/mīṣ lā uradda,* "if the land proves to be too large, it shall not be curtailed; if too small, it shall not be increased." This formula was later abbreviated to *miṣā mādā,* "small or large," or *lū mād lū ṣeḫer.*[19] In the same way, Lev. 27:12 appears to establish an average value.

Lev. 27 deals with the redemption of consecrated objects. Things capable of being sacrificed (i.e., animals) cannot be redeemed; human beings, who cannot be sacrificed, can be redeemed and are consecrated in the form of a sum of money determined according to an appropriate scale. Other consecrated objects (e.g., nonsacrificial animals,

13. *HAL,* II, 885; *GK,* §135q,r.
14. These are analogous to the forms cited in *GK,* §135r.
15. Speiser.
16. §§63ff.
17. Speiser, 126.
18. See Greenberg, "Some Postulates."
19. Speiser, 136.

houses, devoted property [*ḥērem*] excepted) can be redeemed by the person making the offering for their assessed value plus one fifth as a penalty for rescinding the vow. Consecrated objects can be resold for their assessed value to anyone other than the person offering them.[20]

3. *ma'ᵃrāḵâ/ma'ᵃreḵeṯ*. The nominal form *ma'ᵃrāḵâ*, "battle line," does not need separate discussion. The nominal form *ma'ᵃreḵeṯ* refers to the bread laid out on the table in the tabernacle. In Ex. 40:23 the term *'ēreḵ* refers in general terms to the arrangement of the bread. The nonspecific meaning of *'ēreḵ* is apparent in the lack of precision in the instructions for arranging the bread. Lev. 24:6 gives detailed instructions, describing an arrangement comprising "two rows of six [loaves] each." Despite the size of the loaves, the basic meaning of the root *'rk* indicates a horizontal arrangement. In later books *ma'ᵃreḵeṯ* in the construct phrase *leḥem ma'ᵃreḵeṯ* no longer means "row" in general; it is a technical term for "bread of the Presence."

The arrangement of the bread on the table illustrates on the one hand the use of the term in connection with ordinary meals (see II.1 above); at the same time, however, it suggests at least typologically a different conception of how offerings are made to the deity. Here, in contrast to the way things are generally offered to God, the bread is simply placed on a table. This type of offering is characteristic of Egypt and Mesopotamia, but is unusual in Israel. It is one of several signs that the tabernacle was thought of as the dwelling place of God, for whom drink and bread were provided.

III. Dead Sea Scrolls; LXX. There are 56 occurrences of the root in the Dead Sea Scrolls, 9 of the verb and 47 of *ma'ᵃrāḵâ;* with few exceptions, these are in the War Scroll. Usage is largely identical with that in the Bible, although *'ēreḵ* does not appear. Since the community meal played an important role at Qumran, we again find *'āraḵ* with *šulḥān* as its object (1QSᵃ 2:17; cf. also 1QS 6:4; 1QM 7:3). Once *miqṭereṯ* appears as object (1QM 2:5). The verb also refers to preparing for war (1QM 2:9; 1QH 4:24) and forming up for battle (1QM 2:9, with *milḥāmâ* as obj.). The most frequent form, however, is *ma'ᵃrāḵâ,* "line of battle," which is not surprising in view of the source (46 occurrences in 1QM). 11QT 8:9 refers to the arrangement of the bread of the Presence.

The LXX uses no fewer than 23 verbs to translate the verb, with a preference for *paratássein* (24 times), *etoimázein* (8 times), *synáptein* (5 times), *stoibázein,* and *timán* (4 times each). The noun *'ēreḵ* is translated 27 times by *timḗ* and related words, twice by *próthesis; ma'ᵃrāḵâ* is translated by *parátaxis* (16 times), *ma'ᵃreḵeṯ* by *próthesis* (6 times) and *théma* (3 times).

Firmage — Milgrom

20. For a discussion of the entire subject see Milgrom, 48.

עָרַל *ʿāral;* עָרֵל *ʿārēl;* עָרְלָה *ʿorlâ*

I. Linguistic Matters; LXX. II. Usage: 1. Ethnic Identity; 2. Relationship with God; 3. Lev. 19:23-25. III. Dead Sea Scrolls.

I. Linguistic Matters; LXX. The root *ʿrl,* attested in Akkadian, Aramaic, and Arabic,[1] appears in the Bible as *ʿorlâ,* "foreskin" (16 occurrences), *ʿārēl,* "uncircumcised" (32 occurrences), *ʿrl* qal, "leave uncircumcised," and *ʿrl* niphal, "show oneself uncircumcised" (1 occurrence each). In 1 S. 18:25,27; 2 S. 3:14, *ʿorlâ* refers to the whole uncircumcised member.[2]

Ezk. 32:27 is textually problematic; the reading *mēʿōlām* has been suggested on the basis of the LXX.[3] Also dubious is Hab. 2:16, where some scholars read *rʿl* niphal, "stagger," with *Q* and LXX.[4]

The LXX translates *ʿorlâ* with *akrobystía* (*akatharsía* in Lev. 19:23). It translates the phrase *ʿorlaṯ lᵉḇaḇkem* with *sklērokardía* in Jer. 4:4 and Dt. 10:16, and uses *aperítmētos* or *aperikáthartos* in Lev. 19:23 and 26:41. In Ezk. 32:27 it reads *apó aiṓnos.* The phrase *ʿorlaṯ śᵉpāṯayim* is translated as *álogos* (Ex. 6:12) or *ischnóphōnos* (Ex. 6:30). For *ʿrl* qal it uses *perikatharízō* (Lev. 19:23), for the niphal, *seíomai* (Hab. 2:16).

II. Usage.

1. *Ethnic Identity.* Possession of a foreskin is understood as the mirror image of circumcision. From the end of the patriarchal period on, it is a mark of ethnic difference, barring connubium (Gen. 34:14; cf. Jgs. 14:3). Various groups are referred to as uncircumcised: Shechemites (Gen. 34), Philistines, Babylonians (Isa. 52:1; Hab. 2:16 MT). During Israel's conflicts with the Philistines, "uncircumcised" became a term of opprobrium for the enemy (1 S. 14:6; 17:26,36; 31:4 = 1 Ch. 10:4; 2 S. 1:20). The two hundred members with foreskins that David brought Saul proved that he had been victorious two hundred times in battle with the Philistines. The assignment Saul had given him, intended to result in his death, he carried out successfully (1 S. 18:25,27; 2 S. 3:14).

ʿāral. K. Albrecht, *ʿOrlah (Vorhaut). Giessener Mischnah,* I/10 (1916); O. Eissfeldt, "Schwerterschlagene bei Hesekiel," *Studies in OT Prophecy. FS T. H. Robinson* (1950), 73-81; R. Gradwohl, "Der 'Hügel der Vorhäute' (Josua V 3)," *VT* 26 (1976) 235-40; H. J. Hermisson, *Sprache und Ritus im altisraelitischen Kult. WMANT* 19 (1965); F. Liebrecht, *Zur Volkskunde* (1879), esp. 94-96; A. Lods, "'La mort des incirconcis,'" *CRAIBL* (1943) 271-83; K. L. Schmidt, "ἀκροβυστία," *TDNT,* I, 225-26; → מול *mûl.*

1. *HAL,* II, 885.
2. *HAL,* II, 886.
3. W. Zimmerli, *Ezekiel 2. Herm* (Eng. trans. 1983), in loc.; *BHS,* in loc.
4. *BHS;* but cf. W. Rudolph, *Micha-Nahum-Habakuk-Zephanja. KAT* XIII/3 (1975), 221, who retains the MT.

2. *Relationship with God.* Ezekiel, Deutero-Isaiah, and P identify uncircumcision with cultic impurity (Ezk. 44:7,9; Isa. 52:1; Ex. 12:48). Possession of a foreskin is a sign of breaking the covenant (Gen. 17; Lev. 12:3; Ezk. 44:7). It was obviously not rare for spiritual pride to be rampant among the "circumcised." Boasting of the sign of the covenant, even members of the priesthood forgot that it is also possible to break the covenant by severing fellowship with God through disobedience and impenitence. Such people are circumcised in the flesh, but their hearts are still uncircumcised.[5] "Circumcise your hearts!" was Jeremiah's call to repentance — taken up also in other texts — shortly before the catastrophe of 587 B.C.E. descended on Jerusalem and Judah (Lev. 26:41; Dt. 10:16; Jer. 4:4; 9:24-25; Ezk. 44:7,9). Jerusalem's obdurate resistance to God was due to uncircumcised ears, as Jeremiah called the people's unwillingness to repent (Jer. 6:10). The notion of ears incapable of hearing God's word helps us understand the statement put by P in the mouth of Moses, to the effect that Pharaoh will not listen to him because his lips are uncircumcised (Ex. 6:12,30). This idiom is not intended to mean simply that Moses is not possessed of rhetorical skills. He rather confesses humbly that he does not feel equipped to carry out God's commission.

The inglorious end with which Ezekiel threatens the Phoenicians (Ezk. 28:10) and Egyptians (31:18; 32:17-32) is manifested in their lying in death with the uncircumcised and those slain by the sword; they have a special place in the netherworld, where they must share the fate of Israel's other enemies — Assyria, Elam, Meshech and Tubal (Cilicia and Phrygia), Edom, the princes of the north, and the Sidonians — who wait to receive them. Here speaks an Israelite who applies to foreign nations the image of a knacker's yard where the uncircumcised among his own people, who have broken their ties with the people and with God, and those slain by the sword (i.e., executed) are hastily buried. Their end and their burial are ignominious; they are damned to ignominy for eternity.

3. *Lev. 19:23-25.* The usage found in Lev. 19:23-25 (P) is unique. This text directs that during the first three years after a tree is planted, its fruit must be treated "like foreskins" (v. 23), i.e., the fruit must not be eaten; in the fourth year it is treated as a second tithe (→ עשׂר *ʿeśer*), i.e., the owner has to sell the fruit to himself and spend the proceeds on a feast during a pilgrimage to Jerusalem. Only then is the fruit available for regular consumption. The point of comparison is probably that the fruit is left in place as a foreskin is left in place; just as the uncircumcised are excluded from the cult, so the fruit is excluded from consumption. The rabbis collected most of the detailed regulations in tractate *ʿOrlah* of the Mishnah, the Tosephta, and the Jerusalem Talmud.

III. Dead Sea Scrolls. Usage in the Dead Sea Scrolls is similar to that in the Bible. The uncircumcised, the unclean, and the violent are lumped together in 1QH 6:20. According to 1QH 18:20, "a word was revealed" to one whose ear was uncircumcised. In

---

5. → VII, 433.

1QS 5:5 we read of circumcising the foreskin of impulse. Hab. 2:16 (where the text reads *r'l!*) is interpreted by 1QpHab 11:13 as a reference to the wicked priest, who has not circumcised the foreskin of his heart. For discussion of 4Q184, → VII, 437.

Mayer

עָרַם *'āram;* עָרוּם *'ārûm;* עָרְמָה *'ormâ*

I. Etymology. II. 1. Usage; 2. Synonyms and Antonyms. III. 1. Nonwisdom Contexts; 2. Proverbs; 3. Job. IV. LXX. V. Dead Sea Scrolls.

I. Etymology. Apart from Hebrew, the verb *'āram* is found only in Syriac and Jewish Aramaic.[1] Unique to Hebrew are the derived *qāṭûl* form *'ārûm,* used as an adjective expressing a state,[2] and the subst. *'ormâ.*

II. 1. *Usage.* Except for 1 S. 23:22 and Ps. 83:4(Eng. v. 3), the verb *'āram* is found only in wisdom literature (Prov. 15:5; 19:25; Job 5:13). The adj. *'ārûm* is more common (11 times), used once in Genesis and 10 times in wisdom literature (twice in Job, 8 times in Proverbs). The subst. *'ormâ* occurs twice outside wisdom literature (Ex. 21:14; Josh. 9:14) and 3 times in Proverbs. The verb *'āram* II and its derivatives can therefore be considered wisdom terminology.

2. *Synonyms and Antonyms.* Prov. 15:5 contrasts the → אויל *'ᵉwîl* with one whose conduct is described as *'āram.* Additional semantic evidence can be found in Prov. 19:25, which uses *'āram* in parallel with *bîn da'aṯ* and in contrast with *peṯî ya'rim;* as suggested by Prov. 1:4, the → פתי *peṯî* is to be understood as "the untutored youth who comes to learn from the wisdom teacher."[3] In Job 5:13, however, the verb *'āram,* describing the wise, has negative connotations; the same is true in Ps. 83:4(3), where the subject is Yahweh's enemies.

This variation, which allows *'āram* to have both negative and positive connotations,

---

'āram. O. Bauernfeind, "πανουργία, πανοῦργος," *TDNT,* V, 722-27; M. Dahood, "Hebrew-Ugaritic Lexicography VII," *Bibl* 60 (1969) 337-56, esp. 354-55; M. Görg, "Die 'Sünde' Salomos," *BN* 16 (1981) 42-59, esp. 50-53; K. R. Joines, "The Serpent in Gen 3," *ZAW* 87 (1975) 1-11, esp. 4-8; F. Nötscher, *Zur theologischen Terminologie der Qumran-Texte. BBB* 10 (1956), 61; G. von Rad, *Wisdom in Israel* (Eng. trans. 1972); B. Renz, "Die kluge Schlange," *BZ* 24 (1938/39) 236-41; O. H. Steck, *Die Paradieserzählung. BSt* 60 (1970) = his *Wahrnehmungen Gottes im AT. ThB* 70 (1982), 9-116, esp. 56, 88-91; T. C. Vriezen, *Onderzoek naar de Paradijsvoorstelling bij de oude Semietische volken* (1937).

1. See Brockelmann, *LexSyr,* 549; Levy, *WTM,* III, 700-701; Beyer, 664.
2. *GK,* §84am.
3. W. McKane, *Proverbs. OTL* (1970), 525.

can also be noted in the usage of the adj. *ʿārûm,* as is shown by its synonyms and antonyms. As synonyms we find *ḥāḵām* and *nip̄tāl* (Job 5:12-13); as antonyms, *kᵉsîl* (Prov. 12:23; 13:16; 14:8), *ʾᵉwîl* (12:16), and *peṯî* (14:15,18; 22:3 = 27:12). In the case of *kᵉsîl* and *peṯî,* we are dealing with wisdom vocabulary, since *peṯî* appears outside Proverbs only in Ezk. 45:20; Ps. 19:8(7); 116:6; 119:130; and of the 70 occurrences of *kᵉsîl,* only 3 appear in Psalms, while the rest are distributed throughout Proverbs and Ecclesiastes.[4] With regard to the usage of *ʿārûm,* we must distinguish between its negative connotations in Job 5:12 and 15:15 ("crafty") and its positive connotations in Proverbs, where we find no synonyms but only negatively colored antonyms, indicating that *ʿārûm* should be understood as "prudent."

The synonyms and antonyms associated with the subst. *ʿormâ* suggest connotations comparable to those of the adj. *ʿārûm.* The parallel terms *daʿaṯ ûmᵉzimmâ* (Prov. 1:4), *daʿaṯ mᵉzimmôṯ* (8:12), and *lēḇ* (8:5) indicate that in Proverbs, like *ʿārûm, ʿormâ* has positive connotations; it has negative connotations, however, outside Proverbs (Ex. 21:14; Josh. 9:4). At the same time, too much weight should not be put on the positive connotations of *ʿormâ* in Proverbs; like *mᵉzimmâ, ʿormâ* always stands on the borderline of the pejorative, in part because the educational process was concerned more with the expansion of intellectual ability than with morality. "It did not educate men to change the existing world into something better, but to make their way successfully in the world as it was."[5]

III. 1. *Nonwisdom Contexts.* The earliest occurrence of a derivative of *ʿāram* is in the Covenant Code (Ex. 21:14), in the context of regulations governing asylum. If a homicide is committed with *ʿormâ,* the perpetrator loses the right of altar asylum (v. 14b). Here *ʿormâ* may be understood as "malice aforethought."

The occurrence of *ʿārûm* in Gen. 3:1 belongs to J's special material, since he enriched the pre-J primal history by adding the motif of the serpent.[6] The description in 2:25 of the man and his wife as naked (→ עירום *ʿārôm*) likewise goes back to J, who uses a wordplay involving *ʿārôm* and the description of the serpent as *ʿārûm.* With reference to the serpent, it should be noted that, like all the other beasts of the field, it was made by God and is therefore one of God's creatures.

In the light of the anti-Solomonic bias of J's primal history, the serpent can be interpreted as a figured evolved from the Egyptian goddess Renenutet.[7] The serpent is set apart from the other beasts of the field and appears as a creature endowed with the power of speech, who has an interest in providing the man and his wife with the special nourishment that comes through the knowledge of wisdom. The serpent was given this special status for the purpose of criticizing the notion that the serpent deity, as a symbol

---

4. H.-J. Hermisson, *Studien zur israelitischen Spruchweisheit. WMANT* 28 (1968), 76; T. Donald, *VT* 13 (1963) 287, 291.

5. McKane, *Proverbs,* 165.

6. P. Weimar, *Untersuchungen zur Redaktionsgeschichte des Pentateuch. BZAW* 146 (1977), 155; L. Ruppert, *BZ* 15 (1971) 195-96.

7. See W. von Soden, *WO* 7 (1973/74) 228-40; Görg, 42-59, esp. 53.

associated with the provision of divine wisdom, could be reconciled and made interchangeable with the tutelary deity of Israelite tradition. The serpent thus becomes the symbol of wisdom without Yahweh.[8]

This analysis also explains the negative connotations associated with the use of *'ārûm* in Gen. 3:1 for the crafty cunning of the serpent. It is impossible to determine whether J is borrowing here a traditional appraisal of the serpent,[9] choosing the serpent because its "treacherous, dangerous behavior makes it the archenemy of Palestinian peasants, and as such it was ready to hand in 3:15."[10] The serpent's intelligence is related to "its ability to produce venom (and antithetically its power to heal) or its ability to shed its skin."[11] To this extent, the connotations of *'ārûm* when describing the serpent in Gen. 3:1 are not purely negative, a point also made by its ability to speak and its awareness of the tree of knowledge.[12] By choosing the ambiguous term *'ārûm* to describe the serpent, J calls attention to the dubious nature of the serpent's intelligence, which contrasts with the knowledge of good and evil.

In the Deuteronomistic History the verb *'āram* occurs in 1 S. 23:22 and the subst. *'ormâ* in Josh. 9:4. The text of 1 S. 23:22 belongs to the story of David's rise, which literary criticism assigns to the early monarchy. Saul describes David as *'ārôm ya'rim hû'*. As in Gen. 3:1, *'ārûm/'āram* in this context is to be understood primarily as "crafty, cunning," with negative overtones; at the same time, however, a connotation of "prudent" in the sense of worldly wisdom should not be ruled out.

Comparison of these earliest occurrences of the root *'āram* reveals that they are similar with respect to their primarily negative and only inchoately positive connotations; on the basis of this observation, Mendenhall believes that the use of *'ārûm* in Gen. 3:1 stands at the end of a semantic evolution and represents a rejection of the "intelligence" claimed by wisdom.[13]

We may compare another, probably earlier occurrence of *'ormâ* in Josh. 9:4, where it describes an action analogous to the capture of Jericho.[14] The context of ch. 9 shows that the Gibeonites duped Joshua and the Israelites; *'ormâ* may therefore be interpreted as "trickery" or "craftiness."

The latest occurrence of *'āram* II hiphil is in Ps. 83:4(3), which describes the actions of Yahweh's enemies against his people: *'al- 'ammᵉḵā ya'ᵃrîmû sôḏ*. Here the term *sôḏ* should be understood as "secret discussion" craftily devised, the "deceitful plans of one's enemies."[15]

---

8. Görg, 53; → נחש *nāḥāš*.
9. Joines, 4-8.
10. Steck, 89.
11. C. Westermann, *Genesis 1–11* (Eng. trans. 1984), 239.
12. Renz, 236; W. H. Schmidt, *Die Schöpfungsgeschichte der Priesterschrift. WMANT* 17 (^{3}1973), 211-12.
13. G. Mendenhall, "The Shady Side of Wisdom," *Light unto My Path. FS J. M. Myers* (1974), 319-34, here 328.
14. J. A. Soggin, *Joshua. OTL* (Eng. trans. 1972), 113.
15. Quotations, respectively, from M. Sæbø, *TLOT*, II, 794; H.-J. Fabry, → X, 176.

2. *Proverbs.* All three derivatives of the root *ʿāram* II are found in the book of Proverbs. Prov. 15:5 uses *ʿāram* to characterize a person who heeds admonition (→ יכח *ykḥ*) and thus acts prudently. The context is discipline in the education of children by their parents. Prov. 19:25 takes up the theme of 1:4a, which deals with an untutored youth who is to study with a wisdom teacher and thus become prudent (*ʿāram*). The context of both 15:5 and 19:25 therefore has to do with education. In the background stands a concept of education that identifies with attention to admonitions (15:5) and acceptance of punishment administered by scoffers (19:25). In Proverbs the term *ʿārûm* is paradigmatic of the prudent person, just as *ḥāḵām* typifies the wise. The prudent conceal their knowledge, unlike fools, who broadcast their folly (12:23). They also ignore insults, whereas fools express their anger directly (12:16).[16] The wisdom of the wise assures their way,[17] in contrast to the folly of fools, which misleads (14:8). The prudent do everything intelligently; fools display their folly (13:16). The prudent consider their steps;[18] fools believe everything (14:15). The prudent are crowned with knowledge; fools are adorned with their folly (14:18). The prudent see danger coming and hide;[19] fools go on and suffer for it (22:3 = 27:12).

If we ask what are the typical characteristics of the *ʿārûm* in these passages, they consist in discretion, caution, circumspection, and prudence. The *ʿārûm* personifies the way of life inculcated by the book of Proverbs.[20] This is also apparent in the attributes of *ḥoḵmâ* (14:8) and *daʿaṯ* (12:23; 13:16; 14:8) ascribed to the *ʿārûm.* The subst. *ʿormâ* denotes what the *peṯî* is required to learn (1:4; 8:5). In 8:12 personified Wisdom describes herself as the neighbor of *ʿormâ.* According to Lang, *šāḵantî* is used here with an adverbial accusative (as in Isa. 33:5; Ps. 37:3; 135:21); he translates: "I live in cleverness," i.e., "I know cleverness."[21] According to *BHS,* the text should be emended to *šᵉḵentî,* "prudence is my neighbor." The MT is usually retained and translated "I am the neighbor of prudence."[22]

When we look for a more precise definition of *ʿormâ* in the context of the terminology of Prov. 1:1-5, we may note with von Rad that "a comprehensive term, for which there is no longer any handy word, can be constructed here for the reader by the fact that, to a certain extent, into this prologue a number of known terms have been inserted so that by this cumulation the desired extension of the conceptual range is achieved."[23] The individual terms chosen are in fact differentiated; but they are not conceptually distinct, since they also overlap.[24]

---

16. So *BHS.*
17. See *BHS.*
18. See *BHS.*
19. See *BHS.*
20. Von Rad, 85.
21. B. Lang, *Frau Weisheit* (1975), 86 n. 85.
22. O. Plöger, *Sprüche Salomos. BK* XVII (1984), 85.
23. Von Rad, 13; cf. 27, 53-54.
24. Ibid., 13.

In Prov. 8:5,12, *ʿormâ* appears in the context of personified Wisdom, who addresses the simple and foolish with the imperative to understand *(bîn) ʿormâ* and *lēḇ*. Here the term *lēḇ* must be understood as "acumen" or "prudence," so that *ʿormâ* must be interpreted along the same lines as "(practical) intelligence."[25] In v. 12 personified Wisdom describes herself as the neighbor of *ʿormâ* (see above), which takes on a special accent here by virtue of appearing in parallel with conduct typified by enlightened discretion (v. 12b).

One additional occurrence of *ʿormâ* in Prov. 14:24 is questionable, even though the LXX reads *panoúrgos,* its usual translation of *ʿormâ* (see IV below). The contextual theme of riches and poverty in vv. 20-24 nevertheless gives priority to the MT.[26]

3. *Job.* The verb *ʿāram* II occurs in Job 5:13 in the first discourse of Eliphaz, where it refers to the wise whom God takes in their own craftiness.

There are also two occurrences of the term *ʿārûm,* both in discourses of Eliphaz. In his first exhortation (5:8-16), he speaks of the providence of God, who frustrates the devices of the *ʿᵃrûmîm* (v. 12). In the second response of Eliphaz to Job, he accuses Job of having chosen the language of the *ʿᵃrûmîm* (15:5). In both passages the *ʿᵃrûmîm* are stereotypes, as in Proverbs; but in the context of the crisis of wisdom that is the theme of Job, they appear only in a negative light as the cunning and crafty.

In the Hebrew text of Sirach, we find once more the verb *ʿāram* with positive connotations used in parallel with the verb *ḥāḵam* (Sir. 6:32).

IV. LXX. The LXX usually translates *ʿārûm* with *panoúrgos* and *ʿormâ* with *panourgía* (17 times). In Nu. 24:22 the LXX misread *ʿāḏ-mâ* as *ʿormâ (panourgía);* it made a similar error in Prov. 14:24.[27] There is, however, a semantic shift in the LXX: while *panoúrgos* can also have negative connotations ("wily, malicious"), the *ʿāram* derivatives in Proverbs are positive ("intelligent, prudent"). Since the LXX version of Proverbs uses the derivatives of *panourg-* with particular frequency, their meaning shifts in a positive direction.[28]

In two passages *ʿārûm* (Gen. 3:1) and *ʿormâ* (Job 5:13) are translated by *phrónimos* and *phrónēsis,* respectively, both with negative overtones. In Job 15:5 the LXX has *dynastḗs,* which conveys a more positive sense than *ʿārûm.*

V. Dead Sea Scrolls. The Dead Sea Scrolls use *ʿormâ* primarily with the positive connotations it acquired in Proverbs. In the context of wisdom terminology, CD 2:4 says that *ʿormâ* and *daʿaṯ* serve God, a statement that may be compared to the personification of both terms in Prov. 1:4. New in the scrolls is the construct phrase *ʿormaṯ daʿaṯ* (1QS 10:25), which refers to intelligent knowledge. Also in contrast to OT usage,

---

25. → VII, 419-23. See Plöger, *BK* XVII, 88.

26. McKane, *Proverbs,* 465-66; Plöger, *BK* XVII, 174; contra *BHS* and B. Gemser, *Sprüche Salomos. HAT* I/16 (²1963), 66-67; et al.

27. Bauernfeind, 724 n. 13.

28. Bauernfeind, 724.

ʿormâ can appear as *nomen rectum* in a construct phrase: *m*^{e}*zimmaṯ ʿormâ,* "intelligent thought" (1QS 11:6). These intelligent thoughts of God are concealed from humankind; only the eye of the devout sees them.[29]

The list of the paths of light in the world (1QS 4:2-7) includes *ʿormaṯ kôl* (l. 6), to be understood as prudence in all things. Analogously, the list of characteristics of the sons of darkness (1QS 4:9-11) includes *ʿormaṯ rôaʿ,* "wicked cunning." According to 1QH 1:35, *ʿormâ* is to be increased by the wise and imparted to the simple (1QH 2:9). 1QpHab 7:14 mentions the *ʿormâ* of God, which refers to the mysteries of his prudence, in which he has preordained all ages.

Niehr

---

29. Nötscher, 61.

עֹרֶף *ʿōrep̱*; עָרַף *ʿārap̱*

I. Etymology. II. Noun: 1. Meaning and Occurrences; 2. Related Words; 3. LXX. III. Idioms: 1. Flight; 2. Apostasy; 3. Triumph; 4. Obstinacy. IV. Verb: 1. Meaning, Lexical Field; 2. Firstlings; 3. Homicide; 4. Isa. 66:3; 5. Hos. 10:2. V. Sirach, Dead Sea Scrolls.

ʿōrep. D. C. Benjamin, *Deuteronomy and City Life* (1983), 198-210; G. Brin, "The Firstling of Unclean Animals," *JQR* 68 (1977/78) 1-15; C. M. Carmichael, "A Common Element in Five Supposedly Disparate Laws," *VT* 29 (1979) 129-42; H. Christ, *Blutvergiessen im AT* (1977), esp. 86-91; B. Couroyer, "'Avoir la nuque raide', ne pas incliner l'oreille," *RB* 88 (1981) 216-25; H. J. Elhorst, "Eine verkannte Zauberhandlung (Dtn 21,1-9)," *ZAW* 39 (1921) 58-67; C. H. Gordon, "An Accadian Parallel to Deut. 21,1ff.," *RA* 33 (1936) 1-6; S. H. Hooke, "The Theory and Practice of Substitution," *VT* 2 (1952) 2-17; B. Janowski, *Sühne als Heilsgeschehen. WMANT* 55 (1982); A. Jirku, "Drei Fälle von Haftpflicht im altorientalischen Palästina-Syrien und Deuteronomium cap. 21," *ZAW* 79 (1967) 359-60; S. E. Loewenstamm, "*ʿeglāh ʿ*^{a}*rûp̱āh,*" *EMiqr,* VI, 77-79; H. McKeating, "The Development of the Law on Homicide in Ancient Israel," *VT* 25 (1975) 46-68; R. P. Merendino, *Das deuteronomische Gesetz. BBB* 31 (1969), esp. 234-43; E. Merz, *Die Blutrache bei den Israeliten* (1916), 48-55; J. Milgrom, "ʿEgla ʿArufah," *EncJud,* VI, 475-77; R. Patai, "The ʿEgla ʿarufa or the Expiation of the Polluted Land (Dt 21,1-9)," *JQR* 30 (1939) 59-69; R. Press, "Das Ordal im alten Israel," *ZAW* 51 (1933) 121-40, 227-50; A. Roifer, "The Breaking of the Heifer's Neck," *Tarbiz* 31 (1961/62) 119-43; M. Tsevat, "The Canaanite God Šälaḥ," *VT* 4 (1954) 41-49, esp. 46-47; A. C. Welch, "Remarks on the Article of H. J. Elhorst in ZAW 1921," *ZAW* 42 (1924) 163-64; R. Westbrook, "Lex talionis and Exodus 21,22-25," *RB* 93 (1986) 52-69; Z. Zevit, "The *ʿEgla* Ritual of Deuteronomy 21:1-9," *JBL* 95 (1976) 377-90.

I. Etymology. Heb. *ʿōrep̱,* "neck," is related to Arab. *ʿurfah,* "mane," and Syr. *ʿurpāʾ,* "cockscomb."[1] Otherwise in Aramaic and Syriac "neck" is *qᵉḏāl(āʾ)* or *ṣawwāʾr.* Aram. *ʿurpîn* (pl.) is found only once, as a gloss on *qᵉḏālîn.*[2] Akkadian uses *kišādu* (cf. Eth. *kĕsād*). The verb *ʿārap* is probably a denominative from *ʿōrep̱;*[3] it was formerly[4] entered as an independent root, related to Arab. *ǵarafa,* "cut up." On a third root *ʿrp* → ערפל *ʿᵃrāp̱ēl.*

II. Noun.

1. *Meaning and Occurrences.* The noun *ʿōrep̱* occurs 33 times in the OT. The meaning "back of the neck" is clear from statements like "They have turned their *ʿōrep̱* to me, and not their faces" (Jer. 2:27).

2. *Related Words.* The noun *ṣawwāʾr,* "neck," is similar in meaning but is used differently. A yoke is placed on the *ṣawwāʾr,* not the *ʿōrep̱;* a necklace is likewise placed on the *ṣawwāʾr;* cf. "falling on someone's neck" with *ṣawwāʾr* (Gen. 33:4; 45:14; 46:29).

The noun *gārôn,* "throat," denotes the part of the body used for speaking (Isa. 58:1; Ps. 115:7; 149:6) or swallowing (Ps. 5:10[Eng. v. 9]; Jer. 2:25, thirst); but occasionally it also means "neck," where a chain is placed (Ezk. 16:11). The *gargᵉrôṯ* is also the place for a necklace (Prov. 1:9; 3:3,22; 6:21).

3. *LXX.* The LXX uses a variety of translations: 8 times *nṓtos,* "back"; 10 times *tráchēlos,* "neck" (also used for *ṣawwāʾr, gargᵉrôṯ,* and *gārôn* in the sense of "neck"). The expression *qᵉšēh ʿōrep̱*[5] is translated by *sklērotráchēlos* (5 times + Prov. 29:1, where the LXX reads *miqqᵉšēh ʿōrep̱,* and Sir. 16:11).

III. Idioms. Many stereotyped expressions use *ʿōrep̱.*

1. *Flight.* The syntagm *pānâ ʿōrep̱,* "turn the back (of the neck)," describes flight from the enemy, e.g., "The Israelites will turn their backs to their enemies" (Josh. 7:12; cf. v. 8 with *hāpaḵ*). The idiom also uses the hiphil, e.g., Jer. 48:39 with reference to Moab (cf. 49:24, *hipnᵉṯâ lānûs,* "turned to flee"). It also uses *nāṯan:* Yahweh will make *(wᵉnāṯattî)* the enemies turn their backs to Israel (Ex. 23:27; cf. 2 S. 22:41 = Ps. 18:41[40]).

2. *Apostasy.* Metaphorically, *pānâ ʿōrep̱* denotes apostasy: the inhabitants of Judah "turned their backs to me and not their faces" (Jer. 2:27; 32:33 + "and would not listen and accept correction"); *nāṯan* is also used: "Our ancestors have been unfaithful . . .

---

1. *LexSyr,* 549.
2. Jastrow, 1122.
3. *HAL,* II, 887.
4. *KBL*[2], 738.
5. See III.4 below.

and have turned away *(sbb)* their faces from the dwelling of Yahweh and turned their backs *(wayyitt^enû 'ōrep)*" (2 Ch. 29:6). Conversely, in Jer. 18:17 Yahweh threatens: "With my back and not with my face will I look at them *('er'ēm)*" (LXX, Vulg., and Syr. read *'ar'ēm,* "I will show them my back").

3. *Triumph.* A hand on the neck of the enemy (Gen. 49:8) signifies victory. Job complains that God has seized him *('āḥaz)* by the neck and dashed him to pieces (Job 16:12).

4. *Obstinacy.* Expressions like *q^ešēh-'ōrep,* "stiff-necked," express obstinacy and stubbornness. The following variants are found:

a. The expression *q^ešēh-'ōrep,* "stiff-necked," occurs 6 times, always with *'am;* all occurrences are in Exodus and Deuteronomy, with reference to the golden calf. In this context Israel is called "a stiff-necked people" (Ex. 32:9; 33:3,5; 34:9; Dt. 9:6,13). The word *q^ešî,* "hardness," in Dt. 9:27 is probably elliptical for *q^ešî 'ōrep,* i.e., "stubbornness." Cf. also the division of the expression in Isa. 48:4: "Because I knew that you are obstinate [*qāšeh,* 'hard'], and your neck *('ōrep)* has iron sinews, and your forehead is of brass."

b. The expression *'ōrep qāšeh* appears only in Moses' farewell discourse (Dt. 31). V. 27 reads: "For I know well your recalcitrance *(m^erî)* and stubbornness ['hard, stiff neck']." These words, like the whole discourse in vv. 24-29, clearly refer to the episode of the golden calf (cf. also *mamrîm* in v. 27 with Dt. 9:7,24).[6]

c. The syntagm *hiqšâ 'ōrep* denotes apostasy and disobedience: "they stiffened their necks" (Jer. 7:26; 17:23; 19:15; Neh. 9:16-17,29). Occasionally we find expansions such as "like the necks of the fathers" (2 K. 17:14) or parallels such as "they walked in the stubbornness of their evil hearts" (Jer. 7:24) or "they did not incline their ears" (Jer. 7:26; 17:23), "they did not listen" (Jer. 7:26; 17:23; cf. 19:15; + "to my commandments," Neh. 9:16,29). The expression is also used of individuals: Zedekiah "stiffened his neck and hardened (*'mṣ* piel) his heart against turning to Yahweh" (2 Ch. 36:13). It also appears as an exhortation: "Do not stiffen your necks" (Dt. 10:16; 2 Ch. 30:8; cf. Ps. 95:8, *'al-taqšû l^ebabkem*). Dt. 10:16 offers a further parallel: "Circumcise the foreskin of your heart."

According to most commentators, the expression "stiff-necked" is based on the notion of a recalcitrant, stubborn animal. Some think of an animal being ridden, others of oxen balking at the yoke.[7] This interpretation, however, cannot be accepted: in such situations, an animal is more likely to jerk its neck than to stiffen it. Linguistically, it should be noted that the expression is never used of animals; furthermore, a yoke is not placed on the *'ōrep* but on the *ṣawwā'r.* Closer examination shows that the combination *qšh* + *'ōrep* stands in contrast to "incline one's ear," "listen," and the like (e.g., Zec. 7:11; Neh. 9:29; Jer. 17:23; 19:15). Stiffening one's neck therefore means refusal to incline one's ear (2 K. 19:16; Ps. 45:11[10]; Dnl. 9:18; etc.).[8]

---

6. M. Zipor, "The Impact of the Golden Calf Story in Moses' Sermons in the Book of Deuteronomy," *FS M. Goldstein* (1987).

7. See Couroyer.

8. Ibid., 223-25.9. See I above.

IV. Verb.

1. *Meaning, Lexical Field.* The denominative[9] verb *'ārap̱* occurs 6 times (Ex. 13:13; 34:20; Dt. 21:4,6; Isa. 66:3; Hos. 10:2). It is debated whether the verb means "cut off the head" or "break the neck." Both interpretations are represented in early exegesis. For example, Mish. *Soṭa* 9.5 interprets it as "sever with a knife," and the LXX translates it in Dt. 21:4,6 with *neurokopeín,* "sever the sinew"; the other Greek versions also use compounds of *kopeín.* On the other hand, in Isa. 66:3 the LXX has *ho apokténnōn,* "whoever kills" (also Symmachus in Ex. 13:13); Syr. uses *qeṭal,* "kill" (except in Dt. 21:4,6, where it has *neḵas* = *šāḥaṭ*).

The lexical field includes *mālaq,* "wring off (the head)" (only in Lev. 1:15 and 5:8, with reference to sacrifice of a bird), and → שׁחט *šāḥaṭ* (78 occurrences in the OT), which denotes both ritual and nonritual slaughter and is interpreted traditionally as slitting the throat. According to Zevit, *mālaq* is used for sacrifice on the altar, *šāḥaṭ* for slaughter beside the altar.[10] It is also possible that the terms are used for different sacrificial animals.[11]

2. *Firstlings.* According to Ex. 13:13 and 34:20, every firstborn *(peṭer)* donkey must be redeemed[12] with a sheep; if the owner is unwilling to redeem it, its neck must be broken *('ārap̱).* P does not mention the alternative in Nu. 18:15; cf. Lev. 27:27 — here, however, the subject is redemption of nonsacrificial animals in general.[13] Whether the alternative replaces what had originally been a sacrifice remains uncertain. Since redemption is preferred, however, the alternative is more likely to be a sanction for the possibility that the owner does not want to redeem the firstling, but to keep it.

3. *Homicide.* Dt. 21:1-9 provides an atonement ceremony for cases of homicide by person or persons unknown. To make atonement, a heifer *('eglâ)* is to be killed by *'rp* in an uncultivated wadi.[14] The question is whether *'ārap̱* means "cut the throat" or "break the neck"; in other words, whether the rite is bloody or unbloody.[15] The ritual is unique in the OT. Ugaritic texts show that the community is held responsible for such a homicide; in these cases, however, the point at issue is reparations, which is not the case in Dt. 21.[16]

Many scholars see in Dt. 21:1-9 a modification of an ancient ritual. According to Merz, the blood of the heifer is intended to deceive the soul of the victim into believing that is the blood of the murderer. According to Steuernagel, the punishment of the murderer is inflicted vicariously on the calf.[17] Bertholet and Duhm consider the heifer a

---

10. P. 384.
11. Haran, cited by Zevit, 384 n. 39.
12. → פדה *pāḏâ.* Others read *wa'araḵtô,* "you shall value it" (cf. Lev. 27:27), following LXX Ex. 34:20 *timḗn dṓseis* (13:13 *lytrṓseis*); see A. Kahana, *Biblia Hebraica* (Kiev, 1913) *ad loc.*
13. See Brin, 2 n. 4.
14. → כפר *kipper;* → נחל *naḥal.*
15. Carmichael, 133.
16. *RS* 17, 230; 17, 158; 20, 22. See Roifer, 122-26.
17. *Das Deuteronomium. HKAT* I/3 (1900), 1, 78.

sacrifice to the spirit of the victim.[18] Elhorst thinks the rite was originally a sacrifice to chthonic gods.[19] Von Rad thinks in terms of "a magical procedure for getting rid of sin" and compares the procedure to the scapegoat ritual (as do medieval Jewish exegetes).[20] According to Elhorst, the elders' washing of their hands over the slain animal is a magical act to transfer the guilt of the community to the animal.[21] Others connect the slaying of the calf with the elders' oath: may the same befall us if we do not speak the truth.[22] According to Roifer, the pollution of the land, which is God's heritage (v. 1), must be transferred to an uninhabited locale; this transfer is accomplished by the symbolic repetition of the murder in a new locale. A magical pre-Israelite apotropaic ritual became a Yahwistic sacrifice of atonement. Later, under the influence of Deuteronomistic ideas, breaking the animal's neck replaced the sacrifice. Carmichael thinks the ceremony has a didactic purpose.[23]

4. *Isa. 66:3.* Isa. 66:3 contains a series of seven (or eight?) participial clauses arranged in pairs. One can translate: "Whoever slaughters an ox is like one who kills a man; whoever sacrifices a lamb, like one who breaks a dog's neck" — a condemnation of legitimate sacrifice. Another possible translation — "Whoever slaughters an ox at the same time kills a man; whoever sacrifices a sheep at the same time breaks a dog's neck" — would represent a polemic against syncretism.[24]

5. *Hos. 10:2.* In Hos. 10:2 we find a metaphorical usage: "He will break down *(ʿrp)* their altars and destroy *(yᵉšōḏēḏ)* their pillars." The statement may be ironic: as in a cultic act, the altars will "have their necks broken."[25] Zorell reads *yiśrōp̱,* "he will burn up"; Nyberg derives *ʿārap̱* from Arab. *ġarafa,* "cut off."[26]

V. Sirach, Dead Sea Scrolls. In Sir. 16:11 we find the expression *maqšeh ʿōrep̱:* anyone who is stiff-necked shall not go unpunished.

The OT expression *qšy ʿwrp* appears several times in the Dead Sea Scrolls: "stiffness of neck and hardness *(kibbûḏ)* of heart" in a catalog of vices (1QS 4:11); "whoever circumcises the foreskin of his attitude and his stiff neck" as a description of conversion (1QS 5:5); "whoever answers his neighbor with stiffness of neck" (1QS 6:26); *wrwḥ ʿwrp qš[h]* (1QH fr. 12:4).

---

18. Bertholet, *Deuteronomium. KHC* V (1899), 64-65; B. Duhm, *Die bösen Geister im AT* (1904), 21.
19. Pp. 61-62.
20. *Deuteronomy. OTL* (Eng. trans. 1966), 136.
21. Contra Zevit, 386.
22. Janowski, 165; but cf. Roifer, 122 n. 11.
23. Carmichael, 129ff. For still other interpretations see Christ, 86-89; Janowski, 163-68.
24. Westermann, *Isaiah 40–66. OTL* (Eng. trans. 1969), 413-14, citing a possible dog sacrifice in Carthage; cf. Justin *Epitome* 19.1.10; R. N. Whybray, *Isaiah 40–66. NCBC* (1975), 281-82.
25. Wolff, *Hosea. Herm* (Eng. trans. 1974), 174.
26. Zorell, *LexHebAram,* 630; H. S. Nyberg, *Studien zum Hoseabuche* (1935), 72. See I above.

"Lay your hand on the neck of your enemies," say 1QM 12:11 and 19:3; in 1QM 9:2 we find the expression *whsbw ʿwrpm* used as a term for flight.

The verb appears only in 11QT 63:1-8, quoting Dt. 21:1-9.

Zipor

עֲרָפֶל *ʿarāpel*

I. Etymology. II. Occurrences. III. Early Versions and Postbiblical Literature.

I. Etymology. Outside the OT, the noun *ʿarāpel* occurs in Ugar. *ǵrpl* along with *ʿrpt,* "cloud";[1] in Sam. *ʿarpēl,* in Syr. *ʿarpᵉlā',* in Jewish Aram. *ʿarpîlā',* and in Mand. *'arpilā.*[2] In all these languages and dialects it suggests something like "thick clouds, darkness."

The etymological derivation of the word is disputed. Some have analyzed the quadriliteral as a combination of *ʿrp,* "drop," and *'pl,* "be dark, be eerie," or as a diminutive of *ʿrp* or *ʿarîpā* + the diminutive suf. *-l.*[3] Others have suggested a noun formed with the ending *-al* (with /a/ reduced to /e/).[4] Ružička derives the word from Arab. *ǵamala,* a by-form of *ǵamana;* a secondary shift of /m/ to /ph/ produced *ǵafala,* with the meaning "cover."[5] Contact dissimilation led in turn to a regressive interchange between /ph/ and /r/. Others, too, have often proposed an Arabic etymology.[6] Loader thinks that *ʿarāpel* derives from a root *ʿrp,* related to *ʿrb,* "be shadowy"; *ʿarāpel* means something like "cloudy shade," and the denominative verb *ʿrp,* "drop," derives from this noun.[7] Another theory is that of Vollers, who "with assurance" analyzes *ʿarāpel* as a compound with *'ēl,* "God," roughly similar to "Homeric θεῖος."[8] He also notes Assyr. *irpu,* cited by other scholars as *erpu, erpetu, urpu,* or *urpatu,* which means

---

ʿarāpel. A. van den Born, "Zum Tempelweihspruch (1 Kg viii 12f.)," *OTS* 14 (1965) 235-44; M. Fraenkel, "Bemerkungen zum hebräischen Wortschatz," *HUCA* 61 (1960) 55-101, esp. 80-81; M. Görg, "Die Gattung des sogenannten Tempelweihspruchs (1 Kg 8,12f.)," *UF* 6 (1974) 55-63; J. A. Loader, "The Concept of Darkness in the Hebrew Root *ʿrb/ʿrp,*" *De fructu oris sui. FS A. van Selms* (1971), 99-107; P. Reymond, *L'eau, sa vie, et sa signification dans l'AT. SVT* 6 (1958), 13-14, 35-41.

1. For the former see *KTU* 1.107, [8], 9, [12], 19; for the latter, 1.2, IV, 8, 29; etc.
2. *MdD,* 38.
3. *GesTh,* 1072; cf. also L. Koehler, *TZ* 2 (1946) 72.
4. Stade, *Lehrbuch der hebräischen Grammatik* (1879), §299; cf. *BLe,* §61i; König, *Lehrgebäude,* II, §60, 9; Meyer, II, 40.
5. R. Ružička, *Konsonantische Dissimilation in den semitischen Sprachen* (1909), 105, 135-36.
6. E.g., *LexSyr,* 549, from *ǵafara,* "cover"; see also *KBL*², 738; *HAL,* II, 888.
7. Pp. 101-2.
8. K. Vollers, *ZA* 17 (1903) 310-11.

"cloud."[9] Dahood rejects the derivation from the root *ʿrp,* on the grounds that Ugaritic clearly distinguishes *ʿrpt,* "clouds," from *ǵrpl,* "dark cloud."[10] The description of Baal as *rkb ʿrpt,* which occurs 14 times in the Ugaritic texts, has a better parallel in Ps. 68:5(Eng. v. 4), which refers to Elohim as *rōḵēḇ bāʿarāḇôṯ,* although this parallel, too, has been challenged.[11] But even though there is an etymological distinction between the Ugaritic words *ʿrpt* and *ǵrpl,* now and then the view is expressed that *ʿrpt,* too, can refer to "dark rain clouds."[12] Nevertheless, almost all scholars translate *ʿarāpel* as "thick darkness," "dark clouds," or the like, notwithstanding its disputed etymology.[13]

II. Occurrences. Our noun occurs 15 times: Ex. 20:21; Dt. 4:11; 5:22(19); 2 S. 22:10 (par. Ps. 18:10[9]); 1 K. 8:12 (par. 2 Ch. 6:1); Isa. 60:2; Jer. 13:16; Ezk. 34:12; Joel 2:2; Zeph. 1:15; Ps. 97:2; Job 22:13; 38:9; also Sir. 45:5. Only in Ex. 20:21; Dt. 5:22; 1 K. 8:12 (par. 2 Ch. 6:1) does it have the article. Isa. 5:30, a difficult passage, has the form *ʿarîpeyhâ.*[14] Forms of the verb *ʿārap* occur twice (Dt. 32:2; 33:28). In the lexical field and the immediate context we often find → עָנָן *ʿānān,* "clouds" (Dt. 4:11; 5:22; Ezk. 34:12; Joel 2:2; Zeph. 1:15; Ps. 97:2; Job 38:9; 86 occurrences in the OT); → חשׁך *ḥōšeḵ,* "darkness" (Dt. 4:11; Isa. 60:2; Joel 2:2; Zeph. 1:15; 82 occurrences in the OT); and *ʾapēlâ,* "darkness" (Joel 2:2 and Zeph. 1:15; only 10 occurrences in the OT). In the broader context we again find *ʿānān* (Ex. 19:9,16; 24:15-16,18; 1 K. 8:10-11; 2 Ch. 5:13-14); *ḥōšeḵ* (Dt. 5:23; 2 S. 22:12; Ps. 18:12[11]; Isa. 58:10; 59:9); and *ʾapēlâ* (Isa. 58:10; 59:9), but also such words as → עב *ʿāḇ(ʿāḇîm),* "cloud" (Ex. 19:9; 2 S. 22:12; Ps. 18:12[11]); → צלמות *ṣalmāweṯ,* "darkness" (Jer. 13:16); and *ʾēš,* "fire" (Dt. 5:22; Ps. 97:3).

The term *ʿarāpel,* "dark clouds, thick darkness," has on the one hand baneful connotations; on the other, it promises life and salvation.[15] The word has its setting in theophany accounts.[16] The cloud enshrouds the deity (Ex. 20:21; Dt. 5:22; 1 K. 8:12) or accompanies the deity ("thick darkness under God's feet," 2 S. 22:10 = Ps. 18:10[9]; or "all around God," Ps. 97:2).

In the Pentateuch *ʿarāpel* appears only in the Sinai/Horeb theophany. According to Ex. 20:21 (E), the people stood trembling in the distance while the "priestly" Moses approached the *ʿarāpel* (with article) in which God was enveiled on the mountain.[17] In E's view Yahweh has his dwelling place in the *ʿarāpel* on the mountain (see also Ex.

9. *GesB,* 620; M. Noth, *Könige. BK* IX/1 (1968), 182; H. Wildberger, *Isaiah 1–12* (Eng. trans. 1991), 223; cf. also *CAD,* IV, 279 *(erēpu)* and 302 *(erpetu); AHw,* I, 243 (*erpetu[m],* "cloud"), in turn cites *ʿarāpel.*

10. M. Dahood, *Bibl* 50 (1969) 356; see also Görg, 57; P. J. van Zijl, *Baal: A Study of Texts in Connexion with Baal in the Ugaritic Epics. AOAT* 10 (1972), 331, and n. 7.

11. Cf. A. S. Kapelrud, *Baal in the Ras Shamra Texts* (1952), 61; G. del Olmo Lete, *Mitos y Leyendas de Canaan* (1981), 605.

12. E.g., J. C. de Moor, *The Seasonal Pattern in the Ugaritic Myth of Baʿlu. AOAT* 16 (1971), 98.

13. E.g., W. F. Albright, *Yahweh and the Gods of Canaan* (1968), 201: "storm clouds."

14. See Wildberger, *Isaiah 1–12,* 223.

15. Noth, *BK* IX/1, 182; *HAL,* II, 888.

16. Reymond, 13-14; S. Terrien, *The Elusive Presence* (1978), 194; Gamberoni, → IV, 31.

17. G. Beer, *Exodus. HAT* I/3 (1939), 105.

19:3 and Sir. 45:5, which alludes to the same event). In the proclamation of the Ten Commandments in Dt. 5, we read that on the mountain Yahweh uttered the words out of "the fire" *(hā'ēš),* "the cloud" *(heʿānān),* and "the thick darkness" *(hāʿărāpēl)* (v. 22). Here we find a combination comparable to Dt. 4:11, which speaks of "a mountain blazing up to the very heavens,"[18] "darkness" *(ḥōšek),* "cloud" *(ʿānān),* and "thick darkness" *(ʿărāpel).* These elements are commonly described as manifestations of Yahweh's original nature as a storm god;[19] possibly, however, "fire," "cloud," and "darkness" were added at a later date as a gloss on the word *ʿărāpel.*

The autonomy of this word is apparent above all in 1 K. 8:12 (= 2 Ch. 6:1), in Solomon's prayer at the dedication of the temple. The origin of this passage is obscure. The LXX not only includes (following v. 53) an expansion of the prayer but also cites a source: *hḗlion egnṓrisen eṇ ouranǭ kýrios . . . ouk idoú haútē gégraptai en biblíǭ tḗs ǭdḗs?;* ever since Wellhausen, almost all exegetes have emended this to read: "The sun in the heavens did Yahweh create, but he wished to dwell in darkness, and said: Build me a house, a house of my dwelling place, that I may dwell there forever — behold, it is written in the Book of the Upright" (*sēper hayyāšār* for *sēper haššîr,* "Book of Songs").[20] Van den Born instead derives *egnṓrisen* from *hôḏîaʿ,* which he views as a corruption of an original *hôʿîḏ:* "Yahweh placed . . ."; his translation differs at other points as well: "He instructed it to dwell outside the dark: I have built you a house as a habitation, a place to dwell month by month."[21]

It is clear that these words are an ancient hymn that has been incorporated here. With sovereign authority, Yahweh appoints the sun its place in the firmament of heaven;[22] he himself, however, dwells in "the deep darkness" (with article); Albright erroneously interprets the second colon as a question: "Doth he desire to tent in the storm clouds?"[23] This reading is consonant with the separate chamber in the temple, the *dᵉḇîr* (NRSV "inner sanctuary"), which is in total darkness, having no windows.[24] The nature of the *dᵉḇîr* also chimes with "heavenly" reality: the name of Yahweh — Yahweh himself — dwells within the temple. Yahweh's dwelling in the *ʿărāpel* may also suggest his manifestation as a mountain god and a rain-bringing storm god, who stands in contrast to the astral deities.[25]

This passage thus brings together two previously separate elements: the deity's dwelling in the thick darkness ("a term for the *deus absconditus*")[26] and in the temple.

---

18. On this use of the accusative see *GK,* §118q.
19. E.g., Steuernagel, *Das Deuteronomium. HKAT* I/3 (²1923), 66.
20. Wellhausen, *Die Composition des Hexateuchs und der historischen Bücher des ATs* (⁴1963), 269; but see also A. Rahlfs, *Septuaginta-Studien,* III (1911), 262; H. St. J. Thackeray, *The Septuagint and Jewish Worship* (²1923), 76-79; J. A. Montgomery and H. S. Gehman, *Kings. ICC* (1951), 189-92; D. W. Gooding, *Textus* 7 (1969) 21-25.
21. Pp. 237-38.
22. G. Hentschel, *1 Könige. NEB* (1984), 56.
23. *Yahweh and the Gods of Canaan,* 201.
24. K. Möhlenbrink, *Der Tempel Salomos. BWANT* 59 (1932), 132, 137f.
25. Noth, *BK* IX/1, 182; Würthwein, *Die Bücher der Könige. ATD* 11/1 (²1985), 88-89.
26. Von Rad, *TDNT,* II, 382.

The temple and its furnishings (1 K. 7: the pillars Jachin and Boaz, the molten sea, the wheeled cauldrons) exhibit the influence of Jebusite and Phoenician ideas. What had previously been a Canaanite sanctuary along with its cult, rituals, and myths was now — in the view of a later writer — occupied as his own sanctuary by Yahweh, who had not lived in a house since the day he brought Israel up from Egypt (2 S. 7:6). Previously, of course, he had moved about with a tent as his dwelling place; but his true, original dwelling place was the *ʿarāpel* ("a constant phenomenon").[27]

This notion is confirmed by 2 S. 22:10 (= Ps. 18:10[9]), in the context of a relatively ancient theophany (or perhaps better epiphany) description (vv. 8-15).[28] This epiphany is introduced by an earthquake accompanied by smoke, a devouring fire, and flames. The deity rides on a cherub,[29] flying on the wings of the wind, having come down from the heavens, which have "bowed down." During this descent, the *ʿarāpel* was under the deity's feet. Thus the *ʿarāpel* indicates the actual appearance of God; it is described and paraphrased in terms such as: a canopy of darkness, dark water and thick concealing clouds, and hail, lightning, and thunder in which is heard "the Most High, his voice" (vv. 12-15). The *ʿarāpel* is both manifestation and representation of the hidden God. Of course it is impossible to ignore in this hymn "the allusions of this description to the Sinai theophany" (Ex. 19),[30] but they do not define the special character of the *ʿarāpel*. In consequence, *ʿarāpel* is associated not with the (Sinai) theophany (or epiphany) but with the (veiled) manifestation of God wherever he appears or reveals his presence.

We encounter the same idea in Ps. 97:2, which celebrates God's kingship in a theophany (or epiphany) description recalling Ps. 18. Now, however, the "thick darkness" is not only under God's feet but "all around him." As accompanying phenomena, the psalm again mentions earthquake, fire, lightning, and thunder. In other religions *epopteia* ("vision of the deity") often constitutes the solemn high point of the cult; here, by contrast, Yahweh manifests himself "as one who is veiled."[31] Despite this concealment, however, righteousness and justice are the foundations of his throne.

Job 22:13, too, appeals to God's hiddenness: the final discourse of Eliphaz quotes Job as asking, "What does God know? Can he judge through the deep darkness?" The following verse states that thick clouds enwrap him. Here *ʿarāpel* appears as a massive wall behind which God has concealed himself. In contrast to Ps. 97:2, the cause of human justice seems unable to penetrate to God's presence. In Job 38:9 *ʿarāpel* serves metaphorically as a "swaddling band" (hapax legomenon) for the sea, in parallel with the clouds, which are the sea's "garment." Here *ʿarāpel* represents a barrage against the power of the sea and a sign of God's power.

In the prophetic books *ʿarāpel* is primarily a phenomenon accompanying the "day of Yahweh," which is described as a day of darkness *(ḥōšeḵ)*, gloom *(ʾapēlâ)*, clouds

---

27. Van den Born, 236.
28. Kraus, *Psalms 1–59* (Eng. trans. 1988), 260-61.
29. → כרוב *kerûḇ*.
30. Kraus, *Psalms 1–59*, 260.
31. A. Weiser, *Psalms. OTL* (Eng. trans. 1962), 632.

(ʿānān), and finally *ʿarāpel* (Joel 2:2; Zeph. 1:15). In Zeph. 1:14-15 these descriptions of the "day of Yahweh" are preceded by others such as "day of wrath" and "day of distress and anguish." Here we see that the word and concept *ʿarāpel* has ceased to function as a unique and independent element in the manifestation and representation of the hidden God in epiphany or theophany, having become allied with other phenomena associated with God's power.

Ezk. 34:12 speaks of a "day of clouds and thick darkness," although here too the idea of a "day of Yahweh" hovers in the background.[32] We are possibly dealing with familiar vocabulary associated with eschatology in popular usage.[33] In Jer. 13:6 — a verse of unusual beauty even for Jeremiah[34] — we again see clearly the outlines of a baneful "day of Yahweh." This threat of judgment calls on the people to give glory to Yahweh before he brings darkness; they are looking for light, but God sends impenetrable gloom *(ṣalmāweṯ)* and makes it *ʿarāpel.*

In a description of Zion's future glory, finally, Isa. 60:2 contrasts disaster for the nations with salvation for Israel: darkness *(ḥōšeḵ)* will cover the earth and *ʿarāpel* the peoples, whereas for Zion, Yahweh himself will arise and manifest his glory. Although the notion that God vouchsafes his own people "light" (i.e., himself) also appears elsewhere in the OT (e.g., Ex. 10:23),[35] only here is it expressed in this unique way, suggestive of a theophany.

III. Early Versions and Postbiblical Literature. The LXX translates *ʿarāpel* 9 times with *gnóphos* (Ex. 20:21; 2 S. 22:10 par. Ps. 18:10[9]; 1 K. 8:12 par. 2 Ch. 6:1; Isa. 60:2; Ezk. 34:12; Ps. 97:2; Job 22:13; also Sir. 45:5), 3 times with *homíchlē* (Joel 2:2; Zeph. 1:15; Job 38:9), twice with *thýella* (Dt. 4:11; 5:22), and only once with *skótos* (Jer. 13:16; 115 occurrences in the OT). The word *thýella* occurs also in Ex. 10:22, again alongside *skótos gnóphos,* so that many have voiced the suspicion that in this verse *ʿarāpel* should be added to the MT, after the pattern of Dt. 4:11 and 5:22. (In the NT the word occurs only once, in Heb. 12:18, which reflects Ex. 19:12,16,18; Dt. 4:11.) The other words are less common in the LXX than *skótos: gnóphos* occurs 28 times, *homíchlē* only 10 (cf. also 2 Pet. 2:17). The translation of the Vulg. is also not uniform. Most often (12 times) we find *caligo* (Ex. 20:21; Dt. 4:11; 5:22; 2 S. 22:10 par. Ps. 18:10[9]; Isa. 60:2; Jer. 13:6; Ezk. 34:12; Ps. 97:2; Job 22:13; 38:9; 2 Ch. 6:1), twice *turbo* (Joel 2:2; Zeph. 1:15), and once *nebula* (1 K. 8:12); *nubes* is used in Sir. 45:5. Noteworthy is the difference in translation between 1 K. 8:12 and its parallel 2 Ch. 6:1. As noted above, Sir. 45:5 is a parallel to Ex. 20:21.

The word has not yet been found in the Dead Sea Scrolls, but it does appear in rabbinic literature.[36]

Mulder

---

32. Zimmerli, *Ezekiel 2. Herm* (Eng. trans. 1983), 216.
33. Van den Born, *Ezechiel. BOT* XI (1954), 203.
34. B. Duhm, *Das Buch Jeremia. KHC* XI (1901), 123.
35. Whybray, *Isaiah 40–66. NCBC* (1975), 230.
36. See the lexicons of Levy and Jastrow, s.v.

עָרַץ *ʿāraṣ;* עָרִיץ *ʿārîṣ;* מַעֲרָצָה *maʿ^a^rāṣâ;* עָרוּץ *ʿārûṣ*

I. 1. Etymology, Meaning; 2. Occurrences, Translations. II. 1. Verb; 2. Nouns. III. Later Usage. IV. Theological Significance.

I. 1. *Etymology, Meaning.* The etymology of Heb. *ʿāraṣ* is unclear. On the one hand, we may consider Ugar. *ʿrẓ,* "the terrible one," an epithet of the god ʿAthtar, and possibly Arab. *ʿariṣa,* "be aroused" (with *ṣ* instead of *ẓ*); on the other hand, we may consider Arab. *ʿaraḍa,* "thrust forward"; Jewish Aram. *ʿ^a^raʿ,* Syr. *ʾēraʿ,* "encounter" (but cf. Syr. *ʿrṣ,* "thrust," with *ṣ!*), and Egyp. Aram. *lʿrqh,* "toward." With respect to its original meaning, the Hebrew formative root belongs to the semantic field of "fear," not "be strong."[1]

2. *Occurrences, Translations.* With the exception of the ancient hymn fragment Ps. 89:6-19(Eng. vv. 5-20), in which the root appears in v. 8(7), derivatives of this root appear only in later documents, beginning with Isaiah: Isaiah, Jeremiah, Ezekiel, Job, Psalms; then in Deuteronomy and a Deuteronomistic section of Joshua.

The extraordinary variety the LXX exhibits in translating the root can be summarized in three categories: (1) "fear" (*phobeín, ptoeín, tarássein,* etc.); (2) "be mighty, exalted" (*andreíos, dynástēs, krataíos,* etc.); (3) "act unjustly" (*adikeín, katadynastheúein, loimós,* etc.). The Vulg. distinguishes only the first two: *metuere, expavere, formidare,* etc., vs. *robustus, fortis, praevalere, potentiam ostendere,* etc. — although *tyrannus* (Job 15:20) and *violentus* (Job 27:13) suggest the wickedness of the powerful.

II. 1. *Verb.* Verbal forms occur in the qal (11 times), hiphil (3 times), and niphal (once). The semantic bipolarity of the qal and hiphil is striking: intransitively and passively, forms of both stems mean "feel fear"; transitively and actively, they mean "engender fear in someone." With respect to the qal, a possible explanation might be that it still denotes the originally undifferentiated concept of a sudden jump, which can be both the cause and the result of fear (cf. the ambiguity of the Eng. word "terror"). The reason for the bipolarity in the hiphil is that it functions either as a causative (Isa. 8:13, *maʿ^a^rîṣ,* "who inspires fear") or as a declarative (possibly as a denominative from *ʿārîṣ*)[2] (8:12, *taʿ^a^rîṣû,* "you acknowledge to be fear-inducing," i.e., "you fear").

The Deuteronomistic exhortations to Israel to be fearless in battle against enemy peoples (Dt. 1:29; 7:21; 20:3; 31:6; Josh. 1:9) use the verb in the qal together with forms of the more common roots *yrʾ, ḥtt,* and *ḥpz,* "fear." The rhetorical peculiarity of our words lies in the emphasis it lends to a statement by virtue of its lower frequency.

---

1. Contra P. Joüon, *Mélanges de la Faculté Orientale. . . à Beyrouth* 5 (1910), 443-45, and rabbinic scholars (see III below).

2. See II.2 below.

On the basis of its etymology and use elsewhere, we can recognize its specific semantic nuance as denoting faintheartedness manifested in a physical response: "start, shrink back."

In his oath of purgation (Job 31:34), Job avows that he has never shrunk back *(ʾeʿᵉrôṣ)* from the multitude; elsewhere (13:25) he complains that his enemy wants to startle *(taʿᵃrôṣ)* him like a windblown leaf. In Ps. 10:18 the meaning of the form *laʿᵃrōṣ* can be either active or passive: "so that no man on earth may strike terror any more," or "so that no man on earth need fear."[3]

The qal is used in an active sense in describing the day of Yahweh (Isa. 2:19,21): Yahweh rises to terrify *(laʿᵃrōṣ)* the earth. Here terror is correlated with the appearance in majesty of the lord of the universe. As a result of such usage — sovereign power strikes terror — the dominant notion "be powerful, rule" became associated with the word. A taunt song challenges Babylon to inspire terror *(taʿᵃrōṣî)* once more with its enchantments and sorceries (Isa. 47:12).

Isa. 8:12-13 capitalizes rhetorically on the bipolarity of the hiphil forms: "Do not fear" *(lōʾ taʿᵃrîṣû)* what the people fear, God says, for it is Yahweh who "instills fear in you" *(maʿᵃrîṣᵉḵem)*. Isa. 29:23 borrows the language of this oracle, using *yaʿᵃrîṣû* in parallel with *yaqdîšû*, "sanctify" — a usage that paves the way for a spiritualization of the notion of "fear of God" (Ps. 89:8 [7]).

In the niphal the verb is used in parallel with *nôrāʾ*, "awesome": Yahweh "is feared" *(naʿᵃrāṣ)* in the council of the holy ones (Ps. 89:8[7]).

2. *Nouns.* The noun *ʿārîṣ* is a *qaṭṭîl* form (with compensatory lengthening), i.e., an intensive form expressing an amplification of the root concept. It means primarily someone terrifying, hence powerful and intimidating, a tyrant. It denotes the victorious warrior, whom none can despoil of his booty (Isa. 49:25, par. to *gibbôr*, "mighty"; also in v. 24[4]). The *ʿārîṣîm* are foreign nations, advancing to pillage and slay (Ezk. 28:7 and 31:12 par. to *zārîm*, "strangers"; 32:12 par. to *gibbôrîm;* 30:11). The prophet here calls the Babylonian armies waging war against Tyre and Egypt *ʿārîṣê gôyim*, "the most terrible of the nations." In Isa. 29:5 *ʿārîṣîm* (par. to *zārîm* [1QIsᵃ, *zēḏîm*, "insolent"]) refers to the enemies besetting Jerusalem.

In Isa. 25:3,5, the identity of the *ʿārîṣîm* in this apocalyptic hymn is impossible to determine. For the semantic content of the word, the synonyms (*zārîm* [or *zēḏîm*][5] in vv. 2 and 4; *ʿam-ʿāz*, "ruthless nation," in v. 3) and antonyms (*dal*, "poor," and *ʾeḇyôn*, "needy," in v. 4) are significant. In a similar context (29:20), we find the synonyms *lēṣ*, "scoffer," and *šōqᵉḏê ʾāwen*, "evildoers," and the antonyms *ʿᵃnāwîm*, "meek," *ʾeḇyônê ʾāḏām*, "the neediest" (v. 19), and *ṣaddîq*, "one in the right" (v. 21).

Someone who feels threatened within his own community calls his powerful perse-

---

3. For the former see NRSV; similarly LXX; Vulg. *iuxta Hebraeos;* Rashi; Kraus, *Psalms 1–59* (Eng. trans. 1988), 190. For the latter, Ibn Ezra; B. Duhm, *Die Psalmen. KHC* XIV (²1922), 33; et al.

4. *BHS.*

5. See *BHS.*

cutors *ʿārîṣîm* (Jer. 15:21, par. to *rāʿîm,* "wicked"; Job 6:23, par. to *ṣār,* "enemy"); they rise up against him and seek his life (Ps. 54:5[3]; 86:14, par. to *zārîm* or *zēḏîm).*[6] Finally, the human tendency to view one's opponents as morally inferior leads to the identification of *ʿārîṣ* with *rāšāʿ* in transpersonal reflections on human destiny (Ps. 37:35; Job 15:20; 27:13).

The word *maʿ^{a}rāṣâ* (Isa. 10:33) is generally understood in the sense of "violence," although it may be the name of an implement.[7] Whether *ʿārûṣ* (Job 30:6) is connected with our root remains disputed (possibly: Arab. *ʿrḍ,* "gully"); if so, the text can be translated "In the dreadful wadis. . . ."

III. Later Usage. In the Dead Sea Scrolls the verb appears only in texts that replicate Deuteronomy (1QM 10:4; 15:8). The *ʿārîṣîm* are identified with the "wicked" and "scoffers" (1QH 2:10-11), and finally with the "unbelievers who violate the covenant" (1QpHab 2:6) and the "fellowship of Belial" (1QH 2:21).

Rabbinic linguistic tradition posits two basic meanings: "break to pieces" and "be strong."[8] In addition, however, it explains and uses the hiphil in the sense of "praise," i.e., "confess God's power."[9] Note the translations of Isa. 29:23 in the Targ. *(yēmrûn taqqîp)* and Vulg. *(praedicabunt).*[10]

IV. Theological Significance. The *ʿārîṣîm* may gain riches (Prov. 11:16; Job 27:16) and strike root like a succulent green tree (Ps. 37:35),[11] but they will not endure (Ps. 37:36; Job 15:20). Their children will starve or perish; their riches will devolve upon the just and innocent (Job 27:14-17). For the power of an individual to tyrannize over others involves a blasphemous arrogance (Job 15:20,25) that Yahweh will lay low (Isa. 13:11). Yahweh alone can redeem from the grasp of an *ʿārîṣ* (Jer. 15:21), since Yahweh stands beside his protégé like a "dread warrior" (Jer. 20:11; in this phrase *ʿārîṣ* refers to *gibbôr* and not directly to Yahweh).[12] Israel must not fear hostile powers (Dt. 20:3; Isa. 8:12), since Yahweh is with Israel. Instead, Israel is to fear the power of Yahweh (Isa. 8:13), for whoever confesses Yahweh's sovereign power will recognize Yahweh's holiness.

Kedar-Kopfstein

---

6. See *BHS.*
7. Rashi.
8. Ibn Janāḥ, *Sefer ha-shorashim* (ed. Bacher) (1896), 387; D. Kimchi, *Sefer ha-shorashim* (1847), 280.
9. *Pirqe d'Rabbi Eliezer* IV, etc.
10. Cf. Kimchi in loc.
11. On the text see *BHS.*
12. Contra *GesB,* 619.

עֶרֶשׂ *'ereś;* מִטָּה *miṭṭâ;* יָצוּעַ *yāṣûa'*

I. Beds in the Ancient Near East and Israel. II. Differentiation and Etymology. III. Hebrew OT and Sirach: 1. Sleeping Beds; 2. Sickbed and Bier; 3. Luxury Beds; 4. Adultery and Prostitution; 5. 2 S. 17:28. IV. 1. Dead Sea Scrolls; 2. LXX.

I. Beds in the Ancient Near East and Israel. Cuneiform texts distinguish various types of "beds."[1] Gods had their beds in temples.[2] Names are given for individual parts of bedsteads, accessories, and decorations.[3] In the ancient Near East a bed was a piece of luxury furniture. Its basic form was a rectangular frame, with cords and transverse braces supporting several cushions, as fragments from Ai, Khirbet el-Meshash, and Tell en-Nasbeh illustrate. The Assyrian bed with curved head (in the shape of a demon)[4] is attested from the 8th through the 5th century; such beds were presumably exported to Palestine and copied there, as clay models from Beer-sheba and Ashdod show, as well as a stele from Memphis.[5] Mittmann argues for a distinctive basic type used in the Syro-Palestinian region.[6] The model clay bed from tomb 1002 at Lachish exhibits two supports of different shape (a distinctive basic form?). The six-foot bronze bed from Tell el-Farah South dates from the Persian period.[7]

Beds served for sleeping or reclining, as divans or sofas for sitting during feasts and orgies (with arms supported by the head and foot), as sickbeds, for love and sex. They were also objects of magic.[8]

Only kings and wealthy individuals had beds of ivory (Am. 3:12; 6:4), dining couches of gold and silver (Est. 1:6), divans, and lounges. The pieces in question were probably beds ornamented with ivory or silver and gold. Ordinary individuals slept on

---

'ereś. D. Barthélemy, *Critique textuelle de l'AT,* I. *OBO* 50/1 (1982); H. Gese, "Kleine Beiträge zum Verständnis des Amosbuches," *VT* 12 (1962) 417-38; M. Görg, "Die 'Sänfte Salomos' nach HL 3,9f.," *BN* 18 (1982) 15-25; C. D. Isbell, *Corpus of the Aramaic Incantation Bowls. SBLDS* 17 (1975); R. Kilian, "Die Totenerweckungen Elias und Elisas — eine Motivwanderung?" *BZ* 10 (1966), 44-56; C. Levin, *Der Sturz der Königin Atalja. SBS* 105 (1982); H. G. May, "A Supplementary Note on the Ivory Inlays from Samaria," *PEQ* 65 (1933) 88-89; S. Mittmann, "Amos 3, 12-15 und das Bett der Samarier," *ZDPV* 92 (1976) 149-67; W. Rudolph, "Schwierige Amosstellen," *Wort und Geschichte. FS K. Elliger. AOAT* 18 (1973), 157-62, esp. 157-58; A. Salonen, *Die Möbel des Alten Mesopotamien nach sumerisch-akkadischen Quellen. AnAcScFen* 127 (1963), esp. 107-73; A. Schmitt, "Die Totenerweckung in 2 Kön 4,8-37," *BZ* 19 (1975) 1-25; H. Weippert, "Möbel," *BRL*², 228-32.

1. Salonen, 110-21.
2. Clay models, ibid., 16-19.
3. Ibid., 146-73.
4. K 2411, II, 19; Mittmann, 155-56.
5. *BRL*², 229-30.
6. Pp. 161ff.
7. *BRL*², 229-30.
8. Isbell, text 66.3 (p. 146).

the ground on spreads or rugs, covered with a cloak (Jgs. 4:18; Ex. 22:26-27). In Mesopotamia people slept on matting and straw.

A bed was a rectangular wood frame with four legs, about three feet wide and six feet long, strung with cords that supported a mat or mattress.[9] It included a panel at the foot and a semicircular headboard. The bed was covered with a sheet and pillows or cushions, over which a spread (*massēḵâ* II) was laid. One probably climbed onto (*'ālâ 'al*) a bed with the help of a footstool (Gen. 49:4, *miškāḇ;* 2 K. 1:4,6,16, *miṭṭâ;* Ps. 132:3, *'ereś*); cf. Ugar. *l'ršh y'l.*[10]

II. Differentiation and Etymology. Biblical Hebrew uses five terms for sleeping furniture; they cannot be differentiated because, in addition to being used in parallelism, they enter into many syntagmatic forms.

The most common word, *miškāḇ,* occurs 46 times plus 6 times in the Aramaic sections of Daniel. It denotes sleeping accommodations, usually in the form of a mat or mattress on which the sleeper lies. The term can also refer to a bier (2 Ch. 16:14) or tomb (Isa. 57:2; Ezk. 32:25).

The word *miṭṭâ,* "couch, bed," occurs 29 times in the Hebrew OT plus Sir. 48:6; it refers to a bed with a wooden frame. It can also refer to a litter (1 S. 19:15) or bier (2 S. 3:31). One Ugaritic text attests to a word pair *'rṣ* par. *mṭt* (cf. 1 S. 28:23).[11] The etymology *miṭṭâ* < **minṭâ,* "place where one stretches out" = "couch" (cf. Ger. *Liege*),[12] is analogous to Gk. *klínē* < *klínein.*

There are 11 occurrences of *'ereś,* "bed, couch, divan, sofa," the common Semitic term. The root appears in Akk. *eršu,* "bed,"[13] *uršu,* "bedroom," and *mar(a)šu,* "divan, couch." Ugar. *'rš* (10 occurrences) refers to the bridal bed, and the bed as the locus of conception and birth.[14] In one text a sick man is told to take his bed (and walk); the word pair *bt* par. *'rš* is used, as in Ps. 132:3 and Cant. 1:16-17.[15]

Within the Aramaic language group, the root occurs in Samaritan, Christian-Palestinian, Syriac, and Mandaic. Alongside Jewish Aram. *'arsā',* "bed, bier," we also find *'ᵃrîsâ,* "crib, cradle," with frame and trestle. The meaning appears to have undergone further development in South Semitic: Arab. *'arš/'urš,* "throne," and *'arīš,* "trellis"; Eth. *'arīš,* "bower, tent." Heb. *'ereś* is feminine (like the Syriac and Mandaic cognates), as the pl. *'arśôṯām* (Am. 6:4) shows. A masc. *'rśyh* is attested in 4Q184 5. Usually *'ereś* denotes a more luxurious bed with frame, cushions, and the like. Ps. 6:7(Eng. v. 6) and Am. 6:4 use *'ereś* and *miṭṭâ* in parallel. As an etymology it is reasonable to postulate a verb *'rš,* "lie, rest," or (more likely) a connection with Arab. *'rš,* "erect a trellis, roof over."

The noun *yāṣûa',* "couch, bed," occurs 5 times in the OT plus Sir. 31:19 (= 34:19);

---

9. *AuS,* VII, 187-88.
10. *KTU* 1.17, I, 38.
11. *KTU* 1.14, I, 29-30.
12. → נטה *nāṭâ;* W. Rudolph, *Joel-Amos-Obadjah-Jona. KAT* XIII/2 (1971), 159.
13. *AHw,* I, 246b; Salonen, 110, 123ff.; Mittmann, 158, 161.
14. For the former see *KTU* 1.17, I, 38; for the latter, 1.17, II, 41-42.
15. *KTU* 1.14, II, 43ff. = IV, 21ff.

41:22; 47:20; it derives from *yṣ'*, "spread out a couch" (Isa. 58:5; Ps. 139:8; cf. Arab. and OSA *wḍ'*), as does the noun form *maṣṣā'* (Isa. 28:20).

III. Hebrew OT and Sirach.

1. *Sleeping Beds.* In Ps. 6:7(6) *miṭṭâ* and *'ereś* in parallel refer to the psalmist's bed for the night. David's refusal to climb onto his bed *('ereś yāṣûa')* expresses his indefatigable search for a dwelling place for Yahweh. Job complains about sleepless nights on his couch that pursue him like a persecution mania (Job 7:13); the same theme reappears in Job 17:13 *(yāṣûa')*.

Prov. 26:14 chastises the lazy person who turns over in bed without getting up, who is like a door turning on its hinges while otherwise staying in place. Sir. 31(34):19 warns gluttons and drunks against soiling the bed.

A wealthy Shunammite woman provided a sumptuous room for Elisha in a walled upper chamber, with a bed, table, chair, and lamp (2 K. 4:10); guests would ordinarily spend the night on the roof on straw or in a tent. A desperate mother laid her child suffering from sunstroke on Elisha's bed (2 K. 4:21,32). In 1 K. 17:19 (post-Dtr), Elijah lays the son of a Zarephathite widow on his own bed to perform a magical healing ritual.

2. *Sickbed and Bier.* A bed is often a sickbed. In 1 K. 1 Elijah's oracle of judgment against Ahaziah is repeated three times (vv. 4,6,16): he will never leave the sickbed *(miṭṭâ),* for he must die. In the story of David's flight in 1 S. 19, Saul gives orders to execute David on his sickbed (v. 15); Michal, however, covers David's flight by placing the teraphim in his bed (v. 13). Only after following the urging of his entourage and the medium at Endor does Saul sit on her bed (1 S. 28:23) and eat his last meal.[16] In the context of an individual hymn of thanksgiving, Ps. 41:4(3) promises that Yahweh will sustain the righteous on their sickbed and heal their infirmities.

The dying Jacob sits on the head of his *miṭṭâ* (Gen. 47:31 J), then sits up to bless his grandsons (48:2 E); finally, he draws his feet up into his bed and dies (Gen. 49:33). When death occurs, the bed (or just the bedding?) serves as a bier, as in the state funeral for Abner at Hebron (2 S. 3:31). Dt. 3:11 calls the huge tomb of Og, the king of Bashan, at Rabbah of the Ammonites an *'ereś barzel,* "iron sarcophagus."

3. *Luxury Beds.* Kings and wealthy individuals in the northern and southern kingdoms lay on beds of ivory *(miṭṭôṯ šēn)* in winter and summer palaces, indulging themselves with sofas for dining or lounging (Am. 6:4), a new form of "high civilization" (cf. Akk. *^{iṣ}ereš šinni* in the tribute inventory of Ben Hadad II to Adadnirari III); they lay at table, surfeiting with wealth and luxury. The *māšāl* in Am. 3:12 attacks the high society of the northern kingdom, who sit on the corner or foot of the couch *(miṭṭâ)* and recline on the head (or cushion?) of the bed (*'ereś*).[17] Sir. 48:6 associates this prophetic

---

16. See IV.2 below.

17. On "corner" or "foot" → פאה *pē'â.* For text-critical discussion see H. W. Wolff, *Joel and Amos. Herm* (Eng. trans. 1977), 196ff.; Mittmann, 155-56.

criticism of kings and aristocrats with Elijah. Even the bed of Pharaoh offered no protection against the plague of frogs (Ex. 7:28 J). Ahab lay down on his bed or divan with his face to the wall, angered because Naboth refused to sell his vineyard (1 K. 21:4). The king's palace had a *ḥᵃḏar hammiṭṭôṯ,* a bedroom or a closet for bedding (2 K. 11:2 = 2 Ch. 22:11). In it Jehosheba hid her nephew Joash from Athaliah for six years (or else this room was where the princes were executed).[18]

Ishbaal was murdered and beheaded while lying on his couch in his bedchamber (2 S. 4:7); similarly, conspirators killed King Joash on his bed, after he had been severely wounded during the Aramean invasion (2 Ch. 24:25).

The court narrative of Ahasuerus's banquet in the palace garden at Susa proudly mentions couches of gold and silver (Est. 1:6). On the *miṭṭâ* where Esther is reclining, Haman begs for his life — an act the king interprets as an assault and punishes with execution (Est. 7:8). In Cant. 3:7 *miṭṭâ* refers to the palanquin or litter of Solomon, a processional device used to carry in the bride.[19] The lovers in Cant. 1:16 speak rapturously of their couch with green coverlets in a palace of cedar and juniper.

4. *Adultery and Prostitution.* Beds are mentioned in texts dealing with adultery and prostitution. In the Blessing of Jacob, Gen. 49:4 (alluded to in 1 Ch. 5:1) attacks Reuben, the son of Leah, for sleeping with Jacob's concubine Bilhah (*miškāḇ* par. *yāṣûaʿ*). Prov. 7:16 warns against the perfumed bed *(ʿereś)* of a prostitute, possibly a worshiper of Astarte. Ezk. 23:40-41 (secondary) describes the preparations of the apostate prostitutes Oholah and Oholibah: they send for men, bathe, paint their eyes, deck themselves with ornaments, arrange their couch, set their table with incense and oil.

Sir. 41:22 declares the bed *(yāṣûaʿ)* of a servant girl taboo; 47:20 blames Solomon's polygamy for the division of the kingdom *(yāṣûaʿ* par. *miškāḇ).*

5. *2 S. 17:28.* Textually problematic is 2 S. 17:28. The supplies brought by David's faithful vassals following Absalom's putsch include vessels, food, and **ערשת משכב**, "sleeping gear"; the LXX corrects *ʿrśt* > *ʿśrt,* "ten"; the MT has only *miškāḇ*.[20]

IV. 1. *Dead Sea Scrolls.* A syntagm *yᵉṣûʿê ʿarśî* occurs in 1QH 9:4, in the context of a lament (not entirely certain because of a gap in the text). In the long psalm 1QS 10, the psalmist expresses his desire to extol God always, even when lying in bed (l. 14, *miškaḇ yāṣûaʿ*).

In 4Q184 we have a polemic against prostitution, the way to "the eternal fire" (l. 7); there is no place for it among those "who gird themselves with light" (l. 8). The prostitute's bed is referred to in ll. 5-6 by the terms *ʿrś, yṣwʿ,* and *mškb.*

---

18. An interpretation proposed most recently by E. Würthwein, *Die Bücher der Könige. ATD* XI/2 (1984), in loc.

19. Görg, 20.

20. Barthélemy, 282ff.

2. *LXX.* The LXX translates *miṭṭâ* (24 times) and *'ereś* (9 times) with *klínē,* "bed, litter." In Am. 6:4 *strōmnḗ,* "carpet, cover," translates *'ereś;* Am. 3:12 reads *hiereís* (originally a transcription?).

In 1 S. 28:23 *miṭṭâ* is translated *díphros,* "palanquin"; the translator interpreted the bed as Saul's (royal) palanquin, which had been brought along. In Gen. 47:31 and Am. 3:12, the LXX reads *miṭṭâ* as *maṭṭeh,* "staff, tribe."

The LXX usually translates *yāṣûa'* and *miškāḇ* with *koitḗ,* "couch, marriage bed," once with *strōmnḗ;* Sir. 47:20 paraphrases with *spérma* to make inoffensive a text felt to be obscene. In Am. 3:12 Aquila uses *krábbatos* for *'ereś.*

Angerstorfer

עֵשֶׂב *'ēśeḇ*

I. 1. Semantics; 2. Semitic; 3. OT Occurrences; 4. LXX. II. OT Usage: 1. Fertility; 2. Food; 3. Destruction; 4. Transience.

I. 1. *Semantics.* The noun *'ēśeḇ* is a collective term for all grasses[1] and plants that sprout (*pāraḥ,* Ps. 92:8[Eng. v. 7]; *ṣāmaḥ,* Gen. 2:5) in the rainy season but wither (*yāḇēš,* Ps. 102:12[11]; cf. v. 5[4]) in summer. Other terms reflect their bright green color (→ ירק *yereq*) or luxuriant growth (→ דשא *deše'*). We therefore find the appositions *deše' 'ēśeḇ* (Gen. 1:11,12) and *yereq 'ēśeḇ* (Gen. 1:30; 9:3) (cf. *yereq deše'* in Ps. 37:2) and parallelisms with *deše'* (Dt. 32:2) and with *yereq deše'* (2 K. 19:26 = Isa. 37:27). Ex. 9:25 uses *'ēśeḇ* collectively for low vegetation in contrast to *'ēṣ,* "trees," or woody plants (cf. also Ex. 10:15).

2. *Semitic.* The noun appears in most Semitic languages, with some variation of the sibilant: Akk. *išbabtu,* "grass or the like"; Biblical Aram. *'iśbā';* Jewish Aram. *'iś/sbā';* Syr. *'ēsbā';* Palmyr. *'b[y]'* (abs. pl.).[2] Arab. *'ušb* means "fresh, green, juicy, soft, or tender herbs or herbage"; secondarily it means "pasture."[3] For OSA *'śbn* (sg.?) and *'śbt* (pl.?), Biella gives the meaning "fodder" or "offspring (?)"; for the latter, Beeston offers "pastureland."[4]

No verbal root *'śb* is attested in Hebrew or the various Aramaic dialects, and so the lexeme in Semitic is unlikely to be deverbative. Delitzsch proposed deriving it from

'ēśeḇ. A. E. Rüthy, *Die Pflanze und ihre Teile* (1942), 29-37.

1. → חציר *ḥāṣîr.*
2. On Akkadian see *AHw,* I, 393a; R. C. Thompson, *A Dictionary of Assyrian Botany* (1949), 15ff. On Palmyrene see *DNSI,* II, 890; *CIS,* II, 3913; II, 123.
3. Lane, I/5, 2050; Wehr, 614.
4. Biella, 386; Beeston, 21.

Akk. *ešēbu,* "sprout," but the verbal meanings of Akk. *ešēbu* (D), "plant (a park) with many plants," and Arab. *ʿašiba,* "be grassy, grass-covered," are clearly denominative.[5]

3. *OT Occurrences.* The lexeme occurs 33 times in the OT, primarily in poetic texts; except for the unique fem. pl. form *ʿiśᵉḇôṯ* in Prov. 27:5, it is always a collective singular. Only once does it occur with a suffix: *ʿeśbām,* Isa. 42:15. Biblical Aram. *ʿiśbāʾ* occurs 4 times in the book of Daniel (4:22,29,30[25,32,33]; 5:21).

4. *LXX.* The LXX translates *ʿēśeḇ* 25 times with *chórtos,* in Exodus (5 times) and Zec. 10:1 with *botánē,* and once each with *chortásmata* (Dt. 11:15), *chlōrón* (Dt. 29:22), *ágrōstis* (Mic. 5:6), *chlóē* (Ps. 104:14), and *pambótanon* (Job 5:25).

II. OT Usage.

1. *Fertility.* Since *ʿēśeḇ* refers specifically to plants dependent on rain, their growth and death are totally contingent on precipitation. Until there was rain on the earth, according to the creation account of J, no "herb of the field" *(ʿēśeḇ haśśāḏeh)* could grow (Gen. 2:5). The opening of the Song of Moses (Dt. 32:2) compares the invigorating effect of wisdom teaching to the refreshing drops of rain that promote the growth of grass and young plants. A similar metaphor most likely lies behind Mic. 5:6 (probably postexilic), where the dew and showers that moisten the grass symbolize the blessing vouchsafed to the nations by Yahweh through Israel. According to Prov. 19:12, the favor a king shows his subjects is like dew on the grass. The luxuriant growth of plants during the rainy season symbolizes fertility and vitality. According to Ps. 72:16 (a royal psalm), people blossom *(yāṣîṣû)* like the grass in spring under the rule of the ideal sovereign.[6] (Instead of the textually difficult *mʿyr,* the correct reading may be *ʿmyr[w],* reversing the order of the initial consonants: "may [his] sheaves blossom" like the grass of the field; the comparison would then refer to abundance of grain mentioned previously in this verse.)[7] Job 5:25 also uses *ʿēśeḇ* as a symbol of fertility: Eliphaz says that the offspring of those who submit to God's discipline are like the grass of the field. Ps. 92:8(7) (a hymn tending toward a "judgment doxology") says of the wicked and evildoers that, though they sprout and flourish like grass, they are ultimately doomed to destruction.

2. *Food.* The OT also uses *ʿēśeḇ* in the sense of food for human beings and animals. A distinction must be made between cultivated plants (primarily grain) and wild plants, or between crops grown from seed and pasturage.

In P's creation account (Gen. 1:29-30), *ʿēśeḇ* is a blessing provided by God. In J's story of Eden, however, it is lent negative overtones by the curse pronounced by Yahweh. By means of 3:18b, an interpolator has emphasized the agricultural labor re-

5. Cf. F. Delitzsch, *Prolegomena eines neuen hebräisch-aramäischen Wörterbuch zum AT* (1886), 87; *AHw,* I, 253b; Wehr, 614.

6. Subject "people" supplied; cf. NRSV. See also *AuS,* I, 333.

7. *BHS* and Kraus, *Psalms 60–150* (Eng. trans. 1989), 76.

quired to cultivate the plants of the field *(ʿēśeḇ haśśāḏeh),* an inferior diet imposed as a punishment in place of the delicious fruit provided by the trees in the garden of Eden (2:16; cf. the different usage in 2:5, where it contrasts with *śîaḥ haśśāḏeh*). According to P's creation account, humans and animals were totally vegetarian from the beginning, an expression of their peaceful way of life, which will return at the eschaton (Isa. 11:6-7; 65:25; Hos. 2:20[18]). When P allots food to humans, the use of the paronomastic attribute *zōrēaʿ zeraʿ* to qualify *ʿēśeḇ* in Gen. 1:29 probably refers not to propagation by seed but to the nutritional value of the seeds produced by grasses and other plants (grains and legumes). All these plants, which the earth brings forth in abundance (the connotation of *ʿēśeḇ*) at God's command, are available for human use, whereas in the case of the animals P emphasizes green plants (*yereq ʿēśeḇ,* 1:30). Only after the deluge does P permit the eating of meat (9:3), as a concession to sin; but again all "green plants" (*yereq ʿēśeḇ;* oddly here; cf. their allotment to animals in 1:30) are designated as human food.

In Ps. 104, a creation psalm, v. 14 calls attention to the fact that God causes the grass *(ḥāṣîr)* to grow for the cattle and *ʿēśeḇ* "for people to cultivate"; cultivated plants grown from seed in contrast to wild plants, especially — as the mention of *leḥem* immediately afterward shows — grain.

Only Yahweh, the creator and ruler of the forces of nature, can send rain at the right time; it is therefore ultimately Yahweh who gives human beings their bread and the field its vegetation (Zec. 10:1). If *lāhem* should be emended here to *leḥem,*[8] then the words *ʿēśeḇ baśśāḏeh* that follow refer by contrast to animal food. This prepositional phrase appears with the same meaning in Dt. 11:15, a similar context, where as food for livestock *(liḇᵉhemteḵā)* it contrasts with the grain, wine, and oil that v. 14 names as the basic human foods.

Pejorative overtones of *ʿēśeḇ* as "animal fodder" may be the point of Ps. 106:20 (an historical psalm): Israel is accused of exchanging the glory of God for the image of an ox (*šôr;* used only here with reference to the golden calf) that eats grass. The lexeme also has this connotation in Dnl. 4:22,29,30(25,32,33); 5:21: to punish his pride, King Nebuchadnezzar is driven from human society and is made to eat "grass like oxen" (Aram. *ʿiśbāʾ kᵉṯôrîn*); this bestial way of life is intended to express his profound humiliation.

The pl. *ʿiśśᵉḇôṯ,* which occurs only in Prov. 27:25, probably refers to the wild medicinal herbs and other useful plants gathered on the mountains in the spring (or wild plants used as cattle fodder).[9]

3. *Destruction.* Hail and locusts were feared plagues that could damage or even destroy vital agricultural crops. In the seventh plague of Egypt (a combination of J and P), hail strikes down "all the plants of the field" (*kol-ʿēśeḇ haśśāḏeh,* as in Gen. 2:5 [J]; cf. Gen. 3:18b; Ex. 10:15b), distinguished in v. 25 from the "trees of the field" *(ʿēṣ*

8. *BHS;* K. Elliger, *Das Buch der zwölf kleinen Propheten. ATD* 25 (⁶1967), 154.
9. *AuS,* I, 326, 335.

haśśāḏeh). In the next plague, what the hail left standing falls victim to locusts, which devour "every plant in the land" (*kol-'ēśeḇ hā'āreṣ,* Ex. 10:12,15a; the genitive construction is divergent, as are the contrasting *kol-pᵉrî hā'ēṣ* and *kol-yereq bā'ēṣ* in v. 15a,b). Ps. 105:35 looks back on this plague; here too *'ēśeḇ* appears with *'ereṣ,* this time with a preposition. In Amos's vision of a plague of locusts (Am. 7:1-2), too, these voracious insects destroy the late sowing *(leqeš),* the green of the land *('ēśeḇ hā'āreṣ).*

No less catastrophic was drought, when there was no rain (Jer. 14:4) and "all the green of the field" withered (12:4; probably the correct reading [cf. Gen. 2:5], with LXX *pás ho chórtos toú agroú* rather than MT *'ēśeḇ kol-haśśāḏeh*), so that the wild animals languished for lack of grass (*'ên-'ēśeḇ,* Jer. 14:6).

Deutero-Isaiah's prophecy of deliverance and return from Babylon (Isa. 42:14-17) illustrates Yahweh's unexpected intervention, which stands the situation on its head, by describing him as laying waste mountains and hills and drying up "all their herbage" (v. 15), an image of the fate awaiting the still strong and vigorous enemies of Israel. Israel, too, is threatened with radical devastation of the land if it transgresses the covenant: the curse in Dt. 29:22(23) speaks of sulfur and salt covering the land so that it cannot support any vegetation (*kol-'ēśeḇ;* LXX *pán chlōrón*).

4. *Transience.* In the natural course of events, however, the greenery that sprouts so luxuriantly in the spring withers and perishes in the heat and drought of summer, symbolizing the mortality of transient human beings. The same symbolism is found with → חציר *ḥāṣîr* and → ציץ *ṣîṣ* (Ps. 37:2; 90:5-6; 103:15-16; Isa. 40:6,8; 51:12; Job 14:2).

In Ps. 102:5(4) the psalmist, seriously ill, feels like grass "stricken" (*hûkkâ;* cf. Ps. 121:6; Isa. 49:10; Jon. 4:8) by the sun and withered (*wayyiḇaš;* possibly a gloss) — an image that reappears in v. 12(11), which laments the transience of life. The inhabitants of the cities destroyed by Sennacherib are likened in their prostrate impotence (2 K. 19:26 = Isa. 37:27) to the plants of the field, the tender vegetation, and the grass on the housetops, brought to a violent end by the east wind (reading *qdym* with 1QIs^a for MT *qāmâ*), which blows with scorching heat in April and May.[10]

Maiberger

10. *AuS,* I/2, 323-26.

עָשָׂה *'āśâ;* מַעֲשֶׂה *ma'aśeh*

I. 1. Etymology; 2. Homonymous Roots; 3. Occurrences. II. Qal: 1. Make; 2. Idols; 3. Create; 4. Produce; 5. God as Subject; 6. Abstract Objects; 7. Do Good and Evil; 8. Carry Out; 9. Act; 10. With *le;* 11. Yahweh's Acts in History; 12. Locutions. III. Niphal. IV. *ma'aśeh:* 1. Work; 2. Deed. V. 1. LXX; 2. Dead Sea Scrolls.

I. 1. *Etymology.* Ugar. *'šy* appears to have the same double meaning as Heb. *'āśâ:* "do, make." Occurrences include: *grš d'šy lnh,* "he drives away whoever wants to do something to him";[1] *'š bt bqrb hlkh,* "construction worker in his palace";[2] *šd 'šy,* "cultivated field";[3] *yn 'šy,* "prepared wine"[4] (cf. 1 S. 25:8; another interpretation is "pressed wine," reflecting Middle Heb. *'śh,* "press"; see I.2.a below).

In Phoenician the root appears to occur only in personal names.[5] In the Mesha inscription, however, there are 5 occurrences, all with the meaning "make": a *bāmâ,* a cistern, a wall, a cistern, a road.[6] The Lachish Letters also contain several occurrences, as do the letters from Arad.[7] In Old South Arabic a verb *'sy* (with *s,* not *š*) is found with the meaning "make, build, acquire, buy, offer (sacrifice)."[8] Aramaic uses *'bd,* Akkadian *epēšu.*

2. *Homonymous Roots.* a. A verb *'āśâ* II, "squeeze, press," is used in Ezk. 23:3,8,21 (piel; obj.: breasts). It is found also in Middle Hebrew (*gēṭ me'uśśeh,* "forced bill of divorce") and Jewish Aramaic (pael = "squeeze, knead"). Some scholars connect this root with Ugar. *yn 'šy,* "pressed wine" (but see I.1 above). Dahood registers the pual *'uśśêṯî* in Ps. 139:15 here: "I was pinched off," but derivation from *'āśâ* I ("I was

---

'āśâ. H. J. Boecker, *Redeformen des Rechtslebens im AT. WMANT* 14 (²1970); D. Edelman, "Saul's Rescue of Jabesh-Gilead (1 Sam 11,1-11)," *ZAW* 96 (1984) 195-209; D. R. Hillers, *Treaty-Curses and the OT Prophets. BietOr* 16 (1964); M. R. Lehmann, "Biblical Oaths," *ZAW* 81 (1969) 74-92, esp. 80-82; H. D. Preuss, *Verspottung fremder Religionen im AT. BWANT* 12 (1971); G. von Rad, "Das Werk Jahwes," *Studia Biblica et Semitica. FS T. C. Vriezen* (1966), 290-98; M. Reisel, "The Relation Between the Creative Function of the Verbs — ברא — יצר — עשה in Is 43,7 and 45,7," *Verkenningen in een stroomgebied* (1975), 65-79; W. Schottroff, *Der althebräische Fluchspruch. WMANT* 30 (1969); E. Sjöberg, "Neuschöpfung in den Toten-Meer-Rollen," *ST* 9 (1955) 131-36; idem, "Wiedergeburt und Neuschöpfung im palästinischen Judentum," *ST* 4 (1950) 44-85; J. Vollmer, "עשׂה *'śh* to make, do," *TLOT,* II, 944-51.

1. *KTU* 1.17, I, 29, 47; II, 19. Cf. L. Delekat, *UF* 4 (1972) 23; M. Dijkstra and J. C. de Moor, *UF* 7 (1975) 176-77; but *WUS,* no. 2109: "disturb," Akk. *ešu.*
2. *KTU* 1.4, V, 14, 30, 37; *WUS,* no. 2113. *KTU* reads *'ḏbt* instead of *'š bt.*
3. *KTU* 4.282, 7, 10, 14; cf. Dijkstra and de Moor, *UF* 7 (1975) 177.
4. *KTU* 1.17, VI, 8.
5. Benz, 385.
6. *KAI,* 181.3, 9, 23, 24, 26.
7. For Lachish see *KAI* 194.3; 196.9, 11; 197.8; 198.1. For Arad, *KAI,* 1.8; 5. 6; 21.3; 40.15.
8. Biella, 374-75.

made"; pual as pass. of the qal) is equally possible.[9] The Arabic verb *ġšy,* "press," appears not to exist.[10]

b. The verb *ʿāśâ* III is associated with Arab. *ġašiya,* "cover, veil." Driver finds it in Ezk. 17:17 ("Pharaoh with his mighty army and great company will not protect him in war"), but derivation from *ʿāśâ* I is nevertheless possible ("treat punitively").[11] In Prov. 13:16 *kol-ʿārûm yaʿaśeh bᵉdaʿaṯ* might be translated "the clever conceal their knowledge" (cf. 12:23, *ʾāḏām ʿārûm kōseh dāʿaṯ*),[12] but "act with knowledge" (cf. NRSV "do all things with intelligence") is equally possible. This root might also occur in Isa. 59:6a *(lōʾ yiṯkassû bᵉmaʿaśêhem),*[13] but v. 6b supports the usual meaning "work." Reider finds a *maʿaśeh* meaning "cloud" in Ps. 104:13.[14]

c. Some texts where the verb might mean "turn toward" are listed by *HAL* under *ʿāśâ* IV (cf. Arab. *ʿašā* with the same meaning).[15] This root is suggested in the following texts. In 1 S. 14:32 the meaning would be "the troops turned to the spoil" (or read *wayyaʿaṭ* [from *ʿyṭ*], "rushed at"; Reider suggests Arab. *saʿā,* "run").[16] In 1 K. 20:40 "your servant turned this way and that" makes sense,[17] but "was busy here and there" remains possible. Ruth 2:19 can easily be translated, "Where have you been working?" Driver suggests, "If he turns to the north, I cannot see him" in Job 23:9 (cf. NRSV, "I turn to the right . . ."); another interpretation is, "[If I go] to the north, I do not see his works."[18] Driver also cites Isa. 5:4, where the usual meaning "yield" is preferable, as well as Prov. 6:32, where "commit, do" makes good sense.[19]

3. *Occurrences.* Etymological uncertainty makes it impossible to state the number of occurrences precisely. *HAL* lists 2,527 occurrences of the qal and 99 of the niphal; there is one possible occurrence of the pual (see I.2.a above). According to *HAL,* the noun *maʿaśeh,* "work," occurs 220 times.[20]

II. Qal. Like Gk. *poieín* and Lat. *facere,* *ʿāśâ* combines the two meanings "do" and "make." Both meanings appear in a wide range of finer nuances. Here we can point out only some of the most important.

---

9. M. Dahood, *Psalms III: 101–150. AB* 17A (1970), 294.

10. Cited by *HAL,* II, 890, 892. Cf. Lane, I, 2261-62.

11. G. R. Driver, *Bibl* 35 (1954) 153. Cf. W. Zimmerli, *Ezekiel 1. Herm* (Eng. trans. 1979), 357.

12. I. Eitan, *A Contribution to Biblical Lexicography* (1924), 57-58; Driver, *VT* 4 (1954) 243.

13. I. Eitan, *HUCA* 12/13 (1937/38) 83.

14. *VT* 4 (1954) 284.

15. Kopf, *VT* 9 (1959) 270.

16. *HUCA* 24 (1952/53) 85.

17. Cf. J. Barr, *Comparative Philology and the Text of the OT* (1968), 246.

18. See, respectively, G. R. Driver, "Difficult Words in the Hebrew Prophets," *FS T. H. Robinson* (1950), 54; EÜ.

19. Driver, "Difficult Words," 54. Cf. Kopf, 270.

20. *HAL,* II, 616; Vollmer (*TLOT,* II, 945) lists 235.

1. *Make.* There are numerous instances of the meaning "make." God makes garments for Adam and Eve after the fall (Gen. 3:21); people make implements of war (1 S. 8:12); Noah makes the ark (Gen. 6:14-16; 8:6); Abraham "makes" (i.e., builds) an altar (13:4; cf. 35:1,3; Ex. 20:24-25) and asks Sarah to make cakes (Gen. 18:6); Jacob and Laban make a heap of stones (*gal,* 31:46); Jacob makes booths for his cattle (33:17). The Israelites are to make a *miqdāš* for Yahweh (Ex. 25:8); the text goes on to state in detail how the tabernacle and all its appurtenances are to be made (vv. 10ff.) and then describes the actual construction (Ex. 36–39). A potter makes a vessel (Jer. 18:3-4) — here *'āśâ* becomes a catchword: just as the potter "makes" his vessel as seems good to him, so Yahweh can "do with" (*'āśâ l^e,* v. 6) his people. Jonah makes a booth (Jon. 4:5); Zechariah makes a golden crown for the high priest Joshua (Zec. 6:11); the bridegroom makes golden chains for the bride (Cant. 1:11); Solomon makes a palanquin (Cant. 3:9-10); Haman makes a gallows (Est. 5:14; cf. 7:9). A garden is "made" (planted, Am. 9:14); books are "made" (written, Eccl. 12:12).[21] A *b^{e}rēḵâ '^{a}śuyâ* is an artificial pool (Neh. 3:16). People "hold" a feast (*mišteh,* Gen. 19:3; 21:8; 26:30; 29:22; 40:20; Jgs. 14:10; 2 S. 3:20; 1 K. 3:15; Isa. 25:6 [Yahweh's messianic banquet]; Job 1:4; Est. 1:3,5; 2:18; only once *nāṯan,* Ezr. 3:7). A sacrifice is "prepared" (1 K. 18:23,25); in an extended sense, *'āśâ* comes to mean "offer" (like Akk. *niqê epēšu*[22]): it is used with *'ōlâ* (Lev. 9:7,22; Nu. 6:16; 29:2; Dt. 12:27; Jgs. 13:16; 1 K. 8:64; 2 K. 5:17; 10:24-25; Ezk. 43:27; 45:17; 46:2,12; Ezr. 3:4-5; 2 Ch. 7:7; elsewhere *he'^{e}lâ, hiqrîḇ, šāḥaṭ*), *minḥâ* (Nu. 6:17; 28:31; 1 K. 8:64; Ezk. 45:17; 46:15), and *'iśśārôn,* "tithe" ("offer," Nu. 28:21).

2. *Idols.* Especially significant in this respect are texts that speak of making idols. The Decalogue forbids making a *pesel* or a *t^{e}mûnâ* to worship (Ex. 20:4; Dt. 5:8, with textual variants). Dt. 4:15-16 grounds this prohibition in the fact that the people saw no form at Horeb (here the expression is *pesel t^{e}mûnaṯ kol-sāmel*). The OT nevertheless includes several accounts that describe the making of such images by the Israelites. Shortly after the establishment of the covenant, the Israelites made the golden calf (*'ēgel massēḵâ,* Ex. 32:4,8; cf. v. 35). Jgs. 17:4-5 describes how Micah has a silversmith make idols *(pesel ûmassēḵâ);* v. 5 speaks of his making an ephod and *t^{e}rāp̄îm* as well. In 18:24 Micah accuses the Danites: "You have taken the gods that I made." The choice of words characterizes the "gods" as the work of human hands.[23] The prophet Ahijah censures Jeroboam for making "other gods" (referring to the bull images at Bethel and Dan); these are further described as "cast images" *(massēḵâ),* "provoking me [God] to anger (*k's* hiphil)" (1 K. 14:9). By his action the king has "done evil" *(hēra' la'^{a}śôṯ)* and scorned Yahweh. Similar is 2 K. 17:29: "Every nation [settled in Samaria] made gods of its own." Amos speaks of *kôḵaḇ '^{e}lōhêḵem* (an astral deity?) and "your images *(ṣelem),* which you made for yourselves" (Am. 5:26). Hosea grieves that

21. See P. A. H. de Boer, *A Tribute to A. Vööbus* (1977), 85-88.
22. *AHw,* I, 225b, 5g.
23. Preuss, 65.

the people of the northern kingdom have made *ʿaṣabbîm* of silver and gold (Hos. 8:4), as well as a cast image *(massēḵâ)* of silver and *ʿaṣabbîm,* which are nothing but the work of artisans *(maʿaśēh ḥārāšîm).* All these instances involve an element of arbitrary self-assertion. Hab. 2:18 asks sarcastically: "How can an idol maker trust in what has been made, though they are only idols *(ʾelîlîm)* that cannot speak?" In similar contexts, Ezekiel uses the word *ṣelem:* "From their beautiful ornaments they made abominable images *(ṣalmê ṯôʿaḇōṯām),* their detestable things *(šiqqûṣ)*" (Ezk. 7:20; cf. also 16:17: using God's gifts to make idols is outrageous).

That these idols are nothing more than the work of human hands is underlined by the numerous texts that call them (with some variation) *maʿaśēh yāḏayim* (Isa. 2:8: "They bow down [*hištaḥᵃwâ*] to the work of their hands, which their own fingers have made [*ʿāśâ*]"; cf. also Jer. 1:16; Mic. 5:12). In Hezekiah's prayer in Isa. 37:14-20, the king says that the kings of Assyria have destroyed the gods of the nations, "though they were no gods, but the work of human hands, wood and stone" (v. 19). Especially impressive is the criticism in Jer. 10: "Their idol[24] is but wood, a tree cut from the forest, worked with an ax by the hands of an artisan" (v. 3); "they are beaten silver . . . and gold, . . . the work of the artisan *(ḥārāš)* and the goldsmith *(ṣōrēp),* . . . the product of skilled workers *(ḥᵃḵāmîm)*" (v. 9); "they are worthless *(heḇel),* a work of delusion *(maʿaśēh taʿtuʿîm)*" (v. 15; cf. 51:18). Two very similar passages in the Psalms (115:3-8 and 135:6,15-18) expand on this idea: Yahweh can "do" whatever he pleases, whereas idols *(ʿaṣabbîm)* are only silver and gold, the work of human hands (115:4; 135:15); they cannot speak, see, hear, smell, or move. "Those who make them *(ʿōśêhem)* are like them" (115:8; 135:18).

3. *Create.* "Making" takes on theological significance when Yahweh is the agent. Most of these texts refer to the creation of the world. In all periods, in fact, *ʿāśâ* was the commonest verb for "create"; it was not supplanted by the use of *bārāʾ* in the P sections of Gen. 1–5, Deutero-Isaiah, and Trito-Isaiah. P's creation account uses *ʿāśâ* 8 times, *bārāʾ* only 5. Whether a subtle theological distinction is involved or the text is a revision of an original *ʿāśâ* account may remain an open question.[25] It is noteworthy that God says "Let us *make* humankind" (Gen. 1:26) but then *creates* them (1:27: 3 times *bārāʾ*). Thus 3 of the 6 occurrences of *bārāʾ* refer to the creation of humankind; a fourth appears in the combination *bārāʾ laʿaśôṯ* (2:3). Gen. 6:6 has *ʿāśâ,* but v. 7 *bārāʾ.* Deutero-Isaiah equates *yāṣar, bārāʾ,* and *ʿāśâ* (Isa. 45:7).[26] God makes the earth and the heavens (Gen. 2:4 [J]; contrast 1:1 [P]; also 2 K. 19:15 par. Isa. 37:16, when Hezekiah invokes God in his prayer, and in Jeremiah's prayer after purchasing a field [Jer. 32:17]). God will also make a new heaven and a new earth (Isa. 66:22; contrast 64:17 with *bārāʾ*).

In the Psalms we find the formulaic divine epithet *ʿōśēh šāmayim wāʾāreṣ:* 115:15

---

24. On the text see the comms.
25. → ברא *bārāʾ.*
26. See Reisel.

(with the commentary in v. 16 that the heavens are Yahweh's heaven, whereas the earth he has given to human beings); 121:2 (the mighty helper); 124:8 ("our help"); 134:3 (bestower of blessings from Zion); 146:6 (expanded: ". . . the sea, and all that is in them"; helper). Gen. 14:19 preserves an earlier formula: *qōnēh šāmayim wā'āreṣ.*[27] Deutero-Isaiah includes the universal statement: "I am Yahweh, maker of all things" (Isa. 44:24). Expanding on these words, 45:7 says: "Former *(yōṣēr)* of light and creator *(bôrē')* of darkness, maker *('ōśeh)* of weal and creator *(bôrē')* of woe" — in sum, "I am Yahweh, doer of all these things *('ōśēh kol-'ēlleh).*" Wildberger rightly calls this verse "the most radical renunciation of dualism known to the Bible."[28] Individually, Yahweh made the stars (Ps. 104:19; 136:7-9), the sea (Ps. 95:5), the sea and the dry land (Jon. 1:9), as well as humankind (Isa. 17:7: "people will regard their Maker"; Job 4:17: "Can a man be pure before his Maker?") or the earth with its people and animals (Jer. 27:5: "By my great power . . . and I give it to whomever I please"). God made the poor, and those who oppress the poor insult their Maker (Prov. 14:31; 17:5). God made the rich and the poor, and therefore they live side by side (Prov. 22:2). Job 41:25(33) appears to say that the crocodile was "made without fear" ("wholly intrepid").[29] Job twice calls God "my maker" (32:22, *'ōśēnî;* 35:10, *'ōśay;* cf. also *'ōśēhû* in Isa. 27:11). PNs such as *'aśāh'ēl, 'aśāyâ(û),* and *'el'āśâ* bear witness to the same notion of creation.[30]

4. *Produce.* More generally, *'āśâ* can mean "produce, yield": fruit trees yield fruit (Gen. 1:11-12; Jer. 12:2; 17:8; Ps. 107:37; Hos. 9:16), vines yield grapes (Isa. 5:2), fields yield food (Hab. 3:17 — or rather in this case they fail to do so; cf. *qemaḥ* in Hos. 8:7); cows and sheep produce milk (Isa. 7:22). Trees put forth branches (Job 14:9; Ezk. 17:8,23); the prosperous wicked put on fat (Job 15:27). Isa. 19:15 is difficult: the import of the verse clearly is that Egypt will be able to accomplish nothing (lit. "no work" [*ma'aśeh*]).

With an abstract object, *'āśâ* often has the meaning "perform": wonders (*môpēṯ,* Ex. 11:10), signs (*'ôṯ,* Ex. 4:17,30; Nu. 14:11,22), signs and wonders (Dt. 34:11; elsewhere often with *nāṯan* or *śîm*), "signs and deeds" (*'ōṯōṯ . . . ma'aśeh,* Dt. 11:3).

When the object is → חיל *ḥayil,* the meaning of *'āśâ* is determined by the meaning of *ḥayil* in the passage in question. In military contexts *'āśâ ḥayil* means "do great deeds," i.e., win a victory (Nu. 24:18; 1 S. 14:48). Ps. 60:14(12) says: "With God we shall do great deeds; it is he who treads down our foes"; according to Ps. 118:16, the right hand of Yahweh is exalted and effects *ḥayil.*

It is equally clear, on the other hand, that Dt. 8:17-18 deals with the acquisition of wealth, which comes not though one's own efforts but with God's help. Ezk. 28:4 says that Tyre amassed great wealth. Ruth 4:11 is ambiguous. Here *'āśâ ḥayil* parallels *qārā' šēm.* The former can mean "acquire wealth" (RSV "prosper"), the latter either "gain respect" (RSV "be renowned") or "bestow a name." Labuschagne interprets *ḥayil* as "po-

27. → קנה *qānâ.*
28. *Beiträge zur alttestamentliche Theologie. FS W. Zimmerli* (1977), 524.
29. G. Hölscher, *Das Buch Hiob. HAT* I/17 (1937), in loc.
30. Noth, *IPN,* 172.

tency, fertility" (NRSV "produce children"); this fits the context, which speaks of numerous descendants, but is linguistically improbable despite Job 21:7 and Joel 2:22.[31] The reference is possibly to the power that having a large family bestows.[32] Prov. 31:29 is also not entirely clear; it is usually translated, "Daughters (= women) have done excellently," but the reference may be to acquiring wealth.

We find *ʿāśâ* in the sense of "acquire" with *kāḇôḏ,* "wealth" (Gen. 31:1), *nep̱eš,* "living beings," i.e., people, slaves (Gen. 12:5), male and female singers (Eccl. 2:8), chariots and horsemen (1 K. 1:5), *miqneh wᵉqinyān,* "cattle and goods" (Ezk. 38:12), and *pᵉʿullaṯ śeḵer,* "reward" (Prov. 11:18, what one gains through wickedness or righteousness).

Wealth makes itself wings and flies away (Prov. 23:5); God draws a laugh from Sarah (*ṣᵉḥōq,* with an allusion to *yiṣḥāq;* Gen. 21:6); Israel brings its present fate *(zōʾṯ)* upon itself by its apostasy (Jer. 2:17; cf. 4:18, *ʾēlleh*). "Make a name for oneself" means "become famous" (Gen. 11:4; Isa. 63:12; Jer. 32:20; Dnl. 9:15; Neh. 9:10; even of God: Isa. 63:14).

In addition, *ʿāśâ* means "celebrate" or "observe" a festival or ritual": *pesaḥ* (Ex. 12:48; Nu. 9:2,4-6,10,13-14; Dt. 16:1; Josh. 5:10; 2 K. 23:21; Ezr. 6:19; 2 Ch. 30:1-2,5; 35:1,16-17), *ḥag* (Ex. 34:22; Dt. 16:10; 1 K. 8:65; 12:32-33; Ezr. 3:4; 6:22; Neh. 8:18; 2 Ch. 7:8-9; 30:13,21; 35:17), the sabbath (Ex. 31:16; Dt. 5:15). One keeps a vow (Jer. 44:25), observes a time of mourning (*ʾēḇel,* Gen. 50:10; Ezk. 24:17; *mispēḏ,* Jer. 6:26; Mic. 1:8).[33]

5. *God as Subject.* Frequently *ʿāśâ* refers to something God brings to pass in his governance of the world. His doing is characterized by abstract objects describing the nature of his actions. He does great things *(gᵉḏōlôṯ):* Ps. 71:19 ("Who is like you?"); 106:21 (in Egypt) — cf. *higdîl laʿᵃśôṯ,* Joel 2:20; Ps. 126:2-3. He does wonders (*pele'* or *niplāʾôṯ*): Ex. 3:20; Isa. 25:1; Ps. 72:18; 77:15(14); 78:4,12; 86:10; 98:1; 105:5 (cf. also Dt. 11:3-4: "signs and deeds").[34] The usual verb with → מופת *môp̄ēṯ* is *nāṯan,* but in Ex. 11:10 and Dt. 34:11, at Yahweh's command, Moses performs *(ʿāśâ)* wonders. God does *nôrāʾôṯ* (Isa. 64:2[3]). God works *ṣᵉḏāqôṯ:* Ps. 103:6 — in this context, probably "victories." Ezekiel in particular speaks of Yahweh as executing *šᵉp̄āṭîm,* "judgments": Ezk. 5:10,15; 11:9; 25:11; 28:22,26; 30:14,19; cf. also Ex. 12:12; Nu. 33:4. Israel's enemies execute God's judgment: Ezk. 16:41; 2 Ch. 24:24. Yahweh also executes vengeance *(nāqām, nᵉqāmâ):* Jgs. 11:36; Ezk. 25:17 (here together with *nāṯan,* as in v. 14; cf. *ʿāśâ binqāmâ* in v. 15); Mic. 5:14(15); Ps. 149:7 (along with *tôḵēḥôṯ,* "punishments"). He can make a full end *(kālâ):* Isa. 10:23; Jer. 30:11; 46:28 (to the nations, but not to Israel); Ezk. 11:13; Nah. 1:8-9; Zeph. 1:18; he refrains occasionally: Jer. 4:27; 5:18. Here the emphasis is on the object that defines the nature of Yahweh's act.

31. C. Labuschagne, *ZAW* 79 (1967) 364-67.
32. Cf. Parker, *JBL* 95 (1976) 23 n. 1.
33. See II.1 above on sacrifice.
34. → פלא *plʾ.*

6. *Abstract Objects.* As objects we also find nouns that denote a kind of behavior. Thus *ʿāśâ ṣᵉḏāqâ ûmišpāṭ* describes Abraham's manner of life (Gen. 18:19, par. "keep the way of Yahweh"). The statement that David executed or administered *mišpāṭ ûṣᵉḏāqâ* (2 S. 8:15 par. 1 Ch. 18:14) probably refers to the king's obligation to maintain order.[35] Reigning as king, Yahweh too executes "righteousness and justice" in Jacob (Ps. 99:4).

The expression *ʿāśâ ḥeseḏ ʿim,* "exercise *ḥeseḏ* in dealing with," appears frequently. When used of humans, it usually refers to social loyalty, mercy, and kindness. The mutuality of the relationship is often stressed: to do *ḥeseḏ* is to render service in return or to perform an act of gratitude (Gen. 21:23; Josh. 2:12,14; Jgs. 1:24; 8:35; 1 S. 15:6; 2 S. 2:5-6; 1 K. 2:7; Ruth 1:8; cf. Zec. 7:9 [+ *raḥᵃmîm*]; Ps. 109:16). On the other hand, God shows *ḥeseḏ* to those who love him (Ex. 20:6; Dt. 5:10; 1 K. 3:6 [par. *šāmar*]; Jer. 32:18). God also shows *ḥeseḏ* to his anointed (Ps. 18:51[50]). Other verbs used with *ḥeseḏ* are *nāṣar* (Ex. 34:7), *šāmar* (Dt. 7:9,12), *zāḵar* (Ps. 25:6; 98:3; cf. Ps. 109:16, *lōʾ zāḵar ʿᵃśôṯ ḥeseḏ*), and *rāḏap* (Prov. 21:21).

It is also possible to do *ḥōnēp,* i.e., act wickedly (Isa. 32:6), or *ḥāmās,* i.e., act violently (Isa. 53:9). "Commit an outrage *(nᵉḇālâ)*" refers to a socially destructive or godless act (Gen. 34:7; Dt. 22:21; Josh. 7:15; Jgs. 19:23-24; 20:6 [+ *zimmâ*]; 2 S. 13:12; Jer. 29:23; Job 42:8).

7. *Do Good and Evil.* An action performed can be characterized as "good/evil in the eyes of Yahweh" — in other words, as something Yahweh perceives as good or evil, something that pleases or displeases him. Instances of doing something "good" in the eyes of Yahweh are rather rare (Dt. 6:18; 2 Ch. 14:1); much commoner is the expression "do whatever is good in one's own eyes," i.e., "do as one pleases" (Gen. 16:6; Jgs. 19:24; 1 S. 1:23; etc.). But the expression "do evil in the eyes of Yahweh" is quite frequent (Nu. 32:13; Dt. 4:25; 9:18; 17:2; 31:29; Jgs. 2:11; 3:7,12; 4:1; 6:1; 10:6; 13:1; 1 S. 15:19; etc., in the Dtr History; Isa. 65:12; 66:4; Ps. 51:6[4]).

Simple *ʿāśâ ṭôḇ* (or *ṭôḇâ*) usually means "do good," i.e., act rightly: "Depart from evil, and do good" (Ps. 34:15[14]; 37:27); "Trust in Yahweh, and do good" (Ps. 37:3); "There is no one on earth so righteous as to do [only] good and never sin *(ḥāṭāʾ)*" (Eccl. 7:20 — here "doing good" is associated with *ṣdq* and contrasted with "sinning" [or "making a mistake"]). The negated expression appears in Ezk. 18:18: "do what is not good"; cf. also "do what is good and right *(yāšār)*" (Dt. 12:28; 2 Ch. 31:20). According to Hillers, *ʿāśâ ṭôḇâ* in 2 S. 2:6 is comparable to Akk. *ṭābūta epēšu,* "conclude a compact of friendship."[36] David hopes to replace Saul as the feudal overlord of Jabesh-gilead.[37]

Similarly, *ʿāśâ raʿ* means "do evil," i.e., act wrongly: "You say, 'All who do evil are good in the eyes of Yahweh'" (Mal. 2:17); "The face of Yahweh is against those who

35. H. H. Schmid, *Gerechtigkeit als Weltordnung. BHT* 40 (1968), 85.
36. D. Hillers, *BASOR* 176 (1964) 46-47.
37. Cf. D. Edelman, *ZAW* 96 (1984) 202.

do evil" (Ps. 34:17[16]); "Fools do not know how to keep from doing evil" (Eccl. 4:17[5:1]); "The desire to do evil grows in the human heart, for a sinner *(ḥōṭe')* can do evil a hundred times and still live a long life" (Eccl. 8:11-12). Perhaps these idioms imply the notion that people effect or "make" good or evil. The expression *ʿāśâ rāʿâ* can refer to a specific act of wickedness: "How could I [Joseph] do this great wickedness and sin against God?" (Gen. 39:9; cf. Jer. 26:19); "My people have committed two evils" (Jer. 2:13); "You have done all this evil" (1 S. 12:20). Nu. 24:13 uses "do good or bad" in the sense of "do anything at all."

In Eccl. 3:12 *ʿāśâ ṭôḇ* most likely means "make (for oneself) something good [or: happiness]," i.e., "enjoy oneself." Gk. *eu prắttein,* often cited as a parallel, is not entirely comparable.[38]

8. *Carry Out.* The verb *ʿāśâ* can refer to the carrying out of a command. The directives concerning construction of the tabernacle use the command *w^eʿāśîṯā,* "you shall make" (Ex. 25:11,13,17-18; also *w^eʿāśû,* 25:8,10; *ʿ^aśēh,* 25:19,40; *taʿ^aśeh;* and *taʿ^aśû*); the carrying out of the directives is then itself described with forms of *ʿāśâ* (*wayyaʿaś,* Ex. 36:8; 39:1,6; etc.; or *ʿāśâ,* 36:11,14,22; etc.). Here, of course, something is always "made." Elsewhere, however, the execution formula *wayyaʿaś* or *wayyaʿ^aśû ḵēn* means simply "do" (Gen. 29:28; 42:20,25; 45:21; Ex. 7:20; 8:13[17]; 14:4; 16:17; 17:6; Nu. 5:4; 8:3,20; Isa. 20:2; Jer. 38:12); also with Yahweh as subject (Ex. 8:9,20[13,24]). Gen. 6:22 is more expansive: "Noah did this; he did all that God commanded him" (cf. Gen. 7:5; 21:1; 50:12; Ex. 7:6,10; 12:50; 19:8; 39:43; 40:16; Lev. 8:4-5; 9:6; 16:34; Nu. 1:54; 17:26[9]; 20:27; 23:26; 32:31; Dt. 34:9). In this context Ex. 19:8 and 24:7 are theologically significant: "Everything that Yahweh has spoken we will do, and we will be obedient"; similar is Dt. 5:27: "Speak, we will listen and do it." These words express the people's readiness to accept the covenant and fulfill its obligations. Jeremiah refers to this obligation when he says: "Listen to my voice, and do all that I command you; so shall you be my people" (Jer. 11:4; cf. v. 6: "Hear the words of this covenant and do them"; and v. 8: ". . . the words of this covenant, which I commanded them to do, but they did not"). Additional instances of "doing what was commanded" are Jer. 32:23; 35:10,18; 40:3; 50:21; Ezk. 9:11; 12:7; 24:18; Ruth 3:6.

In Joel 2:11 a vast army carries out Yahweh's *dāḇār,* i.e., his orders or will. According to Ps. 103:20-21, angels carry out the *dāḇār* and the *rāṣôn* (will) of God. At the same time, Yahweh himself watches over his word to perform it (Jer. 1:12). In Mic. 2:1 people devise plans and carry them out.

Similar are texts in which *ʿāśâ* is made concrete by such objects as *ḥōq, miṣwâ, mišpāṭ, tôrâ,* and *piqqûḏîm* (cf. Akk. *amāta epēšu*).[39] To "do" the ordinances, the commandments, the statutes, the torah is to fulfill them, to translate them into action.

We find *ʿāśâ* with *mišpāṭîm* in Lev. 18:4; Ezk. 5:7; 11:12; 18:17; 20:11,13,24; with

38. Cf. R. Braun, *Kohelet und die frühhellenistischen Popularphilosophie. BZAW* 130 (1973), 53-54.

39. *AHw,* I, 225b.

ḥuqqôṯ/ḥuqqîm in Lev. 18:30; 25:18; Ezk. 20:11,13. In combination with *šāmar,* "observe," we find *'āśâ* with *mišpāṭîm* in Lev. 19:37; 20:22; 25:18; Ezk. 11:20; 18:9; 20:19,21; 36:27; with *ḥuqqôṯ* in Lev. 19:37; 20:8,22; Ezk. 37:24.[40] All these texts are in the Holiness Code or Ezekiel. Numerous texts in Deuteronomy also present various combinations: 4:6; 5:1; 6:1,3,24; 7:11-12; 8:1; 11:22,32; 13:1(12:32); 16:12; 17:19; 19:9; 23:24(23); 24:8; 26:16; 28:1,13,15; 29:28(29); 30:8; 32:46. We find *'āśâ* with *miṣwâ/miṣwôṯ* as object in Lev. 26:14-15 (cf. 4:13,22,27; 5:17); Nu. 15:22,40;[41] Dt. 6:25; 15:5; 27:10; 28:1,15; 30:8 (but 23 times with *šāmar* in Deuteronomy); Ps. 119:166; Neh. 10:30(29); 1 Ch. 28:7; 2 Ch. 14:3(4) (and 30:12 with reference to the king's command); we find it with *tôrâ* in Nu. 5:30; Josh. 22:5; 2 Ch. 14:3(4) (common elsewhere with *nāṣar* and other verbs); with *piqqûḏîm* in Ps. 103:18 and in a very unusual construction in Ps. 111:8 (pass. ptcp.: "performed with faithfulness and uprightness").

9. *Act.* Doing can also be qualified by a wide range of other objects, notably sin: *ḥṭ'* (Nu. 5:6-7; Isa. 31:7; Ezk. 18:21), *peša'* (Ezk. 18:22,28), *'āwel/'awlâ* (Lev. 19:15,35; Dt. 25:16; Ezk. 3:20; 18:24,26; Zeph. 3:5,13; Ps. 37:1; cf. Ps. 119:3, *pā'al*), *'āwen* (Isa. 32:6; cf. Prov. 30:20, *pā'al;* also *pō'ᵃlê 'āwen*), *riš'â/reša'* (Ezk. 18:27; Mal. 3:15,19[4:1]; Prov. 16:12), *šeqer* (Jer. 6:13; 8:10; Prov. 11:18), *tō'ēḇâ* (Lev. 18:27,29-30; 20:13; Jer. 6:15; 8:12; 32:35; 44:4,22; Ezk. 8:6,9,13,17; 16:47,50-51; 18:12-13; 22:11; 33:26,29), *'ōšeq* (Jer. 22:17), *rᵉmîyâ* (Ps. 52:4[2]; 101:7), *zimmâ/mᵉzimmâ* (Jer. 11:15; 23:20; 30:24; Hos. 6:9; Ps. 37:7; Prov. 10:23).

Positively appraised objects are remarkably rare: *'ᵉmeṯ* (Ezk. 18:9), *'ᵉmûnâ* (Prov. 12:22).

To this category belong in a sense the expression *'āśâ šālôm,* "make peace" (Isa. 27:5; cf. Akk. *salīma epēšu*) and its opposite *'āśâ milḥāmâ,* "wage war" (Gen. 14:2; Dt. 20:12,20; Josh. 11:18; 1 K. 12:21; Prov. 20:18; 24:6; 1 Ch. 5:10,19; 22:8; often with *'āraḵ* as well), although the meaning here is close to "bring about, create." In such cases the primary emphasis is on the qualifying object; for more detailed analysis the reader should therefore consult the entries for the words in question.

10. *With lᵉ.* The expression *'āśâ lᵉ* means "make into, cause to become." God will make Abraham a great nation (Gen. 12:2; cf. Nu. 14:12). The idol maker makes wood into a god (Isa. 44:17; cf. v. 19) or gold and silver into an image of Baal (Hos. 2:10[8]). The secretary Jonathan's house was made into a prison, i.e., equipped as a prison (Jer. 37:15). Jer. 8:8 declares that "the false pen of the scribe" has made the law a lie. The verb can also have this meaning without *lᵉ:* Jeroboam made men from among all the people priests (1 K. 12:31); God makes the winds messengers (Ps. 104:4). But Ps. 135:7; Jer. 10:13; 51:16 should probably be translated: "He makes lightnings for the rain" (so NRSV).

---

40. See Elliger, *Leviticus. HAT* I/4 (1966), 237 n. 7.

41. Noth, *Numbers. OTL* (Eng. trans. 1968), 114: "one of the very latest sections of the Pentateuch."

In other cases *ʿāśâ lᵉ* means "do something to someone." Here *ʿāśâ* covers a wide range of nuances. In Isaiah's Song of the Vineyard, the friend (= God) says: "What more could I have done for my vineyard than I have done?" (Isa. 5:4), and continues: "I will tell you what I will do to my vineyard" (v. 5). Cf. Est. 6:6: "What shall be done for [here: *bᵉ*] the man?" (how is he to be treated?). "What have you done to us?" Abraham asks Abimelech (Gen. 20:9). The Israelites reproachfully ask Moses the same question, referring to his bringing them out of Egypt (Ex. 14:11). "Do not do anything to him," says Yahweh to Abraham, when Abraham is on the point of sacrificing Isaac (Gen. 22:12; cf. Dt. 22:26: "You shall do nothing to the young woman"). Jacob is to take refuge with Laban until Esau forgets "what you have done to him" (Gen. 27:45). The Israelites must not forget what Amalek did to them (Dt. 25:17; cf. 1 S. 15:2). "Yahweh is with me, I do not fear — what can mortals do to me?" asks the psalmist (Ps. 118:6; cf. 56:5,12[4,11]). Or: "If you sin, what have you done to God?" (Job 35:6).

An element of reciprocity is often expressed, e.g., "As he has done, so shall it be done to him" (Lev. 24:19; cf. Dt. 19:19: "Then you shall do to him just as he meant to do to his brother"). Ob. 15 addresses Edom: "As you have done, it shall be done to you." Prov. 24:29 cautions against private vengeance: "Do not say, 'I will do to him as he has done to me.'" Here too belongs the oath formula *kōh yaʿᵃśeh ʾᵉlōhîm lî wᵉḵōh yōsîp̱. . . .* "So may God do to me and more, if . . ." (2 S. 3:35; see II.12 below).

Somewhat comparable is the construction with *ʿim* or *ʾēṯ*. The expression *ʿāśâ ṭôḇ ʿim,* "deal well with," means to treat as a friend (Jgs. 9:16; 1 S. 24:19[18]; 2 S. 2:6; Ps. 119:65). Conversely, *ʿāśâ rāʿâ ʿim* means "treat badly, do harm to" (Jgs. 15:3). Here again we find the element of reciprocity, especially in Gen. 26:29: "You will do us no harm, just as we have not touched *(nāḡaʿ)* you and have done to you nothing but good" (cf. also Jgs. 11:27).

11. *Yahweh's Acts in History.* Sometimes, especially in exilic and postexilic literature, *ʿāśâ* refers to Yahweh's governance of history and intervention in human affairs; in these cases it is constructed absolutely or with *zōʾṯ* or *ʾēlleh* as its object. "Yahweh does nothing without revealing his secret through the prophets," we read in the Amos tradition (Am. 3:7 [Dtr]; cf. v. 6, where *ʿāśâ* means "inflict [a disaster]"). In Am. 9:12, too, it is Yahweh who "does this," i.e., brings the event to pass. Isa. 28:21 (probably secondary)[42] speaks of Yahweh's "strange deed," here expressed by *figura etymologica: ʿāśâ maʿᵃśeh* (par. *ʿāḇaḏ ʿᵃḇōḏâ*). What Yahweh plans to do is unique, totally unexpected. Isa. 33:13 (Dtr) uses "what I have done" in parallel with "my might." In Isaiah's oracle to Sennacherib (37:22-32), Yahweh asserts that since long ago *(mērāḥôq)* and from days of old he has planned *(yāṣar)* to destroy the cities of the Assyrian king (v. 26). God thus predetermines the course of events, a notion especially central to Deutero-Isaiah (see below).

In Jeremiah we find the question: "Why *(taḥaṯ meh)* has Yahweh done all these things to us?" (5:19; cf. 30:15); the answer is: on account of the people's apostasy. Jer-

42. O. Kaiser, *Isaiah 13–39. OTL* (Eng. trans. 1974), 250.

emiah prays: "Although our iniquities testify against us, act [on our behalf: intervene, help] for your name's sake" (14:7). When Nebuchadnezzar attacks, Jeremiah says: "Perhaps Yahweh will act with *('ēṯ)* us according to his wonders and will make him withdraw from us" (21:2). Or, more generally: "Thus says Yahweh, who does *('āśâ)* it, Yahweh, who shapes *(yāṣar)* it and establishes it" (33:2; NRSV, following the LXX, supplies "the earth" as obj.).[43] The use of several verbs associated with creation with reference to historical events comes to the fore in Deutero-Isaiah.[44]

Ezekiel emphasizes that Yahweh both speaks his word and "does" it, i.e., fulfills it, brings it to pass (12:25; 17:24; 22:14; 36:36; 37:14). And what he does, he does not without cause (14:23). "I have dealt with you as you have done, you who have despised the oath, breaking the covenant" (16:59). Further, what he does, he does not for Israel's sake but for the sake of his holy name (36:22).

Yahweh does great things *(higdîl la'ᵃśôṯ),* resulting in fecund abundance (Joel 2:20-21; cf. *'āśâ gᵉḏōlôṯ*).

Deutero-Isaiah is convinced that Yahweh is at work everywhere. Israel's imminent deliverance will convince the world that the hand of Yahweh has "done" (accomplished) it and that the Holy One of Israel has "created" *(bārā')* it (Isa. 41:20). Yahweh is on the point of "doing" (effecting) a new thing, the deliverance of his people (43:19). The whole natural world is to rejoice because he has acted, i.e., he has redeemed his people and glorified himself in them (44:23). No idol has done this (48:5); Yahweh has done it for his own sake (48:11). He does (fulfills) his purpose (*ḥēpeṣ,* 46:10); cf. 48:14, where Yahweh's chosen agent Cyrus fulfills his *ḥēpeṣ;* and 55:11, where Yahweh's word accomplishes what he purposes *('ᵃšer ḥāpaṣtî).* The same idea also appears frequently elsewhere (Ps. 115:3; 135:6, *kōl 'ᵃšer-ḥāpēṣ*).

The clause in Mal. 3:17,21 is ambiguous: "on the day when I act" or ". . . that I make [= bring about]." The former interpretation refers to Yahweh's action in history, the latter to the day he establishes to intervene; cf. Ps. 118:24: "This is the day that Yahweh has made" or ". . . on which he has acted, intervened."

Yahweh also acts in the lives of individuals. The thanksgiving hymn concluding Ps. 22 ends by declaring that generations yet unborn will be told that Yahweh has done it, i.e., intervened to help the suffering worshiper (v. 32; cf. 52:11[9]). Ps. 37:5 urges trust in Yahweh, "for he will act." Conversely, in Ps. 39 the psalmist is silenced, knowing that Yahweh has done it, i.e., brought about the distress (v. 10[9]). Job, too, knows that God's hand "has done all this" (12:9) — or does the verb refer to the act of creation? Or, with reference to the wicked: "Who declares their way to their face, who repays them for what they have done?" (21:31), i.e., who can call them to account? "What he desires, that he does" (23:13).

---

43. Contra Rudolph, *HAT* I/12, in loc.: "who effects what comes to pass."

44. T. M. Ludwig, "The Traditions of the Establishing of the Earth in Deutero-Isaiah," *JBL* 92 (1973) 345-57, esp. 355-56.

12. *Locutions.* Among established locutions, one of the most common is the accusation formula *mah-zzōʾṯ ʿāśîṯā* or *meh ʿāśîṯā,* "What have you done?"[45] It is an accusatory question that precedes the legal process proper. With minor variations, it appears in Gen. 12:18; 26:10; 29:25; Ex. 14:11; Jgs. 8:1; 15:11; 2 S. 12:21; Neh. 2:19; 13:17 (cf. also Gen. 20:9; 42:28; Nu. 23:11) and as a more or less attenuated expression in Ex. 14:5; Jgs. 2:2; Jon. 1:10. It also appears in Gen. 3:13 in the story of the fall, where God's question to Adam still preserves something of the forensic character of the locution.

The counterpart in the mouth of the accused is the appeasement formula "What have I done?"[46] Examples are Nu. 22:28 (Balaam's donkey); 1 S. 13:11; 20:1; 26:18; 29:8; and (somewhat differently) Jer. 8:6, where Jeremiah chastises the people because no one says *meh ʿāśîṯî.* When a third party intervenes on behalf of the accused, the formula appears in the 3rd person singular: 1 S. 20:32; cf. also 2 S. 24:17 = 1 Ch. 21:17, where David confesses that he has sinned — but "what have the people done?" Mic. 6:3 places this question, ostensibly a defense, in God's mouth as an accusation.

In Josh. 7:20, in response to the admonition "Tell us clearly *(haggēḏ)* what you have done," the statement "Thus and so *(kāzōʾṯ wᵉḵāzōʾṯ)* I did" appears as an admission of guilt. Also forensic are the verdict and sentence in 2 S. 12:5: "The man who has done this is a child of death," i.e., deserves to die. Here too belongs the oath of purgation in Ps. 7:4-5(3-4): "If I have done this . . . let the enemy pursue and overtake me" (cf. the oath formula discussed above.

Totally different in character is the question *māh ʾeʿᵉśeh,* "What can/should I do?" (also pl.). It appears with varying nuances in Gen. 27:37; 30:30; 31:43; Jgs. 13:8; 1 S. 5:8; 6:2; 10:2; 2 S. 21:3; 2 K. 4:2. Especially interesting is Ex. 17:4, where Moses asks in desperation, "What shall I do with this people?"; cf. Hos. 6:4, where God asks, "What shall I do with you, O Ephraim?"

The oath formula *kōh yaʿᵃśeh lî ʾᵉlōhîm wᵉḵōh yōsîp̱. . .,* "So may God do to me, and more, if . . ." (2 S. 3:35; cf. 1 S. 14:44; 20:13; 2 S. 3:9; 1 K. 2:23; 19:2; 20:10; 2 K. 6:31; similarly 1 S. 3:17), invokes divine intervention against the swearer if the oath is not kept. The formula presumably begins "Thus . . ." because its pronunciation was accompanied by some kind of symbolic action.[47]

The Deuteronomistic framework of the books of Kings uses the formula "The rest of the acts *(yeṯer diḇrê)* of PN and all that he did are written in . . ." (1 K. 14:29; 15:7,23,31; etc.).

III. Niphal. The occurrences of the niphal bring nothing fundamentally new: they are passive forms covering the same semantic field as the qal. The heavens were "made" (i.e., created) by the word of God (Ps. 33:6); the seven-branched lampstand was "made" (Ex. 25:31), as was an altar (Ezk. 43:18). Jer. 3:16 should probably be in-

45. Boecker, 26-31.
46. Ibid., 31-34.
47. Hillers; Schottroff, 161; Lehmann, 80-82; G. Giesen, *Die Wurzel šbʿ, "schwören." BBB* 56 (1981), 143-44.

terpreted along the same lines: a new ark of the covenant shall never again be made.[48] Food is prepared (Ex. 12:16; Neh. 5:18), an offering is prepared or offered (Lev. 2:7-8,11; 6:14[21]), Passover is observed or celebrated (2 K. 23:22-23 par. 2 Ch. 35:18-19; cf. Purim in Est. 9:28).

Commandments *(miṣwōṯ)* are obeyed or fulfilled (Lev. 4:2,13,22,27; 5:17), a sentence *(piṯgām)* against an evil deed is (not) executed (Eccl. 8:11), counsel is (not) followed (2 S. 17:23). A deed is done (Gen. 20:9), *tôʿēḇâ* is "done" or committed (Dt. 13:15[14]; 17:4; Ezk. 9:4). Work *(m^elāʾḵâ)* is performed (Ex. 12:16; 31:15; 35:2; Lev. 7:24; 11:32; 13:51; but cf. Ezk. 15:5: "nothing could be made of it"). Especially frequent in Ecclesiastes are locutions like "what is done" and "the works that are done under the sun," describing the bustle of human activity.

Of particular interest is the locution "This is not done in our country" (*lōʾ-yēʿāśeh ḵēn bimqômēnû,* Gen. 29:26), i.e., that is not the practice among us. "Works *(maʿ^aśîm)* that ought not to be done" (Gen. 20:9) are forbidden or improper acts. The statement "Such a thing is not done in Israel" (2 S. 13:12) illustrates a knowledge of the uniqueness of Israel's legal system.[49] The concept of retribution appears in Ob. 15: "As you [Edom] have done, it shall be done to you"; in Ezk. 12:11 Ezekiel is the example: "As I have done, so shall it be done to them" (here *ʿāśâ l^e* means "do something to"). Other instances are Ex. 2:4; Nu. 15:11; 1 S. 11:7.

IV. *maʿ^aśeh.* The noun *maʿ^aśeh,* like the verb, has a double meaning: on the one hand, "something made, work," on the other, "deed."

1. *Work.* The jewels to which the thighs of the bride are likened are called "the work of a master hand" (Cant. 7:2). A pastry is *maʿ^aśēh ʾōp̱eh* (Gen. 40:17; cf. 1 Ch. 9:31). A garment can be a "work" of goat hair (Nu. 31:20; cf. also Ex. 24:10; 26:1,31,36; etc.). The "precious children of Zion" are likened to the work of a potter in their degradation (Lam. 4:2). The author of Ps. 45 calls the poem his "work" (v. 2[1]). Isa. 29:16 sounds almost proverbial: "Shall the thing made say of its maker *(ʿōśēhû)*, 'He did not make me?'" (par. to "pot" and "potter"). The wicked make garments but cannot cover themselves with what they make (Isa. 59:6a) — then, however, the meaning changes: "Their works are works of iniquity *(maʿ^aśê ʾāwen)*"; here *maʿ^aśeh* clearly means "deed."

Idols are very often called "the work of human hands" or "the work of an artisan" (Dt. 4:28; 27:15; 2 K. 19:18; Isa. 41:29; Jer. 10:3,9,15; 51:18; Hos. 13:2; Ps. 115:4; 135:15; 2 Ch. 32:19), language that represents idols as being powerless.[50] That people should not bow down *(hištaḥ^awâ)* to the work of their hands is stressed frequently (Isa. 2:8; Jer. 1:16; Mic. 5:12[13]). Similar is the description of altars as "works of their hands" in Isa. 17:8. In Ezk. 6:6, too, the context indicates that "your works," which are to be wiped out, are connected with idolatry.

---

48. Contra H. Cazelles, *VT* 18 (1968) 157-58: it will no longer be used.
49. F. Horst, *Gottes Recht. ThB* 12 (1961), 253.
50. Preuss, 65, 129, 173.

Not entirely clear is the statement that the Israelites provoked *(hiḵʿîs)* God "through the work of their hands" (Dt. 31:29; 2 K. 22:17; Jer. 25:6-7; 32:30; 44:8; 2 Ch. 34:25). Since the context speaks of idolatry, the expression probably refers to idols; but the possibility exists that it refers to their deeds in general. Also ambiguous is Jer. 48:7, which says that Moab trusted in its own *maʿᵃśîm* and treasures; either *maʿᵃśeh* means "what has been acquired, wealth," or it should be emended to *māʿuzzayiḵ,* "your fortresses," with the LXX.

Just as *ʿāśâ* means "bring forth" in general, so *maʿᵃśeh* means "produce, fruits." Thus Ex. 23:16 speaks of the "firstfruits of the field." Isa. 32:17 uses *maʿᵃśeh* and *ʿᵃḇōḏâ* in parallel: both refer to the fruits of righteousness, namely peace and security. Hab. 3:17 speaks of the produce of the olive tree, and Isa. 65:22 of the "produce of the hands of the elect."

Here too belong certain passages in which *maʿᵃśeh* means something like "pattern" (Nu. 8:4; 1 K. 7:28-33; 2 K. 16:10) or "design" (1 K. 7:8,17,19,22).

Everything created is God's "work." The heavens are the work of God's fingers (Ps. 8:4[3]), human beings the work of God's hands (v. 7[6]). The heavens are the work of God's hands; they will perish, but God will endure (102:26-27[25-26]). God rejoices in these works (104:31) and the heavens proclaim them (19:2[1]). The earth is satisfied with the fruit of God's work (104:13; the text is uncertain: the parallelism suggests rain). All God's works are called on to praise God (103:22). According to Isa. 60:21; 64:7(8), the people are the work of God's hands. When Ps. 145:9-10 says that divine compassion is over all God's works, the context indicates that this refers to the faithful (similarly Ps. 138:8). Job 14:15 calls a mortal the work of God's hands. According to Prov. 16:11, even "the weights in the bag" are God's work: "honest balances" are divinely ordained.

2. *Deed.* a. *General.* When *maʿᵃśeh* refers to deeds or actions, the reference is occasionally to conduct as such and its manner. For example, Israel is warned not to do as the Egyptians and Canaanites do and follow their *ḥuqqōṯ* (Lev. 18:3); they are also told: "You shall not worship their [the nations'] gods or follow their practices," i.e., imitate their conduct (Ex. 23:24; some exegetes interpret *maʿᵃśeh* as referring to idols, but this idea would hardly be expressed with *kᵉ*). See also Ps. 106:35: "They learned from their [the nations'] practices"; Mic. 6:16: "You have followed . . . all the works of the house of Ahab and lived according to their counsels *(mōʿᵃṣôṯ)*"; 1 S. 8:8: "the deeds that they have done since I brought them up out of Egypt"; also Jer. 7:13; 2 Ch. 17:4. Ezk. 16:30 accuses Israel: "You did all these things like the deeds of a whore *(kᵉmaʿᵃśēh ʾiššâ-zônâ).*"

Some references are to continuing action: Hezekiah prospered (*ṣlḥ* hiphil) in every work that he undertook (2 Ch. 31:21; 32:30; cf. Ps. 1:3 with *ʿāśâ*). Yahweh will make Egypt stagger "in all its doings" *(bᵉḵol-maʿᵃśēhû),* and so for Egypt there will be no future (*lōʾ-yihyeh . . . maʿᵃśeh,* "nothing will be done") (Isa. 19:14-15). God saw what the Ninevites did, how they turned from their evil ways (Jon. 3:10).

At other times the word denotes an isolated act: "You have done a deed that ought not to be done" (Gen. 20:9); "His [David's] deeds have been of good service to you [Saul]"; "He told him all that the man of God had done" (1 K. 13:11); "What deed is this that you have done?" (Gen. 44:15). According to Job 33:17, God can turn a person aside from an evil deed.

God observes the deeds of mortals (Ps. 33:15), knows their works and their thoughts (Isa. 66:18), and will never forget any of their deeds (Am. 8:7). People become unclean through their acts (Ps. 106:39). God repays (*šlm* piel) all according to their work (Ps. 62:13[12]; cf. Lam. 3:64); the psalmist prays that God will repay the wicked according to their work (Ps. 28:4). Cf. also Neh. 6:14: "Remember them according to these things that they did."

Another meaning of *ma'ᵃśeh* is "work, labor." "Six days you shall do your work" (Ex. 23:12; cf. 20:9 with *'āḇaḏ* and *'āśâ mᵉlā'ḵâ*). A *yôm ma'ᵃśeh* is a working day (Ezk. 46:1). A man returns from his work in the field (Jgs. 19:16; cf. Ex. 5:4,13; 1 Ch. 23:28). Noah will relieve his father from his work (Gen. 5:29; par. *'iṣṣāḇôn*). We read frequently that God will bless his people "in the work of their hands" (Dt. 2:7; 14:29; 15:10; 16:15; 24:19; 30:9; cf. Ps. 90:17; Job 1:10; negated: Eccl. 5:5[6]); this refers to both the work itself and its fruits. The noun can also mean "occupation" (Gen. 46:33; 47:3) or "business" (1 S. 25:2).

In Prov. 16:3 *ma'ᵃśeh* means activity in general: "Commit *(gōl)* your work to Yahweh, and your plans will be established." This meaning is especially common in Ecclesiastes: "I saw all the deeds that are done under the sun" (1:14; cf. 4:3; 8:9); "I carried out great works" (2:4: built houses, planted vineyards, etc.); "I considered all my doing" (2:11). There is a proper time for every matter *(ḥēp̄eṣ)* and activity (3:17). People can enjoy their work (3:22). In Sheol there is no work or thought or knowledge or wisdom (9:10).

b. *God's Governance of History.* Several poetic texts (esp. in laments) describe God's governance of history as his "work" *(pō'al):* Dt. 32:4; Ps. 44:2(1); 64:10(9); 90:16; 95:9; 111:3; Job 36:24.[51] On occasion, *pō'al* appears in conjunction with *ma'ᵃlāl* and *'ᵃlîlâ* (Ps. 77:12-13[11-12]) or with *ma'ᵃśeh* (92:5; 143:5). This terminology refers primarily to God's saving acts, especially in connection with the exodus. The Deuteronomistic History uses *ma'ᵃśeh* for this concept. We read, for example, that Israel "served" Yahweh until the death of Joshua, during the lifetime of the generation that had "known all the work that Yahweh did for Israel" (Josh. 24:31; Jgs. 2:7); then came a generation "that did not know the work Yahweh had done for Israel" (Jgs. 2:10). Ex. 34:10 (a Dtr interpolation) and Dt. 11:7 also speak of seeing the works of Yahweh. This refers to the saving acts of God, as in Ps. 77:12-13(11-12), which, however, uses different terminology.

In Isaiah, however, this terminology refers to what Yahweh is doing in the present or will do in the future: "They do not regard the deeds *(pō'al)* of Yahweh, or see the work of his hands" (Isa. 5:12). Those so attacked reply with scorn: "Let Yahweh speed his work, that we may see it" (v. 19). Another time the prophet proclaims that Yahweh will rise up "to do his deed and to work his work *('ᵃḇōḏâ)*" (28:21).[52] And soon he will fin-

---

51. See von Rad.
52. → X, 383.

ish all his work on Mt. Zion (10:12). According to Wildberger, Isaiah is influenced here by the creation terminology of cultic language; according to von Rad, he is influenced by passages that speak of God's acts in history (Ps. 44:2[1]; 64:10[9]; 90:16; 95:9; etc.).[53] Kaiser believes all these passages are late.[54] We may note that *pō'al* replaces *ma'ᵃśeh* in this sense in Hab. 1:5; 3:2; Isa. 45:11. But *ma'ᵃśeh* appears again in a late addition to the book of Jeremiah, Jer. 51:10: "Let us declare the work of our God" — referring to the fall of Babylon.

In other (late) texts, *ma'ᵃśeh* denotes the working of divine providence in creation, God's "silent governance of fortunes."[55] Ps. 145:4,10 speak of God's works of creation, using *ma'ᵃśeh;* then v. 17 declares: "Yahweh is just in all his ways, faithful in all his doings." Here *ma'ᵃśeh* refers to God's activity in general, especially in human lives. The same is true in Sir. 38:8, which says that the pharmacist makes medicines "so that God's works will not cease." According to Job 37:7, in the rainy season God "seals" human hands (i.e., makes activity cease), "that all may know his work" (cf. also Sir. 17:8).

For Qohelet, the concept of "God's work" takes on fundamental significance. "[God] has made everything suitable for its time . . . yet human beings cannot find out the work that God has done from the beginning to the end" (Eccl. 3:11). "I saw all the work of God, that no one can find out the work that is done under the sun" (8:17; cf. 7:13; 11:5). God's governance is hidden from human eyes; it is unsearchable. This is the fundamental problem posed by Qohelet.

V. 1. *LXX.* In the majority of cases, the LXX translates *'āśâ* with *poieín* and *ma'ᵃśeh* with *érgon.* Other translations of the verb include *gígnesthai* (for the niphal, but also for the qal), *ergázesthai, prássein, chrán/chrásthai, synteleín, plássein, hetoimázein, kataskeuázein,* and even *hamartánein;* for the noun we find *poíēma, poíēsis,* and *ergasía.* A few other translations also appear.

2. *Dead Sea Scrolls.* The Dead Sea Scrolls have little new to offer. The Temple Scroll in particular, with over one hundred occurrences of *'āśâ* and (only!) three of *ma'ᵃśeh,* remains entirely within the framework of OT usage.

"To do truth/faithfulness (*'ᵉmeṯ),* righteousness, and justice" summarizes the ethical ideal of the Qumran community (1QS 1:5; 5:3-4; 8:2). One can also speak of "fulfilling God's ordinances *(ḥuqqîm)*" (1QS 1:7; 5:20; cf. 5:22) and "doing what he has commanded" (1QS 1:16). The members of the community are *'ôśê hattôrāh* (1QpHab 7:11; 8:1; 12:4). The Damascus Document uses the expression "do according to the exact interpretation of the Torah *(kᵉpērûš hattôrâ)*" (CD 4:8; 6:14). We also find expressions such as "do what is good" (1QS 1:2), "do *ḥeseḏ*" (of God: 1QH 16:8-9 [par. *ḥnn*]; CD 20:21, following Ex. 20:6), "do evil" (1QS 1:7), "do *rᵉmîyâ*" (1QS 7:5), "do what one considers right *(yāšār bᵉ'ênāyw)*" (CD 3:6; 8:7; 19:19; cf. Dt. 12:8). Other combina-

53. H. Wildberger, "Jesaja's Verständnis der Geschichte," *Congress Volume, Bonn 1962. SVT* 9 (1963), 94ff.; von Rad, 294.

54. O. Kaiser, *Isaiah 1–12. OTL* (Eng. trans. ²1983), in loc.; idem, *Isaiah 13–39,* in loc.

55. Von Rad, 296.

tions already found in the OT are *'āśâ g^e^bûrâ* (1QM 16:1), *'āśâ ḥayil* (1QM 6:6; 11:5,7; 12:11; 19:3), *'āśâ n^e^qāmâ* (CD 8:11), *'āśâ m^e^lā'ḵâ* (CD 10:14), and *'āśâ š^e^pāṭîm* (1QS 8:11; 1QH 15:19).

Theologically significant but not entirely clear is the expression *'^a^śôṯ ḥ^a^ḏāšâ* (1QS 4:25), which refers to what comes after the "visitation" *(p^e^quddâ),* apparently a new creation. In 1QH 13:11-12 the same notion is expressed by the words *liḇrô' ḥ^a^ḏāšôṯ* (an allusion to Isa. 43:19; 48:6).[56] It is also significant that God "made" Belial (1QM 13:11).

Typical of Qumran is the statement "without him [God] nothing was done/takes place" (1QS 11:11; 1QH 1:8,20; 10:9) — in other words, nothing takes place that is not predestined by God.

On the whole, the meaning of *ma'^a^śeh* also remains unchanged, although the meaning "act, deed" (both human and divine) predominates. In 1QM 5:4-14, where the weapons of the sons of light are described, there are 10 occurrences of "work of an artisan" or the like. Those to whom God's wonders are told (1QH 1:33; 3:23) and to whom God shows *ḥeseḏ* (11:30) are termed "his work." God's righteousness was revealed "before all his works" (14:16); he executes judgment "before all his works" (15:20) and "provides for" *(klkl)* all his works (9:36). He rules over "all the work," i.e., all creation (1QH 10:8), and knows the inclination *(yēṣer)* of every creature (1QH 7:13) — or does this refer to "deeds?"

God's deeds are great (1QM 10:8; cf. 1QH 10:11 with *pele'*) and wondrous (1QH 7:32; 11:4); they are done with might (1QS 1:21; 1QH 4:32). There is frequent mention of "the deeds of your truth/faithfulness *('^e^meṯ)*" (1QS 1:19; 1QH 1:30; 10:17; 1QM 13:1,2,9; 14:12).

God knew all the deeds of his works before creating them (1QH 1:7) — note the continuation: " . . . without you nothing is done" (see above) — and established a norm for their deeds (1:9).

At the beginning of the Damascus Document, the listeners are called on to understand *(bîn)* God's actions (1:1). God in turn understands the actions of mortals (1:10; cf. Ps. 33:15). Human deeds are grounded in God's predestination (1QS 3:25; 4:16). To God belong all works of righteousness (1QH 1:26-27; cf. 4:31); human deeds are *r^e^mîyâ* (1:27; cf. 4:17) and are carried out in folly (1QH 4:8,17), unlike the deeds of God (4:20). Human deeds are further characterized by such attributes as *reša'* (1QS 2:5), *peša'* (3:22), *r^e^mîyâ* (4:23; 1QH 1:27; 4:17), *'āwel/'awlâ* (1QS 8:18; 1QH 16:11), *ḥōšeḵ* (1QS 2:7; 1QM 15:9), *'ep̱'eh* (1QH 3:17), and *niddâ* (1QS 5:19; CD 2:1). But God acts "for the sake of his mercy and not according to our [wicked] deeds" (1QM 11:4); God "judges their deeds in his truth and mercy" (1QH 6:9; cf. 18:13). Those who enter into the covenant, accordingly, are to be examined as to their understanding and their deeds (1QS 5:21,23,24); this examination is to be repeated continually (1QS 6:14,17,18; cf. 3:14; CD 13:11). In such contexts the Damascus Document uses the expression *bhwp' ma'^a^śāyw,* "when his deeds are revealed."

Ringgren

---

56. H. Ringgren, *The Faith of Qumran* (1963), 164-65; Sjöberg.

עֶשֶׂר *ʿeśer;* עשר *ʿśr;* מַעֲשֵׂר *maʿaśēr*

I. Number. II. Tithe: 1. Egypt; 2. Mesopotamia; 3. South Arabia; 4. Ugarit. III. 1. Early Israel; 2. Gen. 14:20; 3. Deuteronomy; 4. P and Later. IV. Outside the OT: 1. Rabbinic Literature; 2. Dead Sea Scrolls; 3. LXX. V. Summary.

I. Number. The word for "ten" is common Semitic. Heb. *ʿeśer,* fem. *ʿaśereṯ, ʿaśārâ,* occur 56, 68, and 50 times, respectively; the forms *ʿāśār,* fem. *ʿeśrēh,* appear only in compounds for the numbers 11-19 (211 and 135 times, respectively). There are 315 occurrences of *ʿeśrîm,* "twenty," and 8 of *ʿaśereṯ,* "group of ten." Derivatives are *ʿāśôr,* "set of ten" (days, strings) (17 occurrences); *ʿaśîrî,* "tenth" (20 occurrences as an ordinal, 8 as a fraction); and *ʿiśśārôn,* "tenth [fraction]" (31 occurrences). Whether *maʿaśēr,* "tithe," and its associated verb *ʿāśar* (2 occurrences in the qal, 3 in the piel, 2 in the hiphil) are connected with the word for "ten" is presently disputed, but highly likely (see II.4 below).

II. Tithe.

1. *Egypt.* A stele found at Naukratis in Egypt, dating from the first year of Nectanebo I (380 B.C.E.), decrees that the temple of Neith of Sais is to receive a tithe of

---

ʿeśer. N. Airoldi, "La cosiddetta 'decima' israelitica antica," *Bibl* 55 (1974) 179-210; J. M. Baumgarten, "The First and Second Tithes in the Temple Scroll," *Biblical and Related Studies. FS S. Iwry* (1985), 5-15; idem, "On the Non-Literal Use of *maʿăśēr/dekatē,*" *JBL* 103 (1984) 245-51; W. Boochs, *Finanzverwaltung im Altertum* (1985); W. Bunte, *Maaserot/Maaser Scheni. Die Mischna* I/7-8 (1962); H. Cazelles, "La dîme israélite et les textes de Ras Shamra," *VT* 1 (1951) 131-34; F. Crüsemann, "Der Zehnte in der israelitischen Königszeit," *WuD* 18 (1985) 21-47; M. A. Dandamajew, "Das Tempelzehnte in Babylonien während des 6.-4. Jh. v.u.Z.," *Beiträge zur Alten Geschichte und derem Nachleben. FS F. Altheim* (1969), 82-90 = *Vestnik drevnej isotrii* 92 (1965) 14-34; O. Eissfeldt, *Erstlinge und Zehnten im AT. BWANT* 22 (1917); idem, "Zum Zehnten bei den Babyloniern," *Abhandlungen zur semitischen Religionsgeschichte und Sprachwissenheit. BZAW* 33 (1918), 163-74 = *KlS,* I, 13-22; G. Giovinazzo, "Le decime *(ešru)* nella Mesopotamia neo-babilonese e achemenide" (diss., Naples, 1985); H. H. Guthrie, "Tithe," *IDB,* IV, 654-55; M. Haran, "מַעֲשֵׂר," *EMiqr,* V, 204-12; F. Horst, *Das Privilegrecht Jahwes. FRLANT* 45 (1930), 51-56 = *ThB* 12 (1961), 73-79; M. S. Jaffee, "Mishnah's Law of Tithes" (diss., Brown, 1980); H. Jagersma, "The Tithes in the OT," *OTS* 21 (1981) 116-28; M. Lichtheim, "The Naucratis Stela," *Studies in Honor of G. Hughes. SAOC* 39 (1976), 139-46; E. Lipiński, "Banquet en l'honneur de Baal," *UF* 2 (1970) 75-88; J. Pedersen, *ILC,* III-IV, 307-13; E. Salonen, *Über den Zehnten im Alten Mesopotamien. StOr* 43/4 (1972); W. Schmidt and A. Erler, "Zehnten," *RGG*[3], VI, 1877-80; E. Schürer, *History of the Jewish People in the Age of Jesus Christ,* rev. G. Vermes et al., II (Eng. trans. 1979), 257-74; R. de Vaux, *AncIsr,* I, 200-201; II, 380-82, 403-5; M. del Verme, "Le decime del Fariseo orante," *Vetera Christianorum* 21 (1984) 253-83; cf. idem, *RivB* 32 (1984) 273-314; M. Weinfeld, "The Change in the Conception of Religion in Deuteronomy," *Tarbiz* 31 (1961) 1-17; idem, "The Covenant of Grant in the OT and in the Ancient Near East," *JAOS* 90 (1970) 184-203; A. Wendel, *Das Opfer in der altisraelitischen Religion* (1927); M. Wischnitzer, "Tithe," *EncJud,* XV (1971), 1156-62.

the port's turnover and of the goods produced.[1] On the so-called Famine Stele, from the Ptolemaic period, the duty on goods in transit via Elephantine is set at 10 percent.[2]

2. *Mesopotamia.* In Mesopotamia tithes contributed to temples are attested in the Sumerian, Old Babylonian, and Late Babylonian periods (*zag-10, ešrētum, ešru,* respectively). The tithes were contributed by various occupational groups, private individuals, and towns, as well as by the kings. They could consist of gold and silver, agricultural produce, or articles made by artisans. Secular imposts are attested at the Old Assyrian trading colonies in Cappadocia: the merchants had to give 10 percent of their wares to the local ruler. Salonen believes this represents an ancient temple practice, which gradually led to acceptance of a tenth as the appropriate amount of the impost.

3. *South Arabia.* Pliny the Elder reports that in South Arabia the priests levied a tithe as a contribution due their god.[3] Inscriptions speak of statuettes dedicated as tithes *('šr)* or paid for from tithes. One text speaks of a cultic meal *('lm)* paid for out of tithes.[4]

4. *Ugarit.* In Ugaritic texts the verb *'šr* occurs particularly in three contexts: twice it is followed by *šqy,* "drink," and once in a text where *dbḥ dbḥ,* "slaughter an animal" (or "offer a sacrifice[?]"; cf. Prov. 9:2) and *'šr 'šrt* occur together.[5] This *'šr* has been connected with Eth. *'ašara,* "hold a banquet," and *'āšūr,* "banquet"; Cazelles translates it "drink offering."[6] The expression *'šr 'šrt* appears also in another text in a context that speaks of offering sacrifices to repel an enemy attack; here it must denote some sort of cultic act.[7]

III. 1. *Early Israel.* In the OT (except for Lev. 27:32), *ma'ᵃśēr* has no explicit connection with "ten." Eissfeldt treats tithes simply as a subcategory of firstfruits.[8] Guthrie undertakes to arrange the texts in chronological order and thinks that the earliest instances are of North Israelite origin. The only examples (Gen. 28:22; Am. 4:4), however, have to do with Bethel, which was located on the ever-shifting boundary. Both occurrences, moreover, are probably associated with the literature of the South (Gen. 28:22: JE; Am. 4:4: Judahite redactor).

2. *Gen. 14:20.* A noteworthy early instance, from the time of David,[9] is the *ma'ᵃśēr* Abraham gave Melchizedek (Gen. 14:20) — not in the North, but in the region of Jeru-

---

1. *LexÄg,* IV, 360-61; Lichtheim.
2. *LexÄg,* I, 6.
3. *Natural History* 12.63.
4. For sources see Biella, 387.
5. For the former see *KTU* 1.3, I, 9; 1.17, IV, 30-31. For the latter, 1.16, I, 40.
6. *LexLingÄth,* 967. But cf. Lipiński, 79.
7. *KTU* 1.119, 32-33.
8. → ראשׁית *rē'šîṯ.*
9. Westermann, *Genesis 12–36* (Eng. trans. 1985), 192.

salem or further to the southeast.[10] Abraham's "tithe" is usually understood not as tribute but as a spontaneous gift from his "revenue," i.e., his booty.

Closer examination reveals the nature of this gift to be very complex. The king of Sodom and his defeated allies were grateful to Abraham for rescuing them and went to meet him (in the Valley of Shaveh, possibly Kidron, or at any rate a valley accessible from both Shalem and Sodom). Their gratitude finds expression in the double blessing pronounced by Melchizedek, once blessing El Elyon, once blessing Abraham in the name of El Elyon. Abraham's spontaneous reaction is to deliver a tithe of all his booty (which belonged to him, not to the five kings) into the hands of Melchizedek — either for him personally or for the god he worshiped. This booty included prisoners from the army of Chedorlaomer and his allies (as v. 21 shows). Although Abraham's tithe was given to El Elyon, the king of Sodom feels obliged to intervene and define how the tithe is to be treated: "Give me the *nepeš* [i.e., the human spoils], but take the goods for yourself" (v. 21). Abraham rejects this proposal; he wishes to keep none of the goods except the necessary provisions for his men. What is left for El Elyon may have been a tenth of the total. According to Airoldi, this passage reflects the establishment of a covenant, accompanied by a meal.[11]

A tithe is also mentioned in Gen. 28:22; 1 S. 8:15; Am. 4:4. In the first passage, Jacob promises at Bethel to give a tithe (*'śr* piel) of everything God gives him. There are no further details. The second passage appears in the context of the "Law of the King" in 1 S. 8. Samuel says that the king will take a tithe (*'śr* qal) of the fields and vineyards and give it to his officers and courtiers. This text is clearly talking about a kind of tax; possibly it is aimed at preventing abuse of the right to tax. The Amos passage speaks of sacrifices and "tithes on the third day." Here the tithe appears to be comparable to an offering. Here too Airoldi interprets *ma'ᵃśēr* as a sacrificial meal.[12]

3. *Deuteronomy.* The Covenant Code speaks only of firstfruits (Ex. 22:28-29, *bᵉḵôr;* 23:19, *rē'šîṯ, bikkûr*) of grain, wine, flocks, and herds; not until Deuteronomy do we find detailed regulations concerning tithes (12:6-7,11-12,17-18; 14:22-29; 26:12-15). A North Israelite origin of these verse is hardly ascertainable.[13]

According to 14:22, "all the yield of the seed that grows on the earth" is to be tithed (*'śr* piel); in consequence of cultic centralization, "the *ma'ᵃśēr* of grain, wine, and oil," as well as "the firstlings of herds and flocks," is to be eaten in the presence of Yahweh at the chosen place (v. 23; it is not clear whether the firstlings constitute part of the tithe). The *ma'ᵃśēr* is not a gift to the temple or an individual, but a joyful meal in thanksgiving to God for a good harvest.[14] Although v. 23 contains the typical Deuteronomic requirement that the meal be eaten at the single place chosen by God,

---

10. R. Tournay, *RB* 67 (1960) 24-25.
11. Pp. 193-94.
12. Pp. 187ff.
13. Contra Guthrie, see N. Lohfink, *Bibl* 44 (1963) 492; E. Nielsen, *Law, History, and Tradition* (1983), 77-89.
14. Airoldi, 195ff.

this requirement is mitigated by the recognition that the central sanctuary can be too far away to permit observance of the harvest festival. In this case the *ma'ᵃśēr* can be sold; but the income must be set aside to provide a festive meal at the sacred place at a later date. This would be possible during one of the pilgrimage festivals, but the concern with too great a distance seems to imply the possibility of a substitute site located closer; v. 27 suggests that the celebration can also be held at home, since the Levites "resident in your towns" must not be neglected. (On the evidence of Dt. 12:17, Wendel concludes that the tithe cannot be consumed in one's hometown; but v. 21 makes clear that flesh may be eaten in one's hometown if the chosen place is too far away.) The mention of the Levites in 14:17 appears to be a later addition, and vv. 28-29 include the Levites among the needy, with *gērîm,* orphans, and widows, for whom every third year "the full *ma'ᵃśēr*" (not a second *ma'ᵃśēr*) is to be withheld (cf. also 26:12-15).

4. *P and Later.* Later the tithe becomes an obligatory contribution to support the priests and the temple. In the texts mentioned, it appears that the Levites received each year only a portion of the tithes and every third year a portion of tithes for the needy, while according to Dt. 18:4 the priests received the firstfruits and certain portions of the offerings (v. 3).

Eissfeldt's chief concern is to counter the view of Wellhausen and others that, in the process of reshaping the tradition (P and the Chronicler), the priesthood gradually increased its share. He stresses that no essential change took place in the period from J to Chronicles. Weinfeld assumes a totally contrary evolution: what had previously been sacral, Deuteronomy made the prerogative of the owner.[15] In similar fashion, Horst characterizes the festive meal as the consequence of a secularizing tendency.[16]

Eissfeldt also rejects the identification of firstfruits with tithes.[17] According to Dt. 14:28; 26:10,12; 18:4; 2 K. 4:42, firstfruits and tithes appear at least in part to have the same function. It should be noted that tithes are not always collected from the goods of the owner, but only when they come into the owner's possession for the first time: they are firstfruits. Naturally the owner does not know at the outset what the income will be (including the yield of the land: Lev. 27:30, etc.); an estimate is therefore necessary.

In Nu. 18:21 we meet for the first time the statement that God has given to the Levites for a possession "the whole tithe in Israel." The statement appears surprisingly after a long discussion (vv. 11-19) of the firstfruits *(rē'šîṯ),* which the Aaronic priests are to receive as compensation for the risk they incur in dealing with holy things.[18] These firstfruits include not only "the best of the oil and the wine and the grain" (v. 12), which Dt. 14:23 reserves for the celebration of the donor, but also the firstborn of cows, sheep, and goats (v. 17) and even of humans (of course redeemed by monetary payment, v. 15). This situation, which provides so lavishly for the priests, cannot be the original context of vv. 21-24, which allot the *whole* tithe to the Levites, especially since

15. "Change," 31.
16. *Gottes Recht. ThB* 12 (1961), 78.
17. *Erstlinge,* 157.
18. Noth, *Numbers. OTL* (Eng. trans. 1968), 133ff.

v. 26 adds that the Levites must contribute a tithe of their tithe as a *t^erûmâ* for Yahweh, which probably means that it devolves upon the priests.

Lev. 27:30-33 prescribes that "all tithes, . . . the seed from the ground and the fruit from the tree," belong to Yahweh; in cases of necessity, these tithes may be redeemed for 120 percent of their value. "This redemption has nothing to do with the optional temporary conversion of tithes of produce into cash provided for in Dt. 14:24ff."[19] In the case of tithes of animals (note: "every tenth one"), v. 32 forbids redemption; v. 27, however, permits it for unclean animals not suitable for sacrifice.

Lev. 27:32-33 came into being as a kind of codicil after animal tithes were included among the firstfruits assigned to the priests. This is also presupposed in 2 Ch. 31:5-12, whereas Mal. 3:8 still mentions animal tithes (assuming that the unfit sacrifices in 1:8 are not the same thing); only the normal tithes of produce are mentioned in Neh. 10:37(36); 12:44; 13:5,12, although 12:44 designates these tithes as support for "Levites and priests" (more precisely in 10:39[38]: for the Levites, and a tenth of the tithes for the priests).

IV. Outside the OT.

1. *Rabbinic Literature.* Rabbinic literature[20] distinguishes firstfruits not only from the "first" tithe (Nu. 18:21-32) and the priestly *t^erûmâ* in 18:11-12, but also from the two other *t^erûmôṯ* and the "tithe of the tithe" (18:26), also distinguishing the latter from the "second" (or "third," according to Targ^J I on Dt. 26:14, where the tithe for the needy is the "second") tithe intended for the meal of the tither (Dt. 14:22; Lev. 27:3).

2. *Dead Sea Scrolls.* The Temple Scroll from Qumran uses *ma'^aśēr* with the meaning "a tenth" (58:5: "a tenth of the people"; 58:13: of the spoils of war, a tenth belongs to the king, a thousandth to the priests, and a hundredth to the Levites). The regulations governing tithes differ in part from those in the rabbinic system. In 37:10 we read of places prepared for the offerings, firstfruits, and tithes (not further specified) of the priests. The Levites are accorded tithes of corn, wine, and fresh oil in 60:6; in a parenthetical clause, 60:9 speaks of a tithe of (wild) honey — otherwise the context deals entirely with offerings of bagged game, one in a hundred or one in fifty. 11QT 60 deals with what the rabbis call the "first tithe"; 11QT 43 deals with the "second tithe" (Dt. 14:22ff.; 26:12-13), but without using the word *ma'^aśēr.*

Apart from this specialized usage, the number ten plays an important role at Qumran. The *milḥāmâ* literature in particular uses a decimal system to divide the community (1QM 2:13-16; 4:3-5,17). This organization is also maintained in "times of peace" (1QS 2:22; 1QSa 1:15; 2:1; CD 13:1-2). The neophyte is required to study the "ordinances of the covenant" *(ḥuqqê habb^erîṯ)* for ten years. After ten years, whoever transgresses the ordinances of the community is excluded without probation (1QS 7:22). The ancient Jewish *minyān* is called to mind when a judicial panel of ten is ap-

19. Elliger, *Leviticus. HAT* I/4 (1966), 392.
20. St.-B., IV/2, 650ff., 668ff.

pointed for the community and when the presence of at least one priest is required when ten men of the community council are together (1QS 6:3; cf. l. 6 and 1QSa 2:22).

3. *LXX.* With few exceptions, the LXX translates all forms derived from this root with *dékatos* and its compounds. The noun *maʿᵃśēr* is represented by *epidékatos* (18 times) and *dékatos* (13 times), as well as *dékas, ekphórion,* and *aparchḗ* (once each).

V. Summary. The chronological sequence of the tithing laws is hard to determine, because laws dating from various periods were preserved by the tradition even when they were no longer observed. Haran, who dates P (Nu. 18:21) before Deuteronomy, may have rectified the order (although he has to ignore the royal tithe); but Cazelles's contention that *maʿᵃśēr* has nothing to do with "ten" creates difficulties (cf. Airoldi, who interprets the Dtn passages as referring to a "prepared meal"). Taking into account the Mesopotamian data (see I.2 above) and the biblical texts, we must keep the following points in mind: (1) every human group must set aside a certain portion of private incomes for common concerns; (2) the temple cult is a concern that had to be financed by such contributions; (3) spontaneous (or honorific) contributions like the Gk. *leitourgía* (the banquet in Dt. 14:23?) might have sufficed initially, but legal regulation gradually became necessary; (4) the number "ten" has no sacral character (unlike seven or forty), but is prominent when one counts on one's fingers, and a tenth is roughly what an individual can afford; but the tenth was calculated only approximately and over the course of time came to be considered a tax in the general sense;[21] (5) as many social and economic concerns became secularized, tithes were reserved for cultic and priestly purposes and the term lost its association with a fixed percentage.

North

---

21. Baumgarten, *JBL* 103 (1984) 245-51.

עָשָׁן *ʿāšān*

I. Etymology. II. OT Usage: 1. Ex. 19:18; 2. Gen. 15:17; 3. Relationship to *qᵉṭōreṯ;* 4. "Columns of Smoke." III. 1. Dead Sea Scrolls; 2. LXX.

ʿāšān. A. Demsky, "A Note on 'Smoked Wine,'" *Tel Aviv Journal* 6 (1979) 163; G. F. Hasel, "The Meaning of the Animal Rite in Genesis 15," *JSOT* 19 (1981) 61-78; J. Jeremias, *Theophanie. WMANT* 10 (1965); O. Kaiser, "Traditionsgeschichtliche Untersuchung von Genesis 15," *ZAW* 70 (1958) 107-26 = *Von der Gegenwartsbedeutung des ATs* (1984), 107-26; E. C. Kingsbury, "The Theophany *Topos* and the Mountain of God," *JBL* 86 (1967) 205-10; J. Licht,

I. Etymology. The root *ʿšn* with the meaning "smoke" (verb and noun) appears in Pun. *mʿšn,* "cremation urn"; Arab. *ʿaṯana* means "rise" (of smoke). Probably related is the pael *tnn* (< *ʿtn*), "smoke," found in many Aramaic dialects. The root *ʿšn* is not found in Akkadian or Ugaritic; instead we find Akk. *qaṭāru* and Ugar. *qṭr* with the double meaning "smoke" (i.e., emit smoke) (G stem) and "cure by smoking" (D stem).[1]

II. OT Usage.

1. *Ex. 19:18.* In the OT *ʿāšān* is especially striking as a phenomenon accompanying the Sinai theophany (Ex. 19:18): "Mount Sinai was wrapped in smoke. . . . The smoke went up like the smoke of a kiln, and the whole mountain shook violently." Surprisingly, this phenomenon is described elsewhere (58 times in theophanic contexts) as → עָנָן *ʿānān,* "cloud"; nothing is said of smoke in connection with the pillar of cloud and fire that accompanied the people (Ex. 13:21; but cf. Isa. 4:5 in an eschatological context). The smoke in Ex. 19:18 has often been taken to suggest a volcanic eruption, but the closest volcano active in historical times is near Tadra Hala al-Badr, southeast of Elat. Now since the OT occasionally identifies Midian with Sinai (Ex. 2:15–14:19; Nu. 25:15; Hab. 3:7),[2] one might seek to locate Sinai there. But the attempts to identify this volcano with the site of the theophany must be considered failures.[3] There is a consensus, however, that the text describes the theophany in the colors of a volcanic eruption.

Ps. 104:32 alludes to the smoking mountain of Ex. 19:18: "He looks on the earth and it trembles, he touches the mountains and they smoke." Ps. 144:5 prays for a repetition of the event: "Bow your heavens and come down, touch the mountains so that they smoke."

2. *Gen. 15:17.* Gen. 15:17 tells how "a smoking fire pot and a flaming torch [*lappîḏ:* better 'flare']" passed between the pieces of the sacrifice. The text "recalls unmistakably the Sinai volcano."[4] Because Yahweh makes a covenant with Abraham immediately afterward, it is reasonable to suppose that the flaming fire represents Yahweh's presence. This presence, as the context implies, is numinous; but it is not terrifying, as in Ex. 19:18.[5]

The Sinai event may also find an echo in the smoke from God's nostrils in Ps. 18:9(Eng. v. 8) (= 2 S. 22:9), accompanied by fire, darkness, hail, and thunder; but the context here speaks of a manifestation of divine anger (v. 8[7]). The same is true in Dt. 29:19(20) and Ps. 74:1: God's anger is kindled (lit. "smokes") against apostates and his

---

"Die Offenbarung Gottes beim Aufenthalt am Berg Sinai," *Studies in the Bible and the Ancient Near East. FS S. E. Loewenstamm* (1977), 251-67; H. Torczyner (Tur-Sinai), "Zur Bedeutung von Akzent und Vokal im Semitischen," *ZDMG* 64 (1910) 269-311, esp. 270.

1. → קטר *qṭr.*
2. Cf. Ptolemy *Geography* 6.7.2; see R. North, *TAVO-B* 32 (1979) 66-67; E. A. Knauf, *ZDMG* 135 (1985) 16-21.
3. W. Phythian-Adams, *PEQ* 62 (1930) 135-49, 192-209; G. Hort, "Musil, Madian and the Mountain of the Law," *FS G. Silcher* (1955), 81-93.
4. O. Procksch, *Genesis. KAT* I (^{3}1924), 104.
5. On Gen. 15 in general see Kaiser and Hasel; also G. J. Wenham, *JSOT* 22 (1982) 134-37.

people. Ps. 80:5(4) says elliptically that God "smokes" (i.e., is angry) while his people pray. According to Isa. 65:5, those who worship idols are "like smoke in my nostrils, an ever-burning fire" — probably meaning that they provoke God's anger (on this locution see also Jer. 17:4; Dt. 32:22).

3. *Relationship to qᵉṭōreṯ.* The noun *ʿāšān* never appears in parallel with *qᵉṭōreṯ*[6] — Isa. 6:4 (the temple filled with smoke) could be a possible exception, but may be influenced by the theophany motif. The smoke of incense and sacrifice is "a pleasing odor,"[7] whereas *ʿāšān* expresses rather something unpleasant. Smoke comes out of the crocodile's nostrils (Job 41:12[20]). According to Prov. 10:26, a lazy servant is "like vinegar to the teeth and smoke to the eyes."

Smoke is also a symbol of transitoriness and evanescence: the wicked will "vanish like smoke" (Hos. 13:3; Ps. 37:20 [reading *kᵉʿāšān* with 4QpPs 37]; 68:3[2]). In Ps. 102:4(3) the psalmist laments that his days have passed away like smoke. A similar image is present in Isa. 51:6: even if heaven and earth vanish like smoke and wear out like a garment, God's salvation and deliverance will be forever. In Isa. 34:10 the smoke that symbolizes the destruction of Edom goes up forever — "It is clear enough that [the author] thought of the end of Edom in a similar way to the destruction of Sodom and Gomorrah."[8] According to Isa. 9:17(18), "the wickedness [of the people] burned like a fire . . . and kindled the thickets . . . so that they swirled upward in a column of smoke" — in other words, their wickedness provoked the devastating anger of Yahweh. In Isa. 14:31 smoke from the north attests to the devastation wrought by the advancing foe. In Nah. 2:14(13) the chariots go up in smoke. Quite concretely, according to Josh. 8:20-21, the inhabitants of Ai see the smoke of their burned city rising to the sky. In Jgs. 20:38,40, the Benjaminites erroneously interpret the smoke rising from Gibeah, burned by the Ephraimites, as a smoke signal.

4. *"Columns of Smoke."* What Cant. 3:6 means by *tîmᵃrôṯ ʿāšān,* "columns of smoke," is unclear; the context suggests incense burning around the "litter of Solomon." In Joel 3:3 "blood, fire, and columns of smoke" are signs announcing the day of Yahweh.[9]

III. 1. *Dead Sea Scrolls.* The Dead Sea Scrolls remain within the framework of OT usage. The power of the enemy is dispersed like smoke (1QM 15:10); evil will disappear like smoke and vanish forever (1Q27 fr. 1, 1:6). The reading of 1QH 9:5 is uncertain.

2. *LXX.* The LXX translates *ʿāšān* almost exclusively with *kapnós;* we occasionally find *atmís* (Hos. 13:3) and the verbal *kapnízesthai.* The verb is translated with *kapnízesthai* (3 times) or *orgízesthai* (twice); in Dt. 29:19 we find *ekkauthḗsetai (orgḗ).*

North

---

6. → קטר *qṭr.*
7. → ניחוח *nîḥôaḥ.*
8. O. Kaiser, *Isaiah 13–39. OTL* (Eng. trans. 1974), 358.
9. → יום *yôm.*

עָשַׁק *ʿāšaq;* עֹשֶׁק *ʿōšeq;* עֵשֶׁק *ʿēšeq;* עָשְׁקָה *ʿošqâ;* עָשׁוֹק *ʿāšōq;* עֲשׁוּקִים *ʿᵃšûqîm;* מַעֲשַׁקּוֹת *maʿᵃšaqqôṯ*

I. Root, Derivatives: 1. Differentiation; 2. Forms; 3. Distribution; 4. Semantic Domain; 5. Ancient Near East; 6. Translations. II. Meanings and Settings: 1. Active; 2. Stative. III. Semantic and Social Development. IV. Theological Implications. V. Later Influence.

I. Root, Derivatives. *HAL* distinguishes three different roots: *ʿśq,* "quarrel" (only Gen. 26:20); *ʿšq* I, "oppress"; and *ʿšq* II, "be strong" (only Job 40:23; possibly related to *ḥzq*[1]). Because *ʿśq* and *ʿšq* II are so rare and because the differentiation of dentals and sibilants is often nothing more than a question of dialect (as in Jgs. 12:5),[2] we shall deal primarily with the root *ʿšq* I of *HAL.*

Guttural, sibilant, and plosive constitute a phonetic matrix that probably expresses aggression by its very nature.[3] Similar phonetic combinations are: *šdd,* "deal violently with"; *šḥṭ,* "slaughter"; *šḥq,* "rub away"; *šḥt* piel, "destroy"; *šmd* hithpael, "destroy"; *šsʿ* piel, "cleave."

2. *Forms.* Verbal and substantival forms are represented about equally in the OT. The verb appears 27 times in active lexemes, always in the qal; in 19 of these cases the verb has a personal object, in 4 a material or abstract object, and in 4 no object. The hithpael of *ʿśq,* "quarrel" (Gen. 26:20), is easy to associate semantically with the qal of *ʿšq.* As Jer. 21:12 shows, the hapax legomenon *ʿāšōq* in Jer. 22:3 is a normally formed active agent noun, contrasting with all the lexemes expressing a state, result, or situation. With these latter we can associate the fully intransitive *hēn yaʿᵃšōq nāhār,* "Behold, the river is rising" (Job 40:23) (or: "is oppressed"? [cf. NRSV "is turbulent"]; following the LXX, Fohrer emends to *yišpaʿ,* "flows abundantly").[4] Naturally the qal passive participle, which occurs 8 times, and the pual participle (Isa. 23:12), as well as the great majority of the nouns, are stative in orientation: *ʿōšeq,* "oppression" (15

ʿāšaq. W. B. Bizzel, *The Social Teachings of the Jewish Prophets* (1916); L. Epsztein, *Social Justice in the Ancient Near East and the People of the Bible* (Eng. trans. 1986); E. Haag et al., eds., *Gewalt und Gewaltlosigkeit im AT. QD* 96 (1983); T. Hanks, *God So Loved the Third World* (1983); P. Joüon, "Verbe עָשַׁק 'retenir' (le bien d'autrui), secondairement 'opprimer,'" *Bibl* 3 (1922) 445-47; Y. I. Kim, "The Vocabulary of Oppression in the OT" (diss., Drew, 1981); J. Milgrom, "The Missing Thief in Lev 5, 20ff.," *RIDA* 22 (1975) 71-85; J. Miranda, *Communism in the Bible* (Eng. trans. 1982); J. D. Pleins, "Biblical Ethics and the Poor" (diss., Univ. of Michigan, 1986); J. Pons, *L'oppression dans l'AT* (1981); E. Tamez, *The Bible of the Oppressed* (Eng. trans. 1982); L. Wallis, *Sociological Study of the Bible* (^{4}1922).

1. But see F. Hesse, → IV, 301.
2. *BLe,* 191 n. 1.
3. P. P. Saydon, *Bibl* 36 (1955) 294.
4. G. Fohrer, *Das Buch Hiob. KAT* XVI (1963), 523.

times); *ʿošqâ* (only Isa. 38:14 [MT *ʿāšᵉqâ*]);[5] *ʿᵃšûqîm* (3 times) and *maʿᵃšaqqôṯ* (twice), both abstract plurals: "oppression, extortion." The PN *ʿēšeq* (1 Ch. 8:39: a descendant of Saul) might derive from *ʿšq*.[6] Thus we find a total of 28 "active" words alongside 32 "stative" words.

3. *Distribution.* The distribution of these lexemes in the OT is noteworthy. No trace of the root appears in the historical books of any era, i.e., Genesis, Exodus, Joshua, Judges, Kings, Chronicles (except 1 Ch. 16:21 [= Ps. 105:14] and a personal name of uncertain derivation in 1 Ch. 8:39; see above), Ezra, and Nehemiah. The two occurrences in the books of Samuel (1 S. 12:3,4) are virtually lost in the total of 55 chapters. In other words, narrative literature does not use this root. By contrast, it occurs 9 times in Psalms, 7 times each in Isaiah, Ezekiel, and the Minor Prophets, 6 times in Jeremiah, and 5 times each in Proverbs and Ecclesiastes. Thus these books contain 46 of the 60 occurrences. Other occurrences are 4 in Leviticus and 3 each in Deuteronomy and Job. The data suggest two conclusions: (1) *ʿšq* appears primarily in cultic and didactic texts; the prophetic and legal passages must be examined to see how they relate to this observation; (2) attempts to date the texts using *ʿšq* generally bring us to the postexilic period.

4. *Semantic Domain.* The root *ʿšq* and its derivatives always denote negatively construed actions and states. Many of these actions are forbidden (e.g., Lev. 19:13; Dt. 24:4) or characterized as reprehensible (e.g., Lev. 5:21,23[Eng. 6:2,4]) and injurious to the person affected (e.g., Dt. 28:29,33). Frequently *ʿšq* conduct or its result appears in lists of detestable acts (e.g., Ezk. 18:10-18; 22:23-31) and feared afflictions (e.g., Ps. 146:7-9). Thus *ʿšq* belongs to the semantic domain associated with threats to life and well-being. Our word group denotes circumstances inimical to life.

5. *Ancient Near East.* Outside the OT, the root is attested primarily in the Aramaic dialects. Its earliest occurrences, with the meaning "act with violence," are probably in the Nerab inscription (par. to *nûs* haphel, "carry off") and in Sefire III.[7] Isolated occurrences, with the meaning "oppress," appear in the Aramaic Qumran fragments, Jewish and Christian Aramaic documents from Palestine, and Syriac and Mandaic texts.[8] In Egyptian, *ʿšq* may be an Aramaic loanword.[9] Arab. *ʿašiqa,* "love passionately," is possibly related.[10] It is unlikely that Akk. *ʿešqu,* "mighty, massive," has anything to do with *ʿšq*.[11]

---

5. On the omission of the *metheg* and other emendation, see H. Wildberger, *Jesaja 28–39. BK* X/3 (1982), 1444; B. Duhm, *Das Buch Jesaia. HKAT* III/1 (1892), 281, reads the qal impv. of *ʿšq,* "make an effort."

6. Contra *HAL,* II, 897; Noth (*IPN,* no. 1120) claims that the theory that it represents a sigh lamenting oppression is "untenable"; *PNU,* 29: "strong."

7. *KAI* 226.8; 224.20, respectively. See R. Degen, *Altaramäische Grammatik* (1969), 68, 79.

8. See Beyer, 272; Brockelmann, *LexSyr,* 552; *MdD,* 41b.

9. *WbÄS,* I, 230.

10. Wehr, 614.

11. *AHw,* I, 257.

6. *Translations.* The LXX often renders *'šq* and its derivatives with words from the stem *(a)dik-: adikeín* appears 15 times (even in Gen. 26:20, possibly representing *ya'ašōqû 'ōṯô*), plus *apadikeín* in Dt. 24:14. Nominal forms are represented 8 times by *ádikos, adikía,* or *adíkēma.* This Greek lexical field is associated with the legal realm: "injustice."[12] In second place stand Greek equivalents on the stem *dyn-: (kata) dynasteúein* and *dynastía,* "rule," are represented 11 times. This word family is associated with the political realm. The forms *sykophanteín, sykophántēs,* and *sykophantía* also appear 11 times representing words in the *'šq* group. They refer to false accusation, oppression, and extortion, terms from the realm of ethics.[13] Other translations are unique: *bíą ágein,* "act violently" (Isa. 42:4); *aitía,* "guilt" (Prov. 28:17); *apostréphein,* "divert (funds)" (Dt. 24:14 A; Mal. 3:5); *diarpázein,* "loot" (Mic. 2:2); *ekpiézein,* "extort" (Ezk. 22:29); *thlíbein, thlípsis,* "oppression" (Ezk. 18:18). In general the emphasis is on "injustice" and "violence." More specific meanings such as "carry off," "loot," or "slander" appear only rarely. The Vulg. prefers *opprimere* and its derivatives.

II. Meanings and Settings.

1. *Active.* The active verbal forms make the strongest impression in their variety and specificity; from them derive the nouns.

a. *Civil Law.* In Lev. 19:11-14, a series of prohibitions, *'šq* must have a meaning equivalent to the other forbidden acts. V. 11 mentions *gnb,* "steal," *kḥš,* "deal falsely," and *šqr,* "lie," side by side. V. 12 is a priestly and ethical expansion (misuse of God's name). V. 13 — shifting to the singular — now adds three further prohibitions: *lō'-ṯa'ašōq 'eṯ-rē'aḵā welō' ṯigzōl lō'-ṯālîn . . . ;* → גזל *gāzal* means "steal," while *lîn pe'ullaṯ śāḵîr* refers to illegally withholding a laborer's wages (cf. Dt. 24:14-15; absent from the Covenant Code). Then *'šq* means "exploit, extort": delaying payment (Dt. 24:15) is a form of economic exploitation. Elsewhere, too, *'šq* appears in the context of economic transgressions against individuals: 1 S. 12:3-4 (→ לקח *lāqaḥ*), Am. 4:1 (*rṣṣ,* "crush"; cf. 1 S. 12:3-4; Dt. 28:33; Hos. 5:11), Ezk. 22:29 (→ גזל *gāzal;* cf. Lev. 5:23[6:4]; 19:13; Jer. 21:12 [completely synonymous]; 22:3; Mic. 2:2; Ps. 62:11[10]; Eccl. 5:7[8]), Mic. 2:2 (→ חמד *ḥmd, gzl, nś'* [taking real property]). Proverbial literature also uses socioeconomic vocabulary when discussing *'šq* (Prov. 14:31; 22:16; 28:3; Eccl. 4:1; cf. Hos. 12:8[7]). And who are the exploiters of the weak? Well-to-do Israelites! This is clear in the proverbial texts (in Prov. 28:3, should *rāš* be emended to *rāšā'* with LXX?);[14] it is stated trenchantly in Mic. 2:1-10 ("personnel belonging to the military occupation and royal administration") and Ezk. 22:23-29 (princes, priests, officials, prophets).[15] Often the active participle suffices to identify the agent: Jer. 21:12; Am. 4:1; Mal. 3:5; Ps. 72:4; 119:121; Prov. 14:31; 22:16; Eccl. 4:1.

b. *Cultic Community.* Now the charge of exploitation and extortion is not simply a

---

12. G. Schrenk, *TDNT,* I, 149-63.

13. C. H. Hunzinger, *TDNT,* VII, 759.

14. See O. Plöger, *Sprüche Salomos. BK* XVII (1984), 331, 333; he retains the MT.

15. See, respectively, H. W. Wolff, *Micah* (Eng. trans. 1990), 75; W. Zimmerli, *Ezekiel 1. Herm* (Eng. trans. 1979), 465ff.

matter of civil law. Such intimidation of a neighbor falls within the competence of the cultic community. The root *ʿšq* is grounded in the ethos of this community, not in the earlier norms of clan life (cf. *gnb, rṣḥ, nʾp*). The rules in context refer to the cultic community (Lev. 19:12; Jer. 7:6; Ezk. 18:5-18; 22:6-12). The use of *ʿšq* in the sacrificial torah (Lev. 5:20-26) confirms its cultic associations. The "neighbor" to be protected (Lev. 19:11-13) is any member of the community. The "people" (Ezk. 18:18) is Israel, as constituted in the local congregation and in the temple community (Jer. 7:1-11). In admonitions against exploiting fellow believers (cf. Lev. 25:25, "a brother in difficulty"), *ʿšq* can always be used in a more general sense ("oppress, wrong") in contrast to "doing good" (Ezk. 18:18; Mic. 2:1; Zec. 7:9-10). Economic abuse of a neighbor then becomes (in times of crisis? under the pressure of foreign rule and internal class conflicts?)[16] an example of inhumane and godless conduct in general (Ps. 72:4; 119:121-122; *ʿōšēq,* "malefactor"). Because on the national level economic exploitation affects large numbers and because it is the hallmark of all foreign rule, *ʿšq* can also be applied to the nation and the land (Ps. 105:14 = 1 Ch. 16:21; Isa. 52:3-5).

2. *Stative.* a. *Participle.* The state of the *ʿāšûq,* who suffers *ʿōšeq,* arouses concern, pity, a desire to help. No one gloats over the lot of the *ʿᵃšûqîm.* The voices heard in the OT are those of the oppressed. As a rule, the qal passive (and pual) participle denotes an exploited group. In the curses inspired by the experiences of the 6th century (Dt. 28:15-68), we find predictions of a typically parenetic mixture of corporal and politico-economic punishment. The word *ʿāšûq* (in combination with *gāzûl* or *rāṣûṣ*) frames a passage describing violent treatment and exploitation at the hands of foreigners (vv. 29-34; why was the word not used in Lamentations?). The word has similar political overtones in Jer. 50:33 (vocabulary of captivity); Hos. 5:11 (MT, varying from LXX; the earliest occurrence of *ʿāšûq?*); Ps. 103:6 (promise of "vindication and justice"); Eccl. 4:1 ("tears of the oppressed" as a symbol of affliction). The catalog of the wretched in Ps. 146:7-9, beginning with *ʿāšûqîm,* reads like a timeless picture of affliction. The only individual, "spiritualized" usage is found in Prov. 28:17: "Someone burdened with bloodguilt" (semantic bedrock? — more likely figurative usage). The question is whether the three other occurrences of *ʿᵃšûqîm* (Am. 3:9; Job 35:9; Eccl. 4:1a), generally understood as an abstract, might not also be interpreted personally.[17] In Eccl. 4:1a the expression *hāʿᵃšûqîm ʾᵃšer naʿᵃśîm,* ". . . that are practiced," appears to suggest impersonal usage.

b. *Noun.* The noun *ʿōšeq* oscillates between concrete and abstract meaning. In Lev. 5:23(6:4) and Eccl. 7:7, *ʿōšeq* is palpably concrete (see also the proverbs cited in Ex. 23:8 and Dt. 16:17). Eccl. 5:7 and Jer. 22:17 illustrate the same usage. In the case of *bāṭaḥ bᵉʿōšeq* (Jer. 30:12; Ps. 62:11), there is room for doubt whether the locution refers to ill-gotten gains or an "exploitative attitude." The expression *dibber ʿōšeq* (Isa. 59:13; Ps. 73:8) admits only the latter interpretation. The practice of exploitation or its

16. H. G. Kippenberg, *Religion und Klassenbildung im antiken Judäa* (1978).

17. For Amos see H. W. Wolff, *Joel and Amos. Herm* (Eng. trans. 1977), 190; for Job see G. Fohrer, *Das Buch Hiob. KAT* XVI (1963), 472, with emendation.

mechanism is the subject of Jer. 6:6 and Isa. 54:14 (cf. Am. 3:6, "disaster in a city"; Jer. 6:7; Ps. 55:10-12[9-11]). In the *figura etymologica* in Ezk. 18:18 and 22:29,[18] the noun merges with the verb; "making gain *beʿōšeq*" refers to the attitude of the exploiter. Finally, Ps. 119:134 shows the word used in a very general sense, "the evil people do me" (cf. vv. 29,37,39,115,128,133,153,163; the word *rāʿâ,* "evil," does not occur in this psalm). The context of the abstract noun *maʿᵃšaqqôṯ* (Prov. 28:16) is textually problematic.

III. Semantic and Social Development. Although the scanty extent of the evidence makes it impossible to write a history of the term, a few stages of semantic development can be identified. (a) In Israelite society, characterized by division of labor and marked class distinctions (beginning with the late monarchy? [Jer. 21:12; 22:3,17]; earlier? [Hos. 5:11; 12:8(7); Am. 4:1; Mic. 2:2]), economic exploitation of the weak was forbidden. (b) The proponents of this ideal of social justice were prophetic and priestly circles. The locus of admonition and indictment was primarily liturgical. (c) Words belonging to the *ʿšq* group, together with → גזל *gāzal,* → ינה *yānâ,* → ענה *ʿānāh,* and others, play a role in admonitions addressed to the community. In such contexts *ʿšq* refers to the various economic mechanisms and circumstances, as well as the corresponding attitudes of the economically powerful, that threaten the lives lived by the poor. (d) Particular times of crisis (exile, natural catastrophes, extortion by foreign rulers) made such exploitation notorious within the early Jewish community as the worst kind of disaster and affliction. The social history of the Jewish communities is discussed elsewhere.[19]

IV. Theological Implications. It is theologically significant that in the ancient Near East and especially in Israel the economically weak individual enjoyed divine protection. Here age-old clan traditions of the solidarity linking the tutelary deity with his people and the ideal of the king who cares like a father for his people, which evolved from these traditions, combined fruitfully with experiences of affliction and oppression specific to Israel.

In Ps. 146:7-9 the "righteous" whom Yahweh loves (v. 8c) stand in the midst of underprivileged groups, and are therefore poor themselves (antonym: the "wicked" [*ršāʿîm*] in v. 9c). The "exploited" *(ʿᵃšûqîm)* stand thematically at the head of the list; they shall receive justice *(mišpāṭ).* They are followed by the hungry, prisoners, the blind, and those who are bowed down (vv. 7-8); the traditional "strangers, orphans, and widows" come after the "righteous." Yahweh cares for them all in specific ways, but justice (v. 7a) is the general promise to marginal groups. The king (Ps. 72:1-4) and each individual Israelite (Lev. 19:13; Prov. 14:31; etc.) have a religious obligation to protect those who are socially disadvantaged. In ancient Israel the setting in which a sense of this obligation was inculcated was worship (Ezk. 18; 22; Zec. 7; Ps. 146; etc.).

---

18. *GK,* §117p, q.
19. → ענה II *ʿānâ* II.

V. Later Influence. The *'šq* word group did not play a significant role in the post-OT period: in the LXX it was leveled to *adikeín,* etc.; in the Dead Sea Scrolls, Apocrypha, Pseudepigrapha, and NT, it is scantily attested and has no specifically economic overtones. It has nevertheless influenced the theology of poverty in both Judaism and Christianity.[20] This influence is manifested especially in the exegetical work emanating from the countries of the Third World.[21]

Gerstenberger

---

20. → ענה II *'ānâ* II.
21. Hanks, Tamez, etc.

עָשַׁר *'āšar;* עָשִׁיר *'āšîr;* עֹשֶׁר *'ōšer*

I. Root; Distribution. II. 1. Forms and Occurrences; 2. Parallel Words and Phrases. III. General Usage: 1. Verb; 2. Adjective; 3. Noun. IV. Theological Aspects. V. Dead Sea Scrolls and LXX.

'āšar. H. A. Brongers, "Rijkdom en armoede in Israel," *NedTT* 29 (1975) 20-35; H. Bückers, *Die biblische Lehre vom Eigentum* (1947); T. Donald, "The Semantic Field of Rich and Poor in the Wisdom Literature of Hebrew and Accadian," *OrAnt* 3 (1964) 27-41; H. Donner, "Die soziale Botschaft der Propheten im Lichte der Gesellschaftordnung in Israel," *OrAnt* 2 (1963) 229-45; J. W. Gaspar, "Social Ideas in the Wisdom Literature of the OT" (diss., Catholic University of America, 1947); R. Gordis, "The Social Background of Wisdom Literature," *HUCA* 18 (1943/44) 77-118; J. Gray, "Feudalism in Ugarit und Israel," *ZAW* 64 (1952) 49-55; F. Hauck and E. Bammel, "πτωχός," *TDNT,* VI, 888-94; F. Hauck and W. Kasch, "πλοῦτος," *TDNT,* VI, 323-25; F. Horst, "Das Eigentum nach dem AT," *Gottes Recht. ThB* 12 (1961) 203-21; J. Kelly, "The Biblical Meaning of Poverty and Riches," *TBT* 33 (1967) 2282-91; K. Koch, "Die Entstehung der sozialen Kritik bei den Profeten," *Probleme biblischer Theologie. FS G. von Rad* (1971), 236-57; H.-J. Kraus, "Die prophetische Botschaft gegen das soziale Unrecht Israels," *EvT* 15 (1955) 295-307 = his *Biblisch-theologische Aufsätze* (1972), 120-33; A. Kuschke, "Arm und reich im AT," *ZAW* 57 (1939) 31-57; J. A. Lucal, "God and Justice," *TBT* 32 (1967) 2221-28; M. Lurje, *Studien zur Geschichte der wirtschaftlichen und sozialen Verhältnisse im israelitisch-jüdischen Reiche. BZAW* 45 (1927); E. Marmorstein, "The Origins of Agricultural Feudalism in the Holy Land," *PEQ* 85 (1953) 111-17; P. A. Munch, "Das Problem des Reichtums in den Ps 37.49.73," *ZAW* 55(1937) 36-46; N. Peters, *Die soziale Fürsorge im AT* (1936); G. von Rad, *Wisdom in Israel* (Eng. trans. 1972), 74-96; M. Schwantes, *Das Recht der Armen. BBET* 4 (1977); F. Selter, "Besitz, πλοῦτος," *Theologisches Begrifflexikon zum NT,* I (1967), 101-4; U. Skladny, *Die ältesten Spruchsammlungen in Israel* (1962); W. Thiel, *Die soziale Entwicklung Israels in vorstaatlicher Zeit* (1980); H. E. von Waldow, "Social Responsibility and Social Structure in Early Israel," *CBQ* 32 (1970) 182-204; G. Wanke, "Zu Grundlagen und Absicht prophetischer Sozialkritik," *KuD* 18 (1972) 2-17; H. W. Wolff, "Herren und Knechte," *TTZ* 81 (1972) 129-39.

I. Root; Distribution. The root *ʿšr* (or *ʿšr* I; a root *ʿšr* II may appear in Ps. 65:10[Eng. v. 9][1]) is found in Southwest Semitic (e.g., Arab. *ʿašara,* "be abundant") and above all in Northwest Semitic. Apart from the OT and later Hebrew, the root — verb and substantives — is attested in Aramaic *(ʿtr/ʿtyr)* and Syriac (*ʿtr,* with several derivatives); reference may also be made to Mandaic.[2] The general sense of the root appears to be that something (or some state) is present in unusual abundance.

II. 1. *Forms and Occurrences.* The *ʿšr* word family is represented in the OT by a verb and especially by two nouns. The verb *ʿšr* appears 17 times: twice in the qal (Hos. 12:9[8]; Job 15:29), 14 times in the hiphil (including Ps. 65:10[9],[3] as well as Ps. 49:17[16] and Zec. 11:5,[4] where qal forms may be intended[5]), and once in the hithpael (Prov. 13:7). The occurrences of the verb are distributed as follows: once in the Pentateuch (Gen. 14:23), twice in the Deuteronomistic History (1 S. 2:7; 17:25), 4 times in the Prophets, and 7 times in wisdom literature (6 in Proverbs plus Job 15:29), or 8 if Ps. 49:17(16) (besides 65:10[9]) is included. There is one occurrence in apocalyptic literature (Dnl. 11:2).

The adj. *ʿāšîr,* often used as a noun,[6] appears 23 times (including Isa. 53:9; see below); Prov. 10:15a and 18:11a are identical (cf. also 19:1a with 28:6a). It appears 8 times as subject, once (Eccl. 10:20) as object. Its occurrences are distributed as follows: once in the Pentateuch (Ex. 30:15), 3 times in the Deuteronomistic History (2 S. 12:1,2,4), 3 times in the Prophets (Isa. 53:9; Jer. 9:22[23]; Mic. 6:12), 13 times in wisdom literature (9 in Proverbs and 3 in Ecclesiastes, plus Job 27:19)), or 14 if Ps. 49:3(2) is included (besides Ps. 45:13[12]). It also appears in Ruth 3:10.

The noun *ʿōšer* with its 37 occurrences (12 as subj. and 11 as obj.) is the commonest word based on the root *ʿšr.* Its occurrences in 2 Ch. 1:11-12 and 9:22 parallel those in 1 K. 3:11,13 and 10:23, albeit with minor changes. These occurrences are distributed

---

Isa. 53:9aβ. W. F. Albright, "The High Place in Ancient Palestine," *Volume du Congrès, Strasbourg 1956. SVT* 4 (1956), 242-58, esp. 244-46; B. Barrick, "The Funerary Character of 'High Places' in Palestine," *VT* 25 (1975) 565-95, esp. 580-85; G. R. Driver, "Isa. 52:13–53:12: The Servant of the Lord," *In Memoriam P. Kahle. BZAW* 103 (1968), 90-105, esp. 95; K. Elliger, "Nochmals Textkritisches zu Jes 53," *FzB* 2 (1972) 137-44, esp. 141-43; K. F. Euler, *Die Verkündigung vom leidenden Gottesknecht aus Jes 53 in der griechischen Bibel. BWANT* IV/14 (1934), 73-75; H. S. Nyberg, "Smärtornas man," *SEÅ* 7 (1942) 5-82, esp. 56-58; H. W. Wolff, *Jesaja 53 im Urchristentum* (1952), esp. 41, 77.

Additional bibliography: → אביון *ʾeḇyôn;* דל *dal;* הון *hôn;* חסר *ḥāsēr;* יקר *yāqar;* ענה *ʿānâ.*

1. See *HAL,* II, 898, citing Ugaritic.
2. For later Hebrew see Jastrow; Levy, *WTM,* s.v. For Aramaic see *DNSI,* II, 898; Beyer, 666; also E. Kautzsch, *Die Aramäismen* (1902), 109. For Mandaic see *MdD,* 43b, 188a, 347a. See also *BLe,* §61nα; and the inscription from Khirbet el-Qom, no. 3, discussed by K. Jaroš, *BN* 19 (1982) 31-40.
3. See I above.
4. See below.
5. JM, §§54c, 63c.
6. *BLe,* §61nα.

as follows: once in the Pentateuch (Gen. 31:16), 4 times in the Deuteronomistic History, 8 times in the Chronicler's History, twice in the Prophets (Jer. 9:22[23]; 17:11), and 15 times in wisdom literature (9 in Proverbs and 6 in Ecclesiastes), or 18 if the Psalms are included (49:7[6]; 52:9[7]; 112:3). It also occurs once in apocalyptic literature (Dnl. 11:2) and in Est. 5:11.

Reviewing the overall distribution of the word family, with a total of 77 occurrences (not including *'āśār* in 1 K. 22:49, which should probably be read *'āśâ*),[7] we note its relatively wide literary distribution and especially the clear preponderance of its occurrences in wisdom literature, 35 in all (including Ps. 49:38[37]).

The most disputed text is Isa. 53:9, where many scholars (esp. of an earlier era) have considered the expression *w^{e}'eṯ-'āšîr* to be corrupt. The form in 1QIs^{a} is noteworthy: a pl. *'^{a}šîrîm* (probably original; cf. also LXX and Targ.) has been changed to a singular (MT).[8] The anomalous form וָאעְשִׁר in Zec. 11:5, which exhibits a wealth of variants in the earliest textual tradition, might even suggest the noun *'āšîr*.[9] It is usually read and understood as *wā'a'šîr (K)*.[10]

2. *Parallel Words and Phrases.* The word family belongs to a relatively rich lexical field, within which it has a series of synonyms or parallel words as well as antonyms, occurring in more or less fixed phrases.

In parallel with the qal of the verb, "be(come) rich," we find *māṣā' 'ôn,* "gain wealth" (Hos. 12:9[8]), and *qûm ḥayil,* "wealth endures" (Job 15:29). In parallel with the hiphil, "enrich," we find *gāḏal,* "be(come) great" (Jer. 5:27b; cf. *šāmēn,* "grow fat," in v. 28a); *hiśbîa',* "satisfy" (Ezk. 27:33); and *yirbeh*[11] *k^{e}ḇôḏ bêṯô,* "the glory of his [viz., the rich man's] house increases" (Ps. 49:17[16]). As an antonym we actually find only a single verb: → רוּשׁ *rûš,* "be poor" (Prov. 10:4; 1 S. 2:7, where the hiphil ptcp. of *yrš* is generally emended to *mērîš* [hiphil ptcp.];[12] and Prov. 13:7, where the hithpael of *'šr* is contrasted with the hithpalel of *rûš,* "pretend to be poor"). A substantival antonym, *'îš maḥsôr,* "man of want," appears in Prov. 21:17. Twice the verb uses *'ōšer,* "wealth," as cognate object (1 S. 17:25; Dnl. 11:2).

The adj. *'āšîr,* "rich," often used as a noun, has mostly antonyms, primarily various terms for "poor": *'eḇyôn* (Ps. 49:3[2]), *dal/dāl* (Ex. 30:15; Prov. 10:15 [pl.]; 22:16; 28:11; Ruth 3:10), *rāš/rā'š* (2 S. 12:1,3; Prov. 14:20; 18:23; 22:2,7; 28:6). In Prov. 10:15 *rēš,* "poverty," appears as an antonym of *hôn,* "wealth, possessions." Other antonyms are: *'ōḇēḏ,* "laborer" (Eccl. 5:11[12]); *yōš^{e}ḇîm,* "inhabitants" (Mic. 6:12); *seḵel,* "folly" (or *sāḵāl,* "fool"[13]) (Eccl. 10:6). In the problematic text

---

7. See *BHS.*

8. See III below.

9. M. Sæbø, *Sacharja 9–14. WMANT* 34 (1969), 73-74.

10. See *BHS;* also W. Rudolph, *Haggai-Sacharja 1-9-Sacharja 9–14-Maleachi. KAT* XIII/4 (1976), 202; *HAL,* II, 897.

11. H.-J. Kraus, *Psalms 1–59* (Eng. trans. 1988), 480, reads *yarbēh* (hiphil).

12. *HAL,* II, 442.

13. → סכל *skl;* M. Sæbø, *TLOT,* III, 1270.

Isa. 53:9, the parallel word is *r^ešāʿîm,* "wicked";[14] in Eccl. 10:20 it is *meleḵ,* "king."

Unlike the adj. *ʿāšîr,* the noun *ʿōšer,* "wealth," appears in several combinations in which the parallel word lends *ʿōšer* a positive characterization. This is true especially of *kāḇôḏ,* "glory, splendor." This noun can be combined with *ʿōšer* simply by means of *wᵉ,* "and," either in a dyad (*ʿōšer wᵉkāḇôḏ,* Prov. 3:16; 8:18a [while v. 18b presents as parallels *hôn ʿāṯēq ûṣᵉḏāqâ,* "enduring wealth and righteousness";[15] cf. Ps. 112:3]; 1 Ch. 29:12; 2 Ch. 17:5; 18:1; 32:27) or in a triad including *ḥayyîm,* "life" (Prov. 22:4) or *nᵉḵāsîm,* "possessions" (Eccl. 6:2 [cf. the dyad in 5:18(19): *ʿōšer ûnᵉḵāsîm*]; 2 Ch. 1:11,12). It appears also in the construct phrase *kᵉḇôḏ ʿošrô,* "the splendor of his riches," i.e., "his immense riches" (Est. 5:11; cf. 1:4). This last locution expresses immensity of wealth, a notion conveyed elsewhere by *rōḇ,* "abundance" (Ps. 49:7[6]), *lārōḇ,* "in abundance" (2 Ch. 17:5; 18:1; 32:27), or *gāḏôl,* "great" (1 S. 17:25; Dnl. 11:2). Other synonyms or terms used in positive parallelism are: *ḥoḵmâ,* "wisdom" (1 K. 10:23; cf. Prov. 14:24); *ḥayil,* "riches" (Ps. 49:7[6]); *kesep/zāhāḇ,* "silver/gold" (Prov. 22:1); *yᵉqar tip'ereṯ,* "majestic splendor" (Est. 1:4). Antonyms are relatively few: *ʾiwweleṯ,* "folly" (Prov. 14:24b; *ʿošrām* in v. 24a need not be emended);[16] *rêš,* "poverty" (30:8; cf. *rāš,* "poor," in 13:8).

III. General Usage. Our examination of the larger lexical field has cast some light on the general usage of the verb and the nouns derived from the root *ʿšr.*[17] This usage covers a wide range of senses, from positive to neutral to sharply negative descriptions and assessments of wealth. Of particular importance are wisdom usage (where all the occurrences of verb and the adj. *ʿāšîr* as well as most occurrences of the noun *ʿōšer* appear in the earlier Solomon collections) and prophetic usage. Both are theologically significant, albeit in different ways.[18]

1. *Verb.* In the case of the verb, it is clear first of all that being or becoming rich can be viewed as an aspect of human life that is simply assumed (Gen. 14:21-23; Ezk. 27:33; Dnl. 11:2) or represented as a desirable goal (1 S. 17:25). It is something over which the individual has control, something that represents a challenge (Prov. 10:4). Second, however, it is equally clear that being or becoming rich is subject even more often to limits and restrictions — imposed, if not otherwise, at least by death (Ps. 49:17-18[16-17]). But wealth can also be squandered by a foolish lifestyle (Prov. 21:17). Positively, wisdom instruction associates wealth with honest labor, wisdom, and righteousness (10:4; 23:4; 28:20); as a result, the act-consequence doctrine can conclude that the riches of the wicked/ungodly *(rāšāʿ)* cannot endure or can ascribe

---

14. See III below.
15. B. Gemser, *Sprüche Salomos. HAT* I/16 (^{2}1963), 44.
16. O. Plöger, *Sprüche Salomos. BK* XVII (1984), 166-67, 174, contra *BHK*^{3} and *BHS.* See Sæbø, *TLOT,* I, 57-58.
17. See II.2 above.
18. See IV below.

wealth to God's intervention (1 S. 2:7) and blessing (Prov. 10:22).[19] Against this background, any association of riches with unrighteousness (and godlessness) becomes increasingly disquieting, leading to the problem of theodicy and the social criticism voiced by the prophets in their oracles of judgment (Jer. 5:17; Hos. 12:[8]; also Ezk. 27:33; Zec. 11:5, as well as Ps. 49).[20]

2. *Adjective.* The conclusions reached by examining the use of the verb are largely confirmed by the use of the adj./subst. *ʿāšîr,* except that the many antonyms[21] tend to present a sharper contrast between the rich and the poor. We find a naive acceptance of the existence of rich and poor, coupled with a certain perceptible concern for the poor (Ex. 30:15; 2 S. 12:1,2,4; Ps. 49:3[2]; Prov. 22:2,7; Ruth 3:10). Other passages, however, paint a negative picture of wealth, expressing not only its impermanence (Job 27:19) but also its inadequacy and injustice (Eccl. 5:11[12]; Prov. 18:23; 22:16; 28:6,11); this picture is painted in even darker tones by the prophets (Mic. 6:12; Jer. 9:22). The wealthy scoundrel becomes a kind of stock figure,[22] a development that could argue for keeping *wᵉʾeṯ-ʿāšîr* in Isa. 53:9b as a collectively understood parallel to *ʾeṯ-rᵉšāʿîm* in v. 9a.[23]

3. *Noun.* As already emphasized,[24] the noun *ʿōšer,* "wealth," appears in a series of locutions that lend it a positive character, especially with reference to kings (see the texts in 1 Kings, 1 and 2 Chronicles, Esther, and Daniel). In this context the significance of wisdom deserves special mention, because it leads to wealth (Prov. 3:16; 8:18; 14:24; but contrast Eccl. 9:11). The same is true of "humility" *(ʿᵃnāwâ)* and "fear of Yahweh" *(yirʾaṯ yhwh)* as well as "righteousness" (*ṣᵉḏāqâ,* Prov. 22:4; Ps. 112:3); this association leads once more to the act-consequence doctrine,[25] which, however, is relativized by Ecclesiastes (4:8; 5:12-13[13-14]). Wealth is also relativized when it is called less important than a good name (Prov. 22:1; cf. LXX) and when the text warns against trusting *(bāṭaḥ)* in riches (Prov. 11:28; Ps. 52:9[7]). Jeremiah is even more caustic in his threat of judgment on those who amass wealth unjustly (Jer. 17:11). Prov. 30:8 is remarkably evenhanded in its attitude toward wealth and poverty, and Qohelet can speak of riches positively as a gift of God (Eccl. 5:18[19]; 6:2).

IV. Theological Aspects. The theological profile of what the OT has to say about wealth is complex, including its use of the *ʿšr* word group. Above all, the OT treatment of wealth goes hand in hand with its treatment of poverty and the poor. There are many intersecting lines of approach, especially since voices representing many different mi-

---

19. K. Koch, *ZTK* 52 (1955) 2ff.; von Rad, 124ff. See IV below.
20. See the bibliog. at the beginning of this article.
21. See II.2 above.
22. Skladny, 19ff., 39ff., 62ff.
23. Nyberg, Barrick, contra *BHS* and to some extent Elliger.
24. See II.2 above.
25. See III.1 above.

lieus are heard. But the various theological aspects may be summarized under the following points:

1. Wealth is simply presupposed and accepted as a fact of human life; it is something positive and desirable.

2. Wealth is viewed as the consequence of human activity, depending in the first instance on the industry and sagacity of the individual and made the individual's responsibility.

3. But wealth cannot simply be an individual concern; it is equally a concern of the community in the context of changing economic and social circumstances. For it is not irrelevant how wealth is acquired or how it is managed, because it must not offend against "justice" and "righteousness." The question of wealth becomes an ethical question of gradually increasing importance, both in wisdom teaching and in prophetic preaching.[26]

4. The question of wealth is not simply an ethical question; in the Hebrew "synthetic view of life," it is often a religious question, and we note an increasing tendency to ground the phenomenon and problem of wealth on a religious foundation. This tendency finds classical expression in the Song of Hannah: "Yahweh makes poor and makes rich; he brings low, he also exalts" (1 S. 2:7). It is developed more pointedly in Prov. 10, where v. 4 says that "the hand of the diligent makes rich," then v. 15 praises the advantage of wealth as the "fortress" of the rich, and finally v. 22 propounds a radical theological correction: "The blessing of Yahweh makes rich, and [one's own] toil adds nothing to it."[27]

5. Especially among the sages, the intersection of God's blessing and God's righteousness with the unrighteousness and godlessness of the rich raises the problem of theodicy; it also leads to extensive social criticism in the indictment and judgment discourses of several prophets.

In short, the *ʿšr* word group paints a rather conflicted picture of wealth and what it means to be rich, including from a theological perspective.

V. Dead Sea Scrolls and LXX. This word family does not appear in the Dead Sea Scrolls, although the question of rich and poor had to be important for the self-understanding of the Qumran community, since their theology was shaped in a major way by an awareness of human need.[28]

The treatment of the *ʿšr* words in the LXX is remarkably uniform: of the 77 occurrences of the word family in the MT, 76 are translated by *ploûtos,* which also represents several of the synonyms listed previously.[29]

Sæbø

---

26. See III above.

27. Plöger, 120-21.

28. → I, 41; also F. M. Cross Jr., *The Ancient Library of Qumran and Modern Biblical Studies* (1958); M. Hengel, *Property and Riches in the Early Church* (Eng. trans. 1974); idem, *Judaism and Hellenism,* 2 vols. (Eng. trans. 1974); → ענה (II) *ʿānâ* (II), VI.1.

29. See *TDNT,* VI, 323.

עשתרת *ʿštrt (ʿaštōreṯ);* *עַשְׁתֶּרֶת **ʿašterėṯ;* עַשְׁתָּרֹת *ʿaštārōṯ;* עַשְׁתְּרָתִי *ʿaštᵉrāṯî*

I. Etymology. II. *ʿṯ/ štr:* 1. Ebla, Mari; 2. Babylonia; 3. Ugarit; 4. Deir ʿAllā; 5. South Arabia. III. *ʿṯ/štrt:* 1. Ugarit; 2. Egypt; 3. Phoenicia. IV. OT: 1. Singular; 2. Plural. V. **ʿašteret.* VI. Toponyms: 1. Ending; 2. Og; 3. Identification.

I. Etymology. Most scholars derive Hebrew forms with the consonants *ʿštrt* as well as the DNs *ʿṯ/štr(t)* from the Sem. root *ʿṯ/šr,* "be rich" (Arab. *ġaṯara,* "be covered with rich vegetation"; *ʾarḍ ʿaṯūr,* "irrigated land"; Heb. *ʿšr* I, "become rich"; *ʿōšer,* "wealth";

ʿaštōreṯ. W. F. Albright, *Yahweh and the Gods of Canaan* (1968), 115-17, 197-212; M.-T. Barrelet, "Les déesses armées et ailées," *Syr* 32 (1955) 220-60; idem, "Deux déesses syrophéniciennes sur un bronze du Louvre," *Syr* 35 (1958) 27-44; A. Cooper, *RSP,* III (1981), 358, 403-6; E. Cumont, "Astarte," *PW,* II (1896), 1776-78; M. Delcor, "Astarté et la fécondité des troupeaux en Deut. 7, 13 et parallèles," *UF* 6 (1974) 7-14; idem, "De l'Astarté cananéenne des textes bibliques à l'Aphrodite de Gaza," *FolOr* 21 (1980) 83-92; idem, "Le hieros gamos d'Astarté," *RSF* 2 (1974) 63-76; O. Eissfeldt, "Astarte," *RGG,* I ([3]1957), 661; G. Fohrer, "Astarte," *BHHW,* I (1962), 142-43; T. S. Frymer, "Ashtoreth," *EncJud,* III (1971), 738-39; H. Gese in H. Gese, M. Höfner, and K. Rudolph, *Die Religionen Altsyriens, Altarabiens und der Mandäer. RdM* 10/2 (1970), 62-63, 151-52, 161-64; J. Gray, "Ashtaroth, Ashtoreth," *IDB,* I (1962), 254-55, 255-56; idem, *The Legacy of Canaan. SVT* 5 ([2]1965), 169ff.; E. Gubel, "An Essay on the Axe-Bearing Astarte and Her Role in a Phoenician 'Triad,'" *RSF* 8 (1980) 1-17; W. Helck, *Betrachtungen zur grossen Göttin und den ihr verbundenen Gottheiten* (1971); idem, *Die Beziehungen Ägyptens zu Vorderasien im 3. und 2. Jt. v. Chr.* ([2]1971), 456-60; J. Henninger, "Zum Problem der Venussterngottheit bei den Semiten," *Anthropos* 71 (1976) 129-68; W. Herrmann, "Aštart," *MIO* 15 (1969) 6-55; idem, "*ʿṯtrt-ḫr,*" *WO* 7 (1973/74) 135-36; T. Klauser, "Astarte," *RAC,* I (1950), 806-10; J. Leclant, "Astarté à cheval d'après les représentations Égyptiennes," *Syr* 37 (1960) 1-67; idem and R. Stadelmann, "Astarte"; "Astartepapyrus," *LexÄg,* I (1975), 499-509, 509-11; F. Løkkegaard, "A Plea for El, the Bull, and Other Ugaritic Miscellanies," *Studia Orientalia J. Pedersen* (1953), 219-35; M. J. Mulder, *Kanaänitische Goden in het OT* (1965), 43-51; A. L. Perlman, "Asherah and Astarte in the OT and Ugaritic Literatures" (diss., Berkeley, 1978); J. Plessis, *Études sur les textes concernant Ištar-Astarté* (1921); M. H. Pope, "ʿAṯtar"; "ʿAṯtart, ʿAštart, Astarte," *WbMyth,* I (1965), 249-50, 250-52; G. Ryckmans, "ʿAṯtar-Ištar: nom sumérien où sémitique," *FS H. von Wissmann* (1962), 186-92; R. Stadelmann, *Syrisch-palästinensische Gottheiten in Ägypten* (1967), 96-110; J. G. Taylor, "The Song of Deborah and Two Canaanite Goddesses," *JSOT* 23 (1982) 99-108; M. Weippert, "Über den asiatischen Hintergrund der Göttin 'Asiti,'" *Or* 44 (1975) 12-21; U. Winter, *Frau und Göttin. OBO* 53 (1983), 544-51.

On VI: F.-M. Abel, *Géographie de la Palestine,* II ([3]1967), 255; W. Borée, *Die alten Ortsnamen Palästinas* ([2]1968), 46-49; S. Cohen, "Ashteroth-Karnaim," *IDB,* I (1962), 255; K. Elliger, "Astaroth," *BHHW,* I (1962), 142; K. Galling, "Astaroth," *BRL*[1], 41-42; cf. *BRL*[2], 111ff.; D. Kellermann, "ʿAštārōt — ʿAštərōt Qarnayim — Qarnayim," *ZDPV* 97 (1981) 45-61 (with bibliog.); W. Schatz, *Genesis 14. EH* 23, Theologie 2 (1972), 169-70; M. Wüst, *Untersuchungen zu den siedlungsgeographischen Texten des ATs,* I. *Ostjordanland* (1975), 48-55.

ʿāšîr, "rich"; Aram. *ʿtr,* "wealth"[1]). To explain *ʿṯ/štr(t),* a form with an infixed /t/ and metathesis of /t/ and /ṯ/ must be postulated.[2] It is also surprising that the DN *ʿṯ/štr(t)* appears primarily in languages (Ugaritic, Phoenician, Aramaic, Old South Arabic, Ethiopic) in which the verbal root *ʿšr* is not attested. OSA *ʿultr,* which *HAL* still cites under *ʿšr,* is no longer registered as an independent root by Beeston and Biella; the /ǵ/ instead of /ʿ/ in the supposed Arabic cognate *ǵaṯara* is also a problem. If, however, *ʿṯ/štr(t)* is a secondary feminine form related to Mesopotamian Eštar/Ištar,[3] we may ask with Ryckmans whether the word is a Semitic form at all; if it is, it would have to be treated as a quadriliteral derived from a root with an unknown basic meaning.

II. *ʿṯ/štr.* The grammatically masculine form of the divine name, *ʿṯ/štr,* is found in Eblaite, Akkadian, Ugaritic, and Old South Arabic, as well as in the Moabite compound *ʿštr kmš.*[4] It appears also as a theophorous element in Old Mariotic, Old Akkadian, Amorite, Ugaritic, and Phoenician-Punic.[5] In the form *ʿtr* it may appear in Amorite; it clearly appears in Aramaic (Sefire, 8th century B.C.E.: *ʿtrsmk;* Luristan: *ʿtrmṣrn*) and Palmyrene.[6]

1. *Ebla, Mari.* At Ebla ^{d}*aš-tár* appears also in the specified forms ^{d}*aš-tár* sa-za$_{x}$^{ki}, "Aštar of the administrative center," and ^{d}*aš-tár ti-in*^{ki}.[7] Old Akkadian and some Old Babylonian personal names use ^{d}*aš-tár* as a theophorous element along with ^{d}*eš*$_{4}$*-tár;* the latter form is also familiar outside the realm of onomastics. Immediately before *aš-tár* = ^{d}*inanna*(MUŠ), the "Ebla Vocabulary" contains an entry *áš/iš-tár:tá* = ^{d}EN.TE.[8] Whether this reflects a form */ʿaṯtarat/, as claimed by Archi, remains to be seen.[9] On the feminine cf. ^{d}*eš*$_{4}$*-tár bé-el-ti-šu,* "Eštar his Lady," in the later inscription of Ibbiṭ-Lim.[10]

If the predicate in the Old Mariotic PN *eš*$_{4}$*-tár-dam-qá* reflects a 3rd person masc. stative in /-a/, "Eštar is good," Eštar would be a masculine god here.[11] Whether the name of one of the deities to whom archaic temples in Mari were dedicated is really to

1. Ahiqar 207, etc.
2. Perlman, 104, et al.
3. Herrmann, "Aštart," 46.
4. *KAI* 181.17.
5. For Amorite see *APNM,* 171-72; I. J. Gelb, *Computer-Aided Analysis of Amorite. AS* 21 (1980), 97-98. For Ugaritic, *PNU,* 113-14. For Phoenician-Punic, Benz, 385-86.
6. For Amorite see *APNM,* 173. For Sefire see *KAI* 222A.1, 3, 14. For Luristan, J. C. L. Gibson, *TSSI,* II, 57-58. Cf. also G. Garbini, "ʿAtar dio aramaico?" *RSO* 35 (1960) 25-28; P. Grelot, *Documents araméens d'Égypte* (1972), 466. For Palmyrene, *PNPI,* 46-47, 108.
7. H.-P. Müller, *ZDPV* 96 (1980) 14-15.
8. G. Pettinato, *Testi lessicali bilingui della biblioteca L. 2769. Materiali epigrafici di Ebla* IV (1982), 290.
9. A. Archi, *AAAS* 29/30 (1979/80) 167-171, esp. 168b.
10. G. Pettinato, *AAAS* 20 (1970) 73-76, esp. 75.
11. See R. Jestin, *RA* 46 (1952) 196, no. 44; I. J. Gelb, *RA* 50 (1956) 10; H. Limet, *Syr* 52 (1975) 49.

be read ^{d}EŠ$_4$-DAR-*ra-at,* a feminine form of Eštar, as Dossin claims, cannot be discussed here.[12]

2. *Babylonia.* Bottéro deduces a masc. *eš$_4$-tár* from Old Akkadian personal names (cf. also *eš$_4$-tár-la-ba,* "Eštar is a lion" [contrast the fem. in *si-la-ba-at*], etc.).[13] The conservative nature of family religion probably allows us to conclude that previously a masc. Eštar played the more important role; cf. also the PN *I-nin-la-ba,* "Innin is a lion."[14] That Ištar a goddess of love and war should bear a name that is grammatically masculine is best explained by the theory that originally this deity was androgynous; this theory may also account for her cruel aspects and the aggressive nature of her vitality.[15]

Mediated by the Old Assyrians, the cult of Ištar came to Asia Minor,[16] where Ištar became associated with Hurrian deities.[17] Ištar of Nineveh could even be summoned from Sidon, one of her cultic centers, to the Hittite kingdom, with the hope that she would intervene there.[18] At Emar, too, the names Aštar and Eštar are now attested, as well as Aštartu and ideographic forms of the name.[19]

Having become an appellative, *ištartu* means "the goddess" in the combination *ilu* and *ištaru,* usually with a pronominal suffix, denoting the personal gods of a family.[20] The pl. *ilū u ištarātū* becomes a meristic collective term for "gods." From the pl. form *ištarātŭ* with its feminine ending may derive Neo-Bab. *ištartu,* "(personal) goddess."[21]

3. *Ugarit.* The role played by *ʿṯtr* at Ugarit is minor. In the Baal myth, he is to occupy Baal's throne while Baal is in the underworld; but his inadequacy even physically is quite clear: his characterization as *rẓ,* "formidable," is atavistic and ironic.[22] In the PN *ʿṯtrum* the otherwise masculine god is also "mother."[23]

Egyp. *ʿá-s-tá-ra* is discussed in III.2 below. The combination Aram. *ʿatar* (< *ʿattar* < *ʿaṯtar*) + *ʿattā* (< *ʿanat*) results in Aram. *ʾtrʿtʾ,* the name of the Hellenistic goddess Atargatis, the Dea Syria of Lucian.[24]

---

12. Dossin, in A. Parrot et al., *Les temples d'Ishtarat et de Ninni-Zaza. Mission archéologique de Mari* 3 (1967), 307, 329-30. See the critical comments of W. von Soden, *OLZ* 64 (1969) 565; and M. Krebernik, *ZA* 74 (1984) 165.

13. J. Bottéro, *Le antiche divinità semitiche* (1958), 40-42. Cf. J. J. M. Roberts, *The Earliest Semitic Pantheon* (1972), 37-39, 101-2 n. 290.

14. *MAD,* III (^{2}1973), 160.

15. On Ištar see now C. Wilcke and U. Seidel, *RLA,* V (1976-80), 74-89.

16. See H. Hirsch, *Untersuchungen zur altassyrischen Religion. BAfO* 13/14 (^{2}1972), 17, 20, 25-26.

17. E. von Schuler, *WbMyth,* I, 179-80.

18. Weippert, 20, citing *KBo* II, 9, i, 4; II, 36, ro. 14.

19. Private communication from W. von Soden.

20. *CAD,* VII, 273-74, s.v. *ištartu* 2.

21. *CAD,* VII, 271, s.v. *ištartu.*

22. *KTU* 1.6, I, 44ff.

23. *PNU* 46; see II.5 below.

24. *KAI* 239.3. See W. Röllig, *WbMyth* I, 244-45.

4. *Deir ʿAllā.* In the Canaanite-Aramaic inscription from Tell Deir ʿAllā on the upper Jordan (8th/7th century B.C.E.), I, 14(16) (in the context of a description of well-being) reads *qqn šgr wʿštr,* "the *qqn* plant (?) of *šgr* and *ʿštr.*"[25] The juxtaposition of the DNs *šgr* and *ʿštr* corresponds on the one hand to that of the Ugaritic DNs *š ʿṯtr š šgr* in a list of sacrifices and on the other to the appellative *nomina regentia* in the Heb. phrase *šᵉgar-ʾalāpeykā wᵉʿaštᵉrōṯ ṣōʾnekā* in Dt. 7:13; 28:4,18,51.[26] Caquot and Lemaire propose such an appellative sense for *šgr wʿštr:* "the increase of your cattle and sheep";[27] but in Dt. 7:13, etc., *šᵉgar* and **ʿašteret* are disambiguated semantically by *nomina recta,* which do not appear at Deir ʿAllā.

5. *South Arabia.* The presumably great importance of *ʿṯtr* in the ancient Semitic pantheon is still reflected in the role played by *ʿṯtr(m)* or *ʿtr,* associated with the planet Venus, in the religion of ancient South Arabia (but cf. also *ʾmʿṯtr,* if the fem. divine name means "Mother [is] Aṯtar";[28] Ugar. *ʿṯtrʾum* is discussed in II.3 above).

III. *ʿṯ/štrt.* Except for the questionable *áš/iš-tár:tá* from Ebla and ^{d}EŠ$_4$-DAR-*ra-at* from Mari (see II.1 above), the fem. DN *ʿṯ/štrt* appears only in Northwest Semitic, namely Ugaritic, Phoenician-Punic, and Hebrew; Canaanite Astarte was known in Egypt since Amenhotep II (15th century B.C.E.). Outside Egypt, *ʿṯ/štrt* appears as a theophorous element in personal names primarily in Phoenician and Punic; forms of these names later passed into Greek and Latin.[29]

1. *Ugarit.* In Ugaritic rituals and lists of deities, *ʿṯtrt* plays a relatively important role; in the syllabic list of deities RS 20.24, 24,[30] ^{d}IŠ$_8$.DAR$^{iš\text{-}tar}$ corresponds to the entry *[ʿ]ṯtrt* in *KTU* 1.47, 25. In the myth of Baal, however, Astarte takes a back seat to *ʿnt,* Baal's "sister." The comparison of the beauty *(nʿm* par. *tsm)* of *Ḥry,* courted by *Krt,* to that of *ʿnt* and Astarte may reflect their erotic and sexual function.[31] In another text[32] *ʿṯtrt ṣwd̊[t],* "Astarte the hun[tress]," plays a martial role, bringing to mind *Krt*'s invocation of her in his curse against his son *Yṣb*[33] and the role of the horse as an attribute of Astarte and *ʿnt.*[34] Thus if Astarte, like Ištar and *ʿnt* — and in contrast to the more motherly *ʾṯrt,* the consort of the high god El — is a goddess of both love and war (Herrmann's emphasis on the latter role probably being too one-sided), she embodies

---

25. H.-P. Müller, *ZAW* 94 (1982) 217-18, 229-30.
26. Cf. *KTU* 1.148, 30-31; and V below.
27. Deir ʿAllā I, 14; A. Caquot and A. Lemaire, *Syr* 54 (1977) 201.
28. On *ʿṯtr* see M. Höfner, *WbMyth* I, 497-501, 547-48; idem, *RdM* 10/2, 268-72, 276-77, 283, 290-91. On *ʾmʿṯtr* see *CIH* 544.2, and possibly Nami 19.5.
29. Leclant, *LexÄg,* I, 501; Benz, 386-87.
30. *Ugaritica* V (1968), 45.
31. *KTU* 1.14, III, 41-42.
32. *KTU* 1.92, 2; Hermann, 7-16.
33. *KTU* 1.16, VI, 55-57 (cf. 1.2, I, 8; also 40).
34. *KTU* 1.86, 6; on 1.2, VI, 27-30, see Herrmann, 16-17.

opposing expressions of vitality: the joy and terror of life spring from the same source. Neither lists of deities[35] nor myths associate *ʿṯtr* and *ʿṯtrt* in any way.

In *Krt*'s curse mentioned above, Ugar. *ʿṯtrt* is referred to as *šm bʿl;* the parallel in the Phoenician inscription of Eshmunazar has long been recognized.[36] With reference to *ʿṯtrt ḫr*[37] = ᵈ*ištar*(IŠ₈.DAR) *ḫur-ri* from (?)Šuksu (Tell Sūkās) near Ugarit,[38] compare now Phoen. *lʿštrt ḥr* on a bronze statuette in the Seville Archaeological Museum representing a seated naked goddess, "Astarte of the cave," or the widely attested "Hurrian" or "Syrian" Ištar, now Northwest Semitic Astarte.[39] The term *ʿṯtrt šd,* "Astarte of the field,"[40] = ᵈ*ištar-ṣêri ma-mi-ta*[41] now has a parallel in *bʿl šd,* "Baal of the field,"[42] and possibly also in Phoen. *šd/r̊ qdš* as an epithet of Eshmun.[43] This usage makes untenable the theory that the attribute reflects the notion that goddesses become *šd ỉlm,* "the field of El/the gods," through sexual intercourse.[44] "Astarte the hun[tress]"[45] comes *bmdbr,* "from the steppe" (cf. Cant. 3:6), not from the field; the two should probably not be identified.[46]

2. *Egypt.* In her Egyptian guise, the goddess never loses her erotic and sexual aspect, even in the Astarte papyrus.[47] In Egypt, too, Astarte appears as a mounted female warrior and charioteer; her identification with Sekhmet, the lion-headed goddess of war, may have played a role. A mounted goddess on the rock relief east of the temple of Seti I bears the caption *ʿá-śi-tá;*[48] a naked *ʿá-tá-ya [ ] śu-[k]ə-ší,*[49] mounted and shooting at a Nubian, appears on stele 1308 suppl. of the Turin Museum (18th Dynasty), identified by Helck with Ugar. ᵈIŠ₈.DAR *ḫur-ri* (see 1 above).[50] Therefore ᵈIŠ₈.DAR *ḫur-ri* can probably be connected with *ʿá-śi-tá-ya ḫú-rú,* the "Hurrian" or "Syrian Asiti" in the votive inscription of the *ptḫ-ʿnh* (probably a temple official at Memphis),

---

35. With reference to *Ugaritica* V, III 9, ro. 8-9 (p. 584), see now *KTU* 1.148, 30-31.
36. *KAI* 14.18.
37. *KTU* 1.43, 1.
38. RS 18.01, 3, 6 (*PRU,* IV, 230); RS 16.173, 9′ (*PRU,* III, 171); cf. RS 17.410, 7′ (*PRU,* VI, 35).
39. For the former see M. Dietrich et al., *UF* 7 (1975) 526-27. For the latter, see, among others, F. M. Cross, *HTR* 64 (1971) 189-95; Herrmann, "*ʿṯtrt-ḥr,*" 135-36; J. Teixidor, *HTR* 68 (1975) 197-98; *TSSI,* III (1982), no. 16, 3-4.
40. *KTU* 1.91, 10; 1.148, 18; 4.182, 55, 58.
41. RS 17.352, 12; 17.367, 2′ (*PRU,* IV, 122, 124).
42. *KTU* 4.183, I, 1.
43. *KAI* 14.17.
44. *KTU* 1.23, 13, 28.
45. *KTU* 1.92, 2.
46. Contra Herrmann, "Aštart," 19-20.
47. On the role of Astarte in Egypt, see *RÄRG,* 55-57; Stadelmann; Leclant; Helck; and Herrmann, "Aštart." On the Astarte papyrus see A. Gardiner, *FS F. L. Griffith* (1932), 74-85; R. Stadelmann, *LexÄg,* I (1975), 509-11; on a Hittite parallel see A. H. Sayce, *JEA* 19 (1933) 56-59.
48. Helck's transliteration.
49. But cf. *LexÄg,* I, 507 n. 71.
50. Helck, *Beziehungen,* 458. Cf. Weippert, 14-17.

and above all with *ʿá-s-tá-ra ḫá-rú,* the "Hurrian" or "Syrian Astara" with the epithet "Lady of the Heavens, Lady of the Two Lands," on a stele in Copenhagen, both dating from the period of Amenhotep III. An Astarte with an Egyptian tiara and spear appears on a Late Bronze seal from Bethel;[51] Gubel describes a 7th-century scarab in the Hamburgisches Museum für Kunst und Gewerbe with an enthroned, clothed Astarte (?) bearing an ax over her shoulder.[52]

3. *Phoenicia.* The earliest Phoenician mention of Astarte is the *ʿštrt ḥr* on the bronze statuette in Seville (see III.1 above). Astarte was the object of particular devotion at Sidon, where King Tabnit and his father (late 6th century B.C.E.) bore the primary title "priest of Astarte" and only secondarily "king of the Sidonians."[53] Josephus describes Ittobaʿal as priest of Astarte.[54] The funerary inscription of Eshmunazar (early 5th century) calls his mother "priestess of Astarte," followed by "queen"; both built temples, including a temple for *[ʿštr]t* and for (a different?) *ʿštrt šm bʿl.*[55] In the temple of Eshmun at Sidon, a votive inscription was found reading *lʿštrt lʾdny lʾšmn,* "for Astarte [and] for [the donor's] Lord Ešmun."[56] Also illustrative of the Sidonian cult of Astarte, besides a Phoenician seal from the 7th century,[57] are 1 K. 11:5,33; 2 K. 23:13 (Jgs. 10:6); and Lucian *De Dea Syria* 4. Evidence for the worship of Astarte at Tyre includes: the Akkadian treaty of Esarhaddon (680-669) with Baal of Tyre, in which the curse on whoever breaks the treaty mentions *ᵈas-tar-tú,*[58] clearly a warlike figure and apparently identical with *ᵈiš-tar;*[59] the Phoenician "throne of Astarte" inscription from Tyre (2nd century);[60] another Phoenician inscription, dating from 222, probably from Umm al-ʿAwāmīd, near Tyre ("for Astarte in the sanctuary of the deity of *ḥmn*");[61] a Greek inscription from Tyre mentioning the goddess Ἀστρονόη together with Herakles (= Melqart);[62] three texts in Josephus;[63] and Philo of Byblos.[64] Additional Phoenician and Punic texts mentioning Astarte are listed elsewhere.[65] On Rhodes a certain *bʿlmlk* refers to himself as *mqm ʾlm mtrḥ ʿštrny,* "he who arouses/exalts the deity, the bridegroom (?) of Ἀστρονόη (?)."[66] In a Punic inscription from Pyrgi (500 B.C.E.), the tem-

51. *ANEP,* no. 468.
52. Inventory no. 1964.324.
53. *KAI* 13.1-2.
54. *Against Apion* 1.18 §123.
55. *KAI,* 14.14-15, 16, 18; see III.1 above.
56. P. Magnanini, *Le iscrizioni fenicie dell'oriente* (1973), 12.
57. N. Avigad, *IEJ* 16 (1966) 247-51; Weippert, 13.
58. IV, 18.
59. R. Borger, *Die Inschriften Asarhaddons. BAfO* 9 (1956), 107-9, esp. 109.
60. *KAI* 17.1.
61. *KAI* 19.4.
62. R. Dussaud, *RHR* 63 (1911) 331-39.
63. *Ant.* 8.5.3 §146; *CAp.* 1.18 §118 ("Heracles and Astarte") and §123.
64. Cited by Eusebius *Praep. evang.* 1.10, 31.
65. Magnanini, *Iscrizioni,* 234; M. G. Guzzo Amadasi, *Le iscrizioni fenicie e puniche delle cononie in occidente* (1967), 19-95.
66. *KAI* 44.2.

poral phrase *bym qbr ʾlm* refers to "the day of the god's burial," but *k ʾrš bdy,* "because Astarte required it of me," does not suggest a sacral marriage of the king with Astarte.[67]

The caption on a relief in the Winchester College collection identifies the goddess *qdš,* often represented standing on a lion, with Astarte and ʿAnat.[68] Therefore the PN *ʿbdlb(ʾ)t* on the spear point from al-Khaḍr near Bethlehem (12th-11th century) may also refer to Astarte; cf. the Ugaritic PN *ʿbdlbìt* and the toponym *bêṯ lᵉḇāʾôṯ* in Josh. 19:6 (15:32).[69] As is well known, both Eštar (see II.1 above) and Ištar were pictured as lions or depicted mounted on lions.[70]

The double deity *mlkʿštr,* "King(-god) and Astarte" (or: "Astarte is king") is mentioned frequently at Umm al-ʿAwāmīd near Tyre in the 3rd and 2nd centuries B.C.E. and appears also in Carthage, Leptis Magna (Lybia), and Cadiz (Spain).[71] Other texts[72] identify this deity as *ʾl ḥmn,* "the god of Ḥammon,"[73] and therefore possibly the predecessor of Baal Hammon, worshiped in Sam'al,[74] Malta,[75] Carthage, and throughout Africa. It is possible that *ḥmn* can be identified with Umm al-ʿAwāmīd (cf. *ḥammôn* in Josh. 19:28).[76]

IV. OT. Apart from 1 S. 31:10, the OT texts that mention Astarte all appear in Deuteronomistic polemic; these texts (and CD 5:4, which echoes the Dtr language) convey virtually no specific information about the religious notions associated with the divine names.

1. *Singular.* The sg. **ʿaštart* > **ʿašteret* (MT *ʿaštōreṯ* uses the vocalization of *bōšeṯ*) appears only in 1 K. 11:5,33; 2 K. 23:13 (LXX and Josephus: *Astártē*). In 1 S. 31:10 most exegetes read *bêṯ ʿašteret* for *bêṯ ʿaštārôṯ* (LXX *eis tó Astarteíon* is not specific).[77] The phrase *bêt ʾᵉlōhêhem* in 1 Ch. 10:10a expresses detached repugnance.

If the "house of Astarte" into which 1 S. 31:10a says the Philistines put Saul's armor after he was slain was located at Beth-shan, as v. 10b suggests, the deity is the Egyptianized, warlike Astarte, possibly represented on a stele in Egyptian style from Beth-shan dating from the 13th century B.C.E.: a slim, clothed goddess with a tall coni-

---

67. See, respectively, ll. 8-9, 6. Contra Delcor, "Hieros gamos," 2; cf. *TSSI,* III, 145-47, 151-59, esp. 154, with additional bibliog.
68. I. E. S. Edwards, *JNES* 14 (1955) 49-51, pl. 3; cf. *ANEP,* nos. 471, 474; cf. 470, 472, 473.
69. See *KAI* 21; *KTU* 4.63, III, 38.
70. With reference to *ʿṯtr,* possibly cf. also *lbỉ* in *KTU* 1.24, 30.
71. *KAI* 71.2; masc.: *lʾdn* in l. 1 and *lʿbdm* in ll. 2/3.
72. *CIS,* I, 8, 1; etc.
73. Cf. *KAI* 19.4.
74. *KAI* 24.16.
75. *KAI* 61.3-4.
76. But see also H.-P. Müller, *Rechts- und Wirtschaftsurkunden: Historisch-chronologische Texte. TUAT* I/6 (1985), 640.
77. On the form, see Josephus *Ant.* 6.14.8 §374; for a different approach see O. Eissfeldt, *KlS,* II, 276 n. 1; cf. H. J. Stoebe, *Das erste Buch Samuelis. KAT* VIII/1 (1973), 522.

cal *atef* crown and horns.[78] Ashkelon, whose temple of *ouraníē Aphrodítē* Herodotus calls the earliest sanctuary of the goddess,[79] is too far from the battlefield "on Mount Gilboa" (1 S. 31:1,8; cf. 2 S. 1:21); a location different from that given in v. 10b would have been stated explicitly in v. 10a. Antipathy toward Saul (1 Ch. 10:13ff.) and a knowledge of Philistine religion motivate the Chronicler to have Saul's head brought "into the temple of Dagon" (1 Ch. 10:10b) instead of having his body brought to Beth-shan, as described in 1 S. 31:10b, especially since 1 Ch. 10:9 = 1 S. 31:9 draws attention to the fate of Saul's head. The effect is to heighten the edifying horror of the scene.

According to 1 K. 11:5 (Dtr[N?]), Solomon, led astray by his foreign wives, worshiped Astarte of the Sidonians and Milcom of the Ammonites; in an oracle of disaster spoken by Ahijah the Shilonite, v. 33a (Dtr[N_2?]) repeats the charge, adding Chemosh of Moab from v. 7. The MT of v. 7 says that Solomon built a high place for Chemosh and "Milcom" (reading *ûlᵉmilkōm* for *ûlᵉmōleḵ,* on the basis of *kaí tō̧ basileí autṓn* in v. 5 LXX, *kai tō̧ melchom* or the like of the Lucianic recension, and vv. 5 and 33 of MT); v. 6 LXX says that he built a high place for Astarte as well.

The use of *'āz* in v. 7 led Noth to see here an "official statement concerning the building program of the king"; instead of *šiqquṣ* he therefore reads *'ᵉlōhîm* — reflecting vv. 5a and 33 MT and *eidṓlō̧* in v. 5 LXX instead of *bdelýgmati* in v. 6 (cf. v. 33).[80] The statement of location in v. 7aβ, absent from v. 5 LXX, is a secondary addition based on the more precise information in 2 K. 23:13.[81] The pre-Deuteronomistic text of v. 7aαb thus records an example of the syncretistic religious politics that Solomon practiced for the non-Israelite elements of his domain — not, as the Deuteronomists would have it, for his wives. It was the Deuteronomists who added *ʿaštōreṯ 'ᵉlōhê ṣiḏōnîm/n* before Chemosh and Milcom in vv. 5 and 33; the LXX followed them in v. 33 (cf. v. 6), using for Astarte *bdelýgmati = (lᵉ)šiqquṣ* from v. 7aαb cj. (vv. 5a,33) instead of *eidṓlois = (lᵉ)'ᵉlōhê.* Therefore we have no information concerning any role played by Astarte in Solomon's religious politics.

In 2 K. 23:13 the Deuteronomists (N?) return to all three deities, again with Astarte in first place, in describing Josiah's defilement of the high places, which he locates *ʿal-pᵉnê yᵉrûšālēm* (cf. Zec. 14:4) *'ᵃšer mîmîn lᵉhar-hammišḥâ* (for MT *hammašḥîṯ*),[82] "opposite Jerusalem, south of the Mount of Olives"; Würthwein disputes (probably rightly) the historicity of this location for the time of Josiah.[83]

In short, 1 K. 11:5,33 and 2 K. 23:13 bear witness only to the important role played by Astarte in the exilic period, possibly on the Mount of Olives. The LXX's use of *bdélygma* for Astarte shows the same antipathy toward the goddess displayed by *bêṯ 'ᵉlōhêhem* in 1 Ch. 10:10a.

---

78. *WbMyth,* I, "Syrien," fig. 7. But cf. Stoebe.

79. *History* 1.105.

80. M. Noth, *Könige. BK* IX/1 (1968), 246; cf. E. Würthwein, *1 Könige. ATD* 11/1 (^{2}1985), 134.

81. Würthwein, 131, contra Noth, 241.

82. See *BHS, HAL,* II, 899.

83. *Die Bücher der Könige. ATD* 11/2 (1984), 460.

2. *Plural.* The pl. *'aštārōṯ* represents the wholesale condemnation of foreign gods by the Deuteronomists. Especially the meristic combination — functionally comparable to the Akk. pl. *ilū u ištarātū* — of *habbᵉ'ālîm* and *hā'aštārōṯ* in Jgs. 10:6; 1 S. 7:4 (LXX *Astarṓth* in both verses); 10:12, plus the substantially similar *labba'al* (sg.!) *wᵉlā'aštārōṯ* in Jgs. 2:13 (LXX *Astártai*) and the isolated *'štrt* (pl.) in CD 5:4, refers to the totality of the detested idols. The Deuteronomists restrict the plural to the period of the judges, a usage apparently continued by CD 5:4. That the expression *'eṯ-habbᵉ'ālîm wᵉ'eṯ-hā'ᵃšērōṯ* in Jgs. 3:7 (cf. 2 Ch. 33:3) accomplishes the same purpose shows how little the identity of the individual goddess mattered to the Deuteronomists. Similarly, the LXX uses *Astártē* for *'ᵃšērâ* in 2 Ch. 15:16 and *Astártai* for *hā'ᵃšērîm* in 24:18. See below for discussion of 1 S. 7:3 and 12:10.

The Deuteronomistic descriptions of Israel's idolatry stand in the interest of a theodicy in the light of Yahweh's judgments; they establish the calculability of his actions. From the beginning, the Israelites worshiped "Baal and the Astartes" (Jgs. 2:13 — Dtr[H?]); throughout the period of the judges they continued to do what was evil in the eyes of Yahweh (10:6). Here the Deuteronomists seize the opportunity to anticipate the association of foreign gods with Sidon, Moab, and Ammon in 1 K. 11:33 and 2 K. 23:13, rounding out the list with *wᵉ'eṯ- 'ᵉlōhê 'ᵃrām* at the beginning and *wᵉ'ēṯ 'ᵉlōhê pᵉlištîm* at the end. But at the end of the period of the judges, when Samuel admonished them to put away the foreign gods (on this locution cf. Gen. 35:2; Josh. 24:23; Jgs. 10:16), the Israelites put away "the Baals and the Astartes" (1 S. 7:3-4 — Dtr[N?]). This action paved the way, by divine providence, for deliverance from the Philistine danger. In v. 3 the phrase *wᵉ('eṯ-)hā'aštārōṯ,* "and (especially) the Astartes," after "the foreign gods" sounds like an afterthought; it is probably a late Deuteronomistic or post-Deuteronomistic addition, obviously reflecting a contemporary concern. In the same vein 1 S. 12:10 (Dtr[H + N?]), looking back over the period of the judges, recalls that, when the Israelites lamented that they had worshiped "the Baals and Astartes" (cf. Jgs. 10:10), this confession motivated Yahweh to intervene against the enemies of Israel — successfully, as experience proved in the time of the judges (v. 11); the Deuteronomists expect this confession to result in similar intervention in the exilic present.

In 1 S. 7:3 and 12:10, the LXX has *tá álsē* and *kaí toís álsesin* instead of *wᵉ('eṯ)hā'aštārōṯ*. In both texts it may have read *w't-h'šrwt:* in Dt. 12:3 *kaí tá álsē autṓn* represents *wa'ᵃšērêhem.* In contrast to 2 Ch. 15:16 and 24:18 (see above), we have here a confusion resulting from lack of interest in the distinction between the goddesses (cf. the toponym *Asērṓth* for *'aštārōṯ* in 1 Ch. 6:56[61] LXX), whose mutual assimilation was well advanced.

Again, a decision whether the "queen of heaven" of Jer. 7:18; 44:17-19,25 was Astarte or some other female deity was of no interest to the Deuteronomist, who at least edited the passages. Since in a syncretistic milieu similar or identical notions can be associated with related gods bearing different names, the question has little religio-historical meaning. Immediately before and during the exilic period, besides the Canaanite Astarte and the Egyptianized Astarte, Ištar, who is called *šarrat šammê,* "queen of heaven," in a Babylonian list of gods, may have contributed to the picture of the goddess, who may also have been a counterpart to the *bʿl šmm/n,* "Baal of heaven," so popular in Syria during the 1st millennium B.C.E.[84] The same is true of the *ouraníē Aphrodítē* of Ashkelon mentioned by Herodotus.[85] According to Hermopolis Papyrus 4:1 (ca. 500 B.C.E.), a *mlkt šmyn,* "queen of heaven," had a temple along with the god Beth-El near the Jewish military colony at Syene;[86] it must also remain an open question whether this goddess is specifically identical with Astarte.

V. *ʿašteret̲. The appellative **ʿašteret̲* appears in the phrase *ʿašt^e rôt̲ ṣōnek̲ā,* "issue/increase of your flock" (almost certainly not "fertility of your flock")[87] (Dt. 7:13; 28:4,18,51), each time in parallel with *š^e gar ʾ^a lāpeyk̲ā,* "offspring of your cattle." According to Delcor, this usage represents a demythologization of the two divine names found in the combination *ʿt/štr* and *šgr.*[88] Behind **ʿašt^e rôt̲ ṣōʾn* stands the role of Astarte as the "Lady of the Animals," more precisely the "Shepherdess of Goats"; the picture of a goddess on an ivory tablet from a tomb in Minet al-Beiḍa offers a visual representation.[89] In the appellatives **ʿašteret̲* and *šeger,* this analysis claims, divine names have become terms for the gifts bestowed by the deities. A meaning "dams" for *ʿašteret̲* is harder to defend, since the parallel *šeger* is hard to interpret as either a synonym or an antonym.[90] Whether the *šgr* of Deir ʿAllā I, 14 is a goddess is still unclear.[91] Ugar. *šgr (mud)*[92] and Heb. *šeger* in the (pleonastic?) expression *pet̲er šeger b^e hēmâ,* "firstlings of the offspring of cattle," in Ex. 13:12 (and *šgr,* "young cattle (breeding)," in Sir. 40:19) do not denote brood animals. The correspondence of the fem. **ʿašteret̲* in Dt. 7:13 and elsewhere to the masc. *šeger* make direct derivation from a root *ʿšr* problematic, quite apart from other arguments against such an etymology (see I above).

In Dt. 7:13 and 28:4, the gifts of Astarte and *šgr* are so clearly among the consequences of Yahweh's blessing that in the present form of the texts any echo of the earlier deities appears to have been lost. In case of disobedience, a curse will strike the womb, the ground, and the offspring of the cattle (28:18); according v. 51aβ, Yahweh will make all *š^e gar-ʾ^a lāpeyk̲ā w^e ʿašt^e rōt̲ ṣōʾnek̲ā,* "the fruit of your livestock" (cf. vv. 4,18) and "the fruit of your ground" the spoil of the Neo-Babylonians.

VI. Toponyms. The toponyms *ʿaštārôt̲* and *(b^e)ʿešt^e râ* (Josh. 21:27) bear witness to the importance of the Astarte cult.

---

84. On Astarte see Gese, 191-92; for Ištar see *Anum,* IV, 171.
85. *History* 1.105; see IV.1 above.
86. *TSSI,* II, 137-38.
87. E. König, *Hebräisches und aramäisches Wörterbuch zum AT* (1910), s.v.
88. Delcor, "Astarté," 14; *KTU* 1.148, 30-31; now also Deir ʿAllā I, 14; see II.4 above.
89. *ANEP,* 464; cf. 465.
90. Cf. *GesTh,* 1083; cf. *KBL*², 745; *HAL,* II, 899.
91. Müller, *ZAW* 94 (1982) 230 n. 106.
92. *KTU* 1.5, III, 16-17.

1. *Ending.* The fem. pl. *ʿaštārôṯ* of the MT contrasts on the one hand with the masc. sg. of Eb. *aš-tár*^ki[93] (cf. also *aš-tár-LUM*^ki and *aš-tá*-LUM^ki[94]), on the other above all with the fem. sg. of *ʿ-s-[ta-]r-tum* (in an Egyptian execration text from the 18th century),[95] *ʿa-s-tá-r-tu* (Thutmose III, Amenhotep III, list of place names from the temple of Amarah in the Sudan),[96] ^uru*aš-tar-te/ti,*[97] ^uru*as-tar-tu* (in a bas-relief of Tiglath-pileser III from Nimrud),[98] *(b^e)ʿešt^erâ* (Josh. 21:27; gentilic *ʿašt^erāṯî* in 1 Ch. 27:14),[99] *ʿštr* (1QapGen 21:28), and Modern Arabic *tell ʿaštara.* The correctness of MT */-ôṯ/* may nevertheless be supported by the LXX equivalent (uniformly *Astarṓth* except *Asērṓth* in 1 Ch. 6:56) and the fact that the ending in the corresponding form *ʿ^anāṯôṯ* is additional to the morpheme for the feminine singular. In the case of *bêṯ l^eḇāʾôṯ* (see III.3 above; Josh. 19:6; but *Baith-labath* in LXX A) and *bêt ʿ^anôṯ* (Josh. 15:59), if a localizing function is served by */-ôṯ/* as well as by the alternative *b^e*- in *b^eʿešt^erâ,* it is doubly realized.[100] More likely *b^eʿešt^erâ* is a contraction of **bêt ʿešt^erâ,*[101] used as a stabilized adverbial. Since MT */-ôṯ/* appears also in toponyms that do not derive from the names of goddesses, we cannot draw general conclusions concerning its function. The retention of feminine divine names in the plural in toponyms may show that observant use of a plural of majesty was better preserved in the toponymic tradition than in the OT narrative tradition, especially since a true numerical plural is unlikely in a genuine toponym: only one local instantiation of the goddess is worshiped in a given place. But why does none of the extrabiblical texts preserve a plural of majesty? The frequent occurrence of the pl. *ʿaštārôṯ* in Deuteronomistic material suggests the possibility that singular toponyms were distorted by the Deuteronomists or under Deuteronomistic influence, as a way of denouncing the despised polytheism with reference to the particular deity in question (cf. also *b^eʿālôṯ* in Josh. 15:24 and 1 K. 4:16 [?] alongside *baʿ^alâ* and the Dtr replacement of *ʾ^elōhê* with *šiqquṣ* in 1 K. 11:7). The same antipathy later (?) may have occasioned the change of **bêṯ ʿašteret* to *bêṯ ʿaštārôṯ* in 1 S. 31:10 (see IV.1 above).

2. *Og.* In an addition to an earlier formula in Josh. 9:10,[102] the Deuteronomist refers to *ʿaštārôṯ* as the dwelling place of King Og of Bashan, where the Egyptian and Akkadian transcriptions as well as Ugar. *ʿṯtrth*[103] can be localized for other reasons.[104] Josh. 12:4; 13:12,31 add *ʾeḏreʿî* (= *derʿa*) as a second royal city of Og, using the information

93. G. Pettinato, *AfO* 25 (1974/77) 7.
94. F. Pomponio, *UF* 15 (1983) 155.
95. Helck, *Beziehungen,* 55.
96. Ibid., 129; Kellermann, 54.
97. EA 197:10; 256:21.
98. B. Meissner, *ZDPV* 39 (1916) 261-63.
99. Kellermann, 48-49.
100. Contra Borée.
101. Abel, 263; *BHK.*
102. Wüst, 48 n. 170.
103. *KTU* 1.100, 41.
104. Kellermann, 53-56; also M. Astour, *JNES* 27 (1968) 32; idem, *RSP* II (1975), 313-14; M. Tsevat, *UF* 11 (1979) 759-78.

in Nu. 21:33 and Dt 3:1 (cf. v. 10) to accommodate the text to the MT of Dt. 1:4. According to Josh. 12:6, Moses gave the land east of the Jordan, formerly possessed by Sihon of Heshbon and Og, to the half-tribe of Manasseh; further details appear in Josh. 21:27 and 1 Ch. 6:56, where *(b^e)'ešt^{e}râ* and *'aštārôṯ* respectively appear after *gôlān babbāšān.* Dt. 3:11,13 associate Og and Bashan with the *r^{e}pā'îm;* Josh. 12:4 and 13:12 do the same with Og and *'aštārôṯ.* Therefore Gen. 14:5 transfers Chedorlaomer's victory over the *r^{e}pā'îm* to **'aštārôṯ,*[105] which this late text calls *'ašt^{e}rôṯ qarnayim* (cf. 1QapGen 21:28-29, *'štr' dqrnyn*), either because the author pictured Astarte as having a pair of horns (cf. Philo of Byblos, who describes Astarte as having the head of a bull)[106] or because Am. 6:13 suggested that *qarnayim* was the name of another town (modern Sheiḫ Sa'ad; cf. 1 Mc. 5:26,43-44; 2 Mc. 12:21,26; Bab. *Sukka* 2a; also Jub. 29:10, where *qarānā'îm, 'asṭarôs,* and other towns are listed together) or region,[107] which he chose to connect with **'aštārôṯ.*

3. *Identification.* Most scholars identify the *'aštārôṯ* of Dt. 1:4; Josh. 9:10; 12:4; 13:12,31; 1 Ch. 11:4 (= *[b^e]'ešt^{e}râ* in Josh. 21:27) with Tell Ashtarah; Tell Ashari has also been suggested.[108] Since the mention of *'ašt^{e}rôṯ qarnayim* in Gen. 14:5 is due solely to conflation, identifying it as a separate location (*GTTOT:* Tell 'Ashtarah) is not indicated, although Eusebius knows two towns with this name.[109]

H.-P. Müller

105. See more recently C. Westermann, *Genesis 12–36* (Eng. trans. 1985), 196.
106. Cited by Eusebius *Praeparatio evangelica* 1.10.31.
107. On the Assyrian province of *qarnini,* see E. Forrer, *Die Provinzeinteilung des assyrischen Reiches* (1920), 62-63.
108. *GTTOT,* §302, p. 124; §355, p. 214.
109. *Onomasticon* 6.4ff.; 12:11ff. See *GTTOT,* §355, p. 214; Kellermann, 56-61.

עֵת *'ēṯ;* עַתָּה *'attâ*

I. Extrabiblical Texts. II. Etymology. III. OT Occurrences. IV. Philology: 1. Meaning; 2. With Prepositions; 3. Construct Phrases; 4. Other Constructions; 5. Plural; 6. *'attâ.* V. Theological Usage: 1. The Hebrew Concept of Time; 2. Creation; 3. History. VI. LXX. VII. Hebrew Sirach and Dead Sea Scrolls.

'ēṯ. K. Aartun, *Die Partikeln des Ugaritischen,* I. *AOAT* 21/1 (1974), esp. 13-14; J. Barr, *Biblical Words for Time. SBT* 1/33 (^{2}1969); idem, *The Semantics of Biblical Language* (1961), esp. 46-88; T. Boman, *Hebrew Thought Compared with Greek* (Eng. trans. repr. 1970); S. G. F. Brandon, *History, Time and Deity* (1965); idem, *Time and Mankind* (1951); H. A. Brongers,

I. Extrabiblical Texts. The common OT noun *'ēṯ* means "time" — a specific time, a span of time, or time in general (see IV below). It is attested with certainty only in Hebrew, Phoenician, and Punic.[1] A connection with Akk. *inu/ittu (enu/ettu),* "time," is often assumed but remains highly questionable.[2]

"Bemerkungen zum Gebrauch des adverbialen *wᵉ'attâ* im AT," *VT* 15 (1965) 289-99; E. Brunner, *Eternal Hope* (Eng. trans. 1954), 42-58; J. L. Crenshaw, "The Eternal Gospel (Eccl. 3:11)," *Essays in OT Ethics. FS J. P. Hyatt* (1974), 23-55; O. Cullmann, *Christ and Time* (Eng. trans. ²1962); G. Delling, "καιρός," *TDNT,* III, 455-64; idem, "χρόνος," *TDNT,* IX, 581-93; G. R. Driver, "Isaianic Problems," *FS W. Eilers* (1967), 43-57; G. Ebeling, "Time and Word," *Future of Our Religious Past. FS R. Bultmann* (Eng. trans. 1971), 247-66; W. Eichrodt, "Heilserfahrung und Zeitverständnis im AT," *TZ* 12 (1956) 103-25; J. A. Emerton, "Some Linguistic and Historical Problems in Isaiah VIII.23," *JSS* 14 (1969) 151-75, esp. 156-62; M. Filipiak, "Kairologia w Ekl 3,1-15," *Roczniki Teologiczno-Kanoniczne* 20/1 (1973) 83-93; J. Finegan, *Handbook of Biblical Chronology* (1964); K. Galling, "Das Rätsel der Zeit im Urteil Kohelets (Koh 3,1-15)," *ZTK* 58 (1961) 1-15; idem, "Stand und Aufgabe der Kohelet-Forschung," *TRu* 6 (1934) 355-73; E. Jenni, "עֵת *'ēt* time," *TLOT,* II, 951-61; idem, "Time," *IDB,* IV, 642-49; idem, "Zur Verwendung von *'attā* 'jetzt' im AT," *TZ* 28 (1972) 5-12; A. Lacocque, "La conception hébraïque du temps," *BCPE* 36 (1984) 47-58; I. Lande, *Formelhafte Wendungen der Umgangssprache im AT* (1949), esp. 46-52; A. Laurentin, "*We'attah — Kai nun;* formule caractéristique des textes juridiques et liturgiques (à propos de Jean 17,5)," *Bibl* 45 (1964) 168-97, 412-32; J. A. Loader, *Polar Structures in the Book of Qohelet. BZAW* 152 (1979), esp. 29-35; idem, "Qohelet 3, 2-8, a 'Sonnet' in the OT," *ZAW* 81 (1969) 240-42; O. Loretz, "*k't ḥyh* — 'wie jetzt ums Jahr' Gen 18,10," *Bibl* 43 (1962) 75-78; idem, *Qohelet und der alte Orient* (1964), esp. 186-88, 251-54; D. Lys, "Par le temps qui court," *ETR* 48 (1973) 299-316; J. Marsh, *The Fulness of Time* (1952); idem, "Time, Season," in A. Richardson, ed., *A Theological Word Book of the Bible* (1950), 258-67; J. Muilenburg, "The Biblical View of Time," *HTR* 54 (1961) 225-71; H.-P. Müller, "Notizen zu althebräischen Inschriften, I" *UF* 2 (1970) 229-42, esp. 234-35 n. 62; idem, *Ursprünge und Strukturen alttestamentlicher Eschatologie. BZAW* 109 (1969); J. M. Rodríguez Ochoa, "Estudio de la dimensión temporal en Prov., Job y Qoh.," *EstBíb* 22 (1963) 33-67; C. von Orelli, *Die hebräischen Synonyma der Zeit und Ewigkeit genetisch und sprachvergleichend dargestellt* (1871); E. Otto, "Altägyptische Zeitvorstellungen und Zeitbegriffe," *Die Welt als Geschichte* 14 (1954) 135-48; M. Perani, "La concezione del tempo nell'AT," *Sacra Doctrina* 23 (1978) 193-242; idem, "Relievi sulla terminologia temporale nel libro di giobbe," *Henoch* 5 (1983) 1-20; G. Pidoux, "A propos de la notion biblique du temps," *RTP* 2 (1952) 120-25; H. D. Preuss, *Jahweglaube und Zukunftserwartung. BWANT* 87 (1968); G. von Rad, *Wisdom in Israel* (Eng. trans. 1972), esp. 138-43; C. H. Ratschow, "Anmerkungen zur theologischen Auffassung des Zeitproblems," *ZTK* 51 (1954) 360-87; J. Schreiner, "Das Ende der Tage," *BiLe* 5 (1964) 180-94; M. Sekine, "Erwägungen zur hebräischen Zeitauffassung," *Congress Volume, Bonn 1962. SVT* 9 (1963), 66-82; J. van Seters, *In Search of History* (1983); W. von Soden, J. Bergman, and M. Sæbø, "יוֹם yôm," *TDOT,* VI, 7-32 (bibliog.: 7-8); G. Stählin, "νῦν (ἄρτι)," *TDNT,* IV, 1106-23; P. Tachau, *"Einst" und "Jetzt" im NT. FRLANT* 105 (1972); S. Talmon, "The Calendar Reckoning of the Sect from the Judean Desert," *ScrHier* 4 (²1965) 162-99; W. Vollborn, *Studien zum Zeitverständnis des ATs* (1951); S. J. de Vries, *Yesterday, Today and Tomorrow* (1975); C. F. Whitley, *Koheleth, His Language and Thought. BZAW* 148 (1979), esp. 30-33; J. R. Wilch, *Time and Event* (1969) (bibliog., 172-80); R. Yaron, *"Ka'eth ḥayyah* and *koh leḥay," VT* 12 (1962) 500-501; F. Zimmermann, *The Inner World of Qohelet* (1973), esp. 44-49.

1. *DNSI,* II, 896.
2. *AHw,* I, 382b, 405-6; *CAD,* I/1, 153b, 304-10; cf. Wilch, 155-60; Jenni, *TLOT,* II, 952; *HAL,* II, 899-900.

Heb. *ʿēṯ* is rare in ancient texts apart from the Bible. Especially noteworthy is the noun *ʿt* as an accusative expression of time in Lachish ostracon no. 6: *yrʾ yhwh ʿt ʾdny hʿt hzh šlm,* "May Yahweh cause my lord to see weal at this time."[3] In some cases, however, the context suggests that the most natural course is to interpret *ʿt* as a defective writing of *ʿattâ,* "now" (Ezk. 23:43; Ps. 74:6).[4] Cross and Freedman propose a pronunciation **ʿat(t)* < **ʿant* by assimilation of the *n;* cf. Ugar. *ʿnt,* "now," and Biblical Aram. *keʿeneṯ,* "now" (Ezr. 4:10-11; 7:12).[5] This interpretation applies, for example, to *wʿt,* "and now," in preexilic texts from Murabbaʿāt, Lachish (ostracon no. 4), and Tell Arad.[6] In particular, note the expression *ʿt kym,* probably meaning "now on this very day, right now," in the Lachish ostraca,[7] where it appears in the blessing formula "May Yahweh cause my lord to hear good news" *(yšmʿ yhwh ʿt ʾdny šmʿt šlm),* used as a greeting.

The noun *ʿt* occurs sporadically in Phoenician and Punic.[8] A Phoenician text from Sidon reads *ngzlt bl ʿty,* "I was snatched away before my time" (cf. Heb. *belōʾ ʿēt*).[9] Two Punic texts use *ʿt* for precise dating: the first, from Carthage, speaks of "the time of lord *ʾdnbʿl*"; the second, from Malta, reads "in the time of the lord of the elite company."[10] Finally, note a 1st-century-C.E. Neo-Punic inscription from Leptis Magna, which is difficult to interpret: *ytnʾ l ʿbd bṣpʿt kl ḥʿt,* "They authorized him to use (?) the tunic (?) at all times" (cf. the OT expression *beḵol-ʿēt*; see IV.1.a below).

II. Etymology. Despite protracted and intensive investigation on many fronts, the etymology of the noun *ʿēṯ* must be considered a mystery.[11] I shall summarize the most important etymological theories put forward to date.

Scholars who presuppose a triliteral root come to very different conclusions. Some suggest a root III *w/y,* such as *ʿdh* I, "pass," or *ʿnh* I, "answer, respond."[12] Others think of a root with a reduplicated second radical, *ʿtt;*[13] but such a root is not attested in OT

---

3. *KAI* 196.1; for discussion and alternative interpretations, see Müller, "Notizen," 234-35 n. 2; also *DNSI,* II, 896, where other occurrences are listed.

4. See Müller; L. A. Bange, *A Study of the Use of Vowel-Letters in Alphabetic Consonantal Writing* (1971), 127; F. M. Cross and D. N. Freedman, *Early Hebrew Orthography. AOS* 36 (1952), 52-53.

5. *UT,* no. 1888. See also *DNSI,* I, 526-28.

6. For Murabbaʿat see *DJD,* II (1961), 96, no. 17, l. 2 (8th century B.C.E.); for Lachish, *KAI* 194.2; for Arad, *TSSI* (repr. 1973), I, 49-54.

7. Müller, "Notizen," 234-35; *KAI* 192.3; 194.1; 195.2-3.

8. *DNSI,* II, 896; *KAI,* III, 20; *Karthago, Revue d'archéologie africaine* 12 (1963/64), 52; *CRAIBL* (1968) 12; Tomback, 259.

9. *KAI* 14.2-3. See IV.2.a.(3) below.

10. For the first see *CRAIBL* (1968) 117, l. 2. For the second, M. G. Guzzo Amadasi, *Le iscrizioni fenicie e puniche delle colonie in occidente* (1967), 23, no. 6, l. 4.

11. For surveys and discussions, see particularly Barr, *Biblical Words,* 110-34; Wilch, 155-60; also *GesB,* 628a; *TLOT,* II, 951-52; *HAL,* II, 899-900.

12. For the former see, e.g., *GesTh,* 1083b, 990b-94b; for the latter, e.g., J. Levy, *ChW,* 572; F. Delitzsch, *Prolegomena eines neuen hebräisch-aramäischen Wörterbuchs zum AT* (1886), 115.

13. E.g., P. Kahle, *Der masoretische Text des ATs* (^{2}1966), 68.

Hebrew. Still others suggest a root I *y,* specifically *y'd,* "appoint."[14] In the light of Akk. *'idtu,* "agreement," a root *'dt* has also been proposed.[15] Akk. *inu/ittu (enu/ettu),* "time," has suggested a root *'nt,* which is attested in Aramaic.[16]

At the same time, others have considered the possibility of derivation from a biliteral root. Apart from occasional references to *'(w)d* I (cf. Arab. *'āda,* "turn back"; found in OT Hebrew only in the piel, polel, and hithpolel), *'n* (+ a fem. ending *-t*) has been the primary object of discussion.[17] This approach connects Heb. *'ēṯ* and Aram. *k'n/k'nt/k't,* "now," with an Ugar. noun *'nt,* ostensibly used adverbially to mean "now."[18]

Today one may observe a tendency to favor derivation from the root *y'd,* "appoint," with the primary meaning of *'ēṯ* being "appointed time" (**'idt* > **'itt* > *'ēṯ*).[19] If this explanation is correct, *'ēṯ* is related etymologically to Heb. *'ēḏâ* I, "assembly," and *mô'ēḏ,* "meeting place, assembly; agreed time, appointed time."[20]

III. OT Occurrences. The Heb. noun *'ēṯ,* pl. *'ittîm/'ittôṯ,* is normally feminine; the exceptions are questionable.[21] There are 296 occurrences in the OT, concentrated in the following books (excluding Ezk. 23:43 *K* and Ps. 74:6 *K*): Ecclesiastes, 40 (31 in ch. 3); Jeremiah, 36; Psalms, 22; Deuteronomy and Ezekiel, 18 each; Daniel and 2 Chronicles, 16 each; 2 Kings and Isaiah, 11 each (8 in Isaiah 1–39); Genesis, Judges, and Job, 10 each; 1 Chronicles, 9.

Two derivatives are found in the OT. The adj. *'ittî,* "opportune," is a hapax legomenon found only in Lev. 16:21; the proposed emendation *'āṯîḏ* is not convincing.[22] The adv. *'attâ* occurs 433 times (including Ezk. 23:43 *Q* and Ps. 74:6 *Q*), 272 times in the expression *w^e'attâ.*[23] Its occurrences are notably concentrated in the narrative books: 1 Samuel, 46; Genesis, 40; 2 Samuel, 30; 2 Chronicles, 29; Judges, 24; 1 Kings, 23; 2 Kings, 22; Exodus, 20; Joshua, 19; Numbers, 15. They are less frequent in the prophetic and poetic books: Isaiah, 29; Job, 18; Jeremiah, 16; Psalms, 13; Hosea, 12; Ezekiel, 8.

In all probability the masc. PN *'attay* (only 1 Ch. 2:35-36; 12:12[Eng. v. 11]; 2 Ch.

---

14. E.g., von Orelli, 47.
15. E.g., H. Bauer and P. Leander, *Grammatik des Biblisch-Aramäischen* (1927), §51z.
16. E.g., Delitzsch, *Wörterbuch,* 34, 116.
17. For derivation from the former see, e.g., Jastrow, 1128a; from the latter, Wilch, 158-60; Aartun, 14.
18. *DISO,* 125; *KBL*², 1086b; *KTU* 1.19, III, 48, 55-56; IV, 6; cf. *UT,* no. 1888, and 102 n. 3; but see *WUS,* no. 2065.
19. *BLe,* §61j; J. C. de Moor, *The Seasonal Pattern in the Ugaritic Myth of Ba'lu. AOAT* 16 (1971), 149; E. Vogt, *LexLingAram,* 85b; *TLOT,* II, 952; *HAL,* II, 900.
20. → יעד *yā'aḏ.*
21. Emerton, 159, citing Driver. See D. Michel, *Grundlegung einer hebräischen Syntax,* I (1977), 58-59.
22. Contra Wilch, 138, et al. See *BLe,* §61w,x.
23. On formation and usage see *VG,* I, 464hα; JM, §§32f, 93g; K. Beyer, *Althebräische Grammatik* (1969), 55; *HAL,* II, 901-2. See esp. Stählin; Lande; Laurentin; Brongers; Jenni, "Zur Verwendung."

11:20) is not connected etymologically with ʿēṯ.[24] Also highly dubious is the association of ʿēṯ with the noun ʿōnâ, as "(time of) sexual intercourse" (Ex. 21:10).[25]

IV. Philology.

1. *Meaning.* It is immediately obvious that ʿēṯ in the OT always refers to time. This is made clear by its various contexts and its frequent use with prepositions (*ʿaḏ,* "until," and *min,* "since," temporal *b*^{e}, *l*^{e}, and *k*^{e}, and occasionally *ʾel-;* see IV.2.a-d below) and temporally functioning adjectives (e.g., *qārôḇ,* "near" [Isa. 13:22]; *rāḥôq,* "distant" [Ezk. 12:27 pl.; see IV.5 below]). By means of genitive modification and other constructions (see IV.5 below), a specific time can be defined or appraised in the cycle of nature, in human life, or in history. The derived adj. *ʿattâ,* "at this time," i.e., "now" (see IV.6 below), further clarifies the picture. But precise definition of this term for time remains difficult and can be approximated only by comparison with other temporal expressions.

Although occasionally *ʿēṯ* can parallel → יום *yôm,* "day" (e.g., Ezk. 7:7,12; cf. also the expression "in those days and at that time" in Joel 4:1[3:1]; Jer. 33:15; 50:4,20), in essence *ʿēṯ* is not a natural division of time; neither does it imply per se a special situation in the course of history — contrast, e.g., → אחרית *ʾaḥ*^{a}*rîṯ,* "end," but also "time to come, future"; → עד *ʿaḏ,* "eternity"; → עולם *ʿôlām,* "long time, age"; → קדם *qeḏem,* "ancient time"; → קץ *qēṣ,* "end, limit," also "end time"; and → ראש *rōʾš* (and derivatives) in the sense of "beginning (of a certain time period)." Temporal terms of this nature appear also in many prepositional and adverbial constructions (along with words like *ʾāz,* "then"). By itself, *ʿēṯ* does not denote a certain length of time — neither an extended period (chiefly expressed by locutions with *yôm/yāmîm; ʿaḏ/ʿôḏ; ʿôlām;* → דור *dôr,* "cycle, lifetime, generation"; or *ḥeleḏ,* "lifetime," but also "world") nor a brief "moment" (for which one finds, e.g., *peṯaʿ,* → רגע *regaʿ,* or Biblical Aram. *šāʿâ*). In itself, *ʿēṯ* is no more defined temporally than → מקום *māqôm* is delimited spatially. Rather it is related semantically to the most general temporal terms of the OT, above all → מועד *môʿēḏ,* "agreed time" or "festival (time)." We even find occasionally *môʿēḏ* in parallel with *ʿēṯ* (e.g., Jer. 8:7; cf. also 2 K. 4:16,17; 2 S. 24:15), but *ʿēṯ* does not share the cultic associations of *môʿēḏ.* There are also several less frequent temporal terms of a general nature, e.g., **ʾōpen,* "(proper) time" (only Prov. 25:11); *ʾ*^{e}*šûn,* "(incipient) time" (only Prov. 20:20 *Q;* 7:9 cj.); *z*^{e}*mān,* "specific time, hour" (4 times in the Hebrew OT: Eccl. 3:1 par. *ʿēṯ;* Est. 9:27,31; Neh. 2:6; also Sir. 43:7 par. *môʿēḏ*); and Biblical Aram. *z*^{e}*mān* (11 times) and *ʿiddān,* "(specific) time" (Dnl. 2:8,9,21; 3,5,15; 4:13,20,22,29[16,23,25,32]; 7:12,25).

Insofar as it is legitimate at all to speak of the basic meaning of a noun, for *ʿēṯ* one might propose in the first instance "(a definite point in) time of/for [something]."[26] But it must be stressed that in a number of passages nothing is said explicitly concerning

24. See *IPN,* 191; *PNPI,* 108a; *HAL,* II, 903.
25. → ענה I *ʿānâ (I),* III.8.
26. Cf. *TLOT,* II, 952.

any determination of the point in time or its relationship to something specific (for examples see IV.4 below).

2. *With Prepositions.* Like most of the temporal terms cited above, *ʿēṯ* is used most often in combination with a variety of prepositions. Such prepositional locutions, in part formulaic, normally function as temporal adverbs and serve to locate an event at a certain time or in a certain period.[27]

a. *b^e*. Comparison of the prepositions used with *ʿēṯ* with those used with the two other most common terms for time in the OT shows that *ʿôlām* most often appears in combination with *l^e* or *ʿaḏ,* whereas *b^e* takes precedence in the case of both *ʿēṯ* and *yôm.*

(1) In the case of *b^e* + *ʿēṯ,* the most frequent usage is the formulaic phrase *bāʿēṯ hahîʾ,* "at that time," with 68 occurrences: Deuteronomy, 15; 2 Chronicles, 8; Judges and Jeremiah, 7 each; 2 Kings, 5; Joshua, 4; 1 Kings, Isaiah, and Zephaniah, 3 each; Genesis, 1 Chronicles, and Daniel, 2 each; and one each in Numbers, Joel, Amos, Micah, Ezra, Nehemiah, and Esther. We also find such expressions as *bāʿēṯ,* "at the proper time" (Eccl. 10:17); *bāʿēṯ hazzōʾṯ,* "at this time" (Est. 4:14); pl.: *bāʿittîm,* "in (these) times" (Dnl. 11:6); *bāʿittîm hāhēm,* "in those times" (Dnl. 11:14; 2 Ch. 15:5). Cf. also *ʿēṯ* with other prepositions: *ʿaḏ hāʿēṯ hahîʾ,* "until that time" (Dnl. 12:1; Neh. 6:1); *min-hāʿēṯ hahîʾ,* "from that time on" (Neh. 13:21).

(2) The expression *bāʿēṯ hahîʾ,* comparable especially to *bayyôm hahûʾ,* "on that day," refers in most cases (52 times)[28] to a time or period in the past. In the narrative sections of the Pentateuch, the Deuteronomistic History, and the Chronicler's History, the expression is used with the consecutive imperfect as an introductory or a connective formula (e.g., *way^ehî bāʿēṯ hahîʾ,* "and it happened at that time" [Gen. 21:22; 38:1; 1 K. 11:29]; *wayyakkû ʾeṯ-môʾāḇ bāʿēṯ hahîʾ,* "and at that time they smote Moab" [Jgs. 3:29; cf. Josh. 6:26; 11:10,21; Jgs. 12:6; 21:14; 1 K. 8:65 (text?); 2 Ch. 13:18; etc.]) or with the perfect as a defining or linking statement of time (e.g., *bāʿēṯ hahîʾ ʾāmar yhwh ʾel-y^ehôšuaʿ,* "at that time Yahweh said to Joshua" [Josh. 5:2]), but chiefly in annalistic style (e.g., *bāʿēṯ hahîʾ ḥālâ ʾ^aḇîyâ,* "at that time Abijah fell sick" [1 K. 14:1; cf. 2 K. 16:6; 18:16; 20:12; 24:10; 2 Ch. 16:7; 28:16; etc.]). Only exceptionally does the expression occur in retrospective nominal clauses (e.g., Nu. 22:4; Jgs. 4:4; 14:4).

In the context of Deuteronomy, with its linear presentation of sacred history,[29] *bāʿēṯ hahîʾ* is used to mark the interval between the "now" *(ʿattâ)* or "today" *(hayyôm)* of the speaker and specific events that took place in the earlier period of the history of God's people (e.g., "And I [Moses] spoke to you at that time [*bāʿēṯ hahîʾ,* the revelation at Horeb] and said . . ." [Dt. 1:9; also 1:16,18; 2:34; 3:4,8,12,18,21,23; 4:14; 5:5; 9:20; 10:1,8][30]). But the same formula can also appear in the promises and threats of the prophets, usually with the imperfect (e.g., "At that time gifts will be brought" [Isa.

---

27. See *BDB,* 773; *TLOT,* II, 953-57; *HAL,* II, 900-901.
28. *TLOT,* II, 953.
29. H. D. Preuss, *Deuteronomium. EdF* 164 (1982), 185-90.
30. Ibid., 62, 179-80, 184, 196.

18:7; also such passages as Jer. 3:17; 4:11; 8:1 *Q;* 31:1; Am. 5:13 (gloss?);[31] Zeph. 3:20 (v. 19 with act. ptcp.); also with *ʾāz* in 3:4]). Especially noteworthy is the double expression *bayyāmîm hāhēm/-mâ ûḇāʿēṯ hahîʾ* (see above). The prophetic usage with a future-directed imperfect reappears in such texts as Dnl. 12:1 (twice).

(3) Quite different in nature is the expression *bᵉ* + *ʿēṯ* + suffix (*bᵉʿittô,* etc.). It occurs 15 times, usually referring to a time set by nature (e.g., for rain or fruit) or the right moment for something (rain: Lev. 26:4; Dt. 11:14; 28:12; Jer. 5:24; Ezk. 34:26; harvest: Hos. 2:11[9]; Job 5:26; fruit: Ps. 1:3; food: Ps. 104:27; 145:15; day and night: Jer. 33:20; constellations: Job 38:32; God's intervention: Isa. 60:22; a word: Prov. 15:23; see V.2.a below).

The negative form appears twice: *bᵉlōʾ ʿēṯ,* "not at the time of" menstruation (Lev. 15:25); *bᵉlōʾ ʿitteḵā,* "not at your time," i.e., "before your time" (dying, Eccl. 7:17).[32] In Job 22:16, again with reference to dying, many mss. read *bᵉlōʾ ʿēṯ* (MT *wᵉlōʾ-ʿēṯ*). A Phoenician text has the analogous *bl ʿty.*[33] There is a single occurrence of the positive expression *bāʿēṯ,* "at the right time" (Eccl. 10:17).

The generalizing expression *bᵉḵol-ʿēṯ,* "at any time, at all times," occurs 15 times (Ex. 18:22,26; Lev. 16:2; Ps. 10:5; 34:2[1]; 62:9[8]; 106:3; 119:20; Job 27:10; Prov. 5:19; 6:14; 8:30; 17:17; Eccl. 9:8); cf. *bᵉḵol-ʿēṯ ʾᵃšer* (Est. 5:13); *ʿim* + *kol* + pl. (1 Ch. 29:30). In most cases this formula expresses a pedagogical generalization of wisdom instruction (e.g., "Let your garments always be white," Eccl. 9:8) or the cultic fervor of the worshiper (e.g., "My soul is consumed with longing for your ordinances at all times," Ps. 119:20; "I will bless Yahweh at all times," Ps. 34:2[1]). Comparable to this expression is *kl ḥʿt* in a Neo-Punic text.[34]

Finally, there are some 35 occurrences (15 in Jeremiah) of a construct phrase made up of *bᵉ* + *ʿēṯ* + a noun, infinitive, or verbal clause. These phrases are used to define a particular time or period: with a noun, e.g., *bᵉʿēṯ qāṣîr,* "in time of harvest" (Jer. 50:16); cf. Jgs. 10:14; Isa. 33:2; 49:8; Jer. 2:27,28; 8:12; 10:15; 11:12; 14:8; 15:11 (twice); 18:23; 51:18; Ezk. 21:30,34(25,29); 35:5 (twice); Zec. 10:1; Ps. 37:19,39); with an infinitive construct, e.g., *bᵉʿēṯ yaḥēm haṣṣōʾn,* "at the time when the flock is in heat" (Gen. 31:10); cf. Gen. 38:27; 1 S. 18:19; Jer. 11:14; Zeph. 3:20 (text uncertain[35]); with a verbal clause, e.g., *bᵉʿēṯ-pᵉqaḏtîm,* "at the time I punish them" (Jer. 6:15); cf. Job 6:17; 2 Ch. 20:22; 24:11; 29:27 (see IV.4, 5 below).

b. *lᵉ*. As in the case of *bᵉ*, use of the prep. *lᵉ* with *ʿēṯ* + a noun, infinitive, or verbal clause (20 instances in the sg.) defines the time or period of an action or event. The following are examples: with a noun, *lᵉʿēṯ ʿereḇ,* "in the evening" (Gen. 8:11; 24:11; Isa. 17:14; Zec. 14:7; *lᵉʿēṯ ziqnâ,* "in the time of old age" (Ps. 71:9; cf. 1 K. 11:4; 5:23); cf. Ps. 21:10 (text?); Ruth 2:14; Eccl. 9:12; 1 Ch. 12:23(22); 20:1; with an infinitive, *lᵉʿēṯ*

31. H. W. Wolff, *Joel and Amos. Herm* (Eng. trans. 1977), 249-50.

32. H. W. Hertzberg, *Der Prediger. KAT* XVII/4 (1963), 137, 141.

33. *KAI* 14.2-3, 12 (cf. I above); see J. C. Greenfield, "Scripture and Inscription," *Near Eastern Studies in Honor of W. F. Albright* (1971), 260.

34. *KAI* 126.9 (see I above).

35. See *BHS*.

bô' haššemeš, "at the time of sunset" (Josh. 10:27; 2 Ch. 18:34); cf. 2 S. 11:1; Ps. 32:6 (text?); 1 Ch. 20:1; with a verbal clause, *l^e'ēṯ tāmûṭ raglām,* "the time when their foot shall slip" (Dt. 32:35; see IV.4, 5 below).

Occasionally, however, the prep. *l^e* with *'ēṯ* serves to introduce an independent dative object, e.g., *l^e'ēṯ kāzō'ṯ,* "at such a time as this" (Est. 4:14b); cf. Jer. 8:15; 14:19; Job 38:23; Dnl. 8:17.

c. *k^e*. The prep. *k^e* is used with *'ēṯ* 22 times, with no clear difference in meaning between *b^e*, *l^e*, and *k^e*. There are 5 occurrences of the expression *kā'ēṯ,* which is comparable to *kayyôm,* "now" (Nu. 23:23; Jgs. 13:23; 21:22 [possibly to be read *kî 'attâ*[36]]; Isa. 8:23[9:1] [text?[37]]; Job 39:18); cf. also *k^{e}mô 'ēṯ* (Ezk. 16:57; possibly to be read *k^{e}mô 'attā[h]*[38]). The expression is used 9 times in combination with *māḥār,* "tomorrow," 8 of which are in the formula *kā'ēṯ māḥār,* "at this time tomorrow" (Ex. 9:18; 1 S. 9:16; 20:12; 1 K. 19:2; 20:6; 2 K. 7:1,18; 10:6) and once in the synonymous *māḥār kā'ēṯ hazzō'ṯ* (Josh. 11:6).

The meaning of the expression *kā'ēṯ ḥayyâ* (Gen. 18:10,14; 2 K. 4:16,17) is disputed. Departing from earlier explanations, Yaron cites the analogous Akkadian expression *ana balāṭ,* "at this time next year."[39] "The phrase occurs only in Gen. 18:10,14; and 2 Kings 4:16,17 in the OT, each time in the same context; this is a certain sign that the phrase, otherwise unknown, was passed on in this particular narrative of the birth of a child (it is there in Gen. 17:21, in the same context, but somewhat altered)."[40] It should be noted, finally, that the combination *k^e* + *'ēṯ* + noun or infinitive also occurs: with a noun, Dnl. 9:21; with an infinitive, 1 S. 4:20 (text?); 2 Ch. 21:19.

d. *Other Prepositions.* I shall not go into further detail here about the other prepositions used with *'ēṯ*: *'aḏ,* "until" (12 times: Josh. 8:29; 2 S. 24:15; Ezk. 4:10,11; Mic. 5:2[3]; Ps. 105:19; Dnl. 11:24,35; 12:1,4,9; Neh. 6:1); *min,* "since" (8: Isa. 48:16; Ezk. 4:10,11; Ps. 4:8[7]; Dnl. 12:11; Neh. 13:21; 1 Ch. 9:25; 2 Ch. 25:27); and *'el,* "to" (once: 1 Ch. 9:25).

3. *Construct Phrases.* When used as a *nomen regens* in a construct phrase, *'ēṯ* normally denotes a specific time or period the nature of which is defined by the following noun, infinitive, or verbal clause. In most cases (65 times), the *nomen rectum* is a substantive. Often the phrase denotes a time defined by the course of nature: *'ēṯ (hā)'ereḇ,* "evening time" (Gen. 8:11; 24:11; Josh. 8:29; 2 S. 11:2; Isa. 17:14; Zec. 14:7); *'ēṯ ṣoh^{o}rāyim,* "noon" (Jer. 20:16); *'ēṯ malqôš,* "season of the spring rain" (March-April,[41]

36. See *BHS*.

37. Driver, 43-49; Emerton, 156ff.; but cf. H. Wildberger, *Isaiah 1–12* (Eng. trans. 1991), 384ff.

38. W. Zimmerli, *Ezekiel 1. Herm* (Eng. trans. 1979), 333.

39. → IV, 343-44.

40. C. Westermann, *Genesis 12–36* (Eng. trans. 1985), 280; cf. also R. Kümpel, *Bausteine biblischer Theologie. FS G. J. Botterweck. BBB* 50 (1977), 162.

41. *AuS,* I/2, 302ff.

Zec. 10:1); *ʿēṯ (haq)qāṣîr,* "time of the grain harvest" (April-June;[42] Jer. 50:16; 51:33); *ʿēṯ tᵉšûḇaṯ haššānâ,* "time of the turn of the year" (1 Ch. 20:1); *ʿēṯ ziqnâ,* "time of old age" (Ps. 71:9; cf. 1 K. 11:4; 15:23); *ʿēṯ niddâ,* "time of menstruation" (Lev. 15:25); cf. also *ʿēṯ dōḏîm,* "age for love" (Ezk. 16:8); *ʿēṯ hazzāmîr,* "time of pruning (the grapes)" (meaning unclear; possibly "vintage time" or "time of singing") (Cant. 2:12).

But such phrases can also refer to times that are not inherent in the course of nature but are determined independently, either by human beings as a regular element of everyday life (e.g., *ʿēṯ hāʾōḵel,* "mealtime," Ruth 2:14) or of cultic practice (e.g., *ʿēṯ minḥaṯ-ʿāreḇ,* "time of the evening sacrifice," Dnl. 9:21), or by God for human weal or woe. Examples of the latter include: *ʿēṯ marpēh/ʾ,* "time of healing" (Jer. 8:15; 14:19); *ʿēṯ šālôm,* "time of peace" (Eccl. 3:8); *ʿēṯ rāṣôn,* "time of (God's) favor" (Isa. 49:8); cf. also *ʿēṯ pāneyḵā,* "time of your appearance/personal presence" (Ps. 21:10[9]); contrast *ʿēṯ ʾappᵉḵā,* "time of your anger" (Jer. 18:23); *ʿēṯ nᵉqāmâ,* "time of (God's) vengeance" (Jer. 51:6; cf. 46:10, "day of vengeance"); *ʿēṯ pᵉquddâ,* "time of punishment" (Jer. 8:12; 10:15; 46:21; 50:27; 51:18 [cf. 6:15; 49:8; 50:31]); *ʿēṯ ṣārâ,* "time of trouble" (Isa. 33:2; Jer. 14:8; 15:11; 30:7; Ps. 37:39; Dnl. 12:1; with suf.: Jgs. 10:14; Neh. 9:27 [cf. 2 K. 19:3, etc.: *yôm-ṣārâ;* Job 38:23: *ʿēṯ-ṣār;* Jer. 15:11; Am. 5:13; Mic. 2:3; Ps. 37:19; Eccl. 9:12: *ʿēṯ rāʿâ;* with suf.: Jer. 2:27,28; 11:12]); *ʿēṯ milḥāmâ,* "time of war" (Eccl. 3:8); *ʿēṯ qēṣ,* "time of the end" (Dnl. 11:35,40; 12:4,9; cf. also 8:17: *ʿeṯ-qēṣ;* 8:19: *môʿēḏ qēṣ*); *ʿēṯ ʿᵃwōn qēṣ,* "time of final punishment" (Ezk. 21:30,34[25,29]; 35:5); *ʿēṯ ʾarṣô,* "time of (judgment upon) his land" (Jer. 27:7); *ʿēṯ môʿēḏ,* "appointed time" (2 S. 24:15); *ʿēṯ ʾêḏām,* "time of their calamity" (Ezk. 35:5); and *ʿēṯ gôyim,* "time of the nations" (Ezk. 30:3; cf. 16:57).

In Ps. 31:22(21) *bᵉʿēṯ māṣôr,* "in the time of affliction," has been a commonly accepted emendation ever since Wellhausen and Duhm (alternatively: *bᵉʿēṯ māṣôq,* "in the time of tribulation"); but the MT is preferable: *bᵉʿîr māṣôr,* "in a fortified city," fits easily into the context: *bᵉsēṯer pāneyḵā . . . bᵉsukkâ,* "in the shelter of your presence . . . in a booth" (v. 21[20]).[43] For *ʿᵃṯereṯ* in Jer. 33:6, an unexplained hapax legomenon, Rudolph has proposed the plausible emendation *ʿēṯ rewaḥ,* "restoration."[44]

Related to construct phrases comprising *ʿēṯ* + a noun are the some 25 occurrences of *ʿēṯ* + an infinitive construct (most commonly *bôʾ* [5 times] or *yāṣāʾ* [4 times]). Here too we are often dealing with the temporal fixation of a natural event, e.g., *ʿēṯ bôʾ haššemeš,* "at sunset" (Josh. 10:27; 2 Ch. 18:34); *ʿēṯ yaḥēm haṣṣōʾn,* "the time when the flock is in heat" (Gen. 31:10); *ʿēṯ bôʾ,* "the time of coming (of the turtledove?)" (Jer. 8:7); *ʿēṯ ledeṯ,* "time of delivery" (Gen. 38:27; Job 39:1); *ʿēṯ mûṯ,* "time to die" (1 S. 4:20). But the reference can also be to a human activity: *ʿēṯ ṣēʾṯ haššōʾᵃḇōṯ,* "the time when women go out to draw water" (Gen. 24:11); *gōren ʿēṯ hiḏrîḵâ,* "the time when a threshing floor is trodden" (Jer. 51:33); *ʿēṯ hēʾāsēp hammiqneh,* "time for the animals to be gathered" (Gen. 29:7); other examples include 1 S. 18:19; 2 S. 11:1; 2 K. 5:26;

42. *AuS,* III, 4-5.
43. Contra H.-J. Kraus, *Psalms 1–59* (Eng. trans. 1988), 360. See *BHS.*
44. W. Rudolph, *Jeremia. HAT* I/12 (³1968), 214; cf. *BHS; HAL,* II, 906.

Isa. 48:16; Jer. 11:14; Eccl. 3:4b,5aβ; 1 Ch. 20:1; 2 Ch. 28:22. Finally, the time of a divine activity can be fixed: *'ēṯ qabbᵉṣî 'eṯkem,* "the time when I gather you [Israel]" (Zeph. 3:20); *'ēṯ bô'-ḏᵉḇārô,* "the time when his word comes (to pass)" (Ps. 105:19); see also Hag. 1:2; Ps. 32:6; 2 Ch. 21:19. The construction *'ēṯ* + infinitive construct with *lᵉ* is discussed below (see IV.4).

Some texts, primarily from the exilic or postexilic period, contain the combination *'ēṯ* + a verbal clause. This construction may use either the perfect (*'ēṯ pᵉqaḏtîw,* "the time when I punish him," Jer. 49:8; also 6:15; 50:31; Mic. 5:2[3]; Ps. 4:8[7];[45] Dnl. 12:11; 2 Ch. 20:22; 29:27) or the imperfect (*'ēṯ tāmûṭ raglām,* "the time when their foot shall slip," Dt. 32:35; also Nu. 23:23; Hos. 13:13; Job 6:17; 2 Ch. 24:11). Sometimes we find a relative clause: *'ēṯ 'ᵃšer šālaṭ hā'āḏām,* "the time when one person exercises authority over another" (Eccl. 8:9); also 2 Ch. 25:27 and Ps. 4:8(7).

Only rarely does *'ēṯ* appear in a construct phrase with an active participle (e.g., *[bᵉ]'ēṯ môlîḵēḵ baddāreḵ,* "the time when he [Yahweh] led you [Israel] in the [right] way," Jer. 2:17; also Ezk. 27:34).

4. *Other Constructions.* Several texts place more emphasis on *'ēṯ* as an independent element of a clause. The actual constructions vary considerably.

Some 30 times *'ēṯ* is modified by a following infinitive construct with *lᵉ,* not rarely functioning attributively. Examples are: *'ēṯ liḏrôš 'eṯ-yhwh,* "the (right) time to seek Yahweh" (Hos. 10:12); *'eṯ-bēṯ yhwh lᵉhibbānôṯ,* "the time to build Yahweh a temple" (Hag. 1:2); cf. Hag. 1:4; Ps. 102:14; 119:126; Job 39:2; Eccl. 3:2-8a (23 times).

Sometimes an independent *'ēṯ* is the object of a preposition. With *bᵉ* it denotes the right or best time to do something, e.g., *bā'ēṯ yōḵēlû,* "[your princes] feast at the proper time" (Eccl. 10:17).[46] The expression *kā'ēṯ* means "about this time," "now" (Jgs. 13:23; 21:22; see further IV.2.c above). There are also isolated instances of related constructions using the preps. *min* and *'aḏ* or *'el* (*mē'ēṯ 'aḏ-'ēṯ,* "from time to time," Ezk. 4:10,11; *mē'ēṯ 'el-'ēṯ,* "from one appointed time to the next," 1 Ch. 9:25; *[wᵉ]'aḏ-'ēṯ,* "until the time [appointed by God]," Dnl. 11:24).[47]

Totally unique is the construction *(wᵉ)hā'ēṯ gᵉšāmîm* in Ezr. 10:13, which to all appearances means "it is the time of heavy rain."[48] The language peculiar to Ecclesiastes occasionally treats *'ēṯ* as an independent entity: *kî-'ēṯ wāpega' yiqreh 'eṯ-kullām,* "time and change happen to them all" (9:11); the heart of the sage knows *'ēṯ ûmišpāṭ,* "time and judgment" (8:6; hendiadys? cf. LXX).[49] Cf. also *'ēṯ lᵉḵol-ḥēpeṣ,*[50] "there is a time for every matter" (3:1,17).

Finally, note that the coming of the time referred to by *'ēṯ* is generally expressed by the verb → בוא *bô'* (e.g., Isa. 13:22; Jer. 27:7; 46:21; 49:8 [hiphil]; 50:27,31; 51:33;

45. Not in Lisowsky, 1140a-42a.
46. On *bᵉ'ittô* see IV.2.a above.
47. See IV.2.d above.
48. *GK,* §141d; Brockelmann, *Synt,* §14b.
49. → פגע *pega';* → משפט *mišpāṭ.*
50. → V, 100.

Ezk. 7:7,12; Hag. 1:2), occasionally by → נגע *nāga'* hiphil, "arrive" (Cant. 2:12). Note also that *'ēṯ* can appear as the object of verbs like *ḥśk l^e^*, "reserve" (Job 38:23), → ידע *yāḏa'*, "know" (Job 39:1,2; Eccl. 8:5; 9:12), → קוה *qāwâ* piel, "hope for" (Jer. 8:15; 14:9), and → שׁמר *šmr,* "observe."

5. *Plural.* The pl. of *'ēṯ* is generally *'ittîm* (15 times), occasionally *'ittôṯ* (3 times; see III above). The occurrences of the pl. *'ittîm* are almost all in late texts. As a rule it is easy to determine the meaning from a parallel text using the singular. An exception is the expression *rabbôṯ 'ittîm* (Neh. 9:28), generally taken to mean "many times," appearing in a liturgical context;[51] it can be compared to such expressions as *p^e'āmîm rabbôṯ* (Eccl. 7:22, etc.).[52] Cf. also Aram. *z^emān,* especially *zimnîn t^elāṯâ b^eyômā',* "three times a day" (Dnl. 6:11,14[10,13]).

A clearly numerical plural occurs in some texts, especially in the expression *l^e'ittîm m^ezummānîm,* "at appointed times" (Ezr. 10:14; Neh. 10:35; *b^e'ittîm m^ezummānôṯ,* Neh. 13:31). But the numerical character of the plural is often attenuated, so that the individual points in time included in *'ittîm/-ôṯ* are comprehended in a totality. Ezekiel prophesies *l^eyāmîm rabbîm ûl^e'ittîm r^eḥôqôṯ,* "for many years ahead and for distant times" (12:27); Job longs for God's *'ittîm,* "times (of judgment)," in parallel with *yāmāyw,* "his days" (24:1). There are 3 occurrences of *'ittîm* as a *nomen rectum* in a construct phrase: Isa. 33:6 speaks of *'^emûnaṯ 'itteyḵā,* "the stability of your times" (text?);[53] Dnl. 9:25 says that Jerusalem will be rebuilt *ûḇ^eṣôq hā'ittîm,* "in oppression of times" (NRSV "in a troubled time"); Dnl. 11:13 describes a situation *l^eqēṣ hā'ittîm,* "at the end of times." In the MT the pl. *'ittôṯ* occurs twice as a *nomen rectum: l^e'ittôṯ baṣṣārâ* (Ps. 9:10[9]; 10:1) means "in times of drought";[54] possibly, however, the reading of the LXX is correct: . . . *haṣṣārâ,* "in times of trouble." The expression *bā'ittîm,* "in the(se) times," occurs only in Dnl. 11:6; it is usually connected with v. 7, but this can hardly be correct.[55]

In some cases an association (probably original) with astrologically determined times comes through clearly (cf. *y'ryḥ 'twt,* "the moon marks the seasons," Sir.^M 43:6): the sons of Issachar "have understanding of the times" (*yôḏ^e'ê ḇînâ la'ittîm,* 1 Ch. 12:33[32]); the sages "know the times (determined by God)" (*yōḏ^e'ê hā'ittîm,* Est. 1:13). This meaning explains the shift "to a more content-filled term"[56] in the pl.: "times" = "fate, lot, destiny." This meaning is especially clear in Ps. 31:16(15): "My times [*'ittōṯāy;* = 'my lot'] are in your hand." In parallel with the mighty rule of David, 1 Ch. 29:30 speaks of "the events *(hā'ittîm)* that befell *('āḇ^erû)* him and Israel and all the kingdoms of the earth." The same "saturation with content" can be seen, for exam-

---

51. W. Rudolph, *Esra und Nehemia. HAT* I/20 (1949), 164; Barr, *Biblical Words,* 122-23; Jenni, *TLOT,* II, 957; but cf. Ps. 31:16(15) (see below).
52. → פעם *pa'am.*
53. See O. Kaiser, *Isaiah 13–39. OTL* (Eng. trans. 1974), 337, 344.
54. See *HAL,* II, 901.
55. Cf. *BHS;* NRSV; O. Plöger, *Das Buch Daniel. KAT* XVIII (1965), 152, 155.
56. Jenni, *TLOT,* II, 957.

ple, in Isa. 33:6; Ps. 9:10(9); 10:1. (Albright has proposed associating *ʿittôṯ* with Akk. *ʿanatu-ettu,* ascribing to it the meaning "omens.")[57] We may note that pre-Islamic poetry uses Arab. *dahr,* "time," similarly as a term for "fate": "time and its content."[58]

6. *ʿattâ.* The adv. *ʿattâ,* "now," "nevertheless," "henceforth," etc., occurs 433 times in the OT.[59] Although this adverb appears frequently in the OT narrative books (see III above), it is noteworthy that it is not normally found in the narrative sections but in conversations and speeches (including letters), oracles, and prayers — in other words, in direct discourse. In these contexts, *ʿattâ* serves to activate a speech situation.[60] Within a passage of discourse, this activation usually affects an entire clause (the next rhetorical unit). This holds true for most of the 272 occurrences of *weʿattâ:* in some 220 cases, following mention of circumstances that divert from the actual situation of the discourse, *weʿattâ* returns to this situation to introduce a reaction. This reaction may be a consequence ("so . . . now/therefore"), e.g., "And Yahweh God said: The man has become like one of us, knowing good and evil; and now, lest he reach out his hand . . ." (Gen. 3:22).[61] More rarely the meaning may be adversative ("nevertheless"), e.g., Isa. 64:7; Hag. 2:4.[62] In some 40 texts simple *ʿattâ* (without *we*) is used similarly (e.g., 1 S. 9:6).

It is relatively common, however, for *ʿattâ* to function as a temporal adverb modifying a predicate. It can mark a contrast with what has gone before, e.g., *ʿaḏ-ʿattâ,* "until now"; the temporal starting point may be named (Gen. 46:34; Ex. 9:18; 2 S. 19:8b[7b]; 2 K. 8:6; Ezk. 4:14; Ruth 2:7) or not (Gen. 32:5[4]; Dt. 12:9). It contrasts explicitly with *(mē)ʾāz,* "then" (e.g., Josh. 14:11; 2 S. 15:34; Isa. 16:13-14; 48:7; Hos. 2:9[7]) and appears in the formulaic expression *ʿattâ yāḏaʿtî,* "now I know" (Gen. 22:12; Ex. 18:11; Jgs. 17:13; 1 K. 17:24; Ps. 20:7[6]; cf. Zec. 9:8). In etymologies of names it means "henceforth" (Gen. 26:22; 29:32,34); negated it means "no longer" (Isa. 29:22 [twice]; Gen. 11:6; 26:29; etc.). Finally, in the context of an invective or lament, it contrasts the present with the past ("formerly . . . but now": Isa. 1:21; 16:14; Ezk. 19:13; 26:18; Ps. 119:67; etc.). In this function, however, *ʿattâ* can also contrast with the future, e.g., *mēʿattâ,* "from now on" (e.g., Isa. 48:6; 2 Ch. 16:9; Jer. 3:4); *mēʿattâ weʿaḏ-ʿôlām,* "now and forever" (8 times, e.g., Isa. 9:6; Mic. 4:7); in exhortations (Dt. 32:39; Jgs. 9:38; 1 K. 19:4; etc.); in prophetic declarations of the imminent future (Isa. 33:10 [3 times]; 43:19; 49:19; Jer. 4:12; 14:10; etc.); and in isolated occurrences in the historical books (e.g., Ex. 5:5; 6:1; Jgs. 8:6,15). Finally, *ʿattâ* can have this function even in

57. See the comments of Barr, *Biblical Words,* 123; H.-J. Kraus, *Psalms 1–59* (Eng. trans. 1988), 195, 364.

58. J. Pedersen, *RHPR* 10 (1930) 353-54; H. Ringgren, *Studies in Arabian Fatalism. UUÅ* 1955:2, 30-43.

59. See III above. On its use in the OT see esp. Lande, 46-52; Laurentin, 168-95, 413-32; Brongers, 289-99; Jenni, "Zur Verwendung," 5-12; idem, *TLOT,* II, 957-58; *HAL,* II, 901-2; also Stählin, 1099-1117; Tachau, 21-70.

60. See Jenni, *TLOT,* II, 957-58; idem, "Zur Verwendung."

61. On the other texts see Jenni, "Zur Verwendung," 8 n. 15 and 17.

62. See Brongers, 295.

the bipolar contrast between past and future (e.g., introductory *w*[e]*'attâ* in Deutero-Isaiah, "but now," Isa. 43:1; 44:1; 49:5).[63]

V. Theological Usage. The theological foci of the OT use of *'ēṯ* are in fact few and far between. In many individual texts the noun plays a role in the theology of creation, but a coherent theory of this role appears only in Ecclesiastes (see V.2a, b below). Its use in the theology of history is more varied, but only exceptionally does it constitute a real focus (see V.3.a-c below).

1. *The Hebrew Concept of Time.* The philological survey presented above (esp. IV.1) has shown that throughout the OT *'ēṯ* always refers to time, even if sometimes in an attenuated sense. As one of the temporal terms of the OT, it is theologically comprehensible only in the overall context of the so-called Hebrew understanding of time.

As is well known, the OT understanding of time has been a subject of lively discussion ever since von Orelli's pioneering study in 1871; the most important contributions have been those of Pedersen, Delling, Vollborn, Marsh, Pidoux, Ratschow, Eichrodt, Boman, Muilenburg, Sekine, Barr, Wilch, and Jenni; see also such studies as those of Nilsson and Brandon.

The primary focus of this discussion has been the tension observable in the OT between the revelations of Yahweh that alter the course of history together with the associated historical encounters with deliverance and judgment experienced by Israel on the one hand, and the notion of Yahweh as the eternal God, exalted above the world and its history, on the other. This tension has led — or misled — scholars to postulate for the OT a special conception of time, fundamentally opposed to ours. They have described the Western understanding of time as linear and chronological, while describing the OT conception as punctiliar, realistic, saturated, concentrated, psychological, etc. Nevertheless, Eichrodt in particular showed that the linear and chronological conception is by no means foreign to the OT.[64] Quite the contrary: throughout the OT we find a mode of thought informed by an awareness of the relationship between the present and the past or future.[65]

Recent scholarship is naturally also inclined to recognize the uniqueness of the OT understanding of time. It has become increasingly clear, however, that the appropriate way to examine and define this uniqueness is not through comparative (and often tendentiously etymological) word studies or analyses of grammatical structure (including speculations about different so-called tense systems), such as Boman's attempt to grasp the difference between the Hebrew and Greek ideas of time.[66] Instead, the indi-

---

63. Tachau, 34-41; for a complete list of texts, see Jenni, "Zur Verwendung," 10-12.

64. Cf. already Brunner.

65. This phenomenon is described by such later scholars as Jenni, "Time"; Barr, *Biblical Words;* and Wilch; it is also noted in OT theologies like those of W. Zimmerli, *OT Theology in Outline* (Eng. trans. 1978), 17-32; C. Westermann, *Elements of OT Theology* (Eng. trans. 1982), esp. 9-15; W. H. Schmidt, *Faith of the OT* (Eng. trans. 1983), 1-4, 84-88; cf. also H. W. Wolff, *Anthropology of the OT* (Eng. trans. 1974), 83-92.

66. See esp. the criticisms of Barr, *Semantics,* 46-88.

vidual terms referring to time must be studied primarily within the context of the texts and locutions in which they occur.[67]

Naturally this holds true also for any study of the OT term *ʿēṯ,* which, despite its general nature, normally refers to "the appointed time for something," thus resembling in meaning such terms as Egyp. *tr* and *nw* and Gk. *kaíros.*[68] A survey of the relevant texts and locutions makes clear, however, that *ʿēṯ* per se does not denote time having a definable content or quality.[69] The actual content or quality of the time in question can be determined only from the particular context.[70] Only contextual examination of the term *ʿēṯ* is in a position to reveal the specific character of the OT conception of the appointed or right time and its unique relationship to God, whom the faith of Israel believes to be present in creation and in the history of God's people and world.[71] In the OT texts the various times observed in the created order — times of day, seasons, the hours of the daily round — as well as the present, past, and future in the history of God's revelation to Israel are set forth as times appointed by God and bearing witness to God.

2. *Creation.* a. *Survey.* As already noted (see IV above), a series of OT texts uses *ʿēṯ* as a term for times or periods in the diverse domains of Yahweh's created order.

The changing times of day, such as evening (Gen. 8:11; 24:11; Josh. 8:9; 2 S. 11:2; Isa. 17:14; Zec. 14:7), noon (Jer. 20:16), and sunset (Josh. 10:27; 2 Ch. 18:34), are perceptible to humans; but the significant fact theologically is that the OT ascribes these times of day to the creative activity of the one God, Yahweh. He alone leads forth the constellations *(mazzārôṯ)* "at their appointed time" (Job 38:32; cf. Ps. 148:6); because of his covenant with day and night, they come regularly "at their appointed time" (Jer. 33:20). Because Yahweh brings about the times of day, they are appropriate as times for cultic functions — e.g., the time of the evening sacrifice (Dnl. 9:21).

The constant recurrence of the seasons and their associated times in the cycle of nature are due to the hand of the creator — e.g., the time of the turn of the year (1 Ch. 20:1),[72] of heavy rain (Ezr. 10:13) and spring rain (Zec. 10:1), the time when migratory birds arrive (Jer. 8:7), when the flocks are in heat (Gen. 31:10), when goats give birth (Job 39:1), when grain and wine abound (Ps. 4:8[7]). Among other things, the recurrent theme of Yahweh's sovereign authority over the life-giving rain "in its season" in promises of blessing underlines dependence on Yahweh (Lev. 26:4; Dt. 11:14; 28:12; Ezk. 34:26; cf. Jer. 5:24). Israel's hymns extol Yahweh for giving all his earthly creatures their food "in due season" (Ps. 104:27; 145:15). The times of the year and of the

---

67. For Egyptian see esp. Otto and the comments of Brunner, as well as E. Hornung, *Geschichte als Fest* (1966).

68. See IV.1 above. For the Egyptian see Otto, 136-39; for the Greek, VI below.

69. Contra such scholars as von Orelli, 63; Pedersen, *ILC,* I-II, 487-91; Vollborn, 26; Marsh, *Theological Word Book,* 258; idem, *Fulness,* 28; Muilenburg, 235-36; Ebeling, 253-54.

70. As Wilch in particular has shown (e.g., 32-33, 102); for criticism, see Jenni, *TLOT,* II, 956.

71. See Schmidt, *Faith of the OT,* 53-88.

72. → X, 247-48.

day are appointed by God; they can be understood and managed only through insight into (God's) wisdom (cf. Est. 1:13; 1 Ch. 12:33).

But this brings us already into the realm of the various times associated with human life, for several of the times just mentioned, though independent of humanity, are critical for human life — the time of birth (Eccl. 3:2), of love (Ezk. 16:8), of delivery (Gen. 38:27), of menstruation (Lev. 15:25), of aging (Ps. 71:9; cf. 1 K. 11:4; 15:23), and of death (1 S. 4:20; Eccl. 3:2). This is probably also implicit in the use of the phrase *b*ᵉ*lō' 'ēṯ* for premature death — cf. Akk. *ina ūm lā šīmtišu,* "on a day that was not his fate."[73] These times delimit human life, but behind them stands Yahweh. This implies that human beings encounter God at work in the determined and determining times of their own lives (cf. the Egyptian temporal terms that also suggest spatial proximity, esp. *hȝw* and *rk*).[74]

Something similar also holds true for the times established by human beings in response to those inherent in nature, e.g., mealtime (Ruth 2:14), the time when the animals are gathered each day (Gen. 29:7) or women go out of the city to draw water (Gen. 24:11), the time of the grain harvest (Jer. 50:16; 51:33; cf. Isa. 28:23-29; Job 5:26), threshing (Jer. 51:33), or pruning grapes (Cant. 2:12) — in short, the right times for the various activities of human life (Eccl. 3:2-8; see V.2.b below). What is theologically significant is that these times of human activity, and thus the fate of all human beings, are in the hand of God (Ps. 31:16[15]; see IV.5 above).

Naturally this includes the notion of the right time for people to act (e.g., Prov. 15:23) and for the events that befall them (Eccl. 3:8). These events are either times of God's favor (Isa. 49:8; Ps. 69:14[13]) and presence (Ps. 21:10[9]) or times of misfortune, e.g., distress (Jgs. 10:14; Isa. 33:2; Jer. 14:8; 15:11; 30:7; Ps. 37:39; Dnl. 12:1; Neh. 9:27) or evil (Jer. 2:27,28; 11:12; 15:11; Am. 5:13; Mic. 2:3; Ps. 37:19; Eccl. 9:12). Such times are divine punishment (Jer. 6:15; 8:12; 10:15; 46:21; 49:8; 50:27,31; 51:18), wrath (Jer. 18:23), and vengeance (Jer. 51:6).

b. *Ecclesiastes.* A consistent view of time from the theological perspective of creation, based on the term *'ēṯ,* is found in the OT only in the book of Qohelet.[75] Although Qohelet's intellectual world may include many elements reflective of Egyptian, Babylonian, and Greek wisdom, his overall conception is best understood on the basis of Israelite wisdom thought.[76]

In fundamental agreement with the thought of ancient Israel, Qohelet frequently emphasizes that "everything happens at its proper time, which God determines."[77] He expresses this view in the introductory statement of his anaphorically formulated *māšāl* concerning the right time: "For everything there is a season *(z*ᵉ*mān),* and a time for every matter *(w*ᵉ*'ēṯ*

73. See IV.2.a.(3) above. For Egypt see S. Morenz, *Egyptian Religion* (Eng. trans. 1970), 76.

74. Otto, 146-47.

75. See, e.g., Galling, "Rätsel"; Ochoa; Loretz, *Qohelet;* F. Ellermeier, *Qohelet,* I/1 (1967), 309-22; Loader; Wilch, 117-28; von Rad, *Wisdom,* 138-43, 228-37; Filipiak; Lys; Wolff, *Anthropology,* 89-92; Zimmermann; Crenshaw; Whitley.

76. A. Lauha, *Kohelet. BK* XIX (1978), 13-14. For bibliog. see N. Lohfink, *Kohelet. NEB* (1980).

77. Loretz, *Qohelet,* 182, 200, 253.

l*ᵉḵol-ḥēpeṣ)*" (3:1; also 3:17; see IV.4 above). The *māšāl* that follows develops this thought in seven bicola, each hemistich of which comprises two antithetically formulated observations (vv. 2-8) related in content (e.g., vv. 2,4,6,8). Qohelet also emphasizes that God, who is always at work in creation, "made everything suitable for its time" (v. 11). This statement should not be understood simply as an echo of the P creation account;[78] it represents a profound analysis of continuous divine activity. In other contexts, too, Qohelet states that "every matter has [its] time and judgment" (*lᵉkol-ḥēpeṣ yēš 'ēṯ ûmišpāṭ,* 8:6; cf. 7:17; 8:9; also Sir. 1:23; 4:20,23; 10:4; 20:1,6-7,19-20; etc.). The wise mind "knows the time and judgment" (*'ēṯ ûmišpāṭ yēḏa',* 8:5; cf. Est. 1:13; 1 Ch. 12:33).

The new element in Qohelet's thought, critical of the earlier wisdom tradition — although he does recognize in part the validity of that tradition — is that the mysteries of God's appointed times are impenetrable not only to the swift, the strong, the intelligent, and the skillful, but also to the wise (cf. 3:11): "Bread is not to the wise, nor riches to the intelligent, nor favor to the skillful; but time and chance happen to them all *(kî-'ēṯ wāpega' yiqreh 'eṯ-kullām)* — for humans do not know *(lō-yēḏa')* their times" (9:11-12). The context prohibits the common interpretation that this refers exclusively to the hour of death;[79] this ignorance is all-embracing, and can be compared, for example, to what Qohelet says about the meaningless suffering of the righteous. Zimmerli has therefore rightly stressed that Qohelet achieved insights incomparably more radical than the rest of Israelite wisdom: "No one can control the moment of his birth or of his death; in like fashion, recognition and therefore also mastery of the particular moment are totally outside the realm of human possibility."[80]

3. *History.* The whole spectrum of times appointed by Yahweh in his constant creative activity are not limited to the realms of nature and everyday life. They can also be viewed from the perspective of a theology of history. The historical revelations of Yahweh to his people and his world, together with his appointed times of deliverance, disaster, and return, are associated with particular moments and periods.

a. *Present.* Many OT texts describe the present as the right time for Yahweh to intervene or the people of God to repent. This present is often expressed simply by *hayyôm,* "today" (esp. the 59 occurrences in Deuteronomy: 5:1,3; 8:19; 11:2,26,32; 15:15; 26:15ff.; etc.);[81] it is also expressed frequently by *(wᵉ)'attâ,* "(and) now" (e.g., Isa. 43:1; 44:1; 49:5; see IV.6 above) and occasionally by *'ēṯ.*

For example, Hosea addresses the people of God in the northern kingdom: "It is time to seek Yahweh" (10:12). Haggai is thinking of the present when he asks Zerubbabel and Joshua the high priest: "Has the time (now) come for you *(hă'ēṯ lāḵem*

78. As claimed by C. Forman, *JSS* 5 (1960) 256-63; cf. the counterargument of K. Galling, *Der Prediger. HAT* I/18 (²1969), 95. → X, 542.

79. E.g., Jenni, *TLOT,* II, 959-60.

80. *OT Theology in Outline,* 162.

81. G. von Rad, *OT Theology,* 2 vols. (Eng. trans. 1962-65), II, 99-106; J. M. Schmidt, *EvT* 30 (1970), 169-200; de Vries, 164-87, 337.

'attem) to live in your paneled houses, while this house [the temple] lies in ruins?" (1:4); the people, by contrast, are looking for this time in the future (v. 2).

As one might expect, the OT uses *ʿēṯ* to focus on the present in liturgical contexts, as in the prayer of an individual: "You [Yahweh] will rise up and have compassion on Zion, for it is time to favor it" (Ps. 102:14[13]). In a similar vein, the great *tôrâ* psalm says: "It is time to act for Yahweh" (119:126; cf. Est. 4:14).

b. *Past.* It is primarily in the theologically important formula *bāʿēṯ hahîʾ*, "at that time," that *ʿēṯ* refers to a time in the past. This formula appears 52 times in the OT (Deuteronomy, narrative portions of the Pentateuch, the Dtr History, and the Chronicler's History).

c. *Future.* With respect to the future, it is noteworthy that *ʿēṯ* does not appear in any formulas comparable to the expression *yôm yhwh,* "day of Yahweh."[82] Some preexilic and exilic texts, however, use *ʿēṯ* in combination with this notion, thus varying *yôm,* "day," as the term for the time of judgment appointed by Yahweh. For example, a prediction of the conquest and destruction of Babylon declares: "Its time is close at hand, and its days will not be prolonged" (Isa. 13:22). Ezekiel speaks similarly of the coming end of the land of Israel, using the definite article: "The time is coming, the day is near" (7:7, repeated with a minor variation in v. 12; cf. also 21:30,34[25,29]; and 30:3, which identifies the day of Yahweh with the "time of the nations"; see also Dt. 32:35; Jer. 46:21; 50:27,31).

The formulaic expression *bāʿēṯ hahîʾ,* "at that time," occasionally functions prospectively, especially in prophetic promises or threats (Isa. 18:7; Jer. 3:17; 4:11; etc.; see IV.2.a above).

Highly significant theologically is the use of *ʿēṯ* in the prophecies of judgment in the book of Jeremiah, for they picture the hour of prospective disaster as a time of God's active intervention: it is the time of Yahweh's "punishment," "wrath" (18:23), "vengeance" (51:6), and "harvest" (51:33); cf. also "the time of his own land" (27:7).[83]

The phrase *beʿēṯ ʿᵃwōn qēṣ,* "at the time of the guilt of the end," occurs 3 times in Ezekiel (21:30,34[25,29]; in 35:5 par. to *beʿēṯ ʾêḏām,* "at the time of their calamity"). It is questionable whether this expression is used in an eschatological sense; the context suggests rather that it refers to "the date at which the sphere of perdition and guilt comes to fruition over the perpetrator in a final, fateful end."[84] What is clear in any case is that this "time of the guilt of the end" is brought about solely by Yahweh's wrath.

The expression *ʿēṯ qēṣ* in the book of Daniel (8:17; 11:35,40; 12:4,9; cf. Hab. 2:3) clearly aims to convey a juxtaposition of the present and the eschatological future; for, although "the time of the final phase" refers primarily to the period of persecution by Antiochus IV Epiphanes, this period is also the time of tribulation that marks the opening phase of the eschaton;[85] the expression *ûḇāʿēṯ hahîʾ,* "and at that time," probably re-

---

82. → יוֹם *yôm.*

83. On "punishment" → פקד *pāqaḏ;* on "wrath" → אַף *ʾap;* on "vengeance" → נקם *nāqam.*

84. Cf. W. Zimmerli, *Ezekiel 1. Herm* (Eng. trans. 1979), in loc.: "in a time of final punishment" (also NRSV); K. Koch, → X, 557.

85. L. F. Hartman and A. A. de Lella, *Book of Daniel. AB* 23 (1978), 231-32, 300-304, 310-13.

fers to the death of Antiochus.[86] But for Daniel, too, all these times of eschatological tribulation are hidden among the mysteries of God.

Only exceptionally do prophetic predictions of salvation use the noun *'ēṯ,* for example, in Deutero-Isaiah: "In the time of favor I will answer you, on a day of salvation I will help you" (Isa. 49:8), where past and future coalesce; and in Trito-Isaiah: "I am Yahweh: in its time/at the right time I will accomplish it quickly" (60:22). In these texts the association of the temporal term *'ēṯ* with Yahweh is explicit.

VI. LXX. The LXX most frequently uses *kairós* to translate *'ēṯ* (198 times + 26 times in Sirach; see VII below); 24 times (+ 5 in Sirach) it uses *hṓra;* other translations include *hēméra* (9 times), *hēníka* (4 times), and *chrónos, eukairía, nún,* and *án* (3 times each).[87] This usage reflects the primary meaning of *'ēṯ:* "the appointed or right time for something"; by no means does it suggest that the LXX translators did not understand the real meaning of *'ēṯ.*[88] The *kairós* notion of the LXX, and thus the OT conception of *'ēṯ,* lives on in the NT.[89]

VII. Hebrew Sirach and Dead Sea Scrolls. In the Hebrew text of Sirach, the noun *'ēṯ* occurs some 40 times; on the whole, its usage reflects that of the OT, especially wisdom literature.[90] Only the construction *l't* without further qualification appears to be new (10:4; 39:30; 48:10; cf. also 12:16). Even in these cases, however, we seem to be dealing with "the appointed or right time."[91]

For the most part, the use of *'ēṯ* in the Dead Sea Scrolls also continues OT usage, as is clear from Wilch's discussion of some forty passages (to which should be added now such texts as 11QT 33:2 [uncertain]; 45:6, as well as the adj. *'ittî* [citing Lev. 16:21]; also 4Q491 1-3, 17; 8-10, I, 11 [pl. *'tym*]; 496, 3, 4; 508, 2, 2; 512, 1-6, 2, 5 [pl. *'tym*].[92] The Temple Scroll does not use *(wᵉ)'attâ,* which does appear 6 times (some textually uncertain) in *DJD,* VII.

Generally speaking, the use of *'ēṯ* in the Dead Sea Scrolls exhibits two opposing tendencies that go beyond OT usage: on the one hand, it is used in cultic rules and regulations, especially in calendrical texts such as CD 10:14-15 and 1QH 12:7-8;[93] on the other, it is used in generalizing statements, such as references to liturgical praise "at all times" (*[bkwl] 'tym,* 1QM 14:13; cf. 4Q491 8-10, I, 11), divine revelations "from time to time" (*'t b't,* 1QS 8:15; *l't b't,* 1QS 9:13; cf. the late OT texts Neh. 8:18; 1 Ch. 12:23[22]; 2 Ch. 24:11; 30:21), or divine counsel "for time eternal" (*l't 'wlm,* 1QSᵇ 4:26; cf. 5:18).

Kronholm

86. Ibid., 306.
87. Wilch, 151-55.
88. Contra Wilch; see the critical discussion by Jenni, *TLOT,* II, 956.
89. Delling; also Cullmann and Finegan.
90. See the analysis by Wilch, 138-43.
91. Ibid., 143.
92. Ibid., 143-51.
93. Talmon; Wilch, 143-45.

עַתּוּד *ʿattûḏ*

I. Occurrences. II. 1. Etymology and Meaning; 2. LXX. III. OT: 1. The Domestic Animal; 2. Commerce; 3. Sacrifice; 4. Metaphorical Usage.

I. Occurrences. The noun appears 29 times in the OT, always in the plural. In the Semitic languages other than Hebrew, the lexeme plays a role only in Akkadian and Arabic. The lexicons give the meaning of Akk. *atūdu,* Old Assyr. *etūdum* or *dūdu,* as "wild sheep, ram"; according to Landsberger, however, the meaning is "wild boar."[1] Arab. *ʿatūd* means "young he-goat."

II. 1. *Etymology and Meaning.* The etymology of *ʿattûḏ* is not entirely certain. Some lexicons postulate a root *ʿtd* II, without suggesting its meaning.[2] Landsberger derives the lexeme from *ʿtd* I, "be ready," considering it a nominal *qiṭṭûl* form analogous to *bikkûr(îm),* "firstfruits," or *bikkûr(â),* "early fig," and *limmûd,* "beginner, disciple," which denote a beginning stage.[3] He relates the term *ʿattûḏ* to sexual maturity, understanding it as referring to a ram intermediate in age between a kid *(g^eḏî)* and a mature ram *(ʾayil),* i.e., between an animal capable of reproducing and a fully developed animal, just as he believes that Akk. *atūdu* denotes a male sheep or goat of a particular age. A similar basic meaning was already suggested by Gesenius, who cited Arab. *ʿatad* (or *ʿatīd*), which refers to "a horse 'ready' to run" and can also mean "strong."[4] Arab. *ʿatūd* denotes a goat more than a year old (possibly also a sheep).[5]

In contrast to Akk. *atūdu,* which refers primarily to a wild sheep, the OT word refers only to the male domestic goat — not (as *HAL* states) a male sheep or ram (an interpretation justified by the context only in Zec. 10:3a, a gloss that interrupts the metaphor): *ʿattûḏîm* appear for the most part in a triad that includes rams *(ʾêlîm)* and lambs *(kārîm,* Dt. 32:14; Isa. 34:6; Jer. 51:40; Ezk. 27:21; 39:18; or *k^eḇāśîm,* Nu. 7:17-88; Isa. 1:11; with *ʾêlîm* alone, Ezk. 34:17; Ps. 66:15), where they represent the "flock," i.e., sheep and goats.

The theory that *ʿattûḏ* emphasizes a particular attribute, obvious sexual maturity (cf. Gen. 31:10,12), is suggested by the observation that Hebrew has three other synonyms for "male goat": *śāʿîr,* "the hairy one," along with *tayiš* and *ṣāp̱îr,* the root meanings of which are unknown. Since Isa. 14:9 and Jer. 50:8 imply that the *ʿattûḏ* is the bellwether

---

1. B. Landsberger, *JNES* 24 (1965) 296 n. 40 ("wild boars of the mountain"); idem, *WO* 3 (1966), 265 n. 5 ("Wildschwein"). Cf. *AHw,* I, 88b: "Wildschaf; Schafbock," Old Assyrian "Widder (der Herde)?"; *CAD,* I/1, 521: "wild sheep [male], wild ram."

2. *GesB:* "he-goat"; *KBL*[2]: "ram and he-goat."

3. B. Landsberger, *Die Fauna im alten Mesopotamien* (1934), 97.

4. *GesTh,* II, 1083-84.

5. Cf. Lane, I/5, 1945: "a yearling goat"; T. Nöldeke, *Beiträge zur semitischen Sprachwissenschaft* (1904), 83.

of the flock (albeit also called *tayiš* in Prov. 30:31), who leads it as its sturdiest member, *ʿattûḏ* probably denotes not just any male goat (like *śᵉʿîr ʿizzîm* in Gen. 37:31), but a particularly robust and valuable animal (a breeding goat).

2. *LXX.* The LXX usually uses *trágos,* "he-goat," to translate *ʿattûḏ* (but also to translate *tayiš* in Gen. 30:35; 32:15[Eng. v. 14]; Prov. 30:31; and *ṣāp̄îr* in Dnl. 8:5,8, 21); in Ps. 50:9 it uses the synonymous *chímaros* (also used for *śāʿîr* in Lev. 4:24; 16:7-8; 16:9-26 [9 times]; and for *ṣāp̄îr* in 2 Esd. = Ezr. 8:35; 2 Ch. 29:21), and in Jer. 51:40 = 28:40 *ériphos,* "young male goat." In Ezk. 27:21 and Zec. 10:3, however, it uses the translation *amnós,* "lamb," and in Prov. 27:26 the synonymous *arḗn.* It translates the sense of the metaphor *ʿattûḏê ʾāreṣ* in Isa. 14:9 with *hoi árxantes tḗs gḗs,* whereas in Jer. 50:8 = 27:8 it erroneously uses *drákontes.*

III. OT.

1. *The Domestic Animal.* The domestic goat[6] of Palestine *(Capra hircus),* which is descended from the Near Eastern bezoar goat *(Capra aegagrus),* is usually black (hence the comparison of the bride's hair to a flock of goats in Cant. 4:1 and 6:5; cf. also 1 S. 19:13). Animals with hair of a different color or displaying markings were the exception; the modest wage claimed by Jacob from Laban (Gen. 30:31-34) presupposes that striped *(ʿᵃquddîm),*[7] spotted *(nᵉquddîm),* and speckled *(bᵉruddîm)* goats (31:10,12) were not exactly common (the LXX adds *krioí,* "rams," to *trágoi;* 30:35 refers to the speckled [NRSV "mottled"] goats as *tᵉyāšîm ṭᵉluʾîm*).

These animals are probably the result of mutation or crossbreeding with other species of goats.[8] The various Hebrew words for the he-goat may therefore refer to different breeds, although Feliks assigns them all to *Capra hircus mambrica.*[9]

Even though the flesh of goats was not as fat as that of sheep,[10] the *ʿattûḏ* had sufficient fat: the Song of Moses (Dt. 32:14) lists it as a fat animal along with lambs and rams.

2. *Commerce.* These animals were of substantial commercial importance. Many were imported from Arabia, which was a prime source of sheep and goats (Ezk. 27:21; as tribute, 2 Ch. 17:11). According to Prov. 27:26, *ʿattûḏîm* provided the price of a field.

3. *Sacrifice.* a. *Sacrifice of Well-Being.* Most often (18 times) the *ʿattûḏ* is mentioned in sacrificial contexts, especially in the postexilic period (the *atūdu* in Gilg. XI, 51 was

6. → עז *ʿēz.*

7. *HAL,* II, 873: "a twist in the tail."

8. This subject and the domestication of the goat are discussed by B. Brentjes, *Die Haustierwerdung im Orient* (1965), 22-29; and G. Cansdale, *Animals of Bible Lands* (1970), 44-48.

9. J. Feliks, *The Animal World of the Bible* (1962), 16.

10. *AuS,* VI, 99.

probably also a sacrificial animal[11]). Cultic texts describe the ordinary he-goat as being used only for a sin offering. (Except in Gen. 37:31, where the LXX translates *śᵉʿîr ʿizzîm* with *ériphos aigṓn,* although elsewhere it always uses *chímaros ex aigṓn* for the sacrificial animal, the *śāʿîr* is mentioned only in this context [Lev. 4:23; 16:9-26], esp. in the expressions *śᵉʿîr ʿizzîm* [Lev. 4:23; 9:3; 16:5; 23:9; Nu. 7:16-87; 15:24; 28:15,30; 29:5-25; Ezk. 43:22; 45:23] and *śᵉʿîr ḥaṭṭāʾṯ* [Lev. 9:15; 10:16; 16:15,27; Nu. 28:22; 29:28-38; Ezk. 43:25; 2 Ch. 29:23], whereas the *ṣāp̄îr* [possibly a loanword from Aram. *ṣᵉp̄îrāʾ;* cf. Ezr. 6:17] appears only twice, in postexilic texts [Ezr. 8:35; 2 Ch. 29:21]; the *tayiš* is never mentioned as a sin offering.) By contrast, the *ʿattûḏ* was offered specifically as a sacrifice of well-being (RSV "peace offerings").

Reflecting postexilic cultic theology, the account of the consecration of the altar at Sinai describes offerings of all kinds by the leaders of the twelve tribes of the Israelites on each of twelve days, including various animals for the different sacrifices to be offered on the altar: burnt offering, sin offering, and sacrifice of well-being *(zeḇaḥ haššᵉlāmîm).* Each sacrifice of well-being involved two oxen, five rams, five *ʿattûḏîm,* and five yearling lambs (Nu. 7:17-83), for a total of sixty *ʿattûḏîm* (v. 88). According to Lev. 3:1-17, the sacrifice of well-being (*zeḇaḥ šᵉlāmîm;* P was the first to link the two words[12]) was an ox or a male or female sheep or goat (*ʿēz,* the most general term). The animal's blood was sprinkled around the altar and its fat burned.

b. *Burnt Offering.* Non-P texts (in part earlier than P) mention the *ʿattûḏ* along with *bāqār* and *ṣōʾn* (cattle, sheep, and other goats) only in the context of the burnt offering *(ʿōlâ);* no specific cultic schema is detectable in the listing and terminology of these sacrificial animals.[13]

In Ps. 66:15, for example, the psalmist promises to offer fatlings as a burnt offering of thanksgiving, along with rams, bulls, and *ʿattûḏîm.* Two texts critical of the cult speak of the "blood of *ʿattûḏîm.*" Isaiah bitterly criticizes a misconstrued, soulless sacrificial ritual *(zᵉḇāḥîm* and *ʿōlôṯ),* which is totally repugnant to Yahweh; he detests burnt offerings and the blood of bulls, lambs, and *ʿattûḏîm* (1:11). Since the value of sacrifice resides in a proper attitude, in worship and adoration, not in feasting and manipulating the deity, Ps. 50:7-15, a Levitical judgment discourse on the theme of the proper worship of God, points out that the whole world with all its animals belongs to Yahweh. He is not dependent on the bulls and *ʿattûḏîm* of Israel (v. 9); contrary to a naive notion of sacrifice and God (cf. Dnl. 14:6 LXX = Bel 6), his life is not sustained by eating the flesh of bulls or drinking the blood of *ʿattûḏîm* (Ps. 50:13).

4. *Metaphorical Usage.* a. *Leader.* The *ʿattûḏ* that goes at the head of the flock as its leader serves as an image of the king going at the head of his people. Isa. 14:9 refers metaphorically to the rulers of the earth (LXX *hoi árxantes tḗs gḗs*) as *ʿattûḏîm.* (The phrase *kol-ʿattûḏê ʾāreṣ* is defined more precisely by the following *kōl malḵê gôyim.*

---

11. W. von Soden, *ZA* 53 (1959) 232.

12. This sacrifice is discussed by R. Rendtorff, *Studien zur Geschichte des Opfers in alten Israel. WMANT* 24 (1967), 149-68, 237-38.

13. Ibid., 117-18.

The male goat [*ṣāp̄îr*] in Dnl. 8:5,8,21 symbolizes Alexander the Great; Prov. 30:29-31 speaks of a king striding before his people like a lion, a rooster, or a he-goat [*tayiš*].) The lead goat is the first to rush out when the corral is opened; the oracle against Babylon interpolated secondarily into the book of Jeremiah (50:1–51:58), which summons Israel to flee the destruction of the threatened city and leave the land of the Chaldeans (50:8), therefore uses the *'attûḏ* (LXX *drákōn!*) as a model of quick and courageous action.

The *'attûḏ* can maintain his position and assert his authority only if he ruthlessly fights off his competitors; he therefore serves also as a prototype of brutality and oppression. In Ezekiel's parable of the good shepherd, the *'attûḏ* and the ram in v. 17 (possibly a gloss[14] on the fat and sturdy sheep that push the weaker sheep away from food and water) therefore represent the wealthy leaders of Israel, who rob the weaker Israelites of their rights and property (cf. also Mt. 25:33, where the goats [*eríphia*] symbolize the unjust). Zec. 10:3 employs the same image: Yahweh, the true shepherd, cares for his flock and punishes the *'attûḏîm,* as the false shepherds (the brutal leaders of Israel) are called in a gloss.

b. *Sacrificial Feast.* In the image of "Yahweh's day of sacrifice" (according to Gressmann, a prophetic inversion of the festal eschatological banquet),[15] when the Lord will take vengeance on his foes, the *'attûḏîm* and other sacrificial animals embody the enemies of God, doomed to destruction.

For example, at the great sacrificial feast *(zeḇaḥ gāḏôl)* that Yahweh will celebrate to punish Gog (Ezk. 39:17-20; the motif predates Ezekiel[16] [cf. Zeph. 1:8]), the enemies from the north will be slaughtered like sacrificial animals — oxen, bulls, rams, lambs, and *'attûḏîm* — and all the birds (cf. Rev. 19:17-18) and wild animals (cf. Isa. 56:9; Jer. 12:9) are invited to the sacrificial meal. Isa. 34 (secondary, probably dating from the late exilic or early postexilic period)[17] similarly compares the judgment on Edom to a colossal sacrificial feast *(zeḇaḥ . . . wᵉṭeḇaḥ);* here too the multitude of sacrificial animals illustrating the enormous magnitude and monstrous frenzy of this bloody orgy must include the *'attûḏîm* whose blood will drip from the sword of Yahweh (Isa. 34:6; cf. Jer. 46:10). Probably from this source, the description of Babylon's punishment in the book of Jeremiah incorporated this image (albeit somewhat attenuated) in Jer. 51:34-39. (Its position following the concluding formula suggests that this element is secondary.) Yahweh will take vengeance on this city for the blood spilled in Jerusalem, as though leading lambs, rams, and *'attûḏîm* to the slaughter *(liṭᵉḇôaḥ)* (v. 40; cf. also 50:27).

Maiberger

---

14. W. Eichrodt, *Ezekiel. OTL* (Eng. trans. 1970), 473 n. b.
15. H. Gressmann, *Der Ursprung der israelitisch-jüdischen Eschatologie* (1905), 141.
16. W. Zimmerli, *Ezekiel 2. Herm* (Eng. trans. 1983), 308-9.
17. H. Wildberger, *Jesaja 28–39. BK* X/3 (1982), 1341.

עתק *ʿtq*; עָתִיק *ʿāṯîq*; עַתִּיק *ʿattîq*; עָתֵק *ʿāṯēq*; עָתָק *ʿāṯāq*

I. Etymology. II. OT: 1. Verb; 2. Adjectives. III. LXX.

I. Etymology. The basic meaning of the root *ʿtq* appears to be "move forward, advance" (in space or time). The verb occurs in Ugaritic: "one, two days pass";[1] "and they [the troops?] move on";[2] somewhat obscure is the shaphel participle: "[a goddess?] who causes to go past, who removes."[3] The much-discussed words *kklb bbtk nʿtq . . . uḫštk lntn/lbky ʿtq* probably also convey the sense of advancing or enduring: "like a dog in your house we shall grow old . . . or shall your sepulchre become a lasting wailing *(ntn)*/weeping?"[4] It is unnecessary to postulate a root *ʿtq* II, "speak loudly, howl."[5] The meaning "advance" is normal in other languages as well: Akk. *etēqu,* "pass"; Arab. *ʿatuqa* and *ʿataqa,* "grow old"; Imperial Aram. *ʿtq,* "old"; Syr. *ʿtq,* "advance," "grow old," "be impudent."[6]

II. OT.

1. *Verb.* The root *ʿtq* occurs 20 times in the MT (17 times in Hebrew, 3 in Aramaic). In the case of the verb, the basic meaning is often quite apparent, as in the two instances of the qal: Job 14:18, "A rock can move from its place [e.g., on account of a landslide]," a theme that reappears in 18:4: "Should a rock move from its place . . . because of you?"[7] The hiphil expresses the same meaning: "the one [God] who removes mountains" (9:5); this meaning develops into "set out, move on" (elliptical for "move one's tent"[8]) (Gen. 12:8; 26:22). Twice the verb is used figuratively: "Words have departed from them" (Job 32:15); "The proverbs of Solomon that the officials of Hezekiah copied [or: 'collected'; lit. 'moved from elsewhere, transferred']" (Prov. 25:1). Ps. 6:8(Eng. v. 7) is obscure: *ʿāšᵉšâ . . . ʿênî ʿāṯᵉqâ;* the meaning "swollen . . . is my eye, protruding" is more likely than "My eye is dimmed, . . . entirely worn out."[9] In Job 21:7 the meaning "grow old" is generally assumed, e.g., "Why do the wicked live on, grow

ʿtq. D. Pardee, "A Note on the Root *ʿtq* in CTA 16 I 2, 5 (UT 125, KRT II)," *UF* 5 (1973) 229-34; J. Sanmartín, "Lexikographisches zu ug. *ʿtq* (KTU 1.16 I 2-5, 15-19, II 38-42)," *UF* 10 (1978) 453-54.

1. *KTU* 1.6, II, 5, 26.
2. *KTU* 2.36, 17.
3. *KTU* 1.16, VI, 1-2, 13.
4. *KTU* 1.16, I, 2, 4 = I, 16, 18-19 = II, 38, 41. Trans. of Sanmartín, 454; similarly Pardee, 233: "to grow old . . . to pass on."
5. Contra M. Dietrich and O. Loretz, *UF* 12 (1980) 190; B. Margalit, *UF* 15 (1983) 103.
6. See II.2 below.
7. See I above.
8. *BDB,* 801.
9. For the former see *HAL,* II, 905, citing L. Delekat, *VT* 14 (1964) 54; for the latter, H.-J. Kraus, *Psalms 1–59* (Eng. trans. 1988), 159.

old (*'āṯ^e^qû*), and achieve superiority in power (*gam gāḇ^e^rû ḥayil*)?"[10] Since here — as elsewhere in Job (5:5; 15:29; 20:15,18; 31:25) — *ḥayil* must mean "wealth, possessions," the second hemistich must be understood as "when they grow old, their wealth increases," which sounds rather banal, or as "they live to a great age and their wealth increases," in which case the verb *'tq* conveys a meaning that is not inherent and for which the OT has other means of expression (cf. 42:17: "And Job died, old and full of days"). More appropriate to the context is the meaning "advance," i.e., "achieve success," which is also suggested by the parallels cited by Fohrer: Jer. 12:1-2, "Why does the way of the wicked prosper? . . . You plant them, and they take root; they grow *(hlk)* and bring forth fruit"; and Ps. 73:3ff., esp. v. 12, "Such are the wicked; always at ease, they increase their wealth *(ḥayil)*."

2. *Adjectives.* The adjectives occupy the same semantic domain as the verb. Both *'āṯîq* and *'āṯēq* (one occurrence each) mean "displaced from the ordinary," i.e., "fine," "abundant": "fine clothing" (Jer. 23:18), "abundant wealth *(hôn)*" (Prov. 8:18).

The adj. *'attîq* occurs twice. Isa. 28:9 uses it in a periphrastic expression for "young children": "those removed (*'attîqê*) from the breast." The text of 1 Ch. 4:22 is difficult: among the sons of Shelah are listed "Joash and Saraph, who worked for Moab and were 'inhabitants' of Lehem,[11] *w^e^hadd^e^ḇārîm 'attîqîm*." Most exegetes translate the final two words as "and the matters/records are ancient";[12] but it is also possible that this is a marginal gloss, "and the words have been moved," i.e., words have been omitted or transposed here.[13]

There are four occurrences of the adj. *'āṯāq,* "insolent" ("freed from traditions, emancipated"[14]); it is used in cultic contexts to describe the language of the arrogant wicked (1 S. 2:3; Ps. 31:19[18]; 75:6[5]; 94:4). In Ezk. 35:13 a proposed emendation of MT *w^e^ha'tarṭem* finds a denominative verb *'tq* hiphil, "make insolent" (addressing Mt. Seir): "You have magnified (yourselves) with your mouths against me and have made your words impudent against me."[15]

Aram. *'attîq yômîn/yômayyā'* (Dnl. 7:9,13,22), "ancient of days," expresses the eternity of God. A parallel to this expression is found in the divine title *rĕ'ĕsa mawā'ĕl,* "head of days," in the Similitudes of Enoch (1 En. 46:1,2; 47:3; 55:1; 60:2; 71:10,12,13,14). The Ugaritic expression *'b šnm* (in the phrase *qrš mlk 'b šnm*), translated "father of years," has also been cited as a parallel.[16] This interpretation is disputed, however; Pope translates it "father of the eldest" and views it as expressing the

---

10. G. Fohrer, *Das Buch Hiob. KAT* XVI (1963), 335-36.
11. Translation following M. Dijkstra, *VT* 25 (1975) 672.
12. Including Dijkstra.
13. W. Rudolph, *Chronikbücher. HAT* I/21 (1955), 36.
14. *HAL,* II, 905.
15. See W. Zimmerli, *Ezekiel 2. Herm* (Eng. trans. 1983), 227.
16. → I, 245; F. M. Cross, *Canaanite Myth and Hebrew Epic* (1973), 16. See *KTU* 1.1, III, 24; 1.2, III, 5; 1.3, V, 8; 1.4, IV, 24; 1.5, VI, 2; 1.6, I, 36; 1.17, VI, 49.

great age (and concomitant debility) of El.[17] According to Gordon and Jirku, *'b šnm* means "father of [the god] Šnm."[18] Aistleitner interprets *šnm* as "the name of El's exalted heavenly dwelling place," translating *qrš mlk 'b šnm* as "the domain of the king and father, the *šnm*."[19]

III. LXX. Of the 20 occurrences of *ʿtq,* the LXX translates 8 with the verb *palaioún;* Prov. 25:1 uses *engráphein,* and Job 18:4 uses *katastréphein.* The adj. *ʿattîq* is represented by *apospán* and *athoukieín, ʿāṯāq* by *adikía, anomía,* and *megalorrēmosýnē.* To date the root has not been found in the Dead Sea Scrolls.

Schmoldt

---

17. → I, 6; M. Pope, *El in the Ugaritic Texts. SVT* 2 (1955), 34-36.

18. C. H. Gordon, *JNES* 35 (1976) 261-62; A. Jirku, *ZAW* 82 (1970) 278-79. Both cite *KTU* 1.114.

19. *WUS,* no. 312.

עָתַר *ʿāṯar;* עָתָר *ʿāṯār*

I. 1. Distribution; 2. Etymology. II. Semantics: 1. Niphal; 2. Qal and Hiphil; 3. Derivatives; 4. Setting. III. Theology. IV. Dead Sea Scrolls.

I. 1. *Distribution.* The root *ʿtr* is scantily attested in the OT (23 occurrences); it appears primarily in Ex. 8–10, Ezra/Chronicles, and Job. This root with the meaning "entreat" has not been found elsewhere in the environs of Israel. Jewish tradition retains the ancient sense (Sir. 37:15; 38:14). The more commonly used synonyms are → פלל *pll,* → זעק *zāʿaq,* → קרא *qr',* and → שׁאל *š'l.*

The LXX uses *(pros)eúchesthai* for the active stems (11 times; used 80 times for *pll*) and *(eis/ep)akoúein* (otherwise used primarily for *šmʿ, 'zn, ʿnh* I, and *qšb*) for the niphal.

2. *Etymology.* Etymological association with Arab. *ʿatara,* "slaughter, sacrifice," and Ugar. *ǵtr,* "kill, slaughter, sacrifice, ask," is possible;[1] there is probably no connec-

---

ʿāṯar. R. Albertz, "עתר *ʿātar* to pray," *TLOT,* II, 961-62; D. R. Ap-Thomas, "Notes on Some Terms Relating to Prayer," *VT* 6 (1956) 225-41; W. Fuss, *Die deuteronomistische Pentateuchredaktion in Ex 3–17. BZAW* 126 (1972); F. Hesse, "Die Fürbitte im AT" (diss., Erlangen, 1951).

1. For Arabic see J. Wellhausen, *Reste arabischen Heidentums* (^{2}1897), 142; for Ugaritic, M. Dietrich, O. Loretz, and J. Sanmartín, *UF* 7 (1975) 138.

tion with Arab. *'aṭara,* "be fragrant" (cf. Ezk. 8:11, *'āṯār,* "fragrance"), or Arab. *'aṯara,* "lie" (possibly suggested by Prov. 27:6). By a similar process of semantic development, *zbḥ tôḏâ,* "sacrifice of thanksgiving," resulted in *tôḏâ,* "prayer of thanksgiving."[2] But Heb. *'tr* no longer has any connection with "sacrifice" or "burn incense."

II. Semantics.

1. *Niphal.* The use of the niphal is striking: Yahweh "was (successfully) entreated" (*wayyē'āṯer;* always with *l^e* — *commodi* or *auctoris?*[3] [Gen. 25:21; 2 S. 21:14; 24:25; Ezr. 8:23; 2 Ch. 33:13; other niphal forms in Isa. 19:22; 1 Ch. 5:20; 2 Ch. 33:19; possibly Prov. 27:6]). The niphal thus appears four times in the Chronicler's History (special material in liturgical contexts). As a rule, the qal of *'tr* is not used to describe the actual entreaty, but rather *bqš, z'q, ḥlh,* or *pll.* The sequence *'tr* niphal + *šm'* in 2 Ch. 33:13 is unique: *'tr* precedes the hearing of the prayer. The liturgical prelude is described in vv. 12-13a (cf. Ezr. 8:21-23a). In other words, *'tr* niphal means that God, influenced by liturgical prayer, alleviated Israel's affliction. The other niphal texts are similar. In 2 S. 21:14 and 24:25, the same language is used to describe God's concern for (over?) the land following certain cultic acts. In Isa. 19:22 the return of the Egyptians to Yahweh evokes Yahweh's pardon. In Gen. 25:21 Isaac's prayer (only here *'tr* qal) prompts the alleviation of Rebekah's affliction (is the qal here an artificial back-formation from the niphal?). As a rule, the theological schema of prayer (or worship) followed by Yahweh's intervention is represented by such verb pairs as *z'q* — *šm'* (Neh. 9:27,28[4]) or *qr'* — *'nh/yš'/šm'* (Ps. 3:5[Eng. v. 4]; 17:6; 18:7[6]; 34:7[6]; 55:17[16]; 57:3-4[2-3]; 91:15; 119:146; 138:3). The use of *'tr* niphal probably reflects the (regional?) usage of a few redactors.

2. *Qal and Hiphil.* Except in Gen. 25:21, active forms of *'tr* are never associated syntactically with the niphal. They refer to the act of entreaty, usually with the addressee specified (always God; twice with *l^e* and 8 times with *'el*), and in appropriate cases the party or parties on whose behalf prayer is offered (*b^e'aḏ,* Ex. 8:24[28]; *l^enōḵaḥ,* Gen. 25:21; *l^e,* Ex. 8:5[9]) and concern expressed (Ex. 8:4[8]; 8:25[29]; 9:28; 10:17; Jgs. 13:8). The actual prayer is quoted in Jgs. 13:8; v. 9 describes God's response. In all these texts the ritual setting is discernible. Job 22:21-27 and 33:14-26 contain elements of a ritual of penance and restitution.[5] The theme of God's favorable response belongs to the semantic field (*šm',* Job 22:27; cf. Jgs. 13:8; *rṣh,* Job 33:26; cf. God's intervention in Ex. 8:26-27[30-31]; 10:18-19).

Why is *'tr* chosen instead of one of its synonyms? Ex. 8–10, with 8 occurrences of *'tr,* provides the most ready answer. In the second, fourth, seventh, eighth, and tenth plagues (a separate stratum of tradition? literary dramaturgy?[6]), the strict schema of

---

2. → IV, 24.
3. Brockelmann, *Synt,* §107e; *GK,* §121f.
4. For Dtn see Fuss, 39.
5. K. Seybold, *Das Gebet des Kranken im AT. BWANT* 99 (1973), 82-98.
6. B. S. Childs, *Book of Exodus. OTL* (1974), 133-37; contra M. Noth, *History of Pentateuchal Traditions* (Eng. trans. 1972), 65-71.

Pharaoh's hardness of heart is abandoned. Pharaoh entreats Moses to pray for him. The hiphil and qal of *ʿtr* are used for Pharaoh's entreaty and Moses' prayer (Ex. 8:4-5[8-9],24-26[28-30]; 9:28; 10:17-18); for the latter, we also find *zʿq* (Ex. 8:8[12]) and *prś kappayim* (Ex. 9:29,33). Here *ʿtr* presumably refers to the liturgical prayer of the congregational leader (Moses' successor), which (as in the Passover ritual?) ends with a blessing (Ex. 12:32: "And bring a blessing on me too"; source stratum uncertain[7]).

3. *Derivatives.* The noun *ʿāṯār* occurs only in Zeph. 3:10; it might mean "suppliant"; in any case, the liturgical background is more than clear (v. 9).[8] The noun *ʿāṯār,* "fragrance of incense"(?), which appears only in Ezk. 8:11 (not in the LXX), and the toponym *ʿeṯer,* "place of incense"(?)[9] (Josh. 15:42; 19:7), may derive from a root not otherwise attested in Hebrew (cf. Arab. *ʿaṭara*). For *naʿtārôṯ* in Prov. 27:6, the meaning "deceptive" has been postulated.[10]

4. *Setting.* The tradition recorded in Ex. 1–15 can be envisaged only in the setting of a liturgical community. The plague narratives (Ex. 5–12) have an independent force, serving to strengthen the community (cf. 10:2). The wicked[11] pharaoh's heart is hardened, so that he cannot achieve knowledge of Yahweh and a "humble"[12] way of life. He breaks down in the face of demonstrations of God's power and resorts to the prayers of the community. It would not be surprising if the texts in Job, Samuel, and Genesis borrowed the active forms of *ʿtr* from the late plague cycle. The passive usage in Chronicles could be the product of theological reflection on the efficacy of intercession.

III. Theology. Like → פלל *pll, ʿtr* does not inherently mean "intercede for." It denotes — at a particular time and in a particular liturgical setting (the plague cycle) — the prayer that can move God. Gen. 25:21 reflects the synthesis: Yahweh is a God who answers prayers.

IV. Dead Sea Scrolls. The only occurrence of *ʿtr* in the Dead Sea Scrolls (4Q173 1:4 [4QpPs^b 127]) is uncertain: the text may speak of the *ʿtrwt* ("intercessions") of the Teacher of Righteousness.

Gerstenberger

---

7. Contra Fuss, 160-61.
8. W. Rudolph, *Micha-Nahum-Habakuk-Zephanja. KAT* XIII/3 (1975), 291-92.
9. *HAL,* II, 906.
10. *HAL,* II, 905; cf. Arab. *ʿaṯara,* "lie."
11. → רשׁע *rāšāʿ*.
12. → ענה II *ʿānâ* II.

פֵּאָה *pē'â*

I. Root, Etymology. II. Occurrences: 1. Side, Edge. 2. Edges of a Field; 3. Boundary; 4. Hair; 5. Dead Sea Scrolls and Sirach; 6. Mishnah; 7. LXX.

I. Root, Etymology. A root *p'h* with the basic meaning "split, cut off, cut up" is reflected in Qat. *f'y,* "divide, split," the Minaean causative *sf'y,* "strike, destroy,"[1] and the Biblical Hebrew hapax legomenon *hip'â,* "cut in pieces" (Dt. 32:26, text uncertain).[2] Figurative or resultative meaning is exhibited by Arab. *fa'ā,* "seize, carry off (as booty)," which derives from the removal of precious metal and metal objects from walls and socles as booty. This root may also be present in Arab. *fi'at,* "group, class, military unit," also attested in Ethiopic and Amharic.

Von Soden, however, interprets Akk. *pātu,* "edge," and *pūtu,* "front," as feminine forms of the monoconsonantal root *pû,* "mouth."[3] Besides the Aramaic languages (Jewish Aram. *pāṯā',* Syr. *pa'ṯā'*), *pē'â* with the meaning "side, edge," appears in Ugaritic as *p't/pìt;* four of its occurrences are in the phrase *p't mdbr,* "edges of the desert."[4] Several texts are obscure, including *pìt 'dm* in an incantation, which is more likely to mean "forehead of the man" than "corner."[5] Like Akk. *pātu* and *pūtu,* the related lexemes Heb. *pē'â* and **pōṯ,* "front," have influenced each other mutually, as the textual apparatus associated with individual biblical texts illustrates. Dhorme defines the basic meaning as "side, direction, focal point";[6] probably two homophonous roots have coalesced.

II. Occurrences. The noun *pē'â* occurs 84 times in the OT; 48 of these occurrences are in the so-called draft constitution of Ezk. 40–48, and 26 are in H and P. It refers indiscriminately to the sides or edges of an object (a room, a piece of furniture) or a space (a field, a tribal territory). Occasionally *pē'â* functions as a synonym of → גבול

---

pē'â. W. Bauer, *Pea (Vom Ackerwinkel). Die Mischna,* I/2 (1915); R. Brooks, *Support for the Poor in the Mishnaic Law of Agriculture: Tractate Peah. BJS* 43 (1983); E. Dhorme, *L'emploi métaphorique des noms de parties du corps en hébreu et en akkadien* (1923); H. Gese, "Kleine Beiträge zum Verständnis des Amosbuches," *VT* 12 (1962) 417-38; E. A. Knauf, "Supplementa Ismaelitica," *BN* 22 (1983) 25-33; S. Mittmann, "Am 3, 12-15 und das Bett der Samarier," *ZDPV* 92 (1976) 149-67, esp. 158-59; S. D. Ricks, "A Lexicon of Epigraphic Qatabanian" (diss., Graduate Theological Union, Berkeley, 1982); G. A. Wewers, *Pea; Ackerecke. Übersetzung des Talmud Yerushalmi,* I/2 (1986).

1. According to Biella, 403, and Beeston, 47, the root is *fy'.*
2. Ricks, 193.
3. *GaG,* §54b; *AHw,* II, 849a.
4. E.g., *KTU* 1.14, III, 1; IV, 30.
5. *KTU* 1.107, 32.
6. P. 71.

$g^e\underline{b}\hat{u}l$, "border," or as an expanded preposition to indicate a direction. It also has a specialized use in the context of trimming beards and hair.

1. *Side, Edge.* In late strata of P, *pē'â* refers to the locations of the frames on the long sides of the tabernacle (Ex. 26:18,20 [= 36:23,25]). Ex. 27:9-13 (= 38:9-13) regulates the mounting of hangings on the long and short sides of the courtyard. In Ex. 25:26 (= 37:13) *pē'â* refers to the four corners at the legs of the table for the bread of the Presence. The meaning of the lexeme in Am. 3:12 is uncertain;[7] it has something to do with a bed (*miṭṭâ,* par. to → עֶרֶשׂ *'ereś*). Amos's *māšāl* attacks the high society of Samaria, who at their parties sit on the corner/edge/foot of a bed or recline against the head or cushions (?) of a couch. "Splendor of the couch" is the translation of *HAL.*[8]

2. *Edges of a Field.* The term denotes the edges of a grain field, which must remain unreaped (Lev. 19:9; 23:22); no minimum width is given. Clearly *pē'â* represents an ancient legal institution, probably cultic in origin,[9] for the purpose of poor relief, a function that survives in the Mishnah.

3. *Boundary.* In lists *pē'â* serves as a synonym of $g^e\underline{b}\hat{u}l$, "border," qualified by a direction. Josh. 18:12-20 defines the borders of Benjamin, 15:5 the eastern border of Judah. The list in Ezk. 47:15-20 defines the boundaries of the whole territory of the twelve tribes outside the sanctuary. Ezekiel's so-called draft constitution sketches a map of the new Israel. In similar fashion Nu. 34:3 defines the southern boundary in the description of the boundaries of Israel's inheritance (Nu. 34:3-12) in the promised land.

The list of tribes in Ezk. 48:1-29, which outlines a new allocation of territory for each tribe with boundaries in each direction, uses *pē'â* 18 times. V. 8 singles out the "offering"[10] as a thirteenth tribal territory. Ezk. 48:16 defines the dimensions of the new Jerusalem in each direction; 48:30-34 lays out the gates on each of the four sides of the city. Ezk. 47–48 alone contains 44 occurrences of *pē'â* (more than half the total).

The same term is used to define the boundaries of pastureland in each direction — that of the "prince"[11] in Ezk. 45:7 and that of the Levitical cities in Nu. 35:5, two thousand cubits on each side. In Ezk. 41:12 *pē'â* describes the situation of the broad-room building facing the temple on the west. Here *pē'â* functions as an expanded preposition. A unique usage appears in Ezra's prayer (Neh. 9:6-37), where v. 22 categorizes the kingdoms and peoples as the "peripheral territory" or (more likely) "edge of the field" (to be harvested) for the tribes of Israel.

---

7. On the text see H. W. Wolff, *Joel and Amos. Herm* (Eng. trans. 1977), 196-98; Mittmann, 155-56.

8. *HAL,* III, 908.

9. K. Elliger, *Leviticus. HAT* I/4 (1966), 257.

10. → תרומה *t^erûmâ.*

11. → נשׂיא *nāśî'.*

4. *Hair.* The noun *pē'â* appears as a technical term in the context of beard trimming and hairdressing. The syntagm *qᵉṣûṣê pē'â,* "trimmed at the edge (of the hair)," describing Arab bedouin in judgment oracles of the book of Jeremiah (Jer. 9:25[Eng. v. 26]; 25:23; 49:32), refers to an Arab hairstyle "in which they also shave under the temple."[12] It is attested iconographically.[13]

In Lev. 19:27a the Holiness Code forbids trimming the edges of the hair or cutting the edges of the beard; 21:5 repeats the latter prohibition explicitly for priests. This prohibition is probably aimed at offerings of hair for the dead, using hair cut from the head.[14] In the regulations concerning leprosy in Lev. 13–14, 13:41 declares that loss of hair from the edge of the face (receding hair, frontal baldness) does not make the individual unclean. In a judgment oracle against Moab, Jer. 48:45 (conflating Nu. 21:28 and 24:17) describes fire as destroying the *pē'â* of Moab; the parallelism with *qoḏqōḏ,* "crown (of the head)," suggests the temples covered with a fringe of hair, synonymous with *raqqâ.* The dual form in Nu. 24:17 reinforces the meaning "temples." The ancient versions (LXX, Vulg., Targ., Syr.) translate the expression as "rulers of Moab," suggesting metaphorical usage.

5. *Dead Sea Scrolls and Sirach.* In the Dead Sea Scrolls *pē'â* occurs only in 1QM 11:6 (quoting Nu. 24:17). A later reflex of the "temples of Moab" occurs in Sir. 33:12a (Heb.; LXX 36:12a): *r'š p'ty mw'b* (although LXX, Vulg., and ms. B read *'wyb,* "enemy," instead of *mw'b*).

6. *Mishnah.* The Mishnah tractate *Pe'ah* defines the "edge of the field" as a minimum of 1/60 of the crop in the case of food crops (grain, legumes, vegetables, onions) and trees (fruit trees, grapevines, nut trees). Gleanings, leavings, the tithe for the poor, and *pē'â* are rabbinic institutions of poor relief. These contributions are left behind by the landowner or distributed directly in the case of crops that are difficult to harvest (grapes, nuts, dates).

7. *LXX.* The LXX has a wide range of translations for *pē'â,* which are not distributed consistently among the various books. The equivalents are the pl. of *méros,* "region," *klítos,* "side" (a specialized LXX term?), and *therismós,* "harvest" (used for "edge of the field" in Lev. 19:9, while Lev. 23:22 ventures a translation: *tó loipón toú therismoú*). In the context of directions, *pē'â* is translated by a preposition *(prós, apó, héōs, katá, hōs),* simply left untranslated, or represented by an article (esp. in Ezk. 47–48). Unique are *eísodos* (Ezk. 47:20), *archēgós* (Nu. 24:17; corrupt text?), and *katénanti phylḗs* (Am. 3:12). In the context of beard and hair, the LXX uses *ópsis* (Lev. 19:27; 21:5) and *kómē* (Lev. 19:27).

Angerstorfer

---

12. Herodotus *History* 3.8.
13. Knauf, 30-33.
14. Elliger, *HAT* I/4, 261.

פאר *p'r;* תִּפְאֶרֶת *tip'eret̲;* פְּאֵר *pᵉ'ēr*

I. Occurrences. II. Usage: 1. Secular Usage; 2. Glorification of an Individual or a People; 3. Theological Usage. III. Sirach and Dead Sea Scrolls. IV. LXX.

I. Occurrences. The verb *p'r* occurs 6 times in the piel (Isa. 55:5; 60:7,9,13; Ps. 149:4; Ezr. 7:27) and 7 times in the hithpael (Ex. 8:5; Jgs. 7:2; Isa. 10:15; 44:23; 49:3; 60:21; 61:3 + Sir. 48:4; 50:20). There are also 7 occurrences of the noun *pᵉ'ēr* (Ex. 39:28; Isa. 3:20; 61:3,10; Ezk. 24:17,23; 44:18). The noun *tip'eret̲/tip'ārâ* occurs much more frequently (51 times), so that it is the actual focus of this article. There are also 23 certain and 4 uncertain occurrences in the Dead Sea Scrolls.

There are no direct equivalents in the other languages of the ancient Near East.[1]

II. Usage.

1. *Secular Usage.* Secular usage is particularly prominent in the case of the noun *pᵉ'ēr.* It always denotes a headdress, possibly a turban. In Ex. 39:28 it refers to the headdress of Aaron and his sons; its meaning in Ezk. 44:18 is similar (the headdress of the Levitical priests). Elsewhere *pᵉ'ēr* is the headdress of a bridegroom (Isa. 61:10), women (3:20), or people in general (Isa. 61:3;[2] also Ezk. 24:17,23).

The vestments of Aaron and his sons are also the subject of Ex. 28:2,40, where *tip'eret̲* appears in combination with *kbd.* Both texts express the notion that these vestments serve to adorn or glorify their wearers. It is also possible, however, that the vestments emphasize the glory and honor of the sanctuary.[3] Est. 1:4 speaks of the splendor and pomp of King Ahasuerus. Ezk. 23:26,42 refer to the jewelry of the whores Oholah and Oholibah. Jer. 13:20 characterizes a flock as being beautiful, while Isa. 44:13 can be interpreted as "beauty of a human being."[4] In Ezk. 24:25 *tip'eret̲* serves to reinforce *mᵉśôś* and conveys no independent meaning.

In Proverbs, apart from 28:12, *tip'eret̲* is always used in a secular sense, as something that brings honor to a person. Thus gray hair is the crown of glory of old age (16:31; cf. 20:29b). Wisdom in general is a beautiful crown (4:9), fathers are the glory of their children (17:6), the glory of youths is their strength (20:29), and it redounds to one's glory to overlook an offense (19:11). Jgs. 4:9 says that Barak will not receive glory if Deborah goes into battle alongside him. In a rhetorical question Isa. 10:15 asks whether an ax "vaunts itself" over the one who wields it.

---

p'r. E. E. Platt, "Jewelry of Bible Times and the Catalogue of Isa 3:18-23," *AUSS* 17 (1979) 71-84, 189-201; D. Vetter, "פאר *p'r* pi. to glorify," *TLOT,* II, 963-64; W. Zimmerli, "Zur Sprache Tritojesajas," *Gottes Offenbarung: GSAT. ThB* 19 (1963), 217-33, esp. 226ff.

1. On the problems raised by suggested etymologies, see the bibliog. in Vetter, 963.
2. See II.3 below.
3. F. Michaeli, *Le livre de l'Exode. CAT* II (1974), 249.
4. K. Elliger, *Deutero-Jesaja. BK* XI/1 (1978), 429.

Ex. 8:5(Eng. v. 9) with *hiṯpā'ēr 'ālay* does not fit in this category. It is unclear whether we are dealing here with a formula of politeness or Moses' acknowledgment of Pharaoh's superior position;[5] the latter might also be meant ironically.

2. *Glorification of an Individual or a People.* Several texts have to do with the glory and resultant pride and arrogance of a particular people or a king. The latter is true in Isa. 10:12, which attacks the haughty pride of the king of Assyria. Isa. 13:19 speaks of Babylon as the glory of kingdoms.[6] Isa. 20:5 censures the boasting of Israel's Egyptian allies; Isa. 28:1,4 speak to the pride of Ephraim, which will be brought low. In contrast to this threat, a later addition in vv. 5-6 declares Yahweh will be a garland of glory to the remnant of his people (Ephraim?). It is probably safe to say that none of the texts from the book of Isaiah listed here goes back to the prophet himself.[7]

Jgs. 7:2 criticizes and checks Israel's self-glorification. According to Zec. 12:7, Yahweh will restrain the pride of Jerusalem by giving victory first to Judah in the time of salvation, and only then to Jerusalem. Jer. 48:17 declares that the glory of Moab will be brought low by Yahweh's intervention. The glory brought the temple by its magnificence is the subject of 1 Ch. 22:5; 2 Ch. 3:6; Ezr. 7:27.

3. *Theological Usage.* In the realm of theological usage, two aspects attract our attention. Some texts speak of the glory that Yahweh bestows on an entity, others of the glory and honor that are Yahweh's. Dt. 26:19 mentions Yahweh's promise to set Israel high above all nations in praise *(tᵉhillâ),* fame *(šēm),* and glory *(tip'ereṯ).* The people as a whole is also the subject of the (early?[8]) text Ps. 149:4, which speaks of the pleasure Yahweh takes in his people, whom he will crown with victory and adorn *(yᵉpā'ēr).*

Jerusalem is the subject of Isa. 52:1; Jer. 33:9; Ezk. 16:12,17, each with a different emphasis. According to Jer. 33:9, the good Yahweh does the city will give the nations occasion for joy, praise, and glory (cf. Dt. 26:19). In an oracle of judgment against faithless Jerusalem, Yahweh recalls how he had adorned her with ornaments, including a beautiful crown (*'ᵃṭereṯ tip'ereṯ,* Ezk. 16:12). Jerusalem removed these ornaments in her faithlessness and turned them into cult objects (16:17). Isa. 52:1 likewise speaks of adorning Jerusalem, summoning her to put on beautiful garments *(biḡḏê tip'artēḵ)* to celebrate her incipient deliverance (similar in context to 61:3). The glory of Zion is also the subject of 60:7,9,19,21; 62:3. Here, however, the glorification of Zion or the temple (60:7) ultimately serves the glory of Yahweh, as 60:21 makes clear. See also 62:3, which presents Jerusalem as a crown of beauty in which Yahweh takes pleasure. Westermann notes the parallel with Babylon.[9]

---

5. For the former see B. S. Childs, *Book of Exodus. OTL* (1974), 128; Vetter, 963. For the latter see Michaeli, *CAT* II, 72.

6. The problems occasioned by the mention of Babylon here are discussed by Wildberger, *Isaiah 13–27* (Eng. trans. 1997), 12-14.

7. Wildberger, *Isaiah 1–12* (Eng. trans. 1991), 423.

8. H. Schmidt, *Die Psalmen. HAT* I/15 (1934), 257.

9. *Isaiah 40–66. OTL* (Eng. trans. 1969), 375, citing Stummer.

The other texts focus on the honor of Yahweh. Ps. 71:8 praises the glory of Yahweh *(tᵉhillâ* and *tip'artekā),* in consequence of Yahweh's deliverance in the context of the lament. Ps. 96:6 is similar: here *tip'eret* appears in conjunction with *'ōz, hāḏār,* and *hôḏ.* Here we may see a reference to Yahweh's theophany and its cultic representation.[10]

Praise of Yahweh's glory also stands in the foreground in 1 Ch. 29:11,13; along with *tip'eret,* v. 11 speaks of *gᵉḏullâ, gᵉḇûrâ, nēṣaḥ,* and *hôḏ,* while v. 13 speaks of *šēm tip'artekā.* In the context of an historical retrospect, Ps. 78:61 describes Yahweh as delivering his glory to captivity — probably a reference to the capture of the ark by the Philistines. Here again *'ōz* appears in the lexical field; the parallelism suggests that *tip'eret* should be understood more in the sense of "strength." The same combination appears also in Ps. 89:18(17), which should likewise be interpreted as speaking of the power and might that Yahweh is to his people. According to Jer. 13:11, Yahweh wishes that his people would cling to him as his fame, praise, and glory *(šēm, tᵉhillâ, tip'eret)* — but they refused.

Yahweh is the subject of *p'r* (hithpael) in Isa. 44:23 and 49:3. Both texts speak of Yahweh's glorification of himself; according to 44:23, this is accomplished through the redemption of Israel (the impf. indicating continuous or recurrent action[11]), and according to 49:3, by the servant of God.

The theological orientation of Prov. 28:12 is at variance with these texts: it deals neither with the glorification of Yahweh nor with that of the people or Zion, but rather with the great joy (*rabbâ tip'eret;* better than "great glory") ensuing when the *ṣaddîqîm* triumph, in contrast to the way people go into hiding with the wicked prevail.

It is clear that the focal point of the theologically oriented texts is the exilic and postexilic period, with special emphasis on the texts in Deutero- and Trito-Isaiah. We also note a concentration of texts in hymns of praise and assurances of salvation; we may therefore safely conclude that the root *p'r* is used especially to express Yahweh's salvific acts on behalf of his people together with his glorification in the light of these acts — ultimately even when the glory of Israel or Zion is the subject of *p'r.*

III. Sirach and Dead Sea Scrolls. Except for 38:6, it is noteworthy that Sirach never uses *p'r* to express the glory and honor of Yahweh, but always to express the glory of human beings. It is one's glory to fear the Lord (9:16; 10:22) and not to depart from the right way (31:10 = 34:10 LXX). Sirach speaks of the honor of Adam (49:16; possibly we may see here "some communication of the glory of the Most High"[12]), the glory of Joseph (49:15), the boasting of Goliath demolished by David (47:4), and the honor of generations past (44:7). Sir. 11:4 (ms. B) and 38:15 warn against arrogance. It is appropriate, however, to be proud after the manner of Elijah (48:4). In combination with *'ᵃṭeret, tip'eret* appears in 6:31 as a symbol for wisdom. The vestments of the high

---

10. A. A. Anderson, *Psalms. NCBC,* 2 vols. (1972), II, 683.
11. Elliger, *BK* XI/1, 452.
12. J. Marböck, *Weisheit in Wandel. BBB* 37 (1971), 148.

priest are described in 45:8 and 50:11, while 50:20 says that after blessing the Israelites the high priest showed himself glorious.[13] Only 38:6 refers directly to the glory of God: God gave skill to human beings that they might glorify him in his power.

The Dead Sea Scrolls use the root *p'r* primarily in theological contexts. There are two exceptions: 1QH 8:22 (cf. 4Q501 1:5; 11QPs^a 22:4) uses *p'r* in a celebration of creation to describe tree boughs(?), probably to indicate their special beauty; 1QM 7:11, describing the vestments of the priests during battle, uses *pry* for an article of clothing, probably a turban.

Other texts deal particularly with the glory and honor of God: 1QS 10:12 (with *qdš* and *kbd* in the lexical field); 1QS 11:15; 4Q511 1:4; 11QPs^a 22:5-6 (with *ṣdq* in the lexical field); 1QM 14:13, where *'rtkh* should probably be supplied with *tp-;* 1QSb 5:19, in conjunction with *hdr.* This last text should be compared especially with 1Q19 13:2, where *tip'eret* is used in the same environment as *hdr* and *kbd.* God's glory rests on lands and seas (11QPs^a 18:7); he will magnify his glory in the face of those who hate his people (4Q160 3-4 2:4). 4QShirShab^a (4Q400) 1:2 extols the God of knowledge, the glory of God's power, the God of gods, the Lord of the saints. The wise understand themselves as heralds of God's glory (4Q510 1:4; cf. 11QPs^a 18:1).

The subject of 4QDibHam (4Q504) 4:12 (cf. Hag. 2:7-9) is the glory *(kbd)* of the people of God, of Zion, the holy city, and *bêt tip'artekâ.* The question is whether the expression that interests us is to be understood as referring to the temple or, like "the holy city," standing in apposition to Zion.[14] The syntactic shape of the clause probably makes its interpretation as an apposition more likely. The crucial point, however, is that once again this verse uses the root *p'r* for the beauty and glory of an entity associated with Yahweh. The same is true in 1QH 13:17, in a hymn of praise: God is extolled for embellishing (*p'r* piel) a man with grandeur. CD 6:7 describes the glory of the converts of Israel. The community clearly connects its own self-understanding with the *tip'eret* of God (11QPs^a 22:5). It understands itself as a community that proclaims God's majesty (18:2), thereby offering true worship (18:7-8). It knows that God bestows his favor on those who give him glory (18:14). Finally, generations of the devout will be God's *tip'eret* (22:4). Overall, it is surprising to find the otherwise infrequent notion of proclamation associated so closely with the root *p'r.*

Some obscure passages, which do not contribute to our investigation, should also be mentioned: 1QH 4:1; 1QM 14:13; 1Q16 3:4.

IV. LXX. A look at the LXX demonstrates the semantic variety of the root *p'r;* it is represented by a wealth of different translations, among which derivatives of *dóxa* stand out.

Hausmann

---

13. For a more detailed discussion see O. Rickenbacher, *Weisheitsperikopen bei Ben Sira. OBO* 1 (1973), 98.

14. M. Baillet, *RB* 68 (1961) 224.

פִּגּוּל *piggûl*

I. 1. Etymology; 2. Occurrences. II. 1. Lev. 7:18 and 19:7; 2. Ezk. 4:14; 3. Isa. 65:4. III. 1. LXX; 2. Dead Sea Scrolls.

I. 1. *Etymology.* The etymology of *piggûl* is unknown. Gesenius notes that both Arab. *faǧala,* "putrefied food," and Eth. *faḥala* may be cited for comparison.[1] Barth proposes Arab. *ǧafala* (with metathesis), "drop dung," as an etymological parallel.[2] Görg has undertaken the interesting notion of connecting the word with Akk. *bugurru* (or *buqurru* or *pug/qurru*), which means "an edible organ of a sacrificial animal" or "a piece of meat,"[3] and Egyp. *grg,* "lie," which can mean "to all appearances not only spoken untruth but also anything wrong, loathsome, or perverted."[4] The combination of noun and article *(pꜣ grg)* could be compared to Heb. *piggûl.* It would be wrong to reject out of hand Görg's theory that "phonetic and semantic contamination may have taken place, i.e., an Egyptian loanword denoting an improper or loathsome circumstance became linked with an inherently neutral term for a specific sacrificial portion through phonetic similarity, despite the latter's Semitic origin and semantic difference."[5] König theorizes that the original meaning was "disintegration = putrefaction" (Ezk. 4:14) and that later the word came to be used as an *abstractum pro concreto,* in the sense of "putrefied meat."[6]

A denominative verb *pgl* is used in the piel in Middle Hebrew and in the pael in Jewish Aramaic and Samaritan in the sense "set a sacrificial portion aside for consumption beyond the prescribed term, thus making it abominable."[7]

2. *Occurrences.* The noun *piggûl* occurs 3 times in the singular (Lev. 7:18; 19:7; Ezk. 4:14) and once in the plural (Isa. 65:4).

II. 1. *Lev. 7:18 and 19:7.* In Lev. 7:18 and 19:7, Elliger translates *piggûl* as "filth"; Kornfeld prefers "unfit."[8] Both Leviticus passages deal with meat from a sacrifice of

---

piggûl. M. Görg, "Piggul und pilaegaeš — Experimente zur Etymologie," *BN* 10 (1979) 7-11; B. Levine, *"Piggûl," EMiqr,* IV (1971), 435-36; W. Paschen, *Rein und Unrein. SANT* 24 (1970).

1. *GesTh,* 1090b. On the Arabic cf. Lane, VI, 2342c-43a; *HAL,* III, 909-10, cites *fağula,* "be limp, withered." The Ethiopic was already rejected by A. Dillmann, *LexLingÄth,* 1347.
2. J. Barth, *Wurzeluntersuchungen zum hebräischen und aramäischen Lexicon* (1902), 36-37.
3. For the former see *CAD,* II, 307a; for the latter, *AHw,* I, 136b.
4. Görg, 9; *WbÄS,* V, 189-90.
5. P. 10.
6. E. König, *Hebräisches und aramäisches Wörterbuch zum AT* (1936), 356.
7. *HAL,* III, 909-10.
8. K. Elliger, *Leviticus. HAT* I/4 (1966), in loc.; Kornfeld, *Levitikus. NEB* (1983), in loc., following EÜ.

well-being (*zeḇaḥ šᵉlāmîm;* RSV "peace offerings") that is not eaten until the third day. But the conclusion that this gives us the basic meaning of *piggûl* may well be a fallacy.[9] Leviticus describes only the special circumstances under which the sacrificial flesh becomes an abomination. It refers to sacrificial flesh that has not yet been consumed on the third day; its holiness changes from that moment on to dangerous uncleanness, on which account it must be burned (7:17).

2. *Ezk. 4:14.* In Ezk. 4:9ff. Yahweh orders Ezekiel to use human dung as fuel to bake bread made from a variety of grains and lentils (cf. the prohibition in Lev. 19:19; Dt. 22:9). The prophet refuses indignantly, declaring that never in his life has he eaten an animal that died of itself *(nᵉḇēlâ)* or was torn *(ṭᵉrēp̄â)* and that *bᵉśar piggûl* has never come into his mouth. In his translation Zimmerli leaves *piggûl* untranslated, because he suspects rightly that the term originally had "a more general meaning which extended beyond" that suggested by the Leviticus passages.[10]

3. *Isa. 65:4.* Isa. 65:1-7 is an invective and threat attacking alien cults and idolatry; vv. 3-4 mention the offering of sacrifices in gardens, the burning of incense on bricks, the eating of swine's flesh, and "the broth of abominable things in their vessels." The Heb. text *ûpᵉraq piggūlîm kᵉlêhem* requires two emendations: with 1QIs[a], LXX, Targ., and Vulg., *Q mᵉraq,* "broth, soup," should replace *K pᵉraq,* "chunk"; and, with 1QIs[a], Targ., and Vulg., the prep. *bᵉ-* (omitted by haplography) should be added to *kᵉlêhem,* yielding the translation "the broth of abominable things is in their vessels." Elliger's emendation of *kᵉlêhem* to *makkoltām* ("their food," following 1 K. 5:25[Eng. v. 11]) can hardly be correct.[11] The *Ketib* probably envisions actual chunks of the three-day-old sacrificial flesh (following Lev. 7:18; 19:7), while the "broth of abominable things" may recall the blood soup *(haimatía)* of the Lacedemonians in Sparta, as suggested by Robertson Smith.[12] In either case the text deals with food antithetic to the cult of Yahweh.

III. 1. LXX. In Lev. 7:18 the LXX translates *piggûl* with *míasma,*[13] in 19:7 with the adj. *áthytos* (only here in LXX), "unfit for sacrifice." In Ezk. 4:14 it translates *bᵉśar piggûl* with *kréas héōlon* (*héōlos,* "stale, flat"; only here in the LXX). In Isa. 65:4 *memolymména* clearly represents *piggulîm* in the rather free translation: "and sacrificial broth, all their vessels are befouled [with it]." Except in Isa. 65:4, where it retains *piggûl,* the Targ. always translates it with *mᵉraḥaq,* "abominable."

2. *Dead Sea Scrolls.* There are only 3 occurrences of *pgwl* in the Dead Sea Scrolls: 11QT 47:14,18; 52:18. The meaning is somewhat more general than in the OT. Maier

---

9. As does *GesB,* 632.

10. W. Zimmerli, *Ezekiel 1. Herm* (Eng. trans. 1979), 150, quotation 171.

11. K. Elliger, *Die Einheit des Tritojesaja. BWANT* III/9 (1928), 21.

12. W. Robertson Smith, *Religion of the Semites* (1899, repr. 1956), 343-44 n. 3. Cf. Pollux 6.57.

13. F. Hauck, *TDNT,* IV, 646: "ritual . . . moral defilement."

translates *pgwl* as "profane" (cf. Jerome, who in the Vulg. uses *profanus* in Lev. 19:7; Isa. 65:4); Yadin as "abominable." 11QT 14:14,18 offer a rigorous interpretation of the law of purity: even the skins of clean animals can be used for transporting goods to the holy city only if they come from animals that have been sacrificed; the skins of animals slaughtered profanely *('wrwt zbḥy pgwlyhmh)* outside the city are considered abominations. 11QT 52:17-18 emphasizes once more that clean but blemished animals may be slaughtered and eaten; but the slaughtering must take place at least 30 *ris* (about 4 mi.) from the sanctuary, for the flesh is the product of profane slaughtering (*bśr pgwl;* cf. Ezk. 4:14).

D. Kellermann

פָּגַע *pāga';* פֶּגַע *pega';* מִפְגָּע *mipgā'*

I. Occurrences. II. Cognates. III. Etymology and Lexical Field. IV. Usage: 1. Qal; 2. Niphal; 3. Hiphil. V. LXX. VI. Derivatives: 1. *pega';* 2. *mipgā'.* VII. Personal Name. VIII. Dead Sea Scrolls.

I. Occurrences. The verb *pāga'* occurs 46 times in the OT: 39 times in the qal, once (Isa. 47:3) in the niphal (cj. for the qal), and 6 times in the hiphil (if the ptcp. in Job 36:32 should not be changed to a noun). Derivatives include the nouns *pega'* (once) and *mipgā'* (once plus a cj.). The root appears also in the theophorous PN *pag'î'ēl* (5 times).

II. Cognates. The root is attested only in Northwest Semitic, especially the Aramaic branch, and in Arabic: Pun. and Imperial Aram. *pg',* qal "encounter," piel "fulfill(?) (a vow)";[1] Syr. *p^ega'* (always with the prep. *b*), "encounter (a person), reach (a place), come upon, befall (illness, misfortune), attack, resist"; Middle Heb. *pāga',* "come upon, meet," often "attack,"[2] niphal "be stricken," often "be beset (by evil spirits or demons)"; Jewish Aram. *p^ega',* "encounter, meet";[3] Arab. *faǧa'a,* "inflict suffering and grief, afflict, . . . II, torment, torture, distress."[4] A related root *faǧa'a* puts more emphasis on the aspect of surprise, being closer in meaning to Syr. *p^ega'* and Middle Heb. *pāga':* I and III, "come unexpectedly (upon someone), confront (someone) suddenly, (with *bi*) take by surprise, attack (someone)."[5]

Garbini has identified a specialized meaning of *pg'* as a sacrificial term in Neo-Punic inscriptions: on account of its basic meaning "encounter, reach," he compares

1. *DNSI,* II, 900-901.
2. Levy, *WTM,* IV, 7.
3. Ibid.
4. Wehr, 697.
5. Ibid.

Pun. *pg'* to the synonymous Hebrew root *qrb,* the hiphil of which means "offer (sacrifice)" and concludes that the piel means "offer."[6]

III. Etymology and Lexical Field. The Sem. root *pg'* describes movement toward a place (object) or person. This movement may be unintentional (Syr. *men pᵉg'ā*) or intentional; if the latter, it is usually sudden and violent; cf. Arab. *faǧ'atan* or *fuǧā'atan,* "unexpectedly, suddenly." Finally, positive, negative (hostile), and neutral intention or effect must be differentiated. The verb "strike" or "hit" approximates most closely the basic meaning and variety of usage of Heb. *pāga'*.

The senses conveyed by the qal (G stem) can be categorized as follows:

1. unintentional
   1.1 neutral
      1.1.a place: (1) hit = arrive at; (2) hit = touch
      1.1.b person (animal): hit upon = meet, encounter (cf. the related root *pāgaš*)
   1.2 negative
      1.2.a person: strike out at = attack
      1.2.b animal (beast of prey [bear]): strike down = slay
2. Intentional (only of persons)
   2.1 negative
      2.1.a strike down (by sword) = kill
      2.1.b strike down (by sword or pestilence) = kill (God as subj.)
      2.1.c hit = jostle, upset, get rid of
   2.2 positive: strike = press someone to do something (for the benefit of another person), i.e., importune.

For the most part (in Syriac always), the object is introduced by *bᵉ*.

IV. Usage. 1. *Qal* 1.1.a.(1). The story of the holy site of Bethel recounts how Jacob unintentionally and unknowingly comes to *(bᵉ)* this place (Gen. 28:11).

1.1.a.(2). The verb *pāga'* has a specialized meaning in the idiom *pāga' gᵉḇûl bᵉ* used in Josh. (15)16–19 to define the borders of the tribal territories (except in the case of Judah and Benjamin).

Depending on the actual topography, many different verbs expressing motion or change of place are used to describe the course of a boundary *(gᵉḇûl): yāṣā', hālaḵ, 'āḇar, 'ālâ, yārad, sāḇaḇ, pānâ, tā'ar, šûḇ.*[7] When the boundary touches a particular place, 9 times *pāga' bᵉ* is used (LXX *synápsei* [except Josh. 16:7, *eleúsetai*]). The place may be a city (Jericho, 16:7; Dabbesheth, 19:11), a mountain (Tabor, 19:22; Car-

6. G. Garbini, "Terminologia sacrificiale fenicia: pg'," *BeO* 21 (1979) 109-13. Cf. J. G. Février, *JA* 243 (1955) 60; 255 (1967) 62: "sacrifice."

7. See O. Bächli, *ZDPV* 89 (1973) 3-5.

mel, 19:26), a watercourse (the wadi east of Jokneam, 19:11 [only here is *pāga‘* surprisingly construed with *'el,* possibly a scribal error for *pōneh 'el* — cf. 15:7; Simons prefers to follow the LXX, deleting *ûpāga‘* and reading "Dabbesheth, near [*'el*] . . ."];[8] also [as the obj. of *pāga‘*] the rivers Libnath [19:26] and Jordan [19:34]), or a tribal territory (Asher, 17:10; 19:34; Zebulun, 19:27,34; Issachar, 17:10; Judah, 19:34).

1.1.b. It is also by chance that Jacob discovers Mahanaim, "God's camp," where "angels of Elohim" meet him (Gen. 32:2: *wayyip̱g^e‘û-ḇô*); the account does not characterize this encounter as either hostile (like 32:25ff.) or friendly; cf. the question in Josh. 5:13 in an analogous situation.

After their futile negotiations with Pharaoh, the Israelite supervisors come upon Moses and Aaron (Ex. 5:20). Also unexpected, although predicted by Samuel, is the encounter of Saul with a company of prophets at Gibeah (1 S. 10:5). The ethos of the Covenant Code requires whoever happens upon a stray ox or donkey belonging to an enemy to bring it back to its owner (Ex. 23:4).

The meaning of *pāga‘* is obscure in Isa. 64:4a(Eng. v. 5a), which appears out of place in the context of a communal lament and is therefore probably secondary; it is also textually corrupt. Following LXX *synantḗsetai* and Vulg. *occuristi, HAL* associates it with the meaning "meet." In the same vein, Westermann translates: "Would that you would meet those who do right."[9] He interprets this wish as a secondary interpolation expressing the pious hope that God will find righteous people on earth when he tears open the heavens and comes down (63:20[64:1]).[10] An otherwise unattested meaning "meet halfway, accommodate, look after" has also been proposed;[11] cf. EÜ: "Would that you would meet halfway those who do what is right."

1.2.a. An encounter between two enemies may be accidental, but its negative consequence are predictable. For example, an avenger of blood may kill a murderer whenever they meet. To avoid being killed or captured, Rahab urges the Israelite spies to flee to the hills so that their pursuers may not come upon them (Josh. 2:16).

1.2.b. An encounter with a beast of prey also has evil consequences. According to the simile in Am. 5:19 (probably proverbial), whoever flees from a lion runs inescapably into disaster, being met by a bear. The context — the calamitous day of Yahweh — presupposes that the meeting with the bear refers less to the accidental encounter (Vulg. *occurat ei ursus; GesB* glosses *pāga‘* here as "come upon, encounter") than to the deadly blow of the bear's paw (LXX *kaí empésę autǭ hē árkos; HAL,* "assault someone," is too weak).

2.1.a. Often *pāga‘* occurs with the specialized meaning (always with *b^e*) "strike down," i.e., "kill with the sword." This is clear from 1 K. 2:32, where the statement that Joab "attacked" two men is made more precise in synonymous parallelism: *wayyahargēm baḥereḇ,* "and he killed them with the sword." This manner of death is also intended by the Midianite princes Zebah and Zalmunna when they say to Joshua, "Come

8. J. Simons, *GTTOT,* §329, p. 181; §332, p. 188 n. 173.

9. C. Westermann, *Jesaja 40–66. ATD* 19², 310 (not in Eng. trans., which follows RSV).

10. Westermann, *Isaiah 40–66. OTL* (Eng. trans. 1969), 396.

11. *GesB.*

and kill us" (Jgs. 8:21; cf. v. 20). Because Saul's servants refused to kill the priests of Nob, Doeg the Edomite slays them (par. *mûṯ* hiphil, 1 S. 22:17-18). At David's command, one of his young men strikes down the man who dared to kill Saul, the anointed of Yahweh (par. *wayyakkēhû,* 2 S. 1:15). When Solomon, to consolidate his rule, settles accounts with his enemies and the enemies of David, he sends Benaiah to strike down Adonijah (1 K. 2:25), Joab (2:29,31,34 [*wayyipga'-bô wayᵉmiṯēhû*]), and Shimei (2:46).

In the extended sense, *pāga'* means "slay" (by the sword or other means). In Jgs. 15:12, when the men of Judah bind Samson to give him into the hands of the Philistines, he asks them not to "strike him down" (Vulg. *occidatis;* NRSV "attack"); they therefore promise not to "kill" him (*mûṯ* hiphil). The verb has the same meaning in Jgs. 18:25, where Micah and his followers are warned that if they make trouble the aroused Danites will strike them (LXX *apantḗsōsin;* Vulg. *veniant ad;* NRSV "attack") and they will "lose their lives" (*'āsap̱ nep̱eš).*

2.1.b. Only once is God the subject of *pāga':* in Ex. 5:3 the Israelites fear that Yahweh will slay them "with pestilence or sword" (EÜ "punish"; LXX impersonal: *mḗpote synantḗsę̄ hēmín thánatos ḗ phónos*) if they do not go into the wilderness to sacrifice to him.

2.1.c. The verb *pāga'* can also refer to hostile, vexatious behavior in order to "be done with" someone and drive him or her away. In Ruth 2:22, for example, Naomi advises Ruth to glean only with the young women of Boaz: in another field she might be "bothered" (LXX simply "encountered": *apantḗsontaí soi;* but cf. Vulg. *resistat tibi*), i.e., "jostled" and driven from her source of food (*GesB:* "set upon with intent to injure"; *HAL:* "molest a woman").

2.2. In a positive sense *pāga'* can mean to "elbow someone in the ribs" (figuratively) to get attention in order to importune them (God or a human being: with *bᵉ*) for something, to "press" for something (cf. Arab. *faǧa'a,* "afflict, annoy").

The wicked find it profitless, however, to serve the Almighty and assault God with their prayers (Job 21:15). When an irrevocable sentence has been pronounced upon the apostate people, it is pointless for Jeremiah to importune God with entreaties (Jer. 7:16). In Jer. 27:18 Jeremiah challenges the false prophets to demonstrate the truth of their words by entreating God not to allow the temple vessels left behind in 597 B.C.E. to go to Babylon as well.

Abraham asks the citizens of Hebron to entreat Aaron to sell him the cave of Machpelah as a burying place for Sarah (Gen. 23:8). Ruth tells Naomi not to press her to return to Moab (Ruth 1:16).

2. *Niphal.* The niphal is not attested in the MT. There is a possible occurrence in Isa. 47:3b, where many scholars vocalize MT *'epga'* (qal) as *'eppāga'* (niphal). Others follow the Vulg. in reading the 3rd person sg. qal impf. or propose a different verbal root *(pr').* Since the noun *'āḏām* has also come under suspicion, the many conjectural emendations and proposed translations must be evaluated strictly on the basis of the context.

Ch. 47 is the only poem in Deutero-Isaiah belonging to the genre of oracles against foreign nations. Its subject matter is the fall of Babylon. The one certain observation is that Yahweh will take vengeance on the city (v. 3b). Consequently the following *wᵉlō' 'epga' 'āḏām* is probably a qualification of this action. Following the Vulg. *(et non resistet mihi homo)* and Symmachus *(kaí ouk antistḗsetaí moi ánthrōpos), BHS* proposes the 3rd person sg. qal impf. *yipga'* (*HAL:* "and no one can come pleading with me"). The niphal *'eppāga',* however, seems more persuasive.[12] This is also the preference of *HAL:* "I will not (be made to) yield to any petition" (cf. Jer. 27:18). This is also the translation proposed by Köhler: "'I take vengeance inexorable,' says [reading *'āmar* for *'āḏām*] our redeemer."[13]

3. *Hiphil.* The hiphil conveys two distinct meanings:

a. Causative: "cause to strike." Yahweh causes the punishment for the iniquity (*'āwōn)* of Israel to strike *(bᵉ)* the servant of God (Isa. 53:6), so that he suffers vicariously for the people.

b. Transitive in the sense of the qal: "entreat passionately (on behalf of someone)," i.e., intercede for someone.[14] This second sense appears in v. 12 of the same poem, where the servant intercedes for *(lᵉ)* the transgressors. Delitzsch speaks here of an intensive equivalent to the qal: "press forward with entreaty."[15] Jeremiah interceded with *(bᵉ)* Yahweh on behalf of the enemy (Jer. 15:11). This is also the sense in Jer. 36:25 (contrary to *HAL,* which distinguishes "2. intercede for [someone]" and "3. urge someone [with entreaties]"), where Elnathan, Delaiah, and Gemariah implore the king not to burn the scroll. In Isa. 59:16 the context suggests that the ptcp. *mapgîa'* refers to intervention with deeds rather than words.[16]

The participle in Job 36:32 is discussed in VI.2 below.

V. LXX. The LXX usually translates the qal of *pāga'* (in part imprecisely or erroneously) with *apantáō* (14 times) or *synantáō* (8 times). It makes a more precise distinction only in 1 K. 2, where it uses *anairéō* 4 times (and *apantáō* 6 times — cf., e.g., v. 31 with v. 34) for "strike down (with the sword),"[17] and Josh. 17 and 19, where it uses *synáptō* consistently (7 times; but *érchomai* in Josh. 16:7) for "border on."[18] When the meaning is "implore,"[19] it uses *empíptō* (Am. 5:19), *laléō* (Gen. 23:8), and *prosérchomai* (Jer. 7:16) — along with 3 instances of *apantáō*.

VI. Derivatives.

1. *pega'.* The noun *pega'* means a "stroke" or "blow" in a negative sense. It may be (a) unintentional, a stroke of fate or a mishap, or (b) intentional, in the form of a hostile

12. Proposed by H. Oort, *Textus Hebraici emendationes* (1900).

13. L. Köhler, *Deuterojesaja stilkritisch untersucht. BZAW* 37 (1923), 32. This reading is also adopted by C. Westermann, *Isaiah 40–66. OTL* (Eng. trans. 1969), 186; similarly B. Duhm, *Das Buch Jesaja. HKAT* III/1 (⁵1968), 355; G. Fohrer, *Das Buch Jesaja. ZBK* XIX/3 (1964), 104; EÜ.

14. G. Bergsträsser, *Hebräische Grammatik,* 2 vols. (1918-29), II, §§19-20.

15. F. Delitzsch, *Isaiah. KD* (Eng. trans. 1954), II, 340.

16. Cf. ibid., 404.

17. See IV.2.1.a above.

18. See IV.1.1.a.(2) above.

19. See IV.2.2 above.

and life-threatening attack. In Middle Hebrew *pega'* means "what befalls someone, incident, *týchē*," while *pig'ā'* means "attack, trouble."[20]

a. According to Eccl. 9:11, human efforts and hopes are often thwarted by the unforeseen and unpredictable factors of time and *pega'* (LXX *apántēma*), i.e., chance,[21] that can befall anyone.

b. When Solomon had defeated all his political opponents, he did not need to fear any adversary *(śāṭān)* or malicious attack *(pega' rā')* (1 K. 5:18[14]).

2. *mipgā'*. The derived noun *mipgā'* with *m* preformative denotes the place *(mem locale)* where painful blows strike. In Job 7:20 long-suffering Job asks why he has become the focus of God's attacks (LXX *katenteuktḗ*). Perhaps we have here the same metaphor as in 16:12 (cf. also Lam. 3:12), where Job feels like a target *(maṭṭārâ)* for the arrows of God's wrath (cf. 6:4; Ps. 38:3[2]).

Many scholars suggest the same meaning also in the difficult text Job 36:32, emending the hiphil ptcp. *mapgîa'* to *mipgā'*. The passage probably means that God takes (reading *niśśâ* for *nissâ*)[22] the lightning (*'ôr;* same meaning in 37:3,15) in his hands and commands it (reading *'ālāyw* for *'āleyhā*) to strike its "mark" (cf. Wis. 5:21; Bar. 6:62). The notion that Yahweh hurls lightning bolts against his enemies is not attested elsewhere in the OT; the causative meaning of the hiphil ("cause to strike") probably rules it out here as well.

VII. Personal Name. The root *pg'* also appears in the theophorous name *pag'î'ēl* (LXX *Phagaiēl*), leader *(nāśî')* of the tribe of Asher (Nu. 1:13; 2:27; 7:72,77; 10:26).

This verb is probably also an element of the theophorous name *pg'qws,* which occurs twice (no. 5 and 9) on ostracon no. 6043 from Ezion-geber, dated by paleographic evidence from the 6th century B.C.E. and interpreted by Albright as "Entreat Qaus," "Qaus is my prayer," or "Qaus is entreated."[23] In the short form *pg'* the name may also occur in l. 4 of Samaria ostracon no. 1, as well as in four Thamudic inscriptions from the Persian period.[24] Noth is unable to assign an intelligible meaning to the biblical name *pag'î'ēl.*[25] A meaning "El is terrible," based on Arab. *fāǧî',* is considered highly unlikely by *HAL,* which suggests instead "the one pleading with El." According to Schult, theophorous names do not always express praise or thanks to God; on the basis of Arab. *faǧa'a,* "inflict suffering and grief," he therefore proposes the meaning "God has afflicted with grief."[26]

---

20. Levy, *WTM,* IV, 7.
21. A. Lauha, *Kohelet. BK* XIX (1978), 172: "fate."
22. G. Fohrer, *Das Buch Hiob. KAT* 16 (1963), 479.
23. Reading uncertain; so read by W. F. Albright, *BASOR* 82 (1941) 13.
24. Cf. Ryckmans, I, 177: *fāği',* "terrible."
25. M. Noth, *IPN,* 254, no. 1128.
26. H. Schult, "Vergleichende Studien zur alttestamentlichen Namenkunde" (diss., Bonn, 1967), 114.

VIII. Dead Sea Scrolls. A 3rd person fem. sg. verbal form *wtpg'* appears once in the hymns (1QH fr. 4:16).[27] In another passage (1QH 17:5) we find the nominal form *pwg'wt,* not attested in the OT (probably par. to *n^e^gî'îm,* "afflictions," in l. 8); cf. the suffixed Christian Palestinian nominal form *pgw'ty,* "adversity," for *magg^e^pōṯay* in Ex. 9:14.[28]

In 4Q504 (4QDibHam^a^) 1-2, 4:12-13, the combination *'ên śāṭān w^e^'ên pega' rā',* "adversary" and "malicious attack," is borrowed from 1 K. 5:18(4) and contrasted with *šlwm wbrkh,* "peace and blessing."[29]

Mental and physical disabilities were clearly ascribed to demonic influence, since 4Q510 (4QShir^a^) 1:6 speaks of "those who strike unexpectedly" (*pwg'ym* [act. ptcp.]). (Cf. Middle Heb. *p^e^gā'îm/n* or *p^e^gô'în,* "assailing demons, tormenting spirits";[30] alongside demons [*šdym*], Targ. Est. II on 1:2 speaks of *pg'ym*[31].) There is also a verbal form *ypg'w* in 4Q511 11:4: "to confound the spirit of understanding, to ravage their heart." According to 11QPs^a^ 27:10, David composed four songs *(šyr)* "to sing over the 'stricken'" (pass. ptcp. *pgw'ym;* cf. also the fragmentary *wpgw'*[ ] in 4:2 of the same document, with presumably the same form and meaning; also *hpgw'ym* in 4Q511 11:8), those possessed or assailed by evil spirits (cf. Middle Heb. *pāga'* niphal, "be assailed by tormenting spirits, demons"[32]). Seybold interprets the expression as referring to "struck" and stringed instruments.[33] Ps. 91, probably already used at Qumran to ward off demons, is called by rabbinic tradition *šyr šl pg'ym/pgw'yn.*[34]

Maiberger

---

27. S. Holm-Nielsen, *Hodayot. AcThD* 2 (1960), 264: "and this affecteth Thy servant."
28. F. Schulthess, *Lexicon Syropalaestinum* (1903), 154.
29. See VI.1.b above.
30. Levy, *WTM,* IV, 7.
31. St.-B., IV/1, 501: "assailers."
32. Levy, *WTM,* IV, 7.
33. K. Seybold, *Die Psalmen. Urban Taschenbuch* 382 (1986), 201 n. 3.
34. For Qumran see J. P. M. van der Ploeg, "Un petit rouleau de psaumes apocryphes (11QPsAp^a^)," in G. Jeremias et al., eds., *Tradition und Glaube. FS K. G. Kuhn* (1972), 128-39, esp. 128-29. For rabbinic tradition see Bab. *Shebuot* 15b; Jer. *Erubin* 10.26c; Jer. *Shabbat* 6.8b.

פָּגַר *pāgar;* פֶּגֶר *peger*

I. *pāgar:* 1. Etymology and Meaning; 2. OT Usage; 3. Gen. 15:11. II. *peger:* 1. Semitic; 2. OT Usage; 3. Dead Sea Scrolls; 4. LXX. III. Ezk. 43:7,9: 1. Corpse; 2. Stela; 3. Sacrifice.

I. *pāgar.*

1. *Etymology and Meaning.* The lexemes *pāgar,* "be faint, tired," and *peger,* "corpse," probably have nothing to do with each other etymologically (contra *GesB* and *HAL,* which treat the latter as a derivative of the former). Obermann defined Heb. *pāgar* as a denominative from Sem. *pgr,* "unanimated, immovable matter; a lifeless, rigid mass"; in Hebrew, Aramaic, and Akkadian, this became "corpse," and in Ugaritic, "stone, heap of stones, altar." He therefore derived the meaning "be petrified" for the piel.[1]

Arabic may cast some light on the basic meaning of *pāgar.* Here *fağara* means "cleave"; the derivative *fağr,* for example, means "daybreak"; cf. also OSA *fgr,* "let water flow freely."[2] Intransitively, *fağara* reflects a "breach" of morality: "act immorally, sin, live licentiously."[3] Both aspects are also attested in Jewish Aramaic and Middle Hebrew. Transitively, *p^egar* means "destroy, demolish"[4] (cf. *pa/igrā',* "damage, loss," which has no etymological connection with *pa/igrā',* "corpse"). With respect to the basic meaning "cleave, break," the intransitive verb refers in the first instance to a physical breakdown, but it can also refer to psychic and moral breakdown. The latter sense is probably reflected in Jewish Aram. *p^egar,* "be idle, indolent";[5] cf. Syr. *b^egar,* "be weak, feeble, decrepit, exhausted."

A form *tpgr* (3rd person fem. sg. impf. pael?) appears in a fragmentary context in the Deir ʿAllā texts; it may mean "to be weak, to be faint (?)."[6]

2. *OT Usage.* This is also the meaning of the Hebrew verb *pāgar,* which appears only twice (in the piel, 1 S. 30:10,21). When David was pursuing the Amalekites, two

---

pāgar. M. Dietrich, O. Loretz, and J. Sanmartín, "*PGR* im Ugaritischen," *UF* 5 (1973) 289-91; R. Dussaud, "Deux stèles de Ras Shamra portant une dédicace au dieu Dagon," *Syr* 16 (1935) 177-80; J. H. Ebach, "*PGR* = (Toten-)Opfer?" *UF* 3 (1971) 365-68; K. Galling, "Erwägungen zum Stelenheiligtum von Hazor," *ZDPV* 75 (1959) 1-13; D. Neiman, "*PGR:* A Canaanite Cult-Object in the OT," *JBL* 67 (1948) 55-60; J. Obermann, "Votive Inscriptions from Ras Shamra," *JAOS* 61 (1941) 31-45, esp. 38-40.

1. P. 39 n. 14.
2. Biella, 400.
3. Wehr, 697.
4. *WTM,* IV, 7-8.
5. Ibid., 8.
6. Combination V, fr. c,3. See *ATDA,* 307; cf. 175 and 256-57.

hundred men stayed behind at Wadi Besor because they were too "weakened" or "exhausted" (*piggᵉrû* [intransitive][7]) to continue chasing the enemy.

3. *Gen. 15:11.* The noun *peger* in Gen. 15:11 is probably derived from transitive *pāgar,* "cleave, break," meaning "something broken off, piece." This meaning is supported by the context and the fact that elsewhere *peger* refers only to a human corpse.[8] Abram "cuts in two" or "divides" *(wayᵉbattēr)* the sacrificial animals and lays the pieces *(beṯer)* over against each other (v. 10). When the text goes on to say that birds of prey came down on the *pᵉgārîm,* in the context of this particular ritual (cf. Jer. 34:18) the term probably conveys the meaning of "pieces" *(peger* used as a synonym for *beṯer;* the LXX therefore adds to *tá sṓmata* the explanatory *tá dichotomḗmata autṓn)* rather than "carcasses" (NRSV; cf. Vulg. *cadavera*), which would be superfluous here.

II. *peger.*

1. *Semitic.* The noun *peger* is found in Northeast and Northwest Semitic, but not in Southwest Semitic (Arabic, Ethiopic).

a. *Body.* In Akkadian, *pagru(m)* means "body," either living (but only of a human being; in Old Babylonian, *pagru* also serves as the reflexive pronoun) or dead (either of a human being ["corpse"] or an animal ["carcass"]).[9] The lexeme has the widest semantic range in Syriac, where it has also given rise to several derivatives (e.g., *eṯpaggar,* "was incarnate").[10] In the OT Syr. *pagrā'* is used mostly for the dead body of a human being (*gᵉwîyâ,* 1 S. 31:12) or an animal (*nᵉḇēlâ,* Lev. 7:24; 11:8,11,24,25,27). In Mandaic a dualistic ideology devalued the body, considering it the prison of the soul; therefore *pagra* usually conveys the notion of the material and mortal body.[11]

b. *Corpse.* In Old Aramaic, Imperial Aramaic, and Palmyrene, by contrast, *pgr* is used only for a dead body.[12] The formulaic expression *pgr . . . 'l pgr,* "corpse upon corpse," appears in two treaties from Sefire in connection with a battle.[13] In Jewish Aramaic, too, *pa/igrā'* means only "corpse."[14] The same is true of Heb. and Middle Heb. *peger.* We are probably dealing here with a semantic development somewhat similar to that of Eng. "corpse," which originally could mean simply "body," living or dead.

2. *OT Usage.* For "body" Hebrew uses → גויה *gᵉwiyyâ;* like Akk. *pagru,* this word denotes both the living body of a human (Gen. 47:18; Neh. 9:37) or of a heavenly being (Ezk. 1:11,23; Dnl. 10:6) and the dead body of a human (1 S. 31:10,12; cf. *gûpâ* par. in

7. *HP,* 52, 54.
8. Contra *HAL,* III, 911: "b) of animals Gn 15:11."
9. *AHw,* II, 809.
10. R. Payne Smith, *Thesaurus Syriacus,* 2 vols. (1879-1901), II, 3033-34.
11. *MdD,* 359.
12. *DNSI,* II, 901.
13. *KAI* 222B.30; 223B.11; context damaged.
14. *WTM,* IV, 8.

1 Ch. 10:12) or animal (Jgs. 14:8-9, where *mappelet* is also used for an animal carcass). By contrast, → נבלה *nᵉbēlâ* refers only to the dead body of a human or animal.

a. *Pejorative Connotations.* The noun *peger* (18 times) refers only to a human corpse; each instance involves death by violence, so that in Hebrew this term has pejorative connotations. The collective sg. or the pl. *pᵉgārîm* frequently parallels the "killed" (*hᵃrugîm,* Isa. 14:19) or "slain" (*ḥᵃlālîm,* Isa. 34:3; Jer. 41:9; Ezk. 6:5; Nah. 3:3) or appears in conjunction with the verb "smite" (*nkh* hiphil, 2 K. 19:35 = Isa. 37:36; Jer. 33:5; 41:9).

The corpses in question are disfigured and dishonored, simply "cast out" (Am. 8:3; Isa. 34:3; cf. Isa. 14:19; Jer. 36:30) without burial, so that their stench rises (Isa. 34:3); they are thrown unceremoniously into a cistern instead of being laid to rest in a tomb (Jer. 41:9), given to the birds and wild animals for food (1 S. 17:46), strewn about everywhere (Nah. 3:3), trampled underfoot (*peger mûbās,* Isa. 14:19; the text is clearly corrupt; the suggested image of "trampled carcass"[15] is probably inaccurate because of the animal carcass), abhorrent to all (Isa. 66:24). The noun *peger* appears primarily in the context of battle; the violent death is usually the result of God's punishment.

b. *Violent Death.* Victims of battle are the subject of 1 S. 17:46 (*peger* used collectively for the corpses of the Philistines) and 2 Ch. 20:24 (the corpses of the Ammonites, Moabites, and inhabitants of Mt. Seir; *BHS* emends *pᵉgārîm* in v. 25 to *bᵉgāḏîm,* probably correctly [Vulg. *vestes;* LXX *skýla*]). Jer. 41:9 deals with the corpses of victims of a perfidious murder.

In a secondary passage describing the borders of Jerusalem, Jer. 31:40 mentions a "valley of corpses" (*ʿēmeq happᵉgārîm).* The topographical information suggests a location on the western or southern edge of city; it is probably identical with the Valley of Ben-Hinnom. Weiser believes that *happᵉgārîm wᵉhaddešen* is probably a later gloss on *hāʿēmeq;*[16] the entire phrase is omitted by the LXX. The name probably derives from the corpses of children sacrificed to Moloch on Topheth (Isa. 30:33; Jer. 7:31; 19:5; 32:35).[17] Therefore, according to Jer. 7:32 (cf. 19:6,11), this valley will be called the Valley of Slaughter (*gêʾ hahᵃrēḡâ)* and the dead will be buried in Topheth.

c. *Divine Punishment.* The other texts where *peger* occurs all have to do with divine punishment. Because the Israelites constantly complained during their wandering in the wilderness, they would be punished by not being allowed to enter the promised land: their dead bodies will "fall" in the wilderness (Nu. 14:29,32; *yippᵉlû* has negative connotations here).[18] Breaking the covenant and sinning are punished by death: in Lev. 26:30, a secondary passage cursing the disobedient,[19] God threatens to destroy their high places and incense altars and to heap their corpses on the corpses of their idols (*pigrê gillûlêḵem).* Since *peger* probably also means "memorial stela" (Obermann

15. H. Wildberger, *Isaiah 13–27* (Eng. trans. 1997), 42, 71.
16. A. Weiser, *Jeremia. ATD* 20/21 (⁶1969), 290.
17. See also the theory of Ebach discussed below (III.3).
18. → נפל *nāpal.*
19. K. Elliger, *Leviticus. HAT* I/4 (1966), 377.

translates *pigrê gillûlêḵem* as "the stone-heaps of your idols"; Galling: "heap your stelae on the stelae of your idols; Kornfeld interprets the expression as "shattered statues and images"), Noth believes that the text plays on the ambiguity of the term.[20] Metaphorical usage is more likely, however, since Jer. 16:18 also speaks of the "corpses" or "carcasses" of "their detestable idols" *(niḇlaṯ šiqqûṣêhem),*[21] and polemical texts often mock idols as "dead" objects (Ps. 115:4-8; 135:15-18; Dt. 4:28; Isa. 44:9-20; Dnl. 14:7; Ep. Jer. 6:70-72 [v. 70: "the gods are like a corpse [Gk. *nekrǭ*]"; Wis. 15:5: "the lifeless form of a dead image" [Gk. *nekrás eikónos eídos ápnoun*]). In Ezk. 6:5, too, Yahweh threatens to lay the corpses of the idolaters in front of their idols *(gillûlêhem)* (probably a secondary addition based on Lev. 26:30, repeating what has already been said in v. 4b; not in LXX).

Because of the sins of Jerusalem, during the Chaldeans' siege of the city Yahweh slew its inhabitants in his anger and wrath, filling the houses with corpses (Jer. 33:5). The word of the Lord appended to the fourth vision of Amos also speaks of God's dire punishment: dead bodies are cast about everywhere (Am. 8:3).

In oracles against the nations, *peḡer* also signalizes horrific slaughter. In the terrible punishment visited on Edom, corpses are cast out so that their stench rises to the heavens (Isa. 34:3); when Nineveh is destroyed the "heap of corpses" *(kōḇeḏ pāḡer)* is so huge that people stumble over it (Nah. 3:3). A taunt song mocking the king of Babylon describes the tyrant's wretched and ignominious end: his body lies unburied under a heap of corpses and is trampled underfoot (Isa. 14:19). The sudden destruction of the Assyrian army (by an epidemic?), bordering on a miracle, is interpreted as divine punishment for Sennacherib's arrogance: the angel of the Lord struck down 185,000 men, so that the enemy was "all dead bodies" (*peḡārîm mēṯîm,* tautology for emphasis, 2 K. 19:35 = Isa. 37:36). Particularly grandiose and vivid is the eschatological vision of the final destruction of God's enemies in Isa. 66:24, a very late addition at the end of Trito-Isaiah: their corpses litter the countryside and will be "an abhorrence [*dērā'ôn;* cf. Dnl. 12:2] to all flesh."

3. *Dead Sea Scrolls.* There are 4 occurrences of *peḡer* in the Dead Sea Scrolls; its usage is similar to that in the OT. In the eschatological battle, the corpses of the enemy will be "smashed" *(rûṭṭešû)* by the hand of God and lie unburied (1QM 11:1; cf. 4QM[a] 14-15:9), so that the sons of light must cleanse their garments of the blood of the "guilty corpses" *(pigrê hā'ašmâ)* (1QM 14:3; cf. also 4QpNah 2:6, commenting on Nah. 3:3 in the light of Am. 8:3).

4. *LXX.* The LXX uses a variety of translations for *peḡer* and *peḡārîm.* The most frequent is *tá kṓla* (Lev. 26:30 [twice]; Nu. 14:29,32,33; Isa. 66:24; 1 S. 17:46 [collective: *tó kṓla*]); *nekroí* is also used several times (Isa. 34:3; Jer. 33:5; 2 Ch. 20:24; Isa. 14:19

---

20. See III.2 below; Obermann, 39 n. 14; Galling, 11; W. Kornfeld, *Levitikus. NEB* (1983), 107; M. Noth, *Leviticus. OTL* (Eng. trans. [2]1977), 200.

21. For "corpses" see Elliger; for "carcasses" see NRSV.

[sg.]). Twice we find *tá sṓmata* (2 K. 19:35 = Isa. 37:36; also Gen. 15:11) and once each *peptōkṓs* (Am. 8:3) and *ptṓsis* (Nah. 3:3). In 2 Ch. 20:25 the LXX reads *skýla* (cj.). The texts Jer. 31:40; 41:9; and Ezk. 6:5 are not represented in the LXX.

III. Ezk. 43:7,9. Considerable debate surrounds the meaning of *peg̱er* in the passage in Ezekiel's temple vision where the glory of the Lord fills the new temple and the Israelites are commanded never again to defile this holy dwelling place of Yahweh "by their whoring" *(bizᵉnûṯām)* and "by the *pig̱rê* of their kings *bāmôṯām*" (Ezk. 43:7). Not only is the meaning of *pᵉg̱ārîm* controverted, but so is that of the synsemantic expression *bāmôṯām,* which is syntactically awkward. Since the construct phrase *ûpig̱rê malḵêhem* in clear parallelism with *zᵉnûṯām* reappears in v. 9, but without the addition of *bāmôṯām,* the latter is either redundant or to be supplied in v. 9 on the basis of v. 7 (Zimmerli even suggests deleting *bmwtm* as dittography with the following *bttm*).[22]

The LXX paraphrases *peg̱er* with *kaí en toís phónois,* "with the murders" *(tṓn hēgouménōn);* Fohrer therefore conjectures *ûḇᵉhargām* for *ûpig̱rê,* reads *bᵉṯôḵām (en mesǭ autṓn)* instead of *bāmôṯām,* and translates the passage: ". . . with their whoring and their killing in their midst," interpreting "whoring" as cultic sins and "killing" as ethical sins.[23] The Vulg. associates *peg̱er* with Aram. *pᵉg̱ar,* "destroy, demolish":[24] *et in ruinis regum suorum;* but this makes little sense. The Vulg. also resolves the syntactic tension of *bmwtm* (which, like the Masoretes, it derives from *bāmâ,* "hill, high place") by introducing a copula: *et in excelsis.*

1. *Corpse.* The problem presented by *bāmôṯām* is that "high places" would seem to be out of place in association with the temple precincts, while the conjectural emendation *bᵉmôṯām* is a superfluous tautology in conjunction with *pᵉg̱ārîm,* "corpses"; Ehrlich therefore proposed deleting the word as a gloss.[25] The traditional translation "by the corpses of their kings" led to the theory that the temple was defiled by the presence of several royal tombs in the close vicinity (specifically those of Manasseh [2 K. 21:18 = 2 Ch. 33:20] and Amon [2 K. 21:26]), but no literary or archaeological evidence supports this theory.

Since the meaning "corpse" for *peg̱er* makes no sense in Ezk. 43:7,9, we appear to be dealing here with a secondary term or a homonym, whose unknown meaning scholars have attempted to deduce with the aid of Ugaritic and Akkadian.

2. *Stela.* The word *pgr* appears in two memorial inscriptions from the temple of Dagon at Ugarit; Dussaud translates it as "sacrifice," Obermann as "altar, stone altar." Comparing this usage with three analogous early Phoenician votive inscriptions, Neiman arrives at the meaning "stela" and interprets Ezk. 43:7 as "With the stelae of

---

22. W. Zimmerli, *Ezekiel* 2. *Herm* (Eng. trans. 1983), 409.
23. G. Fohrer, *Ezechiel. HAT* I/13 (1955), 243, 244.
24. See I.1.a above.
25. A. B. Ehrlich, *Randglossen zur Hebräischen Bibel* V (1912), 148.

their kings (they desecrated) their high places,"[26] since they added these memorial stones dedicated to the gods to the cultic inventory of the *bāmâ*.

Albright prefers the reading *b^e^bāmôṯām,* understanding it as a reference to "a special funerary installation separate from the royal tombs themselves," where the memorial stelae of the kings were set up.[27] According to Galling, the text has to do with memorial stelae set up "within my walls" (reading *b^e^ḥômōṯay* [cf. Isa. 56:5] for *bāmôṯām,* which fits better with the text that follows) for the ancestor cult of departed kings (like those in the stela sanctuary at Hazor), evoking an atmosphere of death that is condemned here (cf. Zimmerli: "by the memorials of their kings at their death").[28]

Etymologically, *peger* in the sense of "memorial stela" could be considered a secondary development from *peger,* "corpse."[29] The same holds true for the third proposed translation: "sacrifice for the dead."

3. *Sacrifice.* In Akkadian, *pagrā'um, pagrûm* means "a sacrifice to Dagan (?)," who appears at Mari as *be-el pa-ag-re-e,* "lord of the *pagrê* sacrifices."[30] For Ugar. *pgr, WUS,* after the analogy of Arab. *fağr,* gives the meanings "1. daybreak" and accordingly "2. morning sacrifice (?)."[31] In the Mari texts *pagrā'um* denotes a specific kind of sacrifice (in his glossary, Finet assigns the lexeme the meaning "death" in the sg. and "sacrifice of the dead" in the pl.); Ebach therefore proposes "sacrifice for the dead" as the meaning of Ugar. *pgr,* in part because of Heb. *peger,* "corpse."[32] (Dietrich, Loretz, and Sanmartín also see in *pgr* a sacrifice, not further specified.) On account of the par. *z^e^nûṯ* (in the sense of cultic impurity), he suggests consideration of this meaning for Ezk. 43:7,9 (probably also for Jer. 31:40 and possibly for Gen. 15:11), especially because this term was infected with the odium of syncretism, since it denoted a sacrifice originally offered to a non-Israelite god.

Maiberger

---

26. Neiman, 59. See *UT,* no. 2005: *pgr,* "monument, stela." For the Phoenician inscriptions see *KAI* 1, 4, and 6.

27. W. F. Albright, *Volume du Congrès, Strasbourg 1956. SVT* 4 (1957), 247-48.

28. K. Galling, *ZDPV* 75 (1959) 12; Zimmerli, *Ezekiel* 2, 409.

29. Neiman, 60.

30. *AHw,* II, 809a; *HAL;* but cf. *ARM,* X, 63, 15: "lord of the dead."

31. No. 2189.

32. Finet, *ARM,* XV, 238; Ebach, 368.

פָּדָה pāḏâ; פְּדוּת p^eḏûṯ; פִּדְיוֹן pidyôn

I. Semitic. II. OT: 1. Pre-Deuteronomic Texts; 2. Deuteronom(ist)ic Texts; 3. Exilic Texts; 4. Postexilic Texts. III. Early Judaism, LXX, Dead Sea Scrolls.

I. Semitic. The root *pdy* (III weak) is well attested in Akkadian as *padū/pedū,* "spare, release"; the Assyrian king is often called *lā pādū,* "merciless."[1] It is rare in Ugaritic; Whitaker cites 12 occurrences of *pdy* (plus 2 of *pdyn*), primarily proper names; many appear to be Hurrian.[2] The root appears to be unknown in Aramaic (apart from an Israelite name in the Murašu archives).[3] It is well attested with the meaning "buy, pay, redeem" in Old South Arabic, however, as well as in later Semitic languages: Arabic (a *fedu* offering "to deliver a person or an animal from imminent destruction"), Ethiopic, and Punic.[4]

---

pāḏâ. M. A. Anat, "Determinism and Redemption," *BMiqr* 23 (1978) 425-29 (Heb.); C. Barth, *Die Errettung vom Tode in den individuellen Klage- und Dankliedern des ATs* (1947), 133-37; E. Beaucamp, "Alle origine della parola 'redenzione,'" *BibOr* 21 (1979) 3-11; idem, "Aux origines du mot 'rédemption,'" *Laval théologique et philosophique* 34 (1978) 49-56; J. L. Cunchillos, "Rachat. I. AT," *DBS,* IX, 1045-54; G. I. Davies, "The Hebrew Text of Exodus VIII 19 (Evv. 23): An Emendation," *VT* 24 (1974) 489-92; R. Duval, "Exode et altérité," *RSPT* 59 (1975) 217-41; F. García López, "'Un peuple consacré,' analyse critique de Deutéronome VII," *VT* 32 (1982) 438-63, esp. 445-55; H. Goeke, "Das Menschenbild der individuellen Klagelieder" (diss., Bonn, 1971), 172ff.; H. Gross, "Selbst- oder Fremderlösung," *Wort, Lied und Gottesspruche. FS J. Ziegler. FzB* 2 (1972), II, 65-70; F. K. Heinemann, "Erlösung im AT," *Theologie der Gegenwart* 25 (1982) 42-55; B. Janowski, "Auslösung des verwirkten Lebens," *ZTK* 79 (1982) 25-59; idem, *Sühne als Heilsgeschehen. WMANT* 55 (1982); A. Jepsen, "Die Begriffe des Erlösens im AT," *Solange es heute heisst. FS R. Herrmann* (1958), 153-62; H. W. Jüngling, "Ich mache dich zu einer ehernen Mauer," *Bibl* 54 (1973) 1-24; H.-J. Kraus, "Erlösung. II. Im AT," *RGG*³, II, 586-88; M. R. Lehmann, "Identification of the Copper Scroll Based on Its Technical Terms," *RevQ* 5 (1965/65) 97-105; L. de Lorenzi, "Gesù λυτρωτής," *RivB* 8 (1960) 10-41, esp. 15-16; A. A. Macintosh, "Exodus VIII 19, Distinct Redemption and the Hebrew Roots פדה and פדד," *VT* 21 (1971) 548-55; J. Mejía, "La liberación, aspectos bíblicos: evaluación critica," *Teologia* (Buenos Aires) 10 (1972/73) 25-61; W. F. Meyer, "Semantic Significance of פָּדָה in OT Hebrew" (diss., Wisconsin, 1974); J. Nuñes Carreira, "O exodo e a linguagea de libertaçao," *Didaskalia* 7 (1977) 239-58; J. Pirenne, "RShW, RShWT, FDy, FDyT and the Priesthood in Ancient South Arabia," *Proceedings of the Seminar for Arabian Studies* 6 (1976) 137-43; O. Procksch, "λύω," *TDNT,* IV, 328-35; A. Schenker, "*kōper* et expiation," *Bibl* 63 (1982) 32-46; J. J. Stamm, *Erlösen und Vergeben im AT* (1940), 7-30; idem, *Das Leiden des Unschuldigen in Babylon und Israel. ATANT* 10 (1946), 68-69; idem, "פדה *pdh* to redeem, liberate," *TLOT,* II, 964-76; C. Stuhlmüller, *Creative Redemption in Deutero-Isaiah. AnBibl* 43 (1970); R. J. Thompson, *Penitence and Sacrifice in Early Israel Outside the Levitical Law* (1963); J. Untermann, "The Relationship of Repentance and Redemption in Jeremiah" (diss., Berkeley, 1983).

1. For Akkadian see *AHw,* II, 808; on the Assyrian see Seux, 210.
2. See *WUS,* no. 2194-98; Whitaker, 521.
3. F. Vattioni, *Bibl* 50 (1969) 365.
4. On Old South Arabic see Beeston, 43; Biella, 401. On Arabic, A. Jaussen, *Coutumes des arabes au pays de Moab* (1908), 361-62. On Ethiopic, *LexLingÄth,* 1378-80. On Punic, *KAI,* II, 92, 114; Benz, 97, 389.

The root appears 70 or 71 times in the OT,[5] often several times in the same verse. The verb is found in the qal (51 times), niphal (3 times), hiphil, and hophal (once each). Substantival use of the root is uncommon: it occurs 2 or 3 times in the form *pᵉḏûṯ,* 4 times as *pᵉḏûyim (Q: pdym),* once in the form *piḏyôn,* and twice in the variant *piḏyôm.* The root also appears in several PNs: *pᵉḏāh'ēl, pᵉḏāyâ, pᵉḏāyāhû,* and *pᵉḏāhṣûr.* The PN *p(e)d(a)yahu* is found on seals.[6]

The root frequently parallels → גאל *gā'al* (Lev. 27:27; Isa. 35:9-10; 51:10-11; Jer. 31:11; Hos. 13:14; Ps. 69:19[18]) and once → נצל *nṣl* (Isa. 50:2), found also in Jer. 15:21.[7] Other semantic relations are discussed at → בכור *bᵉḵôr,* → יצא *yāṣā',* → ישע *yšʿ,* and above all → כפר *kipper* (see Ex. 21:30).[8]

II. OT. The original meaning is certainly juridical, as Old South Arabic and Ugaritic usages show. The Ugaritic text *KTU* 3.4 contains a document of release from a legal obligation.[9] But the theophorous names with *pdy* suggest also a broader meaning such as "set free."[10] As always in prebiblical civilization, the meaning is both secular and religious, i.e., cultic.

1. *Pre-Deuteronomic Texts.* We may identify as pre-Deuteronomic the following texts: Ex. 21:8,30; 34:20 (3 times); very probably: 1 S. 14:45; 2 S. 4:9; 1 K. 1:29; Isa. 29:22; Hos. 7:13; 13:14; Mic. 6:4; probably: Ex. 8:19(23).

The two texts from the Covenant Code (Ex. 21:8,30) contain customary law. V. 8 deals with the redemption (hiphil) by a third party of a female slave or concubine whose master does not wish to marry her.[11] V. 30 deals with the payment *(piḏyôn)* the owner of a goring ox must give as ransom *(kōper)* for his own life if his failure to restrain it results in someone's death.[12]

With minor stylistic variations, the same law appears in Ex. 13:13. Although the law appears here in a context that has undergone Deuteronomistic redaction, the text does not treat the subject in the same way as Dt. 15:19 and must therefore be considered pre-Deuteronomic; it should possibly be assigned to E. There is no recognizable theologi-

---

5. On *pᵉḏûṯ* in Ex. 8:19(Eng. v. 23), see *HAL,* III, 913; Macintosh; and Davies.
6. P. Bordreuil and A. Lemaire, *Sem* 26 (1976) 52; Vattioni, no. 45, 235; also Arad ostracon 49:15: see R. Lawton, *Bibl* 65 (1984) 343-44.
7. See H.-W. Jüngling, *Bibl* 54 (1973) 8, who compares Jer. 1:18-19 and 15:20-21.
8. See, respectively, II, 126; VI, 234, 242, 245; VI, 445-46, 457; VII, 289-303.
9. See Yaron; on the meaning "obligation" or "corvée," see O. Loretz, *UF* 8 (1976) 449; M. Heltzer, *Sem* 30 (1980) 6-12.
10. Stamm, *TLOT,* II, 973.
11. H. Cazelles, *Études sur le Code de l'Alliance* (1946), 18; S. M. Paul, *Studies in the Book of the Covenant in the Light of Cuneiform and Biblical Law. SVT* 18 (1970), 53-54; Stamm, *TLOT,* II, 966.
12. Cazelles, 57, 152; Paul, 109, cf. 80-82; on the relationship with the laws of Eshnunna (§§53-54), see J. J. Finkelstein, *The Ox That Gored* (1981), 14-15; with the Code of Hammurabi, ibid., and V. Korošec, *RIDA* 8 (1960) 23; with Hittite law, R. Haase, *RIDA* 14 (1967) 36-47; outside the Near East, B. C. Jackson, "Travels and Travails of the Goring Ox," *Studies in Bible and in the Ancient Near East. FS S. E. Loewenstamm* (1978), 41-56.

cal variation. The Covenant Code treats the redemption of the firstborn in Ex. 22:28b-29.[13]

We are dealing here with the Israelite application of a general practice. The existence of the Ugaritic theophorous names with *pdy* requires us to add Ex. 34:19-20 to these texts. This short piece of "ritual" legislation clearly has not undergone Deuteronomic redaction;[14] if it had, its syntactic structure would be very different (cf. Dt. 15:19-23). The Israelite must redeem *(tipdeh)* the firstborn *(bᵉḵôr)* or break the neck of the *peṭer reḥem* ("that which opens the womb") of a cow or a donkey — probably not the firstborn itself, but an article of value (on the basis of a Mari text).[15] The *bᵉḵôr* and the *peṭer reḥem* belong to the deity, but they may or must be redeemed. Consecration is not sacrifice. The text does not specify precisely what is given to the deity.

This is also the case in 1 S. 14:45, where the people *(ʿam)* redeem or set free Jonathan, who is condemned to death by virtue of Saul's vow. It is the deity, however, who releases (a better translation than "redeems" or "delivers") the intended victim, as David reaffirms with his oath. The same formulation appears in 1 K. 1:29 with regard to David's successor. Isa. 29:22 says the same of Abraham, without adding "from every danger." This is the theologoumenon to which Hos. 7:13 alludes: it is God who releases from evil.

The same theologoumenon is also present in Akkadian theophorous names with *paṭāru* and Egyptian personal names with *nḥm m.*[16] But these verbs evoke the notion of magic or force.[17] When the biblical author chose the legal term *pāḏâ* rather than *pṭr* or *yšʿ*, it was probably to avoid charging the God of Abraham with acting in such a way. He chose a verb from the field of contract law, though reserving the setting of a price. The essential point is to make the God of Abraham, Israel, and David the sole agent in this act of release. In Isa. 29:22 it is the God of the house of Israel who released (or redeemed) Abraham — without saying how and from what. It is still the same religious perspective of releasing or redeeming an individual from danger, oppression, or obligation with respect to a third party.

In Hosea the meaning becomes more theological, since he speaks of a collective redemption. But the text, with the masc. pl. suf., still refers to a number of individuals rather than a people as such. Both passages use the 1st person sg. qal perfective of *pāḏâ*. Grammatically, as in the previous instances, this would express an affirmation of God's positive desire to redeem. The context, however, which speaks of rebellion and lies against God, leads many translators (TOB, NJB, *NEB,* etc.) to read 7:13 as a refusal on the part of God and treat it as a question expecting a negative answer. Others,

---

13. For a detailed analysis, see M. Caloz, "Exode XIII,3-16 et son rapport au Deutéronome," *RB* 75 (1968) 5-62.

14. H. Cazelles, "L'alliance du Sinaï en Ex 34,10-27," *Mélanges bibliques et orientaux en l'honneur de M. Delcor. AOAT* 215 (1985), 57-68.

15. For the former see *DBS,* VIII, 467-91; for the latter, H. Cazelles, "Consecration d'enfant et de femmes," *Miscellanea Babylonica. FS M. Birot* (1985), 45-50.

16. See *AN,* 169, 191; H. Ranke, *Die altägyptischen Personnenamen* (1935), I, 208.

17. *Šurpu,* II, 134-84; E. Reiner, *Šurpu. BAfO* 11 (1958), 17-18.

however, concurring with the early versions, maintain the positive sense (Osty and Trinquet, Rudolph, Andersen and Freedman, Mays, Hauret, Wolff). The same divergence is manifested in Hos. 13:14, where *pāḏâ* appears in parallel with *g'l;* the context speaks of stillbirth and Sheol. Many likewise see a rhetorical question in the parallel "I will be your plague, O Death, I will be your destroyer *(qōṭeḇ),* O Sheol," reading with the LXX *(poú) 'ayyēh* instead of *'ᵉhî.* But everyone who follows this line recognizes that the LXX does not solve the problem.[18] MT *'ᵉhî* fits quite naturally into the series of verbs, but the question "Where?" is out of place. Death and Sheol are personified, as are the destructive powers; Hosea is reasserting the traditional affirmation of God's power over all other powers, even death (likewise personified in Isa. 28:15).[19] This does not mean that God will in fact redeem, since v. 15 announces the ruin of Ephraim, but only that God has the power to do so (perfective used in a modal sense).

In every era the theology of sacral history crystallizes around the exodus from Egypt. I would hesitate to read *pᵉḏûṯ* in Ex. 8:19(23),[20] since the verse probably speaks of a "miraculous separation" rather than a redemption "between my people and your people." But the *diastolḗ* of the LXX can mean "payment,"[21] and *bên* is used in the realm of transactions. We would have here a gratuitous act of collective redemption by God; the verb *šyt* could be used in the sense of "imposing" a payment or obligation (Ex. 21:22; Nu. 12:11).

This theology of deliverance through a gratuitous act of God's power finds more precise expression in Mic. 6:4. The authenticity of this verse is less controverted than that of others;[22] it displays indisputable evidence of pre-Deuteronomic origin. The parallel "bring up out of Egypt" differs from the Deuteronomic "bring out of Egypt";[23] the equal treatment of Moses, Aaron, and Miriam as deliverers is hardly compatible with the total dominance of Moses in the texts of Deuteronomy and P. "I delivered you from a house of slavery" refers to an administration in which all — particularly the officials — were branded as Pharaoh's "servants." In Deuteronomy the expression takes on the sense of a "land of slavery" for Israel.

2. *Deuteronom(ist)ic Texts.* The relevant Deuteronomic texts are Dt. 7:8; 9:26; 13:6(5); 15:15; 21:8; 24:18. The Deuteronomistic texts are 2 S. 7:23 and Isa. 1:27, together with (less certainly) Jer. 15:21 and 31:11.

We read in Dt. 7:8 that "Yahweh brought you out with a mighty hand and redeemed you from the house of slavery, from the hand of Pharaoh king of Egypt." The same theme expressed in the same language reappears in 9:26; 13:6(5); 15:15 ("Remember: when you were a slave in the land of Egypt, Yahweh your God redeemed

---

18. See H. W. Wolff, *Hosea. Herm* (Eng. trans. 1974), 221.

19. But cf. F. I. Andersen and D. N. Freedman, *Hosea. AB* 24 (1980), 639-40; E. Jacob, *Osée. CAT* XIa (1965), 93-94.

20. See H. Cazelles, *Studien zum Pentateuch. FS W. Kornfeld* (1977), 46 n. 32.

21. LSJ, 413a, 4.

22. J. L. Mays, *Micah. OTL* (1976), 130.

23. See J. Wijngaards, *VT* 15 (1965) 91-102.

you"), in a pericope that is taken from the Covenant Code but given different content and form. In 21:8 the *pāḏâ* of Yahweh establishes an atoning sacrifice *(kipper)* for Israel, to absolve the people from the guilt of blood shed by unknown persons. Finally, in connection with the taking of a pledge, 24:18 recalls that Yahweh gratuitously redeemed Israel when it was a slave in Egypt. We see here how the legal and theological (sacral history) meanings overlap. This is also recalled by the prayer of David (2 S. 7:23, Dtr).[24]

There are two occurrences of *pāḏâ* in Jeremiah. Jer. 15:21 concludes one of the "confessions of Jeremiah."[25] One might see in it an oracle of Jeremiah from the period of his exile under King Jehoiakim. God will make Jeremiah a bronze wall, impregnable to his enemies: "I will deliver you *(hiṣṣaltîḵā)* out of the hand of the wicked, and redeem you *(pᵉḏiṯîḵā)* from the grasp of the ruthless." Again we are dealing with deliverance by God's power and individual redemption, but the images employed make the prophet a symbol of the people. Ittmann believes this verse is a later restatement of 20:13b.[26] Hubmann, however, sees in vv. 20-21 a further development of the text evoked by a new crisis in Jeremiah's life.[27]

Jer. 31:11 is in the Book of Comfort, one of the most important collections in the composition of the book of Jeremiah. On the one hand, it makes allusions to the fall of Judah; on the other, it contains early oracles from the period of high hopes following the fall of Assyria and Josiah's reconquest of some northern areas. Böhmer rejects Jeremianic authenticity on the basis of the parallel use of *gā'al* (twice in Deutero-Isaiah).[28] But the root *g'l* also appears in the juridical section of Jer. 32 (vv. 7-8). Nonetheless, the pericope with the twin themes of the restoration of Samaria and the cult in Zion (Jer. 31:1-6; authentic) does fit with Deuteronomistic theology.[29]

3. *Exilic Texts.* The exilic texts are all in Deutero-Isaiah. Ezekiel never uses *pāḏâ* and uses *g'l* only once (as a noun), and then with the meaning "kin" rather than "redemption." Ezekiel, too, looks for a return brought about by God's power, but he puts more emphasis on the presence of God in the midst of the people.

By contrast, Deutero-Isaiah frequently uses *g'l* for the deliverance of Israel from those who would wreak vengeance on it, while using *pdh* only twice: Isa. 50:2 and 51:11.[30] In 50:2 it appears in a juridical context as the subst. *pᵉḏûṯ*, par. to *hiṣṣîl.* "You were sold because of your sins." There was a bill of divorce, but God's hand proved to

---

24. P. Kyle McCarter, *II Samuel. AB* 9 (1984), 240; M. Weinfeld, *Deuteronomy and the Deuteronomic School* (1972), 42, 326-29.

25. On its literary structure, see H. Mottu, *Les "Confessions" de Jérémie* (1985), 83-100; see also the analysis by W. Thiel, *Die deuteronomistische Redaktion von Jeremia 1–25. WMANT* 41 (1973), who is not certain that the verse is Dtr.

26. N. Ittmann, *Die Konfessionen Jeremias. WMANT* 54 (1981), 44-49, 54-55.

27. F. D. Hubmann, *Untersuchungen zu den Konfessionen. FzB* 30 (1978).

28. S. Böhmer, *Heimkehr und neuer Bund* (1976), 69.

29. On the authenticity of Jer. 31:1-6 see ibid., 81-82. See also H. Weippert, *Die Prosareden des Jeremiabuches. BZAW* 132 (1973).

30. On *g'l* → II, 354. On *pdh* see *DBS,* IX, 1052-53.

be not too short to set free. In a similar fashion, in 51:11 those "set free" by Yahweh return to Zion. Neither text uses *pdh* in strict parallelism with *g'l*.

There is good reason for wanting to date Isa. 1:27 in the same period (Isa. 1 betrays evidence of Deutero-Isaianic redaction): "Zion shall be set free by justice [*mišpāṭ;* cf. 40:14; 42:1,3], and those who return to it [*šāḇeyhâ,* 'captives'?] by righteousness." But such ideas appear also in Trito-Isaiah, although *pdh* never occurs there.

4. *Postexilic Texts.* The postexilic prophets do not use *pdh,* with the exception of two texts already bearing apocalyptic coloration that draw on the theology of Deutero-Isaiah. In the "Little Apocalypse" of Isaiah (35:10), those set free by Yahweh return filled with joy to Zion. According to Deutero-Zechariah (Zec. 10:8), those who have been set free are full of joy and await the "signal of the one who gathers them."

P uses *pāḏâ* frequently (15 times), but the occurrences are concentrated in four pericopes (Lev. 19:20; 27:27-29; Nu. 3:46-51; 18:15-17). Except for Lev. 19, they all appear to belong to expansions (P^S) of the basic P document, which adapt the historical legal text to the conditions of the restored cult in the second temple.[31]

The subject is always payment for a release. The most interesting instance is Lev. 19:20 (Holiness Code): it deals with the guilt offering to be presented by a man who has had sexual relations with another man's slave, a woman who has been neither ransomed *(nipdāṯâ)* nor freed *(ḥupšâ).* This text is purely juridical.

The three other passages deal with the redemption of the firstborn, which is legitimated theologically on the grounds that they are holy (*qōḏeš,* Nu. 18:17). Israel is described as a holy people, consecrated to God, in Deuteronomy, the Holiness Code (Lev. 17–26), Ezekiel, and P.[32] Nu. 3 (P^S) permits the enrollment of the Levites (contrary to Lev. 1:49 [P^G]; cf. 1:47). The Levites belong to Yahweh (Nu. 3:45) and are looked upon as the ransom price of the firstborn of Israel; even the amount owed is calculated precisely (3:48-50). Nothing is said about the Levites being "holy." Only the priest *(kōhēn)* is *qōḏeš;* in this legislation the Levites are cleansed and given to the priest Aaron and his sons to minister in the sanctuary (Nu. 8:19).

In the schedule presented in Lev. 27, one of the latest texts of the Pentateuch, unclean animals can be redeemed (*pdh,* 27:27); but persons or animals that have been devoted to Yahweh by *ḥērem* (→ חרם *ḥāram*) cannot be redeemed, since they belong to Yahweh absolutely (vv. 28-29).

After the return from exile and the restoration of the temple liturgy, the Psalms also take up this theme. The 16 occurrences of the root in the Psalter are not concentrated in any of the collections; the meaning is somewhere between "redeem" and "set free."

In this regard Ps. 49, a wisdom psalm, is the most interesting. The text is difficult and badly preserved,[33] especially v. 9(8). One person cannot "ransom" another, not even by paying God the price (*kōper:* v. 8[7]); nor can persons ransom themselves,

31. On Nu. 1 see *DBS,* VII, 842, 851.

32. *DBS,* X, 1424-29.

33. H.-J. Kraus, *Psalms 1–59* (Eng. trans. 1988), 478ff.; J. van der Ploeg, *OTS* 13 (1963) 139; L. G. Perdue, *JBL* 93 (1974) 533-42.

whatever price they offer (v. 9[8]). Only Yahweh can ransom a life (*nep̱eš,* v. 16[15]; cf. Hos. 13:14) and "take" *(lāqaḥ)* a person from the power of Sheol (the same verb is used of Enoch in Gen. 5:24 and Elijah in 2 K. 2:10). It is a frequent theme in the Psalms that God sets people free, whether in the past (Ps. 78:42, from the foe [*ṣar;* cf. 2 S. 4:9]; Ps. 111:9: "he sent *p*ᵉ*ḏûṯ*") or in the present (Ps. 25:22). Ps. 130 makes clear that God sets Israel free from all its iniquities (v. 8), for his *p*ᵉ*ḏûṯ* is plenteous.

Most often it is an individual or an individual's life (see the discussion of Ps. 49 above) that is the object of Yahweh's liberating act (Ps. 26:11; 31:6[5]; 55:19[18]; 71:23). One may be set free from enemies (69:19[18]) or oppression (119:134). In 34:23(22) and 44:27(26), it is the psalmist whom God sets free. Along the same lines Nehemiah reminds God that he set his servants the Israelites free by his power (Neh. 1:10); in the Chronicler's version of the prayer of David (1 S. 7), 1 Ch. 17:21 reaffirms that God "redeemed" or "set free" his people to make them his own.

The three occurrences in the book of Job (5:20, from death; 6:23, from oppressors; 33:28, from the Pit) fit with the usage of the Psalms. It is surprising that *pdh* is not found elsewhere in protocanonical wisdom literature. It appears only in the concluding prayer of Sirach (51:2): "You have preserved my body from destruction."

III. Early Judaism, LXX, Dead Sea Scrolls. The root does not appear in either the Hebrew or Aramaic sections of Daniel. It is highly unlikely that it was in the Hebrew text used by the LXX; in Pr. Azar. 66 (= LXX Dnl. 3:88) *lytroún* more likely represents *prq* (as in 4:24) or *šêziḇ* (as in 6:27[MT 28]).

The LXX varies widely in its translation of *pdh.* Most commonly it uses *lytroún* and its compounds (47 times), which it also uses 7 times to represent *kpr.* In addition, it uses *rhýesthai,* "restrain, save" (5 times: e.g., Job 5:20; 6:23; Isa. 50:2), *allássein,* "give in exchange" (3 times: Ex. 13:13 [twice]; Lev. 27:27), and *aphorízein, synágein,* and *sṓzein* (once each). In three passages it resorts to paraphrase.

While the LXX prefers *hiláskesthai,* "reconcile, atone," and *hagiázein,* "sanctify, consecrate," for *kipper* (and twice for *kōp̱er*), it clearly understands *pāḏâ* in the sense of *lytroún* and its compounds, which in classical Greek imply a payment or ransom.[34] It thus preserves the original meaning, even though in some cases it notes that God's redemption is gratuitous and therefore translates in a theological sense.[35]

The verb *pāḏâ* occurs 13 times in the Dead Sea Scrolls, the subst. *p*ᵉ*ḏûṯ* 14 times (almost exclusively in the *milḥāmâ* texts), and *pdwyym* once (4Q511 36:3). While *kipper* predominates in the Rule texts (1QS, CD) and the Temple Scroll, *pāḏâ* is concentrated in the *Hodayot,* where it has the same meaning as in the Psalms. God frees the *nep̱eš* of the poor (1QH 2:32,35) and saves the hymnodist from the Pit (3:19). In 1QM 1:12; 14:5, *ʿm pdwt ʾl,* "people of God's redemption," appears to be a self-designation of the Qumran community. The term *pdwt* in 1QM is to be understood (with Carmignac) as a

34. For examples see *TDNT,* IV, 332.

35. *TDNT,* IV, 333-34; S. Daniel, *Recherches sur le vocabulaire du culte dans la Septante* (1966), 325, and the notes on the Hexapla.

"liberation" of the people by God, a pure gift of grace.[36] The usage of *pāḏâ* in the Temple Scroll is fundamentally comparable to Deuteronom(ist)ic usage: God redeems Israel from the house of slavery (54:16), from the hand of those who hate it (59:11), and increases its number (l. 12). God pardons his people, whom he has redeemed (63:6).

The root *pdh/pd'* appears about 100 times in rabbinic literature.[37] The juridical meaning predominates in applying biblical texts that deal with the redemption of consecrated objects or the firstborn. Midrash and Talmud also speak of the freeing of Israel.[38] The Jewish conception of redemption from guilt and error developed around *kpr* rather than *pdh*.

Cazelles

---

36. See F. Nötscher, *Zur theologischen Terminologie der Qumran-Texte. BBB* 10 (1956), 188-89.
37. Kasowski, *Thesaurus Mischnae* (rev. ed. 1967), s.v.
38. Jastrow, 1136-37.

פֶּה *peh*

I. Ancient Near East: 1. Akkadian; 2. Ugaritic; 3. Phoenician, Hebrew, Aramaic. II. Occurrences and Distribution. III. Semantic Survey: 1. Orifice; 2. Bodily Organ; 3. Organ of Communication; 4. Idioms. IV. Specific Usages: 1. Bodily Organ; 2. Organ of Communication. V. Theological Usage: 1. Yahweh's Mouth; 2. Prophets; 3. Worshipers. VI. Wisdom: 1. General; 2. Wise vs. Foolish; 3. Power; 4. Ethical Ideal. VII. 1. LXX; 2. Dead Sea Scrolls.

---

peh. M. Bernaert, *Cœur — langue — mains dans la Bible. Cahiers Évangile* 46 (1983); W. Bühlmann, *Vom rechten Reden und Schweigen. OBO* 12 (1976); E. Cortese, *Da Mosè a Esdra* (1985); M. Dahood, "Hebrew-Ugaritic Lexicography, VIII," *Bibl* 51 (1970) 391-404, esp. 395-96; P. Dhorme, "L'emploi métaphorique des noms de parties du corps en hébreu et en akkadien, IV," *RB* 30 (1921) 517-40; P. Fronzaroli, *Studi sul lessico commune semitico. AANLR* 19 (1964), 255, 269; T. H. Gaster, "A Canaanite Magical Text," *Or* 11 (1942) 41-79; B. de Geradon, "Le cœur, la bouche, les mains," *BVC* 1 (1953) 7-24; idem, *Le cœur, la langue, les mains* (1974); J. H. Greenberg, *The Languages of Africa* (1963); R. Grelot, "La bouche du gloire," *Sem* 35 (1985) 61-65; A. R. Johnson, *The Vitality of the Individual in the Thought of Ancient Israel* ([2]1964); C. J. Labuschagne, "פֶּה *peh* mouth," *TLOT,* II, 976-79; A. Lemaire, *Inscriptions hébraiques,* I. *Les ostraca* (1977); H. Michaud, "Les ostraca de Lakiš conservés à Londres," *Syr* 33/34 (1956/57) 39-60, esp. 55-56; W. H. Schmidt, "Anthropologische Begriffe im AT," *EvT* 24 (1964) 374-88; R. Sollamo, *Renderings of Hebrew Semiprepositions in the Septuagint. AnAcScFen Dissertationes Humanarum Litterarum* 19 (1979), esp. 224-34; J. H. Tigay, "'Heavy of Mouth' and 'Heavy of Tongue,'" *BASOR* 231 (1978) 57-67; H. W. Wolff, *Anthropology of the OT* (Eng. trans. 1974).

I. Ancient Near East. Heb. *peh,* "mouth," represents a monoconsonantal root found in all Semitic languages, but expanded variously in some: Akk. and Amor. *pû* (also Old Akk. *pā'um, pīum*), Ugar. *p,* Phoen. *py,* Arab. *fū* (const.; abs. usually expanded to *fam*), OSA *f* (only with the meaning "command"), Aram. *pum* (expanded), Eth. *'af.*

1. *Akkadian.* In Akkadian literature *pû* appears in many expressions that have analogues in Biblical Hebrew. For example, the Old Akkadian formula *ina pîm u lišānim* emphasizes the parallelism between mouth *(pû)* and tongue *(lišānu).*[1] The familiar biblical expression *môṣā' peh* (Dt. 8:3) corresponds to Akk. *ṣît pî,* "that which issues from the mouth."[2]

2. *Ugaritic.* Ugaritic uses the monoconsonantal form *p.* The frequent use of synonyms and parallel terms that Ugaritic has in common with Hebrew is especially clear in the case of *p,* which parallels *lšn,* "tongue," *šnt,* "teeth," and *špt,* "lip(s)."[3] The Aqhat Epic frequently repeats the formula *bph rgm l yṣ'* par. *bšpth ḥwt(h),* "The word came forth from his mouth, the utterance from his lips."[4] The expression *bph yṣ',* "come forth from the mouth," recalls the Deuteronomic formula just cited.[5] In all these texts, *p, špt,* and *lšn* denote organs of speech.

In two passages from the myth describing the battle between Baal and Mot,[6] Schmidt notes the parallelism between *p* and *npš,* whose meaning "throat" is close to that of *peh,* and points out the relevance of these texts to Isa. 5:14.[7] In these myths *p(eh)* is an organ of the body used for eating or devouring; used metaphorically, it describes the activity of Sheol, which devours like a monster.[8] Ugaritic also uses *p* as an element in personal names.[9]

3. *Phoenician, Hebrew, Aramaic.* The term "mouth" appears as *py* in a few Phoenician inscriptions and in the expression *bpy* in extrabiblical Hebrew; it appears as *pm* in Aramaic. All these occurrences date from the period of the OT.

A 7th-century incantation in Phoenician script from Arslan Tash applies to the god Ḫoron (or his consort — the text is not clear) the epithet *'š tm py,* "whose mouth [utterance] is perfect [true]").[10] This may be compared to Akkadian magical texts that speak

---

1. *AHw,* I, 556a, 4a.
2. For other analogues see Dhorme, 533-39; and *AHw,* II, 872-74; for PNs see *APN,* 128, 254.
3. M. Dahood, *Psalms III: 101–150. AB* 17A (1970), 454; M. Dahood, *RSP,* I, 309-11, nos. 455-58.
4. *KTU* 1.19, II, 26; III, 7, 21, 35.
5. See I.1 above.
6. *KTU* 1.5, I, 7 par. II, 4.
7. P. 377.
8. H. Wildberger, *Isaiah 1–12* (Eng. trans. 1991), 204-5; J. B. Burns, *VT* 22 (1972) 245-46; M. Dahood, *Bibl* 51 (1970) 395.
9. F. Gröndahl, *PNU,* 170.
10. *KAI* 27.16.

of a deity's purity of mouth or utterance; the epithet probably expresses the idea that the deity is lord (or lady) of the magic words.[11]

In ll. 3-5 of Lachish ostracon 16, Michaud reconstructs the following text: *šlḥ ʿ[bdk d]br bpy q[šbyhw] hnbʾ,* "[Your servant] sent: [S]ay through the mouth of Qe[šabyahu] the prophet."[12] If this reconstruction is right,[13] we have here a Hebrew inscription with a formulation resembling that found in prophetic literature.

In the story of Ahiqar, we find two expressions typical of wisdom literature that resemble in part expressions in Proverbs. In 7:97-98, we find the admonition to "guard one's mouth," because it can be the cause of trouble. The continuation (l. 99) points out that one can use one's mouth for the benefit of others, "because the ambush of the mouth is worse than the ambush of war" *(ky ʿzyz ʾrb pm mn ʾrb mlḥm).* In 10:156, *pm* parallels *lšn* in a reflection typical of religious wisdom: *yʾpk ʾl ʾpkʾ wynsh lšn*[*h*], "God will pervert the mouth of the perverse [liar] and tear out [his] tongue."[14]

II. Occurrences and Distribution. The 505 occurrences (not 500[15]) of the noun *peh* in the OT are distributed quite uniformly among the various sections: 101 in the Tetrateuch (Genesis 21, Exodus 23, Leviticus 8, Numbers 49), 110 in Deuteronomy and the Deuteronomistic History (Deuteronomy 23, Joshua 27, Judges 15, Samuel 20, Kings 25), 99 in wisdom literature (Job 36, Proverbs 56, Ecclesiastes 7), 95 in the remaining books (Psalms 68, Song of Songs, Lamentations, Esther, and Daniel a total of 9, Chronicler's History 18). The word is normally in the singular *(peh;* const. *pî);* the plural appears only twice (Jgs. 3:16; Prov. 5:4: *pēyôṯ/pîyôṯ*). In 1 S. 13:21 *pîm* denotes a unit of weight.[16] Two texts use the reduplicating form *pîpîyôṯ,* "cutting edges" (Isa. 41:15; Ps. 149:6).

In the biconsonantal form *pum,*[17] the word appears 6 times in the Aramaic sections of Daniel.

III. Semantic Survey. The noun *peh* is used in a variety of linguistic domains; it can belong to an object, an animal, a human being, a cultic image, or even God when the text speaks of God anthropomorphically.

1. *Orifice.* In the broadest sense, *peh* denotes an orifice, in a variety of forms. The orifice normally connects an interior with an exterior. It may be the mouth of a well (Gen. 29:2,3,8,10), the opening of a jar or sack (Gen. 42:27; Zec. 5:8), the entrance to a cave or a city (Josh. 10:18; Prov. 8:3), etc.

---

11. See Gaster, 41-44, 62-63.
12. Pp. 55-56.
13. But see Lemaire, 131.
14. For Biblical Aramaic see II below. For other occurrences of *p(m)* in West Semitic see *DNSI,* II, 916-17; Tomback, 261-62.
15. Contra Labuschagne, *TLOT,* II, 976.
16. E. A. Speiser, *BASOR* 77 (1940) 18ff.; R. Gordis, *JBL* 61 (1942) 209ff.; H. J. Stoebe, *Das erste Buch Samuelis. KAT* VIII/1 (1973), 255.
17. See I.1 above.

2. *Bodily Organ.* In the narrower sense, in the case of animals and human beings, *peh* normally denotes the orifice in the front of the head that connects with the stomach (cf. Gk. *stóma,* "mouth" — *stómachos,* "stomach"). In this sense the mouth is the organ that serves for eating and drinking (Jgs. 7:6; Ezk. 2:8; Ps. 78:30; Prov. 19:24; Neh. 9:20). This organ is associated with such adjacent organs as the lips, tongue, gums, and teeth.

In the extended sense, *peh* can also refer to the earth, which is described as a monster that devours human beings, animals, and objects (Gen. 4:11; Nu. 16:30,32; Dt. 11:6). By association, a sword is also said to have a *peh;* its blade devours the flesh of the enemy (Dt. 32:42). The expression *l^e^p̱î-ḥereḇ,* "by the edge of the sword," is especially common in the historical books (Josh. 6:21; 8:24; Jgs. 1:8; 4:15; 18:27; 1 S. 22:19; 2 S. 15:14; 2 K. 10:25).

3. *Organ of Communication.* In the OT the *peh* is the normal organ of linguistic communication. This usage reflects the basic meaning precisely, for language is an expression of thoughts, which emanate from within the individual. The actual organs of speech are the lips and tongue,[18] but the biblical text often transfers this function to the mouth *(peh).* In this sense *peh* refers to the mouth of a human being or of God (Gen. 45:12; 1 K. 8:15,24), rarely of an animal (Nu. 22:28). By metonymy, *peh* as an organ of communication can refer to what issues from the mouth (speech, words, commands, etc.; Nu. 14:41; Dt. 32:1; Ps. 19:15[Eng. v. 14]; Eccl. 10:12-13), whether the person is speaking directly or transmitting a message (Ex. 4:15-16; Jer. 15:19).

Finally, the mouth is also used for kissing (1 K. 19:18). This is a special form of communication, which transmits a feeling. Although the mouth that gives a kiss is an external organ, the kiss represents love, the language of the heart (Job 31:27; Cant. 1:2).

4. *Idioms.* Finally, we note various fixed expressions using *peh,* such as *k^e^p̱î, l^e^p̱î,* and *'al-pî,* "according to" (Ex. 16:21; Lev. 25:52; Nu. 26:54; Josh. 18:4; 2 K. 23:35; Prov. 22:6); these are connected only indirectly with the basic meaning of the word, referring to the norm established by speech (that which issues from the mouth).

There are also special cases in which *peh* refers to a limit or end (2 K. 10:21; 21:16; Ezr. 9:11: "from one end to another." In this context we may note the possible etymological connection between *peh* and → פאה *pē'â,* "side, edge."[19]

IV. Specific Usages.

1. *Bodily Organ.* As an organ of the body — for now disregarding its function — the mouth is associated more or less closely with other parts of the body. The primary association of the mouth is with the head — or better, considering the biblical perspective on the nature of human beings, the face, i.e., the organs adjacent to or constituting the mouth.[20] Especially important is the association of *peh* with *lāšôn* and *śāp̱â.*[21] Such as-

18. → שׂפה *śāp̱â;* → לשׁון *lāšôn.*
19. See VII.1 below; also *TLOT,* II, 976; *GesTh,* 1086-87.
20. See Johnson, 40-50; Wolff, 74-79; → פנים *pānîm.*
21. See III.3 above.

sociations are very common in poetic texts, where *peh* parallels these organs: *peh* par. *lāšôn* in Isa. 57:4; Jer. 9:7(8); Ps. 10:7; 37:30; 39:2(1); 50:19; 66:17; 73:9; 78:36; 109:2; 126:2; Job 15:5; 20:12; 33:2; Prov. 10:31; 15:2; 26:28; 31:26; cf. Ex. 4:10; *peh* par. *śāpâ* in Isa. 11:4; 29:13; Mal. 2:6,7; Ps. 51:17(15); 59:8,13(7,12); 66:14; 119:13; 141:3; Job 8:21; 15:6; 23:12; (33:2-3); Prov. 4:24; 10:32; 13:3; 14:3; 16:10,23; 18:6,7,20; 27:2; Eccl. 10:12.

In some cases "tongue" and "lips" alternate with or complement "mouth" (Dt. 23:24[22]; Mic. 6:12; Zec. 14:12; Ps. 5:10[9]; 39:2[1]; 51:16-17[14-15]; 59:13[12]; 63:6; Prov. 18:20-21; 21:23). In Isa. 6:7 *peh* and *śāpâ* are interchangeable: "He touched my mouth with it and said, 'This has touched your lips.'" In Isa. 11:4 *rûaḥ śāpâ* has the same meaning as *rûaḥ peh* in Ps. 33:6. In addition, the mouth is associated with the palate (*ḥēk*, Ezk. 3:26-27; Job 29:9-10; Prov. 8:7-8), so that by synecdoche *ḥēk* stands for the mouth (Hos. 8:1; Job 20:12-13; 33:2); the teeth (→ שֵׁן *šēn,* Mic. 3:5; Zec. 9:7; Ps. 58:7[6]; Lam. 2:16); the throat (*gārôn,* Ps. 5:10[9]); the cheeks (→ לחי *lᵉḥî,* Job 16:10); the forehead (→ קרן *qeren,* 1 S. 2:1); the eyes (→ עין *ʿayin,* Gen. 45:12), and the ears (*ʾōzen,* Jer. 9:19[20]; Ps. 78:1; cf. Ps. 54:4[2]). One text uses "mouth" in parallel with "head" *(rōʾš)* (Prov. 10:6; cf. v. 11).[22] More distant is the association of "mouth" and "flesh" (*bāśār,* Ps. 145:21; Eccl. 5:5).

Second, we note the association of the mouth with the "inner parts" of the human body *(qereb)*. What the mouth speaks comes from within (Ps. 5:10[9]). The most important organ in this respect is the heart,[23] which is frequently associated with the mouth: "The word . . . is in your mouth and in your heart" (Dt. 30:14). The mouth and lips may move, but it is the heart that speaks (1 S. 1:12-13). There is therefore a vital relationship between these organs, whether harmonious (Ps. 17:3; 19:15[14]; 37:30-31; 49:4[3]; 66:17-18; 141:3-4; Job 15:12-13; 22:22; 31:27; 33:2-3; Prov. 4:4-5,23-24; 16:23; Eccl. 5:1) or not (Isa. 29:13; Ezk. 33:31; Ps. 55:22[21]; 78:36-37; cf. also Prov. 15:14,28; 1 S. 2:1). With the belly *(beṭen)* the mouth has a more organic and physical connection[24] than with the heart (Ezk. 3:3; Prov. 18:20). Also evident is the connection between *peh* and *nepeš;* the basic meaning of the latter is "throat," but in this context it normally refers to an individual's vital breath (Ps. 63:6[5]; Prov. 21:23).

Finally, we come to the association of the mouth with other members of the body, especially the hand.[25] Several texts speak of raising the hand to the mouth to eat or drink (Jgs. 7:6; 1 S. 14:26,27; Ezk. 2:8-9; Prov. 19:24; 26:15). Other texts speak of putting one's hand over one's mouth (*śîm yāḏ ʿal-peh:* Jgs. 18:19; Mic. 7:16; Job 21:5; 40:4)[26] to indicate silence; Jgs. 18:19 uses *ḥāraš,*[27] "be silent," as a synonym. In P we find the characteristic formula "at the command of . . . under the direction of" (*ʿal-pî* X

22. See the observations of W. McKane, *Proverbs. OTL* (1970), 422; O. Plöger, *Sprüche Salomos. BK* XVII (1984), 121.

23. → לב *lēḇ.*

24. See III.2 above.

25. → יד *yāḏ.*

26. For Egyptian parallels see R. Couroyer, *RB* 67 (1960) 197ff.

27. → דמה II /דמם *dāmâ/dāmam.*

b^e yad Y: Ex. 38:21; Nu. 4:37,45,49; 9:23; 10:13; Josh. 22:9), which expresses deputation and mediation, a perfect coordination of mouth and hand. The mouth describes an action, the hand puts it into effect (Jer. 44:25; Ps. 144:7-8,11). The collaboration of Yahweh's mouth and hand is the subject of 1 K. 8:15,24 par. 2 Ch. 6:4,15. Yahweh's hand touches or rests on the mouth of a prophet (Jer. 1:9; Ezk. 33:22; cf. Isa. 51:16). Yahweh punishes with his hand those who do not heed the commands of his mouth (1 S. 12:15).

2. *Organ of Communication.* As an organ of communication, the mouth participates in various functions and activities, all related to language. From the biblical perspective, the primary function of the human mouth (like the mouth of Yahweh) is speech. This function is fundamental to our understanding of the various nouns and verbs the OT uses for the words uttered by the mouth.

First, there are terms denoting the communication of ideas: the verb *dbr* piel, "speak" (with a human subj.: Gen. 45:12; Jer. 32:4; 34:3; Ps. 49:4[3]; 63:12[11]; 66:14; 144:8,11; 145:21; with God as subj.: Nu. 12:8; Isa. 1:20; 40:5; 58:14; Jer. 9:11[12]; Mic. 4:4), and its corresponding noun *dāḇār,* "word" (with a human subj.: Ps. 36:4[3]; Prov. 18:4; Eccl. 10:13; with Yahweh as subj.: Jer. 9:19[20]; Ezr. 1:1; 2 Ch. 36:21-22). This same function of generalized speaking — without further qualification — is expressed by the verb *'āmar,* which, surprisingly, is never used in conjunction with *peh.* Instead, the noun phrase *'imrê peh* is used frequently, of both human beings (Dt. 32:1; Ps. 19:15[14]; 54:4[2]; 78:1; Prov. 4:5; 5:7; 6:2; 7:24; 8:8; Job 8:2; 23:12) and God (Hos. 6:5; Ps. 138:4). Other words used with *peh* are: *š'l,* "ask" (Gen. 24:57 [humans]; Josh. 9:14; Isa. 30:2 [God]); *'nh,* "answer" (Dt. 31:21; 2 S. 1:16; cf. Job 15:6; Prov. 15:28), and its noun *m'nh* (Job 32:5; Prov. 15:1); *nb'* hiphil, "cause words to gush forth" (Ps. 59:8[7]; 78:2; Prov. 15:2,28); *spr* piel, "tell" (Ps. 71:15; cf. 50:16); *mll,* "utter" (Job 8:2); *nāqaḇ,* "designate" (Isa. 62:2, with Yahweh as subj.); *hgh,* "utter" (Ps. 37:30; cf. Prov. 15:28); *ngd* hiphil, "declare" (Gen. 43:7; Ps. 51:17[15]; cf. Dt. 17:10; Isa. 48:3); *yd'* hiphil, "cause to know" (Ps. 89:2[1]); *ṣiwwâ,* "command" (Isa. 34:16, the mouth of Yahweh commands [*kî-p̱î hû' ṣiwwâ*]). In the light of these examples, the parallelism between *'al-pî yhwh* and *ka'ašer ṣiwwâ yhwh* is easy to understand (Nu. 3:16,51; 4:49; 36:5-6; cf. Josh. 17:4: *'el-pî*), as are the parallelism between *ṣiwwâ* and *śîm b^e pî* (2 S. 14:19; Ezr. 8:17) or *nāṯan b^e pî* (Dt. 18:18) and the association of "rebel" *(mārâ + peh)* and "command" *(ṣiwwâ)* (Josh. 1:18; 1 K. 13:21). The mouth of Yahweh is also associated with his commands (*pî yhwh — miṣwaṯ yhwh,* 1 K. 13:21; Job 23:12; cf. also Dt. 8:2-6).[28] In a similar fashion, *peh* is associated with *tôrâ:* the law or instruction of Yahweh is called *tôraṯ pîḵā* (Ps. 119:72; cf. Job 22:22); the *tôrâ* must be in the believer's mouth and must not depart from it (Ex. 13:9; Josh. 1:8; Mal. 2:6,7). A parallel expression is *'ēḏûṯ pîḵā* (Ps. 119:88; the suf. refers to Yahweh). In this context we may also note the phrase *mišpaṭ peh* (Ps. 105:5; 119:13; 1 Ch. 16:12).

Second, there are utterances of the mouth that serve to convey feelings or emotions:

---

28. See also V.1 below.

hll piel, "praise" (Ps. 63:6[5], obj.: Yahweh; Prov. 27:2, obj.: a human being; cf. also Ps. 34:2-3[1-2]; 109:30; 63:12[11] in comparison with v. 6[5]), and the noun *t^ehillâ,* "praise" (71:8, *yimmālē' pî t^ehillāṯeḵā,* "my mouth is filled with your [God's] praise"; cf. 34:2[1]; similarly the mouth declares praise: 51:17[15]; cf. 40:4[3]; 71:14-15); *ydh* hiphil, "give thanks" (109:30 par. with *hll;* cf. also 138:4, where thanksgiving is a response to promises uttered by Yahweh's mouth); *brk* piel, "bless" (32:4; 63:5-6[4-5]; 145:21, obj.: God; 62:5[4] condemns the two-faced who bless with the mouths while cursing in their hearts; cf. Prov. 11:11); *qll,* "curse" (Job 3:1, "Job opened his mouth and cursed his day"; cf. Ps. 62:5[4]); *rāṣâ,* "be pleased" (49:14[13] says that the rich are pleased with great words, whereas in 119:108 the psalmist prays that Yahweh will be pleased with the words of his mouth; similarly in 19:15[14] the psalmist prays that Yahweh will take pleasure [*rāṣôn*] in the words of his mouth [*'imrê-pî*]); *ḥnn* hithpael, "implore" (Job 19:16, *b^emô-pî 'eṯḥannen-lô*); *qārā',* "call" (Ps. 66:17, *'ēlāyw pî-qārā'ṯî,* obj.: Yahweh; Prov. 18:6, *ûpîw l^emah^alumôṯ yiqrā',* describing fools). Here too belongs the expression *peh ḥālāq,* "flattering mouth" (Prov. 26:28).

Finally, if we stay in the realm of communication, we come to a series of expressions using *peh* that are ambiguous: the context determines which of the two meanings discussed above they convey. Such expressions include several that mean "open one's mouth": *pāṣâ peh* (Jgs. 11:35-36; Job 35:16; cf. Lam. 2:16; 3:46), *pāṯaḥ peh* (of human beings: Ezk. 21:27[22]; Ps. 38:14[13]; 39:10[9]; 78:2; 109:2; Prov. 24:7; 31:8,9,26; Job 3:1; 33:2; Dnl. 10:16; cf. Isa. 53:7; of God: Ezk. 3:27; 33:22), and *pā'ar peh* (Ps. 119:131; Job 16:10; 29:23). These three verbs appear frequently with *peh* in other contexts; here we shall consider only combinations that remain in the realm of communication. Other expressions are: *'āḇar pîw,* "transgress with one's mouth" (Ps. 17:3); *šāmar peh,* "guard one's mouth" (Mic. 7:5; Prov. 21:23); *sāḵar peh,* "cover one's mouth" (Ps. 63:12[11]); *śîm yāḏ l^epeh,* "lay one's hand on one's mouth" (Job 40:4; cf. Prov. 30:32 without *śîm*); *bāhal 'al-pî,* "speak very quickly" (Eccl. 5:1[2]); *ḥāśaḵ peh,* "restrain one's mouth" (Job 7:11). Such expressions usually denote an activity that can be qualified in terms of the antithesis "prudent/stupid."[29]

These various usages have enabled us to observe the broad semantic range of the lexeme *peh.* In the human domain, the lexeme is both psychological and physical: sometimes it refers to psychological qualities (emotions, intellect), sometimes to physical qualities (a part of the body with its own characteristic functions). The instances associated with the psychological realm of communication are replete with overtones of wisdom and ethics. They illustrate personal conduct as expressed through the mouth. In other cases, the language takes on a religious sense, especially when Yahweh invades the psychological domain, the human heart and mouth — always, when a human being becomes a mouthpiece to express God's thoughts and God's will.

V. Theological Usage. Here we shall consider only those passages where the mouth is associated with Yahweh — whether they speak directly of Yahweh's mouth, describe

29. See VI below.

Yahweh as speaking through another's mouth, or mention the mouth of someone engaged in dialogue with Yahweh.

1. *Yahweh's Mouth.* The primary texts that speak of Yahweh's mouth are those that use the expression *pî yhwh* by itself (47 instances) or with a preposition (*kᵉpî yhwh,* 1 Ch. 12:24[23]; *mippî yhwh,* Jer. 23:16; 2 Ch. 36:12; cf. 2 Ch. 35:22, *mippî ʾᵉlōhîm*). The expression *pî yhwh* is an anthropomorphism; it means literally "mouth of Yahweh," but it is usually understood figuratively as referring to what is in or comes from the mouth of Yahweh. The expression appears frequently in legal and prophetic contexts, especially in the Deuteronomistic and P traditions.

Dt. 8:3, a text from the time of Josiah before Deuteronomistic redaction, uses the expression *kol-môṣāʾ pî-yhwh,* which has clear precursors in Akkadian and Ugaritic literatures.[30] At first glance, this expression means precisely "what comes from the mouth of Yahweh"; but in the narrower context, the words represent a structural nucleus of the catechetical unit Dt. 8:2-6 and refer to the expression *miṣwōṯ yhwh,* which occurs several times in this pericope (vv. 2,6). In this case, therefore, "everything that comes from the mouth of Yahweh" means first and foremost Yahweh's commandments.[31]

The Deuteronomistic and P traditions use the expression *pî yhwh* to denote Yahweh's commandment, instruction, or mandate (Ex. 17:1; Lev. 24:12; Nu. 3:16,39, 51; 4:37,41,45,49; 9:18,20,23; 10:13; 13:3; 33:2,38; 36:5 [all P]; and Dt. 34:5; Josh. 15:13; 17:4; 19:50; 21:3; 22:9; 2 K. 24:3 [all Dtr]). This meaning is clearly confirmed by the passages that use the expression *pî yhwh* in conjunction with expressions that refer explicitly to Yahweh's commandment (e.g., *ṣiwwâ* or *mišmereṯ*[32]) or to a law established by Yahweh. In the majority of these texts, Moses (or less frequently Joshua) is charged with interpreting the will of Yahweh and seeing to it that the commandments are obeyed. Thus Moses appears as the mediator of God's will, acting as a middleman between God and God's people.

Not to accept Yahweh's will is to rebel against him. For example, Balaam finds it more important to acknowledge God's will than to carry out the intentions of Balak. No matter what rewards Balak offers, Balaam will not transgress the commandment of Yahweh: *lōʾ ʾûḵal laʿᵃḇōr ʾeṯ-pî yhwh* (Nu. 22:18; 24:13 — texts introduced by later redactions[33]). The expression *ʿāḇar ʾeṯ-pî-yhwh* is synonymous with *ḥāṭāʾ,* "sin," as Saul's confession to Samuel shows (1 S. 15:24 [Dtr]).

The Deuteronomistic and P traditions in particular contain many accounts of the people's rebellion against the will of Yahweh. Dt. 1:26,43; 9:23; 1 S. 12:14,15; 1 K. 13:21,26 (typically Dtr texts) use the verb *mārâ,* "rebel," in conjunction with the expression *pî yhwh* to describe Israel's opposition to a divine command. The same situation appears in Nu. 20:24 and 27:14 (P); the wording is slightly different, but the mean-

30. See I.1,2 above.
31. F. García López, *Bibl* 62 (1981) 50-53.
32. See IV.2 above.
33. Cortese, 144.

ing is identical. In the Deuteronomistic traditions, the expression *mārâ* or *ʿāḇar* + *pî yhwh* often appears in conjunction with negated *šāmaʿ*, *šāmar,* or *ʾmn* hiphil, which also express the people's disobedience toward God and God's commandments. In Dt. 9:23 and 1 S. 12:14-15, we find *himrâ ʾeṯ-pî yhwh* in parallel with *lōʾ šāmaʿ beqōlô,* illustrating the fundamental association of → קוֹל *qôl* with *peh.*[34]

In the prophetic domain, the expression *pî yhwh* appears in Josh. 9:14 as the object of *šāʾal* (cf. Nu. 27:21; Isa. 30:2); in Isa. 1:20; 40:5; 58:14; Jer. 9:11(12); Mic. 4:4 as the object of *dibber;* and in Isa. 62:2 as the object of *nāqaḇ* (cf. also Isa. 34:16, *ṣiwwâ* + *peh* with reference to Yahweh).

Josh. 9:14 may allude to oracular practice in which Yahweh was consulted by the casting of lots,[35] so that the expression *pî yhwh* is equivalent to "oracle of Yahweh." Nu. 27:21 describes the oracular use of Urim to allow Yahweh to speak to the people. In such situations the divine response was not articulated; the priest had to interpret it so that the people could recognize the divine revelation. In the expression *ûpî lōʾ šāʾālû* (Isa. 30:2), the "mouth of Yahweh" probably refers to the prophet, sent to King Hezekiah to convey a message from God, which Hezekiah refused to hear.[36]

Isa. 1:20; 40:5; 58:14; and Mic. 4:4 use the expression *kî pî yhwh dibber* as a concluding messenger formula to validate the prophecy as a word spoken by Yahweh's own mouth. Jer. 9:11(12) uses *dibber* + *pî yhwh,* but in a different formulation, to refer to those prophets, recognized for their wisdom (cf. 8:8-9), who had the responsibility of proclaiming God's will to the people.

2. *Prophets.* The mouth of a prophet is an extension of the mouth of Yahweh. Jeremiah thinks of himself as Yahweh's mouth. If he turns back to Yahweh, he can serve once more as Yahweh's mouth (Jer. 15:19).

With Yahweh as subject, the expressions *śîm deḇārîm bepeh* and the equivalent *nāṯan deḇārîm bepeh* are characteristic of prophetic literature. The former appears in the Balaam story (Nu. 22:38; 23:5,12) and is repeated in Isa. 51:16; 59:21. Like the other prophets, Balaam receives the word of Yahweh in his mouth. This expression, too, takes on the function of a messenger formula (2 S. 14:3,18-19; Ex. 4:15; Ezr. 8:17). Jeremiah interprets himself as a messenger in the account of his call and later in his prophetic ministry, when he states that Yahweh put his words in his mouth (Jer. 1:9; 5:14; cf. Dt. 18:18); this usage again confirms that the prophets thought of themselves as the mouth of God. The undeniable similarity of Jeremiah's mission to that of Moses is established by the use of identical language (cf. Jer. 1:9 with Dt. 18:18),[37] which further underlines the function of the prophet as mediator.[38]

The functions of the true prophets are clearly different from those of the false prophets, who deliver false oracles (1 K. 22:22-23 par. 2 Ch. 18:21-22) and proclaim

34. See VII.1 below.
35. M. H. Woudstra, *Book of Joshua. NICOT* (1981), 160.
36. On prophets as the mouth of God see V.2 below.
37. F. García-López, *VT* 35 (1985) 1-12.
38. See V.1 above; L. Ramlot, *DBS,* VIII, 1038-40.

visions that issue from their own heart, not from the mouth of Yahweh (Jer. 23:16). According to Mic. 3:5, they listen to the sound of money rather than the mouth of Yahweh.

Finally, the mouth of Yahweh speaks not only through the prophets in person but also through their written words. In at least one case, the mouth of Yahweh is identified with the book of Yahweh, which is also the book of the prophet Isaiah (Isa. 34:16). Ezekiel analogously describes his prophecy as a scroll given him by Yahweh, which he must devour before he can transmit its message to his people (Ezk. 3:2-3). He consumes the scroll and Yahweh opens the mouth of the prophet, so that the words of the scroll can be transmitted to the people (v. 27). This message, whether spoken or written, is at the same time a message both totally God's and totally the prophet's.

These words from the mouth of Yahweh, transmitted by the prophets, are so powerful and effectual that they can be compared to instruments of punishment or even death (Hos. 6:5; Isa. 11:4). The prophetic word is like a devouring fire — a role also played by the mouth (Jer. 5:14) — a deadly arrow (Jer. 9:7[8]), or a sharp sword (Isa. 49:2).[39] The effectual power of the divine word is especially clear in Isa. 55:10-11, which compares it to the rain and snow that fructify the earth. A word from the mouth of God can bring life or death, quite like the blessings and curses associated with the covenant ceremony (Dt. 30:14-15).

3. *Worshipers.* God places his words not only in the mouths of prophets but also in the mouths of worshipers *(nāṯan + bᵉpî):*[40] "a new song, a song of praise to our God" (Ps. 40:4[3]). The praise of God is possible because God opens the lips of the psalmist, inspiring the hymn that is uttered (51:17[15]). The praise of God thus turns out to be a gift of this very God. This explains why the voice of the living God can even be heard in the mouths of children. God is manifest in babes and infants, from whose mouths issues praise (8:3[2] LXX; cf. Mt. 21:16).

The mouth, in harmony with the lips and the tongue (Ps. 51:17[15]; 63:6[5]; 66:17; 126:2), indeed with one's whole being (145:21) — all are set in motion to sing the greatness of the Lord, to tell of God's righteousness and salvation (71:8,15; 126:2; 145:21). If a prayer is to be uttered, the Lord must open the lips of the worshiper; only then will God hearken to the prayers that issue from human mouths (54:4[2]; 119:108).

In prayer a further organ is needed: the heart. Even though the lips move and the mouth opens, it is the heart with which a worshiper prays. The heart moves toward God and the mouth joins it (1 S. 1:12-13; 2:1).

Finally, the mouth of the psalmist, which sings the wonders of Yahweh, is contrasted with the mouth of the wicked, pictured as wild beasts, their mouths open to devour the speaker. In such situations prayer is addressed to God, who can deliver the psalmist (Ps. 22:22[21]; 109:2,30; cf. Am. 3:12 and Job 36:16). This notion brings us close to the domain of wisdom literature.

39. See III.2 above.
40. See V.1 above.

VI. Wisdom. In wisdom literature, *peh* appears frequently in Proverbs and Psalms, less often in Job and Ecclesiastes.

1. *General.* In these books the passages mentioning the mouth can be very general in meaning and intent. In Prov. 4:5; 5:7; 7:24, for example, the "sons" (i.e., pupils) are urged to learn the words of the mouth *('imrê peh)* of their teacher. A similar exhortation, but addressed to the people, appears in Ps. 78:1-2 (cf. 49:2ff.[1ff.]).

2. *Wise vs. Foolish.* In the wisdom texts that mention the mouth, we can observe a clear division between two antithetical classifications: wise vs. foolish and good vs. evil. The former represents an intellectual categorization typical of wisdom thought, while the latter embodies an ethical and religious categorization; but the two frequently overlap, so that the wise or foolish can be identified by their goodness or wickedness.

The group of the good includes the righteous (*ṣaddîqîm,* Prov. 10:6,11,31; 11:9; Ps. 37:30) and the upright (*yᵉšārîm,* Prov. 11:11). The mouth of the righteous utters wisdom (*ḥoḵmâ,* Prov. 10:31; Ps. 37:30). Prov. 8 personifies wisdom, describing the words of her mouth as truth and righteousness. Wisdom hates a lying mouth *(pî tahpuḵōṯ);* in her words there is nothing twisted or crooked (vv. 7-8,13). In this series of ethical values, truth is contrasted with wickedness: truth without deceit and righteousness without wickedness, in the domain of language.

The group of the evil includes the scoundrel and villain (*'āḏām bᵉlîyaʿal, 'îš ʿāwôn,* Prov. 6:12) and the wicked (*rᵉšāʿîm,* Prov. 10:6,11; 11:11; 12:6; 15:28; 19:28; Ps. 36:2ff.[1ff.]). Their mouth is characterized by falsehood (*ʿiqqᵉšûṯ,* Prov. 4:24; 6:12), perversion and lies (*tahpuḵôṯ,* 10:32; *ʿāwôn,* 19:38; Ps. 36:4[3]), and evil in general (*rāʿôṯ,* Prov. 15:28; cf. Ps. 50:19). The hearts of the intelligent are attuned to wisdom and their mouths utter knowledge, whereas the mouths of fools feed on malice and utter folly (Prov. 15:2,14). The wise control their lips and speak with prudence, but the mouths of fools utter arrogance (14:3); "those who guard their mouths preserve their lives; those who open wide their lips come to ruin" (13:3; Job 35:16). "The heart of the wise makes their speech judicious and increases instruction upon their lips" (Prov. 16:23). Eliphaz rejects the views expressed by Job on the grounds that he has not spoken with wisdom; Job's utterances are profitless and his words carry no weight: "Your own mouth condemns you, and not I; your own lips testify against you" (Job 15:2-6).

3. *Power.* The human mouth is not neutral; on the contrary, it is a mighty weapon. Its speech entails serious consequences, good or evil. This is true not just for the individual, but also for society. The mouth of the righteous is a source of life and blessing. Their speech brings prosperity. Fools produce violence and practice it with their mouths. Their speech destroys them and those around them (Prov. 10:6,11,14,31-32; 18:7; Ps. 50:19; Eccl. 10:12-13). The human mouth can foster or destroy solidarity and fellowship with one's neighbor. The speech of the wicked engenders intrigues and slanders their neighbors; such speech becomes a destructive force within society. Contrariwise, the blessings uttered by the righteous serve the prosperity and well-being of the city; their speech is good and constructive, because they are concerned for the wel-

fare of their neighbors (Prov. 11:9,11). The words of the wicked can even be deadly snares. Those who are guilty attempt to pervert justice with their words; they condemn the innocent to death. Those who are innocent can defend and deliver themselves by speaking the truth (12:6; 18:7). Careful attention to one's speech is therefore a matter of life and death: the fruits of the mouth are either beneficent or deadly. Those who guard their mouths refuse to spread poison and take care not to injure others (13:2-3; 21:23; 26:9). All these passages underline the gravity and effectiveness of human language, the potency of the mouth. These observations confirm once again what we have already noted about the power of the word.[41] It is therefore easy to understand the psalmist who uses the language of wisdom to emphasize the dangers that emanate from a wicked mouth and a lying tongue and, faced with such peril, prays for God's speedy intervention and deliverance (Ps. 109:2; 144:8-11; cf. Job 5:15-16).

4. *Ethical Ideal.* If we seek to summarize the ethical ideal espoused by wisdom as expressed in texts that use the word "mouth," we must speak of a "coherent life." The heart, mouth, and hands are the most important foci of human life. The ideal is that there be harmony among these three organs and their functions: thought, speech, and action. But this coherence is often impugned by conflicts between thought and speech (lies), speech and action (hypocrisy), or thought and action (duplicity or powerlessness).[42]

In Prov. 4:20-27 we find a series of links between parts of the human body and major elements of human activity. The description of the heart, mouth, tongue, eyes, ears, hands, and feet seeks to represent the whole personality of the disciple in its corporeal being and in the totality of its life. The heart functions as the center of the individual, regulating the functions of the other parts of the body. From the heart proceeds control over the mouth and tongue, the eyes and what they see, and finally the action of the feet.

Prov. 6:12-14 expounds a contrast between the external organs (mouth, eyes, feet, fingers) and the mind (heart), i.e., a discrepancy between internal activity (intention) and its external manifestations. The misuse of the external organs betrays a perversion of the heart, the center of life, from which proceed thoughts and emotions.[43] By contrast, the heart of the wise makes their speech (mouth) judicious (16:23). This inner connection between mind (heart) and speech (mouth) constitutes a substantial part of the argumentation and fundamental conception of several other wisdom texts: Prov. 15 (esp. vv. 14,28); 16:23; Ps. 141:3-4. It is the properly oriented heart, giving rise to correct moral conduct, in which the law of God resides (Ps. 37:30-31). The ethical ideal of wisdom is ultimately grounded in the relationship of the individual to God, in whom alone is found a perfect unity of heart, lips, and speech.

VII. 1. *LXX.* In general the LXX translates *peh* with *stóma,* a word with essentially the same range of meanings as *peh.* In five cases it uses *peristómion,* which strictly

41. See V.2 above.
42. See de Geradon, 31, 36; Bernaert, 5-6.
43. B. Gemser, *Sprüche Salomos. HAT* I/16 (1963), 39.

means "that which surrounds the mouth"; in the broader sense it denotes the oral cavity as a whole (cf. Ex. 28:32; 36:30 [= 39:23]; Job 30:18; also Job 15:27). When the LXX uses other translations, these variants still remain within the semantic domain of *peh* (see IV above). They fall into two groups. In the first, *peh* is translated by *glṓssa* (Jgs. 7:6), *cheílos* (Prov. 6:2), or *prósōpon* (Ps. 17:8; 54:21[19]; Prov. 2:6), i.e., words for other parts of the body that are associated with the mouth. In the second, *peh* is translated by words that refer to communication: *eipeín* (Gen. 45:21); *lógos* (1 S. 15:24); *próstagma* (Lev. 24:12; Nu. 9:18b,20,23b; 33:38; 36:5; Josh. 15:13; 17:4; 19:50; 21:3; 22:9; Job 39:27); *rhḗma* (Ex. 17:1; Nu. 14:41; 22:18; 24:13; 27:14; 33:2; Dt. 1:26,43; 9:23; 34:5; 1 K. 13:26; Job 16:5; 23:12); *phónos* and *phōnḗ* (Ex. 17:13; Nu. 21:24; Dt. 13:16[15]; 20:13; Nu. 3:16,39,51; 4:37,41,45,49; 9:20; 10:13; 13:3; Am. 6:5).

A curious but noteworthy translation appears in Ps. 132:2, where *peh* is represented by *ǭa*, "fringe," which is finally still within the semantic domain of *peh.*[44]

Apart from such variants, various idioms with *peh* have their own special translations: e.g., *kᵉḇaḏ peh* (Ex. 4:10) is represented by *ischyóphōnos, higdîl peh* (Ob. 12) by *megalorremoneín,* and *mārâ 'eṯ-peh* (Nu. 20:24) by *paroxýnein.* In most cases such variants convey a more precise meaning while still remaining in the semantic domain of *peh.* This is always true of terms signifying communication, since in these passages *peh* does not denote the mouth in the strict sense but rather speech, commandments, or the voice — that which issues from the mouth.

In 1 S. 15:24 *pî yhwh* is translated by *tón lógon kyríou;* here the LXX avoids an anthropomorphism that might occasion a misunderstanding on account of the parallel expression *dᵉḇāreyḵā (šᵉmû'ēl).* The same purpose is at work in the passages where the LXX often simply omits the expression *'eṯ-pî,* e.g., Josh. 9:15.[45]

2. *Dead Sea Scrolls.* Various forms of *peh* occur 138 times in the Dead Sea Scrolls: 39 in 1QH, 31 in 1QS, 20 in CD, 17 in 11QT, 13 in 1QSa, 4 in 1QM, and 14 in other documents. In more than three-quarters of its occurrences, *peh* is introduced by a preposition: *lᵉ* (35 times), *'al* (33 times), *bᵉ* (17 times), *min* (11 times), or *kᵉ* (9 times); the meaning is quite similar to that found in Biblical Hebrew: "according to. . . ." We likewise find the same idioms that appear in the OT: *'al pî haddᵉḇārîm* or *'al pî hattôrâ* (1QS 6:24; CD 7:7; 19:4; 20:28). There are also expressions characteristic of the Qumran materials, such as *'al pî hārabbîm* (1QS 6:21; 8:19; 9:2), a phrase that probably corresponds to the expression *'al pî rāḇ yiśrā'ēl* (1QS 5:22).

In 1QS 6:26 we note the formula *bᵉ'amrôṯ 'eṯ pî rᵉ'ēhû,* denoting rebellion against the will of another; this formula recalls Dt. 1:26,43; 9:23, where the rebellion is against Yahweh.[46] Another important text is 1QS 10:21-22, where heart *(lēḇ),* mouth *(peh),* lips *(śāp̄â),* and tongue *(lāšôn)* appear together referring to a series of personal decisions, a usage reminiscent of wisdom literature. In 1QS 10:23 *peh* parallels *lāšôn,* in a

---

44. See III.4 above.
45. See R. G. Boling, *Joshua. AB* 6 (1982), 258.
46. See V.1 above.

formula found also in the *Hodayot: b^{e}hôḏôṯ 'epṯaḥ pî* par. *w^{e}ṣiḏqôṯ 'ēl t^{e}sappēr l^{e}šônî tāmîḏ* (cf. 1QH 11:4,33).

According to 1QM 14:6 (a thanksgiving text), God personally opens the mouth of the faithful so that they may give thanks and opens the mouth of the dumb to sing God's praises. This text alludes to Ezk. 33:22; cf. also Ps. 39:10(9).

In the *Hodayot* (1QH) the term *peh* bears a higher theological significance than in the other documents.[47] God stands at the center of many expressions using *peh.* The text speaks of God's "mouth" (3:5), God's "glorious mouth" (*b^{e}pî k^{e}ḇōḏ^{e}ḵā,* 6:14), and God's "truthful mouth" (*'^{e}meṯ piḵâ,* 11:7). In this last text we also find a parallelism between God's mouth and hand: "I know that truth is in your mouth, and in your hand is righteousness." God's mouth issues words of instruction (6:9) and establishes the temporal order (12:9). It motivates repentance (6:14) and proper conduct (4:21). It is God who places prayer and praise in the mouth of the psalmist (9:11; 11:4; cf. also 11:33). A similar expression with *śîm* appears in 8:16: *śamtâ b^{e}pî k^{e}yôreh gešem,* "You have placed in my mouth [something] like the early rain," referring to the Teacher of Righteousness, who plays an important role here as the mediator of instruction.[48] It is God who places true teaching in the human mouth and understanding in the human heart, as similar parallel formulations assert in 2:17-18. This explains the question asked in 10:7 and 12:32: "How shall I speak if you do not open my mouth?" The psalmist's mouth is open to sing God's praise, for God created the breath on the tongue *(rûaḥ b^{e}lāšôn)* and the "fruit of the lips" *(p^{e}rî ś^{e}pāṯayim),* and God gives a rhythm for words and a cadence for puffs of breath from the lips (1:28,30-31; cf. 11:24-25).

Alongside these many passages referring to God and the psalmist, the *Hodayot* contain a series of texts that speak of the mouth of those "who seek after trickery" (2:34): people who look for God in the mouth of prophets of deceit, attracted by delusion (4:16). In 7:11 we find a lovely parallelism between mouth and tongue: "There is no mouth for the spirit of destruction, and no reply in the tongue for all the sons of guilt." In 8:35, however, the tongue is clearly treated as part of the mouth.

Several passages in the Temple Scroll exhibit the use of *peh* in the context of vows. The priestly laws governing vows prescribe that one must keep a vow that has been spoken by one's mouth (11QT 53:13; cf. ll. 10 and 15). A clear relationship between *śāpâ* and *peh* is presupposed. 11QT 54:4-5 also discusses vows, using a formula that connects the verb *yāṣā'* directly with *peh: kwl ndr . . . 'šr . . . 'l npšh yqwmw 'lyh kkwl 'šr yṣ' mpyh,* "Every vow of a widow or a divorcee, everything by which she binds herself formally, will hold good according to everything that has issued from her mouth." These texts are based in turn on Nu. 30:10(9) and Dt. 23:22ff.(21ff.). The occurrences of *peh* in the Aramaic texts of the Dead Sea Scrolls are discussed elsewhere.[49]

García-López

---

47. See V.3 above.
48. See M. Delcor, *Les Hymnes de Qumran* (1962), 206.
49. See Beyer, 669.

פוח *pwḥ*

I. Etymology. II. 1. Occurrences; 2. Phraseology; 3. LXX. III. Usage: 1. Blow Vigorously; 2. Speak Vigorously. IV. Sirach and Dead Sea Scrolls.

I. Etymology. The onomatopoetic root *pwḥ,* originally monosyllabic,[1] acquired the counterpart → נפח *npḥ* at an early date. There is no monosyllabic equivalent in Ugaritic, but the root is represented by Syr. *pāḥ*[2] and Middle Heb. and Jewish Aram. *pûaḥ;* cf. Arab. *fāḥa,* "diffuse an aroma," and *faḥḥa,* "howl (storm)." We may also cite Akk. *puḫpuḫḫû/u,* "roar of battle."[3] Ugar. *ypḥ,* "witness,"[4] plays a role in the discussion; it is noteworthy that the Ugaritic equivalent of Heb. *npḥ* is *npḫ* (with *ḫ*). We must think in terms of a close relationship exhibiting a striking semantic development. The argumentation also relies on Syr. *paḥ,* "grow faint (voice), labor."[5]

II. 1. *Occurrences.* The verb occurs 15 times, 3 in the qal and 12 in the hiphil. It is often maintained, however, that *yāp̱îaḥ* in Prov. 6:19; 14:5,25; 19:5,9 is a separate noun meaning "witness."[6] This possibility may also be considered in Ps. 12:6(Eng. v. 5) and Hab. 2:3. The form *hāp̄ēaḥ* in Isa. 42:22 is the hiphil infinitive absolute, but derives from *pḥḥ.*

2. *Phraseology.* The verb *pwḥ* appears frequently in fixed expressions. For example, *pûaḥ hayyôm* occurs twice and *yāp̄îaḥ kᵉzāḇîm* 5 times. As prepositions introducing

---

pwḥ. J. Barth, *NSS;* P.-R. Berger, "Zu den Strophen des 10. Psalms," *UF* 2 (1970) 7-17; B. Blake, "'Until the Day Break and the Shadows Flee Away,'" *ExpT* 47 (1935/36) 45; W. Bühlmann, *Vom rechten Reden und Schweigen. OBO* 12 (1976), esp. 93-100, 160-67; M. Dahood, "Some Ambiguous Texts in Isaias (30,15; 52,2; 33,2; 40,5; 45,1)," *CBQ* 20 (1958) 41-49; G. Gifford, "Songs of Songs II.17 (IV.6) and Isaiah XL.3," *ExpT* 47 (1935/36) 381; S. E. Loewenstamm, *"yāpeᵃḥ, yāpiᵃḥ, yāpîᵃḥ," Leš* 26 (1962) 205-8, 280; P. D. Miller, "Yāpîaḥ in Ps xii 6," *VT* 29 (1979) 495-500; J. Obermann, "Survival of an Old Canaanite Participle and Its Impact on Biblical Exegesis," *JBL* 70 (1951) 199-209; D. Pardee, "Ypḥ 'Witness' in Hebrew and Ugaritic," *VT* 28 (1978) 204-13; F. H. Pickering, "'Until the Day Break and the Shadows Flee Away,'" *ExpT* 48 (1936/37) 44; J. S. Sibinga, "Une citation du cantique dans la secunda Petri," *RB* 73 (1966) 107-18; W. von Soden, "*n* als Wurzelaugment im Semitischen," *Studia Orientalia in Memoriam C. Brockelmann* (1968), 175-84; A. Strobel, *Untersuchungen zum eschatologischen Verzögerungsproblem. NovTSup* 2 (1961); D. Winton Thomas, "'Until the Day Break and the Shadows Flee Away,'" *ExpT* 47 (1935/36) 431-32; C. Virolleaud, "L'alphabet sénestrogyre de Ras-Shamra," *CRAIBL* (1960) 84-90.

1. Von Soden, 176; Meyer, II, 133.
2. *LexSyr,* 559.
3. *AHw,* II, 876.
4. *UT,* no. 1129.
5. *LexSyr,* 561-62.
6. See *NSS,* 189, 233.

the object, we find l^e (twice), b^e (once), and *'al* (once). Only in Ezk. 21:36 and possibly in Ps. 12:6(5) is Yahweh the subject; in Hab. 2:3 the subject appears to be *ḥāzôn*.

3. *LXX*. The LXX translation strives for uniformity in the choice of words, while at the same time seeking to capture the meaning accurately. The following words may be noted: *diapneúein* (3 times), *ekkaíein* (5 times), *emphysán, enkaleín, epideiknýein, anatéllein,* and *katakyrieúein* (once each).

III. Usage. Usage embraces the domain of strongly blowing wind (expressed verbally) with a figurative extension to the domain of speech (exhale > express). It is not out of the question to see an emphasis on the forensic realm. If so, usage in the sense of "testimony" cannot be ruled out. The semantic focus has led one lexicon hesitantly to distinguish *pûaḥ* I and *pûaḥ* II.[7]

1. *Blow Vigorously.* The basic meaning of *pûaḥ* is found in Cant. 4:16, where the quality of the blowing wind is intended to elucidate the nature of what is expressed figuratively in a lyrical context. A descriptive poem (4:12-15) is followed antithetically by a poem of desire,[8] appealing urgently to the beloved to enjoy the fruits of the garden (the woman who is speaking). The concrete symbols of the north wind and south wind are commanded to come (*'wr:* cf. Jer. 25:32; *bw':* cf. Hos. 13:15) and blow *(pwḥ).* The choice of words suggests a violent tempest; the use of the same parallelism in Sir. 43:16-17 reinforces this interpretation. In the context of the Song of Songs, the point is the intensity of the lovers' desire. Keel and Krinetzki shift the point to quiet pleasure, hardly doing justice to the unbridled explosivity expressed.[9] For the hiphil of *pwḥ,* close examination shows that the action reflected in the verb cannot be described simply as wafting an aroma abroad;[10] the meaning has an element of being caught up and swept along violently: "tear through, roar through." In the garden the entire force of the wind, penetrating every corner, will be activated to capture all its fragrances, and, abundant as the rain that pours down[11] on everything (Nu. 24:7; Jer. 9:17; 18:14; Ps. 147:18; Job 36:28), to catch up the lover and carry him to the garden.

The expression *pûaḥ hayyôm* appears only in Cant. 2:17 and 4:6: "Until the day *yāpûaḥ* and the shadows flee *(nûs).*" Since Cant. 2:17ab and 4:6ab are identical, some have suggested that 4:6 is repeated secondarily from 2:17 and is also out of place (it should follow v. 7 or v. 8).[12] But such theories cannot be substantiated; it is more likely that we are dealing with evidence that this topos was popular in love poetry.

---

7. *HAL,* III, 916-17.
8. G. Krinetzki, *Kommentar zum Hohenlied. BBET* 16 (1981), 22, 153.
9. O. Keel, *Song of Songs* (Eng. trans. 1994), 181; G. Krinetzki, *Das Hohe Lied* (1964), 175.
10. W. Rudolph, *Das Hohe Lied. KAT* XVII/2 (1962), 151.
11. → נזל *nāzal.*
12. Cf. H. Ringgren, *Das Hohe Lied. ATD* 16 (^{3}1981), 272; et al. O. Loretz (*Die althebräische Liebeslied. AOAT* 14/1 [1971], 26, 28) suggests v. 7; Graetz (*Schir ha Schirim* [1885], 157) favors v. 8.

To establish the meaning of *pûaḥ hayyôm,* we may examine other passages that describe the advancing day. The "passing of the day" is expressed by *ʿbr yôm (yāmîm)* (Zeph. 2:2 [disputed]; Gen. 50:4; Job 17:11; etc.), *pnh hayyôm (yāmîm)* (Jer. 6:4; Ps. 90:9), and *rph hayyôm* (Jgs. 19:9). While the majority of such passages use verbs of motion *(ʿbr, pnh),* Jgs. 19:9, like the passages in the Song of Songs, is figurative. Most exegetes see here an allusion to the otherwise unspecified departure of the day and the lengthening of shadows; others, however, find a description of the breaking day.[13] Pope explains that the reference is to the time when "the amative activity ends."[14] Meteorological considerations cast doubt on this interpretation of *yāpûaḥ hayyôm.* The expression probably refers to the effect of the *rûaḥ hayyôm* mentioned also in Gen. 3:8. "During the summer, a pleasant west wind regularly begins to blow in the course of the morning; toward evening it becomes stronger."[15] Dalman already observed that this wind reaches its greatest strength around 2 p.m.; according to him, the passages in the Song of Songs must be assigned to this time of day.[16]

Indeed, the use of *pûaḥ* itself points in this direction, since, as noted above, the verb has an element of tempestuous activation. When the invigorating wind of late afternoon relieves the paralyzing heat of the day, the spirit of enterprise is aroused. This interpretation is reinforced by the similes of the gazelle and the young stag, which in ancient Near Eastern literature symbolize quickness, playfulness, and above all a passionate enjoyment of life.[17] In such a spirit, in 2:17, the woman calls to her beloved; in 4:6, similarly, the beloved says that he will hasten to the mountain of myrrh and the hill of frankincense when the quickening wind blows. The mountain and hill represent metaphorically the enticing, intoxicating aura of the woman.[18]

Ezk. 21:33-37(28-32) (secondary) is a "drastic oracle of judgment."[19] It incorporates some language typical of Ezekiel, but clearly differs at many points from Ezekiel's usage. "The fire of my wrath *ʾāpîaḥ* against you" takes up the theme of fiery judgment on the wicked (Job 20:26; cf. 15:34; Dt. 32:22; Jer. 15:14; 17:4), echoing Ezk. 22:21,31; *npḥ* appears in 22:21 in the sense of "kindle." The use of a different verb appears to be intentional. The point of vv. 35b-37(30b-32) is to describe the concentrated, inexorable momentum of God's wrath, which will lead to a bloodbath. In such a context, the frequently neutral *npḥ* is too vague; by contrast, *pwḥ* expresses the raging of a tempest — here describing figuratively the fire of divine anger.

2. *Speak Vigorously.* Other texts depart even further from the initial imagery. Prov. 29:8 still has to do with tempestuous energy, but the context reveals a new accent: a

---

13. Berger, 14; Sibinga, 108-9; Loretz, *Liebeslied,* 19.
14. M. Pope, *Song of Songs. AB* 7C (1977), 365.
15. Keel, Küchler, and Uehlinger, *Orte und Landschaften der Bibel,* I (1984), 51.
16. *AuS,* I/2, 511-12.
17. See the texts cited by O. Keel, *ZBK* 18, 95-96.
18. Cf. Loretz, *AOAT* 14/1, 28.
19. Fuhs, *Ezechiel 1–24. NEB* (1984), 115.

form of speech is involved. "Scoffers *('anšê lāṣôn)* set aflame *(yāp̱îḥû)* a city *(qiryâ).*" The *'anšê lāṣôn* are contrasted to the *ḥ*ᵃ*ḵāmîm,* and a community *(qiryâ)* is affected. The purpose of the *'anšê lāṣôn* is to stir up unrest and vilification, which rage through the city like a tempest, churning it up. The hiphil of *pwḥ* is used to express the tempestuous agitation of the disastrous result.

The expression *yāp̱îaḥ k*ᵉ*zāḇîm* is common to Prov. 6:19; 14:5,25; and 19:5,9. Gemser accepts Gordon's arguments, seeing in *yāp̱îaḥ* a substantive synonymous with *'ēḏ,* "witness."[20] In all his translations, however, he retains the hiphil of *pwḥ* ("one who breathes out lies"). As Dahood argues convincingly in the case of Ps. 27:12, *yāp̱aḥ* can stand in synonymous parallelism with *'ēḏ.*[21] The parallelism in Prov. 19:5 is well suited to establishing this meaning in Proverbs as well *('ēḏ š*ᵉ*qārîm lō' yinnāqeh w*ᵉ*yāp̱îaḥ k*ᵉ*zāḇîm lō' yimmālēṭ),*[22] but 12:17a *(yāp̱îaḥ '*ᵉ*mûnâ yaggîḏ ṣeḏeq)* and the chiasmus in 14:5 suggest the contrary. While retention of the hiphil of *pwḥ* in all the texts remains a possibility, there is a real question whether the tautology in 6:19a and 14:5b, which is inescapable if *yāp̱îaḥ* is used synonymously with *'ēḏ,* actually represents the author's intention. In 19:5 a clear decision appears impossible.

It is clear that in the texts just discussed the meaning of *pwḥ* hiphil shifts in the direction of verbal utterances. The verb *dibber* is frequently used to express the speaking of *k*ᵉ*zāḇîm* (Jgs. 16:10,13; Hos. 7:13; Zeph. 3:13; Dnl. 11:27). The language of wisdom appears to have evolved a different terminology. The similarity to *'ēḏ šeqer* (Prov. 6:19; 14:5; Ex. 20:16; Dt. 19:18) or *'ēḏ š*ᵉ*qārîm* (Prov. 12:17; 19:5,9) as well as *'ēḏ ḥāmās* (Ex. 23:1; Dt. 19:16; Ps. 35:11) or *'ēḏ k*ᵉ*zāḇîm* (Prov. 21:28) is unmistakable. This brings us into the realm of social disintegration and its concomitant iniquity (*'āwen,* 19:28). This is also the theme of 19:5,9. Prov. 6:19 emphasizes that the utterance of lies sows discord among brothers, disrupting family ties. Since a witness usually appears in court, life itself can be at stake in case of a guilty verdict (14:5); one who speaks lies as a false witness is rightly called *rāšā'*. Now it remains to ask whether — as several translations suggest — this language refers to a quiet, secretive act, a whisper in the background. The forensic situation itself indicates that a false witness appeared in public. The consequences of false utterances do not suggest lies spoken behind someone's back. If someone who utters (*pwḥ* hiphil) *'*ᵉ*mûnâ* speaks justice *(ṣeḏeq)* (12:17) and an *'ēḏ '*ᵉ*meṯ* saves lives (14:25), then the actions of the destructive counterpart are presumably equally public. We may assume that we are dealing with a vigorous advocacy of lies and an argumentative insistence on an unjust claim. This analysis suggests that the wisdom-related phrase *yāp̱îaḥ k*ᵉ*zāḇîm* should be understood as meaning "one who vigorously utters lies."

The combination *yāp̱aḥ laqqēṣ* (Hab. 2:3) is unique in the OT. On the basis of 1QpHab, the verb should be interpreted as a simple hiphil,[23] and not, as the MT seems to suggest, as a verbal adjective or jussive. The point of the passage is that the prophet

---

20. B. Gemser, *Sprüche Salomos. HAT* I/16 (²1963), 38; Gordon, *UT,* no. 1129.
21. M. Dahood, *CBQ* 20 (1958) 47-48 n. 21.
22. See Delitzsch, *Proverbs of Solomon. KD,* 2 vols. (Eng. trans. 1955), I, 148.
23. Rudolph, *Micha-Nahum-Habakuk-Zephanja. KAT* XIII/3 (1975), 212.

is "vehemently and impatiently"[24] looking for the fulfillment of his vision. Keller rightly includes *pwḥ* among the terms Habakkuk uses for "speak"[25] ("it pants for the end"[26] catches the urgency but does not do justice to the element of speech). The vision vehemently proclaims the end, and it does not lie *(wᵉlō' yᵉkazzēḇ)*. The meaning is close to that of Prov. 14:5. Later, Hab. 2:3 came to be understood primarily in an eschatological sense.[27]

Ps. 10:5 also belongs to the series of texts in which *pwḥ* hiphil denotes vigorous verbal expression, here with aggressive overtones. A forensic setting is not out of the question. But there is no evidence to support the theory that the text "originally had to do with breathing as a form of magic."[28]

The expression *yāp̄îaḥ lô* in Ps. 12:6(5) is among the problematic passages. Comparing Hab. 2:3, Delitzsch translates it as "him who languisheth for it [God's deliverance]."[29] Kraus agrees that the text refers to such an individual, who is sorely beset.[30] Another theory is that the expression refers to a "witness" who interceded on behalf of the oppressed poor.[31] The words can also be understood to mean that Yahweh vouchsafes his aid to the poor, when "he" (understood collectively) "cries out for it" *(lô* referring to *yešaʿ)*.

IV. Sirach and Dead Sea Scrolls. Sir. 4:2 warns against "grieving the poor."[32] This usage diverges from what we have observed elsewhere.

The context of 1QS 7:14 shows that the verb must denote some windlike motion that blows clothing about.[33] If the genitals are exposed, the person in question is to be punished for thirty days.

Reiterer

---

24. Jeremias, *Kultprophetie und Gerechtsverkündigung in der späten Königszeit Israels. WMANT* 35 (1970), 85.
25. C.-A. Keller, *ZAW* 85 (1973) 159.
26. Molin, *Die Söhne des Lichtes* (1954), 14.
27. See Strobel.
28. H. Gunkel, *Die Psalmen. HKAT* II/4 (^{4}1926), 38.
29. *Psalms. KD* (Eng. trans. 1955), I, 192, 195-96.
30. H.-J. Kraus, *Psalms 1–59* (Eng. trans. 1988), 206-7, 209-10.
31. Miller, *VT* 29 (1979) 499-500.
32. Sauer, "Jesus Sirach," *JSHRZ* III/5, 513.
33. See III.1 above.

פוץ pûṣ; תְּפוּצָה tᵉpûṣâ; נָפַץ nāp̱aṣ; פזר pzr

I. Etymology. II. The Verb in the OT: 1. Occurrences; 2. Overflow, Spread; 3. Scatter; 4. Scatter Flocks; 5. Scatter People; 6. Exile, Diaspora. III. Nouns: 1. *tᵉpûṣâ;* 2. *bat̲-pûṣay.* IV. 1. Dead Sea Scrolls; 2. LXX. V. *pzr.*

I. Etymology. Etymologically, *pûṣ* is related to Arab. *fāḍa(i),* "overflow, spread."[1] Since this Arabic verb is mediae *y,* in contrast to the Hebrew mediae *w,* and since there is also a by-form *npṣ* in Hebrew, there is every reason to think that we are dealing with a biconsonantal root that has been expanded in a variety of ways.

II. The Verb in the OT.

1. *Occurrences.* In the OT the verb appears 13 times in the qal, 16 times in the niphal, and 36 times in the hiphil. Whether a noun *tᵉp̱ûṣâ* occurs in Jer. 25:34 is dubious.[2] The word *pûṣay* in Zeph. 3:10 has not been explained satisfactorily.[3]

2. *Overflow, Spread.* a. The basic meaning "overflow" is found in Prov. 5:16, where the disciple is admonished to drink from his own well: "Should your spring flood the street?" V. 18 identifies this well with the disciple's wife: the text thus belongs to the category of warnings against strange women. "One's own well" probably symbolizes wisdom or personal faith.[4] The same meaning probably appears in Zec. 1:17: "My cities shall again overflow with prosperity."[5] Job 40:11 uses the hiphil figuratively: Job is to pour out the overflowings of his anger *(ʿeḇrôṯ ʾap̱).*

b. The meaning "spread" is found in 2 S. 18:8: the battle spread throughout the whole region. Job 38:24 belongs here also: the east wind spreads over the earth (intransitive hiphil). But in 1 S. 14:34 we already hear overtones of the meaning "scatter": "Disperse yourselves." Spreading sometimes includes division: the families of the Canaanite spread abroad and divided (Gen. 10:18; cf. 9:19 with *npṣ*). The people scattered throughout Egypt to search for straw (Ex. 5:12). Troops leave their commander and disperse (1 S. 13:8; 2 K. 25:5 = Jer. 52:8; cf. 1 S. 13:11 with *npṣ*).

---

pûṣ. G. Widengren, "The Gathering of the Dispersed," *SEÅ* 41-42 (1977) 224-34; idem, "Yahweh's Gathering of the Dispersed," *In the Shelter of Elyon. FS G. W. Ahlström. JSOTSup* 31 (1984), 227-45.

1. Kopf, *VT* 8 (1958) 191.
2. See III.1 below.
3. See III.2 below.
4. See H. Ringgren, *Sprüche. ATD* 16/1 (³1980), 30.
5. K. Elliger, *Das Buch der zwölf kleinen Propheten. ATD* 25/2 (⁶1967), 116; and W. Rudolph, *Haggai-Sacharja 1–8-Sacharja 9–14-Maleachi. KAT* XIII/4 (1976), 72-73; F. Horst (*Die zwölf kleinen Propheten. HAT* I/14 [³1964], 220), however, interprets *pûṣ miṭṭôḇ* as "wretched, scattered."

3. *Scatter.* The hiphil in particular denotes the scattering of fine, light material. In the parable of the farmer in Isa. 28:23-29, v. 25 uses the verbs *hēp̄îṣ* and *zāraq* for the scattering of seed. Mountains are turned into chaff, scattered by the wind (Isa. 41:16), an image representing the destruction of Israel's foes. Yahweh will scatter the faithless Israelites like chaff driven by the west wind (Jer. 13:24; cf. 18:17). In Hab. 3:14 the enemy storms *(s'r)* forward to scatter Israel. In the last two passages, the objects of the verb are persons; but the origin of the image is clear. Job 37:11 is somewhat ambiguous: God spreads or scatters "the clouds of light." We should probably read *'ānān* (abs.) and interpret *'ôr* as "lightning," as in v. 3: the clouds scatter their lightning bolts. If this is correct, Ps. 18:15(Eng. v. 14) (= 2 S. 22:15; cf. also the petition in Ps. 144:6) would mean that God "sends forth and scatters (in all directions)" his arrows of lightning. Otherwise the suffixes must refer to unspecified enemies.

4. *Scatter Flocks.* In the language of shepherding, a specialized meaning developed: a flock is dispersed and the animals are scattered. This usage is usually figurative. In Ezk. 34:5 Yahweh says: "Because they had no shepherds, my sheep were scattered and became food for all the wild animals" — obviously a reference to Israel. Zec. 13:7 calls on a sword to strike the shepherd, that the sheep may be scattered. The precise reference of these words is unknown. According to Elliger, the author is picturing a messianic figure (cf. the NT quotation in Mark 14:27).[6] Or does the text refer to the wicked shepherd of 11:5? According to Jer. 10:21 (cf. 23:1-2), the shepherds (i.e., leaders) of Israel were stupid, and their flock was scattered. Micaiah ben Imlah sees Israel scattered on the mountains "like sheep without shepherds" (1 K. 22:17 = 2 Ch. 18:16).

5. *Scatter People.* This meaning can then be applied to human beings in various situations. The people of Babylon wanted to build a tower so that they would not be scattered over the face of the whole earth (Gen. 11:14), but God intervened and scattered them (vv. 8-9). The Blessing of Jacob describes the tribes of Simeon and Levi as being scattered in Israel. Vanquished enemies are scattered (1 S. 11:11; cf. Isa. 33:3 with *npṣ* par. *ndd*). After the fall of Jerusalem, all the Judeans face the danger of being scattered (Jer. 40:15). Here we recall in particular the ancient ark formula in Nu. 10:35: "Arise, Yahweh, let your enemies be scattered, and your foes flee *(nûs)* before you." Ps. 68:2(1) echoes these words.

6. *Exile, Diaspora.* In the great majority of the passages using the niphal or hiphil, *pwṣ* refers to the diaspora in exile (3 times in Deuteronomy, once in Isaiah, 3 times in Jeremiah, 13 times in Ezekiel [+ 3 times with reference to Egypt], and once in Nehemiah). According to Dt. 4:27, Yahweh will scatter the Israelites among the nations if they practice idolatry. In Dt. 28:64 the scattering is a consequence of not keeping the commandments; 30:3 speaks of gathering the scattered. In Ezekiel, where the occurrences of this usage are especially numerous, scattering is threatened

6. *ATD* 25/2 ([6]1967) 175-76.

(12:15, "that they may know that I am Yahweh"; 22:15 par. *zrh;* 20:23 par. *zrh* in an historical retrospect; cf. also Jer. 40:15). The primary emphasis rests on the imminent gathering of the scattered "from all the lands/nations where they have been scattered" (Ezk. 11:17; 20:34,41; 28:25; 29:13; 34:12 [all niphal]; 11:16; 36:19 par. *zrh;* cf. v. 24; cf. also Jer. 30:11). Egypt is also threatened with being scattered (29:12-13; 30:23,26 par. *zrh*). In a penitential prayer to Yahweh, Neh. 1:9 recalls Yahweh's promise to gather the scattered Israelites. Isa. 11:12 (probably postexilic) prophesies that God will assemble *('āsap)* the outcasts *(ndḥ)* of Israel and gather (*qbṣ* piel) the scattered *(n^e^pûṣôṯ)* of Judah. According to the eschatological prophecy in Isa. 24:1, Yahweh is about to scatter the inhabitants of the earth in the context of a universal catastrophe.

According to Widengren, "gathering the scattered" was one of the duties of the Assyrian king. It does not necessarily follow, however, that the OT notion is dependent on the Assyrian; it may well have arisen from the historical situation.

III. Nouns.

1. *t^e^pûṣâ.* The only occurrence of *t^e^pûṣâ* (Jer. 25:34) is dubious. The MT form *ûṯ^e^pôṣôṯîḵem* is grammatically impossible and is very difficult to place in the syntax of the context. The shepherds are called upon to wail and cry out because the days of slaughter have come; the words that follow appear to mean something like "and you will be scattered and fall." The word is omitted by the LXX. We are possibly dealing with a corrupt form of *npṣ,* "smite."[7]

2. *baṯ-pûṣay.* Equally problematic is *baṯ-pûṣay* in Zeph. 3:10: "From beyond the rivers of Cush, *'^a^ṯāray baṯ-pûṣay* bring me an offering *(minḥâ)*." The untranslated expressions have resisted all attempts at explanation. If *'^a^ṯāray* is associated with *'tr,* "pray," it could mean "my suppliants." Gerleman has suggested that *baṯ-pûṣay* could mean (collectively) "the daughter of my scattered ones," to be interpreted as a variant of "my suppliants."[8] Rudolph interprets *pûṣay* as an abstract plural meaning "dispersion."[9] The conjectural emendation *batt^e^pûṣâ* has some merit. In any case the verse remains obscure.

IV. 1. *Dead Sea Scrolls.* There are only 5 occurrences in the Dead Sea Scrolls. The War Scroll speaks of "God's power to scatter the enemy" (1QM 3:5; similarly 4QM[a] [4Q491] frs. 8-10, I, 14 and 4QShir[a] [4Q510] 1:3, with *pzr*). An aspect of the community's theology stands behind 4QPrFêtes[c] (4Q509) 3:4, where the temporally defined *(t^e^qûpâ)* situations of scattering and gathering may refer to ecclesiological eras.

7. W. L. Holladay, *Jeremiah* 1. *Herm* (1987), 677.
8. G. Gerleman, *Zephanja* (1942), 57.
9. *Micha-Nahum-Habakuk-Zephanja. KAT* XIII/3 (1975), 292.

2. *LXX.* The LXX usually translates *pwṣ* with *diaspeírein* or *diaskorpízein.* Only rarely do we find such other translations as *diacheín* (Zec. 1:17), *hyperekcheín* (Prov. 5:16), *speírein* (Isa. 28:25), or *skorpízein* (Ps. 18:15[14]).

V. *pzr.* Only in one passage (Est. 3:8, pual ptcp.) does the partially synonymous root *pzr* refer to the diaspora of the Jewish people. A similar meaning is probably also conveyed by Jer. 50:17: Israel is like a sheep separated from the flock (qal pass. ptcp.), pursued by lions. An interpolation explains the figure: the lions are Assyria and Babylon. Then v. 19 predicts the return of the sheep. In Yahweh's battle with Rahab, he "scattered his enemies" (Ps. 89:11[10]: piel). Joel 4:2(3:2) speaks of God's judgment on the shepherds who have scattered (piel) Israel; God scatters (piel) the bones of the ungodly (Ps. 53:6[5]), an image of total annihilation; cf. Ps. 141:7, where the psalmist laments, "Our bones have been scattered [niphal] at the mouth of Sheol."

Finally, *pizzar* can mean "distribute" in the sense of "give abundantly": the subject may be God (Ps. 112:9 par. *nāṯan*) or a human being (Prov. 11:24, "One who gives freely grows all the richer"). This may also be the meaning of Jer. 3:13, if we may follow *BHS* in reading *dôḏayiḵ* instead of *d^{e}rāḵayiḵ:* "You have scattered your favors among strangers." Holladay keeps the MT and translates: "You have spent your strength."[10] Finally, Ps. 147:16 says that Yahweh scatters frost like ashes.

Ringgren

---

10. *Jeremiah* 1, 59.

פַּז *paz* → זָהָב *zāhāḇ*

פזר *pzr* → פוץ → *pûṣ*

פַּח *paḥ*

I. 1. Etymology; 2. Occurrences; 3. Meaning. II. Usage. III. 1. Dead Sea Scrolls; 2. LXX.

I. 1. *Etymology. HAL* treats Heb. *paḥ* as a primary noun of the form *qall.* The word appears throughout Aramaic (Jewish Aramaic, Christian Palestinian, and above all Syriac[1]) as *paḥḥā',* with the meaning "snare." Fraenkel therefore lists Arab. *faḫḫ* as one of the Aramaic loanwords in Arabic.[2]

Akk. *pāḫu,* cited by several lexicons, has nothing to contribute to the etymology of Heb. *paḥ* and is therefore rightly not mentioned by *HAL.*[3] In Egyptian, however, there is a word *pḫꜣ,*[4] which appears in Demotic as *pḫ* and in Coptic as *paš* or *faš* and means "trap, snare, noose"; it cannot be divorced from Heb. *paḥ,* which is therefore an Egyptian loanword.[5] The meaning "trap (for birds)" in Egyptian appears to be a secondary development from the original meaning of *pḫꜣ,* "panel, stick." The Egyptian trap must therefore have been made of wood, whereas in Hebrew the *paḥ* was probably most characteristically a kind of net. It is tempting to consider *paḥ* an onomatopoetic form, but its demonstrable Egyptian origin argues against such a derivation.

A separate root *paḥ* II has been posited, an Egyptian loanword derived from *pḫꜣ* as discussed above.[6] But it is impossible to separate *paḥ* I and II; we must assume instead that Heb. *paḥ,* "hammered plate," has retained the original Egyptian meaning, while *paḥ,* "snare for birds," represents a specialized semantic development.

The word occurs twice in the OT with the meaning "plate." In the description of how the ephod was made, Ex. 39:3 states that plates of gold *(paḥê zāhāḇ)* were hammered thin so as to be cut into gold threads, which were worked into the blue, purple, and crimson yarns and the twisted linen, in skilled design. In Nu. 17:3(16:38) Yahweh demands that the censers used illegitimately by the followers of Korah be hammered into thin plates as a covering for the altar.

---

paḥ. G. Fohrer, "Falle," *BHHW,* I, 463; G. Gerleman, "Contributions to the OT Terminology of the Chase," *Bulletin de la Société Royale des Lettres de Lund 1945-46,* IV (1946), 79-90; P. Hugger, *Jahwe meine Zuflucht* (1971), esp. 173-76; I. Scheftelowitz, "Das Schlingen- und Netzmotiv," *RVV* XII/2 (1912) 1-12; J. Schneider, "παγίς, παγιδεύω," *TDNT,* V, 593-96; G. Stählin, *Skandalon. BFCT Monographien* 24 (1930), esp. 98-104; E. Vogt, "'Ihr Tisch werde zur Falle' (Ps 69,23)," *Bibl* 43 (1962) 79-82; H. Wildberger, "Schlinge," *BHHW,* III, 1702-3.

1. Brockelmann, *LexSyr,* 562a.
2. S. Fraenkel, *Die aramäischen Fremdwörter im Arabischen* (1886, ²1962), 119.
3. Cf. *GesB; KBL*²; Brockelmann, *LexSyr,* 562a. See *AHw,* II, 811b: "sleeve" (with a question mark).
4. *WbÄS,* I, 543.
5. See F. Calice, *Grundlagen der ägyptisch-semitischen Wortvergleichung. WZKMBeih.* 1 (1936), 148-49, no. 605.
6. See *HAL,* III, 922; M. Ellenbogen, *Foreign Words in the OT* (1962), 130.

2. *Occurrences.* The noun *paḥ* occurs 25 times in the OT; there is a concentration in the Psalter, with 9 occurrences (8 if *peḥām* or *paḥᵃmê* is read instead of *paḥîm* in Ps. 11:6; otherwise Ps. 69:23[Eng. v. 22]; 91:3; 119:110; 124:7 [twice]; 140:6[5]; 141:9; 142:4[3]). Elsewhere it occurs 3 times in Isaiah (8:14; 24:17,18) and Jeremiah (18:22; 48:43,44), twice each in Hosea (5:1; 9:8), Amos (3:5 [twice]), Job (18:9; 22:10), Proverbs (7:23; 22:25), and once each in Josh. 23:13 and Eccl. 9:12. It appears also in Sir. ms. A 9:13. Apart from Ps. 11:6, the plural *paḥîm* appears in Job 22:10; Prov. 22:5; Jer. 18:2; Sir. 9:13.

There is a single occurrence (Isa. 42:22) of a denominative verb in the hiphil, meaning "be trapped." The MT reads *hāp̱aḥ,* an infinitive absolute; proposed emendations are the hophal inf. abs. *hupaḥ* and the finite verb form *hupaḥû.*[7]

3. *Meaning.* While there is no consensus concerning the precise meaning of *môqēš* (trigger of a snare for birds, boomerang, bait, net),[8] *paḥ* can be defined with some precision. It is true that the two terms are sometimes used in parallel (Josh. 23:15; Isa. 8:14; Ps. 69:23[22]; 141:9) with no apparent distinction; but we can see from Prov. 7:23; Ps. 124:7; Eccl. 9:12, and above all Am. 3:5, that a *paḥ* was used to trap birds. We may therefore identify the *paḥ* with the triggered net used as a snare for birds represented in contemporary art and still in use today.[9] It consists of two frames, generally curved, each covered with a net. The baited snare is set half opened. When a bird alights on the net resting on the ground, the two halves come together and the bird is trapped.

II. Usage. In the OT the noun *paḥ* is used only figuratively and only in poetic texts. In this metaphorical usage, the emphasis is usually the elements of trickery and ruin.

The expression *hāyâ lᵉpaḥ* used figuratively can be translated "be someone's ruin." In his farewell discourse, for example, Joshua warns Israel against the dangers of life among foreign nations (an obvious allusion to the exile). If Israel turns back and joins foreign nations, they will be "a snare and a trap" (Josh. 23:13) — in other words, they will be the ruin of Israel. In Ps. 91:3 the psalmist knows that God can deliver from the snare of the fowler *(mippaḥ yāqûš),* i.e., from the machinations of the enemy (cf. also Ps. 124:7), and therefore prays to be protected from the snare and trap (or bait) of the wicked (cf. Ps. 141:9). In Ps. 69:23(22),[10] the psalmist entreats God to intervene and inflict on the enemy the punishment they deserve by turning their table into a snare and their sacrificial banquet (reading *wᵉšalmêhem*) into bait. The comparison of a table *(šulḥān)* to a snare *(paḥ)* is clear if one keeps in mind that for ordinary people an animal hide or straw mat placed on the ground served as a table and that the rich in northern Syria and Asia Minor often used folding tables.[11] The construction of net snares re-

7. See, respectively, *KBL*², 758; K. Elliger, *Deutero-Jesaja. BK* XI/1 (1978), 272-73; *BHS.*
8. → VI, 288.
9. See *AOB,* 58, with fig. 182; O. Keel, *Symbolism of the Biblical World* (Eng. trans. 1978), figs. 110-19a. For modern use see G. Dalman, *AuS,* VI, 338-39, with figs. 60-63.
10. See Vogt.
11. H. Weippert, *BRL*², 230.

sembles that of such tables. This construction is clearly reflected in Ps. 141:9 if the MT is not emended: "Keep me from the hands of the snare *(mîḏê paḥ)* that they have laid for me." This clearly alludes to the "two nets or flaps of the snare, which snap together suddenly to trap the surprised bird."[12] When the psalmist says in Ps. 142:4b(3b) that a snare has been hidden in the path, the image represents insidious defamation and malicious accusation; in Ps. 140:6(5), similarly, the arrogant set a snare for the psalmist. The faithful worshiper can feel confident of not having strayed from God's precepts even though the wicked have laid a snare (Ps. 119:110; cf. Prov. 22:5).

In Bildad's second reply, Job 18:9 says that a snare is waiting for Job to bring about his downfall. Job 18:8-10 lists a whole palette of devices used to trap birds and animals, not all of which can be identified precisely. In the third reply of Eliphaz, too, Job is warned that snares (22:10, pl.) have been set around him.

In Isa. 24:17-18 the author depicts the fate of all the inhabitants of the earth on the day of judgment in words whose style, including alliteration, betrays the powerful voice of an eloquent apocalyptist:

> Panic and pit and snare *(paḥaḏ wāpaḥaṯ wāpaḥ)*
> are upon you, inhabitant of the earth!
> Thus shall be: Whoever flees
> the sound of terror
> shall fall into the pit.
> And whoever climbs out of the pit
> shall be caught in the snare!

This prophecy of inescapable universal judgment, which again mentions the net snare as the last and surest trap, reappears in the same words in Jer. 48:43-44, this time with reference to Moab. A human being can also be a trap to others, i.e., be their ruin (cf. also 1 Mc. 5:4). Hos. 9:8 belongs in this context. Hosea describes how the people show their hostility to him: "Snares like the fowler's snare are on all his ways." The LXX misunderstands the text and reverses the relationship: according to the LXX, the prophet is a *pagís skoliá,* whereas the MT probably refers to the priests and the royal house as a snare *(paḥ)* for Hosea.

Sir. 27:26 illustrates the doctrine of retribution: "Whoever digs a pit will fall into it, and whoever sets a snare will be caught in it." In Hos. 5:1-2 the prophet calls on the priests, heads of families, and the royal house to fulfill their shared responsibility. He uses three images from hunting to characterize them as destroyers of Israel's freedom. They have been a snare at Mizpah, a large net (used to trap lions and gazelles [Ezk. 19:8; Sir. 27:2]) spread upon Tabor, and at Shittim (cj.) a concealed pitfall to capture game. The images indicate that those responsible for the people led them astray and brought about their downfall at these three places. To set snares means to rob people of their freedom and endanger their lives. Unfortunately we know nothing about the precise historical situation.

---

12. Vogt, 82.

Eccl. 9:12 points out that fate strikes human beings as unpredictably as a bird or fish is caught in a snare or net. The unexpected disaster falls on them suddenly *(piṯʾōm).* Prov. 7:23 speaks of the strange woman and her victim: the man attracted to the prostitute acts "like a bird rushing into a snare, not knowing that it will cost its life." Even blunter is Sir. 9:3: "Do not go near a loose woman, or you will fall into her snares."

Even Yahweh can be a snare to his own people. With its image of trap and snare, Isa. 8:14 presumably alludes to the encirclement of Jerusalem first by the Assyrians and then by the Babylonians. Yahweh has become "a snare and a trap which has seized the inhabitants of the city."[13] In this context also belongs Am. 3:5, a difficult text: "Does a bird '. . .' to earth if no bait has been set out? Does the snare spring up from the ground when it has taken nothing?" "The two . . . events are, as it were, simply two aspects of the same reality: just as the closing of the net and the entrapment of the prey constitute only a single event seen by two different subjects, so prophecy and the word of Yahweh constitute a single entity."[14]

III. 1. *Dead Sea Scrolls.* The noun *pḥ* occurs ten times in the Dead Sea Scrolls. Some usages derive from the OT; for example, CD 4:14 cites the *paḥaḏ wāpaḥaṯ wāpaḥ* of Isa. 24:17, then interprets it as the three nets *(mṣwdwt)* of Belial, namely, fornication, wealth, and defilement of the temple. The text of 1Q22 1:8 (Words of Moses) draws on Josh. 23:13 when Moses says that the idols of the land of Israel will become "a sn[are and] trap" *(lp[ḥ w]mwqš).* The use of *pḥ* in combination with *ṭmn* for the secret laying of a snare appears in Ps. 140:6(5); 142:4b(3b); Jer. 18:22b, as well as 1QH 2:29 and 1QH fr. 3:4,8. Not based directly on OT usage are the images of the psalmist as a snare for the wicked in 1QH 2:8 (but cf. Hos. 9:8 LXX) and the opening of the snares of the pit *(pḥy šḥt)* in 1QH 3:26. Also new are the images in 1QH fr. 3:4,8: "my steps upon their hidden snares" and "they hide snare upon snare" *(wpḥ lpḥ yṭmwnw).* Particularly unusual is the prayer to be delivered "from the snares of judgment according to your mercy" (1QH 18:25).

2. *LXX.* The LXX regularly uses *pagís,* "snare, trap, noose," to translate *paḥ;* Jerome likewise regularly uses the Latin equivalent *laqueus.* The concrete image of the snare for birds is not recognized. The word *pagís* also translates such words as *môqeš.*

In Ezk. 29:4 the LXX reads *ḥaḥîm,* "hooks," as *paḥîm (pagídas),* clearly by mistake. In Isa. 42:22, clearly because of a misunderstanding on the part of the LXX, the Syr. and Vulg. *(laqueus iuvenum omnes)* read *happaḥ* for *hāpaḥ.* The verb *pagideúō,* a neologism either of Koine or of the LXX itself, appears in 1 S. 28:9, rendering *miṯnaqqēš,* "lay a snare," and in Eccl. 9:12, where *pagideúontai* = *yûqāšîm.*

D. Kellermann

---

13. O. Kaiser, *Isaiah 1–12. OTL* (Eng. trans. ²1983), 193.
14. H. Gese, *VT* 12 (1962) 427.

פָּחַד *pāḥad;* פַּחַד *paḥad* I and II

I. Roots. II. Heb. *pḥd* and *pāḥad:* 1. Semantics; 2. Verb; 3. *pḥd 'el;* 4. Noun; 5. Numinous Dread; 6. Fear of God. III. *pāḥad yiṣḥāq.*

I. Roots. There are at least three roots *pḥ/ḫd/d* in Semitic. (1) The Hebrew verbal root *pḥd* (< *pḥ/d* I), "experience dread, tremble," and the noun *paḥad* I appear only in Hebrew and Jewish Aramaic, except for an unintelligible syllabic passage in a series of Ugaritic incantations *(lip-ḫu-tu-ma),*[1] the obscure PN *ypthd* on a silver bowl from Halla Sultan Tekké (Cyprus, 13th century B.C.E.),[2] and the damaged beginning of a line in the Deir ʿAllā inscription.[3] (2) The concrete noun represented by the consonants *pḫd* appears in Heb. *paḥ^a^ḏāw,* "its [Behemoth's] thighs," in Job 40:17; /d/</ḏ/ instead of the regular Heb. /z/</ḏ/ is an Aramaism. It appears also in Targumic Aram. *paḥ(ᵃ)ḏîn,* "testicles"[4] (cf. also the Vulg. of Job 40:12[=17]: *testiculorum eius*), Syr. *puḥdā,* "thigh, leg," OSA *fḫḏ,* and above all Arab. *faḫiḏ, faḫḏ, fiḫḏ* (fem.), "thigh," with a denominative verb and other derivatives; cf. Egyp. *ḫpdwy,* "buttocks," with metathesis of *p* and *ḫ.* Other possible derivatives of the same root include the word *pḥd*ʾ (reading uncertain), "the clan," from Hatra, Palmyr. *pḥ(w)z, pḥd,* "clan," and Arab. *faḫiḏ* (masc.), "subdivision of a tribe."[5] (3) Akk. *puḫādu(m),* fem. *puḫattu(m),* lamb," and Ugar. *pḫd,* "lambs (collec-

---

pāḥad. B. J. Bamberger, "Fear and Love of God in the OT," *HUCA* 6 (1929) 39-53; J. Becker, *Gottesfurcht im AT. AnBibl* 25 (1965); Y. Braslavi, "*pḥd yṣḥq* and the Blessing of Ephraim and Manasseh," *BethM* 14 [7/2] (1962), 35-42; L. Derousseaux, *La crainte de Dieu dans l'AT* (1970); J. Haspecker, *Gottesfurcht bei Jesus Sirach* (1967); J. Hempel, *Gott und Mensch im AT. BWANT* 38 (1936), esp. 4-33; D. R. Hillers, *"Paḥad Yiṣḥāq," JBL* 91 (1972) 90-92; P. Joüon, "Crainte et peur en Hébreu biblique," *Bibl* 6 (1925) 174-79; K. Koch, "*păḥăd jiṣḥaq* — eine Gottesbezeichnung?" *Werden und Wirken des ATs. FS C. Westermann* (1980), 107-15; N. Krieger, "Der Schrecken Isaaks," *Jud* 17 (1961) 193-95; A. Lemaire, "À propos de *paḥad* dans l'onomastique ouest-sémitique," *VT* 35 (1985) 500-501; idem, "Les Benê Jacob," *RB* 85 (1978) 321-37; idem, *Inscriptions hébraïques,* I (1977), 287-89; idem, "Le 'pays de Hépher' et les 'Filles de Zelophehad' à la lumière des ostraca de Samarie," *Sem* 22 (1972) 13-20; B. Levine, *"pḥd yṣḥq," EMiqr,* VI, 451-52; S. E. Loewenstamm, *"ṣlpḥd," EMiqr,* VI, 738; M. Malul, "More on *paḥad yiṣḥāq* (Genesis xxxi 42, 53) and the Oath by the Thigh," *VT* 35 (1985) 192-200; S. Morenz, "Der Schrecken Pharaos," *Liber amicorum. FS. C. J. Bleeker. Numen Sup* 17 (1969) 113-125; E. Puech, "'La crainte d'Isaac' en Genèse xxxi 42 et 53," *VT* 34 (1984) 356-61; C. H. Ratschow et al., "Gottesfurcht," *RGG*³, II (1958), 1791-98; K. Romaniuk, "Furcht. II. AT und NT," *TRE,* XI (1983), 756-59; J. M. Sasson, *RSP,* I (1972), 438-39; H.-P. Stähli, "פחד *pḥd* to shake," *TLOT,* II, 979-81; G. Wanke, *TDNT,* IX, 197-205.

1. *RS* 17.155 with duplicate 15.152; *Ugaritica,* V, 32, h.
2. Puech, 358, 361 n. 19; but see also Lemaire, "À propos de *pāḥad.*"
3. I, 10[12].
4. J. Levy, *Chaldäisches Wörterbuch,* II (rep. 1966), 258.
5. For Hatra see *NESE,* III (1978), 73-74. For Palmyrene see *DNSI,* II, 904, with bibliog.

tively)," however, appear to reflect a nominal root with the consonants *pḫd* II, which has no Hebrew isogloss.[6]

The theory that *pḫd* > *pḫz/d,* "clan," is related to the other concrete noun from the root *pḫd* II (Akk. *puḫādu(m),* "lamb"; Ugar. *pḫd*) presupposes a very broad metonymic semantic variation.[7] Furthermore, instead of Akk. *puḫādu(m)* we would expect a form with /*z*/ as its third radical, contra Albright, Gordon, Segert, and Dahood.[8] Dahood not only agrees with Albright and Gordon in associating the meaning "flock" with Ugar. *pḫd* but also proposes the meaning "pack [of dogs]" for Heb. *paḥaḏ* in such passages as Isa. 24:18.[9] On the basis of Job 40:17, Puech suggests the meaning "thigh" for Ugar. *pḫd.*[10]

The word *pḥz* in the phrase *mn pḥzy bny 'š* ("on account of the arrogance of the sons of man") in the Deir ʿAlla inscription does not derive from any of the three roots discussed above, but rather from *pḥz,* "swell up, seethe; be insolent," found in Hebrew, Jewish Aramaic, Syriac, and Arabic.[11] Cf. Middle Bab. *pa/eḫīdu* for a kind of flour.[12]

II. Heb. *pḥd and paḥaḏ.*

1. *Semantics.* The complex signification of the Hebrew verb *pḥd* I is "feel dread" and its somatic manifestation "tremble." Trembling may occasionally be the result of joy (Isa. 60:5; Jer. 33:9). As the modifier *tāmîḏ* shows, the piel denotes continuous, lifelong fear (Isa. 51:13) or the fear of God (Prov. 28:14; Sir. 37:12); without the adverb it means "terrify" (1QS 4:2). The causative hiphil means "cause to dread" (Job 4:14). The object of the dread is introduced by *min* or *mippᵉnê.*

The Hebrew noun *paḥaḏ* denotes the experience of dread (Dt. 28:67; cf. *qôl happaḥaḏ,* "the sound of terror," Isa. 24:18; *qôl pᵉḥāḏîm,* Job 15:21; similarly Jer. 30:5) or the "trembling" it occasions (Job 4:14, par. to *rᵉʿāḏâ,* "trembling"). But it may also denote whatever causes the "dread" and "trembling," the object of terror, the thing feared (Isa. 24:17 = Jer. 48:43; etc.; Job 3:25; 22:10; etc.).[13] When *paḥaḏ* denotes the experience of dread rather than its somatic manifestation, its locus is the heart (Dt. 28:67; cf. the use of the verb in Isa. 60:5; Ps. 119:161; Sir. 7:29; 1QS 4:2). Insofar as the verb in the qal and piel has a transitive connotation, "be in dread of, fear," a genitive depending on the noun *pāḥaḏ* can be construed as an objective genitive if it refers to the thing feared[14] and as a subjective genitive if it refers to the person fearing.

---

6. M. Dietrich and O. Loretz, *UF* 17 (1985) 99-103, esp. 100-101, with bibliog.

7. Hillers, 92.

8. W. F. Albright, *From the Stone Age to Christianity* (^{2}1957), 248 n. 71; Gordon, *UT,* no. 2035; S. Segert, *Basic Grammar of the Ugaritic Language* (1984), 198; Dahood, *Ugartic-Hebrew Philology. BietOr* 17 (1965), 69.

9. Cf. J. Sasson, *RSP,* I, 439.

10. P. 359 n. 5.

11. Deir ʿAlla II, 8. See H.-P. Müller, *ZAW* 94 (1982) 233; contra J. Hoftijzer and G. van der Kooij, *ATDA,* 277; and *HAL,* III, 923, s.v. *paḥaḏ* I, 3.

12. *AHw,* II, 811.

13. See II.4 below.

14. Contra Stähli, 413.

In Ps. 53:6(Eng. v. 5); 91:5; Job 3:25; 39:22; Prov. 1:26-27,33; 3:25; Cant. 3:8, objectification of the *paḥaḏ* concept leads to the connotation "danger."[15] If the object of dread is to be specified, an appropriate genitive or suffix is appended to *paḥaḏ,* so that the noun once again means the experience of dread or the trembling caused by the feared thing. Expressions like *paḥaḏ 'ôyēḇ* (Ps. 64:2[1]; 4QpNah 2:5), *pḥdy mwt* (Sir. 9:13), or *paḥaḏ yhwh*[16] present the "enemy," "death," or Yahweh as an object of terror. Terror of Yahweh is mentioned in Isa. 2:10,19,21; the people hide from Yahweh when he rises (vv. 19,21) on his day (v. 12), not of course from their own terror. In the *figura etymologica pḥd paḥaḏ* (Dt. 28:67; Ps. 14:5 = 53:6[5]; Job 3:25; Sir. 9:13 [pl.]), *paḥaḏ* can mean either the experience of dread (Dt. 28:67, par. to the experience of seeing, just as *ûpāḥaḏtā laylâ wᵉyômām* in v. 66bα means the continual experience of dread that is the opposite of assurance of life [v. 66bβ]) or the object of dread, the terrifying danger (Job 3:25). Job 15:21 and Sir. 9:13 use the plural with an intensifying function.

The concentration of occurrences of *pḥd* in exilic and postexilic literature may be due to the use of other lexemes in earlier periods to express the emotion-laden concept, whereas after the exile a need was felt for a more specific term.[17] This theory requires a detailed analysis of the semantic field, which is beyond the scope of this article.

The rendering of the Hebrew verbs meaning "fear" in the LXX is discussed extensively elsewhere, as are synonyms and antonyms of the root *pḥd.*[18] Akkadian parallels include *puluḫtu,* which means both "fear" as a human experience and the "fearsomeness" of deities; the latter phenomenon is also expressed by *melemmu(m),* the "dreadful radiance" associated with deities, demons, kings, and temples.[19] Egyptian parallels are *nrw, snḏ,* and *š't.*[20]

The shift of /ḏ/ to /d/ (although found also in Ugaritic) shows that the Hebrew noun *paḥaḏ* II < **pḫḏ* in the expression *gîḏê paḥᵃḏāw,* "the sinews of its thighs" (Job 40:17; see I.[2] above), is one of the Aramaisms characteristic of the secondary passages in the book of Job, especially in the speeches of Elihu. The LXX did not translate the consonants *pḥd,* clearly because it could not make sense of the word, whereas the Vulg. interpreted them on the basis of contemporary Aramaic, treating them (like the Targ.) as Aramaic. Lacau's claim that Egyp. *ḫpdwy* (dual), "buttocks," is an isogloss is morphologically and semantically plausible.[21] The word's phonological categorization, apart from the consonantal metathesis, must remain an open question.

2. *Verb.* The meaning "experience dread" or "tremble," conveyed above all by the verb *pḥd,* corresponds to one of the basic features of human and animal life.

---

15. See most recently *HAL,* III, 922, 1b.
16. See II.4-6 below.
17. Wanke, 200.
18. See Wanke; also Stähli, 413, with bibliog. For synonyms and antonyms see Joüon; Wanke; Stähli, 413.
19. Stähli, 413; *AHw,* II, 878/9, 643.
20. See Morenz, 114-15; also II.5 below.
21. P. Lacau, *Les noms des parties du corps en égyptien et en sémitique* (1970), 79.

In an admonition that has overtones of a purpose clause, Sir. 9:13 speaks of the creaturely fear of human beings in the face of death: keep far from one who has the power to kill, *w'l tpḥd pḥdy mwt,* "lest you be haunted by the fear of death."[22] According to Sir. 41:12, one should "tremble" more for one's name than for a thousand hordes of gold, since its influence is more enduring. The horse is an animal that "laughs at fear" *(yiśḥaq l^epaḥaḏ).* The ostrich (?) treats its young "carelessly" *(b^elî-pāḥaḏ),* conduct that the author of Job considers foolish.

Except for these passages, the creaturely fear experienced by human beings, usually without any explicit object, attracts our attention only in religious contexts. That Yahweh is the life and salvation of the faithful precludes fear (Ps. 27:1; Isa. 12:2). Yahweh led Israel "in safety, so that they were not afraid" (Ps. 78:53). Contrariwise, in a prophecy of doom we hear a "cry of terror" and *paḥaḏ,* the opposite of *šālôm* (cf. 49:5 in an oracle against the Ammonites). Deutero-Isaiah admonishes the people not to fear (Isa. 44:8), above all not to be continually in dread (51:13, piel), because Yahweh is about to intervene in history. But dread *laylâ w^eyômām,* "by night as well as by day,"[23] cast a pall on the life of Israel under the Neo-Babylonians, as we learn from Dt. 28:66f., a Deuteronomistic description of disaster in the context of a curse on Israel if it does not observe the Deuteronomic law.

In the orderly world of wisdom tradition, ethical conduct guarantees sleep without fear (Prov. 3:24), above all a life without sudden panic (*paḥaḏ piṯ'ōm,* v. 25). According to the doctrine of retribution, terror is the lot of the wicked, because God avenges the righteous (Ps. 14:5 = 53:6[5]); "terrifying sounds are in their ears," for unexpectedly *(baššālôm)* the destroyer comes upon them, and *paḥaḏ piṯ'ōm* reveals the wicked for what they are, as Job's antagonist Eliphaz asserts (Job 15:21; 22:10). In a parody of the norm, however, Job finds *šālôm mippāḥaḏ,* "prosperity free from fear," in the houses of the wicked (21:9), while he himself is beset by dread, the danger that, as a sage, he had always feared (3:25). On the other hand, in Deutero-Isaiah's description of Yahweh's salvation, the heart of the redeemed Israelites "trembles" and "swells" (Isa. 60:5). Jer. 33:9 (post-Dtr) describes "all the nations of the earth" as trembling *(pḥd)* and quaking *(rgz)* because of all the good *(ṭôḇâ)* and prosperity *(šālôm)* Yahweh has provided.

In the Dead Sea Scrolls, by contrast, the prevalence of creaturely fear appears to be a mark of the present aeon: 1QH 2:36 and 1QS 1:17 articulate the concern that "fear" may lead the members of the community to unfaithfulness. According to 1QS 10:15, *pḥd w'ymh* are characteristic of this present "place of distress and grief"; cf. the fear of the nations and of the rule of the Kittim voiced in 1QpHab 3:4-5; 4:7.

3. *pḥḏ 'el.* Creaturely fear that seeks refuge in Yahweh *('el-yhwh)* has a religious purpose and is therefore positive. The prophecy of Israel's return following judgment in Hos. 3:5 (an early addition to Hosea)[24] equates the future *ûpāḥ^aḏû 'el-yhwh w^e'el-*

22. See II.4 below.
23. *HP,* 224.
24. J. Jeremias, *Der Prophet Hosea. ATD* 24/1 (1983), 57.

ṭûḇô ("they shall go trembling to" > "seek refuge[25] with Yahweh and his goodness") with *yāšûḇû* ("they shall return") and *ûḇiq(q)ᵉšû 'eṯ-yhwh 'ᵉlōhêhem* ("and they shall seek Yahweh their God"). We may compare Jer. 36:16: *pāḥᵃḏû 'îš 'el-rē'ēhû,* "they turned to one another in alarm." Jer. 2:19aβb, which echoes Hos. 3:5 and sounds like an afterthought following the concluding words in v. 19aα, returns secondarily to the theme of v. 17 and expands on it by lamenting that Israel did not in fact return trembling to Yahweh (reading *wᵉlō' pāḥaḏtî 'ēlay*[26]). Despite the change in word order, Mic. 7:17bβ (MT) appears also to echo Hos. 3:5, formulated as a conclusion to Hos. 1–3.

4. *Noun.* The noun *paḥaḏ* is often used to objectify "the fearsome," the danger that arouses creaturely dread. According to Eliphaz (Job 22:10), *paḥaḏ piṯ'ōm,* a sudden onset of fear like that which attacks Job, is the consequence of his "wickedness" and "iniquities" (v. 5). By contrast, the observant need fear no terrors (Prov. 3:25); they are secure *(ša'ᵃnan)* from *paḥaḏ rā'â,* "the peril of evil" (1:33), as well as from *paḥaḏ lāylâ,* "that which brings terror in the night" (Ps. 91:5), i.e., the nocturnal horror against which the men in the bridal procession are armed with their swords (*mippaḥaḏ ballêlôṯ,* Cant. 3:8).[27] Those threatened by terror and danger can see themselves in the pronominal suffix (subjective gen.) of the expression *paḥdᵉḵem,* "the danger that threatens you," in the wisdom admonition in Prov. 1:26-27. In the lament in Ps. 31:12(11), the phrase *paḥaḏ limyuddā'ay,* "a horror to my acquaintances," uses *lᵉ* plus a dependent participle to designate those affected.

The cause of dread can be stipulated more specifically when it is appended to *paḥaḏ* as a genitive, as we have already seen in *paḥaḏ rā'â* (Prov. 1:33) and (formally) in *paḥaḏ lāylâ* (Ps. 91:5). Above all, in the petition in Ps. 64:2(1), *paḥaḏ 'ôyēḇ* means "dread evoked by an enemy." We may compare *mpḥd 'wyb,* "from fear of the enemy" (4QpNah 2:5), and *mpḥd hwwt r[š'y]m,* "from fear of the terror of the wi[cke]d" (1QH 2:36), as well as *[p]ḥd ḥpš,* "the terror evoked by the abyss" (Deir 'Alla I, 10 [12]), *pḥdy mwt,* "the terror aroused by death" (Sir. 9:13), and *hkty'ym 'šr pḥdm [w'y]m[t]m 'l kwl hgw'ym,* "the Kittim, who provoke fear and dread among all the nations" (1QpHab 3:4-5).

5. *Numinous Dread.* Another cause of creaturely dread, again usually expressed by *paḥaḏ,* is the numinous, above all the deity as the quintessence of "terror," the *mysterium tremendum.*

The archaizing curse formula *paḥaḏ wāpaḥaṯ wāpaḥ 'āleyḵā,* "panic, pit, and snare upon you," with its magically effective assonance, appears twice: in Jer. 48:43 in an oracle against Moab and again in Isa. 24:17 in an eschatological oracle against "the inhabitants of the earth" (cf. the quotation in CD 4:14). At one time the forces of doom,

25. L. Kopf, *VT* 9 (1959) 257.
26. Cf. *BHS.*
27. See III below.

paḥaḏ, etc. may have been mobilized directly by the formulaic nominal clause, without reference to a deity appointing and governing them. The stability of such formulas is indicated by the allusions in Job 22:19 *(paḥîm* par. *paḥaḏ pit'ōm)*, Lam. 3:47 *(paḥaḏ wāpaḥaṯ)*, and Sir. 9:13 *(w'l tpḥd pḥdy mwt . . . d' ky byn pḥym ts'd*, "lest you be haunted by the fear of death . . . know that you are stepping among snares").

More specifically, the deity is described as arousing numinous terror in the context of the holy war, by means of such genitive phrases as *paḥaḏ yhwh*, "the terror Yahweh inspires" > "the terror Yahweh represents" (1 S. 11:7; Isa. 2:10,19,21; 2 Ch. 14:13 [14]; 17:10), or *paḥaḏ 'elōhîm* (2 Ch. 29:29).[28] In Ex. 15:16 the absolute use of *('êmāṯâ wā-)paḥaḏ*, reinforced by *bigḏōl z'rô''ḵā*, "by the great (might) of your arm," serves the same function, as do the noun *paḥaḏ* in Isa. 19:16 and Jer. 49:5 and the verb *pḥd* in Isa. 19:17 and 44:11 (cf. the malediction in Mic. 7:17) in oracles against enemies. For those who have been saved by the "terror" visited on the enemy, the beneficiaries of the *paḥaḏ*, it clearly represents a "positive experience of God's presence," such as is also the goal of the action denoted by *pḥd 'el*.[29] The use of *paḥaḏ* with a genitive of the deity may be compared to Akk. *[a]t-rat puluḥtašu*, "immense was my dread of him > his dreadfulness," in parallel with *kabtat qātšu*, "heavy was his hand [sc. upon me]"[30] (cf. also Isa. 19:16). In Job 25:2 the "dread" inspired by Yahweh, like the preceding *hamšēl*, "dominion," functions virtually as an attribute.

The frequency with which the subj. *paḥaḏ* appears in the context of war with the predicate *npl 'al*, "fall upon" (Ex. 15:16; 1 S. 11:7; etc.), and later *hyh 'al*, "come upon" (2 Ch. 14:13[14]; 17:10; 19:7; 20:29), bespeaks the overwhelming spontaneous experience of the numinous in these circumstances (for *paḥaḏ 'al* see Dt. 2:25; 11:25; Isa. 24:17 = Jer. 48:43; Jer. 49:5; 1 Ch. 14:17; for *paḥaḏ 'el*, see Job 31:23 cj.; see below). It falls upon the Israelites, so that they come out as one and thus derive an advantage from their dread (1 S. 11:7); above all, however, it falls upon the enemy, making them still as a stone (Ex. 15:16) and putting them to shame *(ḥoggā'*, Isa. 19:17; *yeḇōšû*, 44:11), so that they are scattered (Jer. 49:5). In the context of a day of Yahweh on which war is waged against everything high and exalted, the refrain in Isa. 2:10,19,21 calls on its hearers to hide in the rock and in the dust.

Around the motif of the dread inspired by Yahweh crystallized the ideological construct that God alone is the protagonist in a holy war.[31] Jgs. 7:16-22 shows how a militarily decisive divine terror could be inspired artificially (cf. 1 S. 4:4-8; Josh. 6).[32] Phenomenologically, the association of *paḥaḏ yhwh* with war suggests that Gk. *phóbos*, the son of Aries, himself becomes a god of war.[33]

---

28. On 2 Ch. 19:7 and Ps. 36:2(1) see II.6 below.

29. Contra Koch, 108. See II.3 above.

30. Ludlul iii.1-2.

31. See, e.g., the discussion of Am. 2:14-16 in G. von Rad, *Holy War in Ancient Israel* (Eng. trans. 1991), 109ff.; F. Stolz, *Jahwehs und Israels Kriege. ATANT* 60 (1972), 187-91.

32. See H.-P. Müller, *VT* 14 (1964) 183-91.

33. Homer *Iliad* 13.298-300; Hesiod *Theog.* 933-36; for a general discussion of *phóbos* in war, see H. Balz, *ThWNT,* IX, 187f.; *EWNT,* III, 429.

The exilic and postexilic period developed systematically an ideology of war that had previously been rather archaic,[34] giving a central place, contrary to all political experience, to the Israelite faith in divine election. In the course of this development, the dread formerly inspired by Yahweh became associated with Israel (*paḥdᵉḵā, -ḵem,* "the dread of you," Dt. 2:25; 11:25; cf. *paḥdām,* Ps. 105:38; Est. 9:2) or David (*paḥdô,* 1 Ch. 14:17) (cf. also *paḥaḏ hayyᵉhûḏîm,* Est. 8:17; *paḥaḏ mordᵒḵay,* 9:3). At the same time, the scope of this dread became universal (1 Ch. 14:17; 2 Ch. 20:29 [cf. 17:10]). The suffixes in *paḥdᵉḵā, -ḵem, paḥdām,* and *paḥdô,* as well as the genitives in *paḥaḏ hayyᵉhûḏîm* and *paḥaḏ mordᵒḵay,* are objective genitives specifying who is to be feared. With respect to David and Mordecai as inspirers of terror, compare Egyp. *nrw.f,* "the dread of him (Pharaoh), the dread that he inspires," *snḏ.f,* "the fear of him," and *šʿt.f,* "the horror of him."[35]

This numinous dread is individualized when individuals react with fear *(pāḥᵃḏû)* at the reading of the prophecies of disaster in Jeremiah's scroll (Jer. 36:16); ominously, the king and his servants fail to display such fear when the scroll is burned (v. 24). Similarly, the individual sinners are gripped by fear *(pāḥᵃḏû)* before the entrance liturgy (Isa. 33:14). That an almost physical *paḥaḏ ʾl* would assail Job if he transgressed is presupposed in Job's oath of purgation (Job 31:23 cj.; reading *paḥaḏ ʾēl yeʾᵉṯeh ʿālay*);[36] for *ʾth* with *paḥaḏ* as subject see also 3:25 and (indirectly) Prov. 1:27. Dread of God's presence also assails Job on account of God's arbitrariness (*mippānāyw ʾebbāhēl,* "at his presence I am terrified," par. *wᵉʾepḥaḏ mimmennû,* "and I am in dread of him," Job 23:15); conversely, again in an almost physical sense, he threatens his antagonists with "dread of him [Yahweh]" (13:11). More experiential are the *paḥaḏ* ("dread") and *rᵉʿāḏâ* ("trembling") that also assail someone visited by the spirit (of wisdom), as described by the rather mannered account in 4:14; at the same time, a **rîḇ ʿᵃṣāmôṯ* (cf. Akk. *rību* I, "earthquake") evokes dread (*pḥd* hiphil).

6. *Fear of God.* Wisdom literature and its related traditions use the piel of *pḥd* absolutely as a general term for conduct in accordance with the religious standards of wisdom: *mᵉpaḥēḏ tāmîḏ,* "constantly reverent" (Prov. 28:14; Sir. 37:12; cf. the use of Gk. *phoboúmenos, -oi* [Acts 10:2,22,35; 13:16,26] along with *sebómenos* [Acts 13:43 on] for Gentile adherents of Judaism). The piel inf. in *lpḥd lbbw bmšpṭy ʾl,* "to establish in his heart fear of God's judgments," denotes one of the virtues of the "sons of light" or the "spirits of light" behind them (1QS 4:2ff.), by means of which they evoke conduct that accords with the religious standards of wisdom. Consonant with this development, in 2 Ch. 19:7 *paḥaḏ yhwh* is already reduced to "fear of Yahweh," with *pḥd* as a grammatically transitive term, associated here with the care required of judges in fulfilling their duties. The opposite, *ʾên-paḥaḏ ʾᵉlōhîm,* "no fear of God" (Ps. 36:2[1]), however, conveys a general religious meaning. In Sir. 7:29 the qal impv. *pḥd ʾl,* "fear God," par-

34. F. Schwally, *Semitische Kriegsaltertümer,* I (1901).
35. Morenz, 114-15.
36. A different emendation is suggested by *BHK,* none by *BHS.*

allels respect for the holiness of priests. Fear of God's "judgments" as in 1QS 4:2-3 (cf. 1QH fr. 4:9) appears also in Ps. 119:120, with only a rhetorical distinction between these judgments and God's "words" as an object of fear in v. 161.

III. *pāḥaḏ yiṣḥāq.* The phrase *pāḥaḏ yiṣḥāq* (Gen. 31:42) or *pāḥaḏ 'āḇîw yiṣḥāq* (v. 53b) most likely derives from the root *pḥd* I rather than *pḫd,* if only because the former is well attested in Hebrew, albeit mostly in late texts, whereas the latter, except for Job 40:17, appears only in later languages. Only in Aramaic and idioms influenced by Aramaic can the /*ḏ*/ in Proto-Sem. **pḫḏ,* which can be deduced from Arab. *faḫiḏ,* become /*d*/;[37] the same shift could also occur in Ugaritic, but **pḫd,* "thigh" or "clan," is not attested in that language. On the basis of this argument, the noun *paḥaḏ* would denote the "fearsome one" (see II.4 above); the possessive gen. *yiṣḥāq* identifies the beneficiary of a numinous terror that prevails over enemies (see II.5 above): "the fearsome one of Isaac." But because religious formulas (esp. ancient or archaizing formulas) are polysemous, we cannot rule out the possibility that Isaac himself is the one who arouses fear, as in genitive phrases like *paḥaḏ yhwh;* thus the phrase could mean "the fear evoked by Isaac."[38] Anyone who has a fearsome God is also fearsome.

It would appear, furthermore, that the term and concept are not as isolated in the OT as Alt assumed.[39] The personal or tribal name *ṣlpḥd,* to be read *ṣēl paḥaḏ* on the basis of LXX *Salpaad,* can be explained as "Shadow of the Paḥad" that protects the family or tribe.[40] Comparable is Akk. *puluḫti ṣillīka,* "the fearsomeness of your shadow,"[41] the theophorous element of which obviously is a deity in whom the panic "terror" emanating from another god, such as an El, has become an independent figure, a tutelary numen of the family or tribe in the inevitable military conflicts of the group. Although erroneously citing Arabic, Westermann is probably correct in viewing the words *'elōhê 'aḇrāhām ûpaḥaḏ yiṣḥāq* in Gen. 31:42 as a secondary addition based on v. 53b.[42] In any case, the peaceful nature of the patriarchal stories is most likely due to secondary reworking.[43] The expressions *paḥaḏ lāylâ* (Ps. 91:5) and *paḥaḏ ballêlôṯ* (Cant. 3:8), then, may indicate that a fearsome deity of a small group has been reduced to the status of a minor demon.[44] Related in meaning are the *balhôṯ ṣalmāweṯ (ṣalmûṯ?),* "terrors of deep darkness," which the adulterer does not fear (Job 24:17), as well as the *meleḵ ballāhôṯ,* "king of terrors" (18:14), especially since the association of Cant. 3:8 and Job 24:17 with marriage and sexual intercourse also suggests a background in familial religion.

---

37. Hillers, 92.

38. For bibliog. see A. Alt, *Essays on OT History and Religion* (Eng. trans. 1966), 26 n. 63.

39. Ibid., 26.

40. Lemaire, "Pays de Hépher," 20; idem, *Inscriptions,* 288; also *HAL,* III, 1030, where my interpretation is misrepresented, and Puech, 356-57, 360 n. 10.

41. *AHw,* II, 879a.

42. C. Westermann, *Genesis 12–36* (Eng. trans. 1985), 497.

43. M. Rose, *BZ* 20 (1976) 197-211.

44. See II.4 above; H. Gunkel, *Genesis* (^{6}1964), 349; idem, *Die Psalmen. HKAT* (^{5}1968), 406.

Of course neither the PN *ṣlpḥd* nor Cant. 3:8 suggests any particular association with Isaac. According to late texts such as Nu. 26:33; 27:1; Josh. 17:3 (1 Ch. 7:15), the former is a descendant of Manasseh-Gilead-Hepher; at least his daughters Hoglah and Tirzah (Nu. 26:33; 27:1; 36:11; Josh. 17:3) correspond to localities in central Palestine.[45] Both observations are at odds with the localization of Isaac in the far south. In any case, though, the association of *paḥad̠* as a deity with a genitive of appellative nature and with a personal name is grounded in the familial function of the numen.

The narrator of Gen. 31:53b displays great interest in familial religion. May we conclude, then, that the interpretation of a numinous familial *paḥad̠* as the god *'āḇîw yiṣḥāq,* "of his father Isaac," is simply a construct of this narrator, which was later abbreviated from *paḥad̠ 'āḇîw yiṣḥāq* to *paḥad̠ yiṣḥāq* and now has the feel of an independent divine name, to fill out v. 42? For the oath in the marriage contract recorded in v. 50, appropriation of a familial numen embodying the "fearsome one" and handed on from Isaac to Jacob would fit with the preceding aggressive situation. For vv. 50 and 53b as elements of a familial history appear to be earlier than "the tribal pact in vv. 51-53a,"[46] with its confrontation between the God of Abraham and the God of Nahor in v. 53a, who represent for the narrator the later nations of Israel and Aram. Furthermore, since the list of divine appellatives in Gen. 49:24-25 does not include a *paḥad̠ yiṣḥāq,* the more general question of Alt's "God of the fathers" does not arise here.[47] Köckert has disputed (on insufficient grounds) the assumption that the familial religion of the patriarchal narratives exhibits authentic pre-Israelite nomadic traditions.[48]

The translation of *paḥad̠ yiṣḥāq* as "kinsman of Isaac" has no semantic basis in Aram. (?), Palmyr., and Arab. *pḥd/z/* or *faḫid̠,* "clan."[49] Koch's theory "that Jacob swears by the thigh or procreative member of his father Isaac" relies entirely on such late semantic isoglosses as Targumic Aram. *paḥ^a^d̠în,* "testicles," and the Vulg. of Job 40:17, which clearly depends on the Aramaic; in earlier Hebrew prior to Aramaic influence, we would expect /z/ rather than /d/ as the third radical of a phonological isogloss of Aram. **paḥad̠* corresponding to Arab. *fahid̠,* "thigh."[50] Citing Koch, Malul therefore considers *paḥad̠,* "thigh," in Gen. 31:42,53 to be an Aramaic word, overlooking the fact that, appropriately to the narrative situation, the Aramaic expression in v. 47 is placed quite naturally in the mouth of Laban, not Jacob.[51] The same objection can be made to the translation "clan of Isaac."[52] Moreover, if *paḥad̠ yiṣḥāq* in 31:42 derives from *paḥad̠ 'āḇîw yiṣḥāq* in v. 53b, the only relevant narrative context (that of v. 53b) lends no support to Koch's theory. On the contrary: although on the literal level Jacob invokes a curse on himself should he

---

45. See also N. H. Snaith, *VT* 16 (1966) 124-27; Lemaire, "Pays de Hépher"; idem, *Inscriptions,* 287-89; A. Demsky, *ErIsr* 16 (1982) *70-*75.
46. Westermann, *Genesis 12–36,* 499, citing Gunkel.
47. "The God of the Fathers," *Essays on OT History and Religion,* 1-66, esp. 25-27.
48. M. Köckert, *Vätergott und Väterverheissung* (1987).
49. Contra Albright, *From the Stone Age,* 248, see Hillers et al.
50. P. 113.
51. Pp. 194ff., citing Koch.
52. Puech, 356.

break his oath, so that he would be attacked by the "terror" of v. 53b, on the pragmatic level of the narrative, especially after Jacob has become the representative of Israel and Laban the representative of the Arameans, the *paḥaḏ yiṣḥāq* is a "terror" to the enemies of Jacob and Israel; secondarily, in v. 42 it acts as the guarantor of the prosperity of both parties, in accord with the tendency of the patriarchal narrative. According to Koch, the "terror" Isaac suffers would have to be called **paḥaḏ ʿal-yiṣḥāq* and would therefore have no bearing on our understanding of the formula.[53] For the swearing by the "thigh" of Koch's interpretation, the patriarchal narrative uses *yārēḵ* (24:2,9; 47:29); the absence of the expression **śîm yāḏ taḥaṯ yārēḵ* in 31:53 is not without significance.

As a synonym of *paḥaḏ* in its function as a divine appellative we find *môrāʾ*, "fearsome one," in Ps. 76:12(11), where it parallels *yhwh ʾᵉlōhêḵem,* a usage that recalls the juxtaposition of *ʾᵉlōhê* (twice) and *paḥaḏ,* each time with a genitive denoting the worshiper. Thorion-Vardi points out that *mwrʾ* appears as a divine appellative in 1QpHab 6:5.[54]

H.-P. Müller

53. Koch, 108. See II.5 above.
54. T. Thorion-Vardi, *RevQ* 46 (1986) 282.

פַּחַת *paḥaṯ*

I. Etymology. II. Occurrences and Meaning: 1. OT; 2. Ancient Versions; 3. Dead Sea Scrolls. III. Lev. 13:55.

I. Etymology. The noun *paḥaṯ* is generally derived from the verb *pḥt,*[1] which occurs in many Semitic languages (Jewish Aramaic, Syriac, Samaritan, Akkadian), but not in Biblical Hebrew. Among its meanings are "hollow out" and "pierce." Arabic has a verb *faḥata,* "dig, pierce"; Akkadian has a verb *patāḫu(m)* with roughly the same meaning,"[2] like Syr. *pḥt* (pael). The basic meaning of the noun in Hebrew is probably "pit." It occurs with this meaning in other Northwest Semitic languages as well, like Sam. *pḥth*[3] or Syr. and Aram. *peḥtā* or *paḥtā*.

paḥaṯ. A. Schwarzenbach, *Die geographische Terminologie im Hebräischen des ATs* (1954), 40-41.

1. *BLe,* 458; *HAL,* III, 924.
2. See Wehr, 693; *AHw,* II, 846-47.
3. *LOT,* II, 517.

II. Occurrences and Meaning.

1. *OT.* The word *paḥaṯ* appears in the singular in 2 S. 18:17; Isa. 24:17,18 (twice); Jer. 48:28,43,44 (twice); and Lam. 3:47; it appears in the plural in 2 S. 17:9. A hapax legomenon *peḥeṯeṯ* is found in Lev. 13:55.[4] A conjectural reading *paḥaṯ* has been proposed in Am. 3:5 (for *paḥ*)[5] and, more cogently, in Job 39:22 (for *paḥaḏ,* with some Heb. mss. and Syr.; cf. LXX). From 2 S. 18:17 we can conclude that *paḥaṯ* is masculine, although 17:9 reads *'aḥaṯ* rather than *'aḥaḏ;* in Syriac the word is sometimes masculine, sometimes feminine.

The verbs used in 2 S. 18:17; Isa. 24:18; and Jer. 48:44 *(hišlîḵ 'el, nāpal 'el,* and *'ālâ min)* show clearly that *paḥaṯ* refers to a "hole" or "pit" (e.g., in a forest[6]); in mountainous terrain it might be called a gorge (as in 2 S. 17:9; Jer. 48:28). The word acquires a more specialized meaning when it refers to a "pitfall" or "bird snare" (Isa. 24:18; Jer. 48:44).[7] The latter suggestion is not so likely, because in Am. 3:5 *paḥ* should probably be deleted (with the LXX) rather than emended to *paḥaṯ.* The meaning "pitfall," however, is more obvious: it is suggested by the alliterative proverb (Isa. 24:17-18; Jer. 48:43-44) in which *paḥaṯ* comes between *paḥaḏ* ("terror") and *paḥ* ("snare"). According to Schwarzenbach, the image is that of game fleeing the noise of the beaters and falling into a pit. If it escapes from the pit, it is trapped in a snare. It is possible, however, that this proverb does not draw directly on the language of hunting, in which *paḥaṯ* means "pitfall," but refers simply to a "hole" into which a fugitive suddenly falls. Furthermore, there are other words for "pitfall" in the OT: *šaḥaṯ* (Ezk. 19:4,8; Ps. 7:16[Eng. v. 15]; 9:16[15]; etc.), *šûḥâ* (Jer. 18:20,22; etc.), or *šîḥâ* (Ps. 57:7[6]; 119:85; etc.).[8]

The wording of the text in Jer. 48:28 poses problems for the translator: the inhabitants of Moab are urged to leave their towns and dwell among the rocks, like the doves that nest *be'eḇrê pî-paḥaṯ,* "on the sides[9] of the mouth of a gorge." Citing Eissfeldt, Schwarzenbach suggests deleting *pî* as a kind of catchword filling out a line, but this emendation is unnecessary, as Rudolph correctly observes.[10] We may also note van Selms's conjectural reading *pîpaḥaṯ* = Akk. *papaḫḫu,* "mountainous terrain"; but this is a Hurrian loanword.[11]

The proverb used in Isa. 24:17-18 and — with minor modifications — in Jer. 48:43-44 in a prophecy against Moab attracts immediate attention by virtue of its alliteration and assonance.[12] It is probably one of the stock proverbs of ancient Israel, referring to the dread, destruction, and inexorable fate associated inevitably with judgment — in

---

4. See III below.
5. G. Dalman, *AuS,* VI, 339.
6. → יער *ya'ar* III.2.a.
7. For the former meaning see Schwarzenbach; for the latter, Dalman, *AuS,* VI, 335, 339.
8. But see G. Gerleman, *Bulletin de la Société Royale des Lettres de Lund 1945-1946* 4 (1946) 86-87; K. Galling, *BRL*², 152.
9. B. Gemser, *VT* 2 (1952) 351.
10. O. Eissfeldt, *VT* 2 (1952) 87-92; W. Rudolph, *Jeremia. HAT* I/12 (³1968), 278.
11. A. van Selms, *Jeremia. POT,* 3 vols. (1972-74), III, 31. Cf. *AHw,* II, 823.
12. A. Weiser, *Jeremia. ATD* 20/21 (⁶1969), 401: "a secondary addition."

this case, the coming judgment of God (cf. Am. 5:19). The juxtaposition of *paḥaḏ* and *paḥaṯ* in Lam. 3:47 probably reflects this wordplay.

2. *Ancient Versions.* The LXX usually translates *paḥaṯ* with *bothýnos;* 2 S. 18:17 has a double translation, both *bothýnos* and *chásma.* In 2 S. 17:9 LXX^{BA} read *bounós,* "hill" (which often translates *giḇʿâ*), but the Lucianic recension reads *aulṓn,* "gorge."[13] Some have suggested that *bounós* is here a scribal error for *bothýnos.*[14] In Lam. 3:47 LXX^{BA} have *thymós* while other LXX mss. use *thámbos,* "wonder." The Syr. usually translates the word with *gûmāṣā* (2 S. 18:17; Isa. 24:17-18; Jer. 48:43-44). In Jer. 48:28 the Syr. telescopes the last three words[15] into *geḏānpā,* "reef, cliff." In 2 S. 17:9 it has *ʾāṯrāwāṯā,* "spaces," and in Lam. 3:47 *gûmāṣā* appears in a different place. The Targ. also usually uses *qûmṣā* or *kûmṣā* to translate *paḥaṯ.* In the Vulg., finally, we usually find *fovea;* only in Jer. 48:28 do we find *foramen* and in Lam. 3:9 *laqueus.*

3. *Dead Sea Scrolls.* CD 4:14 cites Isa. 24:17: "Panic, pit, and snare against you, inhabitants of the land." CD 11:13-14 prohibits assisting an animal that gives birth on the sabbath; even if it falls into a well *(bôr)* or a pit *(paḥaṯ),* a member of the community must not help it get out on the sabbath (cf. Mt. 12:11; Lk. 14:5).

III. Lev. 13:55. The law governing leprosy[16] speaks of "leprous" spots on clothing (Lev. 13:47-59). When the garments, skins, or whatever are clearly unclean, they are to be burned in fire; in questionable cases they are to be washed. If the result is negative, the item in question is still unclean and is to be burned in fire (v. 55): "There is *peḥeṯeṯ* on the bare spot on the front or on the back." The word is generally translated "erosion," "(eroded) depression," or the like.[17] The text is probably referring to traces of mildew. Elliger believes that the word is one of the new technical terms from a fairly late period.[18]

Mulder

13. See Josephus *Ant.* 7.9.6 §218.
14. As early as I. F. Schleusner, *Novus Thesaurus,* I (1820), 583.
15. See II.1 above.
16. → צרעת *ṣāraʿaṯ.*
17. For the former see K. Elliger, *Leviticus. HAT* I/4 (1966), 186; for the latter, *GesB, KBL*², *HAL.*
18. P. 173.

פַּטִּישׁ *paṭṭîš* → מַקֶּבֶת *maqqeḇeṯ*

פָּטַר pāṭar; פָּטִיר pāṭîr; פֶּטֶר peṭer; פִּטְרָה piṭrâ

I. Etymology. II. Occurrences. III. Meaning: 1. Architecture; 2. Cult; 3. General Usage. IV. LXX. V. Dead Sea Scrolls.

I. Etymology. In discussing the origin of the verb *pāṭar,* we may cite the Akk. verb *paṭāru,* "release," and the noun *ipṭiru,* "ransom."[1] In Akkadian personal names the element *paṭāru* sometimes has the meaning "release."[2] Elsewhere, analogously to Heb. *peṭer reḥem,* scholars assert that it has taken on the meaning "split (the womb)" with reference to the firstborn;[3] Stamm, however, rejects this interpretation.[4] But the Heb. verb *pāṭar* can be explained as a technical architectural term on the basis of the meaning "split"; Noth therefore also cites Arab. *faṭara,* "split."[5] Heb. *peṭer reḥem,* "splitting of the womb," belongs accordingly in this context. The element of separation present in Akk. *paṭāru,* "release," makes itself heard in the noun *paṭrum,* "deserter,"[6] and in the verbal meaning "escape" of Heb. *pāṭar* (1 S. 19:10; Sir. 32:11).

The root *pṭr* appears in Ugaritic in the orthographic variants *pṭr/bṭr/pẓr.*[7] It is used, for example, in the expression *bṭr bd mlkt,* "exempt from service, to the attention of the queen"; it also has the meaning "extirpate."[8] In the El Amarna tablets, the verb *paṭāru* is attested with the meaning "release, depart," or "yield."[9] A subst. *pṭrh* appears in Phoenician; according to Lidzbarski, it refers to the status of a released or redeemed slave.[10] A PN *pṭr* is also found.[11] In Imperial Aramaic we find the verb *pṭr* I with the

---

pāṭar. A. van den Born, "Erstgeburt," *BL*² (1968), 424-25; H. Cazelles, "Premiers-Nés. II. Dans l'AT," *DBS,* VIII (1972), 482-91; H. Gese, "Ezechiel 20, 25f. und die Erstgeburtsopfer," *Beiträge zur alttestamentliche Theologie. FS W. Zimmerli* (1977), 140-51; J. Halbe, *Das Privilegrecht Jahwes. FRLANT* 114 (1975), 176-85; G. C. Heider, *The Cult of Molek. JSOTSup* 43 (1985), 252-58; O. Kaiser, "Den Erstgeborenen Sohn deiner Söhne sollst du mir geben," *Denkender Glaube. FS C. H. Ratschow* (1976), 14-48; W. Zimmerli, "Erstgeborene und Leviten," *Near Eastern Studies in Honor of W. F. Albright* (1971), 459-69; repr. in *Studien zur alttestamentliche Theologie und Prophetie. ThB* 51 (1974), 235-46.

1. For the verb see *AHw,* II, 849-51; for the noun, *AHw,* I, 395; *CAD,* VII, 171-73.
2. K. L. Tallqvist, *APN,* 301.
3. Ibid., 301; see also idem, *Neubabylonisches Namenbuch* (1905), 327.
4. J. J. Stamm, *AN,* 169-70, but cf. 128.
5. M. Noth, *Könige. BK* IX/1 (²1968), 102; also previously *GesB,* 640, and now *HAL,* III, 925.
6. *AHw,* II, 851.
7. See the survey in J. Sanmartín, *UF* 11 (1979) 724 n. 24.
8. For the former see *KTU* 4.382, 1.2; for the latter, 1.108, 34.
9. EA, I, 1491.
10. See *CIS,* I, 102a; *LidzEph,* III, 109-10. Cf. *DNSI,* II, 909; *KAI,* 49.34.
11. Benz, 390.

meaning "separate" (?).[12] Beyer lists the verb with the meaning "remove, depart" along with a subst. *pṭr,* "loss," and a second subst. *pṭwryn,* "separation."[13]

II. Occurrences. In the OT the verb occurs 8 times in the qal and once in the hiphil; there are 11 occurrences of the noun *peṭer* and one of the subst. *piṭrâ.* Except for Ezk. 20:26, the substantives appear only in the Pentateuch (8 times in Exodus, 3 times in Numbers), while the verb appears 5 times in the Deuteronomistic History, twice in the Chronicler's History, and once each in Psalms and Proverbs. To date, the use of the substantives extends from the early period of the monarchy in the primary covenant recognizing Yahweh as Israel's God (Ex. 34:19-20) through the exilic (Ezekiel, Holiness Code) and postexilic period (P^S). The verb *pāṭar* makes its first appearance in texts of the exilic period.

III. Meaning.

1. *Architecture.* The verb is used as a technical architectural term in 1 K. 6, in the account of the building of the temple. The construct phrase *pᵉṭurê ṣiṣṣîm* appears in vv. 18, 29 (> LXX), and 32. There is still no consensus concerning the meaning of the verb. Noth's assumption that the root is associated etymologically with Arab. *faṭara,* "split," leads him to suggest "burst" or "open" floral forms, i.e., calyces, to be pictured as long rows of botanical ornamentation.[14] Others think instead in terms of floral hangings, an interpretation that can be associated with the meaning "set free."[15]

2. *Cult.* The subst. *peṭer* is found already as a technical cultic term in Ex. 34:19-20, in the prerogative law of Yahweh. The theory that this passage is a Deuteronomistic interpolation from Ex. 13 must be rejected.[16] Here *peṭer* occurs for the first time in the construct phrase *peṭer reḥem.* Ex. 34:19-20 is not a single literary unit: its core is vv. 19aα,20bα, so that we should read *kol-peṭer reḥem lî kōl bᵉḵôr bāneyḵā tip̱deh.*[17] Thus we observe a terminological distinction between *peṭer reḥem,* referring to the firstborn of an animal, and *bᵉḵôr,* which refers to a firstborn human being.[18] The phrase *peṭer reḥem* is not used of humans because it defines the firstborn with respect to the mother; in the circumstances of polygyny, such a definition would create problems concerning the status of the firstborn.[19] Therefore the phrase could not become the standard term for primogeniture; the predominant terms are *rē'šîṯ 'ôn* and especially *bᵉḵôr.* Ex. 34:19-20 stipulates that all the firstborn belong to Yahweh and that every firstborn son must

---

12. Cf. *DNSI,* II, 908.
13. Beyer, 667.
14. M. Noth, *BK* IX/1², 97, 102, 125-26; cf. T. A. Busink, *Der Tempel von Jerusalem,* I (1970), 272-74.
15. *GesB,* 640; E. Würthwein, *Die Bücher der Könige. ATD* 11/1 (²1985), 60-61.
16. Contra E. Kutsch, *ZTK* 55 (1958) 7-8, see Halbe, 179-80; Kaiser, 46-47.
17. Halbe, 177.
18. Zimmerli, 237.
19. Cf. Cazelles, 483; M. Tsevat, → II, 125-26.

be redeemed.[20] The firstborn of every animal is to be sacrificed, while a substitute sacrifice is offered for a human being. The later Covenant Code text Ex. 22:28(Eng. v. 29) is already more ambiguous; as a consequence, it could be understood (and was) as referring to child sacrifice.[21]

Following its initial appearance in the prerogative law of Yahweh, the construct phrase *peṭer reḥem* does not reappear until the exilic period, this time in texts that also refer to firstborn humans. The explanation for this change is that altered social circumstances (monogamy) now precluded any misunderstanding concerning the status of the firstborn designated as *peṭer reḥem*. In Ex. 13:2 and Nu. 3:12, *peṭer reḥem* appears in epexegetic combination with *b^e^ḵôr*, since the construct phrase was appreciated for its archaic ring, but by itself was felt to be inappropriate to the material.[22]

In contrast to the ancient legislation in Ex. 34:19-20, 13:11-16 connects the setting apart of the firstborn for Yahweh with the event of the exodus: in Egypt Yahweh killed all the firstborn of both humans and animals; therefore every firstborn male animal must be sacrificed and every firstborn son must be redeemed (v. 15). Since Ex. 34:19-20 already bears witness to differing sacrificial practices with respect to humans and animals, the new element in 13:15 is the appeal to the slaying of the Egyptian firstborn to explain the sacrifice. Detailed comparison of 13:11-16 with 34:19a,20abα demonstrates the secondary nature of the former text with respect to a law governing the firstborn virtually congruent with 34:19-20.[23]

The priestly requirement in Ex. 13:2 that all the people consecrate *(qiddēš)* their firstborn to Yahweh is incorporated into Nu. 3:12 and interpreted as an elective act[24] on the part of Yahweh (cf. 8:16), just as it is likewise Yahweh who consecrates to himself all the firstborn in Israel (v. 13). The notion of redeeming firstborn sons is extended here in vv. 12-13, since Yahweh accepts the Levites as substitutes for all the firstborn. The reason stated is the same as in Ex. 13:12-13. What is new is the acceptance of the Levites as a substitute for the firstborn, a principle that reappears in Nu. 8:16-18. Here, however, the fem. form *piṭrâ* in the sense of a collective noun is chosen instead of the usual subst. *peṭer*.[25]

The substance of these texts assures us of two aspects of the religio-political situation in the postexilic period: First, the Levites are no longer degraded to the status of servants in the sanctuary; instead, divine election bestows on them the prerogative of the service. Second, the ancient requirement that the firstborn be set apart for God is fully reestablished in a more radical sense. No longer does the sacrifice of an animal redeem a firstborn son: the entire tribe of Levi substitutes for every individual Israelite as an offering to God.[26]

---

20. → פדה *pāḏâ*.
21. Zimmerli, 239.
22. Halbe, 181 n. 24.
23. Ibid., 181-84, 185.
24. → לקח *lāqaḥ*.
25. *HAL*, III, 925.
26. Zimmerli, 245.

According to Nu. 18:15, the *peṭer reḥem* is given to the priests as their share of the offering. The firstborn of human beings and of unclean animals must be redeemed. Except in the case of cows, sheep, and goats, a firstborn animal is redeemed by payment of a sum of money.

The only occurrence of *peṭer reḥem* in the book of Ezekiel (20:26) also presupposes the practice of redemption as required by Ex. 34:19-20, but indicates that the Israelites have neglected this practice, since they have made all their firstborn "pass through fire" as a sacrifice to idols. It is disputed whether the use of *peṭer reḥem* in this context, as in Ex. 34:19-20, refers to animals or human beings. It is probably safe to assume that the passage deals with child sacrifice, which was very much in vogue during the Assyrian period (cf. 2 K. 16:3).[27] The use of the archaizing expression *peṭer reḥem* in this passage in Ezekiel suggests polemical use of a cryptic mythological idea.[28] Or possibly the attack on unjust ordinances bespeaks an intention to rule out the notion that Yahweh required the killing of the firstborn, since there is no regular child sacrifice in the OT.[29] In the light of Ezk. 20:28,40, one may also ask whether 20:25-26 may refer to an animal sacrifice that was impracticable or was offered at the wrong site.[30]

3. *General Usage.* In the sense of "release," the verb *pāṭar* has a variety of connotations and appears in diverse contexts.

It is used intransitively in its earliest occurrence (1 S. 19:10), in the account of David's rise, to describe David's escape from Saul: *wayyipṭar mippᵉnê šā'ûl.* Some scholars read a niphal form here on the basis of postbiblical usage of the word, especially in the Dead Sea Scrolls.[31] But since the qal also appears with the same meaning in Sir. 32:11, it can be retained in 1 S. 19:10.[32] The intransitive use of the verb in 1 S. 19:10 and Sir. 32:11 calls to mind the noun *paṭērum,* "deserter," in the Mari texts.

Used transitively, the qal of *pāṭar* means "release, set free." It can be used figuratively, as in Prov. 17:14, where it refers to the release of a torrent of water, a usage analogous to Akk. *nagbē puṭṭuru,* "open the springs."[33] In the expression *pôṭēr mayim rē'šîṯ māḏôn, pôṭēr* is not an abstract noun of the *qôṭēl* type; it should be construed instead as a *casus pendens.*[34]

In the context of Levitical service in the second temple, *pāṭar* means exemption from such service granted by the priests (2 Ch. 23:8). This exemption is also mentioned

---

27. W. Zimmerli, *Ezekiel 1. Herm* (Eng. trans. 1979), 344, 411-12; H. Spieckermann, *Juda unter Assur in der Sargonidenzeit. FRLANT* 129 (1982), 106; P. Maiberger, "Gen 22 und die Problematik des Menschenopfers in Israel," *BiKi* 41 (1986) 104-12, esp. 109-10.

28. Halbe, 181 n. 24.

29. Kaiser, 25, 44-47; → VIII, 387-88.

30. J. Garscha, *Studien zum Ezechielbuch. EH* XXIII/23 (1974), 119-20.

31. *BHK;* Stoebe, *Das erste Buch Samuelis. KAT* VIII/1 (1973), 357.

32. Cf. *BHS.*

33. *VAB,* VII, 6, 45; 212, 1; cf. *HAL,* III, 925.

34. Contra B. Gemser, *Sprüche Salomos. HAT* I/16 (²1963), 112; G. R. Driver, *Bibl* 32 (1951) 196; and W. McKane, *Proverbs. OTL* (1970), 505, see *GK,* §116w; see also the thorough discussion by W. Gross, *BN* 35 (1986) 30-72.

in 1 Ch. 9:33a, where the phrase *liškōṯ pᵉṭûrîm* denotes the chambers assigned to the exempt division. Rudolph sees a contraction between v. 33a and 33b, since he takes *pᵉṭûrê* as a *plurale tantum,* translating the whole phrase as "recess in the chambers."[35]

The only occurrence of the hiphil is in Ps. 22:8(7), with a prepositional object: *hipṭîr bᵉśāpâ,* "they make a cleft with their lips," a reference to opening the mouth wide as a gesture of derision.

IV. LXX. The LXX uses *dianoígon mḗtran* or *prōtótokos* (Ex. 34:19) to translate *peṭer (reḥem).* Similarly, *bᵉḵôr peṭer reḥem* (Nu. 3:12) is translated by *prōtótokos dianoígōn mḗtran,* as is the hapax legomenon *piṭrâ* in Nu. 8:16. In Prov. 17:14 the LXX reads *lógoi* for *mayim* and translates *pāṭar* as *exousían didónai.* In 2 Ch. 23:8 the verb is translated by *katalýein;* the LXX interprets the *liškôṯ pᵉṭûrîm* of 1 Ch. 9:33 as *diatetagménai ephēmeríai.* The intransitive use of *pāṭar* in 1 S. 19:10 is represented in the LXX by *apérchesthai.* In Ps. 22:8(7) the LXX translates the hiphil of *pṭr* with *en cheílesin.*

V. Dead Sea Scrolls. In the Dead Sea Scrolls, the niphal of *pṭr* appears with the meaning "go away" (1QS 7:10,12). The form *pᵉṭûrî[m]* in 4Q491 fr. 1-3, 8 recalls the usage in 1 Ch. 9:33.[36] The obscure context prohibits a more precise definition of its meaning. The verb *pāṭar* in the sense "be exempt from" (having to pay) is attested in a letter from En-gedi.[37]

Niehr

35. W. Rudolph, *Chronikbücher. HAT* I/21 (1955), 90.
36. See M. Baillet, *DJD,* VII, 15.
37. J. T. Milik, *DJD,* II, no. 46, 9.

פלא *pl';* פֶּלֶא *pele'*

I. 1. Occurrences; 2. Basic Meaning; 3. LXX. II. Verb: 1. Niphal; 2. Hiphil. III. Nouns: 1. *niplā'ōṯ;* 2. *pele'* and *pil'î.* IV. Dead Sea Scrolls.

pl'. R. Albertz, "פלא *pl' ni.* to be wondrous," *TLOT* II, 981-86; G. Bertram, "θαῦμα," *TDNT,* III, 27-42; D. Grimm, "Die hebräische Wurzel *pl'* und ihre nominalen Ableitungen im AT" (diss., Halle/S., 1977) (cf. *ZAW* 90 [1978] 306-7); idem, "'Jahwe Elohim, der Gott Israels, der allein Wunder tut,'" *Jud* 35 (1979) 77-83; J. Haspecker, *Wunder im AT* (1965); F. Nötscher, *Zur theologischen Terminologie der Qumran-Texte. BBB* 10 (1956); G. Quell, "Das Phänomen des Wunders im AT," *Verbannung und Heimkehr. FS W. Rudolph* (1961), 253-300; J. J. Stamm, *Beiträge zur hebräischen und altorientalischen Namenkunde. OBO* 30 (1980); H. J. Stoebe, "Anmerkungen zur Wurzel *pl'* im AT," *TZ* 28 (1972) 13-23; F.-E. Wilms, *Wunder im AT* (1979).

I. 1. *Occurrences.* In the OT the word group *pālā'* is attested only in Hebrew. The verb occurs 57 times in the niphal, 11 times in the hiphil, and once in the hithpael. Of the occurrences of the niphal, 42 are instances of the participle in the nominalized plural form *niplā'ôṯ* (except in Ps. 131:1 and Job 42:3, where *niplā'ôṯ* is used as an adj.). The piel and hiphil forms denoting technical cultic procedures constitute a special group.[1] The qal is found only in personal names and as a substitute for the hiphil (*pᵉlā'yâ,* Neh. 8:7; 10:11; *pᵉlāyâ,* 1 Ch. 3:24; the short form *pallû',* Gen. 46:9; Ex. 6:14; Nu. 26:5,8; 1 Ch. 5:3; its derivative *pallu'î,* Nu. 26:5;[2] the form *'ᵉlîplēhû* in 1 Ch. 15:18,21 and conjectured in Nu. 16:1 is problematic[3]). Derivatives are the noun *pele'* and its associated adj. *pil'î* (fem. *pil'îyâ; Q pelî,* fem. *pᵉlî'â*). The noun occurs 13 times, including 2 instances of the pl. *pᵉlāyôṯ* and one of *pᵉlā'îm;* in late mss. it appears also as a suffixed form in Ps. 77:12(Eng. v. 11); 88:13(12); 89:6(5).[4] The adjective occurs twice. The hapax legomenon *miplā'ôṯ* may be a scribal error for *niplā'ôṯ.* The niphal occurs 4 times in Sirach (twice as the nominalized form *niplā'ôṯ*), the hiphil 3 times, and the feminine plural of *pele'* 3 times.

Outside the OT, the word group basically appears only in Hebrew and in late Aramaic, under Hebrew influence.[5] Possibly Jewish Aram. *pil'ᵃṯā',* "parable, riddle," and the corresponding Syr. *pēlē'tā'* should be included here.[6] The verb occurs in the Ugaritic PN *ya-ap-lu* and in Punic.[7] The supposition of occurrences in other languages, such as Ugaritic or North Arabic *(fa'l,* "omen," deriving from *pālā'),* is highly uncertain.[8]

2. *Basic Meaning.* To determine the basic meaning of the root *pālā',* we must rely on its occurrences in the OT. Köhler proposed "be different, striking, remarkable," but this definition is too general.[9] The texts all deal with extraordinary phenomena, transcending the power of human knowledge and imagination. Seen from this perspective, the usual translation of the niphal as "be marvelous" comes close to the basic meaning.

Stoebe has objected that "the statement this translation makes refers to an attribute statically inherent in an object or action that is in itself different, remarkable, and therefore marvelous," and that "this interpretation does not comport with the essence of what the OT means when it speaks of marvels."[10] He concludes instead that "*pl'* incor-

---

1. See I.2 below.
2. See *IPN,* 36, 38, 191; *HAL,* III, 927, 928.
3. See *IPN,* 32; *KBL*³, 56, 927.
4. But see III.2 below.
5. Jastrow, 1174, 1181.
6. Ibid., 175; *LexSyr*², 569.
7. For Ugaritic see *PNU,* 336; cf. Stamm, 188. For Punic see Plautus *Poenulus* 1017; *DNSI,* II, 911.
8. For Ugaritic see *HAL,* III, 927; for North Arabic, *GesB,* 641.
9. L. Köhler, *TZ* 1 (1946) 304; *KBL*¹, 759.
10. P. 14.

porates the element of an efficacy proceeding from or associated with the agent."[11] In fact, the texts do not deal with circumstances presented simply as being extraordinary, but rather with certain goals impossible for humans to attain by their own devices or with actions and events directed toward them or affecting them that they are nevertheless unable to influence. In other words, they deal with acts and effects transcending human knowledge and imagination and hence above all transcending the powers of human agency. To this extent Stoebe is absolutely correct.

It must be noted, however, that the word group *pālā'* does not describe the act or effect as such, but rather qualifies it as transcending human knowledge or power. In other words, we must distinguish between the basic meaning and its application to specific subjects. The former requires a stative definition such as "be inscrutable, incredible." Only from this perspective can we explain the construction of niphal forms with comparative *min* or the function of the hiphil. Primarily, then, an observation is made concerning a line that human beings cannot cross but that can be crossed from the other side. The word group thus also marks the contrast between the finitude of what is possible on one side of the line and the infinite range of what is possible on the other side. In particular cases the latter can extend to include other human beings; but for the most part it applies to superhuman forces and powers, especially to God. The texts are concerned above all with the insurmountable contrast between what is possible for human beings and what is possible for God — in other words, with God's otherness and superiority, which humans experience as inscrutable and unattainable.

From this perspective it is easy to see how Quell can ascribe to the noun *pele'* (meaning the whole word group) a "characteristic note that is genuinely sacral and numinous, bringing it extremely close to the fundamental term for the divinity inherent in God, the holy."[12] But the word group does not refer solely to God. Some texts using the niphal of the verb clearly attest that it can be used also in the secular sphere of human relations and that this usage cannot represent a secondary semantic development. In these instances Quell speaks only of a "divine numinosity" or a "numinous tinge";[13] quite apart from the vagueness of the term "numinous," however, this interpretation is unquestionably overdrawn. The word group does not possess a genuinely theological meaning, even though it is used almost always with reference to God; it should not, therefore, be traced as a whole to the sacral realm.

Stoebe and Quell notwithstanding, I shall stand by my conclusion that the basic meaning involves a stative qualification. In placing all the emphasis on the aspect of effective agency, Stoebe is relying on the specific contexts in which the basic meaning is instantiated. Of course, this aspect is very important if we wish to comprehend the actual usage of the word group.

The interpretation of the piel and hiphil forms used by P as technical cultic terms in conjunction with the noun *neḏer* (piel, Lev. 22:21; Nu. 15:3,8; hiphil, Lev. 27:2; Nu.

---

11. P. 15.
12. P. 294.
13. P. 296.

6:2 [possibly to be read as a piel[14]]) is totally obscure. Some scholars derive them from the same root *pālā',* usually presupposing the dubious basic meaning "be different, special" ("fulfill a special vow"); consistently with his interpretation of the root, Stoebe suggests that the vow is put into effect.[15] Others propose another root: a by-form of *pālâ* ("separate a vow") or a totally different root meaning "pledge."[16] All these proposed etymologies and interpretations are totally hypothetical, since the context offers no clue for a more precise definition. In any case, a connection with the word group under discussion here is highly uncertain.

Also problematic is the theory of a connection with the root *pālâ.* The hiphil forms of this root in Ex. 8:18(22); 9:4; 11:7 can only mean "separate, make a distinction." The root appears in other Semitic languages with the same meaning or a modification of it.[17] This meaning can hardly be harmonized with that of the hiphil of *pālā'* ("make inscrutable, incredible"). The two roots must therefore be treated as distinct. At most, they might share the common notion of an insurmountable limit. Formally, however, there has been a mutual assimilation of the two roots, since some occurrences of the verb *pālā'* are formed after the analogy of a verb with a weak third radical (niphal, Ps. 139:14; hiphil, 4:4[3]; 17:7; a hybrid form in Dt. 28:58). In the Samaritan Pentateuch, conversely, *pālâ* is assimilated to *pālā'* in Ex. 9:4; 11:7. The same holds true in Middle Hebrew. In Aramaic the two verbal classes are totally merged. In the case of the niphal in Ex. 33:16, one may therefore ask whether it should be translated "be distinct" *(pālâ)* or "prove to be marvelous" *(pālā'* with comparative *min).* The former is probably preferable, since a niphal of *pālā'* with a direct human subject is unlikely (such a form appears in Ps. 139:14, but the text is clearly corrupt[18]).

3. *LXX.* The LXX generally uses *thaumásia* to translate the pl. *niplā'ôṯ* and noun *pele'* (sg. and pl.); more rarely it uses *thaumastá,* and occasionally other expressions such as *exaísia* (also translating *miplā'ôṯ*), *éndoxa,* or *hypéronka* (in Ex. 15:11 *térata* and in Job 37:14 *dýnamis*). The niphal is represented by *thaumastoún* (pass.), *adynateín/adýnatos,* or *hypéronkos (eínai),* in Jer. 32:17,27 by *(apo)krýptein* (pass.); the hiphil is represented by *thaumastoún* or *thaumásia/thaumastá poieín,* in Dt. 28:59 by *paradoxázein,* and in Isa. 29:14 by *metatithénai* (a finite verb form for the inf. abs. [and *pele'*]; *éndoxos* for the inf. abs. in 2 Ch. 2:8; *térata* in Isa. 28:29 [erroneously connected with v. 29a]). For the hithpael (Job 10:16) we find *deinṓs olékein.* The adj. *pil'î* is represented by *thaumastós* (Jgs. 13:18) or verbally by *thaumastoún* (pass., Ps. 139:6).

---

14. See *BHS.*
15. Pp. 15-16.
16. See *GesB,* 641-42; *HAL,* III, 927; Albertz, *TLOT,* II, 981-82, 983; → נדר *nāḏar* I.3.
17. *HAL,* III, 930; Jastrow, 1181; *MdD,* 373; cf. *AHw,* II, 817.
18. See II.1 below.

II. Verb.

1. *Niphal.* Fundamental to our understanding of the word group are the passages using the niphal of the verb (apart from *niplā'ōṯ* as a subst.[19]), always (except for Ps. 139:14) constructed with the prep. *min* or the prepositional expression *bᵉ'ênê*. The construction with *min* in particular clearly bespeaks a limit. These texts deal with phenomena that can be noted and observed and on occasion used for one's own purposes, but cannot as such be explained or accounted for adequately and therefore are not subject to human decision and control. But these phenomena are not simply observed from a neutral distance: they affect and confront individuals directly, either as tasks and obstacles beyond one's imagination or ability, or as events and forces to whose effects one is exposed.

This spectrum of meanings is clearly recognizable in the few texts that refer to the realm of human society or the secular world. There are legal cases, for example, where the local authorities feel themselves incompetent to reach a decision, so that they must seek the assistance of a different court (Dt. 17:8-9). Amnon is tormented with desire for Tamar, but under the circumstances does not know how to approach her (2 S. 13:1-2). Only someone craftier than he is can help him (vv. 3-5). In the love of Jonathan, on the other hand, David experienced something far transcending the normal experience of human love, something mysterious that affected him all the more profoundly (2 S. 1:26). Prov. 30:18-19, a numerical saying, deals in the first instance with the limits of human knowledge, at least in the first two phenomena (v. 19a). The third (v. 19bα), however, is accessible to human beings and therefore efficacious. This is true especially of sexual relations (v. 19bβ), which reside entirely within the domain of human behavior and exercise an extremely powerful effect. Here the normal relationship between a man and a woman is understood as the ultimate and most profound mystery; possibly the text has in mind the act of intercourse at the beginning of a marriage, which is experienced as foundational. The numerical saying as a whole thus expresses the idea that human beings are surrounded by a world of mysteries that surpass understanding, but can be experienced as beneficial forces or powerfully effectual phenomena.

All the other texts deal with the relationship between God and human beings. Their primary thrust is that there are no limits on God's ability to help people in distress or in difficult circumstances where they do not know which way to turn. As a word from God in the form of a rhetorical question, it gives the human party assurance for the future. It may be addressed to an individual (Gen. 18:14) or to a group such as the city of Jerusalem (Jer. 32:27 [cf. v. 17]) or postexilic Israel (Zec. 8:6b). This assurance, however, presupposes that those addressed are ready to embrace an event that runs counter to their own expectations and abilities (Zec. 8:6a), in other words, to rely totally on God's actions. When help does come, it can only be praised and celebrated as an extraordinary marvel (Ps. 118:23; here spoken by the congregation in the context of an individual thanksgiving liturgy).

---

19. See III.1 below.

Wisdom literature and the Psalms also contain more general statements. Sir. 39:20 declares that everywhere in every age God acts with unimaginable ascendancy, intervening to save and to supply every need (cf. v. 33). It is important to recognize this ascendancy and not to question it from the perspective of one's own ideas (v. 21). Job must therefore confess that it surpasses the limits of his understanding when he tries to debate with God about his fate and God's actions (Job 42:3aβb). In Ps. 131:1, conversely, the psalmist emphasizes that he does not strive to attain high goals and thus transgress the limits of his own possibilities; he renounces all willfulness and trusts totally in God (v. 2). In Ps. 139, too, the psalmist expresses total reliance on God, who created him and preordained his entire life (vv. 13,15-18). God has shown himself thereby to be incomprehensibly great (v. 14a, reading *niplêṯā* instead of *niplêṯî*[20]), and the psalmist concludes from his personal experience that all God's works are inscrutable (v. 14bα). But he views this only as a cause for rejoicing. The form *nôrā'ôṯ,*[21] used adverbially, suggests rather that there is also an ominous element in God's ascendancy.

God's work is also at issue in Dt. 30:11. Obedience to the law does not transcend what is possible for Israel and consequently for the individual Israelites, because it has been brought very near them and placed in their hearts (v. 14). Obedience to the law is within the realm of the possible because God has established the necessary conditions. The same holds true for the much broader claim in Sir. 48:13 that Elisha had unlimited possibilities for action at his disposal.

2. *Hiphil.* The hiphil passages almost without exception refer to God's work; in principle, therefore, God is the grammatical or logical subject of the verbal form. But the verb forms do not serve to describe God's actions as such, but rather to characterize the action portrayed in each particular context as unfathomable to human beings or at variance with human understanding. This is quite clearly the case when the infinitive construct of another verb follows (Jgs. 13:19; 2 Ch. 26:15), but is inherently true in other cases as well. In individual laments, for example, the verb expresses a plea for or assurance of God's favor and help *(ḥeseḏ)* in apparently hopeless circumstances (Ps. 4:4[3] [emended]; 17:7; 31:22[21]). Because the psalmist's situation is hopeless, this can mean only that God must intervene or has intervened in a totally extraordinary way. The same holds true for the prophecy of new salvation and prosperity for Israel as a whole in the face of the devastating consequences of a plague of locusts (Joel 2:26; cf. v. 25). In more general terms, Uzziah is said to have received quite astonishing help in the military field (2 Ch. 26:15), which naturally came from his god (cf. v. 7).

Isa. 28:29, too, probably refers to a specific situation. Taken literally, vv. 23-29 are a didactic wisdom text concerning the intelligent activity of farmers, in which they are mysteriously guided by God (v. 26). This refers undoubtedly to the divine order of the

---

20. See *BHS.*

21. → VII, 302.

universe, which determines all of human life while remaining unfathomable to the human mind. Nonetheless, the passage is probably a parable intended to illustrate the fact that God always acts appropriately in dealing with human beings and exhibits concern for the maintenance of a rational order, even though at present this divine governance conflicts with human understanding.[22]

Text-critical problems make the meaning of Jgs. 13:19bα somewhat ambiguous. It can refer to the promise of Samson's birth as a whole, emphasizing that even a woman's barrenness is no obstacle to God when Israel must be delivered (in apposition with *lᵉyhwh* in v. 19aβ[23]). But the words may also be treated as a nominal clause referring to the ascending of the divine messenger in the flame from the altar (v. 20), indicating that God wondrously brought this about as well (MT).

In the hymnic exhortation to praise God that concludes the "glorification of the ancestors" in Sirach, 50:22 makes a very general statement to the effect that God works in an inscrutable and mysterious way throughout the whole world.

But the end of God's actions is not inevitably salvation. In an equally inscrutable way, God can proceed to punish and destroy Israel if it does not diligently observe the divine law (Dt. 28:59; cf. v. 58). Isa. 29:14 expresses the same idea. Because Israel's worship is only outward (v. 13), God will react in a way that even the wisest would have thought impossible. The construction with *yāsap̱* (text emended) is intended to indicate that, although God always deals with Israel in amazing ways, this can also mean disaster, in which case Israel perceives God only as ominous (this possibility is emphasized by the unusual elliptical construction with a repeated infinitive and *pele'*). Here too belongs the only instance of the hithpael. Job 10:16 challenges God: Job, who believes he has been treated unjustly, is forced to accuse God of consigning him to perdition in a totally incomprehensible and appalling fashion (cf. v. 15).

Only rarely does the hiphil refer to human actions. Solomon desires to build a temple that will transcend the limits of human architecture (2 Ch. 2:8[9]). The text clearly presupposes that the temple befits the greatness of God, so that ultimately it is God who realizes Solomon's intentions, thus expressing his efficacious power.[24] Two disparate texts appear in Sirach. According to 31:9 (34:9), a rich person who lives blamelessly and does not succumb to the temptations of wealth has accomplished something virtually impossible (cf. vv. 1-8). On the other hand, there have been kings in Israel who committed unbelievable sins (48:16).

The personal names formed with the qal of verb share the meaning of the hiphil.[25] They are clauses declaring that God has acted extraordinarily for the benefit of the persons in question. The immediate reference is probably to their auspicious birth, so that the names are expressions of thanksgiving. But such names probably also express confidence that God always acts in this manner and that those bearing these names will experience God's beneficence throughout their lives.

---

22. → VI, 175-76.
23. See *BHK*.
24. See also Stoebe, 18.
25. See I.1 above.

III. Nouns.

1. *niplā'ôṯ*. a. *General.* With two exceptions, the nominalized ptcp. *niplā'ôṯ* refers to mighty acts of God that are humanly inexplicable and indescribable, but are experienced as extremely efficacious events that shape human lives. The term is an expression covering the range of God's mighty acts. Its primarily formulaic nature is particularly clear in those texts where it is followed by a stereotyped relative clause with a perfect form of *'āśâ* (Ps. 78:4; 105:5 [1 Ch. 16:12]; Neh. 9:17) or where it appears as the object of *'āśâ* in an equally stereotyped participial construction (Ps. 72:18; 86:10; 106:21f.; 136:4; Job 5:9; 9:10). That we are dealing with an inclusive abstract term for God's mighty acts is underlined by the observation that it occurs only in the plural. Since the majority of the word's occurrences are in the Psalms, we may assume that its usage was shaped by the cult; its particular locus is in hymns and songs of thanksgiving. All the occurrences of the term outside the Psalter are in exilic or postexilic texts. This is probably true as well for the psalms in question. The nominalization of the participle is therefore probably a relatively late phenomenon.

b. *Specifics.* The *niplā'ôṯ* are generally God's mighty acts on behalf of all Israel, through which it was delivered from afflictions in the past and preserved as a people. The word refers above all to the great events of the early period of Israel's sacred history (Ex. 34:10; Ps. 78:4,11,32; 136:4 [cf. vv. 10-22]; Neh. 9:17; with reference to Egypt: Ex. 3:20; Jgs. 6:13; Ps. 106:7,21-22; cf. Mic. 7:15; with reference to the occupation: Josh. 3:5; including the patriarchs: Ps. 105:2,5 [1 Ch. 16:9,12]). These events were foundational to Israel's existence and are therefore of outstanding and enduring significance. But these mighty acts are not limited to the early period. Ps. 111 shows clearly that the *niplā'ôṯ* of v. 4 are to be found throughout Israel's entire history; they are signs that God steadfastly maintains the covenant[26] (vv. 5,9) and constantly sees to the protection of Israel. In Ps. 96:3 (1 Ch. 16:24) and 98:1, which echo the message of Deutero-Isaiah, the reference is to the new exodus and the ingathering of the diaspora. The word can also express the hope or plea that God will alleviate affliction and intervene to save in the present as before or in Israel's early history (Jer. 21:2; Mic. 7:15). The *niplā'ôṯ* as signs of God's constant intervention to save and to preserve appear also in laments and thanksgivings of the individual, where they bespeak the fundamental conviction that help and salvation will put an end to the psalmist's own affliction (Ps. 9:2[1]; 26:7; 40:6[5]; 71:17; 86:10). When the psalmist speaks with emphasis of all God's wondrous deeds or God's innumerable deeds, or claims to have proclaimed them since childhood (71:17), the reference is naturally to God's deeds on behalf of Israel. At the same time, however, God intervenes directly — and equally indescribably and efficaciously — in the personal lives of individuals. Ps. 107 calls on various groups to bear witness to their deliverance from specific afflictions as demonstrations of God's extraordinary saving work (vv. 8,15,21,31).

According to Ps. 119, it is the → תורה *tôrâ* that bestows perfect salvation on those

---

26. → ברית *b^e^rîṯ*.

who obey it. Therefore its effects (v. 18) and its precepts themselves (v. 27, par. to *piqqûḏîm*) can be called *nip̠lā'ôṯ*.

But God's mighty acts are not of significance solely for Israel. According to Ex. 34:10, they are marvelous throughout the world. They should therefore be proclaimed to all peoples (Ps. 96:3 [1 Ch. 16:24]; 105:1-2; Ps. 98:1 should also be interpreted in this sense). As a result, according to Ps. 96:6-9 and 98:3-5, the peoples in turn worship and praise the God of Israel as king of all the world (cf. also Ps. 86:9-10). In addition, the *nip̠lā'ôṯ* mentioned in Ps. 145:5 are God's universal work of salvation to protect all the oppressed and devout (vv. 14,18-19), so that "all flesh" will sing God's praises (v. 21). This praise is sung not just by human beings but by all God's works (v. 10): the whole creation is included (Ps. 96:11-12; 98:7-8). Thus the works of creation themselves may be called *nip̠lā'ôṯ* (Ps. 107:24; Job 37:5 [here *nip̠lā'ôṯ* is used adverbially or the text must be emended],[27] 14,16 [*mip̠lā'ôṯ*];[28] Sir. 42:17; 43:29 [the following word should probably be read as *gbwrtw* rather than *dbryw*]) and be listed before the mighty acts on behalf of Israel (Ps. 136:4-9). Quite generally, then, one can say that God alone does wondrous things (Ps. 72:18), demonstrating thereby that he alone is God (86:10 [cf. v. 8]; 96:3-5).

The Psalms and the book of Job also use other terms to refer to God's mighty acts in the immediate context of *nip̠lā'ôṯ;* they are largely synonymous with *nip̠lā'ôṯ,* but also bring out certain elements inherent in the word. Above all we note *g^e^ḏōlôṯ* (Ps. 71:19; 106:21; Job 5:9; 9:10; 37:5; cf. *g^e^ḏullâ* in Ps. 145:6), *g^e^ḇûrôṯ* (145:4; cf. *g^e^ḇûrâ* in 71:18), *'^a^lîlôṯ* (78:11), *ma'^a^śîm* (107:24; 145:4; cf. Ex. 34:10), *t^e^hillôṯ* (Ps. 78:4), and *mōp̠^e^ṯîm* (Ps. 105:5 [1 Ch. 16:12]); the aspect of menace is brought out by *nôrā'ôṯ* (Ps. 106:22; 145:6; cf. Ex. 34:10) and the aspect of loving favor by *ḥ^a^sāḏîm* (Ps. 106:7; cf. 107:8,15,21,31). God's *nip̠lā'ôṯ* are also an expression of majesty and power (*kāḇôḏ:* Ps. 96:3 [1 Ch. 16:24]; Ps. 145:5 [emended[29]]; *šēm* (9:3[2]); *'^e^zûz* (78:4; 145:6) as well as of salvific action and righteousness (*y^e^šû'â,* 96:2; 98:2; *ṣ^e^ḏāqâ,* 71:19; 98:2; 145:7). In contrast to all these terms, the defining aspect of *nip̠lā'ôṯ* is that of being humanly unfathomable and unattainable.

Thus the fundamental notion conveyed by *nip̠lā'ôṯ* is that of a beneficent act on the part of God, beyond human understanding and therefore unfathomable, but experienced as liberating and saving (according to Ps. 107:10-16,17-22, even in cases of affliction the victims have brought on themselves). This notion is challenged, however, in the book of Job. While Eliphaz is convinced that God's *nip̠lā'ôṯ* are just and salutary (5:8-9; cf. vv. 1-7,10-27), Job, citing Eliphaz's own words (9:10), stresses that he must consider God's actions totally preposterous: for no reason at all, God is determined to destroy him (vv. 11-35). For Job, God's *nip̠lā'ôṯ* are incomprehensible and unfathomable only in a horrendous sense. A mediating position is stated at the end of the Elihu discourses. Observing the world of natural phenomena, Job should see that God, al-

27. G. Fohrer, *Das Buch Hiob. KAT* XVI (1963), 480.
28. See I.1 above.
29. See *BHS*.

though not accessible to human beings, is nevertheless righteous; all Job can do is submit (37:5,14,16;[30] cf. v. 23).

Only two passages associate *niplā'ôṯ* with a human being; both refer to Antiochus IV Epiphanes. According to Dnl. 11:36, he exalts himself above all gods and even speaks *niplā'ôṯ* against the most high God, i.e., the God of Israel. In other words, he makes himself the only god and believes that he personally has unlimited possibilities at his disposal. Here too *niplā'ôṯ* means divine omnipotence; but this omnipotence is arrogated and perverted by a mortal and therefore can lead only to disaster. The same is true in Dnl. 8:24. Here *niplā'ôṯ* functions as an adverbial modifier of *yašḥîṯ,* which is itself probably a dittography of *hišḥîṯ* in v. 24b; read instead *yᵉdabbēr* as in 11:36 or better *yāśîaḥ.*[31]

c. *Collectively.* The *niplā'ôṯ* are not isolated phenomena to be considered individually. We are dealing instead with particular manifestations of God's work in general; as such, they are of fundamental significance, pointing beyond themselves. This is illustrated above all by the verbs that have *niplā'ôṯ* as their object, directly or indirectly.

It is frequently emphasized, especially in formulaic passages,[32] that God has done, does, or will and can do *niplā'ôṯ* (*'āśâ,* Ex. 3:20; 34:10; Josh. 3:5; Jer. 21:2; Ps. 40:6[5]; 98:1). This means basically that God does in fact act; the resulting reality makes God's action patent. But more is involved than simple observation. The essential point is that all who experience or hear of this reality can appeal to it and have recourse to it, confident that God will also act with power in other circumstances. The same is true of the statement that God manifests *niplā'ôṯ* (*rā'â* hiphil, Ps. 78:11; Mic. 7:15 [emended]). In Ex. 34:10 their fundamental significance is further emphasized by the use of the creation verb *bārā'*[33] along with *'āśâ.*

God's mighty acts do not automatically engender confidence and hope on the part of human beings. They must meet with a readiness to accept and rely on them as manifestations of God's enduring benevolence and power to act. Thus the desert generation is accused of not considering (*śāḵal* hiphil, Ps. 106:7) the mighty acts that they had experienced firsthand, not believing in them (*'āman* hiphil, Ps. 78:32), not remembering them (*zāḵar,* Neh. 9:17), or forgetting them (*šāḵaḥ,* Ps. 78:11; 106:21-22). In other words, they treated them simply as events of the past rather than putting ongoing trust in them. The same is true of the hope for a new intervention by God voiced in Jer. 21:2. This passage presupposes that the people are not ready to rely entirely on God; therefore God's intervention on their behalf would accomplish nothing. Therefore Israel can only be called upon to remember God's mighty acts in the past so that they will understand their dependence on God in the present and future (Ps. 105:5 [1 Ch. 16:12]; cf. Ps. 105:4). Similarly, Job is urged to consider (*bîn* hiphil) in depth the phenomena of the natural world so as to arrive at a proper attitude toward God (Job 37:14). What is

30. See the discussion of these verses above.
31. *BHS.*
32. See III.1.a above.
33. → II, 247-48 (IV.2).

more, Ps. 119:18 says that God will see to it that the psalmist beholds (*nāḇaṭ* hiphil; cf. *śîaḥ* in v. 27) the wondrous things of the *tôrâ* in order to keep it. This leads to the even more far-reaching statement of Ps. 111:4: God has produced in Israel a remembrance *(zēḵer)* of his mighty acts, thus personally establishing the necessary conditions for them to be appropriated and remain effectual.

But such remembrance is transmitted and preserved by human agents who recount (*sāp̄ar* piel) God's mighty acts to others. Those recounting these stories may be the generations of Israel (Jgs. 6:13; Ps. 78:3-4) or a group speaking for Israel as a whole (Ps. 75:2[1] emended), who also are to address all the nations in this role (Ps. 96:3 [1 Ch. 16:24]). Or they may be individuals who publicly proclaim or vow to proclaim God's mighty acts after being delivered from their own afflictions (Ps. 9:2[1]; 26:7). In 71:17-18 the afflicted psalmist attests that he has proclaimed these mighty acts since his youth, and therefore is confident that now in his old age he will be delivered, so that he can proclaim (*nāḡaḏ* hiphil) this to the coming generation as a new demonstration of God's saving work (v. 18 emended[34]). The psalmist in 40:2-13(1-12), delivered from affliction, finds God's wondrous deeds so boundless in number that it is impossible to recount them individually (*nāḡaḏ, dāḇar* piel: v. 6[5]). According to Sir. 42:17, the same holds true for God's work of creation in the realm of nature.

This latter notion is of course only one more expression of the fact that we are dealing with events that simply cannot be represented adequately by human words. To recount them can only mean to glorify them as something ineffable and unfathomable, thank God for them, and praise God. This is expressed by the verbs *yāḏâ* hiphil (Ps. 107:8,15,31; cf. 9:2[1]; 75:2[1] emended) and *śîaḥ* (105:2 [1 Ch. 16:9]; Ps. 145:5 emended). Other verbs of similar meaning appear in the contexts of these verses, making clear that the real emphasis is on the aspect of praise and glory. The natural place for such praise and glory and for the public proclamation of God's mighty acts, however, is the cult. The psalms cited quite clearly reflect a cultic observance (26:6-7; 107) or at least were shaped after the pattern of cultic observances. This observation, too, supports the conclusion that the development of *nip̄lā'ôṯ* as a substantive took place specifically in the cult.

2. *pele' and pil'î.* The noun *pele'* has fundamentally the same meaning as *nip̄lā'ôṯ;* directly or indirectly, it refers exclusively to the work of God. Here too we are dealing with an inclusive generalizing term for this work. It appears primarily in the singular, but is to be understood collectively. There is thus no reason to treat the plural found in late mss. in Ps. 77:12(11); 88:13(12); 89:6(5) as original; the plural forms in the versions represent merely the collective sense of the Hebrew. Even more clearly than in the case of *nip̄lā'ôṯ,* which is plural in form, this usage is an abstraction from the particular event. Again most of the occurrences are in the Psalter and related texts; all are probably exilic or postexilic. There are a few occurrences, however, in other and earlier

34. See *BHS.*

contexts (Isa. 9:5 [date disputed]; 29:14 [preexilic]; Dnl. 12:6). These occurrences suggest that the noun is not a specifically cultic term or a late formation.

Like *niplā'ōṯ,* it denotes in the first instance the mighty acts of God on behalf of Israel (Ps. 77:12,15[11,14]), especially in the context of the exodus from Egypt (Ex. 15:11; Ps. 78:12; cf. 77:15,21[14-15,20]). Within the overall context of the psalm, 89:6 refers to the divine election of David (cf. vv. 20-38). Here and in Ps. 77, God's mighty acts are also an expression of God's power as creator and sole lord of the world (77:17-20[16-19]; 89:7-19[6-18]; cf. Ex. 15:11a and, in a context referring only to creation, Sir. 43:25). Isa. 25:1 refers to a saving act in the future (cf. v. 2; the association with *'ēṣôṯ* is discussed below in connection with Isa. 9:5[6]).

The noun *pele',* too, frequently parallels other terms for God's mighty acts (*tᵉhillôṯ, nôrā'* used adjectivally, Ex. 15:11; *ma'ᵃśeh,* Sir. 43:25;[35] *ma'ᵃlālîm,* Ps. 77:12[11]; cf. also v. 13[12]; *'ōz,* 77:15[14]; in 89:6[5] *'ᵉmûnâ* as a term for the constancy of God's saving work; in 78:1, inclusion of *'ᵃlîlôṯ* and *niplā'ôṯ* in v. 11). The verbs used with *niplā'ôṯ* again express the enduring significance of the event (*'āśâ,* Ex. 15:11; Ps. 77:15[14]; 78:12; Isa. 25:1; *zāḵar,* Ps. 77:12[11]; *yāḏâ* hiphil, Isa. 25:1; Ps. 89:6 emended [with the heavens or heavenly beings as subj.]).[36] In Ps. 119:129 it is the ordinances of the *tôrâ* that are experienced as *pᵉlā'ôṯ* and must therefore be kept *(nāṣar).*[37]

The remaining texts provide rather different accents. According to Ps. 88:11, 13(10,12), God does not work wonders for the dead or in the netherworld; as a result, such works cannot be praised and proclaimed there. Furthermore, God's work can also be calamitous (Isa. 29:14;[38] stated indirectly in an adverbial construction in Lam. 1:9). The meaning of the noun in Dnl. 12:6 is ambivalent. It refers to the afflictions described previously, but these are harbingers of the final defeat of all evil and the beginning of a new reign of God. In other words, we are dealing with events that lead ultimately to salvation, but which those who remain faithful to God can experience only as totally mysterious and therefore baneful. Similar to this ambiguity is the general statement of Sir. 11:4 that God's works *(ma'ᵃśîm)* are unfathomable and can lead to unexpected changes of fortune (cf. vv. 5ff.). The future ruler announced in Isa. 9:5(6) will possess limitless potential *(pele' yô'ēṣ)* to bring about final, perfect peace. Here the verb *yā'aṣ* means the planning and determination of actions that are then carried out; the same is true of *'ēṣôṯ* in 25:1.[39]

Sir. 3:21 uses the noun adjectivally with *min.* It is generally assumed that in Job 11:6 *kiplā'îm* or *pᵉlā'îm (pᵉlāyîm)* should be read instead of *kiplayim.*[40] The text would then mean that wisdom *(ḥoḵmâ),* bestowed by God, leads to understanding otherwise inaccessible to human beings and as a result to success *(tûšîyâ).* But the fact that no other

35. See III.1.b above.
36. These verbs are discussed in III.1.c above.
37. See III.1.b above.
38. See II.2 above.
39. See *BHS.*
40. See *BHS.*

passage uses the word group *pālā'* to make such a statement casts doubt on the proposed emendation.

The adj. *pil'î* in Jgs. 13:18 characterizes the divine messenger as a mysterious and powerful figure, underlining the mysterious nature of the event described in this chapter (cf. v. 19[41]). In Ps. 139:6 the psalmist, known perfectly and completely to God (*da'at̲* as God's knowledge, vv. 1-2,4), confesses that this transcends the bounds of comprehension; it can only mean that the psalmist is wholly at God's mercy (vv. 5,7-12).

IV. Dead Sea Scrolls. The word group plays an important role in the Dead Sea Scrolls. The verb occurs some 20 times in the hiphil (12 times in 1QH). Only the nominalized participle of the niphal is attested (some 30 occurrences of *nip̲lā'ôt̲,* 12 in 1QH; rarely also *nip̲lā'îm*). The noun *pele'* occurs some 45 times (19 times in 1QH). The word group refers in general terms to God's work of creation and salvation. Most of the occurrences are in psalmic texts. The usage and lexical field therefore often exhibit a close relationship with the occurrences of the word group (esp. *nip̲lā'ôt̲*) in the OT psalms.

Nevertheless, the notions of election, sin, dualism, and eschatology specific to the Qumran community determine the understanding of how God accomplishes his saving work. Only rarely, for example, do the scrolls mention God's mighty acts in the early history of Israel (1QM 11:9; cf. 11:1-10). What is critical is instead God's work in the community itself, since only within it does true salvation begin; for it is there that God mysteriously and unfathomably takes away sin and guilt (CD 3:18; cf. 2:14–3:17,19). In 1QH the word group refers primarily to the individual as a member of the community (5:15; 9:7,27; 11:3). But God's saving work evidenced within the community is not relevant simply to the individual; as in the OT psalms, it is to be proclaimed to all of God's works and to all human beings (1:33-34; 3:23; 6:11-12). It is of universal significance beyond the Qumran community.

In the hymnic portion of 1QM, the word group refers also to the eschatological inauguration of universal salvation, when the powers of evil will be destroyed (13:9; 14:5,9; 15:13; 18:7,10 [18:10 supplemented by 1Q33 1:4 draws on Isa. 29:14, but interpreted positively[42]]). In other words, what is at issue is salvation for the entire world; meanwhile, however, this salvation can be experienced only within the Qumran community.

In contrast to the OT, the most frequently used noun is *pele'* (always in the sg.). This noun also expresses most clearly the characteristic notions of community, especially in verbs referring to knowing *(bîn, yāḏa', śāḵal).* It emphasizes on the one hand that human beings cannot understand the mighty acts of God by their own power (1QH 7:32). On the other hand, it attests that God has nevertheless given understanding of them to those who belong to the community, thus incorporating them into the salvation bestowed on the community (1QH 11:4; *nip̲lā'ôt̲,* 10:4).

---

41. See II.2 above.
42. See II.2 above.

Especially characteristic are the approximately 10 occurrences of *pele'* in conjunction with the noun *rāz* (with verbs of knowing, 1QH 7:27; 11:10; cf. 1:21; 1QS 11:5; similarly *sôḏ,* 1QH 12:11-12).[43] Less often *rāz* occurs with *niplā'ôṯ* (1QM 14:14; cf. 1QS 11:19); cf. also the hiphil of the verb in 1QpHab 7:8. This combination puts particular emphasis on the aspect of mystery inherent in the word group *pālā'* and thus also on the paradox of a knowledge that transcends the limits of human ability but is nevertheless bestowed on humans. Such knowledge is given above all to the "Teacher of Righteousness" (probably referred to in 1QH 2:13; 4:28), who transmits it in turn to the members of the community. According to 1QS 9:18, it is the function of a *maśkîl* to mediate this knowledge.

It is appropriate to the weightiness of the noun *pele'* that God is referred to directly as *'elōhîm pele'* (4QCant^a 1:8; 4QCant^b 10:7). God's servants are described similarly (1QH 5:21). Occurrences of *pele'* are especially frequent in 4QShirShabb 39 and 40,[44] where it describes certain elements of the heavenly cult (40:24, 6-7). This text also speaks of the seven *diḇrê pele'* with which heavenly beings are to bless particular groups of human beings (39:1,16ff.). The term *'elōhê pele'* is attested here as the title of an angel.[45] The phrase *pele' yô'ēṣ* in 1QH 3:10 is discussed elsewhere.[46]

Conrad

---

43. On both nouns see Nötscher, 71-77.
44. Strugnell, *Congress Volume, Oxford 1959. SVT* 7 (1960), 318-45.
45. Ibid., 332.
46. → VI, 183-85 (IV.2).

פָּלַג *pālag;* פֶּלֶג *peleg;* פְּלַגָּה *p^{e}laggâ;* פְּלֻגָּה *p^{e}luggâ;* מִפְלַגָּה *miplaggâ*

I. 1. Ancient Near East; 2. Meaning; 3. LXX; 4. Dead Sea Scrolls. II. Secular Usage: 1. Verb; 2. Nouns. III. Religious Usage: 1. *peleg;* 2. *p^{e}luggôṯ.*

I. 1. *Ancient Near East.* The root *plg* appears in the OT as both a verb and a noun, with several derivatives. It is also found in Middle Hebrew, Jewish Aramaic and Egyp-

---

pālag. A. D. Crown, "Judges V 15b-16," *VT* 17 (1967) 240-42; I. Engnell, "'Planted by the Streams of Water,'" *FS J. Pedersen* (1953), 85-96; G. Morawe, "Peleg," *BHHW,* III (1966), 1411; P. Reymond, *L'eau, sa vie et sa signification dans l'AT. SVT* 6 (1958), 70, 129; A. Schwarzenbach, *Die geographische Terminologie im Hebräischen des ATs* (1954), 61-62; N. M. Waldman, "On הפליג, עבר, and Akkadian Parallels," *Gratz College Annual of Jewish Studies* 2 (1973) 6-8; H.-J. Zobel, *Stammesspruch und Geschichte. BZAW* 95 (1965), 49.

tian Aramaic, Palmyrene, Nabatean, Samaritan, Syriac, Christian Palestinian, and Mandaic texts, as well as in Akkadian, Ugaritic, Phoenician, Arabic, Ethiopic, and Coptic sources. Taking the basic notion of division as its point of departure, ancient Near Eastern usage exhibits semantic bifurcation: (a) the predominant meaning "divide" or "part, half,"[1] as well as the meaning "district" found in Phoenician;[2] (b) the meaning "ditch, canal" exemplified by the Akkadian parallel *palgu,*[3] which reappears in Ugaritic texts with the meaning "wadi"[4] and again in the analogous Arab. *falǧ,* "cleft," and *falaǧa,* "cleave," as well as Eth. *falag,* "wadi."

2. *Meaning.* The range of meanings of the root in the ancient Near East reflects its meanings in the OT. Of the 26 occurrences in the OT, 7 involve personal names (Gen. 10:25; 11:16,17,18,19; 1 Ch. 1:19,25). Among the other 19, there are 2 occurrences of the verb in the piel (Ps. 55:10[Eng. v. 11]; Job 38:25) and 2 in the niphal (Gen. 10:25; 1 Ch. 1:19). Nouns such as *peleg* occur 15 times; the commonest meaning is "ditch, channel, wadi" (11 times, 12 counting Ps. 55:10 cj.). There are 4 occurrences of the meaning "division, contingent" (*pᵉlaggâ,* Jgs. 5:15-16; *pᵉluggâ,* 2 Ch. 35:5; *miplaggāh,* 2 Ch. 35:12). The 4 occurrences of the verb mean "cleave, groove" (Ps. 55:10[9]; Job 38:25) or "be divided" (Gen. 10:25; 1 Ch. 1:19).

3. *LXX.* The LXX clearly had no precise notion of the meaning of the root. Apart from the translation *diaíresis* in three passages with the meaning "division" (Jgs. 5:15; 2 Ch. 35:5,12), the LXX translations are totally heterogeneous. For the nouns, we find such equivalents as *diéxodos, hormḗ, hórmēma, áphesis,* and *potamós;* only Gen. 10:25 and 1 Ch. 1:19 agree in using *diamerízō* to translate the verb. The proper name is transliterated as *Phalek.*

4. *Dead Sea Scrolls.* In the Dead Sea Scrolls the root appears as a verb and in nouns; some of the latter mean "wadi, channel," others mean "division."[5] The proper name appears in CD 20:22.

II. Secular Usage.

1. *Verb.* All the forms of the verb refer to the secular process of dividing or employ it metaphorically. Job 38:25 refers to the cutting off of an area by digging a channel for water; Gen. 10:25 and 1 Ch. 1:19 have to do with the division of humankind into various peoples. Even the figurative image of a divided tongue (Ps. 55:10[9]), which represents the impossibility of speaking the truth, is based on a wholly secular notion.

---

1. *DNSI,* II, 911-12; *MdD,* 360b, 373b.
2. *DNSI,* II, 913; *KAI* 18.3.
3. *AHw,* II, 815-16.
4. *KTU* 1.100, 69; M. Dietrich, O. Loretz, and J. Sanmartín, *UF* 7 (1975) 122, 125.
5. Kuhn, 130, 177.

2. *Nouns.* a. *Watercourse.* Analogously to the meaning found in Job 38:25, the noun used in a secular sense means "ditch, wadi, channel." It is always used in conjunction with "water" or "oil." The phrase *palgê mayim* refers literally to a ditch or channel distributing water through a region (Ps. 1:3; Isa. 32:2); early on, however, it became a popular metaphor, especially in wisdom poetry. It serves to describe a flood of tears (Lam. 3:48; Ps. 119:136) or a torrent of words (Ps. 55:10[9] cj.). But it can also symbolize the possible yearning of a married woman for other men (Prov. 5:16). The phrase *palgê (pᵉlaggôṯ) šemen* should be understood analogously: in proverbial language it represents a figurative term for wealth and abundance (Job 29:6; 20:17 cj.).[6]

b. *Division.* In the sense of "part" or "division," the nouns are also used primarily in secular contexts. Already in the Song of Deborah the noun *pᵉlaggôṯ* refers to the divisions of an Israelite tribe (Jgs. 5:15f.); in 2 Ch. 35:5,12, analogously, *pᵉluggôṯ* and *miplaggôṯ* refer to the divisions of an Israelite clan.

c. *Proper Name.* As a proper name, the noun *peleg* refers to a son of Eber, who is considered a descendant of Shem (Gen. 10:22-25). The comment explaining the name shows that it is to be understood as a simple personal name.[7]

III. Religious Usage.

1. *peleg.* The use of the root *plg* and its derivatives in the cultic sphere and in theological contexts first appears in postexilic texts. The primary emphasis is on the association of the noun *peleg* in the sense of "watercourse" with Yahweh, his city Jerusalem, and its sanctuaries. The "watercourse" of Yahweh is the source of all blessing (Ps. 65:10[9]); "watercourses" make glad Jerusalem, the city of God (Ps. 46:5[4]); at the eschaton, they will be found on all the heights (Isa. 30:25). These texts incorporate an ancient mythologoumenon (cf. Isa. 33:21; Ezk. 47:1-12; Joel 4:18[3:18]; Zec. 14:8). In Isa. 32:2 the phrase *palgê mayim* serves to characterize the salvation that the eschatological king will bring; Prov. 21:1 uses it as a graphic image describing how Yahweh guides the king's thoughts. The phrase is used analogously in Ps. 1:3 as a metaphor for the devout (cf. Ps. 92:13-15[12-14]).

2. *pᵉluggôṯ.* The form *pᵉluggôṯ* appears only in 2 Ch. 35:5; it may possibly be explained as a mispointing of the noun *pᵉlaggôṯ* (Jgs. 5:15-16; Job 20:17) influenced by the Biblical Aramaic word *pᵉluggâ* (Ezr. 6:18). It has an indirect tie to the cult: the divisions of clans mentioned here belong to priestly families.

Schunck

---

6. See G. Fohrer, *Das Buch Hiob. KAT* XVI (1963), 324-25.
7. C. Westermann, *Genesis 1–11* (Eng. trans. 1984), 526.

פִּלֶגֶשׁ *pilegeš*

I. 1. Etymology; 2. Occurrences, Meaning, LXX. II. The Position of a Concubine.

I. 1. *Etymology.* We can give no satisfactory explanation for the origin of *pilegeš* (Gk. *pállax, pallakís;* Lat. *pellex;* Jewish Aram. *palqeṯā;* Syr. *palqā;* Arabic in the fem. PN *bilqīs*). Scholars have sought its home in both the Semitic and the Indo-European language families and have put forward many conjectures about mutual influence.[1] Suggested etymologies include the Hebrew root *plg,* "divide, cleave," or a back-formation from Gk. *pallakís, pallakḗ, pállax,* originally "youth" or "girl," or from the same source *plgs,* "marriageable." On the basis of the Indo-European elements *pi-* ("at, on, toward") and *legh-* ("to lie down") and the nominal ending *š,* Rabin concludes that the word is Philistine in origin, while Görg thinks in terms of Egyptian influence and proposes the basic meaning "someone next to a person."[2]

2. *Occurrences, Meaning, LXX.* The noun occurs 37 times in the OT: Gen. 22:24; 25:6; 36:12 (4 times); 12 times in Judges, all but one in the story of the Levite's concubine (chs. 19–20); 8 times in 2 Samuel; once in 1 Kings; once in Ezekiel; twice in the Song of Solomon; once in Esther; 5 times in 1 Chronicles; once in 2 Chronicles. It means "concubine, mistress." The following are named as having had concubines: Nahor, Abraham, Jacob, Eliphaz, Gideon, David, Saul, Rehoboam, King Ahasuerus, Caleb, and Manasseh. The term occurs once in a "boasting song" (Cant. 6:8-9); but it is noteworthy that it is not found in legal texts (although such texts as Lev. 18:8,11,18 clearly presuppose polygyny), wisdom literature, or prophetic literature (Ezk. 23:20 is uncertain and refers to male *pilagšîm*).

The LXX equivalent is always *pallakḗ/pallakís,* except in Ezk. 23:20 *(toús Xaldaíous)* and Est. 2:14 *(tṓn gynaikṓn).* In addition, Gen. 46:20 (echoing 1 Ch. 7:14) mentions a *pallakḗ* of Manasseh; Job 19:17 speaks of Job's concubines, who are unknown to the MT.

---

pilegeš. J. P. Brown, "Literary Contexts of the Common Hebrew-Greek Vocabulary," *JSS* 13 (1968) 163-91, esp. 166-69; M. Ellenbogen, *Foreign Words in the OT* (1962), 134; L. M. Epstein, "The Institution of Concubinage among the Jews," *Proceedings of the American Academy for Jewish Research* 6 (1934/35) 153-88; M. Görg, "Piggul und pilægæš, Experimente zur Etymologie," *BN* 10 (1979) 7-11, esp. 10-11; G. Jasper, "Polygyny in the OT," *Africa Theological Journal* 2 (1969) 27-57; H.-W. Jüngling, *Richter 19. AnBibl* 84 (1981); S. Levin, "Hebrew *pilegeš,* Greek *pallakē,* Latin *pellex,*" *General Linguistics* 23 (1983) 191-97; H. Lewy, *Die semitischen Fremdwörter im Griechischen* (1895, repr. 1970); E. Neufeld, *Ancient Hebrew Marriage Laws* (1944), esp. 118-32; W. Plautz, "Monogamie und Polygamie im AT," *ZAW* 75 (1963) 3-27; C. Rabin, "The Origin of the Hebrew Word *Pīlegeš,*" *JTS* 25 (1974) 353-64.

1. See Ellenbogen, 134.
2. For a survey of scholarship see Rabin.

II. The Position of a Concubine. It would seem that the OT gave little thought to the legal and social position of a *pileḡeš*. The texts in question deal with the concubines of patriarchs, kings, a Levite, one of the "major judges," and a tribal ancestor. Among all these passages, the early narrative in Jgs. 19–20, incorporated into the Deuteronomistic History, constitutes an exception. Only here are several terms from the realm of family law — *lāqaḥ lô 'iššâ* (take to wife), *ḥōṯēn* (father-in-law), *ḥāṯān* (son-in-law) — used in conjunction with *pileḡeš*, suggesting a marriagelike relationship that does not correspond to the picture painted by other texts. In addition to Jgs. 19:1,27, the combination *'iššâ pileḡeš* (like *'iššâ zônâ* in Jgs. 11:1; 16:1; *'iššâ nᵉḇî'â* in Jgs. 4:4; and *'iššâ 'almānâ* in 2 S. 14:5) appears also in 2 S. 15:16; 20:3, being used for the ten concubines (probably from the royal harem) David left behind in Jerusalem to look after the house when he fled from Absalom. When he returned, since they had been violated publicly by Absalom, he had them shut up as widows until their death.

That *pileḡeš* status differed from ordinary marriage is shown by the difference in terminology; the difference is underlined by two further observations. First, wives and concubines are mentioned together (Jgs. 8:31; 2 S. 5:13 [only here are concubines mentioned first]; 19:6[Eng. v. 5]; 1 K. 11:3; Cant. 6:8,9 [queens and concubines]; 2 Ch. 11:21). Second, a man has two or more primary wives; an additional wife is not necessarily a *pileḡeš* (Gen. 4:19; 26:34; 28:9; 36:2; 1 S. 1:2; 1 Ch. 4:5,18; 8:8; 2 Ch. 24:3). This distinction is not contradicted by the use of the phrase *nᵉšê 'āḇîw* for Jacob's two concubines, Bilhah and Zilpah, in Gen. 37:2, since 35:22 clearly classifies Bilhah as *pileḡeš 'āḇîw*. Jacob's wife Rachel gives him Bilhah as a concubine with the same formula (30:4; *nāṯan lô lᵉ'iššâ* is a technical term referring to marriage, but legally always reflects the perspective of the male leadership of the family) and for the same reason as Leah gives him Zilpah (30:9). Each wife, being barren, expects that Jacob will beget offspring with her *šipḥâ*, offspring that she can later adopt. There is a similar account of Sarah's *šipḥâ* Hagar in 16:1-3 and of Abimelech's wife and his *'ᵃmāhôṯ* (20:17). These observations suggest that a concubine had a lower social status than a wife. The theory that concubines were always former maids or slaves is not persuasive. They were often of non-Israelite origin (Jgs. 19:1; 8:31; 1 Ch. 1:32; 7:14).

The OT also does not pay much attention to the legal position of concubines. If Ex. 21:10-11 deals with a slave taken as a concubine, the man must not deprive his wife (in this case a slave) of food, clothing, or sexual intercourse (?) when he takes another woman. If he does not fulfill his obligations, the wife is released without payment; in other words, the rights of the first woman are protected, not those of the second. Lev. 18:18 prohibits taking a wife's sister as a concubine.

Dt. 21:15-17 protects the hereditary rights of the firstborn son in the circumstances of polygyny. All in all, a concubine appears to have been exposed to the caprice of her "husband" and, if she was a slave belonging to the wife, to the latter's power of decision as well. For the benefit of Isaac, the sons of Abraham's concubines were not allowed to inherit but were compensated with gifts (Gen. 25:6). But this does not necessarily imply that the sons of concubines were subordinate in status. Tamar appears to be the daughter of one of David's concubines (1 Ch. 3:9); she is the only such daughter identified by name. It was wrong for her brother Amnon to disgrace her (2 S. 13). In the eyes of the OT, the function of concubinage clearly derives from the desire for many descendants. Except in the case of the Levite's concubine, who dies an early violent death (Jgs. 19), and the ten concubines David leaves behind in Jerusalem, whose function has nothing to do with procreation (2 S. 15:16; 16:21-22; 20:3), almost all the concubines mentioned are said to have borne children, primarily sons. This appears to be the most important point the OT authors wanted to make. In the case of the royal harem, there was also an element of prestige and the political goals of the ruler. An attack on the harem was tantamount to an attack on the throne (2 S. 3:7; 16:21-22; 1 K. 2:22). Est. 2:8-18 shows how the author pictured a Persian harem.

Throughout the entire OT period, in addition to his first wife a male Israelite probably enjoyed the legitimate privilege of taking one or more other wives (Gen. 4:19; 29:23,30; 36:2; Jgs. 8:30; 1 S. 1:2; Jer. 38:23) and/or concubines; there is no recorded prohibition, and *pileḡeš* occurs in both early and late texts. There is no evidence for the opposite possibility of polyandry (Ezk. 23:20 can hardly refer to this practice). There is no explicit criticism of concubinage, and only one text (Dt. 17:17) that criticizes polygyny on religious grounds; but too many (foreign) wives could lead the king into apostasy from Yahweh to foreign gods (1 K. 11:3).

In brief, we can observe two tendencies: (a) in the period of the patriarchs and judges, concubinage was probably perceived as a natural institution, while later it tended to be reserved to kings; (b) even though polygyny was not criticized explicitly (except by Dt. 17:17), Deuteronomistic texts and texts influenced by the Yahwist appear not to have viewed it in a positive light. We might suppose that polygamy is blamed at least in part for the negative fate of the families in question and for the fall of rulers, because it results in contention, jealousy, violence, and death.

The word *pileḡeš* does not appear in the Dead Sea Scrolls.

Engelken

פָּלַט *pālaṭ;* מָלַט *mālaṭ;* פָּלִיט *pālîṭ;* פָּלֵ(י)ט *pālêṭ;* פְּלֵ(י)טָה *pᵉlêṭâ;* מִפְלָט *miplāṭ*

I. Cognates: 1. West Semitic *plṭ;* 2. East Semitic; 3. West Semitic *mlṭ.* II. 1. Etymology and Basic Meaning; 2. Statistics; 3. Distribution; 4. Related Terms; 5. LXX. III. Semantic Field: 1. Verbs; 2. Nouns. IV. 1. Poetry; 2. Wisdom; 3. Remnant; 4. Apocalyptic. V. Dead Sea Scrolls.

---

pālaṭ. R. Bach, *Die Aufforderung zur Flucht und zum Kampf im alttestamentlichen Prophetenspruch. WMANT* 9 (1962), esp. 15-50; C. Barth, *Die Errettung vom Tode in den individuellen Klage- und Dankliedern* (1947), esp. 124-40; G. Fohrer, *TDNT,* VII, 970-80; G. F. Hasel, "Remnant," *IDBSup,* 735-36; idem, *The Remnant. Andrews University Monographs. Studies in Religion* 5 ([3]1980); idem, "The Origin and Early History of the Remnant Motif in Ancient Israel" (diss., Vanderbilt, 1970); V. Herntrich, "λεῖμμα. B. Der 'Rest' im AT," *ThWNT,* IV, 200-215; J. Mejia, "La liberación," *Theología* 10 (1972/73) 25-61; W. E. Müller and H. D. Preuss, *Die Vorstellung vom Rest im AT* ([2]1973); W. J. Rosłon, "Zbawienie czlowieka w Starym

I. Cognates.

1. *West Semitic plṭ.* The Ugaritic root *plṭ,* "free, save," appears in poetry and personal names.[1] In the Legend of Aqhat, ʿAnat challenges El in verbal battle: "And summon [Aqhat] and let him save you *(ypltk),* son of Danel, and let him help you *(yʿdrk)* [to escape] from the hand of Virgin ʿAnat."[2] The parallelism of *plṭ* and *ʿdr,* "save, help," corresponds (but in reverse order) to Heb. *ʿāzar* par. *pālaṭ* in Ps. 37:40.[3] Ugar. *plṭ* appears in several PNs: *palaṭ (plṭ),*[4] either a one-word name meaning "savior" or a hypocoristicon;[5] *yapluṭ (yplṭ),*[6] "(God) saves/saved," corresponding to Heb. *yaplēṭ* (1 Ch. 7:32-33);[7] *yapluṭánu (yplṭn),* a simple name consisting of a *yaqṭul* form of the verbal root plus suffix.[8]

In Phoenician the lexeme *plṭ* appears in the PN *palaṭbaʿal (plṭbʿl),* "Baal saves/is savior."[9] The root *plṭ* appears also in Ammonite personal names. A 7th-century seal contains the name *plṭw,* which is vocalized as *palṭô* or *palṭû*[10] and means "salvation"; the final *-w* is a hypocoristic ending. On another seal from the same period we find the PN *palṭi (plṭy),* "my salvation," corresponding to the simple Hebrew forename *palṭî* (Nu. 13:9; 1 S. 25:44), which has the same meaning.[11] The simple name *palaṭ (plṭ),* "salvation," likewise has a Hebrew equivalent in *pēlēṭ* (1 Ch. 2:47; 12:3).[12] Also Ammonite is the clause name *ʾdnplṭ,*[13] in which *plṭ* is either a verb in the piel or a masc. sg. noun, meaning, respectively, either "Adon [the lord] saves" or "Adon is savior."[14] In

---

Testamencie" (diss. habil. Acad. Teol., Warsaw, 1970); E. Ruprecht, "פלט *plṭ* pi. to save," *TLOT,* II, 986-90; J. F. A. Sawyer, *Semantics in Biblical Research. SBT* 2/24 (1972); H. Schult, *Vergleichende Studien zur alttestamentlichen Namengebung* (1967), esp. 114-16; D. M. Warne, "The Origin, Development and Significance of the Concept of the Remnant in the OT" (diss., Edinburgh, 1958).

1. *WUS,* no. 2223; *UT,* no. 2048.
2. *KTU,* 1.18, I, 13; on the text see Whitaker, 316.
3. See H. L. Ginsberg, *Or* 7 (1938) 3; M. Dahood, *Psalms I: 1–50. AB* 16 (1966), 232.
4. *KTU,* 4.374, 7.
5. *PNU,* 57.173.
6. *KTU,* 4.214, IV, 4; 4.222, 2; 4.638, 1-2.
7. See *IPN,* 199.
8. *KTU,* 4.215, 5; see *PNU* 58; also S. Segert, *A Basic Grammar of the Ugaritic Language* (1985), 188.
9. Z. S. Harris, *Grammar of the Phoenician Language. AOS* 8 (1936), 137. See *KAI* 11, where the translation "Baal is my savior" does not agree with the form of the name, which would have to be *plṭybʿl;* cf. Benz, 176.
10. For the former see P. Bordreuil, *Syr* 50 (1973) 190-91; for the latter, K. P. Jackson, *The Ammonite Language of the Iron Age. HSM* 27 (1983), 71.
11. P. Bordreuil and A. Lemaire, *Sem* 26 (1976) 53; Jackson, 72. *HAL,* III, 931, has mistakenly assigned this to epigraphic Hebrew.
12. Bordreuil and Lemaire, 60; Jackson, 73; *IPN,* 156. *HAL,* III, 931, also erroneously assigns this personal name to epigraphic Hebrew.
13. M. Lidzbarski, *Handbuch der nordsemitischen Epigraphik* (1898), 209; F. Vattioni, *Bibl* 50 (1969) 370, no. 98.
14. L. G. Herr, *The Scripts of Ancient Northwest Semitic Seals. HSM* 18 (1978), 59, no. 2; Jackson, 72.

Moabite the root *plṭ* is attested only in the theophorous PN *kmšplṭ* (cf. such Moabite theophorous clause names as *kmšṣdq, kmšnṭn, kmšyḥy,* and *kmšm'š*[15]), where *plṭ* again can be understood as a verb or a noun, the name meaning accordingly "Chemosh saves" or "Chemosh is savior."[16]

The Yaudic verb *plṭ* (pael), "save," appears in the inscription on the Panammu statue (ca. 730 B.C.E.) in the sentence: "On account of the [right]eousness of his father, the gods of *y'dy* saved him *(plṭwh)* from annihilation."[17] The Aramaic of the Elephantine papyri uses *plṭ* in the PNs *plṭw,* "salvation"; *plṭh,* "[divine name] saved"; *plṭy,* "Yh set free," or better "Yhwh has saved/is savior."[18] The usage of *plṭ* in Middle Aramaic is discussed in the context of the Dead Sea Scrolls (see V below). In Palmyrene the noun *blṭ* from the root *b/plṭ* appears in the hypocoristic PN *blṭy,* "savior."[19] Mandaic uses various forms of the root *plṭ* (peal, pael, and etpael) in the sense of "escape, separate."[20] The Syriac verb *plṭ* has the meaning "escape" in the peal and "save, deliver" in the pael.[21]

Classical Arabic uses *falaṭa* IV, "deliver, set free," and *falaṭa,* "deliver, escape."[22] Whether OSA *blṭ,* "a coin," belongs here is dubious.[23] Ethiopic uses the root *plṭ* in the sense of "separate"; it appears as *fälätä* in the Harari dialect and as *fällätä* in Amharic.[24]

2. *East Semitic.* In Akkadian the verb *plṭ* appears as a foreign word of West Semitic origin in the PN *palaṭay.*[25] This category also includes other personal names of West Semitic origin, mostly found in Assyrian legal documents: *pal-ṭi-i, pal-ṭí-ía-u,* and *pal-ṭí-iá-u.*[26] These correspond to the Hebrew PNs *palṭî, pᵉlaṭyâ,* and *pᵉlaṭyāhû.*[27] Between the 15th and 13th centuries we find the Akkadian PNs *ia-ab-lu-ṭá-nu* and *ia-ab-lu-ṭá-na,* both of Northwest Semitic origin containing the lexeme *plṭ.*[28] From the same pe-

15. Herr, 155-58.
16. N. A. Giron, *Textes araméens d'Egypte* (1931), 30.
17. See P.-E. Dion, *La langue de Ya'udi* (1974), 36-43; *DNSI,* II, 915; *KAI* 215.2.
18. On *plṭw* see *AP,* 13:15; M. H. Silverman, *Or* 39 (1970) 490-91 n. 3, with bibliog. On *plṭh* see *AP,* 82:10; W. Kornfeld, *Onomastica Aramaica aus Ägypten* (1978), 68. On *plṭy* see *AP,* 40:1; *BMAP,* 6, fr. b. On the former meaning see Kornfeld, 69; on the latter, *HAL,* III, 931; *IPN,* 38 n. 156.
19. *CIS* 4212, 2; *PNPI,* 76, translates it as "life," apparently assuming a connection with the noun *balāṭu.*
20. *MdD,* 374.
21. *LexSyr,* 573.
22. Lane, I/7, 2730ff.; C. Barth, 32.
23. Cf. Biella, 43; A. K. Irvine, *JRAS* 1964, 22-23, proposes a different etymology.
24. See Dillmann, *LexLingAeth,* 1344-45; Leslau, *Contributions,* 42; idem, *Etymological Dictionary of Harari* (1963), 63; idem, *Hebrew Cognates in Amharic* (1969), 99.
25. *CBS* 4993, 26; 10350 = *pa-la-ṭa[a-a];* M. D. Coogan, *West Semitic Personal Names in the Murašû Documents* (1976), 33, 82.
26. See R. Borger, *TUAT* I/4 (1984), 412; *APN,* 179; cf. S. Parpola, *CT* 53, no. 46, ll. 4, 27.
27. *IPN,* 156.
28. D. Sivan, *Grammatical Analysis and Glossary of the Northwest Semitic Vocables in Akkadian Texts of the 15th-13th C.B.C. from Canaan and Syria. AOAT* 214 (1984), 259. On the former name see *PRU,* III, 202 (16.257, III, 57); on the latter, *PRU,* III, 37 (16.287, 3).

riod comes the word *pu-la-ṭu,* "save," which appears in a polyglot lexical text from Ugarit and is identified with Akk. *šūzubu,* "save."[29] Besides these occurrences, *plṭ* is used in one of the Amarna letters: "and scarcely a single house survived *(pa-li-iṭ-mi)*."[30] The use of the verb *plṭ* in this letter probably bespeaks West Semitic influence.

In many of its meanings, Akk. *balāṭu,* "life," overlaps semantically with Heb. *plṭ* and is therefore conjoined with the Hebrew term.[31] Because *balāṭu* usually has to do with life or survival, it is also used in the sense of "escape" or "save." In the Atrahasis Epic (17th century B.C.E.), the water god Enki gives Atrahasis the command: "Save life *(napišta bulliṭ)*,"[32] or more appropriately to the context: "Preserve the life [of the people and animals on the ship]."[33] Later the enraged war god Enlil asks: "How did the man escape destruction *(kī ibluṭ awēlum)?*"[34] This scene is repeated almost word for word in the eleventh tablet of the Gilgamesh Epic. Enki commands: "Let life be preserved *(napišti bulliṭ)*"; later the enraged Enlil insists: "None shall escape destruction *(a-a ib-luṭ amēlu)*."[35]

Akkadian legal terminology also uses *blṭ* in the sense of "escape." The Code of Eshnunna (early 2nd millennium) requires that under certain circumstances a thief or an adulteress "shall die and not be spared *(imât ul iballuṭ)*."[36]

Although Akk. *blṭ* has a wide range of meanings, semantically and from the perspective of comparative Semitic philology much of its usage is quite similar to that of West Semitic *plṭ*. Therefore the Akkadian verb *balāṭu* may be considered an East Semitic revival of the common Semitic root *plṭ*.

3. *West Semitic mlṭ.* In comparison to *plṭ,* the word *mlṭ* I is much more restricted, appearing outside Hebrew and Aramaic only in South Semitic. The root is clearly used in various Ethiopic dialects. In the Harari dialect we find the verb *(a)mäläṭa,* "escape,"[37] which derives from the root *mlṭ,* "scrape off, pull off."[38] In Tigre we find *mälṭa* (= *mälča*), "escape."[39] Amharic has the derivative *amälläṭä,* "escape."[40] It is most unlikely that the Palmyrene noun *mlṭ',* "sheepskin,"[41] is connected with Heb. *mlṭ.* In Modern Hebrew we find *mlṭ* in the sense of "save" (piel) and "be saved, escape" (niphal,

29. *RS* 20.123; *Ugaritica* V, no. 137, II, 20, p. 243.
30. EA 185:25, 33.
31. P. Fronzaroli, *AANLR* 8/19 (1964) 248-49; 8/20 (1965) 250, 263, 267. See *AHw,* I, 99.
32. Atrahasis iii.1.24.
33. H. A. Hoffner in *Cuneiform Studies in Honor of S. N. Kramer. AOAT* 25 (1976), 241-45.
34. Atrahasis iii.6.10.
35. See, respectively, Gilg. xi.2.26 (cf. H. Schmökel, *NERT,* 94: "ensure life"); l. 173 (*ANET*[3], 95).
36. See *TUAT* I/2, 34, 36; *ANET*[3], 162. For the thief see Code of Eshnunna, §12, 40; for the adulteress, §28, 37 (*ANET*[3], 162).
37. Leslau, *Etymological Dictionary of Harari,* 107-8.
38. Dillmann, *LexLingAeth,* 154.
39. Leslau, *Contributions,* 30.
40. Leslau, *Hebrew Cognates in Amharic,* 97.
41. *DISO,* 152.

hithpael).[42] In Jewish Aramaic there is an itpeal form of the root *mlṭ,* used in the sense of "be saved, escape."[43]

II. 1. *Etymology and Basic Meaning.* Heb. *plṭ* belongs to the stock of common Semitic roots; it has the basic meaning "escape." The qal, which appears only in Ezk. 7:16, means "escape" from mortal danger, in other words, run away to safety.

The Hebrew verb *mlṭ* I has been associated with or derived from Arab. *malaṭa,* "depilate," V "be bald," and Eth. *maláṭa,* "strip, be naked."[44] It is more likely that *mlṭ* II (hithpael), "be bald" (Job 19:20), is associated with the Arabic forms and should be treated as a separate verb distinct from *mlṭ* I.[45] We may assume that *mlṭ* I is a variant of *plṭ.*[46] The comparative material in other West Semitic languages (see I.1-3 above) supports this derivation, as does the usage of the Hebrew stems. Thus the basic meaning of *mlṭ* I is "escape" (from danger).

2. *Statistics.* a. *plṭ.* The root *plṭ* occurs 80 times in the OT.[47] The qal form occurs once in the MT (Ezk. 7:16). The piel form is most frequent, with 24 occurrences; the hiphil occurs only twice (Isa. 5:29; Mic. 6:14). In Job 23:7 the MT reads *ʾapallᵉṭâ,* a piel form. Hölscher and Driver, followed by others, point *ʾplṭh* as *ʾeplᵉṭâ,* a qal form meaning "escape."[48] Fohrer rightly rejects this repointing, and *BHS* does not adopt it.[49] Some emend the piel of *plṭ* in Mic. 6:14 to a hiphil form or the hiphil form in the first portion of the verse to a piel.[50] Both emendations are unnecessary; the MT should be retained.[51]

The root *plṭ* has four nominal derivatives. The most common is the fem. noun *pᵉlē(ê)ṭâ* (a *qᵉṭîlâ* form),[52] found 28 times in the OT. The masc. *qāṭîl* form *pālîṭ,* which occurs 19 times, derives from an adjective form. The masc. *qaṭil* form *pālē(ê)ṭ* occurs 5 times (Nu. 21:29; Isa. 66:19; Jer. 44:14; 50:28; 51:50), only in the plural.[53] The masc. verbal noun *miplāṭ,* "place of refuge," with a *ma-* preformative, appears in the MT only in Ps. 55:9(Eng. v. 8).[54]

Many scholars repoint the piel ptcp. *mᵉpallᵉṭî,* "my deliverer," in Ps. 18:3(2) as

---

42. G. Dalman, *ANH,* 237.

43. Ibid.

44. For the association see *GesTh,* 791. For the derivation see *LexHebAram,* 441; cf. G. R. Driver, in *Wisdom in Israel and in the Ancient Near East. FS H. H. Rowley. SVT* 3 (1955), 80.

45. With *HAL,* II, 589; and E. Kutsch, *VT* 32 (1982) 464-84, esp. 474-82.

46. With *KBL*², 529; and Fohrer, 972; Ruprecht, 421, is noncommittal.

47. A. Even-Shoshan, *A New Concordance of the OT* (1985), 944-45, 663.

48. G. Hölscher, *Das Buch Hiob. HAT* I/17 (²1937), 56; G. R. Driver, *AJSL* 52 (1935/36) 160; *BHK;* M. Dahood, *Bibl* 50 (1970) 397; Ruprecht, 421; et al.

49. G. Fohrer, *KAT* XVI, 363. Cf. *HAL,* III, 931.

50. On the former see, e.g., *BHK;* for the latter, *BHS.*

51. With *HP,* 107; W. Rudolph, *Micha-Nahum-Habakuk-Zephanja. KAT* XIII/3 (1975), 116-17; *HAL,* III, 931.

52. Meyer, II, 28.

53. *BLe,* 464.

54. *HAL,* II, 618.

miplāṭî, "my refuge," or delete it *metri causa.*[55] The is also true of the same participle in Ps. 55:9(8) and 144:2. The reading *mplṭ ly* in 11QPs[a] 23:13 = Ps. 144:2, which can be translated "a deliverer for me"[56] or as a noun meaning "a refuge for me," does not point persuasively to the original meaning of the Hebrew text. Repointing makes it possible to understand these three piel participles as instances of the verbal noun *miplāṭ.* The need for this repointing nevertheless remains dubious.

b. *Personal Names.* The root *plṭ* appears in a number of masculine PNs: *peleṭ,* "deliverance"; *palṭî,* "my deliverance"; *pilṭāy,* "Y[ahweh] is my deliverance"; *palṭî'ēl,* "God is my deliverance"; *p[e]laṭyâ,* "Yah[weh] has delivered"; *yaplēṭ,* "may [God] deliver" or "God delivered"; *'elîpeleṭ* and *'ēlpeleṭ,* "God is deliverance."[57] Several of these names appear in other Semitic languages as well (see I.1-2 above).

c. *mlṭ.* If we restrict our attention to *mlṭ* I, the verb *mlṭ* occurs 94 times in the OT.[58] The niphal occurs 62 times, the piel 28 times, and the hiphil and hithpael twice each.

3. *Distribution.* A survey of the distribution shows that *plṭ/mlṭ* occurs only 10 times in the Pentateuch: 5 times as the niphal of the verb *mlṭ* in Genesis, and 5 times as a nominal form of *plṭ* (3 times in Genesis, once each in Exodus and Numbers). The highest concentration of occurrences of *plṭ* derivatives is in the Major and Minor Prophets (9 in Ezekiel; 8 each in Isaiah and Jeremiah; 2 each in Micah, Joel, and Obadiah; and one in Am. 9:1), poetry (20 in the Psalms), and the historical books (4 in Ezra; 3 each in Judges, 2 Samuel, 2 Kings, and 2 Chronicles; one each in Joshua, Nehemiah, and 1 Chronicles). Derivatives of *mlṭ* occur most frequently in the prophetic literature (14 times in Jeremiah, 4 times in Ezekiel, 3 times in Amos, once each in Joel, Zechariah, and Malachi), followed by the historical books (17 times in 1-2 Samuel, 8 times in 1-2 Kings, twice in Judges, once in 2 Chronicles), wisdom literature (11 times in Job, 3 times each in Proverbs and Ecclesiastes), poetry (8 times in the Psalms), twice in Daniel (11:41; 12:1), and once in Esther (4:13). Thus we see that derivatives of *plṭ/mlṭ* are concentrated in the historical books, the Major and Minor Prophets, and poetry.

4. *Related Terms.* The verbs *plṭ* and *mlṭ* are used in lexical fields that include a large number of related terms: *nṣl* hiphil, "deliver"; *nûs* qal, "flee"; *brḥ* qal, "flee"; *yṣ',* "go out"; *nwḥ* piel, "leave alone"; *yš',* "help, save."[59]

The various nominal forms of the root *plṭ* are associated particularly with the lexical field of the OT remnant motif:[60] *pālîṭ/pālēṭ* par. *śārîḏ,* "escaped one"; *p[e]lêṭâ/p[e]lēṭâ* par.

---

55. For the former see *BHK;* Dahood, *Psalms I,* 101; W. G. E. Watson, *Classical Hebrew Poetry. JSOTSup* 26 ([2]1986), 265. For the latter, *BHS.*

56. J. A. Sanders, *The Dead Sea Psalms Scroll* (1967), 79.

57. See *IPN,* 38 and n. 1, 156, 199.

58. *HAL,* II, 589; Even-Shoshan, 663-64, if the hithpael form in Job 19:20 is assigned to a separate root.

59. See esp. Fohrer, 970-72, 978-79.

60. See Hasel, *Remnant Motif,* 176-80, 185-86, 197-98; see IV.3 below.

šᵉʾērîṯ, "remnant"; *šᵉʾār,* "remnant"; *ytr* niphal, "be left over"; *yeṯer* (cj. Ezr. 9:8);[61] and *ʾaḥᵃrîṯ,* "remnant."[62]

5. *LXX.* The LXX uses 17 different Greek words to represent *plṭ/mlṭ* and their derivatives. Forms of *sǭzein,* "preserve, save," translate *mlṭ* 49 times (niphal 37 times, piel 11 times, hiphil once) and *plṭ* 12 times (piel once; otherwise only verbal nouns: *pᵉlêṭâ* 5 times, *pālîṭ* 4 times, *pālêṭ* and *miplāṭ* once each); *anasǭzein,* "recover," translates *plṭ* forms 20 times (qal once, *pālîṭ* 10 times, *pᵉlēṭâ* 6 times, *pālêṭ* 3 times) and *mlṭ* 3 times (niphal twice, piel once); *diasǭzein,* "preserve through," translates *mlṭ* 24 times (niphal 20 times, piel 4 times) and *plṭ* with its substantives 11 times (piel twice, hiphil once, *pālîṭ* twice, *pᵉlêṭâ* 5 times, *pālêṭ* once); *perisǭzein* translates the niphal of *mlṭ* once. Six times the noun *sōtēría,* "salvation, protection, well-being," translates *pᵉlêṭâ.* By drawing so heavily on *sǭzein* and its derivatives, the LXX clearly exhibits a shift from the Hebrew notion of escape to that of salvation and deliverance, so that the escaped of the MT become the saved in the LXX.[63]

The verb *rhýomai* translates *plṭ* 10 times and *mlṭ* 8 times (piel 6 times, niphal twice);[64] *exaireín* translates *mlṭ* 5 times (piel 4 times, niphal once) and *plṭ* piel 4 times. A form of *diapheúgein* is used once (Prov. 19:5) to translate the niphal of *mlṭ* and twice to translate *pālîṭ.* The niphal of *mlṭ* is represented once each by *dialanthánein* (2 S. 4:6) and *heurískein* (2 K. 23:18), and the hiphil by *tíktein* (Isa. 66:7). The piel of *plṭ* is represented 4 times by *rhystḗs,* once each by *exágein* (Job 23:7) and *hyperaspistḗs* (Ps. 40:18[17]), and the hiphil once by *ekbállein* (Isa. 5:29).

III. Semantic Field.

1. *Verbs.* The roots *plṭ* and *mlṭ* piel frequently appear in parallel with the hiphil of → נצל *nṣl.* The sequence of *nṣl* hiphil, "deliver (from the power or clutches of someone)" followed by *mlṭ,* "save," appears in the people's description of their victory (2 S. 19:10[9]) and in a prophetic promise of Yahweh's eschatological salvation (Jer. 39:17-18). In hymns we find the sequence *plṭ* piel + *nṣl* hiphil (Ps. 18:49[48]; 22:9[8]; 31:2-3[1-2]) and *nṣl* + *plṭ* (71:2); it is always God who is or will be the agent of salvation. It is hard to identify any difference in meaning. "Deliverance" (*nṣl* hiphil) is "salvation," as is "rescue" (*plṭ* piel). The same semasiological correspondence appears in God's words addressed to the council of the gods: "Rescue (*plṭ* piel) the weak and the needy, deliver (*nṣl* hiphil) them from the hand of the wicked" (Ps. 82:4).

The causative sense of *mlṭ* hiphil is used in the context of childbirth (Isa. 66:7): a son is "delivered" from the mother's womb, and is thus "given life."[65] The piel of *mlṭ*

61. *HAL,* II, 452.

62. G. F. Hasel, "'Remnant' as a Meaning of *ʾAḥᵃrît,*" *Archaeology of Jordan and Other Studies. FS S. H. Horn* (1986), 511-24.

63. See Fohrer, 973.

64. W. Kasch, *TDNT,* VI, 999.

65. *HP,* 107.

has a concrete factitive sense in Isa. 34:15, where it refers to the "laying" of eggs.[66] In Job 21:10 *plṭ* piel is used for the calving of the cow of the wicked. These instances of childbirth or calving, together with the account of the escape of Ishbaal's murderers in 2 S. 4:6 ("then Rechab and his brother Baanah escaped [*mlṭ* niphal]"), have led Rudolph to suggest that the basic meaning of *mlṭ* niphal is "get out of confinement."[67] But the evidence for this meaning is weak, because no texts explicitly mention "confinement" and only two passages use the niphal in the specialized sense of "give birth" or "calve." The most sensible course is therefore to stay with "escape" as the basic meaning of *plṭ/mlṭ* (see II.1 above).

The hiphil of *mlṭ* in Isa. 31:5 is problematic. The MT vocalization is *wᵉhimlîṭ*, "rescue."[68] The reading of 1QIsᵃ is *hplyṭ*, which does not change the meaning; but the great number of questionable variants in 1QIs means that this does not necessarily represent the earliest reading. With changing the consonantal text, Stade repointed the hiphil forms *wᵉhiṣṣîl* and *wᵉhimlîṭ* as infinitive absolutes: *wᵉhaṣṣēl* and *wᵉhamlēṭ*.[69] The Vulg. renders the four verbs in Isa. 31:5 as *protegens et liberans transiens et salvans*. Although Stade's revocalization is the most attractive emendation and has been generally accepted, one must recall that syntactically in Hebrew an introductory infinitive absolute can be followed by consecutive perfects with frequentative future meaning (Josh. 6:13; 2 S. 13:9), so that no emendation of the MT is really imperative.[70]

In Job 41:11(19) we find the only occurrence of *mlṭ* in the hithpael, with the meaning "sparks of fire flash forth."[71] The reading of 11QtgJob is *blšny 'šh yrṭwn'*, "they run with tongues of fire." If "sparks (of fire)" is the correct translation of the subj. *kîḏōḏ* in the Hebrew text, then the context suggests that the hithpael of *mlṭ* should be translated "spew forth (sparkle)."[72]

The qal of → נוס *nûs*, "flee," frequently parallels the niphal of *mlṭ*. The normal sequence is *nûs* followed by *mlṭ*: the former expresses the act of fleeing from conflict with others, while the latter expresses the success or failure of the flight itself with the notion of escape. David flees *(nûs)* from Saul and succeeds in escaping or saving himself (*mlṭ* niphal, 1 S. 19:10; cf. 1 K. 20:20) by finding a safe refuge. In Am. 9:1c we read: "Of them no fugitive *(nās)* shall flee *(nûs)* and no escapee *(pālîṭ)* shall escape (*mlṭ* niphal)." An oracle against Egypt declares: "The swift cannot flee away *(nûs)*, nor can the warrior escape (*mlṭ* niphal)" (Jer. 46:6; the jussives *'al-yānûs* and *'al-yimmālēṭ* emphasize the impossibility of flight and escape).[73] The parallelism of *nûs* and *mlṭ* appears also in oracles against Moab (Jer. 48:6) and Babylon (Jer. 51:6). The ptcp.

66. Wildberger, *Jesaja 28–39. BK* X/3 (1982), 1329.
67. P. 421.
68. *HASL*, II, 589.
69. B. Stade, *ZAW* 6 (1886) 189; followed by *BHK, BHS*, etc.
70. See Wildberger, *BK* X/3, 1237. Cf. esp. *GK*, §113t.
71. G. Fohrer, *Das Buch Hiob. KAT* XVI (1963), 525; M. H. Pope, *Job. AB* 15 (³1973), 335: "flames of fire escape."
72. See *HAL*, II, 589; cf. König, *Wörterbuch*, 226: "emerge"; *BDB*, 572: "slip forth, escape." Cf. M. Dahood, *Bibl* 46 (1965) 327, who reads *kîḏôḏê 'ēš*, with no change of meaning.
73. *GK*, §107b; R. P. Carroll, *Jeremiah. OTL* (1986), 762.

nimlāṭâ denotes a female fugitive, just as the parallel *nās* in Jer. 48:19 denotes a male fugitive.[74] The promise of salvation to Israel in Zec. 2:10-11(6-7) includes the command to flee *(nûs)* in haste from the land of the north and escape *(mlṭ* niphal).[75]

Playing on the assonance with Lot's name,[76] the account of Lot's deliverance uses the niphal of *mlṭ* 5 times for his escape (Gen. 19:17,19,20,22); once (v. 20) it parallels *nûs*. Here again *nûs* appears to stress the act of flight, while *mlṭ* stresses the result: safe refuge in the city. The remnant notion plays an important role in this context. Yahweh is the driving force that effects Lot's survival.[77]

The sequence *mlṭ* niphal + *nûs* (1 S. 30:17; 2 S. 1:3ff.; Am. 2:15-16) also shows that *nûs* denotes the process and *mlṭ* the final result of salvation and security. Am. 2:13-16, a prophetic oracle threatening Israel with Yahweh's punishment, uses the piel of *mlṭ* 3 times: the brave, the swift, and the rider "cannot save" his life *(nep̄eš)* (the result of flight), and even the stout of heart among the mighty shall "flee away" *(nûs)* naked.

The niphal of *mlṭ* is related in meaning to the qal of → ברח *bāraḥ,* "run away, flee,"[78] but they are not true synonyms. The verb *brḥ* is similar in meaning to *nûs*.[79] Both terms emphasize the action of running away, in contrast to the niphal of *mlṭ,* as their occurrences in parallel show (1 S. 19:12,18; 22:20). The sequence of actions is illustrated clearly in 19:12: David "set out (*hlk* qal) and fled away *(brḥ)* and escaped *(mlṭ* niphal)" — the beginning of the action *(hlk),* the action itself *(brḥ),* and its result *(mlṭ)* are expressed by three verbs that are almost synonymous but nevertheless have distinct semantic nuances. The action *(brḥ)* and result *(mlṭ)* of running away are mentioned again in the same context: "and David fled *(bāraḥ)* and escaped *(wayyimmālēṭ)*" (v. 18). The same distinction between similar terms also appears in 1 S. 22:20 (sequence: *mlṭ* niphal + *brḥ*). We may conclude that the niphal of *mlṭ* conveys the resultative aspect of flight, "deliverance" and "escape" (cf. Jgs. 3:26; Ps. 124:7).

Prophetic oracles against the nations use the niphal or piel of *mlṭ* with *nep̄eš* as object (Jer. 48:6; 51:6,45; Zec. 2:10-11[6-7]) in the genre of the "summons to flight," identified by Bach.[80] This prose genre uses → יצא *yāṣā',* "go/come out," in parallel with *mlṭ* piel with *nep̄eš:* "Come out of her (*yṣ'* qal), my people, and save (*mlṭ* piel) your lives, each of you" (Jer. 51:45). The first verb denotes the beginning and action of flight, the second the result, salvation.

The verb *mlṭ* piel, "let alone," appears in 2 K. 23:18 in parallel with → נוח *nûaḥ,* "be at rest": "And he said, 'Let him rest *(hannîḥû);* let no one move his bones.' So they let

74. For the former see *BLe,* §62y; for the latter, Rudolph, *Jeremia. HAT* I/12 (³1968), 276; Carroll, 786.

75. W. Rudolph (*Haggai-Sacharja 1–8-Sacharja 9–14-Maleachi. KAT* XIII/4 [1976], 89 n. 3) points out that *nûs* means not only "flee" but also "depart in haste" (cf. Isa. 30:16).

76. H. Gunkel, *Genesis* (Eng. trans. 1997), 210.

77. Hasel, *IDBSup,* 735.

78. *HAL,* I, 156.

79. E. Jenni, *Or* 47 (1978) 351-59; B. Grossfeld, *ZAW* 91 (1979) 107-23.

80. See pp. 20-21.

his bones alone (*mlṭ* piel), with the bones of the prophet." Leaving the bones alone or undisturbed means that they will continue to be inviolate and secure.

The extended semantic field of *plṭ* piel includes also the common verb → ישׁע *yšʿ* hiphil, as in Ps. 37:40: "Yahweh helps (*ʿzr* qal) them and rescues (*plṭ* piel) them; he rescues (*plṭ* piel) them from the wicked, and saves (*yšʿ* hiphil) them, because they take refuge in him." Here we see that the first *plṭ* piel extends beyond the action of Yahweh in the first part of the sentence, and furthermore that Yahweh's salvation (*yšʿ* hiphil) means more than rescue by Yahweh. It is a substantial consequent act on the part of God, presupposing divine rescue (*plṭ* piel). The same usage can be observed in Ps. 71:2-4.[81]

2. *Nouns.* We now turn to the usage of the nominal derivatives of *plṭ* (see II.2.a above). The adjectival forms *pālîṭ* and *pālêṭ* both have the basic meaning "escapee." The subst. *pālêṭ* appears in various contexts in semasiological association with *śārîḏ,* "survivor," a term associated with the remnant concept (Josh. 8:22; Jer. 42:17; 44:14; Ob. 14,17-18; Lam. 2:22). In Jer. 44:28 *pālîṭ* and *šeʾērîṯ* are parallel. The substs. *pālîṭ/pālêṭ* usually refer to "escapees" from historical catastrophes: Ephraim (Ezk. 7:16; 24:26-27; 33:21), Judah (Ob. 14; Ezk. 6:9; 24:26), Jerusalem (Ezk. 7:16; 24:26-27; 33:21), Moab (Nu. 21:29), Babylon (Jer. 50:28), Ramoth-gilead (2 K. 9:15), the nations (Isa. 45:20; 66:19). Sometimes they are associated with the wars of Yahweh (Nu. 21:29; Josh. 8:22) or prophetic oracles of judgment (*pālîṭ,* Am. 9:1; Isa. 45:20; Jer. 42:17; 44:28; Ezk. 6:8-9; 7:16; Ob. 14; *pālêṭ,* Isa. 66:19; Jer. 44:14; 50:28; 51:50).

The fem. subst. *pelêṭâ (pelēṭâ),* "escapee," refers to inhabitants of Judah (Isa. 37:31-32 = 2 K. 19:30-31) or Israel (Isa. 4:2; 10:20), Israelites (2 Ch. 30:6), Benjamin (Jgs. 4:2; 10:20), Moab (Isa. 15:9), Jerusalemites (Ezk. 14:22), the postexilic community (Ezr. 9:8,13,15; Neh. 1:2), Amalek (1 Ch. 4:43), as well as objects such as "fruit of the field" (Ex. 10:5). This substantive, too, is linked firmly with the OT notion of the remnant (see IV.3 below): cf. the use of *pelêṭâ* parallel to *šeʾērîṯ,* "remnant" (→ שׁאר *šʾr;* Gen. 45:7; Isa. 15:9; 37:32 = 2 K. 19:31; 1 Ch. 4:43; Ezr. 9:14); *šeʾār,* "remnant"; the nominalized niphal ptcp. *nišʾārîm,* "those left over" (Gen. 32:9[8]; Ex. 10:5; Isa. 4:2-3; Neh. 1:2-3); and in conjunction with *ʾaḥarîṯ* (Am. 9:1; see IV.1.a below).

The terms in the semantic field of the *plṭ* nouns always refer more or less to a remnant, those left over, or the like. The *plṭ* nouns themselves, however, like the verbal forms, emphasize repeatedly that this remnant is a remnant that has *escaped* from a war, a battle, or the like.[82] Thus the positive notion of surviving a military action is emphasized. Finally, this escape can express the salvation accomplished by God.

IV. 1. *Poetry.* The greatest concentration of occurrences of *plṭ/mlṭ* is found in the Psalms (8 occurrences of *mlṭ,* 21 of *plṭ*). We observe at the outset that the subject is almost always God or Yahweh (except in Ps. 33:17; 89:49[48] with *mlṭ* piel; 82:4 with *plṭ*

81. On the difference between *plṭ* piel and *yšʿ* hiphil, see *HP,* 122-23.
82. Herntrich, 202; Hasel, "Remnant Motif," 179-80.

piel; 56:8[7] and 32:7 [see below] are problematic). Yahweh is addressed repeatedly as "my deliverer" (*plṭ* piel ptcp., 18:3[2]; 40:18[17]; 70:6[5]; 144:2). In association with the covenant notion, we read that Yahweh "delivered" (*plṭ* piel) Israel's ancestors because they trusted in God (22:5[4]). Contrariwise, trusting (*mlṭ* piel) in an animal like a warhorse will not bring deliverance (33:17). Because of his righteousness *(ṣᵉḏāqâ),*[83] God will deliver (*plṭ* piel, 31:2[1]; 71:2) those who trust in him (22:5-6[4-5]) and love him (91:14). A cry for help[84] to Yahweh prompts divine deliverance (22:5-6[4-5] with *plṭ* and *mlṭ;* 107:19-20 with *mlṭ*). The suffering or afflicted individual cries, calls, or beseeches: "Deliver me" (*plṭ* piel, 31:2; 43:1; 71:2,4) or "Deliver my life *(nep̱eš)*" (*plṭ* piel, 17:13; *mlṭ* piel, 116:4). The psalmist's life is threatened by the wicked (17:9; 37:40), the hand of the wicked (71:4), the wrathful adversary (18:49[48]), strife (→ ריב *rîḇ*) with the people (18:44[43]). The psalmist prays for deliverance from an ungodly people and those who are deceitful (43:1), turns to God with the plea that God will be his judge and give judgment on his behalf (7:9-10; 9:5; 26:1). God delivered in the past (18:44,49[43,48]; 22:5-6[4-5]) and will deliver in the future (37:40b). The use of the terms *plṭ* and *mlṭ* shows that God is the delivering savior of all who are oppressed, afflicted, persecuted, suffering, or falsely accused. Therefore those who are in peril may turn to God with a plea for help: "In your righteousness deliver me" (31:2[1]; 71:2). Deliverance leads to thanksgiving (22 with *plṭ/mlṭ* in vv. 5-6,9[4-5,8]) and praise (22:23,26[22,25]; 107:32 [*mlṭ* in v. 20]; 40:10-11[9-10] [*plṭ* in v. 18]).

The MT of Ps. 32:7 reads *ronnê pallēṭ,* "Shout (cries of joy) of deliverance." Budde emended *rny,* a hapax legomenon, to *māginnê,* "with shields of deliverance."[85] Dahood proposes vocalizing *rny* as *ronnî,* "my refuge," from the root *rnn,* "find refuge, rest," which he also postulates for Ps. 63:8(7).[86] Leveen emends *rny* to *'dny,* "Lord," and translates: "Rescue me, O Lord, and encompass me."[87] Not uncommonly the inf. abs. *pallēṭ* is read as an imperative or emended to the verbal noun *pālîṭ.*[88] All these emendations are highly dubious. A literal translation of the MT, "You will encompass me with joyful shouts of salvation," cannot be rejected out of hand.[89]

2. *Wisdom.* The root *plṭ* (Job 23:7) and especially *mlṭ* also belong to the Israelite language of forensic justice. The prologue of Job speaks of Job's servants who have escaped the natural catastrophes of lightning and whirlwind (Job 1:16,19) as well as attacks by Sabean and Chaldean marauders (vv. 15,17). They survived to tell their tale of disaster. In Job's statement of his case (cf. Jer. 15:2), he asks whether he has said to any of friends, "Save me (*mlṭ* piel) from an opponent's hand?" (Job 6:23). Eliphaz declares (22:30): "He [God] will deliver the innocent; they will escape because of the cleanness

83. → צדק *ṣdq.*
84. → זעק *zā'aq.*
85. Followed by Kraus, *Psalms 1–59* (Eng. trans. 1988), 367; cf. *BHS, HAL,* III, 931.
86. Dahood, *Psalms I,* 196.
87. J. Leveen, *VT* 21 (1971) 55.
88. Cf. Dahood, *Psalms II: 51–100. AB* 17 (1968), 99; *BHS.*
89. P. C. Craigie, *Psalms 1–50. WBC* 19 (1983) 264.

of their hands."[90] In his reply (23:1-17), Job says: "Truly I shall be acquitted (*plṭ* piel) by my judge" (v. 7). Zophar declares that the wicked work evil, and therefore "they will not escape with their treasures" (20:20). Job describes how he has cared for the needy: "I delivered the poor who cried for help" (29:12).

Poetic wisdom maintains that "a false witness will not escape" (Prov. 19:5). Conversely, we are assured that in the forensic domain "the offspring of the righteous will escape" (11:21).[91] Those who trust in their own wits *(lēḇ)* are fools, but those who walk in wisdom "come through safely" (28:26).

Ecclesiastes contrasts the one who pleases God, who escapes (*mlṭ* niphal) the strange woman, with the sinner, who is taken and led astray by her (7:26). Wickedness *(rešaʿ)* cannot deliver (*mlṭ* piel) one who practices it *(baʿal).*[92] In 9:15 *mlṭ* piel, "deliver," is used for the sage who could have delivered the city but was forgotten or despised. People must use wisdom to protect their lives and thus deliver themselves and others.

3. *Remnant.* Theological usage employs the *plṭ/mlṭ* word group in particular to express the OT "remnant" concept. In the Pentateuch forms of *plṭ/mlṭ* have a high profile in this motif. The Abram-Lot cycle tells of a single "escapee" *(pālîṭ)* from a battle, who reports the abduction of Lot to Abram (Gen. 14:13). The same cycle repeatedly uses the verb *mlṭ* for Lot's flight from a natural catastrophe to save his life (19:17,19,20,22). The text speaks explicitly of "saving one's life *(nep̱eš).*" What is at stake is survival in a perilous situation and hence the escape of a remnant ordained by God. The fundamental motif of the remnant concept is the preservation of life according to God's plan; here it makes its first appearance in the OT.[93]

In Gen. 32:9(8) the story of Jacob and Esau refers to the "escape" *(pᵉlēṭâ)*[94] of the portion of Jacob's divided camp that is "left" *(hanniš'ār)* in the family conflict. In the recognition scene in the Joseph saga, Joseph says to his brothers: "God sent me before you to preserve for you a remnant *(šᵉ'ērîṯ)*[95] on earth and to keep you alive as a great deliverance *(pᵉlēṭâ)*" (Gen. 45:7). The correlation *šᵉ'ērîṯ* par. *pᵉlēṭâ,* "remnant" par. "deliverance," ties "deliverance" securely to the remnant concept. It is associated with the preservation of life, which is imperiled by famine. The surviving remnant embodies life (45:5), the traditions of divine election, and the Israel that will spring from it.[96]

---

90. On the textual problems, see N. M. Sarna, *JNES* 15 (1956) 118-19; R. Gordis, *JNES* 4 (1945) 54-55.

91. Following the LXX, O. Plöger (*Sprüche Salomos. BK* XVII [1984], 140-41) emends to "offspring/seed of the righteous," reading: "Those who sow righteousness will be saved."

92. For the many proposed emendations, see *BHK* and *BHS;* contrast A. Lauha, *BK* XIX, 746: "Text-critically and substantially, the verse is unexceptionable."

93. See Hasel, *Remnant,* 50-134, on the origin of the remnant motif in the realm of life and death, with the safeguarding of life, in the literature of the ancient Near East — i.e., in Sumerian, Akkadian, Ugaritic, Hittite, and Egyptian texts. → שׁאר *š'r.*

94. Cf. Yiddish and Ger. *Pleite; HAL,* III, 932; Ruprecht, 424.

95. Müller and Preuss, 54, contra O. Procksch, *Genesis. KAT* I (^{2}1924), 415.

96. Hasel, *Remnant,* 157-59.

In the Saul-David cycle of 1 Samuel, David is often the subject of *mlṭ:* he repeatedly escapes to save himself from Saul's assaults and persecutions (19:10-12,17-18; 22:1; 23:13; 27:1). In the struggle for succession, when Adonijah attempted to seize the throne (1 K. 1:1-10), the prophet Nathan counseled Bathsheba: "Save (*mlṭ* piel) your own life and the life of your son Solomon" (1 K. 1:12), in order to secure Solomon's succession.

The story of Elijah contains a wealth of remnant terminology: *ytr* niphal (1 K. 19:10,14), *š'r* hiphil (19:18), *mlṭ* niphal (18:40; 19:17 [twice]). The Israelite remnant is not a heterogeneous mob of fugitives from the religious struggle, an historical remnant securing the future existence of the people. It is a remnant of believers, a group faithful to Yahweh, which represents the true Israel of God and maintains its existence. For the first time in the OT a distinction is made within corporeal Israel, a distinction based on religious fidelity and leading to a new Israel bound to Yahweh.

Amos speaks frequently of a remnant (Am. 3:12; 4:1-3; 5:1-3,14-15). The cycle of oracles against the nations culminates in a prophecy of judgment against Israel (2:13-16). The day of Yahweh for which Israel has been hoping (5:18) is "that day" on which "the mighty shall not save (*mlṭ* piel) their lives . . . and those who are swift of foot shall not save themselves (*mlṭ* piel, but changed to a niphal with the LXX), nor shall those who ride horses save (*mlṭ* piel) their lives" (2:14-15). In God's judgment there is no escape for all Israel, any more than for the worshipers of Baal (cf. 1 K. 19:17).[97] In 9:1 Yahweh declares: "Those who are left *('aḥªrîṯ)* I will kill with the sword; not one of them shall flee away, no escapee *(pālîṭ)* shall find refuge (*mlṭ* niphal)." The negative force of the remnant concept for the corporeal nation of Israel (cf. 3:12; 4:1-3; 6:9-10) is clearly spelled out. But it does not mean the end of all the inhabitants of Israel.[98] A remnant of those who are faithful to Yahweh (5:14-15) will be spared. (Several exegetes have questioned the authenticity of vv. 14-15,[99] but the majority defend it with cogent arguments.)

The remnant notion is widespread in the book of Isaiah. Derivatives of *plṭ* (4:2; 5:29; 10:20; 15:9; 37:31-32 = 2 K. 19:30-31; 45:20; 66:19) and *mlṭ* (20:6; 31:5; 34:15; 37:38; 46:2,4; 49:24-25; 66:7) appear frequently. Isa. 4:2-3 speaks of "that day" on which "the survivors *(pᵉlēṭâ)* of Israel" and "whoever is left in Zion and remains in Jerusalem" *(hanniš'ār* par. *hannôṯār)* will be holy, i.e., "everyone who has been recorded for life in Jerusalem." Here for the first time the OT speaks of a "holy remnant," or, as another passage describes it, "holy seed" (6:7). The prophetic oracle of judgment (5:26-29) concludes by comparing the enemy to a lion that brings her prey — defeated Israel — "safely home" (*plṭ* hiphil, v. 29). The people will not be spared! Later, however, the prophet give assurance that Yahweh will strip the enemy of its prey by restoring the people of God and rescuing them from the enemy (49:24-25).

Isa. 10:20-23 (date and authenticity disputed by modern scholars) is the theological

---

97. Fohrer, 981.
98. Hasel, *Remnant,* 190-207.
99. E.g., H.-W. Wolff, *Joel and Amos. Herm* (Eng. trans. 1977), 234, 250.

locus classicus of the remnant concept. The "survivors *(pᵉlēṭâ)* of the house of Jacob" and the "remnant *(šᵉʾār)* of Israel" (v. 20) are those who rely on Yahweh and do not seek refuge in political powers. They return to their mighty God and trust faithfully in him (vv. 21-22). The juxtaposition of the deliverance of the faithful remnant and the imminent judgment that spells the end of the nation (vv. 22-23) means that Israel will cease to exist as a nation, but God will continue to carry out his plan with a faithful remnant. In the future, Yahweh of Hosts will "protect and deliver *(hiṣṣîl)*" Jerusalem, "spare and rescue *(himlîṭ)* it" (31:5).[100]

The promise of salvation in 37:31-32 (= 2 K. 19:30-31) stresses the growth of the remnant: "The surviving remnant *(pᵉlēṭâ hanniš'ārâ)*[101] of the house of Judah shall again take root downward and bear fruit upward. For from Jerusalem a remnant *(šᵉʾērîṯ)* shall go out, and a band of survivors *(pᵉlēṭâ)* from Mount Zion." This historical remnant provides the basis for the eschatological remnant, which comprises those yet to come who are truly faithful to God. Yahweh will send these "survivors" to the nations, and "they shall declare my glory among the nations" (66:19-20).

Joel takes up this theme. On the eschatological day of Yahweh, "everyone who calls on the name of Yahweh shall be saved (*mlṭ* piel); for in Mount Zion and in Jerusalem there shall be escape *(pᵉlēṭâ),* as Yahweh has said, and among the survivors *(sᵉrîḏîm)* shall be those whom Yahweh calls" (3:5[2:32]). All who call on[102] God single-heartedly and turn to him will be saved. This passage does not say that Jerusalem/Zion will be saved as one nation among others;[103] it speaks of the deliverance of a remnant, those who are called by Yahweh and are faithful to him. Obadiah also speaks of the day of Yahweh that is near against all nations (v. 15), a day on which the whole world will be judged. Like Joel, Obadiah proclaims: "On Mount Zion there shall be escape *(pᵉlēṭâ)*" (v. 17).

The promise of salvation of Zechariah's third night vision calls on Israel to flee from Babylon and escape (Zec. 2:10-11[6-7]).

The book of Jeremiah uses forms of *plṭ/mlṭ* for the historical remnant of survivors of a military catastrophe as well as for the eschatological remnant of the age of salvation. Jeremiah tells Ebed-melech, who trusts in Yahweh, that he will be saved on that day (*mlṭ* niphal, 39:18 [twice]). The Judeans who go to Egypt will die by the sword, famine, and pestilence: "there shall be no remnant (*śārîḏ:* collective) or survivor (*pālîṭ:* collective) from the disaster that I am bringing upon them" (42:17). The historical remnant has its future not in Egypt but in Judah (44:14). Nevertheless, a small number of "those who escape *(pālîṭ)* the sword" will return[104] to Judah (44:28). In apocalyptic language the prophet proclaims that on the day of Yahweh flight *(mānôs)* shall fail the leaders of the nations and there shall be no escape *(pᵉlēṭâ)* (25:35).[105] The eschatological day of judgment brings the nations to an end.

---

100. On proposed emendations see III.1 above.
101. See S. Iwry, *Textus* 5 (1966) 34-43, for the variants in 1QIsᵃ.
102. On *qārā' bᵉ* see *GK,* §119k.
103. Contra Wolff, *Joel and Amos,* 60-61.
104. → שׁוּב *šûḇ.*
105. See the discussion of Jer. 51:6,45 in IV.4 below.

The theme of an end from which there is no escape is common in the prophetic oracles against the nations. They declare repeatedly that there shall be no escape for Egypt (Jer. 46:6), Moab (48:8,19; cf. Isa. 16:13), or the inhabitants of the coastlands (Isa. 20:6). Other texts use related remnant terminology instead of *plṭ/mlṭ:* Syria (Isa. 17:1-6), Philistia (14:28-32), Arabia (21:13-17), Babylon (14:22-23).

Here we may mention the unique phrase "survivors of the nations" (*pᵉlîṭê haggôyim,* Isa. 45:20), which does not refer to Israelites who have escaped from the nations[106] but to an eschatological remnant of the pagan nations that worship idols, who have escaped Yahweh's judgment. These survivors of the nations are offered salvation. The historical remnant of the nations is called to become a faithful remnant. They are to turn to Yahweh, the only God (v. 22), for only in Yahweh are righteousness and strength (v. 24). Here the remnant concept becomes universalistic, transcending nationalistic particularism.

In the book of Ezekiel derivatives of *plṭ/mlṭ* appear in the form of the masc. verbal noun *pālîṭ* (6:8-9; 7:16; 24:26-27; 33:21-22), the fem. subst. *pᵉlēṭâ* (14:22), and the verbs *plṭ* qal (7:16) and *mlṭ* niphal (17:15 [twice],18) and piel (33:5). The "escapee" *(pālîṭ)* should generally be interpreted not as a refugee or deportee but as a survivor who has escaped from battle and the devastation of war (6:8).[107] During their exile among the nations, these people who have escaped the sword realize their guilt and turn to Yahweh (6:8-10). Ezk. 14:22 describes how "survivors" of the fall of Jerusalem join the exiles as a sign of consolation in the face of catastrophe, that they may know Yahweh (v. 23).

Ezk. 33:21-22 describes the arrival of an escapee from Jerusalem, who tells the prophet of the city's fall. The prophet "will speak and no longer be silent; he will be a sign to them, and they shall know that I am Yahweh" (24:27). The purpose of the actions (judgment and word of revelation) and of the actors (escapees and the prophet) is to bring the people to knowledge of Yahweh. Those who know and acknowledge Yahweh have a future. In Yahweh is salvation.

4. *Apocalyptic.* The prophetic oracles against Babylon in Jer. 50–51, which exhibit marked eschatological and apocalyptic features, are characterized as "early apocalyptic."[108] Babylon exhibits universalistic features going far beyond the 6th-century historical enemy of Israel, so that it may be considered the archetype of the archenemy of the people of God in all ages to come. Three times the people of God are summoned to flee from Babylon. All those faithful to God who dwell in Babylon are to save their lives (*mlṭ* niphal, Jer. 51:6 [LXX 28:6]) and thus find protection from the judgment that will be visited on the guilt of Babylon. The call to depart resounds: "Come out of her, my people; save your lives (*mlṭ* niphal), each of you" (Jer. 51:45 [not in LXX]). "You

---

106. J. L. McKenzie, *Second Isaiah. AB* 20 (1968), 82-84; J. Morgenstern, *JSS* 2 (1957) 225-31.

107. Contra G. Hölscher with W. Zimmerli, *Ezekiel 2. Herm* (Eng. trans. 1983), 191-92.

108. D. L. Christensen, *Transformations of the War Oracle in OT Prophecy. HDR* 3 (1975), 249-80.

survivors *(pᵉlēṭîm)* of the sword, go, do not linger!" (Jer. 51:50; cf. 50:29 for the *pᵉlēṭâ*). Here the remnant concept plays an important role. The people of God in the form of the faithful survivors must rise up and escape from Babylon before its fall.

The vision of the future of Dnl. 11:40-45 describes military campaigns in the apocalyptic eschaton: for a while the Edomites, Moabites, and the leaders (MT *r'šyt;* the Syr. reading *šrk'* has led some to emend this to *šᵉ'ērîṯ,* "remnant," but the emendation is not compelling)[109] of the Ammonites will escape (*mlṭ* niphal, v. 41) from the hand of the king of the north, whereas for Egypt "there will be no escape" (*pᵉlēṭâ,* v. 42). According to Dnl. 12:1, at the eschaton, after a time of anguish, there will be deliverance for the remnant that has remained faithful to God. "Everyone who is found written in the book," having faced heavenly judgment,[110] "shall be delivered" (*mlṭ* niphal). The promise of the eschatological salvation of the remnant shows that the Danielitic parallel schema of peril–supernatural intervention–salvation or deliverance typical of the apocalyptic visions of Dnl. 7–12 is maintained here as well. To the deliverance of the surviving remnant is added as an eschatological event the resurrection of those who have fallen asleep (12:2), so that all who have been faithful will experience eternal life.[111]

V. Dead Sea Scrolls. In the Hebrew texts from Qumran, *plṭ/mlṭ* appear in verbal forms; *plṭ* is also attested in nominal derivatives. It has been claimed that the qal of *mlṭ* appears for the first time in a previously unknown psalm from 11QPsᵃ, an "apostrophe to Zion" (= 4QPsᶠ):[112] "Who has ever perished (*'bd* qal) in unrighteousness? Who has ever escaped (*mlṭ* qal, with the meaning 'survive';[113] or possibly a piel meaning 'save') in injustice?" As a specialized meaning, the hiphil of *mlṭ* is also used in the sense of "give birth" in 1QH 3:9, par. to the niphal of *plṭ,* "deliver from spasms" (1QH 3:10).

The remaining occurrences in the Qumran Hymn Scroll (1QH) reflect the usage of OT love poetry (see IV.1 above). A hymn extols God's protection of the poor: "You have preserved (*plṭ* piel) the life of the poor" (5:18). "Your peaceful protection is present to save (*plṭ* inf. const.) my life."[114] Those who trust in God "will be saved (*plṭ* piel) forever" (9:29; cf. 6:32).

The Damascus Document speaks of the steadfast who "escaped (*mlṭ* niphal) to the land of the north" (CD 7:14) and the sons of Seth who "escaped (*mlṭ* niphal) at the time of the first visitation" in the past. At the visitation to come, "these [the poor ones of the flock] will escape (*mlṭ* niphal)" (19:10). Then God will "leave (*ytr* piel) a remnant *(pᵉlēṭâ)* for the country to fill the face of the world with their offspring" (2:11-12). For the wicked, however, there will be "no remnant *(šᵉ'ērîṯ)* or survivor *(pᵉlēṭâ)*" (2:6-7; cf.

---

109. *BHK; BHS;* L. Hartman and A. DiLella, *Daniel. AB* 23 (1978), 260.

110. G. W. Nickelsburg, *Resurrection, Immortality, and Eternal Life. HTS* 26 (1972), 11; cf. J. J. Collins, *The Apocalyptic Vision in the Book of Daniel. HSM* 16 (1977), 136.

111. G. F. Hasel, *ZAW* 92 (1980) 267-84, esp. 267-80.

112. J. Starcky, *RB* 73 (1966) 353-71.

113. J. A. Sanders, *DJD,* IV, 87.

114. Cf. E. Lohse, *Die Texte aus Qumran* (²1979), 149: "to save my soul."

1QM 1:6 with the same formula and 1QS 4:14 with the very similar formula *śārîḏ/ p^eleṭâ;* also 1Q27 fr. 1, I, 4 with *mlṭ* niphal).

The benedictions of the Community Rule (1QSb) pray that God will "save" (*plṭ* piel) the one who is blessed (1:7). Derivatives of *plṭ/mlṭ* do not appear in the Temple Scroll. Neither does the Qumran community ever use them to describe itself as a remnant, as it uses *š^e'ērîṯ* (1QM 14:8: "but we are the rem[nant *(š^e'ē[rîṯ])* of your people]").

Aramaic texts from Qumran make frequent use of the verb *plṭ* peal/pael in the sense of "escape, release."[115] The verb *plṭ* appears three times in the Genesis Apocryphon. The survivors of the flood give thanks to the Most High for saving them from destruction (pael, 12:17; cf. Jub. 7:34). In a dream God tells Abraham that, for the sake of Sarai, his life will be spared (peal, 19:20; cf. Gen. 12:13). The story of Lot tells of a shepherd "who had escaped from captivity" (peal, 1QapGen 22:2). The pael of *plṭ,* "release," is used in 11QtgJob 39:3 for the life that birth brings into the world.[116] The books of Enoch contain an apocalyptic passage that says that at the last judgment "the truthful shall be saved" (peal, 4QEn^c = 1 Enoch 10:17).[117] These Aramaic occurrences in the Dead Sea Scrolls correspond to forms of Heb. *plṭ.*

Hasel

115. Beyer, 668.
116. Ibid., 296; B. Jongeling, C. J. Labuschagne, and A. S. van der Woude, *Aramaic Texts from Qumran. SSS* 4 (1976): "usher in."
117. Beyer, 238.

פלל *pll;* תְּפִלָּה *t^epillâ;* פְּלִילִים *p^elîlîm;* פְּלִילָה *p^elîlâ;* פְּלִילִי *p^elîlî;* פְּלִילִיָּה *p^elîlîyâ*

I. Etymology, Distribution: 1. Root; 2. OT; 3. Versions; 4. Extracanonical Literature. II. Noun and Verb: 1. *t^epillâ;* 2. Hithpael; 3. Other Stems and Nouns; 4. Personal Names. III. Cult: 1. Prayer; 2. Corporate Worship; 3. Theology. IV. Later Developments. V. Dead Sea Scrolls.

pll. A. Aejmelaeus, *The Traditional Prayer in the Psalms. BZAW* 167 (1986) 1-118; R. Albertz, "Gebet II. AT," *TRE,* XII, 34-42; D. R. Ap-Thomas, "Notes on Some Terms Relating to Prayer," *VT* 6 (1956) 225-41; S. E. Balentine, "The Prophet as Intercessor," *JBL* 103 (1984) 161-73; P. A. H. de Boer, *De voorbede in het OT. OTS* 3 (1943), esp. 124-30; E. S. Gerstenberger, *Der bittende Mensch. WMANT* 51 (1980); M. D. Goldman, "The Root PLL and Its Connotation with Prayer," *ABR* 3 (1953) 1-6; A. Gonzalez, *La oración en la Biblia* (1968); K. Heinen, *Das Gebet im AT* (1971); idem, "Das Nomen *t^efillā* als Gattungsbezeichnung," *BZ* 17 (1973) 103-5; F. Hesse, "Die Fürbitte im AT" (diss., Erlangen, 1949; rev., 1951); C. Houtman, "Zu 1. Samuel

I. Etymology, Distribution.

1. *Root.* Homonymous roots meaning "pray" are not found in the Semitic languages; it is therefore virtually impossible to trace the etymology of *pll.* Several conjectures have been put forward: (a) The root is related to Arab. *falla,* "dent, break."[1] In this case *pālal* might have referred originally to cultic self-mutilation (cf. 1 K. 18:28).[2] (b) The root is related to *npl,* "fall"; this etymology suggests a basic meaning "fall down."[3] Derivations from the juridical realm find more support: (c) Akk. *palālu,* "guard, keep under surveillance," points to a judicial action.[4] (d) Palache takes as his point of departure a hypothetical original meaning "cleave, break, separate," associated with all *pl* roots, and postulates its development into "judge, demand, judgment, plead, pray."[5] (e) More neutrally, Speiser identifies a reconstructed *pālal,* "appraise, evaluate," as the starting point of historical development. All etymological theories, however, boil down ultimately to attempts to constrain the clear usage of a word group within the corset of a preconceived theology.[6]

Because the search for the origin of the root has been fruitless, we should seriously consider the possibility of taking the noun *tᵉpillâ* as given and the hithpael of the verb as a derivative of the noun. The denominative process may have been furthered by the phonetic resemblance to *hiṯnappēl* (cf. the points of semantic contact in Jer. 42:2; Dt. 9:18,25; Ezr. 10:1; and several Qumran texts) as well as the general tendency of cultic language to use hithpael forms (e.g., *npl,* see above; *ḥnn,* 1 K. 8:33,47,59; *ydh,* Neh. 1:6; 9:2-3; Ezr. 10:1; *šḥh,* Ex. 4:31; Josh. 5:14; Isa. 44:17; Ps. 95:6; *qdš,* Ex. 19:22; Isa. 66:17; 2 Ch. 29:5,15,34; etc.). The hithpael often expresses "a more indirect application to the subject,"[7] so that *hiṯpallēl* means "intercede for oneself." Against this etymology, one might argue that *tᵉpillâ* does not look like a primary noun.

2. *OT.* The vast majority of occurrences of the root comprise the hithpael of the verb and the noun *tᵉpillâ.* They appear 155 times in the OT. All the other forms of *pll* occur a

---

2,25," *ZAW* 89 (1977) 412-17; N. Johansson, *Parakletoi* (1940); E. Kutsch, "'Trauerbräuche' und 'Selbstminderungsriten' im AT," in K. Lüthi, E. Kutsch, and W. Dantine, *Drei Wiener Antrittsreden. ThS* 78 (1965), 25-42; G. C. Macholz, "Jeremia in der Kontinuität der Prophetie," *Probleme biblischer Theologie. FS G. von Rad* (1971), 306-34; J. L. Palache, *Semantic Notes on the Hebrew Lexicon* (1959); H. Graf Reventlow, *Gebet im AT* (1986); J. F. A. Sawyer, "Types of Prayer in the OT," *Semitics* 7 (1980) 131-43; J. Scharbert, "Die Fürbitte im AT," *"Diener in Eurer Mitte." FS A. Hofmann* (1984), 91-109; E. A. Speiser, "The Stem *PLL* in Hebrew," *JBL* 82 (1963) 301-6; E. F. de Ward, "Superstition and Judgment," *ZAW* 89 (1977) 1-19.

1. Wehr, 725.
2. De Boer, with modifications.
3. K. Ahrens, *ZDMG* 64 (1910) 163.
4. *AHw,* II, 813; Johansson; Hesse; J. Levy, *WTM,* IV, 53.
5. P. 59.
6. Heinen; Macholz; J. Barr, *The Semantics of Biblical Language* (Oxford: Oxford University Press, 1961).
7. *GK,* §§54-55.

total of only 11 times. In addition, four personal names are formed with *pll.* The two primary forms *(pll* hithpael and *tᵉpillâ)* enjoy a tightly circumscribed and clearly defined semantic field: "pray" and "prayer."

3. *Versions.* The ancient versions confirm the highly specific usage of the two primary forms of *pll.* The LXX uses *eúchesthai* 8 times for the hithpael, otherwise *proseúchesthai;* these are the standard terms for cultic prayer in Hellenistic Judaism and the early Christian congregations.[8] Usage is fluid, but Greek, like Hebrew, generally uses other verbs for informal prayer, e.g., *déomai* and *krázein.*[9]

In the Latin tradition the primary equivalent to *pll* appears to be *orare/oratio;* other expressions (*rogare, supplicare, implorare, petere, precari,* and their derivatives) appear occasionally (see the Vulg. of Ex. 10:17; 1 K. 1:12; Zeph. 3:10; Job 33:25-26; Ezr. 10:1; Ex. 12:32; 1 K. 1:17,27; Dt. 3:23; 2 K. 24:10; 4 K. 1:13; 1 Ch. 4:10). The Aramaic languages generally use the roots *bʿʾ, ḥnn,* and *ṣlʾ* for prayer (Dnl. 6:14,12, 11[Eng. vv. 13,11,10], respectively; Ezr. 6:10).[10]

The LXX of 1 S. 2:25 extends the cultic meaning even to the piel *(proseúchesthai).* Thus few passages remain that fall outside this semantic field: Ezk. 16:52 (*diaphtheírein,* "destroy"); Ps. 106:30 (*exiláskein,* "atone"); Gen. 48:11 (*stereísthai,* "be deprived of"). Besides the verbal forms, we may cite the rare substs.: *pᵉlîlîm* (Ex. 21:22, *metà axiṓmatos,* "as may seem good"; Dt. 32:31, *anóētos,* "ignorant"; Job 31:11 [different text]); *pᵉlîlî* (Job 31:28, *ʿāwôn pᵉlîlî, anomía hē megístē,* "capital offense," possibly a free translation of "offense to be punished by the judge"; so in many modern translations); *pᵉlîlâ* (Isa. 16:3, *sképē,* "protection"); *pᵉlîlîyâ* (Isa. 28:7, not in the Greek text). The ancient translators shared our modern uncertainty.

4. *Extracanonical Literature.* Extracanonical Hebrew literature makes little use of *pll* as a verb. It has its accustomed form (hithpael) and meaning, e.g., in Sir. 36:22; 38:9; 51:11. The Dead Sea Scrolls use *hiṯnappēl.* On the other hand, we find new derivatives such as Jewish Aram. *palpēl,* "dispute," and Middle Heb. *pilpēl,* "examine." Levy connects both these forms with *pilpēl,* "peppercorn."[11] Thus the hithpael of *pll,* "pray," so important in several strata of the OT, later vanishes from the literature.

The noun *tᵉp̱illâ,* on the contrary, appears in Sirach (e.g., 7:10,14), the Dead Sea Scrolls (e.g., 1QH 12:4; 1QM 15:5; but not in 11QT), and rabbinic literature. In the Mishnah and later writings it refers to ritual prayer, especially the Eighteen Benedictions.[12]

---

8. H. Greeven and J. Herrmann, "εὔχομαι," *TDNT,* II, 775-808; H. Schönweiss, "Gebet," *Theologisches Begriffslexikon zum NT,* I, 421-24.

9. For the former see U. Schoenborn, *EDNT,* I, 286-87; for the latter, W. Grundmann, *TDNT,* III, 898-903.

10. See also C. Brockelmann, *LexSyr,* 82b, 243a, 628a; Beyer, 745.

11. *WTM,* IV, 57.

12. See I. Elbogen, *Der jüdische Gottesdienst in seiner geschichtlichen Entwicklung* (³1931, repr. 1967), 27-60, 247-49, and s.v. *tᵉp̱illâ.*

The word *tᵉpillîn,* "prayer bands," appears to be related, at least in the popular mind.[13] Others derive this noun from *tpl,* "hang down,"[14] or *tpl,* "be insipid."

II. Noun and Verb. Occasionally (e.g., 2 S. 7:27; 1 K. 8 = 2 Ch. 6) the noun and the verb appear conjoined, belonging to the same semantic field. Their distribution is illuminating: the verb occurs just 6 times in the Pentateuch. In Deuteronomistic sections of the historical books 1 Samuel–2 Kings, there are 27 occurrences of the verb and 10 of the noun *tᵉpillâ.* The Chronicler's History uses the hithpael 20 times and the noun 14 times. In the prophetic books (exclusive of Daniel), the verb occurs 19 times and the noun 9. The Psalms have a concentration of 31 occurrences of *tᵉpillâ* but only 3 occurrences of the hithpael. Job, Proverbs, Daniel, and Lamentations together have 4 hithpaels and 9 occurrences of *tᵉpillâ.* This survey shows that the word pair "prayer/pray" came into common use in the Deuteronomistic period. The passages in the prophets and Psalms, too, must generally be dated in the exilic period.

1. *tᵉpillâ.* a. The absence of the noun from the Pentateuch is no accident. It betrays the hand of a deliberate redactor: the patriarchs spoke with God directly and personally (Gen. 18:22b-32; Ex. 32:11-13; 33:11-23), not through congregational mediation. The noun *tᵉpillâ* denotes formalized cultic prayer emanating from the worshiping community. In individual laments the psalmist presents a personal petition to God (*tᵉpillāṯî,* "my prayer"; often par. to *tᵉḥinnâ, rinnâ, šawʿâ, ʾimrê pî, taḥᵃnûn, maśʾaṯ kappayim,* and always with the 1st person sg. suf., referring to the psalmist: Ps. 4:2[1]; 6:10[9]; 17:1; 35:13; 39:13[12]; 54:4[2]; 55:2[1]; 61:2[1]; 66:19-20; 69:14[13]; 84:9[8]; 86:6; 88:3,14[2,13]; 102:2[1]; 141:2,5; 143:1; Jon. 2:8[7]). In these contexts *tᵉpillâ* either is the only term for prayer (Ps. 4:2[1]; 35:13; 66:19,20; 69:14[13]; 84:9[8]; cf. Jon. 2:8[7]) or stands first in a series of two or more synonyms (Ps. 39:13[12]; 54:4[2]; 55:2[1]; 86:6; 88:3[2]; 102:2[1]; 141:2; 143:1). Only in four cases does another word come first (Ps. 17:1 and 61:2[1], *rinnâ;* 6:10[9], *tᵉḥinnâ;* 88:14[13], *šawʿâ*). This observation clearly demonstrates the special significance of *tᵉpillâ* as a term meaning "prayer."[15]

Furthermore, the formulaic character of these petitions and comparison with other texts, especially in Akkadian, indicate that we are dealing with what was originally liturgical material from the circumscribed realm of the family cult.[16] The prayer presumes a life-threatening affliction.[17] Set in the framework of fasting and self-depreciatory ritual (Ps. 35:13-14),[18] it seeks to gain the attention of the angered personal tutelary deity. The focus can be shifted to the affliction of the people and their prayer (Ps. 80:5[4]).

---

13. H. G. Kuhn, "Gebetsriemen," *BHHW,* I, 525-26.
14. Jastrow, 1687.
15. Cf. Heinen.
16. Gerstenberger.
17. → צרר *ṣrr.*
18. Kutsch.

The noun *tᵉpillâ* appears frequently in pleas for a favorable hearing (invocation and petition in a lament: Ps. 4:2[1]; 17:1; 39:13[12]; 54:3-4[1-2]; 55:2-3[1-2]; etc.).[19] This element is the core of the liturgical prayer.[20] It is accompanied by such verbs as "call," "cry," "call for help" (→ קרא *qārā'*, זעק *zā'aq*, שׁוע *šw'*); only exceptionally (Ps. 5:3[2]; 32:6) do we find the hithpael of *pll,* which is used in other strata. In practice the language of collective cultic prayer knows only the noun. Lam. 3:8,44 — a prayer of an individual — shows that the way to God through *tᵉpillâ* can be blocked.

b. The Deuteronomic History reveals a changed situation. Now *tᵉpillâ* denotes primarily a prayer of the community on any occasion. This holds true already for the Deuteronomistic prayer of David in 2 S. 7:18-29. Conceived as a thanksgiving consequent to God's promise of a dynasty, it is edifying and exemplary in nature; its polished insistence on Yahweh's exclusivity and its use of the communal tradition formula (esp. in v. 22b) reveal its true origin.[21] The communal background is even more evident in the great prayer of Solomon at the dedication of the temple (1 K. 8:23-53 = 2 Ch. 6:14-42).[22] Here Solomon is not anticipating the situation of the early Jewish community at the time of the second temple; instead, the community is retrojecting its new temple theology into the period of Solomon.[23] The temple is the house of prayer (Isa. 56:7) for individual concerns and the prayer of the whole community (cf. 1 K. 8:38 and the context, vv. 31-51). The *tᵉpillâ* is set in a liturgical framework; communal prayer comprehends all the concerns of the community — praise, thanksgiving, and petition (cf. the use of *tᵉpillâ* in psalm superscriptions: 17:1; 86:1; 90:1; 102:1[superscription]; 142:1[superscription]). In 1 K. 8 (vv. 28,29-30,38,45,49,54) *tᵉḥinnâ* is an established explanatory remark. The word pair still appears as a formula in the NT (Eph. 6:18; Phil. 4:6; Heb. 5:7).

In 2 K. 19–20 — in various redactional versions — we find at least three situations for prayer, as suggested by the prayer at the dedication of the temple. Here too the content and structure of the prayers (although uttered in their present context by Hezekiah and Isaiah, respectively) point to communal use: derision of the living God is an exilic motif; designation of the community as a "remnant" (v. 4 = Isa. 37:4; v. 31 = Isa. 37:32; cf. Isa. 46:3; Jer. 8:3; 42:2,15,19; 44:12,14) reflects the self-understanding of the early Jewish adherents of Yahweh. Vv. 15-19 are a typically Deuteronomistic prayer, and 2 K. 20:5 responds to Hezekiah's petition: "I have heard your prayer."

c. The Chronicler's History and Daniel also use the noun. Here *tᵉpillâ* denotes primarily the penitential prayer of the community. The associated ritual acts (putting on sackcloth, placing ashes or dirt on one's head, and lamentation [cf. Neh. 9:1-2 and already 2 K. 19:1-2])[24] are mentioned expressly. The penitential texts Neh. 1:5-11 and Dnl. 9:4-19 are referred to specifically as *tᵉpillâ.* For Ezr. 9:6-15 and Neh. 9:5-37, the

---

19. H. Gunkel and J. Begrich, *Intro. to Psalms* (Eng. trans. 1997), 152, 154.
20. Aejmelaeus.
21. T. Veijola, *Die ewige Dynastie. AnAcScFen* B 193 (1975), 78-79.
22. See III.2 below.
23. E. Würthwein, *Das Erste Buch der Könige. ATD* 11/1 (²1985), 97-100.
24. Kutsch.

genre is implicit (cf. Ezr. 10:1; structure and content for Neh. 9). Of course *t*^{e}*p̱illâ* is not an exclusive technical term: *t*^{e}*ḥinnâ* and *taḥ*^{a}*nûnîm* also appear (2 Ch. 6:19,21; 33:13; Dnl. 9:3,17,23), and a variety of verbal expressions mean "pray."[25]

It is important to note the identity of those who utter the prayers. We still find private prayers on behalf of an individual (2 Ch. 33:9-13). Alongside these, we observe a marked concentration on the leader of the congregation and official personnel. A spokesperson utters the text on behalf of the assembled congregation. We even read in 2 Ch. 30:27 that the priests addressed "their" prayer to heaven. But there is at least as much emphasis on the roots of this prayer in corporate worship.[26] The corporate "we" pervades many texts.[27] Liturgical codification of the texts and rites appears to be at an advanced stage. As "leader of praise," a descendant of Asaph is to "begin the thanksgiving in prayer" (Neh. 11:17).

d. In comparison to the concentrations in the Psalms, the Deuteronomistic History, and the Chronicler's History, the remaining occurrences of *t*^{e}*p̱illâ* are of secondary importance. Isa. 37:4; 38:5; Jer. 7:16; 11:14 belong in the Deuteronomistic context. Otherwise there is only a single occurrence of *t*^{e}*p̱illâ* in Proto-Isaiah: *hirbāh t*^{e}*p̱illâ* (Isa. 1:15 [unique]; cf. Isa. 23:16; Job 40:27). The second temple is both a house of prayer and a house of sacrifice (Isa. 56:7; 2 Ch. 7:12-15). Thus the prophetic writings as a whole take no notice of our word, although cult and temple are often central themes.

Occurrences are also rare in wisdom literature, where the word refers apparently to individual prayer in the setting of corporate worship (e.g., Prov. 15:29). The ritual background is evident (Job 16:15-16; Prov. 15:8). Prayer *(t*^{e}*p̱illâ)* is a remedy for violence (*ḥāmās,* Job 16:17), has a place alongside sacrifice (Prov. 15:8), and can be vitiated by wicked misconduct (28:9; cf. 21:27).

To sum up: the noun *t*^{e}*p̱illâ* always refers to a ritual prayer, but various social and cultic structures are presupposed. The congregation conjoins the prayer of the individual with that of the larger community in corporate prayer, which becomes increasingly codified, is implemented by "servants of the cult," and includes penitential elements.

2. *Hithpael.* The usage of the verb in the hithpael is largely but not entirely parallel to that of the noun. The act of praying and the fixed liturgical prayer are two different things.

a. In the Psalms the relatively few texts using the hithpael of *pll* stand out. Ps. 5:2-3(1-2) is an invocation with a petition that God will hear "my words, "my sighing," and "the sound of my cry." There follow a unique divine appellative ("my King and my God") expressing the psalmist's trust in God and an asseveration of the psalmist's intent to pray (*pll,* v. 3c[2c]). In Ps. 32:5-6 confession of sin and assurance of forgiveness are followed by the conclusion: "Therefore all the faithful pray *(pll)* to you." Ps. 72:15

---

25. See below.

26. See III.2 below.

27. J. Scharbert, "Das 'Wir' in den Psalmen," *Freude an der Weisung des Herrn. FS H. Gross. SBB* 13 (1986), 297-324.

urges intercession (*pll;* par. to *brk,* "bless") for the king. All three texts are formal and liturgical, possibly late compositions.

In the Psalter as a whole, the verb *pll* plays no role. Other terms are used for the act of prayer: "cry," "call," etc.[28] The Deuteronomistic (?) narrator of 1 S. 1–2, who views Hannah's vow and prayer as belonging to the genre of solemn cultic invocations, makes extensive use of *pll* hithpael (1 S. 1:10,12,26,27; 2:1). The verb also appears in the story of Jonah (Jon. 2:2[1]; 4:2), but not in the psalm of Jonah (2:3-10). Groups can also turn to God in prayer (Jer. 29:7,12; Neh. 4:3[9]; ironically or maliciously: Isa. 16:12; 44:17; 45:14,20). When the verb appears in the context of prayer texts, it suggests a situation in the ritual of the cult. It can refer to all types of prayer: vow, lament, thanksgiving, intercession of an individual or a group.

b. Passages in which a leader prays to Yahweh in the name of the people have attracted special attention. They are claimed to prove that the primary meaning of *pll* is "intercede on behalf of." The army of great prayer figures is impressive. The prophet Abraham intercedes for Abimelech (Gen. 20:7,17). Twice Moses averts peril threatening the people (Nu. 11:2; 21:7; intercessory situations without *pll:* Ex. 32:12ff.,30ff.; Nu. 12:10ff.; in Dt. 9:20,25-26, *pll* is used in an allusion to Ex. 32). Next to Moses, Samuel is the great intercessor (1 S. 7:5; 8:6; 12:19,23; cf. Jer. 15:1; Ps. 99:6). David and Solomon intercede vicariously for the people (2 S. 7:27; 1 K. 8:28ff. = 1 Ch. 17:25; 2 Ch. 6:19ff.). The Deuteronomist — using *pll* — extends the notion of the royal intercessor to Hezekiah (2 K. 19:15,20; 20:2; cf. Isa. 37:15,21; 38:2; 2 Ch. 30:18; 32:20). But Hezekiah's prayers in 2 Ch. 32:24 and 33:13 belong to the genre of individual prayer for deliverance from sickness (cf. Isa. 38:10ff.). The sequence of prophetic intercessors is continued through an anonymous figure from the northern kingdom (1 K. 13:6), Elisha (2 K. 4:33; 6:17-18), and finally Jeremiah, whom many consider the intercessor par excellence (Jer. 7:16; 11:14; 14:11; 32:16; 37:3; 42:2,4,20). In the domain of wisdom literature and P, Job (Job 42:8,10), Daniel (Dnl. 9:4,20), Ezra (Ezr. 10:1), and Nehemiah (Neh. 1:4,6; 2:4) are so described.

Does this mean that *pll* refers to the activity of a mediator or intercessor? By no means. Apart from the grammatical and semantic problems occasioned by attempts to reduce the communal *pll* texts to the common denominator of intercession and to identify the office responsible for making intercession (prophet? cult prophet? priest? sage?), the regnant interpretation[29] ignores the fact that the intercessory figures — especially Moses, Samuel, and Jeremiah — have been stylized by the postexilic community. The intercessors reflect the cultic practice and communal structure of the restoration period. Moses the lawgiver and prophet is manifested in priests and Levites. His voice is heard in liturgical readings and corporate prayer (cf. Ps. 90:1). Samuel prays on behalf of the community at critical moments (1 S. 7:5; 8:6; cf. 1 S. 15:25-26). When Jeremiah's very life and vocation are under attack and the situation is hopeless, he fights for the survival of the community (Jer. 7:16; 11:14; 14:11, intercession is forbidden; cf. 32:16ff.; 15:1).

---

28. → צעק *ṣā'aq;* קרא *qārā'.*
29. De Boer, Hesse, Macholz, Reventlow.

3. *Other Stems and Nouns.* The occurrences of the piel and the other nouns derived from *pll* cannot in fact be connected with the hithpael and *tᵉpillâ.* Whether another root *pll* or *pl* should be postulated remains an open question.[30] The scarcity of the evidence, as well as the uncertainty of the OT texts and the ancient versions, does little to encourage a quick decision.

The frequently proposed basic meaning "judge, determine"[31] is highly dubious, probably being inspired by modern notions of order. Ps. 106:30: according to Nu. 25:7-8 Phinehas executes apostates; he does not issue a judicial verdict. Ezk. 16:52: Judah "surpasses" Israel in sin, disgrace, and punishment (cf. Ezk. 23:35; Jer. 3:11). Gen. 48:11: Jacob cries out, "I never would have believed [? *lō' pillālṯî*] that I would see you again." And 1 S. 2:25a is a proverb whose text and meaning are obscure.[32] The noun *pālîl* and its derivatives might have a juridical sense in certain texts such as Ex. 21:22;[33] Job 31:11,28; Isa. 16:3; 28:7. Dt. 32:31 remains opaque, and other explanations achieve the same degree of (im)probability.[34]

4. *Personal Names.* Personal names that include the element *pl* are difficult to interpret. The names *pālāl* (Neh. 3:25), *pᵉlalyâ* (Neh. 11:12), *'eplāl* (1 Ch. 2:37), and *'ᵉlîpal* (1 Ch. 11:35) can be interpreted on the basis of the hypothetical meanings of the root; they may also be understood as formations unconnected with *pll.*[35] The only sure observation is that in names with theophoric elements the verb cannot mean "pray."

III. Cult. The hithpael of *pll* and the noun *tᵉpillâ* belong to the language of Israel's cult. The original setting of the noun appears to be Israelite "occasional worship," whereas the hithpael of *pll* and other hithpael forms come into prominence only in the Deuteronomic and Deuteronomistic periods. What cultic theory and practice does this usage reflect?

1. *Prayer.* a. Prayer is human speech addressed to a deity.[36] It must therefore be formalized and ritualized according to religious rules. Posture, gestures, tone of voice, accompanying ceremonies, music, place, and time — all are prescribed by norm and custom for specific kinds of prayer:[37] Ps. 5:4(3), morning prayer and sacrifice; vv. 2,8(1,7), invocation and proskynesis; Ps. 35:13-14, mourning rituals; Neh. 1:4; Job 16:15-17, penitential ceremonial; Isa. 44:17, caricature of idolaters; 1 K. 8:22, elevation of hands; etc. Numerous similar rituals, many still practiced today, are familiar

---

30. For the former see *GesB;* for the latter, Levy, *WTM.*
31. *GesB,* 643-44: *pll* I; *HAL,* III, 933: *pll* A; H.-P. Stähli, *TLOT,* II, 991.
32. See de Ward.
33. Justified doubts are noted by Speiser, 302-3; Budde, *ZAW* 11 (1891) 107-8, proposes the conjectural emendation *bannᵉpālîm,* "for the miscarriage."
34. E.g., Speiser, de Ward, and Levy.
35. *HAL,* s.v.; *IPN,* 187-88.
36. F. Heiler, *Prayer* (Eng. trans. 1932).
37. Ap-Thomas, 225-30; Albertz, 34-35.

from ancient Near Eastern sources.[38] The point of *pll* hithpael is thus to describe the recitation of a prayer correctly and in conformity to the required ceremonial.

b. Neither *tᵉpillâ* nor *pll* hithpael defines a prayer with specific content or liturgical form. Quite the contrary: our expressions presuppose the widest possible range of liturgical prayer: lament and petition (Isa. 38:2-5; 2 Ch. 33:12-13,18-19; for the most part also in the Psalms and 1 K. 8); praise and thanksgiving (2 S. 7:18-27; Ps. 42:9[8]; Neh. 11:17; 2 Ch. 20:22,27); vow (1 S. 1:10-11). In one text the pl. *tᵉpillôṯ* denotes the various prayer genres collectively (Ps. 72:20).[39]

c. Prayer always involves a personal appearance before the deity, in a smaller or larger company, with or without the aid of a liturgist. The suffixed noun *tᵉpillāṯî,* "my prayer," occurs 22 times, primarily in the Psalms.[40] An additional 8 occurrences use the 2nd or 3rd person sg. suffix to refer to the person doing the praying (1 K. 9:3; Isa. 38:5; Ps. 109:7; 2 Ch. 33:18-19). Prayer is a most personal and individual act on the part of a worshiper, even when it is liturgical in form. It is fundamentally God's "song," vouchsafed to comfort the believer (Ps. 42:9[8]). It is not collectivized even when it is uttered by the congregation (Ps. 80:5[4]; 1 K. 8:45,49); although it is possible to speak of "our prayer" (Jer. 42:2; Neh. 4:3[9]; Dnl. 9:18), this expresses the solidarity of the congregation taking part in the liturgical action.[41] Whether God "hears"[42] and grants the prayer depends on the individual or congregation. Woe to those who "make many prayers" (*hirbâ tᵉpillîm,* par. to *pāraś kappayim,* "stretch out [their] hands"), while their hands are full of blood (Isa. 1:15).

d. That ritual specialists should take over responsibility for the text and mode of prayers and even recite them vicariously on behalf of the individual and the group is a widespread phenomenon.[43] To view it as a process of "ossification and mechanization" is inappropriate.[44] The structure of the community, its religious organization, and the cultic occasion determine how the liturgical functioning of various figures is perceived: the head of a clan (Gen. 20:7; a later interpolation makes Abraham a "prophet" [*nāḇîʾ*]), a man of God (1 K. 13:6, although the LXX does not use *hiṯpallēl*), a king (1 K. 8:22-23), a prophet (Jer. 42:2ff.), a priest (2 Ch. 30:27), or a governor (Neh. 1:4ff.). There is an unmistakable tendency to set the liturgist apart from the congregation as an intercessor endowed with special powers (*hiṯpallēl bᵉʿaḏ* or *ʿal,* Gen. 20:7; Nu. 21:7; Dt. 9:20; 1 S. 7:5; 12:19,23; 1 K. 13:6; Jer. 7:16; 11:14; 14:11; 29:7; 37:3; 42:2,20; Ps. 72:15; Job 42:8,10; Neh. 1:6; 2 Ch. 30:18). Here remnants of a magical notion of prayer (cf. 1 S. 12:16-17; 2 K. 4:33-34) appear to be preserved well into the theocratic community of the postexilic period. The *tᵉpillâ* proper is the prayer of the afflicted individual, the worshiping congregation or com-

38. O. Keel, *Symbolism of the Biblical World* (Eng. trans. 1979), 308-23.
39. See II.1.b above.
40. See II.1.a above.
41. Reventlow, 295-98.
42. → שׁמע *šāmaʿ.*
43. Heiler, 65-73.
44. Contra ibid., 65, etc., see Reventlow, 228-64; Gerstenberger, 67-73, 134-60.

munity, or the leader praying in solidarity with the congregation. We need to view OT "intercession" with a critical eye.

Many scholars have asserted that "intercession" was a specific function of a prophet and that the precise meaning of *hitpallēl* is "intercede on behalf of."[45] Unfortunately, no manuals for prophets have been preserved. The intercessory function is probably a late accretion to the picture of a prophet.

2. *Corporate Worship.* A positive statement of this point emerges from examination of the use of *pll* hithpael. Contemporaries did not seem to feel that this usage — almost always in late texts — required explanation. Engaging in prayer (*lᵉhitpallēl,* without attribute) is stereotypical (1 S. 1:12,26; 12:23; 2 S. 7:27; 1 K. 8:54; Isa. 16:12). Prayer is offered in holy places and in cultic contexts (Dt. 9:18,25-26; 1 S. 1:9ff.; 7:5-6; 2 K. 19:14-15; Isa. 16:12 [the Moabites!]) or privately with reference to the temple and its congregation (2 K. 20:2; Jon. 2:2,4,8-9[1,3,7-8]; Dnl. 6:11[10]). The congregation is at times clearly the active subject (Jer. 29:7,12ff.; Ps. 32:6; 72:15; Dnl. 9:18; 2 Ch. 7:14-15) — here and there, in fact, texts using *pll* cite liturgical material in the 1st person pl.: "we have sinned" (1 S. 7:6, following "I will pray for you [pl.]" in v. 5; Dnl. 9:5ff. following "I prayed" in v. 4); "we have broken faith with our God" (Ezr. 10:2; cf. v. 4, addressed to Ezra as he lies prostrate in prayer: "take action, for it is your duty and we are with you"); "I pray . . . and confess the sins of the people of Israel, which we have sinned against you" (Neh. 1:6; cf. v. 11: "the prayer of your servant and the prayer of your servants"; also 4:3[9]). There could be no more vivid demonstration of the interplay between corporate prayer and prayer in the mouth of a liturgist.

The text with the highest concentration of *pll* hiphil (9 occurrences, together with 6 occurrences of *tᵉpillâ*) is the literarily and redactionally complex prayer of Solomon at the dedication of the temple (1 K. 8:22-54 = 2 Ch. 6:12–7:1a; cf. the liturgical corrections such as 6:13). The passage emphasizes the congregational setting (1 K. 8:14,22,55,65).[46] The festal assembly takes place within the temple (vv. 5-11). The liturgist steps up to the altar, spreads his hands, and utters the great intercessory prayer (v. 22). His primary concern is to assure that all the prayers Israel offers to Yahweh in the holy place will be heard (v. 30). Seven typical situations for prayer are listed (vv. 31-51). When an individual or the congregation addressed God in prayer in or facing the temple, "then hear in heaven" (vv. 32,34,36,39,43,45,49). A variety of verbs refer to the act of supplications: "pray" (*hitpallēl),* but also "come" (*bô',* vv. 31,41,42), "turn" (*šûḇ,* vv. 33,35,37,48), "confess" (*ydh,* vv. 33,35), "plead" (*hithannēn,* vv. 33,47), "spread one's hands" (*pāraś kappayim,* v. 38). But *hitpallēl* is the predominant term (vv. 33,35,42,44,48; once *yihyeh tᵉpillâ,* v. 38). The text envisions small congregations and the great congregation engaged in occasional worship and festival observance, in Jerusalem and in the diaspora. The "congregation of Israel" in its various manifestations is the body responsible for prayer and the worship that is its setting.

45. Hesse, Scharbert, Reventlow, etc.; see the criticisms of Balentine and Sawyer.
46. → קהל *qāhāl.*

Solomon functions solely as liturgist for the congregation. This agrees totally with the liturgical reality we can deduce from the Psalms. When narrative and prophetic literature pictures mighty figures of prayer, this legendary exaggeration serves edifying and pedagogical purposes.

In the nonsacrificial worship of exilic and postexilic Israel, prayers (together with readings from Scripture and homilies) became the dominant element of all religious ceremonies. The hithpael of *pll* and *tᵉpillâ* signalize this development.

3. *Theology.* In the prayer of the exilic and postexilic periods the traditions of individual and corporate prayer, of the festival and temple congregations, and of the prayers of godly individuals endowed with extraordinary powers coalesce. This is why the prayer of Israel is infinitely rich and theologically complex. The prayer tradition has preserved concepts of God emanating from different eras. Considered as a whole, however, Israel's prayer always presents a partnership in solidarity with God, communicating delight in life, thanksgiving, and longing for help. It is also a way of influencing Yahweh, of appeasing an angry deity, an attempt to persuade an indifferent God, as well as lament and reproach. The noun *tᵉpillâ* can denote any kind of prayer.[47] In the later period, when *pll* became by far the favorite term, penitence and petition become dominant, at least in corporate worship (1 S. 7:5-6; Ezr. 10:1ff.; Neh. 1:4ff.; 9 [without *pll*]; Dnl. 9). The shock of the fall of Jerusalem and its consequent theocratic theology resulted in a sense of unworthiness that left its mark on prayer (cf. also the Dtr theology of history).

IV. Later Developments. The OT prayer traditions, especially the tradition of liturgical prayer denoted by the hithpael of *pll* and *tᵉpillâ*, profoundly influenced the Jewish and Christian religious communities. This holds true not only formally for the survival of many liturgical forms, but also for the fundamental theological and ethical values informing the prayer of Israel.

Gerstenberger

V. Dead Sea Scrolls. In the Dead Sea Scrolls the verb has been identified 6 times, the nouns *tᵉpillâ* and *pᵉlîlîm* once each. There appears to be no notable divergence from OT usage. An Apocryphon of Moses describes Moses as an intercessor who prays *(hiṯpallēl)* before Yahweh and pleads *(hiṯḥannēn)* for mercy (2Q21 1:4). In the context of a congregational hymn (?), 1QH 17:18 illustrates the intimate connection between proclamation of God's mighty acts and intercessory prayer (cf. also 12:4). The contexts of the noun *tᵉpillâ* at Qumran show clearly that the community had collections of prayers and hymns for specific times of day, festivals, and other occasions:[48] *tplt lywm hkypwrym* (1Q34 2:5), *tplh lmwʿyd* (4QPrFêtes[c] [4Q509] fr. 10, IV, 8). A series of superscriptions indicating the occasion of various psalms includes the words *tplt mnšh*

---

47. See III.1.b above.
48. P. W. Skehan, *CBQ* 35 (1973) 195-205.

mlk yhwdh, "prayer of Manasseh, king of Judah, when the king of Assyria took him captive" (4Q381 33:8). The community had a repertory of prayers and hymns for war (*tplt mwʿd hmlḥmh,* 1QM 15:5; cf. 4QM^a [4Q491] frs. 8-10, 1:17). Finally, the reinterpretation of the cult by the Qumran Essenes, with its new sacrificial system, is evident in CD 11:21: "The sacrifice of the wicked is an abomination, but the prayer of the just is an agreeable offering." The word *p^{e}lîlîm* in 4Q158 9:5 is a citation of Ex. 21:22.

Fabry

פָּנָה *pānâ*

I. Etymology, Meaning, Occurrences. II. Turn: 1. Local; 2. Temporal; 3. Persons. III. Theological Usage: 1. Yahweh; 2. Israel. IV. LXX. V. Dead Sea Scrolls.

I. Etymology, Meaning, Occurrences. The root *_pan,_ probably originally a biliteral (cf. Ugar. *pn*)[1] occurs in all the Semitic languages.[2] In Ethiopic it appears only as a verb. In Hebrew it is treated as a hollow verb. Because the noun *pānîm,* "face," is much more frequent, most scholars assume that the verb *pn(h)* derives from the subst. *_pan._[3] Von Soden, too, believes that *panû(m),* "turn," is a denominative from *pānu* I, "front, pl. face."[4]

We may assume the basic meaning "turn" in all the Semitic languages; also associated with this meaning are Eth. *fanawa,* "send," and Arab. *faniya,* "pass away"; cf. Tigr. *fanna,* "be transitory." Heb. *pānâ* may originally have meant "turn one's face," then "turn" in general.[5] This theory may be supported by the observation that the turning of the face is denied explicitly when the text speaks of turning someone's back (Jer. 2:27; 32:33). But other texts speak of turning the back (Josh. 7:12; Jer. 48:39) or the

pānâ. O. Bächli, "Von der Liste zur Beschreibung," *ZDPV* 89 (1973) 1-14; P. Dhorme, "L'emploi métaphorique des noms des parties du corps en hébreu et en akkadien, III," *RB* 30 (1921) 374-99; J. A. Fitzmyer, *The Aramaic Inscriptions of Sefîre. BietOr* 19 (1967), esp. 110-11; P. Fronzaroli, *Studi sul lessico comune semitico I/II. AANLR* VIII/19 (1964), esp. 255, 269; E. Lipiński, "Peninna, Iti'el et l'athlète," *VT* 17 (1967) 68-75; W. W. Müller, "Altsüdarabische Beiträge zum hebräischen Lexikon," *ZAW* 75 (1963) 304-16; F. Nötscher, *"Das Angesicht Gottes schauen" nach biblischer und babylonischer Auffassung* (1924, ^{2}1969); J. Reindl, *Das Angesicht Gottes im Sprachgebrauch des ATs. ETS* 25 (1970); A. S. van der Woude, "פָּנִים *pānîm* face," *TLOT,* II, 995-1014; J. Ziegler, "Die Hilfe Gottes 'am Morgen,'" *Alttestamentliche Studien. FS F. Nötscher. BBB* 1 (1950) 281-88; → פָּנִים *pānîm.*

1. *WUS,* no. 2230.
2. Fronzaroli, 255, 269; *HAL,* III, 937.
3. Dhorme, 376 n. 3; Nötscher, 4, citing H. Holma, *Die Namen der Körperteile im Assyrisch-Babylonischen* (1911), 13.
4. *AHw,* II, 822b.
5. Nötscher, 3.

shoulder (1 S. 10:9) without mentioning the face. Roughly two-thirds of all the passages with the qal have a human subject (to which should be added some 13 in which Yahweh is the subj.); the subject is always human with the hiphil, and with 5 instances of the piel (plus 3 with Yahweh as subj.); only in 15 texts does *pānâ* have an inanimate subject. This observation suggests taking the implicit basic meaning "turn one's face" as our starting point.

The verb occurs 116 times in the qal and 8 times each in the piel and hiphil. Two texts (Jer. 49:8; Ezk. 9:2) are cited for the hophal, but this was probably not the original reading. Elsewhere when Ezekiel uses *pānâ* to describe the position of the gate (e.g., 8:3), the form is the qal participle, so that 9:2 should probably be read *happōneh* also. In Jeremiah turning to flee is expressed by means of the hiphil (46:5,21; 49:24), so that 49:8 also should probably be vocalized as *hapnû*. In neither text does the meaning of the clause require a hophal.

II. Turn.

1. *Local.* In many cases *pānâ* denotes an anticipated or incipient change of place. The change may be indefinite, when it is not clear where the road might lead (Gen. 24:29). One may also turn deliberately in all directions to be sure the coast is clear (Ex. 2:12) before carrying out an intended action. Frequently, however, someone turns in a specific direction before setting out. For example, the Philistines raiders turn in the direction they intend to go (1 S. 13:17-18). Conversely, the "daughters of Jerusalem" do not know in what direction the beloved has gone, whom they wish to seek in the company of the bride (Cant. 6:1).

An impersonal subject may also be used with *pānâ* to indicate direction. The course of a boundary may be defined in this way (Josh. 15:2,7). The observer follows the boundary as it moves. In architectural descriptions *pānâ* likewise serves to indicate direction; for example, it defines the orientation of the oxen supporting the bronze sea (1 K. 7:25). In Ezekiel's temple visions, the gates are "turned" in the direction from which one approaches the building or the gates (Ezk. 8:3; 9:2; 11:1; 43:1; 46:1,12,19; 47:2). Their exterior or facade "faces" east. In the case of the altar (43:17), the steps leading up to it are on the east side of its base. The person describing the layout appears to be standing inside the temple. Ezk. 10:11, describing the movement of Yahweh's chariot throne, also fits with this oriented vision. The wheels are not allowed to turn in any direction they choose. The direction the front wheel faces determines the direction of the others.

In the Deuteronomistic view, by describing the route and the destination toward which Israel must turn at God's command, Yahweh guided the occupation of the promised land. The men Moses sent to spy out the land (Nu. 13:1, at Yahweh's command) turned toward the hill country (Dt. 1:24), explored it, and returned with their report. The Lord had already decreed the beginning of the occupation, commanding the Israelites to go up into the hill country of the Amorites (Dt. 1:7). After the spies reported, when the people murmured and refused to believe, Yahweh revoked the command to enter into the promised land and decreed that Israel should turn once more to the wilderness and set off in the direction of Sea of Reeds (Dt. 1:40; Nu. 14:25), which they did (Dt. 2:1). After the people had spent many days fruitlessly circling Mt. Seir, Yahweh opened the way to Transjordan (v. 3); Israel adopted the new route ordained by their God, heading out along the road to the wilderness of Moab (v. 8) and then turning north toward Bashan (3:1; cf. Nu. 21:33). All these changes of route, commanded by God, are concrete signs of God's guidance. Even Israel's departure from the place chosen to celebrate Passover (Dt. 16:7) was governed by God.

Elijah, too, even when not actively carrying out his prophetic ministry, is subject to the authority of God's guidance: Yahweh orders him to go to Wadi Cherith to escape the famine (1 K. 17:3).

Texts use *pānâ* deliberately to mark turning points in the course of a narrative. When someone turns from one locus of action to another, a new scene begins. The men who are God's messengers turn to go toward Sodom (Gen. 18:22); in the account of the plagues, Pharaoh turns away to express his indifference (Ex. 7:23), and Moses turns and leaves without waiting for Pharaoh's answer (10:6). When the queen of Sheba turns to go home (1 K. 10:13), her sojourn with Solomon is over. In the story of the golden calf, Moses' turning as commanded by Yahweh (Ex. 32:15) signals more than a simple change of scene: the narrative takes a decisive turn, the image is destroyed, the tablets of the law are shattered as a sign that the covenant has been broken (cf. also Dt. 9:15ff.). Moses' next encounter with God is followed by a redemptive turning (Dt. 10:5) that marks an act of great significance for Deuteronomistic theology: Moses places the tablets in the ark of the covenant.

When Saul turns and sees the Amalekite (2 S. 1:7), he makes the decision to end his life. Abner's dispute with Asahel turns to disaster for the latter: he is slain. When Naaman the Aramean turns away disillusioned and angry (2 K. 5:12), he is in danger of losing his chance to be healed. With the statement that he will turn elsewhere, Abraham's servant forces a decision (Gen. 24:49). By turning back, both the Danites and Micah indicate that nothing more can be done (Jgs. 18:21,26).

When the occupation of the land west of the Jordan is complete, Joshua releases the East Jordanian tribes to go to their territories (Josh. 22:4), documenting from the Deuteronomistic perspective that they have fulfilled Moses' commission (Dt. 3:18ff.). For Deuteronomistic theology it is also important not simply to state (2 K. 23:16) that there were tombs in the vicinity of Bethel from which bones were taken to defile the altar at Bethel, but to ascribe the initiative to Josiah: he turns, sees the tombs, and burns the bones on the altar, "according to the word of the Lord that the man of God proclaimed" (1 K. 13:2).

In battle, when the combatants turn and look about them, it is clear that the situation has shifted against them (Josh. 8:20; Jgs. 20:40; 2 Ch. 13:14) or in their favor (2 Ch. 20:24). If the situation is unfavorable and victory is out of reach, they turn their backs to the enemy (Josh. 7:12; Jer. 48:39) or turn to flee (Jgs. 20:42,45,47; Isa. 13:14; Jer. 46:5,21; 49:8,24; Nah. 2:9[Eng. v. 8]). The same thing happens when the Lord visits his punishment on his enemies.

The expression "wherever he turns" (1 S. 14:47; 1 K. 2:3 [2nd person]) means "whatever he undertakes." When people turn toward their vineyard (Job 24:18), the intent is to work it, to see and harvest its fruit. In a similar vein, Qohelet (2:11-12) turns in his mind toward all the works he has done, considers the effort expended, and then turns to wisdom. He concludes that there is no real advantage or gain in either.

The interpretation of Hag. 1:9 is difficult. The prophet tells his listeners that they "turn to much, and lo, to little." The context, which speaks of sowing and reaping, suggests the expected harvest. The words may mean "you looked forward to much." Or they may refer in general to everything undertaken.

We come finally to the piel, which has the meaning "clean up" and is also important in theological usage.[6] Laban cleans his house (Gen. 24:31) to make room for the servant and his small caravan. A house is to be cleaned out before the priest comes to examine its "leprosy"[7] (Lev. 14:36), so that its furnishings will not become unclean and hence unusable.

2. *Temporal.* Turning (toward or away) naturally implies a temporal aspect, a before and after. Sometimes, though, it is the time periods themselves that "turn" and thus occasion a specific situation. One formula speaks of the coming of evening (Gen. 24:63; Dt. 23:12), when the day declines (Jer. 6:4), turning to depart, or the turn of morning at break of day (Ex. 14:27; Jgs. 19:26; Ps. 46:6[5]). At this hour of dawn the fate of Israel was decided at the Sea of Reeds and catastrophe was averted by God's help. This notion of divine help at dawn was then incorporated into the theology of the Holy City in one of the Zion psalms (Ps. 46:6[5]).[8] With the coming of evening, the Deuteronomic theory of the purity of Israel's camp allows someone who has become unclean to wash with water and reenter the camp (Dt. 23:12[11]), so as not to have to remain outside the camp during the baneful night. But the psalmist associates the disaster consequent on God's anger with the turning point of all his days (Ps. 90:9): they will come to an end. Aware of how transitory life is, the psalmist appeals to the eternal God to have compassion on him, to deliver him from guilt, and to make glad the days of his life.

3. *Persons.* Turning clearly takes on special overtones when one turns toward a person. The result can be beneficial, as in the case of Merib-baal, to whom David showed favor because he did obeisance (2 S. 9:8). This turning to show favor should bring help in distress (cf. Jer. 47:3). This is the purpose of Job's repeated request (Job 6:28; 21:5). Job's friends should hear him, listen to his arguments, put themselves in his position, take his words seriously, and not argue at cross-purposes. In relationships between states and nations, observance of treaties (Ezk. 17:6) — but not false reliance (Ezk. 29:16) — should mark ties of favor.

But turning to someone is not always beneficial. Abner turns and slays Asahel (2 S. 2:20). Elisha turns to the small boys who have been jeering at him and curses them, bringing about their destruction (2 K. 2:24). Someone who gives a bribe is not interested in another's welfare but in private advantage. As Prov. 17:8 avers, bribes always

---

6. See III below.
7. → צרעת *ṣāra'aṯ.*
8. → II, 227-28.

seem to succeed. Before passing judgment, one should address the situation and examine it thoroughly, as Aaron did in the case of Miriam (Nu. 12:10) and the priests did in the case of Uzziah (2 Ch. 26:20).

Looking back over the varied uses of the verb *pānâ,* we can probably summarize them as follows: *pānâ* expresses a change in the course of an event or act, the beginning of an action, a purposeful orientation. What all this means specifically is expressed by the statements of the particular context. This summary applies to the qal and hiphil. In the piel, however, *pnh* takes on the meaning "clean up, clean out." In large measure if not predominantly, the meaning of the verb can be expressed by the statement that someone or something "turns."[9] The subsequent text describes or reveals the result and consequences. Similar observations may be made with respect to theological usage.

III. Theological Usage.

1. *Yahweh.* The Holiness Code (Lev. 17–25) is followed by a promise of blessing if Israel is obedient; here Yahweh promises his people: "I will turn toward you" (26:9; NRSV "I will look with favor upon you"). Vv. 9-13 expand on what this means: Yahweh will make his people fruitful and multiply them, will place his dwelling in their midst, walk among them, not abhor them, and make them walk erect once more after delivering them from slavery in Egypt. All these blessings are inherent in God's favor and are bestowed with it. The same is true of the oracle addressed to the mountains of Israel, to which the Lord will turn once more (Ezk. 36:9). They will be verdant and yield fruit for Israel, so that the people may return. They will be tilled and sown. Many human beings and animals will live there, and the towns will be rebuilt. When Yahweh turned away, the land fell victim to the judgment of desolation. His turning again in favor brings new life.

In order to deliver his people, God can also turn to an individual, as in the case of Gideon (Jgs. 6:14). There follows a mandate commissioning him to deliver Israel. The Lord refutes Gideon's objection and declares his willingness to give a sign that he is with his elect. When Yahweh turns to someone, it is a serious promise of favor and constancy, so that the person in question can rely on Yahweh's help. In Solomon's prayer at the dedication of the temple, therefore, before his specific petitions, he says: "Turn to [NRSV 'regard'] your servant's prayer and his plea, O Lord my God" (1 K. 8:28). The psalmists address the same plea to their God with the same basic expectation. One afflicted psalmist, suffering from a sense of guilt and persecution by enemies, pleads for God's grace and forgiveness, asking to be delivered from fear and to be saved (Ps. 25:16). A worshiper who is unjustly persecuted prays for mercy (69:17[16]), a favorable hearing, God's presence, and deliverance: "Do not hide your face from your servant" (v. 18[17]). Another who is poor and needy finds in God's gracious favor the promise of new strength and, quite generally, effectual help (86:16). Also the scribe who would follow the teachings of the Lord looks for God to turn in

9. *HP,* 22.

gracious favor (119:132) and vouchsafe instruction, steady his steps, redeem him, and grant him salvation: "Make your face shine upon your servant" (v. 135). A sick worshiper, praying that God will not hide his face and thus prolong the petitioner's distress (102:3[2]), expresses confidence that the Lord regards the prayer of the destitute (v. 18[17]).

Insofar as sacrifice represents humble submission and a plea for forgiveness, coupled with a forthright effort to do God's will, Yahweh turns to accept it (cf. Mal. 2:13) and graciously favors those who offer the sacrifice. This explains why, when Korah, Dathan, and Abiram revolt, Moses prays that Yahweh will not turn to accept (NRSV "pay attention to") their offering (Nu. 16:15). But if Yahweh addresses the obduracy of his people, their guilt and their sin, then they are in imminent danger of being destroyed. Moses seeks to avert this destruction through his intercession (Dt. 9:27).

If Yahweh turns away (*pnh* piel, Zeph. 3:15) the enemies who have beset and oppressed his people, he clears the ground for them once more, as he did at the time of the occupation (Ps. 80:10).

As for Yahweh's turning in favor toward his people, at the end of the Elisha story (2 K. 13:23) the author (probably Dtr) manages to strike a positive balance, but against a menacing background: the Lord turns once more toward Israel on account of his covenant with Israel's ancestors; he is not yet ready to reject and destroy Israel. Later, however, this author must record Yahweh's turning away and its consequences (2 K. 17).

2. *Israel.* Israel should always turn toward their God, as a psalmist who has experienced deliverance counsels in a hymn of thanksgiving (Ps. 40:2-12[1-11]): happy are those who trust in the Lord, who do not turn to the proud and to faithless liars (v. 5[4]). Trust and confidence are in fact required of those who turn to someone in expectation of being accepted and receiving help. When the people, suffering hunger after the exodus from Egypt, respond to the word of Moses communicated through Aaron, it is in this expectation that they turn to the wilderness, to Yahweh, who also appears in his *kāḇôḏ* (Ex. 16:10). When the Israelites assemble against Moses and Aaron, the latter turn toward the tent of meeting, i.e., toward Yahweh, who again appears in his glory (Nu. 17:7) and punishes the people until Aaron makes atonement for them.

In an oracle of salvation that is also addressed to other nations (Isa. 45:22), the prophet promises salvation to all who turn to Yahweh. Because Yahweh is the only God, there is no other who can save. It is indispensable to turn to him. In a later period, when faith came to picture a more transcendent God surrounded by hosts of angels, people in distress were apparently wont to turn to "the holy ones" (angels) who could serve as mediators between the supplicant and God (Job 5:1). Eliphaz probably looks on the appeal as a last recourse, which he nonetheless rejects.

Deuteronomistic theology is forced to conclude that Israel's heart has turned away from its God (Dt. 30:17) and turned to other gods (31:18) to serve them. Then Israel breaks the covenant and is therefore under the curse. On that day, the Lord will surely hide his face. The Song of Moses (32:1-43) bears witness (31:20-21) against the people, unfolding God's gracious favor as well as the injustice and peril of idolatry.

Hos. 3:1b is clearly a Deuteronomistic addition, interpolating an interpretive gloss that interrupts the flow of the symbolic action by drawing a premature conclusion. It is an expansion of the word "adulteress" *(m^e^nā'āpeṯ),* referring to Israel: Yahweh's love for his faithless people, who have turned to other gods, is here understood as pedagogic. The symbolic action, however, speaks of depriving Israel of communion with God and its benefits (v. 4). To turn to other gods is to transgress the first commandment of the Decalogue. Lev. 19:4 therefore demands: "Do not turn to (other) gods [NRSV 'idols']."

Jer. 2:27 and 32:22 use an eloquent image to describe the apostasy from Yahweh implicit in idolatry: "They turn their backs to me and not their faces." In 2:27 we may also have an allusion to magical ceremonies associated with the worship of foreign gods. Such practices are clearly behind Dt. 29:17(18), which warns everyone not to turn away from the Lord and bless themselves in their idolatry with a blessing intended to contravene the curse brought on by transgression of the covenant. Isa. 8:21-22 also warns against turning to dark forces, including ghosts and wizards (v. 19). For those who do so there will be no dawn, no hope. Lev. 19:31 and 20:6 accordingly forbid turning to mediums and soothsayers. They render those who resort to them unclean, depriving them of the possibility of turning to Yahweh, who will turn his face against them and cut them off from among the people. The people should instead consult their God and take refuge in him (Isa. 8:19). God has told Israel how it is to live; and wisdom, too, admonishes Israel not to turn to iniquity (Job 36:21). Nevertheless, those surrounding the Suffering Servant must confess that they have turned to their own way and gone astray (Isa. 53:6). This passage may suggest — as in the case of Israel's leaders (56:11) — that every individual is pursuing his or her own advantage.

It is difficult to determine the precise meaning of 1 S. 10:9: "And it came to pass [reading *wyhy* instead of *whyh*], when he [Saul] turned his shoulder to leave Samuel. . . ."[10] The text appears to say that Saul turned his back on Samuel. Is it intended to suggest that he was already at odds with Samuel and hence with the prophet and with Yahweh?

The theological meaning of *pnh* in the piel requires special mention. Theological texts make use of the meaning "clean up, remove." Isa. 40:3 promises that a way will be prepared in the wilderness for the return of the exiles to Jerusalem. The impv. *pannû* refers in the first instance to the removal of obstacles. The road is to be constructed by the heavenly powers to whom the imperative is clearly addressed. It is the way of Yahweh, on which he will return to Zion with his liberated people. Isa. 57:14 cites the imperative of 40:3. Here it is to be understood figuratively: purge your lives and conduct of everything that obstructs the coming of salvation. Isa. 40:3 is cited once again in 62:10: now those already dwelling in Jerusalem are called on to remove the obstacles that "prevent the many Israelites still abroad from returning to Jerusalem."[11]

---

10. See ibid., 59 n. 93.
11. C. Westermann, *Isaiah 40–66. OTL* (Eng. trans. 1969), 379.

IV. LXX. The LXX predictably uses the roughly synonymous *stréphein* and its compounds to translate *pānâ* (some 42 times). Equally often (some 45 times), however, it uses *blépein* and its compounds. In these cases the translator is probably influenced by *pānîm.* Job 5:1 uses *horán,* as though the text has to do with a vision of angels — a sign that Job is innocent? It is noteworthy that *blépein* also appears in the Ezekiel texts referring to the orientation of a gate or building. A series of passages, including the Psalms in which the supplicant appeals to God (24[MT 25]:16; 39[40]:5[4]; 68[69]:17[16]; 85[86]:16; 101[12]:18[17]; 118[119]:132), use *epiblépein:* the afflicted psalmist looks up to God, and Yahweh looks upon his people (Ezk. 36:9).

With verbs of motion *pānâ* is frequently translated interpretively on the basis of its context and changed into a longer expression beginning with "turn." Examples include Ezk. 29:16, *akoloutheín;* Dt. 29:18(17), *ekklínein;* Ps. 89(90):9, *ekleípein;* 2 K. 2:24; 23:16, *ekneúein;* Isa. 56:11, *exakoloutheín;* Lev. 19:4, *epakoloutheín;* Josh. 15:7, *katabaínein;* Jer. 6:4, *klínein;* Dt. 30:17, *methistán;* Nu. 17:7, *hormán;* Isa. 53:6, *planásthai;* Nu. 16:15, *proséchein.* In temporal statements *pānâ* is translated with *tó prós (hespéran)* (Dt. 23:11[12]) and *tó prós (prōí)* (Ps. 45[46]:6[5]).

To translate the piel, the LXX uses *aposkeuázein* in Lev. 14:36, *hetoimázein* in Gen. 24:31 and Isa. 40:3, and *hodopoieín* in Isa. 62:10 and Ps. 79:10(MT 80:9). In other words, it associates Yahweh's "cleaning up" not with the expulsion of the nations from the promised land but with God's guidance of Israel along the way to Canaan.

V. Dead Sea Scrolls. The Qumran community found in Isa. 40:3 an important insight into its self-understanding and the mission entrusted to it by God. It saw itself "set apart from the midst of the habitation of the men of wickedness to go into the wilderness and the prepare the way of the Lord. . . . This is the study of the law that he commanded through Moses, to act in compliance with all that has been revealed from time to time, and according to what the prophets have revealed through his holy spirit" (1QS 8:13-16). Preparing the way means that the men of the community "walk uprightly each with his neighbor in all that has been revealed to them" (9:19). The Damascus Document warns the members of the community not to reject and forsake God's precepts and turn aside in the stubbornness of their hearts (CD 8:19; 19:33). In the *Hodayot* the worshiper cites Gen. 1 to designates the time to praise God: in the evening and in the morning (1QH 12:5-6). In 1QH 8 it appears that the teacher of righteousness thanks God for choosing him to carry out the critical task of instructing the community; he says: "And by my hand you have opened their spring with (its) channels . . . to turn according to a reliable measuring line" (8:21). He pictures the community as a plantation, to which he vouchsafes teaching and instruction according to God's will.

Schreiner

פִּנָּה *pinnâ*

I. Etymology; Occurrences. II. Meaning: 1. Architecture; 2. Sociology; 3. Theology. III. LXX. IV. Dead Sea Scrolls.

I. Etymology; Occurrences. The etymology of *pinnâ* is uncertain. There are three possibilities: (1) it may derive from a root **pnn* not attested in Hebrew, which can be interpreted as a by-form of → פנה *pānâ,* "turn (back)";[1] (2) we may be dealing with an independent root meaning "divide," analogous to Arab. *fanna* II, "make different, mix";[2] (3) it may represent a nominal extension of Heb. → פנים *pānîm.*[3]

The word occurs 30 times in the OT: 18 times in the singular, 11 times in the pl. form *pinnôṯ,* and once in the pl. form *pinnîm* (Zec. 14:10). It is distributed as follows: twice in Exodus; 4 times in the Deuteronomistic History; twice in Isaiah; 3 times in Jeremiah; twice each in Ezekiel, Zephaniah, and Zechariah; once in Psalms; twice in Job; 4 times in Proverbs; 3 times each in Nehemiah and Chronicles.

II. Meaning.

1. *Architecture.* The vast majority of occurrences (23) are in structural contexts. Here *pinnâ* denotes the point where the straight of a street (Prov. 7:8,12; 2 Ch. 28:24) or a wall changes direction, with a sharp bend in contrast to a curve (*ḥāmûq,* Cant. 7:2). In particular, there was a prominent and familiar angle in the city wall of Jerusalem, probably on the north or northeast side (Neh. 3:24,31,32); on the northwest side (facing the new city?) there was a corner gate referred to as *šaʿar happinnâ* (2 K. 14:13; Jer. 31:38; 2 Ch. 26:9). Only in Zec. 14:10, where the site of eschatological Jerusalem is probably described in terms of the city's greatest extent, is the gate called *šaʿar happinnîm.* The widely accepted theory that we are dealing here with a gloss (and a corrupt text to boot) is dubious. More likely we have here a deliberately archaizing expression intended to conjure up the preexilic city. This interpretation is supported by

---

pinnâ. J. Jeremias, "Der Eckstein," *Angelos* 1 (1925) 65-70; idem, "Eckstein — Schlußstein," *ZNW* 36 (1937) 154-57; idem, "Κεφαλὴ γωνίας — Ἀκρογωνιαῖος," *ZNW* 29 (1930) 264-80; idem, "λίθος," *TDNT,* IV, 268-80; L. Köhler, "Zwei Fachworte der Bausprache in Jesaja 28,16," *TZ* 3 (1947) 390-93; J. Lindblom, "Der Eckstein in Jes 28,16," *Interpretationes ad Vetus Testamentum Pertinentes. FS S. Mowinckel. NoTT* 56 (1955) 123-32; U. Maiburg, "Christus der Eckstein," *Vivarium. FS T. Klauser. JAC Erganzungsband* 11 (1984), 247-56; H. Merklein, *Das kirchliche Amt nach dem Epheserbrief. SANT* 33 (1973), esp. 144-52; H. Muszyński, *Fundament, Bild und Metapher in den Handschriften aus Qumran. AnBibl* 61 (1975); J. van der Ploeg, "Les chefs du peuple d'Israel et leurs titres," *RB* 57 (1950) 40-61; K. T. Schäfer, "Lapis summus angularis," *FS H. Lützeler* (1962), 9-23; idem, "Zur Deutung von ἀκρογωνιαῖος," *Neutestamentliche Aufsätze. FS J. Schmid* (1963), 218-24.

1. *GesB,* 650; *HAL,* III, 944.
2. Wehr, 728.
3. Cf. A. S. van der Woude, *TLOT,* II, 995.

the explicit words "at the location of the former gate" *(šaʿar hāriʾšôn),* especially since Neh. 3 makes no more mention of this corner gate. By synecdoche, in the sense of "corner tower, bastion," *pinnâ* could also mean "fortress, battlement" (Zeph. 3:6).[4] There is no evidence that *pinnâ* was a technical term for the salients of a stepped wall like that found at Arad.[5]

Six texts use *pinnâ* in conjunction with *ʾarbaʿ* for the four corners of a house (Job 1:19), the altar (Ex. 27:2; 38:2), the altar ledge (Ezk. 27:2; 38:2), and the stands for wheeled basins (1 K. 7:34).

For the theological meaning of the word, scholars (primarily NT scholars) have extensively debated whether the phrase *rōʾš/ʾeḇen pinnâ* denoted only the copestone of a building[6] or was used exclusively for the cornerstone of the foundation, the foundation stone.[7] The evidence of the OT does not permit a decision one way or the other as to the architectural meaning of the term. Prov. 21:9; 25:24 *(pinnaṯ-gāg);* and Zeph. 1:16 *(happinnôṯ haggᵉḇōhôṯ)* clearly require the meaning "capstone (of a roof), pinnacle" (cf. also Zeph. 3:6; 2 Ch. 26:15). On the other hand, Job 38:6 clearly refers to a "cornerstone." In Jer. 51:26 it is not clear whether *lᵉpinnâ* stands in synonymous parallelism with *lᵉmôsāḏôṯ*[8] and means "cornerstone" or is intended as an antithetical merism denoting the totality from cornerstone to "pinnacle."

2. *Sociology.* In Jgs. 20:2; 1 S. 14:38; Isa. 19:13 (par. *śārîm*); Zec. 10:4; and possibly Zeph. 3:6 (par. *gôyîm*), *pinnâ* is used figuratively for the leadership of society. The metaphor *pinnôṯ kol-hāʿām* can thus mean both the "pillars of the community" and the most exalted pinnacles, "high society." It can hardly be demonstrated that a specific function or office was associated with this title.[9]

3. *Theology.* In the context of an oracular threat against illusory trust in (anti-Assyrian) alliances (on the part of Hezekiah against Sennacherib?), Isa. 28:16 clearly presents a *pinnaṯ yiqraṯ mûsāḏ* (par. *ʾeḇen bōḥan*) as an alternative. The uncertain temporal reference of the main verb *(hinᵉnî yissaḏ)* makes it difficult to interpret this "precious cornerstone of the foundation" (or possibly: "corner where one foundation wall meets another"):[10] Are we dealing with an elective act of Yahweh in the past (the selection of Zion as the foundation of the temple and the navel [= keystone] of the earth or the Davidic monarchy)? Or does the text refer to a future act (preservation of a "remnant" of the faithful [cf. Qumran] or the messiah)? Or — if the oracle is exilic or even postexilic — might it not refer to the community of returnees and the new temple? Or, as v. 16bβ ("one who trusts will not panic") would suggest, is faith in the present hour

---

4. W. Rudolph, *Micha-Nahum-Habakuk-Zephanja. KAT* XIII/3 (1975), 286.
5. Cf. R. de Vaux, *AncIsr,* I, 233.
6. J. Jeremias et al.
7. Esp. Schäfer; see the survey of the discussion in Merklein, 144-52.
8. See R. Moses, → VI, 113.
9. Van der Ploeg, 51, 60.
10. Köhler.

likened here to the cornerstone set into the foundation (LXX *eis tá themélia*), which undergirds the stability and alignment of the whole building and alone gives it endurance (cf. Isa. 7:9)?[11]

Ps. 118 is the reflex of a dynamic liturgical thanksgiving ritual with several changes of speaker, in which an individual who has been delivered from death expresses thanksgiving to God in the temple, in and with the congregation. V. 22 interprets the worshiper's deliverance as a communal confession of faith, using the image of a stone that — although rejected by presumably expert builders — God's miraculous intervention has nevertheless made the cornerstone (*lerō'š pinnâ,* with *rō'š* probably to be understood not vertically as the topmost stone but horizontally as the foremost; cf. Ezk. 16:25,31; Isa. 51:20). This image has a complex history of interpretation:[12] Jewish exegesis and (frequently) critical Christian exegesis interprets the "I" of the psalm collectively as standing for Israel, which recalls in a national thanksgiving observance the miraculous reversal of its fate when all appeared to be lost — possibly following the completion of the city wall under Nehemiah in the face of general hostility or after the victories of the Maccabees. There has been an increasing tendency, however, to interpret the "I" individually — not so much as a specific historical figure like a king (Hezekiah, Josiah, Jehoiachin) or the coming messiah, but as an "exemplary I." On the basis of personal experience, the speaker of the psalm bears witness to God's typical way of dealing with human existence: God restores to life and fellowship those who seem to be rejected and makes proclamation of their deliverance the focus of congregational worship for the purpose of "edification."

III. LXX. The LXX usually uses *gōnía* or *(akro)gōniaíos (líthos)* to translate *pinnâ,* less frequently *kampḗ* (Neh. 3:24,31) or *klíma* (Jgs. 20:2). By the addition of *ep' autǭ* in Isa. 28:16 ("one who trusts *in him*"), the LXX promotes a messianic interpretation, which is suggested in Ps. 118:22 as well as by inclusion of an explicative *hoútos* ("*this one* has become the cornerstone").

IV. Dead Sea Scrolls. The noun *pinnâ* occurs 33 times in the extant Dead Sea Scrolls; 30 of these occurrences are in the Temple Scroll. The phrase *pny hmgdl* in 1QM 9:13 is uncertain: "corners *or* front of the tower." All but two of the occurrences refer to structural elements. In particular, the Temple Scroll uses the noun for the corners of the altar, of the ideal new temple, and courts arranged in order of increasing holiness.

In 2Q23 1:6,[13] an apocryphal prophetic woe pronounced upon the wicked inhabitants of a city, whose name has not been preserved (Jerusalem?), threatens them with being overthrown *m'bn pnh,* which must mean "from the pinnacle stone" (cf. 2 Ch. 25:12). Only in what is probably the earliest section of the Community Rule (1QS 8:7)

---

11. On the various interpretations of the cornerstone oracle see, e.g., O. Kaiser, *Isaiah 13–39. OTL* (Eng. trans. 1974), 252ff.; H. Wildberger, *Jesaja 28–39. BK* X/3 (1982), 1075ff.

12. On earlier interpretations see H. Hupfeld and W. Nowack, *Die Psalmen,* II (^{3}1888), 521ff.; on recent proposals see H.-J. Kraus, *Psalms 60–150* (Eng. trans. 1989), 399-400.

13. M. Baillet, *DJD,* III, 82-83.

do we find an example of figurative theological usage. Here Isa. 28:16 is given a quasi-ecclesiological interpretation and made to refer to the foundation of the community, which understands itself as the "precious cornerstone" consisting of the ones maintaining the true faith.[14]

Oeming

---

14. See Muszyński, 174-93; C. Dohmen, *RevQ* 11 (1982/84) 86-87.

פָּנִים *pānîm*

I. Etymology. II. Distribution. III. Nominal Usage: 1. Objects; 2. Cosmic Entities; 3. Animals; 4. Humans; 5. Yahweh; 6. Construct *pānîm.* IV. Idioms and Collocations: 1. *pānîm bᵉ/ʾel-pānîm;* 2. *bqš pānîm;* 3. *hēʾîr pānîm;* 4. *ḥlh pānîm;* 5. *nśʾ/hdr pānîm;* 6. *ntn/śym pānîm;* 7. *sbb/swr/šwb pānîm;* 8. *ksh/str pānîm;* 9. *rʾh/ḥzh pānîm.* V. Semantic and Theological Assessment. VI. Prepositional Usage: 1. *lipnê;* 2. *millipnê;* 3. *mippᵉnê;* 4. *(mē)ʿal-pᵉnê;* 5. *ʾeṯ/mēʾēṯ-pᵉnê;* 6. *ʾel- pᵉnê;* 7. Other Prepositions; 8. Adverbial Usage. VII. LXX. VIII. Dead Sea Scrolls.

---

pānîm. S. E. Balentine, "A Description of the Semantic Field of Hebrew Words for 'Hide,'" *VT* 30 (1980) 137-53; idem, *The Hidden God* (1983); J. Barr, "Theophany and Anthropomorphism in the OT," *Congress Volume, Oxford 1959. SVT* 7 (1960), 31-38; W. W. Graf Baudissin, "'Gott schauen' in der alttestamentlichen Religion," *ARW* 18 (1915) 173-239; repr. in F. Nötscher, *"Das Angesicht Gottes schauen" nach biblischer und babylonischer Auffassung* (²1969), 193-261; J. Böhmer, "Gottes Angesicht," *BFCT* 12 (1908) 323-47; P. A. H. de Boer, "An Aspect of Sacrifice," *Studies in the Religion of Ancient Israel. SVT* 23 (1972), 27-47, esp. 27-36; G. C. Bottini, "'Pose la sua faccia tra le ginocchia,'" *SBFLA* 32 (1982) 73-84; W. H. Brownlee, "'Son of Man Set Your Face,'" *HUCA* 54 (1983) 83-110; J. Carmignac, "Le complément d'agent après un verbe passif dans l'Hébreu et l'Araméen de Qumrân," *RevQ* 9 (1978) 409-27, esp. 421-27; E. Dhorme, "L'emploi métaphorique des noms des parties du corps en hébreu et en akkadien. III. Le visage," *RB* 30 (1921) 374-99; L. Díez Merino, "Il vocabolario relativo alla ricerca di Dio nell'Antico Testamento," *BeO* 24 (1982) 129-45; 25 (1983) 35-38; J. F. Drinkard, "*ʿal pĕnê* as 'East of,'" *JBL* 98 (1979) 285-86; M. Fishbane, "Form and Reformulation of the Biblical Priestly Blessing," *FS S. N. Kramer = JAOS* 103 (1983) 115-21; M. D. Fowler, "The Meaning of *lipnê* YHWH in the OT," *ZAW* 99 (1987) 384-90; C. T. Fritsch, "A Study of the Greek Translation of the Hebrew Verbs 'to see,' with Deity as Subject or Object," *FS H. M. Orlinsky = ErIsr* 16 (1982) 51*-57*; O. Garcia de la Fuente, "'David buscó el rostro de Yahweh' (2 Sm 21,1)," *Aug* 8 (1968) 477-540; Y. Gil, *"kî qāran ʿôr pᵉnê mōšeh," BethM* 30 (1984/85) 341-44; M. I. Gruber, "The Many Faces of Hebrew נשא פנים 'lift up the face,'" *ZAW* 95 (1983) 252-60; E. G. Gulin, "Das Antlitz Jahwes im AT," *AnAcScFen* B 17/3 (1923), 1-30; B. Halpern, "Yhwh's Summary Justice in Job xiv,20," *VT* 28 (1978) 472ff.; M. Haran, "The

I. Etymology. The noun *pānîm* is the Hebrew form of the common Semitic subst. **pan,* "face":[1] Akk. *pānu(m),* "front," pl. "face";[2] Ugar. *pnm,* "face";[3] Phoenician, Punic (noteworthy is the designation of the goddess Tinnit as *pn bʿl,* "countenance of Baal"),[4] Moabite, and Imperial Aramaic;[5] Arab. *finā',* "forecourt"; Syr. *penîṯā,* "side, region"; OSA *fnwt,* "front, in front of."[6] The verb → פנה *pānâ* may be a denominative from *pānîm.*[7] Heb. *pānîm* never occurs in the singular and should be considered a *plurale tantum.*

In Ugaritic and Hebrew the following appear in parallel with *pānîm: ṣr,* "back" (Ps. 97:3); *ymn,* "right side" (Ps. 16:11; 44:4[Eng. v. 3]); *ksl,* "back, loins" (Job 15:27); *p't,* "side" (Lev. 13:41); *pʿm,* "foot, pace" (Ps. 57:7[6]; 85:14[13]); *tmwnh,* "image, likeness" (Ps. 17:15).[8] Of particular interest is that many collocations with *pn(m)* appear also in Hebrew. In Ugaritic we find the expression *ytn pnm ʿm,* "turn one's face toward" (cf. Heb. *śym/ntn pānîm 'el/ʿal*), with reference to sending or going;[9] cf. also *wbhm pn bʿl*[10] (cf. Heb. *śym/ntn pānîm bᵉ,* "turn one's face toward") and the prepositional expression *lpn-,* "before, in(to)/from the presence of." In Aramaic, *lpn-* appears frequently with the meaning "in the presence of, in the opinion/judgment of."

Akkadian above all has many expressions closely related to Heb. *pānîm* collocations. As in Hebrew, the subst. *pānu(m)* means "face, front, top, appearance." Also as in Hebrew, it is used in connection with persons, objects, and cosmic entities (the heav-

---

Shining of Moses' Face," *In the Shelter of Elyon. FS G. W. Ahlström. JSOTSup* 31 (1984), 159-73; A. Jirku, "'Das Haupt auf die Knie legen,'" *ZDMG* 103 (1953) 372; A. R. Johnson, "Aspects of the Use of the Term פָּנִים in the OT," *FS O. Eissfeldt* (1947), 155-59; H.-J. Kraus, *Theology of the Psalms* (Eng. trans. 1986), esp. 38-40; S. C. Layon, "'Head on Lap' in Sumero-Akkadian Literature," *JANES* 15 (1983) 59-62; S. Layton, "Biblical Hebrew 'to Set the Face' in Light of Akkadian and Ugaritic," *UF* 17 (1986) 169-81; R. W. L. Moberly, *At the Mountain of God. JSOTSup* 22 (1983); J. Morgenstern, "Moses with the Shining Face," *HUCA* 2 (1925) 1-27; F. Nötscher, *"Das Angesicht Gottes schauen" nach biblischer und babylonischer Auffassung* (²1969); J. Reindl, *Das Angesicht Gottes im Sprachgebrauch des ATs. ETS* 25 (1970); F. Schnutenhaus, "Das Kommen und Erscheinen Gottes im AT," *ZAW* 76 (1964) 1-22; K. Seybold, *Der aaronitische Segen* (1977); idem, "Reverenz und Gebet," *ZAW* 88 (1976) 2-16; D. C. T. Sheriffs, "The Phrases *ina IGI Dn* and *lipĕnēy Yhwh* in Treaty and Covenant Contexts," *JNSL* 7 (1979) 55-68; R. Sollamo, *Renderings of Hebrew Semiprepositions in the Septuagint. AnAcScFen Dissertationes humanarum litterarum* 19 (1979); M. Tsevat, "קרן עור פניו," *FS H. M. Orlinsky = ErIsr* 16 (1982) 163-67; E. Vogt, "Die vier 'Gesichter' *(pānīm)* der Keruben in Ezechiel," *Bibl* 60 (1979) 327-47; C. Westermann, "Die Begriffe für Fragen und Suchen im AT," *KuD* 6 (1960) 2-30.

1. P. Fronzaroli, *AANLR* VIII/19 (1964), 255, 269.
2. *AHw,* II, 818b-822a.
3. *WUS,* no. 2230; *UT,* no. 2059.
4. *KAI* 78.2, with commentary.
5. *DNSI,* II, 918-20; cf. Biblical Aram. *'ᵃnaf.*
6. Beeston, 45.
7. *HAL,* III, 937.
8. M. Dahood, *RSP,* I, 313-16.
9. Del Olmo Lete, 610.
10. *KTU* 1.12, i, 33.

ens, stars, the surface of the deep). Used figuratively it expresses purpose or intention: *ana ālim pānūšu,* "he intends (to go) to the city" (cf. 2 Ch. 32:2, *pānāyw lammilḥāmāh*). We also find fixed idioms such as "the beaming *(nawārum)* of a face," "cause someone's face to beam" *(p. nummuru),* "seek/behold someone's face" *(p. amāru),* "exercise oversight" *(p. wabālum;* cf. *nś' pānîm),* "direct one's face" *(p. nadānu),* "lower one's face" *(p. quddudu),* "turn one's face toward/away from" *(p. suḫḫuru).* Each of these expressions can have a variety of meanings. As semiprepositions we find such expressions as *ana pān-,* "to, for, opposite," and *ina pān-,* "in view of, in the presence of, before."

In the OT only two proper names incorporating *pānîm* occur: the PN *pᵉnû'ēl* (1 Ch. 4:4; 8:25 *Q*) and the toponym *pᵉnû/î'ēl* (Gen. 32:31-32[30-31]).

II. Distribution. The table on p. 592 (based on Lisowsky) displays the distribution of *pānîm* separately and with its associated prepositions (including *lip̱nê* in 1 K. 6:17; excluding *millip̱nî* in 1 K. 6:29 and *pny* [*Q pî*] in Prov. 15:14).[11] The total in each OT book also includes the occurrences that will be cited below of *pānîm* with other prepositions. Under *'ēṯ* we count both the sign of the accusative and the preposition without distinction. Under *'al* we also include the combination with *kōl ('al-kol-pᵉnê).*

In addition to the prepositional phrases counted in the table, we find *lᵉpānîm* (used adverbially in the sense of "earlier"; including *millᵉpānîm* in Isa. 41:26) (22 times), *'el-mûl* (8), *mimmûl* (2), *mē'ēṯ* (6), *('el-)nōḵaḥ* (6), *negeḏ* (4), *minnegeḏ* (1), *mē'im* (2), *'al-lip̱nê* (1), and *lappānîm* (1).

Formally speaking, the prepositions (except for *bᵉ*) can be divided into two categories: one of which expresses turning toward the object of the preposition, the other of which expresses turning away from the object. The first category comprises *lᵉ, 'el, 'ēṯ, 'al, 'el-mûl, nōḵaḥ,* and *negeḏ;* the second comprises *min* and its compounds. Substantively, it is interesting to note that the use of *pānîm* tends to echo the content of the book in question: Genesis emphasizes *'al (pᵉnê-hā'āreṣ, hā'ᵃḏāmâ),* the "cultic" books (Exodus, Leviticus, Numbers, Deuteronomy) *lip̱nê* (Yahweh, cultic objects), Esther *lip̱nê (hammeleḵ),* Ezekiel, Psalms, and Job *pānîm* without any preposition.

III. Nominal Usage. The word *pānîm* appears as a noun some 400 times in the OT (402 according to Reindl);[12] in most cases it is related to another substantive or a proper name, whether as part of a construct phrase, by means of a possessive suffix, or, in a few instances, through the immediate context. A tenth of its occurrences are associated with objects, more than half with anthropoid beings (including animals and hybrids such as cherubim and seraphim). Somewhat more than one-quarter of the texts refer to Yahweh. It appears semantically inappropriate to postulate for *pānîm* a "literal" or original meaning in one or another of these groups.

---

11. See, respectively, M. Noth, *BK,* IX/1, 100, 102; O. Plöger, *Sprüche Salomos. BK* XVII (1984), 177.

12. P. 8.

	Total	*'el*	*b^e*	*'ēṯ*	*lý*	*millý*	*min*	*'al*	*me'al*	None
Gen	141	1	—	8	56	5	15	28	5	20
Ex	128	2	—	5	62	3	17	9	1	21
Lev	107	4	—	5	76	4	5	5	—	6
Nu	119	2	1	—	83	3	10	13	—	4
Dt	132	3	5	3	67	5	26	9	1	10
Josh	91	1	3	—	51	2	22	9	—	—
Jgs	46	1	—	—	22	—	15	2	—	2
1 S	98	—	—	5	62	3	12	8	1	4
2 S	73	1	—	6	41	1	8	8	—	7
1 K	100	—	—	10	56	3	9	15	3	4
2 K	73	—	—	4	32	2	14	7	6	7
Isa	89	—	—	1	27	2	29	4	1	23
Jer	128	—	—	2	44	4	45	9	6	16
Ezk	155	18	4	4	37	2	5	17	—	64
XII	72	—	2	4	27	3	15	8	3	9
Ps	133	—	—	5	49	6	21	3	—	48
Job	70	2	1	1	16	—	11	11	—	24
Prov	42	—	1	1	22	—	1	1	—	15
Ruth	2	—	—	—	—	—	—	1	—	—
Cant	2	—	—	—	1	—	—	—	—	1
Eccl	21	—	—	—	10	5	1	1	—	4
Lam	11	—	—	—	3	—	3	—	—	3
Est	37	—	—	1	30	4	—	—	—	2
Dnl	33	—	—	3	15	1	—	4	—	10
Ezr	10	—	—	—	7	1	—	—	—	2
Neh	31	1	—	—	23	1	3	—	—	2
1 Ch	63	—	—	—	40	4	10	2	—	5
2 Ch	119	1	—	4	71	9	10	8	1	14
OT	2,126	37	17	72	1,030	73	307	182	28	327

1. *Objects.* In conjunction with objects, *pānîm/p^enê* denotes the part or side facing the observer: the facade of the temple (Ezk. 41:14,21; 46:1) or of a gateway (Ezk. 40:6,15,20), the face of the moon (Job 26:9), the front of a garment (Job 41:5[13]), a battlefront (2 S. 10:9; 11:15; 1 Ch. 19:10), the crux of a situation (2 S. 14:20). In Eccl. 10:10 *pānîm* denotes the cutting edge of a weapon.[13]

2. *Cosmic Entities.* We find *pānîm/p^enê* in combination with various terms denoting elements of the geographical domain. The phrase *p^enê hā'^adāmâ* (Gen. 2:6; 8:13; Ps.

13. A. Lauha, *Kohelet. BK* XIX (1978), 186.

104:30; Prov. 24:31 — *pānāyw*) refers to the surface of the earth or of the land, which can be watered or dried, made habitable or fertile. The expressions *pᵉnê 'ereṣ/hā'āreṣ* (Gen. 19:28; 41:56; Ezk. 34:6), *pᵉnê ṯēḇēl* (Isa. 14:21; 27:6), and *pᵉnê* + city names (Gen. 19:28) do not add any nuances to the nouns they appear with. In Job 38:30 *pᵉnê ṯᵉhôm* is the "surface of the abyss," which can become hard like stone. In Cant. 7:5(4) *pᵉnê dammāśeq* indicates direction. The expression *pᵉnê-X,* referring to elements of the cosmos, can be the object of a verb: renewing (*ḥdš* piel, Ps. 104:30) or laying waste (*'wh* piel, Isa. 24:1) the face of the earth.

3. *Animals.* In conjunction with animals (lion: *'aryēh,* Ezk. 1:10; 10:14; 1 Ch. 12:9; *kᵉpîr,* Ezk. 41:19; eagle: Ezk. 1:10; 10:14; ox: Ezk. 1:10; flocks [of sheep]: Gen. 30:40) and cherubim (Ex. 25:20; 37:9; Ezk. 10:14,21), *pᵉnê* refers to the front of the head. In Prov. 27:23 *pᵉnê ṣō'neḵā* denotes the appearance or condition of the flock.

4. *Humans.* a. *Anatomical Meaning.* In conjunction with proper names or other substantives denoting persons, *pānîm/pᵉnê* often refers to the face in the anatomical sense: the face of Jacob (Gen. 50:1), Moses (Ex. 34:25 [twice]), a young man (2 K. 4:29,31), a number of individuals (Isa. 13:8; Nah. 2:11), a human figure (Ezk. 1:10; 10:14; 41:19), Daniel (Dnl. 9:3; 10:15), Haman (Est. 7:8), someone dead (Job 14:20). In Gen. 31:2,5, *pānîm* refers to Laban's facial expression. In Ezk. 21:3(20:47), without further specification, *kol-pānîm* refers to the face of hypothetical witnesses of a blazing fire that shall be scorched.

In its literal sense the human face is the object of the verbs "wash" (Gen. 43:31), "look on" (*nbṭ* hiphil, Ps. 84:10[9]), "cause to shine" (*ṣhl* hiphil, Ps. 104:15), "change" (*šnh* piel, Job 14:20). Spitting in someone's face (*yrq bᵉpānîm*) is a sign of disrespect (Nu. 12:14; Dt. 25:9). One wraps (*lwṭ*) one's face in one's mantle as a token of fear (1 K. 19:13) or shame (2 S. 19:5 [here *lā'aṭ*]), a sign of condemnation to death (*ḥph,* Est. 7:8), or in order to avoid recognition (*ksh,* Gen. 38:15; *śîm sēṯer,* Job 24:15). Moses covers his face with a veil (*wayyittēn 'al-pānāyw masweh,* Ex. 34:33; cf. vv. 34-35) not as a person involved in the official cult but as a private individual, insofar as he is not involved in proclaiming the word of Yahweh. The shining (→ קרן *qrn*) of his face in the presence of the Israelites is the justification of his authority.[14]

b. *Expressing Emotion.* As the subject of certain verbs, *pānîm* in its literal sense is used in idioms that express emotions reflected in the face or in gestures involving the face. After Eli's words of comfort, "Hannah's face was no longer the same" (1 S. 1:18). Worry (*ra',* Gen. 40:7; Neh. 2:2) may make a face downcast; lack of proper nourishment (*zō'ᵃpîm,* Dnl. 1:10) can mar it. It can be angered by a backbiting tongue (Prov. 25:23), reddened by tears (Job 16:16), made pale (*hwr,* Isa. 29:22[15]) by affliction, made "green" by terror (Jer. 30:6), or convulsed (*r'm,* Ezk. 27:35) by an appalling sight. Faces "gleaming" with terror (*qbṣ pā'rûr;* NRSV "pale")[16] is among the traditional

14. Haran, 163.
15. H. Wildberger, *Jesaja 28–39. BK* X/3 (1982), 1135.
16. H. W. Wolff, *Joel and Amos. Herm* (Eng. trans. 1977), 46.

motifs characterizing the day of Yahweh (Joel 2:6; Nah. 2:11[10]). Cain's anger shows in his face, which is downcast (*npl,* Gen. 4:5,6; cf. v. 7: *śᵉʾēṯ* and *nśʾ pānîm;* see IV.5 below); this gesture breaks the bond established by the eyes. To throw oneself on the face (*npl ʿal/ʾel- pᵉnê,* Gen. 50:1) of someone who has just died is a mark of grief. By contrast, falling on one's face before (a manifestation of) the deity is an expression of fear and awe (*ʿal,* Gen. 17:3,17; Lev. 9:24; Nu. 17:10[16:45]; 20:6; Jgs. 13:20; 1 K. 18:39; Ezk. 1:28; 3:23; 9:8; *ʾel,* Josh. 5:14; Ezk. 43:3; 44:4). It is also a mark of respect for the king (2 S. 9:6). It can denote anger or shame (Nu. 14:5; 16:4) as well as humble entreaty (Nu. 16:22; Josh. 7:6,10; Ezk. 11:13). By falling on his face, Dagon acknowledges the sovereignty of Yahweh (1 S. 5:3,4, reading with the LXX *ʿal-pānāyw* instead of *lᵉpānāyw*). The summons to entreat Yahweh *ûp̱ᵉnêhem ʾal-yeḥpārû* (Ps. 34:6[5]) coupled with the injunction to look on him in radiant joy suggests that shame, expressed by *ḥpr* (often par. *bwš*), is reflected visibly in facial contortions.

c. *Figurative Usage.* As the object of certain verbs, *pānîm* retains something of its literal meaning while also taking on a metaphorical and general sense; such expressions refer to acts related to the expression or appearance of the face and the emotions experienced by the possessor of the *pānîm,* who is often the subject of the verb. The expressions *šyt* (Nu. 24:1) and *kwn* hiphil (Ezk. 4:3,7) *pānîm* mean "turn one's face toward." A fixed gaze (*ʿmd* hiphil, 2 K. 8:11) bespeaks sadness; a stony face (*ʿzz* hiphil, Prov. 7:13; 21:29, *bᵉpānāyw),* impudence. The face is lifted (*rwm* hiphil, Ezr. 9:6) in prayer. Figuratively, Yahweh causes his face to fall (*npl* hiphil *bᵉ,* Jer. 3:12) in anger on someone or shows (*rʾh* hiphil, Jer. 18:17) someone his back rather than his face in punishment. A face may be covered with shame (*bwš* hiphil, 2 S. 19:6[5]) or be full of disgrace (*mlʾ* piel, Ps. 83:17[16]). Joy makes a countenance cheerful (*ṭwb* hiphil, Prov. 15:13). "Putting off a sad countenance" (*ʿzb pānîm,* Job 9:27[17]) drives away care.

d. *Synecdoche.* In several fixed constructions (e.g., with the verbs *bqš, hdr, ḥlh, ksh, nśʾ, rʾh,* and *šwb;* see IV below) as well as elsewhere, *pᵉnê* denotes the actual person identified by the *nomen rectum:* Isaac (Gen. 27:30, although *mēʾēṯ pᵉnê* appears to be simply prepositional), Joseph (44:26), the poor (Lev. 19:15; Isa. 3:15), the aged (Lev. 19:32; Lam. 5:12), one's neighbor (Prov. 27:17), servants (2 S. 19:6), the eminent (Prov. 19:6), sages (Prov. 17:24), priests (Lam. 4:16), authorities (2 K. 18:24; Job 34:19), the king (1 S. 22:4; 2 S. 14:24 [*pānay*],28,32; 2 K. 3:14; 25:19), Solomon (1 K. 10:24; 12:6), the anointed (Ps. 84:10[9]; 132:10), Pharaoh (Ex. 10:11), Job (Job 42:9), the wicked (Ps. 82:2). In the majority of these texts the translation "face" or "countenance" is unwarranted. Especially expressive is 2 S. 17:11, where *pāneyḵā* ("you yourself") is the subject of the verb *hlk.*

The expression *nkr* (hiphil) *pānîm* indicated partisanship or favor in the forensic domain (Dt. 1:17; 16:19; Prov. 24:23; 28:21); *kpr* (piel) *pᵉnê-X* means "placate with gifts" (Gen. 32:21[20]); *ṭḥn pᵉnê-X* (Isa. 3:15) means "exploit" (the poor); *qdm* (piel) *pᵉnê-X* (Ps. 17:13; 89:15[14]; 95:2) means "come before, come into the presence of"; *šḥr* (piel) *pānîm* (Prov. 7:15) means "seek"; *šrt* (piel) *ʾēṯ pᵉnê-X* (Est. 1:10) means "at-

17. M. Dahood, *JBL* 78 (1959) 303-9.

tend." In Job 40:13 Yahweh challenges Job to bind the wicked in the netherworld *(ḥbš pᵉnêhem).* Prov. 27:17 declares that one individual "sharpens" another's wits (knowledge? conduct?) *(ḥdd pᵉnê-rēʿēhû).*

When the text has to do with someone in authority, *r'h ('eṯ-) pᵉnê-X* (see IV.9 below) emphasizes the importance of having occasional or regular access to such a person (Gen. 32:21[20]; 33:10; 43:3,5; 44:23,26; Ex. 10:28; 2 S. 3:13; 14:24,28,32; 2 K. 25:19). In the majority of texts cited in this section, *pānîm* represents the presence of the object as the terminus and goal of the verb, the subject of which is not the person whose *pānîm* is involved. In the expressions *qwṭ* (niphal) *bipnêhem* (Ezk. 6:9, "be loathsome in one's own sight"; cf. 20:43; 36:31) and *ʿnh bᵉp̱ānāyw* (Hos. 5:5; 7:10, "testify against oneself[?]"), *pānîm* denotes the prepositional object of the verb, which is effectively identical with the subject.

5. *Yahweh.* The noun *pānîm* is of particular importance in conjunction with Yahweh as the subject of statements in Ex. 33, which belongs to the rhetorical unit Ex. 32–34 and concentrates on the various modes of Yahweh's presence. It is not impossible to distinguish a variety of textual strata, but this approach does not do justice to the unity of the theological problem dealt with by the text as it stands. Following the destruction of the golden calf and the exemplary punishment of the people, Yahweh promises to send "his messenger" in front of Moses (*mal'āḵî yēlēḵ lᵉpāneyḵā,* 32:34; cf. 33:2). Yahweh has determined not to forsake his people entirely; but the presence of his *mal'āḵ* instead of his presence *bᵉqirbᵉḵā* (33:3,5) is viewed as a less than perfect aid, albeit not as fraught with peril (cf. 32:34). In the tent of meeting Moses uses his chance to talk with Yahweh *pānîm 'el-pānîm* (33:11; see IV.1 below) to ask once more whom Yahweh will send (v. 12). The response, *pānay yēlēḵû* (v. 14), is deliberately vague. Moses demands a more precise answer in two mutually supplementary statements: *'im-'ên pāneyḵā hōlᵉḵîm,* "if you do not go with the people," we shall not go (v. 15), and only *bᵉleḵtᵉḵā ʿimmānû* will it be known that Yahweh helps his people (v. 16). On the evidence of Akk. *ālik pānî,* Speiser argues that the primary meaning of the expression is "go before," "act as leader," a meaning that would also make sense in 2 S. 17:11.[18]

In Ex. 33:14,15, *pānîm* serves to express in some undefined sense the personal presence of Yahweh, whether it substitutes for the personal pronoun "you"[19] or is meant to be understood as a reference to Yahweh's cultic presence. Ex. 33:18-23 states more precisely the sole form of Yahweh's presence to which every person (cf. v. 20, *'āḏām*) has access. Moses' request to be allowed to see God's glory (v. 18) receives a threefold answer (v. 19): Yahweh will make *kol-ṭûḇî* pass before Moses (*ʿbr* hiphil anticipates *baʿᵃḇôr kᵉḇōḏî* and *ʿaḏ-ʿoḇrî* in v. 22). In v. 19 *wᵉqārā'ṯî ḇᵉšēm yhwh* (MT preserves *yhwh* as subj.) would mean that Yahweh proclaims his own name as the basis for Moses' invocation in 34:5 (where it is unlikely that the subj. is Yahweh). Yahweh an-

18. E. A. Speiser, "The Biblical Idiom *Pānîm Hōlᵉḵîm,*" *Seventy-fifth Anniversary Volume of JQR* (1967), 515-17. See III.4.d above.

19. See III.4.d above.

nounces his decision to be gracious and merciful to whomever he will in his freedom. The gifts bestowed by Yahweh, the invocation of his name (the possibility of knowing his attributes as described in 34:6-7), and his free decision to bestow them go hand in hand with seeing only his back *('ᵃḥōrîm)* and stand in contrast to seeing his face (vv. 20,23), which no mortal is allowed to do.

In Dt. 4:37 the liberating act of Yahweh *bᵉp̄ānāyw bᵉḵōḥô* reflects the "trials, signs and wonders, war, mighty hand, and outstretched arm" of v. 34 (likewise introduced by *bᵉ*) and supplements Yahweh's appearance in the voice speaking "out of the fire" (vv. 33,36). The expression *bᵉp̄ānāyw* does not denote a mode of manifestation distinct from *bᵉyāḏ* and *bizrôaʿ*. While the latter expressions stress the power and might of the one who appears, *bᵉp̄ānāyw* stresses the personal aspect of the divine act and implies that the only mode in which Yahweh manifests himself is his intervention in history.

The context of Isa. 63:9 is an historical retrospect within the communal lament 63:7–64:11; here *pānāyw hôšîʿām* (it was Yahweh himself who saved them) establishes a contrast between messengers (reading with LXX *ṣir,* instead of *ṣār, ûmal'āḵ*) with their normal modality of action (alliances; cf. Isa. 18:2; Prov. 13:17) and Yahweh, who saves through *(bᵉ)* his love and pity. In Lam. 4:16, also, the words *pᵉnê yhwh* assign to Yahweh ultimate responsibility for the punishment inflicted on the inhabitants of Jerusalem.[20]

6. *Construct pānîm.* When *pānîm* appears as *nomen rectum* in a construct phrase, the emphasis of the expression is on the *nomen regens;* the word *pānîm* often loses all overtones of the meaning "face." The expressions *maśśô' pānîm* (2 Ch. 19:7) and *hakkāraṯ pānîm* (Isa. 3:9) (cf. *nkr pānîm* and *nś' pānîm*) mean "respect for persons, partiality." In *yᵉšûʿôṯ pānāyw* (Ps. 42:6,12[5,11]; 43:5), *pānāyw* functions as a possessive pronoun ("my salvation"). The countenance is the locus of expression for psychological states such as shame (44:16[15], "shame covered my face"). In the expression *bōšeṯ pānîm,* however, *pānîm* emphasizes the possessive: "our/his/her own shame" (Jer. 7:19 with possessive suf.; Dnl. 9:7,8; Ezr. 9:7; 2 Ch. 32:21); here "shame" is an authentic recognition of guilt, of responsibility and failure.

The enemy who has no mercy (Dt. 28:50) and the king who destroys the nation of the righteous (Dnl. 8:23) are *ʿaz-pānîm.* "Hardness of countenance" *(ʿōz pānîm)* is a negative trait that wisdom can alter by making the face shine (Eccl. 8:1). The hardness of Ezekiel's face *(nāṯattî 'eṯ-pāneyḵā ḥᵃzāqîm,* Ezk. 3:8), however, is a gift bestowed by Yahweh to enable him to withstand an impudent *(qᵉšê pānîm)* and stubborn people (2:4). The phrase *rōaʿ pānîm* (Eccl. 7:3) describes a sad expression from which a wise heart can benefit.

The light of a face appears in two passages with a human person as subject. The spontaneous association of light and life (Ps. 36:10[9]; 56:14) allows Prov. 16:15 to say that the light of a king's countenance, like a cloud, promises rain (cf. also the same association in Job 29:23,24), a source of life for his subjects. A king's gesture of pleasure or displeasure promises favor or punishment. Some psalms use the phrase *'ôr pānîm*

---

20. H.-J. Kraus, *Threni. BK* XX ([3]1968), 71, 79-80.

with reference to Yahweh. In Ps. 4:7b(6b) the petition "let the light of your countenance shine ['lift up,' reading *nś'* for *nsh*] upon us," i.e., "turn your shining face toward us," is a reaction to the lament in v. 7a(6a).

There are military overtones to *'ôr pāneyḵā* in Ps. 44:4(3) (". . . gave them victory"), in parallel with "arm" and "right hand." In Ps. 89:16(15) Yahweh's protective presence is expressed by the parallel expressions "walk in the light of your countenance" and *tᵉrû'â* ("festal shout"), the people's acclamation of God's victory. In Ps. 90:8 the light *(mᵉ'ôr)* of Yahweh's countenance illuminates the human heart so that it can recognize its sins.

The expression *leḥem (hap)pānîm* (Ex. 25:30; 35:13; 39:36; 1 S. 21:7[6]; 1 K. 7:48; 2 Ch. 4:19; cf. Nu. 4:7, *šulḥan happānîm*) denotes the loaves offered to Yahweh by Israel in recognition of the fact that he is the giver of life. Yahweh's acceptance of these offerings then establishes enduring table fellowship between Yahweh and the people.[21]

IV. Idioms and Collocations.

1. *pānîm bᵉ/'el-pānîm.* The explanation of the name Peniel in Gen. 32:31(30) — "for I have seen Elohim *pānîm 'el-pānîm*" — may have displaced a different name and a different explanation in the pre-Israelite narrative;[22] in the present story of Jacob and Esau, however, it is an organic element, anticipated by the thrice-repeated *pānîm* in 32:21(20) *(kpr pānîm, r'h pānîm, nś' pānîm)* and taken up again in 33:10 ("I come into your presence as into the presence of an Elohim"; see IV.9 below). In this language we hear echoes of the uncertainty, fear, and hope that accompanied Jacob's encounters with the numinous at Bethel and the Jabbok. The concluding observation *wattinnāṣēl napšî* (32:31[30]) underlines God's presence as the agent of Jacob's deliverance more than Jacob's amazement at having survived the encounter. This perception is emphasized in the whole account of Jacob's encounter with Esau (Gen. 33; see v. 4).

Gideon's terrified exclamation (Jgs. 6:22) establishes a distinction between the *mal'āḵ,* seen *pānîm 'el-pānîm,* and *'ᵃḏōnāy yhwh.* The comforting answer "Do not fear, you shall not die" (v. 23) confirms that it is the *mal'āḵ,* not Yahweh himself, whom Gideon has seen in his vision.

When the text involves not "seeing" but "speaking," "conversing," or "coming into court with," *pānîm bᵉ/'el-pānîm* expresses the intimate association that exists between participants in an event that always involves Yahweh as subject. In Ex. 33:11 it is Moses who enjoys this familiarity. It distinguishes Moses from all the other prophets (cf. Nu. 12:6-8) and is the essence of his final accolade in Dt. 34:10.

In Dt. 5:4 this expression underlines the identification of Moses' audience with the generation at Horeb ("Yahweh spoke with you personally [*pānîm bᵉpānîm*] . . ."); this statement stands in tension with v. 5, which presumes Moses' mediation. Vv. 24-26 revert to this tension and attempt to resolve it. The promises in Ezk. 20:40-44 are conditioned by an inescapable judgment *pānîm 'el-pānîm* (v. 35), the consequence of

---

21. → VII, 527.
22. C. Westermann, *Genesis 12–36* (Eng. trans. 1985), 519.

which will be the cleansing of the people to rid them of the rebels dwelling in their midst.

2. *bqš pānîm.* The expression *biqqēš ('eṯ-) pānîm* means to seek out a person with authority (1 K. 10:24 par. 2 Ch. 9:23, Solomon; Prov. 29:26, a ruler) to learn their wisdom or to request their favor. This meaning appears also in the expression *biqqēš pᵉnê yhwh.* Yahweh promises to hear his people, to forgive them and to heal them, if they humble themselves, pray, "seek my face," and turn from their wicked ways (2 Ch. 7:14). Here *biqqēš pānîm* does not exclude the possibility of a cultic ceremony, but it does not per se designate such a ceremony.[23] The association with "this place" (v. 15) is explained by the transfer to the temple of Solomon's vision at Gibeon.

In Hos. 5:15, too, *ûḇiqšû pānāy* does not refer to a cultic act (although v. 6 alludes to such a ceremony) but rather to the attitude Yahweh expects of his people. When this attitude is not present, Yahweh retreats to his "place" like a lion to its den. Successful seeking of Yahweh presupposes conversion (*bqš* par. *šwb* in Hos. 3:5; 7:10) and is inspired by distress (5:15; cf. Ps. 78:34, where the verbs *šwb, drš,* and *šḥr* piel express the same idea). Those who seek the face of (the God of) Jacob (*bqš* ptcp. + *pāneyḵā,* Ps. 24:6) constitute a specific category of persons *(dôr):* they have clean hands and pure hearts (v. 4) and inquire into *(drš)* the will of Yahweh. Here *bqš* and *drš* do not function as "technical terms for a pilgrimage to the sanctuary";[24] they summarize the condition of inward composure required of the faithful who would enter the temple. They relate to an element that precedes the pilgrimage. "Seek the face of Yahweh" is therefore a commandment that obtains always and everywhere.

The words *ḇaqqᵉšû pānāyw tāmîḏ* par. *diršû yhwh* (Ps. 105:4) point to a fundamental attitude embracing all aspects of the relationship between human beings and God: to know God (as expressed by the verbs "meditate on, seek, remember") and to worship God ("give thanks, call on God's name, make God known, sing, sing praises, glorify," vv. 1-5). It is easy to understand why this was the psalm chosen for the celebration of the entrance of the ark into the tent of meeting (1 Ch. 16:8-22; cf. v. 11). But to seek God does not necessarily mean to find God. In response to the command *baqqᵉšû pānāy* (Ps. 27:8a; text?), the psalmist's statement of intent (*'eṯ-pāneyḵā 'ᵃḇaqqēš,* v. 8b) does not preclude uncertainty as to meeting God (*'al-tastēr pāneyḵā,* v. 9), fear of being "given up" to adversaries (v. 12), and doubt (*lûlē',* v. 13) as to the chance to see God's goodness. The psalmist's naive sense of security (vv. 1-6) engendered by having found refuge in the temple (v. 4) is followed in vv. 7-14 by a realism fraught with fear.

In 2 S. 21:1 it is most unlikely that *biqqēš 'eṯ-pᵉnê-yhwh* refers to making inquiry of Yahweh through a personal oracle.[25] The standard use of *š'l* for consulting an oracle[26] and the meaning of *bqš* in 1-2 Samuel[27] suggest that the text describes an urgent peti-

23. Contra Reindl, 164-74.
24. Kraus, *BK,* XV/1⁵, 346.
25. Contra A. S. van der Woude, *TLOT,* II, 1010.
26. → II, 238.
27. García de la Fuente, 529.

tion by David on behalf of the people, to which Yahweh responds by stating the reason for their punishment (cf. the similar meaning of *biqqēš 'eṯ-hā'*ᵉ*lōhîm* in 2 S. 12:16, David's prayer for [*b*ᵉ*'aḏ*] his son, and Ex. 33:7).[28] It is clear, furthermore, that in relationships between human beings and Yahweh, no distinction can be drawn between asking the reason for a punishment — we are not dealing with a theoretical question on the part of an observer — and praying that it be mitigated or revoked.

3. *hē'îr pānîm.* The expression *hē'îr pānîm,* "make one's face shine," appears 8 times with Yahweh as subject and addressee of a volitive form. Nu. 6:25 and Ps. 67:2(1) use the jussive; they are prayers, respectively, for Yahweh's all-embracing blessing on an individual and the fertility of the land. The other 6 texts use the imperative. Ps. 31:17(16) is a confident petition spoken by an unjustly persecuted psalmist; *hā'îrâ pāneyḵā 'al* appears in immediate conjunction with deliverance and salvation (*nṣl* par. *yš'*). "Let your face shine, that we may be saved" (Ps. 80:4,8,20[3,7,19]) is a repeated refrain that divides the psalm into three sections, increasing in dramatic intensity; it comprehends all the psalmist's petitions: show yourself, come to our aid, restore us, return to us, look on us, avenge us, protect us, champion us. In Ps. 119:135 *hā'ēr pānîm b*ᵉ recognizes the inability of humans to fulfill the commandments if Yahweh does not personally create the necessary conditions for their fulfillment (vv. 133-134). In Dnl. 9 Daniel turns his face to Yahweh to pray (v. 3); he acknowledges the "shame of his own face and the face of the people" (vv. 7-8), confesses that they have not entreated the favor (*ḥillâ pānîm,* v. 13) of Yahweh, and prays that Yahweh will *hā'ēr pāneyḵā* upon the sanctuary (v. 17). The allusions to the destruction of Jerusalem and the sanctuary indicate that Daniel is not praying for a mystical or cultic revelation of Yahweh but for the chance to rebuild life in the land. The light of Yahweh's face is the all-encompassing sign of God's favor. The "shining" face of the one who receives wisdom (Eccl. 8:1) is a reflection of this gracious presence of God in the human world (cf. Ex. 34:29-30).

4. *ḥlh pānîm.* The expression *ḥillâ ('eṯ-) pānîm* occurs 16 times in the OT, plus twice in Sir. 33(30):20d,22a (ms. E). Three times it refers to a human face, 13 times to the face of God (*p*ᵉ*nê yhwh* 11 times, *p*ᵉ*nê 'ēl* once [Mal. 1:9], direct address to Yahweh once [Ps. 119:58]). The uncertain etymology of → חלה *ḥālâ* prohibits any certain conclusions concerning the meaning of the expression. Because the semantic shift from "weak, sick" to "make soft, mild" is problematic, as is the treatment of Yahweh as the passive subject of an action that involves a certain degree of constraint (as evidenced by use of the piel), Seybold associates *ḥlh* here with *ḥlh* II, "be sweet, pleasant," attested in Hebrew in the nominal forms *ḥ*ᵃ*lîyâ* and *ḥelyâ.*[29]

In secular usage Ps. 45:13(12) expresses the wish that the king's bride may receive the homage of the nations; Job 11:19 expresses the assurance that many will entreat

---

28. M. Görg, *Zelt der Begegnung. BBB* 27 (1967), 158.
29. Seybold, "Reverenz," 4, 14.

Job's favor. Prov. 19:6 observes the human propensity for ingratiating conduct: people selfishly seek the favor of one who possesses wealth or power *(nāḏîḇ)*.

The expression *ḥillâ pᵉnê yhwh* is used in situations where someone seeks favor with God to prevent the imposition of a punishment already determined (Ex. 32:11; Jer. 26:19; cf. Yahweh's response in each case: *wayyinnāḥem yhwh ʿal/'el-hārāʿâ,* "and Yahweh changed his mind about the disaster" [Ex. 32:14; Jer. 26:19]), to find help in danger (1 S. 13:1), or to avert the consequences of a punishment (1 K. 13:6; 2 K. 13:4; 2 Ch. 33:12).

The subject of *ḥillâ pānîm* is a person of some note: a charismatic leader (Moses, Samuel), a king (Hezekiah, Jehoahaz, Manasseh), or an anonymous "man of God." In later texts, however, the subject of *ḥillâ* may be a group: emissaries from Bethel seeking guidance concerning observance of a festival (Zec. 7:2), non-Israelites who join with Israel *lᵉḥallôṯ 'eṯ-pᵉnê yhwh* (Zec. 8:21,22, par. to *biqqēš yhwh,* apparently meaning nothing more than "visit the temple"), priests admonished by Yahweh to fulfill their cultic duties punctiliously (Mal. 1:9).

The expression *ḥillâ pᵉnê yhwh/'ēl* appears frequently in cultic contexts, but should not be equated with Moses' intercession on behalf of the people with the prayer of the man of God for Jeroboam (*ḥal-nā'* . . . *wᵉhiṯpallēl,* 1 K. 13:6), Saul's burnt offering (1 S. 13:12), the correct sacrifices required of the priests (Mal. 1:9), or the penitential rites observed by Manasseh (2 Ch. 33:12,13, *wayyikkānaʿ* . . . *wayyiṯpallēl*). Jer. 26:19; Zec. 7:2; 8:21,22 provide no details about what *ḥillâ pānîm* involved. Section *ḥēṯ* of Ps. 119 suggests interpreting *ḥillîṯî pāneyḵā* (v. 58) as assurance of enjoying Yahweh's favor by virtue of having observed his laws. Dnl. 9:13 sets *ḥillâ pānîm* in parallel with turning away from iniquities and obeying the voice of Yahweh. Only the sequence of verbs in 2 K. 13:4 (*wayᵉḥal* [Jehoahaz] . . . *wayyišmaʿ* [Yahweh]) points to a concrete act of prayer. In the remaining texts *ḥillâ pᵉnê yhwh/'ēl* expresses the purpose of the petition or the cultic act, namely gaining Yahweh's favor.

5. *nś'/hdr pānîm.* The expression *nāśā' pānîm* (usually without *'eṯ,* except in Job 42:9) has a purely physical sense in 2 K. 9:32 (Jehu raises his face to look up); there are emotional overtones in 2 S. 2:22 (raising one's face to look someone in the eye). Job will lift up his face in prayer (Job 22:26). In Mal. 1:9 and Job 11:15, *nāśā' pānîm min-* means "turn one's face away" (in the latter passage *mûm* means "what is worthless"; cf. Dt. 32:5).

Elsewhere *nāśā' pānîm* has a figurative meaning. Positively, it means "show consideration for" (as in the petition *yiśśā' yhwh pānāyw 'ēleyḵā* [Nu. 6:26]), concretely "forgive" (Gen. 32:21[20]) or accept (a petition [Gen. 19:21; 1 S. 25:35] or a gift [Mal. 1:8]). In contrast, the enemy has no respect for the old (Dt. 28:50) or the priests (Lam. 4:16). In these texts (with the exception of Nu. 6:26), *pānîm* denotes the person receiving the favor; the subject of *nś'* is the one who bestows the favor. There appears to be no difference between *nāśā' pānîm lᵉ* and *nāśā' pᵉnê X;* Grube's translation of the former as "smile" is based on insufficient evidence.[30]

30. Grube, 253-54.

The recipient of the favor need not be the same person as the subject of *pānîm.* Yahweh shows Job his favor by forgiving Job's "friends" (Job 42:8,9); Elisha shows favor to the king of Judah by his regard for the king of Israel (2 K. 3:14).

Negatively, *nāśā' pānîm* means "show partiality," especially in legal contexts (Lev. 19:15; Ps. 82:2; Prov. 18:5). Yahweh is the model of impartial justice, showing favor to none and refusing to be bribed (Dt. 10:17; Job 34:19), a model that the priests castigated in Mal. 2:9 do not emulate in teaching the Torah. Job charges his enemies with having unjustly shown partiality toward Yahweh in arguing Job's case (Job 13:8); he is confident, however, that Yahweh will punish them for secretly having shown partiality (v. 10). Elihu asserts that he will not show partiality in the discussion (32:21).

The use of *nś' pᵉnê kol-kōper* in Prov. 6:35 is exceptional in that the *nomen rectum* is an object rather than a person. The reading *nś' pāneyḵā lᵉḵōper,* syntactically identical with Gen. 19:21, is more probable. The deceived husband will not show friendship to the seducer, not even for a bribe. This reading agrees with the 2nd-person admonition in v. 35b. Dahood reads *pny,* with a *yōḏ* of the 3rd person sg., and translates: "No gift of any kind will appease him."[31] On the same grounds he translates Job 41:2(10): "Who can stand before it?"[32]

The meanings of the verbal expression *nś' pānîm* are reflected in the nominal phrase *nᵉśû' pānîm.* Positively, it describes the quality of a person whose accomplishments have gained the king's favor (Naaman, 2 K. 5:1). A neutral sense ("dignitary") appears in Isa. 3:3. In two texts the parallelism with "the prophet who teaches lies" (Isa. 9:14 [15]) and "the violent" (Job 22:8) suggests a pejorative sense for *nᵉśû' pānîm:* an individual who has gained special status by crooked dealing.

The expression *hdr pānîm*[33] has a positive meaning in Lev. 19:32 and Lam. 5:12 (niphal) ("respect the countenance of an elder"); used in parallel with *nś' pānîm* ("show improper partiality"), it has a negative sense (*lō' ṯehdar pᵉnê ḡāḏôl,* "you shall not defer to the great," Lev. 19:15).

6. *ntn/śym pānîm.* The expression *ntn ('eṯ-) pānāy bᵉX,* "set one's face against X," appears as a fixed idiom with Yahweh as subject. The expression has its locus between the formula *'îš 'îš mibbᵉnê/mibbêṯ yiśrā'ēl 'ᵃšer,* which introduces a case, and the sentence, which is pronounced by means of the extermination formula "I will cut that person off from the midst of their people." In the Holiness Code *ntn pānāy bᵉ* condemns the eating of blood (Lev. 17:10), child sacrifice (20:3), and the consultation of mediums and wizards (20:6). In Ezk. 14:8 it condemns consultation of a prophet by people who have committed the sin of idolatry. Lev. 26:17 and Ezk. 14:8 use the words in a more general sense to introduce a threatened punishment.

When Yahweh is not the subject of *ntn pānîm,* the words express a physical movement ("turn one's face toward the ground," Dnl. 10:15) or a metaphorical movement

31. M. Dahood, *Bibl* 51 (1970) 399.
32. Also NRSV; MT reads: "Who can stand before me?"
33. → III, 340-41.

associated closely with the literal sense ("turn to the Lord," Dnl. 9:3). In 2 Ch. 20:3 *ntn pānîm lᵉ* + infinitive construct expresses not physical movement (such as visiting the temple) but a decision to inquire of Yahweh *(drš).* In Ezk. 3:8 the subject of *ntn* is not identical with the person whose face is mentioned: Yahweh makes the prophet's face hard against his enemies.

The expression *śîm pānîm bᵉ* with Yahweh as subject parallels *ntn pānîm bᵉ* with the same meaning in Lev. 20:5 (cf. v. 3) and Ezk. 15:7b. Jer. 21:10 and 44:11 add the formula *lᵉrāʿâ,* while retaining "handing over" or "exterminating" as a punishment. The words *śîm pānîm bᵉ* mean that Yahweh has decided to punish ("I have turned my face against") as distinct from the concrete form of the punishment prescribed.

When Yahweh is not the subject, *śîm pānîm* may be used either literally (putting one's face between one's knees, 1 K. 18:42) or figuratively (turning one's face [i.e., attention] in a certain direction, deciding): *śîm pānîm lᵉ* + infinitive construct. For example, Hazael decides to go up against Jerusalem (2 K. 12:18[17]). Jer. 42:14-15 draws a clear distinction between the deceptive desire to go to Egypt, the decision to set out (*śôm tᵉśimûn pᵉnêḵem,* v. 15), and the actual arrival there; Jer. 44:12 is similar. In Dnl. 11:17 the "king of the north" sets his mind to establish his reign over the whole kingdom; in 1 K. 2:15 *śîm pānîm ʿal* expresses the supposed expectation of the people — not their decision, for it was not in their power to decide — that Adonijah would accede to the throne. This expression may lie behind the elliptical forms *dereḵ hēnnâ pᵉnêhem,* "the way thither is their goal" (Jer. 50:5), and *pānāyw lammilḥāmâ,* "his intention was to fight" (2 Ch. 32:2).

The use of *śîm pānîm* with the accusative of direction in Gen. 31:21 (Jacob "turns" toward the hill country of Gilead) and its occurrences in conjunction with verbs of motion in Jer. 42:17; 44:12; 2 K. 12:18(17); and Dnl. 11:17 (where *lāḇôʾ* is part of a special syntagm, not a verb of motion) has led Brownlee to postulate for *śym/śwm pāneyḵā ʾel/ʿal* in Ezk. 6:2; 13:17; 21:2(20:46) *(dereḵ),*7(2); 25:2; 28:21; 29:2; 35:2; 38:2 the character of a formula connected with travel. Brownlee maintains that Ezekiel actually journeyed with a group of refugees from Jerusalem through Israel, Transjordan, Phoenicia, and Egypt. The oracles against Magog bear witness to his presence in Babylon, to which they contain veiled allusions. This hypothesis rests on a lexicographically dubious foundation; it assumes many textual emendations and transpositions as well as a hyper-realistic understanding of Ezekiel's ministry. The purpose of the expression is probably merely to single out the recipient of the message by means of a vivid, seemingly archaic formula, intended to recall the importance of visual contact between the prophet and the recipient of his message (cf. Nu. 22:41; 23:13; 24:2).

In Isa. 50:7 we are not dealing with the fixed expression *śîm pānîm;* here *śîm* means "make into, alter."

7. *sbb/swr/šwb pānîm.* The expression *sbb* (hiphil) *pānîm* occurs 9 times; it means "turn to" someone physically (Jgs. 18:23) with a positive gesture (e.g., of blessing, 1 K. 8:14 = 2 Ch. 6:3) or contrariwise "turn one's face away from" *(min)* with a gesture of resentment (1 K. 21:4), sorrow or despair (2 K. 20:2 = Isa. 38:2), scorn (2 Ch. 29:6), or challenge (2 Ch. 35:22). Only in Ezk. 7:22 is Yahweh the subject of *hēsēḇ pānîm.*

When he averts his face, it means that he has ceased to defend his people; he gives the enemy free rein to profane the sanctuary. A similar meaning attaches to *hēsîr pānîm* in 2 Ch. 30:9. Hezekiah expresses confidence that Yahweh will not turn his face away if Israel returns to him. Here the hiphil of *swr* appears to have replaced the more usual *histîr* on purely linguistic grounds.[34] The text does not really allude to "removal of idols" and a resulting confrontation with Yahweh.[35]

The expression *hēšîḇ pānîm* occurs some 10 times in the OT. When the subject of the verb is identical with the possessor of the *pānîm,* it may have a positive literal meaning ("turn to," Dnl. 11:18,19) or a negative figurative meaning ("turn away from [evil]," Ezk. 14:6). When this is not the case, *hēšîḇ pānîm* has a negative meaning, literal ("repulse," 2 K. 18:24 = Isa. 36:9) or figurative ("refuse, reject") — denial of a specific request (1 K. 2:16,17,20) or total rejection of an individual, the king (Ps. 132:10 = 2 Ch. 6:42). The specific meaning is conveyed by the expression *pānay* ("my face, my self") or *pᵉnê-X* ("the face of X").

8. *ksh/str pānîm.* The expression *ksh pānîm,* "cover one's face," occurs some 11 times.[36] When the expression is used literally (piel), the face may be covered with a veil (Gen. 38:15; Ezk. 12:6), wings (Isa. 6:2), or fat (i.e., grow fat, Job 15:7). A lazy farmer's field is covered or overgrown (pual) with thorns (Prov. 24:31). In the figurative sense a face may be covered (piel) with dishonor (Jer. 51:51), shame (Ps. 44:16[15]), confusion (Ps. 68:8[7]), or darkness (Job 23:17). In Job 9:24 it is Yahweh himself who covers (enshrouds) the faces of the judges, so that they are blind to unrighteousness.

The expression *histîr ('eṯ-)pānîm (min-),* "hide one's face," occurs 29 times in the OT and 4 times in deuterocanonical literature. The subject is always Yahweh, with three exceptions: Moses hides his face in the presence of God (Ex. 3:6), the servant does not hide his face from insult (Isa. 50:6), and the people hide their faces so as not to have to look at the servant (53:3). The gesture is a way of taking precautions against persons or objects perceived as dangerous or repulsive.

Yahweh's hiding of his face (often with *min* + personal obj.) is not simply a punishment: it signifies a radical disruption of the relationship with God. The "house of Jacob," having scorned the signs given by Yahweh, must live out its history against the background of silence on the part of Yahweh, who is hiding his face (Isa. 8:17). The punishments named in Ezk. 39:23,24 are framed by a repeated statement that Yahweh hid his face from Israel, although this action is not identified as a punishment. This text and Isa. 59:2 are based on the sequence sin–hiding of Yahweh's face–punishment. When Yahweh hides his face, the sinner is lulled into a false sense of security, expecting to go unpunished (Ps. 10:11), the prophets are unable to instruct the people (Mic. 3:4), the people themselves are unable to call on his name and are therefore surren-

---

34. Balentine, 109.
35. Reindl, 123.
36. See also III.4.a above.

dered to the power of their iniquities (Isa. 64:6). Yahweh's hiding of his face is his most extreme reaction, preceding the kindling of his anger and forsaking of Israel (Dt. 31:17-18; cf. 32:20; Jer. 33:5).

The relationship between God and human beings is imponderable (Job 34:29) and is not conditioned absolutely by human righteousness or sinfulness. The righteous psalmist is certain that Yahweh does not hide his face from the poor (Ps. 22:25[24]); for mysterious reasons, however, the face of Yahweh is hidden from the psalmist. Other psalmists ask anxiously why they have been so incomprehensibly forsaken and how long this state will endure (13:2[1]; 44:25[24]; 88:15[14]); with the cry "Do not hide your face" (27:9; 69:18[17]; 102:3[2]; 143:7) they give voice to their emotions: "hear me, answer me, do not forsake me, do not reject me, do not forget me, be with me, save me, deliver me." The psalmist is terrified at the prospect of Yahweh's hiding his face (30:8[7]), knowing that the most wondrous works of creation return to dust when Yahweh hides his face (104:29). The psalmist, cut off from Yahweh's face (143:7), must go down into the pit.

The question "How long?" and the petition "Do not hide your face" frequently occur side by side in the Psalms — not in the context of a confession of sin but in an affirmation of Yahweh's faithfulness despite persecution by enemies (e.g., Ps. 44:18-23[17-22]; 69:19[18]; 143:9b); the usage reveals the psalmist's awareness that the relationship with Yahweh is unfathomable.

The statement that Yahweh will never again hide his face (Ezk. 39:29) summarizes all Yahweh's promises, marking an end to a brief separation of Yahweh from his people (Isa. 54:8). When Yahweh no longer hides his face, Job will see clearly the nature of his sin (Job 13:24). Then Yahweh can "hide his face" (Ps. 51:11[9]) from human sin, and the sinner is set free. In later texts we find the assurance that Yahweh will not hide his face from the person who wholeheartedly does what is true (Tob. 13:6). We may also note Tobit's prayer to Yahweh (3:6) and his admonition to Tobias (4:7) not to turn his face from him or from the poor, so that Yahweh will not turn his face away from Tobias. Sir. 18:24 admonishes the reader to think of the day of wrath, when Yahweh will turn away his face.

9. *r'h/ḥzh pānîm.* With reference to human beings, the expression *rā'â ('eṯ/'el-) pānîm* has three meanings: actually to see someone's face (Gen. 31:2,5; Ex. 34:35; Dnl. 1:10); to meet someone (Gen. 32:21[20]; 33:10; 46:30; 48:11); or to enjoy access to an exalted individual (Joseph, Pharaoh, the king), occasionally (Gen. 43:3,5; 44:23,26; Ex. 10:28,29; 2 S. 3:13) or regularly (2 S. 14:24,28,32). The texts of the third group express the refusal of a meeting. The phrase *rō'ê pᵉnê hammeleḵ* is the title of officials with access to the king, listed by 2 K. 25:19 par. Jer. 52:25 together with *sārîs, pāqîḏ,* and *sōp̄ēr* (cf. also Est. 1:14).

In the majority of its OT occurrences, *rā'â ('eṯ/'el-) pᵉnê yhwh* (qal, often repointed as a niphal[37]) is a technical term for a cultic encounter with the deity. Each of the three

37. See the discussion in Reindl, 147-48.

liturgical calendars (Ex. 23:14-19, Covenant Code; Ex. 34:18-26, Yahweh's prerogatives; Dt. 16:1-17, Dtn version of the calendar) uses the expression twice. Following the regulations governing the festival of unleavened bread, Ex. 23:15 and 34:20 conclude with identical words: "They shall not see my face empty-handed." With slightly different words, Dt. 16:16 concludes the regulations governing the festivals: "He [i.e., every male Israelite] shall not see the face of Yahweh empty-handed." Using almost identical language, Ex. 23:17, 34:23, and Dt. 16:16a decree the obligation of every male to visit the sanctuary ("see the face of Yahweh") three times a year. The association of this precept with the description of the three most important festivals suggests that the texts are thinking of a (or: the) central sanctuary.

Dt. 16:16 identifies the sanctuary with the Jerusalem temple. Ex. 34:24 likewise thinks in terms of a distant central sanctuary, stating that "no one shall covet your land when you go up to see the face of Yahweh your God three times in the year." Every seventh year Dt. 31:11 requires the law to be proclaimed to all the people who have come to the (Jerusalem) sanctuary during the festival of booths "to see the face of Yahweh."

Only four times does *rā'â ('eṯ-)pᵉnê yhwh* appear outside the context of liturgical regulations. In Isa. 1:12, an accusation of cultic worship that ignores justice (vv. 10,17), the relationship between "seeing the face" and presence in the temple is emphasized by the mention of "courts"; in 1 S. 1:22 this relationship is established by the concluding phrase "and he will dwell there." The interchange of qal and niphal is not evident here, but the construction with *'eṯ* suggests an active form. Ps. 42:3(2) voices an intense yearning, not found in other texts, to behold the face of Yahweh. The cultic aspect is present in the allusion to the temple (v. 5[4]), the assurance of appearing before the altar of God (43:4), and liturgical praise *(ydh)*. In Job 33:26 *rṣh* and *tᵉrû'â* point to a liturgical context for "seeing his face." When Yahweh shows his back instead of his face (Jer. 18:17, with *r'h* vocalized as a hiphil), his conduct represents his response to the people (Jer. 2:17): he refuses all possibility of help.

The expression *ḥāzâ pᵉnê yhwh* appears in just two psalms, where it is difficult to determine the meaning of the cultic element. In Ps. 11 the innocent psalmist appears to seek refuge from persecution in the temple (vv. 1aβ,4). The psalmist's desire to see the enemy punished (v. 6; within the confines of the temple?) contrasts with an assurance that the upright will see his (God's) face (*yāšār yeḥᵉzû pānāyw* [for *pānêmô*], v. 7). The interpretation of Ps. 17:15, "I shall behold your face in righteousness," is made difficult by the parallel in v. 15b: "When I awake *(bᵉhāqîṣ)*, I shall be satisfied by your likeness *(tᵉmûnâ)*." Both terms point to "cult-related concepts."[38] The use of *ḥāzâ* instead of *rā'â* is not sufficient argument to exclude a cultic theophany, although we risk a *petitio principii*. In any case it is incontestable that in both psalms this expression conveys "the experience of God's gracious favor in an act of saving deliverance."[39]

---

38. H. F. Fuhs, *Sehen und Schauen. FzB* 32 (1978), 273.
39. Ibid., 274.

V. Semantic and Theological Assessment. A study of *pānîm* based on syntactic and semantic categories rather than directly on thematic categories makes it possible to confirm some conclusions regarding its meaning that earlier studies have made increasingly clear. It is impossible to trace any direct dependencies of the biblical expressions with respect to the meaning or setting of corresponding expressions in ancient Near Eastern usage. On the purely linguistic plane, some of these expressions represent borrowings; but their meaning can be determined only from their actual OT context. It is impossible, therefore, to associate *pānîm* collocations with conjectural rituals concerning which the OT provides no information — e.g., understanding *ḥillâ pānîm* as stroking the face of a divine image or connecting "covering their faces with fat" (Job 15:27) with ritual anointing, *nāśā' pānîm* with a gesture of judicial reprieve, or "the light of the countenance" with the cult of astral deities. Discussion of the possible origin of such expressions (secularization of a cultic concept or elevation of a secular concept to the cultic or theological domain) derives from a highly detailed division into categories rather than the normal process of linguistic development; such discussion is therefore ultimately fruitless. In all probability the *pānîm* expressions have their origin in the broad semantic potential of *pānîm.* The face is that part of the human body, and hence of the person, which is most capable of manifesting differentiated appearances; it is only logical, therefore, that language should take the term *pānîm* as a point of departure in numerous collocations and idioms that refer to interpersonal relations as well as relations between human beings and God. To hide one's face, to show, turn, or avert it, to lift, lower, cover, harden it, to make it gentle or dark or bright — these are natural expressions of human comportment; language may therefore draw on them in a variety of idioms, the absence of which — rather than their obvious presence — requires explanation.

It is therefore appropriate to return to Reindl's argument that the *pānîm* expressions (not just the *p^e^nê-yhwh* expressions) represent not concepts but idioms and develop it further.[40] The word *pānîm* did not develop until there emerged from it a precise theological or anthropological concept that could be utilized in turn for various expressions by means of verbs or prepositions. The word *pānîm,* "face," with its variety of possible overtones, can be used, and is used, in many expressions whose meaning does not depend exclusively or primarily on some postulated technical (e.g., theological) sense inferred from *pānîm* but rather on the collocation as a whole, with its context taken into account. This approach makes clear that certain expressions (e.g., *nāśā' pānîm, sbb pānîm*) did not develop as fixed idioms with a unique meaning, but could be used literally and figuratively, positively and negatively.

Only two *pānîm* expressions acquired a technical cultic sense: *rā'â ('eṯ-)p^e^nê yhwh* ("visit the sanctuary") and the prepositional phrase *lipnê yhwh* (see VI.1.b below), which qualifies theologically the majority of cultic acts (but not such acts only) that are performed in some sense in the presence of Yahweh. It is not impossible that the ancient Near Eastern cult of images influenced the development of both expressions. But

40. Pp. 198ff.

it is also probable that the potential of the term *pānîm* for describing interpersonal relations also contributed to the development of both expressions.

As an organ more expressive than the hand and more inclusive than the eye — which, however, belongs to it — the *pānîm* was well suited to represent the entire human person by a kind of synecdoche. This is the case when *pānîm* is the subject in the expressions discussed in III.4.d and in some of the meanings of the collocations listed in IV. Because of its ability to express emotions and reactions, *pānîm* denotes the subject insofar as it turns *(pnh)* to "face" others, i.e., insofar as it is the subject of relationships. The term *pānîm* describes relationships. The relationship is syntactically explicit when the subject of the verb is not identical with the subject of *pānîm.* When the two coincide, either there is a syntactic signal expressing the relationship (e.g., the face is hidden from [*min*] someone) or the immediate context points to the nature of a relationship (Ex. 33). The relationship encompasses the present of both parties and the action of at least one of them. The mode of presence includes seeking *(biqqēš pānîm),* behavior that may be general (seeing, observing, being in someone's presence) or particular, positive (appeasing, showing favor or favoritism, seeking or receiving benevolence) or negative (opposing, refusing, rejecting), and finally even refusal to meet (averting one's face, hiding from someone).

The semantic possibilities of *pānîm* also make it a suitable term to use in connection with Yahweh. It is no more and no less anthropomorphic than any other term used in theological discourse; neither does it presuppose any particular adaptation of a technical theological kind. Applied to Yahweh, *pānîm* says no more and no less than when applied to human beings. The semantically constitutive elements of *pānîm* that make it appropriate for discourse about Yahweh are the same that apply to human beings: real personal presence, relationship, and meeting (or refusal to meet). All the fundamental relationships between God and human beings can be described by *pānîm* and its associated expressions.

It does not appear expedient, however, to see in the expression *pᵉnê yhwh* as such an aspect of Yahweh's special presence or relationship with human beings, such as a mediated presence in contrast to immediate presence, or a presence that brings comfort or punishment. In Ps. 21:10(9) *ʿēṯ pāneyḵā* is the "time of presence," when Yahweh will reveal himself; the notion of punishment derives from the verse as a whole (cf. vv. 9-11[8-10]). In specific cases a translation like "anger" in texts such as Ps. 9:4(3); 34:17(16); 80:17(16); Eccl. 8:1; Lam. 4:16, as well as Ps. 21:10(9),[41] can be appropriate. Its systematic application, however, could easily forget the complex and profuse shades of meaning of *pānîm.*

Insofar as *pānîm* bespeaks presence, its purpose is to underline the positive aspect of the interpersonal relationship. The negative aspect of the relationship is expressed by separation from *pānîm.* The idiom *nāṯan pānîm bᵉ* is an exception. The expression *śîm pānîm ʾel/ʿal* acquires its negative overtones only from the oracle it introduces.

---

41. W. F. Albright, *Yahweh and the Gods of Canaan* (1968), 117; M. Dahood, *Bibl* 51 (1970) 399; but cf. F. J. Morrow Jr., *VT* 18 (1968) 558-59.

When associated with Yahweh, *pānîm* is a fertile term that occupies a mediating position between the danger of a materialistic conception of the deity conveyed by images, which the OT systematically rejects, and the danger of a nominalism that reduces the divine presence to an abstraction. Ex. 33 bears witness to the difficulties created by the incorporation of *pānîm* into the theological conceptuality of Israel, Ps. 17:15 *(pānîm* par. *t*ᵉ*mûnâ)* to its theological value in harmonizing the different notions.

No one has yet presented a persuasive case for viewing *pānîm* as a hypostasis;[42] the extant OT material does not appear to support such an argument.

VI. Prepositional Usage. The construct form *p*ᵉ*nê* is an element of several semiprepositions.

1. *lip̱nê.* a. *General.* The various meanings of *lip̱nê* derive from the combination of *l*ᵉ with *pānîm* in the sense of "presence" and the meaning of the verb used with the preposition. In the static spatial sense, *lip̱nê* means "before" with such verbs as *ḥnh, yṣb* hithpael, and *ʿmd* (Gen. 41:46; 43:15; Ex. 8:16[20]; 9:13; 14:2) or verbs describing an action performed in someone's presence (Ex. 11:10). In the dynamic spatial sense, *lip̱nê* introduces the person (or thing) in whose presence a movement terminates, with such verbs as *ntn* (Ex. 30:6), *ʿmd* hiphil (Lev. 27:8), *qrb* hiphil (Ex. 29:10), and *śîm* (40:26). "Before" can also refer to the relationship between two persons in motion, one of whom precedes the other: Gen. 24:7 *(šlḥ);* Ex. 13:21 *(hlk);* Dt. 9:3 (*ʿbr;* cf. v. 1); 1 S. 10:8 *(yrd);* cf. also 1 S. 8:11 *(rwṣ).*

Depending on the verbs used and the circumstances, the static and dynamic spatial senses of *lip̱nê* can take on various shades of meaning in which physical presence "before" someone or something is no longer the central element but only a possible concomitant. When the king or some other important personage is involved, *ʿmd lip̱nê* (Gen. 41:46; 43:15; Ex. 9:10; 1 S. 16:22; 1 K. 10:8; 2 Ch. 29:11; with *ʾeṯ-p*ᵉ*nê,* 1 K. 12:6) or *hyh lip̱nê* (1 S. 19:7; 29:8; 2 K. 5:2) means "be at someone's disposal." This meaning emerges from the difference in status between the persons in a particular relationship. In military contexts *yṣb* (hithpael) *lip̱nê* (Dt. 9:2), *ʿmd lip̱nê* (Jgs. 2:14), and *qwm lip̱nê* (Lev. 26:37; Josh. 7:12,13) mean "resist, withstand." The expression *yṣʾ lip̱nê* means "go forth at the head of" (1 S. 8:20) or "go forth against" (1 Ch. 14:8; 2 Ch. 14:9). Other combinations include *nws lip̱nê,* "flee from" (Josh. 7:4; 2 S. 24:13; cf. also *pnh lip̱nê* [Jgs. 20:42]); *npl lip̱nê,* "fall before" (1 S. 14:13; 2 S. 3:34); and *ngp* (niphal) *lip̱nê,* "be struck down (by enemies)" (Lev. 26:17; 1 S. 4:2; 7:10; 2 S. 10:15). The combination *śym lip̱nê* can mean "expound (the law to the people)" (Ex. 19:7; 21:1).

In addition, *lip̱nê* can indicate that the person in whose presence something takes place is of high rank (2 S. 2:14), supervises another (1 S. 3:1), or has the option (Eccl.

42. Contra G. Pfeifer, *Ursprung und Wesen der Hypostasenvorstellungen im Judentum. AzT* I/31 (1967), 69, who views *pānîm* as a form of Yahweh's manifestation, somehow associated with cultic objects, when guiding the people; cf. the critical remarks of A. S. van der Woude, *TLOT,* II, 1005; idem, III, 1362-63.

9:1) or right to pass judgment in certain situations (Dt. 25:2; Est. 5:14). The expression *'kl lip̄nê* (2 K. 25:29) means "be permitted to dine at the table of the victor," i.e., "be granted a reprieve"; *hlk* (hithpael) *lip̄nê* (1 S. 12:2) means "act in the presence of someone [Yahweh, the people]" in such a way as to be assured of a positive response. This meaning comes close to "in the opinion of, in the judgment of" (1 S. 20:1; 2 K. 5:1), but does not emphasize the right to pass judgment. In expressions like "grant or find mercy and favor" (Gen. 43:14; 1 K. 8:50; 2 Ch. 30:9; Est. 2:17), *lip̄nê* underscores the status of the person showing mercy and favor.

The expression *ntn lip̄nê* (in contrast to simple *ntn lᵉ*) emphasizes the aspect of giving disposition over something of importance (the land, Dt. 1:8; enemies, Dt. 23:15[14]); *lᵉpāneyḵā* (without a verb) emphasizes directly the element of free disposition (Gen. 13:9; 20:15; 24:51; 47:6); cf. also *npl* (qal/hiphil) *tᵉḥinnâ lip̄nê,* "make/receive a request" (Jer. 36:7; 37:20; 42:2,9). When the word introduced by *lip̄nê* refers to an event rather than a person or object, *lip̄nê* (often with the inf. const.) expresses temporal priority with respect to another event, whether in the past (Gen. 13:10; 1 S. 9:15) or the future (27:7), or simply priority in the context of a recurrent situation (laws and customs such as not giving the younger daughter in marriage before the elder, 29:26).

b. *Yahweh.* The use of *lip̄nê* with Yahweh does not differ from its general usage except in the frequent occurrence of particular meanings. The temporal meaning is found only in Isa. 43:10: "Before me no god was formed." The dynamic spatial meaning in a military context is also rare: *kbš* (niphal) *hā'āreṣ lip̄nê yhwh* (1 Ch. 22:18); *šbr* (niphal) (the Cushites) *lip̄nê yhwh* (2 Ch. 14:12[13]). Both texts repeat *lip̄nê* and add another agent (the people, the army) cooperating with Yahweh to bring about the defeat. The dynamic spatial meaning with both terms in motion (one preceding [*lip̄nê*] the other) may be present in a literal sense in Josh. 4:13: forty thousand armed men go (across the Jordan) *lip̄nê yhwh;* but the image appears to have more to do with marching in the watchful presence of Yahweh. In 6:8 *'br* is not connected with *lip̄nê yhwh:* the priests carry the trumpets *lip̄nê yhwh* (before or in the presence of Yahweh). Figuratively, a windstorm (1 K. 19:11), pestilence (Hab. 3:5), fire (Ps. 50:3; 97:3), righteousness (Ps. 85:14[13]), a "messenger" (Mal. 3:1), and Yahweh's "reward" (Isa. 40:10 par. 62:11) go before Yahweh when he reveals himself. "Honor and majesty" (Ps. 96:6 par. 1 Ch. 16:27) and wisdom (Prov. 8:30) are *lip̄nê yhwh* as his servants.

In the static spatial sense, Abraham (Gen. 18:22 [cf. 19:27, *'eṯ-pᵉnê*]), the people (Dt. 4:10; 1 S. 6:20), and a member of the heavenly court (1 K. 22:21 par. 2 Ch. 18:20) are described as standing before Yahweh. Moses' speaking *(dbr, 'mr) lip̄nê yhwh* (Ex. 6:12,30) is a deferential variant of "speak to."

The commonest use of *lip̄nê yhwh* (or *lip̄nê* + suf. referring to Yahweh) in the static or dynamic spatial sense is in cultic contexts. P localizes *lip̄nê yhwh:* immediately before the ark (Ex. 16:33; Lev. 16:13; Nu. 17:22[7]), the curtain in front of the ark (Lev. 4:6,17), the table with the bread of the Presence (Ex. 25:30), the lamp (Ex. 27:21; Lev. 24:3), the altar in the tent of meeting (Lev. 4:18) and before the tent (Lev. 1:11; 16:18), the space in front of the tent (Ex. 29:11). The majority of cultic acts take place *lip̄nê yhwh:* the raising of the elevation offering in the hands of the priests (*hēnîp tᵉnûpâ,* Ex. 29:24,26; Lev. 7:30; 8:27,29; 9:21; 10:15; 14:12,24; 23:20; Nu. 6:20; 8:11,21), the offering of the sacrificial gifts (*hiqrîb,* Lev. 3:1,7,12; 6:7[14]; 9:2; 10:1,19; 12:7; Nu. 3:4; 6:16; 16:17; 17:3[16:38]; 26:61; 1 Ch. 16:1; Ezk. 43:24), the slaughtering of the sacrificial animals (*šḥt,* Ex. 29:11; Lev. 1:5,11; 4:4,15,24; 6:18[25]), the burning of the incense offering (Lev. 16:13), the ritual of atonement (*kpr,* Lev. 5:26[6:7]; 10:17; 14:18,29,31; 15:15,30; 19:22; 23:28; Nu. 15:28; 31:50), the sacrifice of well-being (*zbḥ,* Lev. 9:4; 1 S. 11:15; 1 K. 8:62; 2 Ch. 7:4), the burnt offering (*ʿōlâ,* Jgs. 20:26; 2 S. 6:17), Moses' sacrifice at the ordination of Aaron and his sons (Ex. 29:11), and the consecration of the Levites (Nu. 8:10). To enter the sanctuary is to "go *lipnê yhwh*" (Ex. 28:35); in fact, any priestly ministry could be so designated (cf. Ex. 28:30). In a more general sense service to Yahweh is called *ʿmd lipnê yhwh* (1 K. 17:1; 18:15; 2 K. 3:14; 5:16 [in an oath formula]; Jer. 15:19; cf. Ezk. 44:15), a formula that emphasizes the element of faithfulness to God.

Outside P, other texts describe the sacrifices at Bethel (Jgs. 20:26) and Gilgal (1 S. 11:15), the transfer of the ark to Jerusalem (2 S. 6:17), and Solomon's dedication of the temple (1 K. 8:62) as taking place *lipnê yhwh.*

Not just the rituals of the official cult but also private religious acts are performed *lipnê yhwh:* the prayers of Hannah (1 S. 1:12), David (2 S. 7:18), and Hezekiah (2 K. 19:15), the prayer and fasting of Nehemiah (Neh. 1:4), the pouring out of the psalmist's heart (Ps. 62:9[8]; 102:1), worship (Ps. 22:28[27]), self-humiliation (2 Ch. 34:27). None of these gestures presupposes a cultic act associated with the sanctuary.[43]

Some gestures include a formal cultic act in certain situations but not always. Eating *lipnê yhwh* is a precisely circumscribed cultic act (Dt. 12:7,18; 14:23,26; 15:20; Ezk. 44:3), but Ex. 18:12 and 1 Ch. 29:22 suggest an observance that is not strictly liturgical. The same is true of "rejoicing *lipnê yhwh,*" which accompanies such meals (Dt. 12:12,18; 16:11; 27:7) but is also found independently of them (Lev. 23:40; Isa. 9:2[3], *lᵉpāneykā, lipnê yhwh ʾᵉlōhêkem*). "Weeping *lipnê yhwh*" may have been a ritual of expiation after a defeat (Dt. 1:45; Jgs. 20:23,26). In Nu. 11:20, however, wailing *lᵉpānāyw* (before Yahweh) is a gesture of supplication and simultaneously of protest (cf. vv. 4,10). Religious gestures outside the cult include the blessing of Isaac (Gen. 27:7), Joshua's curse over the ruins of Jericho (Josh. 6:26), and the making of covenants (David and Jonathan, 1 S. 23:18; David and the elders of Hebron, 2 S. 5:3 par. 1 Ch. 11:3; Josiah, the people, and Yahweh: 2 K. 23:3 par. 2 Ch. 34:31). In Jer. 34:15,18, the covenant *lᵉpānay* is a covenant with Yahweh himself. Jgs. 11:11 (cf. v. 8), too, appears to allude to a covenant *lipnê yhwh* between Jephthah and the elders of Gilead; it is therefore dubious whether the phrase *lipnê yhwh* by itself can be considered a characteristic mark of covenant making. For example, Dt. 29:14(15) shows clearly that *lipnê yhwh* is not an absolute prerequisite for making a covenant.[44]

---

43. M. D. Fowler, *ZAW* 99 (1987) 384-90.

44. See Sheriffs, 62, who compares *lipnê yhwh* to *ina IGI* + DN.

"Dying *lipnê yhwh*" can include cultic presence (Lev. 10:2; Nu. 3:4; 1 Ch. 13:10?), but it can also bespeak a punishment from Yahweh (Nu. 14:37; 20:3). To live *lipnê yhwh* (Gen. 17:18; Hos. 6:2) is to recognize that life depends solely on Yahweh. Recognition that Yahweh is the effective cause of everything appears in a wish uttered on behalf of the king: "May he be enthroned forever before God" (Ps. 61:9[8]).

The phrase *lipnê yhwh* can also express the viewpoint of Yahweh and his assessment of persons and situations (Gen. 6:11; 7:1; 10:9; Lev. 16:30; Dt. 24:4; Eccl. 2:26). Whatever is at odds with the nature and work of Yahweh cannot endure (*'md lipnê yhwh,* 1 S. 6:20; Jer. 49:19 par. 50:44; Ps. 76:8[7]; Ezr. 9:15). Only heaven and earth (Isa. 66:22) and those who turn to Yahweh (Jer. 15:19) can stand before him (*'md lipnê yhwh).* Because institutions and individuals can be established only before Yahweh (*kwn lipnê yhwh,* 2 S. 7:26; 1 K. 2:4; 1 Ch. 17:24; Jer. 30:20; Ps. 102:29[28]), it is important that Yahweh be reminded (*zkr* [niphal] *lipnê yhwh,* Nu. 10:9) of people's need for him. This is the significance of objects that are carried or gestures that are performed as a *zikkārôn* (Ex. 28:12,29; 30:16; Nu. 10:10; 31:54). The expression *sēper zikkārôn lᵉpānāyw* (Mal. 3:16) reflects the same notion.

Pennacchini's proposal to interpret *lipnêhem* in Job 21:8 as a prepositional expression serving as a substantive ("progenitors," as a parallel to "progeny") eliminates the parallelism between *lipnêhem* and *lᵉ'ênêhem.*[45]

2. *millipnê.* The meaning of *millipnê* adds to that of *lipnê* a nuance of separation or removal. Its use in a temporal sense is rare: *millᵉpānênû,* "before us" (Eccl. 1:10). In a spatial sense it is used with verbs that signify departure from someone's presence (*yṣ',* Gen. 4:16; 41:46; 47:10; Ex. 35:20; *nws,* 1 Ch. 19:18), driving or taking away (*grš,* Ex. 23:28; *yrš* hiphil, Dt. 11:23; *swr* hiphil, 2 S. 7:15; *šlk* hiphil, Ps. 51:13[11]; *krt,* 1 K. 8:25 par. 2 Ch. 6:16), or hiding (*str* niphal, Jer. 16:17). Verbs expressing fear or respectful distance are also used with *millipnê: z'q* (1 S. 8:18), *kn'* niphal (par. *kn'* niphal *mippānay,* 1 K. 21:29), *ḥyl* (1 Ch. 16:30), *yr'* (Eccl. 3:14). Movement, expressed by verbs such as *qwm,* can be defined more precisely by *millipnê* (1 K. 8:54; Ezr. 10:6). In Gen. 23:4,8, *millipnê* appears to be pleonastic in conjunction with *qbr,* but the meaning is probably "apart from the living."

We also find *millipnê* used to express the notion that something comes from Yahweh or a human authority: anger (Nu. 17:11[16:46]; 2 Ch. 19:2), vindication (Ps. 17:2), a messenger (Ezk. 30:9). The fire that comes forth *millipnê yhwh* either means that he has accepted a burnt offering (Lev. 9:24) or portrays him as the source of a punishment (Lev. 10:2).

3. *mippᵉnê.* The expression *mippᵉnê* emphasizes the prepositional sense of *min,* while the nominal meaning of *pānîm* vanishes almost entirely. It expresses separation or physical distance and may be used with verbs either intransitive (*brḥ,* Gen. 16:6,8; *nws,* Gen. 36:6; Ex. 4:3; *ns',* Ex. 14:19; *sbb,* 1 S. 18:11) or transitive (*grš,* Ex.

---

45. B. Pennacchini, *Euntes Docete* 29 (1976) 505; cf. M. Dahood, *Bibl* 47 (1966) 411.

23:29; Ps. 78:55; *yrš* hiphil, Ex. 34:24; *str* hiphil, 2 K. 11:2; *swr* hiphil, Jer. 4:1; *ʿṣr*, 1 Ch. 12:1). The idiom *qwm mippᵉnê* means to stand upright before a person of rank. In connection with verbs and/or in contexts that suggest fear, repugnance, or the need to flee or find refuge (Gen. 7:7; 27:46; 45:3; Ex. 1:12; Nu. 20:6; 22:3; Dt. 5:5; 7:19; 28:60; Josh. 2:9; Jgs. 11:33; Jer. 1:17), *mippᵉnê* introduces the person or thing from which one seeks to escape while simultaneously indicating the reason for flight or terror.

A causal sense without the notion of spatial separation appears in Gen. 6:13 ("because of them"); 47:13 ("because of the famine"); Ex. 3:7 ("on account of their taskmasters"); and 9:11 ("because of the boils"); cf. also Josh. 6:1; 1 K. 5:17(3); 8:11; Jer. 7:12; 14:16; 26:3; Hos. 11:2; Ps. 38:4,6(3,5); 44:17(16); 55:4(3). The prepositional meaning appears clearly in expressions such as *mippᵉnê ʾᵃšer* (Ex. 19:18; Jer. 44:23).

The phrase *mippᵉnê yhwh* conveys the three meanings just discussed: physical distance (Gen. 3:8; Nu. 10:35), spiritual distance (Ex. 9:30; 10:3; 1 K. 21:29), and causality (Jgs. 5:5; Jer. 4:26). More emphasis on the presence of Yahweh may be possible in Ps. 68:2(1); cf. the emphasis on *pānîm* in the next four verses.

The meaning "(human) presence" is suggested by the context in Gen. 45:3; 1 Ch. 12:1; Lam. 2:3.

4. *(mē)ʿal-pᵉnê.* In the expression *ʿal-pᵉnê, pᵉnê/pānîm* + suffix can be a substantive and *ʿal* can simply mean "on" (e.g., Gen. 50:1; Ex. 20:20; 2 K. 4:29; Jer. 13:26; Job 4:15).

As a prepositional phrase, *ʿal-pᵉnê* + personal noun means "face to face with," "near," in the physical or moral presence of someone: Gen. 11:28 (during the lifetime of?); Ex. 4:21; 11:10; 33:19; 34:6; Nu. 3:4b ("under the supervision of"); 2 S. 15:18; 2 K. 13:14; Ps. 9:20(19). In Gen. 16:12 and Nah. 2:2(1), the meaning is "against"; in Gen. 32:22(21), "before" (spatially). In Job 6:28 and 21:38, the emphasis is more on the element of challenge than hostility. In Dt. 21:16 and probably Gen. 25:18 as well, *ʿal-pᵉnê* means "at the expense of," "in preference to" (cf. also Gen. 16:12).

With reference to Yahweh, *ʿal-pᵉnê* emphasizes the impudence of acting contrary to his will in his very presence (Isa. 65:3; Jer. 6:7; Job 1:11; 2:5 [emended]). Zorell categorizes these texts (with the exception of Jer. 6:7) as examples of adverbial usage.[46] For certain Hebrew morphemes, the prepositional/adverbial distinction is not adequate (see VI.8 below). Both presence and confrontation are expressed in the commandment, "You shall have no other gods in my presence *(ʿal-pānāy)* [and hence as my rivals]" (Ex. 20:3 par. Dt. 5:7).[47]

With objects, *ʿal-pᵉnê* means "on, over" (Lev. 16:14; 2 Ch. 34:4), even when the point is the view of a low area from a higher location (Gen. 18:16; 19:28; Nu. 21:20; 23:28). The phrase appears frequently with *ʾereṣ*, "land"; *ʾᵃḏāmâ*, "ground, soil"; *śāḏeh*, "field"; *mayim*, "water"; *miḏbār*, "wilderness"; and *tᵉhôm*, "deep." Except in

46. *LexHebAram*, 656.
47. See the comms.

cases where *pānîm* as a substantive can mean "surface" (Gen. 1:29; 7:18,23),[48] *'al-pᵉnê* means simply "over" (Gen. 1:2; 8:9; 11:4,8,9; Ex. 16:14; 32:20; 33:16).

With toponyms, *'al-pᵉnê* means "near, opposite, in the direction of" (occasionally "east of"[49]): Gen. 23:19 (Mamre); 25:18 (Egypt); Nu. 21:11 (Moab); 33:7 (Baal-zephon); Dt. 32:49 (Jericho); Josh. 17:7 (Shechem); Jgs. 16:3 (Hebron); 1 K. 11:7 (Jerusalem); cf. also Josh. 13:25; 18:14; 19:11; 1 S. 26:1,3; 2 S. 2:24; 1 K. 17:3,5.

With structures or objects associated with the temple, *'al-pᵉnê* means "in front of" or sometimes "at the head of" (1 K. 7:6,42; 8:8; 2 Ch. 3:17; Ezk. 42:8).

The expression *mē'al-pᵉnê* refers to separation from persons (Gen. 23:3) and often their violent removal from the land or the earth (Gen. 4:14; 6:7; 7:4; Ex. 32:12; Dt. 6:15; 1 S. 20:15; 1 K. 9:7; 13:34; Jer. 28:16; Am. 9:8; Zeph. 1:2,3). With the exception of 2 Ch. 7:20, *mē'al-pᵉnê yhwh* appears almost exclusively in the vocabulary of Jeremiah and in Deuteronomistic texts, always following verbs that denote rejection: *šlḥ,* 1 K. 9:7; Jer. 15:1; *šlk* hiphil, 2 K. 13:23; 24:20; Jer. 7:15; 52:3; 2 Ch. 7:20; *swr* hiphil, 2 K. 17:1,23; 23:27; 24:3; Jer. 32:31; *nṭš,* Jer. 23:39.

5. *'eṯ/mē'ēṯ-pᵉnê.* The phrase *'eṯ-pᵉnê X* denotes spatial (Gen. 33:18; figuratively, Prov. 17:24) or personal proximity (1 S. 2:11; 22:4; 1 K. 12:6). The precise meaning (guarding, supervising, protecting) depends on the context. The combination *mē'ēṯ-pᵉnê* adds the element of separation from a place or a person (Gen. 27:30; 43:34; Ex. 10:11; 2 K. 16:14). With Yahweh, *'eṯ/mē'ēṯ-pᵉnê* denotes Yahweh's nearness or distance. In these expressions *pānîm* is synonymous with "presence." The lament of Sodom and the sin of Eli's sons are great *'eṯ-pᵉnê yhwh* (Gen. 19:13; 1 S. 2:17). Abraham returns to the place where he stood *'eṯ-pᵉnê yhwh* (Gen. 19:27); Samuel serves in the presence of Yahweh (1 S. 2:18). The tempter goes out *mē'ēṯ pᵉnê yhwh* (Job 2:7 par. *mē'im* in 1:12). In Ps. 16:11; 21:7(6), joy finds expression *'eṯ-pāneyḵā* ("in your presence"). In Ps. 140:14(13) the dwelling of the upright *'eṯ-pāneyḵā* suggests participation in the temple liturgy; it also suggests dwelling in the land in contrast to the banishment that the psalmist prays Yahweh will inflict on his enemies (v. 12[11]).

6. *'el-pᵉnê.* In conjunction with objects or places, *'el-pᵉnê* signifies direction ("toward"), without emphasis on the front of that object or place (Lev. 6:7[14]; 9:5; 16:2; Nu. 17:8[16:43]; 20:10; Ezk. 41:4,12,15; 44:4). The prepositional sense is strengthened when the expression appears together with *mûl* (Ex. 28:27; Nu. 8:2,3) or *nōḵaḥ* (Nu. 19:4). In all these texts we are often dealing with objects to which respectful reverence is due: the head covering of the priest, the altar of sacrifice, the tent of meeting, the lamp, the sacrificial offering, the court of the temple, the temple, the rock of Moses. The expression *'el-pᵉnê* bespeaks a respectful distance in dealing with these objects (but cf. Neh. 2:13).

Used with a personal object, *'el-pᵉnê* appears to emphasize strongly the person to

---

48. See III.2 above.
49. Drinkard.

whom an action is addressed: Yahweh (Ex. 23:17;[50] Job 13:15); the king (2 Ch. 19:2); the wicked (Dt. 7:10). In such texts as Lev. 6:7(14); 9:5; Josh. 5:14; 2 S. 14:22; Ezk. 41:25; 42:3, *'el* may have taken the place of *'al*.

7. *Other Prepositions.* The expression *bip̱nê* indicates opposition. With *'md* and the hithpael of *yṣb,* it means "withstand" (Dt. 7:24; Josh. 10:8; 21:44). It also appears with "testify (against)" (Hos. 5:5; Job 16:8).

Both *nōḵaḥ pᵉnê* (Jer. 17:6; Lam 2:19; Ezk. 14:3,4,7) and *neḡeḏ pᵉnê* (Isa. 5:21; Hos. 7:2; Lam. 3:35; 1 S. 26:20 [*minneḡeḏ*]) mean "before, in the presence of" or (1 S. 26:20) "away from the presence of." In the context of Lam. 3:35 and 1 S. 26:20, Yahweh's presence is in the land of Judah. There is no difference in meaning between these expressions and *lip̱nê, 'el-pᵉnê,* or *millip̱nê*.

In Ex. 10:10 *neḡeḏ pᵉnêhem* should not be taken as a prepositional expression; *pānîm* appears in place of "you," and the meaning of the statement is, "You have some evil purpose in mind."

The idiom *'el-'ēḇer pānāyw* (Ezk. 1:9,12; 10:22) means "straight ahead."

8. *Adverbial Usage.* Used adverbially, *pānîm* appears in a variety of expressions. In a spatial sense *pānîm wᵉ'āḥôr* means "front and back," in the description of a scroll (Ezk. 2:10). In military contexts (1 Ch. 19:10; 2 Ch. 13:14; 2 S. 10:9, *mippānîm ûmē'āḥôr*), it refers to a line of battle that is dangerously close in every direction. Figuratively (ethically), in a dynamic spatial sense, it means "go backward rather than forward" (*lᵉ'āḥôr wᵉlō' lᵉp̱ānîm,* Jer. 7:24).

Elsewhere *lᵉp̱ānîm* has a temporal sense, referring to a period in the past, generally not precisely defined, when a people lived in a particular region (Dt. 2:10,12,20; 1 Ch. 4:40), a city was a capital (Josh. 11:10) or had a different name (Josh. 14:15; 15:15; Jgs. 1:10,11,23), customs were different (Jgs. 3:2; 1 S. 9:9; Ruth 4:1) or did not exist (Neh. 13:5), or an event took place (1 Ch. 9:20). With reference to Yahweh, *(mil)lᵉp̱ānîm* refers to the time of Yahweh's initial acts (Isa. 41:26, his foreknowledge of the future; Ps. 10:26[25], creation).

VII. LXX. In the LXX *prósōpon* is the term most commonly used to translate *pānîm;* it embraces all the latter's meanings almost without exception: face, side, front, surface. It is used for objects, cosmic elements, animals, persons, and Yahweh. It can be used literally or figuratively, and can occur in prepositional phrases and fixed idioms. The most important of these are always represented by the same verb. Thus *biqqēš pānîm* is regularly translated *zēteín tó prósōpon; śîm pānîm* is *stērízein t.p.; histîr pānîm* is regularly *apostréphein t.p.* (but twice *krýptein*); *ḥillâ pānîm* is *litaneúein, therapeúein,* or *deísthai; rā'â pānîm* is *horán* or *blépein t.p.; nāśā' pānîm* is *thaumázein t.p.; pānîm 'el-pānîm* is *prósōpon prós prósōpon*.

When *pānîm* is the subject of a verb (Ex. 33:14,15; Dt. 4:37; Isa. 63:9), the LXX

50. But see IV.9 above.

prefers *autós*. In cultic regulations with *r'h pānîm* (Ex. 23:17; 34:23; Dt. 16:16), the LXX, like the MT, uses a passive form: *ophthḗsetai enṓpion/enantíon*.

In the majority of cases *lip̱nê* is translated as an ordinary preposition (*enṓpion,* 218 times; *enantíon,* 181 times; *énanti,* 153 times; *émprosthen,* 80 times).

Literal translations, hebraizing rather than idiomatic, include *pró prosṓpou* (67 times) and *katá prosṓpou* (65 times). Other semiprepositions are usually translated by *prósōpon* plus a preposition.[51] This is true of *mippᵉnê,* which is rendered 194 times by *apó prosṓpou,* 21 times by *ek prosṓpou,* 11 times by *pró prosṓpou,* 29 times by *apó,* and 15 times by *diá* plus an accusative. We find *millip̱nê* represented by *apó prosṓpou* 34 times, by *ek prosṓpou* 10 times; *'al-pᵉnê* is represented by *epí prosṓpou/prósōpon* 29 and 28 times, respectively, by *katá prósōpon* 20 times; *mē'al-pᵉnê* is represented by *apó prosṓpou* 11 times, *'el-pᵉnê* by *katá prósōpon* 10 times. In all these cases nonidiomatic translations account for 50 to 66 percent of the total. For the remaining semiprepositions, the paucity of the evidence prohibits drawing any conclusions. Freer translations are common in the Hexateuch, Isaiah, Proverbs, and Job.

Including its prepositional and adverbial uses, *pānîm* is represented by 45 different expressions (counting the numerous collocations with *prósōpon* as a single expression).[52]

VIII. Dead Sea Scrolls. As a substantive and in various adverbial expressions, *pānîm* appears more than three hundred times in the Dead Sea Scrolls. For the most part its meanings and usages correspond to the spectrum found in the OT, e.g.: *nāśā' pānîm* (1QS 2:4,9; 1QH 14:19; 1QSb 3:1,3, alluding to Nu. 6:26); *hē'îr pānîm* (1QH 4:5,27; 3:3; 1QSb 4:27); *ḥillâ pānîm* (1QH 16:11); *histîr pānîm* (CD 1:3; 2:8); *'al-pᵉnê mayim* (1QH 3:13,26; 5:8; 6:24); *mal'aḵ pānîm* (1QSb 4:25-26).[53] In 1QM *pānîm* appears at times to take on a special technical sense when it designates the front rank of the eschatological army (5:3,8; 7:12; 9:4; etc.; cf. *pᵉnê hammigdāl,* "front of the tower," a military formation). According to 1QM 5:5,11, *pānîm* refers to the gleaming surfaces of the weapons of the "sons of light."

Simian-Yofre

---

51. See Brockelmann, *VG,* 383; Sollamo, 1.
52. For a discussion of *prósōpon* in general, see E. Lohse, *TDNT,* VI, 768-80.
53. For adverbial use see Carmignac.